HANDBOOK OF
Child and Adolescent Psychiatry

VOLUME FOUR

HANDBOOK OF
Child and Adolescent Psychiatry

Joseph D. Noshpitz / Editor-in-Chief

VOLUME FOUR

Varieties of Development

NORMAN E. ALESSI

EDITOR

John Wiley & Sons, Inc.
New York • Chichester • Weinheim • Brisbane • Singapore • Toronto

ABF 4610

ISBN 0-471-55079-5 (vol. 1)
ISBN 0-471-55075-2 (vol. 2)
ISBN 0-471-55076-0 (vol. 3)
ISBN 0-471-55078-7 (vol. 4)
ISBN 0-471-17640-0 (set)

Printed in the United States of America

10 9 8 7 6 5 4 3 2 1

DEDICATION

This set of volumes grows out of an attitude that reflects the field itself. To put it succinctly, the basic theme of child and adolescent psychiatry is hope. Albeit formally a medical discipline, child and adolescent psychiatry is a field of growth, of unfolding, of progressive advance; like childhood itself, it is a realm of building toward a future and finding ways to better the outcome for the young. But within the field, an even greater theme inspires an even more dominant regard. For, beyond treating children, child and adolescent psychiatry is ultimately about rearing children. This is literally the first time in human history that we are on the verge of knowing *how* to rear a child. While people have reared children since we were arboreal, they did it by instinct, or by cultural practice, or in keeping with grandma's injunctions, or by reenacting the memories, conscious and unconscious, of their own childhood experiences. They did what they did for many reasons, but never because they really knew what their actions portended, what caused what, what was a precondition for what, or what meant what.

At this moment in history, however, things are different. The efforts of researchers, neuroscientists, child developmental specialists—in short, of the host of those who seek to understand, treat, and educate children and to work with parents—are beginning to converge and to produce a body of knowledge that tells us what children are, what they need, what hurts them, and what helps them. Hard science has begun to study the fetus, rating scales and in-depth therapeutic techniques have emerged for the mother with the infant in her arms, increasing precision is being achieved in assessing temperament, in measuring mother/infant fit, and in detecting the forerunners of person-

ality organization. Adolescence and the intricacies of pubertal transformation are being explored as never before. Indeed, a quiet revolution is coming into being: the gradual dissemination of knowledge about child rearing that, within a few generations, could well alter the quality of the human beings who fall under its aegis.

If children—all children—could be reared in a fashion that gave them a healthier organization of conscience, that preserved the buds of cognitive growth and helped these to flower (instead of pinching them off as so many current practices do), that could recognize from the outset any special needs a child might have in respect to impulse control or emotional stability—and could step in from the earliest moments in development with the appropriate tactics and strategies, anodynes and remedies, techniques of healing and practices of enabling to allow the youngster to better manage his or her inner life and interpersonal transactions—consider what fruit this would bear.

Today this is far more than a dream, far more than a wistful yearning for a better day to come. The beginnings are already accomplished, much of the initial work has been done, the directions of future research are becoming ever more evident. As the heretofore cryptic equations of development are beginning to be found and some of their solutions to be discerned, the once-mystical runes are being read—and are here inscribed in page after page of research report and clinical observation.

Some of the initial changes are already well under way. As with all science, first a process of demystification must occur. Bit by bit, we have had to unlearn a host of formulaic mythologies about children and about parenting that have been part of Western civilization for centuries.

We have indeed begun to do so. We have been able to admit to the realities of child abuse, first to the violence directed toward children and then to their sexual exploitation. And we have had to admit to children's sexuality. Simply to allow those things to appear in print, to become part of common parlance, has taken immense cultural energy, the overcoming of tremendous defensiveness; after all, such things had been known but not spoken of for generations. Right now the sanctity, the hallowed quality of family life, is the focus of enormous cultural upheaval. There is much to suggest that the nuclear family set in the bosom of a body of extended kin relationships that had for so long served as the basic site for human child rearing is no longer the most likely context within which future generations of our children will grow. The quest is on for new social arrangements, and it is within this milieu that the impact of scientific knowledge, the huge and ever-increasing array of insights into the nature of childhood, the chemistry of human relationships, the psychodynamics of parent-child interplay—in short, within the area of development that this work so carefully details—that we find the wellsprings of hope. As nursery schools, kindergartens, grade schools, and high schools become more sophisticated, as the psychiatric diagnostic manuals become more specific and more differentiated, as doctors become better trained and better prepared to address human issues with dynamic understanding, as what children need in order to grow well becomes ever more part of everyday cultural practice, the realization of this hope will slowly and quietly steal across the face of our civilization, and we will produce children who will be emotionally sounder, cognitively stronger, and mentally healthier than their parents. These volumes are dedicated to advancing this goal.

Joseph D. Noshpitz, M.D.
Editor-in-Chief

PREFACE

Some 16 years ago the first two volumes of the *Basic Handbook of Child Psychiatry* were published, to be followed shortly by volumes III and IV, and then, in 1985, by the fifth volume. More than a decade has passed since that volume was released, during which time the field of child psychiatry has advanced at a remarkable pace. Indeed, it has even changed its name to be more inclusive of the teenage years. New advances in neuroscience, in genetics, in psychoanalytic theory, in psychopharmacology, in animal studies—new findings in a host of areas have poured out during these years. It is therefore necessary to revise the handbook, to reorganize it, to update many of the clinical accounts, and to bring it to the level where the active practitioner can use its encyclopedic format to explore the enormous variety of clinical possibilities he or she may encounter.

The focus of this work is on development. It is no exaggeration to look on child development as the basic science of child and adolescent psychiatry. Development is so vital a concern that in this revision, we have abandoned the classical way of presenting the material. Rather than following tradition, wherein development, diagnosis and assessment, syndromes, treatment, and so on are discussed for a variety of related topics, in these volumes the bulk of the material is presented developmentally. Thus, volumes I, II, and III focus on development and syndromes of infancy and preschool, of grade school, and of adolescence, respectively. Within each of these larger sections, the material on development comes first, followed by chapters on syndromes, conceptualized as disturbances of development. While syndromes are described in depth, they are discussed only within the framework of the developmental level under study. Volume IV, entitled *Varieties of Development,* explores a host of ecological niches within which children are reared.

Volumes V and VI will contain sections on consultation/liaison, emergencies in child and adolescent psychiatry, the prehistory of child and adolescent psychiatry, current cultural issues that impinge on young people, forensic issues involving children and youth, and professional challenges facing the child and adolescent psychiatrist. Volume VI will include a most unusually rich banquet of studies on the assessment and evaluation of children, adolescents, and their families, plus reports on the basic science issues of the field and the current status of the various treatment techniques.

The intention of the work is to be as comprehensive and as readable as possible. In an encyclopedic work of this sort, concerns always arise as to how much space to allot to each topic and to which topics should be covered. To deal with such questions, a number of readers reviewed each submission. One editor had primary responsibility for each section; often a coeditor also reviewed submissions. Then the editor of another section reviewed the submissions, exchanging his or her chapters with the first colleague so that someone outside the section read each chapter. In addition, one editor reviewed all submissions with an eye to contradictions or excessive overlap. Finally, the editor-in-chief reviewed and commented on a large proportion of the materials submitted. In short, while the submission process was not juried, a number of readers reviewed each chapter. Each author was confronted with their cumulative critiques and asked to make appropriate changes. Most did so cheerfully, although not always with alacrity.

The writing and review process lasted from about 1990 to 1996. For much of this time, a host of authors was busy writing, revising, and polishing their work. The editors worked unstintingly, suffering all the ups and downs that accompany large projects: many meetings, huge expenses, moments of despair, episodes of elation, professional growth on the part of practically all the participants (a couple of authors who never came through with their material may be presumed to have shrunk), profound disappointments and thrilling break-

throughs, lost causes that were snatched from the jaws of defeat and borne aloft to victory, and, ultimately, the final feeling that we did it!

I speak for all the editors when I say that it was our purpose and it is our earnest wish that these volumes make for better understanding of young people, greater access to knowledge about children and adolescents, a richer sense of what this field of human endeavor entails, and a better outcome for the growth, development, mental health, and happiness of all the young in our land and of those who would help them.

Joseph D. Noshpitz, M.D.
Editor-in-Chief

CONTENTS

Contents

SECTION III / Varieties of Medical Disorder

SECTION IV / Varieties of Culture and Ethnicity

Contents

CONTRIBUTORS

PAUL ADAMS, M.D.
Cofounder, Vice President of Board of Directors, and Coordinator of Faculty, Kentucky Psychoanalytic Institute; Professor Emeritus, University of Texas; Private Practice.

NORMAN ALESSI, M.D.
Assistant Professor of Psychiatry, University of Michigan Medical Center, Ann Arbor, Michigan.

BARBARA J. ANDERSON, PH.D.
Senior Psychologist, Joslin Diabetes Center; Associate Professor of Psychology, Department of Psychiatry, Harvard Medical School, Boston, Massachusetts.

VIJAYA APPAREDDY, M.D.
Medical Director, Columbia Valley Hospital; President, Tri-State Psychiatric Services, Chattanooga, Tennessee.

WILLIAM ARROYO, M.D.
Clinical Assistant Professor of Psychiatry, University of Southern California School of Medicine; Director, Los Angeles County-University of Southern California Child-Adolescent Psychiatric Clinic, Los Angeles, California.

PETER ASH, M.D.
Assistant Professor of Psychiatry and Behavioral Science, Emory University School of Medicine, Atlanta, Georgia.

ROWLAND P. BARRETT, PH.D.
Associate Professor, Department of Psychiatry and Human Behavior, Brown University School of Medicine, Emma Pendleton Bradley Hospital, East Providence, Rhode Island.

WILLIAM R. BEARDSLEE, M.D.
Psychiatrist-in-Chief and Chairman, Department of Psychiatry, Children's Hospital; George P. Gardner-Olga E. Monks Professor of Child Psychiatry, Harvard Medical School, Boston, Massachusetts.

DONALD W. BECHTOLD, M.D.
Associate Professor of Psychiatry, Director of Training in Child Psychiatry, Director of Children's Day Psychiatric Hospital, University of Colorado School of Medicine, Denver, Colorado.

JOSEPH H. BEITCHMAN, M.D.C.M., M.P.H., F.R.C.P., D.A.B.P.N.
Head, Child and Family Studies Centre, Clark Institute of Psychiatry; Professor, Department of Psychiatry and Preventive Medicine and Biostatistics, University of Toronto, Toronto, Ontario, Canada.

MYRON L. BELFER, M.D., M.P.A.
Professor of Psychiatry, Department of Social Medicine, Harvard Medical School, Boston, Massachusetts.

KAREN A. BENES, B.A.
Formerly Research Assistant, Joslin Diabetes Center; Graduate Student, Clinical Psychology, University of Massachusetts, Boston, Massachusetts.

PETER L. BENSON, PH.D.
President, Search Institute, Minneapolis, Minnesota.

IAN A. CANINO, M.D.
Clinical Professor of Psychiatry and Deputy Director of Planning, Division of Child and Adolescent Psychiatry, Director of Community Child Psychiatry, College of Physicians and Surgeons, Columbia University, New York, New York.

GLORISA CANINO, PH.D.
Professor, Department of Pediatrics, University of Puerto Rico School of Medicine; Director, Behavioral Sciences Research Institute, Rio Piedras, Puerto Rico.

ROSARIO CEBALLO, PH.D.
Assistant Professor of Psychology, Department of Psychology, University of Michigan, Ann Arbor, Michigan.

Contributors

RICHARD C. CERVANTES, PH.D.
Senior Research Associate, Behavioral Assessment, Inc., Los Angeles, California.

DONALD J. COHEN, M.D.
Director, Yale Child Study Center, Irving B. Harris Professor of Child Psychiatry, Pediatrics, and Psychology, Yale University School of Medicine; Chief, Child Psychiatry, Children's Hospital, Yale University, New Haven, Connecticut.

STUART ALAN COPANS, M.D.
Associate Professor, Division of Child and Adolescent Psychiatry, Department of Psychiatry, Dartmouth Medical School, Lebanon, New Hampshire; Child and Adolescent Psychiatrist, Brattleboro Retreat, Brattleboro, Vermont; Psychiatric Consultant, Marlboro College, Marlboro, Vermont, and Deerfield Academy, Deerfield, Massachusetts.

TERRY L. CROSS, M.S.W.
Executive Director, Northwest Indian Child Welfare Association, Portland, Oregon.

CHARLES W. DAESCHNER III, M.D.
Director, Pediatric Hematology Oncology Section, Associate Professor of Pediatrics, Department of Pediatrics, Hematology Oncology Section, East Carolina University School of Medicine, Greenville, North Carolina.

DAN DICKASON, M.A.
Research Assistant, Oregon Health Sciences University, Portland, Oregon.

JAMES E. DILLON, M.D.
Clinical Assistant Professor of Psychiatry, Director of Training in Child and Adolescent Psychiatry, University of Michigan School of Medicine, Ann Arbor, Michigan.

CARL B. FEINSTEIN, M.D.
Associate Professor, Johns Hopkins School of Medicine, Kennedy Krieger Institute, Baltimore, Maryland.

PAUL M. FINE, M.D.
Professor, Child and Adolescent Psychiatry, Department of Psychiatry and Behavioral Science, Mercer University School of Medicine, Macon, Georgia.

JOSEPH FISCHHOFF, M.D.
Professor of Psychiatry, Wayne State University School of Medicine, Detroit, Michigan.

JEAN A. FRAZER, M.D.
Instructor of Psychology, Harvard Medical School, Massachusetts General Hospital, Boston, Massachusetts.

RUTH L. FULLER, M.D.
Associate Professor of Psychiatry, Health Sciences Center, University of Colorado School of Medicine, Denver, Colorado.

JOAN P. GERRING, M.D.
Assistant Professor of Psychiatry and Pediatrics, Johns Hopkins University School of Medicine, Baltimore, Maryland.

LINDA J. GUDAS, R.N.,PH.D.
Staff Psychologist, Instructor in Psychiatry, Children's Hospital and Harvard Medical School, Boston, Massachusetts.

JULIE A. GUTHRIE, M.D.
Resident and Clinical Instructor, Department of Psychiatry, Staff Psychiatrist, Ohio State University Psychiatric Health Care, Ohio State University, Columbus, Ohio.

MELVIN J. GUYER, PH.D., J.D.
Professor, Department of Psychiatry, Adjunct Professor, Department of Psychology, University of Michigan Medical Center, Ann Arbor, Michigan.

FADY HAJAL, M.D.
Medical Director, Stony Lodge Hospital, Ossining, New York; Clinical Associate Professor in Psychiatry, Cornell University Medical College, White Plains, New York.

JAMES M. HARPER, PH.D.
Professor and Chair, Department of Family Sciences, Marriage and Family Therapy Graduate Program, Brigham Young University, Provo, Utah.

JAMES C. HARRIS, M.D.
Director, Developmental Neuropsychiatry, Associate Professor of Psychiatry, Pediatrics, and Mental Hygiene, Johns Hopkins University School of Medicine, Baltimore, Maryland.

STUART T. HAUSER, M.D. PH.D.
President, Judge Baker Children's Center; Professor of Psychiatry, Harvard Medical School; Codirector, Clinical Research Training Program, Department of Psychiatry, Harvard Medical School, Boston, Massachusetts; Co-Executive Director, Children's Studies, Harvard University, Cambridge, Massachusetts.

SARAH E. HERBERT, M.D.
Assistant Professor, Division of Child and Adolescent Psychiatry, Department of Psychiatry, Emory University School of Medicine, Atlanta, Georgia.

LUIS D. HERRERA, M.D., M.P.H.
Professor of Pediatrics and Psychiatry, University of Costa Rica School of Medicine, National Children's Hospital; President, Board of Directors, Fundación Paniamor, San José, Costa Rica.

Contributors

E. MAVIS HETHERINGTON, PH.D.
James M. Page Professor of Psychology, Department of Psychology, University of Virginia, Charlottesville, Virginia

S. SUMIKO HIFUMI, B.A.
Research Assistant, Neuropsychiatric Institute, University of California at Los Angeles, Los Angeles, California.

LIZBETH A. HOKE, PH.D.
Instructor in Psychiatry, Harvard Medical School and Beth Israel HealthCare, Boston, Massachusetts.

MARGARET H. HOOPES, PH.D.
Professor Emerita, Department of Family Sciences, Marriage and Family Therapy Graduate Programs, Brigham Young University, Provo, Utah; Private Practice, Yelm, Washington.

THOMAS M. HORNER, PH.D.
Private Practice, Ann Arbor, Michigan.

VERONICA ICHIKAWA, PH.D.
Private Practice, Berkeley, Michigan.

ALAN M. JACOBSON, M.D.
Medical Director, Joslin Diabetes Center; Professor of Psychiatry, Harvard Medical School, Boston, Massachusetts.

DOROTHY STEVENSON JENKINS, PH.D.
Program Associate, Employee Assistance Program, Detroit Public Schools, Detroit, Michigan.

PETER S. JENSEN, M.D.
Chief, Child and Adolescent Disorders Research Branch, National Institute of Mental Health, Rockville, Maryland.

JOHN P. KEMPH, M.D.
Professor and Chief, Division of Child and Adolescent Psychiatry, University of Florida, Gainesville, Florida; Professor and Dean Emeritus, Medical College of Ohio, Toledo, Ohio.

WUN JUNG KIM, M.D., M.P.H.
Associate Professor, Director of Child and Adolescent Psychiatric Residency Training, Medical College of Ohio, Toledo, Ohio.

PENELOPE KRENER KNAPP, M.D.
Professor, Psychiatry and Pediatrics, Chief, Division of Child, Adolescent, and Family Psychiatry, University of California at Davis, Davis, California.

GERALD P. KOOCHER, PH.D.
Chief Psychologist, Associate Professor, Children's Hospital and Harvard Medical School, Boston, Massachusetts.

ROBERT KROLL, PH.D.
Head, Department of Speech Pathology, Clarke Institute of Psychiatry, University of Toronto, Toronto, Ontario, Canada.

DAVID B. LARSON, M.D., M.S.P.H.
President, National Institute for Healthcare Research; Adjunct Professor, Duke University Medical Center, Durham, North Carolina; Adjunct Professor, Northwestern University Medical School, Chicago, Illinois; Adjunct Professor, Uniformed Services University of the Health Sciences, Bethesda, Maryland.

JAMES F. LECKMAN, M.D.
Neison Harris Professor of Child Psychiatry and Pediatrics, Yale Child Study Center, New Haven, Connecticut.

JUDY L. LUPART, PH.D.
Professor of Educational Psychology, Department of Educational Psychology, Faculty of Education, University of Calgary, Calgary, Alberta, Canada.

SARAH C. MANGELSDORF, PH.D.
Associate Professor of Psychology, Department of Psychology, University of Illinois, Urbana-Champaign, Illinois.

SPERO M. MANSON, PH.D.
Professor, Department of Psychiatry; Director, National Center for American Indians and Alaska Natives, Mental Health Research, Denver, Colorado.

KEVIN S. MASTERS, PH.D.
Assistant Professor, Utah State University, Logan, Utah.

ÅKE MATTSSON, M.D.
Professor of Psychiatry and Clinical Pediatrics, Director, Division of Child and Adolescent Psychiatry, Department of Psychiatry, East Carolina University School of Medicine, Greenville, North Carolina.

ROSE McDERMOTT, PH.D.
Postdoctoral Fellow, University of California, San Francisco, California.

MELANIE L. McGRATH, PH.D.
Assistant Professor of Psychology, Tulane University, New Orleans, Louisiana.

VONNIE C. McLOYD, PH.D.
Professor of Psychology, Department of Psychology, Research Scientist, Center for Human Growth and Development, University of Michigan, Ann Arbor, Michigan.

SHIRLEY McSHARRY, M.S.W.
At the time of her death, Ms. McSharry was a Research Associate at the University of Utah School of Medicine, Salt Lake City, Utah.

Contributors

DEBRA MEKOS, PH.D.
Assistant Professor, Johns Hopkins University School of Public Health, Baltimore, Maryland.

DAVID A. MRAZEK, M.D., F.R.C.PSYCH.
Chairman, Psychiatry and Behavioral Sciences, Children's National Medical Center; Acting Chairman and Professor of Psychiatry, Behavioral Sciences, and Pediatrics, George Washington University School of Medicine, Washington, D.C.

JOSEPH D. NOSHPITZ, M.D.
Clinical Professor of Psychiatry and Behavioral Science, George Washington University; Private Practice, Washington, D.C.

ALLEN OLIVER, D.MIN.
Director, Highlands Community Ministries Counseling Services; Adjunct Professor of Marriage and Family Therapy, Presbyterian Theological Seminary; Adjunct Professor, University of Louisville; Private Practice, Louisville, Kentucky.

HELEN C. PANARITES, M.D.
Assistant Professor of Psychiatry, Department of Psychiatry, Emory University School of Medicine, Atlanta, Georgia.

LIZETTE PETERSON, PH.D.
Professor of Psychology, University of Missouri.

THEODORE A. PETTI, M.D., M.P.N.
Arthur B. Richter Professor of Child Psychiatry, Indiana University; Psychiatric Consultant, Indiana Division of Mental Health.

ANDRES J. PUMARIEGA, M.D.
Professor and Chair, Department of Psychiatry and Behavioral Sciences, James H. Quillen College of Medicine, East Tennessee State University, Johnson City, Tennessee.

MARK RIDDLE, M.D.
Associate Professor of Pediatrics and Psychiatry, Director, Division of Child and Adolescent Psychiatry, Department of Psychiatry and Behavioral Sciences, Johns Hopkins University School of Medicine, Baltimore, Maryland.

LISA MARIE ROCCHIO, PH.D.
Associates in Psychotherapy, North Kingstown, Rhode Island.

ELINOR B. ROSENBERG, M.S.W.
Clinical Faculty, University Center for the Child and the Family, University of Michigan, Ann Arbor, Michigan.

MARY JANE ROTHERAM-BORUS, PH.D.
Professor of Psychiatry, Department of Psychiatry, Division of Social and Community Psychiatry, University of California, Los Angeles, California.

PEDRO RUIZ, M.D.
Professor and Vice Chair for Clinical Affairs; Medical Director, Mental Sciences Institute, University of Texas/Houston Health Science Center, Houston, Texas.

WILLIAM H. SACK, M.D.
Professor of Psychiatry, Director, Division of Child and Adolescent Psychiatry, Oregon Health Sciences University, Portland, Oregon.

CINDY M. SCHAEFFER, M.A.
Doctoral Candidate, Clinical Psychology, University of Missouri, Columbia, Missouri.

JON A. SHAW, M.D.
Professor and Director, Division of Child and Adolescent Psychiatry, University of Miami School of Medicine, Miami, Florida.

JEANNE SPURLOCK, M.D.
Clinical Professor, George Washington University and Howard University, Washington, D.C.

ANNIE G. STEINBERG, M.D.
Assistant Professor, Departments of Psychiatry and Pediatrics, University of Pennsylvania School of Medicine, Philadelphia, Pennsylvania.

HANS STEINER, DR. MED. UNIV.
Professor of Psychiatry, Division of Child Psychiatry and Child Development, Stanford University School of Medicine, Stanford, California.

FREDERICK J. STODDARD, M.D.
Assistant Clinical Professor of Psychiatry, Harvard Medical School; Chief of Psychiatry, Shriners Burns Institute at the Massachusetts General Hospital, Boston, Massachusetts.

MARGARET L. STUBER, M.D.
Associate Professor of Psychiatry, University of California at Los Angeles; Neuropsychiatric Institute and Hospital, Los Angeles, California.

JONATHAN A. SUGAR, M.D.
Clinical Assistant Professor of Psychiatry, University of Michigan School of Medicine; Private Practice, Ann Arbor, Michigan.

LUKE Y. TSAI, M.D.
Professor of Psychiatry and Pediatrics and Director, Developmental Disorders Clinic, University of Michigan Medical School, Ann Arbor, Michigan.

EMILY B. VISHER, PH.D.
Lecturer, Graduate School of Professional Psychology, John F. Kennedy University, Orinda, California.

JOHN S. VISHER, M.D.
Emeritus Lecturer in Psychiatry, Stanford University School of Medicine, Stanford, California.

Contributors

ANNE S. WALTERS, PH.D.
Clinical Assistant Professor, Department of Psychiatry and Human Behavior, Brown University School of Medicine, Emma Pendleton Bradley Hospital, East Providence, Rhode Island.

NAIMAH Z. WEINBERG, M.D.
Special Expert, National Institute on Drug Abuse, National Institutes of Health, Rockville, Maryland.

ELIZABETH B. WELLER, M.D.
Director, Division of Child Psychiatry, Professor of Psychiatry and Pediatrics, Ohio State University College of Medicine, Columbus, Ohio.

RONALD A. WELLER, M.D.
Professor and Director of Training and Education, Department of Psychiatry, Ohio State University College of Medicine, Columbus, Ohio.

JENNIFER WILD, M.ED.
Research Psychologist, Department of Psychiatry, Charing Cross and Westminster Medical School, London, England.

JOE YAMAMOTO, M.D.
Professor of Psychiatry, University of California at Los Angeles; Neuropsychiatric Institute, Los Angeles, California.

JOYCE WU YEH, PH.D.
Clinical Psychologist, Children's Services; Coordinator, Coastal Asian Pacific Mental Health Services, Department of Mental Health, Los Angeles County, Los Angeles, California.

MAY YEH, M.A.
Graduate Student, Clinical Psychology, University of California, Los Angeles, California.

SECTION I
Varieties of Family Structure

1 / Adoption

Elinor B. Rosenberg and Fady Hajal

Adoption is a social institution with a long history. Historical (Moses, Joseph) and creative (Oedipus, Hansel and Gretel, Babar) literature offer many representations of the plight of orphaned and abandoned children through the ages many of whom were cared for by adoptive families.

The United States leads currently in the number of extrafamilial adoptions. It is estimated that there were 1.3 million adopted children under 18 years of age in the United States in 1985 (Zill, 1985). This constitutes roughly 2% of the U.S. population. It is further estimated that one-third of these adoptions are extrafamilial, where the child is adopted by unrelated adults; the other two-thirds are intrafamilial. In the 1980s there was a shift toward an increase of adoption of foreign-born children as well as of older and special needs children. In the United States, children in need of adoptive homes come from a wide range of classes, religions, ethnic and national origins, and from varied personal circumstances. Many such children are adopted informally within their extended families. Others require placement with nonrelatives. Nonrelative adoptions take place most commonly when the child was conceived out of wedlock in a society where this circumstance carries a social stigma. It occurs also when parents (or one parent) are unwilling or unable to provide adequate care for a child. While most of these children are relinquished in infancy, others are relinquished voluntarily or forcibly taken away from their parents when older. Often their adoption is finalized following multiple placements in foster care or institutions.

Most children currently in adoptive homes and almost all adult adoptees were placed as infants following the traditional mode of confidential adoption. Little or no information was exchanged between adoptive parents and birth parents, with the adoptive agency or private facilitator acting as an opaque wall between the two parties.

Conception, Pregnancy and Birth

For adoptees, relinquishment by birth parents is evidence of their being a problem solved by extrusion—people whose very birth caused difficulty. Therefore, the first piece of autobiographical data for most adopted children is that they were a mistake—people who were not planned and not "meant to be." Other facts around the conception may impact on the way the adoptees feel about themselves and about their predicament. It may matter to them whether they were born out of a loving relationship, a casual relationship, or a relationship of violence. It may matter whether they perceive birth parents to have been irresponsible regarding birth control, victims of a real accident, or simply unable to care for them.

CASE EXAMPLE

A 7-year-old girl had been told that her parents, too young to get married and raise a child, had wanted her to grow up in a good home with both a mother and a father. They arranged for her adoption through an agency. Her retelling of the story included modifications reflecting her feelings about the event. For example, she reported that while her parents were too young to raise children, her mother had wanted to keep her, but her father said she could not. The father forced the crying and begging mother to put her in a box on the doorstep of the agency. A social worker picked her up and carried her in the back of her van with all the other babies she had picked up that day. She then drove them all to their adoptive homes.

It was clearly important to this child to feel that her mother gave her away only when forced to do so. Children are likely to develop many versions of their birth stories as they grow and develop. These initial "facts" and their revisions will require

3

confrontation and processing throughout the life cycle.

In addition to psychosocial factors surrounding conception and pregnancy, biological factors including both genetic endowment and constitutional aspects play a crucial role in the makeup of children relinquished for adoption. These biological factors, previously overlooked as factors in the development of adoptees, have been studied systematically only recently. Prior to these studies children were viewed as a kind of tabula rasa, to be given substance and form by their adoptive parents. From the mid-1960s on, numerous studies have demonstrated the significant role played by genetic factors in human development (Cadoret, 1990). These studies have suggested, for instance, that genetic factors play a significant role in intelligence; in some major mental illness (schizophrenia, bipolar affective disorder); in the formation of antisocial personality disorders; in substance abuse, and in attention deficit disorders. Traits associated with these disturbances present in birth parents may be causally related to the occurrence of an unwelcome pregnancy and to the relinquishment of the baby that ensues. It is important to note that we cannot conclude, however, that adoptees come from a riskier genetic pool; we simply do not have any way of comparing the relinquishing parents' genetic base to other single parents or to the parental population at large.

Most adoptive parents and their children have been given only shards of information about their birth parents. While the question of nature vs. nurture remains an ambiguous one in general, it is more problematic for adoptees deprived of the most basic information about their birth parent and who end up relying on fantasy and conjecture in sorting out these aspects of their being. Adopted children who lived with or know their biological parents also assess their genetic roots.

The fetus is affected by the mother's behavior. Low birthweight and other physical anomalies have been shown to be related to poor nutrition, smoking, and alcohol and drug use during pregnancy. It is less clear whether and how a mother's emotions affect the fetus.

Some developmental investigators argue that bonding between mother and baby begins in utero as the mother and child physically experience each other. No one knows what specific effect that experience has for the baby. One feature unique to adoptees is that the birth mother set upon relinquishing her baby consciously and/or unconsciously experiences anticipatory grief during pregnancy. Yet this grief is a difficult quality to measure, and we do not know what impact it may have on the infant. A reasonable inference may be that the conflictual circumstances of the pregnancy of a relinquishing mother make it more difficult for her to provide a positive physical and emotional prenatal environment for her baby and therefore may place these babies in a higher risk category.

Postpartum Phase

Adopted children have a wide range of preadoption experiences. Physical and emotional separation from their birth mothers is a universal one. The degree of trauma caused by even an infant being separated from the familiar person (her sounds and movements, temperature, scents, etc.) varies among adoptees. In addition, some children experience multiple placements before they reach their adoptive homes. It is not uncommon for permanent adoption to be preceded by time spent in a hospital and/or one or several foster homes. Each of these moves can exacerbate an already prenatally and postnatally stressed, or even traumatized, child. Biological factors, on the other hand, may determine how sensitive any particular child is going to be to the psychosocial aspects of its environment.

Pre- and postnatal stress may impact on children loaded with genetic vulnerabilities with such force that even the most favorable postadoptive circumstances will not completely alleviate the damage done. At the other end of the spectrum, a genetically resilient child may weather similar stresses quite easily. A "good enough" adoptive environment will be sufficient for such a baby to reach and maintain equilibrium. Most children fall somewhere between these two extremes. Having all suffered from maternal loss, they need a consistent, nurturing environment to help them recover.

Adoption and Infancy

Adoptive parents are able to best nurture their children when they have adequately confronted their motivation for adoption and are prepared to deal with the special issues related to adoption for themselves and for their children. They need to love, nurture, guide, and discipline. Infants enter their adoptive homes in varying states of well-being and with their own particular temperaments. Adoptive parents need to educate themselves about their child's special needs, respect these needs, and then do all they can to meet them. They need to give themselves and their children permission to have thoughts and feelings biological families do not have to confront.

All parents have stories of their first experiences with their infants. These stories become part of family lore. These stories represent an expression of the "matching" between parents and child. For example, the baby described as "wanting to be left alone" could be experienced as anything from "admirably independent" through "needing to be gently coaxed into warming up" or "aloof and rejecting." Parents still struggling with their own issues regarding the decision to adopt may be less able to accept a child as he or she is and to offer the kind of help the child needs in joining their family.

The process of integration and matching is more arduous in some families than in others. A critical factor is the degree to which adoptive parents have been able to achieve realistic expectations about the adoption process, namely that adoptive parenting is not exactly like biological parenting but does present added features and likely stresses. For example, a difficult "match" occurs when a couple, not having sufficiently resolved their own infertility, looks to the child to fulfill their notion/fantasy of their idealized biological child and instead are faced with a traumatized, troubled child. The easiest match, on the other hand, is a couple realistic about the special needs of an adopted child who receives a child highly responsive to their efforts. Parents who have accepted the notion that adopting presents special challenges are best equipped to help any child at this early stage of adjustment.

An adopted infant develops a familiarity thanks to predictability and continuity in the new household. This stability contributes to the development of a sense of security that in turn promotes healing of the original trauma. One father reported, "She was a wreck when we brought her home. It took weeks before she settled down and was able to eat and sleep in a comfortable way. It was months before she was calm enough to even notice we were there." Over time, each family will need to make its own adjustments to allow for bonding to develop and for a new real family to begin.

Preschool-Age Children

As children move quickly from one stage of development to another, snugly attached infants all too quickly become striving, demanding toddlers. Eager to make their own choices and exert self-control, toddlers test out whether they continue to be acceptable children to their parents and whether these urges jeopardize the developing relationship. Similarly, behaviors reflecting sexuality and aggression are tests of the parent-child relationship. The parent's ability to accept these aspects of their children's development contributes to furthering self-esteem while supporting the children's healthy initiative and strengthening the parent-child tie. When adoptive parents carry major concerns about the birth parents' lack of control of sexuality and aggression, they may attribute their child's normal expression of sexual and aggressive drives to a direct transmission of these negative traits.

Sometimes parents choose the preschool period as a time to disclose children's adoptive status to them. More recent research has indicated that children under the age of 6 or 7 (preschoolers) lack the capacity to understand the concept of adoptive vs. biological parents (Brodzinsky, Singer, & Braff, 1984; Pickar, 1986). They think in concrete and magical ways. Their concreteness is reflected in the literal way they process language. As a result, the "news" of the adoption at this stage could pave the way for confusion.

CASE EXAMPLE

A 3-year-old boy visited a friend and her new baby sister. There was some discussion of "where babies come from." When back home, he asked if he had come from his mommy's tummy the way his friend's sister had. His adoptive mother explained that the lady who had made him couldn't take care of him so she brought him to Family Services where they found good homes for children who needed them. She warmly told him of how happy they were to have him come home to them. One day, as they drove by the agency, his parents pointed out the building where they received him. They tenderly described what a happy day it had been. Several months later, the parents overheard a conversation their son was having with his friend. He explained to her that while her sister had come from her mommy's tummy, he had come from a building downtown—he was born from the family building. Neither child seemed clear about whether this difference was better or worse!

The content, quality, circumstances, and timing of the disclosure will interact with children's developmental state. When told during the preschool stage, they will make sense of it in any way they can in the realm of concrete and magical thinking. Some interactions are more problematic than others. Disclosure at this stage is a trade-off of trust over comprehension. Parents can be sensitive to these possible confusions and make efforts at clarification. The confusions are not necessarily damaging; most will fall into the category of the "I used to think" that will naturally become clarified in time.

In families with both biological and adopted children, there is an ongoing process of sorting out what is regular or special and which is better. Each may feel the other to be more valued by parents at different times.

School-Age Children

Significant shifts in cognitive abilities take place in children as they enter middle childhood. They become able to comprehend concepts heretofore beyond them. They become increasingly able to understand causal relationships and to think planfully and logically. As a result, they will begin to rework information received from earlier disclosure and to reuse their prior conclusions. Vestiges of earlier themes or beliefs as well as the feelings associated with them may persist, however.

If disclosure of adoption took place during the school-age phase, children are able to understand that they have two sets of parents—one biological and one adoptive. The "news" upsets a basic belief in the inviolability of the parent-child tie. Some children become noticeably distressed at the disclosure and reflect their distress emotionally and behaviorally. Some muster immediate defenses convincing themselves that being adopted is as good as, or even better, than not being so.

In a child's mind-view, when something bad happens, it must be somebody's fault. Adopted children begin to struggle with feelings about the whole cast of characters, including themselves. They experience mixed feelings toward each set of parents and toward themselves. Sometimes they split these feelings by making one party good and the other bad—consistently or alternately. Other parties also may be implicated. Doctors, lawyers, and social workers may be seen as the ones who did good or bad deeds—thus protecting the primary characters in this intense drama children may ponder.

School-age years are a time when fantasies abound for all children. In addition, they experience daily disappointments with their parents. They are past the point where they see their parents as all-knowing and all-powerful. They develop "family romances" in which they fantasize that they are not, in fact, the offspring of these less than perfect people but, rather, were born of some nobility—beautiful, wonderful princes and princesses—and that they somehow ended up with these plain folks. This fantasy provides them a respite from life's daily disappointments and makes the latter more tolerable.

For adopted children, these fantasies are more complicated (Rosenberg & Horner, 1991). When angry or disappointed with their adoptive parents, many conjure up idealized images of their birth parents who would grant them every desire and be perfect parents in every way a child wishes for. But for this fantasy to be possible, adopted children must include in it some plausible explanation of the loss of birth parents that would not compromise their perfection, such as: it must be entirely someone else's fault that they lost the child.

CASE EXAMPLE

An 8-year-old developed an elaborate fantasy to be evoked whenever she felt angry at her adoptive parents.

In this fantasy, she had a mother who looked just like her and a father who looked like the prince in *Cinderella*. They would come into her bedroom and hug her and hold her. They would always bring cookies and candy, read her stories, then take her for rides at the amusement park and on to McDonald's. They said that everything about her was good. She wasn't messy, she wasn't lazy, she wasn't rude. She was perfect and so were they—a far cry from the reality of her everyday life.

Many adopted children find it difficult to develop this kind of comforting fantasy. They are obliged to deal with disappointments and ambivalence toward two sets of parents. The few facts shared with them about their birth parents conjure up disquieting images of inadequate, irresponsible, rejecting people. The commonly offered explanation—"She loved you so much she gave you away so you could have a better life"—is not comforting to children for whom loving and giving away are not compatible. The children's fantasies aim at sorting out responsibility and blame. The fantasy may expand to include biological siblings who were or were not kept. For example, one boy fantasized that he had a twin. He was the bad, throwaway one while his twin brother was the good, "kept" child. Another logical conclusion adoptees reach is that their birth mother was a bad mother who gave away a perfectly good baby. There may be moments of comfort in imagining a bad mother giving away all her good children or even a good mother giving away all her bad children. The notion of some or even one being kept upsets the child's basic insistence on fairness.

Birthdays are a time when members of the adoption circle tend to be particularly aware of each other. Many adopted children begin to feel distressed in anticipation. This distress is different from the usual excitement (and anxiety) biological children experience around their birthdays. Many adoptees think that if ever *she* would think of him, it would be this day. Some consciously, others unconsciously await some sign—a card, a call, a visit—and find themselves disappointed when it does not occur. The aftermath of a birthday can be a time of disappointment, leaving the children with heightened resentment and lowered self-esteem that requires a recovery period.

At times, children blame the adoptive parents to protect themselves. If the children believe the birth parents were "bad," as the offspring of bad people, they may feel tainted with this "badness." One way to defend against these feelings is to conclude rather that they came from good stock and are therefore good people. The "family romance" also may include the belief that the birth parents were indeed nobility and that the child was kidnapped by the adoptive parents for their own selfish needs.

These wishes and fears—common to latency-age adopted children—upset the sense of permanency of the adoptive relationship. If they were abandoned once, might it not happen again? Some children have a need to test this out and may behave in ways that test their parents' patience and limits.

As children enter the school system, their world enlarges. In this wider community, their adoption must be either accepted as a fact of life and disclosed to friends or kept under wraps to be known only by family members. There may be some uncomfortable and even jarring moments when issues of heredity or lineage arise naturally in school programs.

School age is a phase of development in which children seek recognition by producing things—by becoming workers—and begin taking pride in their competence and adequacy. The issue of abandonment that adopted children confront during this phase tends to compromise the feelings of adequacy and call into question their basic human status. They fight feelings of being a castoff as well as fears of being inadequate as they may perceive their birth parents to be. Any less than "good enough" circumstances, such as the presence of a physical anomaly and/or intolerance and rejection on the part of adoptive parents, contributes further to a sense of inferiority and poor functioning.

Adolescence

Adoption issues are ones that are highly resonant with adolescent issues. They interact in a way that exacerbates and sometimes inflames normal adolescent development tasks. For adoptees, it is not enough to integrate internal stirrings with the known external environment. Developing a separate identity within the family and establishing appropriate independence from the family form only one aspect of the charge for adoptees. There is another world for them to process, that of their birth parents and their own fantasies about them.

From the earliest moments of puberty, adoptees wonder who they are and what they would be like as an adult. They scan the environment to find some human reference points with whom to identify. Since adopted children have no visible biological relative, they lack any such reference point. As their bodies change, they imagine how they will turn out and what it means.

The little pubescent adolescents do know about their birth parents is that they were sexually active and usually irresponsible about birth control. As they observe themselves developing sexual characteristics, this knowledge can be a distressing and complicating factor, reflecting both the wish and fear of being like the birth parents.

CASE EXAMPLE

A 14-year-old boy became quite distressed when he found himself having wet dreams. He concluded that the lustfulness behind his wet dreams meant he was an uncontrolled "stud," as he imagined his birth father to be. Partly, he thought this was "cool." In another way, he thought it was gross and irresponsible.

Sexual identifications become complicated as adoptees attempt to integrate their impulses with the usually conflicting identifications with adoptive parents on the one hand and facts and fantasies of birth parents on the other. Depending on current needs, adoptees may identify or deidentify with their impressions of birth parents and/or adoptive parents. At times, they may identify themselves as either asexual or overly responsible to be sure they will not turn out like their birth parents. Attempting to sort out these identifications requires dealing with their wishes and fears as well as feelings of loyalty or disloyalty to both sets of parents.

Some adopted girls seem compelled to repeat their birth mother's experience—perhaps unconsciously feeling it is the only way they can really understand what happened. Unable to cognitively understand how a mother could give a child away, they attempt to understand it experientially. Or becoming pregnant may be based on a wish to undo the birth mother's mistake by now having a baby and keep it to raise.

Another possible conscious or unconscious motivation is to do the one thing their adoptive mother was unable to do. This may be based on competitive feelings and may be a way of surpassing a mother an adoptee may have felt she could not live up to.

Or the pregnancy may, instead, be based on a need to fulfill the adoptive couple's long-term unmet wish to have a baby born in the household. In some ways it may be the ultimate gift to the adoptive parents, which can neither be perceived or appreciated as the circumstances around it are so distressing.

Adopted boys also may be compelled somehow to repeat the primal pregnancy drama. They may be irresponsible as they imagined their birth fathers to have been, and when a pregnancy occurs they may pressure their lover to abort, keep, or place the child depending on where their identification and needs rest. Others may become super-responsible to make up for the past.

Adolescent adoptees need their parents' help in recognizing that their sexuality is a developing part rather than a predetermined part of themselves. Accepting their children's sexuality can be a difficult task for adoptive parents, depending on the feelings they have about birth parents' sexuality.

As adoptees go through the process of identity consolidation again, they wonder "Who am I and who am I like?" Adoptive parents provide one set of possible identifications—in terms of cultural and religious attributes, psychological attributes, social class, lifestyle, career choices, and so on. Concomitantly, adoptees have facts and fantasies of birth parents to integrate cohesively into their self-concept. Although they may intellectually think that relinquishment was a perfectly good decision and one they would emulate, it is difficult for them to accept the decision on an emotional level. The "facts" and personality descriptions of birth parents may produce intense ambivalent feelings about similarities or dissimilarities between them.

CASE EXAMPLE

A younger teenager had been told that her birth mother was very artistic. Her adoptive father was also artistic. While the girl herself had artistic ability, her parents observed that she seem resistant to develop this skill. Feeling overwhelmed by what she felt to be a "choice" between being like an inadequate woman or an adequate man, she fled the conflict by avoiding that part of her personality. In so doing, she denied herself (and her family) the pleasures of her talent.

A bright, handsome, talented 14-year-old boy was notably unsuccessful in all areas of his life. Having been told that his birth parents had been unable to take care of him, he imagined them to be totally nonfunctioning street people. In therapy he reported fearing that if he were to become too successful and prominent, they might discover him and come to him to be salvaged. He referred, as an example, to a local wealthy self-made man who had become the object of innumerable philanthropic requests. To avoid the stress of such reunion and responsibility, he maintained a low profile of mediocrity. As he came to understand this about himself, he was able to function to his own potential.

The struggle to integrate conflicting identity figures does not always involve such negative interferences. Some adoptees may experience getting the best of both worlds. When the worlds are very different, however, it takes extra effort to put them together.

For adoptees, separation and independence have special meanings. Given their relinquishment history, separation-individuation may imply a second abandonment. They fear that the loss of the adoptive parents' child-rearing function may mean the end of the relationship and result in evicting them rather than launching them.

Instead of risking rejection again, adoptees may take it upon themselves to do the leaving. They may do it in a dramatic manner, such as by running away, or more quietly, by becoming aloof and elusive, thus placing parents in the position of constantly taking initiative in the relationship. Some adolescents may fantasize about finding their birth parents so that they can reattach and undo both the original abandonment and what they feel is an impending one.

Late adolescence is a time when, for a variety of reasons, adoptees often begin expressing interest in their biological families, both to learn more about them and also about themselves. However, the confluence of the increased interest in birth parents, of the rebellious and devaluing attitude, and also of the distancing make this stage a difficult one for adoptive parents. They may feel that they are losing their child rather than experiencing a complicated though normal developmental stage. Some parents may feel so rejected and hurt that

they reject in return: "If he doesn't want us, we don't want him." Thus, they fulfill the adolescent's expectation and fear. Other parents may find themselves trying to hold on tighter, thus causing the child to pull away even harder.

This process has the potential to be a recapitulation of the original homecoming and early bonding process setting the stage for a bilateral readoption. Adolescents and parents look each other over anew, feel each other out, reacknowledge explicitly the existence of the birth parents, and reexplore the nature of the tie they wish to establish between them at this stage of their lives. The pushes and pulls during the adolescent years are part of a process of accepting a different model of joining and maintaining a family. Adoptive parents and adolescents alike must accept the family's different parts so that the children can move forward to achieve a sense of independent membership in the family rather than a feeling of being evicted from it. When this occurs, parent and child can be said to have recontracted their family tie with the recognition that their relationship will continue to be a permanent one based on their life experience of caring, nurturance, and companionship if not on blood ties.

Life events such as illness, death, or divorce of adoptive parents have special significance for adoptees. They already carry with them a vulnerability in terms of their legitimacy, their losses, and their concerns about being bad and causing trouble. Some adoptees will navigate these difficult events quite adequately. Those struggling with extra vulnerabilities may be overwhelmed by such events. Remarriages of adoptive parents will present all the usual challenges of blended families. Stepparents will need to be distinguished from adoptive parents. If either adopted parent produces a biological child with the new partner, issues around feeling like second choice or second best may reemerge. Again, the security of the preexisting parent-child relationship will be crucial for adoptees' capacity to weather this life transition.

Young Adulthood

For adoptees, the choices of work and intimacy that take place during this stage of transition are more complicated than for biological children in a family. The tie to family involves both an attachment to the adoptive family and concerns about genealogical continuity.

The question of "Who am I?" continues to be salient in the choice of work and love. Consider the case of a young woman who was determined to become a hairdresser despite her lack of aptitude with hair and her exceptional abilities in other areas. She had been told that her birth mother had dropped out of school and had noticed that many girls who dropped out of school had gone on to beauty schools. The least conflictual process occurs when the fantasies or reported facts regarding birth parents are similar to the circumstances of the adoptive family. An adoptee who had been told that her birth parents were bright college kids who loved each other but were not ready to marry and raise a child imagined that they both went on to successful professional careers very much like her adoptive parents. She had no difficulty pursuing that course herself.

A real fear (conscious or unconscious) that many adoptees have is that they will inadvertently marry a biological relative. One young man reported spending hours trying to figure out a foolproof method of selecting a mate guaranteed not to be related to him.

Some adoptees find themselves discarding one potential mate after another and never being quite sure why. Others may establish a set of exclusion criterion for a safe choice. Given such complications, it is not at all unusual that adoptees take additional time in choosing a mate.

Being "unattached" has different implications for adopted people (no longer children). They must learn through everyday experience that leaving home means neither abandonment nor eviction. They must see that the adoptive family remains an anchoring point for return and refueling. Even when the separation is a rocky one, the bonds will likely remain constant and the emotional tie unbroken. Some adoptees (and parents) may need to "cut off" for a time to test this bond. In a few cases, however, the mutual need for cutoff between parent and adoptee may prove irreparable.

These disquieting issues motivate many young adults to search for their birth parents for some answers. Some seek information only and have no stated wish to have personal contact. Some wish for information as well as reunion with the opportunity to have continuing relationships with both sets of parents. Adoptees pursue these goals with different degrees of intensity. For some, there is a feeling of urgency and a sense that they cannot be complete people without a confrontation with their genetic heritage. Others feel less urgency yet are eager for such information to enrich their sense of well-being. They may decide to search out of four basic motivations: a life cycle transition (as with the birth of a first child), desire for information, hope for a relationship with the birth parent, and wish for self-understanding. By bringing the two parts of themselves together, they hope they can build a sense of self that feels complete to them.

Other adoptees reject the idea of a search. Those who feel angry and rejected may express their discontent in this manner. "If they haven't wanted to look for me, I sure as hell don't want to look for them." Others express being satisfied and comfortable with their lives and do not expect much to be gained from such a search. Still others fear that a reunion might bring on problems for them in feeling obligated to attend to the needs of an additional set of parents.

In whatever ways these issues emerge— whether in discussions with family or friends, in therapy or in support groups—it is important to recognize the legitimacy of the questions and of the discomfort. The difficult processes of integrating one's identity and coming to terms with the lack of genealogical continuity are likely to prolong ordinary young adult tasks of separation, choosing mates, and work. As integration of identity occurs, an engagement to include all members of the adoption circle, first with the adoptive family and sometime later with the birth parents' family, is possible.

Adulthood

As people move on into adulthood, a shifting of generation and of generational roles occurs. Caregiving roles become more mutual.

In making this shift, a complication for adoptees is a sense of continuing to be seen by society as "adopted children" no matter how old they become.

For adoptees, the birth of a child has special meaning. They achieve the opportunity to have a blood relative perhaps for the very first time. Even when the experiences in the adoptive family have been excellent, the procreation of blood kin can be a poignant and highly significant event.

Adoptive parents who have worked through their own reproductive issues and have come genuinely to accept the "difference" of their family will be happy for their children to have this heartwarming experience. Those who have not worked through their issues may find it threatening—experiencing envy and fearing (again) that they may lose their child to a blood relative.

Having, keeping, and raising a child of one's own is likely to stir up old and new feelings about birth parents. During the pregnancy, there may be concerns about what heredity is likely to produce. Adoptees must deal with a fear of the unknown. Some adoptees report overwhelming anxiety about being able to produce a normal child. Spouses and relatives may feel and express similar concerns—all of which may contribute to the urge to search. There may be a benevolent wish to let birth parents know that they have become grandparents and to mark the significance of this milestone. There may be a need to address the relinquishment at a time when it may feel inconceivable to give up a child. Adoptees also may feel empathy for their birth parents' loss.

At some point there arises the task of disclosing the parent's adoption to his or her own children. In doing so, there is likely to be resurgence of the anguish originally experienced in feeling "atypical" or imperfect in some way.

Later Life

Developmental tasks of later life include dealing with changing life circumstances such as loss of parents, declining health, death or divorce of a spouse, grandparenthood, job retirement, or financial strain. All these tasks carry with them added burdens and complications for adoptees.

In addition to the genuine loss of a real relationship, the loss of an adoptive parent involves the relief from some burden of loyalty and feelings of protection toward the parent vis-à-vis longings for the birth parents. Some adoptees postpone a search until adoptive parents, and particularly adoptive mothers, have died. The expressed feeling around this decision is a wish not to hurt the adoptive parents, out of respect and gratitude for their care. There also may be a fear of anger or retribution. Still others may be seeking a "backup" mother to replace the one lost.

Related to the timing of a search at this phase of life may be a feeling that it is "now or never" in regard to the aging birth parents. There also may be some wish to tend to an aging parent in need, as was done or not done for the adoptive parent.

Death or divorce of a spouse may be especially difficult for adoptees as it may trigger their most profound vulnerability, the feeling of abandonment. If accompanied by declining health and financial stress, there may be a revisiting of "abandoned orphan" feelings previously experienced.

Outcome for Adoptees

Adopted children make up from 4 to 15% of the clinical population of inpatient, outpatient, and residential treatment settings, although they constitute only 2% of the population at large (Kadushin, 1980). The fact that they are significantly overrepresented in the inpatient and residential treatment centers—up to 25% in some centers—may be suggestive of the presence of serious dysfunction.

This overrepresentation is so consistently reported and frequently replicated across settings over the years that it is an accepted clinical fact. It is still unclear why such an overrepresentation exists. It is possible that the facts speak for themselves and that adopted children (for whatever reasons) have more emotional and behavioral problems and thus are aptly overrepresented in mental health facilities. But other explanations are also possible. One is that adoptive parents tend to represent a more educated, higher socioeconomic group of people more likely to turn to mental health facilities and are no more overrepresented than other demographically similar parents. Another possibility is that adoptive parents, having successfully turned to agencies for placement of their child, feel more trusting and more ready to seek further help than their nonadoptive counterparts. Some clinicians have suggested other psychological motivations—for instance, a secret wish to return the child to an agency or to have the agency "fix" what they feel are damaged goods.

Clinical studies and research findings suggest differences in the presenting symptomatology between these children and nonadoptees. Adoptees are more likely to present with problems of an "acting out" and externalizing nature such as lying, stealing, running away, impulsivity, and aggression in addition to learning difficulties and attention deficit disorder. Many explanations for these difficulties are offered.

Clinically, adoptees present with some common themes. One theme is a sense of being unwanted, rejected, or abandoned by birth parents. They develop fantasies to explain or explain away these distressing feelings. Adoptees then struggle with why they were unwanted and whose fault it was—their own or their birth parents. Adoptive parents are sometimes pitted against birth parents to determine who is "good" or "bad." During adolescence, adoptees attempt to separate from both adoptive parents and images of birth parents in determining their sense of self and identity. This struggle can be more or less intense, with adoptees identifying with adoptive parents and also with their fantasized images of the birth parents. Others may feel less of a struggle and more easily integrate their biological heritage with their adoptive upbringing. Out of these clinical experiences with referred adoptees, some clinicians conclude that these children are susceptible to a level of psychological risk greater than nonadoptees. In addition, clinicians have identified adoptive parents' unresolved conflicts regarding infertility, idealization of their fantasied biological child, and marital problems as significant factors impinging on the development of the adopted child (Brinich, 1990).

Research studies raise important questions as we try to assess how adopted children fare along the path of development. Unfortunately, research to date has been so flawed methodologically that it provides few definitive answers. These studies suffer from being based on few clinical cases, on anecdotal reports, or on a highly selected sample of volunteers or support group members and generally on samples small in size. Their conclusions are thus derived from the study of a small percentage of the adoptee population at large, primarily those who become known to researchers by being a part of either the clinical population or of preestablished, self-selected support groups. It is difficult to say how representative these two groups of adoptees vis-à-vis the total adoptee population are. We still know very little about the large number of adoptees who do not make their presence known in these ways. More important, there has been no significant research on adoptees once they reach adulthood. They are rarely mentioned in the psychological literature. It may be that adoptive status has been generally overlooked as a significant factor in the emotional life of adult patients.

Clinical Implications of Adoption Issues

It is clear that adoptees face special issues and challenges. They have to confront the fact of their relinquishment, the physical and emotional loss, and of their adoptive status as well as making sense of it in the context of their experience with their adoptive families (Hajal & Rosenberg, 1991).

All adoptees will struggle with the significance of this fact of their lives. According to their varied coping styles, some will "think it out," some will "talk it out," and yet some others will "act it out"; others will use a combination of all these. Adoptive parents provide the most positive context for their child's development when they are clearly committed to the permanency of the relationship and can accept their child's special tasks.

Sometimes it may be unclear whether an adoptee is struggling adequately with his or her special tasks or whether he or she, in fact, needs some extra help. How does a parent or adoptee know that it is necessary to seek such help? Two guidelines may be useful. The first is that adopted children need help when they are arrested in their development and seem unable to progress. For example, if a girl is unable to move beyond the testing of the permanency of the relationship and is mired in a provocative struggle, she needs help with whatever is keeping her stuck. Or, if, in processing the news of adoption, she cannot get beyond blaming her adoptive parents for her relinquishment, she needs someone besides her parents to talk to.

A second guideline is that adopted children need help when they deviate significantly from their own developmental task. That is, instead of a mastery of age-appropriate developmental tasks, a process that naturally includes progressions as well as digressions and regressions, they "opt out." This opting out may take the form of dysfunctional behavior or of persistent disturbance of mood.

Even in the very best of family circumstances, the inherent nature of adoptees' issues make it more difficult for them to discuss their internal conflicts with their adoptive parents. The neutrality of a support group or a therapist is thus sometimes necessary and can be highly effective in helping adoptees get "unstuck" or back on a healthy developmental course.

Members of the adoption circle need and often request clinical services at different points along their developmental courses: a pregnant teenager, an infertile couple with marital problems, adoptive parents referring their 13-year-old son because of school failure, a 60-year-old birth mother with depression. Each referral offers opportunities for remediation of past or current dysfunction and also for prevention of future difficulties.

The clinician's task is to take adoption issues into consideration during the assessment phase as well as when designing and implementing therapeutic interventions. Clinicians run the risk of either minimizing or exaggerating the relevance of adoption issues. Historically, the view of adoption as a perfect solution, from which no special problems were expected, supported a minimizing bias. The majority of mental health practitioners are still woefully uninformed regarding adoption issues. These authors often see referred adopted children who have been in intensive inpatient or residential treatment where adoption and its related issues have never been raised in spite of the fact that clinicians knew that an adoption had occurred.

At the other extreme are clinicians who exaggerate adoption's significance and view all feelings and behavior through an adoption lens. This is particularly true of some specialists who, working predominantly or exclusively with the adoption circle population, become mired in a rigid and narrow view of their clients' experiences. A well-informed and open-minded clinician seeks to assess and understand the individual structure of each participant, their lifelong developmental course, as well as the family and social systems to which they belong.

The Process of Clinical Assessment and Treatment in the Adoption Circle

Clinical work in the adoption circle relies on our basic understanding of individual and family dynamics; in addition it is informed by the particular issues that this alternative family structure evokes. Clinicians use their proven skills while taking into consideration the special tasks of members of the adoptive family system.

The most common clinical presentation is that of an acting-out adolescent adoptee and his or her distraught parents. The presentation may or may not include references to participation in an adoption either as a primary participant or as an extended family member. Generally, relationships to adoption are not mentioned immediately unless specifically asked for. Rather, it is likely to emerge, sometimes as an afterthought, in the assessment stage of clinical work. Occasionally, adoption remains a family secret. In the birth parent's families of origin and procreation, relinquishment remains a secret more frequently. The manner in which the clinician deals with the presence of an adoptive relationship often constitutes a significant therapeutic intervention. By responding matter-of-factly to this information as a significant life event while recognizing everyone's effort at adaptation and coping, the therapist both acknowledges the challenge and diminishes the toxicity of the experience. Some will feel relief that this aspect of their life is (finally) taken seriously. Others may find reassurance in hearing that adoption is not necessarily scarring and pathogenic event.

Assessment of individual needs ought to include, but should not be exclusively based on, exploration of adoption-related issues. Clinicians need to collect data that enable them to understand the personality structure and psychodynamics of the patient and the ways in which adoption issues play a part in both. Such an assessment requires exploration of individual, family, and sociocultural dynamics in their developmental context. Ideally, clinicians would collect relevant data through individual and family interviews. Even when this is not possible, construction of a genogram and ecogram can provide salient information; they also sometimes serve as therapeutic tools.

Special Features of Clinical Work in Adoption

In recent years therapists have begun to address adoption issues in clinical work. Each author suggests basic principles in working with members of the adoption circle (Hartman, 1984; Reitz & Watson, 1992; Rosenberg, 1992; Winkler, Brown, van Keppel & Blanchard, 1988).

ACKNOWLEDGMENT OF THE CIRCLE

Assessment and treatment of any individual or subsystem of the adoption circle must be undertaken with the awareness of the circle as a whole and the ways in which its participants remain part of each other's worlds in fantasy or reality over the course of their lifetime. No one forgets about the existence of the other. Participants need to be encouraged to allow thoughts and feelings about those cut-off, yet significant, people, who remain a ghostlike presence in their lives, lest their suppression proves an interference with their mastery of developmental tasks.

There may be cases where supporting efforts at searching for birth parents or adoptees may be an important part of the therapeutic work. The treatment plan might then also include found members if they need help in adjusting to one another.

NORMALIZATION OF SPECIAL TASKS

An important aspect of a therapeutic approach is the normalization or legitimation of the special developmental tasks of each participant. The recognition that it is legitimate for them to deal with special adoption-related issues lessens the feeling of deviancy and detoxifies the struggle. This kind of normalization can be enhanced through membership in support groups that focus on threads of commonality woven through the fabric of different family and life experiences.

ACCEPTANCE OF THE NEED FOR ALTERNATIVE COURSES

Associated with normalization of special tasks is the acceptance of an alternative course in one's development. For example, birth parents may need to wait longer to bear more children than their counterparts who never relinquished. Children who are adopted at an older age may need a strong holding environment that other children would find overly restrictive. Adoptive parents may feel that their children do not launch into adulthood as easily as their friends' children, since their issues around identity and separation are more complex. Searches and reunions, or some kind of contact between birth parent and adoptees over the years, may be part of the family life. It is natural that an alternative family structure would involve at times alternative courses of development.

SUPPORT OF HEALTHY DEFENSES

Special developmental tasks and an alternative course should not imply that members of the adoption circle do not have the same basic needs as other individuals. Therapists have frequently observed the negative consequences of individual denial and family secrets. With such experience, it is easy to overlook the need for ordinary defenses that vary over time. There is a natural ebb and flow in the salience and intensity of adoption issues for all involved. At times they are primary and must be addressed. At other times individuals need to comfort themselves with a healthy degree of denial or other defenses. The skillful therapist recognizes these needs as they emerge and supports them.

14

MANAGEMENT OF COUNTERTRANSFERENCE

The formation of an adoption circle involves important human and social issues, such as the creation of life; responsibility for children; needs and rights of children, adoptees, and birth parents. The primacy of these issues will stir up a wide range of thoughts and feelings in clinicians that may threaten their clarity and effectiveness. These feelings must be recognized and managed in a way that allows for even-minded assessment and treatment of a very complicated and often highly charged clinical presentation.

TRANSFERENCE

Therapists working with the adoption circle may become the birth parents', adoptive parents', or adoptees' object of transference of feelings toward any of the cast of characters involved. They may be experienced as the social worker (especially if, in fact, they *are* social workers by training) who gives and/or takes children away. They may at times be the overprotective adoptive parent or the rejecting birth parent. A common and powerful transference is the adoptee experiencing therapists (even males) as the birth mother. They may at times be seen as the idealized birth mother who has (finally) arrived to rescue and tend to the adoptee. With a canceled session or vacation, the therapists may quickly become the abandoning one. Adoptive parents may reexperience competitive feelings with birth parents and see a therapist as one who has become the better parent. If not attended to, such transferences can seriously compromise if not destroy the treatment efforts. Proper interpretation, instead, can be highly productive and enhance the outcome.

TERMINATION

The profound losses experienced by all adoption circle members makes termination a crucial phase in treatment. This is a time when work on previous losses will be revisited and reexperienced. In saying "good-bye" to therapists, patients say "good-bye" to others who have been important forces in their lives. Therapists working in the adoption circle need to be sure to allow sufficient time and opportunity for this important work to be completed.

In summary, treatment of members of the adoption circle occurs at many possible points along the life cycle. To be effective, such treatment needs to be undertaken with an awareness of the functioning of the adoption circle and the likely impact of membership in such a circle on the patients' own psychological and social functioning. Such informed clinicians and therapists are best prepared to use their special skills in addition to their established general ones to assist birth parents, adoptive parents, adoptees, and their extended families in their efforts at coping and adaptation.

Sorting out the "facts" of their life in ways that feel so often incongruous and conflictual, adoptees are likely (and accurately) to feel that they have gone through more and "sweated" more than nonadopted people. Through this process, it is hoped that they will come to accept the notion that their adoption was not a matter of good and bad adults or good and bad children. It is, rather, a matter of life circumstances. Mastery requires a genuine acceptance of their life circumstances and the paradoxes they created. Satisfaction can be taken in this mastery with full credence given to wishing it would have been different.

REFERENCES

Brinich, P. (1990). Adoption from the inside out: A psychoanalytic perspective. In D. M. Brodzinski & M. D. Schecter (Eds.), *The psychology of adoption* (pp. 42–61). New York: Oxford University Press.

Brodzinsky, D. M., Singer, L. M., & Braff, A. M. (1984). Children's understanding of adoption. *Child Development, 55,* 869–878.

Cadoret, R. (1990). Biologic perspectives of adoptee adjustment. In D. M. Brodzinski & M. D. Schecter, *The psychology of adoption.* New York: Oxford University Press.

Hajal, R., & Rosenberg, E. (1991). The family life cycle in adoptive families. *American Journal of Orthopsychiatry, 25,* 541–551.

Hartman, A. (1984). *Working with adoptive families beyond placement.* New York: Child Welfare League of America.

Kadushin, A. (1980). *Child Welfare Services* (3rd ed.) New York: Macmillan.

Pickar, J. L. *Children's understanding of parenthood.* Unpublished diss., University of Michigan, 1986).

Reitz, M., & Watson, K. W. (1992). *Adoption and the family system.* New York: Guilford Press.

Rosenberg, E. (1992). *The adoption life cycle.* New York: Free Press.

Rosenberg, E., & Horner, T. (1991). Birthparent romances and identity formation in adopted children. *American Journal of Orthopsychiatry, 61,* 70–77.

Winkler, R. C., Brown, D. W., van Keppel, M., & Blanchard, A. (1988). *Clinical practice in adoption.* New York: Pergamon Press.

Zill, N. (1985). *Findings from a U.S. national survey of child health.* Paper presented at the meeting of the Society for Research in Child Development, Toronto.

2 / Central City Families

Jeanne Spurlock and Ian A. Canino

Central city families are from a variety of racial and ethnic backgrounds. Among them are rural-to-urban migrants (including American Indians), foreign immigrants, minorities, and whites at the lower rungs of the socioeconomic level. Whoever they may be, they are all exposed to a variety of different stressors. Wilson's (1987) depiction of inner cities points to the commonplace stressors experienced by the residents:

. . . The flight of the more affluent families to the suburbs has meant that the central cities are becoming increasingly the domain of the poor and the stable working class. Thus, in major cities such as New York, Chicago, Atlanta, Washington, D.C., Philadelphia, St. Louis and Detroit, not only have public schools become overwhelmingly populated with minority students, but the background of both minority and white students is primarily working or lower class. . . . Changes in societal organization have created situations that enhance racial antagonism between those groups that are trapped in central cities and are victimized by deteriorating services and institutions that serve the city. (P. 136)

Central city families may contain children born within an intact family structure or to a single mother. Regardless of the structure of their family at the time of their birth, many central city children, especially African Americans and Puerto Ricans, are likely to live most of their childhood in a single-parent household or in foster care. Even though we have known single- and two-parent families in the central cities that function reasonably well in spite of a myriad of problems (e.g., poor housing, street violence, underemployment, or unemployment), the families that most often attend our clinics are barely managing. The single mother may or may not have some support (financial and emotional) from her family of origin or the child's father. Some families are totally dysfunctional. Their children are severely neglected or abandoned; a significant number are likely to live on the streets or, in adolescence, become confined to a correctional institution. Poverty and violence—within the homes and in the broad environment—are commonplace.

The antagonisms that exist between the central residents and nonresident business owners, many of whom are recent immigrants from Asian countries, often have added to the unrest of the communities. The unfamiliarity that each group has about the culture of the other group often serves to trigger a range of clashes.

Canino and Spurlock (1994) noted that many of the conclusions drawn by Rutter (1982) in his study of special stresses experienced by families of central city London parallel those experienced by families in the central city communities in the United States. The children we have known were not unlike those whose most characteristic problems were "those beginning early, lasting a long time, and accompanied by many other problems in the family" (P. 357).

Poverty

In recent years the steady move of industry from the cities to suburbia and to foreign shores has heightened the poverty status of central city families. Poverty may have detrimental effects, of monumental proportions, throughout the life cycle of individuals who are classified in this category. To be poor may mean that pregnant women receive inadequate or late prenatal care, which, in turn, may lead to premature birth and/or infant morbidity and mortality. To grow up in an environment in which a high percentage of adults are unemployed or underemployed lends to a tarnishing of a child's notion that schooling is important and serves as a significant stepping stone to adulthood.

Feelings of powerlessness and depression, if not despair, are rooted in part in the joblessness that exists in many pockets of the central cities. The multiple sequelae include the use of alcohol and other drugs to quell the depression and anxieties; then addiction takes over. The most powerless—the children—become easy targets for the parents' anger and despair about the condition in which they find themselves. Thus, the resultant violence (child and spousal abuse) completes one of the circular patterns so prominent in large urban areas. The impact of chronic unemployent on the psyches of central city families was addressed by the Carnegie Council on Children (Keniston, 1977):

Unemployment, low wages and discriminatory barriers to employment that affect parents are directly translated into harmful effects on their children. Young children, whether or not they understand what their parents do, form an impression of whether the work world esteems their parents. A parent does not have to say a word to communicate a feeling of helplessness, powerlessness, worthlessness, or futility to a child. (P. 84)

To be poor in many pockets of the central cities is likely to mean living in unsafe housing in a crime-ridden neighborhood and being subjected to serious injury within the home as well as on the streets. As noted in a report of the predicaments of African Americans (Jaynes & Williams, 1989):

. . . the highest rates of injuries occur in or near the home. Injuries are related to socioeconomic status: poor children are very likely to live in areas in which heavy traffic patterns lead to pedestrian injury . . . there are dilapidated or abandoned structures, and there is dangerous or uncollected litter. Within the house, unrepaired stairwells and inadequate or absent screens or window guards expose children to the risks of falls. Missing smoke detectors along with defective heaters and other household appliances pose fire hazards. Poor homes are almost more likely to contain toxic substances, such as chemicals for pest control or peeling lead paint. (Pp. 405–406)

We would add that the foregoing applies to most poor, central city families, regardless of race or ethnicity.

Poverty also is reflected in the schools. In their study of the history of education in the United States, Bowles and Gintis (1976) determined that the educational system within central city schools ensures the future economic inadequacies of minority students. They found the internal environments, methods of teaching, and attitudes toward students to be much different than that which was found in middle-class, predominantly white schools in the suburbs. Kozol's (1991) recent study of a sampling of central city schools provides vivid illustrations.

The atmosphere within the schools is often not conducive to study and "book learning." Often, children are not encouraged to learn. We have known teachers who tend to "write off" African Americans as early as the third grade. This is not to suggest that there are no teachers who inspire and foster positive self-esteem in their students, who "go that extra mile" in teaching and promoting sound study habits, and who reach out to parents. Unfortunately, many teachers are on the verge of "burnout" because of the conditions within the school (e.g., inadequate supplies and equipment, building code violations, etc.). Thus, some school experiences can heighten risk factors to children, although others can offer increased protection (Canino & Spurlock, 1994). Some children we have known entered school with shaky self-esteem that became further damaged by a series of negative experiences within the school setting. So it has been with children who have had a teacher who has sent a message that their linguistic style is inferior to standard English. Comer (1991) points out that the "almost exclusive focus of school on instruction and curriculum, without attention to issues of relationships and development, is probably at the root of academic underachievement of many students" (p. 1084). Furthermore,

parents often lack education themselves or bear social and psychological scars related to their social status and conditions. They often sense exclusion and feel alienated from the mainstream of society. They often carry some attitudes, values, and ways that are different from those of the mainstream . . . even when they want to prepare their children to succeed in school—a mainstream institution—they are not able to adequately do so. (P. 1086).

As noted previously, the physical health of many central city children may be impaired because the economic status of their parents may not allow for care directed toward health maintenance and disease prevention during the full range of development. Babies are born at risk and may continue to be at risk because of poor nutrition, accidental injuries, and environmental pollution. Poor nutrition often is reinforced by the excessive use of junk and fast foods as an almost steady diet. Iron-deficiency anemia, which often goes undetected for some time because of the absence of routine medical care, is a common finding in these children. Because of low immunization rates, central city children suffer more infectious diseases than their peers from more economically stable families. Although few American children, if any, are free of exposure to lead, the exposure is probably more severe for central city children because of the heavy traffic patterns and old housing with interior lead paint chips, which crawling babies and toddlers often pick up and ingest. Children with high lead blood levels have been reported to score significantly less well on the Weschler Intelligence Scale for Children (Revised) than those with low levels. They also have an impaired attention span and are less competent than children with low levels in the areas of verbal performance and auditory processing (Needleman, Gunnal, Leriton, Reed, Peresie, Maher, & Barrett, 1979).

In a 20-year-long longitudinal study, investigators determined that "perinatal complications were consistently related to later impaired physical and psychological development when combined with consistently poor mental circumstances . . ." (Werner & Smith, 1982, p. 31). The absence of, or late, prenatal care received by many women, particularly African American and His-

panic adolescents, is likely to yield perinatal problems. The potential difficulties inherent in such beginnings are compounded by the hazardous conditions of the external environment. The chronic stressors make a greater impact when internal mediators are impaired, as often happens in children with perinatal problems. In such instances, poor impulse control, sensorimotor deficits, unusual sensitivities, and inability to read caregivers' cues are likely to occur (Murphy & Moriarity, 1976). When mothers cannot read the cues of their infants, as often happens with young mothers who have not had their own developmental needs met, the problems are accentuated. The foregoing is a familiar history of children who present with a symptom picture of a disruptive behavior disorder.

The occurrence of a number of other preventable illnesses is rooted, for the most part, in poverty.

. . . According to the 1989 White House Task Force Report on Infant Mortality, at least 25 percent of infant deaths could be prevented. For every infant who dies, another 10 will be left with permanent disabilities. Twenty-five percent of these disabilities could be prevented, as well. Three in 10 U.S. infants and toddlers go without adequate childhood immunizations and face the nearly unimaginable risks in a civilized society and lifelong disability from preventable childhood disease. (Rosenbaum, Layton, & Liu, 1991, p. 1)

Rosenbaum, Layton, and Liu, writing in a report for the Children's Defense Fund, highlighted several key findings that warrant emphasis.

- In 1988, less than 76% of all infants were born to mothers who received prenatal care within the first 3 months of pregnancy. Black and Mexican American infants were far less likely to be born to mothers who received early prenatal care—61% and 58%, respectively.
- In 1990, well over 25,000 cases of measles were reported. More children died of measles that year than in any year since 1971.
- Too often families cannot get needed health care they need because they lack insurance. Only 83% of all children in families with annual incomes of less than $25,000 were likely to have health coverage.

Physical risk factors are known to be closely linked with and/or strengthen the roots of cognition, emotional, and social disorders. The psychological sequelae, as illustrated by behavior and cognitive disorders, vividly illustrate the connections.

The inadequacy or unavailability (for whatever reason) of health care services in the central city communities are major roots for the chronic illnesses that befall so many of the young. Generally, psychologically as well as physically, strains are set off. Access to services continues to be a problem of considerable significance for children and families of the lower socioeconomic groups in general and for multiproblem children and their families in particular. A number of factors serve as barriers, ranging from eligibility rules, to service program availability, to parents' limited finances and time to avail themselves of the offered services. The health care system's concentration on specialized services rather than on comprehensive care is often a barrier for multiproblem families (Canino & Spurlock, 1994). The overt biases of those providers who view a cultural difference as deviant also serve to discourage a sizable number of inner city families from seeking services from some facilities. In addition, limited hours (during the standard work week—Monday to Friday, 9:00–5:00) of the availability of some services restrict the access for employed parents who cannot take time off from work without a cut in their paycheck. These factors certainly act as barriers to early and effective intervention and cause disease exacerbation and a poor prognosis due to inefficient follow-up.

Poverty thus can create symptoms of depression and powerlessness, exacerbate learning disorders through inadequate and poor schooling, and certainly cause, through disease and poor health care, neurological damage precipitating irritability, impulsivity, and inattention.

The Epidemic of Violence

COMMUNITY VIOLENCE

The availability and open selling of drugs and guns account for a high percentage of violence that takes place in central city communities. News reports constantly address the ready availability of guns and drive-by shootings.

A law enforcement officer (Supenski, 1989) noted that gang fights have come to be deadly to bystanders as well as to the active participants. "Knives are out. Nine millimeters are in. Clubs have become replaced by Colts; bats by Berettas. Death is automated; fast and indiscriminate" (p. 72). Observations reported by Hechinger (1982) have become commonplace in many communities, but perhaps more so in the central cities.

. . . Conflicts that used to end in fistfights are now increasingly resolved with the use of deadly knives and guns. Often shots are fired over the acquisition of material goods—leather jackets, running shoes, stereos—or as a tragic, ritualized response to a verbal slight or "show" of disrespect. "Dissing," the slang expression for any affront to a youngster's "reputation," can be the cause for a teenage death sentence. And such death sentences are carried out with terrifying frequency as disadvantaged young people cut off from the possibilities of mainstream success create their own brutal societies. (P. 150)

Homicide has become the leading cause of death of African American youth and young adults; they were 43% of homicide victims (Hamburg et al., 1989). The ages of the victims and perpetrators have declined to the extent that pre-adolescents are now identified in the statistics (Earls, 1994).

SCHOOL VIOLENCE

Regrettably, violence has spilled over into the schools. There are almost daily reports that a child or adolescent (most often a male) has brought a gun to school. Administrators of some schools have installed metal detectors; others are considering taking similar action. Armed police are stationed in the corridors of some schools; however, their presence has not always prevented a homicide.

One of the authors was asked to confer with a group of school nurses and counselors to help them deal with their growing anxieties about violence. Almost daily they had to comfort students who were experiencing a range of psychological and psychosomatic responses to a recent act of neighborhood violence. Several of the personnel were at the point of burnout. There was no question that they were secondary victims, as teachers and administrators apparently are. Some school systems have organized crisis intervention sessions for students immediately after any incident in which a student has been a victim of violence. Some schools hold safety drills for the purpose of teaching children measures they can take to protect themselves from drive-by shootings (Hechinger, 1992). A few schools are implementing "conflict resolution" teaching approaches to prevent further violence.

FAMILY VIOLENCE

Family violence also must be addressed, even though this pattern of violence is not limited to central city families. Nevertheless, the violence directed toward family members is an acute problem throughout the central cities. This finding is related in part to the stresses that are generated by conditions embedded in poverty (e.g., overcrowded and poorly heated in winter/poorly ventilated in summer housing, inadequate funds for essentials). A child born prematurely and/or one with a chronic illness needs intensive parenting. Such situations can be overwhelming to many mothers, who come to see the child as demanding, as the mothers become increasingly depressed or overtly angry or out of control. Such reactions commonly are seen among adolescent mothers who are not prepared for the responsibilities of parenting (Canino & Spurlock, 1994). Of course, adolescent mothers are not the only child abusers, and stress that provokes the violent response is as varied as is the victimizer's personality pattern. Regarding the latter, Wilking (1979) notes that many investigators have focused on the mother's self-esteem, overidentification of mother and child, poor emotional control and anger, and the nature of the maternal expectations; however, the impact of depression, which is commonplace among mothers of the lower socioeconomic classes who abuse, warrants further exploration.

As noted previously, people often use alcohol and other drugs to cope with depression; then addiction may take over and violence often follows. Often men who beat the women in their lives are under the influence of alcohol. Drinking, however, is not always the sole factor; that is, intoxication may unleash overwhelming feelings of low self-esteem and powerlessness. For these abusers, the sense of power and control is restored through the acts of violence directed toward someone even more powerless. Novelist Gloria Naylor (1982) provides a vivid illustration in an account of the musings of the protagonist, Cora Lee, about the father of her oldest children:

. . . a pot of burnt rice would mean a fractured jaw, or a wet bathroom floor a loose tooth, but that had been their [the children's] fault for keeping her so tied up she couldn't keep the house straight. But she still carried the scar under her left eye because of a baby's crying. Babies had to cry sometimes, and so Sammy and Maybelline's father had to go. (P. 113)

Although a piece of fiction, Naylor's portrayal of Cora Lee is not unlike the situation of many battered women. The impact of violence on a child's development will span from learned conflict-resolution techniques, identification with the aggressor, the development of poor frustration tolerance and certainly, and, most worrisome, tolerance to higher degrees of violence. The case of a young adolescent, known to one of us, is illustrative.

CASE EXAMPLE

Thirteen-year-old Malcolm was a product of a two-parent violent family. His father, a binge alcoholic, was physically and verbally abusive to his wife and occasionally to the older children. Malcolm and three of his five siblings had sustained numerous injuries, ranging from falls from varying heights to ingestion of toxic agents.

Malcolm first became known to the mental health system when he was in the first grade. Referral had been made by the teacher because of the child's abusive behavior toward his peers. Malcolm would/could not listen to reason and tended to view someone else at fault whenever a conflict arose. This characteristic apparently had heightened during the course of years and was readily apparent when referred for psychiatric evaluation at age 13 because of an assault on Jimmy, a same-age opponent on a basketball court. The referral complaint also noted a history of truancy from school and three episodes of overnight absence from his home in the past year.

Malcolm, who wore a sullen expression at the time of the examination, appeared to be older than his stated age. He readily admitted to the assault on the other adolescent, whom he described as a "nerd." He insisted that Jimmy "got what he deserved because he 'dissed' me." In response to the examiner's request for clarification, Malcolm commented about previous encounters with Jimmy, who laughed at his (Malcolm's) erroneous response to a teacher's question; also, Jimmy "looked at me funny" when they passed in the school corridor.

His reports of the wrongdoings of others had a paranoid coloring.

The examiner's inquiries about Malcolm's life history revealed the following pertinent points:

- His mother is the person whom he loves the most, even though she "takes too much stuff" from his father.
- He hates his father, especially when he "comes home drunk"and when he beats his mother and/or his siblings.
- Since he's gotten bigger and stronger, he "won't take anything off nobody," although he can't yet take on his father (the latter in response to examiner's question, "Your father, too?")
- Sometimes he feels sad, "but I fight it off." (Again, he was unable to elaborate.)
- He hasn't given much thought about long-term goals—"Maybe pro-basketball."

Making use of the referral history and information gleaned from the examination, the examiner concluded that the violence within the family provided a model of behavior for Malcolm (and probably for his siblings, as well). A question was raised about the possibility of central nervous system insults as one of the root causes for the impulsivity and aggressive behavior, although a significant origin was a displacement of the anger that stemmed from the father's chronic abusive behavior. Referral was made for a neurological evaluation; conduct disorder was the psychiatric working diagnosis.

Other children whom we have known, who have been exposed to family and/or neighborhood violence, develop multiple fears and anxieties and are clearly victims of posttraumatic stress disorder. So it was for 10-year-old Vivian, who had migrated with her family to an East Coast central city community from a semirural town in the mid-South. Although the family was knowledgeable about acts of violence in the inner cities, members were not prepared for the enormity of the transgressions that took place in their immediate neighborhood and within the school. Before Vivian witnessed a drive-by shooting, she had been an outgoing child. A month later she was described as withdrawn socially and easily startled by loud sounds, and she experienced frequent nightmares about the event. Reluctance to attend school had replaced her past eagerness, and she refused to take the route that would necessitate her going past the site of the shooting. Her three friends who had been with her at the time of the incident experienced similar responses.

In spite of multiple stressors that affect their lives daily, some central city families are able to raise reasonably healthy children. A variety of factors are operative in deflecting and reducing the power of the stressors. Support networks appear to be the key agents. Members of the extended family, including biological, "adopted," and "adopting" kin, serve as protective and stabilizing promoters of growth. A great-aunt served such a role for an African American family of seven—five children and their parents. Before and after school, she was there to be an appropriate disciplinary figure (to train as well as chastise for misbehavior). She also served as mother's counselor during the periods of father's unemployment, which were usually coupled with heavy (but quiet) drinking. Previously, Aunt Mary had been there at periods of crisis for other units of the family clan. When asked about the source of her strength, she spoke of her ties to her religion and the supportive networks within her church. For many ethnic groups, religion and religious leaders are important agents of sustenance.

For other families, the aforementioned support networks are not available, or are overpowered by the intensity of the multiple stressors that create their impact simultaneously and with chronicity. These stressors are more prevalent in some pockets of the central cities than in others. Street violence as well as violence occurring within overly crowded apartment buildings and schools allows for little, if any, respite from the anxieties and fears of the residents. For many children, the chronicity and number of stressful events overwhelm their adaptive capacities. So it was for 8-year-old Aimee, who with her mother had recently migrated to a large central city from a rural community in the West Indies. Nightmares, worries, and concerns for her mother's safety were noted as complaints at the time of the referral to a community mental health center. The history also revealed that Aimee had witnessed several assaults and had herself once been assaulted on her way home from school. A crack raid had occurred in the next apartment the week before the evaluation. The history and Aimee's clinical picture met the diagnostic criteria for separation anxiety disorder and posttraumatic stress disorder (Canino & Spurlock, 1994).

Responses of Children to the Central Environment

RESPONSE TO THE COMMUNITY

Some sociological studies (Mancini, 1980; Rainwater, 1966) have yielded findings that point to specific coping styles of African American center city youth. In our experience, some of these findings are applicable to center city youth, regardless of their ethnic or racial identity. Rainwater (1966) identifies three kinds of survival strategies: "(1) expressive life style wherein an effort is made to make oneself interesting to others in order to be in a better position to manipulate them; (2) violent strategy whereby one forces others to give what one needs; (3) depressive strategy which lends to the development of goals [that] are increasingly constricted to the bare necessities for survival" (p. 107). Mancini's study, which focuses on adolescent males in Roxbury, a center city community of Boston, identified the following styles:

THE COOL GUY:	the together guy
	the supercool guy
THE CONFORMIST:	the all right guy
	the too-good guy
THE TOUGH GUY:	the real tough guy
	the troublemaker
THE ACTOR:	the put-on
	the con artist
THE RETREATER:	the withdrawn kid
	the loner
	(Mancini, 1980, p. 15)

The tough guy, which is akin to Rainwater's violent strategy, could be an African American or Hispanic girl or an Asian or Hispanic guy—all members of a particular gang. Children and adolescents who handle their conflicts through aggressive behavior are not necessarily involved with a gang. Often aggressive behavior is first noted in the immediate environment of the home. Since the family is the first and an important agent of socialization for children, it is not unlikely that a boy who sees his father beat his mother as a means of resolving a conflict will develop a similar pattern. Thus, this child may strike out physically at others (e.g., a teacher, a sibling, a friend, or even his mother) in response to a conflict of any kind. Un-fortunately, the far-reaching consequences of witnessing family violence extends into adulthood, when the former child witness beats his girlfriend or his wife. The retreater fits the description of many center city youth, of whatever race or ethnicity, who respond to their everyday life circumstances with feelings of hopelessness and despair. For some children and adolescents, withdrawn behavior becomes coupled with several precise symptoms (e.g., expressions of worthlessness, changes in sleep patterns, suicidal ideations) of a depressive disorder. The use of alcohol and other drugs is not uncommon and may lend to a dual diagnosis. A 16-year-old Caucasian girl, a recent migrant from a rural community in another state, reported that she drank wine coolers because it made her feel better when she was "down." She has felt "down" since shortly after the family's arrival to the city "where people are so different from us." Thus, self-medication may be the beginning of drug addiction. The beginning also might be "accidental" in that an adolescent is unaware that experimentation with a drug (e.g., crack cocaine) is equivalent to addiction. Since crack heightens sexual urges and diminishes judgment, it follows that the female adolescent is likely to become pregnant; the continued and the earlier use of the drug subjects the infant to intrauterine addiction and withdrawal symptoms at birth and postnatal neglect. Should the substance abuse continue, as it often does, delinquent patterns (e.g., stealing, exchange of sexual favors for drugs) are developed, or accentuated if they have been previously established. This sequence is frequently observed in central city communities. The experiences of an 11-year-old boy, Antonio (Canino & Spurlock, 1994), are illustrative.

CASE EXAMPLE

[Antonio's] mother had begun to use cocaine prior to the time the school referred him to a child psychiatry clinic because of his disturbed and disturbing behavior in his first-grade classroom. At that time he was diagnosed as having an attention deficit hyperactivity disorder; treatment was recommended, and his mother was referred to a drug treatment facility. As happens in so many cases like this, neither the mother nor the clinic followed through. That is, according to the clinic record, the case was closed 6 weeks after the diagnostic evaluation because of failed appointments and the inability to contact the mother.

A second referral took place when Antonio was 11 years of age. This time the referral complaints included assaultive behavior, alleged stealing, and possible drug use. The source of drugs was thought to be his mother's supply. Antonio had been failed at least twice—by his mother and by the service system. Of course, his mother's problems did not occur in a vacuum and probably represent, in part, flaws in systems (including her own family system) from which she sought help.

RESPONSE TO THE SCHOOLS

Children's attainment of academic achievement is dependent, to a considerable degree, on their physical, emotional, and intellectual competence and family support. For those children who are compromised in any one, or all, of these areas, a sense of estrangement from the world of school is likely to develop.

Chronic subclinical malnutrition and neurological deficits are common physical problems in central city children. The clinical manifestations of the latter (which are rooted in the mother's use of alcohol or other substances during pregnancy), ranging from hyperactivity, to impulsivity, to attention deficits, make for mammoth barriers to learning.

Family problems can weigh heavily on children and divert energy and attention away from learning tasks. In order to protect themselves from the turmoil within the home, children find some protection in selective inattention. If and when this defense carries over into the school setting, a learning problem is bound to ensue. If a parent devalues education, and many depressed and "beaten down" parents do, it is likely that a child takes on this same attitude. If school is unimportant, why should a child be attentive to the teacher? On the other hand, scores of central city children are highly motivated to achieve; they, like their parents, illustrate that many families who live in the ghetto "are not of its culture" (p. 173) (Rainwater, 1966). That is, they have middle-class aspirations and desires to participate in the "American dream." Thus, unlike their unmotivated peers, academic failure has untoward psychological repercussions for them.

The emotional response to failure may range from the development of defensive attitudes of avoidance or denial, to aggressive or clowning behaviors. When the latter response occurs, the learning disability often becomes submerged as attention is directed to the child's "misbehavior." The children who "misbehave" are earmarked for suspension, especially in junior and senior high schools. The pattern of dropping out of school, which is commonplace in the center cities, may be rooted in these kinds of behavior; however, the patterns may be much more intricate than appears at first glance, since dropouts often are aided by the system's pattern of pushing some children out (e.g., "writing off" African American males as early as the third grade).

Some youths who fail project sense of devaluation onto the system and shift or reinforce their identification with others who have met with academic failure and then quickly drop out of school. In the course of such a shift, many of these adolescents redirect their energies into self-destructive and delinquent behavior. Unfortunately, most of these individuals get caught within the correctional system, where there is no screening or evaluation of psychological impairment.

RESPONSE TO THE FAMILY

A number of references have been made to the impairment of family functioning as a result of being exposed to multiple stressors, and their dire consequences. In some instances the impairment of parenting has led children to attempt to parent their parents, who may have a chronic illness, be severely mentally deteriorated, or be chronic substance abusers. These children have met with years of neglect, if not abuse, and as a result, they have become distrustful of adults. A sizable number of these children drop out of school. Many of those who remain in school display disruptive behavior in the classroom and do not perceive, or disregard, that there are consequences to their misbehavior. When parents have not had their own dependency needs met, they are likely to make unrealistic demands on their children. Some parents we have known expect a 5- or 6-year-old to assume responsibility for the care of an infant sibling. Schorr and Schorr (1988) provide a vivid illustration:

At 8:30 one evening, Lenore (age 6) arrived at a neighbor's door, her face contorted, cheeks and cream-colored party dress stained with tears. Through the sobs that racked her body, the child finally managed to explain. Her mother, who had gone out early that morning, leaving her in charge of her seven-month-old sister, had called to say she was spending the night away, and the girl should fix a bottle of formula for the baby. The six-year-old was confused about how to prepare the formula and frightened about spending the night alone with the baby. This was not the first time little Lenore had shown up in panic, but this young mother did not seem to recognize that this arrangement could be harmful to both little Lenore and her baby sister. (P. 144)

The family's fragile economy frequently serves as a partial root for a parent to collude with a child's antisocial behavior by asking no questions about the source of money that is used to buy various household appliances, furnishings, and luxury items. So it was for 16-year-old Carlos, who had been arrested for selling drugs. When his mother asked why he had done this and reprimanded him for getting into this "kind of trouble," he responded, "I did it for you and the kids."

For some children, efforts to adapt to family expectations become ego-alien. For many youngsters, the only way to cope is by isolating themselves from the family—by being away from home as much as possible (Wilking, 1979). Some become truant or runaways. For others, affiliation with a gang provides a sense of belonging, an experience that they have known only briefly, if at all. Whether these youngsters are members of a gang or not, they are likely to become involved in delinquent behavior—either to survive or because of their psychopathy.

Treatment

A cursory review of the literature points to a shift in views about the treatability of center city children and families. References reflecting positive outcomes have been supplanted by those recounting insurmountable barriers to the effective psychotherapeutic intervention with the use of "traditional" treatment modalities. The literature is also reflective of the apparent increase in severe psychopathology among center city residents. The contrast of the description of these residents seen in a psychiatric clinic in the 1960s and the 1980s is striking.

We do see patients with a variety of ego states, of achievement striving and levels, and persistent efforts to utilize available energies in the service of personal gratification. Many persons who reveal these variables come from the same environment that do many who are too apathetic, too paranoid, too defeated, too emotionally undernourished to be available for a problem-solving effort which call for a transactional relationship with another human being. (Spurlock & Cohen, 1969, P. 21)

Shaer's (1991) observations and formulations were based on his work with inner city youths who had experienced multiple and chronic traumas.

The children demonstrate a range of problems, but manifest behaviors often clustered around specific deficits. They are often impulsive and action oriented, tending not to use verbal mediation in problem-solving or conflict resolution. . . . Object relations reveal fixations at oral and anal phases with resort to splitting, or, at best, highly ambivalent interactions with others. . . . Concomitant with areas of both social and academic deficits, some areas of ego functioning seem to be extremely advanced, in particular a set of behaviors that have been termed "survival skills." . . . Despite facile friendliness which leads unsuspecting adults into being "conned," there appears to be deficits in the ability to trust. . . . A special quality of hypervigilance is apparent, the child sensitized to nuances in the therapist's emotional state or changes in the environment. What is therapeutically frustrating is the endless re-enactment of traumatic events; verbal interpretations do not lead to a binding of anxiety, but become the trigger for increased physical acting out. (P. 13)

Although limited in number, reports have been published about successful interventions with the use of psychoanalysis (Meers, 1970); psychoanalytically oriented psychotherapy (Spurlock & Cohen, 1969); and a range of other treatment modalities, ranging from cognitive (Canino & Spurlock, 1994; Cohen & Schleser, 1988; Petti, 1991), to advocacy (Benoit, 1988; Canino & Spurlock, 1994).

Parents' delays in seeking mental health services for their children should not be overlooked. Initial help seeking from family and community resources should be considered and evaluated in the course of clinical evaluation and treatment planning (McMiller & Weisz, 1996). Service providers who have discussed the successes in utilizing "traditional" techniques have addressed the multiple family and social problem and the need for services from other sources (e.g., schools, social welfare agencies) in conjunction with psychotherapeutic intervention. A comprehensive service system is certainly the preferred, if not ideal, service for multiproblem families. A number of such programs have been described (Adnopoz, Grisby, & Nagler, 1991; Kaplan, 1986; Schorr & Schorr, 1988), all of which have several common features. One, perhaps, is of particular significance: Therapy is available to all family members in the home setting. The singling out of this one feature is not to negate the importance of other aspects of these programs. Schorr and Schorr (1988) emphasized the following: (1) flexibility of staff and program structures; (2) child evaluated/treated "in the context of the family and the family in the context of its surroundings" (p. 257); (3) staff's establishment of solid personal relationships with the family; (4) "services are coherent and easy to use" (p. 258); (5) adaptation or circumvention of traditional professional and bureaucratic limitations as necessary to meet the needs of the family; (6) ability of professionals to redefine their roles in order to direct efforts to meet often unarticulated family needs.

The references that are focused on family-centered, home-based services do not specifically address cultural sensitivity on the part of the providers; however, attention given to this matter has been widespread (Gibbs, Huang, et al., 1989; Martinez, 1986; Rogler, Blumenthal, Malgady, & Costantino, 1987; Walker & LaDue, 1986; Wilkinson & Spurlock, 1986; Yamamoto, 1986). Canino and Spurlock (1994) discussed the use of prevention strategies within the sociocultural context of central city families.

Cultural sensitivity on the part of clinicians is essential in the implementation of any program that is to have any measure of success. Canino and Canino (1993) address this matter in a discussion of psychiatric care of Puerto Ricans. They point out that the "frequency of substance abuse in Puerto Rican males and of dysthymia in Puerto Rican females, and the frequency of somatic symptoms in the Puerto Rican population as a whole, should alert clinicians to the close relationship between culture and symptom expression" (p. 493).

Conclusion

A variety of racial and ethnic groups are represented among the families in the central cities. Low working-class status or actual poverty, coupled with exposure to multiple stressors, are common features of each group. The sequelae of poverty and the various earmarks of violence that characterize the neighborhoods lend to the numerous health problems, physical and psychological, that are experienced by residents of these communities.

The development and operation of additional comprehensive service systems are recommended as one of the important efforts to meet the needs of residents of central cities. Family centered, home-based programs should be highlighted in the planning. A broad range of services (e.g., traditional psychotherapies, indigenous healer interventions) should be available in sites that would lend to the accessiblity of services. Cultural sensitivity must be a central focus in training programs and continued education programs for providers. Community outreach, in order to inform residents of the nature of and benefits of mental health services, is essential.

REFERENCES

Adnopoz, J., Grisby, R. K., & Nagler, S. R. (1991). Multiproblem families and high-risk children and adolescents; causes and management. In M. Lewis (ed.), *Child and adolescent psychiatry: A comprehensive textbook* (pp. 1059–1066). Baltimore: Williams & Wilkins.

Benoit, M. B. (1988). The role of the mental health practitioner in child advocacy in the school system. In A. F. Coner-Edwards & J. Spurlock (Eds.), *Black families in crises: The middle class* (pp. 139–146). New York: Brunner/Mazel.

Bowles, S., & Gintis, S. (1976). *Schooling in capitalist America: Education and the contradictions of economic life.* New York: Basic Books.

Canino, I. A., & Canino, G. J. (1993). Psychiatric care of Puerto Ricans. In A. C. Gaw (ed.) *Culture, ethnicity and mental illness* (pp. 467–499). Washington, D.C.: American Psychiatric Press.

Canino, I. A., & Spurlock, J. (1994). *Culturally diverse children and adolescents: Assessment, diagnosis and treatment.* New York: The Guilford Press.

Cohen, R., & Schleser, R. (1984). Cognitive development and clinical interventions. In A. W. Meyers & W. E. Craighead (Eds.), *Cognitive behavior therapy with children* (pp. 45–68). New York: Plenum Press.

Comer, J. P. (1991). African American children and the school. In M. Lewis (Ed.), *Child and adolescent psychiatry: A comprehensive textbook* (pp. 1084–1091). Baltimore: Williams & Wilkins.

Earls, F. J. (1994). Violence and today's youth. In R. E. Behrman (ed). *The future of children, 4* (3), 4–23.

Gibbs, J. W., Huang, L. N. & Associates (1989): *Children of color: Psychological interventions with minority youth.* San Francisco: Jossey-Bass Publishers.

Hamburg, B. A., Davis, K. P., Haynes, M. A., Jackson, I. S., Lieberson, S., McAdoo, H. P., Parron, D. L., Rice, D. P., & Robins, L. N. (1989). Black Americans' health. In G. D. Jaynes & R. M. Williams (eds.), *A Common Destiny: Blacks and American Society* (pp. 393–450). Washington, D.C.: National Academy Press.

Hechinger, F. M. (1992). *Fateful choices: Healthy youth for the 21st century.* New York: Carnegie Corporation of New York.

House of Representatives. (1989). *Children and Guns.* Hearing before the Select Committee on Children, Youth and Families. Washington, DC: U.S. Government Printing Office.

Jaynes, G. D., & Williams, R. M. (1989). *A common destiny: Blacks and American society.* Washington, DC: National Academy Press.

Keniston, K. (1977). *All our children: The American family under pressure.* New York: Harcourt Brace Jovanovich.

Kozol, J. (1991). *Savage inequalities.* New York: Crown Publishers.

Mancini, J. (1980). *Strategic styles: Coping in the inner city.* Hanover, NH: University Press of New England.

Martinez, C. (1986). Hispanics: Psychiatric issues. In C. B. Wilkinson (Ed.), *Ethnic psychiatry* (pp. 61–88). New York: Plenum Medical Book Co.

McMiller, W. P., & Weisz, J. R. (1996). Help-seeking preceding mental health clinic intake among African-American, Latino and Caucasian youth. *Journal of the American Academy of Child and Adolescent Psychiatry, 35* (8), 1086–1094.

Meers, D. R. (1970). Contributions of a ghetto culture to symptom formation: Psychoanalytic studies of ego anomalies in childhood. *Psychoanalytic Study of the Child, 25,* 209–230.

Murphy, L. B., & Moriarity, A. E. (1976). *Vulnerability, coping and growth from infancy to adolescence.* New Haven, CT: Yale University Press.

Naylor, G. (1982). *The women of Brewster Place.* New York: Viking Press.

Needleman, H. L., Gunnal, C., Leriton, A., Read, R., Peresie, H., Maher, C., & Barrett, P. (1979). Deficits in psychological and classroom performance of children with elevated dentine lead levels. *New England Journal of Medicine, 300,* 689–695.

Petti, T. A. (1991). Cognitive therapies. In M. Lewis (Ed.), *Child and adolescent psychiatry: A comprehensive textbook* (pp. 831–841). Baltimore: Williams & Wilkins.

Rainwater, L. (1966). Crucible of identity: The Negro lower-class family. *Daedalus.* Richmond, VA: American Academy of Arts and Sciences, pp. 172–216.

Rogler, L. H., Blumenthal, R. G., Malgady, G., & Constantino, R. (1987). What do culturally sensitive mental health services mean? The case of Hispanics. *American Psychologist, 426,* 565–570.

Rosenbaum, S., Layton, C., & Liu, J. (1991). *The health of America's children.* Washington, DC: The Children's Defense Fund.

Rutter, M. (1982). The city and the child. In S. Chess & A. Thomas (Eds.), *Annual progress in child psychiatry and child development* (pp. 353–370). New York: Brunner/Mazel.

Schorr, L. B., & Schorr, D. (1988). *Within our reach: Breaking the cycle of disadvantage.* New York: Anchor Press.

Shaer, I. J. (1991). A theoretical conceptualization of the multiply traumatized inner-city child of poverty. *Newsletter.* Washington, DC: American Psychological Association *1* (1), 12–22.

Spurlock, J., & Cohen, R. S. (1969). Should the poor get none? *Journal of the American Academy of Child Psychiatry, 8,* 16–35.

Supenski, L. J. (1989). Statement of Col. Leonard Supenski, Chief, Crime Prevention Bureau, Baltimore County Police Department, Baltimore, MD. *Children and Guns* (pp. 70–74). Hearing before the Select Committee on Children, Youth and Families, House of Representatives. Washington, DC: U.S. Government Printing Office.

Walker, R. D., & LaDue, R. (1986). An integrative approach to American Indian mental health. In C. B. Wilkinson (Ed.), *Ethnic psychiatry* (pp. 143–194). New York: Plenum Medical Book Co.

Werner, E. E., & Smith, R. S. (1982). *Vulnerable but invincible: A study of resilient children.* New York: McGraw-Hill.

Wilking, V. N. (1979). The street child. In J. D. Call, J. D. Noshpitz, R. L. Cohen, & I. N. Berlin (Eds.), *Basic handbook of child psychiatry* (Vol. I, pp. 301–309). New York: Basic Books.

Wilkinson, C. B., & Spurlock, J. (1986). The mental health of Black Americans. Psychiatric diagnosis and treatment. In C. B. Wilkinson (Ed.), *Ethnic psychiatry* (pp. 13–60). New York: Plenum Medical Book Co.

Wilson, W. J. (1987). *The truly disadvantaged, the inner city, the underclass, and public policy.* Chicago: University of Chicago Press.

Yamamoto, J. (1986). Therapy for Asian American and Pacific Islanders. In C. B. Wilkinson (Ed.), *Ethnic psychiatry* (pp. 89–142). New York: Plenum Medical Book Co.

3 / Child Abandonment

Melvin J. Guyer and Thomas M. Horner

The fostering and "adoption" of abandoned offspring are far from unique to humans, and occur across a broad variety of mammals and birds (Riedman, 1982). The physical abandonment of children, while not as common as many other predicaments in which children find themselves, poses many legal, social, and clinical problems, all of which center on the uncertain and sometimes perilous conditions created by abandonment. In this chapter we consider only the condition of *physical* abandonment. Psychological abandonment, which may entail conditions in which the child is not actually left by the parent and which applies to a range of conditions, is too broad and labyrinthine a category to be covered here effectively. Reports of the frequency of abandonment vary and are inevitably affected by the mechanisms of reporting. Thus, many children who are abandoned escape notice because they are, in essence, passed within networks lying outside the established sociolegal domains in which children ordinarily live. Unformalized fosterings of children, including black-market adoptions, constitute a hidden realm of abandonment, as well.

The definition of an abandoned child has legal as well as psychological aspects that are not altogether congruent. Thus, many runaway teenagers, who from a psychological standpoint might be considered to be functionally abandoned on the basis of their parents having given up on them in one or another of so many ways, are not considered abandoned from any legal standpoint, even though various police and social agencies might be involved in their eventual placement and custody, and even though placement and custody of the adolescents eventually might occur outside the parental domain.

Laws across the 50 states generally define an abandoned child as one who has been willfully abandoned by those who are legally responsible for that child's care and who do not make reasonable and legal provisions for that child once he or she is beyond the abandoning person's control.

Thus, although a child left with a relative or acquaintance followed by the disappearance of his or her parent is given reasonable grounds for *feeling* abandoned, courts are less likely in such cases to immediately recognize that actual or physical abandonment has occurred, particularly if the person receiving the child has at least in part, perhaps with no foreboding of the parent's intentions, accepted responsibility for the child. Yet the court under whose jurisdiction such a child eventually might come would quite likely insert itself as custodian of that child until a determination of parental location and fitness were determined.

Sociolegal and Psychiatric Perspectives

The present era in family law has seen a shift in the balance of parental and state prerogatives with regard to defining and enforcing the standards of child care and with regard to the standards of children's welfare and well-being of children by which the fitness of parents may be weighed judicially. This shift has been decidedly in favor of the state. (See Guyer, 1979, 1982, 1985, 1990; see also Freed & Walker, 1988; Hart, 1991; Horowitz & Davidson, 1984.) In an era in which the independent (and so-called best) interests of children have come to occupy an increasingly powerful status vis-à-vis parents in the courts, courts have become increasingly solicitous of expert child psychiatric opinion concerning such interests. Although the predictive reliability of child psychiatric and related categories of experts has been shown, at least in certain types of cases, to be virtually nil (Horner & Guyer, 1991a, 1991b; Horner, Guyer, & Kalter, 1992, 1993), courts seem to feel more confident in their decision making when they have drawn on what the mental health specialist has to offer in the way of technical or cognate expertise. Through a series of court decisions and legislative enactments that spans the past two decades, courts and social services agents have come to subscribe to certain "minimal standards" by which parenting may be judged to be suitable ("fit") toward child rearing and care and according to which either civil or criminal penalties may be sought when findings of unfitness are made. Obviously, physical abandonment of a child is among the criteria that courts use to determine parental unfitness as well as to terminate parental rights.

Along with infanticide, child physical abandonment is rooted in the most distant origins of human history. Based on either their defective nature or status of being unwanted, children historically have been abandoned during all phases of their development, from birth through adolescence. Four forms of abandonment have predominated: (1) *infanticide,* in which the child is exposed to the elements with the purpose of disposing of it; (2) *sloughing,* in which a child may be left perilously at a site where the abandoning person reasonably expects the child to be found and then cared for; or in which, with the covert or evolving intention of relinquishing the child, a child may be given by its parent(s) into the care of others; (3) *formal abandonment* of the child to community authorities for placement and custody, as in the case of placing a child for adoption or of a parent's request that the court to take possession of an incorrigible youth; and (4) *societal abandonment,* which encompasses the children of families rendered homeless for lack of adequate or humane social policies and programs on the part of local, state, and/or federal agencies and legislative bodies.

Obviously, children may be temporarily, intermittently, or permanently abandoned by those legally responsible for them. Intermittent abandonment, of course, poses intriguing opportunities to examine the interfaces between psychological abandonment (which, as psychotherapists know, can exist within a context of actual nonphysical abandonment) and actual abandonment. Thus, the condition of a mother who regularly leaves her children unattended and unsupervised while she leaves the dwelling (say, to go to work) can conceivably be defined as one of intermittent abandonment. This chapter is devoted only to the conditions of physical abandonment encountered within the four rubrics just enumerated.

INFANTICIDE

Abandonments of children to nature date from ancient times and, until relatively recent times, have been a predictable (if not always acceptable) part of community life. Criminally illegal in the United States and most other countries, the practice nevertheless is encountered from time to time.

In the West, legal prohibitions of child exposure began to take hold in fourth century in the common era, but exposure and abandonment continued to be common. Throughout the medieval period, various attempts to control and suppress infanticide occurred, but it was not until the 18th and 19th centuries in Europe and the United States that legal prohibitions and severe sanctions against infanticide became widely imposed.

In the present era, laws governing infanticide relate principally to investigations of how the child came to be abandoned and to prosecutions of those who are apprehended and found guilty under one or more of several headings of homicide, including reckless homicide, manslaughter, or premeditated homicide. In cases where the child happens to be found alive, investigations generally are made as to the perpetrator of the child's abandonment, so that relevant and appropriate prosecutions may be made and sanctions applied under existing laws governing the abuse or neglect of children.

SLOUGHING

Three general varieties of sloughing occur: anonymous sloughing, covert sloughing, and formal adoption. Sloughing primarily occurs in relation to newborns, infants, and slightly older children.

Anonymous Sloughing: As amply depicted in fairy tale, myth, legend, and recorded history alike (see, e.g., Horner & Rosenberg, 1991; see also Boswell, 1988; Darnton, 1985), anonymous and formal abandonments of children date far back into history. Institutions specifically geared toward rearing such children (i.e., foundling homes, orphanages) did not appear until the High Middle

28

Ages. (See Boswell, 1988.) In ancient times, children reportedly would be left at community refuse sites, as the likelihood that they would be found and taken in would be greater there than if left elsewhere. Today's not infrequently reported findings of children at Dumpster sites thus have their parallels in rather ancient history. The intentions of such abandoners would be plain to any who encountered a child left at the heap, so to speak, although presumably not all who encountered the child would necessarily have taken it in.

As in the case of children abandoned to nature, today's foundlings trigger both the investigatory and prosecutorial machinery in the community, with such children coming under the temporary legal custody of the state. Such children are then given over to one of the state's social agencies for care or through a state agency to private agency contracted by the state for its foster care services.

Covert Sloughing: Covert sloughing varies from ad hoc transfers of children by the birth parent to the care of others (who are usually known to the parent and who also commonly are parental kin) to planful transfers of care, again usually to persons known to the parent, again commonly relatives. The covertly sloughing parent typically shifts the care of her or his children for an indefinite period of time, although abandoning parents commonly state that they always intend to retake possession of the abandoned child(ren). Child psychiatric practitioners become familiar with children sloughed in this fashion through referrals from the recipient caregivers themselves or through Child Protection Services agents who have become involved with such children. Careful distinction must be made in this regard between covert sloughing and informal adoption; the latter may occur with planfulness and without the intention of abandonment in its literal sense. (See Sandven & Resnick, 1990.)

The recipients of covertly sloughed children may not be aware of the parent's intention to disappear, that is, abandon the children. While not infrequent, parents of children brought for medical care sometimes disappear soon after the children are hospitalized. Such cases always result in notification of Child Protection Services agencies. Psychiatric practitioners may become involved in such cases either through an existing pediatric psychiatric consultation-liaison service

or on an outpatient basis as Child Protection Services agents and the courts wish formal appraisals to be made of the child's developmental and mental status. The psychiatric practitioner who is called upon to provide input to the state also can expect in most cases to assess the fitness of the abandoning parent.

FORMAL ABANDONMENT

In the United States, the most common forms of child abandonment are those in which voluntary formal arrangements are made, formally but sometimes informally (e.g., Sandven & Resnick, 1990), between birth parents and either a private agency or broker to place a child into adoptive circumstances. (Historically, children might be sold or indentured. Today's laws in the United States, of course, prohibit the selling of humans.) Over a decade ago, it was estimated that over 1 million women in the United States had surrendered an infant for adoption (Silverman, 1981) and that in one year alone (1982) over a half million children, mostly infants, were relinquished to adoption (Bachrach, 1986). In recent years, the realm of adoption has, at least indirectly and not without considerable controversy, extended itself to include the newest of children transferred from care by the birth parent, the children of surrogate parenting. (See, e.g., Katz, 1986; Miller, 1988; and Neuhaus, 1988.)

Children who have been formally abandoned to adoption come to the attention of psychiatric practitioners as requests are made by adoption agencies or prospective parents for advice concerning placement at infancy, or for advice during early childhood if the child has been difficult or impossible to place as an infant. They also may be consulted as issues surrounding the adoption itself emerge in the affected child's and family's lives. Authorities seem divided as to how, when, and what to tell adopted children about their birth status, although the general contemporary trend seems to be one emphasizing gradual—that is, age-correlated—disclosure and open dealing with the topic.

Although the proportions of adoptees seen in child guidance clinics tend to be greater than in the population as a whole (Hersov, 1977; Kotsopoulos et al., 1988), as a rule, children adopted in early infancy have no greater likelihood of manifesting psychiatric disorder than children raised by their birth parents (e.g., Bratfos, Ettinger & Tau, 1968; Humphrey & Ounsted, 1963), particularly when the adoptive parents are well prepared and supported in the early adoption phase (Bohman & Sigvardsson, 1990); indeed, some authors have asserted that the quality of relationship formations over childhood is of greater psychiatric significance than the mere fact of adoption (e.g., Rutter, 1979; see also Triseliotis & Hill, 1990).

Increasingly in recent years, psychiatric practitioners have been consulted by adoptive agencies faced with parents of adopted children who seek to return them on one or another basis of chronic maladjustment or unhappiness. Affected children are largely those who were adopted following infancy and who had been initially difficult to place. The conditions that they present typically bear psychiatric implications: tempermental difficulty (e.g., attention deficit hyperactivity disorder), frank psychiatric or developmental disability (e.g., pervasive developmental disorder), or behavioral disability (e.g., conduct disorder, oppositional defiant disorder).

Mental health practitioners increasingly are being asked to make diagnostic and, by implication, predictive statements as to the prospect of psychiatric normality at the point of adoptive placement. Thus, if a birth or surrogate mother is known or suspected to have used drugs or alcohol during the child's gestational development, prospective agencies and would-be adoptive parents are questioning whether there is an identifiable pattern of present or likely disability, impairment, or maladjustment on the part of the child.

SOCIETAL ABANDONMENT

With nearly one-third of the over 2.5 million homeless persons in the United States consisting of children and their mothers (see Bassuk & Rosenberg, 1990), it should not go unstated or unrecognized that the homeless children of this and other developed countries are, essentially speaking, abandoned children. Homelessness in the United States is, of course, not new, but rather historically a recurring feature of the economic landscape of American family lives (Katz, 1986).

If, as is now customary in various professional and sociolegal quarters, the parent is the definable critical element of protection and augmentation with respect to the development and maturation of the child, then the communities of persons that effectively comprise society itself must be definable as the proper and necessary ultracontext of child protection. Thus, the children of homeless families certainly may be construed as children who have been abandoned, if not by their specific caregivers then by those whose position and opportunity it would be to provide care. Only recently have mental health professionals and researchers entered the domain (and domains) of the homeless. (See, e.g., Bassuk, 1986; Bassuk & Rubin, 1987; Jones, Levine & Rosenberg, 1991; Klein, Behnke & Peterson, 1992).

The Child Psychiatrist and the Abandoned Child

Abandoned children come to the attention of the child psychiatrist when questions of mental or developmental status arise, when advice is sought with respect to placement, and when parental fitness is in question. The child psychiatrist will have specific things to say concerning the immediate psychological characteristics, needs, and dynamics of the child, which in turn pose tasks related to the placement of the child (e.g., temporary versus permanent foster care, adoption). Most experts agree that formal adoption is the best placement alternative for abandoned children in relation to long-term outcomes, but obviously not all abandoned children can be so placed.

Moreover, beyond the subjective effects of abandonment, which may be either cumulative or acute depending on situational and experiential factors that are prodromal to it, are the effects created by factors intrinsic to the child, factors relating to temperament and endowed behavioral and cognitive capacities. These intrinsic factors account for a number of conditions that are distributed along Axis II of the fourth edition of the *Diagnostic and Statistical Manual of Mental Disorders.*

Thus, some abandoned children present disorders of temperament (e.g., attention deficit hyperactivity disorder) that make any caregiving challenging if not soberingly difficult. Some have mental retardation or borderline intellectual capacity, the etiological features of which, although difficult to differentiate from sociogenic forces in the immediate aftermath of being rescued, are endogenous in nature. Pervasive developmental disorder, with or without evident autism, may be encountered in some of these children. Some, either by dint of the child-rearing circumstances that have culminated in abandonment or by virtue of factors intrinsic to the child, are behaviorally classifiable, including conduct disorder and oppositional defiant disorder. Finally, specific Axis I disorders may be encountered occasionally, as well.

While psychiatric examination of the child in the immediate phase of recovery from abandonment may be useful in achieving preliminary perspectives on the conditions that have culminated in abandonment, assessment following a period of protective placement is crucial in gauging the chronicity of any conditions or characteristics encountered in the acute phase. There should be little doubt that beyond securing a permanently safe and nurturant milieu for abandoned children, guidance and support for those into whose care they are placed is an essential part of the psychiatric consultations that are provided in such cases.

REFERENCES

Bachrach, C. A. (1986). Adoption plans, adopted children, and adoptive mothers. *Journal of Marriage and the Family, 45,* 243–253.

Bassuk, E. L. (Ed.). (1986). *The mental health needs of homeless persons: New directions for mental health services.* San Francisco: Jossey/Bass.

Bassuk, E. L., & Rosenberg, L. (1990). Psychosocial characteristics of homeless children and children with homes. *Pediatrics, 85,* 257–261.

Bassuk, E. L., & Rubin, L. (1987). Homeless children: A neglected population. *American Journal of Orthopsychiatry, 57,* 279–286.

Bohman, M., & Sigvardsson, S. (1990). Outcome in adoption: Lessons from longitudinal studies. In D. M. Brodzinsky & M. D. Schechter (Eds.), *The psychology of adoption* (pp. 93–106). New York: Oxford University Press.

Boswell, J. (1988). *The kindness of strangers.* New York: Pantheon.

Bratfos, O., Ettinger, L., & Tau, T. (1968). Mental illness and crime in adopted children and adoptive parents. *Acta Psychiatric Scandinavia, 44,* 376–384.

Darnton, R. (1985). *The great cat massacre and other episodes in French cultural history.* New York: Random House/Vintage.

Freed, D. J., & Walker, T. B. (1988). Family law in the fifty states: An overview. *Family Law Quarterly, 21,* 417–571.

Guyer, M. J. (1979). The consciously rejected child: Legal and social issues. *Psychiatry, 42,* 338–350.

Guyer, M. J. (1982). Child abuse and neglect statutes: Legal and clinical implications. *American Journal of Orthopsychiatry, 57,* 73–81.

Guyer, M. J. (1985). Commentary: The juvenile justice system. In D. Schetky & E. Benedek (Eds.), *Emerging issues in child psychiatry and the law.* (pp. 159–179). New York: Brunner/Mazel.

Guyer, M. J. (1990). Psychiatry, law, and child sexual abuse. In A. Tasman & S. M. Goldfinger (Eds.), *Review of Psychiatry* (Vol. 10, pp. 367–390). Washington, DC: American Psychiatric Press.

Hart, S. N. (1991). From property to person status: Historical perspective on children's rights. *American Psychologist, 46,* 53–59.

Hersov, L. (1977). Adoption. In M. Rutter & L. Hersov (Eds.), *Child psychiatry: Modern approaches* (pp. 136–162). London: Blackwell.

Horner, T. M., & Guyer, M. J. (1991a). Prediction, prevention, and clinical expertise in child custody cases in which allegations of child sexual abuse have been made. I. Predictable rates of diagnostic error in relation to various clinical decisionmaking strategies. *Family Law Quarterly, 25,* 217–252.

Horner, T. M., & Guyer, M. J. (1991b). Prediction, prevention, and clinical expertise in child custody cases in which allegations of child sexual abuse have been made. II. Prevalence rates of child sexual abuse and the precision of procedures designed to diagnose it. *Family Law Quarterly, 25,* 381–409.

Horner, T. M., Guyer, M. J., & Kalter, N. M. (1992). Prediction, prevention, and clinical expertise in child custody cases in which allegations of child sexual abuse have been made. III. Studies of expert opinion formation. *Family Law Quarterly, 26,* 141–170.

Horner, T. M., Guyer, M. J., & Kalter, N. M. (1993). Clinical expertise and the assessment of child sexual abuse: An empirical study of mental health experts. *Journal of the American Academy of Child & Adolescent Psychiatry, 32,* 925–931.

Horner, T. M., & Rosenberg, E. B. (1991). The family

romance: A developmental-historical perspective. *Psychoanalytic Psychology, 8,* 131–148.

Horowitz, R. M., & Davidson, H. A. (Eds.). (1984). *Legal rights of children.* New York: McGraw-Hill.

Humphrey, M., & Ounsted, C. (1963). Adoptive families referred for psychiatric advice. *British Journal of Psychiatry, 109,* 599–608.

Jones, J. M., Levine, I. S., & Rosenberg, A. (Eds.). (1991). Homelessness. *American Psychologist* (Special Issue), *46*(1).

Katz, A. (1986). Surrogate mothering and the baby-selling laws. *Columbia Journal of Law and Social Problems, 20,* 1–53.

Katz, M. B. (1986). *In the shadow of the poorhouse: A social history of welfare in America.* New York: Basic Books.

Klein, M. E., Behnke, S. E., & Peterson, C. (1992). *Characteristics of sheltered homeless mothers.* Unpublished manuscript. Ann Arbor: University of Michigan Department of Psychology.

Kotsopoulos, S., Côté, A., Joseph, L., Pentland, N., Stavrakaki, C., Sheahan, P., & Oke, L. (1988). Psychiatric disorders in adopted children: A controlled study. *American Journal of Orthopsychiatry, 58,* 608–612.

Miller, S. (1988). Surrogate parenthood and adoption statutes: Can a square peg fit into a round hole? *Family Law Quarterly, 22,* 199–212.

Neuhaus, R. J. (1988). Renting women, buying babies and class struggles. *Society, 25,* 8–10.

Riedman, M. L. (1982). The evolution of alloparental care and adoption in mammals and birds. *Quarterly Review of Biology, 57,* 405–435.

Rutter, M. (1979). Maternal deprivation, 1972–1978: New findings, new concepts, new approaches. *Child Development, 50,* 283–305.

Sandven, K., & Resnick, M. D. (1990). Informal adoption among black adolescent mothers. *American Journal of Orthopsychiatry, 60,* 210–224.

Silverman, P. R. (1981). *Helping woman cope with grief.* Beverly Hills, CA: Sage.

Triseliotis, J., & Hill, M. (1990). Contrasting adoption, foster care, and residential rearing. In D. M. Brodzinsky & M. D. Schechter (Eds.), *The psychology of adoption* (pp. 107–120). New York: Oxford University Press.

4 / Childhood Bereavement

Julie A. Guthrie, Ronald A. Weller, and Elizabeth B. Weller

Epidemiology

In the United States, nearly 1 out of every 25 children (over 1 million) experiences the death of at least one parent before the age of 18 (Statistical Abstract of the United States, 1990). Even more children experience the loss of siblings, grandparents, other family members, and friends. Thus, childhood bereavement is not rare. The frequency of its occurrence and its clearly stressful nature suggest that bereavement in childhood may have a significant impact on the developing child. However, interest in studying childhood bereavement systematically is a relatively recent development. For many years psychoanalytic theory suggested that childhood bereavement did not exist. It was believed that children did not have the capacity to grieve because of their immature and underdeveloped egos (Freud, 1960; Wolfenstein, 1966).

To study and understand the process of be-reavement in children and adolescents most effectively, it must be understood that a child's concept of death changes during development—children may understand death differently from adults and differently from children at other stages of development. Nagy (1948) described 3 developmental stages children experience in developing a mature, adult concept of death. Young children under age 5 perceive death as a reversible process, like sleep or separation. Children ages 5 to 9 tend to personify death as a wicked death man, ghost, or "boogey man" with the power to cause death. Children ages 9 and above understand death to be an inevitable, universal, and irreversible event.

Definitions of the terms "bereavement," "grief," and "mourning" are necessary to understanding the processes that occur following a death. *Bereavement* is the actual deprivation or loss of a loved person, while *grief* is the intense distress and emotional disturbance that immediately follow the experience of loss (bereavement) and accompany mourning. *Mourning* involves a wide array of psychological processes initiated by the loss of a loved person (Bowlby, 1960a).

Bereavement in Infancy

The consequences of bereavement occurring in infancy and early childhood continue to be widely debated among mental health professionals. Currently no prospective long-term studies report on the impact of parental death on infants or young children.

Bowlby (1960b) described a predictable sequence of reactions manifested by infants or young children when separated from the mother. This sequence begins with protest, likened to separation anxiety, where children try to reunite with the mother using whatever means are available. This stage is followed by despair, sometimes also called grief and mourning, in which children have a persistent preoccupation and longing for the mother's return but with fading hopefulness. Finally, in the detachment phase, children become apathetic and withdrawn, and are emotionally detached and emotionally divested from the mother.

Kranzler, Shaffer, Wasserman, and Davies (1990) found that preschool-age children have the capacity to grieve, a finding that also is contrary to earlier psychoanalytic theory. In their study of parent-bereaved children ages 3 to 6, bereaved children expressed more feelings of depression and anxiety than normal children in the 6 months following parental death. A gender difference was noted as well, as bereaved boys exhibited significantly more behavior disturbance than normal controls.

Bereavement in Childhood

There are a few prospective studies of bereavement in normal children. Of these, methodologic shortcomings may limit their generalizability. Elizur and Kaffman (1982, 1983) examined grief reactions in father-bereaved prepubertal children living on a kibbutz in Israel. Information was gathered from the children's mothers and teachers. Sleep disturbance, social withdrawal, and restlessness were commonly observed. Family conflict and preexisting emotional disturbance in the child predicted a more troubled emotional response during the early months of bereavement. The expanded social (and financial) support system of the kibbutz is not typical of families in the United States, where often both parents work. Thus, the death of either parent can cause the loss of both emotional and financial support that can be devastating for surviving family members. Because of this, Elizur and Kaffman's findings may have limited application to the more heterogeneous population of bereaved children in the United States.

Van Eerdewegh, Bieri, Parrilla, and Clayton (1982) reported dysphoria, social withdrawal, temper tantrums, and sleep disturbance in children ages 2 to 17 one month after the death of a parent. At 13 months after the death there was a significant drop in school performance, but other symptoms were less frequent than at the initial interview. More psychopathology was found in children of psychiatrically ill mothers. However, this information was not obtained directly from the children but was gathered from parents and teachers. Internalizing symptoms such as sadness, anxiety, guilt, or suicidal ideation may be less apparent to others and therefore underreported by parents who are unaware of their presence (Weller & Weller, 1984). Van Eerdewegh et al. (1982) did not separate prepubertal children and adolescents. Thus, age-related differences in the course of bereavement could not be determined.

Studies of bereavement in adults have described a variety of psychological and physical sequelae including depression, anxiety, and an increased risk of morbidity and mortality (Clayton, Halikas, & Maurice, 1972; Parkes, 1987; Rees & Lutkin, 1967; Zisook, Shucter, & Shuckit, 1985). These studies have provided a useful framework for studying bereavement in children.

Two of the authors (E.W. and R.W.) conducted a prospective, longitudinal, and comprehensive study of 38 bereaved prepubertal children and their surviving parents in order to better describe acute bereavement in children and to determine the course of bereavement in the first year follow-

33

ing the death of a parent. Children and parents were interviewed using standard structured interviews, clinical rating scales, and self-report inventories at 2, 6, and 12 months after parental death. Normal children and hospitalized depressed children matched for age, sex, and socioeconomic status served as controls.

Weller, Weller, Fristad, and Bowes (in press) reported on depressive symptomatology in this group of 38 bereaved children 2 months following parental death. The bereaved children reported more depressive symptoms than the normal children but significantly fewer depressive symptoms than the depressed children. Dysphoria and loss of interest best differentiated bereaved children from normal children. Nearly two-thirds of bereaved children reported suicidal ideation, although none reported a suicide attempt, compared to 42% of the depressed children, who reported at least one suicide attempt. Both depressed and bereaved children tended to endorse more symptoms of depression than the parents endorsed for their children. Family history of depression or preexisting untreated psychiatric disorder in the child were both associated with increased depressive symptomatology in the bereaved child. Age and sex of the child and type of death (anticipated or unanticipated) were not significant predictors of depression in bereaved children.

Guthrie, Weller, Fristad, and Weller (1991) evaluated depressive symptomatology 2 months after parental death in this same group of bereaved children and their surviving spouse-bereaved parents to determine if there were similarities in the type or severity of depressive symptoms experienced by the bereaved children and their parents. There was a significant correlation in the severity of depression in bereaved children and their surviving parents. A history of depression in either parent and severity of depression in the surviving parent were the strongest predictors of depression in the bereaved child.

Bereavement in adults often results in social withdrawal and an impaired capacity to perform expected duties at work or at home. Bereaved children might be expected to show less interest in play or declining school performance, but there is little research investigating the effects of bereavement on a child's "work." Fristad, Gallerston-Jedel, Weller, and Weller (1988) studied the effect of parental death on peer relations, self-esteem, and school performance in these bereaved prepubertal children during the year following parental death. Bereaved children reported no impairment in self-esteem and peer relations compared to normal controls. Depressed children and their parents reported significantly more problems with peer relations, self-esteem, and school performance than bereaved children and their parents. At 2 months postparental death, bereaved children showed more behavior problems at school and were less interested in school than normal controls. This did not change significantly at the 6-month and 12-month follow-up.

Anxiety has been described as part of an acute reaction to separation in children (Arthur & Kemme, 1964; Bowlby, 1960). Sanchez, Fristad, Weller, and Weller (1989) evaluated anxiety symptoms in the bereaved children 2 months following the death of a parent. Bereaved children reported more symptoms of anxiety than normal children, although the difference was not significant. Bereaved children reported significantly fewer symptoms of anxiety than depressed children. Parents of both bereaved and depressed children reported significantly fewer anxiety symptoms than did the children themselves.

Sood, Weller, Weller, Fristad, and Moye (1987) investigated somatic complaints in the bereaved children 2 months postparental death. The number of somatic complaints for all groups was low, and there were no statistical differences between groups. Bereaved parents consistently reported fewer somatic complaints in their children than the children did themselves. Stomachaches and headaches were the most frequently endorsed somatic complaints in bereaved children. Current somatic complaints in the surviving parent were associated with increased somatic complaints in the bereaved child.

Knowledge of the expected longitudinal course of bereavement is necessary to differentiate normal from complicated or pathological bereavement and to determine if intervention is appropriate. Fristad, Grosshans, Weller, and Weller (1988) evaluated the bereaved prepubertal children longitudinally to determine the natural course of bereavement. Depressed children endorsed significantly more severe symptoms than bereaved children at each interview. Although bereaved children endorsed more severe symptoms than normal children, this did not reach statistical significance. Half the children experienced the most intense symptomatology at 2 months postparental death; one-third experienced their most severe symptomatology at 6 months; and one-sixth experienced peak symptomatology at 12 months.

In addition to the readily observable psychological and physical symptomatology during bereavement in children, there is also evidence of neuroendocrine abnormalities. Weller, Weller, Fristad, and Bowes (1990) evaluated 18 acutely bereaved children and adolescents using the dexamethasone suppression test (DST). Seven children (39%) had a positive test. Nonsuppressors reported more depressive symptoms than suppressors, and all symptoms of depression from the third revised edition of the *Diagnostic and Statistical Manual of Mental Disorders* occurred more frequently in nonsuppressors, but the difference was nonsignificant. Suicidal ideation was significantly correlated with post-dexamethasone cortisol levels.

Bereavement in Adolescence

Few prospective controlled studies have investigated bereavement during adolescence. Gregory (1965) was one of several authors to study data gathered on a sample initially studied as 10th graders. He found a higher incidence of delinquent behavior in bereaved adolescents compared to controls. However, the age of the adolescent at the time of parental death was not given. Characteristics of bereavement during adolescence cannot be determined without this critical information.

Van Eerdewegh, Clayton, and Van Eerdewegh (1985), in a follow-up study of 105 bereaved children ages 2 to 17, recognized the importance of considering adolescents separately from prepubertal children so that age-dependent differences in the course of bereavement could be determined. Bereaved adolescents, ages 13 to 17, showed a propensity similar to that observed in prepubertal bereaved children to develop dysphoria, social withdrawal, and deteriorating school performance. Temper tantrums were increased in bereaved prepubertal children compared to normal children. However, temper tantrums in be-

reaved adolescents were not more frequent than in normal adolescents.

Effects of Childhood Bereavement in Adulthood

Several studies have attempted to determine the long-term effects in adulthood of bereavement in childhood or adolescence. Results have varied widely and often have been contradictory. These studies are primarily retrospective studies of adult psychiatric patients. Unfortunately, retrospective information is often inaccurate, particularly in a psychiatric population that may be suffering from cognitive distortions (Akiskal & Weller, 1989). It is difficult to find appropriate control subjects and to control for a lifetime of intervening experiences. Furthermore, important variables such as the quality of the home environment and adjustment of the surviving parent following the death may not be considered.

In a follow-up study to Gregory's work, Markusen and Fulton (1971) prospectively studied the same group of 10th graders when they reached their 20s. Bereaved males tended to have a greater incidence of legal offenses than the control group. Bendiksen and Fulton (1976) evaluated this same cohort while in their 30s. The bereaved group had sustained more major medical illness and more emotional distress than the controls, but this time there was no difference between the groups with respect to legal offenses. Specific information about the course of bereavement and the type, duration, and occurrence of symptoms was not available. Furthermore, variables such as age of the child at the parent's death, type of death, psychosocial adjustment of the child prior to the death, and availability of other support systems (such as surviving parent) following the death were not considered.

Breier et al. (1988) investigated the impact of early parental loss on subsequent adult psychopathology and the factors that may influence development of psychopathology in adulthood. They interviewed 90 subjects who had experienced parental death or permanent separation from a parent during ages 2 to 17. Of these subjects, 77%

had a lifetime history of psychiatric disorders, predominantly major depression. All but 4 were euthymic at the time of the interview. Furthermore, those subjects with a prior history of psychopathology showed increased hypothalamic-pituitary-adrenal axis activity with elevated levels of cortisol and beta-endorphin at the time of the study, despite the fact that nearly all subjects were free of psychiatric symptoms at that time.

This same study also found that inadequate caregiving by the surviving parent was the most powerful predictor of subsequent psychopathology. A nonsupportive relationship with the surviving parent and a relationship where the child felt responsible for the emotional well-being of that parent were both strong predictors of psychopathology in adulthood for these bereaved children. Age of the child at the time of separation, sex of the deceased or absent parent, and family history of psychopathology were not predictors of maladaptive childhood grief or subsequent adult psychopathology.

Clinical Implications

Research to date has identified a number of depressive and anxiety symptoms that seem to be a part of the normal bereavement process. It is important to distinguish symptoms of normal bereavement from those that are part of a well-defined psychiatric disorder. There are still many unanswered questions, particularly how to identify bereaved children and adolescents destined for a poor outcome. Theoretically, those who develop a well-established psychiatric disorder may require more intensive intervention to achieve healthy adjustment to the loss. Several psychiatric disorders should be considered routinely in evaluating uncomplicated bereavement.

MAJOR DEPRESSION

According to the fourth edition of the *Diagnostic and Statistical Manual of Mental Disorders* (*DSM-IV*; American Psychiatric Association, 1994), normal grief can be differentiated from depression by the absence of morbid preoccupation with worthlessness, marked psychomotor retardation, prolonged and marked functional impairment, and prominent suicidal ideation. When present, these factors may indicate that bereavement is complicated by a major depressive episode. Thirty-seven percent of bereaved prepubertal children satisfied symptom criteria for major depressive episode 2 months after parental death (Weller et al., 1988). Symptoms of guilt/worthless feelings and fatigue best discriminated bereaved children from depressed children. Thoughts about death and dying are quite common among bereaved children. These ideas most likely represent a longing to be reunited with the dead person and are not true suicidal thoughts, which may account for the fact that bereaved children have fewer feelings of worthlessness than depressed children. If true suicidal wishes are present, or if the child has attempted suicide, the possibility of bereavement complicated by a major depressive episode should be considered and intervention for the protection of the child or adolescent may be necessary.

ADJUSTMENT DISORDER WITH DEPRESSED MOOD

In children, adjustment disorder with depressed mood is diagnosed when a psychosocial stressor results in symptoms of depression that are insufficient in number to meet criteria for a diagnosis of major depressive episode. However, in *DSM-IV* uncomplicated bereavement is classified as a V code, a condition that is a focus of attention or treatment but is not considered a psychiatric diagnosis, even though a child may be reacting to the death of a significant person.

SEPARATION ANXIETY DISORDER

Separation anxiety disorder is defined in *DSM-IV* as "excessive anxiety concerning separation from those to whom the child is attached." Such anxiety is beyond that expected for the child's developmental level. This anxiety can be manifested by a variety of fears, including:

1. Fear of harm befalling important figures or fear that they will not return
2. Fear that the child will be the victim of kidnapping, death, or other violent separation
3. School refusal in order to stay with attachment figures
4. Refusal to sleep without being near attachment figures
5. Fear of being alone

6. Nightmares involving separation
7. Feigning physical symptoms in order to avoid separation from attachment figures
8. Distress in situations of impending separation
9. Distress when away from home or separated from attachment figures

DSM-IV requires that at least 3 of these 9 symptoms be present for a minimum of 2 weeks to diagnose separation anxiety. If a bereaved child meets these criteria, anxiety disorder also should be diagnosed.

POSTTRAUMATIC STRESS DISORDER

Posttraumatic stress disorder (PTSD) arises in response to a psychologically distressing event that is outside the range of normal human experience. Death of a loved one and subsequent bereavement are universal human experiences. Therefore, posttraumatic stress disorder is not a normal sequela of bereavement. An exception to this might be a child who loses a significant person due to murder or suicide. Posttraumatic reactions in children are similar to those in adults, although there are some developmental differences. For example, children are less likely to have "flashbacks" but will relive the trauma in their play or fantasies. Children or adolescents who manifest symptoms of posttraumatic stress disorder may need help in expressing their feelings using puppets, play therapy, or other indirect techniques when there are feelings of rage or revenge that may be frightening to the child (Pynoos & Nader, 1990).

Clinical Interventions

Uncomplicated bereavement is considered to be part of the normal human experience, and intervention may not be necessary. Freud (1957/1917), in fact, felt that intervention might be harmful. Most often the surviving parent informs the child of the parent's death. As described earlier, children of different ages understand death in different ways. Regardless of the child's developmental level, it is important to explain death in simple, clear, and unambiguous language. Death should never be likened to sleep, as this can create sleep phobia in the children, who may worry that they, their brothers and sisters, or their surviving parent

also might die when going to sleep. Comparing death to sleep also may perpetuate the misunderstanding that death, like sleep, is a reversible process.

Once children begin to process this information, they may have questions about what happens next, specifically, what happens to the body. Most children have had experiences where a family pet has died and been buried, and many are aware that people also can be buried when they die. Often parents worry about what effects funeral attendance will have on their children. Opinions differ on this subject. Some have reported that funeral attendance is traumatic to children (Furman, 1974; Showalter, 1976), but many reports in this area are anecdotal. Weller, Weller, Fristad, Cain, and Bowes (1988) interviewed 38 bereaved prepubertal children and their surviving parents regarding participation in and reaction to funeral activities. Most children were expected to go and wanted to attend the funeral home visitation and funeral services. Most parents (90%) and children (79%) reported the child's reaction as "basically controlled" (i.e., little or no crying). Factors associated with children having atypical reactions (either markedly withdrawn or upset) included helping with funeral arrangements and attending the funeral despite not wanting to go. Other factors that predicted an atypical reaction were knowing someone who had died before and believing that death meant that a person "was buried." Children who attended the funeral did not show any increased psychiatric symptomatology 2 months postparental death compared to bereaved children who did not attend their parents' funeral.

Often when a child's parent dies, the child is deprived not only of the care of the deceased parent but of the surviving parent, as well. Parents who have lost a spouse are coping with their own loss and may not be able to emotionally support the bereaved child, provide day-to-day caregiving, or meet the child's physical needs. Both the bereaved child and the surviving parent will benefit from the intervention of another adult, for example, a relative or a family friend, whom the child can trust to take care of him or her until the parent is able to resume parenting responsibilities. The death of a parent results in many changes both for the child and for the family. Typically the surviving parent becomes completely responsible for the financial, emotional, and physical needs of the family. There may be less time and money for activities or vacations that the family enjoyed when both parents were alive. The family may need to move and change schools to obtain less expensive housing or to be nearer to relatives. The surviving parent may date or remarry. All these disruptions may create anger and resentment in children who perceive that their wants and needs are not considered important. Often parents are not aware of difficulties that their children may be having. Adults involved in the children's care (e.g., parents, relatives, or teachers) should encourage them to talk about their feelings and help them to understand that the feelings may be normal.

Parents, for a variety of reasons, may be hesitant to discuss death with their children. They believe it will be upsetting to the children or fear they will not be able to control their own emotional reaction. In the authors' experience, for some bereaved children and parents, the process of being interviewed about their bereavement made discussion of their grief easier and more acceptable. Books on bereavement may help the child to understand the process and give the family a vehicle that allows them to discuss their thoughts and feelings. Bereavement support groups may be helpful for both the parent and the child. Unfortunately, there are very few bereavement support groups for children.

Children may develop a more complicated or maladaptive course of bereavement that interferes with their ability to function at school or at home.

In this situation, professional intervention is indicated. Children should be evaluated carefully for the presence of an underlying major depression or anxiety disorder. If indicated, the surviving parent also should be referred for psychiatric evaluation and treatment. Individual psychotherapy may help children work through the difficulties of the bereavement and improve their ability to function. If children have had a prior episode of depression, or when individual psychotherapy has not provided improvement, antidepressant medication might be considered.

Conclusion

Every year many children suffer the loss of a loved one. Recent research of bereavement in children and adolescents indicates that children are capable of grieving and do react to bereavement. Acutely, most experience an initial period of sadness, anxiety, or impaired school performance, but the symptoms gradually diminish. A child's ability to adjust to the loss of a parent may be related in part to the adjustment of the surviving parent and the stability and support in the environment. Further investigation is needed to describe more fully both the acute and perhaps more important long-term effects of bereavement in children and adolescents.

REFERENCES

Akiskal, H. S., & Weller, E. B. (1989). Mood disorders and suicide in children and adolescents. In H. I. Kaplan & B. J. Sadock (Eds.), *Comprehensive textbook of psychiatry* (Vol. 5, p. 1988). Baltimore: Williams & Wilkins.

American Psychiatric Association. (1994). *Diagnostic and Statistical Manual of Mental Disorders* (4th ed.). Washington, DC: Author.

Arthur, B., & Kemme, M. L. (1964). Bereavement in childhood. *Journal of Child Psychology and Psychiatry, 5,* 37–49.

Bendiksen, R., & Fulton, R. (1976). Death and the child: An anterospective test of the childhood bereavement and later behavior disorder hypothesis. In R. Fulton (Ed.), *Death and identity* (pp. 274–287). Bowie, MD: Charles Press.

Bowlby, J. (1960a). Grief and mourning in infancy and early childhood. *Psychoanalytic Study of the Child, 15,* 9–52.

Bowlby, J. (1960b). Separation anxiety. *International Journal of Psycho-analysis, 41,* 89–113.

Breier, A., Kelsoe, J. R., Kirwin, P. D., Beller, S. A., Wolkowitz, O. M., & Pickar, D. (1988). Early prenatal loss and development of adult psychopathology. *Archives of General Psychiatry, 45,* 987–993.

Clayton, P. J., Halikas, J. A., & Maurice, W. L. (1972). The depression of widowhood. *British Journal of Psychiatry, 120,* 71–78.

Elizur, E., & Kaffman, M. (1982). Children's bereavement reactions following death of the father: The first four years. *Journal of the American Academy of Child Psychiatry, 21* (5), 474–480.

Elizur, E., & Kaffman, M. (1983). Factors influencing the severity of childhood bereavement reactions.

American Journal of Orthopsychiatry, 53 (4), 668–676.

Freud, A. (1960). Discussion of Dr. John Bowlby's paper. *Psychoanalytic Study of the Child, 15,* 53–62.

Freud, S. (1957). *Mourning and melancholia.* In J. Strachey (Ed.), *The standard edition of the complete psychological works of Sigmund Freud* (Vol. 14, pp. 237–259). London: Hogarth Press. (Originally published 1917.)

Fristad, M., Gallerston-Jedel, R., Weller, E., & Weller, R. (1988). *Peer relations, school performance, and self-esteem in bereaved children.* Paper presented at the 35th annual meeting of the American Academy of Child and Adolescent Psychiatry, Seattle, WA.

Fristad, M. A., Grosshans, B., Weller, E. B., & Weller, R. A. (1988). *Children's bereavement during the first year post-parental death.* Paper presented at the 36th annual meeting of the American Academy of Child and Adolescent Psychiatry, New York.

Furman, E. (1974). *A child's parent dies.* New Haven, CT: Yale University Press.

Gregory, I. (1965). Anterospective data following childhood loss of a parent: I. Delinquency and high school dropout. *Archives of General Psychiatry, 13,* 99–109.

Guthrie, J. A., Weller, R. A., Fristad, M. A., & Weller, E. B. (1991). *Comparison of depressive symptoms in bereaved children and their parents.* Paper presented at the 144th annual meeting of the American Psychiatric Association, New Orleans, LA.

Kranzler, E., Shaffer, D., Wasserman, G., & Davies, M. (1990). Early childhood bereavement. *Journal of the American Academy of Child and Adolescent Psychiatry, 29* (4), 513–520.

Markusen, T., & Fulton, R. (1971). Childhood bereavement and behavioral disorders: A critical review. *Omega, 2,* 107–117.

Nagy, M. (1948). The child's theories concerning death. *Journal of Genetic Psychology, 73,* 3–27.

Parkes, C. M. (1987). *Bereavement: Studies of Grief in Adult Life* (2nd ed.). Madison, CT: International Universities Press.

Pynoos, R. S., & Nader, K. (1990). Children's exposure to violence and traumatic death. *Psychiatric Annals, 20* (6), 334–344.

Rees, W. D., & Lutkin, S. G. (1967). Mortality of bereavement. *British Medical Journal, 4,* 13–16.

Sanchez, L., Fristad, M. A., Weller, E. B., & Weller, R. A. (1989). *Anxiety symptoms in bereaved children.* Paper presented at the 142nd annual meeting of the American Psychiatric Association, San Francisco, CA.

Showalter, J. E. (1976). How do children and funerals mix? *Journal of Pediatrics, 89,* 139–145.

Sood, B., Weller, E. B., Weller, R. A., Fristad, M. A., & Moye, J. (1987). *Somatic symptoms in bereaved children.* Paper presented at the 140th annual meeting of the American Psychiatric Association, Chicago, IL.

Statistical Abstract of the United States (110th ed.). (1990). Washington, DC: Bureau of the Census.

Van Eerdewegh, M. M., Bieri, M. D., Parrilla, R. H., & Clayton, P. J. (1982). The bereaved child. *British Journal of Psychiatry, 140,* 23–29.

Van Eerdewegh, M. M., Clayton, P. J., & Van Eerdewegh, P. (1985). The bereaved child: Variables influencing early psychopathology. *British Journal of Psychiatry, 147,* 188–194.

Weller, E. B., & Weller, R. A. (Eds.). (1984). *Current perspectives on major depressive disorders in children.* Washington, DC: American Psychiatric Press.

Weller, E. B., Weller, R. A., Fristad, M. A., & Bowes, J. M. (1990). Dexamethasone suppression test and depressive symptoms in bereaved children: A preliminary report. *Journal of Neuropsychiatry and Clinical Neurosciences, 2* (4), 418–421.

Weller, E. B., Weller, R. A., Fristad, M. A., Cain, S. E., & Bowes, J. M. (1988). Should children attend their parent's funeral? *Journal of the American Academy of Child and Adolescent Psychiatry, 27* (5), 559–562.

Weller, R. A., Weller, E. B., Fristad, M. A., & Bowes, J. M. (1991). Depression in recently bereaved prepubertal children. *American Journal of Psychiatry, 148* (11).

Wolfenstein, M. (1986). How is mourning possible? *Psychoanalytic Study of the Child, 21,* 92–123.

Zisook, S., Shucter, S., & Shuckit, M. (1985). Factors in the persistence of unresolved grief among psychiatric outpatients. *Psychosomatics, 26* (6), 497–503.

5 / **Children in the Military**

Jon A. Shaw and Peter S. Jensen

The military community includes approximately 1.6 million children of active-duty personnel (*Defense Medical Information System,* 1990). Roughly 90% of these children are under 15 years of age, while 30% are less than 4 years of age. As there are so many children in military families, it is important to attempt to understand the influence of the military community on their development.

While children in the military community experience the same developmental and maturational processes as other children, they also experience a unique social and facilitating environment. The family living on a military installation resides in a highly structured community, an authoritarian society, with clearly delineated patterns of conduct expected not only of the soldiers but of their dependents, as well.

In recent years the traditional military family has undergone an increasing diversification. Approximately 10% of the military forces are women. In 1991, 7% of army families were dual-career families—both parents are members of the armed forces. Six percent of families in the army are single-parent families (Plewes, 1991).

Over the years, there has been considerable controversy regarding the psychological health of the children of the military. Lagrone (1978) suggested that behavioral problems were more prevalent in children and adolescent military dependents than among their civilian counterparts and suggested the presence of a military family syndrome. In contrast, Morrison (1981), in a prospective study, found few differences between the diagnostic spectrum of mental disorders of children and adolescents in the military and their civilian peers. Likewise, Kenny (1967) noted that military children have lower delinquency rates, higher achievement scores, and a higher median IQ. Similarly, a study comparing illicit drug use between military and civilian students reveals less usage among the military population (Frenkel, Robinson, & Finman, 1974). Jensen (1992) criticizes the stereotyping of the "military brat" which he feels is the product of presupposition and misattribution, and stresses the need for empirical research. He concludes that while the military child is exposed to a number of unique and repeated stressors, this is offset by strong social and community support systems.

Jensen, Xenakis, Wolf, Degroot, & Bain (1991) examined a community-based sample of 213 6- to 12-year-old military children and their parents. The parents and teachers were asked to complete a behavior checklist on each child. In addition, the parents completed a stressful life events inventory and a checklist of their own symptoms while the children were assessed using self-report depression and anxiety scales. There was no evidence to support the notion of increased or elevated psychopathology in military children.

When attempting to understand the extent of psychopathology in military children, an important consideration involves family factors, including socioeconomic status and parental mental health. For example, Kenny (1967) found that officers' children tended to be better adjusted compared to enlisted soldiers' children. Officers and higher-ranking enlisted soldiers report more life and career satisfaction than other soldiers. It may be that families of enlisted and lower-ranking soldiers experience more stressors than officers' families, partly as a function of income, differences in the soldier-parents' control over geographic assignment, educational advantages, and widely differing work situations (Jensen, Lewis, & Xenakis, 1986). Furthermore, it is likely that the effects of military life on children may be mediated through its effects on parents. For example, Pedersen (1966) studied boys' responses to the fathers' absence and found that adverse effects on the child could be mediated by maternal difficulties during the course of fathers' absence. Similarly, Pedersen and Sullivan (1964) found that parental attitudes about family mobility mediated children's responses to the effects of geographic dislocations.

Evidence from a number of studies indicates that the majority of military personnel cope reasonably well and are satisfied with military life, although this finding varies as a function of a number of lifestyle factors (Soefel & Savell, 1978; Stumpf, 1978). For example, a study (Fernandez-Poi, 1988) of military wives found that self-report of symptoms of psychological distress were no different from their civilian counterparts. The author rightfully wonders what protective factors reduce the responses to the unique stressors of military life.

Overall results provide no evidence of a military family syndrome (LaGrone, 1978). Rather, they support other recent findings that personality characteristics of military children and their parents (Rosen & Corcoran, 1978) do not differ in any important ways from those of civilian families. In cases in which military children do seem to show evidence of impaired functioning, the effects of nonspecific and military unique stressors upon the parents, the parent's own functioning levels, and socioeconomic status/rank should be examined.

Military Community Supports

A variety of factors operate to reduce psychologic dysfunction in military families. Divorce is less common in military than civilian families (Morrison, 1981; Williams, 1976), and child abuse is less common (Jensen et al., 1986) Military families, by definition, do not experience unemployment or even the lowest levels of poverty. The military provides free access to health care, social work, legal services, mental health counseling, and day care. Education and intelligence standards, and the screening out of those with criminal histories, severe psychiatric difficulties, or personality disorders also make the military a select population. In addition, the relative geographic isolation of many military posts has resulted in a philosophy of "taking care of their own." Every imaginable social and recreational facility is available for families. Thus, communal life often has the quality of an extended family with shared values, loyalties, and commitment to a particular lifestyle.

Stressors in the Military Community

Specific psychosocial risk factors associated with military life influence the developmental and life experiences of children. Stressors that generally are judged to be disruptive are frequent family moves, life experiences in foreign countries, intermittent father/mother absence, war and combat stress, and early military retirement. We will briefly review the current literature regarding the impact of these stressors on children in the military.

GEOGRAPHIC MOBILITY

Children in a military family are members of a community in which there is a high expectation of mobility. Darnauer (1976) noted that the average

military adolescent 16 to 18 years of age had experienced 5.8 family moves. A study of military high school graduates found that they had attended on the average nine schools prior to graduation (Strickland, 1970).

There is conflicting evidence as to whether geographic mobility has adverse effects on children and their families. Studies of military children have consistently failed to find any predictable relationship between emotional and behavioral problems and the frequency of family moves. Tooley (1970) has written that "moving house seems to improve family adjustment or individual adjustment, almost as often as it disturbs it" (p. 373).

The predominant factors determining the child's adaptation to frequent family moves are parental attitudes and identification with the military, the intrinsic adaptive capacities of the family, and the child's personality structure, level of psychosocial development, and coping repertoire. Children who are in periods transition, such as early school age children cautiously entering into peer-related activities and adolescents struggling to emancipate themselves from their parents, appear to be more vulnerable to the effects of family moves (Shaw, 1986). Consider the following case.

CASE EXAMPLE

A young adolescent girl was referred for evaluation shortly after her arrival in Germany because of a sudden change in her behavior manifested by delinquency and a history of a runaway with a boy. It was evident that a number of features peculiar to the army community in Germany contributed to the present crisis; the overcrowding and cramped space of apartment accommodations extenuated the oedipal concerns of this physically precocious adolescent girl and her father. The moral values and standards of conduct of her new peer group were less well defined and regulated in the absence of a stable peer group and a readily visible jurisdictional system. The need to reestablish status and popularity valence in the new peer group led this girl to sacrifice desperately and uncritically her regulated patterns of individual conduct for a sense of belonging to a group. It seemed that a dependent posture aligned to any peer group irrespective of its explicit value system was preferable to the regression and conflict associated in this girl's mind with maintaining a dependent posture in the family. She literally fled into the new group attempting to escape the regressive pull of the family.

Yet other adolescents may negotiate the crisis with firmer consolidation of a sense of continuity and sameness with a new sense of confidence in their adaptive skills and a greater understanding and acceptance of the life cycle and the human situation.

Shaw (1979) compared 30 adolescents (mean age 15.5 years) averaging 2.1 family moves with a group of 26 adolescents (mean age 15.4 years) who had averaged 9.5 family moves. Adolescents with frequent family moves reported themselves as more boring, changeable, distant, insecure, complaining, unhappy, inconsistent, critical, and less intimate than their low-move peers. Male adolescents were more likely to describe moves as important and easy, while females described them as unimportant and difficult.

Jensen et al. (1986) summarized the current literature noting that while geographic mobility may present problems for both military children and parents, these difficulties are generally time-limited.

TRANSCULTURAL EXPERIENCES

Not only must children adapt to family moves, they must adjust frequently to new cultures. It is estimated that there are over 140,000 school-age children of military personnel in overseas areas. Children moving overseas experience a discontinuity in their social network, the lack of availability of extended family, and the "culture shock" of changing customs and standards of conduct and norms. Subsequent to a move, youths may find themselves confronting a social and legal system that is not always well defined or congruent with their own upbringing. In one country, prostitution may be legal, while in another a boy and a girl holding hands may be abrasive to the sensitivities of the host country. The ready availability of drugs and other temptations may be attractions difficult for adolescents to resist. The impact of this experience on children is variable and not well known.

TRANSIENT FATHER ABSENCE

Operation Desert Storm was unique in that in addition to the children who experienced paternal absence, a fair number of children experienced maternal absence and, in some instances, children experienced dual parent absence. As of yet we have not found any systematic literature on the effect of these absences (Jensen & Shaw, 1996). The studies that we will be reporting reflect the effects of father absence. Pedersen (1966) found that by the age of 15, 90% of the children in a control group receiving outpatient medical care had experienced a long-term separation from their fathers. The recurring cycle of departure, interim absence, and reunion with the father represents a varying stress on the growing child. A child's specific reaction to father absence is determined by the child's gender, stage of development, the length of father absence, the mother's capacity to expand her parental role, the quality of the relationship with the father, and the availability of male surrogates. Father is perceived as the model for masculine behavior for boys' sexual development and also represents the model of male behavior for developing girls.

The doll play of young boys experiencing prolonged father absence in World War II was less aggressive and masculine when compared to that of controls (Bach, 1946). In the Norwegian sailor study (Lynn, 1959), boys who experienced father absence were found to exhibit immaturity, impaired masculine identification, poor peer adjustment, and compensatory masculinity. The Genoan sailor study (Herzog & Suid, 1971) of similar-age boys failed to find any differences in masculine identification and peer adjustment between boys with an absent father and a control group. The differences in these studies' findings may represent the impact of cultural factors. The Norwegian mothers were described as isolated from social contacts, overprotective, and emphasizing obedience. Certainly family ambience, the capacities of the mother, and the availability of surrogates are crucial variables.

Baker et al. (1968) studied boys 5 to 8 years of age whose military fathers departed for a 1-year unaccompanied noncombat tour overseas. Most of the boys demonstrated unhappiness at their father's departure. Some subsequently exhibited management problems, increased masculine strivings, and poor peer adjustment. Reunion with the father was generally associated with improvement in eating and sleeping behavior and more effective involvement in school. It is evident, however, that the impact of father's absence is determined as much by the elements that are present before and after separation as it is by father absence itself. The effects of the reunion were influenced by the quality of the prior son-father relationship and the marital relationship. Those boys whose relationship with the father was compromised often blossomed in father's absence.

A study of the effects of transient father absence on 213 military children 6 to 12 years of age revealed higher rates of self-reported anxiety and depressive symptoms (Jensen et al., 1989). Interestingly, these symptoms were not apparent to parental and teacher observers. These findings disappeared when maternal psychiatric symptoms and intercurrent stressors were controlled. This fact provides support for Pedersen's (1966) observation that a psychologically healthy mother may be able to counter the effects of father absence.

CHILDREN DURING WAR

The children of fathers who have been assigned to a combat area are under unusual stress. While there are anecdotal accounts reflecting this experience, there appear to be few controlled studies. Children of fathers who were held prisoner during the Vietnam conflict for extended periods uniformly performed below the test norms in both personal and social adjustment (Dahl et al., 1976). Children of fathers who had returned home demonstrated less nervous symptoms and better community adjustment than those whose fathers continued to be away from home.

A study of war-born children whose fathers were absent during the first year of life demonstrated poor peer relationships and greater difficulties with sleeping, eating, and elimination behavior (Stolz et al., 1968). The war-separated fathers tended to be more severe, annoyed, and less accepting of their war-born child when compared to a sibling.

The mobilization of forces for Operation Desert Storm, the recent war in Iraq, resulted in a massive deployment of military personnel with sudden disruption of family lives for tens of thousands of children. For the army alone, it has been reported that over 16,000 soldiers who were single parents were deployed overseas. Approximately 3,700 of these single parents were women. Nine thousand dual-military career families were deployed necessitating that those with children suddenly had to find other resources to care for their children (DMIS, 1991). Rosen, Teitelbaum, & Westhuis (1993) studied 1,798 children and their 934 non-

deployed parents whose spouses who had been deployed to Operation Desert Storm and found that over half of the children experienced sadness and disciplinary problems. Jensen, Martin, & Watanabe (1996) studied 383 children and the remaining caregiving parent while the other parent went to participate in Operation Desert Storm. Compared to nondeployed families, the children and their caregivers reported higher levels of depression and more intervening stressors, such as loss of income, family relocation, marital tensions, and so on. Boys were found to be more vulnerable than girls, but this was probably related to the fact that most of the deployed parents were fathers. Younger children were more vulnerable than older children. Both studies while describing distress related to parental deployment noted that the severity of dysfunction was rather mild to moderate and did not usually require therapeutic intervention.

A discussion of the effects of war on children is presented in Chapter 7.

MILITARY RETIREMENT

The advantages of early military retirement may be offset by the impact of this experience on the emerging adolescent. The midlife career change not infrequently results in further geographic relocation, loss of occupational prestige, and a sense of decreased psychological well-being. Just as adolescents are struggling to resolve their own identity conflicts, they also may encounter a father who is experiencing uncertainty in his own social, economic, and occupational identity.

Summary

Children's adaptation to the psychosocial stressors intrinsic to the military community are best understood within the context of crisis theory. Frequent family moves, transcultural experiences, transient father absence, and the effects of war and early military retirement represent crisis situations that are temporarily upsetting, not always in an unpleasant sense, and require reorganization and mobilization of an individual's adaptive capacities. In this context these experiences imply neither good nor ill. Some individuals have higher levels of adaptation with effective coping and problem-solving patterns of behavior. Others achieve a less adaptive equilibrium. In those instances, where the parents have identified with the military way of life and assimilated the shared network of values and loyalties, many stresses can be significantly mitigated if not offset by the other psychosocial advantages of membership in this community.

REFERENCES

Bach, G. R. (1946). Father-fantasies and father typing in father-separated children. *Child Development, 17,* 63–80.

Baker, S. L., Fisher, E. G., Cove, L., Master, F. D., Fagen, S., & Janda, E. J. (1968). Impact of father absence on personality factors of children. *American Journal of Orthopsychiatry, 37,* 269.

Dahl, B. B., McCubbin, H. I., Elester, E. R. (1976). War-induced father absence: comparing the adjustment of children in reunited, non-reunited and reconstituted families. *International Journal of Sociology of the Family, 6,* 99–108.

Darnauer, P. F. (1976). The adolescent experience in career army families. In H. McCubbin, B. Dahl, & E. Hunter (Eds.), *Families in the military system* (pp. 42–66). Beverly Hills, CA: Sage.

Defense Medical Information System (1990). Office of the Assistant Secretary of Defense, Health Affairs, Pentagon, Washington, D.C.

Fernandez-Poi, B. (1988). Does the military family syndrome exist? *Military Medicine, 153,* 418–420.

Frenkel, S. L., Robinson, J. A., & Finman, B. G. (1974). Drug use: Demography and attitudes in a junior and senior high school population. *Journal of Drug Education, 4,* 179–185.

Herzog, E., & Suid, W. C. (1971). *Boys in fatherless families.* U.S. Dept. of Health, Education and Welfare, Publication No. (OCD) 72-33, Office of Child Development, Children's Bureau.

Jensen, P. S., Martin, J., & Watanabe, T. (1996). Children's response to parental separation during Operation Desert Storm. *Journal of the American Academy of Child and Adolescent Psychiatry, 35* (4), 433–441.

Jensen, P. S. (1992), Resolved: Military family life is hazardous to the mental health of children: Debate forum. *Journal of the American Academy of Child and Adolescent Psychiatry, 31,* 984–987.

Jensen, P. S., & Shaw, J. A. (1996). The effects of war and parental deployment upon children and adolescents. In R. J. Ursano & A. E. Norwood (Eds.), *Emotional Aftermath of the Persian Gulf War.* Washington, D.C.: American Psychiatric Press Inc.

Jensen, P. S., Grogan, D, Xenakis, S., & Bain, M., (1989). Father absence: Effects on child and maternal psychopathology. *Journal of the American Academy of Child Psychiatry, 2,* 171–175.

Jensen, P. S., Lewis, R., & Xenakis, S. (1986). The military family in review: Context, risk and prevention. *Journal of the American Academy of Child and Adolescent Psychiatry, 25,* 225–234.

Jensen, P. S., Xenakis, S., Wolf, P., Degroot, J., & Bain, M. (1991). The military family syndrome revisited: By the numbers. *Journal of Nervous and Mental Disease, 179,* 102–107.

Kenny, J. (1967). The child in the military community, *Journal of the American Academy of Child and Adolescent Psychiatry, 6,* 51–63.

Lagrone, D. M. (1978). The military family syndrome. *American Journal of Psychiatry, 135,* 1040–1043.

Lynn, D. S. (1959). The effects of father absence on Norwegian boys and girls. *Journal of Abnormal Social Psychology, 59,* 258–262.

Morrison, J. (1981). Rethinking the military family syndrome. *American Journal of Psychiatry, 138,* 354–357.

Pedersen, F. A. (1966). Relationship between father absence and emotional disturbance in male military children dependents. *Merrill Palmer Quarterly, 12* (4), 321–331.

Pedersen, F. A., & Sullivan, E. J. (1964). Relationship among geographic mobility, parental attitude and emotional disturbance in children. *American Journal of Orthopsychiatry, 34,* 575–580.

Plewes (1991). Personal Communication.

Rosen, H., & Corcoran, J. F. (1978). The attitude of USAF officers too mental illness: A comparison with mental health professionals. *Military Medicine, 145,* 681–685.

Rosen, L. N., Teitelbaum, J. M., & Westhius, D. J. (1993). Children's reaction in the Desert Storm deployment: Initial findings from a survey of army families. *Military Medicine, 158,* 465–469.

Shaw, J. A. (1979). Adolescents in the mobile military community. In S. O. Feinstein & P. O. Giovacchini (Eds.), *Adolescent psychiatry: Developmental and clinical studies* (Vol. 7, pp. 191–198). Chicago: University of Chicago Press.

Shaw, J. A. (1987). Children in the military. *Psychiatric Annals, 17,* 539–544.

Shaw, J. A., & Pangman, J. (1975). Geographic mobility and the military child. *Military Medicine, 140* (6), 413–416.

Stoltz, L. (1968). *Father relations of war born children: The effects of postware adjustment of fathers on the behavior and personality of first children born while fathers were at war.* New York: Greenwood Press.

Strickland, R. C. (1970). *Mobility and achievement of selected dependent junior high school pupils in Germany.* Ph.D. diss. University of Miami, Miami, FL.

Stumpf, S. S. (1978). Military family attitudes toward housing benefits and the quality of military life. In E. J. Hunter & D. S. Nice (Eds.), *Military families: Adaptation to change* (pp. 3–16). New York: Praeger Publishers.

Tooley, K. (1970). The role of geographic mobility in some adjustment problems of children and families.

Journal of the American Academy of Child Psychiatry, 9, 366–378.

Williams, J. (1976). Divorce and dissolution of the military family. In H. McCubbin, B. Dahl, & E. Hunter (Eds.), *Families in the military system* (pp. 209–236). Beverly Hills, CA: Sage.

Woelfel, J. C., & Savell, J. M. (1978). Marital satisfaction, job satisfaction and retention in the army. In E. J. Hunter & D. S. Nice (Eds.), *Military families: Adaptation to change* (pp. 17–31). New York: Praeger Publishers.

6 / **Children in Stepfamilies**

John S. Visher and Emily B. Visher

In the past 30 years, the United States has been experiencing a silent revolution in family styles and practices. Remarriage of adults with children from previous relationships is one of the most striking ways that the world has changed for families. Remarriage as a social institution has always existed, but until recently it generally followed the death of a spouse. However, with the escalating divorce rate of the past three decades, the remarriage rate has also soared, and most stepfamilies now form following divorce rather than death. Today in the United States, approximately 50% of first marriages end in divorce, and a significant percentage of divorced adults do remarry.

A stepfamily is defined as a household in which there is an adult couple at least one of whom has a child from a previous relationship. The census requires a narrower definition of a stepfamily, counting only one primary-residence family. A broader definition is more appropriate for psychological purposes, however, because children often have two households, in each of which similar stresses occur regardless of the children's living arrangements.

In 1990, approximately 50% of marriages were remarriages for at least one of the adults, with 60% of the divorced persons who remarry having children from their previous marriage. Demographers are predicting that 35% of children born during the 1980s will live with a stepparent before they are 18 years of age (Glick, 1989).

Although stepfamilies and first-marriage families often are considered to be similar because there are children living with two adults, clinical impressions and empirical research both document that the dynamics of remarriage families are unique. Stepfamilies can be considered to be families in transition from former households to an integrated stepfamily household. They are comparable in many respects to families that are emigrating from one culture to another, and when individuals do not progress at the same rate toward this goal, symptoms can occur and the family can become dysfunctional (Landau-Stanton, 1985).

Stresses in families in the process of emigrating toward stepfamily integration often are mistakenly viewed as arising from intrapsychic difficulties rather than from problems of adjustment to a new environment. Thus, in treating stepfamilies, it can be important to deal with adjustment problems as the initial focus of therapy, at times coupled with specific treatment programs for other difficulties. For example, when an adolescent in a stepfamily is hospitalized for drug addiction, often two households must be involved in the treatment process, if the teenager is a member of more than one household. Both households need to be approached directly so that each receives a clear message and so that there is less opportunity for either household to sabotage the treatment plan. Contacts with both families also allows for necessary therapeutic work with both parents and stepparents, all of whom have varying degrees of responsibility for raising the child.

Stepfamily Characteristics

Stepfamilies are different in many significant ways from first-marriage families. The following are major stepfamily characteristics that create important stepfamily tasks:

1. *The stepfamily begins after many losses and changes.* All individuals have experienced important losses.
2. *There are often incongruent individual, marital, and family life cycles.* Individuals in stepfamilies come together at different places in their developmental cycles.
3. *Children and adults all come with previous family experiences and expectations.* All come with ways of doing things from former families.
4. *Parent-child relationships predate the new couple.* In first-marriage families, the couple is together for a period before the children are born. In remarriage, the opposite situation occurs.
5. *There is a biological parent elsewhere in actuality or in memory.* An influential person is present elsewhere, who can affect the stepfamily's decisions and integration.
6. *Children are often members of two households.* Many children are members of two households since they may have contact with each of their biological parents.
7. *There is little or no legal relationship between stepparent and stepchild.* Social and institutional support mechanisms for stepfamilies are lacking.

Significant Research in Stepfamily Relationships

Research into stepfamily relationships proliferated during the 1980s and 1990s, and several factors appear to be especially important in looking at children's adjustment: the type of stepfamily, the age and sex of the children, and the length of time since the remarriage. Knowing what is normative in stepfamilies provides therapists with data that often can be used to alleviate guilt and a sense of failure on the part of stepfamily members.

An outstanding difference between stepfamilies and first-marriage families lies in the lack of positive correlations among marital satisfaction, parenting styles, and parent/child relationships and stepparent/stepchild relationships. In stepfamilies, the couple relationship may be very good while the other relationships are filled with tension (Crosbie-Burnett, 1984; Hetherington & Arasteh, 1988; Hetherington, Stanley-Hagen, & Anderson, 1989; White & Booth, 1985). In fact, if the marital relationship is very strong initially, the children's adjustment may be less satisfactory (Brand & Clingempeel, 1987). Clinically this seems to be related to an increased sense of parental loss experienced by the children as they now share their parent with the new spouse and perhaps with other children, as well. Indeed, the greater the number of children in the household, the more problematic is children's adjustment. (Hetherington et al., 1989; Santrock & Sitterle, 1987; Zill, 1988). Helping the remarried parent maintain warm relationships with his or her children at the same time that the parent is attempting to develop a solid adult couple bond is often a major therapeutic task.

Residential arrangements can make a difference. For example, girls living primarily with their fathers have a more difficult adjustment than those living primarily with their mothers (Brand & Clingempeel, 1987; Clingempeel & Segal, 1986). Generally speaking, however, children have greater self-esteem and a more satisfactory life adjustment when contact with both parents is maintained (Hetherington et al., 1989).

As for stepparent/stepchild relationships, they require a longer time to develop than people usually expect. Stepparents need to give themselves and their stepchildren enough time to slowly form a caring relationship before taking more of a disciplinary or parental role (Hetherington & Clingempeel, 1988; Visher & Visher, 1996). Research indicates that there are many satisfactory roles for the adult and the stepchild involved (Crosbie-Burnett, 1984; Mills, 1984).

Many studies support the clinical observation that stepchildren develop warm relationships with stepfathers more often and more easily than they do with stepmothers (Hetherington et al., 1989). When children are young, the stepparent's personality does make a difference to the formation of these relationships; however, by the time children have become teenagers, in newly created stepfamilies there is no correlation between the personal characteristics of the stepparents and the forming of positive relationships. By that age stepparent acceptance or nonacceptance by the children is a major ingredient of what will develop between the children and their stepparents (Hetherington et al., 1989). Frequently warm and caring stepparents are especially difficult for children to accept because of the loyalty conflict that can result if the biological parent of the same sex as the stepparent is distant emotionally or geographically. Stepparents become the convenient target of much anger from stepchildren that is displaced from biological parents because children fear more parental loss if they show anger to their parents (Visher & Visher, 1988).

Children have been found to take longer to adjust to the remarriage than to the divorce of their parents (Hetherington et al., 1989). The most difficult period in remarriage families usually is the first two years, although many stepfamilies take longer to become integrated and functioning in a satisfactory manner, particularly if there are older children (Papernow, 1991). The process is one of going from a lack of connection between individuals in the family unit to a sense of connectedness and belonging in the stepfamily.

Many older adolescents (15 to 18 years of age) leave the household earlier than adolescents of similar age in first-marriage families (White & Booth, 1985). Even though they may not have accepted the changes, they frequently develop warm relations with their stepparents later on when they have become more independent.

Two years after a divorce, only 50% of children continue to have contact with their nonresidential parent (Furstenburg, 1987). Because approximately 90% of mothers still obtain physical custody of their children (Glick, 1989), it is ordinarily the biological father who is no longer an active part of the child's life. At times this withdrawal may be due to lack of interest, but often it occurs because of the pain of not having more contact with the children or feelings of helplessness to influence what happens to them. Sometimes the custodial parent interferes with the contact because of anger or fear of further loss. Some also believe the myth that, after a remarriage, children will do better if the connection is broken between the children and the noncustodial parent.

The impact on children of continued contact with the nonresidential biological parent has received attention, and empirical research suggests that contact with a nonresidential biological father is neutral or may actually enhance the ability of children, especially boys, to form a good relationship with a stepfather (Furstenburg, 1987). For nonresidential mothers and stepmothers, the findings are somewhat different; contact with nonresidential mothers may impede children's relationships, particularly for girls with their stepmothers (Brand & Clingempeel, 1987). However, this negative influence dissipates over time.

A number of clinicians have reported that children who do not have at least minimal contact with their nonresidential parent often become highly disturbed after a remarriage and often may be very hostile to the stepparent. Frequently they build elaborate fantasies about their absent biological parent, and their self-esteem is low (Visher & Visher, 1996). This observation is certainly congruent with Bowen's theory that family "cut-offs" are detrimental to families. Thus it appears that it can be advantageous in the long term for children to have continued contact with their nonresidential parent.

Relationships between siblings, half siblings, and stepsiblings take time to form, with more difficulty occurring the more complex the stepfamily structure and the more children involved (Hetherington et al., 1989). The influence of grandparents and stepgrandparents also may be impacting the stepfamily, and working with grandparents directly or through their "adult children" (the parent or stepparent) may be necessary if the relationships are negative ones.

Age-Related Reactions to Divorce and Remarriage

Children of different ages react quite differently to divorce and remarriage (Visher & Visher,

1996). Infants appear to have little awareness of family changes, provided they receive continuity of care from a nurturing individual. If the child spends time with each biological parent, the child tends to accept this pattern. Sometimes questions arise regarding how old a child should be before a regular visitation is arranged. We believe that each instance needs to be decided individually; but, if both parents provide satisfactory care, there should not be a barrier to visitation.

Preschool children often try to explain their situation by convincing themselves that they had some control over their parent's divorce; perhaps they come to believe that a parent left because of something they did wrong, such as having angry thoughts, or that there is something wrong with them and therefore they are to blame for the parent's departure. We have sometimes thought that it may be easier for children to blame themselves than to not have any control of what happens in their lives. Parents who are able to "give permission" for their children to participate in and enjoy having two households provide the best possible situation for the children.

The ages from 6 to 12 are difficult because of feelings of guilt. Children often feel they have to take sides and to find that one of the adults is responsible for their pain. They have no sense of being in charge of their lives. If they stop feeling guilty, they may have to deal with the sadness which accompanies acceptance of loss and the reality of less control. Children of this age can also be angry at their parents, but this anger is frequently displaced onto a stepparent, who is blamed for everything that has happened. It tends to be less threatening to be angry with a stepparent, since they are willing to have that person leave; in fact, children sometimes try to take charge of their lives by making the stepparent so uncomfortable that they will leave and the child's original parents will get back together. Because parents often feel guilty about the pain that their children are experiencing, they may have difficulty setting limits for children, and the parent and stepparent have difficulty working together.

Adolescents who are trying to establish their own identity and become independent of the family tend to break away earlier in stepfamilies (White & Booth, 1985). They have their own developmental tasks and are frequently unmotivated to work with their parent and stepparent to form a new family unit. Teenagers in stepfamilies may have had the experience of having had an important role when living with their patient during the single-parent phase, then feel rejected when a stepparent joins the household and takes over some of the responsibilities formerly carried by the young person in the single-parent household. Teenagers may be depressed over not having had any control over what has happened to their original family and they may be angry about what is now being expected of them. Their anger is frequently expressed in rebellion and uncooperativeness, just as it is by adolescents in first-marriage households. With adolescent's emerging sexuality, observing the new couple relationship, and living in close proximity to stepsiblings of the opposite sex can cause some tension. At times teenagers will attempt to control these feelings in themselves by being distant or hostile to those who stimulate in them these uncomfortable emotions.

Specific Therapeutic Interventions

WORKING DIRECTLY WITH CHILDREN

With younger children, assisting the adults in dealing more effectively with their family can be the primary way of helping. However, as children become elementary and high school ages, direct therapeutic help is more likely to be needed. A number of interventions are important, some similar to those that are helpful with adults and others that are more directly applicable to young people. The following list reflects common feelings and situations that arise for children and interventions that are important:

- Validation of feelings
  Children, like adults, need reassurance that the feelings they are having are "par for the course" and to be expected.
- Help mourning losses
  Nearly all children experience anger and grief at the time of a divorce or remarriage of their parents.

Helping them deal with these feelings is of great importance (Visher, 1996a).

- Help controlling what can be controlled
Children can control many things, such as what they wear, what courses to take, what sports to play. In some cases, the parenting adults may need help allowing and encouraging this independent decision-making ability. Feeling more "in charge" of such issues can reduce the sense of helplessness at not having control over the death or divorce and remarriage of one's parents.

- Removal of responsibility for the adults' behavior
Children may be able to let go of guilt more easily once they feel less helpless. Believing their behavior led to their parents' divorce or withdrawal does guard against feelings of total helplessness. Gaining positive control can reduce anger, anxiety, and depression, and also diminish acting-out behavior. If the parent has disappeared, it is helpful to reassure the children that the reasons are inside that adult and *not* possible to know, and that the withdrawal of the adult is not because there is something wrong with the child or because he or she did something to antagonize the adult.

- Help getting out of the middle
Younger children may not have the cognitive or psychological maturity to deal with hostile parents. By the time they are adolescents, however, with therapeutic help many teenagers are able to let their parents know that they are unwilling to be messengers between households or to be "in the middle" in other ways.

- Talking rather than acting out
Children tend to act out their feelings rather than talk about them. With help they may be better able to recognize the emotions behind the behavior and learn to communicate verbally rather than behaviorally.

- Groups for children
Counselors and therapists are beginning to recognize how helpful organized school groups can be for children who have experienced divorce and remarriage of their parents. Such groups can be an excellent adjunct to therapy. Information about Banana Splits, Shapes, Rainbows for All Children, and other supportive group programs in the schools can be obtained from Stepfamily Association of America, Inc., 215 Centennial Mall S. #212 in Lincoln, Nebraska 68508 (800/735-0329).

WORKING WITH STEPFAMILY ADULTS

Because of their "executive" positions in the household, adults exert a profound influence on the lives of children. After a remarriage, adults often need assistance in learning how to encourage the development of a well-functioning stepfamily. In a study of step couple's responses to their therapy experiences, Elion (1990) found that the following interventions were considered by the couples to be the most helpful: validation and the enhancement of self-esteem; education about what to expect in stepfamilies and information on ways to handle typical situations; reduction of helplessness; and strengthening of the couple relationship (in large part this was an outgrowth from the first three types of interventions). Elion's work has recently been expanded and corroborated through a large study of couple's responses to stepfamily therapy (Pasley, Rhoden, Visher, & Visher, 1996). This recent research replicates Elion's study and also provides information about what was *unhelpful* to them in their therapy: Therapists who did not understand stepfamily dynamics could make the family situation worse rather than better. The following sections outline ways in which therapists can provide stepfamilies with the help that these studies suggest is particularly valuable.

Validation and Enhancing Self-Esteem: It is important to validate the fact that life has moved on past the divorce and single-parent household phase. Including the stepparent in therapy sessions is one important way to validate the couple and help the integration process in the family. It gives the stepparent legitimacy in the eyes of the children and at times even in the eyes of the children's parents. Many adults, particularly stepmothers, seek clinical help because they believe there is something wrong with them because of their feelings. They think that they have failed in some manner because the fragility of the family system and the complex interrelationships within the household contribute to produce a higher degree of family tension. An understanding therapist who validates the existence of the new unit and the viability and rewards possible in this type of family allows the self-esteem of the remarried parent and the stepparent (and indirectly, the children) to increase. As the adults feel more adequate, they will be able to deal more effectively with the turmoil that may be present in their stepfamily at the time.

Providing Information and Education: Stepfamily adults often need a road map to help them navigate the journey to satisfactory family integration. Helpful basic information includes the following:

- The length of time the process may take.
- The uniqueness of stepfamily structural and emotional characteristics. (It will not fit into a first-marriage family mold.)
- A primary couple relationship is central to the viability of the family and is a valuable model for the children in their future lives.
- Instant love is an unfortunate myth. It takes time to build relationships.
- There are many satisfactory roles for stepparents, not just that of a parent.
- The remarried parent needs to be *active* with his or her children. The stepparent cannot assume a disciplinary role until a relationship has developed with his or her stepchildren.
- One-to-one time together for the couple and between each adult and child is especially helpful with the development and maintenance of relationships. These special times need conscious planning as they do not ordinarily "just happen."
- A "parenting coalition" with the adults in the children's other household is important as it reduces children's loyalty conflicts and helps keep them out of the middle between their two households.

Reducing Helplessness: When individuals become anxious and upset, solving problems is difficult for them. Adults in stepfamily households usually have less control than adults in first-marriage families, since there are important parenting figures in other households. Concrete suggestions by the therapist can help the couple to handle situations in a manner that will decrease their feelings of helplessness. They need to keep control where they *do* have it, not relinquish it because they do not have total control.

For example, following the advice of their therapist, one couple arranged to hire a neighborhood baby-sitter for their children when the parent in the other household was late picking them up. This allowed the couple to follow through as planned with their own commitments. They had come to realize that they could not control the other household, but they could work things out so that they were not victims of chronic lateness patterns or unreasonable demands from a frustrated and angry ex-spouse. Modeling one or two

such situations in therapy sessions can act as a good paradigm for the couple in finding solutions to other problems.

Strengthening the Couple Relationship: Working together as an adult team is essential to the well-being of families. In stepfamilies, doing so can be especially difficult because the adults come together amid preexisting parent/child alliances and complex connections to other households. Remarried parents often feel as if they are betraying their relationship with their biological children if they make a primary commitment to their new partner. This commitment, however, is vital for the children, because without it the marriage may not survive and the children will face another major disruption.

If a remarried parent has experienced weak couple bonding and primary parent/child bonding in his or her family of origin, this model can reinforce a parent's clinging to an existing parent/child alliance. Recognition of the possible effects of this earlier experience allows the individuals to view some of their problems from a cognitive, less personal, perspective. Then they can begin to develop a new model in which their relationship is a primary one that can develop and continue to grow both in the present and after the children mature and are on their own.

The tasks of remarried parents are complex. At the same time that they are developing their new couple relationship, they also must respond to the needs of their children. Because of the pulls of partner and children, many remarried parents feel torn and helpless. In actuality, they are the adults with the power in the household because they belong in both the parent/child and the couple subgroups. Reframing their situation in this manner and helping the adults work together to meet the needs of the children can become the focus of therapy.

Well-functioning stepfamilies speak of their need for family meetings to ensure good communication. Therapists can model this type of family interaction in a therapeutic session once the couple has developed a satisfactory relationship. Including the children in sessions with the couple prior to good bonding between the adults can be divisive and work against the establishment of a good couple relationship. Including children with the adults after the couple bond is secure can help bring increased understanding and acceptance between family members.

THE CREATION OF PARENTING COALITIONS

One of the major tasks for adults in stepfamily households is working out some type of parenting coalition in which the adults in the children's two households are cooperative rather than competitive in the raising of the children (Visher & Visher, 1988, 1989). Besides having happier, better-adjusted children, such a working arrangement also benefits the adults because it reduces their feelings of helplessness. It often enables them to let go of the anger and hostility that can hold the children's households together with tight and painful bonds (Visher & Visher, 1989).

In working with the adults, therapists can assist in this important and difficult task of creating a parenting coalition in the following ways:

- Validate the new couple as the primary couple. Usually it is not possible for parents and stepparents to work with a former spouse before they have a deep sense of marital security and a realization that life has moved on to the reality of a new couple.
- Help households "trade assurances" that neither will try to change the children's residential pattern unilaterally. This assurance can help reduce the children's fear of more loss (Ricci, 1980). Sharing in the rearing of children is a difficult emotional task, and parents often fear more loss of relationships with their children. This fear can underlie tension between the households and result in greater loyalty conflicts for the children. A mother, for example, who has not remarried may fear that the children will prefer to remain in their father and stepmother's home. When fear of further loss, rather than residual feelings from the divorce builds up, children can get caught in the crossfire of hostility.
- Settle boundary issues. If there has not been psychological as well as physical separation between former spouses, it is unlikely that a remarried couple will be able to work productively with the children's other household.
- If each couple is working together reasonably well, see the two couples together to work out a satisfactory parenting coalition. If only one parent has remarried, "balance" in the therapy sessions is necessary (Visher & Visher, 1988).
- The Stepfamily Association of America, Inc., with a central office located in 215 Centennial Malls, #212 (800/735-0329), Lincoln, Nebraska, is a good educational resource for stepfamilies. Along with other services to assist stepfamilies, its publication, *Stepfamilies Stepping Ahead*, provides information and action steps the adults can take to help with the integration process in the family.

Conclusion

While it is important to be aware of the anticipated stresses that occur for children and adults during the early years of remarriage family, it is also important for therapists to keep a balanced perspective. Many stepfamily tasks must be accomplished in an environment usually characterized by a swirl of strong, often conflicting emotions. However, it is also important to realize that developmental and individual psychodynamic factors may be present that are not "stepfamily related."

A stepfamily is well worth the initial struggle, since this family system can bring important rewards to all its members. Adults have an opportunity for happiness in a new couple relationship, and researchers have consistently found "that children adapt better in a well-functioning single-parent or stepparent family than in a conflict-ridden family of origin" (Hetherington et al., 1989, p. 304).

Although successful stepfamilies are similar to successful first-marriage families in some ways, it is important to recognize that in other ways they are different. For example, well-functioning stepfamilies are less cohesive than first-marriage families (Bray, 1988; Chollak, 1989) and more complex structurally and emotionally. When stepfamilies have developed their own traditions and ways of doing things, there can be satisfying couple, parent/child, and steprelationships, and when a parenting coalition has been developed, the adults are able to share parental responsibility and the children can experience additional caring in their lives.

In these families there continue to be "family" events that reflect the complexity of the structure: Family composition shifts from week to week or year to year as children move back and forth between households, and family events such as graduations and weddings can be complicated and re-awaken old feelings.

In well-functioning stepfamilies, interpersonal relationships have a high priority and are not taken for granted, and there is a richness and diversity that can be a positive experience for everyone. For children as well as for adults, learning to deal effectively with the complexities in this type of family can bring a feeling of competence and self-esteem that extends far beyond the boundaries of the family.

REFERENCES

Brand, E., & Clingempeel, W. G. (1987). The interdependence of marital and stepparent-stepchild relationships and children's psychological adjustment: Research findings and clinical implications. *Family Relations, 36,* 140–145.

Bray, J. H. (1988). Children's development during early remarriage. In E. M. Hetherington & J. D. Arasteh (Eds.), *Impact of divorce, single-parenting, and stepparenting on children* (pp. 279–298). Hillsdale, NJ: Lawrence Erlbaum.

Chollak, H. (1989). *Stepfamily adaptability and cohesion: A normative study.* Unpublished Ph.D. diss. The Graduate School of Education, University of Pennsylvania.

Clingempeel, W. G., & Segal, S. (1986). Stepparent and stepchild relationships and the psychological adjustment of children. *Child Development, 57,* 474–484.

Crosbie-Burnett, M. (1984). The centrality of the steprelationship: A challenge to family theory and practice. *Family Relations, 33,* 439–463.

Elion, D. (1990). *Therapy with remarriage families with children: Positive interventions from the client perspective.* Unpublished master's thesis, University of Wisconsin, Stout.

Furstenburg, F. F. (1987). The new extended family: The experience of parents and children after remarriage. In K. Pasley & M. Ihinger-Tallman (Eds.), *Remarriage and stepparenting: Current research and theory* (pp. 42–61). New York: Guilford Press.

Glick, P. C., (1989). Remarried families, stepfamilies, and children: A brief demographic profile. *Family Relations, 38,* 24–27.

Hetherington, M., & Arasteh, J. (1988) *Impact of divorce, single-parenting and stepparenting on children.* Hillsdale, NJ: Lawrence Erlbaum.

Hetherington, M., & Clingempeel, W. G. (1988, March). *Coping with remarriage: The first two years.* Symposium presented at Southeastern Conference on Human Development, Charleston, SC.

Hetherington, M., Stanley-Hagen, M., & Anderson, E. (1989). Marital transitions: A child's perspective. *American Psychologist, 44,* 303–312.

Isaacs, M. B., & Leon, G. H. (1988). Remarriage and its alternatives following divorce: Mother and child adjustment. *Journal of Marital and Family Therapy, 14* (2), 163–173.

Landau-Stanton, J. K. (1985). Adolescents, families and cultural transition: A treatment model. In M. P. Mirkin & S. Koman (Eds.). *Handbook of Adolescents and Family Therapy.* New York: Gardner Press.

Mills, D. M. (1984). A model for stepfamily development. *Family Relations, 33,* 365–372.

Papernow, P. (1993). *Becoming a stepfamily: Patterns of development in remarried families.* San Francisco: Jossey-Bass.

Pasley, K., Rhoden, L., Visher, E., & Visher, J. (1996). Stepfamilies in therapy: Insights from adult stepfamily members. *Journal of Marriage and Family Therapy, 22,* (3), 343–357.

Ricci, I. (1980). *Mom's house, Dad's house: Making shared custody work.* New York: Macmillan.

Santrock, J. W., & Sitterle, K. (1987). Parent-child relationships in stepmother families. In K. Pasley & M. Ihinger-Tallman (Eds.), *Remarriage and stepparenting: Current research and theory* (pp. 273–299). New York: Guilford Press.

Visher, E., & Visher, J. (1988). *Old loyalties, new ties: Therapeutic strategies with stepfamilies.* New York: Brunner/Mazel.

Visher, E., & Visher, J. (1989). Parenting coalitions after remarriage: Dynamics and therapeutic guidelines. *Family Relations, 38* (1), 65–70.

Visher, E., & Visher, J. (1996). *Therapy with Stepfamilies.* New York: Brunner/Mazel.

Wallerstein, J. S., & Kelly, J. B. (1980). *Surviving the break-up: How children and parents cope with divorce.* New York: Basic Books.

White, L. K., & Booth, A. (1985). The quality and stability of remarriages: The role of stepchildren. *American Sociological Review, 50,* 689–698.

Zill, N. (1988). Behavior, achievement, and health problems among children in stepfamilies: Findings from a national survey of child health. In E. M. Hetherington & J. D. Arasteh (Eds.), *Impact of divorce, single-parenting, and stepparenting on children.* Hillsdale, NJ: Lawrence Erlbaum.

7 / Children of War

Jon A. Shaw and Peter S. Jensen

Recently there has been increasing awareness and sensitivity to the plight of children in a warring world. In the last few decades the nature and intensity of war has changed significantly. As armed conflicts around the world have become increasingly characterized by low-intensity and episodic conflict with the employment of guerrilla armies, the civilian population has been victimized at an accelerating rate. Dyregrov, Raundalen, Lwanga, and Mugisha (1987) have suggested that 80 to 90% of all casualties of war around the globe are civilians. UNICEF (1992) has noted that "In the last decade, more than 1.5 million children have been killed in wars. More than 4 million have been physically disabled . . . 5 million children are in refugee camps because of war; a further 12 million have lost their homes" (p. 15). Cairns (1996) has noted that much of the armed violence that children have been exposed to occurs not as a derivative of war, that is, a conflict between two nation states, but rather the violence occurs within a political context in which there is an intergroup struggle. Thus, Cairns prefers the concept of "political violence" to war. While there is some legitimacy to this claim, it is apparent that the concept of political violence is rather vague. We will be using *war* as a generic for armed conflict.

In his monograph *Children of War,* Rosenblatt (1983) states that "there are places in the world . . . [where] children have known nothing but war in their experiences. The elements of war, explosions, destructions, dismemberments, eruptions, noises, fire, death, separation, torture, grief, which ought to be extraordinary and temporary for any life are for these children normal and constant." He relates his conversations with the children of these wartorn lands. A 15-year-old Palestinian girl notes, " I would not bring children into this world"; speaking of the Arabs, an Israeli girl comments, "I hate them without reason"; and a Cambodian child relates, "Peace is worth more than gold" (p. 21). In more recent years we have seen low-intensity wars in Mozambique, Lebanon, Sudan, Central America, Yugoslavia, and subsequent to the disassembling of the Soviet Union.

In the early months of 1991, the United States and its coalition were involved in a high-intensity, high-lethality war against Iraq. This war, lasting approximately 6 weeks, was characterized by unrelenting and sustained air bombardment and the use of massive firepower. While the military mission focused on destroying the political, logistical, and military infrastructure supporting the army of Iraq in its occupation of Kuwait, the sustained bombing and the devastation of life support and economic systems impacted not only on the quality of life but life itself for civilian as well as military inhabitants of Iraq. While most casualties were military, the children of Iraq were and are exposed to all the stressors associated with war. The civilian populations suffer not only during the time of military action but also during the long days of its aftermath.

What are the psychological consequences of war and armed conflict on children and adolescents? During war, an enormous diversity of stressors are imposed on participants. How do children experience the exposure to death and injury of loved ones; bodily and life threat; the loss of family and community; and the sense of unsafety and uncertainty that pervades their lives (Shaw, 1987)?

Psychological Reactions to War

There are relatively few studies of the effects of military action on children. Most reports have been limited to a clinical descriptive approach. There is evidence, however, that children who have been victimized by war are similar to other victims of overwhelming disastrous life events. Children may manifest posttraumatic stress symptomatology, such as intrusive recollections of thoughts and images of war expressed in traumatic play, storytelling, dreams, music, and other behavioral reenactments, or they may manifest avoidance behaviors such as emotional constriction, reduced interests, and estrangement from others (Baker, 1990; Chimienti, Nasr, & Khalifeb, 1989; Shaw, 1987). Others have described the children of war as manifesting regressive behaviors, episodic aggressive dyscontrol, psychophysiological disturbances, guilt, grief reactions, changes in school performance, personality changes, and various depressive and anxiety symptoms (Baker, 1990; Chimienti et al., 1989; Dyregrov et al., 1987; Raviv & Klingman, 1983; Saigh, 1991; Shaw & Harris, 1994).

It has become apparent that the concept of posttraumatic stress disorder has limited applicability to the understanding of the effects of war on children. The diagnosis of posttraumatic stress disorder traditionally has been applied to the configuration of psychobiological symptoms occurring subsequent to the sudden exposure to a stressor that is beyond the normal range of experience and that is circumscribed and singular in its threat of bodily injury and death. It often is associated with affects of fear, terror, and helplessness. War usually represents a chronic, enduring context in which there are multiple and diverse stressors of a sustained and unrelenting nature.

In a review of the childhood traumas, Terr (1991) has noted the important role of actual trauma as a crucial etiological factor in the development of a number of serious mental disorders of childhood and adulthood. She has described two basic types of traumatic experiences in children: Type I (event stressor) refers to childhood trauma, which is usually characterized by a single, sudden, and unexpected exposure to an overwhelming stressor; Type II (process stressors) refers to prolonged and sustained exposure to repeated stressors such as occurs in child physical or sexual abuse. Type I traumas can cross over to be type II traumas. This pattern is quite common in children who have been exposed over time to the enduring stressors of war.

While the psychological responses to the conditions of war can be divided phenomenologically into immediate and enduring stress reactions, the particular configuration of stress response symptomatology will be mediated by biopsychosocial risk factors, parental responsivity, developmental effects, proximity, and the degree of exposure to the stressors with their particular intensity and

duration, the degree of injury or life threat, the losses of family members, and the disruption of the continuity of community, school, and family (Bloch, Silber, & Perry, 1956; Breslau, Davis, Andreski, & Peterson, 1991; Erikson, 1976; McFarlane, 1987; Newman, 1976; Pynoos et al., 1987). Greenacre (1943/1971) has suggested that trauma in childhood is any event that is "noxious, unfavorable and injurious to development" (p. 158). The exposure to war with its multiple stressors is a significant interference with a child's development. Yet the cognitive immaturity, plasticity, and adaptive capacities of children often have veiled the effects of war. Garmezy and Rutter (1985) noted that, not infrequently in the child's response to stress, "behavior disturbances appear to be less intense than might have been anticipated." A conflicting and controversial literature debates the existence, frequency, and configuration of psychiatric morbidity in children exposed to war.

The responses of children and adolescents to war can be divided into five categories: no or little reaction, immediate reactions, long-term effects, bereavement, and children who have become the pupils of war.

NO OR LITTLE REACTION

It is surprising how often children and adolescents are reported to adapt to the conditions of war with little evidence of manifest distress. Freud and Burlingham (1943) noted that children over 2 years of age who had witnessed air raids over England in World War II were able to distinguish between falling bombs and antiaircraft weaponry and that after 3 years of war, the idea of fighting, killing, and bombing had ceased to be extraordinary and was accepted as a part of everyday life. Gillespie (1942) described as a remarkable feature of the English home front the low incidence of child psychiatric casualties compared to the number anticipated.

There are contradictory reports from Israel regarding the effects of shelling on youths. A study of the dreams and sleep habits of Israeli youths in a border town subject to terrorist activities indicated that they slept longer and had fewer dreams, manifesting fewer horror, sexual, and aggressive themes than did their counterparts in a nonborder town (Rofe & Lewin, 1982). Ziv, Kruglanski, and

Shulman (1974) compared 144 children who had been exposed to wartime shelling with 54 children without such exposure with regard to their peer relationships, aggression, and attitudes toward war, peace, and terrorists. Results indicated that stressed children did not have significantly worse outcomes. Using measurements of anxiety, Ziv and Israeli (1973) discovered that children from frequently shelled kibbutzim were no different from those from nonshelled kibbutzim. There is some evidence that communal solidarity, group cohesion, and common purpose shared by civilian and military participants of war may provide protection against anxiety (Zuckerman-Bareli, 1979).

It appears that in some instances, the stressors of war become a part of children's lives, with little emotional affect evident; it is as if there has been a habituation or adaptational effect. Children's capacity to adapt to the ongoing stresses of war is a subject requiring further investigation. The Ziv and Israeli (1973) study of children in Israel suggests that adaptation may become a mediating variable affecting the manifestations of posttraumatic symptomatology. These authors concluded that shelling may become a somewhat routine "part of life," since no significant trauma directly impacted on the children's lives. Similar findings have been reported by Milgram (1982), who found that anxiety levels in 50 11-year-old children living along the Jordanian border were no different from levels in children living in the middle of the country, where terrorist attacks were very uncommon.

Other Israeli studies have suggested psychological effects, even if somewhat muted. Kristal (1978) compared 66 shelled children ages 10 to 12 with 71 nonexposed peers and found a higher prevalence of bruxism among exposed children. While the groups did not differ in neutral situations, exposed children reported higher anxiety levels after watching a film of a terrorist attack. Thus, a provocative stimulus was required to demonstrate the differences between exposed and nonexposed children.

While results are not conclusive, the predominant opinion among researchers of the effects of war-related stresses on children and adolescents is that children may acclimate to relatively low or moderate levels of war-related stressors, particularly when such stressors do not involve direct physical trauma to the child or immediate family.

IMMEDIATE REACTIONS

Immediate reactions may include transient fear reactions, acute panic states, psychophysiological manifestations, regressive phenomena, sleep and appetite disorders, depression, passive reactions, behavior disturbances, dissociative states, disorientation, confusion, and amnesia (Baker, 1990; Chimienti et al., 1989; Freud & Burlingham, 1973; Punamaki, 1987; Shaw, 1990).

Dunsdon (1941) found that children who remained under fire in Bristol, England, demonstrated 8 times more incidents of psychological distress when compared to those evacuated. Bodman (1941) observed that while only 4% of school-age children experienced psychological distress, 61% of those children in a hospital hit by bombs showed signs of distress several weeks after the explosion and 11% manifested symptoms 7 months after the bombing. This is one of the early studies demonstrating the importance of proximity to the zone of impact as a determinant of psychological distress.

Milgram and Milgram (1976) compared prewar and wartime measurements of anxiety during the Yom Kippur War and demonstrated that the general level of anxiety in fifth and six graders doubled. There was, however, no predictable relationship between wartime stress and anxiety; rather there was a correlation with being a boy and/or being a boy from the upper middle class. However, socioeconomic changes and the effects of mobilization and other uncontrolled variables may have mediated children's response rather than the threat of war per se. Chimienti et al. (1989) noted that children in Lebanon exposed to war conditions of shelling, destruction of home, death, and forced displacement were 1.7 times more likely to manifest regressive, depressive, and aggressive behavior. Saigh (1991) has demonstrated that 24 of 72 Lebanese adolescents exposed to major war-related stressors met diagnostic criteria for posttraumatic stress disorder.

LONG-TERM EFFECTS OF WAR

There is considerable evidence that children of war suffer its emotional consequences long after its immediate impact (Arroya & Eth, 1985; Carlin, 1979, 1980; Dyregrov et al., 1987; Kinzie, Sack, Angell, Clarke, & Ben, 1986, 1989; Lin, Masuda, & Tazuna, 1984).

These children often demonstrate the sustained effects of loss, grief, and bereavement. The children and adolescents often have a sense of a fore-shortened future and a pervasive sense of unsafety in an uncertain world. They have a heightened sense of vulnerability and an increased sense of anxiety that something disastrous could happen at any moment (Punamaki, 1987; Shaw, 1987). Often there is a tendency toward life constriction, avoidant behavior, episodic aggressive dyscontrol, and an enduring sense of pessimism. We know that the devastating effects of severe trauma can continue on to the next generation.

The enduring effects of war may be associated with fixation to the trauma, psychic numbness interfering with resumption of life's tasks, residual symptoms of guilt, rage, self-reproach, pessimism, apathy, emotional lability, episodic aggressiveness, and depression. Pynoos et al. (1987) have suggested that 4 factors associated with the exposure to a traumatic situation affect symptom outcome; these include: (1) life threat and witnessing injury or death and posttraumatic stress disorder; (2) loss and grief reactions; (3) worry about significant others and continued apprehension about separation; and (4) reminders of previous life events and renewal of symptoms.

Recently the flight of refugees from wartorn areas of the world has received increasing attention and study. The massive uprooting and resettlement of refugees with their well-documented medical and emotional problems has become a world health problem.

Studies of adult Southeast Asian and Central American refugees have demonstrated considerable psychological and psychiatric symptomatology (Eth, 1992). Refugees have endured the acute and enduring effects of perilous escape and exposure to violence, mutilation, rape, and starvation (Arroyo & Eth, 1985; Baughan, White-Baughan, Pickwell, Bartlome, & Wong, 1990; Carlin, 1979, 1980; Kinzie et al., 1986, 1989). In a 3-year follow-up, Arroya and Eth (1985) studied 30 refugees, each less than 17 years of age, who had fled Central America and who were referred to a mental health clinic. Many had been separated from their families. Often the parents had preceded the children to this country, with the children left behind with relatives. Children who were left perceived that they were abandoned to the repeated violence of

war. The investigators noted that approximately 33% of these youngsters exhibited posttraumatic stress disorders. Other diagnostic categories included adjustment disorders, separation-anxiety disorder, somatoform disorders, and major depressive disorder and dysthymia. Kinzie et al. (1986) noted that 50% of the Cambodian war refugee children traumatized between 6 and 12 years of age had a diagnosis of posttraumatic stress disorder in young adulthood, with considerable comorbidity. Other prominent diagnoses were major depressive disorder, generalized anxiety disorder, and intermittent depressive disorder. Follow-up 3 years later noted that 48% of 27 of the Cambodians continued to exhibit posttraumatic stress disorder; 41%, depression; avoidant behavior was particularly prevalent (Kinzie et al., 1989).

Patterns of bereavement associated with the loss of loved ones and of language and customs are evident. Entrance into the new culture is associated with personal and ethnic identity conflicts and changing social expectations. While studies have demonstrated the progressive adaptive capacities of many of these individuals and their gradual assimilation into the United States, the residual effects of trauma continue long after their flight. A longitudinal study of the adaptational problems of Vietnamese refugees during their first 3 years in the United States demonstrated a progressive reduction in their rates of unemployment and welfare status; nevertheless, this cohort was reported to continue to exhibit compromised physical and mental health (Lin et al., 1984).

There is evidence that unaccompanied Indochinese refugees settled with ethnic foster care families experience less psychiatric morbidity and school difficulties than Indochinese refugees settled into Caucasian families or group homes (Porte & Torney-Purta, 1987).

BEREAVEMENT ISSUES

Many stressors impact upon a civilian population suddenly caught up in the midst of war. Of them all, however, the most grievous is the loss of loved ones. Gleser et al. (1981) noted that in the Buffalo Creek disaster, the threat to life and bereavement served as the predominant stressors giving rise to the subsequent prolonged pathology. Civilians suffer not only as the innocent victims

56

of war but also as the bereaved of those lost in battle and through cruel mischance. The suffering of those whose most crucial relationships are severed in battle was poignantly described by the Greek tragedian Aeschylus, when he has Clytemnestra describe the capture of a Greek city and how the vanquished "women have flung themselves on lifeless bodies, husbands, [and] brothers, little children are clinging to the old dead that gave them life, sobbing from throats no longer free."

A longitudinal study of 25 Israeli children who had lost their fathers to military action when they were 2 to 10 years of age has documented the sustained effect of parental death on their psychological health. Fifty percent continued to have severe behavior and emotional problems 3.5 years after the father's death. Important determinants affecting the enduring effects of the loss were antecedent marital discord, a conflicted relationship with father, hyperactivity and poor control in the child, the mother-child relationship, availability of father surrogates, and the mother's capacity to cope (Elizur & Kaffman, 1982, 1883). Smilansky (1982) evaluated 206 children who had been orphaned by the Israeli wars and observed that compared to same-age and sex classmates, they were more likely to be shy, quiet, depressed, to give up easily on tasks, and to score lower on group intelligence tests.

In addition to the losses associated with death, there are other losses: separations from loved ones; the loss of homeland, ideals, protective security (shelter, food and confidence regarding one's well-being); and the losses associated with bodily injury. There is a new awareness of biological vulnerability and the limitations of others to protect the self. The premature exposure to death, injury, and the limitations of the parents to provide protection poses an unusual stress for children; unable to ensure their own survival, they find themselves suddenly exposed and afraid in a hostile world. They lose trust in others, the future, and in fate.

CHILDREN AS "PUPILS OF WAR"

The youngsters who are exposed to sudden violence at a time when they are struggling to control their own aggression are in danger of having their own evolving control over their aggression undermined and becoming aggressive themselves. We know that children who are physically abused often grow up to abuse their own children. A number of studies have explored the effects of continued exposure to the violence of war on children's subsequent behavior (Chimienti, Nasr, & Khalifeb, 1989; Liddell, Kvalsvig, Qotyana, & Shabalala, 1994; Punamaki, 1987). There is a general finding that there is an increase in aggressive behavior and that the destructiveness of war may become interwoven in the child's inner fantasy life. This seems to occur through a process of modeling and identification with the aggressors. Others have suggested the possibility that aggressive behavior may evolve as a strategy for managing anxiety (Thomas, 1990). Garbarino, Kostelny, & Dubrow (1991) have raised the possibility, however, that in some instances children exposed to war may respond with a heightened sense of moral development and a commitment to peaceful endeavors. Shaw & Harris (1994) found that child victims in Mozambique in many instances yearned and aspired to peaceful life endeavors.

Sometimes children are not only the passive victims of war; in certain conflicts they have been forced to participate in military activities, to become the "pupils of war" (Dyregrov et al., 1987; Shaw & Harris, 1989, 1994). These children have not only participated in military action but also have killed others.

The peculiar brutality of the "bandidos" in Mozambique is evident in their kidnapping of children from local villages and coercing them into military training and forcing them to fight against their own villagers and families. Failure to comply resulted in the cutting off of an ear, the fingers of one's hand, or even death.

An evaluation of 12 of these children, who had been recaptured by government forces, indicated a high frequency of posttraumatic stress symptomatology and dysphoria (Shaw & Harris, 1994). These children tended to see themselves as victims of war. Nevertheless, they tended to identify with future career patterns where they would be helpers to other "victims." They thought of themselves as future priests, doctors, and bureaucrats. A few imagined working in the mines in South Africa where they would be able to make enough money to support themselves and their families.

With one exception the children indicated they did not want to be soldiers, but rather yearned for peace and freedom from war. Although separated from their families who lived in the country controlled by the "bandidos," most asked to remain in Maputo, the capital of Mozambique, where they would be free from the risk of recapture.

These children were forced to be aggressive and violent in a civil war when all they wanted to do was to take flight from violence. Normal children struggle to achieve control over their aggressive and destructive impulses. They control their impulses by both conscious and unconscious self-regulation. Children who are forced to be aggressive at a time when they are learning to control aggression are traumatized in a particularly cruel manner. Imagine how much more traumatized the children will be who are forced to attack members of their own family and village.

Mediators of the Effects of War

The responses of children to war-related stressors are determined by a number of mediators that are not always well understood and whose effects must be tested empirically. The effects of war on children are a function of the intrinsic characteristics of the child, geographic proximity, intensity and duration of exposure, and the response of family members to the stressful and traumatic effects of war. The child's response to the conditions of war is determined by a number of mediators, including those pertaining to the child, the family, and the sociocultural milieu.

CHILD-SPECIFIC FACTORS

Variables intrinsic to an individual child that are likely to affect ultimate outcomes in children exposed to wartime conditions include developmental age, gender, coping capacity, cognitive level and other developmental effects, temperament, and preexisting psychopathology.

Age and developmental factors may set important limits on children's and adolescents' capacity to respond adaptively to war conditions. Preschool children living within the security of a constantly available and supporting family often mirror the parental response to the stressor. School-age children in a more independent fash-

ion experience posttraumatic symptomatology as the product of their own exposure and affective and cognitive processing. School-age children lack the cognitive capacities available to adults. Their theories of causality are egocentric. Children are rarely able to talk about their frightening experiences. Unable to transform their internal conflicts and feelings into words, they are expressed in action, play, aggressive and regressive activities, and other behavioral states. Their egocentric explanations may lead to self-blame, guilt, and a pattern of maladaptive behavior in which the effects of war and loss may not be able to be resolved without therapeutic intervention.

Adolescents may respond with changes in personality and may exhibit a number of behavioral patterns, including social withdrawal, regressive-dependent behavior, and flight into adulthood with manifestations of inappropriate aggressive and sexual behavior. A number of authors have noted that older children and adolescents who have suffered pronounced effects of war often demonstrate remarkable resiliency. While some evidence suggests that such youths may be at risk for the eventual development of anxiety and depressive symptoms, many also may identify with the "helping professions" (medicine, law, etc.) and prepare themselves for future positions in a society without war or violence (Dyregrov et al., 1987; Shaw & Harris, 1994). However, such findings cannot be understood without long-term studies, since such early responses to war stress could eventually become dysfunctional.

It is apparent that the exposure to the sudden realities of mutilation and death, the realistic limitations of the protective power of loving parents, and the sudden and unexpected impact of violence and brutality may undermine children's illusion of safety. Their reaction to a traumatic situation is greatly influenced by their underlying fantasy life and their interpretation of events. When overt traumatic experiences resonate with an underlying fantasy, the memory traces are more intense and may lead to a fixation on the trauma in contrast to those traumatic experiences that are interpreted as incidental (Greenacre, 1943/1971). This fixation may in turn lead to a compelling need to repeat the traumatic experience in a continuing effort to achieve mastery over the traumatic situation.

A number of children are able to call upon intrinsic coping capabilities during wartime crises and generate new levels of adaptation and coping. For example, during the 1967 Arab-Israeli War, de Shalit (1970) reported that many children responded in a remarkable way, often characterized by self-sacrifice and a desire to help the community. In this situation, children's fears often seemed less than might have been expected.

The opportunity to play an active role and to exert some control over their individual responses to war stressors may have important eventual consequences on children's outcomes. Recent evidence provides further support of the importance of the opportunity to exercise personal control in one's response to war stressors. Baker (1990) studied self-esteem, locus of control, and behavioral symptoms in 796 Gaza and West Bank children, and found evidence of higher levels of positive self-esteem and locus of control since the onset of the Intifada, which allowed the children to respond with more of a sense of mastery to the perceived oppressive Israeli occupation of that territory.

The ability to exert and develop an internal locus of control may be more characteristic of older children, and it may be the adaptive result of a response to stressors. Lifschitz (1975) found that adolescents who had lost fathers during the Six Day War or the Yom Kippur War tended to exercise a more internal locus of control and assert responsibility for their lives, compared to controls.

A child's ability to invoke a variety of cognitive defense mechanisms may enhance adaptive outcomes. For example, Rofe and Lewin (1982) noted that adolescents exposed to moderate levels of bombing stress seemed to evolve a cognitive style, such that they have fewer sleep difficulties than their nonexposed peers. Bodman (1941) noted that among 44 children who had experienced severe bombing of a hospital in which they were being treated, older children tended to describe the event in retrospect as "an adventure." Among the oldest children, reactions were remarkably slight, and adaptive outcomes seem related to their sense of responsibility to care for the younger children.

War-related stressors may unmask latent psychopathology or, perhaps more commonly, may serve as a framing construct for more normal developmental fears. Thus, children who at a given age may be quite normally afraid of dogs or burglars may just as well become afraid of "Arabs" or "Russians." In this sense, the war events may serve as metaphors or "vehicles" for the children to express normal developmental anxieties.

PARENTAL AND FAMILY RESPONSES

Understandably, preschool children often mirror the parental response to wartime stressors. Where there is parental physical injury, significant parental emotional responses, or premorbid parental psychopathology, or excessive intolerance of children's tendency to regress, an emotional contagion may occur that passes on like a "ripple effect" upon the children (Bloch, Silber, & Perry, 1956; McFarlane, 1987; Newman, 1976; Pynoos, Frederick, & Nader, 1987). While these concepts are grounded in a substantial clinical and developmental literature, the actual extent to which parent-child emotional contagion occurs is unclear, and inferences about such factors often are drawn from selected clinical cases.

Highly individualized, specific aspects of the child-parent relationship may be more explanatory of adverse outcomes than generic war events and processes. For example, Lifschitz (1975; Lifschitz et al., 1977) noted that among children who had lost their fathers during the Yom Kippur War, children with an affectionate relationship with the mother were better adjusted. This finding was particularly related to adaptation in boys whom the mothers regarded as similar in characteristics to the deceased father. These findings are not surprising and are quite consistent with findings expected for children who have lost parents under non-wartime conditions.

While parental responses likely mediate important adaptive and maladaptive outcomes in their children, evidence suggests that many adverse outcomes are explained by this phenomenon, particularly in view of the relatively remarkable outcomes in most children exposed to war events and processes. Likely, most parents respond quite appropriately during wartime conditions on behalf of their children. Inferences from clinical samples cannot be applied to the broader populations exposed to these stressors.

SOCIAL AND COMMUNITY CONTEXTS

Beyond the role that child and family characteristics may play in shaping children's reactions to war, the social context of specific war-related events is likely also an important mediator of eventual outcomes. For example, researchers who have studied the effects of the chronic political and social unrest in Northern Ireland have noted that the reported differences in children's behavior in comparative studies between Ireland and England cannot be adequately understood without considering the broader socioeconomic conditions in these two comparisons. For example, unemployment has tended to be much higher in Ireland than England (e.g., 15.4% versus 6.6%). Furthermore, housing conditions are much worse, neonatal mortality is higher, and more families are on welfare (Heskin, 1980). Thus, even if the data suggested (which they do not) that the political unrest in Northern Ireland leads to adverse long-term effects on these children, such concerns must be tempered by the fact that most Northern Ireland children would continue to be "under stress" after the political unrest ceased.

Another contextual factor is the meaning of the war-related tensions within the community. For example, Ziv and Israeli (1973) suggest that Israeli children who have been exposed to bombings may have been protected by a "hero" status, since their situation was well known and met with great sympathy throughout the country.

Other researchers of the effects of war on children in Israel have concluded that the presence of strong social and community supports may buffer the effects of adverse experiences upon children and adolescents. Lifschitz and colleagues (1975, 1977) noted that children who had lost their fathers during the war fared better when they lived in kibbutzim than in less cohesive supportive settings (e.g., the moshav or traditional environments). And among children living in the 150 kibbutzim nationwide across Israel, authors have noted that the incidence of psychological disturbance following the Yom Kippur War was no higher than in the 2 years prior to the war's outbreak (Milgram, 1982). While such positive outcomes may be the result of specific steps taken within the kibbutzim to ameliorate or prevent stressful responses in children during these war tensions, concerns have been raised that such optimistic assessments may be partly related to political motivations (Milgram, 1982). Nonetheless, similar findings have been noted for adults, indicating that under high levels of stress, a higher degree of social supports may buffer the effects of stressful events (Zuckerman-Bareli, 1979), and

additional support for the stress-buffering hypothesis has been found in studies of Palestinian women as well (Punamaki, 1986).

Ayalon (1983) has identified 3 community variables that may mediate child and family responses to terrorist and war-induced stresses. First, the historical and cultural characteristics of the community as well as its previous experience with such traumas may shape its reactions to subsequent traumas. Second, community features such as leadership, community cohesion, and communication can play an important role, particularly during and after the stressful situations. Last, the community's specific anticipatory responses to the possibility of the occurrence of such traumatic events likely shapes responses during and after the traumas.

In addition to these factors, it seems plausible that the community's specific responses after the traumatic situation may further shape eventual outcomes. For example, Ayalon (1983) noted that after a terrorist attack on a school in which many children were significantly injured, traumatized children were treated insensitively by the school system, which tended to regard the children's later concentration difficulties as "taking advantage of the situation." In some instances, responses were punitive: girls who violated the dress codes by wearing slacks to school to cover disfigurement and scarring to their legs were expelled.

Treatment

Almost no literature focuses on the treatment of children and adolescents victimized by war.

One of the few focused efforts is that reported by Shaw and Harris (1994). They describe a treatment-intervention plan for children traumatized by war in Mozambique. These children, separated from their families, villages, and communities, which were controlled by guerilla forces, were treated in a protective school environment in the capital of Mozambique.

It was estimated that treatment would take approximately 3 months while ongoing efforts to plan for reintegration of the children back into their communities took place. The objective was to provide a transitional psychosocial program that would facilitate the children's reorganization of their lives so that they could once again meet the normal developmental expectations of childhood and be effective participants in communal and family life. Phase 1 of the treatment-intervention plan focused on assessment and evaluation procedures. Assessed were the children's: physical and nutritional needs; emotional and mental status (i.e., posttraumatic symptomatology, dysphoria), level of maturity; cognitive capacities; social and family situation; the severity, duration, and type of traumatic experiences; current stressors; coping and adaptive style; an inventory of the child's losses, (loss of community, home, mother/father, siblings, neighbors, body mutilations); and finally each child's definition and understanding of the traumatic situation.

Phase 2 focused on the children's active participation in a therapeutic residential treatment setting in which they could feel safe and protected. The "center" provided an organized program that encouraged participation in a *full* schedule of events, including practical living arrangements, normal schooling, organized play, sports, and group and social activities. The children had an opportunity to express their feelings and to reexperience the traumatic situation through the safety of play, dance, song, drawings, and conversation. A mental health professional familiar with posttraumatic symptomatology worked with the children individually or in a group experience in an effort to facilitate abreaction, reconstruction of the traumatic situation, and "working through." It is important that the children over time talk and act out in play, song, dance, and drawings their understanding and reaction to each of the traumatic events.

All children need to have emotional support from the group. They could do this by sharing experiences and talking about traumatic events with each other in a group setting. Realistic information was provided as to what happened to them, the family and village; how it happened; and what they might expect in the future. Throughout there was an ongoing assessment of the children's emotional response to their rehabilitation program and of their capacity to maintain progressive development.

Phase 3 focused on the reintegration of the children into the community. As children begin to reorganize their lives, to "work through" their traumatic situation, and to enhance their progressive adaptive capacities, plans were being made for a more permanent setting. Emphasis was now on finding an extended solution. Psychosocial evaluation determined the choice of a social setting for each child. Primary emphasis was placed on placing a child with his or her family. If this was not possible, adoption or foster home placement was considered. The plan was implemented under the direction of Neil Boothby under the auspices of Save the Children.

Therapeutic interventions utilized on posttraumatic stress disorders include psychodynamic psychotherapy, behavioral therapy, cognitive-behavioral, group, family and supportive individual psychotherapies, and psychopharmacological approaches.

In general, the task of therapy is to provide opportunities for the expression of painful affects—feelings of helplessness, terror, anxiety, rage; to recognize the meaning of the traumatic situation in one's life; to define losses; and to facilitate restitutive and restoration of defenses that will allow children once again to proceed along developmental lines and to get needs satisfied in a reality-oriented and age-appropriate manner.

Children who have experienced a stress response syndrome either tend to repeat representations of the traumatic experience over and over again or to inhibit/avoid representations to prevent disruptive emotions. "The general rationale of treatment is to prevent either extreme denial, which might impede conceptual and emotional processing or extreme intrusive-repetitiousness, which might cause panic states or secondary avoidance maneuvers" (Horowitz, 1974, p. 773).

A number of therapeutic steps should be taken. The first is to identify the pattern of symptoms, to unravel the pattern of dysfunction, to facilitate the pent-up emotions, fears, and anxieties embedded in the symptom complex and ultimately the meaning of the traumatic situation. The crucial phase of therapy is not the expression of pent-up feelings or abreaction but rather the processing of cognitive distortions and beliefs associated with the trauma. Previous belief systems and cherished convictions, illusions, and delusions regarding one's individual and family life may have to be altered. The conflict between previously held beliefs and the meanings intrinsic to the new reality emergent subsequent to the traumatic situation leads to emotional turmoil and not infrequently to a sense of loss.

A child's response to the traumatic situation may involve regression in which developmental attainments can no longer be sustained nor progression maintained. Early patterns of behavior and conflict may become manifest associated with infantile longings or disavowal of parental figures. The goal of therapy is to provide experiences that are titratable and consonant with each child's capacity to assimilate and integrate the emotionality and meaning of the traumatic experience with all its ramifications and meanings. The incongruity between the child's wishes and the reality of the situation have to be unraveled slowly with awareness that one's childhood beliefs can never be again. The child or adolescent has to come to terms with a new sense of unsafety in the world. Affects are painful; often before children or adolescents can come to terms with the meaning of the experience, they must progress from a sense of loss ultimately through a process of mourning.

Much of the therapy focuses on secondary symptoms associated with denial or the intrusion of representations of the traumatic experience. As Terr (1991) has observed, "terrifying events that render the usual coping and defensive operations useless are often integrated into a child's psyche in a detrimental way" (p. 11).

It is hoped that with the increasing awareness of the suffering of these children, systematic and empirical studies will be undertaken to explicate issues in assessment, phenomenology, comorbidity, and the specific mediators that determine course, outcome, and treatment effects.

REFERENCES

Arroyo, W., & Eth, S. (1985). Children traumatized by Central American warfare. In S. Eth & R. Pynoos (Eds.), *Post-traumatic stress disorders in children* (pp. 103–120). Washington, DC: American Psychiatric Press.

Ayalon, A. (1983). Coping with terrorism. In D. Meichenbaum & M. Jaremko (Eds.), *Stress reduction and prevention* (pp. 293–339). New York: Plenum Press.

Baker, A. M. (1990). The psychological impact of the Intifada on Palestinian children in the Occupied West Bank and Gaza: An exploratory study, *American Journal of Orthopsychiatry, 60* (4), 496–505.

Baughan D. M., White-Baughan, J., Pickwell, S., Bartlome, J., & Wong, S. (1990). Primary care needs of Cambodian refugees. *Journal of Family Practice, 30,* 565–568.

Bloch, D. A., Silber, E., & Perry, S. E. (1956). Some factors in the emotional reaction of children to disaster. *American Journal of Psychiatry, 113,* 416–422.

Bodman, F. (1941, October 4). War conditions and the mental health of the child. *British Medical Journal,* 486–488.

Brander, T. (1941). Kinderpsychiatrische Beobachtungen waehrend des Krieges in Finnland, 1939–1940. *Z. Kinderpsychiatr., 7,* 177–187.

Breslau, N., Davis, G. C., Andreski, M. A., & Peterson, E. (1991). Traumatic events and posttraumatic stress disorder in an urban population of young adults. *Archives of General Psychiatry, 48,* 216–222.

Burke, J., Borus, J., Burns, B., et al. (1982). Changes in children's behavior after a natural disaster. *American Journal of Psychiatry, 139,* 1010–1014.

Cairns, E. (1996). Children and political violence. Cambridge, Mass.: Blackwell Publishers.

Carlin, J. E. (1979). Southeast Asian refugee children. In J. D. Noshpitz (Ed.), *Basic handbook of child psychiatry: Vol. 1, Development* (pp. 290–300). New York: Basic Books.

Carlin, J. E. (1980). *Boat and land refugees: Mental health implications, for recent arrivals compared with earlier arrivals.* Paper presented at the annual meeting of the American Psychiatric Association, San Francisco, CA.

Chimienti, G., Nasr, J. A., & Khalifeb, I. (1989). Children's reaction to war-related stress: Affective symptoms and behavior problems. *Social Psychiatry and Psychiatric Epidemiology, 24,* 282–287.

de Shalit, N. (1970). Children in war. In A. Jaeus, J. Marcus, J. Oren, & C. Rappaport (Eds.), *Children and families in Israel: Some mental health perspectives.* New York: Eardon & Breach.

Dollinger, S. J., O'Donnell, J. P., & Staley, A. A. (1984). Lightning-strike disaster: Effects on children's fears and worries. *Journal of Consulting and Clinical Psychology, 52,* 1028–1038.

Dunsdon, M. I. (1941). A psychologist's contribution to air raid problems. *Mental Health, 2,* 37–41.

Dyregrov, A., Raundalen, M., Lwanga, J., & Mugisha, C. (1987, October). *Children and war.* Paper presented to the annual meeting of the Society for Traumatic Stress Studies, Baltimore, MD.

Earls, F., Smith, E., Reich, W., & Jung, K. G. (1988). Investigating psychophysiological consequences of a disaster in children: A pilot study incorporating a structured diagnostic approach. *Journal of the American Academy of Child and Adolescent Psychiatry, 27,* 90–95.

Elizur, E., & Kaffman, M. (1982). Children's reaction following the death of the father: The first four years. *Journal of the American Academy of Child and Adolescent Psychiatry, 21,* 474–480.

Elizur, E., & Kaffman, M. (1983). Factors influencing

the severity of childhood bereavement reactions. *American Journal of Orthopsychiatry, 53,* 668–676.

Erikson, K. (1976). Loss of community at Buffalo Creek. *American Journal of Psychiatry, 133,* 302–305.

Escalona, S. K. (1975). Children in a warring world. *American Journal of Orthopsychiatry, 45,* 765–772.

Eth, S. (1992). Ethical challenges in the treatment of traumatized refugees. *Journal of Traumatic Stress, 5,* 103–110.

Fredrick, C. (1985). Children traumatized by catastrophic situations. In *Post-traumatic Stress Disorder in Children,* 71–100. Washington, D.C.: American Psychiatric Press.

Freud, A., & Burlingham, D. T. (1943). War and children. *Medical War Books.* New York: Ernst Willard, International Universities Press.

Freud, A., & Burlingham, D. T. (1973). Infants without families. Reports on the Hampstead Nurseries 1939–1945. In *The writings of Anna Freud* (Vol. 3, 543–664). New York: International Universities Press.

Garbarino, J., Kostelny, K., and Dubrow, N. (1991). *No place to be a child.* New York: Lexington Books.

Garmezy, N., & Rutter, M. (1985). Acute reactions to stress. In M. Rutter & L. Hersov (Eds.), *Child and adolescent psychiatry: Modern approaches* (2nd ed., pp. 152–176). Oxford: Blackwell.

Gleser, G. C., Green, B. L., & Winget, C. N. (1981). *Prolonged psychosocial effects of disaster: A study of Buffalo Creek.* New York: Academic Press.

Gersony, R. (1988). Summary of Mozambican refugees' accounts of principally conflict-related experience in Mozambique. *Mozambique Health Assessment Mission.* The Indiana State Board of Health, Division of Media and Publications.

Gillespie, R. D. (1942). *Psychological effects of war on citizen and soldier.* New York: W. W. Norton.

Greenacre, P. (1971). Influence of infantile trauma on genetic patterns. *Emotional growth* (Vol. 1, pp. 260–299). New York: International Universities Press. (Originally published 1943.)

Heskin, K. (1980). *Northern Ireland: A Psychological Analysis.* New York: Columbia University Press.

Horowitz, M. (1974). Stress response syndromes. *Archives of General Psychiatry, 31,* 768–781.

Isaacman, A. (1987, June 28). An African war ensnares the U.S. ultra-right. *Los Angeles Times.*

Kaffman, M., & Elizur, E. (1979). Children's reactions to the death of father: The early month of bereavement. *International Journal of Family Therapy, 1,* 203–229.

Kinzie, J., Sack, W., Angell, R., Clarke, G., & Ben, R. (1986). The psychiatric effects of massive trauma on Cambodian children. *Journal of the American Academy of Child and Adolescent Psychiatry, 25,* 377–383.

Kinzie, J., Sack, W., Angell, R., Clarke, G., & Ben, R. (1989). A three year follow-up of Cambodian young people traumatized as children. *Journal of the American Academy of Child and Adolescent Psychiatry, 28,* 501–504.

Kristal, L. (1978). Bruxism: An anxiety response to environmental stress. In C. D. Spielberger, I. G. Sara-son, & N. A. Milgram (Eds.), *Stress and anxiety* (Vol. 5, pp. 93–101). Washington, DC: Hemisphere Publishing.

Liddell, C., Kvalsvig, J., Qotyana, P., and Shabalala, A. (1994). Community violence and young South African children's involvement in aggression. *International Journal of Behavioral Development, 17* (4), 613–628.

Lifschitz, M. (1975). Long-range effects of father's loss: The cognitive complexity of bereaved children and their school adjustment. *British Journal of Medical Psychology, 49,* 187–197.

Lifschitz, M., Berman, D., Galili, A., & Gilad, D. (1977). Bereaved children: The effects of mother's perception and social system organization on their short range adjustment. *Journal of Child Psychiatry, 16,* 272–284.

Lin, K., Masuda, M., & Tazuma, L. (1984). Problems of eastern refugees and immigrants: Adaptational problems of Vietnamese refugees. Part IV. *Psychiatric Journal of the University of Ottawa, 9,* 79–84.

McFarlane, A. C. (1987). Posttraumatic phenomena in a longitudinal study of children following a natural disaster. *Journal of the American Academy of Child and Adolescent Psychiatry, 26,* 764–769.

McFarlane, A. C., Policansky, S., & Irwin, C. P. (1987). A longitudinal study of the psychological morbidity in children due to a natural disaster. *Psychological Medicine, 17,* 727–738.

Milgram, N. A. (1982). War-related stress in Israeli children and youth. In L. Goldberger & S. Breznitz (Eds.), *Handbook of stress: Theoretical and clinical aspects* (pp. 656–676). New York: Free Press.

Milgram, R. M., & Milgram, N. A. (1976). The effect of the Yom Kippur War on anxiety level in Israeli children. *Journal of Psychology, 4,* 107–113.

Newman, C. J. (1976). Children of disaster: Clinical observations at Buffalo Creek. *American Journal of Psychiatry, 133,* 306–312.

Porte, Z., & Torney-Purta, J. (1987). Depression and academic achievement among Indochinese refugee unaccompanied minors in ethnic and nonethnic placements. *American Journal of Orthopsychiatry, 57,* 536–547.

Punamaki, R. (1986). Stress among women under military occupation: Women's appraisal of stressors, their coping modes and their mental health. *International Journal of Psychology, 21,* 445–462.

Punamaki, R. L. (1987). Children under conflict: the attitudes and emotional life of Israeli and Palestinian children. Tampere: Tampere Peace-Research Institutes, Research Reports.

Pynoos, R., Frederick, C., Nader, K., Arroyo, W., Steinberg, A., Eth, S., Nanez, F., & Fairbanks, L. (1987). Life threat and post-traumatic stress in school-age children. *Archives of General Psychiatry, 44,* 1057–1063.

Pynoos, R. S., & Nader, K. (1988). Psychological first aid and treatment approach to children exposed to community violence: Research implications. *Journal of Traumatic Stress, 1* (4), 445–474.

Raviv, A., & Klingman, A. (1983). Children under stress. In S. Breznitz (Ed.), *Stress in Israel* (pp. 138–162). New York: Van Nostrand Reinhold.

Rofe, Y., & Lewin, I. (1982). The effects of war environment on dreams and sleep habits. In C. D. Spielberger, I. G. Sarason, & A. Milgram (Eds.), *Stress and anxiety* (Vol. 8, pp. 67–80). Washington, DC: Hemisphere Publishing.

Rosenblatt, R. (1983). *Children of war.* Garden City, NY: Anchor Press/Doubleday.

Saigh, P. (1991). *Affective and behavioral parameters of traumatized and non-traumatized adolescents.* Paper presented at the annual meeting of the International Society for Traumatic Stress Studies, May, San Francisco, California.

Shaw, J. A. (1987). Unmasking the illusion of safety: Psychiatric trauma in war. *Bulletin of the Menninger Clinic, 51,* 49–63.

Shaw, J. A., & Harris, J. (1989). *A prevention-intervention program for children of war in Mozambique.* Paper presented at the annual meeting of the American Academy of Child and Adolescent Psychiatry, May, New York City.

Shaw, J. A., & Harris, J. J. (1994). Children of war and children at war: Child victims of terrorism in Mozambique. In R. J. Ursano, B. E. McCaughey, & C. S. Fullerton (Eds.), *Trauma and Disaster* (pp. 287–305). London: Cambridge University Press.

Smilansky, S. (1982). The adjustment in elementary school of children orphaned from their fathers. In C. D. Spielberger, I. G. Sarason, & N. A. Milgram (Eds.), *Stress and anxiety* (Vol. 8). Washington, DC: Hemisphere Publishing.

Terr, L. (1979). Children of Chowchilla: Study of psychic trauma. *Psychoanalytic Study of the Child, 34,* 547–623.

Terr, L. (1983). Chowchilla revisited: The effects of psychic trauma four years after a school bus kidnapping. *American Journal of Psychiatry, 140* (12), 1543–1550.

Terr, L. (1985). Children traumatized in small groups. In S. Eth, R. S. Pynoos, & E. Spencer (Eds.), *Post-traumatic stress disorder in children* (pp. 47–70). Washington, DC: American Psychiatric Press.

Terr, L. (1991). Childhood traumas: An outline and overview. *American Journal of Psychiatry, 148,* 10–19.

Thomas, A. (1990). Violence and child detainees. In B. W. McKendrick and W. Hoffmann (Eds.), *Political violence in South Africa.* Cape Town: Oxford University Press.

Ulman, R., & Brothers, D. (1988). *The shattered self.* Hillsdale, NJ: Analytic Press.

UNICEF (1992). The state of the world's children, 1991. London: Oxford University Press, p. 15.

U.S. Committee for Refugees. (1986, November). *Refugees from Mozambique, shattered land, fragile asylum.*

Ziv, A., & Israeli, R. (1973). Effects of bombardment on the manifest anxiety levels of children living in the Kibbutz. *Journal of Consulting and Clinical Psychiatry, 40,* 287–291.

Ziv, A., Kruglanski, A. W., & Shulman, S. (1974). Frequency of wishes for peace of children during different periods of war intensity. *Israeli Journal of Behavioral Science, 19,* 423–427.

Zuckerman-Bareli, C. (1979). The effects of border tension on the adjustment of Kibbutzim and Moshavim on the northern border of Israel. In C. D. Spielberger, I. G. Sarason, & N. Milgram (Eds.), *Stress and Anxiety* (Vol. 8, pp. 81–91). Washington, DC: Hemisphere Publishing.

8 / Children of Parents with Chronic Illness: The Effects of Parental Depression and Parental Cancer

William R. Beardslee and Lizbeth A. Hoke

For decades it has been well established that severe mental illness in parents is associated with increased risk of psychiatric disorder in offspring

With support of NIMH Grant #RO1 MH48696-02; The William T. Grant Foundation; the Overseas Shipholding Group; and a Faculty Scholar Award of the William T. Grant Foundation to Dr. Beardslee. Dr. Hoke was supported by the Trustees Under the Will of Herman Dana and the American Cancer Society, Massachusetts Division, Inc.

(Buck & Laughton, 1957; Ekdahl, Rice, & Schmidt, 1962; Landau, Harth, & Othnay, 1989; Rutter, 1966); however, psychiatric disorder in these children is rarely recognized or adequately treated (Costello et al., 1988; Keller, Lavori, Beardslee, Wunder, & Ryan, 1991). More recently, studies have suggested that children of parents with serious nonpsychiatric illness, such as cancer, also are at increased risk for mood and behavioral problems and low self-esteem (Lichtman et al., 1984; Siegel et al., 1992). On the other hand, a growing body of literature on resiliency indicates that many youngsters at risk for disorder function well despite adversity (Beardslee & Podorefsky, 1988; Rutter, 1986), suggesting that both risk factors and adaptive strengths must be considered when evaluating the impact of parental illness. It is essential that clinicians treating children understand the ways that parental illness can cause severe stress in families and place children at increased risk for both transient and long-term adjustment problems. Equally important is a knowledge of resiliency, in order that clinicians can support existing strengths and foster adaptive coping as they treat these children and their families.

This chapter presents findings from two widespread and representative chronic illnesses that frequently affect parents with young children and adolescents; one illness is psychiatric—chronic mood disorder—and the other medical—cancer. Even while there is a great deal of heterogeneity within any given diagnosis and across types of illnesses, a comparison of findings about these two illnesses illustrates how different parental disorders affect families in similar ways. In addition, the research on parental mood disorder provides a model for the investigation of parental cancer and other types of nonpsychiatric medical illnesses whose effects on children have not been well studied.

Parental illness disrupts the family on many levels. Serious medical disorders as well as psychiatric disorders frequently can cause symptoms of depression and anxiety in patients (Derogatis et al., 1983). Both psychiatric and nonpsychiatric illnesses can lead to disruptions in the parent-child relationship, reducing the parent's emotional availability to the child and interfering with the parent's ability to engage in child-related tasks (Cox, Puckering, Pound, & Mills, 1987; Siegel, Raveis et al., 1990). Coping with the illness and its consequences also affects the nonill parent and is associated with increased strain in marital relationships (Rounsaville, Prusoff, & Weissman, 1980; Taylor & Aspinwall, 1990). Family members frequently have difficulty communicating and expressing their feelings about the illness, making it hard for them to support one another (Beardslee, 1990; Siegel, Mesagno, & Christ, 1990). Stigmas associated with the disorder may deter families from seeking help and contribute to their feelings of isolation.

When evaluating families with parental illness, it is important to consider the characteristics of the illness, responses of the parent, the children, and the larger family and social environments. A thorough knowledge of psychosocial and biological risk factors for children as well as an understanding of what helps children and families cope when a parent is ill are necessary in order to adequately assess the clinical needs of both parents and children. An awareness of these factors informs the types of interventions prescribed—for example, whether the child is treated directly and/ or whether parents receive some form of therapy or counseling for themselves. Opportunities for early intervention also are improved, thereby increasing the likelihood that negative effects of the parental illness on the family will be curtailed.

Parental Mood Disorders

Over the last two decades, there has been a remarkable growth in knowledge from empirical longitudinal studies of children at risk due to serious parental mood disorder. Despite the employment of different conceptual frameworks and methods, there is a strong consensus in the literature that children of parents with mood disorder fare much more poorly throughout childhood than do children of parents with no disorder. More recently, structured diagnostic interviews scored according to standard criteria and standard systematic assessments of child functioning have facilitated comparisons across studies (Downey & Coyne, 1990). Findings have been documented in several reviews (Beardslee, Bemporad, Keller, & Klerman, 1983; Beardslee & Wheelock, 1994; Downey & Coyne, 1990; Keitner & Miller, 1990; Lee & Gotlib, 1989; Orvaschel, Walsh-Allis, & Ye, 1988; Rutter, 1990; Waters, 1987; Zuckerman & Beardslee, 1987).

Children of parents with affective disorder have rates of diagnosable psychopathology several times higher than comparison samples (Downey & Coyne, 1990). In particular, these youngsters are more likely to develop major depressive disorders during adolescence. The few available longitudinal studies of children at risk for mood disorder demonstrated continued and increasing risk for these children (Hammen, Burge, Burney, & Adrian, 1990). Estimates of the cumulative probability of an episode of psychiatric disorder in the children of unipolar depressed mothers are as high as 80% by late adolescence (Hammen et al., 1990).

Despite their increased risk, these children are undertreated. In one study, less than one-third of children of parents diagnosed with mood disorder received any treatment for their depression (Keller et al., 1991). Epidemiologic studies (Offord et al., 1987) and studies of pediatric practices (Costello et al., 1988) also have identified substantial underrecognition and undertreatment of childhood disorder. The fact that parents with affective disorder frequently do not seek treatment for themselves compounds the problem. Epidemiologic studies have established much higher rates of parental affective disorder in the general population than in parents who present for clinical treatment (Beardslee et al., 1988), and the same powerful negative effects of parental disorder on child outcome have been found in children of parents who do not receive treatment (Beardslee et al., 1983; Beardslee, Keller, Lavori, Staley, & Sacks, 1993).

Impairments in youngsters occur across the life span and involve many areas besides diagnoses (Weissman, Paykel, & Klerman, 1972). Furthermore, several studies suggest that children who develop adjustment problems continue to experience difficulties throughout childhood and adolescence (Billings & Moos, 1983, 1985; Hammen, 1988; Zahn-Waxler et al., 1988).

In infancy, children of parents with mood disorders appear to have disturbances in affiliative and attachment behavior (Gaensbauer, Harmon, Cytryn, & McKnew, 1984) as well as impaired cognitive functioning, more negative emotions, and poorer stress tolerance than infants of parents without mood disorders (Whiffen & Gotlib, 1989). Follow-up studies suggest that these children will experience developmental problems in the preschool years, including cognitive, emotional, and interpersonal difficulties (Sameroff, Seifer, Zax, & Barocas, 1987; Zahn-Waxler,

McKnew, Cummings, Davenport, & Radke-Yarrow, 1984). Higher rates of accidents and medical complaints also have been reported (Brown & Davidson, 1978).

Negative self-perceptions and attributional styles have been found in school-age children of parents with mood disorders (Beardslee & Wheelock, 1994). Zahn-Waxler and colleagues (Zahn-Waxler, Kochanska, Krupnick, & McKnew, 1990) have suggested that increased guilt experienced by young children of depressed mothers may place them at increased risk for depression. When presented with hypothetical situations involving interpersonal conflict, they found that these children responded with excessive guilt feelings, high levels of responsibility, and overarousal.

Adolescents not only are at increased risk for major depressive disorders but are at increased risk for other psychiatric symptoms as well as low self-esteem (Hirsch, Moos, & Reischl, 1985). Compared to children who did not have parents with mood disorders, one study found that adolescents at risk because of parental mood disorder exhibited lower overall adaptive functioning, measured by school and work performance, ability to form relationships, and ability to express feelings (Beardslee, Schultz, & Selman, 1987). A wide range of problem behaviors have been observed in adolescents of depressed mothers, including internalizing and externalizing problems, deficits in prosocial behaviors, and impaired cognitive functioning (Forehand & McCombs, 1988).

Both genetic and psychosocial factors are important in understanding the link between parental mood disorder and poor child outcome. To date, it has not been possible to definitively separate the influence of these two predictors or to determine the relative weight each contributes to the development of childhood mood disorder. Evidence for a genetic component comes from studies of monozygotic twins reared apart, in which increased concordance rates of bipolar illness and, to a lesser extent, increased concordance rates of unipolar illness have been found in twins (Nurnberger & Gershon, 1982). Family history studies have demonstrated that relatives of adults with mood disorder are at increased risk for mood disorder (Gershon et al., 1982) and that the risk goes up as the number of relatives with disorder increases (Tsuang & Faraone, 1990). It is also true that youngsters with mood disorder have higher rates of mood disorder in their relatives (Strober et al., 1988).

Detailed review of the children of parents with affective illness leads to the conclusion that it is not the presence of mood disorder alone that leads to poor outcome in children, but its association with other factors, such as increased chronicity and severity of the disorder, comorbidity in the spouse, poor parenting practices and marital discord. Keller and colleagues (1986) found that more severe and chronic parental illness, as measured by number and duration of episodes, number of times treated and hospitalized, and number of suicide attempts, was strongly related to poor child outcome. Spouses of patients with mood disorder also are more likely to experience a mood disorder and other forms of psychopathology (Coyne et al., 1987; Merikangas, Prusoff, & Weissman, 1988), and comorbidity in parents is associated with poorer outcome in children (Beardslee, Keller, & Klerman, 1985; Weissman et al., 1984).

Poor parenting practices, marital discord, and divorce are well-established risk factors for increased psychopathology and adjustment problems in children (Downey & Coyne, 1990; Keitner & Miller, 1990; Rutter, 1990), and these factors have been associated with parental mood disorder (Downey & Coyne, 1990; Rutter, 1990). Particular attention has been paid to the parenting practices of depressed mothers. Studies of mother-infant interactions suggest that an infant's ability to control and change internal affective states is related to the mother's ability to respond in a positive reciprocal fashion (Tronick, 1989). Mothers who are depressed frequently are less attuned to their infant's affective states, and an early vulnerability to depression may stem, at least in part, from failed emotional communication between an infant and his or her caregivers (Tronick, 1989). Cohn and Tronick (1989) stressed the importance of assessing the quality of mother-child interactions over and above the types of depressive symptoms in the parent, and a variety of negative interpersonal factors between depressed mothers and their children have been identified. These include sustained negative affect (Cohn, Campbell, Matias, & Hopkins, 1990; Field et al., 1985;

Field, Healy, Goldstein, & Guthertz, 1990); less responsivity (Bettes, 1988; Cox et al., 1987; Goodman & Brumley, 1990); a diminished ability to resolve interpersonal conflict in constructive ways (Kochanska, Kuczynski, Radke-Yarrow, & Welsh, 1987); and less structure and discipline (Goodman & Brumley, 1990). While most of these studies were conducted with infants and young children, Gordon and colleagues (1989) also found similar patterns in depressed mothers' interactions with children ages 8 to 16.

Partners of patients with mood disorders experience substantial distress about the illness in the identified patient (Coyne et al., 1987; Krantz & Moos, 1987; Targum, Dibble, Davenport, & Gerson, 1983), and many feel that their ill partner is no longer available to them (Fadden, Bebbington, & Kuipers, 1987). In a study of patients with bipolar illness, spouses also expressed concern about the effect of the parental illness on their children (Targum et al., 1983).

A parental mood disorder can interfere with the whole family's ability to carry out usual functions that help sustain the well-being of family members. Disturbances in communication among family members have been reported (Gotlib & Ruscher, 1988; Hinchliffe, Hooper, Roberts, & Vaughan, 1975), in addition to impaired capacities for problem solving and confusion about roles and responsibilities within the family (Keitner & Miller, 1990).

In summary, it is well established that children of parents with mood disorder are at increased risk for mood disorders and other types of behavior and adjustment problems. The nature of the transmission of disorder is not clearly understood, although studies suggest that risk factors include a combination of impaired parenting practices and interpersonal relationships, along with a possible genetic component, particularly with bipolar illness. It is important to understand that parental mood disorder has profound effects on interpersonal relationships within the family and that it constitutes a constellation of risk factors that must be identified in order to understand how to help children. As the work of Sameroff and colleagues (1987) and Rutter (1986) suggests, it is not any one specific factor but rather the combination of several risk factors that leads to poor outcome in children.

Parental Cancer

In contrast to the research on parental mood disorder, few empirical studies of the effects of parental cancer on children's adjustment have been published. Most of these studies suggest some increased risk for adjustment problems in children of cancer patients; however, the nature and extent of children's impairment is not well defined, nor are the risk factors for developing more long-term or serious difficulties. Only one study has assessed children's adjustment over time (Siegel et al., 1996), and no studies have investigated the types of treatment these children receive. The lack of replicated studies makes it difficult, if not impossible, to know if differences in findings are due to factors related to the heterogeneity of cancer diagnoses, different study samples, and/or different study methodologies.

Nevertheless, there is increasing evidence in the clinical and research literature that children of cancer patients can experience a wide range of adjustment reactions and problems (Hoke, 1996). These include anxiety; depressed mood (Siegel et al., 1992); lower social competence and declining academic performance (Buckley, 1977; Siegel et al., 1992); lower self-esteem (Lewis, 1990; Siegel et al., 1992); somatic symptoms, such as stomachaches and appetite disturbance; trouble sleeping; increased clinging behavior (Buckley, 1977); acting out and anger (Buckley, 1977; Lichtman et al., 1984; Wellisch, 1981); and withdrawal (Adams-Greenly & Moynihan, 1983).

Characteristics of children that influence their responses to the parental cancer have been identified in the clinical and research literature, and include cognitive abilities, level of emotional development or age, and gender (Hoke, 1996). How children understand the parental illness is determined, in part, by their ability to process and integrate information. Studies have shown that children's concepts of illness and death generally tend to move from concrete and personalized to more abstract with increasing age (Bibace & Walsh, 1980; Koocher, 1974). Children's responses also are influenced by the types of developmental tasks they are mastering at the time of the parental illness. Young children, who by nature are dependent on their parents and who may inter-pret the illness in a concrete and personalized way (e.g., may believe something they did caused the illness), have been observed to respond with fear and concerns about their own and their family's safety (Adams-Greenly & Moynihan, 1983; Issel, Ersek, & Lewis, 1990). Preadolescent children are more likely to seek out information about the illness (Lewis, 1990) but also may have difficulty managing their feelings, making it hard for them to understand the information they obtain (Adams-Greenly & Moynihan, 1983). Several authors have suggested that adolescents are more likely than younger children to respond with anger and act-ing-out behaviors when a parent has cancer (Adams-Greenly, Beldoch, & Moynihan, 1986; Buckley, 1977; Issel et al., 1990; Lichtman et al., 1984; Wellisch, 1979). These same authors have hypothesized that adolescents who normally move toward increased independence from their parents experience conflict when the emotional and practical demands of the illness force them to become more involved with their families.

Two studies compared children's responses across age groups. One study of parents with cancer found that preadolescent children were more likely than adolescents and young adults to respond with symptoms associated with stress response syndrome, including intrusive thoughts and feelings and avoidance of their parents' cancer (Compas et al., 1994). On the other hand, adolescents and young adults were more likely to exhibit symptoms of anxiety and depression. The authors hypothesized that younger children may try to minimize the implications of their parents' illnesses, although they cautioned that these findings need replication. In another study of children of terminally ill parents, children ages 10 to 12 reported more anxiety than younger and older children (Rosenheim & Reicher, 1985). These researchers suggested that children in this age range had more realistic understandings of death than younger children but less adequate coping abilities than older children.

Although only one study has examined gender systematically, there is evidence that the gender of both the child and the ill parent can affect the child's response to the parental cancer. Compas and colleagues (1994) found that adolescent girls whose mothers had cancer experienced more depression and anxiety than younger children, boys, or children whose fathers had cancer. Others have observed more distress in daughters of breast cancer patients than in sons, and several possible explanations have been suggested. Mothers with breast cancer may be more apt to look to their daughters for support, creating more stress for their daughters (Lichtman et al., 1984). Adolescent daughters who are experiencing puberty also may suffer more distress because of their identification with their mothers. They may have concerns about their mother's sexuality and body integrity as well as their own (Wellisch, 1981, 1985). Finally, when there is a genetic risk component to the cancer, such as for daughters of breast cancer patients, children may experience heightened fear that they will develop the disease themselves.

Characteristics of the parental illness that affect children's adjustment also have been identified. Studies suggest that children encounter greater difficulties when a parent is terminally ill (Siegel et al., 1992), as compared to children of parents who have not experienced a recurrence of their cancers (Lewis, 1990). There also is some evidence that more severe illness or impairment, as measured by longer duration of illness (Buckley, 1977), poorer prognosis, and more radical surgery (Lichtman et al., 1984), is related to more impairment in children. A recent follow-up study suggested, however, that even for children of terminally ill parents, elevated levels of distress diminish several months after the parent's death (Siegel et al., 1996). Interestingly, a recent study of newly diagnosed cancer patients found that disease characteristics were not as strongly related to measures of distress in patients, their spouses, and children as were measures of family members' perceptions of the severity and stressfulness of the patients' illness (Compas et al., 1994).

As the literature on mood disorders suggests, a parent's own psychological adjustment to the cancer diagnosis is an important factor in the child's experience of, and adjustment to, a parental illness (Hoke, 1996). Adults diagnosed with cancer often suffer from anxiety and depressed moods (Compas et al., 1994; Derogatis et al., 1983). There is some evidence that increased distress in parents with cancer is associated with poorer adjustment in children (Buckley, 1977; Howes, Hoke, Winterbottom, & Delafield, 1994; Lichtman et al.,

1984), although not all studies have found a relationship between parents' and children's responses to the parental illness (Compas et al., 1994).

A cancer diagnosis affects the partner's psychological adjustment, as well, leading to elevated levels of distress similar to that of the patient (Compas et al., 1994; Northhouse & Swain, 1987). One study found that emotional disruption for the spouse can last up to 3 years after diagnosis and treatment (Baider & Kaplan De-Nour, 1984). Coping with the emotional and practical demands of the diagnosis and treatment also can lead to substantial strain in the marital relationship (Taylor & Aspinwall, 1990). The burdens of the illness placed on partners can interfere with their ability to provide consistent discipline and emotional support for their children (Siegel, Raveis et al., 1990), while concerns about the effects of the illness on their children are an added source of distress for parents (Hymovich, 1993).

In summary, the study of parental cancer suggests that these families face many of the same challenges and dilemmas experienced by families with parental mood disorder. A parental medical illness, like a psychiatric illness, affects children and families on multiple levels and places some children at increased risk for developing adjustment problems. However, the investigation of parental cancer and other forms of medical illnesses has received substantially less attention, and many areas need further exploration.

Resiliency and Prevention

It is important to recognize that not all children in studies of parental illness experience difficulties. For example, some studies of breast cancer patients found that most children functioned within the normal range and did not experience major problems (Howes et al., 1994; Lewis, 1990; Lichtman et al., 1984). Many children adjust well despite having a parent who is or has been seriously debilitated.

In recent years there has been an increased interest in identifying characteristics of resiliency in children, that is, qualities and strengths in the children or their environment that help them to cope well when faced with serious life stressors. Rutter (1987) has emphasized a range of factors contributing to resiliency including good physical health; high intellectual ability and easy temperament; the presence of positive relationships, particularly with the parents; and opportunities for involvement outside the home. Inner psychological qualities, such as a sense of control over one's surroundings and high self-esteem, are also important (Garmezy, 1988; Rutter, 1986).

Within this domain is the child's ability to understand the parent's impairments and his or her relationship to the parental illness. Beardslee and Podorefsky (1988) interviewed the most resilient youngsters growing up in homes with severe parental mood disorder and found those children who coped best had close confiding relationships outside the home, were activists and doers—that is, were deeply involved in school, outside activities, and work—and understood that they were not responsible for the parental illness. These children spent a substantial amount of time thinking about the parental illness, but in such a way that it helped them develop a sense of separateness from it. They felt free to carry on with their own lives, despite the parent's severe impairment.

In a study of how children coped with their mother's breast cancer (Issel et al., 1990), children reported several adaptive strategies similar to those identified by Beardslee and Podorefsky (1988). Maintaining normal routines, participating in activities with family and friends, anticipating what might be helpful at home, and being able to sort through one's feelings, either by talking about the illness within the family or thinking about it by oneself, all were described by children as ways they and their families managed their mother's illness.

Certain types of family coping strategies frequently associated with better family functioning (Olson, 1991) have been related to better child adjustment in families with parental mood disorders and parental cancer. These include an ability to adapt flexibly (Howes et al., 1994), and cohesion or supportiveness among family members (Billings & Moos, 1983). More frequent interactions with the well parent, more frequent talking among family members about how they manage the illness (Lewis, Hammond, & Wood, 1993), and sharing information about the illness within the family (Rosenheim & Reicher, 1985) also have been related to better adjustment in children of parents with cancer. Communication between parents and children about the parental illness and its effects on the family is widely endorsed as a way to help children understand the illness, express their feelings, and anticipate future developments (Adams-Greenly & Moynihan, 1983; Buckley, 1977; Lewis et al., 1993; Rosenheim & Reicher, 1985; Siegel, Mesagno et al., 1990; Wellisch, 1981).

In this respect, our experience working with families with parental mood disorders and parental cancer has taught us that it is important to attend not only to the diagnostic and etiologic factors but also to the family's experience of the illness. In families with parental mood disorder, children often are faced with profound misunderstandings and disparate, unintegrated experiences of abrupt and inexplicable behavior, such as hospitalizations, suicide attempts, arguments within the home, and withdrawal of the ill parent. Children of cancer patients and parents with other medical illnesses can have similar experiences as their parents struggle with the symptoms and treatment of the illness as well as their own psychological reactions. Children are at great risk for feeling fearful, confused, and responsible for distress they see in their parents. At the same time, parents often are alone with their fears about how the illness and their responses to it may have irrevocably harmed their children. The parents' and children's needs may conflict as they struggle to cope with the effects of the illness on the family. It is important, then, to attend to the illness experiences of parents and children: the parents' concerns about the impact of the illness on their children, and the children's fears and concerns about their parents.

Recently a number of important institutions have emphasized that children of parents with mental illness represent important populations for prevention initiatives (Institute of Medicine, 1994; National Institute of Mental Health, 1993). While such programs have not been fully evaluated yet, a number of promising approaches exist combining cognitive psychoeducational findings with psychotherapeutic approaches. Beardslee (Beardslee & MacMillan, 1993; Beardslee et al., 1992), has developed a short-term preventive intervention for families with parental mood disorders that is designed to provide parents with information about effects of parental illness on children. The conceptual basis and organization of this intervention stem from research findings about risk factors and resiliency in these children, and thus, its implementation provides one model of how clinical interventions can be informed by empirical study.

The long-term goal of the intervention is to reduce the risk that children in these families will develop serious mood disorder or behavior problems. The short-term goals target a wide range of behaviors related to effects of depression on family functioning and, particularly, the child's functioning. Central to the intervention is the linking of factual information to the unique experiences of each family, in order to increase its understanding of the illness experience. Much of the work takes place with the parents, although the children remain a central focus. Over the course of 6 to 10 sessions, a clinician meets several times with the parents to identify their concerns about the effects of the parental illness on their children and to prepare them to talk with their children about the illness. During an individual session with each child, the clinician assesses the child's concerns about the illness. Finally, the whole family meets together and the clinician facilitates the sharing of information and feelings among the family members, with a particular focus on helping the parents to address their children's concerns.

When compared to parents receiving information in a lecture format, findings showed that parents in the intervention reported greater satisfaction and significantly more behavior and attitude changes related to their illnesses (Beardslee et al., 1992; Beardslee, Salt et al., 1993). Approximately one year later, parents in the intervention continued to report significantly more behavior and attitude changes than parents who attended the lecture (Beardslee et al., in press).

Drawing from their experiences with families with parental cancer, a similar prevention program for children of terminally ill parents has been developed independently by Siegel, Mesagno, and colleague (1990). This intervention, which takes place primarily with the nonill parent and the children, also is designed to help parents better understand their own and their children's reactions to the parental illness and death. Like the preventive intervention for families with parental mood disorders, there is an emphasis on fostering clear and open communication within the family

and helping the surviving parents understand and address their children's emotional needs. Like parents with clinical depression, parents affected by cancer are struggling to assimilate their experience of the illness and talk with their children about it.

Conclusion

The review of parental mood disorders and parental cancer highlights several important considerations both for the design of research investigations of the effects of parental disorder on children and for the clinical evaluation and treatment of children and their families. A family's experience of the parental illness can vary widely within any given diagnosis, and thorough evaluation of the impact of the illness, whether psychiatric or medical, should include the assessment of several domains. First, studies of parental mood disorder and cancer, as well as of other life stressors (Coie et al., 1993), suggest that children's responses to parental illness can be influenced by their gender, cognitive abilities, developmental level or age, characteristics of resiliency, and preexisting qualities that place them at increased risk, such as developmental difficulties, cognitive impairment, or a history of previous psychiatric problems.

Second, characteristics of the illness itself also must be considered: the types of symptoms; the extent of impairment to the parent; side effects and disruptions caused by the treatment, such as time away from the home in the hospital; the course of the illness, such as whether it is episodic or degenerative; and the prognosis, particularly whether the illness is terminal.

Third, it is important to consider the psychological impact of the illness on both the patient and the nonill parent. As studies of cancer patients suggest, medical illnesses as well as psychiatric illnesses can have a negative impact on the ill parent's psychological health. Psychological impairment in the spouse and strain in the marital relationship, both risk factors for children, have been associated with mood disorders and cancer. Furthermore, comorbidity in the spouse frequently is found in mood disorders and other types of psychiatric disorders.

Other characteristics of the family and the

larger social environment can place children at increased risk for psychiatric disorder or protect them from the negative consequences of having an ill parent. Clear communication about the illness and flexibility in managing the changes brought about in the family are associated with better child adjustment. On the other hand, coming from a family with low socioeconomic status is a risk factor for childhood adjustment problems (Coie et al., 1993) because these families have fewer resources. Particularly when a parent is ill, low socioeconomic status can limit the quality of treatment for the ill parent and the availability of resources to help the family cope with the illness. When there are public fears and stigmas associated with the illness, an added psychological burden is placed on family members and access to the usual psychological supports within the family and community may be limited.

When evaluating the impact of parental illness and the etiologic risk factors for children, it is important to understand both the psychosocial influences and what is known about the heritability of the disease. It is also important to understand the relative risks to offspring when a genetic factor is known or suspected. For example, there is a well-established genetic vulnerability in offspring of schizophrenic parents, but the number of children who actually develop schizophrenia is very small (Watt, Anthony, Wynne, & Rolf, 1984). In contrast, a genetic component in unipolar mood disorder is less clearly established, but the risk to children, whether psychosocial or genetic, is much greater. The presence of a genetic risk factor can influence the outcome of the child and also lead to increased distress in the family. Parents and children may feel fearful and helpless if they believe the illness is inherited, and they often are confused about the extent of the genetic influence, overestimating its impact. Clinicians can support parents by helping them to better understand the nature of both psychosocial and genetic risk factors for their children.

The similarities between parental mood disorder and parental cancer suggest a general model for understanding the effects on children of other types of parental illnesses. Such illnesses as parental HIV/AIDS, multiple sclerosis, and diabetes have received little study as they affect children, yet these, too, can have broad implications for families. For example, children born to mothers with HIV/AIDS are at risk for developing the illness themselves and are more likely to experience losses of multiple family members (Belfer, Krener, & Black Miller, 1988). These children also are more likely to experience other risk factors, such as poverty, cultural barriers, social isolation, and having parents who are substance abusers (Spiegel & Mayers, 1991). Therefore, an approach that considers the multiple contexts and meanings of the parental illness is appropriate.

The study of parental mood disorders and parental cancer also suggests that similar interventions may be useful across different types of illnesses. While the investigation of preventive interventions is a relatively new area and additional findings are likely to result from further systematic research, two interventions that show promise have been described in the literature. These interventions include education about the illness and its effects on the family, evaluation of family members' adjustment to the illness, and support of communication and understanding about the illness within the family.

It is clear that parents who are ill are deeply concerned about the effects of the illness on their children. The clinician treating these families must be able to provide accurate information about the illness, evaluate the risk factors for children, assess the need for intervention, support the family's efforts to cope adaptively, and listen empathically to parents' and children's concerns. In this way, it may be possible to help all family members move on with their lives, despite the frightening, often harrowing, experience of severe parental illness.

REFERENCES

Adams-Greenly, M., Beldoch, N., & Moynihan, R. (1986). Helping adolescents whose parents have cancer. *Seminars in Oncology, 2,* 113–118.

Adams-Greenly, M., & Moynihan, R. (1983). Helping the children of fatally ill parents. *American Journal of Orthopsychiatry, 53,* 219–229.

Baider, L., & Kaplan De-Nour, A. (1984). Couples' reactions and adjustment to mastectomy: A preliminary report. *International Journal of Psychiatry and Medicine, 14,* 265–276.

Beardslee, W. R. (1990). The development of a clinician-based preventive intervention for families with affective disorders. *Journal of Preventive Psychiatry and Allied Disciplines, 4,* 39–61.

Beardslee, W. R., Bemporad, J., Keller, M. B., & Klerman, G. L. (1983). Children of parents with major affective disorder: A review. *American Journal of Psychiatry, 140,* 825–832.

Beardslee, W. R., Hoke, L. A., Wheelock, I., Rothberg, P. C., van de Velde, P., & Swatling, S. (1992). Initial findings on preventive intervention for families with parental affective disorders. *American Journal of Psychiatry, 149,* 1335–1340.

Beardslee, W. R., Keller, M. B., & Klerman, G. L. (1985). Children of parents with affective disorder. *International Journal of Family Psychiatry, 6,* 283–299.

Beardslee, W. R., Keller, M. B., Lavori, P. W., Klerman, G. K., Dorer, D. J., & Samuelson, H. (1988). Psychiatric disorder in adolescent offspring of parents with affective disorder in a non-referred sample. *Journal of Affective Disorders, 15,* 313–322.

Beardslee, W. R., Keller, M. B., Lavori, P. W., Staley, J., & Sacks, N. (1993). The impact of parental affective disorder on depression in offspring: A longitudinal follow-up in a non-referred sample. *Journal of the American Academy of Child and Adolescent Psychiatry, 32,* 723–730.

Beardslee, W. R., & MacMillan, H. (1993). Preventive intervention with the children of depressed parents: A case study. *Psychoanalytic Study of the Child, 48,* 249–276.

Beardslee, W. R., & Podorefsky, D. (1988). Resilient adolescents whose parents have serious affective and other psychiatric disorders: The importance of self-understanding and relationships. *American Journal of Psychiatry, 145,* 63–69.

Beardslee, W. R., Salt, P., Porterfield, K., Rothberg, P. C., van de Velde, P., Swatling, S., Hoke, L. A., Moilanen, D. L., & Wheelock, I. (1993). Comparison of preventive interventions for families with parental affective disorder. *Journal of the American Academy of Child and Adolescent Psychiatry, 32,* 254–263.

Beardslee, W. R., Schultz, L. H., & Selman, R. L. (1987). Level of social-cognitive development, adaptive functioning, and DSM-III diagnosis in adolescent offspring of parents with affective disorders: Implications of the development of the capacity for mutuality. *Developmental Psychology, 23,* 807–815.

Beardslee, W. R., & Wheelock, I. (1994). Children of parents with affective disorders: Empirical findings and clinical implications. In W. M. Reynolds & H. F. Johnston (Eds.), *Handbook of depression in children and adolescents* (pp. 463–479). New York: Plenum Press.

Beardslee, W. R., Wright, E., Rothberg, P. C., Salt, P., & Versage, E. M. (In press). Response of families to two preventive intervention strategies: Long-term differences in behavior and attitude change. *Journal of the American Academy of Child and Adolescent Psychiatry.*

Belfer, M. L., Krener, P. K., & Black Miller, F. (1988). AIDS in children and adolescents. *Journal of the American Academy of Child and Adolescent Psychiatry, 27,* 147–151.

Bettes, B. A. (1988). Maternal depression and motherese: Temporal and intonational features. *Child Development, 59,* 1089–1096.

Bibace, R., & Walsh, M. E. (1980). Development of children's concepts of illness. *Pediatrics, 66,* 912–917.

Billings, A. G., & Moos, R. H. (1983). Comparisons of children of depressed and non-depressed parents: A social-environmental perspective. *Journal of Abnormal Child Psychology, 11,* 463–486.

Billings, A. G., & Moos, R. H. (1985). Children of parents with unipolar depression: A controlled 1-year follow-up. *Journal of Abnormal Child Psychology, 14,* 149–166.

Brown, G. W., & Davidson, S. (1978). Social class, psychiatric disorders of mothers and accidents to children. *Lancet, 1,* 378–381.

Buck, C. W., & Laughton, K. B. (1957). Family patterns of illness. *Acta Psychiatrica et Neurologica Scandinavica, 39,* 165–175.

Buckley, I. G. (1977). *Listen to the children: A study of the impact on the mental health of children of a parent's catastrophic illness.* New York: Cancer Care.

Cohn, J. F., Campbell, S. B., Matias, R., & Hopkins, J. (1990). Face-to-face interactions of postpartum depressed and nondepressed mother-infant pairs at 2 months. *Developmental Psychology, 26,* 15–23.

Cohn, J. F., & Tronick, E. (1989). Specificity of infants' response to mothers' affective behavior. *Journal of the American Academy of Child and Adolescent Psychiatry, 28,* 242–248.

Coie, J. D., Watt, N. F., West, S. G., Harkins, J. D., Asarnow, J. R., Markman, H. J., Ramey, S. L., Shure, M. B., & Long, B. (1993). The science of prevention: A conceptual framework and some directions for a national research program. *American Psychologist, 48,* 1013–1022.

Compas, B. E., Worsham, N. L., Epping, J. E., Grant, K. E., Mireault, G., & Howell, D. C. (1994). When mom or dad has cancer: Markers of psychological distress in cancer patients, spouses and children. *Health Psychology.*

Costello, E. J., Costello, A. J., Edelbrock, C., Burns, B. J., Dulcan, M. K., Brent, D., & Janiszewski, S. (1988). Psychiatric disorders in pediatric primary care: Prevalence and risk factors. *Archives of General Psychiatry, 45,* 1107–1116.

Cox, A. D., Puckering, C., Pound, A., & Mills, M. (1987). The impact of maternal depression in young children. *Journal of Child Psychology and Psychiatry, 28,* 917–928.

Coyne, J. C., Kessler, R. C., Tal, M., Turnbull, J., Wortman, C. B., & Greden, J. F. (1987). Living with a depressed person. *Journal of Consulting and Clinical Psychology, 55,* 347–352.

Derogatis, L. R., Morrow, G. R., Fetting, J., Penman, D., Piasetsky, S., Schmale, A. M., Henrichs, M., & Carnicke, C. L., Jr. (1983). The prevalence of psychiatric disorders among cancer patients. *Journal of the American Medical Association, 249,* 751–757.

Downey, G., & Coyne, J. C. (1990). Children of depressed parents: An integrative review. *Psychological Bulletin, 108,* 50–76.

Ekdahl, M. C., Rice, E. P., & Schmidt, W. M. (1962). Children of parents hospitalized for mental illness. *American Journal of Public Health, 52,* 428–435.

Fadden, G., Bebbington, P., & Kuipers, L. (1987). Caring and its burden: A study of the spouses of depressed patients. *British Journal of Psychiatry, 151,* 660–667.

Field, T., Healy, B., Goldstein, S., & Guthertz, M. (1990). Behavior-state matching and synchrony in mother-infant interactions of nondepressed versus depressed dyads. *Developmental Psychology, 26,* 7–14.

Field, T., Sandberg, D. Garcia, R., Vega-Lahr, N., Goldstein, S., & Guy, L. (1985). Pregnancy problems, postpartum depression, and early mother-infant interactions. *Developmental Psychology, 21,* 1152–1156.

Forehand, R., & McCombs, A. (1988). Unraveling the antecedent-consequence conditions in maternal depression and adolescent functioning. *Behavioral Research Therapy, 26,* 399–405.

Garmezy, N. (1988). Stressors of childhood. In N. Garmezy & M. Rutter (Eds.), *Stress, coping and development in children* (pp. 43–84). Baltimore, MD: Johns Hopkins University Press.

Gaensbauer, T. J., Harmon, R. J., Cytryn, L., & McKnew, D. H. (1984). Social and affective development in infants with a manic-depressive parent. *American Journal of Psychiatry, 141,* 223–229.

Gershon, E. S., Hamovit, J., Guroff, J. J., Dibble, E., Leckman, J. F., Screery, W., Targum, S. D., Nurnberger, J. I., Goldin, L. R., & Bunney, W. E. (1982). A family study of schizoaffective, bipolar I, bipolar II, unipolar, and normal control probands. *Archives of General Psychiatry, 39,* 1157–1167.

Goodman, S. H., & Brumley, H. E. (1990). Schizophrenic and depressed mothers: Relational deficits in parenting. *Developmental Psychology, 26,* 31–39.

Gordon, D., Hammen, C., Adrian, C., Jaenicke, C., Hiroto, D., & Burge, D. (1989). Observations of interactions of depressed women with their children. *American Journal of Psychiatry, 146,* 50–55.

Gotlib, I. H., & Ruscher, S. M. (1988). Marital interaction patterns of couples with and without a depressed partner. *Behavior Therapy, 19,* 455–470.

Hammen, C. (1988). Self-cognition, stressful events, and the prediction of depression in children of depressed mothers. *Journal of Abnormal Child Psychology, 16,* 347–360.

Hammen, C., Burge, D. Burney, E., & Adrian, C. (1990). Longitudinal study of diagnoses in children of

women with unipolar and bipolar affective disorder. *Archives of General Psychiatry, 47,* 1112–1117.

Hinchliffe, M. K., Hooper, D., Roberts, J., & Vaughan, P. W. (1975). A study of the interaction between depressed patients and their spouses. *British Journal of Psychiatry, 126,* 164–172.

Hirsch, B. J., Moos, R. H., & Reischl, T. M. (1985). Psychosocial adjustment of adolescent children of a depressed, arthritic, or normal parent. *Journal of Abnormal Psychology, 94,* 154–164.

Hoke, L. A. (1996). When a mother has breast cancer: Parenting concerns and psychosocial adjustment in young children and adolescents. In K. Hassey Dow (Ed.), *Contemporary issues in breast cancer* (pp. 173–181). Boston: Jones and Bartlett Publishers.

Howes, M., Hoke, L. A., Winterbottom, M., & Delafield, D. (1994). Psychosocial effects of breast cancer on the patient's children. *Journal of Psychosocial Oncology, 12,* 1–21.

Hymovich, D. P. (1993). Child-rearing concerns of parents with cancer. *Oncology Nursing Forum, 20,* 1355–1360.

Institute of Medicine. (1994). *Reducing risks for mental disorders: Frontiers for preventive intervention research.* Washington, DC: National Academy Press.

Issel, L. M., Ersek, M., & Lewis, F. M. (1990). How children cope with mother's breast cancer. *Oncology Nursing Forum, 17* (Suppl.), 5–13.

Keitner, E. L., & Miller, I. W. (1990). Family functioning and major depression: An overview. *American Journal of Psychiatry, 147,* 1128–1137.

Keller, M. B., Beardslee, W. R., Dorer, D. J., Lavori, P. W., Samuelson, H., & Klerman, G. L. (1986). Impact of severity and chronicity of parental affective illness on adaptive functioning and psychopathology in children. *Archives of General Psychiatry, 43,* 930–937.

Keller, M. B., Lavori, P. W., Beardslee, W. R., Wunder, J., & Ryan, N. (1991). Depression in children and adolescents: New data on "undertreatment" and a literature review on the efficacy of available treatments. *Journal of Affective Disorders, 21,* 163–171.

Kochanska, G., Kuczynski, L., Radke-Yarrow, M. R., & Welsh, J. D. (1987). Resolutions of control episodes between well and affectively ill mothers and their young children. *Journal of Abnormal Child Psychology, 15,* 441–456.

Koocher, G. P. (1974). Talking with children about death. *American Journal of Orthopsychiatry, 44,* 404–411.

Krantz, S. E., & Moos, R. H. (1987). Functioning and life context among spouses of remitted and nonremitted depressed patients. *Journal of Consulting and Clinical Psychology, 55,* 353–360.

Landau, R., Harth, P., & Othnay, N. (1989). The influence of psychotic parents on their children's development. *American Journal of Psychiatry, 129,* 38–43.

Lee, C. M., & Gotlib, I. H. (1989). Clinical status and emotional adjustment of children of depressed mothers. *American Journal of Psychiatry, 146,* 478–483.

Lewis, F. M. (1990). Strengthening family supports. Cancer and the family. *Cancer, 65,* 752–759.

Lewis, F. M., Hammond, M. A., & Wood, N. F. (1993). The family's functioning with newly diagnosed breast cancer in the mother: The development of an explanatory model. *Journal of Behavioral Medicine, 16,* 351–370.

Lichtman, R. R., Taylor, S. E., Wood, J. V., Bluming, A. Z., Dosik, G. M., & Leibowitz, R. L. (1984). Relationships with children after breast cancer: The mother-daughter relationship at risk. *Journal of Psychosocial Oncology, 2,* 1–19.

Merikangas, K. R., Prusoff, B. A., & Weissman, M. M. (1988). Parental concordance for affective disorders: Psychopathology in offspring. *Journal of Affective Disorders, 15,* 279–290.

National Institute of Mental Health. (1993). *The prevention of mental disorders: A national research agenda.* (Unpublished manuscript.)

Northhouse, L. L., & Swain, M. A. (1987). Adjustment of patients and husbands to the initial impact of breast cancer. *Nursing Research, 36,* 221–225.

Nurnberger, J. I., & Gershon, E. S. (1982). Genetics of affective disorders. In E. S. Paykel (Ed.), *Handbook of affective disorders* (pp. 126–145). New York: Guilford Press.

Offord, D. R., Boyle, M. H., Szatmari, P., Rae-Grant, N. I., Links, P. S., Cadman, D. T., Byles, J. A., Crawford, J. W., Blum, H. M., Byrne, C., Thomas, H., & Woodward, C. A. (1987). Ontario Child Health Study. II. Six-month prevalence of disorder and rates of service utilization. *Archives of General Psychiatry, 44,* 832–836.

Olson, D. H. (1991). Commentary: Three-dimensional (3-D) circumplex model and revised scoring of FACES III. *Family Process, 30,* 74–79.

Orvaschel, H., Walsh-Allis, G., & Ye, W. (1988). Psychopathology in children of parents with recurrent depression. *Journal of Abnormal Child Psychology, 16,* 17–28.

Rosenheim, E., & Reicher, R. (1985). Informing children about a parent's terminal illness. *Journal of Child Psychology and Psychiatry, 26,* 995–998.

Rounsaville, B. J., Prusoff, B. A., & Weissman, M. M. (1980). The course of marital disputes in depressed women: A 48-month follow-up study. *Comprehensive Psychiatry, 21,* 111–117.

Rutter, M. (1966). *Children of sick parents: An environmental and psychiatric study.* (Institute of Psychiatry Maudsley Monograph No. 16.) London: Oxford University Press.

Rutter, M. (1986). Meyerian psychology, personality development and the role of life experiences. *American Journal of Psychiatry, 143,* 1077–1087.

Rutter, M. (1987). Psychosocial resilience and protective mechanism. *American Journal of Orthopsychiatry, 57,* 317–331.

Rutter, M. (1990). Commentary: Some focus and process considerations regarding effects of parental depression on children. *Developmental Psychology, 26,* 60–67.

Sameroff, A. J., Seifer, R., Zax, M., & Barocas, R. (1987). Early indicators of developmental risk: Rochester Longitudinal Study. *Bradley Developmental Psychopathology Research Center, 13,* 383–393.

Siegel, K., Mesagno, F. P., & Christ, G. (1990). A prevention program for bereaved children. *American Journal of Orthopsychiatry, 60,* 168–175.

Siegel, K., Mesagno, F. P., Karus, D., Christ, G., Banks, K., & Moynihan, R. (1992). Psychosocial adjustment of children with a terminally ill parent. *Journal of the American Academy of Child and Adolescent Psychiatry, 31,* 327–333.

Siegel, K., Raveis, V. H., Bettes, B., Mesagno, F. P., Christ, G., & Weinstein, L. (1990). Perceptions of parental competence while facing the death of a spouse. *American Journal of Orthopsychiatry, 60,* 567–576.

Siegel, K., Karus, D., & Raveis, H. (1996). Adjustment of children facing the death of a parent due to cancer. *Journal of the American Academy of Child and Adolescent Psychiatry, 35,* 442–450.

Spiegel, L., & Mayers, A. (1991). Psychosocial aspects of aids in children and adolescents. *Pediatric Clinics of North America, 38,* 153–167.

Strober, M., Morrell, W., Burroughs, J., Lampert, C., Danforth, H., & Freeman, R. (1988). A family study of bipolar I disorder in adolescence—early onset of symptoms linked to increased familal loading and lithium resistance. *Journal of Affective Disorders, 15,* 225–268.

Targum, S. D., Dibble, E. D., Davenport, Y. B., & Gerson, E. S. (1983). The family attitudes questionnaire: Patients' and spouses' views of bipolar illness. *Archives of General Psychiatry, 38,* 562–568.

Taylor, S. E., & Aspinwall, L. G. (1990). Psychosocial aspects of chronic illness. In P. T. Costa & G. R. Vanden Bos (Eds.), *Psychological aspects of serious illness: Chronic conditions, fatal diseases, and clinical care* (pp. 3–60). Washington, DC: American Psychological Association.

Tronick, E. Z. (1989). Emotions and emotional communication in infants. *American Psychologist, 44,* 112–119.

Tsuang, M. T., & Faraone, S. V. (1990). Summary and conclusions. In *Genetics of mood disorders* (pp. 166–176). Baltimore: Johns Hopkins University Press.

Waters, B. G. (1987). Psychiatric disorders in the offspring of parents with affective disorder: A review. *Journal of Preventive Psychiatry, 3,* 191–206.

Watt, N. F., Anthony, E. J., Wynne, L. C. & Rolf, J. E. (Eds.). (1984). *Children at risk for schizophrenia: a longitudinal perspective.* New York: Cambridge University Press.

Weissman, M. M., Paykel, E. S., & Klerman, G. L. (1972). The depressed women as a mother. *Social Psychiatry, 7,* 98–108.

Weissman, M. M., Prusoff, B. A., Gammon, G. D., Merikangas, K. R., Leckman, J. F., & Kidd, K. K. (1984). Psychopathology in the children (ages 6–18) of depressed and normal parents. *Journal of the American Academy of Child Psychiatry, 23,* 78–84.

Wellisch, D. K. (1979). Adolescent acting out when a parent has cancer. *International Journal of Family Therapy, 1,* 230–241.

Wellisch, D. K. (1981). Family relationships of the mastectomy patient: Interactions with the spouse and children. *Israel Journal of Medical Science, 17,* 993–996.

Wellisch, D. K. (1985). The psychologic impact of breast cancer on relationships. *Seminars in Oncology Nursing, 1,* 195–199.

Whiffen, V. E., & Gotlib, I. H. (1989). Infants of postpartum depressed mothers: Temperament and cognitive status. *Journal of Abnormal Psychology, 98,* 274–279.

Zahn-Waxler, C., Kochanska, G, Krupnick, J., & McKnew, D. H. (1990). Patterns of guilt in children of depressed and well mothers. *Developmental Psychology, 26,* 51–59.

Zahn-Waxler, C., Mayfield, A., Radke-Yarrow, M. R., McKnew, D. H., Cytryn, L., & Davenport, Y. B. (1988). A follow-up investigation of offspring of parents with bipolar disorder. *American Journal of Psychiatry, 145,* 506–509.

Zahn-Waxler, C., McKnew, D. H., Cummings, M. E., Davenport, Y. B., & Radke-Yarrow, M. R. (1984). Problem behaviors and peer interactions of young children with a manic-depressive parent. *American Journal of Psychiatry, 141,* 236–240.

Zuckerman, B. S., & Beardslee, W. R. (1987). Maternal depression: A concern for pediatricians. *Pediatrics, 79,* 110–117.

9 / Death and Dying

Gerald P. Koocher and Linda J. Gudas

Grief and Loss Issues in Childhood

All children think about death and experience separations from loved ones. Spontaneous questions about death and loss are expected and predictable. Assessment of what is normal or pathological will generally be matters of gauging the intensity and duration of any grief reaction and the degree to which psychological defense mechanisms are successful in protecting the child from anxiety. Separation and loss syndromes with detailed accounts of childhood grief reactions (Bowlby, 1973) sketch the templates through which patterns of normal adaptation and exaggerated grief reactions may manifest themselves. Children confronting issues of grief and loss must deal with a wide range of difficult, painful, and often confusing feelings. Such losses stir feelings of sadness, anger, insecurity, or fearfulness in the face of events that are difficult for them to comprehend. Adults who would help a child struggle with such concerns often experience a sense of empathy mixed with dread and uncertainty. Most adults who find themselves in the position of counseling bereft children will have already acquired a personal history of loss experiences and cannot help but be influenced by these while sharing in the child's loss. Faced with this potential countertransference relationship, adults may sometimes fail to recognize that the salience or emphasis of loss-related events will differ markedly given the child's developmental level. Clinicians who work with children on such issues will need some understanding of developmental trends and a high degree of personal comfort with their own loss experiences (Koocher, 1980).

This discussion of clinical issues and intervention strategies focuses on three subgroups of children, each with a different context for confronting death. First are children who encounter death in the course of normal life events but who are not confronting a traumatic personal loss (e.g., after finding a dead animal at the roadside, watching a television program involving a death, or through hearsay from a peer). Our discussion of such "normal" childhood experiences includes questions of how death and loss are conceptualized in the least threatening of circumstances, so that the reader may develop a foundation for considering both healthy and pathological reactions in other circumstances. Second, the circumstances of children with life-threatening illness are addressed. In such instances, a variety of special factors, including the child's awareness of his or her own condition, demand special consideration. The third subgroup of children are those who are bereaved by the loss of a parent, sibling, or other significant person in their lives. Although common developmental threads flow through discussion of issues for each of these subgroups, the thrust of clinical work and nature of the interventions proposed necessarily differ.

Conceptions of Death in Normal Children

Wortman and Silver (1989) have called attention to many myths about the mourning process in general, much as Kastenbaum and Costa (1977) did in their overview of psychological perspectives on death. Three oft-held erroneous assumptions include beliefs that children do not comprehend death, that adults do comprehend death, and that even if children were able to understand death, it would be harmful for them to be concerned about it. Such assumptions seem chiefly to reflect defensiveness on the part of their proponents rather than a valid understanding of actual circumstances.

Early classics in what has become a substantial body of literature on children's conceptions of death are the studies by Anthony (1940) and Nagy (1948). Both represented initial attempts to study normal children's conception of death from a systematic developmental perspective, and both also provide support for the theory that such conceptions follow a stepwise progression. While neither study is a paragon of scientific rigor (both had major sampling problems), they represented nearly the whole body of material on the topic for two decades. One result was that many writers simply accepted and repeated these early findings without question or additional investigation (e.g., Kubler-Ross, 1969, pp. 178–179). Additionally, classic psychoanalytic theorists argued that children had neither the intellectual ability to grasp the reality of death nor an adequate formation of object relatedness to mourn, thus halting exploration of mourning in children and undoubtedly affecting the growth of developmental theory of

children's understanding of death (Deutsch, 1937; Miller, 1971; Wolfenstein, 1966).

More recent research has provided firm empirical documentation of the manner in which the death concept develops. The specific concerns and fantasies expressed by children of different ages with respect to death have been found to be reflective of their cognitive understanding about it. A Piagetian framework has been applied to demonstrate how children's responses to questions about death reflect their levels of cognitive development (Koocher, 1981, 1985). Other developmental studies have documented acquisition of the universality and irrevocability of death concepts (Jenkins & Cavanaugh, 1985/86; Orbach, Talmon, Kedem, & Har-even, 1987) as well as highlighting children's own awareness of their potential death (Sourkes, 1982; Spinetta, 1974).

During infancy until approximately age 2, sensorimotor activities dominate the child's experiences. The major cognitive task is the establishment of object permanence. By the middle of the first year of life, recognition and elementary search occurs for lost objects. By 17 months, the child can retain an image and have memory for a lost object (Bowlby, 1980). Ellis (1989) states that the beginning concepts of death can be observed in a child's play (e.g., "All gone" and "Peek-a-boo"). Bowlby's (1973, 1980) research describing protest, despair, and detachment remain the standard for understanding separation and loss in this period.

The egocentrism and magical thinking characteristic of preoperational thought dominate concerns about death in young children. During early childhood (roughly between the ages of 2 to 6), when preoperational thinking is the rule, it is not possible to cognitively take on the "role of the other." As a result, young children's conceptualizations are limited by their own experience and based on the physically observable world. Death is therefore considered solely in terms of the child's own experiences by analogy with sleep, separation, and injury. The preoperational child cannot truly consider "Who do I know who has died?" "What generalizations can I draw from that with respect to myself?" Without a concept of constancy, children are not yet able to regard death as a permanent or irreversible process, and they are most worried about the duration of separation from loved ones that death implies. However, young children can and do express a full range of emotions and feelings related to grief reactions (Kranzler, Shaffer, Wasserman, & Davies, 1990).

With the arrival of concrete operations at about age 6 or 7, children can distinguish self from others, become capable of comprehending the experiences of other people, and thereby begin to sense the permanence of death. At this stage causal and logical explanations are understood, yet thinking remains literal and concrete. The child may still think of death as something that occurs as a specific consequence of illness or injury rather than the outcome of a biological process. When children become capable of concrete operations, they are able to use information gleaned in the media, from friends, and from parents in forming their impressions. Facts become more usable, but not in the abstract sense. The child's predictions become more accurate, although this occurs by means of a gradual testing process over several years. At this stage, youngsters are most concerned with issues of pain and inflicted injury, although separation remains an issue, as well.

The onset of adolescence brings formal operational reasoning and the ability to make use of abstract reasoning. Adolescents can think symbolically, construct theories and metaphors, and analyze both the situation and their own thoughts. For the first time adolescents are able truly to realize that "that which is" may differ from "that which might be." Conceptions of death begin to involve more issues of uncertainty; and abstract reasoning, including theological and philosophical elements, may enter the children's considerations of issues. With the onset of adolescent cognitive functioning (i.e., formal operational thought), a more encompassing comprehension of death as a concept becomes possible.

Guilt feelings about loss can become a significant emotional issue at any age. Younger children may be at particular risk for anxieties of this sort, because they are still trying to grasp the world from a relatively self-centered perspective. By analogy, the more I believe the world revolves around me, the more I fear I may be responsible for what goes wrong. In understanding any particular child's response to a loss event, it will be important to know whether guilt feelings are a part of the reaction.

It has been argued that concepts such as life

and death develop by a natural process through developmental stages little affected by deliberate intervention of an educational nature (Kohlberg, 1968). Such authorities have interpreted Piaget's work as implying that the child's normal maturational sequence cannot be accelerated by direct intervention. Such reasoning has been used to account for the slow development of death education programs in public schools despite the existence of well-crafted developmentally appropriate curricula (Duncan, 1979). At least one experimental design, however, has yielded convincing evidence that 4- to 8-year-old children provided with educational presentations about death make significantly greater gains in understanding the concept than children in a control group that did not participate in the program (Schonfeld & Kappelman, 1990).

In summary, there are distinctly developmental trends in the normal process of acquiring a concept of death. These trends will influence the style and substance of adaptive reactions in the face of a loss and the grief reaction that follows. It will be important for the reader to become familiar with one of the brief (Koocher, 1981; Orbach, et al., 1987) or more detailed (Lonetto, 1980) accounts of these trends prior to beginning therapeutic work on this topic with children.

Addressing Everyday Fears

One strategy for helping the normal child to cope with death and grief issues is education. Death education curricula in schools (see Duncan, 1979) and family discussions of these matters at naturally occurring teaching moments are both important. The parents should not wait until the death of an important person in the child's life to begin thinking about how to communicate on the matter. During the course of normal developments, from storytelling to television watching to family outings, there will be encounters with death. A dead animal on the highway or a story on the evening news might be an appropriate everyday type of occurrence from which to begin a discussion with the child who has noticed and inquired about it. The study by Schonfeld and Kappelman (1990) described earlier provides solid evidence that educational interventions can indeed improve children's understanding of death. It is reasonable to conclude that such interventions also enhance coping potential.

When assessing the reactions and concerns of young children, it is important to avoid adult metaphors. One adult may talk to another about the neighbors who "lost their child last week," but imagine the anxiety and confusion this might induce in a 3-year-old who wonders "Why couldn't they find him?" It is important to understand the concepts and vocabulary from the child's perspective. Special attentiveness to the questions children are asking and the issues of prime concern to them is required.

Unarticulated concerns often include questions such as: "Could that happen to me (or my parents)?"; "Who will take care of me?"; "What will be expected of me?" It is sometimes helpful to have an adult note that these are things all people worry about as the questions are answered in a thoughtful and supportive manner. Discussions of how people cope with sadness, the purpose of memorial services, and what cemeteries and funeral directors are for can all be a part of answering children's questions. Another important thought that will occur to many children will be "Did that happen because of something I did (or thought or wished)?" Some level of assuming personal responsibility or guilt is a routine part magical thinking in early childhood. It is not easily outgrown. Many adults will talk about how a person's acts or words may have led to another's demise. Among adults such talk may be couched in intellectual terms such as stress reactions (e.g., "He worked himself into that heart attack with all that stress at the office."). Children often make similar connections but will be more reticent to express their feelings of guilt. Those attempting to work therapeutically with children around loss issues should be mindful of this.

Rituals and religious services also can be important to children of all ages but only if they are well integrated with family values. A religious funeral service, for example, will probably be of little value to the child whose family has seldom participated in religious services previously, and it may actually be more frightening than reassuring. Fables or similar religious stories raise many potential problems for children whose developmental level makes them prone to literal interpretation in concrete fashion. On the other hand, a child may gain considerable comfort and support from participating in rituals or services involving well-known and liked people and contexts. Parents must carefully assess whether the child's participation in the funeral, for example, meets the child's needs or is being dictated for the vicarious benefit of adults.

One alternative suggestion would be to describe anticipated events to the child as objectively as possible and encourage him or her to express a preference free of guilt. For example, in discussing an upcoming funeral, a parent might tell a child, "There will be a minister (priest or rabbi) talking about the person who died. The body will be in a casket in the room. A lot of people may be crying because they are so sad that the person died. Some people like to go to funerals so they can be with other people when they feel sad, but others would rather not go. What do you want to do?"

A final suggestion for consideration whenever a discussion about death is held with a child, especially a young child, would be a debriefing session. That is to say, the parent should ask the child to restate key elements of the explanation or talk about feelings relative to the discussion or events just passed. Only in this way can the parent immediately become aware of misconceptions and potentially anxiety-arousing communication errors.

Psychotherapy for the Child at Risk for Death

LIFE-THREATENING AND TERMINAL ILLNESS IN CHILDHOOD

Advances in medical therapeutics have transformed diseases that were once uniformly fatal to children into chronic life-threatening conditions. As a result, one must consider both aspects of such conditions in work with seriously ill children. The first involves actual terminal care during an acutely fatal illness. The second and more frequent aspect involves the care of the child with a chronic life-threatening illness. Childhood cancer and cystic fibrosis are good illustrations of the latter. The following pages summarize important treatment approaches arising from this distinction.

Children diagnosed as having standard risk acute lymphoblastic leukemia 30 years ago usually died within 6 months. Today such children have a better than 70% chance of surviving 5 or more years in a disease-free state. In the 1950s most people with cystic fibrosis died in their early teenage years. Today median duration of survival is in the 20s, with approximately 40% of patients surviving to age 40 (Borowitz, Humphrey, & Kagan, 1987). What of the families of such patients? Should they attempt to anticipate the child's death and accommodate to the loss, or attempt to suppress their anxieties about possible death while hoping for the best? Either course may lead to long-term psychological problems. These new concerns form the basis for a host of psychologic stresses, including long-term uncertainty and chronic helplessness (Kazdin, Rogers, & Colbus, 1986; Koocher & O'Malley, 1981). The uncertainty component clearly cannot be overlooked in considering the adaptation of the child, siblings, parents, or extended family members.

The psychologic stresses associated with the uncertainties of long-term survival among children with life-threatening illness have been termed a Damocles syndrome (Koocher & O'Malley, 1981). The quality of life among such patients and their families is often linked to their ability to ignore the uncertainty and adopt an optimistic or hopeful attitude. It would be negligent to stress only the issues of terminal care in this chapter, because the number of long-term survivors grows daily and represents a major challenge for preventive mental health care in pediatrics.

BASIC APPROACHES TO CARE

Because of the threat of death, the practitioner must be sensitive to the whole social ecology of the patient. The family, rather than simply the ill child, must be considered part of the "patient care" locus. The costs of life-threatening illness to all family members in both emotional and financial terms are substantial. The course of the illness is likely to sap the adaptive capacities of the parents, both as individuals and as a couple. Siblings are also likely to experience an extra burden of stress. If the patient does succumb, the surviving family members will have to contend with their grief. The practitioner who does not regard the whole family as "the patient" is likely ultimately to compromise care for the ill family member.

In formulating a service plan or clinic structure for children with terminal or life-threatening ill-ness, teamwork is of critical importance. The most desirable strategy integrates medical and mental health care along with home care and other ancillary services within a single system. Such a system enables the medical and mental health personnel to know each other well and become familiar with the issues each will be encountering. Patients benefit by virtue of the fact that all caregivers interact closely and more efficiently. Families should feel they are not singled out as being "crazy" or "psychiatric cases." Rather, if mental health services are routinely offered to all families, no stigma accrues to those who use the service. Integrating medical and mental health services makes the use of such programs more "normal" for all concerned.

LOCUS OF CARE

Most pediatric patients with life-threatening illness spend the bulk of their lives outside the hospital. There is also an increasing tendency for families to provide home care for children in the terminal phase of their illness. The psychologic issues and needs of pediatric patients and their families are quite different when inpatient care is necessary, and it is important for the practitioner to recognize the distinctions.

Outpatient care is probably more reassuring for the child, who will spend more time in the company of familiar caregivers than would be the case during an inpatient stay. A degree of normality associated with sleeping in one's own home and returning to the familiar family ecology after clinic visits can be quite supportive. In some instances, however, the stresses on family members may be greater in the sense that travel to the clinic, arranging for care of siblings, missing time at work, and other such disruptions can be quite stressful, depending on the duration of the illness and the treatments required. Some parents are reassured and feel more useful when they are able to care for their child at home, whereas others may feel insecure and tense in dealing with the side effects of treatment or other problems of care at home.

During an inpatient stay a child may require more reassurance and emotional support, as a function of the degree to which family members are able to be available and helpful. Some hospitals provide for rooming-in and encourage parents to play a substantial role in caring for their child; in other circumstances this may be discouraged, or the child's condition may dictate less contact with family members. Each hospital admission may have a different meaning for the child and the family. Some may be seen as "routine" therapeutic admissions, while others may generate anxiety that the end is near (appropriately or not).

The important point for the intervener is that each family member must be regarded in the context of the particular current treatment circumstances and the meaning of those events to them. A family that manages well under one set of circumstances may have very different reactions during a subsequent treatment phase. The distinction may well be based on an attribution or perception that is not evident to the physician in charge of the medical case management. This phenomenon underscores the importance of including mental health professionals on the treatment team.

The emotions of clinicians who must care for terminal patients remain an issue, however, at least partially because of the intensity of discomfort in working with children who are so gravely ill. The classic paper by Vernick and Karon (1965) entitled "Who's Afraid of Death on a Leukemia Ward?" illustrates the discomfort effectively. Through the use of life-space interviews, they documented the fact that children clearly knew the seriousness of their illnesses and were eager to have someone to talk with about it. They described the communication barriers often erected by adults to "protect the child" and noted that when a child is passive with respect to discussing these concerns, it is often a reflection of the environment. A number of empirical studies have yielded supportive data (Spinetta, Rigler, & Karon, 1973).

Key Developmental Issues

SEPARATION

The infant who cannot see the parent cannot retain the concept that the parent still exists to provide care (Mahler, Pine, & Bergman, 1994). The infant's reaction of acute distress to the parent's leaving is well recognized. The infant or toddler in the hospital, an unfamiliar setting with strangers as caregivers, seeks parental reassurance and comfort and finds separation even more anxiety producing than the healthy child. Arranging

for parents to sleep in the hospital room with their child and to be integrally involved in their child's care is vital at this age. This includes accompanying and comforting the child during medical procedures. At times the parents' heightened anxiety or withdrawal due to anticipatory grief may cause them to defer basic care of their child to the nursing staff. The consulting mental health professional should assist the parents in openly discussing their emotional reactions and in underscoring the child's need for the parents' ongoing physical care and comfort.

By approximately age 3 the preschooler has established a sense of psychologic autonomy and increasingly can tolerate parental absence (Mahler et al., 1994). The diagnosis of a life-threatening illness and the need for prolonged hospitalization, however, may lead to regressive behavior and an increased need for parental reassurance. The preschool child may perceive death as a type of separation from others. Fears and fantasies about illness and dying may be confused with concern about separation. The parents' presence and active involvement remain essential throughout the childhood years.

The adolescent is concerned about potential family withdrawal related to anticipatory grief, the censoring of medical information, and social withdrawal of peers owing to their anxieties about serious illness. All of these concerns isolate the patient. Acceptance by peers is very important to the adolescent's sense of identity and self-esteem. Separation from normal peer activities poses a difficulty for many adolescent patients.

SYMPTOM MANAGEMENT

The treatment of a life-threatening illness such as cancer requires many painful and noxious procedures, including surgery, bone marrow biopsy, and chemotherapy. In addition to the parents' presence, physical comforting, and reassurance, the treatment team can use other strategies to deal with the anxious anticipation of aversive procedures as well as management of pain.

Every child needs preparation for procedures. An explanation of the procedure, commensurate with the child's age and ability to comprehend, helps the child to anticipate what will transpire and provides an increased sense of control. Play therapy techniques, such as providing the child with a stuffed animal and asking him or her to install an intravenous line using actual equipment prior to a procedure, provides an opportunity to address emotional concerns and bolster coping strategies. The young child, complaining of pain during a procedure, can learn distraction techniques such as deep breathing, squeezing a parent's arm when the pain intensifies, or the use of visual imagery techniques.

Deep muscle relaxation and hypnosis also can be employed with school-age children and adolescents both to aid in reducing anxiety and as a strategy to control chronic pain, such as "phantom pain" following amputation or pain due to an invasive tumor. Psychotherapy also can provide patients with a forum to discuss their emotional reactions and to better understand the emotional context of the pain they are experiencing. The following examples illustrate three approaches to pain management.

CONTROL ISSUES

The diagnosis of a life-threatening illness creates an emotional crisis in a family. The loss of control implicit in the diagnosis is one of the most devastating aspects of the crisis. Parents may experience the loss of ability to protect their child from harm and to positively influence their child's future. Their own feelings of loss of control in this situation may generate intensification of their concern and caregiving behavior, thus helping regain a sense of control when they feel helpless. Often, however, the patient can experience this behavior as infantilizing.

The preadolescent child, who is seeking mastery in many new areas, may experience the loss of control to plan his or her life. The child may displace anger onto schedules or hospitalization that interfere with such plans. Such children may attempt to regain control by testing parental limits. The parents may in turn curtail discipline out guilt or concern for their sick child. Rather than making the child feel special, however, this can make the child feel more out of control.

Although the loss of control is a salient issue for all patients, it has a heightened impact during adolescence. Adolescents strive for greater autonomy in their environment and increasing independence from parents. These gains are impeded by hospitalizations where members of the medical staff make decisions that affect the adolescent's health and daily life. Patients often feel bombarded by intrusive medical practices. The hospital experience can foster passivity and regressive dependence that inhibits adolescents' sense of mastery over their environment. The ability to experience competence through school, social experiences, and planning for the future is also seriously disrupted when treatments or medical conditions make it difficult for the patient to keep up.

Another adolescent task is developing identity and mastery over one's changing body. Body image issues are directly challenged by the physical changes that often accompany illness. For instance, alopecia, a frequent side effect of chemotherapy, is a visible, inescapable reminder to the patient of the disease as well as a possible source of embarrassment and diminution of self-esteem. Comfort and confidence in sexual attractiveness are also severely challenged by the effects of both the disease and its treatment.

Just as with younger children, the loss of control accompanying a hospitalization is also stressful for the adolescent. The patient's daily schedule is disrupted, familiar people and activities are missing, and the result is a loss of control. Some adolescent patients may be especially uncomfortable at some particular time of day, often coinciding with a missed special activity or lonely late-evening hours. Increasing a patient's perception of control can improve his or her ability to cope with disease (Langer & Rodin, 1994; Seligman, 1975). This can be accomplished by permitting patients to wear their own clothes in the hospital or engage in other such normalizing activities.

NORMALIZATION OF THE DISTRESS

The mental health professional can offer important support to the patient, family, and medical staff by consulting with them on the assessment of the patient's developmental level, the meaning of psychologic and psychogenic symptoms, and the care and management of the patient. Indirect consultation may lead to direct patient contact or may allow for improved care without such a referral. The mental health professional also can facilitate creation of a forum to discuss team members' emotional reactions to providing care to patients with life-threatening illnesses.

The mental health professional can best serve the patient and the family when an initial evaluation is made at the time of diagnosis. At this juncture the psychiatric consultant can assess the family's functioning and interactional style and make recommendations for managing predictable stresses. This early intervention can help manage the predictable stress reactions and prevent increased marital tension or sibling problems. Such interventions also can help the family by facilitating clear communication and mutual support. This initial assessment allows for an early intervention when one or more family members seem to be at risk.

Continuity of daily life activity is the key issue for both patients and family. Maintaining a social network through visits, phone calls, and letters is encouraged. Making the hospital room a familiar setting by bringing in personal articles from home also promotes continuity and familiarity. Ensuring that the patient continues to be an active, choice-making, responsible person should be the central priority. This active stance is best introduced to patients as a way of helping them cope with disease and hospitalization. Reinforcing this message by pointing out choices in daily hospital life underscores the realistic options. These choices may include activity room programming, academic tutoring, developing a support network by introducing patients to each other and "veterans" to newly diagnosed patients, allowing patients to participate in decisions concerning medical procedures, and soliciting and responding to patient feedback. These components create an atmosphere in which patients can maintain a sense of control because they understand what is happening to them and know ways to affect and control what happens. This type of milieu should have a positive effect on their ability to cope with disease and hospitalizations.

When Is Psychotherapy Indicated?

Not all children with fatal or life-threatening illnesses are in need of psychotherapy or mental health services. There are two basic paradigms for those who do require such services. First, there is the child or family for whom psychological intervention would have been needed even without the illness, by virtue of preexisting difficulties. Sec-

ond is the child and family struggling with acute stress as a function of the illness affecting a heretofore well-adapted psychosocial system. Both groups will be in need of supportive and crisis intervention treatment services at various points in the treatment of the child's illness.

Most children with chronic life-threatening illnesses will require relatively sophisticated medical care and probably will be treated at or in consultation with major medical centers. In the ideal circumstance, mental health services will be available at these centers through the primary treatment team. Even in the best of circumstances there will be powerful stresses on all concerned with treating such patients (Koocher, 1980) and many opportunities for needless irritations among children, parents, and the treatment staff. The potential difficulties are magnified when the mental health service providers and the medical staff do not know and trust each other's judgment. Additionally, the mental health personnel must become familiar with the natural history of and treatments for the illnesses their patients are struggling with. While mental health centers and practitioners in the community often quite justifiably feel inadequate to the task of serving such families, a variety of models for providing such care has been well described in the literature (Adams, 1979; Kellerman, 1980; Koocher, 1985; Koocher & O'Malley, 1981).

The precise nature of actual intervention strategies and techniques will vary as a function of the individual patient's needs. The basic intervention approach should include consideration of the following clinical questions: What does the child know about the illness? What surface concerns does the child have? What sources of support are available? What sources of stress are anticipated?

Knowing exactly what information has been communicated to the child and family is very important, but it is also critical to recognize that what has been comprehended may differ substantially from what information was allegedly offered. While the nature of the anxieties a child may face is quite complex, some facets are more easily verbalized than others, and these surface concerns should be addressed first. This strategy will establish a climate within which the child later will be able to verbalize more complex worries. Sources of support include the child's own personality and coping abilities as well as the emotional support available from family members. There will be considerable variability across individuals and families with respect to such supports, and the clinician must be sensitive to this. While it is not always possible to predict the timing of stress events associated with the treatment of life-threatening illnesses, the events themselves are well known to those who treat such children (e.g., alopecia among cancer patients, infections, or unexpected hospitalizations). Often it is possible to lessen the psychological stress of such events by preparing the child for them in advance with anticipatory discussions. The clinicial who explores all of these issues with the child will have begun the most important parts of a constructive intervention program.

Telling a child that he or she is dying is probably the most burdensome act an adult can undertake. Still, opening the door to supportive communication in the face of death can be very rewarding and intensely meaningful. If the clinician waits, however, until it is evident that death is near to initiate such discussions, a tragic error has been made. Even young children can be told at diagnosis that their illness is "a very serious disease, people can die from it." This can be followed by other information about how the medical staff plans to "fight the disease," including eliciting the support of the child in the battle. The critical point is that from the very beginning the child be engaged in an emotional climate that encourages supportive discussions of even the most stressful issues.

During the course of treatment for the illness, the clinician might routinely ask what the child is worried about, even asking specifically "Do you ever worry about dying?" If the child answers in the affirmative, the clinician can proceed to discuss the matter. If such fears are denied, the clinician can note, "Well, I'm glad you're not, but if you do get worried I hope you'll let me (or your parents) know so we can talk about it and help."

When a child is clearly entering a terminal trajectory, it is best to meet with the parents and explore the best ways to handle communications on the matter. At times, a child will be open and direct. In that case, most of the clinician's work may focus on helping the family and staff deal with their own concerns about discussing death. In other cases, the child will deny any concern

but show obvious separation anxiety or other symptoms of similar concern. In such cases, it may be wisest to treat the symptoms by helping to see that the child is not alone or by providing similar interventions without confronting the issue of death directly. There are times when the clinician can best facilitate coping by leaving defenses intact. Careful consideration of family values and the level of adaptation operating at any point in time is important. A good rule of thumb is not to disturb a homeostasis unless there is a real problem confronting the parties involved and pressing the issue will facilitate adaptation.

The Bereaved Child

A number of studies have focused specifically on patterns of mourning and bereavement in children. Some have reported descriptions of bereavement in children as young as 3 years of age, although most tend to make only rather gross age distinctions and focus on middle childhood and adolescence. In general, the pattern of bereavement is described as including regression, denial, hopelessness, and occasionally animistic fantasies as a child struggles to cope with the loss of a grandparent, parent, or sibling. Retrospective studies have attempted to link losses in childhood to adult depression and physical illness. Summaries of these studies (Fleming, 1980; Osterweis, Solomon, & Green, 1984) conclude that the course and outcome of childhood bereavement experiences may well influence adult affective disturbance years later, but the nature of the relationship is certainly not clear.

The role of the family in the whole context of grief and loss is critical for children. Children can manifest both cognitive and emotional disruption in the aftermath of a family member's death almost without regard for the specific circumstances of the loss. In some instances, as in the case of a parent's suicide, the reactions may be unusually intense and prolonged. Even the death of a public figure with parent surrogate qualities can evoke a significant mourning response in both children and adults. The authors of an interdisciplinary volume written to discuss children's reactions to the Kennedy assassination well illustrate this point (Wolfenstein & Kliman, 1965). For many children and adults, the public assassination and funeral were akin to losing our country's father figure, and the interviews with the children reported in that volume underscore the point.

At least one author has suggested that the only way to do away with the debilitating consequences of the death of a family member is to do away with death itself (Rosenblatt, 1967). This tongue-in-cheek observation is a rather telling comment with respect to cultural values. The antithesis is well illustrated in Bryer's (1979) paper on the Amish way of death, which underscores the importance of the family as a support system in the face of death. Bryer demonstrates how community orientation, family structure, and cultural attitudes toward life and death can facilitate bereavement within a supportive atmosphere that tends to minimize emotional trauma associated with the loss. In Amish culture death is prepared for throughout life. Although the time of actual passing is certainly a sad one, the coping of survivors seems somehow less trying with such preparation. The importance of the funeral as a family ceremony has been well documented in a variety of cultures, and the welfare of survivors is regarded as of paramount importance to most ethnic groups. At the same time, many families are not well prepared to integrate children into this ceremony, asserting that excluding them is for the children's own protection. For adults to bear their own grief and confrontation with mortality seems difficult enough, and the thought of dealing with a child's worries in addition is frightening to many. Just who is being protected from what is not always clear, although most writers on bereavement in childhood stress the importance of openness, communication, and family support in helping children to cope with loss.

Pathological Bereavement in Children

Expected symptoms associated with grief reactions in childhood may include tearfulness; social and emotional withdrawal; loss of interest in favorite toys or pastimes; decreased attention span; loss of appetite; insomnia or nightmares; decreased effectiveness in school; increases in unfocused activity level; separation anxiety; and expressions of guilt over past activities, especially in relation to the deceased. When these symptoms continue without improvement, the child may be experiencing unresolved or pathological grief.

The natural dependency of childhood, along with the potential for animistic and magical thinking, make children particularly vulnerable to prolonged adverse psychological sequelae following an important loss. At the same time, the absence of any symptoms of acute grief or a sharply truncated reaction may herald premature application of denial or avoidance defenses with the potential for emergence of symptoms at a much later point in time. Dramatic shifts in affect that would seem pathological in an adult are more the norm in children (e.g., being sad one minute and cheerfully asking for a peanut butter sandwich the next).

One key to diagnostic assessment of childhood grief reactions is the presence or absence of anxiety. The child or adolescent who is in the process of adapting to the loss should be able to verbalize some sadness and related feelings in the course of a psychodiagnostic evaluation. Inability to discuss the loss, denial of affect, or anxiety and guilt themes in relation to the deceased or surviving family members would all be indicators that some additional evaluation or psychotherapeutic intervention may be warranted.

Time also can be an important factor in assessing adaptation to loss, but no uniform guidelines apply. While the intensity of the depressive symptoms often will abate substantially over a period of several weeks, so-called anniversary phenomena may trigger renewed symptoms. Arrival of a birthday, holiday, or other family event, for example, may induce a return of sadness, tension, or stress along with thoughts of the deceased person. Usually these recurrences are much less intense than the acute mourning experience. If they persist more than several days following the stimulus event or evoke a heretofore unseen intensity, a diagnostic evaluation is certainly warranted.

The clinician also must be especially sensitive to the principle that the bereaved child cannot be evaluated accurately outside of the family context. Grief reactions in children are subject to both amelioration and exacerbation based on the presence or absence of emotional supports within the surviving family. Behavioral contagion and social learning also play roles in determining a child's response. Religious rituals and family behavior patterns provide opportunities for observational learning and imitation that may be either facilitative or inhibitory with respect to the child's adaptation. Children also may react to mourning, depression, or anxiety in their parents or caregivers even though they have had no personal contact with the deceased individual.

PSYCHOTHERAPEUTIC CARE OF THE BEREAVED CHILD

There are two focal points to the central concern in the psychotherapeutic care of the bereaved child. The first is the need to help the child differentiate his or her fate from that of the deceased. Second is the need of the child to arrive at an acceptable sense of closure with regard to the loss. Doing so may involve feelings of guilt or responsibility for the death as well as magical fears about what actually transpired. Both foci are important issues for any child who experiences a loss, although the need is more acute in the case of pathological bereavement, described earlier in this chapter.

The need to differentiate between the recently deceased and the living is a common cognitive adaptation mechanism among both children and adults. Adults are not immune to magical thinking, especially in times of emotional stress, but children have a particular need to distinguish between real and imagined causes of death. Investigators of cognitive development have long documented the difficulties children of different ages may have in coping with abstractions, and since death is a one-time-only final experience for each of us, it certainly qualifies as an abstract experience when it comes to individual mastery issues.

Lonetto (1980) discusses the cognitive issues quite well, noting that the same phenomena that make abstractions difficult for young children to grasp also make them more tolerant of ambiguities in learning about death. He also illustrates the use of play and drawings as a means of reducing abstraction and ambiguity to a meaningful level

for children in various age groups. Writing from a quite different frame of reference, Rochlin (1953) uses the psychoanalytic model to arrive at similar conclusions. He notes that the child's play is organized to protect the self against fears associated with his or her understanding of death.

Involvement in funerary rituals may be quite helpful and supportive in a family context if such involvement is well explained and consistent with the child's wishes. Vicarious satisfaction of adults is not a proper basis for making the decision whether to involve a child in such activities or not. Introduction of philosophical or religious concepts may tend to confuse and frighten young children, especially in the absence of close family supports (Furman, 1974).

The questions a child may be presumed to worry about in the aftermath of a salient death would include the following: Why (i.e., by what means) did that person die? Will that happen to me (or someone else I care about)? Did I have anything to do with it? Who will take care of me (if the deceased was one of the child's caregivers) now? While the child may not specifically articulate these questions, they are almost always a part of the underlying anxiety that accompanies a prolonged grief reaction. The psychotherapeutic remedy must involve informational, cognitive, and affective components. It may include the need to address significant guilt, even if there is no clear basis for such remorse.

MANAGEMENT OF MENTAL HEALTH RISK

Whether the clinician is considering the needs of the bereaved child, the child with life-threatening illness, or simply children in general, emotional climate is the paramount guarantor of security and adaptation. When the social and emotional context provides a sense of trust and empathic understanding, coping is greatly facilitated. Establishing such a context within the family and in psychotherapy, along with a recognition of salient issues from the child's standpoint, is the most effective base on which to begin dealing with grief and loss in childhood. Each child experiences a death based on many variables, including past involvement with death, associated stressors, and the support of others. No two children will grieve exactly the same way, and professionals must be prepared for individual differences.

REFERENCES

Adams, D. W. (1979). *Childhood malignancy: The psychosocial care of the child and his family.* Springfield, IL: Charles C. Thomas.

Anthony, S. (1940). *The child's discovery of death.* New York: Harcourt, Brace.

Borowitz, S., Humphrey, J., & Kagan, B. (Eds.). (1987). *Cystic Fibrosis Currents, 2.* Spring House, PA: McNeal Pharmaceuticals.

Bowlby, J. (1973). *Separation: Anxiety and anger.* New York: Basic Books.

Bowlby, J. (1980). *Attachment and loss, Volume III: Loss, sadness and depression.* New York: Basic Books.

Bryer, K. (1979). The Amish way of death: A study of family support systems. *American Psychologist, 34,* 255–261.

Deutsch, H. (1937). Absence of grief. *Psychoanalytic Quarterly, 6,* 12–22.

Duncan, C. (1979). *Teaching children about death: A rationale and model for curriculum.* Ph.D. dissertation, Boston College.

Ellis, R. R. (1989). Young children: Disenfranchised grievers. In K. J. Doka (Ed.), *Disenfranchised grief* (pp. 201–211). Lexington, MA: Lexington Books.

Fleming, S. (1980). Childhood bereavement. In R. Lonetto (Ed.), *Children's conceptions of death* (pp. 178–187). New York: Springer.

Furman, E. (1974). *A child's parent dies.* New Haven, CT: Yale University Press.

Jenkins, R. A., & Cavanaugh, J. C. (1985/86). Examining the relationship between the development of death and overall cognitive development. *Omega, 16,* 193–199.

Kastenbaum, R., & Costa, P. T. (1977). Psychological perspectives on death. *Annual Review of Psychology, 28,* 225–249.

Kazdin, A. E., Rogers, A., Colbus, D. (1986). The hopelessness scale for children: Psychometric characteristics and concurrent validity. *Journal of Consulting and Clinical Psychology, 54,* 241–245.

Kellerman, J. (Ed.). (1980). *Psychological aspects of childhood cancer.* Springfield, IL: Charles C. Thomas.

Kohlberg, L. (1968). Early education: A cognitive-developmental view. *Child Development, 39,* 1013–1062.

Koocher, G. P. (1980). Pediatric cancer: Psychosocial problems and the high costs of helping. *Journal of Clinical Child Psychology, 9,* 2–5.

Koocher, G. P. (1981). Development of the death concept in childhood. In R. Bibace & M. E. Walsh (Eds.), *The development of concepts related to health: Future directions in developmental psychology* (pp. 85–99). San Francisco: Jossey-Bass.

Koocher, G. P. (1985). Promoting coping with illness in childhood. In J. C. Rosen & L. J. Solomon (Eds.), *Prevention in health psychology* (pp. 311–327). Hanover, NH: University Press of New England.

Koocher, G. P., & O'Malley, J. E. (1981). *The Damocles syndrome: Psychosocial consequences of surviving childhood cancer.* New York: McGraw-Hill.

Kranzler, E. M., Shaffer, D., Wasserman, G., & Davies, M. (1990). Early childhood bereavement. *Journal of the American Academy of Child and Adolescent Psychiatry, 29,* 513–520.

Kubler-Ross, E. (1969). *On death and dying.* New York: Macmillan.

Langer, E. J., & Rodin, J. (1994). The effects of choice and enhanced personal responsibility for the aged: A field experiment in an institutional setting. In A. Steptoe, & J. Wardle (Eds.), *Psychosocial Processes and Health.* Cambridge, England: Cambridge University Press.

Lonetto, R. (1980). *Children's conceptions of death.* New York: Springer.

Mahler, M. S., Pine, F., & Bergman, A. (1994). Stages in the infant's separation from the mother. In G. Handel & G. Whitchurch (Eds), *The Psychosocial Interior of the Family* (pp. 419–448). New York: Aldine.

Miller, J. B. M. (1971). Children's reactions to the death of a parent: A review of the psychoanalytic literature. *Journal of the American Psychoanalytic Association, 19,* 697–719.

Nagy, M. (1948). The child's theories concerning death. *Journal of Genetic Psychology, 73,* 3–27.

Orbach, I., Talmon, O., Kedem, P., & Har-even, D. (1987). Sequential patterns of five subconcepts of human and animal death in children. *Journal of the American Academy of Child and Adolescent Psychiatry, 26,* 578–582.

Osterweis, M., Solomon, F., & Green, M. (Eds.) (1984). *Bereavement: Reactions, consequences, and care.* Washington, DC: National Academy Press.

Rochlin, G. (1953). Loss and restitution. *Psychoanalytic Study of the Child, 8,* 288–309.

Rosenblatt, B. (1967). Relations of children to the death of loved ones: Some notes based on psychoanalytic theory. In D. Moriarty (Ed.), *The loss of loved ones* (pp. 135–152). Springfield, IL: Charles C. Thomas.

Schonfeld, D. J., & Kappelman, M. (1990). The impact of school-based education on the young child's understanding of death. *Developmental and Behavioral Pediatrics, 11,* 247–252.

Seligman, M. E. P. (1975). *Helplessness.* San Francisco: W. H. Freeman.

Sourkes, B. M. (1982). *The deepening shade: Psychological aspects of lie-threatening illness.* Pittsburgh: University of Pittsburgh Press.

Spinetta, J. J. (1974). The dying child's awareness of death: A review. *Psychological Bulletin, 81,* 256–260.

Spinetta, J. J., Rigler, D., & Karon, M. (1973). Anxiety in the dying child. *Pediatrics, 52,* 841–845.

Spinetta, J. J., Rigler, D., & Karon, M. (1974). Personal space as a measure of a dying child's sense of isolation. *Journal of Counsulting and Clinical Psychology, 42,* 751–756.

Vernick, J., & Karon, M. (1965). Who's afraid of death on a leukemia ward? *American Journal of Diseases of Children, 109,* 393–397.

Wolfenstein, M. (1966). How is mourning possible? *Psychoanalytic Study of the Child, 20,* 93–123.

Wolfenstein, M., & Kliman, G. (Eds.). (1965). *Children*

and the death of a president. Garden City, NY: Doubleday.

Wortman, C. B., & Silver, R. C. (1989). The myths of coping with loss. *Journal of Consulting and Clinical Psychology, 57,* 349–357.

---

10 / Children in Divorce Litigation

Peter Ash

Since 1972, somewhat over 1 million children have seen their parent divorce each year (National Center for Health Statistics, 1991). For most of these children, their parents decide on their custody, and the vast majority of children spend the bulk of their time with their mother. While precise figures are unavailable, a significant number, perhaps one-third to one-half, have trouble deciding themselves and enter into the legal arena, although only a small minority, from 3 to 10%, proceed as far as an actual trial (Foster & Freed, 1980). This chapter focuses on those children whose parents have major difficulties in reaching agreements about child care during and after divorce.

Custody contests usually center on latency and preschool-age children. Adolescents are much less often involved because they usually have a preference, and that preference tends to be decisive. Adolescents may be involved when there are also younger siblings about whom there is more of a question or when parents disagree about whether mental health treatment is indicated for the adolescent.

Legal Background

For many years, custody disputes arose only rarely because courts made use of simplifying rules that governed who would control children after divorce. Roman law gave the father control over his children, a concept that carried over into English and then American law. Courts began separating the issues of child support and custody in the late 19th century, and by the 1920s, with the increasing adoption of the "tender years" doctrine (an evidentiary presumption under which young children's "best interests" are presumed to be furthered in the custody of their mothers), mothers began to be seen as the preferred custodial parent (Derdeyn, 1976). The children's best interest is now the legal test for custody in all jurisdictions in the United States. As the tender years doctrine was increasingly rejected in the 1970s in favor of a sex-neutral standard, custody needed to be decided on a case-by-case basis, and the outcomes of litigation became more uncertain. In the early 1980s joint custody became more common. With the fall of simplifying rules to decide child custody matters and the increasing array of custody options to choose from, psychological questions became more important in deciding contested cases.

At the time of divorce, three major issues need to be decided: who the child will be with when (custody and visitation or access issues), who will make what decisions regarding the child, and who will contribute what portion of child support. There are many steps along the road of deciding these matters: the parents attempt to decide between themselves, their attorneys negotiate, mediation—either court-sponsored or private—is available, a custody evaluation may be sought, various hearings short of trial may be conducted, and, finally, a trial may be required. These steps vary procedurally among jurisdictions, but overall it is important to recognize that there are many potential steps for dispute resolution and only a very limited number of cases are decided by judges. Negotiation takes place in the shadow of Solomon's sword, with an eye to what a judge would likely decide if the case were to go to trial. A full custody trial is very expensive, and many parents cannot afford attorneys for such a trial.

Despite the fact that courts have ultimate formal jurisdiction in contested cases, the courts have acquiesced to parental agreement. Mnookin and Kornhauser (1979) have discussed the ways in which divorce laws provide "a framework in which divorcing couples can themselves determine their postdissolution rights and responsibilities" (p. 950). In their analysis of parents' "bargaining in the shadow of the law," they identified 5 factors that influence negotiations: parental preferences, the bargaining chips each parent begins with (which stem from the outcome the law will impose if no agreement is reached), the uncertainties of potential outcomes, the transaction costs (both of time and money) of contesting custody and visitation, and the strategic behaviors parents use in negotiation. More recently, the increased use of joint custody and divorce mediation, both movements that originated outside of the mental health field, actively emphasize parental decision making. In some jurisdictions, these options are now formally encouraged by statute.

JOINT CUSTODY

Joint custody has multiple definitions. It is sometimes used to refer to arrangements in which each parent has the children for a substantial (more than one-third) portion of the time. It also can mean that the parents alternate possession, of whatever amount, and/or share joint decision making. Under the latter definition, sometimes referred to as joint legal custody, the joint custody label is frequently applied to arrangements that are little different from sole custody. Pearson and Thoennes (1990), in a study of 418 families, found that parents with joint custody were wealthier and reported better cooperation between spouses than sole-custody families, but did not find an association between the children's adjustment and form of custody. While joint custody is an attractive option in cases in which parents agree to it, there is increasing evidence that when courts impose joint custody over a parent's objection, this custody arrangement is associated with more problems for the children involved (Johnston, Kline, & Tschann, 1989; Steinman, Zemmelman, & Knoblach, 1985).

MEDIATION

Mediation in divorce disputes is one aspect of the growing social policy wish to encourage parents to resolve their own disputes and reduce the adversarial nature of divorce proceedings. Divorce mediation grew out of techniques of conflict resolution in industrial disputes. It is often practiced by attorneys and by mediators who mediate other conflicts, as well. In the mental health field, it has been taken up mostly by therapists with a family orientation. There are numerous different approaches (see, e.g., Coogler, 1978; Emery, 1994; Haynes, 1981; Saposnek, 1993), but all emphasize cooperation between parents and parents making their own decisions. Other parameters of mediation vary widely: It may be voluntary or required, one session or extensive, confidential or not, and include property issues or be limited to custody and visitation.

There is a growing but still young literature on the effects of mediation. Pearson and Thoennes (1984) found generally positive rates of parental satisfaction among those who mediated successfully but relatively low rates of use of voluntary mediation services and mixed findings among those who attempted mediation but did not succeed in achieving resolution. Emergy and Wyler (1987), in reviewing the research data, concluded that the data were supportive of the view that mediation diverted a significant number of cases from the adversarial process and was generally preferred by parents, although more by fathers than by mothers (Emery, Matthews, & Wyer, 1991). Many questions remain unanswered, particularly revolving around high-conflict families: Should mediation be required? Should joint custody be imposed? Who should conduct mediation? Are there some families for whom an attempt at mediation does more harm than good? What is the psychological impact on the children?

VISITATION OR ACCESS

Cases may be contested at the time of divorce, when, in the eyes of the law, the parents start relatively equal, or they may start postdivorce, in which case the parent who has had possession since the divorce typically has a presumption in his or her favor. Issues of vision and support tend to predominate in postdivorce cases. While a court can order a custody arrangement and has the authority to make it stick, a court has much more limited powers to enforce visitation arrangements. Such arrangements usually require a modicum of acceptance by both parents in order to be workable. Visitation, as a matter of law, is decided in the best interests of the child; as a matter of practice, visitation usually is treated as a parental right, a right to be withheld only on a showing of serious risk to the child. Ash and Guyer (1986b) found that families who were court-referred for evaluation for contested custody at the time of divorce had a 19% rate of relitigation of custody in the next 2 years, a figure over twice as high as that in control families (7%). Parents who had contested custody at the time of divorce did not relitigate issues of visitation at a higher rate than control families and litigated child support less than controls. This finding contrasted with those families seen in postdivorce visitation disputes, half of whom continued to relitigate visitation in the following 2 years. From the judge's perspective, chronic visitation disputes occur in a small minority of divorce cases but are very time-consuming and seldom rewarding. From the children's—and often the mothers'—perspectives, the major problem is lack of visitation: A survey of a national sample found that 5 years postdivorce, half the children had not seen their fathers in the previous year (Furstenburg, Nord, Peterson, & Zill, 1983). Lack of visitation is a problem that the legal system has had difficulty addressing, although a large-scale study of divorcing families living outside San Francisco in jurisdictions that encouraged joint custody and utilized mandatory mediation for disputing families found that only 14% of children living with their mothers had not seen their fathers in the previous year when assessed 3½ years postseparation (Maccoby & Mnookin, 1992).

Psychological Problems in Disputes

PARENTAL CONFLICT

Few parents divorce because of heated disagreements about how to raise their children, but discrepant views about parenting, especially fathers' concerns about how children are doing with their mothers, and parental hostility have been found the most salient factors in generating legal conflict (Maccoby & Mnookin, 1992). Parents in custody contests often are dealing with their own feelings of loss, rejection, and diminished self-esteem. They tend to be preoccupied with their own needs, and feelings of entitlement are exacerbated. The adversarial legal system, with its emphasis on having an attorney argue one's entitlement, can exacerbate this tendency. This shift to a focus on a parent's own needs clouds the parent's view of his or her children's best interests. Interventions that succeed in helping parents focus on a child's best interest, rather than on the bitterness between the parents, promote parental negotiation and often allow parents to move forward with making their own decisions for their children.

Johnston, Campbell, and Tall (1985) have proposed a typology of impasses that embroil parents and interfere with their devising their own plan for their children's care postdivorce. They describe impasses at the external social level (events such as job loss and interference from members of the extended social network including relatives, attorneys, and, unfortunately, therapists), at the interactional level (marital conflicts, especially perceived attacks on self-esteem or interlocking pathology that forestalls conflict resolution), and at the intrapsychic level (involving psychopathology of one or both parents, especially narcissistic injury caused by rejection or reactivation of unresolved earlier loss or trauma). In these cases, attention to the nature of the impasse, as opposed to therapy with broader goals, is of the most use in helping families resolve the impasse and proceed with planning for their children.

EFFECTS OF PARENTAL CONFLICT ON CHILDREN

There is burgeoning literature on the effects of divorce on children (see Chapter 11), but much of this research has limited applicability to that subgroup involved in litigation, about whom much less is known. In addition to the stresses of divorce, in divorce litigation a child is subjected to the uncertainty of knowing how much he or she will be with each parent. Effective parenting is diminished as parents struggle with their own conflicts. The child is caught in a crossfire of parental conflict that often involves speaking negatively of the other parent or attempts to form a coalition against the other parent. The child may be used as a pawn in the parental battle, and loyalty conflicts are exacerbated. These children have been found to be significantly more disturbed than normals and two to four times as likely to exhibit severity levels comparable to those of children seen for treatment (Ash & Guyer, 1991; Johnston, 1994; Johnston, Kline, & Tschann, 1989).

Children experience the crossfire of parental conflict differently depending on their developmental stages:

CASE EXAMPLE

Jessica, 13 months, and her brother Stephen, 5, visited their father for weekends once a month. On return, Jessica was clingy, ate poorly, and had difficulty sleeping, while her older brother looked forward to the visits but was upset that his new stepmother insisted on being called Mommy. When interviewed, Stephen sadly said that every night he prayed that "Mom and Dad would get back together." Father had filed a motion to take both children for a 4-week summer vacation out of state and saw his ex-wife's discomfort with overnights and the long vacation as further evidence of a controlling, demeaning, and jealous nature. Intervention was directed at helping the father see his daughter's distress as developmentally normal separation anxiety and reframing his motives for agreeing to a new visiting schedule with more frequent but shorter contact with his daughter as "being a sensitive father" rather than "giving in" to his ex-wife. Father's distress about his son's dislike of his new wife was ameliorated somewhat after several father-son sessions in which Stephen was able to express to his father his wishes that his parents get back together, and his father was able to acknowledge Stephen's disappointment that this would not happen.

Children pay a heavy price for their parent's dispute. Johnston, Campbell, and Mayes (1985) studied 44 children ages 6 to 12 who were involved in postseparation and divorce disputes. They found the children were exposed to high levels of parental acrimony and were exhibiting a wide range of symptoms, including anxiety, tension, and depression. Forty percent had somatic symptoms. Their capacity for secure relationships with one or both parents was compromised. Unlike findings reported in most studies of children of divorce, aggressiveness and conduct problems were markedly absent. Younger children were more anxious than older children, but the older children were more likely to form alliances with one parent. The authors identified 4 patterns of coping, in decreasing order of adaptiveness: a tricksterlike method of coping; equilibrating by the child trying to balance his or her own feelings and be fair and equidistant from both parents; merging with one or both angry parents, like a chameleon; and acting in a diffusely disturbed manner. The last two groups showed constriction of affect and problems in ego integration.

CASE EXAMPLE

Amelia, 9, was caught up in a predivorce custody dispute. She had always been seen as a good, responsible girl by her parents. She had told each parent she wanted to live with them, and each was actively encouraging her to tell the court worker her preference. Each parent was also pressuring her to tell about the other parent's dates, and she appeared to do so, but with numerous inconsistencies in her stories. Her somewhat depressed mother described Amelia as "comforting," while her angry father saw her as "withdrawn." When an interviewer described a number of possible custody arrangements, after each one Amelia said, "That sounds good."

Children whose parental conflict includes spouse abuse are at increased risk for difficulties.

CASE EXAMPLE

Robert, 11, was the oldest of five children and had witnessed his father hitting his mother numerous times. There had been no physical abuse of the children. He strongly took his mother's side, was adamant that none of the children should visit their father, and in many ways was acting as his mother's protector. When seen with his father during a court-ordered evaluation, Robert told his father in a steely voice, "One of these days you're going to wake up, and you'll be looking up the barrel of a shotgun, and you'll see me at the other end, and the last thing you're going to think is 'I shouldn't have hit her.'" Robert's father responded, "Naah," and in later discussion clearly did not take the matter seriously.

The question of whether there is any positive gain for children who cope with the distress of a custody contest is an intriguing one. Wolman and Taylor (1991) reported that contested children were more internally control oriented than noncontested children. Contested children displayed less anger, less guilt, and were more concerned with reality testing. At the time of the contest, contested children were less likely to see their families positively, but at follow-up, they were more likely to see their families positively. The authors suggested that these unanticipated positive findings may represent feeling prized in being fought over or that the stress of the custody contest may promote children's resilience.

After most custody disputes are decided, there is little further litigation. Visitation disputes tend to be more chronic, as parents continually return to court as they struggle for much of the child's life over visitation.

CASE EXAMPLE

Bruce, age 7, was the focus of protracted litigation. After each visit with Father, he talked to his mother about the terrible time he spent with Dad and was argumentative for several days and refused to go to bed. When Father came by to pick Bruce up, Bruce said he did not want to go and did so only when forced by his mother, who let him know, resentfully, she had to obey "that damned judge." Father reported that once in the car, Bruce was fine, the visits went well, and at the end, Bruce didn't want to go home, which Father attributed to his ex-wife's "being a lousy mother." The evaluator asked the family to come in and observe what was happening. Mother and Bruce were placed in a room where Father could observe through a one-way mirror. Mother then told Bruce that Bruce's father would come in and she was going to step out. Bruce protested strongly and said he would leave. Father then entered, and Mother left to go behind the observation mirror. After a few minutes, she saw Bruce and his father comfortably playing a board game. Bruce later objected to his father's leaving, and, when Mother reentered, Father was able to observe Bruce start to throw toys at the walls and turn the light off and on. This intervention helped the parents see the difficulty as Bruce's rather than reflecting on the parents' behaviors. They also reported that following this session, Bruce's symptoms around visitation were markedly reduced.

Johnston, Gonzalez, and Campbell (1987), in a study of 56 children involved in postdivorce disputes, found that the extent of the child's involvement in the dispute and the amount of role reversal between parent and child were associated with the level of the child's symptoms at the time of the litigation and that these factors and the level of parental conflict were associated with problems at a 2-year follow-up. The high-conflict children showed a different pattern of symptoms than the pattern typically reported in the divorce literature: High-conflict children showed inhibited as well as impulsive symptoms (children of divorce more typically have impulsive symptoms), and boys did not have higher level of symptoms than girls (the divorce literature typically reports higher levels of symptoms in boys). Children whose parents had high levels of conflict did not display high levels of aggression at the time of the dispute but did display higher levels of aggression at 2-year follow-up, when parental animosity had died down somewhat.

SEXUAL ABUSE ALLEGATIONS

In the last decade, sexual abuse allegations have become an increasingly common complication in postdivorce custody and visitation disputes. While the numbers of such allegations are small—estimated at 2% of cases (Thoennes & Tjaden, 1990)—they represent explosive situations and generate a great deal of legal and mental health expert controversy. As Richard Gardner (1989) put it, "If custody litigation is to be considered 'a bag of worms,' then sex abuse litigation can only be considered as 'a bag of poisonous snakes'" (p. 24).

Cases involving children age 6 and over tend to be easier to sort out because the child interview is likely to be more straightforward than the interview of a preschooler. The case of Tiffany followed an all-too-common pattern.

CASE EXAMPLE

Tiffany's parents had separated abruptly 4 months previously and were in the midst of a bitter divorce when Tiffany, 3, told her mother that her father "touched my 'gina." Mother filed an emergency order for cessation of visitation on the grounds of suspected sexual abuse. The judge, concerned about putting the child "at risk," imposed supervised visitation pending further evaluation. "Pending" meant delay. Mother's attorney recommended an evaluator who opined that Tiffany's one reported statement, coupled with a history of Tiffany's having trouble sleeping after visiting her father and a history that occasionally the girl rubbed her genitals with her finger, was strongly suggestive of sexual abuse. A joint police and child protective service worker interview found Tiffany to say little about her interactions with her father and found she would answer other questions in whatever direction suggested by the interviewers. After the criminal investigation was closed, and 4 months after the allegation originally surfaced, a court order for psychiatric evaluation was entered. Both attorneys expressed the hope that the evaluator would be able "to tell what really happened." When seen, Tiffany missed her father but was angry he had not seen her very much, knew her mother thought it was "scary to see Dad," and said little about her interactions with her father prior to the supervised visits.

When interviewed, a limited number of children provide a compelling story of abuse, but many cases are left undetermined, as it is very difficult to prove something did *not* happen, especially when the data are to come from a 3-year-old child about something that may have happened once many months ago. In the early 1980s, many evaluators, drawing on the experience of abuse allegations in intact families with both parents, believed that in order for an allegation to surface, the family's attempt to shield the activity needed to be surmounted, and so such allegations were almost always true. With experience, it came to be recognized that in postdivorce disputes, especially those involving preschoolers, the allegation was being brought by one parent against the other, and the suspicion that the allegation was false or the parent misinterpreted data out of a complex negative orientation to the other parent needed to be considered. Estimates of rates of false or unconfirmed allegations in cases of preschoolers exceed 50% (Thoennes & Tjaden, 1990). Questions about evaluator bias, appropriate interview technique, and drawing appropriate conclusions from interview data have led to considerable expert and public controversy.

Litigation-Specific Effects

The question of what are the effects of being in litigation per se as differentiated from the effects of living in parental conflict is an intriguing one and much less well studied. Litigation has meanings to children, it tends to exacerbate and polarize the parents, and parental acrimony becomes exacerbated, which may affect others, such as thera-

pists who are reluctant to become involved "until the legal issues are resolved."

CHILDREN'S UNDERSTANDING OF LITIGATION

A very young child may be aware that things are unsettled without any understanding that a judge is going to make an important decision regarding his or her life. Saywitz (1989), in a study comparing children who had been witnesses in abuse cases with children who had not, found that less than 1% of 4- to 7-year-olds could tell accurately what a judge, jury, or court was. She found that small children may hear legal words as pertaining to something they know and think a jury is jewelry, a minor is someone who digs coal, and a court is a place to play basketball. Elementary school-age children seen in custody evaluation have often been told that "Mommy and Daddy can't decide who you'll live with, and a judge will have to help us decide." This understanding can lead to anxiety about having anything to do with the evaluation, and leads some children to refrain from discussing their parents with an evaluator.

Adolescents, on the other hand, usually have a fairly clear idea of what is at stake and respond in terms of the meanings of the possible outcomes for themselves. These meanings may tie in to developmental conflicts, as in the following case example.

CASE EXAMPLE

After Jennifer's parents divorced when she was 8, Jennifer lived with her mother. At age 13, Jennifer had increasing arguments with her mother and asked to go live with her father. Mother agreed, and Jennifer moved to her father's. Nine months later, Father, tired of paying child support while Jennifer was with him and having heard from Jennifer about her arguments with her mother, filed for a legal change of custody, which Mother opposed. A bitter legal fight ensued, during which much of both parents' assets were transferred to the legal profession. Jennifer's adamant insistence to continue living with her father was weighed heavily by the court, and legal custody was changed, despite the court worker's sense that Jennifer's antipathy toward her mother seemed based in large part on developmental conflicts rather than poor parenting on Mother's part. Five months later, Jennifer, at her own initiative, moved back to her mother's.

A similar postjudgment course was seen in several cases of early-adolescent girls but was not seen in similar cases involving early-adolescent boys or girls of other ages. It appears that Jennifer was wrestling with a developmentally common conflict in which early-adolescent girls often find themselves: struggling with wishes to become independent of mother at the same time as wishing to maintain a tie, and expressing this in an angry denunciation of mother. Apparently the girl understood the meaning of the judge's changing custody, independent of the actual living arrangements, as meaning "You can't go back to mother," which precipitated a switch in the girl's ambivalence.

SUGGESTIBILITY OF CHILDREN'S RECOLLECTIONS

The difficulties of sexual abuse cases have sparked research on children's memory and suggestibility. While the findings are complex, results generally support the finding that children are able to recall well, but that younger children, especially preschoolers, are more susceptible to suggestion and misleading questions than older children or adults (Ceci & Brack, 1995). The effect of stress on memory is less clear: High levels of stress at the time of the remembered event have been found to both improve resistance to suggestions and improve free recall (Goodman, Hirschman, Hepps, & Rudy, 1991) and to impair many of the specific, and especially peripheral, details of an event (Christianson & Loftus, 1987).

CHILDREN AS WITNESSES OR PROVIDERS OF INFORMATION

In most jurisdictions, children in divorce litigation seldom take the witness stand in open court, although they frequently provide information as subjects of evaluation or to the judge in his or her chambers. In divorce litigation complicated by sexual abuse allegations, children's stories are closely scrutinized and a child may testify in an associated criminal case. Ceci and Brack (1995) have reviewed many of the difficulties in assessing the validity of such testimony. The effects on a child witness may be indirect and in the future. For example, a child may continue to live with a parent who has strong negative feelings about the

information the child provided and who may act out those feelings toward the child. A child may feel ashamed or responsible for what took place and find it difficult to talk in the public setting that a courtroom represents with the accused parent looking on. In a study of 218 children involved in sexual abuse cases, children's greatest fear about testifying involved facing the defendant (Goodman et al., 1992). The two strongest predictors of the child's courtroom experience were younger age and severity of abuse. Children who testified evidenced greater disturbance 7 months later than children who did not testify. Lack of improvement at 7 months was associated with testifying multiple times, less maternal support, and less corroborating evidence. At the final follow-up, when prosecution ended, these factors were no longer correlated with improvement. Of interest, counseling of the children also was not associated with children's improvement.

The issue of child witness trauma has become the nexus of a social policy debate involving legislatures and the courts in addition to mental health professionals. In 1988 the United States Supreme Court, looking to legal reasoning without going into the question of the child's best interests, held that a defendant's Sixth Amendment "right to confront his accuser" precluded screening the child witness from the defendant without a special showing of need (*Coy v. Iowa*, 1988). Two years later the Court found that the trauma to the child of testifying could override the defendant's right of face-to-face confrontation in particular cases and upheld a statute allowing allegedly abused children to testify in a separate room and have their testimony televised to the judge, jury, defendant, and spectators (*Maryland v. Craig*, 1990). Trauma to the witness, as proved by expert opinion, was given sufficient weight to overcome the defendant's right to a face-to-face confrontation. In 1990 the Court ruled as inadmissible hearsay the testimony of a physician who evaluated a child for sexual abuse using leading questions (*Idaho v. Wright*), but later, in 1992, without any analysis of the trauma of being a witness, the Court allowed others to testify about what the child said regarding her abuse as a "spontaneous utterance" exception to the general bar against hearsay so that the child's statements could be introduced without her having to testify in court at all (*White v. Illi-*

nois, 1992), a holding that may significantly alter the frequency that children will testify in the future.

Roles of Child Psychiatrists

CUSTODY EVALUATION

Difficult cases are often referred for a custody evaluation. Such evaluations are typically solicited by an attorney or by the court. In these forensic evaluations, the child is not a patient of the child psychiatrist. There is no expectation of confidentiality. The purpose is to provide information and recommendations relevant to the legal issue to the parents, the attorneys, or the court, not to make a therapeutic intervention (although the evaluator may recommend therapy). While different authors offer somewhat different suggestions for conducting custody evaluations (American Psychiatric Association, 1988; American Psychological Association Committee on Professional Practice and Standards, 1994; Benedek & Schetky, 1985; Bricklin, 1995; Gardner, 1989; Herman, 1990; Weiner, Simons, & Cavanaugh, 1985), there is growing consensus that the best interests of the children are most likely to be served if the evaluator is impartial, in the sense of being court-ordered or stipulated to by both parents, rather than entering the case at the request of one side. A complete evaluation is extensive and involves interviewing both parents, the children, observing the parents with the children, and providing feedback to both parents, the attorneys, and the courts.

Custody cases that include allegations of sexual abuse present particular problems and require special skills. The American Academy of Child and Adolescent Psychiatry has propounded guidelines for these evaluations (1988). The problem of validating an allegation is particularly marked in these cases and requires special consideration (Benedek & Schetky, 1987a,b; Green, 1986). There remain significant differences over technique, including the use of anatomically correct dolls (Everson & Boat, 1990; Realmuto, Jensen, & Wescoe, 1990).

Many attorneys and parents fear that a custody evaluation is difficult for the child and quite anxi-ety-provoking, and may try on that account to forestall such an evaluation. How the evaluation is presented to the child by a parent is an important factor in how the child feels at the outset of the interview. Conducted properly and empathicly, a forensic interview is rarely detrimental to a child, although interviews conducted as hostile interrogations can certainly arouse anxiety. Interviews in which leading questions are asked run the risk of altering a child's understanding or memory of an event. Many children appear to derive some relief from having an opportunity to express themselves to an interested and empathic listener. In contested custody evaluations, the child interview may well be the first chance the child has had to speak with an unbiased adult. While the subject matter is often anxiety-laden, talking about it or, for a younger child, playing it out often helps the child. It is quite common for parents in such a situation to report that after the child was seen, symptoms they had previously noted were reduced. A forensic evaluation also may bolster a child's sense of having some effect on the outcome and be empowering. This can be a double-edged sword: The child also may feel guilty that he or she caused an outcome that is upsetting to at least one parent, or, at the end of the litigation, a disappointed parent may blame the child for the outcome.

Ash and Guyer (1986a), in a study of 200 disputed cases referred for court-ordered evaluation, found that only 11% of cases were decided by judges. They suggested that the primary role of an evaluation was to help the parents settle their dispute during the evalution (18% of cases) or provide information that functioned as a bargaining chip in parental negotiation (71%), and that court-ordered psychiatric evaluation functioned as an alternative method of dispute resolution.

TREATMENT

When children are involved in litigation, child psychiatrists who work with them can be brought into the dispute. Many child psychiatrists anticipate considerable problems in dealing with the legal system and shy away from legal complications. They see the legal processes as an interference to their treatment; are concerned about having their work subjected to scrutiny by lawyers, judges, or other experts; and find the legal realm unfamiliar and anxiety-provoking. Therapists who feel these ways strongly are best advised to avoid the cases or seek consultation with a professional with more experience in dealing with the legal system. However, the frequency of divorce implies that litigation may arise unexpectedly. The problems associated with litigation are reduced if the child psychiatrist has a clear sense of his or her role: forensic evaluator, therapist focusing on issues in litigation (e.g., having troubles with visitation), or therapist focusing on issues not central to litigation (e.g., pharmacotherapy for attention deficit hyperactivity disorder). Many of the difficulties child psychiatrists get into occur when their role is not clear or when they try to change roles.

Therapists like to think that therapy is confidential. However, given the expansion of courts' working definition of relevance and the fact that the confidentiality of the material is controlled by the parents, assurances of confidentiality in the context of litigation are very difficult to keep (Malmquist, 1994), a problem that has been addresed by an American Psychiatric Association Task Force (1991). The therapist cannot be sure that the treatment records will be protected from discovery. This problem is often unanticipated when parents decide to divorce and contest custody after treatment has begun. Obviously, it is preferable if the therapist can help the parents remain focused on the child's interests or encourage referral to mediation to avoid a custody contest, but such happy outcomes are not inevitable. If a contest develops, even the parents' prior agreement that issues in the treatment will remain confidential are not binding if the parents contest custody and the child's feeling about each parent becomes an issue. In many cases the records can be kept out of litigation, but it is very difficult early in litigation to be sure that this will be the result.

Another relatively common problem occurs when a parent brings a child for treatment, overtly to help the child with the anxiety attendant on a parental divorce or custody contest, and the therapist suspects that the parent is likely to attempt to use the treatment information later in a legal battle. Many therapists become uncomfortable conducting treatment without confidentiality under the specter of later discovery of the records

or possible testimony, and refuse to treat with the rationale that the family "is too stirred up for treatment to be effective," thus depriving the child of needed help during a time of crisis.

If a child or his or her parents anticipate that the details of the treatment may enter into litigation, the expected lack of confidentiality alters the nature of the therapeutic relationship. There is the potential for the child or parents to distort the information they provide in order to affect the outcome of the litigation, emphasizing those aspects that they believe will help their case and minimizing or denying aspects that they perceive as hurting it (Ash & Guyer, 1991). It is very difficult for a therapist to discern the degree of this distortion.

Another role for a child psychiatrist is to provide treatment focused specifically on issues related to the litigation. In the case of contested divorces, it is important to involve the parents. The therapist may find it appropriate to take on the role of case manager, using his or her position as advocate of the child to encourage parents to mediate their dispute or to refer the parents to a marital/divorce treatment focused on helping them reduce their conflict and make decisions for their child. To the extent that the child is reacting to behaviors the parent can change, efforts aimed at improving the two parent-child relationships through parent guidance or family treatment (often with only one parent and the child in the room at the same time) are appropriate. Many interventions with a child of disputing parents are similar to interventions with children of divorce generally, such as those having to do with the child's anxiety about what will happen and coming to terms with the parent's breakup. Additionally, however, children of disputing parents need considerable supportive work in helping the child thread his or her way through the maze of parental conflict. The older the child, the more he or she will be sufficiently separated psychologically from their parents to be helped to stay out of parental conflicts. Typically, children 7 years old and younger have a very difficult time resisting the pull of those parents who directly involve their children in parental battles, although the author has seen some children as young as 5 who successfully resisted a parent's demands for information about the other parent and who resisted pressure to join in talking negatively about the other parent.

Children who have been sexually abused may need treatment not only for the effects of the sexual abuse, but may also need support in preparing to testify (Krieger & Robbins, 1985; Schetky & Benedek, 1989). Important parameters of this role have to do with the degree of coordination with the legal personnel involved, whether the treatment is confidential, or whether the information gained in treatment is likely to enter as evidence. Close coordination with one side may open the child's later testimony to charges of being "put up to it" or otherwise influenced by the therapist. The treatment process can be used to undermine the child's credibility in court, for example, when a child has been treated "for sexual abuse" in a case in which the judge or jury has a serious doubt as to whether abuse actually took place.

To avoid having the treatment used as a pawn in litigation strategies, the most useful approach is to split the therapeutic and forensic functions. The therapist might reasonably point out to the parents and their attorneys that he or she has been focusing on the treatment of the child and has not investigated such issues as the mental health of the parents or their disposition for caring for the child as a single parent, and may propose that an evaluation specifically focused on the issues affecting custody be undertaken by someone else. This helps preserve the confidentiality of the treatment and reflects the fact that most treatment information, while sensitive, is not especially relevant to making a forced choice between parents. As the therapist has not conducted a full custody evaluation, he or she may well not have an opinion on custody "to a reasonable degree of medical certainty," in which case the therapist certainly should refrain from giving an opinion. If a judge insists that treatment information be made available, it is worth remembering that records are sought more frequently than testimony, and record review may show the limits of the therapist's information. The therapist is under no obligation to obtain the additional information that would allow him or her to formulate an opinion on the custody question. Finally, the therapist should strive to maintain a working relationship with each parent, one that can survive the period of acrimonious litigation, so that he or she may be useful to the child in the future.

REFERENCES

American Academy of Child and Adolescent Psychiatry. (1988). Guidelines for the clinical evaluation of child and adolescent sexual abuse: Position statement of the American Academy of Child and Adolescent Psychiatry. *Journal of the American Academy of Child and Adolescent Psychiatry, 5,* 655–657.

American Psychiatric Association. (1988). *Child custody consultation.* Washington, DC: Author.

American Psychiatric Association. (1991). *Disclosure of psychiatric treatment records in child custody disputes.* Task Force Report 9. Washington, DC: Author.

American Psychological Association Committee on Professional Practice and Standards (1994). Guidelines for child custody evaluations in divorce proceedings. *American Psychologist, 49,* 677–680.

Ash, P., & Guyer, M. J. (1986a). The functions of psychiatric evaluation in contested child custody and visitation cases. *Journal of the American Academy of Child Psychiatry, 25,* 554–561.

Ash, P., & Guyer, M. J. (1986b). Relitigation following contested custody and visitation evaluations. *Bulletin of the American Academy of Psychiatry and the Law, 14,* 323–330.

Ash, P., & Guyer, M. J. (1991). Biased reporting by parents undergoing child custody evaluations. *Journal of the American Academy of Child and Adolescent Psychiatry, 30,* 835–838.

Benedek, E. P., & Schetky, D. H. (1985). Custody and visitation—problems and perspectives. *Psychiatric Clinics of North America, 8,* 857–873.

Benedek, E. P., & Schetky, D. H. (1987a). Problems in validating allegations of sexual abuse. Part 1: Factors affecting perception and recall of events. *Journal of the American Academy of Child and Adolescent Psychiatry, 26,* 912–915.

Benedek, E. P., & Schetky, D. H. (1987b). Problems in validating allegations of sexual abuse. Part 2: Clinical Evaluation. *Journal of the American Academy of Child and Adolescent Psychiatry, 26,* 916–921.

Bricklin, B. (1995). *The custody evaluation handbook: Research-based solutions and applications.* New York: Brunner/Mazel.

Ceci, S. J., & Bruck, M. (1995). *Jeopardy in the courtroom: A scientific analysis of children's testimony.* Washington DC: American Psychological Association.

Christianson, S., & Loftus, E. F. (1987). Memory for traumatic events. *Applied Cognitive Psychology, 1,* 225–239.

Coogler, O. J. (1978). *Structured mediation in divorce settlement.* Lexington, MA: D.C. Heath.

Coy v. Iowa. 487 U.S. 1012, 108 S.Ct. 2798 (1988).

Derdeyn, A. P. (1976). Child custody contests in historical perspectives. *American Journal of Psychiatry, 133,* 1369–1376.

Emery, R. E. (1994). *Renegotiating family relationships: Divorce, child custody, and mediation.* New York: Guilford.

Emery, R. E., Matthews, S. G., & Wyer, M. M. (1991). Child custody mediation and litigation: Further evidence on the differing views of mothers and fathers. *Journal of Consulting and Clinical Psychology, 59,* 410–418.

Emery, R. E., & Wyer, M. M. (1987). Divorce mediation. *American Psychologist, 42,* 472–480.

Everson, M. D., & Boat, B. W. (1990). Sexualized doll play among young children: Implications for the use of anatomical dolls in sexual abuse evaluations. *Journal of the American Academy of Child and Adolescent Psychiatry, 29,* 736–742.

Foster, H. H. & Freed, D. J. (1980). Divorce in the fifty states: An overview. *Family Law Quarterly, 14,* 229.

Furstenburg, F. F., Jr., Nord, C. W., Peterson, J. L., & Zill, N. (1983). The life course of children of divorce: Marital disruption and parental contact. *American Sociological Review, 48,* 656–668.

Gardner, R. A. (1989). *Family evaluation in child custody mediation, arbitration, and litigation.* Cresskill, NJ: Creative Therapeutics.

Goldstein, J., Freud, A., & Solnit, A. J. (1973). *Beyond the best interests of the child.* New York: Free Press.

Goodman, G. S., Hirschman, J. E., Hepps, D., & Rudy, L. (1991). Children's memory for stressful events. *Merrill-Palmer Quarterly, 37,* 109–157.

Goodman, G. S., Taub, E. P., Jones, D. P. H., England, P., Port, L. K., Rudy, L., & Prado, L. (1992). Testifying in criminal court: Emotional effects on child sexual assault victims. With commentaries by J. E. B. Myers & G. B. Melton, *Monographs of the Society for Research in Child Development, 57* (Serial No. 229).

Green, A. H. (1986). True and false allegations of sexual abuse in child custody disputes. *Journal of the American Academy of Child Psychiatry, 25,* 449–456.

Haynes, J. M. (1981). *Divorce mediation: A practical guide for therapists and counselors.* New York: Springer.

Herman, S. P. (1990). Special issues in child custody evaluations. *Journal of the American Academy of Child and Adolescent Psychiatry, 29,* 969–974.

Idaho v. Wright. 497 U.S. 805, 110 S.Ct. 3139 (1990).

Johnston, J. R. (1994). High-conflict divorce. *The Future of Children, 4* (1), 165–182.

Johnston, J. R., Campbell, L. E. G., Mayes, S. S. (1985). Latency children in post-separation and divorce disputes. *Journal of the American Academy of Child Psychiatry, 24,* 563–574.

Johnston, J. R., Campbell, L. E. G., Tall, M. C. (1985). Impasses to the resolution of custody and visitation disputes. *American Journal of Orthopsychiatry, 55* (1), 112–129.

Johnston, J. R., Gonzalez, R., & Campbell, L. E. G. (1987). Ongoing postdivorce conflict and child disturbance. *Journal of Abnormal Child Psychology, 15,* 493–509.

Johnston, J. R., Kline, M., & Tschann, J. M. (1989). Ongoing postdivorce conflict: effects on children of joint custody and frequent access. *American Journal of Orthopsychiatry, 59* (4), 576–592.

Krieger, M. J., & Robbins, J. (1985). The adolescent incest victim and the judicial system. *American Journal of Orthopsychiatry, 55,* 419–425.

Maccoby, E. M., & Mnookin, R. H. (1992), *Dividing the child: Social and legal dilemmas of custody.* Cambridge, MA: Harvard University Press.

Malmquist, C. P. (1994). Psychiatric confidentiality in child custody disputes. *Journal of the American Academy of Child and Adolescent Psychiatry, 33,* 158–168.

Maryland v. Craig. 497 U.S. 836, 110 S.Ct. 3157 (1990).

Mnookin, R., & Kornhauser, L. (1979). Bargaining in the shadow of the law: The case of divorce. *Yale Law Journal, 88,* 950–997.

National Center for Health Statistics. (1991). *Vital statistics of the United States, 1987.* Vol. 3, *Marriage and Divorce.* DHHS Pub. NO. (PHS) 91-1103. Public Health Service. Washington, DC: U.S. Government Printing Office.

Pearson, J., & Thoennes, N. (1984). Mediating and litigating custody disputes: A longitudinal evaluation. *Family Law Quarterly, 17,* 497–538.

Pearson, J., & Thoennes, N. (1990). Custody after divorce: Demographic and attitudinal patterns. *American Journal of Orthopsychiatry, 60,* 233–249.

Realmuto, G. M., Jensen, J. B., & Wescoe, S. (1990). Specificity and sensitivity of sexually anatomically correct dolls in substantiating abuse: A pilot study. *Journal of the American Academy of Child and Adolescent Psychiatry, 29,* 743–746.

Saposnek, D. T. (1993). The art of family mediation. Special Issue: Beyond technique: The soul of family mediation. *Mediation Quarterly, 11,* 5–12.

Saywitz, K. J. (1989). Children's conceptions of the legal system: "Court is a place to play basketball." In S. J. Ceci, D. F. Ross, & M. P. Toglia (Eds.), *Perspectives on children's testimony* (pp. 131–157). New York: Springer-Verlag.

Schetky, D. H., & Benedek, E. P. (1989). The sexual abuse victim in the courts. *Psychiatric Clinics of North America, 12,* 471–481.

Shaw, D. S., & Emery, R. E. (1988). Chronic family adversity and school-age children's adjustment. *Journal of the American Academy of Child and Adolescent Psychiatry, 27,* 200–206.

Steinman, S. B., Zemmelman, S. E., & Knoblauch, T. M. (1985). A study of parents who sought joint custody following divorce: Who reaches agreement and sustains joint custody and who returns to court. *Journal of the American Academy of Child and Adolescent Psychiatry, 24,* 554–562.

Thoennes, N., & Tjaden, P. G. (1990). The extent, nature, and validity of sexual abuse allegations in custody/visitation disputes. *Child Abuse and Neglect, 14,* 151–163.

Weiner, B. A., Simons, V. A., & Cavanaugh, J. L. (1985). The child custody dispute. In D. H. Schetky & E. P.

Benedek (Eds.), *Emerging issues in child psychiatry and the law* (pp. 59–75). New York: Brunner/Mazel.

White v. Illinois. 502 U.S. 346, 112 S.Ct. 736 (1992).

Wolman, R., & Taylor, K. (1991). Psychological effects of custody disputes on children. *Behavioral Sciences and the Law, 9,* 399–417.

11 / Alterations in Family Life Following Divorce: Effects on Children and Adolescents

E. Mavis Hetherington and Debra Mekos

The alarmingly high rates of marital separation and divorce and their effects on children and families have created a great deal of concern among researchers and clinicians. We have come to realize that the consequences of marital dissolution do not end when the legal divorce decree is signed, but rather set in motion a series of changes in residential arrangements, economic circumstances, and family alliances that may have long-lasting effects. However, research on children's postdivorce adjustment suggests that these effects are not necessarily harmful in the long term. Instead, how children adapt to this series of family reorganization depends on the characteristics of the individual; the unique changes, stresses, and challenges associated with each stage of the transition; and the familial and extrafamilial resources and supports available to promote adaption to new family roles and relationships. Furthermore, the response to any transition varies with the experiences that have preceded it. A child's response to parental separation and divorce will differ if it involves loss of contact with a warm, supportive parent versus separation from an abusive, rejecting, or disengaged parent or a termination of chronic family conflict and acrimony. Thus, divorce can involve both negative and positive life changes that may undermine or promote the child's psychological and social well-being.

In this chapter we describe the alterations in family life that follow divorce as a means of understanding the diversity in children's adjustments to their parents' marital dissolution. We begin with a brief overview of demographic trends in divorce

rates and then discuss the changes in family life and family relationships that accompany the aftermath of divorce. We review the effects of these changes on children's social and academic adjustment and conclude with a discussion of factors that may mediate the long-term effects of divorce on children.

Demographics of Divorce

Since the early 1900s, the divorce rate in the United States has increased tenfold (Cherlin, 1992). At the beginning of the century, less than 4 in 1,000 marriages ended in divorce, but between 1965 and 1990 the rate of divorce more than doubled. If current trends continue, it is estimated that at least half of all marriages will end in divorce (Cherlin, 1992). Although some argue that the divorce rate has leveled off (Hernandez, 1988), others believe the current rate is an underestimate of the true pattern in that it fails to account for the increasing number of couples who separate but never file for divorce. When these trends are taken into consideration, it is estimated that 66% of all first marriages will end in separation or divorce (Castro-Martin & Bumpass, 1989).

Separation and divorce rates are even higher for black families. In comparison to white couples, black couples are more likely to separate, to remain separated longer before obtaining a divorce, or to never obtain a divorce following separation.

Furthermore, blacks are less likely to remarry (Cherlin, 1992). Thus, following divorce, black children are more likely to spend longer periods of time in a single-parent mother-headed household or a household with a divorced mother and grandmother or cohabitating male than are white children (Cherlin, 1992). Forty percent of white children and 75% of black children will experience their parents' divorce or separation by age 16, and most will reside in a single-parent family (primarily with their mother) for at least 5 years (Bumpass & Sweet, 1989).

What reasons underlie these changing trends in divorce? Furstenberg and Cherlin (1991) argue that women's entry into the workforce and increased economic self-sufficiency coupled with changes in attitudes about divorce and changes in divorce laws brought about the rapid increases of the 1960s and 1970s. The paradox of these historical changes is that divorce has become one of the easiest solutions for dealing with an unsatisfactory marriage, yet our laws and policies remain inadequate in helping families cope with the alterations in family life that precede and follow divorce (Emery, 1994; Furstenberg & Cherlin, 1991; Maccoby & Mnookin, 1992; Scott, 1990).

Alterations in Family Life

CHANGES IN CUSTODIAL ARRANGEMENTS

A critical determinant of how well mothers, fathers, and children adjust after divorce concerns the custodial arrangements for the children. In the large majority of divorces, the mother is awarded custody (Emery, 1988). However, there are times when fathers are awarded joint or sole custody, primarily in the case of male or adolescent chldren, or when mothers are deemed incompetent or do not want custody of their children. About 14% of fathers are awarded either sole or joint custody of their children following divorce (Hetherington & Stanley-Hagan, in press).

Even in cases where joint legal custody of children is established, mothers tend to take on greater responsibility for child care over time, while fathers tend to reduce their contact (Albiston, Maccoby, & Mnookin, 1990; Maccoby &

Mnookin, 1992). It was once believed that joint physical custody, in which children alternate between the mother's and father's residence according to a specified schedule, would encourage fathers to remain involved in their children's lives and would encourage parents to adopt a cooperative coparenting style in which mothers and fathers share equally in the raising of their children (Furstenberg & Cherlin, 1991; Scott & Derdeyn, 1984). Unfortunately, this arrangement has not proven to be the best solution for all families; dual residence appears to work best when interparental cooperation is high or interparental intervention is low. However, when interparental conflict is high the arrangement only serves to deepen and prolong the preexisting conflict (Maccoby & Mnookin, 1992).

The implications of maternal custody arrangements typical of divorced families in the United States is that the bulk of the responsibility for raising and providing for children of divorce falls on the mother. Parenting is difficult enough when two parents divide the responsibility, but in the majority of divorced families, the mother must assume the multiple roles of breadwinner, homemaker, disciplinarian, counselor, and friend to her children at a time when they are experiencing new challenges and stressful life changes themselves. In spite of these difficulties, most mothers and children eventually emerge from divorce as well-functioning individuals and may even be enhanced by their escape from a conflictual marital relationship and strengthened by dealing with adversity (Chase-Lansdale & Hetherington, 1990; Hetherington, 1989).

ECONOMIC CHANGES

One of the primary factors underlying the difficulties faced by custodial mothers and their children is the sharp decline in income they experience as a result of divorce. It has been estimated that 1 year after divorce, custodial mothers retain only 67% of their predivorce income while noncustodial fathers retain 90% of their predivorce income (McLanahan & Booth, 1989). Custodial mothers not only earn less than noncustodial fathers, but they also experience more job instability after divorce. During the first 3 years after divorce, custodial mothers are three times more likely than fathers in two-parent households to be unemployed and are also more likely to experience changes in employment during this time (Garfinkel & McLanahan, 1986; McLanahan & Sandefur, 1994). Fortunately, most divorced mothers eventually return to their predivorce income level, but it is a slow, painstaking process and is usually because of remarriage rather than any substantial career gains of their own (Duncan & Hoffman, 1985).

One of the consequences of income loss and job instability is that single mothers and their children are forced to change residences at least once during the period after divorce. For example, McLanahan (1983) found that 38% of divorced mothers moved during the first year. This percentage dropped to 20% per year afterward but was still 33% higher than the residential mobility rates of two-parent families.

Although biological fathers are legally required to provide for their children, many fathers fail to comply with court-ordered child support arrangements (Emery, 1988; Furstenberg & Cherlin, 1991). According to recent statistics, 61% of divorced mothers with children under age 21 have child support awards, yet only half of those awarded are actually receiving full payment. In other words, less than 25% of custodial mothers receive regular and full child support (U.S. Bureau of the Census, 1989).

CHANGES IN PARENTS' WELL-BEING

Both mothers and fathers, regardless of custodial arrangement, are at risk for physical and psychological disorders during the early phase after divorce (Hetherington & Camara, 1984; Hetherington & Stanley-Hagan, in press). During this period, men and women experience a wide range of emotions, from excitement and optimism about their new lives to anxiety, depression, anger, guilt, and feelings of incompetence as a parent and spouse (Hetherington, Cox, & Cox, 1982; Wallerstein & Kelly, 1980). It is also common for mothers and fathers to show marked alterations in self-concept during this time as they attempt to rebuild their lives and renegotiate family relationships (Hetherington & Stanley-Hagan, in press). Although adjustment to the new family situation eventually occurs, divorced men and women are still more likely to experience depression later in life, to be hospitalized for mental

illness, and to experience impairments in immunological functioning (Bloom, Asher, & White, 1978; Kiecolt-Glaser et al., 1987). One of the critical implications of this is that children are faced with a less physically and emotionally competent parent at a time when they need stability and support the most.

CHANGES IN THE PARENTAL RELATIONSHIP

Although divorce signifies the termination of the marital relationship, in many families the parental relationship between the ex-spouses continues. The existence of a nonconflictual, cooperative relationship between parents, where children do not feel caught in the middle, is critical for children's postdivorce adjustment (Buchanan, Maccoby, & Dornbusch, 1991; Camara & Resnick, 1988; Emery, 1988). Unfortunately, the majority of divorced couples find it extremely difficult to control their anger and resentment in order to maintain a cooperative parental relationship (Hetherington, 1989). Instead, their relationship is often characterized by conflict, primarily over child-rearing practices and finances (Hetherington, et al., 1982). In the long term, many divorced couples deal with the demands of shared parenting by adopting what has been referred to as "parallel parenting" where each parent makes decisions and cares for their children indepenent of what the other parent does (Furstenberg, 1990; Maccoby & Mnookin, 1992). An implicit agreement not to interfere with the other parent's decisions and actions is established; parents rarely see or consult each other, and their primary mode of communication is through their children (Furstenberg & Cherlin, 1991). This type of parental relationship is in stark contrast to a coparenting style in which parents collaborate in the rearing of their children, a style many believe to be optimal for children's adjustment (Camara & Resnick, 1988; Chase-Lansdale & Hetherington, 1990; Maccoby et al., 1990) but that is exceedingly rare, even in families with joint physical custody.

In a recent study of parenting patterns and child custody, Maccoby and her colleagues found that, 1 year after divorce, only 1 in 6 families exhibited a coparenting style (Maccoby & Mnookin, 1992). Even in joint custody families, the most common pattern of parental relations observed was disengagement, with little evidence of cooperation, communication, or conflict between parents. It is also interesting to note that custodial mothers were more satisfied with the arrangement when conflict was low and communication was high, yet custodial fathers were more satisfied when communication was low (Maccoby & Mnookin, 1992). This suggests that part of the problem in establishing a coparenting style is that mothers and fathers have different expectations of what their postdivorce relationship should be.

CHANGES IN PARENT-CHILD RELATIONSHIPS

Because of multiple role demands and stressors, the ability of many divorced mothers to effectively support, control, monitor, and discipline their children diminishes in the immediate aftermath of divorce (Hetherington et al., 1982; Hetherington et al., 1992; Wallerstein & Kelly, 1980). During the first year after divorce, mothers tend to be more irritable, less nurturant, less sensitive, and less supportive of their children's efforts to cope with the day-to-day challenges of adjusting to their new family situation (Hetherington et al., 1982). Custodial mothers have great difficulty monitoring their children's activities and disciplining their children in a consistent and appropriate manner.

Although the parenting of divorced mothers becomes more competent over time, conflictual, mutually coercive relationships with sons are particularly intense and enduring. Mother-daughter relationships are also conflictual immediately after the divorce but gradually may become close and supportive (Hetherington, 1989). However, in adolescence renewed conflict between divorced mothers and daughters frequently emerges, often in response to adolescent daughters' precocious sexual or acting-out behavior (Hetherington et al., 1992). Furthermore, about one-third of adolescents, especially boys, become disengaged from their families. If this disengagement leads to associations with an antisocial peer group, adolescents are likely to become involved in delinquent behavior. However, if a close, supportive relationship with a competent adult outside the family is available, disengagement may be a positive solution to an adverse family situation (Hetherington, 1989).

The relationship between children and their noncustodial father also undergoes transformations during the period following divorce. Noncustodial fathers become either more permissive and indulgent or more disengaged from their children (Hetherington & Stanley-Hagan, in press). They are more likely to assume a recreational, companionate role than the instrumental role of teacher or disciplinarian (Furstenberg & Cherlin, 1991). However, there is little congruence between the quality of father-child relationships before the divorce and the postdivorce noncustodial father-child relationship. Some previously disengaged fathers become very involved with their children after the breakup while some previously involved fathers gradually fade out of their children's lives (Hetherington & Stanley-Hagan, in press). They are more likely to maintain contact with sons than with daughters, but the primary determinant of the noncustodial father's ultimate relationship with his children is the quality of his relationship with the custodial mother (Amado & Booth, 1996; Furstenberg & Cherlin, 1991).

Perhaps the most startling alteration in noncustodial father-child relationships is the drastic decline in contact over time. In a large-scale survey of families in the United States, Furstenberg and colleagues found that 50% of children had not seen their father at all in the past year and only 1 in 6 saw their father on a weekly basis. Furthermore, noncustodial mothers were more likely than noncustodial fathers to maintain regular contact with their children (Furstenberg, Nord, Peterson, & Zill, (1983). Some research suggests that the amount of contact with the noncustodial father has little direct effect on children (Furstenberg, 1990; King, 1994). However, other studies have found that continued contact by a competent, involved father under conditions of low conflict can be a positive support for custodial mothers and their children, specially for sons (Hetherington, et al., 1982; Wallerstein & Kelly, 1980), and for black children (McLanahan & Sandefur, 1994).

Even less is known about the quality of custodial father-child relationships and how they change over time. They appear to fall into two distinct categories: fathers who seek custody of their children and fathers who are awarded custody because the mother is unable or unwilling to care for her children (Hetherington & Stanley-Hagan, in press). Although they complain of some of the same task overload and interference with social relations as custodial mothers do, fathers who seek custody report coping well with single parenthood, possibly because custodial fathers have more resources at their disposal and are more willing to assign household responsibilities to children than custodial mothers are (Chase-Lansdale & Hetherington, 1990). Moreover, because fathers who seek custody tend to have had close relationships with their children prior to divorce, the quality of this relationship may carry over into the new family unit. On the other hand, fathers who assent to custody assigned by the court often have difficulty adjusting to their new family situation (Hetherington & Stanley-Hagan, in press).

MOTHER CUSTODY VS. FATHER CUSTODY

Some research indicates that children are better adjusted when they reside with a same-sex parent (Peterson & Zill, 1986; Warshak, 1986; Zaslow, 1988). For the most part, the coercive cycles of parent-child interaction found in mother-custody families do not occur when boys are placed in the custody of their fathers. Instead, boys in father custody tend to be more socially competent and have fewer behavior problems and higher self-esteem. They do, however, lack an openness in communication and expression of emotion that may be associated with lack of contact with an adult female role model. Daughters in father-custody homes, on the other hand, tend to have more adjustment problems than those in mother-custody homes, and fathers report more difficulty in dealing with adolescent daughters than adolescent sons (Camara & Resnick, 1988; Peterson & Zill, 1986; Santrock & Warshak, 1979). There is, however, recent evidence that adolescents in the custody of fathers are more involved in delinquent activities, perhaps because fathers monitor their children's activities less than mothers do (Buchanan, Maccoby, & Dornbusch, 1992).

In both mother- and father-custody families, authoritative parenting characterized by warmth, support, communication, monitoring, and responsive but firm control is associated with social and cognitive competence and low levels of psychopathology in children (Baumrind, 1991; Hetherington et al., 1992; Steinberg, Mounts, Lamborn, & Dornbusch, 1991). The effects of stressors such as economic disadvantage and conflict between ex-spouses on children's adjustment have been found to be indirect and mediated through their effects on parents' own ability to effectively support and monitor their children (Patterson, 1991). Thus, the quality of parenting serves as an important mediator of the effects of divorce-related stress on children.

CHANGES IN SIBLING RELATIONSHIPS

Deteriorations in the sibling relationship are a common occurrence following divorce, with little evidence of improvement over time (Hetherington, 1989; Hetherington et al., 1992). Male and mixed-sex siblings in mother-custody families are more aggressive and more avoidant of each other than either siblings in nondivorced families or female siblings in divorced families. Girls in divorced families are more likely to ignore or reject their brothers, but are more likely to be involved and nurturant when the sibling is a younger sister. More important, longitudinal research suggests that the negative contentious aspects of sibling relationships have a greater impact on inhibiting children's adjustment of divorce than the positive, supportive aspects of sibling relationships have on fostering adjustment to the marital transition (Hetherington, 1989). When a buffering effect of positive sibling relations occurs. It is most likely to involve female siblings and to appear in adolescence rather than preadolescence (Hetherington et al., 1992).

The quality of the sibling relationship is also affected by the quality of the relationship between the divorced spouses. In both divorced and nondivorced families, the amount of negativity and positivity in sibling interactions has been found to be directly related to the amount reported in the marital relationship as well as the degree to which mothers are satisfied with their family situation (MacKinnon, 1989).

In summary, the alterations in life experiences and family relations that occur as a result of divorce are pervasive, interrelated, and change over time. Most parents and children can adjust to divorce in 2 or 3 years if they do not face new or continued adversity. However, divorce places children at greater risk for encountering negative life experiences such as poverty, family conflict, and inept parenting, and these are associated with problems in children's adjustment.

Effects of Divorce on Children

SOCIAL DEVELOPMENT AND PSYCHOPATHOLOGY

Based on a recent meta-analysis of research on divorce effects, Amato and Keith (1991b) concluded that children from divorced families show poorer social and psychological adjustment than do children from nondivorced families. Children tend to show increases in externalizing and internalizing behavior and decreases in social competence during the crisis period following divorce (Allison & Furstenberg, 1989; Camara & Resnick, 1988; Forehand et al., 1991; Guidubaldi, Cleminshaw, Perry & McLoughlin, 1983; Hetherington et al., 1982; Wallerstein & Kelly, 1980). Furthermore, boys continue to exhibit noncompliant, aggressive, impulsive, antisocial behavior as long as 4 to 8 years after the divorce (Guidubaldi & Perry, 1985; Hetherington et al., 1992; Hetherington, Cox & Cox, 1985).

Most of the research on postdivorce effects on social development has been done with preschool and elementary school–age children. Only recently have researchers begun to examine the effects of divorce on adolescents (Chase-Lansdale & Hetherington, 1990), but the evidence thus far suggests that adolescents from divorced families are also at risk for social adjustment problems. However, the greater vulnerability of boys often found in research with younger children is not seen in adolescence (Hetherington et al., 1992). Instead, by early adolescence, both boys and girls in divorced, mother-custody families are less socially competent and more aggressive and noncompliant than adolescents living in nondivorced families, with adjustment differences between girls in divorced and nondivorced families increasing with age (Baumrind, 1989; Hetherington et al., 1992). This reappearance of adjustment problems in girls at adolescence has been referred to as a "sleeper effect" (Zaslow, 1988). Several studies have documented that adolescent girls from divorced, nonremarried families tend to have lower self-esteem and to be more sexually promiscuous than girls from nondivorced families (Hetherington, 1972; Kalter, 1977; Newcomer & Udry, 1987; Wallerstein, Corbin, & Lewis, 1988).

Research also indicates that adolescents living in divorced families are at greater risk than those in nondivorced families for getting involved with drugs and alcohol and becoming substance abusers (Baumrind, 1988; Dornbusch et al., 1985; Needle, Su, & Doherty, 1990; Steinberg, 1987). Furthermore, adolescents whose parents divorce when they are teenagers are more vulnerable to

drug involvement than adolescents whose parents divorce when they are children. Gender differences in adolescents' susceptibility to substance use are also found. Specifically, parental divorce in adolescence is associated with increased substance use in boys but not girls, whereas parental remarriage is related to increased substance use in girls and decreased substance use in boys (Baumrind, 1988; Needle et al., 1990). These gender effects have been further substantiated in a prospective longitudinal study of divorce where adolescents' adjustment was examined both 1 year prior and 5 months after divorce (Doherty & Needle, 1991). The results showed that divorce during adolescence led to a greater increase in the substance abuse by boys but not by girls.

ACADEMIC ACHIEVEMENT

Based on a comprehensive review of the research up to 1980, Hetherington, Camara, & Featherman (1983) concluded that there were minimal differences between children in nondivorced and divorced single-parent families on achievement test scores. However, they did find that children in single-parent households had lower grade point averages and poorer school attendance, and higher rates of drop-out (among boys). Whether these effects were due solely to family structure or more to the ethnicity or socioeconomic status (SES) of the families could not be determined, however, because race and SES were not controlled for in many of the studies reviewed.

More recent studies, controlling for differences in ethnicity and socioeconomic status, have found that children from divorced families, both black and white, are more likely to show lower levels of academic achievement (Amato & Keith, 1991b; Guidubaldi, Cleminshaw, Perry, & McLoughlin, 1983) and to drop out of school (McLanahan, 1985; McLanahan & Booth, 1989; McLanahan & Bumpass, 1988). For example, Krein and Beller (1988) found that number of years spent in a single-mother household was significantly related to drop-out rates for white and black boys and black girls. Interestingly, when differences in family income were controlled, the effect of divorce on school drop-out still held for boys, but not for girls. Furthermore, the effect was strongest for children living in a single-mother household during the preschool years; family structure during middle childhood and adolescence had little impact on risk for dropping out of school.

The results of one study suggest, however, that these differences in drop-out rates are more a function of social maladjustment than of academic underachievement. Specifically, Zimiles and Lee (1991) found small differences in grades and achievement test scores between adolescents from nondivorced, divorced, and remarried families, yet adolescents who had experienced divorce were three times more likely to have dropped out of school. Furthermore, boys were most likely to drop out if they lived in a divorced, mother-custody family, whereas girls were at greater risk if they lived in a remarried family with a stepfather, suggesting that having a same-sex biological parent in the household may act as a buffer against drop-out. Finally, the results showed that low achievement is a factor in drop-out, but primarily for adolescents in nondivorced families; social and behavioral problems may be more important in understanding dropout rates for adolescents experiencing parental divorce.

WHAT COMES FIRST?

Most of the research on divorce effects in childhood and adolescence is based on assessments of children's behavior after the divorce has occurred, leaving open the possibility that the social and academic problems found in children from divorced families are merely a continuation of prior problem behavior rather than a specific response to the divorce. Some recent evidence indicates that children whose parents will later divorce exhibit some behavior problems prior to the divorce than children in families that will remain intact (Amato & Booth, 1996; Block, Block, & Gjerde, 1986; Capaldi & Patterson, 1991; Cherlin et al., 1991). Two interpretations of these findings are usually made. First, it is likely that family problems leading to divorce have already taken their toll on children's adjustment before the divorce occurred. Second, it is possible that the divorce may be an outcome, in part, of having to deal with a difficult child.

However, a third proposal has been offered that the relation between parental divorce and children's adjustment problems is genetically mediated by the personality characteristics of the par-

ents. Specifically, some argue that irritable, antisocial behavior in parents may be genetically associated with both behavior problems in children and higher rates of divorce in children of divorced parents. McGue and Lykken (1992) have found evidence for genetic links in the intergenerational transmission of divorce. Although very little research has examined a possible genetic basis for divorce, further investigations along these lines may increase our understanding of why continuity in marital discord and marital disruption across generations does occur.

CONSEQUENCES IN ADULTHOOD

Less research has examined the long-term impact of divorce on children when they reach adulthood, but it appears that the effects of divorce may be long-lived, particularly in terms of family formation. A growing number of studies show that children of divorce are more likely to become parents before marriage, to marry early, and to divorce early as adults (McLanahan & Bumpass, 1988; McLanahan & Sandefur, 1994). One possible explanation for this pattern is the impact divorce may have on children's beliefs and expectations regarding marriage. Based on a survey of unmarried college students, Franklin, Janoff-Bulman, and Roberts (1990) found that those from divorced families were more likely to distrust a future spouse and more pessimistic about the success of a future marriage. Furthermore, students from divorced families believed that the success of their marriage would depend more on the qualities of the other person than their own personal attributes, whereas those from nondivorced families believed they were ultimately responsible for the success of their marriage. The effects were strongest for students who reported the greatest degree of continuous conflict between their divorced parents.

There is also emerging evidence that experiencing divorce in childhood may increase the likelihood of mental health problems in young adulthood (Amato & Keith, 1991a; Glenn & Kramer, 1985). Two prospective longitudinal studies, one drawn from a clinic-based sample in the United States (Wallerstein & Blakeslee, 1989) and the other from a nationally representative sample in Great Britain (Chase-Lansdale, Cherlin, & Kiernan, 1995) find elevated levels of emotional disturbance in a small percentage of individuals whose parents divorced when they were children or adolescents. The results of the study by Chase-Lansdale and colleagues are particularly compelling given their ability to control for confounding factors such as the family's economic status and children's behavior problems preceding divorce.

Mediators of Postdivorce Adjustment

INDIVIDUAL DIFFERENCES IN CHILDREN

One of the main findings of research on divorce is that children react to their parents' marital dissolution in a variety of ways. Most children initially exhibit some confusion, anger, anxiety, and behavior problems when dealing with the many changes and challenges associated with divorce. However, in the long run, some appear to be permanently damaged or developmentally delayed, while others seem to be coping well initially but show delayed detrimental effects, and still others adapt rapidly and even benefit from their new family situation (Hetherington, 1989, 1991). The effects of divorce may differ for boys and girls, at different ages, with different temperamental characteristics, and with different pre- and postdivorce family dynamics (Hetherington, Stanley-Hagan, & Anderson, 1989). For example, many researchers have noted that boys exhibit more adjustment problems than girls do following divorce. Zaslow (1988, 1989) reviewed the literature on gender differences and concluded that boys' adjustment problems, however, may be more the result of living in a mother-custody single-parent family than experiencing their parents' divorce. Indeed, boys in father-custody single-parent families do not show the pattern of externalizing problems and low social competence found for boys in mother-custody families (Warshak, 1986). In contrast, girls show poorer psychological adjustment when their mother remarries or when the father is the custodial parent. Furthermore, gender differences in response to divorce are most often found in preadolescent, rather than adolescent, children (Hetherington, 1991; Hetherington et al., 1992).

Research on age differences in children's adjustment to divorce have produced inconsistent findings. Some investigators report that younger children are more adversely affected than older children and adolescents (Allison & Furstenberg, 1989; Kalter & Rambar, 1981). It has been proposed that younger children are more affected because of their limited ability to understand the reasons for their parents' divorce and inability to utilize extrafamilial sources of support (Wallerstein & Kelly, 1980). However, other studies suggest that adolescents are as adversely affected as young children are (Frost & Pakiz, 1990; Needle et al., 1990). In addition, several investigators have found that problems related to experiencing divorce in childhood may not emerge until adolescence (Hetherington, 1972, 1991; Hetherington et al., 1992; Kalter & Rembar, 1981; Newcomer & Udry, 1987).

The major difficulty in interpreting age effects is that most longitudinal studies either focus on a single age group or confound age of the child at the time of divorce with the length of time since the divorce. This methodological flaw makes it difficult to discern whether children exhibit more current adjustment problems because the divorce occurred early in life or because they have been exposed for a longer period to the concomitant stresses found in a single-parent or remarried family.

Children's personality and temperament characteristics are also critical determinants of adjustment to disruptions in family life following divorce. Temperamentally difficult boys are more likely to evoke and to be the target of negative behavior from their divorced custodial mothers, especially if the mother is depressed, under high stress, and has little social support (Hetherington, 1989). Also, as noted earlier, children with adjustment problems prior to the divorce are likely to exhibit increased problems because of the divorce. On the other hand, the experience of divorce may actually strengthen the coping skills of temperamentally easy children in situations where the divorce is only moderately stressful and support is available to the child. This phenomenon has been referred to as a "steeling" or "inoculation" effect, in which children's ability to deal with later stressors is enhanced because of exposure to and successful coping with current stressors (Rutter, 1987). More intelligent children and children with high self-esteem and internal locus of control also may adapt more readily to disruptions in family life

(Hetherington, 1991). Thus, the psychologically poor get poorer and the psychologically rich may get richer when confronting the changes and challenges of divorce.

CUMULATIVE STRESS

Negative life events and prolonged or cumulative stressors following divorce may contribute to the development of behavior problems in children. Divorces characterized by prolonged conflict have more negative effects on children than do less conflictual divorces because of the disruptive effects of discord between the ex-spouses on parenting and parent-child relationships (Buchanan et al., 1991; Camara & Resnick, 1988; Fauber, Forehand, McCombs, & Wierson, 1990; Forehand et al., 1991; Hetherington et al., 1992). At least in the early period following divorce, being caught in the middle of conflicts with divided loyalties between parents presents tremendous difficulties for children and has been linked to increases in depression and delinquency in adolescence (Buchanan et al., 1991).

Both multiple family transitions and cumulative stressors place children at risk for psychological problems. Children who have gone through multiple family transitions show more adjustment problems than children who have experienced a single divorce. For example, Capaldi and Patterson (1991) found that boys who had experienced at least three marital transitions (their mothers' divorce, remarriage, and second divorce), in comparison with those undergoing fewer transitions, had lower self-esteem and academic achievement, were more depressed, and more likely to become delinquent. However, they also found that much of the relation between multiple transitions and boys' maladjustment was accounted for by the mothers' own history of antisocial behavior. They concluded that having an antisocial mother places a child at risk for multiple problems, including the experience of their parents' divorce, ineffective parenting, and delinquency.

SUPPORT SYSTEMS AND
INTERVENTION PROGRAMS

The most effective support for children from divorced families is an authoritative custodial parent (Baumrind, 1991; Hetherington, 1989;

Hetherington et al., 1992; Steinberg et al., 1991). However, support systems outside the family may also play a role in buffering children from the negative consequences of divorce. Child care centers and schools that provide a supportive and stable environment, as well as caring teachers, peers, and grandparents, can offer children the security, comfort, and validation of self-worth necessary to cope with the drastic alterations in family life that accompany divorce (Hetherington et al., 1985, 1992).

Moreover, the past decade has seen a rapid rise in formal intervention and support programs for divorced families. These programs usually focus on one of three levels: coping skills training for children and their parents, divorce mediations, or changes in divorce and child custody laws (Grych & Fincham, 1992). The most widely used interventions, however, are the school-based, child-centered programs designed to alleviate the anger, fear, and misconceptions that children commonly experience after divorce. Evaluation studies indicate that this form of intervention can be helpful in promoting positive child adjustment (Alpert-Gillis, Pedro-Carroll, & Cowen, 1989; Pedro-Carroll & Cowen, 1985; Stolberg & Garrison, 1985). Interventions that focus on increasing parenting skills and reducing family conflict also appear promising, but more long-term evaluation research is needed before any firm conclusions can be made (Grych & Fincham, 1992; Patterson, 1991).

Divorce mediation, whereby spouses negotiate the terms of divorce with the aid of an impartial third party, is designed to reduce conflict and improve the adjustment of parents and children by intervening in the divorce process itself. The basic assumption in mediation is that children and parents will suffer fewer problems if a less conflictual and confrontational alternative to divorce litigation is available (Grych & Fincham, 1992). Although divorce mediation appears to be a positive alternative for children, it may not be best for both mothers and fathers. Recent studies show that fathers greatly prefer mediation over litigation as a means of resolving child custody issues while mothers who go through mediation feel that they have lost more and won less than women who go through litigation (Emery, Matthews, & Wyer, 1991; Emery & Wyer, 1987). However, both men and women report feeling satisfied with the effects of the mediation process on the family, and the process itself greatly reduces the amount of time necessary to reach a settlement, which in the long run may have more positive effects on children's adjustment than parents' perceptions of wins and losses (Emery et al., 1991; Emery, 1994).

Although space limitations preclude a review of legal interventions, innovative efforts have been initiated in some states to collect child support from noncustodial fathers, to assure a minimum income for divorced women and their children, and to promote and protect the rights of noncustodial parents and grandparents (Cherlin, 1988; Emery, 1994; Furstenberg, 1990; Grych & Fincham, 1992; Thompson, Tinsley, Scalora, & Parke, 1989). The direct effects of these legal changes on the psychological well-being of children are for the most part unknown.

Summary and Conclusions

Although many parents and children initially experience separation and divorce as stressful, most eventually adjust to their new life situation if it is not accompanied by sustained or new adversity. In the long run, children are better adjusted in a well-functioning single-parent family with low conflict and an authoritative custodial parent than in a conflict-ridden two-parent household (Amato, Loomis, & Booth, 1995; Barber & Eccles, 1992; Hetherington et al., 1982). Divorce does place children at risk for encountering multiple life stresses, but divorce and remarriage can also remove children from stressful or acrimonious family relationships and provide additional resources for children.

On average, children in divorced families exhibit more problem behaviors than children in nondivorced families. However, the size of the long-term effects of divorce on children's adjustment is modest. Based on clinical impressions and the absence of a comparison nondivorced sample, Wallerstein and Blakeslee (1989) conclude that as many as 33% of children from divorced families sustain deleterious effects. On the other hand, Hetherington et al. (1992) report that by 4 years after the divorce, only 20% of children exhibit serious psychopathology in contrast to 10% in nondivorced families. A meta-analysis by Amato and Keith (1991b) estimates even smaller effect sizes. Overall, the research shows that the vast majority of children are able to adapt to the experience of divorce and emerge as reasonably competent, well-adjusted individuals. However, this in no way negates the importance of understanding and ameliorating the painful experiences many children have in adjusting to their parents' marital dissolution.

Recently, researchers have moved away from a pathogenic model and have begun to focus on the diversity of children's responses to their parents' divorce (Hetherington, 1989; 1991). It is hoped that a greater understanding of factors associated with children's resiliency and vulnerability in coping with their parents' marital transitions will lead to the development of more effective policies and programs aimed at reducing or preventing the adverse outcomes of divorce.

REFERENCES

Albiston, C. R., Maccoby, E. E., & Mnookin, R. R. (1990, Spring). Does joint legal custody matter? *Stanford Law and Policy Review.* 167–179.

Allison, P. D., & Furstenberg, F. F. (1989). How marital dissolution affects children: Variations by age and sex. *Developmental Psychology, 25,* 540–549.

Alpert-Gillis, L. J., Pedro-Carroll, J. L., & Cowne, E. L. (1989). The Children of Divorce Intervention Program: Development, implementation, and evaluation of a program for young urban children. *Journal of Consulting and Clinical Psychology, 57,* 583–589.

Amato, P. R., & Keith, B. (1991a). Parental divorce and adult well-being: A meta-analysis. *Journal of Marriage and the Family, 53,* 43–58.

Amato, P. R., & Keith, B. (1991b). Parental divorce and the well-being of children: A meta-analysis. *Psychological Bulletin, 110,* 26–46.

Amato, P. R., Loomis, L. S., & Booth, A. (1995). Parental divorce, marital conflict, and offspring well-being during early adulthood. *Social Forces, 73,* 895–915.

Amato, P. R., & Booth, A. (1996). A prospective study of divorce and parent-child relationships. *Journal of Marriage and the Family, 58,* 356–365.

Barber, B. L., & Eccles, J. S. (1992). Long-term influences of divorce and single parenting on adolescent family- and work-related values, behaviors, and aspirations. *Psychological Bulletin, 111,* 108–126.

Baumrind, D. (1988, April). *Adolescent exploratory behavior: Precursors and consequences.* Paper presented at the National Institute of Mental Health conference: "Loss of self-regulatory control: Its causes and consequences," Washington, DC.

Baumrind, D. (1989, April). *Sex-differentiated socialization effects in childhood and adolescence in divorced and intact families.* Paper presented at the biennial meetings of the Society for Research on Child Development, Kansas City, MO.

Baumrind, D. (1991). Effective parenting during the early adolescent transition, In P. A. Cowan & E. M. Hetherington (Eds.), *Family transitions* (pp. 111–163). Hillsdale, NJ: Lawrence Erlbaum.

Block, J. H., Block, J., & Gjerde, P. F. (1986). The personality of children prior to divorce: A prospective study. *Child Development, 57,* 827–840.

Bloom, B. L., Asher, S. J., & White, S. W. (1978). Marital disruption as a stressor: A review and analysis. *Psychological Bulletin, 85,* 867–894.

Buchanan, C. M., Maccoby, E. E. & Dornbusch, S. M. (1991). Caught between parents: Adolescents' experience in divorced homes. *Child Development, 62,* 1008–1029.

Buchanan, C. M., Maccoby, E. E., & Dornbusch, S. M. (1992). Adolescents and their families after divorce: Three residential arrangements compared. *Journal of Research on Adolescence, 2,* 261–291.

Bumpass, L., & Sweet, J. A. (1989). Children's experience in single-parent families: Implications of cohabitation and marital transitions. *Family Planning Perspectives, 6,* 256–260.

Camara, K. A., & Resnick, G. (1988). Interparental conflict and cooperation: Factors moderating children's post-divorce adjustment. In E. M. Hetherington & J. D. Arasteh (Eds.), *Impact of divorce, single parenting, and stepparenting on children* (pp. 169–195). Hillsdale, NJ: Lawrence Erlbaum.

Capaldi, D. M., & Patterson, G. R. (1991). Relation of parental transitions to boys' adjustment problems: I. A linear hypothesis. II. Mothers at risk for transitions and unskilled parenting. *Developmental Psychology, 27,* 489–504.

Castro-Martin, T., & Bumpass, L. (1989). Recent trends and differentials in marital disruption. *Demography, 26,* 37–51.

Chase-Lansdale, P. L., & Hetherington, E. M. (1990). The impact of divorce on life-span development: Short and long term effects. In P. B. Baltes, D. L. Featherman, & R. M. Lerner (Eds.), *Life-span development and behavior* (Vol. 10, pp. 105–150). Hillsdale, NJ: Lawrence Erlbaum.

Chase-Lansdale, P. L., Cherlin, A. J., & Kiernan, K. E. (1995). The long-term effects of parental divorce on the mental health of young adults: A developmental perspective. *Child Development, 66,* 1614–1634.

Cherlin, A. J. (1992). *Marriage, divorce, remarriage.* (2nd ed.) Cambridge, MA: Harvard University Press.

Cherlin, A. J. (1988). The changing American family and public policy. In A. J. Cherlin (Ed.), *The changing American family and public policy* (pp. 1–30). Washington, DC: Urban Institute Press.

Cherlin, A. J., Furstenberg, F. F., Chase-Lansdale, P. L., Kiernan, K. E., Robins, P. K., Morrison, D. R., & Teitler, J. O. (1991). Longitudinal studies of effects of divorce on children in Great Britain and the United States. *Science, 252,* 1386–1389.

Doherty, W. J., & Needle, R. H. (1991). Psychological adjustment and substance use among adolescents before and after a parental divorce. *Child Development, 62,* 328–337.

Dornbusch, S., Carlsmith, J., Bushwall, S., Ritter, P., Leiderman, H., Hastorf, A., & Gross, R. (1985). Single parents, extended households, and the control of adolescents. *Child Development, 56,* 326–341.

Duncan, G. J., & Hoffman, S. D. (1985). A reconsideration of the economic consequences of marital dissolution. *Demography, 22,* 485–497.

Emery, R. E. (1988). *Marriage, divorce, and children's adjustment.* Newbury Park, CA: Sage.

Emery, R. E. (1994). *Renegotiating family relationships: Divorce, child custody, and mediation.* New York: Guilford Press.

Emery, R. E., Matthews, S. G., & Wyer, M. M. (1991). Child custody mediation and litigation: Further evidence on the differing views of mothers and fathers. *Journal of Consulting and Clinical Psychology, 59,* 410–418.

Emery, R. E., & Wyer, M. M. (1987). Child custody mediation and litigation: An experimental evaluation of the experience of parents. *Journal of Consulting and Clinical Psychology, 55,* 179–186.

Fauber, R., Forehand, R., McCombs, A., & Wierson, M. (1990). A mediational model of the impact of marital conflict on adolescent adjustment: The role of disrupted parenting. *Child Development, 61,* 1112–1123.

Forehand, R., Wierson, M., Thomas, A. M., Fauber, R., Armistead, L., Kemptom, T., & Long, N. (1991). A short-term longitudinal examination of young adolescent function following divorce: The role of family factors. *Journal of Abnormal Child Psychology, 19,* 97–111.

Franklin, K. M., Janoff-Bulman, R., & Roberts, J. E. (1990). Long-term impact of parental divorce on optimism and trust: Changes in general assumptions or narrow beliefs? *Journal of Personality and Social Psychology, 59,* 743–755.

Frost, A. K., & Pakiz, B. (1990). The effects of marital disruption on adolescents: Time as a dynamic. *American Journal of Orthopsychiatry, 60,* 544–555.

Furstenberg, F. F. (1990). Divorce and the American family. *Annual Review of Sociology, 16,* 379–403.

Furstenberg, F. F., & Cherlin, A. (1991). *Divided families: What happens to children when parents part.* Cambridge, MA: Harvard University Press.

Furstenberg, F. F., Nord, C., Peterson, J. L., & Zill, N. (1983). The life course of children of divorce: Marital disruption and parental contact. *American Sociological Review, 48,* 656–668.

Garfinkel, I., & McLanahan, S. (1986). *Single mothers and their children: A new American dilemma.* Washington, DC: Urban Institute.

Glenn, N. D., & Kramer, K. B. (1985). The psychological well-being of adult children of divorce. *Journal of Marriage and the Family, 47,* 905–913.

Grych, J. H., & Fincham, F. D. (1992). Interventions for children of divorce: Towards greater integration of research and action. *Psychological Bulletin, 111,* 434–454.

Guidubaldi, J., Cleminshaw, H. K., Perry, J. D., & McLoughlin, C. S. (1983). The impact of parental divorce on children: Report of the nationwide NADP study. *School Psychology Review, 12,* 300–323.

Guildubaldi, J., & Perry, J. D. (1985). Divorce and mental health sequelae for children: A two-year follow-up of a nationwide sample. *Journal of the American Academy of Child Psychiatry, 24,* 531–537.

Hernandez, D. J. (1988). The demographics of divorce and remarriage. In E. M. Hetherington & J. D. Arasteh (Eds.), *Impact of divorce, single parenting, and stepparenting on children* (pp. 3–22). Hillsdale, NJ: Lawrence Erlbaum.

Hetherington, E. M. (1972). Effects of father absence on personality development in adolescent daughters. *Developmental Psychology, 7,* 313–326.

Hetherington, E. M. (1989). Coping with family transitions: Winners, losers, and survivors. *Child Development, 60,* 1–14.

Hetherington, E. M. (1991). The role of individual differences and family relationships in children's coping with divorce and remarriage. In P. Cowan & E. M. Hetherington (Eds.), *Family transitions* (pp. 165–174). Hillsdale, NJ: Lawrence Erlbaum.

Hetherington, E. M., & Camara, K. A. (1984). Families in transition: The process of dissolution and reconstitution. In R. D. Parke (Ed.), *Review of child development research* (pp. 398–439). Chicago: University of Chicago Press.

Hetherington, E. M., Clingempeel, W. G., Anderson, E. R., Deal, J. E., Stanley-Hagan, M., Hollier, E. A., & Lindner, M. S. (1992). *Coping with marital transitions: A family systems perspective. Monographs of the Society for Research in Child Development, 57* (Serial no. 227).

Hetherington, E. M., Camara, K. A., & Featherman, D. L. (1983). Achievement and intellectual functioning of children in one-parent households. In J. Spence (Ed.), *Achievement and achievement motives* (pp. 205–284). San Francisco: W. H. Freeman.

Hetherington, E. M., Cox, M. J., & Cox, R. (1982). Effects of divorce on parents and children. In M. E. Lamb (Ed.), *Nontraditional families* (pp. 233–288). Hillsdale, NJ: Lawrence Erlbaum.

Hetherington, E. M., Cox, M. J., & Cox, R. (1985). Long-term effects of divorce and remarriage on the adjustment of children. *Journal of American Academy of Psychiatry, 24,* 518–530.

Hetherington, E. M., & Stanley-Hagan, M. (in press). The effects of divorce on fathers and their children. In M. E. Lamb (Ed.), *The role of the father in child development.* New York: John Wiley & Sons.

Hetherington, E. M., Stanley-Hagan, M., & Anderson, E. R. (1989). Marital transitions: A child's perspective. *American Psychologist, 44,* 303–312.

Kalter, N. (1977). Children of divorce in an outpatient psychiatric population. *American Journal of Orthopsychiatry, 47,* 40–51.

Kalter, N., & Rembar, J. (1981). The significance of a child's age at the time of parental divorce. *American Journal of Orthopsychiatry, 51,* 85–100.

Kiecolt-Glaser, J. K., Fisher, L. D., Ogrocki, P., Stout, J. C., Speicher, C. E., & Glaser, R. (1987). Marital equality, marital disruption, and immune function. *Psychosomatic Medicine, 49,* 13–34.

King, V. (1994). Nonresident father involvement and child well-being: Can dads make a difference? *Journal of Family Issues, 15,* 78–96.

Krein, S. F., & Beller, A. H. (1988). Educational attainment of children from single-parent families: Differences by exposure, gender, and race. *Demography, 25,* 221–234.

Maccoby, E. E., Depner, C. E., & Mnookin, R. H. (1990). Co-parenting in the second year after divorce. *Journal of Marriage and the Family, 52,* 141–155.

Maccoby, E. E., & Mnookin, R. H. (1992). *Dividing the child: Social and legal dilemmas of custody.* Cambridge, MA: Harvard University Press.

MacKinnon, C. E. (1989). An observational investigation of siblings in divorced families. *Developmental Psychology, 25,* 36–44.

McGue, M., & Lykken, D. T. (1992). Genetic influence on risk of divorce. *Psychological Science, 3,* 368–373.

McLanahan, S. (1983). Family structure and stress: A longitudinal comparison of two-parent and female-headed families. *Journal of Marriage and the Family, 45,* 347–357.

McLanahan, S. (1985). Family structure and the reproduction of poverty. *American Journal of Sociology, 90,* 873–901.

McLanahan, S., & Booth, K. (1989). Mother-only families: Problems, prospects, and politics. *Journal of Marriage and the Family, 51,* 557–580.

McLanahan, S., & Bumpass, L. (1988). Intergenerational consequences of family disruption. *American Journal of Sociology, 94,* 130–152.

McLanahan, S., & Sandefur, G. (1994). *Growing up with a single parent: What hurts, what helps.* Cambridge, MA: Harvard University Press.

Needle, R. H., Su, S. S., & Doherty, W. J. (1990). Divorce, remarriage, and adolescent substance use: A prospective longitudinal study. *Journal of Marriage and the Family, 52,* 157–169.

Newcomer, S. F., & Udry, J. R. (1987). Parental marital status effects on adolescent sexual behavior. *Journal of Marriage and the Family, 49,* 235–240.

Patterson, G. R. (1991, April). *Interaction of stress and family structure and their relation to child adjustment.* Paper presented at the biennial meetings of the Society for Research on Child Development, Seattle, WA.

Pedro-Carroll, J. L., & Cowen, E. L. (1985). The Children of Divorce Intervention Program: An investigation of the efficacy of a school-based prevention program. *Journal of Consulting and Clinical Psychology, 53,* 603–611.

Peterson, J. L., & Zill, N. (1986). Marital disruption, parent-child relationships, and behavior problems in children. *Journal of Marriage and the Family, 49,* 295–307.

Rutter, M. (1987). Psychosocial resilience and protective mechanisms. *American Journal of Orthopsychiatry, 57,* 316–331.

Santrock, J. W., & Warshak, R. A. (1979). Father custody and social development in boys and girls. *Journal of Social Issues, 35,* 112–125.

Scott, E. S. (1990). Rational decision-making about marriage and divorce. *Virginia Law Review, 76,* 9–94.

Scott, E. S., & Derdeyn, A. (1984). Rethinking joint custody. *Ohio State Law Journal, 45,* 455–498.

Steinberg, L. (1987). Single parents, stepparents, and the susceptibility of adolescents to antisocial peer pressure. *Child Development, 58,* 269–275.

Steinberg, L., Mounts, N. S., Lamborn, S. D., & Dornbusch, S. M. (1991). Authoritative parenting and adolescent adjustment across varied ecological niches. *Journal of Research on Adolescence, 1,* 19–36.

Stolberg, A. L., & Garrison, K. M. (1985). Evaluation a primary prevention program for children of divorce: The Divorce Adjustment Project. *American Journal of Community Psychology, 13,* 111–124.

Thompson, R. A., Tinsley, B., Scalora, M., & Parke, R. (1989). Grandparents' visitation rights: Legalizing the ties that bind. *American Psychologist, 44,* 1217–1222.

U. S. Bureau of the Census. (1989). *Current Population Reports, Series P-23, No. 154, Child Support and Alimony: 1985.* (Suppl. Rep). Washington, DC: U.S. Government Printing Office.

Wallerstein, J. S., & Blakeslee, S. (1989). *Second chances: Men, women, and children a decade after divorce.* New York: Ticknor & Fields.

Wallerstein, J. S., Corbin, S. B., & Lewis, J. M. (1988). Children of divorce: A ten-year study. In E. M. Hetherington & J. D. Arasteh (Eds.), *Impact of divorce, single parenting, and stepparenting on children* (pp. 198–214). Hillsdale, NJ: Lawrence Erlbaum.

Wallerstein, J. S., & Kelly, J. B. (1980). *Surviving the break-up: How children and parents cope with divorce.* New York: Basic Books.

Warshak, R. A. (1986). Father-custody and child development: A review and analysis of psychological research. *Behavioral Sciences and the Law, 4,* 2–17.

Zaslow, M. J. (1988). Sex differences in children's response to parental divorce: 1. Research methodology and postdivorce family forms. *American Journal of Orthopsychiatry, 58,* 355–378.

Zaslow, M. J. (1989). Sex differences in children's response to parental divorce: 2. Samples, variables, ages, and sources. *American Journal of Orthopsychiatry, 59,* 118–141.

Zimiles, H., & Lee, V. E. (1991). Adolescent family structure and educational progress. *Developmental Psychology, 27,* 314–320.

12 / Foster Care

Myron L. Belfer and Paul M. Fine

Foster care for children as an alternative to traditional care in a family setting has existed for generations (Hacsi, 1995). At its best, it has offered a safe and supportive haven for children who have been deemed "at risk." At its worst, it has been part of a system that has perpetuated a downward spiral in the lives of children. Foster care evokes controversy as a means of caring for children, but alternatives are few and viewed with equal skepticism. With the onslaught of substance abuse and

its consequences, homelessness, and increases in child abuse, foster care is being utilized with increased frequency. Accordingly, it is being subjected to closer scrutiny. This chapter surveys the utilization of foster care, its variations, and its role in relation to the mental health of children. The parameters of practice and training for the psychiatric work with children and adolescents in foster care also are addressed.

Since the mid-1980s, AIDS, homelessness,

teen pregnancy, alcohol abuse, and the widespread crack cocaine epidemic have combined to overwhelm the system. The number of young foster children increased at almost twice the rate of general foster care population (U.S. General Accounting Office [GAO], 1994). Neglect and caregiver absence prompted an estimated 68% of removals, up from 47% in 1986 (GAO, 1994). The GAO (1994) estimated that families where at least one parent was a drug abuser increased from 52% to 78%, and that an increasing percentage, 58% of children in 1991 compared to 43% in 1986, had serious health-related problems in 1991.

No single, comprehensive system tracks all children in public and private foster care. In 1986, 280,000 children were in state-licensed foster care, and at the end of 1991, 429,000 were in state-licensed foster care homes (GAO, 1994). Even these large numbers probably do not reflect the true extent of the use of foster care due to difficulties in collecting the data at all levels of government. As the number of children living in foster care has increased, so have the costs. The federal entitlement program Title IV-B (Child Welfare Services Program) covers a portion of states' foster care expenses related to preventive services. In 1981, the expenditure for Title IV-B was $164 million and in 1991, $273 million. However, the expenditure for Title IV-E (Foster Care and Adoption Assistance), the direct service foster care program, rose from $637 million in 1986 to $2.2 billion. Because federal money for foster care for poor children is guaranteed in the form of an "entitlement" program, states are encouraged to remove children from their families. At the same time, federal assistance for programs that pay for less-expensive preventive measures or for support services aimed at keeping children with their parents has not been keeping up with the need. Some financial relief was realized with the passage in 1988 of the Family Support Act, which retooled the federal-state welfare system. In addition, in 1990 Congress enacted a major new program to help families pay for and obtain child care.

It is important to note that the gains in the 1988 legislation were achieved as a result of solid research findings. Data had been obtained on what kinds of programs effectively moved people from welfare into permanent jobs. In the world of child welfare, comparable data about what works are more difficult to establish. There is a lack of coordination between programs targeted for substance abuse and AIDS on the one hand and with child welfare programs on the other. This impedes development of effective services for children. Moreover, the split jurisdiction over the expenditure of federal funds for child welfare services significantly complicates the appropriations process.

Types of Foster Care

Not all foster care is the same. Some arrangements involve a single child in a conventional, stable family setting for an extended period of time. Other foster care involves a foster mother or foster family caring for multiple children for extended periods of time. Still others involve multiple children for short periods of time. As needs have been identified, specialized foster care for children with a variety of needs or impacted by special problems also have developed (Fine & Pape, 1989; Meadowcroft & Trout, 1990).

Impact of Foster Care

There are mixed opinions (Rice & McFadden, 1988) on the effects of foster care on children. The National Commission on Children in Need of Parents terms it "an unconscionable failure in harming large numbers of the children it purports to serve" (National Commission on Children in Need of Parents, 1979). Fanshel and Shinn (1978), however, found that "in caseworker rating there was little evidence of massive emotional trauma experienced by children on entering foster care. Intense reactions to separation were apparently displayed by only a minority of the subjects." They caution however, that "We are not completely sure that continued tenure in foster care over extended periods of time is not itself harmful to children. On the level at which we were able to measure the adjustment of the children we could find no such negative effect."

Jones and Moses (1984), in a study of former foster children in West Virginia, found that the largest group of respondents were very satisfied with their foster care experience, and over three-quarters of the group expressed satisfaction. In a literature review of the impact of foster care on children, Maluccio and Fein (1985) found that with several exceptions, "researchers have consistently reported that foster care graduates function well and that no negative effect of foster care on the child's adjustment is detected." Festinger (1983), in a study of former foster children, found that on the whole, young adults were quite satisfied with their experience in foster care, and that "by and large those who felt their placement was necessary, and this was a large majority, expressed more satisfaction with their experience than those who felt they had been placed unnecessarily."

There are important behavioral and family differences between children in foster care and those not in foster care (Hulsey & White, 1989). While these differences are evident in both the behavior of the children and the characteristics of their *birth* families, the differences in family characteristics account for a significant proportion of the differences in behavior. The effects of differing family structures and of an unstable family environment, characterized by marital changes and a legal history, appear more important in association with behavior than does placement in foster care (Fanshel, Finch, & Grundy, 1990). Unfortunately, in studies of this type, measures of behavior for foster children occur after placement. Thus, it is not possible to state that for children in foster care, previous family influences are a cause of later behavior problems. It does, however, appear reasonable to assume that children from consistently unstable families would show more dysfunctional behavior, and that these unstable homes would be more frequently associated with children in foster care (Hulsey & White, 1989). It is possible that the experiences of maltreatment and subsequent foster care placement had a lesser impact on later behavior than did the turmoil of an inconsistent and disruptive home life (Hulsey & White, 1989). Elmer (1977) stated that a family with an unstable structure and legal problems may be as potent a factor as abuse in the development of problem behavior. Children kept in foster care have been reported to have better criminal justice outcomes than those sent home (Widom, 1989).

Robertson and Robertson (1972) demonstrated that the impact of the loss of mother as a primary caregiver cannot be differentiated when the foster care situation includes a responsive surrogate mother who provides a safe and predictable environment. Regarding these findings, however, caveats are applicable. Currently, there is a lack of acceptable means to measure the child's psychological adaptation. Yet it remains true that for the child most likely to be in foster care, the child's prior experiences coupled with the outside influences that impact on him or her significantly influence the perceived outcomes attributable to foster care. In addition to the adaptation to a totally new situation, a child who arrives at foster care after multiple psychological and physical traumas has much to overcome. The best of foster care may not be able to overcome adverse prior experiences.

There also is a belief that long-term foster care may be inherently unstable and generally damaging (Steinhauer et al., 1988). Cooper (1978) suggests that while short-term fostering in preparation for adoption has a clear purpose, intermediate and long-term fostering lack a clear definition of task and are so inherently unstable that they promote insecurity for all involved. Current findings raise issues as to whether such a definitive statement can be made (Fein, Maluccio, & Kluger, 1990). Numerous authors have expressed concern about the number of foster children who, more from a lack of adequate planning than from any conscious decision, end up drifting into permanent foster care, abandoned by parents who no longer visit and neglected by agencies supposedly acting on their behalf. But it is important to differentiate these effects of uncertainty in placement and administrative lapses from the effects of permanent foster care that is planned in the best interests of the child and the parent. While well aware of the dangers of indifferent long-term placements, a number of authors hold that for certain children, planned permanent foster care resulting from an appropriate placement and receiving adequate agency support may be the least detrimental alternative available; in selected cases it may even be helpful (Derdeyn, 1977; Fanshel et al., 1990; Fine, 1993).

The factors that influence the impact of foster care on the child relate in part to the characteristics of the foster care situation under scrutiny.

The child placed in the single foster care setting for the first and only time at a young age is not the prototype for the controversy. It is important to realize that the foster care that gains attention occurs where the child often has had multiple foster placements with episodic return to the biologic or "responsible" parent. Such a child often will have had intervening group placements of various types. The child who lives in the uncertain world of child social service agencies, the courts, institutions, and multiple caregivers is in a pathogenic environment to begin with. This situation can induce psychological problems that should not be attributed to the impact of foster care. Foster care is one manifestation of the host of stressful influences on the child.

Most child welfare experts agree that children who have already suffered separation from their birth parents should be spared unnecessary moves while living under substitute care; according to Fanshel (1976) and Fine (1985), any continuity in environment and in relationships with others, particularly surrogate or adoptive parents, should be maintained. Fanshel (1976) reported on the long-term status of changes in children in foster care. After 5 years, 56% of the children had been discharged, 5% placed in adoptive homes, and 3% transferred to state institutions. Almost 10% of the children were discharged more than once. Compared with the oldest category who had left care by the end of the fifth year of the study, among the youngest group of children a greater proportion remained in care. One explanation of the differential outcomes is related to the reasons that the children entered care. Infants often were placed because of the unwillingness of a mother to assume care, whereas in the older group, maladjusted behavior was the reason for entry. The older group thus may have had a longer relationship with the parent than had the infant and therefore may have had a stronger claim for ongoing parental involvement and responsibility. These data tend to contradict a notion originating from earlier research, namely: that unless children leave foster care within the first or second year after entry, they are doomed to spend the rest of their childhood in such care. The implication of the current findings is that even 5 years after a child's entry into care, one need not give up hope of his or her eventual return home or to the home of relatives or friends.

Nonetheless, the intervening period of time may well have placed the child "at risk" for psychological disturbance.

The smallest proportion of children who entered care because of their own behavioral difficulties returned home during the first year; on the other hand, by the end of the study, the smallest proportion of these children remained in care. In contrast, children whose entry into care was due to physical illness of the parent or child left care in large numbers during the first year. The largest proportion of children still in care at the end of 5 years were those who were abandoned. Mental illness of the caregiver accounted for more children coming into foster care than any other category. The implications of this for prevention and crisis intervention are clear, both in the child's family and with the child. Mothers who revealed better parental capacity, as judged by their caseworkers, were more successful in arranging for their children to be returned home.

Foster care can make a contribution to the psychological well-being as well as to the detriment of children. Bryce and Ehlert (1971) reported on 144 foster children and suggested that it was necessary to look much more closely at the status of children in care. They cited Fanshel's 1971 report that suggested that the longer children remained in foster care, the more likely they are to become emotionally disturbed. Yet the child welfare literature on the psychological consequences of foster care is sparse. In regard to the specific issue, the findings of Goldstein, Freud, and Solnit (1973) are particularly relevant. They urged recognition of the child's need for a rapid disposition and attention to the child's sense of investment in caregivers and environment. An understanding of a child's time sense and identifications is an aspect of prevention that must be emphasized to keep the inevitable transient psychological disturbances from becoming significant long-term influences on psychological development.

Zimmerman (1982) reflects that in recent years, child welfare research, theory building, and program development have emphasized decision making, primarily in regard to intake and permanency planning. Concern for limiting the time youngsters spend in foster care and for obtaining permanent homes for them has preempted the concern for the emotional difficulties they bring with them or develop during placement. Although the current focus on decision making (in contrast to the primarily treatment-oriented focus of earlier years) can be applauded, the fact remains that neglected and abused children placed in foster care remain at risk of having behavioral and emotional problems that their caregivers must address. These difficulties have long been documented and have recently been noted as one factor contributing to the disruption of permanent placements.

To be removed from one's own home and placed in foster care is a critical psychological experience. Children and adolescents experience this as an absence of control. Children may attribute causation to themselves and their own behavior; hence that placement, even though a result of their behavior, only proves that they cannot surmount aversive situations and that their actions cause singularly undesirable consequences (Dweck, 1977). From this perspective, placement is in itself "depressogenic" and, unless precautions are taken, becomes an exercise in learned helplessness. Many events and factors in foster care serve to reinforce helplessness in children and adolescents. The repeated unanticipated moves and the visitation with their families and siblings are controlled by others, including relatives, the agency, or the courts. Children often are unable to participate in the normal parent-child negotiations that form a part of healthy psychological and interpersonal development.

Psychological Factors and Psychopathology in the Children

The reported rates for serious psychological, behavioral, and psychiatric problems in foster children vary from 21 to 60%, with most in the range of 35% (Fanshel & Shinn, 1978; Kavaler & Swire, 1983; Kliman, Schaeffer, & Friedman, 1982; Moffat, Peddie, Stulginkas, Pless, & Steinmetz, 1985; Schor, 1982; Simms, 1989). For purposes of rough comparison, a recent estimate of prevalence for moderate to severe psychiatric disorders in the general population is 14 to 20% (Brandenburg, Friedman, & Siiver, 1990). Thus, it appears that children and adolescents who are placed by the state may have more disorders than children in general, but not to an extreme degree.

Certain specific disorders have been found to be frequent among abused and neglected youths, including those in foster care. These include excessive water drinking (Accardo, Caul & Whitman, 1989); hyperphagia (Demb, 1991); psychosocial dwarfism (Taitz & King, 1988); posttraumatic stress disorder, psychic numbing, externalizing responses (Kiser, Heston, Millsap & Pruit, 1991); and depression (Kaufman, 1991). Chernoff et al. (1994) found in their study a 60% incidence of developmental delay, 25% chronic medical problems, and 15% short stature. Learning disabilities and ensuing behavioral and emotional problems also are overrepresented and may not become overt until later in each child's development (Silver, 1989), (Halfon, Mendenca, & Berkowitz, 1995).

For many years, various forms of depression have been observed in foster children (Zimmerman, 1982). Early authors focused on the traumatic effects of separation and loss on children (Kline & Overstreet, 1972; Littner, 1956). More recent articles have directly addressed the issue of depression in young and adolescent foster children (Anderson & Simonitch, 1981; Golden, 1981; Highland, 1979; Kinard, 1982). These authors rely heavily on psychodynamic theory for both explanations of behavior and guides to intervention. Zimmerman (1982) discusses the concept of childhood depression and the sometimes debilitating effects of foster care in light of Seligman's learned helplessness theory reformulated with attribution theory (Peterson & Seligman, 1985). This model attributes depression to the perception of an inability to influence the outcomes of one's life or the inability to avoid negative outcomes.

The application of the learned helplessness model of depression to children has to take into account the cognitive variability of children at different stages of development. Recent research regarding the application of the learned helplessness model to children (Seligman & Peterson, 1986; Van der Kolk, 1987) has produced results indicating that when confronted with uncontrollable events, depressed children show deficits in problem-solving ability. Children in foster care have come from helplessness-inducing environments; thus, their perception of causation or of response consequence may not be well developed or may have developed in a distorted fashion. They may not view themselves as responsible for any action or able to produce any good effect. Or they may hold themselves to be the cause of events that in reality had little to do with them. These cognitive distortions, in turn, limit their interpersonal problem-solving skills and impair their ability to learn from new experiences. Hyperarousal, as seen in posttraumatic stress disorder, also may be seen (Van der Kolk, 1987).

Depression in foster children is an often overlooked explanation for behavioral problems. Many foster parents and social workers tend to view behavioral and emotional problems in foster children as isolated entities resulting from poor early training or from the effects of separation. The learned helplessness model of depression as applied to the children in foster care provides a useful theoretical explanatory model and guide for intervention on both the individual and environmental levels.

Issues in the Support of Foster Parents

Foster parents frequently ask for the removal of children from care at critical times. Bryce and Ehlert (1971) felt that such requests came from three sources: the emotional problems of the children emerging from uncertainty of the placement, frustration of the foster parents, and refusal of other responsible parties to make decisions that would result in more permanent arrangements for the child. The report tends to support the findings of Maas and Engler (1959) and that of Fanshel (1976) regarding the need to make early decisions regarding guardianship and in terminating parental rights. Foster parents face a problem when they are left to rear children who do not belong to them, especially when there is only rare contact with the sponsoring agency. This consequence of uncertainty is by no means a universal finding, for it is well documented (Fine, 1993) that in certain long-term programs and cultural contexts, gifted foster parents are able to communicate permanence. Nevertheless, when foster parents cannot convey to a child that he or she belongs to them, that at times they demand certain things of the child and expect certain things from him or her, problems are likely to ensue. Even when such intensity is possible, some may view it as misleading the child in view of his or her ever-impending departure. If an in-depth meaningful relationship is not provided for children in their younger years, they may be denied experiences necessary for psychological growth.

As a result of their prior experiences of neglect and/or abuse, foster children are more "at risk" of having formed an anxious attachment and being less compliant, more easily frustrated, more aggressive, and more prone to behavioral and antisocial disorders than are children whose family background was less abusive. Egeland and Sroufe (1981) have demonstrated the disturbing effects of patterns of attachment in some foster children, while Kunkel (1983) has described a number of stages of alienation children go through when placed away from their birth homes. Presumably related to their inability to trust others, the manifestations of this alienation will prejudice their ongoing adjustment in and beyond the foster family. Moreover, through the reactions it evokes in others, it may undermine their relationships and even the stability of their placement within the foster family. Poor matching or preparation of child and foster parents prior to placement invites renewed instability and breakdown and undermines the child's chance of finding the stable and tolerant family relationships that have proved beneficial to so many children in care. Many foster children bring with them with all the vulnerabilities that come with being a part of a disadvantaged natural family, including higher rates of mental retardation, poor school performance, conduct disorders, hyperactivity, and emotional disorders. In addition, foster home status in itself carries social stigma that tends to make both adjustment within the new community and achievement of self-esteem more problematic.

Today, foster care programs often are faced with special needs children who come into care with well-established physical, mental, emotional, and behavioral problems. As a result, such youngsters can considerably disrupt the life of the foster family, forcing foster parents, whether they recognize it or not, to function as parent therapists and to provide specialized management in addition to basic care (Fine, 1985). Foster parents often are not paid for this specialized care beyond their basic allowance. Because of the difficulties presented by the care of such special needs children, ongoing training, supervision, and/or support for foster parents are mandatory. Cautley and Aldridge (1973) have stressed that involvement of both foster parents in the matching process and in contracting to provide care for a given child were associated with a positive outcome. Aldridge and Cautley (1975) and Palmer (1979) have stressed the preventive importance of adequate preparation of both children and foster parents prior to coming into placement.

Studies of children's longitudinal responses to marital separation and to being raised in day care have demonstrated that children can form, hold, and benefit from more than one significant attachment simultaneously (Porter & Laney, 1980; Sroufe, 1988). Yet remarkably, this knowledge has remained isolated and has been applied relatively little to the foster care area. Many of the adults involved in the foster care system—biological parents, foster parents, child welfare workers, and mental health consultants—think of a child as being part of one family or of another, but not of two. This either/or paradigm fails to appreciate and utilize knowledge made available through long-term studies of children whose parents have divorced and remarried; it is evident that many children function quite well as members of more than one family. Among the most badly damaged children are those who have flourished in foster families and who are then restored to indecisive, rejecting, and ambivalent parents (Fanshel & Shinn, 1978; Gruber, 1978; Tizard, 1977).

It needs to be recognized that foster parents have individual preferences and that the matching of foster parents with children is crucial to the satisfactory placement of children. Among the most essential issues to be considered is the compatibility of cultural values and the capacity of the foster parent to deal with children with special circumstances. Minority, single-parent, and economically disadvantaged families are significantly overrepresented in foster care populations (Albert, 1994). Some of the most disheartening conflicts that arise in foster care involve the attempt by foster parents to alter already instilled cultural

values and orientation as a part of their goal of getting the child to "adapt." Children's cultural values are part and parcel of their identity; by the same token, the removal of those values may strike at the very core sense of identity that the children need in order to survive the various stresses they face. These values may be the only aspect of the children's lives that they can take with them from placement to placement. Foster parents must be carefully evaluated for their capacity to deal with special needs children. Do they have the extra time needed to make hospital or clinic visits? Do they have the time and capacity to undertake the special training needed to deal with neurologic impairment, AIDS encephalopathy, cancer, the dying child, casework control, and problem families? Do they have the financial resources that allow them to bear the additional costs that will inevitably not be covered? Can they bear the questioning about the disability by schools, neighbors, and friends? Poor matching is a major contributor to the failure of foster care and child psychological morbidity.

Case Management

In the current services climate, in order to ensure the proper treatment of the children in foster care and for the support of foster parents, much emphasis is placed on case management. Case management services are essential to help the children and the foster parents deal with the uncertainties of placement permanence, the workings of the various bureaucracies, and the provision of concrete needs. Within the network of case management services that often surround foster care placements, there is a role for child psychiatrists.

In difficult placements, specific aspects of child and adolescent psychiatry apply directly to case management. These include: a focus on child development, stress reduction, and competent parenting: experience with team approaches in difficult situations; insights into countertransference and the maintenance of objectivity; psychotherapeutic techniques that emphasize competence, inner control, and conflict resolution; family systems applications for crisis intervention; interfacing with psychological and other medical specialties; and access to intensive services such as inpatient evaluations, specialized residential treatment, and psychopharmacology.

Treatment

For most foster children, stable placement is the norm (Fein et al., 1990); this placement, in turn, provides a structured context for most psychiatric evaluation and treatment planning. Agency care workers usually seek psychiatric consultations for children in stable foster homes only when problems are extreme and difficult to manage. When the foster placement is stable, initial considerations for psychiatric treatment include: a clear understanding of the reasons for referral; any special developmental needs of the child; family and network concerns; and the permanency plan, which is usually determined by an agency case manager. Attention to basic safety and security, and opportunities for age-appropriate experiences provide the foundation for a helpful therapeutic experience. Various combinations of individual, family, pharmacologic, and supportive therapies can then be brought in, as required. For children in foster home care, collateral and collaborative relationships with preexisting therapists the school, foster parents, and other supportive adults also are usually necessary. In practice, an important function of the psychiatrist is to ensure that diagnostic closure does not occur prematurely simply because the child is in foster care or has been identified as neglected or abused.

The concepts of vulnerability and resilience are crucial to an understanding of the work with children in foster care, especially those children who are in the most stressful of placement situations. The essential concept is that for any particular individual, developmental vulnerability and resilience derive from a balance among stress, competence, and protective factors (Luthar & Zigler, 1991). Once these factors are ascertained, the environmental conditions then can be influenced to change the vector and trajectory of developmental lines (Garmezy, 1986). Applications of this theory center around assisting individuals to transcend or reduce stress, increase competence, and reinforce self-protective factors such as self-image, self-control, and self-esteem (Fine, 1993; Rae-Grant, Thomas, Offord & Boyle, 1989).

Cognitive therapy for depression has been developed specifically to aid children unlearn the learned helplessness that may be associated with the antecedents of and surrounding foster care (Sacco & Beck, 1985). However, a more appropriate focus might be on the environment of social care that is provided for the child. Foster children need an environment structured to permit them to experience desirable outcomes as a result of their own actions. Negative outcomes are also useful if they occur in a context that helps children analyze their experience, attribute appropriate cause in the specific situation, and develop other ways to behave in order to produce a different outcome. For very young children, basic accomplishments such as riding a tricycle, throwing a ball, or learning to dress themselves are competencies that can elicit positive feedback from parents and siblings. For latency-age children, how to make a friend, what to do when called a name, how to please teachers, and how to study are all cognitive skills that can be taught in the foster care environment.

Adolescents present somewhat different problems in that internal cognitive distortions play a major role in the maintenance of depression and negative outcomes, and such depressive tendencies are less under environmental control (Sacco & Beck, 1985). However, the means of mitigating the helplessness syndrome involve giving adolescent foster children appropriate control of their lives and working to ensure that they develop living and occupational skills (Fine & Pape, 1982; Murphey & Callighan, 1989). That these issues are of concern to foster children and that they wish more legitimate say in their lives is well documented (Festinger, 1983; Zimmerman, 1982). Zimmerman (1982) also conceptualizes foster care as a form of social care and environmental "treatment" for which the theory of learned helplessness provides helpful interventive guidelines. The application of the learned helplessness model does not negate the use of other theoretical approaches to depression, nor does it alter the decision-making permanency planning goals of service providers. Some foster care programs include training to help children develop cognitive skills that mitigate against learned helplessness and depression (Palmer, 1990).

Psychiatrists may encounter foster children within three major contexts. The first and usually most stressful context is a placement in crisis; the second is a stable placement within which specific diagnosis and treatment can occur (Gallagher et al., 1995); the third is therapeutic or treatment foster care, which is a form of residential treatment. Psychotherapy for children and adolescents in the foster care system is often frustrating; in particular, it is frustrated by the foster child's various moves and by the foster parents' varying compliance and participation. Expecially for younger children, the work of mourning requires active and sensitive adult assistance. Psychotherapy with foster children has been described as facilitating the completion of mourning (Kliman & Schaeffer, 1984). In fact, however, it is the foster parents who are most likely to be there for children just when the repressed mourning process is suddenly reactivated—for example, by feelings stirred up by an impending or canceled visit (Steinhauer et al., 1988).

Frequently, the focus of individual psychotherapy is to help children deal with adjustment issues, such as ambivalent attachments, internal dysregulation, change, grief, anger, anxiety, dissociation, and acting out. Simple, concrete, reality-oriented supportive approaches are generally effective, particularly if learning disorders or developmental disabilities are involved.

Psychotherapy can be brief in many instances, although longer periods are required to deal with developmental issues such as conscience development, interpersonal relationship abilities, and patterns connected with traumatization (Pilowsky, 1992; Pilowsky & Kates, 1996). Therapy in these instances is typically an exacting process that proceeds through a generally predictable sequence. Increased experience with graded ethical dilemmas within the accessible environment of the child (Redl & Wineman, 1957) gradually stimulate moral development (Kohlberg, 1978; Jurich, 1979), while techniques to increase relationship capacities have been successfully applied within families and other nurturing environments according to age group (Ekstein, 1966; Scharff, 1989; Stern-Bushweiler & Stern, 1989). Processes of

corrective experiences also have been used to help traumatized children face and modify phasic patterns of inner turmoil (Krugman, 1987).

Specific aspects of child and adolescent psychiatry apply therapeutically during difficult placements. These include: adequate focus on child development and parenting; experience with consultative and team approaches; insights into countertransference and the maintenance of objectivity; psychotherapeutic techniques that emphasize competence, inner control, and conflict resolution; family systems applications for crisis intervention; and intensive services such as inpatient evaluations, specialized residential treatment, and psychopharmacology.

Concepts from family psychotherapy also can apply to the foster care population. Family developmental approaches provide insight into ethnic, cultural, and socioeconomic factors that influence each family and its unique construction of reality (Lindsey, 1991; McGoldrick, Pearce, & Giordano, 1982; Reiss, 1981). Data thus derived may help the psychiatrist match the child's biological family with a congruent foster family, maintain continuity for the child with key attachment figures, train foster care personnel and parents appropriately, and effectively provide aid to marginal families (Bondy, Davis, Hagan, Spiritos, & Winnick, 1990; Fine, 1972; Steinhauer et al., 1988; Taylor Brown, 1991). Network concepts have special application for foster home care. Exceptional foster families can establish extended family-like relationships with less competent families from a similar culture and help them to cope (Fine, 1973; Fine & Pape, 1989; Minuchin & Elizer, 1990). Kates (Kates, Johnson, Rader, & Strieder, 1991) suggests that the network can be broadened to include the case manager and other helping professionals. This network approach is designed to prevent the disintegration of the family once they become involved with the child welfare system.

A special consideration has to be given to getting clearance for any type of clinical intervention. The support of those legally charged with guardianship is essential. Less formal support is needed by those people the child has contact with or turns to for support, including the parents who may be involved. This is particularly true in the use of psychopharmacologic agents and/ or hospital care.

Recent research has explored ways in which psychiatric consultation with the foster parent can be supported and enhanced to assure a more stable and beneficial environment for the child in foster care. The Foster Care Research Project (Steinhauer et al., 1988) compared two models of foster care. In the project, foster parents participated in a group that supplied all of the usual services provided by an agency through individual casework. Families receiving group service had access to emergency psychiatric consultation as well as routine assessments. The Foster Care Research Project (FCRP) differed from other "extended family" models of foster care in several important respects, as reported by Steinauer et al. (1988). These other models were designed as alternatives to residential treatment for disturbed children, whereas the research project was intended to enrich services for regular foster families. Only the project built in an ongoing program consultation with a child psychiatrist and was organized within the framework of an existing child welfare agency. Steinhauer et al. (1988) reported that its experienced clinicians all recognized considerable clinical evidence of indirect benefits for the children. These benefits increased in proportion to the life of the parent groups; moreover, as expected, the group members' high morale and satisfaction did transfer to the children (although the research design did not make this possible to quantify). As agencies are faced with increasingly difficult older children, it is significant that the foster parents rated the groups as providing more support than was offered by individual service.

The value of having a single group meeting format followed by sharing with caregivers was evident from the attitude of the foster youths, who wanted more meetings. Not only could they share and express feelings, but they were able to talk about appropriate means of dealing with issues in their lives. This experience demonstrated that the carefully planned use of group input from foster children at foster parent training conferences can add immeasurably to the immediacy and value of these conferences (Zimmerman, 1988).

Treatment foster care (sometimes called special or therapeutic foster care) is a community-based form of residential treatment that has become prevalent in the social welfare system and often is combined with "wraparound" and other community-based forms of service delivery. Under this model, foster parents function as therapists within the home and are, in turn, supported by social service, mental health, and administrative components. A psychiatrist may assist the work with children in these foster homes, although most frequently they aid in diagnosis and in ancillary treatment for selected cases (Foster Family Based Treatment Association, 1991; Meadow-Croft & Trout, 1990). Certain programs have integrated the psychiatrists as part of the treatment team (Fine, 1993; Kliman et al., 1982).

Training

A good deal of training is necessary to prepare a psychiatrist to deal with treatment issues raised by foster care, to help the children and their families, and to consult with foster parents. Clinical experience should be part of the general training for child psychiatrists and should include certain areas of special emphasis. First, an appreciation of the issues raised by cultural and ethnic diversity is essential. The children and their families and the foster parents may bring expectations derived from various cultural and ethnic heritages. Conflicting attitudes can provoke or intensify conflict and result in symptoms that can be appreciated and dealt with only in the context of economic pressures, minority concerns, and understanding cultural diversity (Ahn, 1990). A related second issue is countertransference: how to function as a clinician in highly charged systems of care where all parties may feel neglected, abandoned, and frustrated by inadequate resources. An acknowledgment of these intrinsic stressors is essential for constructive management and psychotherapeutic work to proceed. On a more formal basis, understanding the psychological implications of foster placement at varying developmental stages is essential (Goldstein, Freud, & Solnit, 1979), and mastering principles of adaptation in stressful environments is key.

Special attention to and experience with the legal and bureaucratic procedures and constraints on treatment and placement options in various localities helps therapists deal with inherent frustrations, gain access to services, and implement comprehensive treatment plans. In such cases, the child psychiatrist must be prepared for active participation in an intricate interlocking set of rules and regulations that relate to child welfare, family reunification, adoption, and ongoing foster care.

New Directions and Concerns in Foster Care

Quality foster care can alleviate some of the most vexing problems associated with children who are at risk, but we need to know more about developmentally based interventions and specific ways to facilitate psychological growth in the stress-filled lives of foster children (Hertzman, 1994). A special challenge for psychiatry then is to stay involved with the evolving needs of children and adolescents in the midst of the social turmoil and to protect their integrity and coping capacities throughout the life cycle.

In this era of heightened concern with the impact of substance abuse, AIDS, and child abuse, great concern exists regarding the development and support of quality foster care. The issues that conspire to undermine the goal of quality foster care include its financing, the training and support available to foster parents, and the complex legal climate surrounding the issues of parental and child rights. In addition, another vital factor is the capacity of sponsoring organizations to recognize and support the need for special psychological and social interventions in order to facilitate the healthy psychological development of children.

Foster care is generally underfunded at the state, agency, and foster parent levels, a situation that leaves foster children vulnerable on a number of fronts. Of central importance is the fact that inadequate financing leads some foster parents to take on more children than they should in settings that may not be sufficient for their mission. The ensuing demands are all too likely to be beyond the capacity of such foster families. This is the

result of the foster care system going from voluntary to involuntary after increased removals in the 1960s (Rosenfeld, et al., 1994). With the possible exception of some specialized programs, this underfunding then further compounds the problem by severely limiting access to supportive services for the foster parent, the biologic parent, and the child (Hughes et al. 1995; Rosenfeld, et al., in press). In the current climate, with the erosion of even the most rudimentary of family systems, children with specialized needs are overrepresented in the foster child population. As a result, many foster parents are chronically overburdened and underappreciated.

In certain instances, the failure of systems to recognize the appropriateness of specialized foster care and move beyond the conventional identification of appropriate foster homes has further eroded the capacity of society to meet the needs of children. Specialized care for abused and neglected children is needed (Flint, et al., 1995). Research is needed to enlist and evaluate the services of certain nontraditional foster parents, such as those who are physically disabled, single male, or gay; and to specify qualities of outstanding foster families that are currently supported. Likewise, mental health agencies are reluctant to become involved in a wholehearted manner with children in foster homes because of issues of client retention, birth and foster parent involvement, and financial or legal technicalities. This, too, is systematically keeping children from getting the care that they need. Research is beginning to show that group interventions, community-based and comprehensive team approaches, treatment focused on learned helplessness, and traditional psychodynamic therapies can help to ease the psychological burden of foster children and their families (Rosenfeld, 1995) and alleviate some burdens of the foster families and attendant personnel.

As long as the capacity to strengthen the family unit and solve social problems that contribute to family instability remains inadequate, foster care in one form or another is here to stay. The goal of mental health professionals should be to emphasize the need for specific clinical services for all involved, recognizing the efficacy of therapy for the children and their families, support for foster parents, and advocacy for those initiatives that will strengthen the social fabric.

REFERENCES

Accardo, P., Caul, J., & Whitman, B. (1989). Excessive water drinking. A marker of caretaker interaction disturbance. *Clinical Pediatrics, 28*, 416–418.

Ahn, H. N. (1990). Cultural diversity and definitions of child abuse. In R. Barth, J. D. Berrick, & N. Gilbert (Eds.), *Social welfare review* (Vol. 1, pp. 29–56). New York: Columbia University Press.

Albert, V. (1994). Explaining the growing number of child abuse and neglect reports and foster care caseloads. In R. Barth, J. D. Berrick, & N. Gilbert (Eds.), *Social welfare review* (Vol. 1, pp. 218–246). New York: Columbia University Press.

Aldridge, M. H., & Cautley, P. W. (1975). The importance of worker availability in the functioning of new foster homes. *Child Welfare, 54*, 444–453.

Anderson, J. L., & Simonitch, B. (1981). Reactive depression in youths experiencing emancipation. *Child Welfare, 60*, 383–390.

Bondy, D., Davis, D., Hagan, S. Spiritos, A., & Winnick, A. (1990). Mental health services for foster children. *Child Psychology, 14*, 28–32.

Brandenburg, N. A., Friedman, R. M., & Silver, S. E. (1990). The epidemiology of childhood psychiatric disorders: Prevalence findings from recent studies. *Journal of the American Academy of Child and Adolescent Psychiatry, 29*, 77–83.

Bryce, M. E., & Ehlert, R. C. (1971). 144 foster children. *Child Welfare, 50*, 499–503.

Cautley, P., & Alridge, M. (1973). *Predictors of success in foster family care.* Madison, WI: Department of Health and Social Services. Cited in P. D. Steinhauer, (1988), The preventive utilization of foster care. *Canadian Journal of Psychiatry, 33*, 459–467.

Chernoff, R., Combs-Orme, T., Risley-Curtiss, C., & Heisler, A. (1994). Assessing the health status of children entering foster care. *Pediatrics, 93*, 594–601.

Cooper, J. D. (1978). *Patterns of family placement: current issues in fostering and adoption.* London: National Children's Bureau. Cited in P. D. Steinhauer (1988), The preventive utilization of foster care. *Canadian Journal of Psychiatry, 33*, 459–467.

Demb, J. (1991). Reported hyperphagia in foster children. *Child Abuse and Neglect, 15*, 77–88.

Derdeyn, A. P. (1977). A case for permanent foster placement of dependent, neglected and abused children. *American Journal of Orthopsychiatry, 47*, 604–614.

Dweck, C. S. (1977). Learned helplessness: A developmental approach. In J. G. Schulterbrandt & A. Raskin (Eds.) *Depression in children: Diagnosis, treatment and conceptual models.* New York: Raven Press.

Egeland, B., & Sroufe, L. A. (1981). Developmental sequelae of maltreatment in infancy. In R. Rizley & D. Cicchetti (Eds.), *Developmental perspectives on child maltreatment.* San Francisco: Jossey-Bass.

Ekstein, R. (1966). *Children of time & space of action & impulse.* New York: Appleton-Century-Crofts.

Elmer, E. (1977). A follow-up study of traumatized children. *Pediatrics, 59*, 273–279.

Fanshel, D. (1971). The exit of children from foster care: An interim research report. *Child Welfare, 50*, 65–81.

Fanshel, D. (1976). Status changes in children in foster care: Final results of the Columbia University Longitudinal Study. *Child Welfare, 55*, 133–171.

Fanshel, D., Finch, S. J., & Grundy, J. F. (1990). *Foster children: A life course perspective.* New York: Columbia University Press.

Fanshel, D., & Shinn, E. B. (1978). *Children in foster care: A longitudinal investigation.* New York: Columbia University Press.

Fein, E., Maluccio, A. N., & Kluger, M. (1990). *No more partings: An examination of foster family care.* Washington, DC: Child Welfare League of America.

Festinger, T. (1983) *No one ever asked us: A post script to foster care.* New York: Columbia University Press.

Fine, P. (1972). An appraisal of child psychiatry in a community health project: Relevance as a function of social context. *Journal of the American Academy of Child and Adolescent Psychiatry, 11*, 279–293.

Fine, P. (1973). Family networks and child psychiatry in a community health project. *Journal of the American Academy of Child and Adolescent Psychiatry, 12*, 675–689.

Fine, P. (1985). Clinical aspects of foster care. In J. J. Cox & R. D. Cox (Eds.), *Foster care: Current issues, policies and practices* (pp. 206–223). Norwood, NJ: Ablex.

Fine, P. (1993). *A developmental network approach to therapeutic foster care.* Washington, DC: Child Welfare League of America.

Fine, P., & Pape, M. (1983). Pregnant teenagers in need of social networks: Diagnostic parameters. In I. R. Stuart & C. F. Wells (Eds.), *Pregnancy in adolescence.* New York: Van Nostrand Reinhold.

Fine, P., & Pape, M. (1989). Foster Families. In J. Spurlock & C. Rabinowitz (Eds.), *Women's progress: Promises and problems* (pp. 35–58). New York. Plenum Press.

Flint, S. S., Yudkowsky, B. K., & Tang, S. S. (1995). Children and medicaid entitlement: What have we got to lose. *Pediatrics, 96*, 967.

Gallagher, M. M., Leavitt, K. S., & Kimmel, H. P. (1995). Mental health treatment of cumulatively/repetitively traumatized children. *Smith College Studies in Social Work, 65*, 205–237.

Garmezy, N. (1986). Children under severe stress: Critique and commentary. *Journal of the American Academy of Child and Adolescent Psychiatry, 25*, 384–392.

Golden, J. M. (1981). Depression in middle and late childhood: Implications for intervention. *Child Welfare, 60*, 457–465.

Goldstein, J., Freud, A., & Solnit, A. J. (1973). Beyond the best interests of the child. New York: The Free Press.

Gruber, A. R. (1978). *Children in foster care: Destitute, neglected, betrayed.* New York: Human Sciences Press.

Hacsi, T., (1995). From indenture to family foster care: A brief history of child placing. *Child Welfare,* LXXIV, 162–180.

Halfon, N. G., Mendonca, A., & Berkowitz, G. (1995). Health status of children in foster care: The experience of the center for the vulnerable child. *Archives of Pediatric and Adolescent Medicine, 149,* 386–392.

Hertzman, C. (1994). The lifelong impact of childhood experiences: A population health perspective. *Daedalus: Journal of the American Academy of Arts and Sciences, 123,* 167–180.

Highland, A. C. (1979). Depression in adolescents: A developmental view. *Child Welfare, 58,* 577–585.

Hughes, D., Newacheck, P., Stoddard, J. J., & Halfon, N. (1995). Medicaid managed care: Can it work for children? *Pediatrics, 95,* 591–594.

Hulsey, T. C., & White, R. (1989). Family characteristics and measures of behavior in foster and non-foster children. *American Journal of Orthopsychiatry, 59,* 502–509.

Jones, M. A., & Moses, B. (1984). *West Virginia's former foster children: Their experiences in care and their lives as young adults.* New York: Child Welfare League of America.

Jurich, A. P. (1979). Coping with moral problems of adolescents in foster care. *Child Welfare, 58,* 187–195.

Kates, W., Johnson, R., Rader, M., & Strieder, F. (1991). Whose child is this? Assessment and treatment of children in foster care. *American Journal of Orthopsychiatry, 6,* 584–591.

Kaufman, J. (1991). Depressive disorders in maltreated children. *Journal of the American Academy of Child and Adolescent Psychiatry, 30,* 257–265.

Kavaler, R., & Swire, M. R. (1983). *Foster child health care.* Lexington, MA: Lexington Books.

Kinard, E. M. (1982). Child abuse and depression: Cause or consequence? *Child Welfare, 61,* 403–413.

Kiser, L., Heston, J., Millsap, P., & Pruit, D. (1991). Physical and sexual abuse in childhood: Relationship with post traumatic stress disorder. *Journal of the American Academy of Child and Adolescent Psychiatry, 30,* 776–782.

Kliman, G., & Schaeffer, M. H. (1984). Summary of two psychoanalytically based service and research projects: preventive treatments for foster children. *Journal of Preventive Psychiatry, 2,* 1–13.

Kliman, G. W., Schaeffer, M. H., & Friedman, M. (1982). *Preventive mental health services for children entering foster home care.* White Plains, NY: Center for Preventive Psychiatry.

Kline, D., & Overstreet, H-M. (1972). *Foster care of children: Nurture and treatment.* New York: Columbia University Press.

Kohlberg, L. (1978). Revisions in the theory and practice of moral development. In W. Damon (Ed.), *New directions in child development: Moral development.* San Francisco: Jossey-Bass.

Krugman, S. (1987). Trauma in the family: Perspectives on the intergenerational transmission of violence. In B. Van der Kolk (Ed.), *Psychological trauma* (pp. 127–152). Washington, DC: American Psychiatric Association.

Kunkel, B. E. (1983). The alienation response of children abused in out-of-home placement. *Child Abuse Neglect, 7,* 474–484.

Lindsey, D. (1991). Factors affecting the foster care placement decision: An analysis of national survey data. *American Journal of Orthopsychiatry, 61,* 272–280.

Littner, N. (1956). *Some traumatic effects of separation and placement.* New York: Child Welfare League of America.

Luthar, S., & Zigler, E. (1991). Vulnerability and competence: A review of research on resilience in childhood. *American Journal of Orthopsychiatry, 6,* 6–22.

Maas, H. S., & Engler, R. E. (1959). *Children in need of parents.* New York: Columbia University Press.

Maluccio, A., & Fein, E. (1985). Growing up in foster care. *Children and Youth Services Review, 7,* 123–134.

McGoldrick, M., Pearce, J. K., & Giordano, J. (1982). *Ethnicity and family therapy.* New York: Guilford Press.

Meadowcroft, P., & Trout, B. (1990). *Troubled youth in treatment homes: A handbook of therapeutic foster care.* Washington, DC: Child Welfare League of America.

Minuchin, S., & Elizer, J. (1990). The foster care crisis. *Family Therapy Networkers,* (January-February), 44–51.

Moffat, M., Peddie, M., Stulginskas, J., Pless, B., & Steinmetz, N. (1985). Health care delivery to foster children: A study. *Health and Social Work, 10,* 129–137.

Murphey, J., & Callighan, K. (1989). Therapeutic vs. traditional foster care: Theoretical and practical distinctions. *Adolescence, 24,* 291–900.

National Commission on Children in Need of Parents. (1979). *Who knows? Who cares? Forgotten children in foster care.* New York: Institute of Public Affairs.

Palmer, S. (1979). Predicting outcome in long-term foster care. *Journal of Social Service Research, 3,* 201–214.

Palmer, S. (1990). Group treatment of foster children to reduce emotional conflicts associated with treatment breakdown. *Child Welfare, 69,* 227–238.

Peterson, C., & Seligman, M. E. P. (1985). The learned helplessness model of depression: Current status of theory and research. In E. E. Beckham & W. R. Leber, *Handbook of depression, treatment, assessment and research.* Homewood, IL: Dorsey Press.

Pilowsky, D. J. (1992). Short-term psychotherapy with children in foster care. *Psychotherapies with children: Adapting the psychodynamic approach.* J. O'Brien et al. (Eds.) Washington, DC: American Psychiatric Press.

Pilowsky, D. J., & Kates, W. G. (1996). Foster children in acute crisis: Assessing critical aspects of attachment. *Journal of the American Academy of Child Adolescent Psychiatry,* in press.

Porter, R. H., & Laney, M. D. (1980). Attachment

theory and the concept of inclusive fit. *Merrill-Palmer Quarterly, 26,* 3–51.

Rae-Grant, N., Thomas, B., Offord, D. R., & Boyle, M. H. (1989). Risk, protective factors and the prevalence of behavioral and emotional disorders in children and adolescents. *Journal of the American Academy of Child and Adolescent Psychiatry, 28,* 262–268.

Redl, F., & Wineman, D. (1957). *The aggressive child.* New York: Free Press.

Reiss, D. (1981). *The family's construction of reality.* Cambridge, MA: Harvard University Press.

Rice, D. L., & McFadden, E. J. (1988). A forum on foster children. *Child Welfare, 67,* 231–243.

Robertson, J., & Robertson, J. (1972). Quality of substitute care as an influence on separation responses. *Journal of Psychosomatic Research, 16,* 261–265.

Rosenfeld, A. A. (1995). Child adolescent mental disorders research. *Archives of General Psychiatry, 52,* 729–731.

Rosenfeld, A. A., Altman, R., Alfaro, J., & Pilowsky, D. J. (1994). Foster care, child abuse, neglect, and termination of parental rights. *Child and Adolescent Psychiatric Clinics of North America, 3,* 877–893.

Rosenfeld, A. A., Altman, R., & Kaufman, I. (1996). Foster care. In R. K. Schreter, S. S. Sharfstein, & C. A. Schreter, (Eds.), *Managing Care Not Dollars,* In press. Washington: American Psychiatric Press.

Sacco, W. P., & Beck, A. T. (1985). Cognitive therapy and depression. In E. E. Beckham & W. R. Leber (Eds.), *Handbook of depression, treatment, assessment and research.* Homewood, IL: Dorsey Press.

Scharff, D. (1989). Transference, countertransference and technique in object relations family therapy. In J. S. Scharff (Ed.), *Foundations of object relations therapy.* Northvale, NJ: Jason Aronson.

Schor, E. L. (1982). The foster care system and health status of foster children. *Pediatrics, 69,* 521–528.

Seligman, M. E. P., & Peterson, C. (1986). A learned perspective on childhood depression: Theory and research. In M. Rutter, C. Izard, & P. Reads (Eds.), *Depression in young people: Developmental and clinical perspectives* (pp.   ). New York: Guilford Press.

Silver, L. (1989). Frequency of adoption of children and adolescents with learning disabilities. *Journal of Learning Disabilities, 22,* 325–327.

Simms, M. D. (1989). The foster care clinic: A community program to identify treatment needs of children in foster care. *Developmental & Behavioral Pediatrics, 10,* 121–128.

Sroufe, L. A. (1988). The role of infant caregiver attachment in development. In J. Belsky & T. Nezworski (Eds.), *Clinical implications of attachment* (pp.   ). Hillsdale, NJ: Lawrence Erlbaum.

Steinhauer, P. D. (1988). The prevention utilization of foster care. *Canadian Journal of Psychiatry, 33,* 459–467.

Steinhauer, P. D., Johnston, M., Snowden, M., Santa-Barbara, J., Kane, B., Barker, P., & Hornick, J. P. (1988). The foster care research project: Summary and analysis. *Canadian Journal of Psychiatry, 33,* 509–516.

Stern-Bushweiler, N., & Stern, D. (1989). A model for conceptualizing the role of the mother's representational world in various mother-infant therapies. *Infant Mental Health Journal, 10,* 142–156.

Taitz, L. S., & King, J. M. (1988). Growth patterns in child abuse. *Acta Paediatrica Scandinavica* (Suppl.), *343,* 62–72.

Taylor Brown, S. (1991). The impact of AIDS in foster care: A family centered approach to services in the United States. *Child Welfare, 70,* 193–209.

Tizard, B. (1977). *Adoption: A second chance.* London: Open Books.

United States General Accounting Office. (1994). *Foster care: Parental drug abuse has alarming impact on children.* GAO/HEHS-94-89.

Van der Kolk, B. A. (1987). *Psychological trauma.* Washington, DC: American Psychiatric Association.

Widom, C. S. (1989). The cycle of violence. *Science, 244,* 160–166.

Zimmerman, R. B. (1982). *Foster care in retrospect* (Vol. 14). New Orleans: Tulane Studies in Social Welfare.

Zimmerman, R. B. (1988). Childhood depression: New theoretical formulations and implications for foster care services. *Child Welfare, 67,* 37–47.

13 / Advanced Intellectual Ability and Giftedness

Judy L. Lupart

CASE EXAMPLE

Susan: By the age of 3 years, Susan's parents knew that she was precocious. Shortly before her second birthday, while the car was stopped at a red light, Susan pointed to the nearby road sign and correctly identified the word "stop." Her parents had read to her consistently from birth. Following this incident, they noted that Susan was able to point out several words on the storybook pages. They provided her with a deck of reading cards. Over the next few months she requested them often, and by the age of 2 years 6 months, she had learned to identify every word on the cards. By the age of 3, Susan could read silently, write, count and read numbers up to 1,000, and even showed some understanding of multiplication. Just before her third birthday, Susan was helping her mother make gingerbread cookies by counting out three raisins for each. When her mother stated that they would have enough dough for four more cookies, Susan instantly replied that they would need to have 12 more raisins.

During the preschool years, Susan's parents made every effort to stimulate and encourage her unending curiosity and desire to learn. In addition to her interests in literacy and mathematics, Susan demonstrated an early passion for singing and playing music. She was able to independently and correctly figure out the keys for several nursery songs on her toy xylophone by the age of 3. She began Suzuki piano instruction following her third birthday and advanced through the program very quickly. By 4 years of age she could read music and demonstrated an ability to accurately name any note and to play new melodies after hearing them only a few times. By 5 years of age Susan was composing her own songs on the computer and was successfully competing at the annual music festival with youngsters who were several years older. Her reading interests were considerable, ranging from classic literature to texts in math and science. As her musical competence developed, she followed a rigorous self-imposed practice schedule of 1 to 3 hours a day.

When Susan began school she was referred for psychoeducational evaluation after 2 months. The psychologist administered the Stanford-Binet (Form L-M) Individual Intelligence test, and Susan's Full Scale IQ measure was 162. The assessment report noted that Susan demonstrated superior verbal abilities and excellent socioemotional development. Concomitant educational assessment carried out by the program specialist indicated that Susan was able to perform above the sixth-grade level in mathematics, reading, and spelling. Not surprisingly, it was concluded that Susan's exceptional learning needs warranted special educational consideration. It was recommended that she receive programming and instruction at a level commensurate with her advanced abilities.

This marked the beginning of a series of struggles with the school for Susan's parents. First they were informed that there were no gifted student programs available until the fourth grade. Despite the assurances of the Resource Team that differentiated programming would be made available for Susan in the regular grade 1 class, it soon became evident that she was expected to follow the same lessons, using the same texts and materials as the other students. When the parents met with the grade 1 teacher at the first parent-teacher interview and were informed that Susan was extremely disruptive and inattentive in class and that she appeared to have difficulty interacting with the other students, they knew they had to take action.

Fortunately, they were referred to the School Division Gifted Educational Consultant, who listened to their concerns and then observed Susan in the classroom setting. Within a week Susan was placed in an ungraded, continuous progress elementary school and an individualized program was planned in cooperation with her parents. By midyear, Susan was showing excellent progress, particularly in mathematics, reading and writing, and she enjoyed several new friendships with same-age and older peers.

Mark: Mark is 17 years and attends grade 12 in a high school in a large city. Mark has a close relationship with his mother, but moved away from home a year ago to escape his father's temper and violent outbursts. Mark now lives with two friends in a duplex close to the school. He still has contact with his mother and siblings, and his mother continues to be involved with the school and serves on several committees.

Mark considers himself to be fairly popular and a "nice guy." Some students judge him by the way he dresses, but this does not concern him. He does not want to succumb to peer pressure to conform to the latest fashion fads. Mark feels that money should not be wasted, and so he will patch his clothes and wear them until they are worn out.

Mark's grades fall within the average range. He was an A student throughout elementary school. However, in junior high, his marks began to drop because, as Mark puts it, he "began to slack off big time." He is content with Cs and Bs, and feels that this will be sufficient to get him into a trade. Mark does relatively well in mechanics and physics, and describes these as his favorite subjects. His current main interests are his friends, playing the saxophone, and dismantling and reassembling cars and mechanical items. Mark's music teacher has suggested that Mark continue to pursue music as a professional career, and Mark is currently a member of an orchestra and a small band. Mark also spends a considerable amount of time writing. His writings are generally unrelated to school topics, so are not handed in for grading. When he does share his products with teachers, they encourage him to pursue academic writing. However, Mark prefers to write for his own enjoyment, and also uses writing as a means for sorting out and solving personal problems.

Although Mark enjoys his music and writing, he has chosen to pursue a career in which he can "work with things." Mark will be returning to high school next year to improve his grade in social studies and to take another mechanics course.

Susan and Mark share the common identity or label of being gifted. However, they present with unique interests and personal characteristics as well as family background and educational experience. Their stories illustrate the diverse nature of giftedness and the complex issues that are related to the study of advanced intellectual ability.

Throughout history, to a large degree, the values of the culture have framed the ways in which eminence might be achieved. Accordingly, society has been interested in individuals who are able to perform at significantly high levels. Historical documents record the lives and accomplishments of persons celebrated for their artistic abilities, military genius, oratorical skills, or philosophical and reasoning talents. Despite the fact that exceptional talents and abilities usually have been recognized, obvious giftedness has not always been well understood. Indeed, up to the beginning of the 20th century, a web of mythical association has been woven around such individuals; in particular, genius has been linked with some notably negative associations, such as insanity and emotional instability. Only in the current century has there been any systematic research into the characteristics of and developmental influences on high ability.

One of the more predominant and enduring problems in the field is establishing exactly what constitutes giftedness; over the course of this century, the issue has been widely debated and actively researched. Terms such as precocity, creativity, talent, and genius have come to be widely associated with giftedness and often are used interchangeably. Intellectual capacity is the most widely recognized and best understood aspect of giftedness; however, other dimensions, such as creativity and talent, have been separately examined under the same rubric. Despite the considerable attention that has been devoted to defining giftedness, a great deal of controversy persists—especially when the definition is tied to funding matters, as it is in many school jurisdictions.

Besides definition, a second problematic area of this field concerns origin, or how individuals come to be gifted. Unlike other areas of exceptionality, where definitive genetic or biological anomalies or correlates can be discerned, giftedness is evidenced by a person's talents and abilities and by what is accomplished through their use. Both genetic and environmental factors play a part in the ultimate expression of giftedness; consequently, much current emphasis is given to the interaction of these elements. Accordingly, researchers seek theoretical and empirical support for the delineation of the involved cognitive and psychosocial processes.

A final concern relates to the permanency or stability of giftedness. Very little is known about its long-term progression. While some theorists view giftedness as something one does or does not have, others emphasize the potentiality for gifted behavior to emerge over time. Early precocity may or may not persist throughout one's life course, and, in contrast, an individual may have been viewed as quite ordinary or even as handicapped in childhood and yet come to be recognized as gifted on the basis of subsequent outstanding achievements. These perspectives represent the predominant investigative areas in giftedness research and, as such, have major implications for the topics addressed here. This chapter provides a general overview of intellectually advanced and/or gifted children and adolescents and a brief summary of their associated developmental and psychosocial characteristics.

Issues Associated with Defining Giftedness

Traditional views about giftedness are associated primarily with intelligence (as measured by an individually administered intelligence test, most often the Weschler Intelligence Scale for Children–Revised or the Stanford-Binet). Individuals who score significantly higher than their same-age peers on intelligence tests are considered to be gifted. Louis Terman translated the original Binet-Simon Scale and published the Stanford-Binet Intelligence Scale, which came to dominate the field (Terman, 1916); his work was highly influential in promoting this narrow view of giftedness. Terman's (1925; Terman & Oden, 1947, 1959) longitudinal study of 1,470 children over a 50-year period has provided, nevertheless, the most comprehensive examination available of gifted individuals and their characteristics. In his study, children ranging from grade 3 to 8 who had measured IQs of 135 or over were identified as gifted. From 1925 through 1959, five volumes of the *Genetic Studies of Genius* were published, providing detailed information concerning the subjects' school performance, careers, and adult accomplishments. Generally the data confirmed the notion that in comparison with the general population, gifted children do fulfill the early promise of significant achievement in terms of occupational status and earned income. The findings also revealed that, contrary to popular belief at the time, gifted youngsters also excel in comparison with the normal population in areas such as general health and physique, mental health, social adjustment, and contentment.

This landmark Terman study solidly entrenched the use of intelligence tests as the primary instrument for identifying giftedness; accordingly, school systems have routinely defined giftedness on a percentage basis (e.g., the top 1 to 3% scorers on individual or group-administered IQ tests), or on the basis of an arbitrary cut-off score on an intelligence test (e.g., 130 IQ).

Recently a number of researchers have challenged the notion of a single index in the form of an IQ score. They assert that intelligence should be considered a multidimensional phenomenon represented by a variety of distinct capacities and abilities (Cattell, 1971; Guilford, 1959). Research efforts were directed at the identification and assessment of a diverse array of possible intellectual functions. The Structure of Intellect Model developed by Guilford (1967), for example, was most influential in positing an expanded view of intelligence. It included both convergent thinking abilities (which most intelligence tests measure) and divergent thinking abilities (which are related to creativity). This work also triggered an interest in the creative aspects of giftedness, and the investigation of its subcomponents, such as creative problem solving and ideational fluency and flexibility, prompted the development of new assessment measures (Torrance, 1966).

Present-day theorists have advanced new theories that focus on the multidimensionality of intelligence (Fogarty & Bellanca, 1995). Gardner (1983) proposed that at least 7 types of intelligence need to be considered: (1) linguistic, (2) musical, (3) logical-mathematical, (4) spatial, (5) bodily-kinesthetic, (6) interpersonal, and (7) intrapersonal. Taking a similar diversified abilities perspective, Sternberg's (1985) triarchic theory includes the interrelated aspects of the individual's internal world, external world, and personal experience. These theories have been influential in expanding both the range of mental functioning that is considered to be intelligent and the ways that we attempt to measure and assess such ability. Finally, there has been a greater recognition of particular aptitudes or special abilities that an individual might demonstrate; accordingly, the inclusion of the term "talent" can be seen in most contemporary definitions of giftedness.

By and large, the issues surrounding the definition of giftedness have centered on the identification of its key dimensions and their measurement. Currently, the traditional definitions of giftedness are being challenged on practical grounds, specifically on the basis of those school identification practices that systematically discriminate against particular subgroups of gifted individuals.

Contemporary critics assert that schools have failed to provide appropriate educational programming and support for a large majority of able students. Indeed, these concerns were significantly elevated by the recent U.S. National Commission on Excellence in Education report that indicated that more than one-half of gifted students do not match their tested ability with comparable achievement at school (National Commission on Excellence in Education, 1983). Hence, current thinking has moved beyond questions concerning the precise nature of giftedness and the critical elements that define it, to more fundamental concerns regarding the purposes for which a definition is used. The matter is not a trivial one, and, as Hardman, Drew, Egan, and Wolf (1990) have noted, the definition of giftedness can, in fact, influence educational practice in a number of significant ways. Definition dictates identification procedure directly in terms of the types of instruments utilized, the scores that must be obtained to qualify for specialized instruction, and the number of students that are ultimately selected. What is recognized as giftedness also determines the types of differentiated education provided, the professional preparation of those teaching them, and the amount of funding required to provide services. If a school's definition of giftedness is based primarily on IQ scores and academic achievement levels, then it is more appropriate to describe this as intellectual giftedness. At the same time, it must be recognized that this definition excludes other areas of talent and/or ability development. At present all dimensions of traditional definitions and associated practice are being carefully reexamined. Current trends suggest that future definitions of giftedness will be multidimensional, more inclusive, and less dependent on standardized testing and single measures, such as IQ tests. These trends are already evident in contemporary definitions of giftedness and talent.

Contemporary Definition of Giftedness

One of the best-known and most commonly used definitions of gifted and talented was provided by the U.S. Office of Education:

Gifted and talented children are those identified by professionally qualified persons who, by virtue of outstanding abilities, are capable of high performance. These are children who require differentiated educational programs in order to realize their contribution to self and society. Children capable of high performance include those with demonstrated achievement and/or potential ability in any of the following areas, singly or in combination.

1. General intellectual ability
2. Specific academic aptitude
3. Creative or productive thinking
4. Leadership ability
5. Visual or performing arts
6. Psychomotor ability (Marland, 1972, p. 2)

This definition captures the view that giftedness can be manifested in a number of areas and requires special educational provision. Even though it has been widely adopted in North American schools, the definition has been criticized on a number of counts. Many of these concerns are associated with the practical decisions that must be made for program development and implementation. It is not clear how much each of the designated components contributes to giftedness, or, for that matter, whether all possible dimensions of high ability have been included. According

to this formulation, it would be possible for an individual to excel in only one dimension in order to be considered gifted; at the same time, it is highly unlikely that an individual would be placed in a gifted program solely on the basis of leadership ability without evidence of scholastic aptitude. The definition does not specify the degree to which a person must excel in one or more areas, nor is the appropriate comparison group suggested. The dimensions are not parallel and independent (Renzulli, 1978). For example, it is virtually impossible to separate intellectual ability and creativity in a given performance assessment. In addition to these concerns, there are further problems concerning the validity and reliability of the associated instruments and the means employed to assess each component area. Techniques for the assessment of intellectual ability and school achievement are fairly well established in most school districts, whereas the measurement of such areas as creativity and leadership is much more difficult to achieve. Those instruments that have been developed have been criticized on both technical and discriminatory grounds. Richert (1991) cites the results of a recent nationwide study and concludes that in the identification of gifted students, there is a significant gap between theory and practice.

Perhaps the most problematic aspect of the traditional definitions is the static view that giftedness is something that a person does or does not have. In contrast, Renzulli (1978) takes a dynamic perspective that emphasizes people's potential for demonstrating gifted behavior given appropriate contextual support. He has suggested an alternative definition of giftedness, which includes three interactive elements: above-average ability, high task commitment, and a high level of creativity. Renzulli's associated "revolving door" identification model is particularly appealing to schools, for it allows for a potential "talent pool" of 20% of the school population and is based on the notion that giftedness emerges out of the intellectually engaging opportunities that are provided at school. In summary, contemporary definitions of giftedness differ from earlier definitions in two respects: the number of dimensions included has been broadened (from a single measure of IQ to multiple assessments in several domains), and the number of individuals likely to be identified has been markedly increased (from 2 to 3% to the current 20 to 25%).

Identification and Prevalence

The number of students who are identified as being gifted is a direct function of the definitions, instruments, and procedures used. Most schools include individually administered IQ tests (such as the Wechsler Intelligence Scale for Children–Revised or the Stanford-Binet) in their procedures, and it is commonly accepted that those students scoring above 130 IQ (2 standard deviations above the mean) are considered to be gifted. Hence prevalence estimates using IQ scores as the primary criteria range between 3 and 5% of the school-age population. The application of multidimensional definitions of giftedness within contemporary schools, however, has substantially increased current prevalence estimates. A wide array of identification measures and procedures including teacher, parent, and peer referrals, self-nomination, individual and group measures of intellectual performance and academic achievement, creativity and leadership assessment, observation, questionnaires, and structured interviews are all currently in use. At the same time, there are wide discrepancies from one district or state to the next in terms of what means are employed and the weight given to any particular measure (Shriner, Ysseldyke, Gorney, & Franklin, 1993; Alvino, McDonnel, & Richert, 1981). On the basis of data obtained from 44 states, the National Center for Education Statistics (1989) found the percentages of gifted and talented students in total school enrollments to range from 1.2 to 9.9%. The median percentage was 3.6%, a figure consistent with normative data. In addition to the multidimensional and pluralistic strategies to improve the general identification of gifted students, many school districts have implemented further measures to counter discriminatory selection and to facilitate specifically the identification of "at-risk" children who are from a cultural minority, economically disadvantaged, handicapped or learning disabled, underachieving, and/or lacking in proficiency in speaking English. Depending on the degree to which these aspects have been incorporated into gifted identification programs, prevalence figures are increased accordingly.

Higher ratios of giftedness have been reported for male children over females at all age levels, most notably at the junior and senior high school levels. The Terman study reported boy-to-girl ratios of 116 : 100 for the main study group and 212.3 : 100 for the adolescent and older children (Shurkin, 1992). There is ample research to verify that a significant number of gifted individuals are firstborn (Olszewski, Kulieke, & Buescher, 1987). Prevalence figures for giftedness increase over the school years, particularly during the grade ranges 4 to 9, which corresponds with the levels at which schools are most likely to offer programs for gifted students. During the adult years there is a significant shift in how giftedness is assessed. Most commonly, there is an association with career and/or financial success or the attainment of prominence in public, political, business or academic fields. It is noteworthy that in adulthood, the primary focus moves from assessed potential for giftedness to the actual achievement of prominence of distinction. It is also of interest to note that in Walberg and Herbig's (1991) study of award-winning writers, scientists, and adolescents, the linkage between the estimated IQ of an individual and significant achievement in adult life is only moderate. However, caution is advised, since much of our current understanding in this area is based on a narrow, IQ-test based definition of giftedness; therefore, when a multidimensional perspective of giftedness is used, it will be of considerable interest to compare figures.

Etiology and Nature of Giftedness

Central to an understanding of the nature and origins of intelligence is the question of the relative contribution of genetics and the environment. Estimates of the "reaction range," or the phenotypical expression of intelligence, vary substantially. Researchers favoring an environmental position claim a wide reaction range of well over 50 IQ points (Hunt, 1971); those favoring the genetic endowment position argue for a narrow reaction range of about 25 IQ points (Cronbach, 1975). Proponents of the genetic perspective have estimated that the respective impact of genetics and environment on intelligence is in the order of 2 : 1 (Eysenck, 1985). The associated prediction of high correlation between child and parental intelligence has been established at .55 to .60 (Humphreys, 1985). The collective results from twin studies, sibling and adoptive studies (Eysenck,

1985; Plomin, 1989), and studies of memory and reaction time (Eysenck, 1986) have clearly established the role of genetics in intellectual development. Recent interest, however, has shifted to an emphasis on those environmental factors that contribute significantly to the full actualization of the gifted child's potential. On the basis of her longitudinal studies of gifted individuals, Freeman (1983) suggests that because of their unique ability to take in and use information and ideas effectively, the degree to which the environment can influence their IQ scores is greater than is true for nongifted peers. In support of this perspective, studies of the family characteristics of gifted children show that their parents tend to be older (Albert, 1980) and better educated (Benbow & Stanley, 1980; Van Tassel-Baska, 1983) than nongifted children. Other studies have demonstrated that families of gifted children tend to emphasize values associated with achievement and success (Olszewski et al., 1987); indeed, the parents typically assume a key role in monitoring and supporting the child's activities (Bloom, 1985; Feldman, 1986). Furthermore, Gallagher (1991) has suggested that the notion of a strong interactive interrelationship between environment and genetics can help resolve some of the puzzling findings in gifted research, such as: the disproportionately high achievement level of males in mathematics, the disproportionate incidence of high learning and language ability in Jewish and Asian populations, and the disproportionately low representation of all other cultural minority group school-age children testing in the gifted range on measures of intellectual ability.

Theoretical perspectives relevant to the question of advanced cognitive ability can be broadly distinguished according to the developmentalist and the information processing positions. Piaget (1983), who represents the developmental perspective, theorized that human intelligence has its roots in biological systems and that the same developmental levels obtain for both biological and cognitive development. Hence, gifted individuals advance more quickly than nongifted individuals through universal, invariant stages of development (Keating, 1975). In particular, a "genotype may offer a more or less broad range of possible accommodations, but all of them within a certain statistically defined 'norm'" (Piaget, 1983, p. 107). Piaget deemphasized the role of teaching and in-

struction on cognitive development and advocated instead a discovery-based learning environment to foster children's intellectual growth. In contrast, neo-Piagetian theorists such as Robbie Case (1985; 1992) have proposed that instructional methodology, based on educational activities appropriate for each stage of intellectual development, can be devised and used to facilitate optimal learning. The collective research carried out by Case and his colleagues (Case, 1992) has convincingly supported the assertion that appropriate educational experiences can significantly influence advanced intellectual development. In support, a developmental model by Horowitz and O'Brien (1985) is most promising; it proposes that although giftedness may be manifested by performance in specific domains (such as mathematics or musical abilities), nevertheless, it is high general intelligence that makes the exceptional performance possible.

Traditional research in the area of information processing has consistently documented the superior performance of gifted children on a variety of memory, attention, and reasoning tasks. These results have been attributed to differences in the individual's knowledge base (Chi & Glaser, 1985) and the efficient deployment of a limited capacity system (Kahneman, 1973). Contemporary information processing theories emphasize the efficiency of metacomponential functioning (cognitive executive processes associated with planning, monitoring, and decision making) as a major distinguishing characteristic of advanced intellectual ability (Sternberg, 1984). One of the few comparative studies of metacognitive functioning, by Borkowski and Peck (1986), confirms that gifted students have superior metacognitive knowledge. Such students consequently require less training to effect learning transfer and wider generalization to new tasks than do children of average intelligence. In general, the information processing research literature indicates that gifted individuals have "fast and easy access to relevant information, are able to view problem situations in qualitatively distinct ways, can use strategies effectively and flexibly, and have better metacognitive skills" than do their nongifted peers (Rabinowitz & Glaser, 1985, p. 76).

In a particularly vivid discussion, Levinger (1979) captures many of the endearing and sometimes disconcerting characteristics often associated with gifted children. She notes, for example, the persistence and delight young gifted children often display in solving complex problems that other children easily give up on. It is not unusual for kindergarten-age gifted students to be engaged for several hours at a time on a problem-solving activity or a particularly interesting task. Some characteristics such as perpetual inquisitiveness and a high need for perfection, however, can be misunderstood and even grating for some parents and teachers.

In contrast to the mental retardation field of study in which it is possible to distinguish subgroups on the basis of distinct etiological factors (such as chromosomal abnormalities), the distinction between gifted and highly gifted individuals is difficult. Early studies by Hollingworth (1942) with highly gifted subjects (i.e., IQs above 155) suggested that these are individuals who may be at significant risk for abnormal psychological development. Moreover, Zigler and Farber (1985) indicate that important differences between gifted and highly gifted individuals may be attributable to factors such as neurophysiological functioning or cognitive style. Giftedness, and particularly extreme giftedness, is distributed across all socioeconomic classes. However, more children identified as gifted come from higher socioeconomic environments (Humphreys, 1985).

Developmental Aspects

In comparison to their same-age peers, gifted individuals are outstanding in one or more areas of human achievement. The actualization of the full potential of any such individual is mediated by a number of factors, which have been summarized by Tannenbaum (1991) as follows. In addition to superior general intellect and distinctive aptitudes in a particular area of performance, a combination of nonintellective aptitudes are also considered to be essential. These include high motivation, positive self-concept, and possession of a good sense of metalearning. The latter attribute is described as a capacity for "fine-tuning their success in an achievement-oriented society" (Tannenbaum, 1991, p. 36). It seems very similar to Sternberg's (1991) notion of practical giftedness, an ability to utilize analytical and synthetic/creative abilities to function optimally in whichever context one is situated. Another factor important to the full development of a potential for giftedness is the environmental context. This refers to both the broad societal conditions (social, political, economic, legal) and to the more immediate milieu involving home, school, and peer group; all of these will interactively influence the degree to which any individual will be challenged and facilitated. Morelock and Feldman (1991), for example, refer to the "transgenerational influences" experienced by the world-renowned Jewish violinist Yehudi Menuhin. The long-established cultural and religious values upheld and modeled by his parents clearly dictated the expressive form of his giftedness. The final factor, "chance," has to do with timing and circumstances that must mesh favorably to enable an individual to make an outstanding achievement. On the basis of his studies of child prodigies, Feldman (1986) similarly contends that truly gifted achievement is a matter of coincidence, "the melding of the many sets of forces that interact in the development and expression of human potential" (p. 11). In the research literature, each of the identified factors is favorably supported from numerous perspectives. Notwithstanding these general factors, the research literature also has shown that over the different psychosocial stages, it is possible to delineate typical developmental patterns and the consequences these may have for the gifted individual and the family.

INFANCY TO PRESCHOOL

The research evidence indicates that intelligence assessments during the infant's first two years have poor predictability (Lewis, 1983; Lewis & Michalson, 1985). The earliest and most reliable indicators of advanced intellectual ability are initially discernible in memory and attention behaviors (Fagan & McGrath, 1981; Freeman, 1985). Once language abilities begin to develop, it is this, rather than any other area of intellectual development, that typically distinguishes the gifted preschooler. Parents often are alerted to a child's advanced intelligence by the child's early use of sophisticated vocabulary, grammatically correct forms, and richness of expression, and, sometimes, too, by an annoying persistence in asking questions. Many parents report that their gifted child learned to read before entering school, and often that this was self-taught. Other domains of ability that are commonly cited by parents include writing, art, music, and math.

Affective factors, such as taking pleasure in learning and a high degree of motivation, contribute to the typical account that gifted preschoolers show good socioemotional adjustment and score higher than nongifted children on self-concept measures (Lewis & Louis, 1991; Lewis & Michalson, 1985).

Parental and familial response to such early indications of advanced intellectual ability varies substantially and can have a significant impact on later school achievement. White (1985) discusses the important teaching role of parents at this stage. It is recommended that parents seek several goals: the provision of learning opportunities geared to the child's level of interest and skill; the mediation of the child's learning and other everyday experiences; and, in matters of social relations, the necessary maintainance of firm control and guidance. As for any child, it is important to establish a nurturing, child-centered home environment for the preschool gifted child; at the same time, however, there are several hazards to avoid. Thus, parents must be careful not to equate advanced cognitive ability with advanced maturity and not to burden the young child prematurely with adult responsibilities and problems. Again, excessive praise and admiration of the young child's abilities can induce an inflated sense of specialness; this is certain to create problems when the child begins school. Finally, an early dependence on external reinforcement may limit the child's ability to derive satisfaction from intrinsically motivating activities such as learning and studying (Rimm, 1991).

ELEMENTARY SCHOOL

The early school years can be particularly trying for young gifted children and their families. Once the child enters school, adjustments and support patterns that have been carefully developed within the home may be disrupted significantly. Most schools offer specialized programs for gifted students only in upper elementary grades; normally, the first three years are spent in regular classroom settings. Beyond the expected boredom and frustration this often creates in the child, there is

the additional risk of behavioral maladjustment. Ironically, behaviors stemming from the lack of appropriate educational challenge in the early years may seriously diminish the child's likelihood of eventual referral for gifted programming in later grades. Special educational alternatives for gifted students range from specialized schools, to enrichment and pull-out classes, to acceleration. Although there is much debate about the relative benefits of one type of program over another, it is generally acknowledged that programming that allows for individual-based pacing and challenge are most effective with respect to achievement levels (Fox & Washington, 1985). Studies of highly advanced or precocious children have shown that parents often provided the initial modeling of training rigor and early mentoring, and thus played a pivotal role in exposing and nurturing the young child within a particular interest area (Bloom, 1985; Bloom & Sosniak, 1981; Feldman, 1979).

A substantial body of research indicates that gifted preadolescent schoolchildren are generally better adjusted than their less intellectually endowed peers (Getzels & Dillon, 1973; Janos & Robinson, 1985; Monks & Ferguson, 1983).

ADOLESCENCE

Beyond the challenges normally experienced when young people move through the transitional life stage of adolescence, gifted individuals may be subject to additional hurdles. Buescher (1991) outlines 3 such barriers. The first is the characteristic denial and camouflaging of one's talents or abilities in an attempt to avoid being seen as "different." During this period, social acceptance by peers tends to take precedence over parental and teacher expectations. Second, gifted adolescents may be paradoxically experiencing a deep sense of personal dissonance arising from the self-analysis of their own talents or special abilities. Such youngsters will set unrealistic and perfectionist goals for themselves, often with the inadvertent support of their parents; the inevitable below-standard performance or even failure that then occurs can have a devastating impact. The perceived discrepancy between talent and performance creates self-doubt and in extreme cases might block efforts for further development of the youngster's talent area. Finally, for gifted adolescents, the search for identity may be especially problematic due to a characteristic intolerance for ambiguity and personal dissonance. Shortcutting this difficult stage by consolidating a premature identity can result in a serious mismatch of talents and abilities or obstruct the youngsters' possibility of fully developing their talent areas.

At the very time that gifted adolescents are experiencing the first major doubts about their talents and ability, the costs of maintaining these capacities and further developing them often escalates, as well. Progress demands long hours of practice and study, deep commitment, and the motivation to persevere, oftentimes at the cost of one's social life. It is during adolescence that these gifted individuals face the major hurdle of moving from a situation in which the gift has organized their life to "the task of beginning to shape the life to organize the gift" (Wallace, 1985, p. 382).

Another area that distinguishes gifted students from their average peers is their advanced moral judgment. This was first noted in Terman's longitudinal studies. A study by Janos, Robinson, and Sather (reported in Janos & Robinson, 1985) confirmed this assertion, showing that in comparison with typical university students, intellectually gifted high school–age individuals demonstrate significantly advanced levels of moral judgment.

In general, adolescence is an ambivalent period for gifted individuals, requiring the resolution of a number of conflicting values and beliefs. Parents, teachers, psychologists, and school counselors can be particularly helpful at this stage by being available and giving support to the students' arduous journey toward self-discovery.

Giftedness At Risk

One of the most pervasive arguments against programs for the gifted is the charge of elitism—that gifted students will form a privileged minority within the school population. Coupled with this sentiment is the egalitarian assertion that gifted individuals are already socially or racially advantaged and therefore should not be provided with special educational programs. Indeed, a recent nationwide survey of school procedures used in the identification and testing of gifted students

led Richert (1991) to conclude that systematic preference has been given to white, middle-class, academic achievers. These criticisms have forced educators to review traditional policies and procedures in respect to gifted education. As a result, increasingly, the schools are beginning to recognize that a number of subgroups of gifted individuals are particularly at risk for psychosocial problems (Janos & Robinson, 1985) and/or school failure (Lupart, 1992; Rimm, Lupart, & Pyryt, 1996).

HIGHLY GIFTED

There is considerable evidence to suggest that highly gifted youngsters are significantly vulnerable to psychosocial difficulties. In part this may well be due to the fact that their extreme abilities sets them so far apart from their peers. Studies indicate that approximately 20 to 25% of the highly gifted population are likely to have such difficulties, as compared to 5 to 7% among the moderately gifted population and approximately 6 to 16% for samples of children assessed as having average intellect (Janos & Robinson, 1985). Where high ability is identified early, and educational programs are appropriately individualized, as in the Study of Mathematically Precocious Youth at Johns Hopkins University (Stanley, 1979), the problem diminishes significantly. Albeit these individuals have the capacity for remarkable achievements and socially valued contributions, it cannot be assumed that they can fulfill this promise on their own. These students need an educational environment that will challenge their outstanding abilities through such tactics as proper class placement and the use of outside resources and mentors. Moreover, counseling support is necessary to "help children evaluate their own situations and sort out 'difference' from 'deviance'" (Janos & Robinson, 1985, p. 183).

CREATIVE GIFTED

Another subgroup of at-risk gifted consists of highly creative individuals. Although there may be some overlap in the characteristics typical for gifted and creative individuals, it is widely acknowledged that children who have a particular aptitude for creativity form a distinct subgroup (Feldman, Csikszentmihalyi, & Gardner, 1994;

Gallagher, 1985). With an ability to think divergently, come up with original formulations and solutions, take a flexible approach to problem solving, and display a greater tendency to take risks and engage in intellectual playfulness, the creative individual is often at odds with schools, where conventional thinking and behavior are the norm (Parke, 1989). One of the unfortunate realities in school testing is that creativity assessment is typically carried out as only one of the measures used to identify students for placement in a gifted program. In fact, the majority of the instruments and methods used are technically inadequate and unreliable (Callahan, 1991). Even if the highly creative individual does get special education placement, the program typically emphasizes intellectual giftedness as opposed to creative giftedness. This combination of factors makes it unlikely that most of the creatively gifted students will be identified and/or provided with the necessary programming; however, they need this to nurture their ability through to innovative or original work in adulthood. It seems rather peculiar that so little attention is given to the development of creative ability in schools, when such capacities are so highly valued and rewarded in adulthood (Wallace, 1985).

GIFTED FEMALES

Terman's longitudinal study revealed that, for the most part, gifted men and women kept abreast of each other right up to the first university undergraduate degree. From that point on, the pursuit of advanced degrees and ultimate success with respect to career achievement distinguished males and females significantly. During the peak years of adulthood, the majority of the males (86%) in Terman's study were involved in professional and managerial occupations, in comparison to only 11% of the female sample. Moreover, the women who did pursue careers chose a limited repertoire of occupations such as teaching, social work, secretarial, library, or nursing. This pattern was noted to be similar in Kerr's (1985) synthesis of several longitudinal studies of gifted females, and by Rudd and McKenry (1980), who carried out a study of male and female career patterns. (They reported that 80% of the women were involved in just 20 out of 500 possible job categories.) A number of external barriers to full actualization of female

potential in adulthood have been identified, including: test and social biases; organizational reward systems; sex-role stereotyping; and conflicting expectations between career, marriage, and family (Kerr, 1985; 1994). Reis (1991) further has suggested that there exist a number of internal barriers with which gifted females typically must deal. The first, fear of success, is associated with the belief that being too successful might jeopardize relations with peers, especially with males. Consequently, to avoid appearing too smart, these women engage in a systematic "holding back." Doing so, unfortunately, can adversely affect confidence. Another internal barrier is what might be called the perfection complex. It involves a persistent belief that one has to be perfect in everything one does. Such thinking often leads to unrealistic expectations of oneself along with a constant striving to achieve at increasingly higher levels. Finally, the imposter syndrome is a condition involving low self-esteem and a view that accomplishments have really been due to external forces such as good luck and not to one's own effort. Hence, these gifted females view their giftedness as an inappropriate or accidental label, agonizing that eventually they will be found out and oftentimes deliberately maintaining their own underachievement and even staging their own failure. Clearly, gifted girls and women need to have additional supports at home and at school to ensure the full actualization of their potential. Appropriate educational programming, particularly encouraging efforts in mathematics and science, and the provision of counseling from early grades would be most helpful in ensuring the future achievement of gifted girls. More than that, as women near adulthood, career counseling and mentorship experiences become essential.

GIFTED HANDICAPPED

Gifted handicapped children form an extremely heterogeneous group, including individuals who are at once gifted and yet burdened with hearing, speech, and/or visual impairment; orthopedic or other health impairment; emotional disturbance; or a learning disability. These students are underidentified within programs for the gifted, for two reasons: (1) schools tend to emphasize student deficit areas; accordingly, referrals focus on the handicap as opposed to any special ability that happens to be present; and (2) even in the case where special ability is recognized, school intervention programs usually are tied to a particular area of exceptionality. Thus, they do not have appropriately trained teachers, nor do they have the diversity of programs and resources to serve children with a dual or multiple exceptionality. As a rule, the family is most instrumental in helping the gifted handicapped child. To begin with, families provide the necessary encouragement, high expectations, guidance, and recognition of successes (Whitmore & Maker, 1985). More than that, effective parents seek out the best possible educational context for their child and place much emphasis on nurturing independence and the development of individual interests (Epstein, 1980). In general, gifted handicapped persons demonstrate an ability to devise creative strategies for overcoming personal limitations. They are likely to have a positive and accurate sense of their stengths and potentials and a high energy level (Whitmore & Maker, 1985). Nevertheless, their limitations may cause feelings of intense frustration, shame, and social discomfort, and lead to emotional/behavioral difficulties (Schiff, Kaufman & Kaufman, 1981). Studies investigating the incidence of suicide, underachievement, and anorexia nervosa among the gifted have suggested that high expectations on the part of parents and teachers and the erroneous assumption that the gifted individual must excel in all areas contribute to the social/emotional difficulties unique to this group (Detzner & Schmidt, 1986; Farrell, 1989; Hayes & Sloat, 1989; McMann & Olivier, 1988; Thoreson & Eagleston, 1983). Taken together, the research and literature concerning the gifted handicapped reveal significant human resources in our society that are allowed to go relatively untapped.

GIFTED MINORITY

Gifted students who have unique needs due to their minority status include those who are culturally diverse, socioeconomically deprived, and/or geographically isolated (Baldwin, 1985). Whether these factors exist singly or in combination, these students are significantly at-risk for academic failure. For example, Richert (1991) notes that minority groups such as blacks, Hispanics, and Native Americans are underrepresented by 30 to 70% in gifted programs and overrepresented by 40 to 50%

in other special education programs. These figures suggest an acknowledged bias and discrimination in school identification and assessment procedures. Other factors may be associated with negative cultural stereotyping. Thus, it is possible that those characteristics and abilities that may be particularly valued by a given subculture may not be similarly valued or may be in conflict with significant values in the dominant society. Gifted children who are disadvantaged due to poverty may lack the school readiness experiences that other students have. They may even lack basic health and medical care; the resulting difficulties could mask the intelligence and special talent areas where they would otherwise have excelled. Other gifted students may simply be at-risk due to their geographic remoteness from current resources, specialized programs and facilities.

SUMMARY

Beyond the problem of adequate identification, it is important for all these students to be offered programming that involves both the parents and the community, plentiful use of mentors and role models representative of the child's ethnic group, hands-on learning activities that foster self-expression, and the availability of counseling services throughout the school years (Van Tassel-Baska, 1989). The great hazard is the tendency to penalize those who do not conform to dominant values and standards by focusing on deficits and weaknesses as opposed to special abilities (Baldwin, 1985). It is most important to move beyond such a narrow view.

Conclusion

Gifted children are identified on the basis of their high achievement and talent or by showing the promise of functioning at high levels of intelligence. Intelligence generally is conceived as a composite of the human functions, including cognition, emotion, and physical capacities. Intelligence can be expressed in numerous ways, including outstanding cognitive ability, academic aptitude, creative behavior, leadership, or ability in visual or performing arts. Current research and theory supports the notion of both genetic and environmental components contributing to the development and expression of intelligence. The full range of these interactive possibilities as it relates to the actualization of gifted individual potential is presently unknown, although significant progress has been seen over the past decade. The importance of parents and school support has dominated recent research investigation, and this will no doubt influence future efforts to nurture giftedness. In these times of great change, the challenge is to ensure that the full spectrum of human potentiality becomes actualized.

REFERENCES

Albert, R. (1980). Exceptionally gifted boys and their parents. *Gifted Child Quarterly, 24* (4), 174–179.

Alvino, J., McDonnel, R. C., & Richert, S. (1981). National survey of identification practices in gifted and talented education. *Exceptional Children, 48*, 124–132.

Baldwin, A. Y. (1985). Programs for gifted and talented: Issues concerning minority populations. In F. D. Horowitz & M. O'Brien (Eds.), *The gifted and talented: Developmental perspectives* (pp. 223–249). Washington, DC: American Psychological Association.

Benbow, C., & Stanley, J. (1980). Intellectually talented students: Family profiles. *Gifted Child Quarterly, 24* (3), 119–122.

Bloom, B. S. (1985). Generalizations about talent development. In B. S. Bloom (Ed.), *Developing talent in young people* (pp. 507–547). New York: Ballantine.

Bloom, B. S., & Sosniak, L. A. (1981). Talent development vs. schooling. *Educational Leadership, 39*, 86–94.

Borkowski, J. G., & Peck, V. A. (1986). Causes and consequences of metamemory in gifted children. In R. J. Sternberg & J. E. Davidson (Eds.), *Conceptions of giftedness* (pp. 182–200). Cambridge: Cambridge University Press.

Buscher, T. M. (1991). Gifted adolescents. In N. Colangelo & G. A. Davis (Eds.), *Handbook of gifted education* (pp. 382–401). Boston: Allyn & Bacon.

Callahan, C. M. (1991). The assessment of creativity. I. N. Colangelo & G. A. Davis (Eds.), *Handbook of gifted education.* (pp. 219–235). Boston: Allyn & Bacon.

Case, R. (1985). *Intellectual development: Birth to adulthood.* New York: Academic Press.

Case, R. (1992). *The mind's staircase: Exploring the conceptual underpinnings of children's thought and knowledge.* Hillsdale, NJ: Lawrence Erlbaum.

Cattell, R. B. (1971). *Abilities: Their structure, growth, and action.* Boston: Houghton Mifflin.

Chi, M. T. H., & Glaser, R. (1985). Problem-solving ability. In R. J. Sternberg (Ed.), *Human abilities: An information processing approach* (pp. 227–250). New York: W. H. Freeman.

Cronbach, L. J. (1975). Five decades of public controversy over mental testing. *American Psychologist, 30*, 1–14.

Detzner, M., & Schmidt, M. (1986). Are highly gifted children and adolescents especially susceptible to anorexia nervosa? In K. Heller & J. Feldhausen (Eds.), *Identifying and nurturing the gifted: An international perspective* (pp. 149–162). Toronto: Hans Huber Publishers.

Epstein, J. (1980). *No music but request,* London: Collins.

Eysenck, H. J. (1979). *The structure and measurement of intelligence.* New York: Springer-Verlag.

Eysenck, H. J. (1985). The nature and measurement of intelligence. In J. Freeman (Ed.), *The psychology of gifted children: Perspectives on development and education* (pp. 115–140). New York: John Wiley & Sons.

Eysenck, H. J. (1986). Toward a new model of intelligence. *Personality and Individual Differences, 7*, 731–736.

Fagan, J. F., & McGrath, S. K. (1981). Infant recognition memory and later intelligence. *Intelligence, 5* (2), 121–130.

Farrell, D. (1989). Suicide among gifted students. *Roeper Review, 1* (3), 134–138.

Feldman, D. (1979). The mysterious case of extreme giftedness. In A. H. Passow (Ed.), *The gifted and talented.* (pp. 335–351). Chicago: National Society for the Study of Education.

Feldman, D. (1986). *Nature's gambit: Child prodigies and the development of human potential.* New York: Basic Books.

Feldman, D. H., Csikszentmihalyi, M., & Gardner, H. (1994). Changing the world: A framework for the study of creativity. Westport, CT: Praeger.

Fogarty, R., & Bellanea, J. (1995). Multiple intelligences: A collection. Arlington Heights, IL: IRI/Skylight Training and Publishing.

Fox, L. H., & Washington, J. (1985). Programs for the gifted and talented: Past, present, and future. In F. D. Horowitz & M. O'Brien (Eds.), *The gifted and talented: Developmental perspectives* (pp. 197–221). Washington, DC: American Psychological Association.

Freeman, J. (1983). Environment and high IQ—a consideration of fluid and crystallized intelligence, *Personal and Individual Differences, 4*, 307–313.

Freeman, J. (Ed.) (1985). *The psychology of gifted children: Perspectives on development and education.* New York: John Wiley & Sons.

Gallagher, J. J. (1991). Issues in the education of gifted students. In N. Colangelo & G. A. Davis (Eds.),

Handbook of gifted education (pp. 14–23). Boston: Allyn & Bacon.

Gardner, H. (1983). *Frames of mind: The theory of multiple intelligences.* New York: Basic Books.

Getzels, J. W., & Dillon, J. T. (1973). The nature of giftedness and the education of the gifted child. In R. M. W. Travers (Ed.), *Second handbook of research on teaching.* Chicago: Rand McNally.

Guilford, J. P. (1959). Three faces of intellect. *Psychological Bulletin, 53,* 267–293.

Guilford, J. P. (1967). *The nature of intelligence.* New York: McGraw-Hill.

Hardman, M. L., Drew, C. J., Egan, E. M., & Wolf, B. (1990). *Human exceptionality: Society, school and family.* (3rd ed.). Boston: Allyn & Bacon.

Hayes, M., & Sloat, R. (1989). Gifted students at risk for suicide. *Roeper Review, 12* (2), 102–106.

Hollingworth, L. S. (1942). *Children above 180 IQ. Stanford-Binet: Origin and development.* New York: World Book.

Horowitz, F. D., & O'Brien, M. (1985). Epilogue: Perspectives on research and development. In F. D. Horowtiz & M. O'Brien (Eds.), *The gifted and talented: Developmental perspectives* (pp. 437–454). Washington, DC: American Psychological Association.

Humphreys, L. G. (1985). A conceptualization of intellectual giftedness. In F. D. Horowitz & M. O'Brien (Eds.), *The gifted and talented: Developmental perspectives* (pp. 331–360). Washington, DC: American Psychological Association.

Hunt, J. M. (1971). Parent and child centers: Their basis in the behavioral and educational sciences. *American Journal of Orthopsychiatry, 41,* 13–38.

Janos, P. M., & Robinson, N. M. (1985). Psychosocial development in intellectually gifted children. In F. D. Horowitz & M. O'Brien (Eds.), *The gifted and talented: Developmental perspectives* (pp. 149–195). Washington, DC: American Psychological Association.

Johnson, C. (1981). Smart kids have problems too. *Today's Education, 70,* 26–29.

Kahneman, D. (1973). *Attention and effort.* Englewood Cliffs, NJ: Prentice-Hall.

Keating, D. P. (1975). Precocious development at the level of formal operations. *Child Development, 46,* 276–280.

Kerr, B. A. (1985). *Smart girls, gifted women.* Columbus, OH: Ohio Psychology Publishing Co.

Kerr, B. A. (1994). Smart girls two: A new psychology of girls, women and giftedness. Dayton, OH: Ohio Psychology Press.

Levinger, L. (1979). The intellectually superior child. In J. Call, J. Noshpitz, R. Cohen, & I. Berlin (Eds.). *Basic Handbook of Child Psychiatry, Vol. 1: Development,* pp. 328–333. New York: Basic Books.

Lewis, M. (Ed.). (1983). *Origins of intelligence: Infancy and early childhood* (2nd ed.). New York: Plenum Press.

Lewis, M., & Louis, B. (1991). Young gifted children. In N. Colangelo & G. A. Davis (Eds.), *Handbook of gifted education* (pp. 365–381). Boston: Allyn & Bacon.

Lewis, M., & Michalson, L. (1985). The gifted infant. In J. Freeman (Ed.), *The psychology of gifted children: Perspectives on development and education* (pp. 35–57). New York: John Wiley & Sons.

Lupart, J. L. (1992). The hidden gifted: Current state of knowledge and future research directions. In F. J. Monks & W. A. M. Peters (Eds.), *Talent for the future: Social and personality development of gifted children. Proceedings of the Ninth World Conference on Gifted and Talented Children.* Maastricht, The Netherlands: Van Gorcum, Assen.

Lupart, J. L., & Pyryt, M. (1996). "Hidden gifted" students' underachievement: Prevalence and profile. *Journal for the Education of the Gifted, 2* (1), 34–52.

Marland, S. (1972). *Education of the gifted and talented.* Washington, DC: U.S. Government Printing Office.

McMann, N., & Olivier, R. (1988). Problems in families with gifted children: Implications for counselors. *Journal of Counseling and Development, 66,* 275–278.

Monks, F., & Ferguson, T. (1983). Gifted adolescents: An analysis of their psychosocial development. *Journal of Youth and Adolescence, 12* (1), 1–18.

Morelock, M. J., & Feldman, D. H. (1991). Extreme precocity. In N. Colangelo & G. A. Davis (Eds.), *Handbook of gifted education* (pp. 347–364). Boston: Allyn & Bacon.

National Center for Education Statistics. (1989). *Digest of education statistics, 1989.* Washington, DC: U.S. Department of Education, Office of Research and Improvement.

National Commission on Excellence in Education. (1983). *A nation at risk: The imperative for educational reform.* Washington, DC: U.S. Government Printing Office.

Oden, M. H. (1968). The fulfillment of promise: 40 year follow-up of the Terman gifted group. *Genetic Psychology Monographs, 77,* 3–93.

Olszewski, P., Kulieke, M., & Buescher, T. (1987). The influence of the family environment on the development of talent: A literature review. *Journal for the Education of the Gifted, 11* (1), 6–28.

Parke, B. N. (1989). *Gifted students in regular classrooms.* Boston: Allyn & Bacon.

Piaget, J. (1983). Piaget's theory. In W. Kessen (Ed.), *Handbook of child psychology (4th ed.). Vol. 1: History, theory, and methods* (pp. 103–128). New York: John Wiley & Sons.

Plomin, R. (1989). Environment and genes: Determinants of behavior. *American Psychologist, 44,* 105–111.

Rabinowitz, M., & Glaser, R. (1985). Cognitive structure and process in highly competent performance. In F. D. Horowitz & M. O'Brien (Eds.), *The gifted and talented: Developmental perspectives* (pp. 75–98). Washington, DC: American Psychological Association.

Reis, S. M. (1991). We can't change what we don't recognize: Understanding the special needs of gifted females. In R. Jenkins-Friedman, E. S. Richert, & J. F. Feldhusen (Eds.), *Special populations of gifted learners: A book of readings* (pp. 29–42). Unionville, NY: Trillium Press.

Renzulli, J. S. (1978). What makes giftedness? Reexamining a definition. *Phi Delta Kappan, 60,* 180–184.

Richert, E. S. (1991). Rampant problems and promising practices in the identification of disadvantaged gifted students. In R. Jenkins-Friedman, E. S. Richert, & J. F. Feldhusen (Eds.), *Special populations of gifted learners: A book of readings* (pp. 43–56). Unionville, NY: Trillium Press.

Rimm, S. (1995). *Why bright kids get poor grades and what you can do about it.* New York: Crown Publishers, Inc.

Rudd, N. A., & McKenry, P. C. (1980). Working women: Issues and implications. *Journal of Home Economics, 72* (4), 26–29.

Schiff, M., Kaufman, A., & Kaufman, N. (1981). Scatter analysis of WISC-R profiles for learning disabled children with superior intelligence. *Journal of Learning Disabilities, 14,* 400–404.

Shriner, J. G., Ysseldyke, J. E., Goracy, D., & Franklin, M. J. (1993). Examining prevalence at the ends of the spectrum: Giftedness and disability. *Remedial and Special Education, 14* (5), 33–39.

Shurkin, J. N. (1992). *Terman's kids: The groundbreaking study of how the gifted grow up.* Boston: Little, Brown.

Stanley, J. C. (1979). Identifying and nurturing the educationally gifted. In W. C. George, S. J. Cohn, & J. C. Stanley (Eds.), *Educating the gifted* (pp. 172–183). Baltimore: Johns Hopkins University Press.

Sternberg, R. J. (1984). Mechanisms of cognitive development: A componential approach. In R. J. Sternberg (Ed.), *Mechanisms of cognitive development* (pp. 163–185). Prospect Heights, IL: Waveland Press.

Sternberg, R. J. (1985). *Beyond IQ: A triarchic theory of intelligence.* New York: Cambridge University Press.

Sternberg, R. J. (1991). Giftedness according to the triarchic theory of human intelligence. In N. Colangelo & G. A. Davis (Eds.), *Handbook of gifted education* (pp. 45–54). Boston: Allyn & Bacon.

Tannenbaum, A. J. (1991). The social psychology of giftedness. In N. Colangelo & G. A. Davis (Eds.), *Handbook of gifted education* (pp. 27–54). Boston: Allyn & Bacon.

Terman, L. M. (1916). *The measurement of intelligence.* Boston: Houghton Mifflin.

Terman, L. M. (1925). *Genetic studies of genius. Vol. 1: Mental and physical traits of a thousand gifted children.* Stanford, CA: Stanford University Press.

Terman, L. M., & Oden, M. H. (1947). *Genetic studies of genius. Vol. 4: The gifted child grows up.* Stanford, CA: Stanford University Press.

Terman, L. M., & Oden, M. H. (1959). *Genetic studies of genius. Vol. 5: The gifted group at mid-life.* Stanford, CA: Stanford University Press.

Thoresen, C., & Eagleston, J. (1983). Chronic stress in children and adolescents. *Theory Into Practice, 22* (2), 48–56.

Torrance, E. P. (1966). *Torrance Test of Creative Thinking: Directions manual and scoring guide, Verbal Test B.* Princeton, NJ: Personnel.

Van Tassel-Baska, J. (1983). Profiles of precocity: The 1982 Midwest talent search finalists. *Gifted Child Quarterly, 27* (3), 139–144.

Van Tassel-Baska, J. (1989). The disadvantaged gifted. In J. Feldhusen, J. Van Tassel-Baska, & K. Seeley (Eds.), *Excellence in educating the gifted.* Denver: Love Publishing Co.

Walberg, H. J., & Herbig, M. P. (1991). Developing talent, creativity, and eminence. In N. Colangelo & G. A. Davis (Eds.), *Handbook of gifted education* (pp. 245–255). Boston: Allyn & Bacon.

Wallace, D. B. (1985). Giftedness and the construction of a creative life. In F. D. Horowitz & M. O'Brien (Eds.), *The gifted and talented: Developmental perspectives* (pp. 361–385). Washington, DC: American Psychological Association.

White, B. (1985). Competence and giftedness. In J. Freeman (Ed.), *The psychology of gifted children: Perspectives on development and education* (pp. 59–73). New York: Wiley & Sons.

Whitmore, J. R., & Maker, C. J. (1985). *Intellectual giftedness in disabled persons.* Rockville, MD: Aspen.

Wolf, J. S. (1990). The gifted and talented. In N. G. Haring & L. McCormick (Eds.), *Exceptional children and youth: An introduction to special education* (5th ed). Columbus, OH: Merrill.

Zigler, W., & Farber, E. A. (1985). Commonalities between the intellectual extremes: Giftedness and mental retardation. In F. D. Horowitz & M. O'Brien (Eds.), *The gifted and talented: Developmental perspectives* (pp. 379–408). Washington, DC: American Psychological Association.

14 / Homeless Youths

Mary Jane Rotheram-Borus and Rose McDermott

Homeless youths often are stereotyped as "Huck Finn" out to seek an exciting adventure. The public forgets that Huck Finn was the son of an alcoholic father who abused him. Most often, runaway

138

and homeless youths come from severely dysfunctional families and are running away from abuse and victimization. Their lives are highly stressful, and homeless youths are overwhelmed by the number and intensity of the problems they confront. It is not surprising that these youths experience significant mental health problems.

This chapter outlines the epidemiology of runaway and homeless youths and the risk factors for mental health problems among these adolescents. When evaluating mental health needs, it is crucial to examine the context of the youths' lives, especially their current living situation and family resources. This chapter reviews the indications of mental health problems of adolescents, including emotional distress, multiple problem behaviors, and problems in establishing ongoing stable social relationships.

Epidemiology of Homeless Youths

The number of homeless youths between the ages of 11 and 18 has risen dramatically in the last 15 years. There were estimated to be 519,500 in 1975 (Brennan, Huizinga, & Elliot, 1979); by 1988, the estimate had risen to between 1 million and 1.5 million (Children's Defense Fund, 1988). In 1987, the United States Mayor's Conference estimated that about 4% of the homeless population were adolescents (Solarz, 1992). Nationally, runaways and homeless youths come from every socioeconomic status; 30% receive public assistance (Shaffer & Caton, 1984). Every year about 300,000 youths receive shelter for 2 to 6 weeks in a national network of temporary residences (General Accounting Office [GAO], 1989).

There are at least 5 categories of homeless youths; most youths simultaneously fit the description of several of these categories. "Runaways" are those children ages 12 to 18 who have left home for at least one night without the permission or knowledge of their parents or caregivers. Adolescents who leave home are more likely to consider themselves homeless than runaways, and this tendency increases with age (Caton, 1986; Council on Scientific Affairs [CSA], 1989). It is unclear how many of these runaways return home voluntarily. One survey suggests that 70% of runaways return home within a week (Opinion Research

Corporation [ORC], 1976), although 5% are reported to leave home for more than a year (Manov & Lowther, 1983). In contrast, the national survey by the General Accounting Office (1989) indicates that about one-third return to their homes, although this appears to be less common in large cities. Many children run away from home more than once; in Shaffer and Caton (1984), 92% of boys and 82% of girls in a shelter ran away previously; between a third and a half ran away more than five times in the past. Most runaways start leaving home before the age of 16. Those adolescents who run away more than once tend to come from more troubled homes, are more likely to stay away from home longer, are less likely to return by themselves, and tend to have more problems with school and the criminal justice system (Shaffer & Caton, 1984).

Homeless youth are often called "throwaway kids" because they have left home at the request of their families. Many of these youths are gay, lesbian, or bisexual (Hunter & Schaecher, 1990). When a family becomes homeless, adolescent children often are not allowed into the shelter with the rest of the family; thus these youths leave home (Brennan et al., 1979). About 10% of runaways fall into this category (Bucy & Obolensky, 1990). However, it is more common for the adolescents' or the parents' problem behaviors (e.g., adolescent drug abuse, parental alcoholism) to lead parents to eject their children from the family home.

"Street kids" are youths who live independently. They often make their living off the drug and sex trade industries. Most adolescents spend only a few nights living on the streets. There are very few hardcore street youths who live longer periods of time on the streets.

"System kids" are those adolescents who have been taken out of their families for their own protection by the state and who run away from a placement in foster care. In many cases, these children are shuffled between foster homes, group homes, and delinquent shelters; these youths often rotate between many types of unsuccessful living situations. About 50% of runaways fall into this category (Robertson, 1989; Shaffer & Caton, 1984).

"Victimized children" are children who have been abused by their parents or caregivers in a systematic way. Many children in shelters could be included in this category. Rotheram-Borus,

Koopman, and Bradley (1989) showed that 37% of runaways had been abused or neglected at home. In this chapter we use the titles "homeless" and "runaway" to signify youths in any of these categories.

The demographic characteristics of homeless youths differ across studies. The modal age for running away is about 15 or 16 years old (ORC, 1976). Although there have been some reports of runaways as young as 9 years old (Rothman & David, 1985), most reports indicate that the majority continue to be older than 15 (Robertson, Koegel, & Ferguson, 1989). There are some indications, however, that increasing numbers of younger adolescents are running away; a 1989 report to Congress reported that 42% of runaways were under the age of 14 (Family and Youth Services Bureau, 1990).

In most cases, homeless and runaway youths stay in the same geographical area as their original home (Shaffer & Caton, 1984; Robertson, 1989). As a result, homeless youths tend to reflect the ethnic composition of the surrounding community. In the national survey, 70% of runaways are white, 19% are black, and 7% are Hispanic (Children's Defense Fund, 1988). Differences in ethnicity can cause language problems in some shelter situations. Eight percent of youths served in shelters in 1988 spoke English as a second language, and half of those were only able to speak Spanish (GAO, 1989).

Apparently an equal number of boys and girls run away, although adolescents in shelters are more likely to be younger and more likely to be female than those who live on the street (GAO, 1989). About 6% of adolescents using shelters identify themselves as homosexual (National Network of Runaway and Youth Services, 1991); some believe this number to be an underestimate because of strong social taboos against acknowledging homosexuality (Bucy & Obolensky, 1990). Few differences have been found in runaway youths based on socioeconomic status (Shaffer & Caton, 1984). However, some religious differences have been found; Shaffer and Caton (1984) found that 45% of runaways are Roman Catholic.

In summary, there are many homeless and runaway youths who are at risk for serious mental health problems. The next section addresses how family problems and the adolescent's living situation exacerbates these risks.

Risk Factors for Mental Health Problems

It is impossible to divorce adolescents' risk factors for mental health problems from the context of their lives. Their living situation is crucial in assessing the likelihood of mental health problems and in evaluating their ability to cope with the challenges they face when homeless. Two aspects of adolescents' lives are essential to understanding their mental health risk factors: the family context from which the adolescents run away and the immediate living environment, a situation characterized by a profound lack of resources.

Context of Runaways' Lives

DYSFUNCTIONAL FAMILIES

Family problems often cause youths to run away from home. Less than 25% of runaways come from two-parent families (Shaffer & Caton, 1984); almost 10% do not have a parental figure (GAO, 1989). Most studies indicate a relationship between large families and running away, especially repeatedly running away; Shaffer and Caton (1984) found almost one-third of runaways came from families with 4 or more children. In one series of studies, 44% of homeless adolescents had lived with mothers receiving public assistance (Rotheram-Borus, Koopman, & Ehrhardt, 1991). Others report a new stepparent in the family (21%), moving to a different residence (55%), or having to enter a new school (43%) in the period shortly before running away (Rotheram-Borus, Rosario, & Koopman, 1991).

The parents' personal problems significantly impact the adolescents. Robertson (1989) found that 60% of runaways report that one or both parents were alcoholics, drug abusers, or convicted criminals. About one-quarter of the mothers are under age 17 when their children are born (Shaffer & Caton, 1984). Runaways are also more likely than nonrunaways to have mothers with psychiatric problems (Shane, 1989). About 37% of these adolescents report that their parents have been increasingly absent from home, with 17% in jail. Almost one-third of the youths' parents have lost a job just before the youths ran away (Rotheram-Borus, Rosario, & Koopman, 1991).

Conflict characterizes the families of homeless youth. About half the runaways reported increased problems between their parents as well as increasing conflict between the adolescents and their parents (Rotheram-Borus et al., 1989). There is also some indication that running away is modeled within an adolescent's environment. Thirty-nine percent have a sibling who has run away, and 16% have a parent who has run away (Shaffer & Caton, 1984). Shaffer and Caton (1984) found about half the runaways had been in foster homes at some point.

Abuse: A staggering number of youths also report abuse and neglect at the hands of their parents. Robertson (1989) reports that 37% of runaways suffer physical abuse; another 10% are sexually abused. Shaffer and Caton (1984) report that half of their New York City sample has received significant and repeated abuse at the hands of a parent, often requiring hospitalization. In addition to overt abuse, many adolescents feel that their parents lack warmth and supportiveness (Englander, 1984).

In summary, Rothman and David (1985) argue that these families tend to be characterized by the following situation: youths have poor relationships with their parents; the parents tend to have their own troubles with marriage, substance abuse, or the criminal justice system; the adolescents feel unwanted and often are used as the scapegoat for other problems in the family; and these children often are physically or sexually abused by family members.

As a result of these factors, the family context of these adolescents provides little support for adolescent runaways. In many cases, the youths would rather face unknown risks on the street than be subjected to known physical and sexual abuses in the family. However, runaways have strong family relations but few avenues for close emotional support or instrumental help. Surprisingly, these runaway adolescents also report being relatively satisfied with the support they receive (Rotheram-Borus, Rosario, & Koopman, 1991). Contrary to popular stereotype, many runaways, especially younger adolescents, maintain some kind of contact with a parent (Shaffer & Caton, 1984).

LIVING SITUATIONS

A homeless adolescent who runs away faces a serious daily challenge in obtaining the resources that are necessary to live. Most youths lack the education or training to gain meaningful employment and have no money. For example, Shaffer and Caton (1984) found about half the homeless youths repeated a grade in school; 10% of the girls and 16% of the boys were functionally illiterate. It is unlikely that these youths will succeed in college.

In many cases, youths lack even the most basic of resources. Many adolescents go hungry at least one day a month, and about half have difficulty obtaining adequate food and clothing (Robertson, 1989). Many more cannot obtain shelter, even in public facilities, which are often filled to capacity; 65% of youths were turned away at one shelter in Los Angeles (Pennbridge, Yates, David, & MacKenzie, 1990). Moreover, adolescents who run away from home often make easy targets for robbery and sexual or physical assault.

Health Problems: Serious health problems are more common in adolescent runaway populations than among nonrunaways (Miller & Lin, 1988; Yates, MacKenzie, Pennbridge & Cohen, 1988). Over 65% report current health problems, yet only one-third have any kind of health coverage (Robertson, 1989). Almost 30% of youths report a major illness or injury just prior to running away. About 20% believe that their health declined after they became homeless and about 20% have an untreated health problem (Robertson, 1989). This situation may be because many of these adolescents believe that without money they cannot obtain medical care. In addition, they tend to be distrustful of authority figures, including doctors (CSA, 1989).

The relationship between stress and mental health problems has been well documented (Dohrenwend & Dohrenwend, 1974). Given the overwhelming stress in these adolescents' lives, it is not surprising that they are at increased risk for multiple mental health problems. Adolescents who are struggling for the next meal will not be receptive to efforts designed to reduce their alcohol and drug use behavior or to improve their performance at school. The immediate needs of adolescents' lives must be met before these other problems can begin to be addressed.

Indications of Mental Health Problems

Mental health problems can take many forms: adolescents' emotional distress; multiple problem behaviors, such as drug and alcohol abuse, pregnancy, conduct disorder, and problems with school and the criminal justice system; and social relationships with peers and adults.

EMOTIONAL DISTRESS

Given the number of stressors, it is not surprising that adolescents feel emotionally distressed. Shaffer and Caton (1984) report that 38% of runaway and homeless youths feel they need help for psychological or emotional problems. However, many of these problems exist prior to the adolescents running away. At least 20% have received some previous psychiatric care; 25% of males and 13% of females have been on some kind of psychotropic medication in the past. Emotional distress and other psychological problems are three times more prevalent in runaway and homeless populations than among their nonrunaway adolescent peer group (Robertson, 1989).

Runaways are frequently depressed. About one-third of the boys and about one-half of the girls request help for depression and/or anxiety (Shaffer & Caton, 1984). Girls are much more likely to report mood disturbances, while boys are more likely to manifest conduct disorders. Girls are more likely to have been hospitalized for a psychiatric disorder (Shaffer & Caton, 1984).

Suicide: Many homeless youths have attempted suicide. Not surprisingly, there is a high correlation between an adolescent feeling depressed and having suicidal ideation. Various studies report between 15% and 50% of runaways have tried to kill themselves at least once (Greenblatt & Robertson, 1993; Robertson, 1989; Rotheram-Borus et al., 1991b; Shaffer & Caton, 1984). Rotheram-Borus et al. (1989) found that almost one-third of adolescent suicide attempts took place within the month just before seeking shelter. Almost 25% of these adolescents have family members who have thought about committing suicide (Rotheram-Borus & Koopman, 1991). It would be difficult to know how many runaway adolescents successfully manage to commit suicide because there are no follow-up studies.

Youths who report high levels of emotional distress are more also likely to have physical complaints and school-related difficulties. They are more likely to have used drugs and gotten into trouble with the criminal justice system. Adolescents with greater emotional problems tend to have experienced more family violence and are more likely to have been raped; they tend to have run away more frequently and are more likely to have lived with their fathers than their mothers (Shaffer & Caton, 1984). In summary, the majority of adolescent runaways experience significant emotional distress that places them at an increased risk for mental health symptoms.

BEHAVIORAL PROBLEMS

Adolescents who run away have a number of behavior problems, including frequently unprotected sexual intercourse that leads to teenage pregnancy and HIV infection, drug and alcohol abuse, and problems at school and with the criminal justice system.

Pregnancy: Pregnancy and teenage motherhood are more common in homeless populations than among nonhomeless youth (American Medical Association Council on Scientific Affairs, 1989). Pregnancy can lead a girl to run away or become homeless. She may be afraid to tell her family about her pregnancy, or they may throw her out of the house when they discover it. However, homelessness itself can place a girl at greater risk for pregnancy; rape and bartering sex may result in pregnancy. Shaffer and Caton (1984) found that 36% of female runaways are pregnant. This study also found that girls who have been abused are less likely to use birth control and less likely to get an abortion if they became pregnant. In another study, half of the runaway girls report being pregnant, one-third while homeless, although only one-third have given birth (Robertson, 1989). Homeless teenagers who are pregnant are at increased risk for low infant birthweight and increased infant mortality due to inadequate prenatal care and poor personal health and dietary care (Sullivan & Damrosch, 1987).

HIV: The HIV pandemic exacerbates the health care needs of homeless adolescents. Almost 4% are estimated to be HIV infected (Stricof,

Novick, & Kennedy, 1990), with estimates as high as 10% among African American homeless youths in San Francisco (Allen et al., 1994). About one-third of runaways are abstinent in any 3-month time frame; however, runaways have more lifetime sexual partners than their nonrunaway peers (Rotheram-Borus et al., 1989). For example, 49% of boys and 12% of girls report more than 10 partners, compared with 7% of boys and 3% of girls in a national sample (Gagnon et al., 1989; Rotheram-Borus et al., 1989). Moreover, sexual intercourse begins at a younger age among runaway youths than among other adolescents (Rotheram-Borus, Koopman, & Ehrhardt, 1991; Yates, Mackenzie, Pennbridge, & Cohen, 1988). Homeless youths are also at high risk for other sexually transmitted diseases, such as gonorrhea, syphilis, and pelvic inflammatory diseases.

Substance Abuse: Problem behaviors also include drug and alcohol abuse. Running away in early adolescence is positively correlated with drug and alcohol use and school dropout status 4 years later (Windle, 1989). Robertson (1989) found that almost 40% of runaway youth meet *Diagnostic and Statistical Manual of Mental Disorders* criteria for substance abuse; this is five times higher than the rate found in nonhomeless runaways. Yates et al. (1988) found that 84% of youths use alcohol and drugs. In New York, 71% report alcohol use, 46% report drug use, and 27% report using either alcohol or drugs at least once per week during the previous 3 months (Koopman, Rosario, & Rotheram-Borus, 1994).

Homeless adolescents with alcohol problems start drinking at a younger age, have greater social impairment as a result of their drinking, and demonstrate more frequent use than nonhomeless adolescents (Robertson, Koegel, & Ferguson, 1989). Those with alcohol problems are also more likely than their homeless peers to have histories of abuse or neglect, including being removed from their homes by authorities; thus, they tend to be more estranged from their families. They also tend to have more chronic histories with homelessness, spend more time in institutional settings, have more difficulty meeting basic survival needs, and generate more of their income illegally. They also are more likely to abuse drugs than homeless adolescents who do not have problems with alcohol, and about one-quarter appear to have substance abuse problems with both alcohol and drugs (Rob-

ertson, et al., 1989). Female runaways recruited from the National Longitudinal Study Youth Survey are more likely to abuse drugs as opposed to alcohol, while males are more likely to manifest a more generalized pattern of substance abuse (Windle, 1989).

Trading Sex for Money or Drugs: Due to lack of food and shelter, many adolescent runaways are forced to resort to the drug and sex trade to make a living. Between 10 and 30% of youths barter sex for money, food, or shelter (Greenblatt & Robertson, 1993; Pennbridge, Freese, & Mackenzie, 1992; Robertson, 1989; Rotheram-Borus et al., 1989). In a review of the existing literature, the American Medical Association (1986) concluded that about one-third of homeless males engage in prostitution, at an average age of 15. In many cases, these youths trade sex for drugs. About half the runaways report having sold drugs for money at some point; another 20% report selling drugs to support their own habit (Robertson, 1989).

Problems with the Law and in School: Problems with school and the criminal justice system place an adolescent at greater risk for other problems later, if they are unable to get a job because of lack of education or a criminal record. The lack of a stable home life or a permanent address makes it extremely difficult for a homeless or runaway youth to attend school. More than half of these adolescents are not enrolled in school at all. Moreover, half have been expelled or suspended from school (Price, 1987). Of those who are enrolled in school, about half have some kind of learning disability or conduct disorder (GAO, 1989). Runaways tend to be below average in their academic performance. In Los Angeles, 25% have repeated at least one grade, and another quarter have been placed in special education classes (Robertson, 1989). Shaffer and Caton (1984) found that 18% exhibit antisocial personalities.

Life on the streets also places many runaways in constant conflict with the criminal justice system. In New York, 21% of males have been in jail just prior to seeking shelter in a public facility (Rotheram-Borus, 1991); in Los Angeles, 56% have spent some time in a detention facility (Robertson, 1989). Shaffer and Caton (1984) report that one-quarter of girls and one-half of boys have been arrested or put in jail at some point in their runaway career.

Mental Health Interventions

The mental and physical health needs of adolescent runaways often are not well met by the existing shelter system. Mental health delivery systems are needed to provide primary prevention for running away, secondary treatment of mental health and problem behaviors among homeless youth, and adequate mental health care for youths with chronic patterns of disturbed behavior.

There are significant needs for prevention programs initiated at three different targets: family advocacy, early interventions with first-time runaways, and stable foster care alternatives for chronic runaways. Family advocacy is crucial to prevent adolescent homelessness. Existing social welfare programs are geared largely toward "traditional" families—those with two parents and their children (Schroeder, 1989). This is not the current reality; stepfamilies are now the modal form of family life in the United States. Family advocacy requires an acknowledgment of changes in the family structure and of the need to provide support services to dysfunctional families in terms of social service programs that reflect the realities of current family life (e.g., after-school child care programs, extended day care, staggered work hours, paid parental leave). The dramatic rise in the numbers of homeless and runaway youths may reflect the need for structural changes in health care management and the social service system supporting families.

Prevention programs also are needed to target early intervention with young runaways before they become chronic runaways (Shaffer & Caton, 1984). Intervention programs need to target youths who have already demonstrated potential risk by running away from home but have not yet established chronic problems. If an adolescent has run away once, there is hope that intervention will prevent a recurrence. By the time that adolescent has run away from home four or five times, running away has become an established coping style, and his or her behavior will be much more resistant to change or prevention. Intensive family work at the time of the first runaway incident may reduce the likelihood of reoccurrence.

Finally, running away can be prevented by establishing well-run, stable foster care alternatives.

Homeless youths often have no viable alternatives for shelter. The length of stay in a runaway shelter typically is dependent on available placements in foster care or group homes (Rotheram-Borus, Rosario, & Koopman, 1991). The shelters that exist are underfunded and understaffed by persons with insufficient training who leave their jobs quickly. The quality of life in foster care is usually low, and adolescents often are shuffled frequently between various group homes and institutional settings. Without a foster care system with a sufficient number of placements in stable, high-quality homes to provide an acceptable alternative to living in the streets, many youths drift between temporary shelters and a life on the street.

Simultaneously, secondary prevention programs must be established to treat the emotional disorders and problem behaviors (substance abuse, frequent unprotected sexual intercourse, truancy, delinquency, conduct disorders) of runaways. The types of interventions needed by these youths are not unique. Interventions that have been developed for emotionally disturbed adolescents are likely to be successful with runaways. However, access to services is a unique problem with an unstable population. In particular, homeless youths who have substance abuse problems with drugs, alcohol, or both must be offered adequate treatment programs. National surveys have reported that only 3 to 20% of adolescent runaways who report drug and alcohol abuse received any kind of treatment. Only 28% receive any help finding a place to live, and less than 23% obtain any medical or mental health care, because they have no access to this care. If services are unavailable, reducing the scope of the problem will be difficult.

In addition, homeless youths are more likely to have been sexually or physically abused, a situation that often requires specialized mental health care. The consequences of this abuse will be reflected in the early initiation of sexual intercourse (Rotheram-Borus et al., 1989) and other problem behaviors. In addition to sex education and access to birth control, abused youths will benefit from therapy for the emotional consequences that arise from such victimization in order to help prevent serious emotional distress, affective disorders, or suicide attempts. Youths who have a history of delinquency also may benefit from similar mental health care. Moreover, they may be in need of legal help in dealing with the court system over past offenses.

One problem in providing this kind of treatment derives from legal and ethical barriers to the handling of emancipated minors. In many states (e.g., Oklahoma), it is impossible to provide care for such conditions as sexually transmitted diseases without parental consent. If a youth has run away from home, he or she is unlikely to be willing to seek such consent, especially if the parent is the one responsible for the abuse he or she is trying to leave. For example, if an adolescent is pregnant and has been thrown out of the home as a result, it is unlikely that she would be able to obtain such consent for an abortion, even if requested. These legal and ethical barriers to health care prohibit access for many adolescents, including homeless youths. Moreover, continuity of health care may be especially difficult to provide to runaways.

As with mental health interventions for acute emotional distress, service delivery systems for chronic mental health problems of runaways must be tailored for youths' lives. Access to services and integrating mental health services with comprehensive care for adolescents is critical. Basic needs for food, shelter, clothing, and health care must be met before mental health problems can be treated effectively. Psychological treatment and counseling for distressed adolescents must be offered on the streets, where homeless youths live, or in reach of easy access. Mental health care has been provided successfully in storefront centers, where adolescents drop in on an irregular basis. Counselors who are young often can identify with youths and serve as role models. Youths' behavior often does not conform to counselors' expectations. Adolescents are not likely to be on time for appointments or verbally disclose their problems without prompting. Youths will not be able to pay for mental health services, and they may not be able to provide identification to enable them to receive Medicaid. Flexibility must be a mainstay for providing mental health care. A mental health service provider must realize that a model of successive approximation must be employed to encourage adolescents to attend counseling. It is hoped that adolescents' adherence to health and mental health behaviors will improve over time to comply with the limits and boundaries that are necessary in shelters. For example, an adolescent may begin by spending one night in foster care, then spend three nights at a later date. Two months later the youth may be able to conform to rules in shelters for several months. This process may progress until the adolescent is able to stay in a stable foster care situation indefinitely.

Moreover, youths need a case manager to help them negotiate the bureaucratic maze that confronts someone seeking Medicaid or other social support services. This strategy may allow adolescents an opportunity to bond with adults whom they can learn to trust and who may even serve as role models.

Homeless youths require comprehensive care. Currently, the mental health care system is too fragmented to provide such full-service care. The initial funding for the national network of runaway and homeless youth shelters in 1972 was based on a model that provided mental health, education, and physical health care in one comprehensive program. The current needs of homeless youth require a return to such a system.

REFERENCES

Allen, D. M., Lehman, S., Green, T. A., Lindegren, M. L., Onorato, I. M., Forrester, W., and the Field Services Branch. (1994). HIV infection among homeless adults and runaway youth, United States, 1989–1992. *AIDS, 8*, 1593–1598.

American Medical Association. (1986). *White paper on adolescent health*. Chicago, IL: author.

American Medical Association Council on Scientific Affairs. (1989). Health care needs of homeless and runaway youths. *Journal of the American Medical Association, 262*, 1358–1361.

Brennan, T., Huizinga, D., & Elliot, D. S. (1979). *The social psychology of runaways*. Lexington, MA: Lexington Books.

Bucy, J., & Obolensky, N. (1990). Runaway and homeless youths. In M. J. Rotheram-Borus, J. Bradley, & N. Obolensky (Eds.), *Planning to live: Evaluating and treating suicidal teens in community settings* (pp. 333–354). Tulsa: University of Oklahoma Press.

Caton, C. (1986). The homeless experience in adolescents years. In E. L. Bussuk (Ed.), *The mental health needs of homeless persons* (pp. 62–70). San Francisco: Jossey-Bass.

Children's Defense Fund. (1988). *A children's defense budget FY 1989: An analysis of our nation's investment in children.* Washington, DC: Author.

Council on Scientific Affairs. (1989). Health care needs of homeless and runaway youths. *Journal of the American Medical Association, 262,* 1358–1361.

Dohrenwend, B. P., & Dohrenwend, B. S. (1974). Overviews and prospects for research on stressful life events. In B. S. Dohrenwend & B. P. Dohrenwend (Eds.), *Stressful life events: Their nature and effects* (pp. 313–331). New York: John Wiley & Sons.

Englander, S. W. (1984). Some self-reported correlates of runaway behavior in adolescent females. *Journal of Consulting and Clinical Psychology, 52,* 484–485.

Family and Youth Services Bureau. (1990) *Annual report to the Congress on the Runaway and Homeless Youth Program, Fiscal Year 1989.* Washington, DC: Author.

Gagnon, J. H., Lindenbaum, S., Martin, J. L., May, R. M., Menken, J., Turner, C. F., & Zabin, L. S. (1989). Sexual behavior and AIDS. In C. F. Turner, H. G. Miller, & L. E. Moses (Eds.), *AIDS: Sexual Behavior and Intravenous Drug Use.* (pp. 73–186). Washington, DC: National Academy Press.

General Accounting Office. (1989). *Homelessness: Homeless and runaway youth receiving services at federally funded shelters.* Washington, DC: Author.

Hunter, J., & Schaecher, R. (1990). Teenage suicide: Lesbian and gay youth. In M. J. Rotheram-Borus, J. Bradley, & N. Obolensky (Eds.), *Planning to Live: Evaluating and Treating Suicidal Teens in Community Settings,* (pp. 297–316). Tulsa: University of Oklahoma Press.

Koopman, C., Rosario, M., & Rotheram-Borus, M. J. (1994). Alcohol and drug use and sexual behaviors placing runaways at risk for HIV infection. *Addictive Behaviors, 19*(1), 95–103.

Manov, A., & Lowther, L. (1983). A health care approach for hard-to-reach adolescent runaways. *Nursing Clinics of North America, 18,* 333–342.

Miller, D., & Lin, E. (1988). Children in sheltered homeless families: Reported health status and use of health services. *Pediatrics, 81,* 668–673.

National Network of Runaway and Youth Services. (1991). *To whom do they belong: Runaway, homeless and other youth in high-risk situations in the 1990s.* Washington, DC: Author.

Opinion Research Corporation. (1976). *National statistical survey on runaway youth, Part 1.* Paper prepared for the U.S. Department of Health, Education and Welfare. Princeton, NJ.

Pennbridge, J. N., Freese, T. E., & MacKenzie, R. G. (1992). High-risk behaviors among male street youth in Hollywood, California. *AIDS Education & Prevention, Fall* (Suppl.), 24–33.

Pennbridge, J. N., Yates, G. L., David, T. G., & MacKenzie, R. G. (1990). Runaway and homeless youth in Los Angeles County, California. *Journal of Adolescent Health Care, 11,* 159–165.

Price, V. (1987). Runaway and homeless street youth. In The Boston Foundation (Ed.), *Homelessness: Critical issues for policy and practice* (pp. 24–28). Boston: Author.

Robertson, M. J. (1989). *Homeless youth in Hollywood: Patterns of alcohol use.* Berkeley, CA: Alcohol Research Group.

Robertson, M. J., Koegel, P., & Ferguson, L. (1989). Alcohol use and abuse among homeless adolescents in Hollywood. *Contemporary Drug Problems, 16,* 415–452.

Rotheram-Borus, M. J. (1991, February). *HIV prevention among adolescents.* Paper presented at the National Conference on Pediatric AIDS, Washington, DC.

Rotheram-Borus, M. J., & Koopman, C. (1991). Sexual risk behaviors, AIDS knowledge, and beliefs about AIDS among runaways. *American Journal of Public Health, 81,* 208–210.

Rotheram-Borus, M. J., Koopman, C., & Bradley, J. (1989). Barriers to successful AIDS prevention programs with runaway youth. In J. O. Woodruff, D. Doherty, & J. G. Athey (Eds.), *Troubled adolescents and HIV infection: Issues in prevention and treatment* (pp. 37–55). Washington, DC: CASSP Technical Assistance Center, Georgetown University Child Development Center.

Rotheram-Borus, M. J., Koopman, C., & Ehrhardt, A. (1991). Homeless youths and HIV infection. *American Psychologist, 46,* 1188–1997.

Rotheram-Borus, M. J., Rosario, M., & Koopman, C. (1991). Minority youths at high risk: Gay males and runaways. In S. Gore and M. E. Colton (Eds.), *Adolescence, stress and coping* (pp. 181–200). New York: Aldine Press.

Rothman, J., & David, T. (1985). Status offenders in Los Angeles County: Focus on runaway and homeless youth. Bush program in Child and Family Policy. Los Angeles: University of California Press.

Schroeder, P. (1989). Toward a national family policy. *American Psychologist, 44,* 1410–1413.

Shaffer, D., & Caton, D. (1984). *Runaway and homeless youth in New York City: A report to the Ittleson Foundation.* New York: Ittleson Foundation.

Shalwitz, J. C., Goulart, M., Dunnigan, K., & Flannery, D. (1990, June). *Prevalence of sexually transmitted diseases (STD) and HIV in a homeless youth medical clinic in San Francisco.* Paper presented at the sixth annual International Conference on AIDS, San Francisco, CA.

Shane, P. G. (1989). Changing patterns among homeless and runaway youth. *American Journal of Orthopsychiatry, 59,* 208–214.

Solarz, A. L. (1992). To be young and homeless: Implications of homelessness for children. In M. J. Robertson & M. Greenblatt (Eds.), *Homelessness: A National Perspective. Topics in Social Psychiatry.* (pp. 275–286). New York: Plenum.

Stricof, R., Novick, L. F., & Kennedy, J. (1990, June). *HIV-1 seroprevalence in facilities for runaway and homeless adolescents in four states: Florida, Texas, Louisiana, and New York.* Paper presented at the fourth annual International Conference on AIDS, San Francisco, CA.

Sullivan, P. A., & Damrosch, S. P. (1987). Homeless women and children. In R. D. Bingham, R. E. Green, & S. B. White (Eds.), *The homeless in contemporary society* (pp. 82–98). Newbury Park, CA: Sage Publications.

Windle, M. (1989). Substance use and abuse among adolescent runaways: A four-year follow-up study. *Journal of Youth and Adolescence, 18,* 331–344.

Yates, G., MacKenzie, R., Pennbridge, J., & Cohen, E. (1988). A risk profile comparison of runaway and non-runaway youth. *American Journal of Public Health, 78,* 820–821.

15 / **Children of Homosexual Parents**

Sarah E. Herbert and Helen Panarites

Our society has seen a significant shift in both the definition and structure of the family. Gay and lesbian parents represent one specific variety of family structure that child psychiatrists will encounter in their clinical practice. It is difficult to estimate the number of children being reared by gay and lesbian parents; indeed, there are inherent limitations in any attempt to do so. For example, a parent may fear that self-disclosure will result in loss of custody; the ensuing secrecy will result in an underestimation of the number of those involved. A "best approximation" is that the number of lesbian mothers is between one and five million (Hoeffer, 1981; Pennington, 1987; Falk, 1989; Patterson, 1992), and the number of gay fathers between one and three million (Bozett, 1988; Patterson, 1992). In sum, researchers have concluded that as many as 6 to 14 million children have gay or lesbian parents (Bozett, 1988; Editors of the Harvard Law Review, 1990; Patterson, 1992).

The majority of children of homosexual parents were conceived within the context of a heterosexual relationship. In fact, the earliest research was instigated by the courts to determine the developmental impact of lesbian mothers retaining custody of their children following divorce. Gay fathers were seldom studied because they rarely sought custody following divorce. Recently, there have been increasing numbers of lesbian couples choosing to conceive children using donor insemi-

nation (McCandlish, 1987; Pennington, 1987). In addition, today gay men and lesbians have greater opportunities to become foster parents and adoptive parents (Pollack & Vaughn, 1987). Therefore, even within the homosexual community, homosexual parents and their families are a more heterogenous and diverse group than before. This fact lends an additional layer of complexity to all the usual developmental questions.

The increasing size of the homosexual parent population dictates that these new family forms must be understood by child clinicians. A first step in this process involves clarifying misconceptions about homosexual parents. Evidence of these misconceptions was reflected in court decisions, parental attitudes, and psychiatric nomenclature. Prior to the removal of homosexuality from the Diagnostic and Statistical Manual of Mental Disorders-III as a diagnostic category, it was believed that gay men and lesbians were burdened with significant psychopathology and would be incompetent parents. In fact, research has shown no major differences in either the mental health of lesbians or their approaches to child rearing when compared to heterosexual women (Mucklow & Phelan, 1979; Pagelow, 1980). Additionally, courts and psychiatrists feared that the homosexual parent or partner would sexually abuse a child in his or her custody. These fears have not been borne out by any research data (Jenny, Roesler, & Poyer, 1994). Existing studies show that child molestation primarily involves heterosexual males and female children (Hutchens & Kirkpatrick, 1985).

Developmental Impact

What developmental impact does homosexual parenting have on children? This is not a simple question because of both the diversity of these family forms and the narrow scope of the research efforts undertaken to date. There is very little empirical data on gay fathers and their children, and few investigations have been done on children adopted into gay families or placed in foster care with gay parents. Research has focused almost exclusively on children raised by their lesbian mothers. As noted, the interest has shifted from children conceived within heterosexual relationships to those conceived via donor insemination.

Using the existing data on children raised by lesbian mothers, and recognizing that this represents only a subgroup of all children with homosexual parents, one can examine the impact of one specific form of parental homosexuality on child development. Obviously, these conclusions will not apply to all homosexual parents, but many common developmental assumptions can be made.

Erikson divided human development into 8 specific stages. The first 5 encompass the time period from infancy through adolescence. The impact of parental homosexuality will be examined using these first 5 stages of Erikson's developmental model (Erikson, 1959).

The first stage, from infancy through age 2, is characterized by the child's struggle with the conflict of "basic trust versus mistrust" of the primary caregiver (Erikson, 1959). The resolution of this conflict is primarily a task dependent on maternal factors such as empathy, responsiveness, and the mother's ability to meet the needs of her baby. How does being raised by a lesbian mother affect this developmental stage? Societal stereotypes suggest that lesbians detest feminine interests and activities. However, studies have shown that lesbian mothers have the same desire to bear and raise children as do heterosexual mothers, and that the maternal attitudes and self-concepts are quite similar for both groups (Mucklow & Phelan,

1979). Thus, the ability to be a good enough mother is a complex product of maternal values, attitudes, and personality, and not of sexual orientation. Like heterosexual women, lesbian mothers may or may not be good enough mothers, but their ability to do so is not related to their sexual orientation.

The second stage, ages 2 to 4 years, is defined by the child's struggle with the conflict of "autonomy versus shame and doubt" (Erikson, 1959). In effect, the child begins to develop self-control of bodily functions and language, is separating from mother, and is testing the boundaries of his or her outer world, while experiencing his or her own sense of vulnerability and inadequacy at the same time. Firm parental limits and consistency without shaming are crucial at this stage for the development of self-control without loss of self-esteem. A study of 3 year-olds raised by lesbian couples showed that the presence of a female co-parent, rather than a father, did not adversely affect separation-individuation; however, it did establish a qualitatively different separation experience (Steckel, 1987). Children of heterosexual parents saw themselves as more aggressive than did children of lesbians and were in turn perceived by teachers and parents as more bossy, domineering, and negative. Children of lesbian parents, on the other hand, saw themselves as more lovable and were regarded by teachers and parents as more affectionate, more responsive, and more protective toward younger children. Given the small sample size, this study is only suggestive of a possible developmental difference (Steckel, 1987).

Another feature of this developmental stage is the establishment of gender identity, which is defined as a clear sense of being male or female (Money & Ehrhardt, 1972). There is no evidence to suggest that children raised by homosexual parents have any difficulty with gender identity development (Green, 1978; Kirkpatrick, Smith, & Roy, 1981).

The third stage, ages 4 to 6 years old, is characterized by the conflict of "initiative versus guilt" and corresponds to Freud's oedipal stage (Erikson, 1959). At this time, children take the initiative in fantasy and action to compete with the same-sex parent in order to win outright the love of the opposite-sex parent. A conflict arises when these fantasies create feelings of guilt in the children, who then develop a fear of specific bodily harm, commonly termed castration anxiety. A resolution occurs with the identification with the same-sex parent, which allows the driving sexual and aggressive forces to be channeled into other avenues. These sublimations become the vehicles for the child's initiative. This identification with the same-sex parent contributes to the development of gender role behavior. Furthermore, this balance of "initiative versus guilt" is crucial for superego development and a sense of moral responsibility.

What is the developmental impact of parental homosexuality at this stage of child development? Erikson's model would predict a negative outcome for children raised by homosexual parents. For example, boys raised by lesbian mothers, who had no available father, would lack the potential for same-sex parental identification and would have difficulty with gender role development. The research, however, has specifically refuted this hypothesis. Significant data were sought concerning the development of gender role behavior in children raised by lesbian mothers. These children were interviewed regarding toy choices and activity preferences. They showed appropriate sex-typed choices and reported typical vocational choices within conventional sex roles (Green, 1978). Furthermore, controlled studies of children ages 5 to 17 raised by lesbian mothers, again found no significant difference in gender role behavior when compared to children of heterosexual single mothers (Golombok, Spencer, & Rutter, 1983; Green, Mandel, Hotvedt, Gray, & Smith, 1986; Hoeffer, 1981; Kirkpatrick, Smith, & Roy, 1981). The lack of gender identity disturbances in boys reared by single or divorced heterosexual mothers supports this conclusion. Daughters of lesbian mothers, however, did show a wider range of gender-behaviors and were less traditionally feminine, but they were not beyond the normal range.

It should be noted that all these children were initially born into a heterosexual household; consequently, during the critical stage when gender identity and gender role behavior are established they had some opportunity for same-sex parental identification. However, one research study found that lesbian mothers were more concerned with providing male role models for their children than the comparison group of single heterosexual mothers (Kirkpatrick, Smith, & Roy, 1981). Other data have shown that when compared to controls,

a higher proportion of the children of divorced lesbians had regular contact with their fathers (Golombok, Spencer, & Rutter, 1983).

What is the result when children are reared from infancy by homosexual parents? Recent studies of children conceived via donor insemination and reared solely by a lesbian couple have likewise shown normal development of gender identity and sex-role behaviors (McCandlish, 1987; Patterson, 1992).

As mentioned before, this stage of "initiative versus guilt" is also the time for superego development. There are no outcome data that specifically examine superego development as such in children raised by lesbian mothers. Behavioral problems and conduct problems, however, were found to be less frequent in these children when compared to a control group of children raised by single heterosexual mothers (Golombok, Spencer, & Rutter, 1983). This finding suggests that parental homosexuality, as an independent variable, has no significant impact on superego development.

The fourth stage, the school-age years, is characterized by the conflict of "industry versus inferiority" (Erikson, 1959). This stage requires an extension of the child's social world into the realm of school. Here the child must interact with peers and begins to develop a sense of self-worth as defined by the rules and values of society. It is during this crucial time, when peer relationships become extremely important, and the child begins to perceive social differences, that feelings of social inferiority can take form.

How does homosexual parenting influence this specific developmental stage? First, there has been concern that the social stigma of being raised by homosexual parents would interfere with the child's peer relationships. Second, one might predict that the social stigma would disrupt the development of self-esteem and create feelings of inferiority.

Studies using parents' and teachers' reports to assess the quality of peer relationships have shown that children of homosexual parents develop normal peer relationships and manifest no significant differences when compared to children reared by heterosexual single mothers (Golombok, Spencer, & Rutter, 1983; Green, Mandel, Hotvedt, Gray, & Smith, 1986). On the other hand, the data obtained from clinical interviews of the children reared by lesbian mothers are much more complicated. In an effort to understand the feelings and struggles experienced by these children, Lewis (1980) interviewed 21 children of lesbian mothers. Although these children had good peer relationships, the process of forming and maintaining these friendships included a need for secrecy and a sense of isolation and differentness (Lewis, 1980). One might hypothesize that the development of this family secret would result in a family system characterized by enmeshment. No clear data, however, have been gathered on homosexual family dynamics.

The children's self-concepts and the development of self-esteem have been investigated. Latency age children of lesbian mothers reported more intense stress reactions, but they also reported a greater overall sense of well-being compared to children of heterosexual mothers (Patterson, 1992). This wide range of emotional experiences is perplexing. A greater tendency for these children to admit feeling angry or upset may be a result of the increased day-to-day stress of living in a homosexual household. On the other hand, it may be a result of greater freedom to talk about emotions, whether positive or negative, encouraged in a household headed by two female parents (Patterson, 1992). These issues must be pursued through further research.

The issue of social stigma is not unique to children with homosexual parents. Many other characteristics make children and their families different: race, religion, mental illness, a parent in prison, and physical disability, among others. The family's strategies for managing this stigma may protect against feelings of inferiority and are crucial to healthy development of self-esteem. As they grew up, the parents of these children had to learn to manage the stigma of homosexuality themselves, and thus may be well prepared to show their children ways to deal with the associated issues. The opposite may also be true; the social ostracism may beget an unhealed wound that always hurts and whose effects are communicated to the children.

Erikson's fifth developmental stage occurs during adolescence and is characterized by the conflict of "identity versus role diffusion" (Erikson, 1959). The developmental tasks include a psychological separation from parents and a strong shift toward peer relationships and peer loyalty. Adolescents begin to explore intimate sexual relationships and thereby enter the final phase of consolidating their sexual identity and sexual orientation. In addition, it is a time of peer conformity and extreme intolerance for those who differ from the peer group.

Research data on adolescents who are being reared by homosexual parents is quite limited. A primary concern has been the development of their sexual orientation. This has been studied by inquiring about the erotic fantasies, romantic crushes and sexual behavior of adolescents raised by lesbian mothers (Green, 1978; Golombok, Spencer, & Rutter, 1983). The available data have shown that these teenagers had typical heterosexual fantasies and heterosexual orientations. These conclusions may be slightly premature since many individuals, expecially women, do not identify their sexual orientation as homosexual until early adulthood. Therefore, further study of the development of these children into adulthood is needed to arrive at a firmer conclusion.

Recent research has suggested that genetic influences may play a role in the development of sexual orientation (Bailey, Pillard, Neale, & Agyei, 1993). This factor is currently the center of considerable controversy, but it would need to be considered when looking at the sexual orientation of the biological children of gay and lesbian parents.

A second concern for adolescent children reared by homosexual parents is the maintenance of self-esteem. Teenaged children of divorced lesbian mothers reported no difference in their level of self-esteem when compared to adolescent children of divorced heterosexual mothers (Huggins, 1989). However, when the group of female adolescents raised by lesbian mothers was compared to female adolescents of heterosexual mothers, one difference in the data was noted. Within the group of female adolescents reared by lesbian mothers, there was a significant split in the levels of self-esteem. This population was clearly divided into smaller groups of females with high self-esteem and females with low self-esteem. When averaged, this led to the conclusion that no difference existed. On examination of the data, high self-esteem among adolescent females was correlated with four specific factors: (1) daughter's awareness of mothers' lesbianism at an early age; (2) mother's living with her lesbian lover; (3) father's acceptance of mother's lesbianism; and (4) daughter's positive view of mother's lesbianism (Huggins, 1989). These findings are consistent with the theory that high self-esteem correlates with a positive identification with the same-sex parent. They also provide suggestions for preventive interventions that may help maintain self-esteem in these adolescents.

Clinical vignettes and case reports indicate that adolescence is a particularly difficult time for children to be informed about parental homosexuality (Javaid, 1983; Weeks, Derdeyn, & Langman, 1975). Examples of specific reactive behavior have included teenage girls becoming pregnant in order to reaffirm their own sexual identity. Boys have reacted by acting out in order to drive away their mother's lover. This latter dynamic is very similar to that which occurs when stepparents enter an established family and are treated as outsiders by the children (Stein, 1988). These, however, are isolated anecdotes about children referred to mental health clinicians; they do not generalize to all adolescents reared by homosexual parents.

Gay Fathers

Most of the previously summarized research involved lesbian mothers and their children. Gay fathers have not been the focus of equivalent research attention since they have not been as likely to gain custody of their children. If the estimate that 20 to 25% of gay men are fathers is accurate, however, there are a substantial number of children affected by this issue. Gay fathers are increasingly being recognized, as more men have become willing to disclose their homosexuality. Gay men have recently had more opportunities to become foster and adoptive parents. What, then, is known about these homosexual fathers and how does their situation resemble or differ from that of lesbian mothers?

In general, gay fathers are similar to heterosexual fathers in their reasons for having children. However, one study found a few differences. Gay fathers placed greater emphasis than did the heterosexual fathers on the function of parenthood in conveying social status and gaining acceptibility as an adult member of the community. The heterosexual men offered more traditional values such as continuing the family name, ensuring security in their old age, and carrying on family traditions (Bigner & Jacobsen, 1989).

In the very little research that has been done on the quality of parenting by gay fathers, when gay fathers are compared to heterosexual fathers, no differences in attitudes toward fathering or parenting styles have been found (Harris & Turner, 1986; Bigner & Jacobsen, 1989, 1992).

There are no studies which shed light on the sexual identity and sexual orientation of children reared by gay fathers. While it is doubtful that the research would show a very different outcome than the studies on lesbian mothers and their children, this work remains to be done (Bigner & Jacobsen, 1989).

The issue of disclosure of parental homosexuality, however, appears to be even more problematic for gay fathers. Fewer of them have custody of their children and, compared to lesbian mothers, fewer disclose their homosexuality to their children. More gay fathers report that their children have difficulties with peers because of parental homosexuality. This is not surprising, as our society has generally been much less tolerant of male homosexuality than female (Bozett, 1989). When disclosure to the children has taken place, the youngsters are frequently more accepting then expected (Bozett, 1989).

Overall, based on the admittedly sparse research, one may conclude that being a gay man is indeed compatible with effective parenting.

Clinical Implications

The clinical implications of these findings raise new issues. The data suggest that children raised by homosexual parents are far more resilient than our theoretical developmental model would have predicted. The concerns of the courts, adoption agencies, and heterosexual parents do not appear to be well-founded. In fact, there is no clear evidence to support any increased risk of sexual identity problems, behavioral problems, or psychiatric disorders among children reared by homosexual parents (Patterson, 1992). The individual parent-child relationship and the quality of parenting far outweigh parental sexual orientation as significant factors affecting child development.

According to the existing studies, the development of self-esteem may be dependent in part on the parents' ability to help their children manage the social stigma of homosexuality. This implies that homosexual parents who have comfortably accepted their own sexual orientation, compared to homosexual parents who feel guilty or embarrassed about their sexual orientation, may be better equipped to help their children cope with the stigma of growing up in a homosexual family.

We know from studies of divorced parents and their children that parents' attitudes toward each other can have a significant impact on the adjustment of the children. Hence, it is not surprising that the impact of divorce and a father's attitude toward a mother's lesbianism can play a significant role in shaping a daughter's development of self-esteem (Huggins, 1989).

Furthermore, clinical experience suggests that a parent's degree of secrecy versus openness may be highly correlated to the development of self-esteem in the children. Unfortunately, many homosexual parents do not disclose their sexual orientation for practical and real reasons; such parents may have legitimate fears that they will lose custody of their children, lose their jobs, or bring their families into disarray. Therefore, they have to balance the advantages and disadvantages of being open about their sexual orientation.

The age at which a child learns of his or her parent's homosexuality may have specific clinical implications. Developmentally appropriate explanations will be necessary to help the child understand the biology of his or her conception, or the concept of sexual orientation. Donor insemination may be a very difficult concept for a young child to understand. On the other hand, a younger child might be able to accept simple explanations about an alternative family more readily than older children. Adolescents may struggle more intensely with the issue of parental homosexuality; after all, their developmental needs are to conform to peer group norms and to consolidate their own sexual identity. Societal stigma or sexual orientation issues may be more salient at this age than at others.

Another implication of this research is that children's development is facilitated rather than hindered, when a lesbian mother is in a stable, loving relationship (Huggins, 1989). Children develop strong and important attachments to both the biological mother and her partner. The presence of two adult parental figures, whether homosexual or heterosexual, is an obvious advantage which provides support during the demanding times of child rearing. This conclusion is contrary to that which the courts had heretofore assumed in their decisions.

Clinical Interventions

Child psychiatrists are occasionally asked to evaluate families with a homosexual parent when child custody is at issue. Given the lack of data suggesting that children are harmed by living with a homosexual parent, it would be important to help the courts understand that homosexuality is not incompatible with effective parenting. In fact, the dissolution or disruption of these families would be just as difficult for children of homosexual parents as divorce would be for children of heterosexual parents.

Advocacy on behalf of their children may be necessary for gay and lesbian parents. Interventions with the school, teachers, and other parents may offer some measure of understanding. Educational books have been used to explain different types of families in classrooms where there is a child with gay or lesbian parents (see Resources for Children of Gay and Lesbian Parents). The level of social ostracism is such, however, that some school libraries and classrooms have been forced to eliminate such books.

Children who feel isolated from peers because of their need to hide the family secret of homosexuality may benefit from a safe place to talk about these feelings. Social activities with other homosexual parents and their children, or participation in a support group for children of homosexual parents might alleviate some of the feelings of isolation and differentness.

If homosexual couples are conflicted about their roles with the children, and the family is not functioning effectively, family therapy may be useful. As noted, inclusion of the homosexual parent's partner into the household creates problems similar to those faced by children of divorce where a heterosexual parent remarries. Clarification of roles may be necessary to help the family function more effectively. However, the issue of homosexuality contributes additional complexity to the definition of roles (Baptiste, 1988). The clinician treating such a family should recognize the special issues which make the situation for homosexual families very different. The parent's partner may function as a stepparent, but there is no legally sanctioned or culturally defined role for him or her. If, moreover, the new partner brings his or her children into the household, there is no word to define the children's relationship to each other. There are few role models and no social support system for these nontraditional families (Stein, 1988).

Effective therapeutic intervention with homosexual families requires that the therapist be knowledgeable about homosexuality and comfortable working with gay or lesbian individuals. It is important to be sensitive to the effects that societal attitudes toward homosexuality have on these families. Yet, it is equally imortant to recognize that not all the family's difficulties stem from parental homosexuality. Many of the issues they bring to therapy are the same as those seen in more traditional families (Baptiste, 1988).

Conclusion

The existing research on children reared by a lesbian mother indicates that there are no significant problems which distinguish them from peers being reared by a divorced heterosexual mother. This statement must be qualified because the existing studies focus almost exclusively on children reared by previously married lesbian mothers. Study of a more diverse population of children being reared by homosexual parents is needed. It has been noted previously that lesbians and gay men are more frequently conceiving children by donor insemination, adopted children, or becoming foster parents. Since little is known about the effect of homosexual parenting on these children, they should be included in future research on this subject.

Longitudinal follow-up of children into their adult years would be an important addition to the current data. Since many of the children studied have been too young to make definitive assessments of sexual orientation, this would provide further important information.

More needs to be known about the most effective and developmentally appropriate way to tell children about the mode of their conception and the sexual orientation of their parents. Delineation of which coping mechanisms would most effectively help children manage the stigma of having homosexual parents would be of great use.

In conclusion, the existing research gives no evidence to support the contention that there is an increased risk of sexual identity problems, behavioral problems, or psychiatric disorders among children reared by homosexual parents (Patterson, 1992).

REFERENCES

Agbayewa, M. (1984). Fathers in the new family forms: male or female? *Canadian Journal of Psychiatry, 29*, 402–406.

Bailey, J. M., Pillard, R. C., Neale, M. C., & Agyei, Y. (1993). Heritable factors influence sexual orientation in women. *Archives of General Psychiatry, 50*, 217–223.

Baptiste, D. A. (1988). Psychotherapy with gay/lesbian couples and their children in "stepfamilies": A challenge for marriage and family therapists. In E. Coleman (Ed.), *Integrated identity for gay men and lesbians: Psychotherapeutic approaches for well-being* (pp. 223–238). New York: Harrington Park Press.

Barret, R. L., & Robinson, B. E. (1990). *Gay fathers.* Lexington, MA: D.C. Heath.

Bell, A. P., & Weinberg, M. S. (1978). *Homosexualities: A study of diversity among men and women.* New York: Simon & Schuster.

Bigner, J. J., & Jacobsen, R. B. (1989). Parenting behaviors of homosexual and heterosexual fathers. *Journal of Homosexuality, 18*, 163–172.

Bigner, J. J., & Bozett, F. W. (1990). Parenting by gay fathers. In F. W. Bozett & M. B. Sussman (Eds.), *Homosexuality and family relations* (pp. 155–176). New York: Harrington Park Press.

Bigner, J. J., & Jacobsen, R. B. (1992). Adult responses to child behavior and attitudes toward fathering: Gay and nongay fathers. *Journal of Homosexuality, 23*(3), 99–112.

Bozett, F. W. (1988). Social control of identity by children of gay fathers. *Western Journal of Nursing Research, 10*, 550–565.

Bozett, F. W. (1989). Gay fathers: A review of the literature. *Journal of Homosexuality, 18*, 137–162.

Cramer, D. (1986). Gay parents and their children: A

review of research and practical implications. *Journal of Counseling and Development, 64,* 504–507.

Crawford, S. (1986). Lesbian families: Psychosocial stress and the family-building process. In Boston Lesbian Psychologies Collective (Eds.), *Lesbian psychologies* (pp. 194–214). Urbana: University of Illinois Press.

Di Bella, G. (1979). Family psychotherapy with the homosexual family: A community psychiatry approach to homosexuality. *Community Mental Health Journal, 15*(1), 41–46.

DiLapi, E. M. (1989). Lesbian mothers and the motherhood hierarchy. *Journal of Homosexuality, 18*(1–2), 101–121.

Editors of the Harvard Law Review. (1990). *Sexual orientation and the law.* Cambridge: Harvard University Press.

Erikson, E. H. (1959). Identity and the life cycle. *Psychological Issues, 1*(1), 1–171.

Falk, P. J. (1989). Lesbian mothers. Psychosocial assumptions in family law. *American Psychologist, 44*(6), 941–947.

Gartrell, N., & Hamilton, J. (1994). Lesbian mother study. Presentation at Women in Medicine Annual Conference.

Golombok, S., Spencer, M., & Rutter, M. (1983). Children in lesbian and single parent households: Psychosexual and psychiatric appraisal. *Journal of Child Psychology and Psychiatry, 24*(4), 551–572.

Green, G. D. (1987). Lesbian mothers: Mental health considerations. In F. Bozett (Ed.), *Gay and lesbian parents* (pp. 188–198). New York: Prager Publishers.

Green, R. (1978). Sexual identity of 37 children raised by homosexual or transsexual parents. *American Journal of Psychiatry, 135,* 692–697.

Green, R. (1982). The best interests of the child with a lesbian mother. *Bulletin of the American Academy of Psychiatry and Law, 10*(1), 7–15.

Green, R., Mandel, J. B., Hotvedt, M. E., Gray, J., & Smith, L. (1986). Lesbian mothers and their children: A comparison with solo parent heterosexual mothers and their children. *Archives of Sexual Behavior, 15*(2), 167–185.

Hall, M. (1978). Lesbian families: Cultural and clinical issues. *Social Work,* 380–385.

Harris, M. B., & Turner, P. H. (1986). Gay and lesbian parents. *Journal of Homosexuality, 12*(2), 101–113.

Herman, S. P. (1990). Special issues in child custody evaluations. *Journal of the American Academy of Child and Adolescent Psychiatry, 29*(6), 969–974.

Hoeffer, B. (1981). Children's acquisition of sex-role behavior in lesbian-mother families. *American Journal of Orthopsychiatry, 51,* 536–541.

Huggins, S. L. (1989). A comparative study of self-esteem of adolescent children of divorced lesbian mothers and divorced heterosexual mothers. *Journal of Homosexuality, 18*(1–2), 123–135.

Hutchens, D. J., & Kirkpatrick, M. (1985). Lesbian mothers/gay fathers. In D. H. Schetky & E. P. Benedek (Eds.), *Emerging issues in child psychiatry*

and the law (pp. 115–126). New York: Brunner/Mazel.

Javaid, G. A. (1983). The sexual development of the adolescent daughter of a homosexual mother. *Journal of the American Academy of Child Psychiatry, 22*(2), 196–201.

Jenny, C., Roesler, T., & Poyer, K. (1994). Are children at risk for sexual abuse by homosexuals? *Pediatrics, 94*(1), 41–46.

Kirkpatrick, M. (1987). Clinical implications of lesbian mother studies. *Journal of Homosexuality, 14*(1–2), 201–211.

Kirkpatrick, M., Smith, C., & Roy, R. (1981). Lesbian mothers and their children: A comparative survey. *American Journal of Orthopsychiatry, 51*(3), 545–551.

Kleber, D. J., Howell, R. J., & Tibbits-Kleber, A. L. (1986). The impact of parental homosexuality in child custody cases: A review of the literature. *Bulletin of the American Academy of Psychiatry and Law, 14*(1), 81–87.

Kweskin, S. L., & Cook, A. S. (1982). Heterosexual and homosexual mothers' self-described sex-role behavior and ideal sex-role behavior in children. *Sex Roles, 8*(9), 967–975.

Lewis, K. G. (1980). Children of lesbians: Their point of view. *Social Work, 25*(3), 198–203.

McCandlish, B. M. (1987). Against all odds: Lesbian mother family dynamics. In F. W. Bozett (Ed.), *Gay and lesbian parents* (pp. 23–36).

Miller, J. A., Jacobsen, R. B., & Bigner, J. J. (1982). The child's home environment for lesbian vs. heterosexual mothers: A neglected area of research. *Journal of Homosexuality, 7*(1), 49–56.

Money, J., & Ehrhardt, A. A. (1972). *Man and woman, Boy and girl.* Baltimore: Johns Hopkins University Press.

Mucklow, R. M., & Phelan, G. K. (1979). Lesbian and traditional mothers' responses to adult response to child behavior and self-concept. *Psychological Reports, 44*(3), 880–882.

Nungesser, L. G. (1980). Theoretical bases for research on the acquisition of social sex-roles by children of lesbian mothers. *Journal of Homosexuality, 5*(3), 177–187.

Pagelow, M. D. (1980). Heterosexual and lesbian single mothers: a comparison of problems, coping, and solutions. *Journal of Homosexuality, 5*(3), 189–204.

Patterson, C. (1992). Children of lesbian and gay parents. *Child Development, 63,* 1025–1042.

Patterson, C. (1994). Children of the lesbian baby boom: Behavioral adjustment, self-concepts, and sex-role identity. In B. Greene & G. M. Herek (Eds.), *Psychological perspectives on lesbian and gay issues: Vol. 1. Lesbian and gay psychology: Theory, research, and clinical applications* (pp. 156–175). Thousand Oaks, CA: Sage Publications.

Pennington, S. B. (1987). Children of lesbian mothers. In F. W. Bozett (Ed.), *Gay and lesbian parents* (pp. 58–74).

Peters, D. K., & Cantrell, P. J. (1991). Factors distinguishing samples of lesbian and heterosexual women. *Journal of Homosexuality, 21*(4), 1–15.

Pollack, S., & Vaughn, J. (Eds.). (1987). *Politics of the heart: A lesbian parenting anthology.* Ithaca, NY: Firebrand Books.

Ricketts, W., & Achtenberg, R. (1987). The adoptive and foster gay and lesbian parent. In F. W. Bozett (Ed.), *Gay and lesbian parents* (pp. 89–111).

Robinson, B. E., & Skeen, P. (1982). Sex-role orientation of gay fathers versus non-fathers. *Perceptual and Motor Skills, 55,* 1055–1059.

Steckel, A. (1987). Psychosocial development of children of lesbian mothers. In F. W. Bozett (Ed.),

Gay and lesbian parents (pp. 75–85). New York: Praeger.

Stein, T. S. (1988). Homosexuality and new family forms: Issues in psychotherapy. *Psychiatric Annals, 18*(1), 12–20.

Tasker, F., & Golombok, S. (1991). Children raised by lesbian mothers. The empirical evidence. *Family Law,* 184–187.

Weeks, R. B., Derdeyn, A. P., & Langman, M. (1975). Two cases of children of homosexuals. *Child Psychiatry and Human Development, 6*(1), 26–32.

Weisner, T. S., & Wilson-Mitchell, J. E. (1990). Nonconventional family lifestyles and sex-typing in six year olds. *Child Development, 60,* 1915–1933.

RESOURCES FOR CHILDREN OF GAY AND LESBIAN PARENTS

Elwin, R., & Paulse, M. (1990). *Asha's mums.* Toronto, Ontario: Women's Press.

Heron, A., & Maran, M. (1991). *How would you feel if your dad was gay?* Boston: Alyson Publications.

Newman, L. (1989). *Heather has two mommies.* Boston: Alyson Publications.

Rafkin, L. (Ed.). (1990). *Different mothers: Sons and daughters of lesbians talk about their lives.* San Francisco: Cleis Press.

Willhoite, M. (1990). *Daddy's roommate.* Boston: Alyson Publications.

RESOURCES FOR GAY AND LESBIAN PARENTS

Barret, R. L., & Robinson, B. E. (1990). *Gay fathers.* Lexington, MA: Lexington Books.

Gay and Lesbian Parents Coalition International (GLPCI). P. O. Box 50360, Washington, DC 20091

Martin, A. (1993). *The lesbian and gay parenting handbook: Creating and raising our families.* New York: HarperCollins.

Pollack, S., & Vaughn, J. (Eds.). (1987). *Politics of the heart: A lesbian parenting anthology.* Ithaca, NY: Firebrand Books.

Schulenberg, J. A. (1985). *Gay parenting.* Garden City, NY: Anchor Press/Doubleday.

16 / Latchkey Children

Lizette Peterson and Cindy M. Schaeffer

The expanding number of children in this country who for part of their day do not have an adult supervisor present have often been labeled latchkey children (Belle, 1994). This term was derived from the key the children wear around their neck or carry in their shoe to allow them entry to an empty house after school (Robinson, Rowland, & Coleman, 1986). Other labels for such children include children in self-care (Coolsen, Seligson, & Garbarino, 1985; Rodman, Pratto, & Nelson, 1985) and children on their own (Peterson & Magrab, 1989). The labels define the population, a group of children who bear the responsibility for and enjoy the freedom of making their own choices, determining their own activities, and ensuring their own safety for some time before school, directly after school, or during the evening hours.

A latchkey population may have existed two decades ago, but if so it was small and was not considered in the child development literature. As recently as the 1960s, only a minority (19%) of mothers of elementary school children were employed full time, and thus most mothers were available to give after-school care. In 1991, in contrast, nearly 60% of mothers of children under age 6 were full-time employees (U.S. Bureau of the Census, 1992). Existing institutionalized after-school care accounts for only a small proportion of children, and estimates of children in self-care range from 2.1 to well over 15 million (Nienhuis, 1987).

Because the phenomenon is so recent, the influence of self-care on long-term cognitive and emotional development is uncertain. Furthermore, the area shows no strong signs of research growth. In addition, very little published research exists that empirically addresses the influence during adolescence and adulthood of having been in self-care as a child. Messer, Wuensch, and Diamond (1989) used a college sample to compare students who were formerly latchkey children to those who were not and found no significant differences between the groups on academic functioning or measures of personality. However, this is a very select and small sample with null findings, so definitive conclusions must await further research. However, a number of recent findings also challenge the early alarm raised by journalists responding to self-care and suggest a more careful consideration of the pros and cons of self-care on a case-by-case basis.

Common Misconceptions

EMOTIONAL TRAUMA

One of the most common erroneous beliefs is that self-care invariably results in some emotional trauma to the child. Such beliefs seem to have

originated with popular press articles with "catchy" titles such as "The Loneliness of the Latchkey Child" (Scherer, 1982), "Latchkey Blues: When Kids Come Home" (Lapinski, 1982), "The Unspoken Fears of Latchkey Kids" (Long & Long, 1982b), and "The Lonely Life of Latchkey Children" (Long & Long, 1982a). Such articles focus on highly selected cases who have been subjected to rather leading interviews and suggested that latchkey experiences lead to fear, depression, and loneliness.

There is no doubt that some latchkey children experience intense fear about being left without parental supervision (Peterson, 1987) and that, for others, loneliness is a real concern. However, studies that have examined random samples of such children find low levels of fearfulness (Rodman et al., 1985) and anxiety due to being home alone (Lovko & Ullman, 1989), and do not find that children typically report being lonely.

How *do* most children feel about being left at home alone? Reactions vary a great deal, depending on the child's situation. The most common negative reaction is boredom (Lovko & Ullman, 1989), which is more common when the child is alone, confined to the home, and does not have preplanned activities or chores. Other children report that they enjoy the time in which they are in charge of the home. They may enjoy the solitude or the ability to engage in activities that are not welcomed when parents are present (e.g., children often mention being able to play their favorite music at their favorite volume on the stereo). Some mention feeling that they are contributing to the family by managing their own care or by taking care of chores in their parents' absence.

Some studies report positive influences on individual development (Batchelder & Winnykamen, 1995) from engaging in self-care. Overall, it appears that in the short-term, the impact of being in self-care is rarely strongly negative and may even be positive for many children.

READINESS FOR SELF-CARE

Ironically, in contrast to the idea that self-care is emotionally damaging is the other most common misconception in this area, the belief that most children are sufficiently prepared for self-care by brief parental discussions and once-yearly presentations by police and fire department officials at school. When a sample of community parents and children were asked independently about the child's ability to deal with day-to-day demands (e.g., answering the telephone) and potential emergencies (e.g., a pipe bursts, a fire occurs), both parents and children rated the child's ability to deal with the situations as good and the child's preparation to be home alone as above average (Peterson, Mori, & Scissors, 1986). However, further testing revealed that these children had only a fraction of the skills and knowledge that they themselves and their parents felt they had. Peterson (1989b) overviewed eight studies in which children's abilities to deal with commonly occurring household tasks were tested. This review noted that none of the 8- to 10-year-old children tested with role-plays had acceptable skills in any of the safety areas tested. Similar results were found when children in self-care were confronted with actual phone calls and package deliveries from strangers; the majority of the children in the sample opened the door to the stranger or revealed on the phone that they were home alone (Kraizer, Witte, Fryer, & Myoshi, 1990). Thus, in contrast to popular belief, most children are insufficiently prepared for self-care. Further, as will be detailed later, most commonly used methods for preparing children for home care are woefully inadequate. There are some workplace programs evolving to examine and train children's self-care, but they have not been extensively evaluated (Colan, Mague, Ronna, & Robert, 1994). Such programs, if empirically validated in the future, may mark a positive change in the health and well-being of latchkey children.

Impact of Self-Care

There are few studies currently on the long-term effects of being in self-care. However, short-term effects have been studied and may offer insight into possible longer-term impact.

CHILDHOOD

Most states regard leaving a very young child without supervision as neglect or abandonment (Missouri Revised Statutes, 1994). Many states regard age 8 as the youngest acceptable age for self-care. Of course, actual decisions concerning self-care should be made on the basis of the environment and the child's cognitive, affective, and social development and not on chronological age. For children 8 to 12 years of age, there are a variety of different kinds of impact of self-care that may be mitigated by their individual skills and circumstances.

Physical Safety: The most important concern for those evaluating the risks of self-care should be the child's physical safety. Unintentional injuries kill more children in the United States than all other causes of death combined, disable over 30,000 children permanently, and necessitate emergency medical treatment for 16 million children each year (Rodriguez, 1990). Children are more likely to be seriously injured at home if they do not have an adult caregiver available (Haller, 1970; Marcus et al., 1960). They may engage in behavior that involves more risk when an adult is not available to ban the activity (e.g., most fireworks, match playing, and flammable solvent injuries occur outside of parental supervision). Children are less able to avoid a hazard than is an adult (e.g., escape from a fire, evaluate the speed of an oncoming car, or avoid a fallen power line) and know less about minimizing the damage when a hazard is contacted (e.g., direct pressure on a cut, cold water on a burn, or cardiopulmonary resuscitation in a near drowning). The entire safety continuum may improve with the presence of a vigilant adult caregiver.

Personal safety is also of growing concern. The magnitude of child sexual abuse is just beginning to be understood, with estimates ranging from 1.4 victims per 1,000 children that are actually reported (American Humane Association, 1984) to around 20% of adult women retrospectively reporting (Finkelhor, 1979; Russell, 1983). Clearly, the absence of concerned parental supervision is one of the most important risk factors for sexual abuse in a child (Finkelhor, 1984).

Thus, perhaps the most important potential impact of self-care is that the child is at greater physical risk for unintentional injury and molestation.

Poor Health Lifestyle: Many parents of children in self-care attempt to ensure their children's safety by insisting that the child remain in the locked apartment or home until the parent returns in the evening. Although this may avoid certain kinds of injury, this strategy also prevents the child from engaging in a variety of important activities that typically fill children's after-school hours. Engaging in active play and sports increases children's cardiovascular fitness (Alpert, Field, Goldstein, & Perry, 1990) and increases their coordination and their self-confidence. After-school activities also often involve more open-peer interaction than is possible during the regimented school day and thus form an important source of children's social skills. Latchkey children who are not allowed to play in the neighborhood miss the opportunities for such physical and social interaction.

Children in self-care relegated to the home most typically do not do their homework or their chores. What do they do? Guerney (1991) found that the primary coping activity among self-care children calling a hotline was watching television. Similarly, Posner and Vandell (1994) found that self-care children watched more television and engaged in fewer social and academic activities than did children in formal after-school programs. In an aptly titled article, Dietz and Gortmaker (1985) asked, "Do we fatten our children at the television set? Obesity and television viewing in children and adolescents" and answer in the affirmative. Combining high-calorie snacks with lack of activity equals a lifestyle with long-term cardiac risk, in addition to diminished physical and social skills.

Cognitive/Affective Costs: As noted earlier, the short-term affective consequences of self-care do not seem as dismal as early articles predicted. However, boredom is a commonly mentioned side effect of latchkeyism. Further, there is some evidence that children's cognitive and emotional needs are not being met on a daily basis. For example, early content analysis of calls on Phone-Friend, the telephone helpline for children, suggests that children need help solving everyday problems (e.g., "I left my book at school. What should I do?"), particularly social problems (e.g., "The boys all make fun of me when I walk by. I have to go that way. What can I do?") and that they have an unmet need for emotional expression (e.g., "I want someone to listen to how I feel") (Guerney & Moore, 1983; Peterson, 1990). The persistent failure to have such needs met may have developmental consequences that have not

yet been realized, and these consequences may become more problematic in adolescence. Indeed, there is some evidence that self-care children display more antisocial behavior problems than children who return home to a parent or who participate in formal after-school programs (Posner & Vandell, 1994). The intensity of the cognitive/affective costs is likely to be related to the extent to which the parents meet these needs after they return home and the degree to which children find alternative ways of meeting their immediate needs. Some studies have suggested that it is the feeling of emotional connectedness with the parent and not just the frequency of control that determines if emotional needs are met (Belle, 1994). In some cases, researchers found that pets assisted children in "feeling good and safe" in their parents' absence (e.g., Guerney, 1991).

TEEN YEARS

For the most part, society does not recognize teenagers as latchkey children. In fact, many adults consider teenage baby-sitters as one solution to the latchkey problem. There are subsequently few data on the influence of lack of supervision past elementary school. However, one study challenges the complacency of this attitude. Steinberg (1986) reported that some teenage latchkey children are at greater risk for antisocial behavior such as early drug and alcohol use and sexual intercourse. Youth who reported home after school, even if there was no adult physically present, fared as well as those with a parent at home. However, teenagers who did not go home but described "hanging out" in the neighborhood were found to engage in more problematic behaviors. The meaning of supervision clearly shifts from childhood to adolescence, but it may be that the importance of having some sort of supervision intensifies rather than diminishes in the older years.

Interventions

Interventions to avoid the negative side effects of a latchkey existence form a continuum ranging from the situation where one parent gives up his or her job to stay home to a choice in which the child is left alone in self-care. This section briefly considers the alternatives between these two ends of the continuum.

PARENTAL SUPERVISION

Some parents manage to work and still be home after school by arranging flexible time, working swing shifts, or working three-quarters of the time. All of these options presuppose that the parent can either work 18-hour days with no diminished capacity for "quality time" or can afford the loss in wages three-quarter time entails. Often such job flexibility is not possible, especially in minimum-wage positions.

CO-OP PARENTING

A variation of parental supervision, co-op parenting allows a parent to take one or two afternoons per week to manage a larger group of children with several parents sharing child care responsibilities. Like parental supervision, this can be a good option in those cases where the parent has the stamina and job flexibility.

AFTER-CARE

In some communities, civic organizations such as the YMCA/YWCA have taken on the latchkey problem and have organized care before and after school. One example, The Adventure Club in Minneapolis, is operated by the local Y in collaboration with the school districts of three participating schools. The Adventure Club's advantages are extensive, from a hot breakfast to exciting activities such as hockey and drama. The fees are reasonable, the environment stimulating and protective (Baden, Genser, Levine, & Seligson, 1982). There is some evidence that children who participate in formal after-school programs have higher grades, better work habits, and better emotional adjustment as compared to children in self- and parent-care (Posner & Vandell, 1994).

Yet some parents cannot afford any fees and others cannot arrange transportation home if the child does not ride the state-supported school bus. Some programs target only those children who require daily care, which may exclude families in need of only temporary or variable after-care (Coleman, Robinson, & Rowland, 1993). Still oth-

ers worry about the large, structured-group atmosphere from 6:45 A.M. to 6:00 P.M. Finally, only a portion of communities currently have good after-care programs available.

NEIGHBORHOOD PARENT

Many children come home to an empty house, but they have arrangements with a parent in the neighborhood that if they need help or company, they can contact him or her. This variation on self-care works best when there is compensation for the person serving as the neighborhood parent, when few children are served by a single adult, and thus when children really feel they can frequently utilize the neighborhood parent. When arranged as a daily intervention, it approaches co-op parenting. When used only as an emergency backup, it becomes more like the next alternative.

PARENTING BY PHONE

For parents whose job allows them the flexibility of receiving frequent calls, parenting by phone can improve a latchkey situation. The child calls as soon as possible after arriving home. This method affords emotional sharing and working out of instrumental problems. Further, in an emergency, the parent is only a few moments away from contact. Some parents even carry beepers to facilitate communication (Kim, 1994). Yet there is no ongoing supervision, and activities may need to be restricted to the home because this limited supervision cannot extend beyond the ring of the telephone.

WELL-PREPARED SELF-CARE

In response to children's need for a variety of self-care skills, many preparation programs have developed over the last decade. It is not possible here to describe each of these programs in detail. However, these interventions rely on the same basic type of teaching techniques, and each has been shown to improve children's skills. Initially, skills are broken down into small steps and the steps are taught through discussion, modeling, and then extensive behavioral rehearsal. Frequent feedback, verbal praise, and rewards for learning are used. In this fashion, preventionists have taught children to avoid stranger abduction (Poche, Brouwer, & Swearingen, 1981), to cross streets safely (Yeaton & Bailey, 1978), to recognize emergencies (Rosenbaum, Creedon, & Drabman, 1981), and to exit fires safely (Jones, Kazdin, & Haney, 1981).

Our laboratory has focused on a broad-spectrum program that teaches children to deal with everyday challenges (e.g., fixing a healthy snack), strangers (at the phone, door, or outside), emergencies (e.g., fires, cuts, burns), and transportation (e.g., bicycle safety). We have successfully used volunteers and parents as teaching agents (Peterson, Mori, Selby, & Rosen, 1988) and have taught children individually (Peterson & Mori, 1985) and in the classroom (Peterson & Thiele, 1988).

These behavioral, intensive methods are quite successful. More didactic methods similar to those advocated by civic groups and by self-help books (Peterson, 1984) and one-time workshops (Peterson et al., 1988) are ineffective and actually may be dangerous as they may result in decreased parental supervision with no concomitant increase in child skills.

RECOMMENDATIONS

Recommendations about how to deal with self-care issues must be tempered by the virtual absence of data on long-term effects and the specificity of short-term effects based on an individual child's temperament; cognitive, physical, social, and affective status; as well as the environment of the community and the child's own home. Many experts, including this author, feel that there is no substitute for adult supervision and that, when possible, continuous and vigilant care by a concerned adult is best. However, when family circumstances dictate that no adult can be present either in the form of an in-home or neighborhood contact, several recommendations can be made.

First, provisions can be made for the child to have adult supervision by proxy, if the home has a telephone. The child can check in with this person on arriving home, discuss any important daily issue, and know that this person is available should a crisis arise. Second, the environment should be as safe as possible. For example, there should be deadlock bolts on doors and windows that securely lock. (Note: The child is in more danger of coming home during a break-in than of being in the home during a break-in and should know not to go into the home if there are signs of forced entry, but

instead go to a public place and call parents or police.) The home should be equipped with a smoke alarm, the water heater should be set at 125°F to avoid scalds, and items in the kitchen that deliver heat (including the microwave, which can heat liquids that can spill, causing third-degree burns), electricity, or that are sharp should be ruled off limits. (For a more complete listing, see Peterson, 1989b.)

Although not all children are aware of all family rules, recent research has shown that families with a larger number of rules have elementary-school-age children who experience fewer minor injuries (Peterson & Saldana, in press), suggesting that if rules are learned and enforced, they may result in some protection against injury. Note these are only correlational data; however, research is still needed on the casual influence of rules on injury.

Third, the child should be completely prepared for common as well as emergency situations through one of the existing behavioral preparation programs. Extensive rehearsal is essential for such children. After ascertaining that the child is completely prepared to be at home alone, parents might want to allow a child to practice with them just outside the home or next door for the first day or two.

Fourth, the self-care time should be clearly structured. Healthful snacks can be left at the front of the refrigerator and a list of activities can be agreed on earlier in the day. The telephone can be used to extend social skills, and special rewards can be available for finishing homework (solitary activities) prior to the parent returning home.

Fifth, the parent must be creative about replacing activities lost to self-care. In many families, the what-happened-today? conversation that once occurred as the child entered the home after school can take place as the child and parent prepare for bed. Sports may move to planned activities in which carpooling is shared or that are relegated to the weekend. Because life for working parents is a steady stream of demands, the struggle for quality time, physical activity, and peer socialization must be engineered rather than taken for granted for a child in self-care.

Sixth, it is optimal for the parent to continually reassess the child's emotional response to self-care as well as to reassess skills. (Most behavioral rehearsal programs suggest booster sessions every 3 to 6 months.) The parent may be able to amplify the positive aspects of the experience by praising the child in front of others concerning his or her responsibility, high skill level, and contribution to the family.

Thus, although self-care may not be the situation of choice, parents can do many things to improve the experience for their children.

Future Issues

Recent survey data suggest that parents worry too little about important risks to children and show too much concern over others. For example, a recent national survey revealed high parental concern over stranger abduction, a very rare event for which most children are at little risk, but parents worried little about injury, a source of great risk to children (Eichelberger, Gotschall, Feely, Harstad, & Bowman, 1990). Parents tend to overestimate children's ability to take care of daily challenges and emergencies; when they do teach safety skills, they rely too much on didactic lecture and too little on behavioral practice. They allocate too little time to practice and do not assess the child's skills directly by asking "show me what you would do if . . ." and listen without coaching. They may be reluctant to pay for quality care either through diminished employment or after-care fees, when they fail to recognize the child's need for such care.

Society continues to worry too little as well about the impact of self-care, as does the behavioral sciences field. Introductory child psychology texts in 1996 tend to cover daycare, homelessness, and stepparenting as special family needs, but most skip the issue of self-care as if daycare needs end when children reach age 5 and enter kinder-garten. A computerized output of "PsycINFO" of the most commonly used key word "selfcare" showed a sharply decreasing trend in recent years, with 10 references in 1990, 10 in 1991, 4 in 1992, 3 in 1993, 3 in 1994, and only 1 in 1995. Similarly, recent research suggests continuing profound disagreement about the supervision needs of children age four, with a concensus that parents, physicians, and the division of Family Service workers may entirely lack a set of community standards for evaluating what is appropriate supervision (Peterson, Ewigman, & Kivlahan, 1993).

In days when drive-by shootings are common, rapes of children under 10 are routinely reported in urban newspapers, and many families have no home to be locked into, perhaps such a casual approach to latchkey existence is predictable. However, it is encumbent upon researchers to continue to study the long-term effects of self-care on children, in order to make better predictions about the cost of our attitudes and decisions.

The bottom line is that children's active needs in this area are unclear. The extent to which appropriate preparation and extensions of parenting such as telephone contact may meet these needs is unknown. Finally, the long-term consequences of failing to meet or only partially meeting children's supervision needs are not yet specified, and probably are the function of dozens of interaction factors, including parenting during the rest of the day, neighborhood support for the child, and the child's own native skills and abilities and affective strengths and weaknesses.

These unknowns stand as challenges to the next decade. Increasing numbers of unprepared children are likely to begin self-care each year, unless positive action is taken to afford other alternatives. It remains to future research to articulate the differing areas of need (or the lack of it) for these other alternatives to self-care for children.

REFERENCES

Alpert, B., Field, T., Goldstein, S., & Perry, S. (1990). Aerobics enhances cardiovascular fitness and agility in preschoolers. *Health Psychology, 9,* 48–56.

American Humane Association. (1984). *Highlights of official child neglect and abuse reporting—1982.* Denver, CO: Author.

Baden, R. K., Genser, A., Levine, J. A., & Seligson, M. (1982). *School Age Child Care: An Action Manual.* Dover, Mass.: Auburn House.

Batchelder, M. L., & Winnykamen, F. (1995). Children in self-care: Homeless in the afternoon or socially provided for? *Journal of Social Distress and the Homeless, 4,* 1–52.

Belle, D. (1994). Support system issues for "latchkey" and supervised children. In F. Nestman & K. Hurrelman (Eds.), *Social networks and social support in childhood and adolescence* (pp. 293–304). New York: Walter de Gruyter.

Colan, N. B., Mague, K. C., Ronna, S., & Robert, J. (1994). Family education in the workplace: A prevention program for working parents and school-aged children. *Journal of Primary Prevention, 15,* 161.

Coleman, M., Robinson, B. E., & Rowland, B. H. (1993). A typology of families with children in self-care: Implications for school-age child care programming. *Child and Youth Care Forum, 22,* 43–53.

Coolsen, P., Seligson, M., & Garbarino, J. (1985). *When school's out and nobody's home.* Chicago: National Committee for Prevention of Child Abuse.

Dietz, W. H., & Gortmaker, S. L. (1985). Do we fatten our children at the television set? Obesity and television viewing in children and adolescents. *Pediatrics, 75,* 807–812.

Eichelberger, M. R., Gotschall, C. S., Feely, H. B., Harstad, R., & Bowman, L. M. (1990). Parental attitudes and knowledge of child safety: A national survey. *American Journal of Diseases of Children, 144,* 714–720.

Finkelhor, D. (1979). *Sexually victimized children.* New York: Free Press.

Finkelhor, D. (1984). *Child sexual abuse: New theory and research.* New York: Free Press.

Guerney, L. F. (1991). A survey of self-supports and social supports of self-care children. *Elementary School Guidance and Counseling, 25,* 243–254.

Guerney, L., & Moore, L. (1983). Phone-Friend: A prevention-oriented service for latchkey children. *Children Today, 12,* 5–10.

Haller, J. A. (1970). Problems in children's trauma. *Journal of Trauma, 10,* 269–271.

Jones, R. T., Kazdin, A. E., & Haney, J. I. (1981). Social validation and training of emergency fire safety skills for potential injury prevention and lifesaving. *Journal of Applied Behavior Analysis, 14,* 249–260.

Kim, J. (1994, July 27). Beepers help keep us in touch. *U.S.A. Today,* pp. B1–B2.

Kraizer, S., Witte, S., Fryer, G. E., & Miyoshi, T. (1990). Children in self-care: A new perspective. *Child Welfare, 69,* 571–581.

Lapinski, S. (1982, September 12). Latchkey blues: When kids come home. *Family Weekly,* pp. 22–23.

Long, L., & Long, T. (1982a, September 20). The lonely life of latchkey children. *People Magazine,* pp. 63–65.

Long, L., & Long, T. (1982b). The unspoken fears of latchkey kids. *Working Mother, 5,* 88–90.

Lovko, A. M., & Ullman, D. G. (1989). Research on the adjustment of latchkey children: Role of background/demographics and latchkey situation variables. *Journal of Clinical Child Psychology, 18,* 16–24.

Marcus, I. M., Wilson, W., Kraft, I., Swander, D., Southerland, F., & Schulhofer, E. (1960). An interdisciplinary approach to accident prevention in children. *Monographs of the Society for Research in Child Development, 25* (Serial No. 76).

Messer, S. C., Wuensch, K. L., & Diamond, J. M. (1989). Former latchkey children: Personality and academic correlates. *Journal of Genetic Psychology, 150,* 301–309.

Missouri Revised Statutes. (1994). Offenses against the family (Vol. 7, p. 7599). S568.030. St. Paul, MN: West.

Nienhuis, M. (1987, February 18). 7.2% of children characterized as "latchkey" in 1984 census survey. *Education Week,* p. 6.

Peterson, L. (1984). The "Safe at Home" game: Training comprehensive prevention skills in latchkey children. *Behavior Modification, 8,* 474–494.

Peterson, L. (1987). Not safe at home: Behavioral treatment of a child's fear of being at home alone. *Journal of Behavioral Therapy and Experimental Psychiatry, 18,* 381–385.

Peterson, L. (1989a). Coping by children undergoing stressful medical procedures: Conceptual, methodological, and theapeutic issues. *Journal of Consulting and Clinical Psychology, 57,* 380–387.

Peterson, L. (1989b). Latchkey children's preparation for self-care: Overestimated, underehearsed, and unsafe. *Journal of Clinical Child Psychology, 18,* 36–43.

Peterson, L. (1990). PhoneFriend: A developmental description of needs expressed by child callers to a community telephone support system for children. *Journal of Applied Developmental Psychology, 11,* 105–122.

Peterson, L., & Magrab, P. (1989). Introduction to the special series: Children on their own. *Journal of Clinical Child Psychology, 18,* 2–7.

Peterson, L., & Mori, L. (1985). Prevention of child injury: An overview of targets, methods, and tactics for psychologists. *Journal of Consulting and Clinical Psychology, 53,* 586–595.

Peterson, L., Mori, L., & Scissors, C. (1986). Mom or dad says I shouldn't: Supervised and unsupervised children's knowledge of their parents' rules for home safety. *Journal of Pediatric Psychology, 11,* 177–188.

Peterson, L., Mori, L., Selby, V., & Rosen, B. N. (1988). Community interventions in children's injury prevention: Differing cost and differing benefits. *Journal of Community Psychology, 16,* 188–204.

Peterson, L., & Thiele, C. (1988). Home safety at school. *Child and Family Behavior Therapy, 10,* 1–8.

Peterson, L., Ewignon, B., & Kivlahan, C. (1993). Judgments regarding appropriate child suspension to prevent injury: The rate of environmental risk and child age. *Child Development, 18,* 499–526.

Peterson, L., & Saldana, L. (1996). Accelerating children's risk for injury: Mothers' decisions regarding common safety rules. *Journal of Behavioral Medicine, 19,* 317–331.

Poche, C., Brouwer, R., & Swearingen, M. (1981). Teaching self-protection to young children. *Journal of Applied Behavior Analysis, 14,* 169–176.

Posner, J. K., & Vandell, D. L. (1994). Low-income children's after-school care: Are there beneficial effects of after-school programs? *Child Development, 65,* 440–456.

Robinson, B. E., Rowland, B. H., & Coleman, M. (1986). *Latchkey kids: Unlocking doors for children and their family.* Lexington, MA: Lexington Books.

Rodman, H., Pratto, D. J., & Nelson, R. S. (1985). Child care arrangements and children's functioning: A comparison of self-care and adult-care children. *Developmental Psychology, 21,* 413–418.

Rodriguez, J. G. (1990). Childhood injuries in the

United States: A priority issue. *American Journal of Diseases of Children, 144,* 625–626.

Rosenbaum, M. S., Creedon, D. L., & Drabman, R. S. (1981). Training preschool children to identify emergency situations and make emergency phone calls. *Behavior Therapy, 12,* 425–435.

Russell, D. E. H. (1983). The incidence and prevalence of intrafamilial and extrafamilial sexual abuse of female children. *Child Abuse and Neglect, 7,* 133–146.

Scherer, M. (1982). The loneliness of the latchkey child. *Instructor and Teacher, 91,* 38–41.

Steinberg, L. (1986). Latchkey children and susceptibility to peer pressure: An ecological analysis. *Developmental Psychology, 22,* 433–439.

U.S. Bureau of Census (1992). Statistical abstract on the United States (112th ed.). Washington, DC: U.S. Government Printing Office.

Yeaton, W. H., & Bailey, J. S. (1978). Teaching pedestrian safety skills to young children: An analysis and one year follow-up. *Journal of Applied Behavior Analysis, 11,* 315–329.

17 / Only Children

James M. Harper and Margaret H. Hoopes

In a family structure with only one child, the lack of interaction with other siblings and the effects of having more interaction with one or two parents without interference or competition with siblings produces a particular type of experience for the child. This chapter examines characteristics of only children and identifies implications for development, clinical assessment, and interventions.

Although early writings about only children focused on negative traits, empirical studies in the last decade indicate that only children are no worse off than their counterparts with siblings (Polit & Falbo, 1987). In many ways they compare more favorably than other children, and in other ways they are very similar to first children.

There are several reasons why the findings of early studies on the only child appear contradictory. In many studies only children were grouped with first- or last-borns because they are both first and last in their families. Many only children come from single-parent families, and the experience of only children in these family structures is different from the experience of only children in two-parent families. In blended families, children may have been only children for a considerable period of time and then acquired new siblings when parents remarried. Only recently have investigators begun to consider these differences in family structure when studying only children (Polit, 1984; Rosenberg, 1993).

In recent years, the number of only children has been increasing worldwide. This situation can be attributed to several factors. Advances in contraceptives, increased entry of women into the work force, and difficult economic times have all led to lower fertility rates in industrialized countries (Westoff, 1978). The increasing divorce rate means that many children are more likely to come from single-parent families today than they were two or three decades ago, and most of these single parents will have only one child (Blake, 1981; Claudy, Farrel, & Dayton, 1979; Falbo, 1977, 1984).

Summary of Recent Empirical Findings Regarding the Characteristics of Only Children from a Developmental Perspective

Studies in the last two decades refute the belief that only children are maladjusted. Consistent with the assumptions of some sibling models (Hoopes & Harper, 1987), most empirical results indicate that only children are not much different from first children. Comparisons of only children with those of other sibling positions on variables of achievement, cognitive functioning, well-being and self-esteem, interpersonal orientation, mental health and dysfunctional issues for one-child single-parent families are summarized in Table 17.1.

As the table indicates, the major differences between only children and other siblings occur in the areas of achievement, language use, and need for affiliation. Only children also appear to be similar to firstborns, which of course makes sense given that all first children are only children for some period of time. The following sections identify studies that have investigated characteristics of only children at different stages of development.

INFANCY AND TODDLERHOOD

In a longitudinal study, Feiring and Lewis (1984) followed only and firstborn children from birth to 3 years of age. They found that mothers of only children touch, bathe, rock, kiss, play, look at, and vocalize with their infants more than mothers of firstborns. Mothers of only children at 24 months of age showed more approval than mothers of firstborns. For firstborn children, earlier child social characteristics are the best predictors of subsequent social development; in other words, sociable infants become sociable children. In contrast, however, the best predictors of subsequent social development in only children seem to be the social characteristics of the mother. Only children who were not sociable at 3 months became more sociable at 20 months, suggesting that mothers were responsible for bringing about this transformation (Feiring & Lewis, 1984).

SCHOOL AGE

The increased verbal skills and adultlike behavior of both only children and firstborns helps them succeed within the school system (Falbo, 1993; Polit & Falbo, 1987). They better understand the expectations of adults because of the increased amount of time they spend with their parents. Only children rate themselves similar to others in academic performance but less proficient in sports and physical activities (Veenhoven & Verkuyten, 1989), possibly because they do not have siblings with whom to practice. For boys in particular where sports plays a large part of the socialization of middle school age males, this may have an impact on their developmental projectory. Only children who do not perceive themselves as proficient in sports and athletic activities may suffer the unfortunate result of being less popular also.

This may be another reason why studies show they turn more to solitary activities.

ADOLESCENCE

Using data collected as part of a national long-term research project on adolescents, Claudy (1984) found few differences between only children and others. Only children received higher scores on cognitive tests, appeared to be more mature and socially sensitive, but were less sociable even though they had social skills. They were more interested in white-collar, scientific, and analytical occupations and activities. They had less intense social lives because they did not seek them out as much. They did not differ in terms of their health. Only children usually worked less in outside employment during high school but had higher long-term occupational and financial expectations.

ADULTHOOD

Groat, Wicks, and Neal (1984) concluded that among a national probability sample of currently married men and women, there were few significant differences between people of only and non-only positions. The clear significant differences that do emerge were higher educational attainment for only children (Falbo, 1993; Polit, Nuttal, & Nuttal, 1980) and adult only children's lack of need to seek out and affiliate with others. Even though these adults have less need to affiliate with others, they did not lack social skills, and their marriages were as stable as sibling counterpart's. Although only children are not different in many aspects from other children, they differ in other ways important to the therapeutic process. For example, their cognitive and affective orientations may require tailored interviewing and interventions. Their identity may be affected by factors that are different from those for other siblings.

Model of Systemic Position Derived from the Clinical Context

Expanding on Bach and Anderson's ideas (1979), Hoopes and Harper (1987) elaborated a model

TABLE 17.1

Recent Empirical Findings Regarding the Characteristics of Only Children

Achievement	Cognitive Functioning	Well-Being & Self-Esteem	Interpersonal Orientation	Mental Health	Dysfunction/Single Parent Families
Only children compare favorably and usually better than people from larger families; higher levels of initiative, more industrious in educational and occupational achievement (Blake, 1981; Claudy, Farrel, & Dayton, 1979; Glenn & Hoppe, 1984). Most overrepresented group in any level of education (Bayer, 1976).	Similar to first children in cognitive functioning, as evident in use of language (Cropley & Ahler, 1975).	Only children are similar to others in terms of self-esteem and well-being. Veenhoven and Verkuyten (1989) found that only children were not less happy nor was their self-esteem lower than children from larger families.	Only children have a more trusting style of interaction and expect others to be helpful and rewarding, possibly because of continual help and nurturing from parents (Falbo, 1984).	Only children do not appear more frequently in categories of mental and emotional illness than people from larger families (Bayrakal & Kope, 1990; Falbo, 1987; Watson & Biderman, 1989; Byrd, 1993).	If only children are at risk it is because of family dysfunction rather than the fact that they are only children.
Not different from first-borns in educational and occupational achievement (Falbo & Polit, 1986, 1987).	Only and first children have larger and more fluent vocabularies than other sibling positions (Falbo & Polit, 1986).	Adult only children find somewhat more pleasure in life than people from larger families (Blake, 1981; Feiring & Lewis, 1984).	Slightly more successful socially, marry better educated partners, less prone to divorce, spend less time with friends than individuals from larger families (Veenhoven & Verkuyten, 1989).	Mower, Miller, and Lawton-Smith (1987) found that only children were the most infrequently referred group for mental health service.	The only child often ends up becoming the substitute mate for the parent (Bayrakal & Kope, 1990).
Only, first, and second children achieve more than individuals from families larger than two children (Mellor, 1990).	Families with only children had more information exchange during meal times in all socioeconomic groups and cultures (Feiring, 1984; Falbo, 1987).		Less of a need to affiliate with others, spend more time in solitary activities, but do not lack social skills or rate themselves lonelier than others (Falbo, 1984).	Some indication that only males may be prone to substance abuse (Stein, DeMiranda, & Stein, 1988).	In single parent families a higher degree of family dysfunction than in single parent families with more than one child (Weirs, 1979).
	Only children appear to be more mature and more cultured in terms of social manners.		Make very close friendships; rated by others as being quite sociable (Falbo & Polit, 1986).	Some evidence that only children are more prone to psychosomatic illness (Sheldrake, Cormack, and McGuire, 1976).	Common problems: fluidity of generational boundaries in which the roles between parent and child were unclear, poorly defined ego boundaries for both the parent and the only child; sometimes the only children bypassed being an adolescent and pretended that they were already adults (Burch, 1985).
	Because only children have been raised primarily around adults, they may be encouraged to act more like adults earlier than children in other sibling positions.			Only and first children were more prone to type A behavior and often suffered from stress related illnesses (Ivancevich, Matteson, & Gamble, 1987).	The well-being of only children in single parent families may be more related to the parent's adjustment than is true of only children who are raised in families where two parents are present (Kalter, Koner, Schreier, & Okla, 1989).
	Only children are rational and analytical; focus on the detail of events and experiences (Falbo, 1984; Hoopes & Harper, 1987).				

of systemic position that identifies characteristic response patterns for the first four sibling positions and the associated family structure and process at the time each sibling is born into the family. In this model, only children are like first children, and both assume a unique role in their family system that is different from those of other sibling positions. The interplay between family structure and processes at the time the child is born and the needs of the system and individual creates a unique response pattern for only children. This response pattern can be subdivided into three categories: family roles assigned according to the needs of the family system, a particular cognitive and affective style formed in a large part by the early interactions in the family, and the identity and well-being of the child. These patterns have been summarized in Table 17.2. (Chapter 23 compares patterns of only children with those of other sibling positions.)

Only children are at the center stage in the family. They carry with them all the hopes and fears of not only their parents but other generations, as well. Everything is being done the first and only time, at least for his or her parents. Sitting up, crawling, first steps, first teeth, first words, and starting school are all met with ecstatic approval from parents, grandparents, and other relatives. At some point in time, however, a family decides to be a one-child family. Once parents decide or discover that they will have only one child, they are more likely to invest energy, time, and approval in that child.

The family role of the only child is to produce outcomes that meet with the family's approval. The security of the only child depends on being on target with others' expectations, especially the parents'. Only children quickly learn that when they achieve, they receive affirmation. Although this can be true of other children in larger families, it is much more emphasized with first and only children.

Burdens may accompany being at center stage. To demonstrate weakness or vulnerabilities may imply that only children fail to represent the family's dream. If parental demands are too harsh, the only child will rebel or shut down. If the power structure in a family denies opportunities for recognition, only children may become highly threatened, lose interest, and withdraw. If the marriage is weak, only children can get caught in coalitions with one parent against the other. Only children feel very responsible to try to compensate for parents' failure and unmet emotional needs.

In terms of interpersonal relationships, only children often feel responsible for outcomes in other people's lives (Lackie, 1984). They may be overly responsible and feel guilty for things over which they have no control. Only children are cautious in forming relationships and do not have high needs for affiliation. They must learn whether they can be safe when they are vulnerable. They want to know that their partner will be there to pick them up if they show weakness and vulnerability. The only child does not lack social skills to create a new relationship but simply may not see the need for using these skills.

The perceptual orientation of only children involves a focus on detail and rational analysis. They focus on explicit, observable behavior, facts, and rule-governed aspects of reality. In gathering information, they often behave as if they must know everything. One detail leads to another, and they often gather much more data than necessary. This emphasis on detail often leads to overload and cognitive compartmentalization. Once only children believe that they understand all the details of a situation, they may go to great lengths to defend their explanation of it. Sometimes it is difficult to get them to consider additional information because they restrict their perceptual field to maintain their own elaborately constructed explanation.

Verbal description is an important part of only children's patterns. They focus on the semantics of language and may confront others about the literal meaning of the words they use. Only children need to feel that their explanations are right, and to these children, being right may become more important than considering new information.

Only children approach feelings through rational cognition. They have to think about their feelings in order to realize their existence and label them. Because emotion is often more implicit, only children may overlook feelings unless they are relevant to some outcome or unless some other family member makes emotional moods explicit. At times they will deny feelings if they believe that discovery of their emotions by others would make them seem weak, vulnerable, or unproductive.

TABLE 17.2

Family Role, Perceptual Orientation and Identity/Well-Being Issues for Firstborn and Only Children

Family Role Patterns for Firstborn and Only Children

Job Assignment	Interpersonal Responsibilities	Social Interactions
1. Responsible for supporting family rules, values, and expectations	1. Responsible for each family member to one parent, often father, but may be mother	1. Interact with individuals
2. Responsible for outcomes, results, products	2. Responsible for that same parent	2. Some performance anxiety in most relationships and social situations
3. Responsible for a central place in the family in order to be productive	3. Responsible for all family members' productivity	3. Feel impelled to respond to others' expectations
		4. Can be direct and engaged
		5. Will encourage others to express ideas and feelings if seen as relevant

Perceptual Orientation Patterns for Firstborn and Only Children

Focus/Awareness	Cognitive Patterns	Affective Patterns
1. Focused on rule-governed aspects of reality	1. Use ideas and facts in a logical and analytical manner to understand	1. Identify and label own and others' feelings easily if relevant
2. Focused on details and parts	2. Perceptually limited, lack of linkages between parts, compartmentalize	2. Integrate and share own feelings if the purpose and outcome is made explicit
3. Aware of some of the implicit environment, but need to be reminded to look	3. Go from parts to the whole	3. Can be lost, confused, and overwhelmed by detail
		4. Sometimes deny feelings

Identity/Well-Being Patterns for Firstborn and Only Children

Self-esteem	Threatened Psychologically	Responses to Threat	What They Need from Others
1. Self-esteem based on doing well in the eyes of others	1. By being "off target" in the eyes of others	1. Experience life as hopeless	1. Recognition and acceptance as being central, "on target," and productive
2. Need to feel productive and successful	2. When ignored by others as central	2. Withdraw, ignore	2. Approval of products
3. Need to be "on target"—right	3. They anticipate other's evaluation of their performance	3. Appear "stony," "black countenance," "unfeeling," "immovable"	3. Exploration of feelings, failures, and helplessness with connections to behavior and logic in a reasonable way without discounting them
4. Need recognition of being central	4. When they encounter too many details, too many people needing assistance, too much disorganization	4. Can be dogmatic	4. Help in making rules, values, and expectations explicit
		5. Can be superrational	5. Obedience to rules

Source: Harper & Hoopes, 1987

Several circumstances can threaten the identity and well-being of only children (Harper & Hoopes, 1990). They are often anxious about their performance and others' approval and become threatened when they feel inadequate at producing some outcome. They also are threatened when they cannot obtain enough information and when too many details overwhelm them. As a result of trying to please their parents, only children often gauge their self-esteem on what they produce and by others' approval. This does not mean that only children have less self-esteem than children from larger families, rather it means that the process through which they gain their self-esteem is different.

Their assigned family role; their cognitive, affective, and interpersonal style; and the processes that affect their identity make only children somewhat unique from those in other sibling positions and most like first children. This characteristic response pattern of only children has important clinical implications.

Clinical Implications and Interventions

Clinicians working with only children need to understand the processes of their family systems. These processes include whether they are in a single or traditional family; what the interaction patterns, boundaries, family rules, and roles are; and how intimacy and dependency needs are met. The only child, the nuclear family, and the larger intergenerational family simultaneously move through stages of development. The issues with which both the family system and the larger intergenerational family are dealing at a given time provide a unique context for the clinician to examine while working with only children.

In working with a symptomatic only child, clinicians should first examine parental expectations, rules, and values to determine if they are realistic. If the family is a two-parent family, clinicians also can assess whether parents agree on rules and values for the family. The ways in which parents respond to the only child's performance and enforce rules affects the child's self-esteem. Many parents of only children are tempted to smother them, not only with physical affection but also with high expectations. When parental expectations are overwhelming, children will give up and fail to achieve.

In working with adolescent and adult only children, therapists should focus on helping their patients establish clear ego boundaries. In helping these patients individuate, clinicians should focus on parents' unresolved emotional issues, such as anger at spouse or parent, fear, sexual fantasies, and intimacy problems. If parents do not deal openly with their anger, for example, their only children often act the anger out by being overly aggressive, being depressed, or fighting their parents' battles with others. These children also may respond to their parents' fantasies and unfulfilled dreams by acting them out. Usually the parents have not openly acknowledged these issues; the clinical task is to make them explicit so the only children are free to let the parents be the parents.

Therapists should assess how only children are like their parents or opposite. The answer may provide additional clues to the parents' unresolved issues. If the family of an only child is dysfunctional, the clinician needs to work to convince the child that he or she is not responsible for causing the dysfunctional outcomes.

Only children who seek therapy are most likely to be "overfunctioners" in their families of origin (Bowen, 1978). It becomes important clinically at each stage of development for clinicians to pay special attention to the ways in which only children feel responsible for the kinds of family processes that occur. When an only child is the identified patient, the clinician should focus on his or her relationship with each parent, paying particular attention to how the behaviors of both parents symbolize productivity.

The family's emotional system—how parents express emotion and whether the family is capable of legitimizing feelings in the only child—should be assessed also. Only children are able to express feeling and emotion when they see it linked to the outcomes upon which they focus. Clinicians can help the parents at each stage of development to find appropriate ways to help legitimize the only child's expression of feeling and to help the child link the emotion to the goals toward which he or she is working.

Since many only children live in single-parent families, clinicians should assess the adjustment of parents. Because the best predictor of the adjustment of only children is the adjustment of their parents (Feiring & Lewis, 1984), clinicians must consider it while simultaneously focusing on the child's adjustment. Consideration of both parent and child adjustment is especially crucial for only-child clients who are in the adolescent stage of development.

In late adolescence, issues of launching from the home need to be addressed, particularly in the single-parent family. If only children have played the role of surrogate spouse, they may feel a responsibility to take care of the needs of their parent. Increased parent-child conflict during this time may be one indication that both parent and child are having difficulty with this developmental task.

In many single-parent families where the father is absent, the only children may assume his responsibilities. They may fight with their father to make him more responsible; become overly responsible for the mother; or try other ways to compensate for the father's lack of responsibility. Possible interventions in such cases include getting the parents to take more responsibility for what happens between the two of them, educating the only children, and working to free them from having to fulfill the parental role.

The following guidelines are useful for clinicians when working with only children. Refer to Table 17.2 for information connected to these guidelines.

- Work to release only children from being overly responsible to and for others.
- Work to validate only children's right to be who they are.
- Reassure them whenever possible that they are on target and that as people, they have your approval.

- Provide more information for them than you would to most patients.
- Help family members understand the children's need for verbal information.
- Legitimize emotions and feelings for only children and help them to make their feelings part of relevant information.
- Help the children understand the relevance of their connection to their parents, their parents' needs and motivations, and their tendencies to be overly responsible for others and for their parents.

Specific guidelines for parental guidance intervention include the following:

- Help parents to make their expectations explicit and reachable.
- Teach parents to let their only children know when they have "done enough." This helps limit the only children's tendency to be obsessive.
- Help parents give increased approval for their children as people, not just approval for what they do.
- Teach parents to provide logical, explicit explanations for discipline and other situations.

Conclusion

The concepts presented in this chapter are useful as a complementary framework to establish therapy approaches. The model explains what happens in the family and how only children develop within that family context. An only child in one family will not behave in a manner identical to that of an only child in another family. Sibling position alone cannot predict how an individual behaves, but these concepts provide a descriptive map that opens up new avenues for understanding the thoughts, behaviors, and feelings of only children in therapy. This descriptive map helps the clinician to intervene at appropriate developmental stages, helps parents and only children function better, and leads to specific types of interventions that are unique to only children.

REFERENCES

Bach, J., & Anderson, A. R. (1979). *A systems model of ordinal position.* Ms., Bach Family Institute, Minneapolis, MN.

Bayer, A. E. (1976). Birth order and attainment of the doctorate: A test of economic hypotheses. *American Journal of Sociology, 72,* 540–550.

Bayrakal, S., & Kope, T. M. (1990). Dysfunction in the single-parent and only-child family. *Adolescence, 25*, 1–7.

Blake, J. (1981). The only child in America: Prejudice versus performance. *Population and Development Review, 7*, 43–54.

Bowen, M. (1978). *Family therapy in clinical practice.* New York: Jason Aronson.

Burch, B. (1985). Identity foreclosure in early adolescence. *Adolescent Psychiatry, 12*, 145–162.

Byrd, B., DeRosa, A. P., and Craig, S. S. (1993). The adult who is an only child: Achieving separation or individuation. *Psychological Reports, 73*, 171–177.

Claudy, J. G. (1984). The only child as a young adult: Results from project talent. In T. Falbo (Ed.), *The single child family* (pp. 211–252). New York: Guilford Press.

Claudy, J. G., Farrel, U. S., & Dayton, C. W. (1979). *The consequences of being an only child.* Palo Alto, CA: American Institute for Research.

Cropley, A. J., & Ahler, K. H. (1975). Development of verbal skills in first-born and only boys. *Journal of Biosocial Science, 7*, 297–306.

Falbo, T. (1977). The only child: A review. *Journal of Individual Psychology, 33*, 47–61.

Falbo, T. (1984). Only children: A review. In T. Falbo (Ed.), *The single child family* (pp. 1–24). New York: Guilford Press.

Falbo, T. (1987). Only children in the United States and China. In S. Oskamp (Ed.), *Annual social psychology* (Vol. 7, pp. 159–183). Beverly Hills, CA: Sage Publications.

Falbo, T. (1993). The academic, personality, and physical outcomes of only children in China. *Child development, 64*, 18–35.

Falbo, T., & Polit, D. F. (1986). Quantitative review of the only child literature: Research evidence and theory development. *Psychological Bulletin, 100*, 176–189.

Feiring, C., & Lewis, M. (1984). Only and first-born children: Differences in social behavior and development. In T. Falbo (Ed.), *The single child family* (pp. 25–62). New York: Guilford Press.

Glenn, M. D., & Hoppe, S. W. (1984). Only children as adults: Psychological well-being. *Journal of Family Issues, 5*, 363–382.

Groat, H. T., Wicks, J. W., & Neal, A. G. (1984). Without siblings: The consequences in adult life of having been an only child. In T. Falbo (Ed.), *The single child family* (pp. 253–289). New York: Guilford Press.

Harper, J. M., & Hoopes, M. H. (1990). *Uncovering shame: An approach integrating individuals and their family systems.* New York: W. W. Norton.

Hoopes, M. H., & Harper, J. M. (1987, 1992). *Birth order roles and sibling patterns in individual and family therapy.* Rockville, MD: Aspen Books.

Ivancevich, J. M., Matteson, M. T., & Gamble, G. O. (1987). Birth order and the Type A coronary behavior pattern. *Individual Psychology, 43*, 42–49.

Jiao, S., Ji, G., & Ching, C. C. (1986). Comparative study of behavioral qualities of only children and sibling children. *Child Development, 57*, 357–361.

Kalter, N., Koner, A., Schreier, S., & Okla, K. (1989). Predictors of children's postdivorce adjustment. *American Journal of Orthopsychiatry, 59*, 605–618.

Lackie, B. (1984). Learned responsibility and order of birth: A study of 1,577 social workers. *Smith College Studies in Social Work, 54*, 117–138.

Lewis, M., & Feiring, C. (1982). Some American families at dinner. In L. M. Laosa & I. E. Sigel (Eds.), *Families as learning environments for children.* New York: Plenum Press.

Mellor, S. (1990). How do only children differ from other children? *Journal of Genetic Psychology, 151*, 221–230.

Mower, B. A., Miller, S. A., & Lawton-Smith, N. (1987). Psychologically referred adolescents: Demographics of a clinical population. *Journal of Early Adolescence, 7*, 217–224.

Polit, D. F. (1984). The only child in single-parent families. In T. Falbo (Ed.), *The single child family* (pp. 178–210). New York: Guilford Press.

Polit, D. F., & Falbo, T. (1987). Only children and personality development: A quantitative review. *Journal of Marriage and the Family, 49*, 309–325.

Polit, D. F., & Falbo, T. (1988). The intellectual achievement of only children. *Journal of Biosocial Science, 20*, 275–285.

Polit, D. F., Nuttal, L. R., & Nuttal, E. V. (1980). The only child grows up: A look at some characteristics of adult only children. *Family Relations, 29*, 99–106.

Rosenberg, B. G. (1993). The only child: Is there only one kind of only? *The Journal of Genetic Psychology, 154*, 269–282.

Sheldrake, P., Cormack, M., & McGuire, J. (1976). Phychosomatic illness, birth order, and intellectual preference. *Journal of Psychosomatic Research, 20*, 45–49.

Stein, S. M., DeMiranda, S., & Stein, A. (1988). Birth order, substance abuse, and criminality. *Individual Psychology, 44*, 500–506.

Veenhoven, R., & Verkuyten, M. (1989). The well-being of only children. *Adolescence, 24*, 155–166.

Watson, P. J., & Biderman, M. D. (1989). Failure of only-child status to predict narcissism. *Perceptual and Motor Skills, 69*, 1346.

Weiss, R. S. (1979). *Going It Alone.* New York: Basic Books.

Westoff, C. F. (1978). Some speculations on the future of marriage and fertility. *Family Planning Perspectives, 10*, 79–83.

18 / Developmental Effects of Parental Alcohol Use

Naimah Z. Weinberg

The impact of parental alcohol abuse and dependence on the development of children is currently receiving increased attention from a number of quarters. The popular media, clinical literature, and research world have all made children of alcoholics and adult children of alcoholics the focus of increasing study, public awareness, and funding.

This chapter provides an overview of the rich and growing body of knowledge on the many effects that parents' alcohol use may have on children. Studies have linked parental alcohol use at least speculatively to almost all common child psychiatric problems, and clinical caseloads are likely to include significant numbers of children of alcoholics. The clinical literature has dealt largely with family process, family roles, and interpersonal consequences related to parental alcohol abuse; research studies have examined a wide array of biologic, psychological, and social outcomes. Recent critical reviews of the literature on children of alcoholics stress the need for more rigorous research methodology in studying this important population.

Population

EPIDEMIOLOGY AND MAGNITUDE OF THE PROBLEM

The number of children of alcoholics under the age of 18 is estimated at 6.6 million (Russell, Henderson, & Blume, 1985), with an additional 22 million adult children of alcoholics. Several methodological issues affect prevalence estimates, however, including sample representativeness, diagnostic criteria, genetic and environmental factors (Russell, 1990). These numbers suggest a problem of significant magnitude; it is estimated

that 1 out of every 8 Americans is a child of alcoholic parents. Moreover, such children are overrepresented in the mental health and general medical systems, with higher rates of injury, poisoning, and admissions for mental disorders and substance abuse, and elevated rates of general hospital admission, length of stay, and total health care costs (Children of Alcoholics Foundation, 1990).

MISCONCEPTIONS ABOUT "CHILDREN OF ALCOHOLICS"

The popular children of alcoholics literature, and some clinical references, depict certain stereotypes regarding the family environment in which these children are raised, and define enduring impairments, particularly in terms of self-esteem and intimate relationships, from which "all" children of alcoholics are thought to suffer. However, there is little research to substantiate these generalizations (Sher, 1991; Woodside, 1988). In addition to lack of methodological rigor, these depictions are generally based on very select and probably unrepresentative samples. Moreover, many of the findings regarding children of alcoholics are nonspecific, possibly characterizing others from "dysfunctional homes"; as Searles and Windle (1990) point out, "no clinical syndrome has been identified that is distinct for adult children of alcoholics" (p. 3). Another point to keep in mind is the heterogeneity of alcoholism, wherein several subtypes probably exist; generalizations based on one group may not apply to others of a different subtype (Sher, 1991). Finally, such unsubstantiated generalizations may be dangerous. The labeling process may itself be detrimental to the self-image and social image of individual children of alcoholics (Emshoff & Anyan, 1991; Sher, 1991), and a failure "to explicitly recognize that most individuals emerge from these environments relatively intact psychologically and emotionally" (Searles & Windle, 1990, p. 3) may result. A balanced view of the individual needs to be maintained.

This work was supported in part by NIAAA grant #F32 AA05312-01.

Developmental Impact

MODEL

The following overview is based on a biopsycho-social model, which recognizes developmental effects of parental alcohol use and misuse on all three realms of child development—biological, psychological, and social—and the existence of very complex interactions among them. An example of this interplay is presented by Rutter (1989) in a discussion of parental psychiatric disorders as risk factors for children's adverse outcomes. Rutter notes two processes whereby familial factors may influence children's risk other than through direct heredity: first, by genetically increasing the child's vulnerability to the deleterious effects of environmental stress, and second, by increasing the likelihood that the child will experience psychosocial stressors due to the secondary effects of the parent's disorder. The field of behavioral genetics also applies a biopsychosocial understanding to the study of alcoholism risk (Tarter, 1991); current thinking has come to look at certain psychological and social constructs, such as temperament, as having a significant biological or heritable substrate. The following review reflects this approach and the complexity of these interactions.

Studies on children of alcoholics have been confounded by a number of methodologic issues. Areas of concern include sample selection and bias; diagnostic criteria and method of ascertainment of parent drinking; the heterogeneous nature of alcoholism; assortative mating patterns among alcoholic parents; choice of control groups, and inclusion or exclusion of comorbid conditions; choice of assessment instruments; failure to control for psychosicial conditions including divorce, poverty, neglect, and socioeconomic status; and failure to take into account biologic insults such as fetal alcohol exposure and early abuse. These complicating factors should be kept in mind through the following review.

PRENATAL ALCOHOL EXPOSURE

Prenatal exposure to alcohol has a variety of effects on the developing fetus. These effects are not limited to fetal alcohol syndrome, but include a broad continuum of defects and deficits. Often

the role of parental alcohol use goes unrecognized as a factor in child impairment.

Fetal alcohol syndrome is a major contributor to disability among children. It is the leading known cause of mental retardation in the United States (Streissguth et al., 1991). The diagnosis of fetal alcohol syndrome is made by the presence of abnormality in each of three categories: growth retardation, central nervous system involvement, and a characteristic facies (Abel, 1990). In addition to mental retardation, central nervous system impairment may manifest as sleep disturbance, altered electroencephalogram and evoked potentials, seizures, cerebral palsy, and impaired sucking reflex: Most patients demonstrate subtle neurodevelopmental problems, including cognitive delays which do not fall in the mentally retarded range; attention problems which do not fit the typical attention deficit-hyperactivity disorder picture; learning disabilities, particularly in math; speech and language problems related to complex speech and comprehension; and problems with reasoning and judgment (Institute of Medicine, 1996). Other associated pathology may include cardiac anomalies, urogenital anomalies, hernias, skeletal defects, neural tube defects, and altered immunologic function.

There is a great deal of variability in the presentation of children affected by prenatal alcohol exposure; fetal alcohol effects and alcohol-related birth defects are terms used when the presenting features do not meet full criteria for fetal alcohol syndrome. Moreover, many children born to alcoholic mothers may not show alcohol teratogenesis (Abel, 1990). A number of factors appear to moderate the outcome; these variables are not fully understood at this time. They include the amount and timing of the alcohol exposure; birth order; genetic factors, which may increase or reduce susceptibility to alcohol damage; the possible genetic effects of paternal alcohol abuse on fetal development; other prenatal influences such as mother's smoking status, general health, age, prenatal care, and nutrition; and features of the postnatal environment, such as caregiving, nutrition, and education. While some alcohol-exposed children may escape unharmed, Streissguth and her group have concluded that even moderate levels of alcohol exposure in children who do not meet criteria for fetal alcohol syndrome can result in persistent neurobehavioral effects (Streissguth et al., 1990), and that no level of alcohol use by pregnant women can be regarded as risk-free. At this time, despite some controversy, the American College of Obstetrics and Gynecology recommends that women abstain from any alcohol use during the entire pregnancy.

Longitudinal studies by Streissguth and her group (1991), looking at the spectrum of outcomes, have found that the deficits from alcohol teratogenesis persist into adolescence and adulthood; an important finding for clinicians is the conclusion that "maladaptive behaviors" represent the greatest difficulty in management. The award-winning book *The Broken Cord* (Dorris, 1989) eloquently describes the "ongoing struggle" of raising a child with fetal alcohol syndrome. As Dorris and other authors note (Smith & Coles, 1991), these multiply handicapped at-risk children often need extensive special services, which may not be forthcoming when based solely on their borderline (not always retarded) IQ scores.

Prenatal alcohol exposure is a very costly problem, to individuals and to society; Abel (1990) has estimated costs in the United States in the range of $250 million per year resulting from the care of children with fetal alcohol syndrome alone. Fetal alcohol syndrome and fetal alcohol effects are also clearly preventable sources of morbidity and disability in children. Therefore, primary, secondary, and tertiary prevention efforts may be directed toward educating the public and health care providers regarding the risks of alcohol use in pregnancy; providing treatment services to alcoholic women of childbearing years; and minimizing morbidity for those children with fetal alcohol damage, by improving the postnatal environment and providing remedial services (Smith & Coles, 1991). The risk of fetal alcohol syndrome actually increases with subsequent pregnancies to alcoholic women who have borne one such child (Abel, 1990); therefore, earlier recognition of children affected by prenatal alcohol exposure also may provide an opportunity for intervention with the mother before more severely affected siblings are born.

ATTENTION DEFICIT HYPERACTIVITY DISORDER

A number of studies have suggested a link between parental alcoholism and hyperactivity in their offspring. (See reviews by Russell et al., 1985;

Sher, 1991; West & Prinz, 1987; Windle, 1990.) Pihl, Peterson, and Finn (1990), in a review of the literature on sons of male alcoholics, note repeated descriptions of hyperactivity, impulsivity, academic disruption, hypersensitivity to auditory and visual stimulation, and difficulty regulating excitement and mood as well as impaired ability to concentrate, pay attention, and control motor behavior. It is possible that direct genetic links exist between attention deficit hyperactivity disorder and parental alcoholism (Cantwell, 1976; West & Prinz, 1987). However, many other factors may contribute to this seeming relationship. In a comprehensive study of psychopathology in children of alcoholics, Reich, Earls, Frankel, and Shayka (1993) did not find clear associations between attention deficit disorder and parental alcoholism. However, strong associations of parent alcohol use with oppositional and conduct disorders and with overanxious disorder were found, the features of which may have been labeled as attention deficit hyperactivity disorder in less rigorous studies. Other findings suggest that hyperactivity symptoms in children of alcoholics may be due to fetal alcohol effects or to cognitive impairments. Thus, a variety of factors—genetic, toxic, and environmental—and the complicated relationship between parental alcoholism and conduct disorder all contribute to a lack of clarity in this area.

Hyperactivity may be a significant risk factor for later substance abuse in children, although conduct disorder again complicates this relationship. Further studies are needed to clarify the relationships among these common and difficult disorders.

CONDUCT DISORDER

There appears to be a relationship between parental alcoholism and the risk of conduct problems and delinquency in their offspring. (See reviews by Pihl et al., 1990; Sher, 1991; West & Prinz, 1987.) In a comprehensive study of psychopathology in children of alcoholics, Reich et al. (1993) found a "very strong connection between parental alcoholism and oppositional and conduct disorders in children" (p. 998). Their study could not determine the nature (biological versus environmental) of the relationship. Current thinking in this complex area suggests that alcoholism and antisocial problems are separate disorders and not simply diverse manifestations of the same genetic vulnerability (Russell et al., 1985), although the possibility of a genetic link is still considered (Sher, 1991; West & Prinz, 1987). The vulnerability to conduct disorders in children of alcoholics appears to be largely environmental, and a number of possible pathways are considered (West & Prinz, 1987; Windle, 1990; see also Dishion, Patterson, & Reid, 1988), including the family effects of poverty and divorce due to parental alcoholism.

COGNITIVE AND NEUROPSYCHOLOGICAL EFFECTS

A number of studies have looked at cognitive, neuropsychological, and neurophysiological differences among children of alcoholics compared to children of nonalcoholics. In terms of academic achievement, it appears that children of alcoholics demonstrate significantly worse school performance (see reviews by Pihl et al., 1990; Sher, 1991; West & Prinz, 1987); parental alcohol abuse may be an unrecognized contributor to specific learning disabilities in children. In terms of actual cognitive abilities, some studies have found reduced overall IQ, with particular impairments in verbal ability and abstraction/conceptual reasoning (Tarter, Hegedus, Goldstein, Shelly, & Alterman, 1984; Tarter, Laird, & Moss, 1990); children of alcoholics nonetheless generally perform within the normal range. Johnson and Rolf (1988) found no difference in IQ, academic performance, or school reports between such children and other middle-class subjects; however, the children of alcoholics and their mothers underestimated the child's abilities to a significant degree, which may have implications for the impaired school performance often seen. Reich et al. (1993) found a possible difference in reading achievement in children with one alcoholic parent and no other significant differences in achievement testing. Thus, the questions of cognitive impairments in children of alcoholics remains unclear. A number of biological, psychological, and social factors associated with parental alcoholism may contribute to cognitive impairment in their children, including prenatal alcohol exposure, neglect (including poor nutrition), higher rates of abuse (especially head injury), and family disruption. Pihl et al. (1990) critique the literature in this area, noting in part the need to study males and females separately and to select study groups carefully. This area

merits further attention, in part because of the associations between cognitive impairments and later conduct problems, which in turn may be associated with later alcoholism in offspring of alcoholic parents.

Several exciting new areas are being explored with regard to neuropsychological findings in COAs. Windle (1990) reviews five cognitive-perceptual personality attributes under study, including the construct of alexithymia. Tarter, Laird, and Moss (1990) elucidate a neuropsychological theory of alcoholism vulnerability, pulling together findings in the neuroanatomic, psychobiological, and behavioral domains. These explorations may hold significance for risk identification and intervention.

ABUSE, NEGLECT, AND INJURY

Although clinical experience has led many people to believe that there is a relationship between parental alcoholism and family violence (child abuse, spouse abuse, and sexual abuse), the dearth of relevant research leads Leonard and Jacob (1988) to conclude emphatically that there is a "desperate" need for more and better research. A number of methodological problems complicate studies of this area, particularly social class issues (Leonard & Jacob, 1988; Russell et al., 1985; Sher, 1991; U.S. Dept. of Health and Human Services, 1993; West & Prinz, 1987). Moreover, much of the available literature deals also with abuse of other substances (Bays, 1990). The known damaging effects of family violence on child development make this an important area for study.

A number of studies have found an increased risk of abuse and neglect in children of substance-abusing parents. (See the review by Bays, 1990.) Many of these studies draw heavily on court records and are found in legal and public policy publications. Alcohol may be a common factor in multigenerational patterns of child abuse. Some studies have found children to be deliberately intoxicated, for sedation or amusement, by substance-using caretakers (Bays, 1990). Even if the children are not themselves abused, children of alcoholic parents are more likely to witness parental abuse, which itself has damaging developmental effects.

The few available studies on child sexual abuse in relation to alcohol use suggest that a substantial proportion of sexual abuse situations involve alcohol abuse by the perpetrator. (See the review by Bays, 1990.) Moreover, in a study of psychiatric diagnoses in incest victims, Sirles, Smith, and Kusama (1989) found that alcohol abuse by the perpetrator was associated with a greater risk of Axis I psychiatric disorder in the victim. Other studies, beyond the scope of this review, have found frequent histories of sexual abuse in female substance abusers, thus implying a painful cycle of alcoholism and sexual abuse in families.

A number of possible factors have been found or speculated to relate parental alcohol use with family violence. There may be the direct effects of alcohol in increasing aggression, through cognitive impairments (reduced inhibition, reduced judgment) and altered expectancies (Leonard & Jacob, 1988). Indirectly, family levels of stress and vulnerability are raised by the adverse impact of such factors as economic distress, other addictions, and concomitant physical and mental illnesses (Bays, 1990). Moderating factors may include the sex of the addicted parent (addicted mothers being more likely to be abusive), presence of violence between parents, lack of financial and social supports, and the presence of a second addicted parent, each of which appears to increase the risk to children (Black & Mayer, 1980). Some children of alcoholics are at increased risk for abuse based on inherited temperament, in utero alcohol exposure, and environmental stress; resulting irritability, dysmorphisms, learning problems, hyperactivity, and anxiety all may affect the parent-child attachment and the child's vulnerability.

The available literature suggests not only that children of substance-abusing parents may be at greater risk for abuse and neglect; substance-abusing parents also have been found less likely to cooperate with interventions or with court-ordered treatment, frequently resulting in eventual termination of parental rights. There are public policy and therapeutic implications of such findings, given that earlier placement in a stable and enriching environment may help mitigate the damage of earlier substance exposure and neglect (Bays, 1990).

In terms of injury, children of alcoholics have been found to have one and a half times the rate of injury and poisonings of other children (Children of Alcoholics Foundation, 1990), and sons of alcoholics have a significantly higher rate of traumatic head injuries (Tarter et al., 1984). Using national survey data, Bijur, Kurzon, Overpeck, and Scheidt (1992) found that children of mothers categorized as problem drinkers had over twice the risk of serious injury compared with children of nondrinking mothers and that children of problem drinking women married to men who were moderate or heavy drinkers had a relative risk of serious injury of 2.7. Such findings have implications for the role of physicians in detecting the sources of injury in children and participating in prevention efforts.

DEPRESSION AND EMOTIONAL FUNCTIONING

Children of alcoholic parents may face an increased risk of developing depressive and anxiety symptoms. (See the reviews by Russell et al., 1985; West & Prinz, 1987.) While one study found significantly more depressive symptoms, and at more extreme levels, in children of alcoholics compared with matched controls (Rolf, Johnson, Israel, Baldwin, & Chandra, 1988), a comprehensive study by Reich et al. (1993) found only a trend toward depression in children with two alcoholic parents, and no significant findings in children with one alcoholic parent, compared with controls. The literature on "depressive spectrum disorder" postulates a range of psychopathological outcomes, including depression and alcoholism, which may run through family pedigrees (reviewed by Russell et al., 1985); in this schema, female offspring may be more susceptible to depression, while males are more susceptible to alcoholism. The sex of the drinking parent may be salient; in one study, children of alcoholic fathers tended to demonstrate more conduct problems, children of alcoholic mothers manifested more emotional disorders, and children with two alcoholic parents showed both conduct and emotional disorders (Steinhausen, Gobel, & Nestler, 1984). Hill and Muka (1996) found significantly higher rates of internalizing disorders in children of alcoholic mothers in comparison with controls, after screening out families with recurrent depression, suggesting that the cotransmission of affective disorders may not be explanatory. In general, this area of research is complicated by the diversity of diagnostic schemes and sampling procedures and by the challenge of separating out the genetic and environment effects.

TEMPERAMENT AND PERSONALITY

The interesting literature on temperament and personality suggests that certain characteristics may differentiate children of alcoholics (and those predisposed to alcoholism) from others in the population. Current thinking does not support the concept of an "alcoholic personality," which is now thought to represent characteristics that are the consequence rather than the antecedents of heavy alcohol use (Vaillant, 1983). However, there may be personality predictors of some types of problematic alcohol use; these include behavioral undercontrol and emotionality, and possibly alexithymia, augmentation-reduction, and external locus of control. (See the reviews by Sher, 1991; Windle, 1990.) The studies on temperament and behavioral genetics (Tarter, 1991) may help in developing the complex models needed to understand vulnerability in offspring of alcoholic parents and perhaps in identifying those at risk for later alcohol problems.

FAMILY PROCESS

A number of clinicians have studied family process in alcoholic families. However, in examining the impact of parental alcohol use on children's development, we do not yet understand how "family interactive processes mediate the relationship between parental drinking and adverse child outcome" (Seilhamer & Jacob, 1990, p. 181). The literature on alcoholic family process is very interesting and has generated important hypotheses; there are some significant limits to the methodology and applicability of this research, as will be discussed.

Steinglass (1982) provides an excellent summary of family systems theory and its application in his studies of alcoholic family process, using the behavioral observation method. (See also Steinglass, 1992, for a more detailed discussion.) A few of his valuable findings concerning alcoholic families will be discussed here. He notes a number of features that are unique to alcohol as a stressor: the chronicity of the problem, the psychobiological activity of the substance, the characteristic on/off cycling (dual-state pattern of behavior), and the consistency (predictability) of a particular alcoholic's response to alcohol. As described by Steinglass, families demonstrate distinct and rigidly predictable patterns of response to intoxicated states in the drinking member, which differ in affect expression and problem-solving capacity from the nonintoxicated state; alcohol may serve several adaptive functions for a family, particularly in maintaining the homeostasis and stability of the family system. For some, for example, the "wet" (intoxicated) system may be more assertive and able to solve problems. These responses may help explain the alcoholic family's investment in homeostasis and resistance to interventions. However, over the long term, these families are unable to progress along the expected life cycle course; the short-term stability comes at the cost of long-term growth and change. These findings have implications for family interventions. Other family process studies, reviewed by Seilhamer and Jacob (1990), have also found differences in parent-child interactions in alcoholic families compared with controls and differences in problem-solving and affective behavior varying with the drinking phase. Furthermore, positive or negative family consequences may differ depending on the drinking pattern and drinking location of the alcoholic spouse.

Seilhamer and Jacob (1990) provide a useful conceptualization of three pathways by which parental alcohol use may affect child outcomes; these include ethanol effects (on mood, behavior, and health), family effects (such as financial strain, marital conflict, social isolation, ritual disruption), and modeling effects (whereby alcohol use is seen, for example, as a coping mechanism). A point that has received little attention is how deviant children may influence the drinking patterns of their caregivers. Based on a series of experiments, Pelham and Lang (1993) concluded that parental alcohol consumption has adverse effects on management of children's deviant behavior, *and* that deviant behavior by children increases parental stress and alcohol consumption.

Other studies have asked whether the family effects of parent alcoholism are modifiable. Moos and Billings (1982) concluded that it is the parent's current drinking, not drinking history, that affects the child's well-being; at follow-up, children of recovered parents were reported to be functioning similarly to controls, while children of relapsed alcoholics had twice the rates of emotional distress. The work of Wolin, Bennett, and colleagues (Bennett, Wolin, & Reiss, 1988; Wolin, Bennett, &

Noonan, 1979) found that children in alcoholic families that maintained family rituals evidenced less behavioral and emotional problems than those from homes where the rituals were disrupted by the parental drinking. These authors suggest that circumstances can moderate the developmental effects; others have questioned these conclusions.

The studies just discussed have important limitations that affect their applicability to clinical interventions (Russell, Henderson, & Blumer, 1985; Seilhamer & Jacob, 1990; Sher, 1991; West & Prinz, 1987). They generally used small sample sizes, with variable (and sometimes unique) methods of ascertainment and study. The lack of control groups means that the specificity of the findings for alcoholic families (versus other dysfunctional families) is unknown. The frequently used method of screening out other psychopathology may render the families unrepresentative of alcoholic families in the general population. Quite significantly, the studies often rely on volunteer families, usually white, middle class, and intact, which again may limit the applicability of such findings to a clinical population. Longitudinal studies are lacking; without a long-term perspective, the ultimate adjustment or maladjustment of these children is unknown. It is hoped that further research will build on these provocative findings to further our work in this important area.

ALCOHOL AND OTHER SUBSTANCE USE, ABUSE, AND DEPENDENCE

It is important for clinicians to recognize that children of alcoholics face an increased risk for alcohol problems themselves. Although the magnitude of the risk varies among studies, the finding has been fairly consistent (Russell, 1990). Alcohol use by such children is characterized by earlier onset of drinking and of problem drinking, and by heavier drinking. (See the review by Russell, 1990; also Weinberg, Dielman, Mandell & Shope, 1994.) Problematic alcohol use by adolescents is further associated with other threats to their safety and well-being, including accidents, suicide, unintended pregnancy, and sexually transmitted diseases.

Yet later alcoholism is not an inevitable result of having an alcoholic parent, and many alcoholics have not had an alcoholic parent. A very complex interplay of genetic and environmental factors

contributes to later alcohol abuse or dependence. Some important methodologic issues further complicate this field; these include the heterogeneity of alcoholism, sex differences, assortative mating by alcoholic parents, and demographic and cohort factors (Russell, 1990).

An array of significant studies have looked at the genetics of familial alcoholsm. Methods have included family, twin, adoption, half sibling, high-risk, genetic linkage, and animal model approaches; excellent reviews of this complex literature are available by Cadoret (1990), Merikangas (1990), Russell (1990), Searles (1990), Sher (1991), and the U.S. Dept. of Health and Human Services (1993). One important finding is the probable significant heterogeneity of alcoholism; alcoholism is not currently thought to be a singular phenomenon, nor carried on one gene. In fact, several typologies of alcoholism have been proposed (Babor et al., 1992); many point to a distinction based on the presence or absence of antisocial features. An excellent discussion of the complexities of gene-environment interactions in the etiology of alcoholism can be found in Searles (1990).

Another exciting area of research seeks biological markers that may distinguish children of alcoholics and/or those at risk for alcoholism. Studies have examined potential differences in biochemistry and hormonal levels, ethanol metabolism, electroencephalograph and event-related potentials findings, and body sway. (See the reviews by Chan, 1990; Sher, 1991; Tarter, Moss & Laird, 1991; U.S. Dept. of Health and Human Services, 1993.)

Environmental influences are also thought to play an important role in the intergenerational transmission of alcohol problems. As noted by West and Prinz (1987), the potential psychosocial effects of parental alcoholism are myriad and pervasive, including disruption of the home environment and parenting functions, risk of financial strain, divorce, poor supervision of children, susceptibility to peer influences, and others. A number of parenting factors have been associated with adolescent use of alcohol and drugs. (See the reviews by Kumpfer, 1989; Hawkins, Catalano & Miller, 1992.) In brief, such variables include parent attitudes toward adolescent drug use, warmth of the parent-child relationship, and family management practices. What is not clear from current studies is whether these parenting variables are themselves associated with parental alcohol and substance abuse.

Other areas of study in risk factor research include examining alcohol expectancies, which are the attitudes with which individuals approach drinking and the outcomes that they expect will result (see the reviews by Sher, 1991; U.S. Dept. of Health and Human Services, 1993); risk perception; moral development; and sensation-seeking.

All of these arenas of etiologic research are thought to hold potential for risk identification and prevention. Given the risks for alcoholism and its significant individual, familial, and societal costs, understanding the etiology of alcoholism in children of alcoholics has important implications for preventive and intervention efforts; it is hoped that further study of risk factors will yield refinement of clinical and preventive approaches.

INTERPERSONAL RELATIONSHIPS

The popular literature on adult children of alcoholics offers descriptions of relationship difficulties and recommendations for treatment based on clinical observation. Yet there is little empirical evidence to support the generalizations put forward by these authors; in fact, recent studies have failed to find certain differences between adult children of alcoholics and control groups. In addition to the lack of methodological rigor, these reports are based on self-referred and overwhelmingly female populations (Searles, 1990), which are unrepresentative of the overall population of adult children of alcoholics that this literature purports to describe.

Given the popularity and frequent acceptance of the adult children of alcoholics literature and movement, it may be helpful for clinicians to have some familiarity with the concepts put forth. The popular literature on their relationships notes interpersonal difficulties, such as lack of trust, a need to feel in control, isolation, and difficulty with establishing intimate relationships (reviewed by Sher, 1991). Specific roles are described, some based on birth order, which are thought to have been adaptive in the family of origin but become rigid and interfering in adult relationships; these include the "hero" (superachiever, responsible child, often the firstborn), "scapegoat" (often the second child), "adjustor," "placator," and "mascot" (often the youngest). Although these are pop-

ularly endorsed, the lack of empirical research leaves unclear the degree to which such roles characterize the general population of adult children of alcoholics and whether such problems are specific to these children in any way that is useful to helping them.

Young children of alcoholics may sometimes experience impairments in their social relationships, but little empirical research is available to test this (West & Prinz, 1987). Sher (1991) provides a review of current social developmental theory, disturbed attachment, and separation as they may apply to the development of children in alcoholic families. Longitudinal studies are needed to examine this question (West & Prinz, 1987).

RESILIENCE

Currently the issue of resilience in children of alcoholics is receiving a surge of attention. In looking at those children who are not significantly damaged by their experiences, we may understand the sources of their strength and be better able to help prevent damage in other children. Aside from interesting case reports, few studies have so far been conducted in this important area (Searles, 1990). Often cited is a study by Werner (1986), which followed a cohort of 698 Hawaiian children, including 49 children of alcoholics, to age 18. Drawing on this and other studies and reports, the features identified as possibly protective in alcoholic homes fall into three domains: child, parent, and environmental. Of the child characteristics, the following features have been identified as protective (Seilhamer & Jacob, 1990; Werner, 1986; see also Rutter, 1979): female sex, easy or affectionate temperament, at least average intelligence and verbal skills, positive self-concept, and an attitude of responsibility, self-help, and internal locus of control. Berlin and Davis (1989) identify an ability to "distance adaptively" from the family as protective. Wolin and Wolin (1993), drawing from their clinical work and studies, describe "7 resiliencies" of survivors of troubled homes: insight, independence, relationships, initiative, creativity, humor, and morality. Kumpfer and Hopkins (1993) also list 7 major self factors that increase resiliency and are associated with specific coping skills: optimism, empathy, insight, intellectual competence, self-esteem, direction, and perseverance.

Parent variables affecting resilience include degree of the alcohol problem, emotional stability and coping style of the parents, and the sex and psychiatric status of the nondrinking parent (if there is one in the home).

Certain environmental features may also be protective. These include birth order, family size, and spacing of children, which affect the degree of attention available to the child in the first 2 years of life; low parental conflict early in life; socioeconomic status; and availability of social supports outside the home. Studies by Bennett and Wolin (Bennett et al., 1988; Wolin et al., 1979) point to the usefulness of maintaining family rituals in protecting from intergenerational transmission of alcoholism.

Clinical Implications

Parental alcoholism is pervasive in society and in clinical populations. Clinicians need to be aware of and educated about addictive processes and ready to integrate current understanding about alcoholism into their work, within whatever theoretical framework they use. Rivinus (1991) provides a comprehensive and useful discussion of the parallel histories of analysis and addictionology, long at odds with and misunderstood by each other. His "new synthesis" draws on a variety of viewpoints (psychoanalysis, behaviorism, self psychology, and others) to form an integrated approach to children of addicted parents.

Clinicians also need to examine their personal views and biases about alcohol and those who heavily use it. DuPont and McGovern (1991) discuss implications that the powerful "mutual aid" (12-step) movement has for medical education as well as the need for the many addicted, recovering, or clinicians who are themselves children of alcoholics to "heal themselves" by facing their own addiction-related issues in their efforts to help others.

Questions regarding parental responsibility and the damaging effects of parental drinking in children raise some as-yet unresolved ethical and legal issues. As more is learned about the effects of prenatal alcohol exposure, for example, will pregnant mothers be held responsible for the damage to their infants, as has sometimes happened with prenatal drug exposure (Wissow, 1990)? Will clinicians be responsible for reporting "prenatal abuse"? Are alcoholic parents inherently "neglectful"? Some of these questions may face clinicians in the future.

Clinical Interventions

At each stage of development, children of alcoholics will present to child psychiatrists and other health care providers with developmental difficulties. Clinicians thus have many opportunities for diagnosis, treatment, and possible prevention of the effects of parental alcohol use on children. A few points should be kept in mind regarding the following review. There is little empirical research to evaluate or demonstrate the efficacy of any of the modalities discussed; research on treatment for children of alcoholics is "almost nonexistent" (Williams, 1990) while the field is in this early stage. Heterogeneitity of alcoholism, nonspecificity of the impact of parental alcoholism, confounding variables such as concurrent parental drug use and other psychopathology all limit generalizations regarding clinical interventions. The following guidelines are drawn from the existing literature, clinical experience, and the preceding review.

EVALUATION AND DIAGNOSIS

The clinician should *ask about alcohol use history* in the parent, child, and extended family *as part of every diagnostic evaluation.* The following instruments may be useful for screening parents or for guidance: MAST, SMAST, CAGE, and T-ACE.

The Michigan Alcoholism Screening Test (MAST; Selzer, Vinokur, & van Rooijen, 1975) is a 24-item, self-administered questionnaire that has been much studied and used in assessing alcoholism in adults. A shortened 13-item version (SMAST) is also available (Selzer et al., 1975). The CAGE (Ewing, 1984) is an acronym for four questions that may be used to screen for alcoholism; they concern cutting down, annoyance, guilt, and eye-openers. The T-ACE (Sokol, Martier, & Ager, 1989) is an adaptation of the CAGE for use with pregnant women; it substitutes a question on tolerance for the one on guilt. An excellent summary on screening instruments (utility, research, and comparative features) can be found in the eighth Special Report to the U.S. Congress on Alcohol and Health (U.S. Dept. of Health and Human Services, 1993).

With children, the CAST, F-SMAST, and M-SMAST have proven useful. The Children of Alcoholics Screening Test (CAST; Pilat & Jones, 1984) is a 30-item inventory for identifying children who are or have been living with an alcoholic parent. It has been shown to have acceptable reliability as a screening instrument (Clair & Genest, 1992) and to be clinically useful and reliable in a child psychiatric population (Staley and el Guebaly, 1991). The F-SMAST and M-SMAST are 9-item questionnaires which have been adapted from the SMAST to screen for parental alcoholism among young adults (Crews & Sher, 1992); both have been shown to be reliable and valid measures.

The clinician should *be particularly alert* to possible parental alcohol problems *in the following presentations:*

Infancy
Dysmorphic presentation
Neurobehavioral deficits
  (poor suck, abnormal
  reflexes, poor arousal
  or habituation)
Disrupted sleep or
  sleep-wake patterns
Developmental delays
Signs of abuse or neglect

Latency
Academic problems and
  cognitive impairment
Chronic physical or sex-
  ual abuse or neglect
Attention deficits
Hyperactivity or other
  conduct problems
Scapegoating of child pa-
  tient (a child becom-
  ing the "identified pa-
  tient" in an alcoholic
  family)
Frequent school ab-
  sences

Preschoolers
Signs of abuse or neglect
Temperament problems
Attentional deficits
Fine and gross motor
  performance decre-
  ments
Dysmorphic features

Adolescence
Continued academic or
  behavioral problems
Sexual abuse and sexual
  acting out
Conduct disorder
Alcohol and substance
  abuse in patient,
  peers, or siblings
Relationship difficulties,
  including choice of significant others with alcohol problems

Clinicians should examine their own possible biases regarding diagnosis and treatment of alcohol problems. Past views of "addictive personalities" and other stereotypes regarding alcoholism need to be reexamined in a more balanced light (see Rivinus, 1991; Vaillant, 1983). Cultural factors, individual and societal biases, family history, and personal drinking patterns also may affect a clinician's objectivity and willingness to probe for and deal with parental alcohol use.

TREATMENT PRINCIPLES AND MODALITIES

Most of the clinical literature on treating children of alcoholics is anecdotal rather than research-based and drawn from treatment of adult patients rather than work with children and adolescents. In fact, a study of alcoholism treatment programs run by the Department of Veteran Affairs found "services to children of alcoholics were nearly nonexistent" (Salinas, O'Farrell, Jones, & Cutter, 1991, p. 545). Although some authors depict "all" children of alcoholic homes to be impaired and in need of treatment, this review takes the approach that treatment should be directed toward a particular psychiatric problem or impairment rather than undertaken solely because a child has an alcoholic parent. Particular treatment modalities will be discussed; however, certain useful principles underlie any therapeutic approach to children once parental alcoholism is identified.

First, the clinician should *label and identify parental alcoholism,* and *refer the alcoholic parent for treatment.* Although it is not known whether recovery of the alcoholic parent promotes improvement in children (Russell et al., 1985; Williams, 1990), it appears preferable to work with parents in recovery, and reduce the risks and stresses associated with alcoholism in the family. If the parent is not physically addicted, a brief intervention may be effective, although long-term abstinence cannot be predicted (U.S. Dept. of Health and Human Services, 1993).

The clinician should *refer family members to support groups* and *to parent training groups.* (See the "Community Resources and Interventions" section later in the chapter.)

He or she also must work with the family to *reduce the number of stressors* as much as possible. This recommendation is based on the research by Rutter (1979) and others, suggesting that stressors potentiate each other as the number of risk factors increases.

While treating the presenting problem with conventional modalities (e.g., treating attention deficit hyperactivity disorder with medication, behavioral interventions, and educational modifications), the clinician should *be aware of the potential impact of parental alcohol problems on the course of treatment* (see Gabel & Shindledecker, 1990). Such parents may be dependent, inconsistent in attendance, unable to follow through on treatment recommendations, and unable to support or tolerate changes in their children (Morehouse & Richards, 1982). The clinician must be prepared to view these issues as meaningful in understanding the child's experience in the home.

Clinicians should *incorporate the following components* into any treatment modality for children of alcoholics (Morehouse & Richards, 1982; Williams, 1990): education regarding alcohol effects; identification and expression of affect; promotion of healthier relationships; and problem-solving and coping skill development and enhancement.

Finally, the clinician should encourage and *support strengths and sources of resilience* in children from alcoholic dysfunctional homes. These avenues may be within the home, such as strengthening family rituals, or outside the family, through identifying stable caring adults and forming healthy supportive relationships with them.

The various treatment modalities include individual, family, and group therapy and community resources and interventions.

Individual Therapy: The preceding principles should be kept in mind particularly in individual treatment of children with alcoholic parents. Some appropriate modifications of the usual clinical approach may be warranted to aid such children. In particular, the clinician has the opportunity to educate children regarding the effects of alcohol use and possibly to help prevent intergenerational transmission of these problems. If the family remains enmeshed in an alcoholic system, the child may benefit from encouragement to find healthy supports outside the family rather than from efforts to fix or join the family of origin (Bennett & Wolin, 1990). The limited capacity of alcoholic parents to benefit from parent guidance should be recognized. Finally, clinicians should

be particularly sensitive to the child's possible transference issues regarding honest communication and trust (Richards, Morehouse, Seixas, & Kern, 1983).

Parental alcohol use may hold particular significance in treating severe psychiatric and behavior disorders requiring hospitalization. Gabel's studies (Gabel & Shindledecker, 1990) have found parental substance abuse to be a powerful predictor of poorer outcomes and of need for out-of-home placements in hospitalized children, even when controlling for child variables such as suicidality and severe aggression. Such findings further support the need for increased awareness of the impact of parental alcohol use and its implications for effective interventions.

Family Therapy: Although several significant studies have explored alcoholic family process, there is surprisingly little empirical literature on alcoholic family treatment (Willams, 1990). Reported studies based on behavioral or family systems theories focus on the presenting alcoholic patient or on the marital dyad; none has included children in the research (Collins, 1990). The lack of adequate control groups and the use of white, middle-class intact families also have limited the applicability of family process studies to family treatment.

Nonetheless, family treatment is a reasonable and favored approach in dealing with families with an alcoholic parent, given the significant interplay between parental drinking and family process. See Steinglass with Bennett, Wokin, and Reiss (1987) for detailed recommendations regarding family treatment with alcoholic families. The clinician should be familiar with the tenets of family systems theory and aware that different patterns of alcohol abuse have different impacts on families (Collins, 1990; Steinglass et al., 1987). Another promising approach is parenting skills training for alcohol and substance abusing parents (Williams, 1990; see "Community Resources and Interventions" later in the chapter); this approach is receiving increased attention as a preventive measure for intervening with children at risk.

Group Therapy: Group treatment is often offered to children and adolescent offspring of alcoholic parents in clinic settings. (For groups offered in school and public settings, see "Community Resources and Interventions.") As reviewed by Williams (1990), the goals of such treatment are to address early drinking problems in children and adolescents and to address dysfunctional behavior and coping. Children may find significant relief and affirmation in such settings and a diminution of their sense of isolation. The four components of group treatment include education regarding alcoholism, affect identification and expression, development of healthy relationships, and improved problem-solving and coping skills.

Formats for group treatment tend to be based on subjective guidelines and vary considerably; little systematic research has been done in this area. Resources for further discussion of current approaches include the National Clearinghouse for Alcohol and Drug Information, Robinson (1989), and Rivinus (1991).

COMMUNITY RESOURCES AND INTERVENTIONS

Clinicians should become familiar with community resources for children and families of alcoholics and feel free to refer to them. They include school-based groups, Alateen and Al-Anon meetings, books and videos for children of alcoholics, and literature and information provided by national organizations devoted to issues concerning children of alcoholics. These resources may be very useful adjuncts to clinical treatment or may be provided when practical barriers or resistance to treatment is high. The clinician can refer a patient to local meetings, consult to school groups, obtain and distribute literature from organizations, and attend a public meeting of Al-Anon or Alateen.

Community resources offer a number of important advantages for children of alcoholics. They are generally free and accessible, and may be more acceptable to family and peers as well as less stigmatizing. Most important, they offer an avenue of support for children and adolescents who may be feeling particularly isolated by the nature of their parent's problem. Some literature suggests that the support and positive identification found in these groups may be especially helpful to those children of alcoholics who are initially less resilient and less able to find their own resources. Such groups may also offer a bridge for resistant patients eventually to engage in other treatment.

Disadvantages or pitfalls of such approaches are reviewed by Emshoff and Anyan (1991) and include issues regarding recruitment and labeling.

The goals of such approaches (Emshoff & Anyan, 1991) are to address the risk factors among children of alcoholics for later alcohol and other life problems, including dysfunctional coping and mood and relationship issues. The intervention components include information and education regarding alcoholism, skill-building, social support, and promotion of positive socioemotional development (Emshoff & Anyan, 1991).

The following resources can be found or established in the community:

School Groups: Many school programs for children of alcoholics have been devised; see Emshoff and Anyan (1991) for a review and Morehouse and Scola (1986) for a list of resources and a description of features and pitfalls. Curriculum materials are also listed in Robinson (1989). The best known of the prevention and educational formats is the CASPAR program, begun in Massachusetts in 1974. It targets group interventions to various age groups, in both school and community settings. Student Assistant Programs (SAPs), modeled on employee assistance programs; the Students Together and Resourceful (STAR) program; and the Stress Management and Alcohol Awareness Program are other intervention models that have been developed and studied (Emshoff & Anyan, 1991).

Parenting Training and Family Skills Training: Many families with a substance-abusing or substance-dependent parent can benefit from specific instruction in parenting skills. Current research suggests that poor parental monitoring of children is a major family risk factor for substance abuse in adolescents and that improving parental monitoring and limit-setting may benefit family members, even if parents are not enrolled in substance abuse treatment. Programs for parents (some of which include the children) are offered in most communities through community colleges and trade schools, community mental health centers, hospitals, schools, and other settings. Exemplary programs such as the Strengthening Families Program are described in the user's guide listed below (Kumpfer, 1993). For referral information, clinicians can contact their local Department of Social Services; the following references also offer information on starting such programs in the community.

Alateen: This is a 12-step self-help program for adolescent family members of alcoholics, offered in many communities. A few studies have evaluated the efficacy of Alateen (see Emshoff & Anyan, 1991; Williams, 1990); there may be some improvement in mood and self-esteem, although group therapy may be more beneficial.

Books, Videos, Pamphlets: Many of these resources are available for children, adolescents, and parents, for use individually or in group settings. These are described and listed extensively in the following sources: Ackerman (1983), Morehouse and Scola (1986), and Robinson (1989).

Further information and resources are available from the following organizations: Al-Anon/Alateen Family Groups Headquarters, Inc., P.O. Box 862, Midtown Station, New York, NY 10018-0862; 212-302-7240; 1-800-344-2666 (U.S.), 1-800-443-4525 (Canada). Children of Alcoholics Foundation, Inc., 555 Madison Avenue, 20th floor, New York, NY 10022, 212-754-0656, 800-359-COAF. *Strengthening America's families: A user's guide* (Kumpfer, 1993); Juvenile Justice Clearinghouse, Box 6000, Rockville, MD 20850, 800-638-8736. National Clearinghouse for Alcohol and Drug Information (NCADI), P.O. Box 2345, Rockville, MD 20847-2345, 301-468-2600, 1-800-729-6686. NCADI offers an extensive catalog of free publications, addressing patient education, research, and prevention, in monograph, booklet, guidebook, and video formats. Audiences include health professionals, educators, parents, children, and adolescents. Three publication series of particular scientific interest are Alcohol Health and Research World, the National Institute of Drug Abuse Research Monograph series, and Alcohol Alert.

OPPORTUNITIES FOR PREVENTION

Clinical Opportunities: Familial alcoholism offers the clinician a rare opportunity for preventive interventions in a clinical setting.

The clinician should *alert* women of childbearing age to the risks of fetal alcohol syndrome and fetal alcohol effects. If significant maternal alcohol use is uncovered in the course of evaluation of a child, efforts should be made to advise the mother regarding risks to future offspring.

He or she also should *warn*, and work with, young children of alcoholics, particularly adolescents, regarding their own heightened risk of alcohol misuse problems. This awareness of risk may help safeguard such children from repeating familial patterns that they don't understand. Forming healthy identifications outside the family also may prove protective.

Community Opportunities: As highly regarded professionals in the general community, child psychiatrists and other mental health professionals can use their influence to *educate the public* and *support public health efforts* to alter the promotion, image, and availability of alcoholic products. Important targets for change include mass media portrayals of alcohol use; alcoholic beverage advertising; and laws regarding liquor sales (price, taxation, hours of sale, location of stores), drinking age, drunken driving penalties, labeling of containers, and server training as well as individual attitudes (Bijur et al., 1992).

Cultural Meanings of Parental Alcoholism

As noted earlier, it is not clear to what degree the stresses faced by a child of alcoholic parents are unique to that situation or are similar to those experienced by children in other "dysfunctional" families. However, one aspect may significantly differentiate the experience of the child in an alcoholic family from that of children of parents with schizophrenia, depression, drug addiction, and other problems: the very mixed messages which coexist in society regarding alcohol use. Alcohol is a legal and heavily promoted product, integral to our society economically. It has roots and cultural significance dating back thousands of years in most cultures. It is associated in the media with sociability, attractiveness, success, and other positive attributes. Only recently have there been community-based efforts to associate alcohol with its potential costs, by groups such as Mothers Against Drunk Driving and Students Against Drunk Driving. The confusion and denial of the alcoholic is reflected in societal attitudes, for example, in the great disparity between the minimal teaching time devoted by most medical school curricula to alcohol issues and the vast number of alcohol-related diseases and alcoholic patients seen in clinical practice.

Stigmatized attitudes regarding alcoholism add to the alcoholic's denial in seeking help. The child in an alcoholic family may note the discrepancy between the happy healthy drinkers on television and the chaos in the home, or may face minimization and denial of parental alcohol problems by those who are in a position to help, such as teachers, counselors, and health care workers. In this sense the experience of being a child of an alcoholic parent may be somewhat distinct.

A final question is whether it is helpful to identify children with an alcoholic parent as "children of alcoholics," with all that such labeling may imply. Whether a distinct syndrome exists for which specific treatment may be offered or not, it is important to keep in mind that many such children do well despite the challenges of their family situation. Their strengths, coping skills, and potential for healthy development should be recognized and nurtured to the fullest extent possible.

REFERENCES

Abel, E. L. (1990). *Fetal alcohol syndrome.* Oradell, NJ: Medical Economics Company.

Ackerman, R. J. (1983). *Children of alcoholics.* New York: Simon & Schuster.

Babor, T. F., Hofmann, M., DelBoca, F. K., Hesselbrock, V., Meyer, R. E., Dolinsky, Z. S., & Rounsaville, B. (1992). Types of alcoholics, I: Evidence for an empirically derived typology based on indicators of vulnerability and severity. *Archives of General Psychiatry, 49,* 599–608.

Bays, J. (1990). Substance abuse and child abuse: Impact of addiction on the child. *Pediatric Clinics of North America, 37,* 881–904.

Bennett, L. A., & Wolin, S. J. (1990). Family culture and alcoholism transmission. In R. L. Collins, K. E. Leonard, & J. S. Searles (Eds.), *Alcohol and the family: Research and clinical perspectives* (pp. 194–219). New York: Guilford Press.

Bennett, L. A., Wolin, S. J., & Reiss, D. (1988). Deliberate family process: A strategy for protecting children of alcoholics. *British Journal of Addiction, 83,* 821–829.

Berlin, R., & Davis, R. B. (1989). Children from alcoholic families: Vulnerability and resilience. In T. F. Dugan & R. Coles (Eds.), *The child in our times: Studies in the development of resiliency* (pp. 81–105). New York: Brunner/Mazel.

Bijur, P. E., Kurzon, M., Overpeck, M. D., & Scheidt, P. C. (1992). Parental alcohol use, problem drinking, and children's injuries. *Journal of the American Medical Association, 267,* 3166–3171.

Black, R., & Mayer, J. (1980). Parents with special problems: Alcoholism and opiate addiction. *Child Abuse and Neglect, 4,* 45–54.

Cadoret, R. J. (1990). Genetics of alcoholism. In R. L. Collins, K. E. Leonard, & J. S. Searles (Eds.), *Alcohol and the family: Research and clinical perspectives* (pp. 39–78). New York: Guilford Press.

Cantwell, D. P. (1976). Genetic factors in the hyperactive syndrome. *Journal of the American Academy of Child Psychiatry, 15,* 214–223.

Chan, A. W. K. (1990). Biochemical markers for alcoholism. In M. Windle & J. S. Searles (Eds.), *Children of alcoholics: Critical perspectives* (pp. 39–72). New York: Guilford Press.

Children of Alcoholics Foundation (1990). *Children of alcoholics in the medical system: Hidden problems, hidden costs.* New York: Author.

Clair, D. J., & Genest, M. (1992). The Children of Alcoholics Screening Test: Reliability and relationship to family environment, adjustment, and alcohol-related stressors of adolescent offspring of alcoholics. *Journal of Clinical Psychology, 48,* 414–420.

Collins, R. L. (1990). Family treatment of alcohol abuse: Behavioral and systems perspectives. In R. L. Collins, K. E. Leonard, & J. S. Searles (Eds.), *Alcohol and the family: Research and clinical perspectives* (pp. 285–308). New York: Guilford Press.

Crews, T. M., & Sher, K. J. (1992). Using adapted short MASTs for assessing parental alcoholism: Reliability and validity. *Alcoholism: Clinical and Experimental Research, 16,* 576–584.

Dishion, T. J., Patterson, G. R., & Reid, J. R. (1988). Parent and peer factors associated with drug sampling in early adolescence: Implications for treatment. In E. R. Rahdert & J. Grabowski (Eds.), *Adolescent drug abuse: Analyses of treatment research,* NIDA Research Monograph 77 (pp. 69–93). Rockville, MD: U.S. Department of Health and Human Services.

Dorris, M. (1989). *The broken cord.* New York: Harper & Row.

Dupont, R. L., & McGovern, J. P. (1991). The growing impact of the children-of-alcoholics movement on medicine: A revolution in our midst. In T. M. Rivinus (Ed.), *Children of chemically dependent parents: Multiperspectives from the cutting edge* (pp. 313–329). New York: Brunner/Mazel.

Emshoff, J. G., & Anyan, L. L. (1991). From prevention to treatment: Issues for school-aged children of alcoholics. In M. Galanter (Ed.), *Recent developments in alcoholism. Vol. 9: Children of alcoholics* (pp. 327–346). New York: Plenum Press.

Ewing, J. A. (1984). Detecting alcoholism. The CAGE questionnaire. *Journal of the American Medical Association, 12,* 1905–7.

Gabel, S., & Shindledecker, R. (1990). Parental substance abuse and suspected child abuse/maltreatment predict outcome in children's inpatient treatment. *Journal of the Academy of Child and Adolescent Psychiatry, 29,* 919–924.

Galanter, M. (Ed.) (1991). *Recent developments in alcoholism. Vol. 9: Children of alcoholics.* New York: Plenum Press.

Hawkins, J. D., Catalano, R. F., and Miller, J. Y. (1992). Risk and protective factors for alcohol and other drug abuse in adolescence and early adulthood: Implications for substance abuse preventions. *Psychological Bulletin, 112,* 64–105.

Hill, S. Y., & Muka, D. (1996). Childhood psychopathology in children from families of alcoholic female probands. *Journal of the American Academy of Child and Adolescent Psychiatry, 35(6),* 725–733.

Institute of Medicine, Committee to study fetal alcohol syndrome. (1996). K. Stratton, C. Howe, & F. Battaglia (Eds.), *Fetal alcohol syndrome: diagnosis, epidemiology, prevention, and treatment.* Washington, DC: National Academy Press.

Johnson, J. L., & Rolf, J. E. (1988). Cognitive functioning in children from alcoholic and non-alcoholic families. *British Journal of Addiction, 83,* 849–857.

Kumpfer, K. (1989). Prevention of alcohol and drug abuse: A critical review of risk factors and prevention strategies. In D. Shaffer, I. Philips, & N. B. Enzer (Eds.), *Prevention of mental disorders, alcohol and other drug use in children and adolescents. OSAP Prevention Monograph 2* (pp. 309–372). Rockville, MD: U.S. Department of Health and Human Services.

Kumpfer, K. (1991). How to get hard to reach parents involved in parenting programs. In D. Pines (Ed.), *Parent training is prevention: Preventing alcohol and other drug problems among youth in the family* (pp. 87–95). Rockville, MD: U.S. Department of Health and Human Services.

Kumpfer, K., & Hopkins, R. (1993). Recent advances in addictive disorders. *Psychiatric Clinics of North America, 16,* 11–20.

Kumpfer, K. L. (1993). *Strengthening America's families: A user's guide.* (1993). Rockville, MD: Office of Juvenile Justice and Delinquency Prevention.

Leonard, K., & Jacob, T. (1988). Alcohol, alcoholism, and family violence. In V. B. Van Hasselt (Ed.), *Handbook of family violence* (pp. 383–406). New York: Plenum Press.

Merikangas, K. R. (1990). The genetic epidemiology of alcoholism. *Psychological Medicine, 20,* 11–22.

Moos, R. H., & Billings, A. G. (1982). Children of alcoholics during the recovery process: Alcoholic and matched control families. *Addictive Behaviors, 7,* 155–163.

Morehouse, E., & Richards, T. (1982). An examination of dysfunctional latency age children of alcoholic parents and problems in intervention. *Journal of Children in Contemporary Society, 15,* pp. 21–33.

Morehouse, E., & Scola, C. M. (1986). *Children of alcoholics: Meeting the needs of the young COA in the school setting.* South Laguna, CA: National Association for Children of Alcoholics.

Pelham, W. E., & Lang, A. R. (1993). Parental alcohol consumption and deviant child behavior: Laboratory studies of reciprocal effects. *Clinical Psychology Review, 13(8),* 763–784.

Pihl, R. O., Peterson, J., & Finn, P. (1990). Inherited predisposition to alcoholism: Characteristics of sons of male alcoholics. *Journal of Abnormal Psychology, 99,* 291–301.

Pilat, J. M., & Jones, J. W. (1984). Identification of children of alcoholics: Two empirical studies. *Alcohol Health and Research World, 9,* 27–36.

Reich, W., Earls, F., Frankel, O., & Shayka, J. J. (1993). Psychopathology in children of alcoholics. *Journal of the American Academy of Child and Adolescent Psychiatry, 32,* 995–1002.

Richards, T. M., Morehouse, E. R., Seixas, J. S., & Kern, J. C. (1983). Psychosocial assessment and intervention with children of alcoholic parents. In D. Cook, C. Fewell, & J. Riolo (Eds.), *Social work treatment of alcohol problems* (pp. 131–142). New Brunswick, NJ: Rutgers Center for Alcohol Studies.

Rivinus, T. M. (1991). Psychoanalytic theory and children of chemically dependent parents: Ships passing in the night? In T. M. Rivinus (Ed.), *Children of chemically dependent parents: Multiperspectives from the cutting edge* (pp. 103–127). New York: Brunner/Mazel.

Robinson, B. E. (1989). *Working with children of alcoholics.* Lexington, MA: Lexington Books.

Rolf, J. E., Johnson, J. L., Israel, E., Baldwin, J., & Chandra, A (1988). Depressive affect in school-aged children of alcoholics. *British Journal of Addiction, 83,* 841–848.

Russell, M. (1990). Prevalence of alcoholism among children of alcoholics. In M. Windle & J. S. Searles (Eds.), *Children of alcoholics: Critical perspectives* (pp. 9–38). New York: Guilford Press.

Russell, M., Henderson, C., & Blume, S. B. (1985). *Children of alcoholics: A review of the literature.* New York: Children of Alcoholics Foundation.

Rutter, M. (1979). Protective factors in children's response to stress and disadvantage. In M. W. Kent & J. E. Rolf (Eds.), *Primary prevention of psychopathology. Volume 3: Social competence in children.* (pp. 49–74). Hanover, N.H.: University Press of New England.

Rutter, M. (1989). Psychiatric disorder in parents as a risk factor of children. In D. Shaffer, I. Philips, & N. B. Enzer (Eds.), *Prevention of mental disorders, alcohol and other drug use in children and adolescents. OSAP Prevention Monograph 2* (pp. 157–189). Rockville, MD: U.S. Department of Health and Human Services.

Salinas, R. C., O'Farrell, T. J., Jones, W. C., & Cutter, H. S. (1991). Services for families of alcoholics: A national survey of Veterans Affairs treatment programs. *Journal of Studies on Alcohol, 52,* 541–546.

Searles, J. S. (1990). Behavior genetic research and risk for alcoholism among children of alcoholics. In M. Windle & J. S. Searles (Eds.), *Children of alcoholics: Critical perspectives* (pp. 99–128). New York: Guilford Press.

Searles, J. S., & Windle, M. (1990) Introduction and overview: Salient issues in the children of alcoholics literature. In M. Windle & J. S. Searles (Eds.), *Children of alcoholics: Critical perspectives* (pp. 1–8). New York: Guilford Press.

Seilhamer, R. A., & Jacob, T. (1990). Family factors and adjustment of children of alcoholics. In M. Windle & J. S. Searles (Eds.), *Children of alcoholics: Critical perspectives* (pp. 168–186). New York: Guilford Press.

Selzer, M. L., Vinokur, A., & van Rooijen, L. (1975). A self-administered Short Michigan Alcoholism Screening Test (SMAST). *Journal of Studies on Alcohol, 36,* 117–126.

Sher, K. J. (1991). *Children of alcoholics: The critical appraisal of theory and research.* Chicago: University of Chicago Press.

Sirles, E. A., Smith, J. A., & Kusama, H. (1989). Psychiatric status of intrafamilial child sexual abuse victims. *Journal of the American Academy of Child and Adolescent Psychiatry, 28,* 225–229.

Smith, I. E., & Coles, C. D. (1991). Multilevel intervention for prevention of fetal alcohol syndrome and effects of prenatal alcohol exposure. In M. Galanter (Ed.), *Recent developments in alcoholism. Vol. 9: Children of alcoholics* (pp. 165–180). New York: Plenum Press.

Sokol, R. J., Martier, S. S., & Ager, J. W. (1989). The T-ACE questions: Practical prenatal detection of risk-drinking. *American Journal of Obstetrics and Gynecology, 160,* 863–870.

Staley, D., & el Guebaly, N. (1991). Psychometric evaluation of the Children of Alcoholics Screening Test (CAST) in a psychiatric sample. *International Journal of the Addictions, 26,* 657–668.

Steinglass, P. (1982). The roles of alcohol in family systems. In J. Offord & J. Harwin (Eds.), *Alcohol and the family* (pp. 127–150). New York: St. Martin's Press.

Steinglass, P. (1992). Family systems approaches to the alcoholic family: Research findings and their clinical applications. In S. Saitoh, P. Steinglass, & M. S. Schuckit (Eds.), *Alcoholism and the family* (pp. 155–171). New York: Brunner/Mazel, Inc.

Steinglass, P., with Bennett, L. A., Wolin, S. J., & Reiss, D. (1987). *The alcoholic family.* New York: Basic Books.

Steinhausen, H., Gobel, D., & Nestler, V. (1984). Psychopathology in the offspring of alcoholic parents. *Journal of the American Academy of Child Psychiatry, 23,* 465–471.

Streissguth, A. P., Aase, J. M., Clarren, S. K., Randels, S. P., LaDue, R. A., & Smith, D. F. (1991). Fetal alcohol syndrome in adolescents and adults. *Journal of the American Medical Association, 265,* 1961–1967.

Streissguth, A. P., Barr, H. M., & Sampson, P. D. (1990). Moderate prenatal alcohol exposure: Effects on child IQ and learning problems at age 7½ years. *Alcoholism: Clinical and Experimental Research, 14,* 662–669.

Tarter, R. E. (1991). Developmental behavior-genetic perspective of alcoholism etiology. In M. Galanter (Ed.), *Recent developments in alcoholism. Vol. 9: Children of alcoholics* (pp. 53–67). New York: Plenum Press.

Tarter, R. E., Hegedus, A. M., Goldstein, G., Shelly, D., & Alterman, A. I. (1984). Adolescent sons of alcoholics: Neuropsychological and personality characteristics. *Alcoholism: Clinical and Experimental Research, 8,* 216–221.

Tarter, R. E., Laird, S. B., & Moss, H. B. (1990). Neuropsychological and neurophysiological characteristics of children of alcoholics. In M. Windle & J. S. Searles, (Eds.), *Children of alcoholics: Critical perspectives* (pp. 73–98). New York: Guilford Press.

Tarter, R. E., Moss, H., & Laird, S. B. (1990). Biological markers for vulnerability to alcoholism. In R. L. Collins, K. E., Leonard, & J. S. Searles (Eds.), *Alcohol and the family: Research and clinical perspectives* (pp. 79–106). New York: Guilford Press.

U.S. Department of Health and Human Services. (1993). *Eighth special report to the U.S. Congress on alcohol and health.* Rockville, MD: U.S. Department of Health and Human Services.

Vaillant, G. E. (1983). *The natural history of alcoholism.* Cambridge, MA: Harvard University Press.

Weinberg, N. Z., Dielman, T. E., Mandell, W., & Shope, J. T. (1994). Parental drinking and gender factors in the prediction of early adolescent alcohol use. *International Journal of the Addictions, 29,* 89–104.

Werner, E. E. (1986). Resilient offspring of alcoholics: A longitudinal study from birth to age 18. *Journal of Studies on Alcohol, 47,* 34–40.

West, M. O., & Prinz, R. J. (1987). Parental alcoholism and childhood psychopathology. *Psychological Bulletin, 102,* 204–218.

Williams, C. N. (1990). Prevention and treatment approaches for children of alcoholics. In M. Windle & J. S. Searles (Eds.), *Children of alcoholics: Critical perspectives* (pp. 187–216). New York: Guilford Press.

Windle, M. (1990). Temperament and personality attributes of children of alcoholics. In M. Windle & J. S. Searles (Eds.), *Children of alcoholics: Critical perspectives* (pp. 129–167). New York: Guilford Press.

Windle, M., & Searles, J. S. (1990). Summary, integration, and future directions: toward a life-span perspective. In M. Windle & J. S. Searles (Eds.), *Children of alcoholics: Critical perspectives* (pp. 217–238). New York: Guilford Press.

Windle, M., & Searles, J. S. (Eds.) (1990). *Children of alcoholics: Critical perspectives*. New York: Guilford Press.

Wissow, L. S. (1990). *Child advocacy for the clinician: An approach to child abuse and neglect*. Baltimore: Williams & Wilkins.

Wolin, S. J., Bennett, L. A., & Noonan, D. L. (1979). Family rituals and the reoccurrence of alcoholism over generations. *American Journal of Psychiatry, 136,* 589–593.

Wolin, S. J., & Wolin, S. (1993). *The resilient self: How survivors of troubled families rise above adversity*. New York: Villard Books.

Woodside, M. (1988). Research on children of alcoholics: Past and future. *British Journal of Addiction, 83,* 785–792.

SECTION II
Varieties of Psychosocial Condition

19 / The Effects of Poverty on Children's Socioemotional Development

Vonnie C. McLoyd, Rosario Ceballo, and Sarah C. Mangelsdorf

Poverty, officially defined as a condition in which the income of an individual or family falls below a standard set by the United States government, rarely comes "alone." Far from being a unitary variable reflecting only insufficient income, it is a pervasive stressor marked by a conglomerate of economic and environmental variables, especially if it is persistent. Scarcity of material resources and services often is conjoined to a plethora of undesirable events (e.g., eviction, physical illness, criminal assault) and ongoing conditions (e.g., inadequate housing, poor health care, dangerous neighborhoods) resulting from inadequate income (Belle, 1984; Pelton, 1989). Poverty also is a marker variable for an array of demographic/person variables, such as low educational attainment, low occupational status, adolescent parenthood, and single parenthood, that are correlates, but not the equivalent, of economic privation.

Although poverty is a well-documented and consistent predictor of children's socioemotional functioning, rarely can its effects be seen as direct. This is so, first, because poverty is an exceedingly multidimensional, global, and, in some ways, distal variable, and, second, because the conceptualization of poverty as a "social address," as when poor children are compared to affluent children, fails to illuminate the intervening structures or processes through which the environment affects the course of development (Bronfenbrenner, 1986). Rather than being direct, relations between poverty and children's socioemotional development typically reflect the operation of some set of poverty-determined or poverty-related elements, often termed mediating variables, on child outcomes or the interaction between these variables (Deutsch,

1973). These mediating variables are more proximal and less distal than poverty per se in the sense that they directly impinge on the child (Baldwin, Baldwin, & Cole, 1990). This approach to understanding relations between poverty and children's development essentially involves dissecting out of the poverty or social class matrix certain process variables and relating them to certain child outcomes (Deutsch, 1973).

The goal of this chapter is to present an analysis of pathways through which poverty influences children's socioemotional development. This analysis assumes that both negative and positive development in poor children are multiply determined. It is guided by a transactional, organismic model that sees development as a product of ongoing, dynamic interactions of the child and the experiences provided by the family and the broader social context, which serve to dissipate or amplify the effects of earlier developmental insults and difficulties (Sameroff & Fiese, 1990). Neither poverty nor mediating variables are seen as having inevitable, certain consequences for children's socioemotional functioning. Linkages exist among these variables only in probabilistic terms determined by mutual influences operating between the child and his or her environment. As Baldwin et al. (1990) point out, it is precisely this fact that makes it possible for poor children to have positive outcomes.

Because of space limitations, this chapter is a selective rather than exhaustive review. It is divided into four major sections. As a backdrop to the discussion of the mechanisms by which poverty influences children's socioemotional development, we begin by summarizing what is known about the incidence, prevalence, and demographic correlates of childhood poverty. In the second section, we describe the relations found to exist between poverty or low socioeconomic status and socioemotional functioning during infancy, childhood, and adolescence. This is followed by a dis-

Preparation of this manuscript was supported in part by a Faculty Scholar Award in Child Mental Health from the William T. Grant Foundation, awarded to Dr. McLoyd. The authors are grateful to Eve Trager, Sheba Shakir, and Gina Barclay-McLaughlin for their bibliographic and editorial assistance.

cussion of two major, proximal variables that appear to mediate these links, specifically parenting and environmental stressors (both discrete and chronic). In the examination of parenting, attention is given to the relation between social class and adult mental health, the influence of maternal mental health and contextual factors such as neighborhood danger and crime on parenting behavior, and, in keeping with the transactional model of development, the influence of child behavior on parenting and parent-child interaction. The final section of the chapter focuses on the implications of research on resilience in poor children for intervention and prevention strategies.

The Incidence, Prevalence, and Demographic Correlates of Childhood Poverty

The official definition of poverty has remained basically unchanged for a generation. A person is defined as living in poverty if his or her cash income from all sources is less than three times the cost of an adequate diet. Currently, there are well over 100 different "poverty lines" reflecting a wide range of family types (as determined by family size, sex, and age of head, number of children under 18, farm versus nonfarm residence, etc.). Many critics claim that the poverty index results in an undercount of the poor because: (1) it has not kept up with increased costs of living due to inflation; (2) it is not adjusted for regional and cultural variations in the cost of food and/or nonfood items; (3) nonfood items typically consume more than two-thirds of all household costs; and (4) money paid in taxes is counted as part of family income when determining specifically who is below the threshold of poverty (pretax income), but the poverty index is based on net, after-tax income (Dear, 1982).

Even using this apparently conservative definition of poverty, the United States is distinguished among Western industrialized countries by the economic plight of its children. During the 1980s, the United States, despite its affluence, had the dubious distinction among Western industrialized countries of having the highest proportion of chil-

dren living in poverty and being the only country in which children constituted the largest age group living in poverty. One of every five American children under age 18 lives in poverty, and 38% of all poor Americans are children (Duncan, 1992). In addition to being worse off than children in other Western industrialized countries, contemporary children in the United States are faring less well than American children two decades ago. Following a period of decline in the rate of poverty among American children from 26% in 1959 to 14% in 1969, the childhood poverty rate rose slightly throughout the 1970s and increased sharply between 1979 and 1984, leveling off at about 22% (Halpern, 1987). Between 1979 and 1985, the rate of poverty for black children 18 years and under increased from 36% to 41%, compared to an increase from 12% to 13% for white children during the same period (Duncan, 1992).

These snapshots of poverty convey only a minor part of the story. Even more telling are data from the Panel Study of Income Dynamics about the persistence and dynamics of poverty across children's lives. This longitudinal study has charted the economic well-being of a nationally representative sample of American families each year since 1968. Duncan and Rodgers (1988) analyzed longitudinal data from the 1968 to 1982 waves of the study (a 15-year period) to characterize patterns of poverty among children who were under the age of 4 in 1968 and for whom data were available for each of the succeeding 14 years. Defining poverty as the ratio of total family income to a needs standard that corresponded to the official U.S. poverty standard for a particular family type, Duncan and Rodgers found that one-third of all children experienced poverty in at least one year, but only about 1 child in 20 experienced poverty over 10 or more years of his or her childhood. An estimated 4.8% of all children experienced poverty during at least two-thirds of their childhood years, and an additional 7% were poor between 5 and 9 of the 15 years. Most childhood poverty in the United States, then, is short-lived rather than persistent, although long-term poverty is not insignificant.

Marked race differences exist in the prevalence and persistence of poverty. In general, black children are two to three times more likely than white children to be poor; this racial disparity widened during the 1980s. Moreover, Duncan and Rodgers

(1988) found that 24% of black children in the Panel Study of Income Dynamics, compared to six-tenths of 1% of nonblack children, were poor for at least 10 of 15 years. Furthermore, 4.9% of black children were poor the entire 15-year period, whereas this was true for none of the nonblack children. In sum, black children accounted for the total number of children who were poor all 15 years and for almost 90% of the children who were poor during at least 10 of 15 years. Fewer than one in 7 (13%) black children lived comfortably above the poverty line all 15 years (family income at least 150% of the poverty level), while over half (56%) of all nonblack children enjoyed this status. This study also found that the persistence of poverty was affected by geographic location, especially among black children. Contrary to popular notion, black children who lived in rural areas, as compared to those who lived in urban areas, and black children who lived in the South, as compared to those who resided outside the South, spent more years in poverty. Similar but weaker trends were found for white children.

The extraordinarily high and increasing incidence of economic hardship among black children is traceable to an array of complex and interrelated factors, including structural changes in the economy that have hit black workers particularly hard (resulting in high rates of joblessness and severe cutbacks in wages), discrimination in the labor market, low wages, and an increasing incidence of female-headed households. The latter trend appears to be closely linked to the deteriorating economic status of black men. Discussion of these factors as contributors to race discrepancies in poverty rates can be found elsewhere (McLoyd, 1990).

Poverty and Children's Socioemotional Functioning

Prevalence estimates of mental health problems, although less precise than those for medical problems as a result of varying methods of assessment and thresholds used in making a diagnosis, suggest that a significant proportion of children under 18 experience emotional and behavioral problems (Butler, Starfield, & Stenmark, 1984). Based on a review of diagnostic data from seven primary care facilities, Starfield et al. (1980) concluded that at least 5%, and as many as 15%, of children seen in one year had one or more psychosocial problems. In a similar study undertaken by Jacobson et al. (1980), between 3 and 10% of children seen in four health care settings during a 1-year period were diagnosed as having a mental disorder. Comparable prevalence estimates have been reported in other studies conducted in pediatric practice settings (Goldberg, Regier, McInerny, Pless, & Roghmann, 1979). In all of these studies, low socioeconomic status was associated with a higher prevalence of emotional and behavioral problems. Links between low socioeconomic status and higher rates of socioemotional problems also have been found in small-scale studies of infants, children, and adolescents in nonhealth care settings. Following is a brief discussion of these studies.

INFANCY

The most intensively studied and theory-grounded marker of socioemotional functioning during infancy is quality of attachment, typically assessed in a standard laboratory procedure known as the Strange Situation (Ainsworth, Bell, & Stayton, 1974). In line with Bowlby's ethological view that the basic function of the attachment system is to promote protective proximity to the object of attachment in the presence of threat or alarm, this procedure is designed to create gradually escalating stress for the infant so that changes in his or her behavior can be observed (Lamb, Thompson, Gardner, & Charnov, 1985). Securely attached infants manifest a smooth balance between exploratory and attachment behavior—they use the mother as a secure base from which to explore, moving freely away from her but keeping track of her whereabouts, and reestablishing brief contact with her from time to time. Following involuntary separation from the mother, these infants greet the mother either by seeking contact or proximity or by distal interaction, whether they exhibit distress as a result of separation or not. Their behavior contrasts with two groups of infants regarded as insecurely or anxiously attached, namely anxious/resistant infants and anxious/avoidant infants. Anxious/resistant infants are overwhelmingly preoccupied with the mother, maintaining greater proximity to her, as if they lack confidence that she will be available when needed. Consequently, their exploration of the environment is greatly truncated. These infants also exhibit ambivalent behavior, mingling proximity/contact seeking with rejecting behavior, especially upon reunion. Anxious/avoidant infants, instead of seeking interaction, avoid or ignore their mothers, especially upon reunion (Lamb, Thompson, et al., 1985).

The distribution of infants across these attachment classifications varies as a function of social class. More specifically, lower-class infants are somewhat more likely than middle-class infants to exhibit anxious attachment (van Ijzendoom & Kroonenberg, 1988). In Egeland and Farber's (1984) study of 212 12-month-old economically impoverished infants and their mothers, 55% of the infants were securely attached, 23% were anxious/resistant, and 22% were anxious/avoidant. Kennedy and Bakeman's (1984) sample of 39 low-income black infants yielded a distribution of 46%, 33%, and 21%, respectively. Forty-seven percent of Lyons-Ruth, Connell, Grunebaum, and Botein's (1990) sample of 32 18-month-old, low-income infants were securely attached, while 53% were anxiously attached (resistant and avoidant combined). These distributions contrast with those found in most American middle-class samples, which yield approximately 65% securely attached, 15% anxious/resistant, and 20% anxious/avoidant infants (Lamb, Gaensbauer, Malkin, & Schultz, 1985).

CHILDHOOD AND ADOLESCENCE

Poverty during early and middle childhood is associated with lower self-confidence, strained peer relations, and higher levels of overall symptomatology, social maladaptation (e.g., shyness, aggressiveness, immaturity, learning problems), and psychological distress (e.g., feelings of sadness, tension, and nervousness). (For a review of this literature, see McLoyd, 1990.) During adolescence, poverty and low socioeconomic status appear to adversely affect self-image (Sarigiani, Wilson, Petersen, & Vicary, 1990), increase the probability of delinquent behavior (Elliott & Huizinga, 1983), and heighten vulnerability to depression (Gibbs, 1986; Lempers, Clark-

Lempers, & Simons, 1989). Researchers have identified a vast array of negative behavioral and cognitive symptoms accompanying adolescent depression. For example, Gibbs (1986) found that low-income adolescent females with high depression scores, compared to their counterparts with low depression scores, were more susceptible to somatic symptoms and problems with memory, concentration, or studying, had poorer self-images, and experienced a greater occurrence of obsessive ideas, compulsive habits, and phobias. Delinquency also is associated with a high incidence of depression, although it is unclear that there is a causal link (Chiles, Miller, & Cox, 1980).

We now turn to a discussion of parenting behavior and acute and chronic stressors as mediators of the link between poverty and children's socioemotional functioning.

Mediators of the Link Between Poverty and Children's Socioemotional Functioning

PARENTING BEHAVIOR

Disparate lines of research provide compelling support for the argument that poor children are at increased risk of socioemotional problems partly because of their increased exposure to nonsupportive and punitive parenting (McLoyd, 1990). The increased probability of such parenting in the context of poverty appears to be, in part, a consequence of the extraordinarily high toll exacted on parents' mental health by poverty and the existence and co-occurrence of difficult life circumstances and events associated with poverty. Compounding the risk of parenting difficulty is aversive behavioral characteristics in the child resulting from prematurity and drug exposure in utero, both of which are linked to poverty. To explicate this line of reasoning, we briefly discuss: the association of social class to adults' mental health and parenting behavior, the relation of parenting behavior to stressors and maternal emotional state, child temperament and behavioral correlates of prematurity and drug-exposure as factors influencing parental behavior, and the relation between parenting behavior and children's socioemotional functioning.

Social Class, Mental Health, and Parenting: Adults who are poor consistently have been found to have more mental health problems than their economically advantaged counterparts (Liem & Liem, 1978; Neff & Husaini, 1980). Among the etiological factors responsible for this relation is an overrepresentation in lower-class life of a broad range of frustration-producing, negative life events and chronic ongoing conditions outside personal control (Liem & Liem, 1978). Stressors in the context of poverty often come in clusters and tend to be highly contagious. Because of limited financial resources, negative life events often precipitate additional crises (Belle, 1984; Makosky, 1982). The negative effects of stressful life events on mental health are more pronounced in lower-class as opposed to middle-class adults (Dohrenwend, 1973). This relation is even stronger when events outside the control of the individual are analyzed separately (Kessler & Cleary, 1980; Liem & Liem, 1978). Poverty appears to weaken the individual's ability to cope with new problems and difficulties, which, consequently, results in more debilitating effects.

Single parenthood, a strong correlate of poverty, is a particularly salient risk factor for poor mental health. Single mothers are at greater risk of anxiety, depression, and health problems than other marital status groups, and this risk is intensified if they are poor and live alone with their children (Guttentag, Salasin, & Belle, 1980). Some of this distress is rooted in the burdens and responsibilities of solo parenting, as evidenced by the fact that the younger the child and the greater the number of children in the household, the stronger the association between marital status and mental health problems (Pearlin & Johnson, 1977). Another factor that contributes to single women's elevated distress is increased exposure to discrete stressors. Even when income is controlled, families headed by single mothers are more likely than two-parent, "male-headed" families to experience stressful life events such as changes in income, job, residence, and household composition, and, for those in the labor force, unemployment (McLanahan, 1983; Weinraub & Wolf, 1983). In addition, single mothers who are poor are more socially isolated than married mothers and generally experience their interaction with the public welfare system as demeaning and dehumanizing (Goodban, 1985). Finally, poor women, compared to economically advantaged women, are more likely to experience the illness or death of children, the imprisonment of husbands, and privation and major losses in childhood that may make coping with new losses even more difficult (Belle, 1984; Brown, Bhrolchain, & Harris, 1975).

Given that parents who are poor experience more environmentally induced emotional distress than their advantaged counterparts, it is not surprising that they tend to be less nurturant, supportive, and sensitive in their interactions with their children than middle-class parents. Numerous studies report that mothers who are poor, as compared to their economically advantaged counterparts, are more likely to use power-assertive techniques in disciplinary encounters and are generally less supportive of their children. They value obedience more, are less likely to use reasoning, and more likely to use physical punishment as a means of disciplining and controlling the child. Data also indicate that lower-class parents are more likely to issue commands without explanation, less likely to consult the child about his or her wishes, and less likely to reward the child verbally for desirable behavior. Poverty also has been associated with diminished expression of affection and lesser responsiveness to the socioemotional needs explicitly expressed by the child. (For a review of this literature, see McLoyd, 1990.)

While it is indisputable that only a small proportion of poor parents are even alleged to abuse their children, strong evidence exists that child abuse occurs more frequently in poor families than in more affluent families (Garbarino, 1976; Pelton, 1989). Indeed, poverty is the single most prevalent characteristic of abusing parents (Pelton, 1989). Several trends appear to defy the argument that the relation between poverty and abuse is spurious because of bias in detection and reporting (due to greater public scrutiny of the poor). First, although greater public awareness and new reporting laws resulted in a significant increase in official reporting in recent years, the socioeconomic pattern of these reports has not changed (Pelton, 1989). Second, child abuse is related to degrees of poverty even within the lower class;

abusing parents tend to be the poorest of the poor (Wolock & Horowitz, 1979). Third, the severest injuries occur within the poorest families (Pelton, 1989).

Discrete and Chronic Stressors, Maternal Emotional State, and Parenting Behavior: The class-linked patterns of parenting just discussed parallel both event-linked and affect-linked patterns of parenting, lending strong support for the argument that differences in the parenting of poor versus nonpoor adults are partly the result of differences in the level of environmental stress and, hence, the degree of emotional distress experienced by these two groups. For example, Gersten, Langner, Eisenberg, and Simcha-Fagan (1977) found the occurrence of undesirable life events to correlate positively with affectively distant, restrictive, and punitive parenting. Similarly, Weinraub and Wolf (1983) reported that mothers who experienced more stressful life events were less nurturant toward their children and, in the case of single mothers, were less at ease, less spontaneous, and less responsive to their children's communications. Even ephemeral, relatively minor hassles produce detectable changes in maternal behavior. Patterson's (1988) observations of mother-child dyads over the course of several days indicate that day-to-day fluctuations in mothers' tendencies to initiate and continue an aversive exchange with their children were systematically related to the daily frequency of hassles or crises the mother experienced.

Research on the relation between stressful life events and the stability and quality of infant attachment also implicates maternal behavior. Infants of mothers who have experienced more stressful life events between the 12th and 18th month of the infant's life, compared to those whose mothers have experienced fewer such events during this period, are more likely to be anxiously attached at 18 months. Furthermore, among economically disadvantaged infants, change from secure attachment (at 12 months) to anxious attachment (at 18 months) is associated with higher frequency of stressful events than stable secure attachment (Vaughn, Egeland, Sroufe, & Waters, 1979). A plausible explanation of these findings is that stress encourages maternal self-involvement and insensitivity to the infant's signals, leading to anxious attachment.

The increased tendency of poor parents to discipline their children in a harsh and inconsistent manner also may be traceable to mental distress resulting from ongoing stressful conditions associated with poverty such as inadequate housing, living in commercial/industrial areas, and exposure to crime. Ongoing stressful conditions appear to be even more debilitating to mental health than discrete negative life events (Belle, 1984; Brown et al., 1975; Makosky, 1982). In some studies of adults, after chronic stressors are controlled, the effects of life events on psychological distress are diminished to borderline significance (Gersten et al., 1977). Increased exposure to chronic stressors may explain why low socioeconomic status is strongly associated with depression and emotional disturbance in women living in urban metropolitan areas but unrelated to mental disorder in women living in small towns (Rutter, 1981).

Perceived neighborhood danger and crime is strongly correlated with neighborhood crime rates (Kriesberg, 1970; Lewis & Maxfield, 1980). In addition to predicting poor mental health among minority women, these perceptions are linked to increased mother-child conflict as reported by mothers and greater use of physical punishment by mothers (Kriesberg, 1970; White, Kasl, Zahner, & Will, 1987). Parents living in dangerous neighborhoods are understandably preoccupied with their children's physical safety. They may resort to a disciplinary style marked by restrictiveness and punitiveness, in part because rules are seen as a main line of defense and because children's violations of rules set by parents can result in grave threats to the children's safety. In the presence of imminent danger, power-assertive disciplinary strategies appear to have more survival value than those that attempt to modify the child's behavior by reasoning, explaining, and negotiating, especially during the preadolescent years. It has been suggested that these adaptations in parenting, while well intentioned and practically sensible, may be detrimental in the long run (Garbarino, Kostelny, & Dubrow, 1991). This issue requires careful study. Note also should be made of the fact that parenting is markedly more burdensome in very dangerous neighborhoods because low levels of social integration and cohesion and reduced availability of resources in the form of formal agencies and informal networks promote an individualistic, rather than a collective, model of parenting and family management. Parents in such contexts often are extremely wary of entrusting their children to the care of others in the neighborhood and, consequently, devote enormous time to supervising, monitoring, and controlling their children's behavior. While adaptive, this child management strategy is very costly to parents' psychological and physical resources (Furstenberg, 1990).

A growing body of data, most from studies of infants and preschoolers, directly ties parental punitiveness, inconsistency, and unresponsiveness to negative emotional states in the parent (McLoyd, 1990). For example, psychological distress encourages parents to adopt disciplinary strategies that require less effort (e.g., physical punishment, commanding without explanation, reliance on authority) rather than more (e.g., reasoning, explaining, negotiating). It also is associated with fewer positive behaviors (e.g., hugs, praise, supportive statements) and diminished responsiveness to children's dependency needs. Parental depression, an affective state experienced more frequently by poor women than nonpoor women, is a critical risk factor for difficulties in parenting and has been linked to physical abuse; use of aversive, coercive discipline; and reduced sensitivity and expression of affection toward the child. (See McLoyd, 1990, for a review of this literature.) In addition, single mothers experiencing greater psychological distress more frequently disclose personal and financial problems to their children (McLoyd & Wilson, 1990). Maternal disclosure of this kind of information is associated with greater psychological distress in children (McLoyd & Wilson, 1992a).

In keeping with Sameroff and Fiese's (1990) notion that children's development is a product of the continuous dynamic interactions of the child and the experiences provided by his or her family and social context, we next turn to the issue of how child characteristics influence and are influenced by parental behavior.

The Influence of Child Characteristics on Parenting: Temperament and Prematurity: Several studies suggest that temperamentally easy children are less likely than children with difficult temperaments to be the target of parental criticism and harshness (Rutter, 1979). When parents are depressed and irritable, they are more likely to direct abusive behavior toward the child with adverse temperamental characteristics. Studies of child abuse also have identified the child's temperament as a factor that appears to elicit maltreatment (Belsky, 1980).

There is growing evidence that child characteristics resulting from prematurity and drug exposure in utero, both strong correlates of poverty, exert notable influence on parental behavior. Every year approximately 7% of infants born in the United States are born prematurely (Meisels & Plunkett, 1988). Prematurity is defined by gestational age of 36 weeks or less and birthweight of less than 2,500 grams. Today infants are born and surviving at much lower birthweights (less than 1,250 grams or 2.5 pounds) and much younger gestational ages than ever before; these infants are described as extremely low birthweight (ELBW). Children born prematurely generally are considered to be at biological and psychosocial risk.

Children born in poverty are overrepresented in premature samples, in large part because of poor or total lack of prenatal care (Randolph & Adams-Taylor, in press). A related factor is that infants born in poverty are more likely to be born to teenage mothers, for whom there is an increased incidence of low birthweight infants (Monkus & Bancalari, 1981). Whether this is due to maternal age per se or to the fact that over 50% of teenage mothers do not receive any prenatal care (Randolph & Adams-Taylor, in press) is not clear.

The sequelae of prematurity, especially extremely low birthweight, are multifaceted. These infants are at great risk for respiratory and neurological problems, including cerebral palsy and seizure disorders. In addition, they are at greater risk for parental abuse and socioemotional problems associated with parental abuse. Some researchers (Frodi, 1981) have suggested that preterm infants are more likely to be victims of abuse than full-term infants because of certain aversive behavioral characteristics. It has been well documented that preterm infants are much more irritable and have more aversive cries than full-term infants (Frodi et al., 1978).

The interaction patterns of preterm infants and their caregivers are quite different from the interaction patterns of full-term infants and their caregivers. (See Meisels & Plunkett, 1988, for a review of this literature.) In general, investigations suggest that preterm infants are less socially responsive and harder to soothe than full-term infants. For example, they have less eye contact with their mothers than full-term infants (Field, 1977). Because eye contact is thought to be central to mother-infant communication, Field cites the lack of eye contact between preterm infants and their caregivers as evidence of interactional deficits. Mothers of preterm infants tend to be more highly stimulating than mothers of normal infants. When the infants withdraw, mothers respond by escalating the level of stimulation. Field suggests that this is a maladaptive response on the part of the mothers because the overstimulation may cause neurologically immature infants to withdraw from social interaction. In contrast, Goldberg and DiVitto (1983) suggest that the high level of maternal stimulation is an appropriate, compensatory response to interacting with a less responsive, less capable infant.

Given the differences in interactional patterns noted between preterm infants and their mothers, it might be expected that attachment relationships also would differ in a preterm sample. Particularly, if the stimulating style of the mothers of preterm infants is viewed as maladaptive, then it might be anticipated that there would be a higher incidence of insecure attachment in preterm infant-caregiver dyads. What is surprising is that the distributions of the secure and insecure relationships in samples of preterm infants have generally been comparable to those found in full-term samples (Easterbrooks, 1989).

In studies in which preterm infants are stratified according to various risk factors, however, differences in security of attachment do emerge. High-risk, sick preterm infants manifest a higher rate of anxious/resistant attachment than healthy preterm infants (Plunkett, Meisels, Stiefel, Pasick, & Roloff, 1986). Plunkett et al. interpret these findings to suggest that chronic illness creates anxiety in caregivers, and this anxiety, coupled with a hard-to-soothe preterm infant, leads to a higher rate of insecure resistant relationships than among healthy infants. Research makes clear that the effects of prematurity depend on the social/economic environment and that birth status cannot be viewed in isolation. Poverty increases both the likelihood that infants will be born prematurely and the probability that prematurity will result in subsequent developmental problems. Among infants born to mothers of low socioeconomic status, proportionately more preterm infants than full-term infants are insecurely attached (Wille, 1991). In their longitudinal research, Ross, Lipper, and Auld (1990) found that prematurity and socioeconomic status had an interactive effect on socioemotional development, with lower-class children who had been born prematurely manifesting significantly more behavior problems at school age than lower-class nonpremature children and middle-class premature children. This finding of an interaction of birth status and socioeconomic status is a common one, particularly in studies of cognitive development. (For a discussion of these issues, see Sameroff, 1986.) It is not surprising that premature infants born into poverty are at greater risk, for if as Sameroff (1986, p. 194) suggests, "the primary causal factor resides not in the child's biomedical history but in the environment, that is, the social context of development," then the socially unresponsive, irritable, and difficult-to-soothe premature infant born into a caregiving environment plagued by the chronic stresses of poverty and inadequate social supports is notably and multiply disadvantaged.

Illegal drug use during pregnancy, particularly ingestion of crack cocaine, has risen dramatically in recent years, especially in low-income urban areas. There is growing but hardly surprising evidence that it poses serious threats to children's physical as well as emotional health. A survey conducted at Boston City Hospital between 1984 and 1988 indicated that 18% of the women who delivered babies there had used cocaine at least once during pregnancy (Zuckerman, Amaro, & Cabral, 1989). Similarly, a study of 1000 babies born in Philadelphia hospitals during the first quarter of 1989 indicated that one in six mothers admitted having taken cocaine during pregnancy (Norris, 1989, cited in Randolph & Adams-Taylor, in press). Given that both of these surveys entailed the use of self-report questionnaires, the actual rate probably was considerably higher.

The consequences of cocaine use during pregnancy are difficult to study systematically particularly because cocaine users frequently use other illegal drugs and alcohol (Randolph & Adams-Taylor, in press; Rodning, Beckwith, & Howard, 1990). In addition, they are likely to smoke and to have poor prenatal care. However, studies that have taken these variables into account generally indicate that prenatal exposure to cocaine is associated with markers of behavioral disorganization in the neonatal period such as tremulousness, irritability, and disturbances in sleep-wake cycles. In addition, these babies tend to have depressed interactive abilities (Chasnoff, Burns, Schnoll, & Burns, 1985) and become easily overstimulated (Bresnahan, Brooks, & Zuckerman, 1991).

Little research has examined the sequelae of drug exposure beyond the neonatal period, and, in any case, it is likely to be difficult to tease apart the proportion of behavioral and psychological problems due to biological vulnerability caused by prenatal exposure to illegal drugs and the proportion due to caregiver dysfunction or to multiple caregivers (Bresnahan et al., 1991). Many infants born to drug-addicted mothers are put into foster care of variable quality, and those infants remaining with mothers who continue to abuse drugs will receive inconsistent care, at best. Recent longitudinal research done by Rodning et al. (1990) has revealed that prenatally drug- (particularly cocaine-) exposed toddlers exhibit less representational play and a constricted range of play events compared to a preterm comparison group. The most dramatic deficits were seen in the child's spontaneous play where self-initiation was required and external structure was not available. In addition, 50% of the drug-exposed infants were rated as insecurely attached to their caregivers. The rate was even higher (88%) when the infants were cared for by mothers who continued to abuse drugs. This finding is not difficult to interpret with a transactional model; drug-exposed infants are highly irritable and easily overstimulated, and drug-addicted mothers have a low threshold for frustration and limited resources for nurturant and involved parenting. Indeed, it would be difficult to imagine how such a dyad could ever attain a "secure" relationship.

In some cases, infants born to drug-addicted mothers remain in the hospital for an extended period until other care arrangements can be made. Referred to as "boarder babies" (Randolph & Adams-Taylor, in press), nothing is yet known about their subsequent socioemotional development, but the outlook can hardly be optimistic.

Parenting Behavior and Children's Socioemotional Functioning: Child-rearing practices that are more prevalent among impoverished parents are predictive of a number of socioemotional problems. Reduced sensitivity and responsiveness to infants' signals by the mother are associated with insecure attachment (Ainsworth et al., 1974). Anxious attachment during infancy is associated with diminished ego resiliency (flexibility and resourcefulness), positive affect, self-esteem, emotional health, and compliance, and more frequent dependency and problem behaviors (e.g., aggression) during the preschool years, although it is unclear whether these latter outcomes are due to the earlier quality of attachment or to the ongoing mother-child relationship (Lamb, Thompson, et al., 1985; Sroufe, 1983). Like maternal insensitivity, child abuse or maltreatment is a strong correlate of anxious attachment (Schneider-Rosen, Braunwald, Carlson, & Cicchetti, 1985), but not if the abusing person was someone other than the mother (Lamb, Gaensbauer, et al., 1985). In addition, children who have been neglected or physically abused, compared to children with no history of neglect or abuse, exhibit more anger, aggression, frustration, and noncompliance in problem-solving situations (Egeland & Sroufe, 1981), behave more aggressively toward their peers and their caregivers, and reciprocate friendly overtures less frequently (George & Main, 1979).

A vast literature exists concerning consequences for children's socioemotional functioning of nonsupportive behavior in parents, defined as low levels of behavior that make the child feel comfortable in the presence of the parent and communicate to the child that he or she is basically accepted and approved. Research consistently shows that children whose parents are nonsupportive have lower self-esteem and more psychological disorders, exhibit more antisocial aggression and behavioral problems, and are more likely to show arrested ego development. (See McLoyd, 1990, for a discussion of this literature.) Patterson (1988) has shown that preadolescent and adolescent children are at high risk of becoming antisocial and highly aggressive if they are temperamentally difficult and have parents who are highly irritable, erratic, and punitive. Adding to this picture is recent evidence that across all social classes, adolescents with nonsupportive parents report more psychological distress and engage in more delinquent activities in comparison to adolescents whose parents are warm, democratic, and firm (Steinberg, Mounts, Lamborn, & Dornbusch, 1991).

Research on specific stressful life events, such as divorce and income loss, provides further evidence of the impact of harsh, insensitive, and inconsistent parenting on children. In particular, this work points to the powerful role of parental behavior as a mediator of the impact of these events on children's socioemotional functioning. For example, depression, aggressiveness, noncompliance, acting out, and peer conflict among children of divorced parents are oftentimes responses to negative changes in parents' socialization practices following divorce (Hetherington, Stanley-Hagan, & Anderson, 1989). Similarly, economic loss leads to higher rates of delinquency, drug use, and socioemotional distress (e.g., moodiness, hypersensitivity, feelings of inadequacy) among adolescents, and more quarrelsome, negativistic, and explosive behavior among younger children due to increasing inconsistent and punitive parenting behavior (Elder, 1979; Lempers et al., 1989).

DISCRETE AND CHRONIC STRESSORS

Like punitive parenting, exposure to discrete and chronic stressors appears to be a significant mechanism by which poverty adversely affects children's socioemotional functioning. In addition to affecting children indirectly by increasing harsh and punitive parenting behaviors, negative life events and chronic conditions may have a direct etiological role in children's psychosocial maladjustment by placing demands on them that exceed their coping resources (Sterling, Cowen, Weissberg, Lotyczewski, & Boike, 1985). Social class does not appear to be closely linked to the frequency of life events (life change) experienced by children or the degree of psychological readjustment required by these events, if the corpus of events at issue includes ones with positive (e.g., outstanding personal achievement) as well as negative connotations (e.g., death of a parent) (Coddington, 1972). However, the preponderance of research clearly indicates that children from lower socioeconomic backgrounds, regardless of race, experience a significantly greater number of negative or undesirable life events (Pryor-Brown, Cowen, Hightower, & Lotyczewski, 1986). More-

over, undesirability of life events, whether conceived in pure terms or in terms of balance between desirable and undesirable events, is a consistent predictor or socioemotional maladjustment (Gersten, Langner, Eisenberg, & Orzek, 1974; Sandler & Block, 1979). Its consistency and, in some cases, power as a predictor of maladjustment exceeds that of life change per se (Gersten et al., 1974). Data also indicate that the adverse effects of clusters of negative life events are multiplicative rather than simply additive (Rutter, 1979).

Sparked by the surge of murder, violence, and gang- and drug-related activities in poor inner-city neighborhoods during the 1980s, there is growing recognition that children's living environment can be a significant, chronic stressor that compounds the psychological distress engendered by negative life events (Zinsmeister, 1990). Low income results in both lesser choice of neighborhood and lesser freedom from neighborhood (Bronfenbrenner, Moen, & Garbarino, 1984). Negative neighborhood characteristics may be a particularly important explanatory factor in the mental health of economically disadvantaged black children, because these children frequently grow up in poor, isolated, urban neighborhoods, whereas this is rarely the case for poor white children (Wilson, 1987). Children are not oblivious to their living environment and, like adults, make judgments of their neighborhoods that are consistent with their neighborhoods' objective characteristics. When asked to evaluate their local neighborhood as "a place to grow up in," children living in poor inner-city areas are most critical, while those living in rural areas and in affluent suburbs are most positive (Zill, 1984). A consistent pattern of findings results when children's evaluations are examined in relation to objective neighborhood indices that reduce the quality of life (e.g., reduced public order and safety, minimum and low-quality health and education services, high rates of unemployment) (Homel & Burns, 1987).

Poor children are more likely than affluent children to live in housing located on commercial/industrial streets. Evidence exists that this ecological factor may be a source of socioemotional difficulties. For example, Homel and Burns (1989) found that children who live in housing located on commercial/industrial streets, compared to children who live in housing located on residential streets, report more worry, fear, and overall distress, especially if they live in neighborhoods (typically poor and urban) characterized by a high level of social problems. They also are more likely to describe themselves as feeling lonely, to report being rejected by peers, and to register dislike of most of their classmates. These differences as a function of geographic location were significant after appropriate controls were introduced for economic, housing, and child characteristics. It is likely that commercial/industrial streets in areas characterized by numerous social problems directly contribute to social and psychological difficulties as a result of being less friendly social environments that offer fewer opportunities for social exchange among children. In addition, they may impact on the child's social experiences indirectly by increasing parents' insistence that children stay in or close to home during free time and by encouraging parental feelings of alienation from the local community (Homel & Burns, 1987).

One of the increasingly salient chronic stressors associated with poverty is living in dangerous, crime-infested neighborhoods resembling "war zones" (Garbarino et al., 1991). For example, a survey of youth in the south side of Chicago indicated that more than 25% had witnessed a homicide by the time they were 17 years old (Bell, cited in Garbarino et al., 1991). Virtually no systematic, empirical investigations have been conducted of the impact of steady exposure to violence, criminal activity, and death on children's socioemotional functioning or the factors that explain variation in children's response. However, numerous poignant and tragic case studies published recently in the popular press liken the effects to the posttraumatic stress symptoms that plague Vietnam combat veterans. Although some therapists report signs of resiliency, they also note that few children growing up in the maelstrom escape unscathed. The children are prone to fear, anxiety, depression, irritability, apathy, poor concentration, and memory lapses. Some respond with aggression, while others withdraw and become inhibited. Many regress to early childhood behaviors and experience somatic ailments that appear to have no organic cause (Kotlowitz, 1991; Zinsmeister, 1990).

A case in point is Lafayette, a 12-year-old black boy who lives with his mother and six siblings in a crime-infested, public housing complex in Chicago. The focus of a journalistic investigation by Kotlowitz (1987, 1991), Lafayette has maneuvered to avoid being hit by the cross-fire of bullets, seen friends shot and adults severely beaten, and stood over a dying teenager who had been gunned down outside his apartment door. He can distinguish a .45 caliber revolver from a .357 Magnum and identify the buildings in his neighborhood where girls have been raped. Lafayette and his 9-year-old brother experience headaches when they hear gunfire, and they sometimes shake uncontrollably when surprised by a loud noise. He attends funerals routinely. When a resident of the project is killed, mimeographed sheets go up in the halls giving details of the funeral. Lafayette's mother has taken out burial insurance on all of her children. Lafayette views peers with suspicion and mistrust, refusing to play basketball with them because he fears they will try to make him join a gang. He sees his future as small and dim. When asked what he wanted to be, Lafayette expresses uncertainty about the prospect of living to see adulthood, saying "If I grow up, I'd like to be a bus driver" (Kotlowitz, 1991, p. x). His mother, who permanently lost the use of two fingers when she was attacked by muggers, worries that he has become unusually withdrawn. Of Lafayette, she says, "He says talking isn't going to help him . . . that everything that goes wrong keeps going on and everything that's right doesn't stay right so why should I talk. He's got a lot of hate built up inside him" (Kotlowitz, 1987, p. 26).

INTERVENTION AND PREVENTION STRATEGIES

The first steps toward both preventing and alleviating socioemotional problems in poor children are awareness of children's socioemotional functioning, appreciation of their current life concerns, and sensitivity to environmental and life circumstances that pose threats to their socioemotional well-being. Toward this end, comprehensive family-centered child development programs in poor communities, with parental consent, could regularly assess children's physical, mental, and emotional development for the purpose of keeping well children well, preventing inchoate difficulties from becoming more serious, and facilitating intervention for distressed children (Lurie, 1974). It is increasingly clear from a small but expanding body of research that resilience in poor children is not an innate characteristic, but depends on a combination of child attributes (e.g., temperament), socialization experiences both within and outside the family (e.g., nurturance and positive relations with family caregivers; mentoring relations with exemplary, nonfamilial adults; parental supervision; regulation of child's peer group activities outside the home) and interactions between these components (Cowen, Wyman, Work, & Parker, 1990; Rutter, 1990; Werner & Smith, 1982).

This means that intervention and prevention strategies that focus exclusively on the child, whether directed toward modification of intrapsychic or behavioral processes, are likely to be severely limited in their effectiveness. Psychiatric interventions for children who are victims of or witnesses to violence, for example, may prove effective in the short run but impotent in the long run if violence is a mainstay of the child's environment (Eth & Pynoos, 1985). Intervention and prevention strategies should seek to both decrease poor children's exposure to acute, and chronic stressors and increase the number of protective factors, such as the availability of mentors and social support (Werner, 1984). These outcomes cannot be achieved without impacting the multiple contexts within which development occurs. In this chapter we have attempted to demonstrate that suboptimal socioemotional functioning associated with poverty is rooted not only in the family context but in the contexts within which parents and child live. That is, in addition to demonstrating that punitive inconsistent parenting is a critical pathway by which poverty adversely affects children's socioemotional functioning, we have underscored the environmental conditions associated with poverty that compromise maternal and child mental health and foster negative parenting. Ultimately, it is these conditions that must be altered in the interests of promoting optimal functioning in both parents and children. In short, it is urgent that we not only help individual parents and children beat the odds imposed by poverty but work toward changing the odds (Schorr, 1989).

Because social and economic stress are often the root causes of maternal depression, psychological distress, and negative parenting, alleviating such stresses is likely to go a long way toward alleviating mental health problems in mothers, enhancing parenting, and contributing to positive socioemotional functioning in children (Belle, 1984; Rutter, 1990). Mental health professionals need to deepen their appreciation of the strong links among these factors and orient their therapeutic efforts accordingly. Needless to say, blaming poor mothers for their economic and psychological plight will exacerbate their psychological problems, heighten mistrust and apprehension, and undercut the professional's role as facilitator and helper. Because typical middle-class therapists or mental health workers have never experienced the stressors that poor women routinely confront, they cannot achieve this level of understanding without concerted efforts to bridge the chasms between them and the poor—chasms engendered by cultural, class, and gender differences. Visits to clients' neighborhoods and homes can help clinicians appreciate clients' ongoing struggle to survive and raise their children in the midst of daunting environmental realities. Treatment that focuses on intrapsychic flaws and parent education, while ignoring the environmental difficulties that undermine psychological and maternal functioning, is likely to be of limited usefulness and, indeed, may engender more, rather than less, passivity, guilt, and depression (Belle, 1984).

Individual therapy for poor women and children, then, needs to be complemented by advocacy activities that help families resolve concrete environmental problems and pressure bureaucracies and social agents to be more responsive to the needs of children and families. Adequate, low-cost housing; employment that provides a living wage; job training that helps women enter nontraditional occupations rather than traditionally "female" jobs that pay low wages; affordable, high-quality child care; and competent legal aid are high-priority needs requiring sustained attention from mental health workers. Belle (1984, p. 147) has thoughtfully argued that clinicians who cannot undertake such efforts "should ally themselves with other service providers in a close working relationship so that all of a client's pressing and interlocking problems can receive attention as part of an overall treatment plan." The importance of a comprehensive, rather than fragmented, piecemeal approach is underscored by Schorr's (1989) research indicating that intervention programs that are successful in changing outcomes for high-risk children typically offer a broad spectrum of services. The prevailing wisdom of these programs is that social and emotional support and immediate, concrete help are usually necessary before a family can make use of interventions with long-range goals.

Mutual help groups for both children and parents can serve useful therapeutic purposes by bringing together individuals with similar experiences, providing support, and bolstering self-

esteem by providing the opportunity to be helpful to others. Mental health workers can play an important role by helping to initiate and sustain such groups (Bell, 1984). Attention also should be devoted to devising creative strategies to stengthen culturally indigenous structures and patterns of relations (e.g., strong kinship bonds, flexible family roles) that have long served to buffer parents and children from the deleterious effects of poverty.

REFERENCES

Ainsworth, M. D., Bell, S., & Stayton, D. (1974). Infant-mother attachment and social development: "Socialization" as a product of reciprocal responsiveness to signals. In M. P. H. Richards (Ed.), *The integration of a child into a social world* (pp. 99–135). Cambridge: Cambridge University Press.

Baldwin, A. L., Baldwin, C., & Cole, R. E. (1990). Stress resistant families and stress resistant children. In J. Rolf, A. S. Masten, D. Cicchetti, K. Nuechterlein, & S. Weintraub (Eds.), *Risk and protective factors in the development of psychopathology* (pp. 257–280). Cambridge: Cambridge University Press.

Belle, D. (1984). Inequality and mental health: Low income and minority women. In L. Walker (Ed.), *Women and mental health policy* (pp. 135–150). Beverly Hills: Sage Publications.

Belsky, J. (1980). Child maltreatment: An ecological integration. *American Psychologist, 35,* 320–335.

Bresnahan, K., Brooks, C., & Zuckerman, B. (1991). Prenatal cocaine use: Impact on infants and mothers. *Pediatric Nursing, 17,* 123–129.

Bronfenbrenner, U. (1986). Ecology of the family as a context for human development: Research perspectives. *Developmental Psychology, 22,* 723–742.

Bronfenbrenner, U., Moen, P., & Garbarino, J. (1984). Child, family, and community. In R. D. Parke, R. Emde, H. McAdoo, & G. Sackett (Eds.), *Review of child development research* (Vol. 7, pp. 283–328). Chicago: University of Chicago Press.

Brown, G., Bhrolchain, M., & Harris, T. (1975). Social class and psychiatric disturbance among women in an urban population. *Sociology, 9,* 225–254.

Butler, J. A., Starfield, B., & Stenmark, S. (1984). Child health policy. In H. Stevenson & A. Siegel (Eds.), *Child development research and social policy* (pp. 110–188). Chicago: University of Chicago Press.

Chasnoff, K. J., Burns, W. J., Schnoll, S. H., & Burns, K. A. (1985). Cocaine use in pregnancy. *New England Journal of Medicine, 313,* 666–669.

Chiles, J., Miller, M., & Cox, G. (1980). Depression in an adolescent delinquent population. *Archives of General Psychiatry, 37,* 1179–1184.

Coddington, R. D. (1972). The significance of life events

as etiological factors in the diseases of children, II: A study of a normal population. *Journal of Psychosomatic Research, 16,* 205–213.

Cowen, E. L., Wyman, P. A., Work, W. C., & Parker, G. R. (1990). The Rochester child resilience project: Overview and summary of first year findings. *Development and Psychopathology, 2,* 193–212.

Dear, R. B. (1982). No more poverty in America? A critique of Martin Anderson's theory of welfare. *Children and Youth Services Review, 4,* 5–33.

Deutsch, C. (1973). Social class and child development. In B. Caldwell & H. Ricciuti (Eds.), *Review of child development research* (Vol. 3, pp. 233–282). Chicago: University of Chicago Press.

Dohrenwend, B. S. (1973). Life events as stressors: A methodological inquiry. *Journal of Health and Social Behavior, 14,* 167–175.

Duncan, G. (1992). The economic environment of childhood. In A. Huston (Ed.), *Children in poverty* (pp. 23–50). Cambridge: Cambridge University Press.

Duncan, G., & Rodgers, W. (1988). Longitudinal aspects of childhood poverty. *Journal of Marriage and the Family, 50,* 1007–1021.

Easterbrooks, A. (1989). Quality of attachment to mother and to father: Effects of perinatal risk status. *Child Development, 60,* 825–831.

Egeland, B., & Farber, E. A. (1984). Infant-mother attachment: Factors related to its development and changes over time. *Child Development, 55,* 753–771.

Egeland, B., & Sroufe, A. (1981). Developmental sequelae of maltreatment in infancy. In R. Rizley & D. Cicchetti (Eds.), *New directions for child development. Vol. 11: Developmental perspectives on child maltreatment* (pp. 77–92). San Francisco: Jossey-Bass.

Elder, G. (1979). Historical change in life patterns and personality. In P. Baltes & O. Brim (Eds.), *Life span development and behavior* (pp. 117–159). New York: Academic Press.

Elliott, D., & Huizinga, D. (1983). Social class and delinquent behavior in a national youth panel. *Criminology, 21,* 149–177.

Eth, S., & Pynoos, R. S. (1985). Psychiatric interventions with children traumatized by violence. In D. H. Schetky & E. P. Benedek (Eds.), *Emerging issues in child psychiatry and the law* (pp. 285–309). New York: Brunner/Mazel.

Field, T. (1977). Effects of early separation, interactive deficits, and experimental manipulations on infant-mother face-to-face interaction. *Child Development, 48,* 763–771.

Frodi, A. (1981). Contributions of infant characteristics to child abuse. *American Journal of Mental Deficiency, 85,* 341–349.

Frodi, A., Lamb, M. E., Leavitt, L. A., Donovan, W. L., Neff, C., & Sherry, D. (1978). Fathers' and mothers' responses to the faces and cries. *Child Development, 51,* 238–241.

Furstenberg, F. F. (1990). *How families manage risk and opportunity in dangerous neighborhoods.* Unpublished manuscript, University of Pennsylvania.

Garbarino, J. (1976). A preliminary study of some ecological correlates of child abuse: The impact of socioeconomic stress on mothers. *Child Development, 47,* 178–185.

Garbarino, J., Kostelny, K., & Dubrow, N. (1991). What children can tell us about living in danger. *American Psychologist, 46,* 376–383.

George, C., & Main, M. (1979). Social interactions of young abused children: Approach, avoidance, and aggression. *Child Development, 50,* 306–318.

Gersten, J., Langner, T., Eisenberg, J., & Orzek, L. (1974). Child behavior and life events: Undesirable change or change per se? In B. S. Dohrenwend & B. P. Dohrenwend (Eds.), *Stressful life events: Their nature and effects* (pp. 159–170). New York: John Wiley & Sons.

Gersten, J., Langner, T., Eisenberg, J., & Simcha-Fagan, O. (1977). An evaluation of the etiological role of stressful life-change events in psychological disorders. *Journal of Health and Social Behavior, 18,* 228–244.

Gibbs, J. T. (1986). Assessment of depression in urban adolescent females: Implications for early intervention strategies. *American Journal of Social Psychiatry, 6,* 50–56.

Goldberg, I. D., Regier, D. A., McInerny, T. K., Pless, I. B., & Roghmann, K. J. (1979). The role of the pediatrician in the delivery of mental health services to children. *Pediatrics, 63,* 898–909.

Goldberg, S., & DiVitto, B. (1983). *Born too soon: Preterm birth and early development.* New York: W. H. Freeman.

Goodban, N. (1985). The psychological impact of being on welfare. *Social Service Review, 59,* 403–422.

Guttentag, M., Salasin, S., & Belle, D. (1980). *The mental health of women.* New York: Academic Press.

Halpern, R. (1987). Major social and demographic trends affecting young families: Implications for early childhood care and education. *Young Children, 42,* 34–40.

Hetherington, E. M., Stanley-Hagan, M., & Anderson, E. (1989). Marital transitions: A child's perspective. *American Psychologist, 44,* 303–312.

Homel, R., & Burns, A. (1987). Is this a good place to grow up in? Neighborhood quality and children's evaluations. *Landscape and Urban Planning, 14,* 101–116.

Homel, R., & Burns, A. (1989). Environmental quality and the well-being of children. *Social Indicators Research, 21,* 188–158.

Jacobson, A. M., Goldberg, I. D., Burns, B. J., Hoeper, E. W., Hankin, J. R., & Hewitt, K. (1980). Diagnosed mental disorder in children and use of health services in four organized health care settings. *American Journal of Psychiatry, 137,* 559–565.

Kennedy, J. H., & Bakeman, R. (1984). The early mother-infant relationship and social competence with peers and adults at three years. *Journal of Psychology, 116,* 23–34.

Kessler, R., & Cleary, P. (1980). Social class and psychological distress. *American Sociological Review, 45,* 463–478.

Kotlowitz, A. (1987, October 27). Urban trauma: Day-to-day violence takes a terrible toll on inner-city youth. *Wall Street Journal,* pp. 1, 26.

Kotlowitz, A. (1991). *There are no children here.* New York: Doubleday.

Kriesberg, L. (1970). *Mothers in poverty: A study of fatherless families.* Chicago: Adline.

Lamb, M., Gaensbauer, T. J., Malkin, C. M., & Shultz, L. (1985). The effects of child maltreatment on security of infant-adult attachment. *Infant Behavior and Development, 8,* 35–45.

Lamb, M., Thompson, R. A., Gardner, W., & Charnov, E. (1985). *Infant-mother attachement: The origins and developmental significance of individual differences in strange situation behavior.* Hillsdale, NJ: Lawrence Erlbaum.

Lempers, J., Clark-Lempers, D., & Simons, R. (1989). Economic hardship, parenting, and distress in adolescence. *Child Development, 60,* 25–49.

Lewis, D. A., & Maxfield, M. G. (1980). Fear in the neighborhoods: An investigation of the impact of crime. *Journal of Research in Crime and Delinquency, 17,* 160–189.

Liem, R., & Liem, J. (1978). Social class and mental illness reconsidered: The role of economic stress and social support. *Journal of Health and Social Behavior, 19,* 139–156.

Lurie, O. R. (1974). Parents' attitudes toward childrens' problems and toward use of mental health services: Socioeconomic differences. *American Journal of Orthopsychiatry, 44,* 109–120.

Lyons-Ruth, K., Connell, D. B., Grunebaum, H., & Botein, S. (1990). Infants at social risk: Maternal depression and family support services as mediators of infant development and security of attachment. *Child Development, 61,* 85–98.

Makosky, V. P. (1982). Sources of stress: Events or conditions? In D. Belle (Ed.), *Lives in stress: Women and depression* (pp. 35–53). Beverly Hills: Sage Publications.

McLanahan, S. (1983). Family structure and stress: A longitudinal comparison of two-parent and female-headed families. *Journal of Marriage and the Family, 45,* 347–357.

McLoyd, V. C. (1990). The impact of economic hardship on black families and children: Psychological distress, parenting, and socioemotional development. *Child Development, 61,* 311–346.

McLoyd, V. C., & Wilson, L. (1990). Maternal behavior, social support, and economic conditions as predictors of psychological distress in children. In V. C. McLoyd & C. Flanagan (Eds.), *New directions for child development: Vol. 46. Economic stress: Effects on family life and child development* (pp. 49–69). San Francisco: Jossey-Bass.

McLoyd, V. C., & Wilson, L. (1992a) Maternal behavior, social support, and economic conditions as predictors of psychological distress in children. In V. C. McLoyd & C. Flanagan (Eds.), *New directions for child development. Economic stress: Effects on family life and child development* (Vol. 46, pp. 49–69). San Francisco: Jossey-Bass.

McLoyd, V. C., & Wilson, L. (1992b). The strain of living poor: Parenting, social support, and child mental health. In A. Huston (Ed.), *Children in poverty* (pp. 105–135). Cambridge: Cambridge University Press.

Meisels, S. J., & Plunkett, J. W. (1988). Developmental consequences of preterm birth: Are there long-term effects? In P. B. Baltes, D. L. Featherman, & R. M. Lerner (Eds.), *Life-span development and behavior* (Vol. 9, pp. 87–128). Hillsdale, NJ: Lawrence Erlbaum.

Monkus, E., & Bancalari, E. (1981). Neonatal outcome. In K. Scott, T. Field, & E. Robertson (Eds.), *Teenage parents and their offspring* (pp. 131–144). New York: Grune & Stratton.

Neff, J., & Husaini, B. (1980). Race, socioeconomic status, and psychiatric impairment: A research note. *Journal of Community Psychology, 8,* 16–19.

Patterson, G. (1988). Stress: A change agent for family process. In N. Garmezy & M. Rutter (Eds.), *Stress, coping and development in children* (pp. 235–264). Baltimore: Johns Hopkins University Press.

Pearlin, L., & Johnson, J. (1977). Marital status, life-strains and depression. *American Sociological Review, 42,* 704–715.

Pelton, L. H. (1989). *For reasons of poverty: A critical analysis of the public child welfare system in the United States.* New York: Praeger.

Plunkett, J. W., Meisels, S. J., Stiefel, G. S., Pasick, P. L., & Roloff, D. W. (1986). Patterns of attachment among preterm infants of varying biological risk. *Journal of the American Academy of Child Psychiatry, 25,* 794–800.

Pryor-Brown, L., Cowen, E., Hightower, A., & Lotyczewski, B. (1986). Demographic differences among children in judging and experiencing specific stressful life events. *Journal of Special Education, 20,* 339–346.

Randolph, S., & Adams-Taylor, S. (in press). The health status of children and adolescents in urban environments. In G. King & W. Davis (Eds.), *The health of black America: Social causes and consequences.* New York: Oxford.

Rodning, C., Beckwith, L., & Howard, J. (1990). Characteristics of attachment organization and play organization in prenatally drug-exposed toddlers. *Development and Psychopathology, 1,* 277–289.

Ross, G., Lipper, E. G., & Auld, P. (1990). Social competence and behavior problems in premature children at school age. *Pediatrics, 86,* 391–397.

Rutter, M. (1979). Protective factors in children's responses to stress and disadvantage. In M. Kent & J. Rolf (Eds.), *Primary prevention of psychopathology* (pp. 49–74). Hanover, NH: University Press of New England.

Rutter, M. (1981). The city and the child. *American Journal of Orthopsychiatry, 51,* 610–625.

Rutter, M. (1990). Psychosocial resilience and protective mechanisms. In J. Rolf, A. S. Masten, D. Cicchetti, K. Nuechterlein, & S. Weintraub (Eds.), *Risk and protective factors in the development of psychopathology* (pp. 181–215). Cambridge: Cambridge University Press.

Sameroff, A. (1986). Environmental context of child development. *Journal of Pediatrics, 109,* 192–200.

Sameroff, A., & Fiese, B. H. (1990). Transactional regulation and early intervention. In S. Meisels & J. Shonkoff (Eds.), *Handbook of early childhood intervention* (pp. 119–149). Cambridge: Cambridge University Press.

Sandler, I. N., & Block, M. (1979). Life stress and maladaptation of children. *American Journal of Community Psychology, 7,* 425–440.

Sarigiani, P., Wilson, P., Peterson, A., & Vicary, J. (1990). Self-image and educational plans of adolescents from two contrasting communities. *Journal of Early Adolescence, 10,* 37–55.

Schneider-Rosen, K., Braunwald, K. G., Carlson, V., & Cicchetti, D. (1985). Current perspectives in attachment theory: Illustration from the study of maltreated infants. In I. Bretherton & E. Waters (Eds.), *Growing points of attachment theory and research. Monographs of the Society for Research in Child Development, 50* (1–2, Serial No. 209).

Schorr, L. (1989). *Within our reach: Breaking the cycle of disadvantage.* New York: Doubleday.

Sroufe, L. A. (1983). Infant-caregiver attachment and patterns of adaptation in preschool: The roots of maladaptation and competence. In M. Perlmutter (Ed.), *Minnesota symposia on child psychology. (Vol. 16: pp. 41–83) Development and policy concerning children with special needs.* Hillsdale, NJ: Lawrence Erlbaum.

Starfield, B., Gross, E., Wood, M., Pantell, R., Allen,

C., Gordon, I. B., Moffat, P., Drachman, R., & Katz, H. (1980). Psychological and psychosomatic diagnosis in primary care of children. *Pediatrics, 66,* 159–167.

Steinberg, L., Mounts, N., Lamborn, S., & Dornbusch, S. (1991). Authoritative parenting and adolescent adjustment across varied ecological niches. *Journal of Research on Adolescence, 1,* 19–36.

Sterling, S., Cowen, E. L., Weissberg, R. P., Lotyczewski, B. S., & Boike, M. (1985). Recent stressful life events and young children's school adjustment. *American Journal of Community Psychology, 13,* 87–98.

Van Ijzendoorn, M., & Kroonenberg, P. (1988). Cross-cultural patterns of attachment: A meta-analysis of the Strange Situation. *Child Development, 59,* 147–156.

Vaughn, B., Egeland, B., Sroufe, L. A., & Waters, E. (1979). Individual differences in infant-mother attachment at twelve and eighteen months: Stability and change in families under stress. *Child Development, 50,* 971–975.

Weinraub, M., & Wolf, B. (1983). Effects of stress and and social supports on mother-child interactions in single- and two-parent families. *Child Development, 54,* 1297–1311.

Werner, E. (1984). Resilient children. *Young Children, 40,* 68–72.

Werner, E., & Smith, R. (1982). *Vulnerable but invincible: A study of resilient children.* New York: McGraw-Hill.

White, M., Kasl, S. V., Zahner, G., & Will, J. C. (1987). Perceived crime in the neighborhood and mental health of women and children. *Environment and Behavior, 19,* 588–613.

Wille, D. (1991). Relation of preterm birth with quality of infant-mother attachment at one year. *Infant Behavior and Development, 14,* 227–240.

Wilson, W. J. (1987). *The truly disadvantaged: The inner city, the underclass, and public policy.* Chicago: University of Chicago Press.

Wolock, I., & Horowitz, B. (1979). Child maltreatment and material deprivation among AFDC recipient families. *Social Service Review, 53,* 175–194.

Zill, N. (1984). *American children: Happy, healthy and insecure.* New York: Doubleday Anchor.

Zinsmeister, K. (1990, June). Growing up scared. *The Atlantic Monthly,* pp. 49–66.

Zuckerman, B. S., Amaro, H., & Cabral, H. (1989). The validity of self-reported marijuana and cocaine use among pregnant adolescents. *Journal of Pediatrics, 115,* 812–815.

20 / Religious Influences on Child and Adolescent Development

Peter L. Benson, Kevin S. Masters, and David B. Larson

The role of religious belief, attitudes, and behavior on child and adolescent development has been a focus of social science research for several decades. Several hundred empirical studies have now been published, providing a base from which important generalizations about religious influence can be drawn. However, significant limitations in methodology permeate this research literature. Nearly all studies are correlational in nature, describing relationships between religious variables and a variety of dependent variables, including social behavior, personality, mental health, and psychopathology. From a technical point of view, the causal role of religion in child and adolescent development can at best be inferred from looking at patterns of relationships across multiple studies. Most empirical studies investigate adolescents ei-

ther during the high school years (grades 9 to 12) or during the college years. Studies of children are relatively less common, and typically they employ interview or case study methods (see, e.g., Coles, 1990) with a focus more on describing the development of religiousness than on documenting the impact of religion.

This review focuses on empirical studies that document relationships between religiousness and a range of constructs that fall under the general umbrella of psychological health and pathology. It is divided into four sections: the national demography of child and adolescent religiousness, religious development, religious influences on social behavior and personality, and religious influences on mental health and psychopathology. Several recent publications provide additional reviews of these areas (Benson, Donahue, & Erickson, 1989; Hyde, 1990; Spilka, Hood, & Gorsuch, 1985). The most complete review of the literature prior to 1970 can be found in *Research on Religious Development* (Strommen, 1971).

The National Demography of Child and Adolescent Religiousness

Recent national opinion polls document that religiousness is normative among American adolescents. Gallup poll data show that 95% of 13- to 18-year-old youths believe in "God or a universal spirit" (Gallup, 1983). Eighty-seven percent pray at least occasionally, and 7 out of 10 report church membership.

HISTORICAL TRENDS

Although some connection to religious belief or practice continues to be commonplace, there is evidence that this connection is in decline. Potvin and his colleagues (1976) compared religious beliefs and practices for adolescents in 1951, 1961–62, and 1975. Decreases across time were documented in three areas: belief in a personal God, weekly attendance at worship services, and daily prayer. Because the three data collections varied somewhat in survey item wording and sample demographics, the conclusion that religiousness declined from the 1950s to the mid-1970s must be viewed with caution.

Trends for the period from 1976 to 1994 are more clear. The most complete examination of trends in adolescent religiousness is found in the annual *Monitoring the Future* project conducted by the Institute of Social Research at the University of Michigan. In the spring of each year from 1976 to 1990, the institute conducted an in-depth study of the attitudes, values, and behaviors of a nationally representative study of high school seniors, under contract with the National Institute of Drug Abuse. This annual monitoring of approximately 16,000 seniors includes several religion measures. As reported in the June 12, 1991, issue of *Education Week,* the percent of students who

attend religious services weekly increased slightly, from 41 to 43%, between 1976 and 1980, and then declined steadily from 1980 to 1990 (30%). A parallel pattern was found with a measure of religious importance. The percent reporting that religion is "very important" or "pretty important" in one's life rose slightly to a high-water mark of 65% in 1980 and then slowly declined over the next decade to 56% in 1990. The reported rate for 1994 was 58% (Donahue & Benson, 1995).

AGE TRENDS

Studies describing age changes in adolescent religiousness are universally cross-sectional in nature. Across many studies within different decades since the 1950s, there is a persistent tendency for religiousness to decline between ages 10 and 18. Because this negative relationship between religion and age has been found so consistently at multiple points in time, it is likely that there is a developmental pattern toward decreasing religiousness. At the same time, however, this decrease may represent for many youths a kind of religious moratorium or period of questioning that produces greater religious maturity during adulthood (Hyde, 1990). Longitudinal research is needed to clarify what factors distinguish those whose abandonment of religion during adolescence remains relatively permanent from those for whom adolescent questioning is a developmental stage triggering expanded or refined religious sentiments in adulthood.

Employing multiple-item indices of religion, Potvin et al. (1976) report significant declines between ages 13 to 15 and 15 to 18 in experiential religion (defined as closeness to God, frequency of prayer, and importance of religion), religious practice, and traditional orthodoxy. Research on students enrolled in Catholic high schools demonstrated that ninth-grade students (ages 14 to 15) were more likely to view the church as important, to attend religious services, to read Scripture, and to value religion than 12th-grade students (Benson, Yeager, Wood, Guerra, & Manno, 1986). In addition to these frequency or quantity measures, significant differences in religious orientation also were reported. In comparison to ninth graders, high school seniors score higher on measures of religious doubt and lower on measures of intrinsic religion (religion as an end in itself), extrinsic religion (religion as a means to other ends), vertical religion (religion understood as a relationship between the individual and God), horizontal religion (religion expressed as love of neighbor), and comforting religion (religion valued for support, comfort, and solace). No age differences were found for liberating religion (religion experienced as freeing and enabling). Ninth graders tend to exhibit higher restricting religion (religion experienced as supplying limits, controls, and discipline) than 12th graders.

Sloane and Potvin (1983) replicated the common overall negative correlation between age and religiousness, but they also reported a significant age-by-denomination interaction. Younger adolescents tended to be more religious than older adolescents among Baptists, Catholics, and mainline Protestants. Among sectarian groups (Pentecostal, Holiness, Mennonite), the reverse was true. No age-by-sex interactions were found.

Recent reexamination of data gleaned from 45,000 public school students in 111 U.S. school district reveals significant grade-in-school differences for both religious importance and church attendance (Benson, 1990). As depicted in Table 20.1, church attendance declines more than religious importance. On both measures, there is a substantial decrease between grades 8 and 9, which coincides, for many students, with the transition from middle school to high school.

TABLE 20.1

Importance of Religion and Church Attendance, by Grade

Grade	Sample Size	Importance of Religion (% "important" or "very important")	Church or Synagogue Attendance (% once a week or more)
6	1,516	54	51
7	7,024	55	53
8	7,380	53	51
9	8,471	48	46
10	8,051	48	41
11	7,009	46	40
12	6,113	46	34

GENDER DIFFERENCES

One of the more persistent findings in the scientific study of religion is that females exhibit greater religiousness than males. This pattern holds for children, adolescents, young adults, and older adults (Argyle & Beit-Hallahmi, 1975). Benson (1991) found significant gender differences in importance of religion, church attendance, frequency of prayer, and frequency of Scripture reading in each of these age periods: 13 to 15, 16 to 18, 20 to 29, 30 to 39, 40 to 49, 50 to 59, 60 to 69, 70 to 79, and 90 and older.

When the measure of religiousness has to do with quantity or amount, the findings typically show greater religiousness commitment by females. Gender differences are more equivocal, however, when religious belief or ideology is considered. Two studies reported no gender differences in orthodoxy (Gallup, 1983; Potvin et al., 1976). One reported higher orthodoxy for boys (Suziedelis & Potvin, 1981). A study of high school students suggests that males and females differ in overall religious orientation, based on Allport's (Allport & Ross, 1967) delineation of extrinsic and intrinsic religion ("the extrinsically motivated person *uses* his religion" for personal gain, "the intrinsically motivated *lives* his religion," p. 434). Boys tend to be more extrinsic than girls while girls tend to be more intrinsic than boys (Benson et al., 1986).

RACIAL/ETHNIC DIFFERENCES

A recent review of this literature documents 4 differences between black and white adolescents (Benson et al., 1989):

1. Blacks tend to place greater importance on religion than do whites.
2. Blacks tend to score higher on intrinsic religion than do whites.
3. Blacks tend to place greater importance on institutional religion than whites.
4. Whites tend to report weekly church attendance more than blacks. In an important extension of this research, Dickinson (1982) reported a significant race-by-gender interaction, with white males attending more than black males, but black females attending more than white females.

Unfortunately, relatively little has been documented about the religious sentiments of other racial-ethnic groups. One study found that Hispanic youths revealed religious patterns more like those of blacks than whites (Benson et al., 1986). Compared to whites, Hispanics placed more value on religion and church and were less likely to be weekly church attenders.

Religious Development

The two forces that have the most profound influence on the shape and force of religiousness are parents and religious institutions. These two influences will be documented first, followed by reviews of what is known about the influence of parochial education and cognitive factors.

FAMILY INFLUENCES

Many studies have found that children and adolescents follow in their parents' religious footprints, adopting their denominational preference more often than switching to another denomination or becoming unaffiliated (Spilka et al., 1985). Argyle and Beit-Hallahmi (1975) found that affiliation among adolescents conformed to parental affiliation 40 to 90% of the time, with liberal Protestant denominations having lower rates of retention and Catholics and Jews having higher rates.

A number of family dynamics have been documented that appear to enhance the religious commitment of children and adolescents. These include the amount of religious activity in the home, the religious modeling done by both mothers and fathers, and the frequency of parent-child communication about religious matters (Benson, Williams, & Johnson, 1987; Hoge & Petrillo, 1978; Ozorak, 1989; Potvin & Sloane, 1985). Religious socialization tends to "take hold" best when families are characterized by closeness or harmony (Benson et al., 1986; Ozorak, 1989). Hoge and Petrillo (1978) suggest that positive religious socialization is enhanced when parents are consistent in providing religious messages.

Overall, the kinds of family dynamics tend to have more influence on religious development than other domains. Benson et al. (1986) estimated several multiple regression equations predicting faith commitment (personal religiousness) and church commitment (institutional religiousness) from their national survey data of Catholic high school seniors. The three key factors predicting church and faith commitment were the student's perception of the importance of religion for mother and father, a positive family life, and the amount of religious activities in the home. The zero-order correlations between the predictors and the criteria were in the .20 to .30 range.

A number of studies have sought to document which parent has the greatest influence on religious development. Although there is some ambiguity in the patterning of results, the most typical finding is that the religious sentiments and practices of the mother are more influential than those of the father (Acock & Bengston, 1987; Benson & Eklin, 1990; Dudley & Dudley, 1986; Hunsberger & Brown, 1984).

Several family factors appear to interfere with the transmission of religious values from parents to children. These include conflict between parent and child (Hunsberger & Brown, 1984), parental discord (Hoge & Petrillo, 1978), and mixed-religion marriages (Spilka et al., 1985).

CONGREGATIONS

Surprisingly, relatively little research has been devoted to the question of how churches and synagogues influence religious development. This would seem to be an important line of inquiry, given the fact that the vast majority of children and adolescents are institutionally involved. Three recent studies have taken an in-depth look at religious education programs within religious denominations, with the goal of identifying the program dynamics that promote religious commitment (Benson & Donahue, 1990; Benson & Eklin, 1990; Kelly, Benson & Donahue, 1986). Across these studies, involving multiple denominations (Catholic, Seventh-day Adventist, Lutheran, Southern Baptist Convention, Methodist, Presbyterian, Christian Church [Disciples of Christ], United Church of Christ), it is found that programs marked by educationally effective practices have a profound influence on religious development. These practices include trained and committed teachers, learner-centered educational processes, positive climate, and a content emphasis on issues of importance to children and adolescents. These dynamics are similar to those found in recent public school research on "what works" in promoting academic achievement. When these effectiveness dynamics are in place in a religious education program, the impact on religious commitment is substantial, rivaling the impact of families (Benson & Eklin, 1990). However, currently many of these dynamics are not found in congregational programs.

PAROCHIAL EDUCATION

The landscape of American schools includes a significant number of private schools (about 28,000), enrolling about 10% of students from kindergarten to the twelfth grade. The majority of these schools have a religious affiliation and/or purpose. Catholic schools represent the largest parochial school sector, although the burgeoning number of evangelical or fundamentalist schools, many of which are not part of a religious denomination, are rivaling the Catholic predominance.

Most of the research on the religious effects of parochial schooling has occurred in Catholic schools, although there is an important literature documenting the impact of Jewish (Bock, 1977; Himmelfarb, 1977) and Seventh-day Adventist schools (Benson & Donahue, 1990). Generally, studies find that parochial education increases religious commitment. This has been particularly well documented with Catholic schools. Greeley and his colleagues (Greeley, McCready, & McCourt, 1976; Greeley & Rossi, 1966) used retrospective accounts by Catholic adults to establish that the number of years of Catholic schooling is positively related to a wide range of pro-religion beliefs and practices. A recent comparison of Catholic students attending Catholic schools found that Catholic school attendance enhanced both faith commitment and church involvement after statistical controls for family and socioeconomic differences were made (Guerra, Benson & Donahue, 1989).

COGNITIVE DEVELOPMENT

Goldman (1964) broke new ground in the scientific study of religion with a series of studies on the development of religious thinking in childhood. Using carefully crafted interviews with 5- to 15-year-olds, he documented that religious ideas move through a series of stages much as Piaget had

established earlier in the general area of cognitive development. Based on samples of British children, he postulated the occurrence of three stages: intuitive, concrete operational, and formal or abstract.

The intuitive stage, surfacing between ages 5 and 7, is marked by religious attributions that are often irrelevant or fanciful. For example, God is someone with an old face, God used magic to part the Red Sea, or the Bible is a significant book because it is thick. The concrete stage, emerging around age 8, is marked by literal and anthropomorphic thinking. The events of the biblical narrative occurred precisely as written; God is a person who made and makes things happen in the physical and human spheres; God has attributes projected from one's understanding of adult power and authority.

The shift from concrete to abstract was placed in the 13- to 14½-age span, with the abstract stage marked by the capacity to recognize the symbolic dimension of religious thinking and to think about religious concepts. Goldman concluded that before the concrete-to-abstract shift can occur in religious thinking, it must have occurred already in general cognitive functioning; the shift to abstract religious thinking occurs more slowly than in other areas of cognitive functioning.

Hoge and Petrillo (1978) sought both to replicate and to extend this line of inquiry. This work documented 3 important findings:

1. Abstract religious thinking among adolescents tends to be negatively related to creedal assent and religious practice, suggesting that the advent of abstract thinking is one factor accounting for the decline in adolescent religiousness documented earlier.
2. Abstract religious thinking is correlated with the general cognitive ability to do abstract thinking.
3. Contrary to Goldman's hypothesis, the discrepancy between level of religious thinking and overall cognitive capacity does not promote rejection of doctrine and church. The level of abstract religious thinking predicts rejection better than does the discrepancy.

A second line of inquiry about religious development can be found in the work of Fowler (1981). Based on in-depth interviews, Fowler posits 4 stages in the development of faith during childhood and adolescence and argues that these stages are invariant and sequential, with growth requiring certain conjunctive prerequisites. These structural developmental concepts are consonant with the thinking of Piaget and with Kohlberg's understanding of moral development (Kohlberg, 1976).

Religious Influence on Social Behavior and Personality

The weight of the evidence on the connection of religiousness to social behavior and personality supports two general conclusions. The first is that child and adolescent religiousness tends to be negatively related to health-compromising and/or antisocial behaviors. The second is that religiousness is positively associated with prosocial behaviors and values. Hence it appears that, in a general sense, religion serves the two functions of prevention of negative choices and the promotion of positive choices. This conclusion, however, is an inference based on the patterning of correlational studies. Direct causal testing of this inference has not been undertaken.

SOCIAL BEHAVIOR

Alcohol and Other Drug Use: Overall, there is a persistent tendency for religion to be inversely related to substance use. This point is elegantly reinforced in Donahue's (1987) reanalysis of data from *Monitoring the Future,* an annual, large sample, cross-sectional survey of high school seniors conducted by the Institute for Social Research at the University of Michigan. Examining the relationship of church attendance and religious importance to 25 measures of substance use (e.g., alcohol, marijuana, cocaine, amphetamines, barbiturates, tranquilizers) for multiple subgroups (gender, race, region) within each year from 1976 to 1985, he calculated 2,200 correlations. A negative correlation between religiousness and substance use was found in all but 14 cases.

Although the negative relationship between religiousness and substance use is highly persistent (found in about 85% of published studies investigating this issue), it tends also to be rather modest. Across a number of studies, the correlation be-

tween religion and alcohol use tends to be in the range of −.10 to −.25 (Benson, Wood, Johnson, Eklin, & Mills, 1983; Benson, 1990; Dudley, Mutch, & Cruise, 1987). With marijuana use, religious measures correlate in the range of −.15 to −.30 (Benson et al., 1983; Donahue, 1987; Rohrbaugh & Jessor, 1975). Correlations with tobacco use are in about the same range of about −.15 to −.30 (Dudley et al., 1987; Vener, Zaenglein, & Stewart, 1977).

Across a wide range of studies, the average correlation of religious importance or church attendance with alcohol, tobacco, and marijuana use is about −.20. The correlation with cocaine, heroin, LSD, amphetamine, and barbiturate use is lower, a finding likely due to range restrictions in which use rates by adolescents tend to be extremely low.

Attributing these effects to religiousness is made problematic by the fact that religious sentiments and practice tend to correlate with other factors (e.g., gender, age, region, education) that also are associated with substance use. A number of studies, using multivariate statistical techniques such as discriminant function analysis and regression analysis, have investigated whether religiousness has an effect on substance use independent of these covariates.

Three studies found that independent effects remain for church attendance and/or religious salience after controlling for these sets of demographic influences: age and gender (Lorch & Hughes, 1985); age, gender, race, region, education, and income (Cochran, Boeghley, & Bock, 1988); region, high school type, gender, race, community size, father presence-absence, parental education, and maternal employment (Benson & Donahue, 1989).

Sexuality: The weight of the evidence in the area of sexuality strongly supports the conclusion that religion has a constraining effect on the likelihood of engaging in premarital sexual intercourse (Benson et al., 1989). It has been estimated that religiousness may decrease the probability of intercourse among adolescents by as much as 50% (Spilka et al., 1985).

Although this pattern has been replicated many times, several recent studies fail to find this "constraining effect" with black adolescents (McCormick, Izzo, & Folcik, 1985; Roebuck & McGee, 1977). One study found that while religiously involved teenage females were more likely to delay the onset of sexual intercourse in comparison to less religious peers, sexually active teens who attend church are less likely to use "medical" methods of birth control (Studer & Thornton, 1987). The interpretation is that religiously active youths are less likely to benefit from "open dialogue, information, and support for birth control use." These findings and interpretations have been challenged by Shornack and Ahmed (1989).

Juvenile Delinquency: Since all religions prescribe moral behavior, it has been assumed that religiousness would be related to reduced probability of delinquency. Somewhat surprisingly, however, several empirical investigations and reviews have failed to demonstrate the expected negative relationship. In an early investigation, Hirschi and Stark (1969) concluded that there was no effect of religiousness on delinquency. This position received support from studies demonstrating that delinquents were no less religious than nondelinquents (Argyle & Beit-Hallahmi, 1975; Lea, 1982; Sanua, 1969). Soon, however, these results were reanalyzed and new investigations were begun.

Jensen and Erickson (1979) found methodological problems in the Hirschi and Stark study that masked the presence of a relationship between the variables. Looking more closely at the correlation between personal church attendance and delinquency, Gartner and colleagues (Gartner, Larson, Allen, & Gartner, 1989) determined that five of six studies reviewed by Argyle and Beit-Hallahmi demonstrated a negative relationship. They found seven additional studies that all confirmed the negative relationship between delinquency and religious commitment, with church attendance standing out as the most potent of the religious variables. Thus, how religiousness is measured may be important when considering its relationship with delinquency. Since delinquency is defined on the basis of engagement in certain behaviors, it is probable that behavioral as opposed to attitudinal definitions of religiousness will show the strongest and most consistent relationship. Indeed, psychologists have demonstrated in a variety of areas that behavior-behavior relationships are much stronger than attitude-behavior relationships. That this would hold true in the area of delinquency and religion is not surprising. When looked at from this behavioral perspective, a con-

sistent negative relationship has been found between religious commitment and delinquency (Gartner et al., 1991).

In their review of adolescence and religion, Benson and colleagues (1989) offered another explanation as to why the relationship between religious attitudes and delinquency may appear to be less than expected. They concluded that religious values may have their greatest effects when their influence is different from that of society at large. Since there is strong general societal rejection of delinquent behaviors (e.g., vandalism, theft, violence, etc.) and since these rejections are communicated through interpersonal relations, primarily family and friends, this may reduce the unique contribution of religiousness in reducing delinquency. In statistical terms, a ceiling effect is produced, resulting in a restriction of range and consequently a small correlation between religious attitudes and delinquency.

It is also likely that the content of religious beliefs is interpreted and communicated to adolescents in very different ways resulting in different effects within the religious community. Investigations in other areas (cf. Donahue, 1985; Masters & Bergin, 1992) have demonstrated clearly that, despite substantial similarities, not all approaches to religion have equal effects. As has been the case with adults, these types of investigations should provide a more basic yet practical understanding of the workings of religion in the lives of adolescents. For example, Forliti and Benson (1986) determined that faith characterized by centrality of commitment and a liberating, accepting message was likely to reduce antisocial behavior while promoting prosocial actions. However, "restricting religion" characterized by limits, controls, and discipline was related to antisocial behavior. The authors hypothesize that this may be due to a natural conflict that develops between the adolescents' need to grow in autonomy and independence while belong held to high behavior standard by authority figures. They also found evidence that adolescents high in restricting religion experienced coercive forms of discipline from their parents.

Finally, a study not directly investigating delinquency provides another possible mechanism through which religion may mediate delinquent behavior. It is known that inclusiveness is often characteristic of delinquent youths. Pearson, Francis, and Lightbown (1986), in a study of 569 British youngsters between the ages of 11 and 17 years, determined that religious attitudes were negatively related to inclusiveness and risk-taking but not related to sensation-seeking. Future efforts that investigate specific behaviors, attitudes, theoretical mechanisms, and ways of being religious will greatly advance our knowledge in this area and provide information of both theoretical as well as practical importance.

Benson (1990) investigated the relationship of religious importance and church attendance to a 20-item index of at-risk behavior. This index counted the number of at-risk involvements in 20 problem areas, including frequent alcohol use, binge drinking, tobacco use, illicit drug use, sexual activity, and antisocial behavior. Both religious variables were negatively related to the score on this index, suggesting that religion inhibits involvement across multiple at-risk domains. This finding held for each grade from 6 to 12, and for both males and females.

Prosocial Behavior: Many studies have found positive relationships between religiousness and measures of prosocial behavior (e.g., kindness, helping, volunteerism, altruism) among children and adolescents. For example, Benson and his colleagues (1987) developed scales measuring both self-reported hours in helping other people and the probability of giving help to persons in distress in several hypothetical situations. Religiousness was moderately related to both measures, in the range of .20 to .30.

Similar but stronger relations were reported by Benson et al. (1986) in a nationwide study of more than 7,500 freshmen and seniors in Catholic high schools with high concentrations of poor students. A similar scale of self-reported altruistic actions correlated .20 to .30 with such measures of religiousness as orthodox Catholic beliefs and the tendency to view religion as liberating. The measures of altruism also correlated .30 to .40 with intrinsic, vertical, and horizontal religious orientations.

Although Batson and colleagues (Batson, 1976; Batson & Flory, 1990; Batson & Gray, 1981) have argued that religious individuals appear more altruistic than they actually are, due to social desirability response sets, and that they help for egoistic

rather than altruistic reasons, a number of authors (cf. Masters & Bergin, 1992) have offered persuasive rebuttals of this position. Therefore, it appears that there is evidence for a consistent positive association between religion and altruism in adolescent samples.

PERSONALITY

Studies looking at the relations between religiousness and various personality dimensions among adolescents are relatively sparse, although some areas have received modest attention; if college-age individuals are included, the literature is more substantial. One construct believed to be particularly important for this age group that has been investigated and produced interesting, though not always consistent, findings is self-esteem. Benson et al. (1989) noted that of seven studies done with adolescents since 1970, there was no evidence of a negative relation between religion and self-esteem but there was very little evidence for a positive relation either. However, Payne and colleagues (1991) along with Watson, Hood and Morris (1985) have noted that the humanistic language of many self-esteem measures is incompatible with orthodox concepts, such as sin and guilt. Consequently conservative Christian beliefs may be confused with a psychological trait—self-esteem—leading to empirical inconsistency.

Utilization of more differentiated conceptualizations and measures of religion also may help to clarify these results. Studies with college students have demonstrated that higher levels of self-esteem have been associated with intrinsic religiousness (Payne, et al., 1991; Wickstrom & Fleck, 1983). Additionally, Bergin and colleagues (Bergin, Masters, & Richards, 1987) found that among Mormon college students, intrinsic religiousness was related to higher levels of personality functioning as measured by the California Psychological Inventory whereas extrinsic religiousness related to poorer functioning. Finally, Forliti and Benson (1986) noted that more central and liberating religion is associated with high self-esteem.

Francis and associates (Francis, Lankshear, & Pearson, 1989; Francis & Pearson, 1985; Francis, Pearson, & Kay, 1982; 1983a,b,c; Francis, Pearson, & Stubbs, 1985; Pearson et al., 1986) have carried out a series of large-sample studies investigating religiousness and personality variables in English adolescents. They have concluded that: (1) introversion is positively related to religiousness; (2) neuroticism is not related to religiousness; (3) neuroticism does not interact with introversion to promote religiousness; (4) psychoticism is negatively related with religiousness; and (5) religiousness may be positively related to immaturity and less insightfulness.

In a study of 167 introductory psychology college students (mean age approximately 19 years), Geist and Daheim (1984) found that Catholic students expressed more verbal hostility than Protestants as measured by the Buss Durkee Hostility Inventory. Further, Catholic men were more resentful than Catholic women and exhibited greater indirect hostility and suspicion than Protestant men. The authors note that these findings are consistent with previous outcomes. However, they caution that neither Catholics nor Protestants are homogeneous groups and further differentiations within groups are needed in order to understand these results more fully.

Religiousness and Mental Health/ Psychopathology

PSYCHOLOGICAL ADJUSTMENT

Adolescence is a time of development, change, and adjustment. Erickson (1963) has noted that adolescents achieve a sense of identity by going through crisis periods requiring them to explore, question, evaluate, and finally formulate their own ways of coping and adapting. While all youths must face their share of difficult experiences, some are particularly burdened by catastrophic events. Most teenagers are able to handle the usual and unusual traumas of adolescence and move capably into adulthood. Some do not. In this section we explore the role of religion as it relates to a few particular areas of adjustment.

Suicide: Suicide is the second leading cause of death among adolescents, trailing behind only automobile and other accidents. Approximately 5,000 suicides are tallied each year in the United States for those in the 15 to 24 age group (Stivers, 1988), and this probably represents a very conservative estimate since many suicidal deaths are erroneously classified as being due to accidents or other causes.

Garfinkel, Froese, and Hood (1982) conducted an interesting archival study of over 1,000 children and adolescents admitted to a large children's hospital in Canada. They matched 505 patients admitted for attempted suicide with a sample of nonsuicidal control patients. Their results demonstrated that the suicidal patients were from families characterized by economic stress, higher rates of medical problems, psychiatric illness, and suicide. They also tended to be hostile and rigid, which interfered in their ability to interact with one another. Suicidal patients were also more likely to be Protestant than Catholic or Jewish. The authors note that it is difficult to separate the religious component from other confounding variables.

Stoddard, Pahlavan, and Cahners (1985) reported 6 case studies of adolescents who attempted self-immolation. They noted that all of the cases were from rigidly religious background, 2 each being Catholic and fundamentalist Christian while 1 each were Jewish and Moslem. How exactly the authors determined that these individuals were "rigidly" religious as opposed to other ways of being religious is not made clear. Nevertheless, they noted that a pattern of behaviors resembling the restricting religious orientation portrayed earlier seemed prominent in the backgrounds of these youngsters. Again, however, it is impossible to separate religious variables from other important factors, such as the poor marital relationships and long-standing psychopathology that also characterized these families.

It has been generally recognized that in cultures where the majority of people subscribe to a formal religion, completed suicides are few and that where there is no formal religion, completed suicides are more numerous (Payne, et al., in press; Stivers, 1988). This pattern seemed to hold true in a study by Berlin (1987) that investigated suicide among American Indian adolescents. A number of factors, including failure to adhere to traditional religious practices and ways of living, were associated with chaotic family structure, adult alcoholism, and high adolescent suicide rates.

Because of the nature of the phenomenon and the intermingling of various other important factors, definitive conclusions regarding the role that religion plays in adolescent suicide are difficult to make. However, overall it is known that religious people tend to commit suicide less often than do the nonreligious (Stack, 1983a,b). Further, Salmons and Harrington (1984) found that religious university students admitted to less suicidal ideation on questionnaires. While some adolescents may interpret religious prescriptions in a demanding and slavish manner that could result in despair and possibly suicidal intent (cf. Bergin, Stinchfield, Gaskin, Masters, & Sullivan, 1988), it seems more common that religious belief acts as a deterrent to suicidal thought and action.

Coping with Disease: Generally adolescence is a time of health and vitality. However, for some teenagers these years present more than their share of crises, as serious illnesses may strike with seemingly sudden and terrible effects. These cases provide perhaps the most stringent test of the adaptive effects of religious belief.

Several studies have highlighted the important role of religious belief in coping with devastating diseases such as cancer. Tebbi and colleagues (Tebbi, Mallon, Richards, & Bigler, 1987) studied 28 adolescent cancer patients who averaged 17 years old. These patients used religion as a source of support in that it provided meaningful interpretations of existence and gave a purpose to living. The authors concluded that religion can provide security in the face of death resulting in less anxiety among the more religious. Similarly, Silber and Reilly (1985) found that more seriously ill adolescents had higher scores on religiosity and spirituality measures. In this regard blacks scored higher than whites, Catholics higher than Protestants, and parochial school students higher than public school students. Gavaghan and Roach (1987) also demonstrated that chronically ill adolescents have more advanced religious development than do their healthy counterparts.

Barbarin and Chester (1984) studied the relationship between the coping strategies used by parents of adolescents with cancer and psychosocial outcomes, such as relations with spouses, friends, and medical staff. The study provides insight into one of the mechanisms through which religion may act as an important agent in both coping and prevention. They found that parents who used religion as an emotion-focused coping style had more supportive relationships with friends and neighbors. The authors suggest that this may be due to a close correspondence between the friends' expectations for the parents' behaviors (i.e., active coping, not feeling hopeless) and their actual behavior. Another plausible explanation is that the more religious parents had a previously established social network that remained dependable and therefore offered support during the time of distress.

The conclusion reached from these studies is that religious beliefs may provide an important source of support during a serious illness. All health care workers should recognize and utilize this fact. From a slightly different perspective. Blotcky and colleagues (Blotcky, Cohen, Conatser, & Klopovich, 1985) recommend early discussion with youngsters and their families regarding specific concerns and religious beliefs. This, they conclude, will lead to fewer treatment refusals and greater compliance with therapeutic programs.

MENTAL ILLNESS

Mental illness is a negative term used to describe psychiatric disturbance. Based on the information just presented, it is tempting to infer that religion reduces incidence and seriousness of mental illness. Indeed, several studies have reported negative relations between religious commitment and variables such as depression and anxiety (Gartner et al., 1991). On the other hand, persons working with psychotic patients may be struck by the abundant religious content of their delusions. Based on this, some have inferred that religious experience and psychosis are positively related. In fact, however, religious delusions can be reliably discriminated from normal religious experience by naive raters (Margolis & Elifson, 1983), indicating that the two experiences are different. Further, Francis and Pearson (1985) found a negative relation between religiosity and psychoticism.

Although these results may appear favorable for the religious perspective, the types of longitudinal research needed to make a clear determination regarding the role of religion in mental illness have not been done (Payne et al., 1991). Short-term and cross-sectional studies do not provide clarification of the issue. Many of these studies were conducted on healthy college students and/or measured variables only tangentially related to mental illness. Further, they provide little information specific to adolescents and children. With few exceptions (notably the work of Francis reported earlier), significant research on those below college age is waiting to be conducted.

Studies that have found a negative relation between religious commitment and mental illness leave unaddressed the issue of causality. For example, it is possible that persons who are mentally disturbed simply drop out of religious as well as other activities. Similarly, those who remain religiously active and mentally healthy are likely to be generally active in a variety of ways. At this point the relation between religion and mental illness is unclear; those studies that have shown an effect favoring religious participation have not clarified the important causal dimensions accounting for this relation.

PREVENTION

The study reported earlier by Barbarin and Chester (1984) provides insight into another possible area where religion may impact the psychological development of adolescents: prevention. Investigating the variables of life satisfaction and psychological hardiness, Hannah and Morrissey (1987) found that Protestant females, compared to Protestant males and Catholic males and females, had the highest scores on both variables. Overall, Protestant high school students were higher in hardiness than Roman Catholic students. The authors suggest that faith that emphasizes personal salvation and responsibility may encourage hardiness and prepare individuals to handle adverse circumstances.

In an interesting study of 199 families (201 children) in Head Start programs, Strayhorn, Weidman, and Larson (1990) found that more religious parents reported more favorable parenting practices, lower self-reported hostility, and greater social support from friends. They also found, however, that ratings of children's behavior in natural settings and videotaped interactions showed no association with parents' religiousness. The authors correctly recognized that the lack of a relationship in preschool children does not rule out the possibility of later effects.

Finally, a longitudinal study of college students by Masters and colleagues (Bergin et al., 1988; Masters, Bergin, Reynolds, & Sullivan, 1991) found that religious influences were highly intermingled with other sociocultural and interpersonal factors in ways that were difficult to separate and analyze individually. Nevertheless, those students whose religious involvement from childhood through adolescence was characterized by continuous development and mild experiences were rated by interviewers as conforming to parental faith without adolescent turmoil and had a tendency to show more favorable psychological profiles. It appears that religion interacted with family life to prepare them for the trials of the teenage and college years in a way that facilitated their growth and development. Those sampled who showed discontinuous religious commitment, sometimes with intense experiences, were more likely to report conflictual parental relations and a generally more troubled life. Troubled personal development and troubled religiousness covaried, however. Some of these students seemed to find healing in their religious faith as they progressed through college. Although the unique contribution of religion to these different outcomes is difficult to ascertain, it seems that religion is likely to play a role in both primary and secondary prevention.

RELIGION AND CLINICAL PRACTICE

There are several ways in which religious belief and activity is relevant to clinical practice. The domain of religious belief can provide insight into key psychological dynamics. For example, there is evidence that an adolescent's images of God reflect self-esteem; youths with high self-esteem tend to understand God as loving, caring, accepting, and forgiving while those with lower self-esteem tend to attribute traits of power and judgments (Benson & Spilka, 1973).

Religious sentiment and practice by children and adolescents is likely to be a positive developmental experience that binds them to the support, nurture, discipline, and boundaries of religious communities. Indeed, religious sentiment and belonging might be considered developmental assets, since they are positively correlated in a number of studies with prosocial behavior and negatively correlated with high-risk behavior (Benson, 1990). The affirmation of such religious activity may function to increase acceptance—by child and parent(s)—of professional care.

Caution is also in order, however. Overly authoritarian religious beliefs can induce dysfunctional levels of guilt or shame or forms of belonging that impede the development of personal autocracy. Although such negative forms of religion tend to be the exception rather than the rule, evidence of such may require the counsel of specialists who have extensive professional experience in explaining the religious domain.

Conclusion

On balance, the weight of the empirical evidence suggests that religiousness is associated with posi-

tive developmental outcomes. This conclusion is based on rather global measures of religious sentiment and practice. Much less is known about the impact of specific religious ideologies.

Most of the research reported here is with mainstream, non-institutionalized adolescents. There is also a strong tendency for these studies to focus on white youth who are connected to schools or congregations. It is much less clear at this point how religion functions in the lives of socially marginalized, alienated, or institutionalized youth.

The role of religion during childhood also requires new research initiatives. This, in turn, will require utilization of observational and interview methodologies which are currently underemployed. Ultimately, the primary need in this field is longitudinal studies. These are needed to better understand the interconnection of religious practice and ideology with life perspectives, behavioral decisions, and mental health.

REFERENCES

Acock, A. C., & Bengston, V. L. (1987). On the relative influence of mothers and fathers: A covariance analysis of political and religious socialization. *Journal of Marriage and the Family, 40*, 519–530.

Allport, G. W., & Ross, J. M. (1967). Personal religious orientation and prejudice. *Journal of Personality and Social Psychology, 5*, 432–443.

Argyle, M., & Beit-Hallahmi, B. (1975). *The social psychology of religion.* London: Routledge & Kegan Paul.

Barbarin, Q. A., & Chester, M. A. (1984). Coping as interpersonal strategy: Families with childhood cancer. *Family Systems Medicine, 2*, 279–289.

Batson, C. D. (1976). Religion as prosocial: Agent or double agent? *Journal for the Scientific Study of Religion, 15*, 29–45.

Batson, C. D., & Flory, J. D. (1990). Goal-relevant cognitions associated with helping by individuals high on intrinsic, end religion. *Journal for the Scientific Study of Religion, 29*, 346–360.

Batson, C. D., & Gray, R. A. (1981). Religious orientation and helping behavior: Responding to one's own or to the victim's needs? *Journal of Personality and Social Psychology, 40*, 511–520.

Benson, P. L. (1990). *The troubled journey: A portrait of 6th–12th grade youth.* Minneapolis: Search Institute.

Benson, P. L. (1991). *Religious development in adolescence and adulthood.* (August). Paper presented to

the annual convention of the American Psychological Association, San Francisco, CA.

Benson, P. L., & Donahue, M. J. (1989). Ten year trends in at-risk behavior: A national study of black adolescents. *Journal of Adolescent Research, 4* (2), 125–39.

Benson, P. L., & Donahue, M. J. (1990). *Valuegenesis.* Silver Spring, MD: North American Division Office of Education, Seventh-day Adventist Church.

Benson, P. L., Donahue, M. J., & Erickson, J. A. (1989). Adolescence and religion: A review of the literature from 1970–1986. *Research in the Social Scientific Study of Religion, 1*, 153–181.

Benson, P. L., & Eklin, C. H. (1990). *Summary report: The national study of mainline Protestant denominations.* Minneapolis: Search Institute.

Benson, P. L., & Spilka, B. (1973). God image as a function of self-esteem and locus of control. *Journal for the Scientific Study of Religion, 12*, 297–310.

Benson, P. L., Williams, D., & Johnson, A. (1987). *The quicksilver years: The hopes and fears of early adolescence.* San Francisco: Harper & Row.

Benson, P. L., Wood, P. K., Johnson, A. L., Eklin, C. H., & Mills, J. E. (1983). *Report on 1983 Minnesota survey of drug use and drug-related attitudes.* Minneapolis: Search Institute.

Benson, P. L., Yeager, R. J., Wood, P. K., Guerra, M. J., & Manno, B. V. (1986). *Catholic high schools:*

Their impact on low-income students. Washington, DC: National Catholic Educational Association.

Bergin, A. E., Masters, K. S., & Richards, P. S. (1987). Religiousness and mental health reconsidered: A study of an intrinsically religious sample. *Journal of Counseling Psychology, 34,* 197–204.

Bergin, A. E., Stinchfield, R. D., Gaskin, T. A., Masters, K. S., & Sullivan, C. E. (1988). Religious lifestyles and mental health: An exploratory study. *Journal of Counseling Psychology, 35,* 91–98.

Berlin, I. N. (1987). Suicide among American Indian adolescents: An overview. *Suicide and Life-Threatening Behavior, 17,* 218–232.

Blotcky, A. D., Cohen, D. G., Conatser, C., & Klopovich, P. (1985). Psychosocial characteristics of adolescents who refuse cancer treatment. *Journal of Consulting and Clinical Psychology, 53,* 729–731.

Boch, G. D. (1977). The Jewish schooling of American Jews: A study of non-cognitive educational effects. *Dissertation Abstracts International, 37,* 4628A.

Cochran, J. K., Boeghley, L., & Bock, E. W. (1988). Religiosity and alcohol behavior: An exploration of reference group theory. *Sociological Forum, 3* (2), 256–276.

Coles, R. (1990). *The spiritual life of children.* Boston: Houghton Mifflin.

Dickinson, G. E. (1982). Changing religious behavior of adolescents 1964–79. *Youth & Society, 13,* 283–288.

Donahue, M. J. (1985). Intrinsic and extrinsic religiousness: Review and meta-analysis. *Journal of Personality and Social Psychology, 48,* 400–419.

Donahue, M. J. (1987). *Religion and drug use: 1976– 1985.* (November). Paper presented at the annual meeting of the Society for the Scientific Study of Religion, Louisville, KY.

Donahue, M. J., & Benson, P. L. (1995). Religion and the well-being of adolescents. *Journal of Social Issues, 51* (2), 145–160.

Dudley, R. L., & Dudley, M. G. (1986). Transmissions of religious values from parents to adolescents. *Review of Religious Research, 28,* 3–15.

Dudley, R. L., Mutch, P. B., & Cruise, R. J. (1987). Religious factors and drug usage among Seventh-day Adventist youth in North America. *Journal for the Scientific Study of Religion, 26* (2), 218–233.

Erickson, E. H. (1963). *Childhood and society.* New York: W. H. Norton.

Forliti, J. E., & Benson, P. L. (1986). Young adolescents: A national study. *Religious Education, 81,* 199–224.

Fowler, J. (1981). *Stages of faith: The psychology of human development and the search for meaning.* New York: Harper & Row.

Francis, L. J., Lankshear, D. W., & Pearson, P. R. (1989). The relationship between religiosity and the short form JEPQ (JEPQ-S) indices of E, N, L and P among eleven year olds. *Personality and Individual Differences, 10,* 763–769.

Francis, L. J., & Pearson, P. R. (1985). Psychoticism and religiosity among 15-year olds. *Personality and Individual Differences, 6,* 397–398.

Francis, L. F., Pearson, P. R., & Kay, W. K. (1982). Eysenck's personality quadrants and religiosity. *British Journal of Social Psychology, 21,* 262–264.

Francis, L. J., Pearson, P. R., & Kay, W. K. (1983a). Are introverts still more religious? *Personality and Individual Differences, 4,* 211–212.

Francis, L. J., Pearson, P. R., & Kay, W. K. (1983b). Are religious children bigger liars? *Psychological Reports, 52,* 551–554.

Francis, L. J., Pearson, P. R., & Kay, W. K. (1983c). Neuroticism and religiosity among English schoolchildren. *Journal of Social Psychology, 121,* 149–150.

Francis, L. J., Pearson, P. R., & Stubbs, M. T. (1985). Personality and religion among low ability children in residential special schools. *British Journal of Mental Subnormality, 31,* 41–45.

Gallup, G. (1983). Teens say religion very important. *Emerging Trends, 5,* 4.

Gartner, J., Larson, D. B., Allen, G. D., & Gartner, A. F. (1991). Religious commitment and psychopathology: A review of the empirical literature. *Journal of Theology & Psychology, 19* (1), 6–25.

Garfinkel, B. D., Froese, A., & Hood, J. (1982). Suicide attempts in children and adolescents. *American Journal of Psychiatry, 139,* 1257–1261.

Gavaghan, M. P., & Roach, J. E. (1987). Ego identity development of adolescents with cancer. *Journal of Pediatric Psychology, 12,* 203–213.

Geist, C. R., & Daheim, C. M. (1984). Religious affiliation and manifest hostility. *Psychological Reports, 55,* 493–494.

Goldman, R. (1964). *Religious thinking from childhood to adolescence.* London: Routledge & Kegan Paul.

Greeley, A. M., McCready, W., & McCourt, K. (1976). *Catholic schools in a declining church.* Kansas City, MO: Shud & Ward.

Greeley, A. M., & Rossi, P. H. (1966). *The education of American Catholics.* Chicago: Aldine.

Guerra, M., Benson, P., & Donahue, M. (1989). *The heart of the matter: Effects of Catholic high schools on student values, beliefs, & behaviors.* Washington, DC: Catholic Educational Association.

Hannah, T. E., & Morrissey, C. (1987). Correlates of psychological hardiness in Canadian adolescents. *Journal of Social Psychology, 127,* 339–344.

Himmelfarb, H. S. (1977). The interaction effects of parents, spouse, and schooling: Comparing the impact of Jewish and Catholic schools. *Sociological Quarterly, 18,* 464–477.

Hirschi, T., & Stark, R. (1969). Hellfire and delinquency. *Social Problems, 17,* 202–213.

Hoge, D. R., & Petrillo, G. H. (1978). Determinants of church participation and attitudes among high school youth. *Journal for the Scientific Study of Religion, 17,* 359–379.

Hunsberger, B., & Brown, L. B. (1984). Religious socialization, apostasy, and the impact of family background. *Journal for the Scientific Study of Religion, 23,* 239–251.

Hyde, K. E. (1990). *Religion in childhood and adolescence.* Birmingham, AL: Religious Education Press.

Jensen, G. F., & Erickson, M. L. (1979). The religious factor and delinquency: Another look at the hellfire hypothesis. In R. Wuthnow (Ed.), *The religious dimension: New directions in quantitative research* (pp. 157–177). New York: Academic Press.

Kelly, F. D., Benson, P. L., & Donahue, M. J. (1986). *Toward effective parish religious education for children and young people: A national study.* Washington, DC: National Catholic Educational Association.

Kohlberg, L. (1976). *Collected papers on moral development.* Cambridge, MA: Center for Moral Education.

Lea, G. (1982). Religion, mental health, and clinical issues. *Journal of Religion and Health, 21,* 336–351.

Lorch, B. R., & Hughes, R. H. (1985). Religion and youth substance use. *Journal of Religion and Health, 24* (3), 197–208.

Margolis, R. D., & Elifson, K. W. (1983). Validation of a typology of religious experience and its relationship to the psychotic experience. *Journal of Psychology and Theology, 11,* 135–141.

Masters, K. S., & Bergin, A. E. (1992). Religious orientation and mental health. In J. F. Schumaker (Ed.), *Religion and mental health.* London: Oxford University Press, 221–232.

Masters, K. S., Bergin, A. E., Reynolds, E. M., & Sullivan, C. E. (1991). Religious life-styles and mental health: A follow-up study. *Counseling and Values, 35,* 211–224.

McCormick, N., Izzo, A., & Folcik, J. (1985). Adolescents' values, sexuality, and contraception in a rural New York county. *Adolescence, 20,* 385–395.

Ozorak, E. W. (1989). Social and cognitive influences on the development of religious beliefs and commitment in adolescence. *Journal for the Scientific Study of Religion, 28,* 448–463.

Payne, I. R., Bergin, A. E., Bielema, K. A., & Jenkins, P. H. (1991). Review of religion and mental health: Prevention and the enhancement of psychosocial functioning. *Prevention in Human Services, 9,* 11–40.

Pearson, P. R., Francis, L. J., & Lightbown, T. J. (1986). Impulsivity and religiosity. *Personality and Individual Differences, 7,* 89–94.

Potvin, R. H., Hoge, D. R., & Nelson, H. M. (1976). *Religion and American youth: With emphasis on Catholic adolescents and young adults.* Washington, DC: United States Catholic Conference.

Potvin, R. H., & Sloane, D. M. (1985). Parental control, age, and religious practice. *Review of Religious Research, 27,* 3–14.

Roebuck, J., & McGee, M. G. (1977). Attitudes toward premarital sex and sexual behavior among black high school girls. *Journal of Sex Research, 13,* 104–114.

Rohrbaugh, J., & Jessor, R. (1975). Religiosity in youth: A personal control against deviant behavior. *Journal of Personality, 43,* 136–155.

Salmons, P. H., & Harrington, R. (1984). Suicidal ideation in university students and other groups. *International Journal of Psychiatry, 30,* 201–205.

Sanua, V. D. (1969). Religion, mental health, and personality: A review of empirical studies. *American Journal of Psychiatry, 125,* 1203–1213.

Shornack, L. L., & Ahmed, F. (1989). Adolescent religiousness and pregnancy prevention: A comment on research by Studer and Thornton. *Journal of Marriage and Family, 51,* 1083–1089.

Silber, T. J., & Reilly, M. (1985). Spiritual and religious concerns of the hospitalized adolescent. *Adolescence, 20,* 217–224.

Sloane, D. M., & Potvin, R. H. (1983). Age differences in adolescent religiousness. *Review of Religious Research, 25,* 142–154.

Spilka, B., Hood, R. W., & Gorsuch, R. L. (1985). *The psychology of religion: An empirical approach.* Englewood Cliffs, NJ: Prentice-Hall.

Stack, S. (1983a). A comparative analysis of suicide and religiosity. *Journal of Social Psychology, 119,* 285–286.

Stack, S. (1983b). The effect of the decline in institutionalized religion on suicide, 1954–1978. *Journal for the Scientific Study of Religion, 22,* 239–252.

Stivers, C. (1988). Adolescent suicide: An overview. *Marriage and Family Review, 12,* 135–142.

Stoddard, F. J., Pahlavan, K., & Cahners, S. (1985). Suicide attempted by self-immolation during adolescence. *Adolescent Psychiatry, 12,* 251–265.

Studer, M., & Thornton, A. (1987). Adolescent religiosity and contraceptive use. *Journal of Marriage and the Family, 49,* 117–128.

Strommen, M. P. (Ed.). (1971). *Research on religious development: A comprehensive handbook.* New York: Hawthorn Books.

Strayhorn, J. M., Weidman, C. S., & Larson, D. (1990). A measure of religiousness, and its relation to parent and child mental health variables. *Journal of Community Psychology, 18,* 34–43.

Suziedelis, A., & Potvin, R. (1981). Sex differences in factors affecting religiousness among Catholic adolescents. *Journal for the Scientific Study of Religion, 20,* 38–50.

Tebbi, C. K., Mallon, J. C., Richards, M. E., & Bigler, L. R. (1987). Religiosity and locus of control of adolescent cancer patients. *Psychological Reports, 61,* 683–696.

Vener, A. M., Zaenglein, M., & Stewart, D. B. (1977). Traditional religious orthodoxy, respect for authority and nonconformity in adolescence. *Adolescence, 12* (45), 43–56.

Watson, P. J., Hood, R. W., Jr., & Morris, R. J. (1985). Religiosity, sin and self esteem. *Journal of Psychology and Theology, 13,* 116–128.

Wickstrom, D. L., & Fleck, J. R. (1983). Missionary children: Correlates of self-esteem and dependency. *Journal of Psychology and Theology, 11,* 226–235.

21 / The Rural Child

Theodore A. Petti

Rural children and adolescents represent a significant and poorly understood minority. The meaning of "rural" defies easy definition (Murray & Keller, 1991; Petti, Benswanger & Fialkov, 1987). The United States Census Bureau (1989) has defined "rural" to include open countryside and areas with 2,500 or fewer residents, excluding suburbs of large cities. "Rural" is generally considered to be synonymous with nonmetropolitan, designated since 1983 as an area that does not contain a central city with a population of at least 50,000 and not related socially and economically to such a city. Rural residents comprise about 24% of the U.S. population and reside on most of the landmass of the country.[1]

The experience of rural life for children depends on the nature of the community and social status of the family. Differences between the environment of a New England village, a Texas ranch, a Carolina farm, and an Appalachian mining town dramatically affect the development of rural youth. Rural culture is enriched by diversity in physical geography, occupations of its inhabitants, wealth and its distribution, subcultures of its own minorities, and proximity to metropolitan areas. Thus, rural children and their families are exposed to a myriad of influences and must be considered a heterogeneous group with unique characteristics depending on the environment within which they have been reared (Blank, Fox, Margrove & Turner, 1995; Kane & Ennis, 1996).

Epidemiology

Significant disparities exist in the epidemiologic data of studies conducted with rural populations. The conclusions range from no differences in the prevalence of most psychiatric disorders to sig-

nificant differences in both increased and decreased rates of psychopathology. Studies of the impact of the farm crisis and economic downswing of the 1980s document the increased prevalence and incidence of depression and suicide in farm families (Anderson, 1990; Fitchen, 1987; Garfinkel, Hoberman, Parsons, & Walker, 1986; Johnson & Booth, 1990; Murray & Keller, 1991).

Few epidemiologic studies of rural children have been conducted. In one rural region, alcohol abuse appears to be well above the national average for middle school students and to increase significantly with age (60% percent of eighth graders reported being drunk at least once). No difference was found in alcohol-induced sickness, reported intoxication, or increase in abuse with age between the sexes (Sarvela & McClendon, 1987). Since major depression often precedes alcohol and substance abuse, these findings may represent an unidentified problem.

A Minnesota study of over 3,600 students attending 82 schools in 52 nonmetropolitan counties (Garfinkel et al., 1986) found 37.6% reporting some form of depression on the Beck Depression Inventory (17.5% with moderate to severe levels) during the month prior to the survey. Severe current depression and suicide attempts at some time were reported by 3 times as many girls as boys. Recent suicide attempts were reported by 2.9% of the students, about 3.5 times the national average. The mean age of the ninth through twelfth graders was 16.3 years, with the suicide attempter group overrepresented among 15- to 16-year-olds. Nonwhite suicide attempters had a rate higher than expected compared to the community base rate.

High-risk factors related to structural changes in the families of youths reporting a suicide attempt in the Minnesota study were identified. They are similar to those found in suicidal youth in urban/suburban studies (Forrest, 1988) and highlight the importance of early awareness of psychiatric disorder in at-risk populations.

Thus, currently available studies suggest that rural youths may be at equal or greater risk for

---

[1] This chapter is an updated, abbreviated version of an earlier work (Petti, Benswanger, & Fialkov, 1987).

developing alcohol abuse and suicidal problems compared to their nonrural peers. They also may be at greater risk in developing other psychiatric disorders, including depression and other syndromes associated with stress.

Misconceptions

Most Americans still retain an idyllic view of rural life. It is characterized by living harmoniously with nature, on a farm away from the stressors of urban chaos. Only about 2% of our population consists of rural farm residents. The proportion of farm families in which farming is the sole employment for both adults is progressively declining (Elder, 1986). About a quarter of farm residents lived within a metropolitan statistical area, and 45.9% of residents designated as rural resided in metropolitan statistical areas in 1988 (U.S. Census Bureau, 1989).

Large numbers of minority groups with special social services needs reside in rural areas and often are isolated from other groups. They are 3 times more likely to live in substandard housing, have lower mean family incomes, and have smaller proportions of working men and women (Murray & Keller, 1991). Far from the prosperity of stable and self-reliant farm families, significant numbers of the impoverished reside in rural areas. Observers increasingly refer to a condition of chronic rural poverty (Fitchen, 1987).

Earlier rural communities were described as composed of small social units with common interests and beliefs as well as relationships based on community ties and kinship. They were considered homogeneous, with an emphasis on conformity to traditional values and adherence to family expectations. The family was considered inviolate and marriage a joint, enduring partnership with clearly defined sex roles (Petti et al., 1987).

In many regions of the nation, the interdependence within rural communities no longer exists. Farm mechanization, increased reliance on the automobile, industrialization, and other changes have resulted in an ongoing process of restructuring rural communities away from traditional community and social support systems (Blank et al., 1995; Murray & Keller, 1991; Petti et al., 1987).

Black rural families in particular have been characterized as receiving considerable support from informal networks. A survey (Gaudin & Davis, 1985) reports significantly smaller, less supportive, and more kin-dominated networks for poor black mothers than those reported by poor white mothers. Networks of the black mothers appeared more durable but were more homogeneous, consisting of fewer individuals from a higher socioeconomic status than their own and containing fewer persons available during times of need. Professional helpers were absent in the networks of both groups. The black disadvantaged families appeared to be characterized as isolated, nuclear units with the mothers having relatively poor access to such basic assistance as baby-sitting, borrowing money, or having someone to listen to them. These findings differ markedly from earlier descriptions of urban black families as being highly supported by strong kinship networks, or the family networks of rural blacks as critical in supplying tangible aid and psychological support (Gaudin & Davis, 1985).

Rural communities have increasingly turned to state and federal agencies, businesses, and corporations in order to meet local needs (Kelleher, Taylor & Reckert, 1992). There has been a "subtle urban transformation" (Murray & Keller, 1991) and a decline in traditional support systems. The continuing outmigration of rural families and the departure of the natural leaders who had helped to integrate the community have accelerated the process. Those who move into the country are often commuters from the metropolitan area who generally fail to turn their attention and energies to rural community problems and issues (Petti et al., 1987).

The continuing economic and social changes evolving from dramatic shifts in the economic environment of rural America (Human & Wasem, 1991) coupled with farm and economic crises of the 1980s (Johnson & Booth, 1990) may lead to collapse of rural communities like that which occurred in the 1920s and 1930s during a similar period of agricultural reorganization (Fitchen, 1987).

In summary, the prevalence of poverty and relative isolation in many rural farm and nonfarm families creates barriers to normal development, particularly for children from disadvantaged families.

The Rural Impact on Development

The literature is sparse regarding the effect of rural residence on development. Few studies specifically address the cognitive, social, or emotional development of rural youngsters. Like their urban counterparts, rural children are the product of diverse factors in their environment.

High rates of rural infant mortality, poverty, unemployment, with increasing rates of psychopathology and lower educational achievement levels of their parents, are high-risk indicators for psychopathologic development of children. From an early age, rural children are forced to learn nonverbal cues in order to understand the thoughts and feelings of their nonverbal parents and other adults (Looff, 1981). With the current emphasis on communication and management of information, the characteristic nonverbal nature of rural residents (Van Hook, 1990) places them at the edge of not being able to engage in the wider society and at risk of increasing their isolation.

For these youngsters, attendance at consolidated schools is a major stressor as peers frequently label them as "different." Without adequate role modeling by their parents to function within the wider world, they develop an internalized sense of worthlessness akin to learned helplessness; this in turn restricts them from successful functioning in the wider society. Thus begins a negative cycle of poor performance, failure, and negative expectations then and for the future (Fitchen, 1987).

However, even in poor rural families, traditional beliefs relating to morality, religion, and political philosophy offer a stability for protected development. Rural folks have characteristically held conservative views on divorce, birth control, and premarital sex and have translated these views into concrete action and community policy. Yet characteristics such as less divorce and fewer mothers employed outside the home in rural as compared to urban residents have been significantly altered by the recent economic downswing and most dramatically by the farm crisis (Johnson & Booth, 1990).

More rural wives are entering the job market than ever before. Their lower educational level results in lower-status jobs; they work a few more hours per week while earning less than those employed in metropolitan areas, and thus limit their economic contribution to the family (Scanzoni & Arnett, 1987). However, their income often means the difference between survival and poverty in their families (Elder, 1986). As farm families shift to rural nonfarm status, and farm wives shift to sole or coprovider roles, husbands have been forced either to seek nonfarm employment or to accept nontraditional responsibilities related to housework and child care (Elder, 1986; Scanzoni & Arnett, 1987).

Ratings comparing interrole conflict between young urban and rural parents (Mertensmeyer & Coleman, 1987) show the latter scoring higher in role conflict and slightly lower in self-esteem. A suggested factor is the dilemma in which need for employment by rural mothers competes with their value of remaining in the home and meeting their expectations as wife and mother, as well as the lowered self-esteem of the males for failing to be adequate breadwinners.

Even the protection afforded by an intact and extended family is steadily being eroded as family members migrate away from the community and economic stressors result in dissolution of marriages and rearing of children outside the traditional nuclear or extended family (Smith & Coward, 1981). Traditional gender-role differentiation has been substantially altered by economic necessity; economic hardship has caused changes in marital communication and happiness as well as engendering thoughts of divorce (Johnson & Booth, 1990). This results in a lack of stability and predictability so crucial for the security of developing children.

The rural family and its place within the community at one time served as the central focus for role definition and identity. As the family has been beset by economic difficulties disproportionate to other sectors of the country, family tensions, violence, and withdrawal from community activities have placed the sense of personal well-being derived from participation in the social structure of the community at risk (Van Hook, 1990). Parents have less opportunity to provide the requisite nurturance. This contributes to the sense of demoralization, guilt, lowered academic functioning, alienation, depression, suicide attempts, and other symptoms of ineffective coping. Socialization into rural occupations has been eroded by the inability to support families solely by such means, which results in an inward-looking demoralization and sense of futility (Fitchen, 1987) or outward-looking and increased emphasis on education as the means for survival (Elder, 1986).

A study of rural farm adolescents from two major agricultural Iowa counties (Van Hook, 1990) found them to be worried about their parents' futures. The youngsters attributed the increasing sense of insecurity for some to the complex nature of the farm crisis and the codes of family and community privacy. Distorted perceptions of the actual family circumstances resulted from barriers in communication. Most reported that life was unfair to their parents whose hard work was unrewarded. However, the majority attempted to assist the family through various sharing and contributing behaviors. Other coping mechanisms involved staying at home or away from home when increased family tensions were present. Coping strategies by a southwestern Pennsylvania sample of teens were found to be optimistic and supportive strategies (Puskar & Lomb, 1993).

Thus, the prevalence of poverty and relative isolation in many rural families creates barriers to normal verbal and, perhaps, social development, particularly for children from disadvantaged families. Rural youth do develop several nonverbal abilities that are not measured in traditional tests. Children from rural "homeless" families may be at even greater risk (Wagner, Menke & Ciccone, 1995).

Cognitive Development

The few available studies of cognitive development in rural children indicate that they lag behind their urban peers on a majority of cognitive measures. These include Piagetian conservation tasks, classification and sorting tests, and memory. Their cognitive style tends to be more concrete, more passive, and less manipulative. They are less advanced in organizing and structuring information. These findings may indicate actual cognitive deficits, deficits in measurement arising from a misperception of the rural environment and the types of skills it fosters, or use of standardized tests inadequate to measure idiosyncratic abilities and strengths (Hollos, 1983).

A critical analysis of reasons for low academic achievement by rural elementary students (Keys, Jacobs, & Celotta, 1990) suggests that many do not possess the preliminary skills and background experiences to be taught. Communication skills have been described as lacking in rural children from disadvantaged backgrounds (e.g., cultural isolation, lowered parental education). The limited feeling-word vocabulary of rural first graders is critical in understanding one aspect of this issue. According to their teachers and from clinician observation, these youngsters were unable to verbally express their own feelings or to recognize the feelings of others. On occasion the children appeared limited to feeling "good or bad" and happy or sad. Described as "one-dimensional emotionality," this limitation was also noted when they described characters in their reading texts (Keys et al., 1990).

Television may be the great leveler in providing a wider worldview. Thus far, television's impact on rural youth has not been well studied. A recent study suggests that TV may have no direct effect on cognitive abilities, but in a complex social-learning type manner may influence achievement test scores (Lonner, Thorndike, Forbes, & Ashworth, 1985).

Clinical Implications of Rural Residence for Children

Among some rural populations, the rates of depression have doubled, and increases in suicide, interpersonal problems, alcohol abuse, domestic violence, and homelessness have been reported (Anderson, 1990). Coupled with the isolated insular nature of rural life and an ethic of self-reliance, rural residents are vulnerable to psychopathologic development when failure, lowered standard of living, and poverty (Bruce, Takeuchi, & Leaf, 1991) must be faced. Rural youths thus are exposed to elevated risk factors for developing psychiatric disorders. The situation is worsened by the rural family's difficulty in seeking assistance.

Although generally tolerant of the idiosyncracies of fellow residents, delinquent or deviant behavior committed by children or teens is traditionally handled in a harsher manner in the country (Petti et al., 1987). Juvenile delinquents adjudicated to rural corrections facilities often are exposed to staff untrained in mental health principles and to aggressive and assaultive role models of city-reared teens. All of this, when combined with inadequate treatment of existing or developing psychiatric problems, may increase the rural delinquents' sense of helplessness and lack of control over their lives and of developing antisocial behavior.

The same can be expected for abused or neglected rural youths, who may be at greater risk than their urban counterparts (Jones, McDanal, & Parlour, 1985). Sexual abuse may be an even more significant rural problem than physical abuse or maltreatment. The social isolation of rural children and the associated lack of social skills in developing and maintaining intimate relationships perpetuate the isolated lifestyle; neglect and sexual abuse facilitate development of psychopathology. Given such factors as distance and paucity of trained professionals, the identification, accurate assessment and appropriate treatment of psychiatric disorders may be difficult to attain in the country (Jones et al., 1985). Management of the sexually abused child in the presence of the traditional rural conservative values typifies the service provision dilemma (Roper, 1991). Similar problems exist for ancillary and critical rural services, such as child welfare and special education (Capper, 1990; Rojewski, 1989).

The increasingly restricted rural economic base, related to the sparse relatively impoverished population, results in continuing paucity of related human services. The children for whom such communities have responsibility are placed at increased risk as services to support their development become scarce or nonexistent. The requirements of children with developmental and other handicapping disabilities that interfere with their ability to learn are more difficult to meet in the country. Almost 75% of the school districts in the United States serve about a third of all children. Yet only about a quarter of all school psychologists provide services in rural settings (Cummings, McLesky, & Huebner, 1985). Country residence means generalist rather than specialist educational services and an inability to provide an equitable opportunity for an acceptable educational experience; the 1987 OSERS (Office of Special Education and Rehabilitation Services) Report on Public Law 94-142 noted rural special education as an area most in need of improvement (Capper, 1990). Capper documents deficits in providing special educational services to handicapped rural youngsters from impoverished families and enumerates reasons for the inadequate efforts to serve them.

Rural education has been described as unique due in part to the families' purported resistance to book learning and formal education. The schools report deficiencies in the overall levels of educational achievement and enrollment of students outside the age of compulsory attendance. In addition, consolidated or small rural schools must accommodate pockets of cultural and social groups, sometimes from large or extended families, with differing styles of learning, linguistic patterns, and educational needs (Petti et al., 1987). Communities and families that formerly controlled or heavily influenced the education of their children have had to give in to a central bureaucracy over which they feel little influence. As changes are proposed and disputed, rural students are vulnerable to loyalty disputes between the school and their community folks. The abilities and needs of individual children are easily overlooked or disparaged. From being central figures with a clear place in the social, athletic, or academic life of the school, many rural youths perceive themselves or are labeled as outsiders and misfits (Fitchen, 1987; Keefe, 1986). Their emotional status is rarely considered as consolidation and change evolve. Change is especially difficult for many rural children and its impact is often neglected (i.e., as busing to other communities occurs, or in response to hospitalization (Strickland, Leeper, Jessee, & Hudson, 1987).

Despite the numerous threats to development of rural juveniles, college students from nonurban areas were found to hold a stronger belief in a just world and a more internalized locus of control orientation than those from urban areas (Witt, 1989). Education in a small school offers a number of benefits (Gotts & Purnell, 1986) to the student (e.g., greater satisfaction, more extensive and responsible participation) and the rural community (e.g., instructional effectiveness, reputation, public support), which are rarely acknowledged.

Clinical and Cultural Implications for Service Delivery

Rural culture and belief systems heavily influence the acceptance and utilization of services (Petti et al., 1987). The strong sense of independence, privacy, and self-reliance conflict with seeking mental health services. Rural males may be at greater risk for psychiatric disorder in the changing rural culture, yet they are significantly less often involved in treatment than their urban counterparts. The relative lack of anonymity in rural settings and homogeneity in the population make traditional sex roles more clearly defined (Gift & Zastowny, 1990). Rural males are aware of the presumably universally negative view of getting help and of help-seeking behavior, as deviating from the prevalent male stereotype and thus making human services for them difficult to access.

Confidentiality is a major concern for traditional reasons, but it is of even greater import in close-knit rural communities (Forrest, 1988). Rural residents are reluctant to seek help for "mental" reasons. Fear of being labeled "crazy" or "weak" keeps them from utilizing mental health facilities, even for severe family or personal problems.

In contrast, the Minnesota Coalition on Health task force report based on surveys of 3,000 farmers and 3,000 rural small business owners and town meetings (*AMA News*, 1987) documented concern about access to mental health and chemical dependency programs and outpatient alternatives to hospital care. Underutilization of certain free services was attributed to fear of the welfare stigma.

There is a growing crisis in the accessibility of rural health care (Blank et al., 1995; Kane & Ennis, 1996; U.S. Congress, 1990). The number of physicians and hospitals serving many rural areas is decreasing due to budgetary constraints. Forced by soon-to-change disparities in reimbursement rates for urban and rural areas, rural hospitals have been closing at an unprecedented rate. This is worrisome since rural professional mental health services often are centered in hospitals or their affiliated mental health centers. Eighteen percent of combined psychiatry and psychology professionals are hospital based in the United States compared to 39.9% in rural areas (Human & Wasem, 1991). In 1988, 49 million persons lived in counties with no psychiatrist (U.S. Congress, 1990). The absence of related health and mental health facilities for consultation and backup makes recruiting child psychiatrists, nurse clinicians, and other core mental health professionals to rural areas especially difficult. The issues concerning recruitment and retention are manifold and have been elaborated upon (Petti & Leviton, 1986). They include those factors pertaining to physicians and other health care professionals (relative scarcity of "civilized" amenities, substandard schools, dearth of related professional services, inaccessibility of continuing education, and isolation from other professionals from the same or related disciplines, lack of employment opportunity for and dissatisfaction of spouse) (AMA Council on Medical Education, 1990) as well as those more specific to mental health.

The latter include the problems of accepting change and outsiders in rural communities, inadequate professional preparation for rural practice, ambiguities about role definition, the dominance of personal dynamics in coloring professional transactions, and the lack of adequate models of service delivery in the country (Brownlee, 1996; Petti et al., 1987; U.S. Congress, 1990). The service mandates and program regulations developed for urban populations do not address the requirements for meeting the needs of sparse population density, inadequate transportation, and scarcity of personnel (Blank et al., 1995; Kane & Ennis, 1996; Petti, 1987).

Child and adolescent psychiatrists in rural areas experience a unique set of stressors (Copans & Racusin, 1983) in common with other child-related professionals. They are unable to practice the comprehensive model of medicine their university training provided. The lack of available support from professionally trained clinical child and educational psychologists, child psychiatric social workers, psychiatric nurse clinicians, and special education teachers leads to decreased job satisfaction and potential burnout. They find they must settle for pragmatic solutions to complex problems. The amount of time they spend providing a wide range of clinical and nonclinical services, often without professional backup, is draining. Frustration is rampant when they are forced to practice at the level of the "generalist," not specialist, and sometimes beyond their perceived level of competence.

Rural mental health centers and their satellites have had fewer full-time equivalent staff than metropolitan centers and fewer specialists in child and adolescent psychiatry. For example, Doan and Petti (1990) compared 9 rural, semirural partial or day-hospital programs to 9 urban area programs in western Pennsylvania. Rural programs were much smaller, concentrated more on serving adolescents compared to children, and were more closely affiliated with the local community mental health center and special education authorities than urban programs. Educational facilities seemed deficient compared to urban programs. Fewer mental health professionals and proportionately more nonprofessional staff were found in rural programs, which also had less access to child psychiatric consultation.

Rural workers have tended to identify more closely with the traditional philosophy of the mental health center, to have a greater sense of mission, to endorse agency and personal activism, and to view their centers as more like a social agency than medical center (Petti et al., 1987). With the restructuring of rural society and the narrowing focus on the ability to pay, Murray and Keller (1991) suggest a movement away from provision of broad, community-based services of the original community mental health center movement. This concern may increase in importance with pressures to restrict medical assistance eligibility and to deliver services to only the most seriously disturbed youngsters. Examples of this phenomenon include rural partial hospital program directors voicing concern about their agencies' isolation from other human services, including mental health (Doan & Petti, 1990) and Epstein's (1990) comments that efforts to refer abused, at-risk children in rural areas are often hampered by inadequate personal contact, communication, and understanding of the roles and functions of relevant agencies and their staffs.

Given the visibility of rural professionals and their patients, the informal patterns of their communication and nature of interagency contacts, rural mental health professionals must learn to balance the prevailing standards of confidentiality and professional responsibility against the demands of the rural system (Brownlee, 1996). Few professionals are trained to work with rural children and their families in the context of the communities within which they reside (Petti, 1987). This fact increases the risk for continuing the cycle of inadequate or inappropriate services for rural youths.

There are many reasons why psychiatrists and other mental health professionals should be encouraged to enter into rural practice. These reasons include opportunities for a range of activities from teaching staff at rural centers, consultation, case management, and administrative consultation (Petti, 1987). Rural folk are also more empathic to prevention measures and their efficacy (Kenkel, 1986). In addition, rural-based psychiatrists are much better able to appreciate more of the context in which their patients exist and to monitor progress and outcome.

Clinical and System Interventions: A View to the Future

Two changes must occur before adequate psychiatric services can be provided to disturbed rural children and their families: There must be an evolution in the understanding of the development and functioning of rural systems, communities, human services providers, families, and children; and policy makers and administrators must develop greater awareness of the singular nature of rural populations. Creation, funding, and implementation of research into rural issues are required as a foundation for any comprehensive and rational approach to delivery of care (Blank et al., 1995; Kane & Ennis, 1996; Merwin, Goldsmith & Manderscheid, 1995). Even model programs that address the public mental health sector have been unsuccessful in adequately addressing the multiple dilemmas that present when rural delivery is considered (U.S. Congress, 1990). The clarion call for innovative approaches must be based on scientifically attained knowledge. The surgence of interest in this area by policy makers, media, researchers, academicians, providers, and the public is propitious. As research evolves, greater attention will be focused on rural issues, and a critical mass of educators and clinicians will become available to provide services and develop approaches to applied clinical issues. Any approach should be founded on the fact that rural and urban existences are more unlike than alike and that providers of care beyond those traditionally associated with the core mental health professions must be developed and nurtured (Petti & Leviton, 1986). Innovative strategies to address the unique needs of rural folk are evolving (Merwin et al., 1995; Sawyer & Moreines, 1995; Sheldon-Keller, Koch, Watts & Leaf, 1996). Training and continuing education for those currently providing services is critical (Merwin et al., 1995). Federal and state initiatives have great potential to provide the required impetus for improving the quality of life by addressing the psychiatric and related needs of rural children and their families. Health care reform will pose major challenges and opportunities for rural delivery of psychiatric services (Shelton & Frank, 1995).

REFERENCES

American Medical Association, Council on Medical Education. (1990). *Educational strategies for meeting rural health physician shortages.* Chicago, IL: Author.

Anderson, L., (1990, July-August). Mental illness in rural America, public hearing held. *Alcohol, Drug Abuse and Mental Health Administration News, 16* (4), 17, 22, 24.

Blank, M. B., Fox, J. C., Hargrove, D. S., and Turner, J. T. (1995). Critical issues in reforming mental health service delivery. *Community Mental Health Journal, 31,* 511–524.

Brownlee, K. (1996). The ethics of non-sexual dual relationships: A dilemma for the rural mental health professional. *Community Mental Health Journal, 32,* 497–503.

Bruce, M., Takeuchi, D., & Leaf, P. (1991). Poverty and psychiatric status. *Archives of General Psychiatry, 48,* 470–474.

Capper, C. A. (1990). Students with low-incidence disabilities in disadvantaged, rural settings. *Exceptional Children, 56* (4), 338–344.

Copans, S., & Racusin, R. (1983). Rural child psychiatry. *Journal American Academy of Child Psychiatry, 22,* 184–190.

Cummings, J. A., McLeskey, J., & Huebner, E. S. (1985). Issues in the preservice preparation of school psychologists for rural settings. *School Psychology Review, 14* (4), 429–437.

Doan, R. J., & Petti, T. A. (1990). A comparison of rural and urban partial hospital programs for children and adolescents. *Journal of Rural Community Psychology, 11* (2), 3–15.

Elder, J., (1986, December). Women's jobs help save many farms. *New York Times,* pp. 23–24.

Epstein, M. (1990, July-August). Networking in a rural community focuses on at-risk children. *Public Health Reports, 105* (4), 428–430.

Fitchen, J. M. (1987). When communities collapse: Implications for rural America. *Human Services in the Rural Environment, 10* (4), 48–57.

Forrest, S. (1988, Summer). Suicide and the rural adolescent. *Adolescence, 23,* 341–347.

Garfinkel, B., Hoberman, H., Parsons, J., & Walker, J. (1986). *The prevalence of depression and suicide attempts in rural Minnesota youth.* Minneapolis: University of Minnesota.

Gaudin, J. M., & Davis, K. B. (1985). Social networks of black and white rural families: A research report. *Journal of Marriage and the Family, 47,* 1015–1021.

Gift, T., & Zastowny, T. (1990). Psychiatric service utilization differences by sex and locale. *International Journal of Social Psychiatry, 36* (1), 11–17.

Gotts, E. E., & Purnell, R. F. (1986). Families and schools in rural Appalachia. *American Journal of Community Psychology, 14* (5), 499–520.

Hollos, M. (1983). Crosscultural research in psychological development in rural communities. In A. W. Childs and G. B. Melton (Eds.), *Rural Psychology.* (pp. 45–71). Lincoln, Nebraska; Plenum Press.

Human, J., & Wasem, C. (1991). Rural mental health in America. *American Psychologist, 46* (3), 232–239.

Johnson, D. R., & Booth, A. (1990). Rural economic decline and marital quality: A panel study of farm marriages. *Family Relations, 39,* 159–165.

Jones, L. R., McDanal, C. E., Jr., & Parlour, R. R. (1985). Children. In L. R. Jones & R. R. Parlour (Eds.), *Psychiatric services for underserved rural populations* (pp. 241–265). New York: Brunner/Mazel.

Kane, C. F., & Ennis, J. M. (1996). Health care reform and rural mental health. *Community Mental Health Journal, 32,* 445–462.

Keefe, S. E. (1986). Southern Appalachia: Analytical models, social services, and native support systems. *American Journal of Community Psychology, 14* (5), 479–498.

Kelleher, K. J., Taylor, J. L., and Rickert, V. I. (1992). Mental health services for rural children and adolescents. *Clinical Psychology Review, 12,* 841–852.

Kenkel, M. B. (1986). Stress-coping-support in rural communities: A model for primary prevention. *American Journal of Community Psychology, 14* (5), 457–478.

Keys, S. G., Jacobs, G., & Celotta, B. (1990, January). Communicating about feelings: A classroom guidance approach for rural disadvantaged students. *School Counselor, 37,* 192–198.

Lonner, W. J., Thorndike, R. M., Forbes, N. E., & Ashworth, C. (1985). The influence of television on measured cognitive abilities: A study with native Alaskan children. *Journal of Cross Cultural Psychology, 16* (3), 355–380.

Looff, D. H. (1981). Assisting Appalachian families. In T. M. Cassidy, M. S. Gordon, & A. Heller (Eds.), *The mountains and valleys are mine: A symposium on rural mental health* (pp. 179–189). Ridgewood, New York: Bren-Tru Press.

Mertensmeyer, C., & Coleman, M. (1987). Correlates of inter-role conflict in young rural and urban parents. *Family Relations, 36,* 425–429.

Merwin, E. I., Goldsmith, H. F., & Manderscheid, R. W. (1995). Human resource issues in rural mental health services. *Community Mental Health Journal, 31,* 525–537.

Minnesota's rural care shortcomings described. (1987, April 25). *American Medical News,* p. 45.

Murray, J. D., & Keller, P. A. (1991). Psychology and rural America: Current status and future directions. *American Psychologist, 46* (3), 220–231.

Petti, T. A. (1987). Practice with rural populations. In R. L. Cohen & M. K. Duncan (Eds.), *Basic handbook of training in child and adolescent psychiatry* (pp. 187–200). Springfield, IL: Charles C. Thomas.

Petti, T. A., Benswanger, E. G., & Fialkov, M. J. (1987). The rural child and child psychiatry. In L. A. Stone (Ed.), *The basic handbook of child psychiatry* (Volume 5, pp. 650–671). New York: Basic Books.

Petti, T. A., & Leviton, L. (1986). Re-thinking rural mental health services for children and adolescents. *Journal of Public Health Policy, 7,* 58–77.

Puskar, K. R., Lamb, J. M. and Bartolovic, M. (1993). Examining the common stressors and coping mechanisms of rural adolescents. *Nurse Practitioner, 18* (11), 50–53.

Rojewski, J. W. (1989). A rural-based transition model for students with learning disabilities: A demonstra-

tion. *Journal of Learning Disabilities, 22* (10), 613–620.

Roper, P. C. (1991). Child sexual abuse—the problem for medical practitioners in small towns. *Medical Journal of Australia, 154* (4), 257–8, 260.

Sarvela, P., & McClendon, E. (1987). Early adolescent alcohol abuse in rural northern Michigan. *Community Mental Health Journal, 23* (3), 183–191.

Sawyer, D. A. & Moreines, S. F. (1995). A model for rural children's mental health services. *Administration and Policy in Mental Health, 22,* 597–605.

Scanzoni, J., & Arnett, C. (1987). Policy implications derived from a study of rural and urban marriages. *Family Relations, 36,* 430–436.

Sheldon-Keller, A. E. R., Koch, J. R., Watts, A. C., & Leaf, P. J. (1996). The provision of services for rural youth with serious emotional and behavioral problems: Virginia's comprehensive services act. *Community Mental Health Journal, 32,* 481–495.

Shelton, D. A., & Frank, R. (1995). Rural mental health coverage under health care reform. *Community Mental Health Journal, 31,* 539–552.

Smith, W. M., & Coward, R. T. (1981). Images of the future. In R. T. Coward & W. M. Smith (Eds.), *Family in rural society* (pp. 225–229). Boulder, CO: Westview Press.

Strickland, M., Leeper, J., Jessee, P., & Hudson, C. (1987). Children's adjustment to the hospital: A rural/urban comparison. *Maternal-Child Nursing Journal, 16* (3) 251–259.

U.S. Bureau of the Census. (1989). Rural and rural farm population: 1988. Series P-20, No. 439. Washington, DC: U.S. Government Printing Office.

U.S. Congress. (1990, September). Office of Technology Assessment. Health care in rural America. OTA-H-434. Washington, DC: U.S. Government Printing Office.

Van Hook, M. P. (1990). The Iowa farm crisis: Perceptions, interpretations, and family patterns. *New Directions for Child Development,* No. 46. pp. 71–86.

Wagner, J. D., Menke, E. M., and Ciccone, J. K. (1995). What is known about the health of rural homeless families? *Public Health Nursing, 12,* 400–408.

Witt, L. A. (1989). Urban-nonurban differences in social cognition: Locus of control and perceptions of a just world. *Journal of Social Psychology, 129* (5), 715–717.

22 / The Sibling of the Psychiatrically Disordered Child

Lisa Marie Rocchio, Carl B. Feinstein, and Vijaya Appareddy

It is estimated that between 5 and 26% of children and adolescents are clinically impaired by a psychiatric disorder (Brandenburg, Friedman, & Silver, 1990). Although clinicians have long suspected that the siblings of psychiatrically disordered youngsters are at risk for the development of emotional problems, there has been a paucity of research and literature on the topic. This chapter reviews the effects on children of having a psychiatrically disordered sibling, utilizing the transactional perspective developed by Sameroff and Chandler (1975). Such an approach provides a context for understanding both genetic and environmental influences as they bear on children. It views developmental outcomes as the product of a continuous interaction between a child and her or his context, where the child and the caregiving environment have mutually altering effects on each other. It is important to recognize at the outset that siblings of psychiatrically ill youngsters may be both positively and negatively affected by this circumstance. Numerous mediating factors come into play in determining the outcome.

As part of this mutual regulatory process, Sameroff (1985) identified 3 broad factors influencing a child's development: the environtype, or external influences affecting the child (such as sociocultural and family factors); the phenotype, or qualities/characteristics displayed by the child; and the genotype, or the biological organization of the child. These factors interact in a nonlinear fashion. The outcome is best predicted by the cumulative effect of numerous influences rather than by the direct effect of any single influence (Sameroff & Fiese, 1990). Employing the transactional model to study the development of children with a psychiatrically disordered sibling allows for examination of the reciprocal influences of the psychosocial and structural factors within the social and family environment, individual characteristics of the well sibling, and genetic factors.

Developmental Impact

ENVIRONTYPICAL INFLUENCES

Family Variables: The environtype is comprised of family and social factors that exert an influence on development. Four subsets of family relationships may be influenced by the presence of a psychiatrically disturbed child: the parent–parent dyad, the parent–well child dyad, the parent–ill child dyad, and finally, the well child–ill child dyad. Each of these subsystems plays a role in the development of the well child in the family. For further discussion of the impact of reciprocal fam-

ily interactions on the sibling of a handicapped child, see Feinstein and David (1987) and Vadasy, Fewell, Meyer and Schell (1984).

The first subsystem to consider is the parents' relationship with each other. For the parent–parent dyad, having a disturbed child constitutes a unique stressor. Concerns over "blame" for the illness, conflicts over responsibility for caregiving, anger over unequal time devoted to parenting, resentment by one parent about the amount of time the other parent spends with the child, reactions of one parent to the other parent's style of child rearing, and other concerns that may arise around division of labor, finances, and child care can all be more volatile and more stressful when there is a child with a mental illness in the home. If the parental relationship is negatively affected, then tension spreads throughout the family system. Parental discord can lead both to differential treatment of the children and to conflicts between the children as they identify with one or the other parent. Researchers have documented that the quality of the parental relationship is predictive of the children's level of general adjustment (MacKinnon, 1988), that distressed families tend to have weak parental alliances when compared to nondistressed families (Gilbert, Christensen, & Margolin, 1984), and that parental conflict is strongly associated with increased psychiatric risk for the children (Rutter & Quinton, 1984).

The second subsystem concerns the relationship between the parents and the psychiatrically disordered child. Parents may treat their children very differently. Self-report data from siblings show that often one child in a family will see herself or himself as being treated differently from a sibling (Plomin & Daniels, 1987). For example, parents may be very lenient or very strict with an ill child as compared to a well child. The perceptions of the sibling of the disordered child as to the fairness or equality of treatment can lead to large developmental differences.

Siblings may come to resent the amount of time and attention paid to the disordered child or may feel neglected or uncared for. This may lead to attention-getting behavior or, conversely, to emotional withdrawal. Alternatively, the sibling may try to typify the "good child" and place a great deal of pressure on herself or himself to succeed. Sometimes this extends to a quest for "perfection" in order to be as distant as possible from the imperfect one. In conjunction with playing out the role of "good child," the sibling may take on a great deal of responsibility within the family and identify with or assume a parental role in interactions with the disordered sibling.

The third subsystem is concerned with the relationship of the parent to the well child. Here, altered demands or expectations often come into play. This may involve pressures such as parental hopes that the well sibling will achieve all that the ill sibling did not. Alternatively, some parents may have decreased aspirations for their healthy child based on experiences with the ill child. Others may actually downplay the accomplishments or successes of the well child, so that she or he does not "outshine" the ill child. Parents may view the disturbed child as a "bad influence" and may strive to insulate the well child. They may fail to acknowledge the inner resources, capacities for independent judgment, or resilience of the well sibling. Additionally, the parents might not have as much time or emotional energy for the well child, who may be expected to "take care of her- or himself." Parents overinvolved or overidentified with the disordered sibling may place unrealistic demands on the well sibling vis-à-vis the disordered child. These demands might include prohibitions against the well child defending herself or himself against the disordered child's aggression or destruction of personal possessions. Or they might involve overinsistence that the well child include the disordered child in her or his peer group, or become the companion and support of the ill child at the expense of her or his independent activities. At the opposite end of the spectrum, some parents may overtly favor the well child, resulting in feelings of guilt in the well child regarding the parents' relative rejection of the ill sibling.

Finally, it is important to consider the subsystem involving the relationship between the well child and her or his psychiatrically disordered sibling. In general, the sibling subsystem is the first social system in which children can experiment with peer relationships and with opportunities to love, support, isolate, scapegoat, and learn from each other. Siblings learn how to negotiate, cooperate, and compete with each other in the context of the family environment. In spite of the importance of this subsystem, much of the clinical research on siblings has focused on sibling rivalry for the mother's attention and little work has fo-cused on healthy and "normal" sibling development (Solnit, 1983).

Psychiatric disorder in a sibling has a direct impact on the well child and on the relationship between the well and disordered siblings. Yater and Klarman (1981) studied the emotional impact of psychiatrically disturbed siblings on well siblings. Emotions and feelings identified by the 60 "well" siblings ranging in age from 7 to 28 years included an increase in "search for meaning" (19%), guilt (17.5%), depression (17.3%), identification with the disturbed sibling (17.2%), anger (15.3%), and withdrawal from the disturbed sibling (13.7%). According to the authors, the item most often agreed to, "search for meaning," suggests an active and hopeful coping style as well as the potential maturity, responsibility, and resiliency to respond to the challenge of growing up with a psychiatrically disordered sibling.

The balance of power in the sibling relationship may be altered as a result of the illness, especially if the older sibling is the identified patient (Daniels-Mohring, 1986). In his discussion of the siblings of mentally retarded children, Trevino (1979) found that while initially the mentally retarded child and the healthy child related to each other on an equal basis, eventually the unimpaired younger sibling became dominant. The well child may assume either an overly responsible or, alternatively, a jealous or envious role in relation to the sibling and may feel guilty about her or his anger at the disordered child's behavioral transgressions or inappropriate emotional responses that ruin potentially enjoyable family experiences. Parents may tolerate regressive or aggressive behaviors in the disordered sibling that are prohibited for the well child. In the face of this, the well child may well experience resentment and rebelliousness. Indeed, at times, the well child may come to resent and blame the parents for the disordered child's problems. These feelings may be intensified when the parents disapprove or fail to acknowledge as legitimate the well child's anger or frustration. In addition, depending on the type of disturbance, the well child may not understand the disordered child's behavior or may be hurt, emotionally traumatized, or embarrassed by the ill child's words and behavior, resulting in self-esteem problems and increased internalized resentment. If the well child perceives a parent reacting harshly, intolerantly, or inappropriately toward the disordered child, she or he may become frightened of or disillusioned and disappointed in the parent, with direct unfavorable repercussions for that relationship or problems in appropriate identification with the parent.

Another relatively common response of the well child is to feel responsible for the sibling's condition and to assume the burden of supporting or protecting the vulnerable one. When the ill child's disorder is particularly severe, the well sibling may assume an excessive and premature parental role. This may interfere with normative, out-of-home peer experience and impede the adolescent separation/individuation process. Finally (particularly if the ill child's disorder involves chronic maladaptive behaviors), the well child may be preoccupied with thoughts and fears that the illness may strike her or him.

Sociocultural Variables: Besides studying the impact on family relationships, it is crucial to examine the development of siblings of psychiatrically disordered children in a social context. Here clinicians working with siblings and families should consider the type and degree of troubled behavior manifested and the "obviousness" of the disorder.

In our culture, there is still a definite stigma associated with mental illness, although it has been mitigated somewhat by the efforts of advocacy groups. Adding to this problem is the ever-present tendency to blame child psychiatric disorders on poor parenting, particularly on inadequate mothering. The well child might be teased about the ill sibling's behavior or might be ashamed to bring friends home for fear of what the sibling might say or do. As a result, the well child's peer relationships may be compromised, thus contributing to problems with social isolation and self-esteem.

PHENOTYPICAL INFLUENCES

The individual characteristics of the well sibling clearly will play an important role in determining that child's developmental outcome. Research on stress and coping has identified a number of "child factors" that contribute to a child's resiliency to stressful conditions. For example, Werner and Smith (1982) found that resilient children with healthy outcomes were more outgoing, had more positive affect, and adapted more easily to change than children who were more disturbed later in

life. Rutter and Quinton (1984) concluded that children with poor temperaments were twice as likely to develop emotional or behavioral problems than their "easy-temperament" counterparts.

A more recent study conducted by Seifer, Sameroff, Baldwin, and Baldwin (1992) explored factors related to improved social/emotional and cognitive functioning. The participants were a group of 50 high-risk children and 102 low-risk children ranging in age from 4 to 13. The authors concluded that improved outcome at age 13 was related to individual characteristics such as good self-esteem and an internalized locus of control. In comparison, poorer outcomes were predicted by such factors as low self-esteem, externalized locus of control, and overconforming values. They also observed an interaction effect, whereby personality trait predictors of poor outcome had a more negative impact on the high-risk group than on the low-risk group. Social support, also identified as a protective factor, may be generated by individual characteristics such as social and communication skills, ability to cooperate, and general sociability. Other characteristics of the well child that may be helpful in ameliorating risk are higher IQ (Rutter, 1983), the ability to empathize with the sibling's situation, and the acquisition of effective problem-solving and coping skills (Seifer & Sameroff, 1987).

GENOTYPICAL INFLUENCES

The degree to which genetic elements affecting the disordered child are shared by his or her siblings plays a significant role in the development of the well child. Three main approaches are used to clarify the role of genetics in mental disorders: family studies, twin studies, and adoption studies (Pardes, Kaufmann, Pincus, & West, 1989). As summarized by Pardes et al. (1989), a substantial number of family studies have shown that the first-degree relatives of patients with psychiatric illnesses are at significantly higher risk for developing the disorder themselves. For example, the risk to relatives or patients with panic disorder is 9 times greater (Crowe, Noyes, Pauls, et al., 1983); the risk to relatives of alcoholics is 10 times greater than controls (Pitts & Winokur, 1966) and 24 times greater for relatives of patients with bipolar affective disorder (Weissman, Gershon, Kidd, et al., 1984). A 1985 study by Kendler, Gruenberg, and

Tsuang examined the risk for psychiatric illness in the first-degree relatives of patients diagnosed with schizophrenia. They found that relatives of patients diagnosed with schizophrenia were 18 times more likely than relatives of surgical patients to be at risk for the diagnosis of schizophrenia. Additionally, the relatives of patients diagnosed with schizophrenia were also at increased risk for meeting criteria from the third edition of the *Diagnostic and Statistical Manual of Mental Disorders (DSM-III)* for other psychiatric disturbances, such as schizoaffective disorder, paranoid disorder, and atypical psychosis.

Twin studies comparing the concordance rates of mono- and dizygotic twins have yielded further support for hereditary influences in psychiatric illnesses. For example, the concordance rate for panic disorder in monozygotic twins is 31% compared to a 0% concordance rate in dizygotic twins (Torgerson, 1983). A study of bipolar affective disorder found a concordance rate of 79% for monozygotic twins and a rate of only 19% for dizygotic twins (Bertelsen, Harvald, & Hauge, 1977). Kendler and Robinette (1983) reviewed the National Academy of Sciences-National Research Council Twin Registry and found a concordance rate for schizophrenia in monozygotic twins of 30.9% ± 3.3% and a rate or 6.5% ± 1.5% for dizygotic twins.

Adoption studies that examine the rates of psychiatric disturbance in children raised away from their biological parents provide evidence of greater alcohol use by the children of alcoholic biological parents (Cadoret, Cain, & Grove, 1980; Goodwin, 1979), and of an increased risk for schizophrenia in biological versus adopted relatives (Kety, Rosenthal, Wender, et al., 1968).

While these data clearly document the role of heredity in psychiatric disorder, they also indicate that genetic effects do not account for all (and in many cases, even most) of the variance between psychiatrically disturbed and mentally healthy individuals (Reiss, Plomin, & Hetherington, 1991). Reiss and colleagues (1991) report on the importance and impact of unshared environmental influences in development. They caution against ignoring the numerous important environmental factors that may differ for different family members.

Thus, when examining the genetic factors that may increase the risk for psychiatric disorder in the siblings of a psychiatrically disturbed child, it is essential to consider also the unshared environment between siblings. The developmental impact on the mentally healthy sibling will clearly be influenced by the interaction of environtype, phenotype, and genotype.

Clinical Implications

The transactional model remains a central analytical tool guiding mental health intervention with siblings of psychiatrically disordered children. Other factors, however, also require the clinician's attention, including the chronicity of the disorder; its severity, type, and age of onset; the age and developmental level of the sibling; and the preexisting strengths and weaknesses within the family prior to the onset of the disorder.

In general, both for parents and for siblings of the afflicted child, chronic mental illness is a more profound stressor than acute or successfully treated conditions. Chronicity may lead to feelings of hopelessness, pessimism, and cynicism, which can make the therapeutic process move more slowly than it otherwise would. Hope and belief in change and in the future can work as catalysts in psychotherapy; lack of hope can be paralyzing. Further, with a chronic illness, there is an increased likelihood that the parents will be more discouraged and perhaps less available to the well sibling. Clearly chronicity can increase the overall stress within the family and have a lasting impact on the development of the well sibling.

CASE EXAMPLE

Sara: Sara, a 19-year-old college student, sought counseling at the student health service to cope with her increasing preoccupation concerning her 21-year-old brother. He had been diagnosed with bipolar affective disorder that had responded poorly to treatment, was forced to leave college, and had undergone multiple psychiatric hospitalizations. He had alienated most of his friends and was unable to continue living independently. Only partially recovered, he had returned home to live with his parents. Sara described a subjective loss of meaning and goal orientation in her life. She had a difficult time focusing on her studies. She was preoccupied with angry feelings directed toward her brother's peers, whom she felt had been fickle friends. Her relationships with family members changed significantly. She assumed enormous responsibility for her brother and became the family moderator and negotiator. She was often in conflict with her parents, defending her brother against their frequent angry remonstrations that he "shape up" and cooperate better with treatment.

The type of disorder and its severity can elicit a variety of reactions from siblings. For example, attention deficit hyperactivity disorder or conduct disorder are conditions in which otherwise normal-appearing youngsters manifest disruptive or defiant behavior problems. Siblings of such children must often contend with both the anger and resentment they may feel toward their disordered sibling as well as high parental expectations directed at themselves. The child with disruptive behavior is often labeled "bad," while the healthy sibling is labeled the "good" child.

CASE EXAMPLES

Bret: Sam and Bret are 13-year-old dizygotic twins. Sam is receiving outpatient treatment for both attention deficit hyperactivity disorder and oppositional defiant disorder. Sam is constantly in trouble and has no friends of his own. He relies on Bret and Bret's friends for social interactions. Bret deeply resents this but is repeatedly urged by his mother to support and protect his brother. Bret is regarded as "better" than his brother and is treated more respectfully by parents, peers, schoolteachers, and administrators. These differential expectations and responses cause Sam to resent Bret's higher status and to compete with negative behavior for his parents' attention.

Jeanine: Jeanine is the 17-year-old sister of Wanda, a 15-year-old girl hospitalized for depression and a suicide attempt by pill ingestion after breaking up with her boyfriend. At hospitalization, Wanda revealed that she was pregnant. During the hospital stay, Jeanine, who was herself a good student, popular, and very active within the church youth group, revealed that she had known for some time that Wanda was using drugs and staying out late with her boyfriend. On more than one occasion she had collaborated in providing Wanda's alibi to keep knowledge of this from their strict and devoutly religious parents. She had privately argued with Wanda about her activities, but shared Wanda's fears of the parents punitiveness and felt she was protecting her. Jeanine was devastated to find out that Wanda was pregnant. Jeanine felt enormously guilty and somehow responsible for the pregnancy, suicide attempt, and hospitalization, believing she should have

told her parents of Wanda's transgressions (although, as it turned out, she only had partial knowledge of Wanda's behavior). The parents, indeed, were shocked and very angry at Wanda's pregnancy and did blame Jeanine.

Jeanine's parents punished her by forbidding her from attending her prom and other events related to her graduation from high school, despite the efforts of the family therapist to dissuade the parents from this course. This was a very hard blow for Jeanine, who, however, tearfully accepted the punishment, believing that she had done wrong.

Siblings of children with severe and chronic psychiatric disorders often have difficulty expressing their thoughts, feelings, and emotions. Anger toward their siblings is often avoided or denied for fear of incurring the disapproval of the parents and of further upsetting the affected sibling. This is particularly the case for siblings of children diagnosed with autism or schizophrenia, where the level of disturbance is particularly high. Healthy siblings may be very attuned to their brother or sister's need for special treatment and help. Consequently, they may be likely to deny their own needs. Additionally, they may be intensely afraid of "being like" their sibling and may be subjected to teasing and taunting by their peers.

CASE EXAMPLES

Cathy and Melissa: June, age 12, is the middle child in a family of three daughters. She has received psychiatric treatment for more than two years for severe psychiatric problems that have included two hospitalizations. Her problems include unrelenting oppositional behavior, sudden mood swings, extremely provocative and abusive verbal interactions, and destruction of family possessions, including those of both sisters. There have also been numerous impulsive self-destructive acts, such as opening the car door while the family was driving on the highway. During several angry encounters she physically attacked her mother. She also has frequent physical battles with her 14-year-old sister, Cathy. She frequently "borrows" Cathy's possessions without telling her and scathingly teases or ridicules her at home and in public.

Cathy feels extremely resentful of June. When June was hospitalized for the second time, Cathy exclaimed, "She ought to go away for good." She hates it when June returns and has recently threatened to run away. Initially, in family therapy sessions, she argued that her parents shouldn't put up with the way June treated them. After a while, she refused to come to these sessions. However, Melissa, her 8-year-old younger sister, is fiercely loyal to June. She refuses to retaliate when she is provoked by June. When June engages in one of her unpleasant confrontations, Melissa tries to see June's side of the argument and to persuade her parents or sister to yield.

The parents' relationship has suffered greatly during the 2-year period. Mother is determined to stick by June, although she is overwhelmed by the many problems. Father believes that June should be "sent away" to residential treatment for the well-being of the rest of the family. Although there is little overt quarreling, Father is spending much time away from home. Mother, Cathy, and Melissa have verbalized fears that a divorce will occur.

There is no doubt that both well siblings are suffering. Cathy is becoming increasingly rebellious. She spends as little time at home as she can manage. Melissa, June's ally, is afraid to bring friends home, fearful that an unpleasant scene will occur. She cries a great deal, expresses hopelessness about all the fighting in the family and about her all-consuming fear that something terrible will happen to June. Her school guidance counselor has expressed concern that Melissa is depressed.

Joey: Joey is the 7-year-old well brother of 10-year-old Billy, a very behaviorally disordered boy with autism. Joey has lived in a household under siege since he was a baby. Billy's behavior includes much destruction of property (including Joey's), nighttime wandering, bizarre stereotypia, unpredictable pinching and biting, and loud and abusive speech. His parents, with only a small amount of respite help, have organized family life around the management of Billy. Outings as simple as trips to the store are tense and embarrassing experiences. Joey's friends don't want to play at his house because of Billy's intrusions. Joey's parents always have expected him to love his brother, to "hang in there," play with Billy, and help him negotiate all aspects of his life at home and in the community. Joey is actually remarkably effective with Billy. His parents are proud of him for this. Billy clearly prefers Joey's presence to any other.

When Billy developed a problem with dangerously self-injurious behavior the family was overwhelmed. They agreed to inpatient treatment in a nearby high-quality program. Joey begged and pleaded with his parents not to "send Billy away." He was reluctant to leave Billy after visits. He appeared depressed and lost interest in both school and peer life. He overtly blamed himself in various unrealistic ways for Billy's hospitalization. His reproach of his parents for their perceived abandonment of Billy made them feel very inadequate and guilty.

John: John is the 14-year-old brother of Paul, an 11-year-old boy with severe chronic anxiety disorder and school phobia. As a result of these problems, and the initial failure of medication and other treatment approaches, Paul did not attend school for a prolonged period. During that interval he received in-home tutoring. At the onset of Paul's school refusal, John was very involved in trying to persuade Paul to go to school. He became very upset, bewildered, and demoralized when Paul continued refusing. His parents gave John the chore of bringing home Paul's homework assignments. However, when Paul failed to do his assignments on a consistent basis, John became angry with his parents for "letting Paul get away with murder."

The relationship between the two siblings, which had been fairly close, now became strained. John began blaming Paul for being "weak" and "acting like a baby." Paul became hostile in return. Although Paul eventually returned to school, 2 years later the two boys were barely on speaking terms.

Katherine: Katherine is a 15-year-old seen in outpatient psychotherapy whose 13-year-old sister, Joanne, was diagnosed with anorexia nervosa. Katherine initially expressed anxious concern about Joanne and talked about how helpless she was to help her or to make her eat. She felt responsible for helping her sister and supporting her mother, who was preoccupied with concerns about Joanne and who often confided in her older daughter. Additionally, Katherine worried that she, too, would develop an eating problem. She exercised a great deal; in spite of her healthy appearance and "normal" body weight, she had a very negative body image. She reported feeling "huge" in comparison to her sister, and wanted to lose weight, but was at the same time guilty and ashamed of her competitive feelings. Katherine clearly was placed in a parentified role in relation to both her sister and her mother and was focusing on them as a way of denying her own problems with self-confidence and body image.

Not only the symptoms and behavior of illness in the psychiatrically disturbed child affect the well sibling. Various aspects of the disordered child's treatment also may have an impact.

CASE EXAMPLES

Beth: Josh is a 6-year-old boy being treated in once-weekly play psychotherapy for explosive and aggressive behavior directed toward his mother and his peers. He greatly enjoys his weekly sessions and talks to his sister, Beth, proudly of the fun he has playing with his "special doctor." Beth, a socially competent and resilient 4-year-old, is perceived by both parents as an "easy child" compared to her brother. However, she has become increasingly upset about not getting these valued visits with the doctor that Josh gets. She complains bitterly about having to accompany her mother weekly to sit in the waiting room; but if she is left behind during Josh's weekly sessions, her complaints are even more impassioned. She wants to see the doctor, too, and demands toys and other compensations so she can be "even" with her brother. Josh and Beth's mother is very concerned about how to handle this problem. In the session, Josh talks about how Beth will have a "fit" if she doesn't get a toy after his appointment.

Kevin: Kevin is a 16-year-old high school student who initially refused to participate in family therapy sessions. Among other issues, the family was dealing with his 12-year-old brother's psychiatric hospitalization, depression and suicidality, and his parents' impending divorce. Kevin denied that his brother was either depressed or suicidal and declared he wouldn't be seen near "that nuthouse." He had significantly detached himself from family activities in the previous two years and complained that therapy was taking time away from being with his friends. He believed his brother did not belong in the hospital and was angry with him for his symptoms, which, he stated, were merely devices to gain his parents' sympathy. As time progressed he began to ally himself with his brother and became overtly angry and rebellious toward his parents.

Clinical Interventions

When working with siblings of psychiatrically disordered children, it is useful to keep several common themes in mind. Often these children have been forced to take on an overly responsible or parentified role in their families and have a difficult time focusing on themselves and taking care of their own needs. They may not have learned how to advocate for themselves and may not know how to ask for or even to identify what they need or want. Adjunct psychotherapy, therapeutic support groups, or family therapy directly can provide them with an opportunity to recognize their own feelings and needs.

Specific individual therapeutic or supportive goals may include enhancing social and communication skills, working to increase social support and assertive behavior, and increasing self-esteem and a sense of self-efficacy. Particularly in cases where parents have been unavailable to the healthy child, the establishment of a trusting and

supportive relationship with an adult can in and of itself be extremely helpful. Family dynamics also must be taken into account, and family therapy should be considered in order to improve lines of communication and to make structural changes in the way family members relate to one another. This approach is particularly helpful when the well child has been acting as a mediator for the family. Family therapy can help the child remove her- or himself from that role. Conjoint interviews with the siblings can help to improve their relationships, increase cooperation, and decrease feelings of resentment and guilt.

Bank and Kahn (1975) point out the enormous and often underrated impact that siblings can have on each other. Siblings often function as an autonomous subsystem within the family and may interact independently, beyond the supervision and monitoring of their parents. According to Bank and Kahn, siblings serve 4 essential functions for each other, independent from their parent's influence: identification and differentiation, mutual regulation, direct services, and forming coalitions in dealing with parents. Therapists working with siblings of psychiatrically disordered children can tap into these functions and use the sibling subsystem as leverage for change within the family and for all of its members.

Bank and Kahn (1975) also point to a wide variety of ways the therapist can utilize the sibling subsystem. The therapist can use relationships between siblings to relabel family problems and to gain important information about the ways the family members interact. Additionally, siblings can be utilized as "consultants" to aid in the treatment of their disordered brother or sister. Siblings can rally around each other to provide encouragement and support as well as understanding.

Kahn and Bank (1981) describe a 3-step process where bringing siblings into therapy can work to ally the siblings and effect change that reverberates throughout the family. In their work, the identified child patient begins in individual therapy, and the first phase involves exploring the sibling relationships. During the second phase of treatment, the patient and her or his siblings are seen together and given an opportunity to express their resentments and to work through their misunderstandings. Once there is sufficient alliance among the siblings, they can use the third phase of therapy to begin confronting their parents in a constructive way and open more direct lines of communication.

Group therapy also can be useful when working with siblings of psychiatrically disordered children (Geronimus & Mielke, 1993). Meeting in a group can provide them with opportunities to detoxify "family secrets" with others who are coping with similar situations. They can share coping strategies, air grievances, and discuss behaviors that have been both helpful and unhelpful. In addition, the group can focus on problem solving for particularly difficult or stressful family situations or interactions. The group context allows for a reduction in the sense of shame that the siblings may feel, a modeling of communication, an increase in self-nurturing behaviors, and an increased sense of their own strengths and weaknesses. In a group format, children sometimes can be given psychoeducational information about their brother or sister's illness and their sibling's condition can become demystified.

Conclusion

In summary, it is clear that the development of siblings of psychiatrically disordered children takes place in the context of a mutually regulated transactional process in which family dynamics, sociocultural variables, and the personal qualities and genetic makeup of the child all work to influence each other. While it is likely that the presence of a psychiatrically disordered child in a family is a risk factor for emotional difficulties or psychiatric symptoms in the well sibling, many youngsters successfully master this developmental complication without harm. No single variable or process determines the well sibling's ultimate adjustment. Similarly, there exist numerous sites for therapeutic or supportive interventions dictated by the unique situation of each family and a variety of ways that the sibling's ongoing healthy development can be enhanced and her or his risk for emotional disturbance reduced.

REFERENCES

Bank, S., & Kahn, M. D. (1975). Sisterhood-brotherhood is powerful: Sibling subsystems and family therapy. *Family Process, 14,* 311–337.

Bertelsen, A., Harvald, B., & Hauge, M. (1977). A Danish twin study of manic depressive disorders. *British Journal of Psychiatry, 130,* 330–351.

Brandenburg, N. A., Freidman, R. M., & Silver, S. E. (1990). The epidemiology of childhood psychiatric disorders: Prevalence findings from recent studies. *Journal of the American Academy of Child and Adolescent Psychiatry, 29* (1), 76–83.

Cadoret, R. J., Cain, C., & Grove, W. M. (1980). Development of alcoholism in adoptees raised apart from alcoholic biologic relatives. *Archives of General Psychiatry, 37,* 561–563.

Crowe, R. R., Noyes, R., Pauls, D. L., and Slymen, D. (1983). A family study of panic disorder. *Archives of General Psychiatry, 40,* 1065–1069.

Daniels-Mohring, D. (1986). Sibling relationships with an older sibling as identified patient. *Dissertation Abstracts International, 47* (12).

Feinstein, C., & Davis, S. E. (1987). The sibling of the chronically ill or disabled child. In J. D. Noshpitz (Ed.) *Basic Handbook of Child Psychiatry, Vol. 5.* New York: Basic Books.

Geronimus, S. R., & Mielke, S. E. (1993). The sibling group: Beginning to meet the needs of child siblings

of psychiatrically hospitalized children. *The Psychiatric Hospital, 24* (1/2), 15–18.

Gilbert, R., Christensen, A., & Margolin, G. (1984). Patterns of alliances in non-distressed and multiproblem families. *Family Process, 23,* 75–87.

Goffman, E. (1963). *Stigma: Notes on the management of spoiled identity.* New York: Simon & Schuster.

Goodwin, D. W. (1979). Alcoholism and heredity. *Archives of General Psychiatry, 36,* 57–61.

Kahn, M. D., & Bank, S. (1981). In pursuit of sisterhood: Adult siblings as a resource for combined individual and family therapy. *Family Process, 20,* 85–95.

Kendler, K. S., Gruenberg, A. M., & Tsuang, M. T. (1985). Psychiatric illness in first-degree relatives of schizophrenic and surgical control patients. *Archives of General Psychiatry, 42,* 770–779.

Kendler, K. S., & Robinette, C. D. (1983). Schizophrenia in the National Academy of Sciences-National Research Council Twin Registry: A 16 year update. *American Journal of Psychiatry, 140,* 1551–1563.

Kety, S. S., Rosenthal, D., Wender, P. H., and Schulsinger, F. (1968). The types and prevalence of mental illness in the biological and adoptive families of adopted schizophrenics. *Journal of Psychiatric Research, 6,* 345–362.

MacKinnon, C. E. (1988). Influences on sibling relations in families with married and divorced parents:

Family form or family quality? *Journal of Family Issues, 9,* 469–477.

Pardes, H., Kaufmann, C. A., Pincus, H. A., & West, A. (1989). Genetics and psychiatry: Past discoveries, current dilemmas, and future directions. *American Journal of Psychiatry, 146,* 435–443.

Pitts, F. N., & Winokur, G. (1966). Affective disorder, VII: Alcoholism and affective disorder. *Journal of Psychiatric Research, 4,* 37–50.

Plomin, R., & Daniels, D. (1987). Why are children in the same family so different from one another? *Behavioral and Brain Sciences, 10,* 1–16.

Reiss, D., Plomin, R., & Hetherington, E. M. (1991). Genetics and psychiatry: An unheralded window on the environment. *American Journal of Psychiatry, 148,* 283–291.

Rutter, M. (1983). Stress, coping and development: some issues and some questions. In N. Garmezy & M. Rutter (Eds.), *Stress, coping, and development in children* (pp. 1–41). New York: McGraw-Hill.

Rutter, M. (1989). Psychiatric disorder in parents as a risk factor for children. In D. Schaffer, I. Philips, & N. B. Enzer (Eds.), *USAP Prevention Monograph 2: Prevention of mental disorders, alcohol and other drug use in children and adolescents* (pp. 157–189). Washington, DC: U.S. Dept. of Health & Human Services.

Rutter, M., & Quinton, D. (1984). Parental psychiatric disorder: Effects on children. *Psychological Medicine, 14,* 853–880.

Sameroff, A. J. (1985). *Can development be continuous?* Paper presented at the annual meeting of the American Psychological Association, Los Angeles, CA.

Sameroff, A. J., & Chandler, M. J. (1975). Reproductive risk and the continuum of caretaking casualty. In F. D. Horowitz, M. Hetherington, S. Scarr-Salapatek, & G. Siegal (Eds.), *Review of child development research, 4,* 187–244. Chicago: University of Chicago Press.

Sameroff, A. J., & Fiese, B. H. (1990). Transactional regulation and early intervention. In S. Meisels & J. Shonkoff (Eds.), *Handbook of early childhood inter-*

vention (pp. 119–149). Cambridge: Cambridge University Press.

Seifer, R., & Sameroff, A. J. (1987). Multiple determinants of risk and invulnerability. In E. J. Anthony & B. J. Cohler (Eds.), *The invulnerable child* (pp. 51–69). New York: Guilford Press.

Seifer, R., Sameroff, A. J., Baldwin, C. P., & Baldwin, A. (1992). Child and family factors that ameliorate risk between 4 and 13 years of age. *Journal of the American Academy of Child and Adolescent Psychiatry, 31,* 893–903.

Solnit, A. J. (1983). The sibling experience. *Psychoanalytic Study of the Child, 38,* 281–284.

Trevino, F. (1979). Siblings of handicapped children. *Journal of Contemporary Social Work, 60,* 488–493.

Torgerson, S. (1983). Genetic factors in anxiety disorders. *Archives of General Psychiatry, 40,* 1085–1092.

Vadasy, P. F., Fewell, R. R., Meyer, D. J., & Schell, G. (1984). Siblings of handicapped children: A developmental perspective on family interactions. *Family Relations, 33,* 155–167.

Werner, E. E., & Smith, R. S. (1982). *Vulnerable but invincible: A study of resilient children.* New York: McGraw-Hill.

Weissman, M. M., Gershon, E. S., Kidd, K. K., Prusoff, B., Leckman, J., Dibble, E., Hamovit, J., Thompson, W. D., Pauls, D., and Guroff, J. (1984). Psychiatric disorders in the relatives of probands with affective disorders: The Yale University-National Institute of Mental Health collaborative study. *Archives of General Psychiatry, 41,* 13–21.

Wyman, P. A., Cohen, E. L., Work, W. C., Raoof, A., Gribble, P. A., Parker, G. R., & Wannon, M. (1992). Interviews with children who experienced major life stress: Family and child attributes that predict resilient outcomes. *Journal of the American Academy of Child and Adolescent Psychiatry, 31,* 904–910.

Yater, S. M., & Klarman, M. (1981). The effect on siblings of psychiatrically disturbed children by means of a questionnaire: A pilot study. *Family Therapy, 8,* 141–148.

23 / Sibling Positions

Margaret H. Hoopes and James M. Harper

Every child is born into a sibling position and develops patterns unique to the position (Adler, 1958; Bowen, 1975; Toman, 1969, 1988). Understanding the specific patterns for each sibling position helps clinicians better match their interviewing styles and interventions to their clients.

Responding to criticism of previous birth order and sibling theories (Ernst & Angst, 1983; Kidwell, 1982; Lamb & Sutton-Smith, 1982; Schachter, 1982; Schvaneveldt & Inger, 1979), we developed a model for sibling positions that focused on the interactional processes in families that lead to the development of sibling position roles. The model provides conceptual descriptions for sibling positions that in turn contribute to the understanding of the development of children within their families.

The model is both a revision and elaboration of the early work of Jerome Bach and Alan Anderson (1979), who developed and applied descriptions of four sibling patterns in therapy, parenting, and supervision. According to Anderson (personal communication, 1978), they observed hundreds of families in therapy as well as their own families and spent thousands of hours observing video therapy tapes of families and individuals focusing on the interaction of family rules and birth order. The result was rudimentary descriptions of each sibling pattern. Because the model was in its early stages and many of the concepts remained intuitive, Bach and Anderson did not develop a published conceptual model connected to theory.

We built on Bach and Anderson's work (Hoopes & Harper, 1984), and after 9 years of observing and doing individual and family therapy, teaching and supervising student therapists, and discussing their observations of families with colleagues, we developed our model (1987, 1992), which is the basis of this chapter. In this model, the term "sibling position" refers to specific roles assigned by the family and assumed by a child as a result of the distinct and unique environment of the family when the child is born. The roles serve the family system and its subsystems. The responses to the family roles combined with a multitude of family and personal variables create characteristic sibling response patterns, repetitions that become observable, identifiable behavioral patterns. A major strength of this model is that it offers an interactional and developmental conceptualization of the formative processes underlying sibling position patterns. We consider the model to be descriptive, not predictive.

Table 23.1 presents the theoretical underpinnings for the concepts and their relationship to the past and present. Table 23.2 identifies the basic concepts from the theories.

The systems perspective is the umbrella for concepts from other theories because it focuses on the family as a whole, on each individual as a subsystem, and on the relationships among family members in all subsystems, including the multigenerational family. Thus, family systems theories provide the background for understanding characteristics of the family system, regardless of the number of individuals involved, differences in individual personalities, and sequence and variability of life events. System concepts that explain how family members interact, how individual and family needs are met, and how families accomplish developmental tasks, provide understanding for how siblings complement each other in order to serve family needs and goals. Because there are exceptions to the traditional two-parent family, we (Hoopes & Harper, 1987) also have modified the sibling concepts to relate to other family forms, such as single-parent and stepfamilies.

TABLE 23.1

Sources of Concepts for the Integrative Conceptual Model for Four Basic Sibling Positions

| Family Context | Family Functioning | |
	Present	Past
Individual (four sibling positions)	Psychodynamic Family Development	Psychodynamic
Nuclear Family	Systems Family Development	Systems Family Development Psychodynamic
Multigenerational Family	Systems Family Development	Systems Family Development Psychodynamic

TABLE 23.2

The Conceptual Model for the Integrative Model for Four Basic Sibling Positions

| Family Units | Theories | | | |
	Systems	Psychodynamics	Individual Development	Family Development
Individuals	Social interaction, responsibilities	Needs, motivation, unconscious emotional processes, perceptual orientation, influence of the past on the present	Identity, stages, tasks, coping skills	Individual development interacts with family development
Nuclear Families	System needs, roles, rules, information processing, alliances, boundaries, interaction patterns	Influence of the past on the present, myths, secrets, themes	Individual development occurs within the family	Identity, stages, tasks, coping skills adapt to meet the needs of individuals as well as the family
Multigenerational Families	Same as above for more than two generations	Intergenerational transmission for more than two generations	Individual development occurs within the multiple generations	Identity, stages, tasks, coping skills adapt to meet the changing needs of individuals, families, and generations

Family Developmental Perspective

The repetitive characteristic response patterns for each sibling position evolve from the interplay between both individual and family development. From a developmental perspective, the basic variables of the systems model include the characteristics of the family environment at the time of a child's birth, the child's developmental needs, and the family system changes that occur over time.

THE CHANGING FAMILY ENVIRONMENT AND
INTERPLAY BETWEEN INDIVIDUAL
AND FAMILY NEEDS

A systems perspective permits the conceptualization of sibling position within the larger context of the nuclear and extended family. Individual family members, marriages, other subsystems, and the nuclear and larger multigenerational family simultaneously move through stages of develop-

ment. The developmental tasks and issues with which each of these various units are coping at a given time provide part of the unique context into which each sibling is born.

Certainly the structure of the family is different when each person enters the family system. When the first child is born, the family usually contains three individuals, one marriage, two parent-child relationships, and one triangle. As other siblings enter the family system, the numbers of these dynamic structural units increase exponentially. In contrast to the family structure at the time the first child is born, the fourth child in the same family encounters six individuals, one marriage, eight parent-child relationships, six sibling relationships, and 11 triangles.

The systems model of sibling position assumes that the interaction of the family system's needs at the time a person is born and the needs of the individual influence the development of the sibling position role. The individual has needs to belong, to be dependent, to make sense and order of the world, and to form an identity unique and separate from that of others. The family system has needs to be productive and stable, but the complexity of the family structure at the time of a child's entry into the family influences which of these system needs will be more apparent to the child. The interface between individual and family needs forms the context in which issues of belonging, loyalty, intimacy, identity, and dependency evolve (Hoopes, 1987).

In the context of this interaction, each new child receives both implicit and explicit messages about how to belong to the family. In this family role assignment, each child focuses on the particular issues and needs of the family at the time he or she was born into it. The family, however, continues to change and evolve so that the system needs and structure are very different when the next child enters the family.

CHARACTERISTIC SIBLING RESPONSE PATTERNS

Individuals and families respond to particular life experiences in their family systems in repetitious ways that become observable, identifiable behavioral patterns. Because of their redundancy, the patterns become characteristic of a particular role or relationship or, in this case, of a sibling role. Although the characteristic response patterns for sibling positions are holistic, for descriptive purposes the patterns can be divided into functional roles in the family system, perceptual orientation, and issues around identity and sense of well-being. Tables 23.3, 23.4, 23.5, and 23.6 describe in detail the patterns of the first four sibling positions (Hoopes & Harper, 1987).

In the tables, descriptions of the family role include job assignment, interpersonal responsibilities, and social interactions. The description of the perceptual orientation includes the focus or awareness of types of information, and cognitive and affective patterns. Last, identity and sense of well-being are divided into what helps a person feel good, what threatens him or her, how the person responds to threat, and what he or she needs from others.

After the fourth sibling, the position patterns begin to repeat, with some variation. For example, a fifth child born into a complex family system would not have the same perceptual orientation

as a first child who was born into a three-person system. However, some of the job assignments may be repeated because the family needs more help and the oldest child usually has moved on into the school system.

Siblings born as twins or other multiple births may receive role assignments characteristic of the order in which they are born, or they may receive blurred and/or blended role assignments. Spacing may influence the characteristic response patterns depending on the length of time between children and how the family system has changed. Gender affects the way in which a role is performed rather than what the role is.

SIBLING POSITION AND INDIVIDUAL STAGES OF DEVELOPMENT

Infancy and Toddlerhood: The interface between the family system's needs and the child's need to belong to the family in a unique way during infancy and toddlerhood has considerable influence in determining each sibling's unique role. Earlier-born siblings typically attain language skills at a slightly earlier age than later-born siblings (Pine, 1995; Polit & Falbo, 1987), probably because of the increased amount of time they spend with adult parents compared to their later siblings. According to the Systems Model of Sibling Position, the perceptual orientation of first and second children is focused on details and parts as a function of being born in smaller family systems that would facilitate learning of language. The best predictors of later social development in first children appears to be the social characteristics of the child during these early ages (Feiring & Lewis, 1984). First- and second-born children also have more time in solitary play compared to later siblings. Hence they learn to entertain themselves or to initiate involvement with adults. Third-born and later siblings have more opportunity to be involved in group social activity within the family structure. The explanation for this lies in the assumption of the sibling position model dealing with the increased complexity of the family structure and process and additional children enter the system. However, it appears that only and first-born toddlers are more sociable than later-born toddlers. One explanation might be that at 2½ years of age (the age of the children in this sam-

TABLE 23.3

Firstborn Siblings

Family Role Patterns for Firstborn Siblings

Job Assignment	Interpersonal Responsibilities	Social Interactions
1. Responsible for supporting family rules, values, and expectations 2. Responsible for outcomes, results, products 3. Responsible for a central place in the family in order to be productive	1. Responsible for each family member to one parent, often father, but may be mother 2. Responsible for that same parent 3. Responsible for all family members' productivity	1. Interact with individuals 2. Some performance anxiety in most relationships and social situations 3. Feel impelled to respond to others' expectations 4. Can be direct and engaged 5. Will encourage others to express ideas and feelings if seen relevant

Perceptual Orientation Patterns for Firstborn Siblings

Focus/Awareness	Cognitive Patterns	Affective Patterns
1. Focused on rule-governed aspects of reality 2. Focused on details and parts 3. Aware of some of the implicit environment, but need to be reminded to look	1. Use ideas and facts in a logical and analytical manner to understand 2. Perceptually limited, lack of linkages between parts, compartmentalize 3. Go from parts to the whole	1. Identify and label own and others' feelings easily if relevant 2. Integrate and share own feelings if the purpose and outcome is made explicit 3. Can be lost, confused, and overwhelmed by detail 4. Sometimes deny feelings

Identity/Well-Being Patterns for Firstborn Siblings

Self-esteem	Threatened Psychologically	Responses to Threat	What They Need From Others
1. Self-esteem based on doing well in the eyes of others 2. Need to feel productive and successful 3. Need to be "on target"—right 4. Need recognition of being central	1. By being "off target" in the eyes of others 2. When ignored by others as central 3. In anticipation of performance evaluation 4. When faced with too many details, too many people needing assistance, too much disorganization	1. Experience life as hopeless 2. Withdraw, ignore 3. Appear "stoney," "black of countenance," "unfeeling," "immovable" 4. Can be dogmatic 5. Can be superrational	1. Recognition and acceptance as being central, "on target," and productive 2. Approval of products 3. Exploration of feelings, failures, and helplessness with connections to behavior and logic in a reasonable way without discounting them 4. Help in making rules, values, and expectations explicit 5. Obedience to rules

Source: Hoopes & Harper, 1987, 1992.

TABLE 23.4

Second-born Siblings

Family Role Patterns for Second-born Siblings

Job Assignment	Interpersonal Responsibilities	Social Interactions
1. To be perceptive and supportive to the implicit elements in family rules and relationships 2. To open clogged channels of communication by making the implicit explicit 3. To monitor the quality of performance 4. To act out the discrepancies between the implicit and explicit to force acknowledgment	1. To have a unique relationship with everyone in the family 2. To be responsible for mother and to mother and father 3. Responsible for affective state of each family member by supporting their emotional needs 4. Work with, fight if necessary with, first sibling. Flush out discrepancies between implicit and explicit rules	1. Tender, sensitive, caring to individuals, or rational, distant, and goal-oriented 2. Can be unaware of personal and others' boundaries

Perceptual Orientation Patterns for Second-born Siblings

Focus/Awareness	Cognitive Patterns	Affective Patterns
1. Focused more on affect, implicit messages, and process than content 2. Aware of symbolic and imaginative meaning 3. Can be focused on the literal meaning of a phenomenon, logical and analytical, with form and structure the outcome 4. Aware of underlying structure, often implicitly	1. Perceive issues in terms of polarities with difficulty of integrating to supply the middle parts 2. Restrict perception sometimes because of missing middle pieces 3. Need to know implicit and explicit to make sense of whole 4. Create images to understand 5. Use underlying structure to complete whole	1. Feel other people's tensions and feelings and absorb them as if their own 2. Sometimes cannot sort out and label own feelings 3. Can become blocked and burdened with details, parts, and emotions 4. Feel as well as think in polarities (mood swings)

Identity/Well-Being Patterns for Second-born Siblings

Self-esteem	Threatened Psychologically	Responses to Threat	What They Need From Others
1. Identity derived from filling emotional gaps or being in touch with underlying structure in a situation 2. Based on having well-defined boundaries in a unique place 3. Clearing discrepancies between implicit and explicit rules, values, feelings, expectations 4. Self-sufficient and purposeful	1. By loss of unique acknowledged place 2. By incongruencies between implicit and explicit rules, feelings, values, expectations 3. By other people's emotional overloads	1. Feel wiped out 2. Polarize to intellect and tasks 3. Polarize to emotional and act irrationally and irresponsibly 4. Appear remote, uninvolved, overly involved, helpless, aimless 5. Look stubborn	1. Acceptance as a person with a place, clear boundaries 2. To have people own their own feelings and expectations by making them explicit 3. To receive feedback from others if they are taking on others' feelings with reminders to let go

Source: Hoopes & Harper, 1987, 1992.

TABLE 23.5

Third-born Siblings

Family Role Patterns for Third-born Siblings

Job Assignment	Interpersonal Responsibilities	Social Interactions
1. Responsible for the dynamics and quality of marital relationships 2. Responsible for the balance in all dyadic relationships 3. To discover and enforce rules about the degree and nature of relationship rules such as closeness, conflict, dependency, intrusiveness, and loyalty 4. To identify family issues	1. To be connected to both mother and father 2. To restore balance in the marital relationship by connecting with each parent 3. Responsible for connecting to all dyadic relationships in the family	1. Negotiate, balance 2. Want to remain detached but connected, so can appear "tentative": one foot in, one foot out 3. Difficulty making a commitment to a relationship, but once committed, very difficult to get out 4. "In and out." Fully there one moment, gone the next—psychologically or physically

Perceptual Orientation Patterns for Third-born Siblings

Focus/Awareness	Cognitive Patterns	Affective Patterns
1. Aware of connections and correlations but not always consciously 2. Focused on issues and relationships in the context 3. Focused on feelings and ideas of people as connections to parts and relationships	1. To derive meanings, looks at connections, correlations, issues, and context 2. Uses connections to get bigger parts to get to the whole 3. Because of lack of information about details and facts, may limit the context prematurely 4. Rearrange and synthesize existing ideas into new forms rather than seek meaning of separate parts	1. Sometimes look unfeeling 2. Feel deeply and can identify and share feelings if they are connected to the context 3. To be relevant, feelings have to be clearly part of a context

Identity/Well-Being Patterns for Third-born Siblings

Self-esteem	Threatened Psychologically	Responses to Threat	What They Need From Others
1. Connected to the stability of the marital relationship 2. Tied to their ability to discover dyadic relationship rules and apply them in maintaining balance	1. By lack of choices 2. By discrepant ideas, feelings 3. By interpersonal conflict, self and others 4. When they perceive they have to make decisions affecting the welfare of others	1. Feel confined and trapped if they do not perceive choices 2. Uncaring, apathetic, ambivalent, carefree 3. Disappear into introspection 4. Turn off feelings and withdraw 5. Inundated and chaotic 6. Stuck, stubborn	1. Appreciation for what they do 2. Recognition that they care 3. Help in creating choices when stuck 4. Recognition of their need for choices 5. Acceptance of their in-and-out behavior 6. Confirmation that they can come back, that they have an enduring connection

Source: Hoopes & Harper, 1987, 1992.

TABLE 23.6

Fourth-born Siblings

Family Role Patterns for Fourth-born Siblings

Job Assignment	Interpersonal Responsibilities	Social Interactions
1. Responsible for family unity and harmony 2. Responsible for family purposes and goals	1. Connect to each family member to assure unity and harmony 2. Responsible for all "garbage" in the family because it disrupts unity and harmony 3. Act out the tensions in relationships; can be quite dramatic	1. Develop pleasant relationships in functional families 2. Feel blamed and burdened by anything "wrong" in family relationships 3. Make relationships easily, although sometimes superficially 4. Impulsive and highly demonstrative with warmth and closeness expressed openly

Perceptual Orientation Patterns for Fourth-born Siblings

Focus/Awareness	Cognitive Patterns	Affective Patterns
1. Focused on the whole field (Gestalt) 2. Focused on purposes and goals of the system 3. Aware of power and responsibility	1. Think in terms of total systems, conclusions, and outcomes 2. Look first at the whole and then the parts 3. Leave out or do not see details, and summarize superficially, prematurely, and dramatically 4. New information accepted only if can be integrated into whole	1. Can be overwhelmed by the size of the "whole" 2. In touch with feelings of self and others 3. Impulsive and demonstrative 4. Collect negative feelings of others as burdens but do not confuse them with their own

Identity/Well-Being Patterns for Fourth-born Siblings

Self-esteem	Threatened Psychologically	Responses to Threat	What They Need From Others
1. Tied to being part of the family and having purposes and goals clear and moving 2. Well-being high when unity and harmony in the family experienced 3. Can have secure sense of self and see themselves as limited in their ability to change things	1. By perception of the size of the whole 2. By disruptive pain in family or relationships 3. By too much pain in the family 4. By sense of being blamed by family for pain	1. Overwhelmed by size of the whole so cuts out parts and people until they can manage it (unconsciously) 2. Irresponsible and helpless, random ineffective behaviors 3. "Cute," "babyish" in acting out 4. Stubborn layers of protection	1. To be told that they are not blamed for pain and tension in the family or relationships 2. Help in assuming their part in conflict so that they do not assume the whole burden 3. Lots of approval 4. For people to own their own feelings and responsibilities

Source: Hoopes & Harper, 1987, 1992.

ple), avoidance of social interaction is a result of later-borns' interactions with older siblings who are typically aggressive (Snow, Jacklin, & Maccoby, 1981).

School Age: During school age, the emphasis for children of all sibling positions is on developing peer social skills and cognitive skills. First and second children typically perform better in school than later-born children (Polit & Falbo, 1987; Skovholt, Moore, & Wellman, 1973). One explanation from the systems model for this better performance is that traditional elementary instruction is designed to fit the style of information processing of first- and second-born children in that teachers begin explaining parts first and then build the whole picture from the parts that have already been explained. Another reason first children are higher achievers in academics is because of their verbal skills (Pine, 1995; Polit & Falbo, 1987). Later-borns, such as third and fourth children, as a group are not as achievement-oriented as first and second children and hence usually do not perform as well in school. However, later-born boys see themselves as more proficient in sports and physical activities (Veenhoven & Verkuyten, 1989).

Adolescence: During adolescence, children of all sibling positions are seeking to master developmental tasks of independence and intimacy with others as well as continue to master more complex cognitive tasks. The ways in which particular sibling positions respond to these development tasks may differ (Musun-Miller, 1995; Nyman, 1995). For instance, when parental expectations seem unrealistic to first-born adolescents, they exhibit underachievement and oppositional behavior. In families that have difficulty expressing emotion, second-born adolescents respond in several ways. They can be in constant conflict with family members who need to be more emotionally expressive, or they may attempt to distract family members from pain through humor or acting out in oppositional ways. When family relationships are conflictual, especially the marriage, third-borns may spend excessive amounts of time away from the family involved with friends and outside activities, such as sports. When the interactional process of the family is dysfunctional, responses of adolescent children to achieving their own developmental tasks become more extreme, and the char-

acteristics patterns of a particular sibling position become more exaggerated or "shut down."

Adulthood: Characteristic response patterns learned as siblings in family systems remain into adulthood and influence the dynamics of relationships, particularly marriage. Several authors have determined that marital dynamics differ based on the combination of the husband and wife's sibling positions (Anderson, 1987; Dastrup, 1986; Hardman, Hoopes, & Harper, 1987; Hoopes & Harper, 1992). The variety of experiences accumulated through the aging process cultivate a broad repertoire of patterns of interaction, but under stress the patterns associated with the sibling roles become exaggerated and can be easily identified.

General Psychopathology and Sibling Position

Although findings have been mixed, it does not appear that sibling position is a major factor in the etiology of most mental illness in children and adolescents, when studies control for the extent to which distribution of birth order varies in the general population (Birtchnell, 1971; Narayan, 1990). However, clinical experience has demonstrated that the descriptive use of the sibling position patterns in therapy is useful in understanding internal motivations and cognitive and emotional processes of children presenting with emotional illness. As stated earlier, the patterns associated with a child's sibling position role either will be totally shut down or will be highly exaggerated as part of the manifestation of any emotional or mental disorder.

However, in a few studies, a specific disorder is associated with a greater prevalence of a particular sibling position. For example, Lacey, Gowers, and Bhat (1991) concluded that females with bulimia are often the oldest or only female child. Earlier research findings (Kayton & Borge, 1967) indicated a higher prevalence of first and only male children who exhibit obsessive-compulsive disorders. However, in a more recent sample, one research team (Pollard, Wiener, Merkel, & Enseley, 1990) questioned whether such was the case. First born children may have more tendency toward narcism (Curtis & Cowell, 1993). Although substance use occurs among adolescents of all sibling positions, it appears that a higher prevalence of alcoholism occurs among last-born children (Barry & Blane, 1977). Self-esteem in adolescents does not appear to be related to sibling position (Gecas & Pasley, 1983), but the sources from which adolescents gain esteem may differ for each sibling position (Hoopes & Harper, 1987). Hyperactivity, attention deficit disorder, and behavior disorders in general are more prevalent in first-born children (Delamater, Lahey, & Drake, 1981), although it is not clear if the researchers in this study controlled for varying distributions of birth orders in the population at large.

Even though sibling position is not a useful predictor of most types of mental and emotional disorders, sibling position patterns can help clinicians understand the internal processes of specific patients. For example, depressed first children likely make many comparisons between their performance and people's expectations and their inability to produce successful outcomes. In contrast, depressed second children are often overwhelmed by the underlying emotion of people they spend time with. Third children, on the other hand, may be focused on their inability to help family relationships, particularly the marriage, function smoothly. Fourth children will be overwhelmed by lack of harmony in the family. Even though such descriptions are more simplistic than the usual reality of depression, they do illustrate that although the symptoms and diagnostic criteria for each case are the same, the underlying processes and perceptual orientation may be quite different.

Clinical Implications

The descriptions of patterns for each sibling position presented in Tables 23.1 to 23.4 do not stand alone as a therapeutic approach, but they are extremely useful as a complementary framework to clinical approaches involving children, adolescents, couples, families, blended families, extended families, and adults (Anderson, 1987; Dastrup, 1986; Hardman et al., 1987; Harper,

1984). The descriptions of patterns can be used in at least four ways in clinical work: to understand the child, to understand the interactional dynamics in marriages and between parents and children, to help assess family system dynamics, and to help match interventions to clients.

For example, to understand the interactional exchanges between a first-child father and a first-child son, a therapist might notice the power struggles between the two. Knowing that first children focus on explicit, analytical information and often lack awareness of implicit processes would help the therapist focus on getting them to acknowledge both their own and each other's emotional process. Their mutual emphasis on productivity and their need to be right would at times escalate the conflict between them.

The following suggestions for working with each of the four sibling positions are drawn from the patterns specified in the tables. These suggestions can be adapted to most therapeutic styles and theories.

First Siblings

1. Validate their right to be who they are and reassure them, whenever possible, that they are "on target." Recognize the intent of first children to be on target even when their actions are not appropriate.
2. Meet their need for information by providing explanations, by giving specific answers to their questions, and by setting explicit, reachable expectations in therapy.
3. Legitimize their emotions by making their feelings part of relevant information and linked to their goals.
4. Demonstrate your understanding of their resistance to some interventions, such as role play and guided imagery, and of their resistance to you, the therapist, by letting them know you recognize their fear of doing something wrong.

Second Siblings

1. Use visual imagery and metaphors to help them understand issues.
2. Rather than giving explanations, ask what they do not understand and then fill in the missing pieces. Give information and pursue questions on two levels, pictorial and content.
3. Help them separate their emotions from those of the people around them. Ask questions such as "Is this what you are feeling, or is this what someone else is feeling?" Remind them to breathe because they literally hold their breath in the presence of another's pain.

4. Help them to share the implicit by asking if there is something that they have forgotten to mention.

Third Siblings

1. Inform them of the importance of the details that they often omit. For example, help them see the relevance of their feelings and connect them to specific contexts.
2. Look to the other side of what third children present in therapy. For example, if they present information about father, ask about mother; if they say they are happy with school, ask about what at school does not please them. Explore with them the underlying principles of how relationships and organizations work.
3. Teach them about their need for having choices, their in-and-out feelings and behavior connected to this need, and this behavior's influence on others. Offer them choices, and avoid taking choices away from third children by cornering them or forcing them to choose.
4. Give them permission to be in and out—verbally recognize their need to take time out so that they can sort out issues. Let them know that you will continue to be available even though they have gone away.

Fourth Siblings

1. Assist them in understanding how they act out family issues and feelings and then become overwhelmed and feel and act helpless. They assume that they cause the pain, so reassure them that they are not responsible for other people's feelings.
2. Help them break the whole into parts. Connect events in their lives to the larger whole. Teach them to develop personal goals apart from the family's goals, because often they fail to state their own preferences or feelings in order to placate others and bring unity to the family. Be alert to fourth children's tendency to cut out people and events in their lives because they are overwhelmed. Often this missing information is crucial to progress in therapy.
3. When they overdramatize, ignore it at times and confront them about it at other times. Comment on the exaggerations or ask them to exaggerate more.
4. Do not justify or allow others to justify behavior and requests to fourth siblings. Teach fourth children that they can assert their own opinions, feelings, and requests without being aggressive or breaking rules. When fourth children are impulsive, set boundaries and limits.

REFERENCES

Adler, B. N. (1958). *What life should mean to you.* New York: Capricorn Books.

Anderson, S. L. (1987). *An interactional analysis of first and third born and first and fourth born sibling position marital dyads.* Unpublished doctoral dissertation, Brigham Young University, Provo, UT.

Bach, J., & Anderson, A. R. (1979). *A systems model of ordinal position.* Ms., Minneapolis: Bach Family Institute.

Barry, H., & Blane, H. T. (1977). Birth positions of alcoholics. *Journal of Individual Psychology, 33,* 62–69.

Birtchnell, J. (1971). Mental illness in subships of two and three. *British Journal of Psychiatry, 119,* 481–487.

Bowen, M. (1975). *Family therapy in clinical practice.* New York: Jason Aronson.

Curtis, J. M., and Cowell, D. R. (1993). Relation of birth order and scores on measures of pathological narcissism. *Psychological reports, 72,* 311–315.

Dastrup, S. L. (1986). *Interaction in marital combinations of identical ordinal position dyads: Based on a systemic approach to sibling positions.* Unpublished doctoral dissertation, Brigham Young University, Provo, UT.

Delamater, A. M., Lahey, B. B., & Drake, L. (1981). Toward an empirical subclassification of "learning disabilities": A psychophysiological comparison of "hyperactive" and "nonhyperactive" subgroups. *Journal of Abnormal Child Psychology, 9,* 65–77.

Ernst, C., & Angst, J. (1983). *Birth order: Its influence on personality.* New York: Springer-Verlag.

Feiring, C., & Lewis, M. (1984). Only and first-born children: Differences in social behavior and development. In T. Falbo (Ed.), *The Single Child Family* (pp. 25–62). New York: Guilford Press.

Gecas, V., & Pasley, K. (1983). Birth order and self-concept in adolescence. *Journal of Youth and Adolescence, 12,* 521–535.

Hardman, R., Hoopes, M. H., & Harper, J. M. (1987). Verbal interaction styles of two marital combinations: Based on a model of four sibling positions. *American Journal of Family Therapy, 15,* 131–144.

Harper, J. M. (1984). The use of sibling position in marital therapy. In R. F. Stahmann & W. J. Hiebert (Eds.), *Counseling in Marital and Sexual Problems* (3rd ed., pp. 81–100). Lexington, MA: D. C. Heath.

Hoopes, M. H. (1987). Multigenerational systems: Basic assumptions. *American Journal of Family Therapy, 15,* 195–205.

Hoopes, M. H., & Harper, J. M. (1984). Ordinal positions, family systems, and family therapy. In M. R. Textor (Ed.), *The book for family therapy: Six schools in therapy and practice* (pp. 264–299). Eschborn, Germany: Fachbuchhandlung für Psychologie.

Hoopes, M. H., & Harper, J. M. (1987, 1992). *Birth order roles and sibling positions in individual and family therapy.* Rockville, MD: Aspen Publishers.

Hoopes, M. H., & Harper, J. M. (1992). *Birth order roles and sibling positions in individual and family therapy* (2nd ed.). Provo, UT: M C Publishing.

Kayton, L., & Borge, G. F. (1967). Birth order and the obsessive-compulsive character. *Archives of General Psychiatry, 17,* 751–754.

Kidwell, J. S. (1982). The neglected birth order: Middle borns. *Journal of Marriage and Family, 2,* 225–235.

Lacey, J. H., Gowers, S. G., & Bhat, A. V. (1991). Bulimia nervosa: Family size, sibling sex, and birth order: A catchment-area study. *British Journal of Psychiatry, 158,* 491–494.

Lamb, M. E., & Sutton-Smith, B. (1982). *Sibling relationships: Their nature and significance across the life span.* Hillsdale, NJ: Lawrence Erlbaum.

Musun-Miller, L. (1993). Sibling status effects: Parents' perceptions of children. *The journal of genetic psychology, 154,* 189–198.

Narayan, C. (1990). Birth-order and narcissism. *Psychological Reports, 67,* 1184–1186.

Nyman, L. (1995). The identification of birth order personality attributes. *The journal of psychology, 129,* 1–9.

Pine, J. M. (1995). Variation in vocabulary development as a function of birth order. *Child development, 66,* 272–281.

Polit, D. F., & Falbo, T. (1987). Only children and personality development: A quantitative review. *Journal of Marriage and the Family, 49,* 309–325.

Pollard, C. A., Weiner, R. L., Merkel, W. T., & Enseley, C. (1990). Re-examination of the relationship between birth order and obsessive-compulsive disorder. *Psychopathology, 23,* 52–56.

Schachter, F. F. (1982). Sibling identification and split parent identification. In M. E. Lamb & B. Sutton-Smith (Eds.), *Sibling relationships: Their significance across the life span* (pp. 123–151). Hillsdale, NJ: Lawrence Erlbaum.

Schvaneveldt, J. D., & Inger, M. (1979). Sibling relationships in the family. In W. R. Burr, R. Hill, F. I. Nye, & I. L. Reiss (Eds.), *Contemporary theories about the family* (pp. 453–467). New York: Free Press.

Skovholt, R., Moore, E., & Wellman, F. (1973). Birth order and academic behavior in first grade. *Psychological Reports, 32,* 395–398.

Snow, M. E., Jacklin, C. N., & Maccoby, E. E. (1981). Birth order differences in peer sociability at thirty-three months. *Child Development, 52,* 589–595.

Toman, W. (1969). *Family constellation: its effects on personality and social behavior.* New York: Springer Publishing Company.

Toman, W. (1988). *Family therapy and sibling position.* Northvale, NJ: Jason Aronson.

Veenhoven, R., & Verkuyten, M. (1989). The well-being of only children. *Adolescence, 24,* 155–166.

SECTION III
Varieties of Medical Disorder

24 / Chronic Illness and Physical Disabilities

Hans Steiner

Psychiatric and pediatric practitioners have increasingly appreciated chronic illness and physical disability as contributors to psychopathologic development in children. Children with chronic illness have twice the risk of psychosocial maladjustment in comparison to normal children, and usually this second handicap poses a significant problem. Illness and disability potentially interfere with the developing organism and make the mastering of developmental tasks much more difficult for those afflicted, leaving a child or adolescent on a deviant trajectory (Pless & Nolan, 1991). In addition, worsening health care coverage for chronic illness and the psychiatric complications associated with it, as well as improved survival rates for the chronically ill, increase the financial burdens borne by the afflicted and their families (Butler, Singer, Palfrey, & Walker, 1987; Newacheck, 1989; Newacheck, Budetti, & McManus, 1984; Siegel, 1987). Thus, chronic illness and disability represent major health problems that place individuals and families at risk for negative outcomes psychologically, socially, academically, and vocationally. Yet it is also a field where child psychiatrists are peculiarly absent (Pless & Nolan, 1991; Sabbeth & Steine, 1990; Steiner, Fritz, Mrazek, Gonzales & Jensen, 1993) but clearly should be more involved, as they have much to offer. Child psychiatrists' involvement appears all the more important, as it has become increasingly clear over the years that the average primary care physician is not particularly well prepared to identify psychiatric morbidity in his or her patients, identifies only a minority of those in need, and refers even fewer for treatment (Costello, Edelbrock, & Costello, 1988; Weiland, Pless & Roghman, 1992). They tend to agree with children's reports more than with those of the parents (Canning, Hanser, Shade, & Boyce, 1992), thus potentially missing as much as one-third of diagnosable pathology. The situation with tertiary care providers is not as clear, as no large-scale studies address these issues. However, from extensive clinical experience it appears that at least some tertiary care practitioners are unwittingly supporting maladaptive attitudes in their patients and families, in order to avoid psychiatric referrals.

As several chapters in this volume deal with the impact of a variety of specific chronic illnesses, this chapter provides an overall evaluation of the field. I define chronic illness and disability, discuss the impact of both on normal development, propose a suitable theoretical model for the study of the field, discuss the epidemiology of chronic illness and the findings of the most important longitudinal population based studies, add some points about the field from clinic-based studies, and suggest directions for future research and investigation. I conclude by discussing implications of the findings for makers of public policy and practitioners in child psychiatry in hopes of stimulating professional interest in participating in the care of children who are in need of our services.

Definitions

Several definitions of chronic illness and disability have been used in the literature (Cadman et al., 1986; Cadman, Boyle, Szatmari, & Offord, 1987; Feinstein & Berger, 1987), with the most common proposed by Pless, Cripps, Davies, and Wadsworth (1989), who defined chronic illness as a "physical, usually non-fatal condition which lasts longer than three months in a given year or necessitates a continuous period in hospital of more than one month" (p. 747). In addition, the condition must be of sufficient severity to interfere to some degree with a child's activities. This definition excludes those who have repeated episodes of acute illness. The interference criterion excludes chronic conditions such as minor allergies and acne, which children tend to outgrow with little impact on their ability to function. Illnesses most commonly included in studies are: blindness and lesser forms of visual impairment; deafness and lesser forms of auditory impairment; speech and language problems; persistent and, at least, moderate pain; asthma; heart problems; epilepsy; convulsions without fever; kidney disease; arthritis; cerebral palsy or other paralyses; muscular dystrophy or other muscle diseases; spina bifida; diabetes; cancer; cystic fibrosis; missing limbs and physical deformities; mental retardation; and autism and phenylketonuria (Cadman et al., 1986, 1987). Disability is defined as a stable form of impairment of either cognitive or physical functioning, most often the result of a chronic illness, chronic trauma, or a birth or genetic defect (Cadman et al., 1987; Feinstein & Berger, 1987).

The Impact of Chronic Illness and Disabilities on Human Development

In order to appreciate fully what patients with chronic pediatric disease and their families have to contend with, it is useful to contemplate briefly the realities of the situation and to examine their potential impact on normal development at the various stages. The issues to be described are readily apparent to all of us who are actively working in environments where we encounter such patients daily: in specially coattended outpatient clinics, jointly run by child psychiatry and pediatrics; on consultation/liaison services; or in the intensive treatment environment of the psychosomatic unit (Steiner, Sanders, Canning, & Litt, 1994). The following discussion is a condensation of many years of experience by many members of our team at Children's Hospital at Stanford of working with such families. While most patients and their families cope with the increased burden of chronic illness and disability, many do so showing signs of strain, and a substantial number of families show signs and symptoms of psychiatric morbidity. This narrative account of what it must be like to grow up under such circumstances cannot substitute for a full-fledged research effort addressing all the issues raised; however, at the present time such an effort is not available. The description of the course of development in children with chronic illness and disabilities is meant to serve as a guideline as we await further confirmatory data to be gathered.

All parents hope and expect that their child will be born and raised healthy and happy. It gives them pause when a child is born with a disability or an illness that is expected to get better and to disappear eventually becomes inextricably established as part of life. As parents begin to understand fully what it means that their child will not recover from a particular problem, even with the best help available, they have to grieve for the wholeness of their offspring; come to terms with many unusual emotional, medical, and financial demands on their resources; and put to rest the notion that their child's development will be an uncomplicated and mostly enjoyable unfolding of potential, as in most other children. Parents have to be able to complete this grieving process in due time, as the child is anxiously observing them during this process, and takes many cues from them as to how to react appropriately to the unwelcome news that he or she is ill for a long time to come.

During the preschool years, the child has almost no understanding of what his or her affliction consists of apart from the parents. The parents function as powerful transducers of information. Thus their emotional reactions to and realistic acceptance of the situation is crucial for the child's continued growth and development. A parent's calm reassurance gets all diagnostic and treatment procedures done, and even the worst tears subside in a soothing embrace. Parents can help by skillful distraction and can hinder by anxious preoccupation. However, beginning in the late preschool years, as the child's body becomes a focus of concern and interest and as it can be represented independently, the child will need more realistic reassurance and support in response to many emerging questions and queries ("Mom, how come I can't have sugar and she can?"). Such a process of comparison continues for many years, and it needs to be handled sensitively and in accord with reality. As the child begins to appreciate his or her own mortality, he or she can understand better the threats emanating from his or her own body. Questions of fairness of fate emerge and need to be dealt with. All this occurs simultaneously with extraordinary challenges the child faces in trying to live a life as close to normal as possible. The demands of the situation reinforce the school child's tendency to be preoccupied with bodily functions, while at the same time not fully understanding them and creating his or her own explanation as to why certain things happen. Some of these explanations are realistic; some of them are not and are driven by cognitive limitations and an egocentric conception of reality. A relapse occurs because a child has been nasty, not because she forgot to take her medicine. Internal changes of bodily function need to be heeded and attended to, anxiously watched as to whether they signal an oncoming relapse, a need for immediate intervention to prevent further worsening, a trial of a new and painful treatment. Procedures need to be carried out on a daily basis and expose private bodily functions to many other people. These procedures also slow down the necessary unfolding of the family's daily schedule. Some of these procedures are frightening and hurtful. They become like painful punctuations of life, leaving the child longing for the interval and wondering if there ever will be a time when this blood draw can be skipped. It is understandable that both child and parent sometimes "forget" to deal with the lowly drudgery of treatment. Compliance with prolonged treatment is a major issue for adults, and it is even more so for children. Most children with chronic illness and disability then face another major stressor: Once they leave their families and enter the realm of school, they have to cope with curiosity and rejection from able-bodied peers. Children's fears about a peer's deficit very often drive them to cruel acts toward the ill child in order to prove to themselves that they themselves, after all, are different—that is, whole and healthy and not ever in danger of becoming like this poor person. Children with chronic illness and disabilities are exposed to more bullying and negative interactions with peers than those not so afflicted. This circumstance is further accentuated by the fact that the ill child is not able to perform many acts of physical achievements that are easy for their peers. Integration into peer groups needs monitoring and facilitation by well-meaning and informed staff who have the time to help. Children with chronic illness miss many days of school because of illness flare-ups or necessary visits to medical personnel. Sometimes these absences are prolonged and painful, and when the child returns to school, he or she once again is out of the mainstream and has much schoolwork to make up. Sometimes the teacher treats an ill child differently, more carefully, and forgives expectations demanded of other pupils; this further leads to isolation and estrangement from the peer group. Friendships also are not easily formed, because many patients struggle with depression, irritability, chronic pain, and are simply not a lot of fun to play with sometimes. At other times, treatments make bizarre symptoms appear most unexpectedly, and they once again scare off potential friends who do not understand. Many of the symptoms and side effects have doctors baffled, so how can a child explain them to peers? Children with chronic illness also are unusually familiar with a whole other world that healthy children hardly experience: hospitals and clinics populated by doctors and nurses and many other unpronounceable professionals. Ill children sometimes become like expert assistants in the process of their own diagnosis and management ("They usually do better if they get my blood from there") and feel very much at home with those who treat them. In fact, the children sometimes call their doctors by their first names and meet up with them in special summer camps, something unheard of for those who are healthy. Doctors and nurses almost become old friends, members of the family, and in many ways become easier to be with than all those other people who do not understand. Peer groups and family groups of children with similar afflictions form and provide shelter and understanding. The waiting rooms of clinics often are transformed spontaneously into a support group setting, sparking new ideas between families and children as to how a problem could be approached better.

As the child progresses through adolescence, many of these issues become more pronounced. Again, the demands of most illnesses interfere substantially with age-appropriate developmental tasks: increasing personal privacy and control, independence from one's family and adults in general, firm establishment of peer bonds, exploration of attractiveness and sexuality, and preparation for personal achievement. Parental support sometimes is rejected, and as part of the normal progression for age, risk-taking behaviors appear. Risk taking also may mean that a child rejects treatments that are life sustaining. The resulting control struggles with parents and the treatment team have an intensity unsurpassed even in cases of drug abuse and blatant self-destruction. During these years, adolescents need to integrate their physical limitations into their self-concept without unrealistically insisting that they now are all better and in no need of further treatment. Very often, the fact that there were no dire consequences after some missed tests or treatments is taken as proof positive that doctors and parents do not know what they are talking about when they are warning of dire consequences to noncompliance with treatment. Sometimes adolescents' refusals to cooperate are couched in terms of ownership of their body and their being in charge of their own life. Other adolescents do not take such a stormy course of action in their pursuit of independence, but instead persist in an adaptive stance characterized by overcompliance, anxious inhibition, preoccupation with somatic function, and failure to venture out from the family at all. Such a stance sends them on a developmental trajectory more consistent with a school-age child's and severely delays the exit from the family. Struggles now involve getting the child to school and keeping him or her there, and often one or even both parents fight this struggle only halfheartedly. Either one of these scenarios can easily trigger, once again, parental depression and grieving, as the parents again must face the fact that life is different for their chronically ill offspring and that obtaining what comes relatively easily to others will be arduous for their child and may be thoroughly unfeasible. And such parental reactions may in turn lead to a further worsening of the patient, who will feel once again that he or she is a burden on the family, and may strengthen the patient's resolve to act independently so as to not to be such a burden regardless, whether this is realistic or not. A vicious cycle is formed.

Sometimes, at any of these stages, the process can derail completely and lead to pretenses on the part of parents and patients that confuse the many doctors, nurses, and researchers who rely excessively on self-report (Tavormina, Boll, Dunn, Luscomb, & Taylor, 1981). An adolescent may pretend to be happier than is realistic, healthier than those who are unafflicted, and hopeful of extreme and unusual treatments. Conversely, he or she can be totally preoccupied with the somatic manifestations of the disease process, to the point of excluding any other pursuits in life, and even to the degree that the child generates false illness data. Such patients are not only oblivious to the psychiatric dimensions of their illness but are hostile and defensive toward those who inquire about their mental health. Very often, anger at parents that will not help, doctors that cannot cure, and peers who will not respond is channeled toward

those who are in charge of the assessment and treatment of the mental health of patients and parents. Needless to say, such a development further adds to the complexity of the situation, creates rifts in treatment teams, and prevents the delivery of much-needed services. It is not surprising that the combined treatment of such patients is not easily achieved and requires many years of collaborative effort and team building between many professionals who regard each other with respect and realistic expectations (Fritz, 1990; Steiner et al., 1993).

Epidemiology of Chronic Illness and Physical Disability

In the last ten years, great strides have been made in the epidemiology of chronic illness and disability. Several population-based studies from different countries are currently available, and their results may be compared to each other and to those of previous investigations (Cadman et al., 1987; Newacheck, 1989; Newacheck, McManus & Fox, 1991; Pless et al., 1989; Pless & Nolan, 1991; Pless, Power, & Peckham, 1993; Wallander & Varni, 1989; Wallander, Varni, Babani, Banis & Wilcox, 1989; Weiland et al., 1992; Weitzman, Walker, & Gortmaker, 1986; Westbom, 1992). Researchers agree that chronic illness and disability in childhood and adolescence are common phenomena. Estimates of the incidence range from 6 to 31.5% of children, depending on the definitions used and the age range studied. Some studies (e.g., Newacheck, 1989) include mental disorders. For this discussion, such studies are tautological and not useful. Simple aggregate estimates of a variety of illnesses (Newacheck, 1989) are also less useful in that they hide shifts in survival rates and the special needs of certain subgroups of chronically ill individuals.

Gortmaker and Sappenfield (1984) used prevalence data at birth and subsequent survival rates to estimate the prevalence of specific disorders in a population of children ages 0 to 20 years. Disorders with onset prior to birth or after birth were estimated using the average age of manifestation. Table 24.1 summarizes their findings. They

TABLE 24.1

Estimated Prevalence of Chronic Diseases and Conditions in Children, Ages 0–20
in the United States—1980

	Prevalence Estimates per 1,000	Range of Prevalence Estimates, per 1,000
Arthritis	2.20	1.00– 3.00
Asthma	38.00	20.00–53.00
Moderate to severe	10.00	8.00–15.00
Autism	.44	.40– .48
Central Nervous System Injury		
Traumatic brain injury	.05	—
Paralysis	2.10	2.00– 2.30
Cerebral Palsy	2.50	1.40– 5.10
Chronic Renal Failure	.08	—
Terminal	.01	—
Nonterminal	.07	—
Cleft Lip/Palate	1.50	1.30– 2.00
Congenital Heart Disease	7.00	2.00– 7.00
Severe congenital heart disease	.50	
Cystic Fibrosis	.20	—
Diabetes Mellitus	1.80	1.20– 2.00
Down's Syndrome	1.10	
Hearing Impairment	16.00	
Deafness	.10	.06– .15
Hemophilia	.15	
Leukemia		
Acute lymphocytic leukemia	.11	
Mental Retardation	25.00	20.00–30.00
Muscular Dystrophy	.06	
Neural Tube Defect	.45	
Spina bifida	.40	
Encephalocele	.05	
Phenylketonuria	.10	
Sickle Cell Disease	.46	
Sickle cell anemia	.28	
Seizure Disorder	3.50	2.60– 4.60
Visual Impairment	30.00	20.00–35.00
Impaired visual acuity	20.00	—
Blindness	.60	.50– 1.00

NOTE: From "Chronic Childhood Disorders: Prevalence and Impact" (p. 5) by S. Gortmaker & W. Sappenfield, 1984. In R. Haggerty (Ed.) *Pediatric Clinics of North America, Vol. 31 Chronic Disease in Children.* Philadelphia: W. B. Saunders. Copyright 1984 by W. B. Saunders. Reprinted by permission.

found a total prevalence rate of 98.32 per 1,000 in their data. The most common chronic illnesses seem to be asthma, seizures, arthritis, and diabetes. The most common disabilities were visual impairment, mental retardation, hearing loss, various forms of birth defects including heart defects, paralysis, and cerebral palsy.

In a study of a birth cohort from 1946 in England and Wales, Pless et al. (1989) found that 106 out of 1,000 children suffered from chronic illness. Aggregate subgroups ordered by organ system, not exact disease distributions, were reported. The distribution was: 58% motor impairment, 22% cosmetic, and 20% sensory. Fifty-four percent were mildly impaired, defined as illness preventing children from taking part in strenuous activities. Thirty-four percent were moderately impaired, defined as illness interfering with activities of daily living. Twelve percent were severely impaired, requiring prolonged periods of absence from school or immobilization. A more recent study (Pless et al., 1993) of a birth cohort from 1958 in Britain provides comparable findings. And a similar survey, based on the reports of mental illness by primary care physicians in Monroe County, New York, showed similar results (Weiland et al., 1992).

Cadman et al. (1987) studied all children born from January 1, 1966, to January 1, 1979, in Ontario, Canada. The researchers interviewed 1,869 families and their 3,294 children ages 4 to 16. Out of 1,000 children, 177 were found to be chronically ill. Twenty-one percent had concomitant chronic illness and disability; 79% had only chronic illness.

Limiting his investigations to adolescents, Newacheck (1989) provides similar data. Studying adolescents between the ages of 10 and 18 and using a randomly chosen representative sample of 15,181 noninstitutionalized subjects from the 1984 National Health Interview Survey, more than 6%, or approximately 2 million nationwide, suffered some degree of disability or limitation of activity. Included in his impaired group were those with mental disorders, the most frequent form of illness found (estimated prevalence: 634,000, or 32%). The most common physical impairments were diseases of the respiratory system (406,000, or 21%), the musculoskeletal system (295,000, or 15%), and the nervous system (115,000, or 6%). The remaining 4% (80,000) suffered from disorders of the ear. The prevalence of disability was associated with sex (more boys than girls, 7.2 : 5.2, $p < 0.01$)

and age (younger significantly more than older, $p < 0.05$). Race and ethnicity did not vary significantly in this age group, but poverty status did; adolescents living below the poverty level were 46% more likely to be limited in their activities than adolescents living above the poverty level. This association was even more pronounced for educational levels. Parents with less than 9 years of education were 90% more likely to attribute disabilities to their adolescents than were those parents who completed college. While this parental report could represent an attribute problem in the reporter, it is unlikely given that other studies have found a similar interaction between socioeconomic status and disability (Cadman et al., 1986; Cadman et al., 1987; Pless et al., 1989). The mediating variable, as Newacheck (1989) points out, could well be reduced use of health care in those whose income is at or below the poverty level. When insurance is not available, physician contact at intervals of 2 to 3 years is three times more likely, with a similar probability of interval between in-hospital services. Newacheck and his group (1991) provided updated information on the subject originating from the 1988 National Health Interview Survey on Child Health, which specifically assessed the prevalence and the impact of chronic conditions in adolescents. Almost a third of adolescents had at least one chronic condition. This means that of the 27 million adolescents (ages 10 to 17) in this cohort, about 9 million were affected. Allergies, asthma, and frequent, severe headaches topped the list. On the average, these adolescents spent 3.4 bed days per year and missed 4.4 days of school related to their conditions during a year. Chronically ill adolescents had a much higher frequency of behavior problems than their healthy counterparts (35%). Multiple chronic conditions occurred in 7% of all adolescents, and they resulted in more time lost in school, more time spent in bed, and more behavior problems. There was a progressive impact between the number of chronic conditions and the number of behavior problems reported. Peer conflict and social withdrawal were the most pronounced problem areas. However, reported problems ranged from anxiety, depression, and hyperactivity to antisocial tendencies. Sex, age, and poverty did not influence the distribution of chronic conditions. Overall, 16% of all chronically ill adolescents were limited in some aspect of their activities. Least affected were those with the most common ailments, such as allergies (12%). Most affected were those with central nervous system involvement, such as cerebral palsy (100%).

Although these studies represent an advance over previous knowledge, several problems remain. Definitions of disability and chronic illness vary from study to study. Age groups studied vary in range, and, more crucially, adolescents and children are not usually reported separately. Disorders are sometimes grouped by organ system, sometimes by etiology of disorder. No grouping by similar course of disorder or age at onset has yet been attempted; both are issues crucial to the impact of chronic illness on child development. No epidemiological study has reported the interaction between family constellation and the impact of chronic illness, both important factors. These limitations notwithstanding, current epidemiological data on chronic illness and disability in Western populations provide convincing evidence that we are speaking of a major health care problem, and that based on Newacheck's newest cross-sectional data, there is little doubt that chronic illness progressively affects behavior in adolescents in negative ways. This raises a crucial question: How does growing up with chronic illness or disability affect the mental health of the child, the siblings, and the parents? The question is complex and requires many answers. Fortunately, at this point, we are in a much better position than 10 years ago to provide some answers, to point to the gaps in knowledge that need to be filled, and to show some opportunities for specific intervention.

A Model for the Study of the Impact of Chronic Pediatric Illness and Disabilities on Human Development

A productive investigation of the complicated interplay of human development and interferences generated by chronic pediatric illness and disability has to be based on a complex model that contains sufficient factors to account for expected and unexpected outcomes. In the opinion of the members of our pediatric–psychiatric team at Stanford, such a model has to based on developmental psychopathological principles and must contain risk

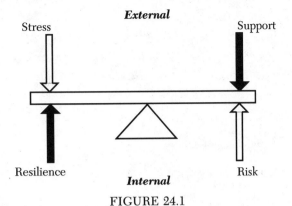

FIGURE 24.1
Risk and resilience model of developmental psychopathology.

and resilience factors. The risk/resilience model of psychopathology (see Figure 24.1) posits that mental health is the result of the interplay between vulnerabilities and stressors and offsetting resistance and support factors, which result in a careful balance, that is, mental health. This balance can be upset by an excessive loading on the stressor-risk side. Balance can be regained by the fortification of offsetting resilience. Conversely, imbalance—psychopathology—also can result from a deterioration of resilience factors, which then can be thrown off balance by even relatively minor and even normative forms of risk and stress. Balance also can be maintained under difficult circumstances, by counterbalancing excessive risk with excessive resilience. In this situation, patients and their families might show only signs of strain in everyday living but may decompensate rapidly and unexpectedly when a relatively minor incident occurs; it becomes the proverbial straw that breaks the camel's back.

Risk and resilience reside in the social environment, the biology and the psychology of the individual. Outcomes will be successfully predicted only if we have examined the full range of these factors as they interact at certain stages of development. All stages of development carry within them their own intrinsic risk for the individual, but they have to be successfully mastered for normal progression. As development unfolds, there is a progressive accumulation of risk and resilience, which determines whether the resulting trajectory is in line with what can be expected given age-appropriate strengths and weaknesses. Some risks and resilience are innately given (e.g., gender and tem-

257

TABLE 24.2

Important Risk and Resilience Factors Related to Psychiatric Illness in Children and Adolescents with Chronic Physical Disease and Disability

Risk	Resilience
Maleness	Femaleness
Poverty	Upper social stratum
Central nervous system involvement	High intelligence
Immature defenses (somatization)	Approach coping
Family conflict and dysfunction	Family cohesion and support
Mulitple handicaps	Single handicap
Severe illness and disability	Mild illness
Parental depression	Parental mental health
Hidden manifestations of disorder	Visible manifestations
Unpredictible disease	Predictible disease
High-technology intervention	
Multiple procedures	

peramental factors), others are acquired at different stages in life (some defense mechanisms and coping strategies), and still others reside in certain environments (poverty). Table 24.2 describes the model of some relevant risk and resilience factors and their relative position in this balance. As will become clear from the general discussion in this chapter and the specific discussions in other chapters addressing specific illnesses, we are at an early stage of understanding the full complexities involved in the field.

The Status of the Field

One of the measures of the maturity of a field is the sheer number of published studies. In this sense, the relationship between chronic illness and disability and psychiatric morbidity has been well studied. When this chapter was first written in 1979, six references were appended to the text (Schowalter, 1979). By the second writing in 1987, the number had increased to 110, but many references were from related fields, not direct studies of chronic illness (Feinstein & Berger, 1987). For the present chapter, a combined computerized and manual search for publications between 1985 and March 1994 yielded more than 400 references. Clearly, interest in this field has increased over the last six years. The ratio of well-designed, controlled studies to descriptive and clinical-anecdotal papers is still about 1 : 4, and thus it is quite apparent that there is still much room for improvement. Our group is currently working on an updated search to appear in 1997. Preliminary results of our efforts are very comparable to the list as reported here.

The methodological limitations of available research are numerous. Most studies are clinic-based, and representativeness of sampled patient populations is unclear. In some studies, multiple illnesses are grouped together to enlarge the sample size, but such groupings may well obscure important special effects on the individual. For instance, asthma and cystic fibrosis often are grouped together, regardless of differing disease courses, which affect psychiatric morbidity quite differently: Asthmatics tend to improve with age, while patients with cystic fibrosis deteriorate to certain death in young adulthood.

Most studies in the field did not employ control groups. In addition, most studies of specific illness report data from children at varying developmental stages without attempting to parse out differential effects in various age groups. This practice must lead to contradictory findings. Samples usually are mixed in terms of age and therefore presumably heterogenous in terms of duration of chronicity. Rare is the use of standardized instruments appropriate to the sample, although it should be mentioned that such instruments are in the developmental stage (Stein & Jessop, 1990; Walker, Stein, Perrin & Jessop, 1990). Many instruments used to measure, for instance, affective disturbances reveal a considerable overlap between pediatric and psychiatric symptoms; for example, anhedonia of depression versus the anergy induced by illness (Burke et al., 1989). Also rare is multimodal assessment obtained from multiple informants. This issue is particularly relevant given the often-contradictory findings in the earlier liter-

TABLE 24.3

Chronic Illness, Physical Disability, and Mental Disorder:
Summary of Data from Prospective Population Basal Studies

Authors	Cohort	Age Range	Follow-up	Instruments	Pediatric Diagnosis	Outcome
Stein & Jessop, 1984a,b; Walker, Stein, Perrin & Jessop, 1990	Population and clinic based; $n = 98$; multisite	5–18 years	No	Pars III; Parent report	Mixed chronic illness without mental retardation	Boys at more risk than girls; no difference by primary psychiatric illness
Pless et al. 1989	Birth cohort in Britain, 1946; $n = 5362$	Up to 36 years	36 years	*Self report;* Eysenk Personality Inventory; observer report; delinquency records; Present State Exam	Mixed chronic illnesses from all systems	*Adolescence:* Boys with Chronic Pulmonary Disease had more habit disorders; girls were more troublesome. Academic achievement significantly lower in both *Adulthood:* Less education; 1.5–2 times more mental disorders than normal; more relationship problems
Cadman et al. 1987	Community based; $n = 3294$ in Ontario 1 year birth cohort	4–16 years	No	Survey Diagnostic Instrument; Observer and self-reports	Full range of chronic illnesses and disabilities	Substantially higher risk for mental disorders; Neurosis and attention deficit hyperactivity disorder most common; high is 2.5–5.1 times as high as in normals

ature concerning the mental health of chronically ill patients. As is the case in cystic fibrosis, those studies using observer-rated instruments usually find a much higher degree of psychiatric morbidity than do those employing self-report instruments (Breslau & Marshall, 1985; Steiner, Rahimzadeh, & Lewiston, 1990), reflecting patients' tendency to deny or be defensive about the full implications of illness. It has been found that such defensiveness is associated with active illness on axis three (Steiner & Harris, 1994) and that degree of defensiveness clearly distinguishes normal adolescents from those with chronic illness (Canning,

Canning, & Boyce, 1992). Another measurement issue that makes it difficult to generalize from studies currently available is the variety of dependent variables used, ranging from school grades to intrapsychic mechanisms of defense. At present there seems to be little agreement as to which variables are most important to study.

Studies of intervention are the most infrequent, no doubt a reflection of problems with definition and measurement that preoccupy researchers in the field. Also, these investigations are usually cross-sectional or have only a very brief follow-up period. There are notable exceptions (Chiarelli,

Tumini, Morgese, & Albisser, 1990; Leibowitz et al., 1985; Levenson, 1992; Nolan, Zvagulis & Pless, 1987; Stein & Jessop, 1991), but they are in the minority.

It is rare that premorbid psychiatric morbidity is assessed, so it is unclear how much of the morbidity in a sample is encountered purely by chance. Research activity in the field also does not parallel the frequency with which certain disorders are encountered. (See Table 24.3.) Thus, there is little information available about the most common forms of impairment (i.e., the chronic effects of trauma as well as visual and hearing problems) while relatively rare illnesses such as cancer are extensively studied. The areas within the field producing the highest volume and quality research are mental retardation, diabetes, cancer and hematological problems, spina bifida, and asthma.

Relatively more is known about the impact of raising a child with chronic illness or disability on a family, especially on siblings (Drotar & Crawford, 1985; Feinstein & Davis, 1987; Stoneman, Brody, Davis, & Crapps, 1988; Tritt & Esses, 1988; Wood et al., 1988). Most studies conclude that there is a profound effect on the patient, siblings, and parents, and, by and large, the impact is negative.

To summarize, it is quite apparent that the field has matured considerably in the past 10 years. While earlier there was a preoccupation with exploring the possibility that chronic illness leads to adverse mental health outcomes, now we are in a position to state that chronic illness and disability put individuals at high risk. We are in the process of refining instruments to measure pathology more appropriately (e.g., Austin & Huberty, 1992; Perrin, Stein, & Drotar, 1991). And rather than duplicating findings, we should concentrate on specific illnesses and interventions that might be useful (Pless & Nolan, 1991).

Review of Population-Based Studies

Given the methodological limitations of virtually all investigations reviewed, general conclusions must be drawn cautiously. Those that can be made are drawn from population-based studies that examine commonalities across illness groups. This noncategorical approach is best exemplified by the work of Stein (Stein & Jessop, 1984a, 1984b, 1990; Stein, Jessop & Riessman, 1983) and Pless (1984; Pless et al., 1989) and their respective groups. (See Table 24.3 for summary.)

STEIN AND JESSOP

Stein and Jessop (1984a,b) studied both a large population-based and a smaller clinic-based sample, examining the relationships between chronic illness and multiple variables relating to the adjustment status of family and child. Variables included: the child's psychological adjustment and functional status; the mother's psychiatric symptoms; the impact of chronic illness on the family; satisfaction with care; judged ability to cope; unmet health needs; health care maintenance; sibling health; and overall burden index. Patients were grouped according to primary pediatric diagnosis. There were virtually no significant differences between diagnostic groups on these measures, but variance within groups was considerable. Stein argues for the validity of this noncategorical approach to chronic illness. However, more sensitive measures of psychopathology, such as psychiatric diagnoses or personality measures that would reveal habitual styles of coping, were not used. Baseline psychopathology and the date of the onset of chronic illness also were not assessed. In addition, the subsamples of different diseases are rather small. Given these limitations, it is not surprising that the results reflect few differences between groups, as most of these methodological problems typically lead to large intragroup variances. It is clear that almost certainly there are many commonalities in terms of how different chronic illnesses affect individuals, but it is also very likely that particular illnesses will impact patients in some specific ways. Still, it is important to realize that chronic illness has an extensive impact on all individuals, regardless of primary disorder.

PLESS

Pless presents data regarding the general impact of chronic illness in a prospective data set (Pless et al., 1989). The data are unique in the field, providing extensive follow-up over 36 years. Although there are problems, particularly with instrumentation, the study deserves detailed discussion because it provides insight into the future of chronically ill and disabled children. Pless's sample consists of one birth cohort in the United Kingdom in one week in 1946, a total number of 5,362 subjects. The assessment included a wide variety of data (medical, social, psychological, and educational) that were collected at intervals of at least 2 years until age 15, then at intervals of 5 years until age 36. Unfortunately, the instruments measuring psychiatric impairment changed between the adolescent and the adult assessment, with a switch from nonstandardized reports by teachers and parents and the Eysenk Personality Inventory, to the Present State Examination, an in-depth structured interview. Nonetheless, the results revealed that the chronically ill group differed from their healthy cohorts in many important aspects; they had higher death rates, especially if they came from lower economic levels, and death rates rose steeply with increasing age. Boys were more likely than age-matched controls to have a high incidence of habitual behavior disturbances and were rated by teachers as more troublesome. The Eysenk Inventory provided no clear picture, although there were some significant differences. This is not surprising, given the simplicity of the instrument, the complexity of the phenomena involved, and patients' noted tendency to distort on self-report instruments. Educational achievement was considerably lowered in both boys and girls, mostly due to the children's lower economic background. This lack of achievement, as in the Isle of Wight Study (Rutter, 1991), was not a function of mental impairment (such subjects were excluded) or absences from class (there was no significant difference on this variable); most likely it was related to emotional impairment. In adulthood, deteriorating health required significantly more days in-hospital (an average of 28 days per year). Educational achievement did not differ at the end of school in the chronically ill group; employment status at age 36 did. This may be a reflection of emotional factors, prejudice, or both. Men had a significantly higher incidence of unemployment at age 36; again, this was most true for those who came from lower socioeconomic backgrounds. Fewer of the chronically ill were married by age 36, and most of those individuals were actively ill between ages 15 and 21. As a rule, chronic illness did not affect fertility in men. (Both groups produced the same number of children.) The fertility of women with chronic illness in childhood declined significantly.

Between the ages of 16 and 26, rates of treated psychiatric problems and reported psychiatric problems were significantly higher in this group than in those who were neither chronically ill in childhood nor reported present illness. Most of this increase stemmed from those who were continuously and chronically ill until age 26, or those who began their course of chronic illness after age 21. The only objective measure of psychiatric morbidity available in this phase of follow-up is patient-reported psychiatric treatment. Thus, it is difficult to determine the meaning of this finding. It may be as much a reflection of the service delivery system in the United Kingdom as it is one of psychiatric risk.

Psychiatric problems elucidated by the Present State Examination given at age 36 present a complex picture that largely supports the view that significant psychiatric morbidity ensues from chronic childhood illness. Women who were chronically ill in childhood had significantly higher symptom scores. How many of these women would fulfill syndromal diagnoses was not reported. Economic circumstances also were worse in the chronically ill group at age 36. Significantly fewer men and women owned their own homes, although there were no differences in reported income. And, as would be expected, significantly more of those chronically ill in childhood were permanently impaired at this age.

The findings from Pless's study (Pless et al., 1989) are complex but permit the conclusion that chronic illness in childhood places the individual at risk for a life that is more economically and emotionally difficult. This conclusion is especially true for those whose illnesses remain active into adulthood, those whose lives are complicated by some form of permanent disability, and those who come from lower socioeconomic backgrounds. It is not clear from this study whether the effect of chronic illness and disability alone leads to increases in psychiatric morbidity, or if the interaction of poor economic status coupled with illness is instead the cause. Particular attention should be paid in future studies to unraveling these two variables. Pless and his collaborators are planning a follow-up of two further birth cohorts from 1958 and 1970. Results should shed further light on representativeness of the original findings for other generations. It is hoped that a more uniform instrumentation will clarify the complexities found in this study.

CADMAN

Cadman and his group (Cadman et al., 1987) also studied a large, population-based sample of 3,294 noninstitutionalized Canadian children ages 4 to 16, selected through an interview survey of 1,869 families. Their instrument was a modified version of the Child Behavior Checklist. The reports were obtained from three sources: parents of all children, self-report of children ages 12 to 16, and teachers' reports for children ages 4 to 11. Categorical diagnoses according to the third revised edition of the *Diagnostic and Statistical Manual of Mental Disorders* (*DSM-III-R*) were developed using threshold values for individual scores. Three diagnostic groupings were explored: neurosis (comprised of affective disorders, anxiety disorders, and obsessive compulsive disorders), conduct disorder, and attention deficit disorder hyperactivity. Groupings were selected for high diagnostic specificity (low rates of false positive cases), ranging from 0.99 to 0.96. Sensitivity was correspondingly low, ranging from 0.1 to 0.78. Unfortunately, somatization disorders, adjustment disorders, and posttraumatic stress disorders were not included, all of which have obvious relevance in chronic illness. Nevertheless, there was a significant association by age and sex-adjusted odds ratio: Children with chronic illness and disability were at highest risk for diagnoses falling within the three categories (4.7 times increased risk for neurosis, 2.5 times for conduct disorder, and 5.1 times for attention deficit disorder hyperactivity). The odds ratio was 3.4 for multiple psychiatric diagnoses. Children with chronic illness but without disability still faced a higher risk than did children who were not chronically ill: The respective ratios are 2.2, 2.2, 2.2, and 2.1. The picture that emerges is fairly clear: Children with chronic illness are at risk for concurrent psychiatric pathology. Parental ratings of the children's social and school adjustment were much less clear. Isolation, low participation, low competence, problems getting along, and not doing well at school were the global categories rated. These findings support the view that, in comparison to healthy children, those with illness and disability fare significantly worse, while those with chronic illness alone do not. This is somewhat surprising given the earlier finding that both chronic illness groups have an increased risk of psychiatric mor-

bidity. Psychiatric disorders tend to be accompanied by disturbances in all of the above areas. However, given that these ratings were obtained from parents only and in a rather global fashion, unclear results might be expected. Also, not examined were interactions with, or primary effects of, socioeconomic status. The authors conclude that "the evidence from population studies convincingly demonstrates an association between chronic health problems and mental health or adjustment problems" (p. 810). No attempts were made in this report to examine the association between specific categories of pediatric and psychiatric disorders. The authors also did not examine the effect of duration of illness as a determinant for either kind or severity of psychiatric disorder. Finally, the report does not permit the examination of developmental factors with regard to the progression of specific syndromes, as there is no follow-up and no assessment of developmental variables other than age.

Selected Findings from Clinic-Based Studies

Many of these studies are discussed in great detail in other chapters, when different authors discuss the impact of specific illnesses on patients and parents. Here I report on only a select few to guide the reader.

Clinic-based studies provide much-needed detail regarding the impact of specific disorders, which should assist the clinician in planning for the problems a particular patient faces. In general, the findings from these studies are complementary. When diversity exists, it is because of the different instrumentations used and different follow-up designs employed. Still, such studies make possible the in-depth exploration of the course of illness interacting with developmental and familial variables. More and better ones are needed in the field.

There has been much debate in the past as to what roles psychosocial factors have in the genesis of somatic illness. One such study is currently in progress and contributes to this area. Mrazek's group investigates prospectively the interaction of development, risk for asthma, and maternal stress and coping (Mrazek, 1988). Preliminary results have been reported and are interesting, indicating a connection between illness onset and familial stress and coping. This series of studies is unique in the field, and we need many more of them to provide additional accuracy in predicting specific risk and resilience factors.

Another group of important questions in the field deals with the issues of how psychosocial factors are involved in the so-called psychomaintenance of disease and recovery. The study of cancer survivors is an example for such an investigation. For instance, several follow-up studies of cancer survivors have reported mixed results: Survivors suffer some forms of distress akin to posttraumatic symptoms for many years after treatment, but function well in terms of interpersonal, vocational, and academic adjustment (Fritz & Williams, 1988; Fritz, Williams & Amylon, 1988; Hernandez, Gary, & Lineberger, 1989; Mulhern, Friedman, & Stone, 1988; Sawyer, Toogood, Rice, Haskell, & Baghurst, 1989; Spirito et al., 1990; Tebbi, Bromberg & Piedmont, 1989; Zevon, Neubauer & Green, 1990). The degree of distress suffered is generally less than that found in clinical psychiatric patients, but it appears highly likely that such distress may be related to subsequent health care seeking or avoiding behaviors, which may complicate recovery. Results are not conclusive, because of methodological problems in the field. Most samples are very small. Many studies used self-report instruments without the concomitant measurement of defensiveness, although it is quite possible that defensiveness may either be a risk or resilience factor in this process. (Canning et al., 1992; Lane, Merikangas, Schwartz, Huang & Prusoff, 1989). It seems that adjustment to cancer is quite variable and probably interacts with preexisting familial and individual pathology to produce a wide range of psychosocial outcomes (Fife, Norton, & Groom, 1987), and it is also quite likely that these outcomes will have important implications for treatment compliance and ultimate outcome.

A special case of interest to the developmental psychopathologist are those illnesses that intermittently become life threatening, in very short order, and without much warning. Diabetes is such a case of a chronic illness, and we could expect that such an illness requires special adjustment.

Fortunately, we know a good amount about the development of the diabetic child and adolescent, due to two mostly complementary data bases. These two ongoing, longitudinal studies of diabetic children deserve special mention because they approach the issues from two very different theoretical frameworks yet offer complementary results and great detail. Kovacs and her group at Pittsburgh have studied a group of 95 diabetic children for 6 years prospectively (Kovacs et al., 1985a,b, 1990a,b; Kovacs, Brent, Steinberg, Paulauskas, & Reid, 1986). Children and families were assessed four times in the first year and every 8 months thereafter by semistructured interview, self-report scales, and consensus *DSM-III-R* diagnosis. Initial responses were most commonly adjustment disorders (64%), while 6% exhibited diagnosable psychiatric disorders, most often depression. Most children recovered within a few months after diagnosis, regardless of preexisting pathology and parental responses. However, long-term follow-up of those with adjustment disorders showed that they had an increased risk for future psychopathology (Kovacs, 1995). Psychiatric diagnoses were more common in low socioeconomic status families and those high in marital distress (Kovacs et al., 1985a). Self-reported coping in this cohort demonstrated normalcy and resiliency (Kovacs et al., 1986). Parental responses to illness onset assessed by observer- and self-rated scales of anxiety and depression showed no significant impact (Kovacs et al., 1985b). Self-reported family characteristics did not relate to diabetic control (Kovacs, Kass, Schnell, Goldston, & Marsh, 1989).

This optimistic picture must be viewed with caution, since most of the measures are self-reported and defensiveness was not assessed. On follow-up (Kovacs et al., 1990a,b), there was some negative effect on adjustment. All children, but girls more than boys, were increasingly anxious and depressed and had more difficulty in coping with the regimen associated with managing the illness after 6 years. Levels of anxiety and depression increased, most especially in those who had more pronounced problems at baseline. Paradoxically, as measured by self-reported distress and depression, mothers tended to fare better the longer their children had been ill. This is perhaps evidence of an increasing acceptance of the child's illness or better parental adjustment as children become increasingly more responsible for their own care. Baseline functioning again predicted future adjustment.

The picture that emerges from these studies is that, after a brief and mostly minor disturbance in adjustment, children and parents recover. Subsequently, however, as year after year of meticulous care is required, the disease takes a toll on a child. In many ways, this course is reminiscent of the reactions of children with cystic fibrosis, where an initial period of good adjustment is followed by gradual increases in pathology as medical crises and complications mount, serving as a reminder of the inevitable outcome.

Another data set on diabetic children ages 9 to 16 is available for comparison. Hauser and his group at Harvard (Hauser et al., 1986, 1990; Jacobson et al., 1986, 1987, 1990; Jacobson, Rand, & Hauser, 1985) studied prospectively a sample of approximately 60 patients over a period of 4 years, focusing on psychological and family variables in relationship to patient adherence to illness management regimens. A comparison group of acutely ill children was studied simultaneously. The design was naturalistic and instruments used were the Family Environment Scale and the Child Behavior Checklist. Analyses in the first year (Hauser et al., 1986; Jacobson et al., 1986, 1987) showed no differences on either scale; means in either group were comparable to reported norms. Further studies of self-esteem, perceived competence, and locus of control again showed no differences for either group. Measuring adjustment to diabetes, the diabetic group fell within the well-adjusted range. Adjustment to diabetes correlated highly with positive psychological characteristics. Thus, the same optimistic picture emerges as in Kovac's study during the first year. After 18 months, compliance with treatment was studied by parent and patient report. High levels of compliance at baseline predicted good compliance at follow-up (Jacobson et al., 1987). Positive psychological characteristics at baseline correlated highly with good compliance at baseline and at follow-up, holding age constant. And finally, adolescents were significantly less compliant than preadolescents. A scale specifically developed to measure self-efficacy in diabetics (Grossman, Brink, & Hauser, 1987; Jacobson et al., 1987) confirmed that high levels of self-efficacy are associated with metabolic control, especially in girls. At the 4-year prospective follow-up, the relationship among maturity, level of defenses, adaptive strength, locus of control, and adjustment at baseline were predictive of adherence throughout the 4 years, although adherence declined somewhat during adolescent years. These same aspects of patient functioning predicted glycemic control. There were no predictors of change in adherence, and subjects' relative position in the group remained stable. Family environmental characteristics also were related to adherence: Conflict was highly negatively correlated and cohesion and organization highly positively correlated with adherence levels in the first year. Cohesion predicted higher levels of adherence at the fourth year follow-up.

Findings from these two data sets are complementary and confirm what has been shown in other cross-sectional studies. Initially, the impact of disease is transient and mild. Those with preexisting pathology and negative family characteristics tend to do more poorly in terms of adjustment to the disorder, including taking care of the disease. Tendencies to do poorly are not corrected by time alone and probably require intervention. If anything, as the disease progresses and patients reach adolescence, the problems of reaction to illness and poor compliance mount. There are clear correlations between negative family and individual characteristics and poor control of illness. This worsening may represent, in part, a reaction to the more complete understanding of the disease, which in turn seems to be a function of cognitive maturation (Allen, Affleck, Tennen, McGrade, & Ratzman, 1984).

By contrast, most chronic illnesses are not immediately life threatening and create more chronic strain on personal and familial resources. A good model for such an illness is juvenile rheumatoid arthritis. This area is also of particular interest, because some recent findings actually suggest some concrete pathways for intervention, which may serve as a model for intervention in other chronic illnesses that present with a similar course. Prior to 1990, the study of juvenile arthritis contained many problems in methodology. Not surprisingly then, studies yielded quite conflicting results (Blalock, deVellis, deVellis & Sauter, 1988; Quirk & Young, 1990; Ungerer, Horgan, Chaitow & Champion, 1988). In 1991 to 1993, however, Moos and his group (Ebata & Moos, 1991; Miller, 1993; Timko, Stovel, Moos & Miller, 1992a,b) published a series of studies, based on prospective follow-up, that clarified the status of these patients. Utilizing a risk and resistance factor paradigm, parents and patients completed self-report questionnaires addressing multiple domains of daily functioning. However, there was no measure of denial or defensiveness, nor were there any objective interviews and exams of patients and parents, independent teacher reports, or peer reports. This would limit the validity of the results, as we know that patients with chronic illness are more likely to represent themselves in a favorable light to themselves and others (Canning et al., 1992; Steiner & Harris, 1994). Still, results supported the view that risk, resistance, and illness factors remained stable over several years. Concurrent risk predicted social outcomes better than risk prior to illness (retrospectively assessed). Lack of maternal depression aided children's adjustment (Timko et al., 1992a). Compared to their nondiseased siblings, patients fared more poorly in terms of mental health, especially when disabled (Timko et al., 1992b). Problems were predominantly evident in social functioning, but appeared also in psychological and family domains. There was a systematic relationship between the patient's level of functioning and the parents': Mothers generally reported higher levels of depression than fathers, but not at "clinical" levels, when the child was not doing well. The findings support a model in which the child's emotional well-being is a predictor of the parent's adjustment. Such a model is also supported by findings of Kovacs et al. (1990a) and Varni and Wallander (1988). Thus, both parents had more difficulty in functioning, fathers less so than mothers, when their child had more difficulty with functional disability and pain. Familial support buffered the development of depression for the parents. When followed longitudinally, each spouse's functioning was affected by the other's baseline functioning. Predominant use of avoidance coping in dealing with the child's illness was associated with the subsequent development of depression in the individual.

These findings suggest specific intervention strategies: Parents should be educated in terms of how to handle pain and disability—they should become "junior members" of the treatment team. The goal should be to facilitate as much independent living in the child, with the help of specific aids, as is possible on a daily basis. Pain manage-ment and self-regulation is important to teach (Varni & Bernstein, 1991). The social problems of the child need to be targeted specifically. Parental use of avoidance coping needs to be monitored carefully and replaced by appropriate approach coping strategies helping the parent deal with those aspects of the illness that can be controlled. And finally, since family variables indicating support had a protective effect in the studies, an addition of family interventions strengthening support should bear dividends. Such an approach, the studies suggest, should be aimed at helping the family to realistically acknowledge the impact of living with a chronic disease on all family members.

Another area of study in this field that yields yet another perspective is the study of disability. Here we usually have the static presence of a deficit that does not present the problems of active disease: There usually is no acute or ongoing and intermittent threat to life. However, on the negative side, there also is much less hope for treatment and recovery. Some prospective data are available on the study of physical handicaps, including two prospective follow-up studies (Breslau & Marshall, 1985; Heller, Rafman, Zvagulis & Pless, 1985), both of which have severe limitations, which makes generalizing from them difficult. Both studies had adequate sample sizes. Instruments were limited to self-report measures and mothers' reports, however, with no measures of defensiveness. Both samples were internally heterogenous in terms of type of handicap, duration of illness, and ages of children examined. Follow-up intervals were 1 and 5 years respectively. In general, findings from the studies were consistent—increased psychiatric morbidity was found in this population. Furthermore, the studies found that severity of illness and central nervous system involvement led to higher chances for behavior problems.

Ever since Rutter's study of children on the Isle of Wight, it has been known that children whose chronic illness involves the central nervous system are at particularly high risk for bad outcome. The model illness for a static disability that affects the central nervous system is mental retardation. This is one of the areas that consistently has produced a fairly high volume of good-quality research, and it, perhaps more than most others discussed up to this point, is ripe for the trial of specific intervention studies. It is clear from the studies in this area that there is a direct relationship between maladjustment and severity of impairment (Gostason, 1985). Even in the absence of overt psychiatric morbidity, some ego disturbances are uniquely present in this population and do not necessarily represent simple developmental lags, yet they distinguish the even mildly impaired from age-matched controls (Levy-Schiff, Dedem, & Sevilla, 1990). Social aspects of development in these children are clearly of great importance in light of the recent tendency to provide education in a mainstream setting. The school experience of mentally retarded children is clearly different from that of normal peers: Subtle and overt rejection and distancing by peers is common, although it seems to be experienced as commonly by psychiatrically impaired children (Gillmore & Farina, 1989). For mentally retarded children, this mild rejection and distancing is evident even in the preschool years, where preference patterns of play have indicated the isolation of developmentally delayed children. It seems that the isolation is based on a child's perceived lower competence, not reputational factors. A comparable study of dyadic relations between the retarded and nonretarded (Cole, Vandercook, & Rynders, 1987) showed that closeness in chronological age made interactions symmetrical, fun, and balanced, suggesting that such distancing and rejection is not ubiquitous but perhaps more evident in public social interactions in certain schools. Evidence for the ability of normals to interact appropriately on a dyadic basis with the mentally impaired is evident as early as ages 3 and 4 (Guralnick & Groom, 1987a,b). The message from this set of studies is clear: While children are able to adjust to interacting with the mentally handicapped in dyadic situations, interactions in more demanding group situations, even from an early age, seem to result in negative consequences for the impaired. Thus, it would seem that mainstream education can be successful only if schools devote appropriate time and personnel to facilitate group interactions between children. Simultaneously, it is clear that adaptive behavior can be changed for the better in even the severely retarded (Felce, de Kock, Thomas, & Saxby, 1986; Matson et al., 1988), and such programs suitably complement efforts at mainstream education. The impact of the retarded on parents and siblings is considerable (Blacher,

Nihira, & Meyers, 1987). This is evident even in subtle aspects of dyadic interactions between mothers and children (Kaiser & Blair, 1987). Some families clearly seem to be at greater risk than others, especially those with fewer psychosocial resources (Mink & Nihira, 1987), such as single-parent families, especially those headed by adolescent mothers (Whitman, Borkowski, Schellenbach, & Nath, 1987). Positive child and family characteristics interact to result in positive outcome (Frey, Greenberg, & Fewell, 1989). However, other admixtures fare considerably less well (Minnes, 1988; Wallander, Varni, Babani, Banis, et al., 1989). Wallander has provided some evidence for a sophisticated, complex, and multifaceted model of the process of familial adjustment to a child's handicap; most likely this model is applicable to a variety of chronic illnesses. It seems that mothers still provide most of the care of mentally retarded children and are the family member at highest risk for developing problems, especially depression, even when the child is very young (Walker, Ortiz-Valdes, & Newbrough, 1989). Employment outside of the home and adequate family psychosocial resources (Wallander et al., 1989a) seem to have a mediating influence. Maternal depression, in turn, is clearly associated with a higher incidence of child behavior problems. These behavior problems also appear in children with other illnesses, but mentally retarded children seem to have a special propensity toward such behavior, given the circumstance of maternal depression (Walker et al., 1989). Family resources beyond those needed for subsistence clearly have a buffering effect in this process of adjustment (Wallander, Varni, Babani, Banis, et al., 1989).

It has been appreciated for some time that siblings also are at risk for problems in families with mentally retarded children (Feinstein & Davis, 1987). Some studies suggest subtle mechanisms by which siblings may be affected. Older siblings, especially sisters, assume parental roles. This in turn decreases appropriate peer interaction and out-of-home activities. Increased child care responsibilities often result in negative sibling interactions. Age and sex therefore seem to interact in significant ways with sibling status to influence outcomes (Stoneman et al., 1988).

A 13-year prospective follow-up of 80 individuals with an average IQ of 53 showed that intellectual abilities remained relatively constant over time. Verbal and numerical skills could be predicted by baseline information, but there was considerable heterogeneity in more complex abilities; for these, prediction was not possible (Palmer, 1987).

Many questions remain open for examination, the most interesting concerning the role of fathers in these families and their effect on the health status of family members. Studies of randomized interventions facilitating mainstream education, long-term health outcomes, and psychosocial status of mentally retarded children and their families are needed. The model culled from the data regarding mothers' role, buffering variables, and problems in children should be tested for predictive and discriminant validity in children with other illnesses, but thus far, results seem consistent and interesting. Mothers who are the primary caregivers adjust very early to a child's deficiencies and thus develop a special relationship with a child. Diminished peer interaction, especially in groups, most likely strengthens these tendencies toward exclusive relationships, as do resentful peers and absent fathers. As the relationship between mother and child intensifies, the mother's resources may begin to fail, resulting in anxiety and depression, which in turn leads to impairment in the child's adjustment. There may be a component of emotional contagion and deficient socialization due to maternal exhaustion, and insufficient exposure to ego-building experiences may contribute to poor outcome. Behavior problems in turn adversely influence the child's adjustment and already precarious peer relationships; this in turn intensifies the relationship with the primary caregiver, and the circle is complete.

General Conclusions for Future Research

Currently we have little conclusive evidence that different pediatric diseases affect children and families differently. There is some evidence from clinic-based studies that this may be so, and to all of us who work in the field, this appears intuitively right. I have attempted to draw a picture of how these disease processes might affect children and

their families differently, but methodological limitations do not permit broad generalizations or adequate comparisons from the currently existing data. It would seem that different diseases that have different courses, prognoses, and responses to treatment lead to different problems, but comparative studies with adequate methodology are lacking. There is little doubt that chronic illness poses an immediate risk for the development of psychiatric disorders and adjustment problems, as well as having implications for future health, economic status, and social functioning. Particularly troubling is the finding that social class interacts with chronic illness and disability to produce much less favorable outcomes. It is likely that the mediating variables here are access to and use of the health care system, especially mental health care. The issue of whether this population should be studied in a categorical or noncategorical fashion is resolved by what questions are to be asked. If a researcher seeks to make a point regarding the psychological cost of chronic illness in general, a noncategorical approach is adequate. Examination of noncategorical variables measuring aspects of adaptation in particular is a promising approach to screening populations at risk. Such variables would indicate risk for the development of psychiatric syndromes, provided that such connections can be shown reliably (Steiner & Feldman, 1994). Since different psychiatric syndromes have different courses, treatments, and outcomes, and since they presumably will require different prevention strategies, the categorical approach is most suitable for studies that focus on issues of specific treatment and risk as well as severity of risk. The issue of whether pediatric diagnostic categories are useful in differentiating children with chronic illness is an open one, as no study to date has presented adequate data to permit firm conclusions. Ordering diseases by organ system is not likely to lead to progress, given the different courses of illnesses affecting the same system (e.g., cystic fibrosis and asthma). A more useful categorization might be through an assessment of the illness's course, prognosis, cost to the family, and visibility or lack thereof as well as amount of familial involvement and developmental phase in which onset occurs. Studies addressing these issues have yet to be conducted on an adequate scale.

But while we are beginning to work on these problems, at this point it seems definitely possible to begin focusing on the implementation and testing of treatment programs. As has been shown by controlled outcome studies (Nolan et al., 1987), the simple addition of a social worker to a pediatric tertiary care clinic does not provide the kind of help these patients and their families need. The models discussed by Kovacs, Varni and Wallander, and Moos suggest more specific targeted approaches to these patients and families, which combine assessment of risk and resistance factors, education in the illness process, confrontation of inappropriate avoidance and denial, and reshaping of family functioning, while acknowledging the impact of living with a chronic disorder. We also can draw on the considerable body of knowledge developed by our colleagues in the adult psychiatric literature addressing needs of adult patients with chronic illness. In the past 10 years, following a NIMH workshop sponsored by the National Institute of Mental Health, considerable research activity has developed in the field of adult medical psychiatry that supports most of the following statements (Levenson, 1992): Psychosocial problems are common in the medically ill, psychological factors do affect medical illness, and medical-psychiatric comorbidity affects health care cost. Psychosocial interventions improve medical outcomes and psychosocial outcomes, and such interventions are cost effective. All these tenets should be attractive to those who are seeking to improve health care and at the same time to contain health care costs. Most likely many of these tenets will apply to the field of pediatric and psychiatric comorbidity. There is a small but dedicated cadre of researchers working in this area (Steiner et al., 1993), and many of them, after years of instrument development and diagnostic work, are now ready to enter into the area of specific testing of screening and treatment programs. Whereas when this chapter was written for the previous edition of this *Handbook,* there was much less information available on the subject of chronic illness and psychiatric comorbidity, now the problems are much more clearly outlined and ready for the systematic study of preventive and curative intervention (Schowalse, 1979).

In conceptualizing treatment, we have to keep in mind that a traditional consultation/liaison model may not be enough to handle the complexities of the situation and do justice to the needs of the patients and the families. Specially integrated in- and outpatient services might be necessary to handle all facets of patient care (Steiner et al., 1994). We might think of new approaches, like effective home health care programs (Stein and Jessop, 1991). A recent report examines the impact of such a program 5 years after random assignment. Discrepancies between intervention and nonintervention groups were apparent even more strongly than on short-term follow-up, and the mental health of the children was better in general, in particular including a reduced tendency to withdraw, coupled with lowered levels of anxiety, depression, and hostility. Peer relationships and dependency were unaffected. Many other areas of intervention are completely untested: the use of psychopharmaca, group and individual explorative psychotherapy, family therapy, and intensive and extensive residential treatment. All these will need to be studied in the near future.

Implications for Practitioners and Public Policy Makers

Most workers in the field would agree that the population of chronically ill children, especially those with disabilities, deserves a great deal of attention from child psychiatry. It is also clear that the link to mental health services is weak (Eiser, 1990; Jaudes & Diamond, 1986; Newacheck, 1989) for reasons that include the availability of services; exclusion of mental health coverage in insurance policies; and pediatrician, patient, and family resistance factors. As these patients are difficult to deal with, approaching them requires considerable skill on the part of clinicians. Still, it is clear that this is a population in great need of our services. Comorbidity is a factor in poor compliance and increased inappropriate health care utilization. The responsibility of the child psychiatrist is to provide the clinical screening for those at high risk. Some patients may not present with full-blown psychiatric disorders but by virtue of their adaptive style are at risk for the development of affective conduct and somaticizing disorders that can further complicate pediatric illness. There is evidence that a number of patients benefit from joint pediatric/ psychiatric management in order to reduce compliance problems, improve chances for remission, and reduce likelihood of future disability. Also, shortly after diagnosis, families and siblings struggle with the impact of illness on their lives. Most illnesses take a toll, and family members need assistance to cope and respond appropriately to a child. Siblings are at high risk for developing problems, regardless of the affected child's primary illness. Families of low socioeconomic background are at particularly high risk.

Although it seems that most families recover from the impact of having a chronically ill child, problems emerge again and again at developmental nodal points, such as transitions into school age, adolescence, and adulthood. Our profession must be prepared publicly to advocate treatment for this group of patients. The current trend in insurance companies is to provide less for those who need the most. More patients are being shifted to the public sector for care as disorders progress and availability of services becomes the primary issue. The net result is the induction of disability, which in turn is extremely costly to society. Prevention of this cycle must start early to be effective. Collaboration with pediatricians is the key, and this is a difficult endeavor.

New systems of mental health delivery also need to be explored. It is clear that routine social service intervention, currently the most frequent mental health care this population receives, seems insufficient to make an impact on the psychiatric problems in these children (Rice, Satterwhite, & Pless, 1977). The model of collaboration that has been most successful in the program at Lucile Salter Packard Children's Hospital at Stanford is one that assumes that patient and family become part of the treatment team of pediatricians and mental health professionals and collaborate as experts to maximize resources and comply with prescribed regimens, these being the best safeguard against progressive disease and permanent disability. Such a model presupposes the close interdisciplinary collaboration of many professionals who address the child's needs. Depending on the primary clinical issues, either the psychiatrist or the pediatrician takes the lead in managing the patient. Intensity of mental health service ranges from simple tracking to intensive inpatient treatment, depending on the severity of the problems. Several model programs have been developed in the United States (Fritz, 1990). It seems that the most effective ones in terms of their impact on this difficult population are those that are fully integrated in the various levels of pediatric hospitals. The staff in these "pediatric psychiatry" programs, a term Fritz has proposed, have the opportunity to develop extensive expertise in the overlap between child psychiatry and pediatrics. Extensive and intensive participation in the ongoing care of these patients and their families does much to circumvent the problems that arise when an ad hoc consultative approach is taken. Patients, families, and pediatricians are sensitive to the fact that chronic illness and disability pose an extraordinary burden on all members of the family. When a psychiatric consultant has to be called in to resolve a crisis and this intervention does not take place in the context of longitudinal involvement, the consultant and the recommendations often are perceived as blaming and critical, an added insult; consultation under these circumstances is usually not effective.

Although diagnosing and treating the chronically ill and disabled child is a challenge from many points of view, it is an area of psychiatric care that we can no longer afford to ignore.

REFERENCES

Allen, D. A., Affleck, G., Tennen, H., McGrade, B. J., & Ratzman, S. (1984). Concerns of children with a chronic illness: A cognitive-developmental study of juvenile diabetes. *Child Care Health Development, 10,* 211–218.

Austin, J. K., & Huberty, T. J. (1992). Development of the child attitude toward illness scale. *Journal of Pediatric Psychology, 18,* 467–480.

Blacher, J., Nihira, K., & Meyers, C. E. (1987). Characteristics of home environment of families with mentally retarded children: Comparison across levels of retardation. *American Journal of Mental Deficiency, 91,* 313–320.

Blalock, S., DeVellis, B., deVellis, R., & Sauter, S. (1988). Self-evaluation processes and adjustment to rheumatoid arthritis. *Arthritis & Rheumatism, 31,* 1245–1251.

Breslau, N., & Marshall, I. A. (1985). Psychological disturbance in children with physical disabilities: Continuity and change in a 5-year follow-up. *Journal of Abnormal Child Psychology, 13,* 199–215.

Burke, P., Meyer, V., Kocoshis, S., Orenstein, D. M.,

Chandra, R., Nord, D. J., & Sauer, J. (1989). Depression and anxiety in pediatric inflammatory bowel disease and.cystic fibrosis. *Journal of the American Academy of Child and Adolescent Psychiatry, 28*, 948–951.

Butler, J. A., Singer J. D., Palfrey, J. S., & Walker, D. K. (1987). Health insurance coverage and physician use among children with disabilities: Findings from probability samples in five metropolitan areas. *Pediatrics, 79*, 89–98.

Cadman, D., Boyle, M. H., Offord, D. R., Szatmari, P., Rae-Grant, N. I., Crawford, J., & Byles, J. (1986). Chronic illness and functional limitation in Ontario children: Findings of the Ontario Child Health Study. *Canadian Medical Association Journal, 135*, 761–767.

Cadman, D., Boyle, M., Szatmari, P., & Offord, D. R. (1987). Chronic illness, disability, and mental and social well-being: Findings of the Ontario Child Health Study. *Pediatrics, 79*, 805–813.

Canning, E. H., Canning, R. D., & Boyce, W. T. (1992a). Depressive symptoms and adaptive style in children with cancer. *Journal for the American Academy of Child Adolescent Psychiatry, 31*, 1120–1123.

Canning, E. H., Hanser, S. B., Shade, K. A., & Boyce, W. T. (1992b). Mental disorders in chronically ill children: Parent–child discrepancy and physician identification. *Pediatrics, 82*, 692–696.

Chiarelli, F., Tumini, S., Morgese, G., & Albisser, A. M. (1990). Controlled study in diabetic children comparing insulin-dosage adjustment by manual and computer algorithms. *Diabetes Care, 13*, 1080–1084.

Cole, D. A., Vandercook, T., & Rynders, J. (1987). Dyadic interactions between children with and without mental retardation: Effects of age discrepancy. *American Journal of Mental Deficiency, 92*, 194–202.

Costello, E. J., Edelbrock, C., & Costello, A. J. (1988). Psychopathology in pediatric primary care: the new hidden morbidity. *Pediatrics, 82*, 415–424.

Drotar, D., & Crawford, P. (1985). Psychological adaptation of siblings of chronically ill children: Research and practice implications. *Journal of Developmental and Behavioral Pediatrics, 6*, 355–362.

Ebata, A. T., & Moos, R. H. (1991). Coping and adjustment in distressed and healthy adolescents. *Journal of Applied Developmental Psychology, 12*, 33–53.

Eiser, C. (1990). Psychological effects of chronic disease. *Journal of Child Psychology and Developmental Psychiatry, 31*, 85–98.

Feinstein, C., & Berger, K. (1987). The chronically ill or disabled child. In J. D. Noshpitz (Ed.), *Basic handbook of child psychiatry, Vol. 5. Advances and new directions* (pp. 122–131). New York: Basic Books.

Feinstein, C., & Davis, S. (1987). The sibling of the chronically ill or disabled child. In J. D. Noshpitz (Ed.), *Basic handbook of child psychiatry, Vol. 5. Advances and new directions* (pp. 91–96). New York: Basic Books.

Felce, D., de Kock, U., Thomas, M., & Saxby, H. (1986). Change in adaptive behavior of severely and profoundly mentally handicapped adults in different residential settings. *British Journal of Psychology, 77*, 489–501.

Fife, B., Norton, J., & Groom, G. (1987). The family's adaptation to childhood leukemia. *Social Sciences in Medicine, 24*, 159–168.

Frey, K. S., Greenberg, M. T., & Fewell, R. R. (1989). Stress and coping among parents of handicapped children: A multidimensional approach. *American Journal of Mental Retardation, 94*, 240–249.

Fritz, G. K. (1990). Consultation-liaison in child psychiatry and the evolution of pediatric psychiatry. *Psychosomatics, 31*, 85–90.

Fritz, G. K., & Williams, J. R. (1988). Issues of adolescent development for survivors of childhood cancer. *Journal of the American Academy of Child and Adolescent Psychiatry, 27*, 712–715.

Fritz, G. K., Williams, J. R., & Amylon, M. (1988). After treatment ends: psychosocial sequelae in pediatric cancer survivors. *American Journal of Orthopsychiatry, 58*, 552–561.

Gillmore, J. L., & Farina, A. (1989). The social reception of mainstreamed children in the regular classroom. *Journal of Mental Deficiency Research, 33*, 301–311.

Gortmaker, S., & Sappenfield, W. (1984). Chronic childhood disorders: Prevalence and impact. In *Pediatric clinics of North America, 31*, 3–18.

Gostason, R. (1985). Psychiatric illness among the mentally retarded. A Swedish population study. *Acta Psychiatrica Scandinavica* [Suppl.], *318*, 1–117.

Grossman, H. Y., Brink, S., & Hauser, S. T. (1987). Self-efficacy in adolescent girls and boys with insulin-dependent diabetes mellitus. *Diabetes Care, 10*, 324–329.

Guralnick, M. J., & Groom, J. M. (1987a). Dyadic peer interactions of mildly delayed and non-handicapped pre-school children. *American Journal of Mental Deficiency, 92*, 178–193.

Guralnick, M. J., & Groom, J. M. (1987b). The peer relations of mildly delayed and non-handicapped pre-school children in mainstreamed playgroups. *Child Development, 58*, 1556–72.

Hauser, S. T., Jacobson, A. M., Lavori, P., Wolfsorf, J. I., Gerskowitz, R. D., Milley, J. E., Bliss, R., Wertlieb, D., & Stein, J. (1990). Adherence among children and adolescents with insulin-dependent mellitus over a four-year longitudinal follow-up: II. Immediate and long-term linkages with the family milieu. *Journal of Pediatric Psychology, 15*, 527–542.

Hauser, S. T., Jacobson, A. M., Wertlieb, D., Weiss-Perry, B., Follansbee, D., Wolfsdorf, J. I., Herskowitz, R. D., Houlihan, J., & Rajapark, D. C. (1986). Children with recently diagnosed diabetes: Interactions within their families. *Health Psychology, 5*, 273–296.

Heller, A., Rafman, S., Zvagulis, I., & Pless, I. B. (1985). Birth defects and psychosocial adjustment. *American Journal of Diseases of Children, 139*, 257–263.

Hernandez, J., Gary, D., & Lineberger, H. P. (1989). Social and economic indicators of well-being among hemophiliacs over a 5-year period. *General Hospital Psychiatry, 11*, 241–247.

Jacobson, A. M., Hauser, S. T., Lavori, P., Wolfsdorf, J. I., Herkowitz, R. D., Milley, J. E., Bliss, R., Gelfand, E., Wertlieb, D., & Stein, J. (1990). Adherence among children and adolescents with insulin-dependent diabetes mellitus over a four-year longitudinal follow-up: I. The influence of patient coping and adjustment. *Journal of Pediatric Psychology, 15,* 511–526.

Jacobson, A. M., Hauser, S. T., Wertlieb, D., Wolfsdorf, J. I., Orleans, J., & Vieyra, M. (1986). Psychological adjustment of children with recently diagnosed diabetes mellitus. *Diabetes Care, 9,* 323–339.

Jacobson, A. M., Hauser, S. T., Wolfsdorf, J. I., Houlihan, J., Milley, J. E., Herskowitz, R. D. Wertlieb, D., & Watt, E. (1987). Psychologic predictors of compliance in children with recent onset of diabetes mellitus. *Journal of Pediatrics, 110,* 805–811.

Jacobson, A. M., Rand, L. I., & Hauser, S. T. (1985). Psychologic stress and glycemic control: a comparison of patients with and without proliferative diabetic retinopathy. *Psychosomatic Medicine, 47,* 372–381.

Jaudes, P. K., & Diamond, L. J. (1986). Neglect of chronically ill children. *American Journal of Diseases of Children, 140,* 655–658.

Kaiser, A. P., & Blair, G. (1987). Mother-child transactions in families with normal and handicapped children. *Upstate Journal of Medical Science Supplement, 44,* 204–207.

Kovacs, M. (1995). Criterion and predictive validity of the diagnosis of adjustment disorder. *American Journal of Psychiatry, 152* (4), 523–528.

Kovacs, M., Brent, D., Steinberg, T. F., Paulauskas, S., & Reid, J. (1986). Children's self-reports of psychologic adjustment and coping strategies during first year of insulin-dependent diabetes mellitus. *Diabetes Care, 9,* 472–479.

Kovacs, M., Feinberg, T. L., Paulauskas, S., Finkelstein, R., Pollock, M., & Crouse-Novak, M. (1985a). Initial coping responses and psychosocial characteristics of children with insulin-dependent diabetes mellitus. *Journal of Pediatrics, 106,* 827–834.

Kovacs, M., Finkelstein, R., Feinberg, T., Crouse-Novak, M., Paulaukas, P., & Pollock, M. (1985a). Initial psychologic responses of parents to the diagnosis of insulin-dependent diabetes mellitus in their children. *Diabetes Care, 8,* 568–575.

Kovacs, M., Iyengar, S., Goldston, D., Obrosky, D. S., Stewart, J., & Marsh, J. (1990a). Psychological functioning of children with insulin-dependent diabetes mellitus: A longitudinal study. *Journal of Pediatric Psychology, 15,* 619–632.

Kovacs, M., Iyengar, S., Goldston, D., Obrosky, D. S., Stewart, J., & Marsh, J. (1990b). Psychological functioning among mothers of children with insulin-dependent diabetes mellitus: A longitudinal study. *Journal of Consulting and Clinical Psychology, 58,* 189–195.

Kovacs, M., Kass, R. E., Schnell, T. M., Goldston, D., & Marsh, J. (1989). Family functioning and metabolic control of school-aged children with IDDM. *Diabetes Care, 12,* 409–414.

Lane, R. D., Merikangas, K. R., Schwartz, G. E., Huang, S. S., & Prusoff, B. A. (1990). Inverse relationship between defensiveness and lifetime prevalence of psychiatric disorder. *American Journal of Psychiatry, 147,* 573–578.

Leibowitz, A., Manning, Jr., W. G., Keeler, E. B., Duan, N., Lohr, K. N., & Newhouse, J. P. (1985). Effect of cost-sharing on the use of medical services by children: Interim results from a randomized controlled trial. *Pediatrics, 75,* 942–951.

Levenson, J. L. (1992). Psychosocial interventions in chronic medical illness. An overview of outcome research. *General Hospital Psychiatry, 14,* 43–49.

Levy-Schiff, R., Dedem, P., & Sevilla, Z. (1990). Ego identity in mentally retarded adolescents. *American Journal of Mental Retardation, 94,* 541–549.

Matson, J. L., Manikam, R., Coe, D., Raymond, K., Taras, M., & Long, N. (1988). Training social skills to severely mentally retarded multiply handicapped adolescents. *Research in Developmental Disability, 9,* 195–208.

Miller, J. J. (1993). Psychosocial factors related to rheumatic diseases in childhood. *Journal of Rheumatology, 20,* 1–11.

Mink, I. T., & Nihira, K. (1987). Direction of effects: Family life styles and behavior of TMR children. *American Journal of Mental Deficiency, 92,* 57–64.

Minnes, P. M. (1988). Family resources and stress associated with having a mentally retarded child. *American Journal of Mental Retardation, 93,* 184–192.

Mrazek, D. (1988). Asthma: Psychiatric considerations, evaluation, and management. In E. Middleton, C. E. Reed, & E. F. Ellis (Eds.), *Allergy: Principles and practice* (3rd ed., pp. 1176–1196). St. Louis: C. V. Mosby.

Mulhern, R. K., Friedman, A. G., & Stone, P. A. (1988). Acute lymphoblastic leukemia: long-term psychological outcome. *Biomedical Pharmacotherapy, 42,* 243–246.

Newacheck, P. W. (1989). Adolescents with special health needs: Prevalence, severity and access to health services. *Pediatrics, 84,* 872–881.

Newacheck, P. W., Budetti, P. P., & McManus, P. (1984). Trends in childhood disability. *American Journal of Public Health, 74,* 232–236.

Newacheck, P. W., McManus, M. A., & Fox, H. B. (1991). Prevalence and impact of chronic illness among adolescents. *American Journal of Diseases of Children, 145,* 1367–1373.

Nolan, T., Zvagulis, I., & Pless, B. (1987). Controlled trial of social work in childhood chronic illness. *Lancet, 2,* 411–415.

Palmer, R. (1987). Courses of development in mentally retarded persons. *Upstate Journal of Medical Science,* [Suppl.], *44,* 212–216.

Perrin, E. C., Stein, R. E., & Drotar, D. (1991). Cautions in using the child behavior checklist: Observations based on research about children with a chronic illness. *Journal of Pediatric Psychology, 16,* 411–421.

Pless, I. B. (1984). Clinical assessment: Physical and

psychological functioning. *Pediatric Clinics of North America, 31,* 33–45.

Pless, I. B., Cripps, H. A., Davies, J. M., & Wadsworth, M. E. J. (1989). Chronic physical illness in childhood: Psychological and social effects in adolescence and adult life. *Developmental Medicine and Child Neurology, 31,* 746–755.

Pless, I. B., & Nolan, T. (1991). Revision, replication and neglect—Research on maladjustment in chronic illness. *Journal of Child Psychology and Psychiatry, 32,* 347–365.

Pless, I. B., Power, C., & Peckham, C. S. (1993). Long-term psychosocial sequelae of chronic physical disorders in childhood. *Pediatrics, 91,* 1131–1136.

Quirk, M. E., & Young, M. H. (1990). The impact of JRA on children, adolescents and their families. Current research and implications for future studies. *Arthritis Care Research, 3,* 36–43.

Rice, N., Satterwhite, B., & Pless, I. B. (1977). Family counsellors in a pediatric specialty clinic setting. *Social Work and Health Care, 2,* 192–203.

Rutter, M. (1991). Isle of Wight revisited: Twenty-five years of child psychiatric epidemiology. *Journal of the American Academy of Child and Adolescent Psychiatry, 28,* 633–653.

Sabbeth, B., & Stein, R. E. K. (1990). Mental health referral: A weak link in comprehensive care of children with chronic physical illness. *Developmental and Behavioral Pediatrics, 11,* 73–77.

Sawyer, M. G., Toogood, I., Rice, M., Haskell, C., & Baghurst, P. (1989). School performance and psychological adjustment of children treated for leukemia. A long-term follow-up. *American Journal of Hematology and Oncology, 11,* 146–152.

Schowalter, J. (1979). The chronically ill child. In J. D. Noshpitz (Ed.), *Basic handbook of child psychiatry: Vol. 1. Development* (pp. 432–435). New York: Basic Books.

Siegel, D. M. (1987). Adolescents and chronic illness. *Journal of the American Medical Association, 257,* 3396–3399.

Spirito, A., Stark, L. J., Cobiella, C., Drigan, R., Androkites, A., & Hewett, K. (1990). Social adjustment of children successfully treated for cancer. *Child and Family Psychiatry, 15,* 359–371.

Stein, R. E., & Jessop, D. J. (1984a). Does pediatric home care make a difference for children with chronic illness? Findings from the Pediatric Ambulatory Care Treatment Study. *Pediatrics, 73,* 845–853.

Stein, R. E., & Jessop, D. J. (1984b). Relationship between health status and psychological adjustment among children with chronic conditions. *Pediatrics, 73,* 169–174.

Stein, R. E., & Jessop, D. J. (1990). Functional status II(R). A measure of child health status. *Medical Care, 28,* 1041–1055.

Stein, R. E., & Jessop, D. J. (1991). Long-term mental health effects of a pediatric home care program. *Pediatrics, 88,* 490–496.

Stein, R. E., Jessop, D. J., & Riessman, C. K. (1983). Health care services received by children with chronic illness. *American Journal of Diseases of Children, 137,* 225–230.

Steiner, H., & Harris, E. H. (1994). Adaptive style in adolescents with psychosomatic illness. *Acta Paedopsychiatrica, 56,* 255–259.

Steiner, H., & Feldman, S. S. (1995). Two approaches to the measurement of adaptive style: Comparison of normal, psychosomatic, and delinquent adolescents. *Journal of the American Academy of Child and Adolescent Psychiatry, 34* (2), 180–190.

Steiner, H., Fritz, G., Mrazek, D., Gonzales, J., Jensen, P. (1993). Pediatric and psychiatric comorbidity: The future of consultation-liaison psychiatry [Editorial]. *Psychosomatics, 34,* 107–111.

Steiner, H., Rahimzadeh, P., & Lewiston, N. (1990). Psychopathology in anorexia nervosa. *International Journal of Eating Disorders, 9,* 675–683.

Steiner, H., Sanders, M., Canning, E., & Litt, I. (1994). The department of pediatric psychiatry at Children's Hospital at Stanford: A model for managing clinical and personnel issues in C-L psychiatry. *Psychosomatics, 35,* 73–79.

Stoneman, A., Brody, G. H., Davis, C. H., & Crapps, J. M. (1988). Childcare responsibilities, peer relations, and sibling conflict: Older siblings of mentally retarded children. *American Journal of Mental Retardation, 93,* 174–183.

Tavormina, J. B., Boll, T. J., Dunn, N. J., Luscomb, R. L., & Taylor, J. R. (1981). Psychosocial effects on parents of raising a physically handicapped child. *Journal of Abnormal Child Psychology, 9,* 121–131.

Tebbi, C. K., Bromberg, C., & Piedmont, M. (1989). Long-term vocational adjustment of cancer patients diagnosed during adolescence. *Cancer, 63,* 213–218.

Timko, C., Stovel, K. W., Moos, R. H., & Miller, J. J. (1992a). Adaptation to juvenile rheumatic disease: A controlled evaluation of functional disability with a one-year follow-up. *Health Psychology, 11,* 67–76.

Timko, C., Stovel, K. W., Moos, R. H., & Miller, J. J. (1992b). A longitudinal study of risk and resistance factors among children with juvenile rheumatic disease. *Journal of Clinical Child Psychology, 21,* 132–141.

Tritt, S. G., & Esses, L. M. (1988). Psychosocial adaptation of siblings of children with chronic medical illnesses. *American Journal of Orthopsychiatry, 58,* 211–220.

Ungerer, J., Horgan, B., Chaitow, J., & Champion, G. (1988). Psychosocial functioning in children and young adults with juvenile arthritis. *Pediatrics, 81,* 195–202.

Varni, J. W., & Bernstein, B. H. (1991). Evaluation and management of pain in children with rheumatic diseases. *Rheumatic Disease Clinics of North America, 17,* 985–1000.

Varni, J. W., & Wallander, J. L. (1988). Pediatric chronic disabilities: Hemophilia and spina bifida as examples. In D. K. Routh (Eds.), *Handbook of pediatric psychology* (pp. 190–221). New York: Guilford Press.

Walker, L. S., Ortiz-Valdes, J. A., Newbrough, J. R. (1989). The role of maternal employment and depression in the psychological adjustment of chronically ill, mentally retarded, and well children. *Journal of Pediatric Psychology, 14,* 357–370.

Wallander, J. L., & Varni, J. W. (1989). Social support and adjustment in chronically ill and handicapped children. *American Journal of Community Psychology, 17,* 185–201.

Wallander, J. L., Varni, J. W., Babani, L., Banis, H. T., & Wilcox, K. T. (1989). Family resources as resistance factors for psychological maladjustment in chronically ill and handicapped children. *Journal of Pediatric Psychology, 14,* 157–173.

Wallander, J. L., Varni, J. W., Babani, L., DeHaann, C. B., Wilcox, K. T., & Banis, H. T. (1989). The social environment and the adaptation of mothers of physically handicapped children. *Journal of Pediatric Psychology, 14,* 371–387.

Walker, D. K., Stein, R. E., Perrin, E. C., & Jessop, D. J. (1990). Assessing psychosocial adjustment of children with chronic illnesses: A review of the technical properties of PARS III. *Journal of Developmental and Behavioral Pediatrics, 11,* 116–121.

Weiland, S. K., Pless, I. B., & Roghman, K. J. (1992). Chronic illness and mental health problems in pediatric practice: Results from a survey of primary care providers. *Pediatrics, 89,* 445–449.

Weitzman, M., Walker, D. K., & Gortmaker, S. (1986). Chronic illness, psychosocial problems, and school absences. Results of a survey of one county. *Clinical Pediatrics, 25,* 137–141.

Westbom, L. (1992). Well-being of children with chronic illness. A population-based study in a Swedish primary care district. *Acta Paedopsychiatrica, 81,* 625–629.

Whitman, T. L., Borkowski, J. G., Schellenbach, C. J., & Nath, P. S. (1987). Predicting and understanding developmental delay of children of adolescent mothers: A multi-dimensional approach. *American Journal of Mental Deficiency, 92,* 40–56.

Wood, B., Boyle, J. T., Watkins, J. B., Nogueira, J., Zimand, E., & Carroll, L. (1988). Sibling psychological status and style as related to the disease of their chronically ill brothers and sisters: Implications for models of biopsychosocial interaction. *Journal of Developmental and Behavioral Pediatrics, 9,* 66–72.

Zevon, M. A., Neubauer, N. A., & Green, D. M. (1990). Adjustment and vocational satisfaction of patients treated during childhood or adolescence for acute lymphoblastic leukemia. *American Journal of Pediatric Hematology Oncology, 12,* 454–461.

25 / Human Immunodeficiency Virus Infection and AIDS

Penelope Krener Knapp

Scope of the Illness

Acquired immunodeficiency syndrome (AIDS) is the result of infection by human immunodeficiency virus (HIV-1), which destroys thymus-derived lymphocytes bearing the CD4 molecule, resulting in secondary immunodeficiency and severe, protean disease manifestations. HIV disease is a socially opportunistic infection, flourishing in host societies that have deficient basic health care distribution. Child psychiatrists, unless their practice is rarefied, deal with minorities, molested and chronically ill children, and sexually active adolescents both heterosexual and homosexual, and are therefore likely to encounter HIV-infected youngsters.

The original definition of AIDS from the Centers for Disease Control was based on 3 criteria: history of a risk factor, laboratory evidence of immunodeficiency, and evidence of HIV-1 infection (Centers for Disease Control, 1987). Using that definition, there were an estimated 10,000 children with HIV infection in the United States in 1991 and, through 1990, 2,786 cases of pediatric full-blown AIDS (Centers for Disease Control, 1991), defined as laboratory evidence of immunodeficiency associated with a previous risk factor and secondary complications such as multiple recurrent bacterial infections or lymphoid interstitial pneumonia. Effective January 1, 1993, the new definition allows AIDS to be diagnosed if there are fewer than 200 CD4 lymphocytes per cubic millimeter and adds pulmonary tuberculosis, recurrent pneumonia, and cervical cancer as indicator diseases. This change greatly increases the official prevalence of AIDS.

The populations most vulnerable to HIV infection through intravenous drug use are those that have the least basic medical care in our society. For adolescents, overlapping risk categories exist: psychiatric symptoms, possible emerging homosexuality drug use, or runaway status, often responded to with fragmented services. Families may experience financial and social depletion as several family members may be infected. In responding to the needs of HIV-positive infants, children, and adolescents, the psychiatrist may carry out direct psychiatric evaluation and treatment of child patients, multidisciplinary consultation, family evaluation, and awareness of ethical issues and caregiver strain.

Epidemiology

FREQUENCY OF OCCURRENCE

At the outset of the AIDS epidemic, in the early 1980s, 97% of cases were among men. Ten years later, 11.5% of adult and adolescent cases reported were among women. The acceleration of the epidemic is shown by the fact that reports of AIDS cases increased 23% from 1989 to 1990, and, based on year of diagnosis, the number of cases increased by 7%. Difference in reports and cases are due to effects of cases reported in 1990 and diagnosed earlier, and cases diagnosed in 1990 but not yet reported. In both comparisons, "the largest proportionate increase occurred among women, blacks and Hispanics, persons living in the South . . . and persons exposed to HIV through heterosexual contact" (*Morbidity & Mortality Weekly Report,* 1991). Risk factors for HIV infection are perinatal transmission, injection of infected blood, and sexual contact with an infected person. The most common route of infection for children (80% of pediatric AIDS cases; Parks & Scott, 1990) is perinatal infection from an infected mother in utero, during delivery, or when nursing. The second most common source of pediatric HIV-1 infection is transfusion, but this is declining. The third source of infection is through adolescent risk behaviors. Preinatal infection rates are highest in areas of high seroprevalence; the geo-graphical distribution of HIV-1-infected women and children mirrors the AIDS epidemic pattern. Cesarean sections have not been shown to reduce risk of HIV transmission (Blanche et al., 1989), although results are conflicting (Italian Multicentre Study, 1988). Breast-feeding has been reported in very few cases to transmit HIV, and instances of HIV-positive mothers who breast-fed their babies and did not transmit the virus have been reported. In the United States, the Public Health Service recommends against an HIV-positive mother breast-feeding, but the World Health Organization supports breast-feeding in developing countries and in very low socioeconomic status environments, because in severe poverty, infant malnutrition is a greater risk than is HIV transmission through breast milk (World Health Organization, 1987). The same principle applies to inner-city poor in the United States. Sexual molestation by an HIV-infected adult is a documented source of HIV infection in children (Gutman et al., 1991). Transmission patterns and some clinical manifestations of HIV disease in children are different from those in adults; the definition of AIDS in children under 13 from the Centers for Disease Control differs from that in adults; multiple recurrent bacterial infections and lymphoid interstitial pneumonia and pulmonary lymphoid hyperplasia are also accepted as indicative of AIDS in children. Racial and ethnic minority children comprise the majority of perinatally transmitted AIDS cases. In 1991 there was an increase of 33.2% of reported cases in women, of 16.7% in children 0 to 4, of 34.8% in children 5 to 9, and of 39.6% among those 10 to 19 years old (*Morbidity & Mortality Weekly Report,* 1991). Prevalence in children under 13 is related to exposure; in 1989, the Centers for Disease Control reported 57% born to mothers who are intravenous drug users or partners of such users, 19% born to mothers who are partners of HIV-infected men, 17% infected by receiving infected blood or blood products, and 7% with unspecified source of infection. However, the percentages change each year; the number of children infected by blood products is not increasing while the number of HIV-positive women with infection associated with intravenous drug use is increasing steadily.

The HIV epidemic is a mosaic of local epidemics with specific characteristics. Ten metropolitan areas in the United States account for 55% of all cases, and the characteristics vary from one area to another: Examples from 6 of the U.S. cities with the highest rates of pediatric HIV infection illustrate this: In New York, New York, Newark, New Jersey, and San Juan, Puerto Rico, pediatric AIDS is related to maternal intravenous drug use. In Miami, Florida, pediatric AIDS is related to heterosexual activity as infected infants' mothers are from parts of the world where heterosexual spread of HIV is common. In Los Angeles, California, pediatric AIDS is related to infants receiving infected blood and blood products.

Because of its variable distribution, it has been said of HIV infection that "geography is destiny." This relates not only to seroprevalence in the community but also to mores that may affect the likelihood of adolescents engaging in risk behaviors related to HIV infection. In seeking to control the epidemic, it would be valuable for public health officials to know what risk behavior patterns exist in different segments of the population, in order to target educational and treatment interventions. Unfortunately, political obstacles exist to doing this. For example, a Centers for Disease Control survey of health habits among 11,631 students in grades 9 to 12 showed that over half had had sexual intercourse but less than half of those had used condoms; nevertheless, in July 1991, the Federal Department of Health and Human Services suspended plans for a large, detailed survey of teenage sex habits after being pressured by conservative politicians who objected to questions about homosexual behavior and other topics.

CLINICAL FEATURES

HIV-1 infection produces extremely varied symptoms because the virus affects multiple systems. Clinical disease may be heralded by nonspecific symptoms such as failure to thrive, generalized lymphadenopathy, hepatosplenomegaly, candidiasis, parotitis, or chronic diarrhea. *Pneumocystis carinii* pneumonia is the most common opportunistic infection, diagnosed by finding the virus in endotracheal aspirates, bronchial washings, or lung tissue. Candida esophagitis is common and is confirmed by endoscopy with biopsy and culture. Lymphocytic interstitial pneumonitis is common; confirmed by lung biopsy, it may be insidious and either static or progressive, resulting in chronic lung disease. Increasingly recurrent bacterial infections are seen. Central nervous system abnormalities have been described in as many as 50 to 90% of HIV-infected children and range from mild developmental delay to progressive encephalopathy. There are other clinical manifestations in the renal, cardiac, or hematologic systems (Parks & Scott, 1990).

Hauger, Nicholas, and Caspe (1991) have provided an excellent current review of guidelines for care of all aspects of HIV infection in pediatric patient population. Fourteen articles summarize the report of the New York State Department of Health AIDS Institute Criteria committee for the care of HIV-infected children providing detailed medical information about the disorder. Children with AIDS are intermittently quite ill, and may endure repeated diagnostic and treatment interventions. The next section addresses certain medical features of HIV infection at different ages and stages with developmental and psychosocial sequelae.

Pregnancy and Birth: HIV and intravenous drug abuse do not inhibit fertility, but immune function is depressed during pregnancy. Although definitive studies confirming the theory that HIV would progress more rapidly during pregnancy have not been done, a pregnancy in an HIV-positive woman is a high-risk pregnancy and deserves early and careful managment. The exact route of perinatal transmission is not clear. The virus has been identified in fetuses at 15 weeks. The infant could be infected during labor and delivery. In rare instances an infant may be infected from the breast milk of an infected woman (Oxtoby, 1988). The estimated risk of an HIV-infected mother giving birth to an HIV-infected infant is 20 to 30% (European Collaborative Study, 1988; Italian Mulitcentre Study, 1988; Thomas & New York City Perinatal HIV Transmission Collaborative Study Group, 1989).

Infancy: Many infants will test positive for HIV antibody at birth, but this may reflect maternal antibodies. The median age of presentation of perinatally acquired infection is 8 to 12 months. Definitive diagnosis can be better made after maternal antibodies disappear, in 9 to 15 months for HIV. Seventy-nine percent of infants are symptomatic by 24 months (Persaud et al., 1992), and longitudinal studies show a bimodal distribution in disease expression, with a subgroup of children showing early immunodeficiency and rapid decline, and the majority having a slowly progressive course and longer survival (Blanche et al, 1990). There have been reports of infants who are HIV infected but antibody negative and reports of infants who become antibody negative when maternal antibodies disappear and then become antibody positive later (Scott et al., 1985). HIV-infected infants frequently remain asymptomatic for the first 4 months of life. Then they may develop anemia, failure to thrive, fever, chronic diarrhea, and thrush. Loss of developmental milestones is common. Until the child is clinically symptomatic, development progresses well, even if the mother is HIV infected (Nozyce et al., 1994a). HIV-1 directly infects cells in the central nervous system, producing both neoplastic involvement and an encephalopathy. Neurological symptoms or evidence of encephalopathy have been noted in 65% of children, and some have neuropsychological deterioration with progressive loss of developmental milestones and cognitive functioning. Adequate nutrition may be a problem. Common childhood infections are more severe. Two incubation period distributions have been found, a short incubation period (median 4.1 months) and a long incubation period (median 6.1 years).

Children: Children are less likely than adults to develop Kaposi's sarcoma and B cell lymphoma, but they develop other malignancies. Bacterial sepsis and lymphoid interstitial pneumonitis are serious problems for HIV-infected children. HIV is neurotrophic and infects a variety of central nervous system-derived cell types with protean neurological manifestations. AIDS encephalitis, the most severe of these infections, affects 7.3% of people with AIDS, with highest prevalence in individuals over 75 years and under 15 years (Janssen, Nwanyanwu, Lelik, & Stehr-Green, 1990). In a study (Persaud et al., 1992) of children diagnosed after age 4, 75% were symptomatic, but 83% of the asymptomatic children had physical signs, such as generalized lymphadenopathy, consistent with HIV-1 infection. Of the symptomatic children, 42% had histories of recurrent infections, and 21% had hematologic abnormalities such as thrombocytopenia, epistaxis, or anemia, as presenting man-

ifestations. The median age of survivors in this study was 8.2 years (range 4 to 14 years). Abnormalities of the cellular and humoral immune systems may prevent normal response to childhood vaccines. The Centers for Disease Control has made specific recommendations for immunization of HIV-infected children. Progression of HIV disease differs in children who received infected blood products and those who were perinatally infected. The progression of HIV disease is faster in those transfused as very small premature infants. Hemophilia patients who are HIV infected develop more normally and remain at an asymptomatic stage of infection longer than perinatally infected infants. However, when clinical AIDS develops, the course of the disease is similar in the two groups.

Adolescents: At highest risk of HIV infection are disenfranchised inner-city youngsters using drugs and engaging in unprotected sex. Underreporting is related to poor medical care for this group and to competing risks for mortality from accidents, homicide, and suicide. Frequency of AIDS in adolescents rises with age; the long incubation period indicates that many 20- to 29-year-olds reported as adult cases were infected as adolescents. The proportion of females to males is higher (1:7) in adolescents than in adults (1:15), indicating heterosexual spread in a population of childbearing age. It is recommended that HIV testing be reserved for patients with risk factors and done with written informed consent of parent(s) or guardian(s).

Psychosomatic Aspects of HIV Infection

CLINICAL ASPECTS

Psychiatric needs of children with AIDs are similar to those of children with cancer or catastrophic chronic illness, except that their families' function also may be compromised by HIV infection. Grandparents or older siblings may be forced into primary parental roles. Forming a therapeutic alliance with a core caregiver who is supported by a multidisciplinary team is most helpful to patients and families over the long course of the illness.

HIV infection is a chronic illness for most children. Those with perinatal infection may live to middle school age or early adolescence. This necessitates multiple clinic visits, many hospitalizations, successions of medications, nutritional and growth compromise, missed school, and, often, developmental delay. Central nervous system involvement may complicate developmental delay.

A review of transmission categories reveals that over 80% of children with AIDS have families with AIDS. Losses and missed childhood experiences result from the illness. Grief and bereavement are common concomitants. Intravenous drug abuse in families of children with AIDS brings with it family dysfunction, poverty, and poor compliance with medical recommendations. The burden of caring for a chronically ill child is thus borne by families that are bereaved or handicapped by AIDS-related illnesses, including AIDS dementia complex or associated substance abuse disorders. Ill parents' clinical course may be accelerated if they only have energy enough for their children's clinic visits or money enough for their children's medications. Provision of social and medical services for the entire family is necessary to support the child's care. Care for children who are orphaned or whose parents are incapacitated is better carried out in foster homes, group homes, or community-based alternatives to inpatient care, but these are generally lacking and should be developed in all communities.

CONSULTATION ISSUES

Decisions about what information to give children and who should give it must be made with reference to the child's level of cognitive development, the family's stage of disclosure to their community, and the relationship between the child and the medical caregiver. Communication must be coordinated among caregivers in several subspecialities who sometimes have a range of training, from volunteers to principal investigators with grants from the National Institute of Mental Health. Forty-five percent of white and 88% of nonwhite children with AIDS acquired the disease from an intravenous drug–using parent. Therefore, the psychiatric consultant must be conversant with substance abuse and with subculture and minority values and customs. The consultation-liaison psychiatrist must be able to help caregivers

of children with AIDS deal with feelings not usually encountered in pediatrics: *contempt* for families whose behavior they blame for the child's illness; *fear* of contagion; *grief* when they care for a child who dies; and *burnout,* the well-described constellation of exhaustion, depersonalization, and feeling of failure. In a national survey of expertise, knowledge, and attitudes of child and adolescent psychiatrists about AIDS, it was found that 52% had provided consultation to or treatment for a minor with HIV infection. The authors noted that there was a tendency for those with less experience to also be less educated about the disease (Brown, Etemad, Brenman, & Dwight, 1991).

Impact of HIV Infection on Children and Adolescents

PSYCHOSOCIAL IMPLICATIONS OF RECENT TREATMENT ADVANCES

Enzyme-linked immunosorbent assay (ELISA) and Western Blot tests detect IgG antibodies. Disadvantages of this type of testing for at-risk newborns is that maternal antibody is also measured, so that a child who is actually free of infection may not be identified as uninfected until as late as 15 months of age. Psychosocial complications of this uncertainty are extensive for so-called boarder babies or AIDS orphans awaiting placement. New tests detecting IgA antibodies, formed only in an infected infant, not in an infected mother, and assays using recombinant antigens may be sensitive and specific means of screening infant sera (Martin et al., 1991).

The progression of HIV disease differs in children who received infected blood products and in those who were perinatally infected. Since transfusion was the first and largest cause of pediatric AIDS, clinical response patterns must shift as the source of infection moves toward predominantly perinatal infection. The age of transfusion affects the course of the disease. Children transfused in the newborn period become symptomatic within 6 months to 3 years, and the progression is faster in those transfused as premature infants. Older children with hemophilia infected through receiving blood products have a more benign course initially, although the final states of the illness are similar and the outcome is equally bleak. Some children with perinatal infection live much longer than the newborns perinatally infected through transfusion; the cohort of the first children infected from infected mothers is now school age, and they live with HIV as a chronic illness. HIV infection is commonly a neurological disorder (Cohen et al., 1991). Patients with encephalitis have neuronal loss, possibly due to decreased neuronal viability as a result of interaction of HIV envelope protein with specific neurotransmitter receptors.

Treatment of the infected person consists of supportive care: passive immunization, antibiotics, and nutrition. The efficacy of intravenous gamma globulin has been established. A study of patients randomized to treatment or control begun in March 1988 has been stopped because an independent review group (the Data Safety and Monitoring Board) determined that a subset of the treatment group (with T4 lymphocyte count greater than 200 cells/mm^3) had fewer infections. However, children with T4 lymphocyte count less than 200 cells per cubic millimeter did not benefit, confirming that early treatment is more effective to prolong life (AIDS Clinical Trials Alert, 1991). Antiretroviral drug therapy with zidovudine (Retrovir, or AZT) reduces morbidity, especially in children with AIDS dementia or encephalopathy. Assessment of neuropsychological functioning should be done with formal testing of perceptual abilities, problem solving, adaptive behavior, language, attention, memory, and learning.

Treatment research approaches whittle away at the problem of HIV infection from every angle. Efforts to develop a vaccine continue, but because of the chimerical behavior of the virus envelope, this vaccine problem is harder than any heretofore solved by virologists and immunologists. The new drugs target the identified stages of the infection process. New delivery systems have been developed for existing drugs. New antibacterials to combat the opportunistic infections are also being developed, and combinations of existing drugs are undergoing clinical trials.

DEVELOPMENTAL PERSPECTIVES

The spread of HIV is a medical epidemic and also a social one. The care provider for patients with HIV infection operates in several dimensions of the epidemic. One dimension is that of the progression of HIV infection within the individual, as a chronic illness eventuating in his or her death. Another dimension is the psychosocial context of the individual person with AIDS. Caring for an HIV-infected person, especially as an outpatient, requires understanding these aspects of the patient's life: What is the person's cultural context and how is illness dealt with in that culture? Is the family intact? Is the family functional, or are family members ill or addicted? Is there a previous illness, such as hemophilia? Has the patient a mental illness or substance abuse disorder as well as HIV infection? How poor or socially isolated is the patient?

Over the course of a protracted illness, the individual patient continues to grow as a person. Children achieve developmental milestones, acquire new knowledge, and become unforgettable parts of the lives of the adults who nurture them. Adult patients whose lives are cut short by a terminal illness compress into the truncated span an intense revisiting of their own most personal issues, and attempt to resolve and complete their relationships and creations.

Adolescents become a special risk group as they evolve into sexual activity and possibly experimentation with drugs. If they have a psychiatric disorder, this risk is compounded. DiClemente, Ponton, and Hartley (1991), describing HIV-related risk factors in psychiatrically hospitalized adolescents, identify cutting practices using shared sharp tools as a special risk behavior in this group. Hospitalized adolescents also exhibit more of other types of HIV-related risk behaviors, such as intravenous drug use, sharing needles, unprotected intercourse, and multiple sexual partners. Risk factors cluster for troubled adolescents; those who had been sexually molested were 1.6 times as likely to report cutting behavior. The child psychiatrist should be aware of double and triple jeopardy for HIV risk as for other psychosocial disorders in this vulnerable group.

Homeless adolescents, now estimated at 1.5 million in the United States (Children's Defense Fund, 1988) are at special risk because of high rates of intravenous drug use and because to survive they must expose themselves to unprotected sex. Although it has been shown possible to track and to make effective AIDS prevention interventions with these youths (Rotheram-Borus, Miller, Koopman, Haignere, & Selfridge, 1991), resources are insufficient to meet the need.

CONSEQUENCES FOR ADOLESCENCE AND ADULTHOOD

HIV antibody testing should be accompanied by pre- and posttest counseling. Suicidal ideation and attempts peak immediately after a person receives news that he or she is HIV positive. Learning of seropositivity is truly a personal crisis. The doctor whom the person will want to discuss this with is most frequently the one who recommended the testing. It might be the child psychiatrist, or it might be a pediatrician or family practitioner who may turn to a mental health professional for advice about how to help the youngster. Anyone seeking voluntary testing is self-defining him- or herself as being in a so-called risk group. Thus pre- and posttest counseling for those who are seronegative is an opportunity for primary prevention.

The pilot work of O'Dowd and her group (personal communication, 1992) at Montefiore Hospital, in the Bronx, New York, addresses suicidality in HIV-infected young adults. In the early findings of a longitudinal study, their outpatient HIV population was surveyed for suicidality. Higher levels of present/recent suicidal ideation were found in populations with AIDS Related Complex and HIV than in AIDS and HIV patients. Possible explanations considered include altered perceptions resulting from organic brain disease in the AIDS population, the refocusing of attention in AIDS Related Complex patients to the real crisis of illness, or demographic differences between groups, as the AIDS patients had a higher proportion of gay males and may be psychologically more stable than the other groups in the studied population.

SPECIFIC PSYCHOSOCIAL INFLUENCES OF HIV INFECTION

Although HIV infection produces chronic illness, it differs from other chronic childhood illnesses in specific ways: It is interrelated with severe psychosocial problems or with other severe illnesses, it is stigmatized, it is likely to affect those with minimal resources, and it uniquely taxes caregivers. The most rapid rate of increase of HIV infection is in intravenous drug users. Among women and children, the epidemic is spreading primarily among such users, their partners, and their infants. Fifty-two percent of women with AIDS are intravenous drug users, and 78% are of peak childbearing age. The demographic and clinical prevalence of pediatric AIDS patients has increased steadily, but the distribution of infections among etiologic risk factors has remained fairly constant, with perinatal (vertical) transmission continuing to account for 80%. Thus, trends in female AIDS cases may predict future trends for AIDS in children, and the epidemic is a family problem. Intravenous drug users, although an identified risk group, still face long waiting lists for drug treatment programs. Some pregnant mothers, knowing that their infants may be removed from their care at birth if they have positive toxicology screens, may postpone prenatal care in order to avoid detection, hoping in the meantime to find a solution to their addiction.

Child psychiatrists may become involved with the high-risk mother-infant pair if a consultation is requested at the time of delivery to assess parenting skills. Application of techniques of evaluating mother-infant bonding and infant neurologic maturity and modulation may assist in identifying infants who will be difficult to parent or mothers who have limited parenting skills. Screening instruments for use by nurses on the postpartum floor may help to identify high-risk mother-infant pairs and direct them for psychiatric consultation. However, if no clinical facilities exist to accept referral, and if there are budgetary constraints which prevent augmenting nursing personnel to meet the patients' needs, there may be administrative resistance even to screening.

Reduction of illicit drug use is the first line of defense against perinatal transmission. However, nationally there is a severe lack of accessible treatment programs, necessary especially for pregnant women. Intravenous drug use treatment plus education on safe sex and injection practices have been shown to be effective in reducing risk of HIV infection (Des Jarlais & Friedman, 1987). Education effectiveness depends on the vehicle of education; knowledge is not enough. Numerous studies show a high level of information is accompanied, especially in adolescents, by ongoing high-risk behavior (Brown & Fritz, 1988). Studies of various educational approaches to change in attitude or behavior show that personal experience (e.g., in workshops and discussion sessions) is more effective than is vicarious experience (e.g., by listening to People with AIDS speakers), which are in turn more effective than lectures or brochures with information only.

Active advocacy is necessary to develop the clinical and outreach treatment programs needed to carry out preventive intervention once high-risk infants and families are identified. Advocacy for the at-risk pediatric patient and for the patient who is ill with AIDS requires proficiency in the tactics of accessing social security, Medicare, health services, legal counsel, and mental health resources. Consultants must be sensitive to the pressures experienced by immediate caregivers: relatives, volunteers, or community workers. To provide emotional support, the caregiver must be trained in counseling, grieving, and active listening skills, and be able to offer friendship along with clinical skill. Practical needs may include providing cooking, shopping, cleaning, transportation, child care, respite care, and personal services to the homebound patient. Families may be isolated, alienated, and lacking support from the rest of their community, or be rejected and discriminated against, so an additional burden falls upon the health care worker. Political awareness requires documenting medical services to satisfy utilization review, particularly for unreimbursed patients.

Children with HIV infection are chronically ill but may have special burdens to bear beyond those of generic chronic illness. Some youngsters with vertical transmission, infected perinatally, may not be diagnosed until they are past infancy, after patterns of failure to thrive and recurrent infections are linked with seropositivity. When hospitalized, often they must stay longer than the other patients on the pediatric service, recovering more slowly from infections and experiencing more complications. In caring for them, nursing staff must be sensitive to the usual issues of separation and apprehension in the hospitalized child, but also to chronic disappointments. HIV-infected children must linger in the hospital but see other children recover and leave. They face the challenge of being cared for by a large number of physicians and nurses. Their families may not visit because of inability to manage the expense of travel to the hospital, because they are ill themselves, or because they are dysfunctional. When

HIV-positive children form attachments to other children in the hospital who have more functional families, their own deprivation is accentuated. They may have bitter days when they expect to go home and then the discharge is postponed because of a relapse or complication. Understanding the complex and intersecting reasons for making a medical decision about readiness for discharge may be too difficult for children who have not achieved the level of formal operations information processing. Therefore, young children may experience the informative contingencies presented by a caring physician as broken promises.

Clinicians and volunteers alike caring for youngsters with HIV infection have difficulty maintaining a balance between overinvolvement, which may deflect energy from other patients, and underinvolvement, which may result in inadequate care. Moreover, patients do not always express their emotional needs in pleasant ways. The clinical and pharmacological management of organic central nervous system sequelae is difficult. Serial diagnostic psychometric assessment is important to corroborate clinical intuition, and if the patient at home develops delerium, it is necessary to furnish adequate medication so that home care workers are not physically and personally drained.

Impact of HIV Infection on the Family

FAMILY INFLUENCES ON THE INDIVIDUAL CHILD'S DEVELOPMENT

The literature on families' accommodation to children's chronic illness is vast. Typically, the child and family are studied once the illness has developed, although conceivably the parenting of a child with vertical infection by HIV, who might remain well for months or years, could be before and after clinical symptoms develop. Because the majority of children with HIV disease have become infected through vertical transmission or through treatment with blood products because of a genetic condition (hemophilia), the family may carry a particular burden of feeling responsible for the child's illness. This will influence their implementation of nurturance and discipline, although if there is ongoing parental pathology, such as substance abuse, this will affect parenting competence as well (Black et al., 1994; Melvin & Sherr, 1993). Separation of family factors which have contributed to HIV exposure from family factors resulting from infection is difficult; Havens et al. (1994) have found that high rates of behavioral and psychiatric morbidity were present both in school-age children with HIV infection and in seroreverted and non-HIV exposed, nonreferred children living in foster placement after exposure to maternal drug addiction.

Developmental compromise commences when children become ill (Papola, Alvarez, & Cohen, 1994) and has been shown to correlate with CT scan brain abnormalities (Wolters et al., 1995). The general picture is consistent with subcortical dysfunction (March & McCall, 1994), which influences the child's availability for all learning, including the social learning which occurs in the family.

Because the child is chronically ill, behavioral and developmental delay may be ascribed entirely to the general features of illness and central nervous system infection treatable by the retrovirus may be overlooked. Standardized testing is necessary, as subtle changes may be missed on mental status examination.

THE INFLUENCES OF THE CHILD'S ILLNESS ON THE FAMILY

Families of children with AIDS often are ill themselves. The infected child may be an orphan or the parents may be ill or addicted. In hemophilia families, transfusion and sexual contact may have infected several family members. Gay couples raising children may be seropositive. Adequate psychiatric care for any child involves working with the family; when the child has AIDS, it requires working with a family that may be ill, bereaved, or blighted by substance abuse and its sequelae. Decisions such as whether to undertake the risk of breast-feeding by a seropositive mother should be made in the context of the family's means to provide the infant with adequate alternative nutrition.

Within households, casual contact such as touching, bathing, dressing, and sharing kitchen and eating utensils does not transmit HIV. The U.S. Public Health Services has issued guidelines for caring for HIV-infected children in day care, foster care, and schools. Children should attend, but special precautions should be taken if they lack control of body secretions, if they mouth toys, if they have cuts with bleeding, or if they bite. Risks to the immunosuppressed child of being exposed to common infections in school or day care should be assessed continually by the child's physician and family in consultation with school and public health officials. A recent study of knowledge and attitudes of child care providers (Coleman, 1992) indicates that they were more cautious and less accepting of children with AIDS than would be predicted by their level of knowledge, indicating that strategies for further education are needed.

Outpatient issues in caring for the child with HIV infection go beyond the usual problems of chronic illness, growth, nutrition, and well-being because of the child's vulnerability to infections and to discrimination, even in a situation where the school is accepting. Decisions about field trips, sleepovers with friends, and the special importance of birthday parties are all charged because of pressure to allow children special experiences but to protect them from ordinary risks, and because there will be fewer birthdays.

HELPING PROFESSIONALS

The HIV epidemic is in its second decade, and it is already clear that it will cut short a generation of young gay men, of families with hemophilia, and of intravenous drug users and their children. The first generation of care providers are also beginning to be lost, either because they themselves are ill or seropositive or because they are exhausted and/or burned out.

Child psychiatrists will increasingly be asked to consult with clinicians and commuity programs whose clients are infected with HIV (Krener & Miller, 1989). To serve these clients, they must deal with untimely death and venture into clinically alien terrains of poverty, chronic illness, and subcultural differences. Training in various therapeutic modalities will insulate them only a little from the erosive losses of caring for dying young people. Their insights into their own countertransference vulnerabilities offer limited protection from the professional self-doubts stirred by serving disenfranchised, addicted, or bereaved clients who are overwhelmed and for whom the consultant cannot command auxiliary services.

To go beyond skills furnished by traditional pediatric and psychiatric training, it is necessary to understand well the elements of liason in hospital settings. The psychiatric consultant must learn from those without the bias of medical training, persons who have worked without pressures of time or reimbursement directly with the children and families whose lives have been mortally infected with the virus. Provision of social and medical services for the entire family is necessary to support the child's care, but current models of health care delivery usually are organized along specialty lines, which practically exclude a parent and child from the same clinic. Orchestration of care among providers on the team caring for the child, and confidence in working in nonmedical settings is necessary for serving children with a chronic illness which threatens the life span and which compromises development (Krener, 1996). Consulting to the special needs of HIV-positive children in schools and daycare settings (Gross & Larkin, 1996) requires the medically trained person to approach such settings with confidence and respect. Contribution of medical knowledge to the educational challenge of AIDS has been shown to be successful (Schonfeld et al., 1995).

Recommendations and Suggestions for Psychiatric Interventions

PRIMARY PREVENTION

The child psychiatrist may have an important role in primary prevention, and also may be consulted at the time a decision is made to test a youth for seropositivity. Enzyme-linked immunosorbent assay (ELISA) tests are run in duplicate on initially positive or borderline sera. Confirmation tests of positive results are performed by Western Blot. HIV antibody testing should be accompanied by pre- and posttest counseling, as this is an opportunity for education of at-risk seronegative persons and for early intervention with those who are seropositive. Suicidal ideation and attempts peak immediately after a person receives news that he or she is HIV-positive; this is a time of personal crisis when the clinician must be available to patients.

Partner notification (contact tracing) by law must be carried out voluntarily, but to be effective it should be complemented by other outreach and educational interventions. Adolescents' therapists and care providers should take a careful history of drug use and sexual activity. It should be determined what substances adolescents use, by what route, and with whom. It is important to emphasize public health aspects, not "being a narc," to persuade youths to disclose contacts. Sexual activity should be queried in more detail than was the clinical custom before this epidemic. The youngster should be asked about his or her sexual preference, number of partners, and specific practices. The therapist should ask whether and how the youngster is able to say no to unprotected sex. Contraception and protection are likewise topics for basic history-taking as a preventive intervention. While barrier contraceptives can protect against HIV infection, the failure rate of condoms is 5 to 15%. History-taking is an opportunity for educational intervention.

As has been shown repeatedly in public health efforts to contain venereal disease, knowledge does not reliably translate into behavioral change. Ponton, DiClemente, & McKenna (1991) have developed and tried an HIV prevention program for psychiatrically hospitalized adolescents in context of a general sex education program. It is multidisciplinary, involves both parents and staff, uses peer group support, and addresses specific risk behaviors by providing not only knowledge but also training in prevention strategies. Rotheram-Borus, Miller, Koopman, Haignere, & Selfridge (1991) have developed an intervention for runaways that emphasizes the development of personal knowledge and acquisition of specific skills to modify risk behaviors. Although the runaway group is highly vulnerable, high-risk behavior patterns were eliminated after a 10- to 15-session intervention through a 6-month follow-up period.

CARING FOR THE ILL CHILD OR ADOLESCENT

Because children affected by HIV infection are exposed through social ailments such as intravenous drug abuse and not only through medical events such as transfusion, those who care for them must be skilled in more than medical care.

For the child to live with a chronic illness, work must be done with the family, which may be ailing or dysfunctional. Coordination with the school is necessary to protect the child from discrimination or avoidable infection. If substance abuse is ongoing in the child's family, social agencies will intervene. No single caregiver can have all of the skills or all of the energy needed to meet the needs of a child with AIDS. Working in multidisciplinary teams buffers one individual's feeling of being unable to give all that is needed. This is essential in hospital and in outpatient work, but in neither setting is reimbursement geared for liaison efforts on a patient's behalf.

When the child goes to a clinic or is hospitalized, the prospect of integrating nursing care with volunteer care may challenge the comfortable division of professional and nonprofessional roles. Nurses and parents may greatly need the volunteer to help sustain the child through procedures and hospital separations. Volunteers are not permitted to read medical charts, and they depend on medical personnel to inform them of all that the child is about to experience, so they can prepare the child. For pediatricians and pediatric nurses, taking care of dying children is a departure from the expected mission of making children well, and depending on an individual without medical training to support them and their patient is a departure from the usual professional expectation of competence and mastery. Medical caregivers' negative feelings about the dsyfunctional families, particularly of infants, may further confuse their therapeutic alliance.

CARING FOR THE CAREGIVER

The health care worker or volunteer who is HIV infected may exist in a state of suspended fear and incomplete grief. Examples are persons who are recovering addicts, gay, or hemophiliac. Identification with the ill person and loyalty to a shared group make them ready to involve themselves in the intense physical and emotional care required. Health care providers may be HIV positive but fear discovery, malpractice, loss of occupation and of their patients at a time when they feel indispensible as health care providers. Mental health providers have countertransference, identification anxiety, and depression. Successive losses with no chance to grieve between bereavements, and the attrition of whole friendship circles and support groups, leach the energies of this special group who might be particularly effective caregivers. Although limited by time and by reimbursement and system constraints in the amount of direct service they can provide to AIDS patients, child psychiatrists can offer individual and group psychotherapy services to other outreach workers and to volunteers

Recognizing symptoms of burnout enables the psychiatric consultant to devise strategies to relieve the stressed caregiver. Group and individual therapeutic support is essential to protect committed care providers whose personal involvement with the epidemic may make them feel there are no outs, not even burnout, and who may live under pressures that may make them more vulnerable and less able to help their clients.

Fear and prejudice have been excited by the HIV epidemic at the highest levels (Gostin, 1990a,b). As noted by the President's Commission on AIDS, the United States is currently the only developed nation that does not have an integrated national policy on AIDS. A recent sampling of lobbyists found that 90% of them had experienced more resistance to adopting policies helpful to HIV-infected infants and children than they had encountered with other policies for children. This was ascribed by 68% of respondents to the possibility that children with AIDS were stigmatized by their association with "identified high-risk populations," namely homosexuals and intravenous drug users (Clemo, 1992). The political reaction to this major epidemiological challenge has been as changeable as the viral envelope itself. No two states have exactly the same response. From a sociological point of view, the AIDS epidemic is now burgeoning as a result of the most tenacious of our unsolved social problems—drug abuse and poverty. From an economic point of view, the victims of the epidemic are being served by the most financially unstable portions of our health care delivery system: public health and community hospitals and clinics. Resources for care of the pediatric patient with HIV infection are therefore impinged upon by the societal attitudes toward the disease; this demands that the physician be aware of the need to contribute to the education of the community as part of the primary and secondary care of patients with HIV spectrum disease.

REFERENCES

AIDS Clinical Trials Alert. (1991, January 16).

Black, M. M., Nair, P., Kight, C., Wachtel, R., Roby, P., & Schuler, M. (1994). Parenting and early development among children of drug-abusive women: Effect of home intervention. *Pediatrics,* Oct (4 part 1), 440–448.

Blanche, S., Rouzioux, C., Moscato, M.-L. G., Veber, F., Mayaux, M.-J., Jacomet, C., Tricoire, J., Deville, A., Vial, M., Firtion, G., De Crepy, A., Douard, D., Robin, M., Courpotin, C., Ciraru-Vigneron, N., Le Diest, F., Griscelli, C., & the HIV infection in Newborns French Collaborative Study. (1989). A prospective study of infants born to women seropositive for human immunodeficiency virus type 1. *New England Journal of Medicine, 320,* 1643–1648.

Blanche, S., Tardieu, M., Duliege, A. M., Rouzious, C., Le Diest, F., Fukunaga, K., Canaglia, M., Jacomet, C., Messia, A., & Griscelli, C. (1990). Longitudinal study of 94 symptomatic infants with perinatally acquired human immunodeficiency virus infection. *American Journal of Diseases of Children, 144,* 1210–1215.

Brown, L. K., & Fritz, G. K. (1988). Children's knowledge and attitudes about AIDS. *Journal of the American Academy of Child and Adolescent Psychiatry, 27,* 504–508.

Brown, L. K., Etemad, J., Brenman, A. J., & Dwight, S. A. (1991). Child and adolescent psychiatrists and HIV disease: A survey. *Journal of the American Academy of Child and Adolescent Psychiatry, 30,* 723–728.

Centers for Disease Control. (1987). Classification system for HIV infection in children under 13 years of age. *Morbidity & Mortality Weekly Report, 36* (7), 225–230.

Centers for Disease Control. (1991, January). U.S. Department of Health and Human Services, *HIV/AIDS Surveillance.* Washington, DC: Department of Health and Human Services. Children's Defense Fund (1988). *A children's defense budget FY 1989: An analysis of our nation's investment in children.* Washington, DC: Author.

Clemo, L. (1992). The stigmatization of AIDS in infants and children in the United States. *AIDS Education and Prevention, 4* (4), 308–318.

Cohen, S. E., Munday, T., Karassick, B., Lieb, L., Ludwig, D. D., & Ward, J. (1991). Neuropsychological functioning in human immunodeficiency virus type 1; Seropositive children infected through neonatal blood transfusion. *Pediatrics, 88,* 58–68.

Coleman, M. (1992). Child care providers and AIDS: A study of knowledge versus acceptance. *AIDS Education and Prevention, 4* (4), 319–327.

Des Jarlais, D. C., & Friedman, S. R. (1987). HIV infection among intravenous drug users: Epidemiology and risk reduction. *AIDS, 1,* 67–76.

DiClemente, R. J., Ponton, L. E., & Hartley, D. (1991). Prevalence and correlates of cutting behavior: Risk for HIV transmission. *Journal of the American Academy of Child and Adolescent Psychiatry, 30,* 735–739.

The European Collaborative Study. (1988). Mother-to-child transmission of HIV infection. *Lancet, 2,* 1039–1043.

Gostin, L. O. (1990a). The AIDS litigation project: A national review of court and Human Rights Commission decisions. Part I: The social impact of AIDS. *Journal of the American Medical Association, 263* (14), 1961–1970.

Gostin, L. O. (1990b). The AIDS litigation project: A national review of court and Human Rights Commission decisions. Part II: Discrimination. *Journal of the American Medical Association, 263* (1), 2084–2094.

Gross, E. J., & Larkin, M. H. (1996). The child with HIV in day care and school. Nursing Clinics of North America. March 31 (1), 231–241.

Gutman, L. T., St. Clare, K. K., Weedy, C., Herman-Giddens, M. E., Lane, B. A., Niemeyer, J. G., & McKinney, R. E. (1991). Human Immunodeficiency virus transmission by sexual abuse. *American Journal of Diseases in Children, 145,* 137–141.

Hauger, S. B., Nicholas, S. W., & Caspe, W. B. (Eds.). (1991). Guidelines for the care of children and adolescents with HIV infection. Report of the NY State Dept. of Health AIDS Institute Criteria committee for the care of HIV-infected children. *Journal of Pediatrics, 119* (1), part 2.

Italian Multicentre Study. (1988). Epidemiology, clinical features and prognostic factors of pediatric HIV infection. *Lancet, 335,* 1043–1045.

Janssen, R. S., Nwanyanwu, O. C., Lelik, R. M., & Stehr-Green, J. K. (1992). Epidemiology of human immunodeficiency virus encephalopathy in the United States. *Neurology, 42,* 1472–1476.

Krener, P. (1996). Neurobiological and psychosocial aspects of HIV infection. In M. Lewis (Ed.), *Child and adolescent psychiatry, a comprehensive textbook,* 2nd ed. (pp. 1006–1015). Baltimore: Williams & Wilkins.

Krener, P. (1991). HIV spectrum disease. In M. Lewis (Ed.), *Child and adolescent psychiatry* (pp. 994–1003). Baltimore: Williams & Wilkins.

Krener, P., & Miller, F. B. (1989). Psychiatric response to HIV spectrum disease in children and adolescents. *Journal of the American Academy of Child and Adolescent Psychiatry, 28,* 596–605.

Marsh, N. V., & McCall, D. W., (1994). Early neuropsychological change in HIV infection. *Neuropsychology, 8* (1), 44–48.

Martin, N. L., Levey, J. A., Legg, H., Weintrub, P. S., Cowan, M. J., & Wara, D. W. (1991). Detection of infection with human immunodeficiency virus (HIV) type 1 in infants by an anti-HIV immunoglobulin A assay using recombinant proteins. *Journal of Pediatrics, 118,* 354–358.

Melvin, D., & Sherr, L. (1993). The child in the family—responding to AIDS and HIV. *AIDS Care, 5* (1), 35–42.

Nozyce, M., Hittelman, J., Muenz, L., Durako, S. J., Fischer, M. L., & Willoughby, A. (1994a). Effect of perinatally acquired human immunodeficiency virus infection on neurodevelopment in children during the first two years of life. *Pediatrics*. December (6 pt 1) 883–891.

Nozyce, M., Hoberman, M., Apadi, S., Wiznia, A., Lambert, G., Dobroszycki, J., Chage, C. J., & St. Louis, Y. (1994b). A 12-month study of the effects of oral zidovudine on neurodevelopmental functioning in a cohort of vertically HIV-infected inner-city children. *AIDS,* May 8 (5), 635–639.

Oxtoby, M. J. (1988). Human immunodeficiency virus and other viruses in human breastmilk: Placing the issues in broader perspective. *Pediatric Infectious Disease Journal*, 7, 825–835.

Parks, W. P., & Scott, G. B. (1990). Pediatric AIDS. In F. A. Oski, C. C. DeAngelis, R. D. Feigin, & J. B. Warshaw (Eds.), *Principles and practice of pediatrics* (pp. 192–195). Philadelphia: Lippincott.

Papola, P., Alvarez, M., Cogen, H. J. (1994). Developmental and service needs of school-aged children with human immunodeficiency virus infection: A descriptive study. *Pediatrics*. December (6, part 1), 914–918.

Persaud, D., Chandwani, S., Rigaud, M., Leibovitz, E., Kaul, A., Lawrence, R., Pollack, H., DiJohn, D., Krasinski, K., & Brokowsky, W. I. (1992). Delayed recognition of human immunodeficiency virus infection in preadolescent children. *Pediatrics*, 92 (5), 688–696.

Ponton, L. E., DiClemente, R., & McKenna, S. (1991). An AIDS education and prevention program for hospitalized adolescents. *Journal of the American Academy of Adolescent Psychiatry*, 30, 729–734.

Rotheram-Borus, M. J., Koopman, C., Haignere, C., & Davies, M. (1991). Reducing HIV sexual risk behaviors among runaway adolescents. *Journal of the American Medical Association*, 2676 (9), 1237–1241.

Rotheram-Borus, M. J., Miller, S., Koopman, C., Haignere, C., & Selfridge, C. (1991). *Adolescents living safely: AIDS awareness, attitudes, actions*. New York: HIV Center for Clinical and Behavioral Studies, Columbia University.

Schonfeld, D. J., O'Hare, L. L., Perrin, E. C., Quackenbush, M., Showalter, D. R., & Chicchetti, D. V. (1995). A randomized, controlled trial of a school-based multifaceted AIDS education program in the elementary grades: The impact on comprehension knowledge and fears. *Pediatrics*, April (4), 480–486.

Scott, G. B., Fischl, M. A., Klimas, N., Fletcher, M. A., Dickinson, G. M., Levine, R. S., & Parks, W. P. (1985). Mothers of infants with acquired immunodeficiency syndrome. Evidence for both symptomatic and asymptomatic carriers. *Journal of the American Medical Association*, 253, 363.

Select Committee on Children Youth and Families. (1989, April 27). *Born hooked: Confronting the impact of perinatal substance abuse*. House of Representatives Hearing. Washington, DC: U.S. Government Printing Office.

Swaz, M., & Rotheram-Borus, M. J. (1992, Fall). Tracking high-risk adolescents longitudinally. *AIDS Education and Prevention Supplement*, 69–82.

Thomas, P. A., & the New York City Perinatal HIV Transmission Collaborative Study Group. (1989, June 4–9). *Early predictors and rate of perinatal HIV disease*. Paper presented at the fifth International Conference on AIDS, Montreal, Quebec.

Trad, P. V., Kentros, M., Solomon, G. E., & Greenblatt, E. R. (1994). Assessment and psychotherapeutic intervention for an HIV-infected preschool child. *Journal of the American Academy of Child and Adolescent Psychiatry*, (November-December), 33 (9), 1338–1345.

Trad, P. V. (1994). A developmental model for risk avoidance in adolescents confronting AIDS. *AIDS Education and Prevention*, 6 (4), 322–338.

Wolters, P. L., Brouwer, P., Moss, H. A., & Pizzo, P. A. (1995). Differential receptive and expressive language functioning of children with symptomatic HIV disease and relation to CT scan brain abnormalities. *Pediatrics* (1), 112–119.

World Health Organization. (1987). Breast-feeding/breast milk and human immunodeficiency virus. *Weekly Epidemiological Record*, 632, 245.

26 / The Allergic Child

David A. Mrazek

Background

There has been long-standing recognition that children who are highly allergic appear to be at a greater risk for a number of psychological symptoms including introversion, anxiety, depression, and dependency. What has been less well-appreciated is that the relationships between the allergic and emotional symptoms are reciprocal, and, most importantly, that the expression of both types of symptoms is clearly the result of the interaction of multiple etiological factors. The reality is that the expression of an eczematous rash is the product of the interactions of antigens, antibodies, cellular mediators (that are reactive to emotional states), and the behavior of scratching. In this case, all four etiological factors must precede the rash, but many other factors can influence the nature of the illness. Once the illness occurs, there is little doubt that a widespread and unattractive eczematous rash is a strong precipitant to depressive episodes and problems with self-esteem. However, an affective disorder rarely develops in the absence of such other etiological factors as a genetic predisposition and some disruption in the familial support system.

There are four common allergic diseases: asthma, eczema, hay fever, and food allergy. The clinical course of each of these illnesses has been linked to emotional factors. Furthermore, when patients with these illnesses have moderate to severe symptoms, they have been observed to be at a modestly increased risk for the development of psychiatric symptomatology. Additionally, psychiatric symptoms such as hyperactivity and inattention have been hypothesized to arise directly as a result of an allergically mediated reaction.

Asthma is discussed in a separate chapter which reviews both the allergic and nonallergic factors that influence the psychiatric status of these children. Atopic dermatitis (i.e., eczema), atopic rhinitis (i.e., hay fever), and food allergy are each reviewed independently. Finally, the status of the link between food sensitivity and behavioral symptoms will be discussed.

Somewhat surprisingly, the complexity of these interactions has been recognized since the beginning of clinical medical reporting. Thus, more than a century ago, Ricketts reported in the *Journal of the American Medical Association* (1892) that for infantile eczema ". . . at times the cause seems to be due to some nervous condition, while at other times there is an indication that it is wholly local."

Atopic Dermatitis

Atopic dermatitis or infantile eczema is a common illness of early childhood characterized by a pruritic skin rash. Sixty percent of children develop their first symptoms in the first year of life and nearly 85% of those affected will have their onset within the first five years of life. Current estimates suggest that as many as 10% of the population may suffer from this condition (Hanifin, 1991). During early childhood, the lesions are most commonly distributed on the face and extensor surfaces of the extremities.

The hallmark of the disorder is that the excoriations of the skin are created by the intense scratching that occurs in response to the pruritus. The prevention of scratching completely eliminates the rash, but treatment must confront the intense pruritic impulses that accompanies the atopic exposure. The absence of any lesions on portions of the body that cannot be scratched provides graphic evidence on the importance of the control of scratching for the management of this problem.

Strong support for an underlying genetic basis for the illness is provided by twin studies that reveal an increased concordance for monozygotic twins (Schultz-Larsen, Holm, & Henningsen, 1986). Furthermore, familial studies have demonstrated that in approximately 40% of the families in which there is a child with atopic dermatitis, another family member also suffers from the disease (Küster, Petersen, Christophers, Goos, & Sterry, 1990). While no neurochemical basis for the pruritus or the concomitant psychological symptoms has been demonstrated, the illness is characterized by increased IgE secretion and diminished cell-mediated immunity (Leung & Geha, 1986).

Furthermore, the exacerbation of symptoms has long been associated with stress. Early studies based on uncontrolled analyses suggested that eczema was linked with early bereavement and loss (Brown, 1972), and that very young children were observed to have clinical flare-ups at times of increased familial tension (Ironside, 1974). It was thought that eczema might occur more frequently in patients with a generalized increase in psychophysiological activity, but this was not the case in a sample of young women with eczema (Koehler & Weber, 1992). In a very small study of eczematous adult patients, a pattern of alexithymic personality and decreased REM sleep was observed, suggesting the utility of sleep studies for examining early patterns of risk in young children (Tantam, Kalucy, & Brown, 1982). A more recent study using a prospective design has also been able to demonstrate a temporal link between the perception of stress and an exacerbation of the skin lesions (King & Wilson, 1991).

The question of the role of the parent-child relationship in both the onset of the illness and its maintenance has been addressed repeatedly. Parental disturbances characterized by problems in maternal sensitivity have been observed, with reports of resolution of the skin lesions with appropriate dyadic therapy (Koblenzer & Koblenzer, 1988). A population of chronically ill children that included a substantial number of children with atopic dermatitis was studied. It was found that both fathers and mothers were particularly desirous of closeness to the affected child, and that they tended to deny the behavioral problems of their children. The mothers of these children were also demonstrated to be more protective (Liedtke, 1990). In the course of a controlled study, a group of preschool children with atopic dermatitis was compared to a sample of same-age children without a chronic illness. The sick children displayed higher levels of behavioral disturbances and, in particular, more dependency fearfulness, and sleep difficulties than did the controls (Daud, Garralda, & David, 1993). Of particular interest, given previous reports of disturbed mother-child relationships, the Daud, Garralda, & David study reported that 86% of these atopic preschool children were estimated to have a secure attachment.

A number of salient psychological issues can become relevant to the mothering of a severely eczematous child. An example was the involuntary rejection by a very successful young mother of her 3-year-old son who developed severe eczema on his face and arms. The interactions that evolved between mother and son were extremely negative and resulted in the mother being unable to care for her child. The boy was chronically uncomfortable and had become increasingly difficult to comfort. His mother, who valued physical attractiveness, found that his facial eczematous lesions made her ashamed of him when others would stare at the severe rash on his face. The dyad was treated simultaneously. The child received extensive skin care which relieved both the chronic pruritus and produced a dramatic resolution in his skin lesions. Simultaneously, the mother received supported psychotherapy. As the child became more attractive, his mother was able to emotionally accept him once again and take a quite active role in providing his physical care.

The positive role of both supportive and behavioral treatment for children with eczema has been repeatedly put forward, but controlled studies have not been available. The use of a cognitive behavioral approach has been reported to be useful in the treatment of adults, but has not been systematically reported to be effective in pediatric patients. Similarly, efforts to prevent eczema have a long history. While recent studies provide some support for early dietary protocols (Zeiger et al., 1989), earlier claims that prolonged breast feeding and avoidance diets could prevent eczema have been critically reviewed (David, 1989).

Atopic Rhinitis

Atopic rhinitis or hay fever is an extremely common, self-limited illness consisting of a cluster of symptoms that include nasal congestion, sneezing, and ocular symptoms such as redness and "watering." Hay fever is believed to represent a classic allergic reaction to a wide range of aero-allergens. Estimates of the prevalence of atopic rhinitis are dependent on the selection criteria and vary from 10% (if strict criteria are employed) to a majority of the population (if very broad historical diagnostic criteria are sufficient to establish "caseness").

Traditionally, clinicians have observed that severe hay fever was associated with a nonspecific range of emotional problems including self-image concerns, fatigue, and poor school performance (Ziering, 1989). School performance has been shown to be particularly affected by the use of sedating antihistamines. This would suggest the avoidance of these agents in the treatment of children with identified school difficulties (Vuurman, van Veggel, Uiterwijk, Leutner, & O'Hanlon, 1993).

A relatively new line of investigation has begun to link a temperamental characteristic defined as "behavioral inhibition" to the diagnosis of hay fever (Bell, Jasnoski, Kagan, & King, 1990). For example, it has been noted that the pedigrees of children with behavioral inhibition contained more first- and second-degree relatives with hay fever than did the pedigrees of socially outgoing children. Additionally, a higher incidence of panic disorder than expected was found in the mothers of these children. In a study of adults, patients with depressive illness were noted to have higher levels of antigen-specific IgE antibodies to inhalants and foods (Sugerman, Southern, & Curran, 1982). Using a questionnaire methodology with college students, Bell, Jasnoski, Kagan, & King (1990) demonstrated correlations between shyness and a history of "professionally diagnosed" hay fever. Future studies using methodologies that ensure accurate diagnosis and are developmentally organized may well lead to a better appreciation of the mechanisms that may link temperament and atopic dermatitis.

Food Allergy

In the early years of childhood, a number of foods have been shown to cause a wide range of allergic reactions that include vomiting, diarrhea, skin rash, wheezing, and, in extreme cases, anaphylaxis. These immunologically mediated reactions should be carefully distinguished from both *food sensitivities* that result from a physiological, but not immunological, mechanism such as a deficiency in lactase and *food aversions* that result from a psychological reaction to exposure to specific foods (Ferguson, 1992). A relatively small subset of foods that include dairy products, eggs, peanuts, tree nuts, and seafood is responsible for more than 90% of the documented allergic reactions. The establishment of a food allergy that is responsible for chronic symptoms has proven to be an extremely challenging task and ultimately requires the use of a double-blind oral provocation challenge (May, 1982; Christensen, 1991). This expensive and somewhat cumbersome technique is still essential to establish the diagnosis definitively as neither skin testing nor assessing immunoglobulin E levels to specified antigens using radioimmune assay testing (e.g., RAST testing) have correlated well with clinical symptoms (Sampson & Albergo, 1984). The concept of pseudo-food allergy has been developed to identify patients who maintain the erroneous belief that they are sensitive to particular foods and who persist in attributing a range of psychological and physical symptoms to the intake of food despite the absence of physiological evidence (Pearson, 1991).

Parental perception of feeding problems and negative reactions to food is often difficult to confirm empirically, despite the fact that parents' reports of feeding problems have been linked to their later accounts of behavioral problems (Forsyth & Canny, 1991). A study of asthmatic children revealed that 56% of their parents reported that the youngsters had experienced food intolerance, and that by far, the most common symptoms were behavioral (Adler, Assadullahi, Warner, & Warner, 1991). Among identified substances were food additives, chocolate, and oranges which rarely trigger IgE-mediated reactions. Skin testing and specific antigen serum levels of IgE of those children with reported chocolate reactions were completely negative; only one child with a reported reaction to oranges was confirmed by skin testing. In contrast, when parental reports of reactions to milk or eggs were compared to skin and RAST testing, they were confirmed in 74% of the cases.

A long-standing controversy has surrounded the hypothesis that food additives or other ingested substances play an etiological role in the expression of attentional problems and hyperactivity (Feingold, 1976; Spring & Sandoval, 1976). Currently, there is little evidence to support this position. A related hypothesis has been that the intake of sugar has a similar effect. This latter question has been examined exhaustively and, again, the balance of evidence provides little support for this belief (Kinsbourne, 1994; Wolraich et al., 1994).

A clinical example is Geoffrey, a 7-year-old boy whose mother became convinced that his hyperactivity was a direct response to eating foods with a high sugar content. On several occasions when he consumed forbidden sweet treats, she was convinced that he immediately became more distractable and oppositional. Consequently, she placed him on a rigid diet with minimal sugar content and his oppositionality worsened to the point that he began to steal candy. The child was enrolled in a double-blind food challenge using objective criteria. On review of the data, there was no difference between his behavior on high sugar content foods versus placebo when sweetness was controlled for using artificial sweeteners. A new behavioral protocol was developed with the mother, who accepted the results of the objective trial, and his hyperactive behavior was treated with methylphenidate. Geoffrey was consequently able to resume a normal diet and the stealing behavior disappeared.

Summary

While an association between atopic status and psychiatric disorder has not been clearly defined, a number of specific issues in the management of children with serious allergies have been established. Specifically, there are narcissistic issues related to parenting children with severe atopic dermatitis particularly in the presence of severe pruritus that requires physical wrapping and restriction of motion. Children with atopic rhinitis may have had an increased likelihood of developing a syndrome of behavioral inhibition; this subsequent pattern of early behavior may be linked to later development of panic disorder. Finally, the psychological factors associated with treatment of food allergy are critical to address directly using double-blind food challenges to provide a rational approach to the diagnostic evaluation and subsequent management of these children.

REFERENCES

Adler, B. R., Assadullahi, T., Warner, J. A., & Warner, J. O. (1991). Evaluation of a multiple food specific IgE antibody test compared to parental perception, allergy skin tests and RAST. *Clinical and Experimental Allergy, 21*, 683–688.

Bell, I. R., Jasnoski, M. L., Kagan, J., & King, D. A. (1990). Is allergic rhinitis more frequent in young adults with extreme shyness? A preliminary survey. *Psychosomatic Medicine, 52*, 517–525.

Brown, D. G. (1972). Stress as a precipitant factor of eczema. *Journal of Psychosomatic Research, 16*, 321–327.

Christensen, L. (1991). Issues in the design of studies investigating the behavioral concomitants of foods. *Journal of Consulting and Clinical Psychology, 59*, 874–882.

Daud, L. R., Garralda, M. E., & David, T. J. (1993). Psychosocial adjustment in preschool children with atopic eczema. *Archives of Diseases of Children, 69*, 670–676.

David, T. J. (1989). Infection and prevention: Current controversies in childhood atopic eczema: A review. *Journal of the Royal Society of Medicine, 82*, 420–422.

Feingold, B. F. (1976). Hyperkinesis and learning disabilities linked to the ingestion of artificial food colors and flavors. *Journal of Learning Disabilities, 9*, 19–27.

Ferguson, A. (1992). Definitions and diagnosis of food intolerance and food allergy: Consensus and controversy. *Journal of Pediatrics, 121*, S7–S11.

Forsyth, B. W. C., & Canny, P. F. (1991). Perceptions of vulnerability 3 1/2 years after problems of feeding and crying behavior in early infancy. *Pediatrics, 88*, 757–763.

Hanifin, J. M. (1991). Atopic dermatitis in infants and children. *Pediatric Clinics of North America, 38*, 763–789.

Ironside, W. (1974). Eczema, darkly mirror of the mind. *Australian Journal of Dermatology, 15*, 5–9.

King, R. M., & Wilson, G. V. (1991). Use of diary technique to investigate psychosomatic relations in atopic dermatitis. *Journal of Psychosomatic Research, 35*, 697–706.

Kinsbourne, M. (1994). Sugar and the hyperactive child. *New England Journal of Medicine, 330*, 355–356.

Koblenzer, C. S., & Koblenzer, P. J. (1988). Chronic intractable atopic eczema. *Archives of Dermatology, 124*, 1673–1677.

Koehler, T., & Weber, D. (1992). Psychophysiological reactions of patients with atopic dermatitis. *Journal of Psychosomatic Research, 36*, 391–394.

Küster, W., Peterson, M., Christophers, E., Goos, M., & Sterry, W. (1990). A family study of atopic dermatitis. *Archives of Dermatological Research, 282*, 98–102.

Leung, D. Y. M., & Geha, R. S. (1986). Immunoregulatory abnormalities in atopic dermatitis. *Clinical Review of Allergy, 4*, 67–86.

Liedtke, R. (1990). Socialization and psychosomatic disease: An empirical study of the educational style of parents with psychosomatic children. *Psychotherapy and Psychosomatics, 54*, 208–213.

May, C. D. (1982). Food allergy: Lessons from the past. *Journal of Allergy and Clinical Immunology, 69*, 255–259.

Pearson, D. J. (1991). Pseudo-food allergy. *Rheumatic Diseases and Clinics of North America, 17*, 343–349.

Ricketts, B. M. (1892). Eczema infantile. *Journal of the American Medical Association, 19*, 740–741.

Sampson, H. A., & Albergo, R. (1984). Comparison of results of skin tests, RAST, and double-blind, placebo-controlled food challenges in children with atopic dermatitis. *Journal of Allergy and Clinical Immunology, 74*, 26–33.

Schultz-Larsen, F., Holm, N. V., and Henningsen, K. (1986). Atopic dermatitis: A genetic-epidemiologic study in a population-based twin sample. *Journal of American Academy of Dermatology, 15*, 487.

Spring, C., & Sandoval, J. (1976). Food additives and hyperkinesis: A critical evaluation of the evidence. *Journal of Learning Disabilities, 9*, 28–37.

Sugerman, A. A., Southern, D. L., & Curran, J. F. (1982). A study of antibody levels in alcoholic, depressive, and schizophrenic patients. *Annals of Allergy, 48*, 166–171.

Tantam, D., Kalucy, R., & Brown, D. G. (1982). Sleep, scratching and dreams in eczema: A new approach to alexithymia. *Psychotherapy and Psychosomatics, 37*, 26–35.

Vuurman, E. F., van Veggel, L. M., Uiterwijk, M. M., Leutner, D., & O'Hanlon, J. F. (1993). Seasonal allergic rhinitis and antihistamine effects on children's learning. *Annals of Allergy, 71,* 121–126.

Wolraich, M. L., Lindgren, S. D., Stumbo, P. J., Stegink, L. D., Appelbaum, M. I., & Kirtsy, M. C. (1994). Effects of diets high in sucrose or aspartame on the behavior and cognitive performance of children. *New England Journal of Medicine, 330,* 301–307.

Zeiger, R. S., Heller, S., Mellon, M. H., Forsythe, A. B., O'Connor, R. D., Hamburger, R. N., & Schatz, M. (1989). Effect of combined maternal and infant food-allergen avoidance on development of atopy in early infancy: A randomized study. *Journal of Allergy and Clinical Immunology, 84,* 72–89.

Ziering, R. A. (1989). Immediate and late side effects of hay fever: Physical and psychosocial problems. *Postgraduate Medicine, 85,* 183–185, 188–189.

27 / The Asthmatic Child

David A. Mrazek

Background

Asthma is the most common chronic illness of childhood. It is characterized by sudden, episodic attacks during which time the child experiences difficulty breathing. The mechanism underlying these attacks is an abrupt bronchoconstriction of the airways with accompanying inflammatory changes that further restrict air exchange. The condition has been known for millennia; descriptions of asthmatic attacks can be found in the writings of Hippocrates. In the twelfth century, Maimonides wrote *The Book of Asthma,* which describes the disease in precise detail. The symptoms of the illness include acute chest tightness accompanied by predominantly expiratory wheezing. Given the commonplace observation that asthma attacks are regularly precipitated by stressful events, it has been studied as a *classic* psychosomatic illness (Mrazek, 1988).

Estimates of its prevalence in childhood are varied, but it is likely that at least 7% of American children will experience some form of asthma (Smith, 1988). The condition varies greatly in both its severity and precipitants. The majority of children with asthma have mild symptoms that can be completely controlled with inhaled medication. At the other extreme of the severity continuum are fatal asthmatic attacks. These frightening deaths appear to be increasing in frequency among children with a severe intractable steroid-dependent form of the illness (Mrazek, 1992). While children

with mild asthma may have relatively few triggers that lead to the sudden onset of symptoms, children with more complex disease often find that exposure to allergens, infectious illness, or stressful life events is sufficient to trigger an asthmatic attack.

Pediatric asthma provides an illustrative model for understanding the interaction between emotional experience and physical illness. There are two classic questions in psychosomatic medicine that are relevant to the study of any illness (Mrazek, 1985): (1) To what extent do early stressful experiences act as a risk factor that leads to the initial expression of the illness? and (2) to what degree do persistent physical symptoms associated with the illness lead to maladaptive patterns of behavior? The vicious cycle of worsening medical symptoms leading to more extreme psychiatric symptoms has been repeatedly described in the literature regarding chronic illness.

Clinical Presentation

Evidence suggests that asthma occurs in children whose genetic vulnerability is such that they develop reactive wheezing in response to environmental experiences. Subsequent to the expression of the illness, children must adapt to their physical symptoms. In the mild case, adapting to normal, expectable, minor illness symptoms during childhood can actually facilitate some aspects of emotional development; the ensuing intensity of caretaking behavior may actually foster a relationship with the primary caretaker (Parmalee, 1989). However, in the case of chronic persistent illness, particularly of a severe nature, the physical symptoms of the illness as well as the persistent anxiety generated by a somewhat uncertain prognosis can lead to psychiatric disturbance. While the most common symptoms are those of anxiety and depression, behavioral problems such as oppositional defiant disorder may easily develop (Mrazek, 1991). When the associated stresses that accompany chronic asthma occur in a child already burdened with additional risk factors for developmental psychopathology, there is an increased probability of psychiatric disturbance (Mrazek, 1992).

Attempts to relate the severity of the asthmatic symptoms to the appearance and intensity of the associated emotional problems have given rise to considerable controversy. The classic epidemiological studies done on the Isle of Wight were not designed to demonstrate the precise interactions between asthmatic symptoms and psychopathology. Nonetheless, a base rate of 13.6% of all asthmatic children was noted to have "definite" psychiatric disturbance, with 42% of the asthmatic children having some co-occurring emotional problem. Among the children classified as being severely asthmatic (based on the criteria that their disease interfered with their ability to function in school or at home), 58% were found to have a co-occurring psychiatric disorder (Graham, Rutter, & Pless, 1967). This initial epidemiological relationship was derived from a relatively small number of identified cases of severe asthma. However, a larger Australian epidemiological study that focused on asthma as the primary index condition reported similar results. In this study, only the most severely asthmatic children had an increased frequency of psychological problems (McNichol, Williams, & Allan, 1973).

Subsequent efforts to evaluate the relationship between severity of asthma and the quality of adaptation in children have raised a number of questions related to measurement. Studies of outpatient samples that used medication requirements as a measure of severity have not always shown a relationship with symptom scores. Norrish, Tooley, & Godfrey (1977) found that in outpatients, the "quality of control" of asthmatic symptoms was statistically associated with emotional disturbance. Using a parental questionnaire to ascertain the presence of behavioral problems in this cohort, 91% of those children who were in poor respiratory control also received high behavioral symptom scores. The discussion of this relationship highlights the possible confounding of emotional difficulties with a range of complex behaviors required to maintain good asthmatic control. However, even when a medication requirement was used as a measure of severity, 57% of children requiring steroids were noted to have behavioral disturbance.

There are several confounding factors that arise when assessing the role of psychological factors in the onset of emotional disturbance of physically ill children. A major one is that the experience of suffering from a chronic illness is in itself a risk factor for emotional difficulties. One traditional strategy to deal with this problem has been to study children shortly after the onset of their symptoms. In a cohort of preschool children with relatively little experience with *chronic* illness, severity was seen to be a strong correlate of emotional disturbance. The sample consisted of 3- to 5-year-olds with severe chronic asthma. Using a semistructured and highly reliable maternal interview assessment, 59% of these children were documented to have had high levels of early behavioral disturbance (Mrazek, Anderson, & Strunk, 1984). These findings suggest that relatively minimal time was required for the experience of severe illness to have an impact on adaptation.

Clinically, the issue of oppositionality in preschool children can be very dramatic. A 3-year-old child who is subject to intense asthmatic attacks that are triggered by overt distress can provide parents with a real management dilemma. Essentially, the parents find themselves in a situation where setting appropriate behavioral limits leads to their child becoming overtly distressed and developing an episode of intense bronchial constriction that may require emergency medical attention. After a few such confrontations have occurred, parents often need help in learning how to cope with these fighting interactions.

A report that questioned the impact of severity on adjustment was conducted in Germany (Steinhausen, Schindler, & Stephan, 1983). Here the study population was primarily an outpatient cohort consisting of predominantly moderately to mildly asthmatic children. Only four severely asthmatic children were included in this sample; but, on the other hand, as measured by parental report, variability of the severity level within this relatively less asthmatic sample was not associated with psychiatric symptomatology.

A recent study with a quite heterogenous sample of asthmatic children reported the highest rate of comorbid psychiatric disturbance to date. Using a direct, semistructured interview with the child, 63% of this cohort met criteria necessary to establish a psychiatric diagnosis. Even children with relatively mild asthmatic symptoms were noted to have ultimately high levels of psychiatric disturbance. While other aspects of this clinical sample were not well-defined, and a bias in ascertainment may have led to these quite high levels of psychopathology, the possibility also exists that the increased sensitivity of the interview with the child may have identified previously undocumented affective and anxiety-based disorders (Kashani, Konig, & Shepperd, 1988).

Etiology

One of the most intriguing aspects in the study of the co-occurrence of asthmatic symptoms and psychological responses is the mechanisms by which these two processes might be linked. Previous conceptualizations have placed the origin of symptoms largely within a psychological context. The emotional experience of limited pulmonary function, the anxiety related to future attacks, and knowledge of future physical limitations are sufficient conceptually to lead to increased anxiety and affective symptomatology. As these symptoms become more persistent or become aggravated by poor compliance or missed school experience, the child may be unable to continue to cope. While these dynamic events provide the framework for the expression of symptoms, the underlying psychophysiological mechanisms have remained obscure.

The parasympathetic nervous system in general and, specifically, the vagal innervation, have a direct influence on the modulation of airway reactivity (Mrazek & Klinnert, 1991). In addition to the parasympathetic system, sensory nerves and sympathetic autonomic feedback are involved in the overall neural regulation of the airways. Panic reactions, chronic anxiety, and affective disorders are emotional disturbances that have been linked to parasympathetic dominance. The comorbidity of these disorders with asthma provides a plausible causal link. Utilizing the protocol of a methacholine challenge, the relative sensitivity of the airway receptors to parasympathetic activation can be studied directly (Cockcroft, Ruffin, Dolovich, & Hargreave, 1977; Juniper, Suda, Kinsman, Souhrada, & Spector, 1978). Furthermore, the efficacy of sympathomimetic or anticholinergic antiasthmatic medications provides pragmatic evidence supporting the nature of these mechanisms (Verstraeten, 1976).

Bronchoconstriction due to parasympathetic innervation can be achieved via either direct activation by the vagus or as a consequence of increased sensitivity of the muscarinic receptors within the airways (Barnes, 1986). Anticholinergic medications have relatively powerful effects in some children while producing a minimal response in others; this suggests that muscarinic receptor sensitivity plays a primary role in only one subset of patients. A similar subtype-specific explanation has been suggested for the variable therapeutic response of asthmatic children to vagotomy.

In asthmatic children, clinical symptoms may be influenced by an increased parasympathetic reflex that is triggered by either sensory stimulation or indirect, sympathetically mediated signals. This exaggerated parasympathetic reflex has been put forward as one explanation for the paradoxical observation that many asthmatic children experience bronchoconstriction at times of intense stress. Normally, stressors elicit the release of sympathomimetics and epinephrine. Consequently, one would expect bronchodilation, but the reverse of that occurs in stress-sensitive asthmatics (Kallenbach, Dowdeswell, Reinach, Millar, & Zwi, 1987). However, this paradox is resolved if the impact of the initial, stress-related sympathomimetic stimulus is to activate a strong reactive parasympathetic response.

Vagal stimulation may potentiate mast cell secretion (Leff, Stimler, Shioya, Tallet, & Dame, 1986). Mast cells contain neuropeptides that may play a role in the regulation of airways. These substances, in turn, have autonomic effects that either stabilize the cell membranes or stimulate the degranulation of mast cells and basophils. Hence, vagal activity may have a direct effect on immunoregulation (Foreman, 1987). Furthermore, other neuropeptides have been shown to influence the membranes of mast cells directly. For example, substance P may stimulate degranulation, having an effect opposite to that of somatostatin, which has been suggested to act as a stabilizing agent (Payan, Levine, & Goetzl, 1984; Goetzl, et al., 1986). Yet another neuropeptide, vasoactive intestinal peptide (VIP), has been demonstrated to be a potent bronchodilator. VIP may be a putative mediator of what is referred to as the sensory or "nonadrenergic, noncholinergic" nerve tracts that regulate the airways. A relative depletion of VIP has been documented in asthmatics (Ollerenshaw, Karvis, Woolcock, Sullivan, & Scheibner, 1989).

The suggestion has been advanced that most cell secretion can be conditioned. This offers a relatively controversial but promising hypothesis regarding the mechanism of the control of airways. It would imply that the central nervous system has direct control over an immunological pathway that is relevant to the regulation of airway diameter. This direct link between the immunologic and the central nervous systems may also work either in conjunction or in competition with more peripheral autonomic regulation of the airways (MacQueen, Marshall, Perdue, Siegel, & Bienenstock, 1989).

Treatment

Many psychotherapeutic modalities have been used to treat the co-occurring psychiatric problems of children with asthma. However, little systematic comparison of the relative efficacy of different interventions has been undertaken. The primary modalities that have been used will be discussed.

EDUCATIONAL APPROACHES

The presentation of accurate information regarding the precipitants that trigger symptoms is a sensible approach to the behavioral management of families with asthmatic children. Specific programs have been developed to achieve these edu-cational objectives (Esquibel, Foster, Garnier, & Saunders, 1984). Programs have been designed to be conducted with individual children using a tutorial model, with families, or within the context of a more traditional group classroom format.

INDIVIDUAL TREATMENT

Historically, a number of individual approaches have been reported to be effective in the management of the psychological symptoms associated with asthma. As early as 1934, Rogerson described the guidelines for such treatment (Rogerson, 1934). Theories postulating a common underlying area of internal conflict have focused primarily on issues of early psychological differentiation between mother and child as well as problems related to separation and loss (Jessner et al., 1955). Despite widespread recognition of these processes, little empirical evidence for a consistent dynamic conflict has been put forward.

In conducting intensive psychotherapy with a 13-year-old severely asthmatic girl, a number of illustrative dynamic issues evolved. This patient had an IQ of 140 and by history was very articulate and successful at school. Unfortunately, her asthmatic symptoms were resistant to conventional treatment and she had required large doses of systemic steroids for her entire life. This had resulted in marked growth retardation and her developing a pronounced scoliosis. Because she was only the height of a 7-year-old, she was frequently treated as if she were much younger. She found this to be both humiliating and enraging.

At the beginning of her treatment, she demonstrated an astonishing degree of denial regarding her physical limitations. She presented herself as a very competent individual and insisted that she would be able to become a professional figure skater. Repeated discussions with her parents, teachers, and friends had been ineffective in modifying this dearly held ambition. However, as she struggled with her physical limitations over the course of her psychotherapeutic treatment, she gradually began to incorporate a more realistic self-image and life goals. While this process was a gradual one and was punctuated by episodic periods of depression as she accommodated to the impossibility of accomplishing some of her previous objectives, the long-term outcome was her development of more adaptive educational objectives and interpersonal communications. After a year of treatment, she had decided to pursue a medical career and was most particularly interested in pediatrics. A concomitant change that occurred over the course of her treatment was that she developed an intense interest in her own illness and became dramatically more compliant with the complex treatment protocol that was required to control her severe asthmatic attacks.

Behavioral treatment has been focused on altering specific maladaptive behaviors that lead to problems in the management of asthmatic children. Furthermore, Kahn developed a counterconditioning approach that was shown to have a short-term effect on improving airway ventilation (Kahn & Olson, 1977). Both positive and negative reinforcement have been shown to have some modest degrees of effectiveness in facilitating proactive and minimizing self-destructive illness-related behaviors (Creer, 1970).

FAMILY THERAPY

Family therapy has been reported to be effective in modifying asthma in children. Two different lines of investigation support the relative effectiveness of this approach. Liebman, et al. focused on the enmeshed nature of some families and advocated the use of a structural family therapy model (Liebman, Minuchin, Baker, & Rosman, 1976). Development of more adaptive and independent behavior on the part of the children with asthma was reported. Lask (1979) also identified a set of abnormal patterns of parenting in some families with an asthmatic child and focused on a different set of issues including pathological denial. When this family therapy approach was used conjointly with routine medical management, more positive symptom scores were achieved (as reflected by decreased wheezing and improved thoracic gas volumes) (Lask & Matthew, 1979).

GROUP THERAPY

Group therapy is a cost-effective method of treating asthmatic children and has the added advantage of utilizing peer support as a strong reinforcer for more adaptive behaviors (Clapham & Sclare, 1958). When compared to control samples, systematic improvement in pulmonary function has been demonstrated in behavioral-oriented group treatments (Hock, Rodgers, Reddi, & Kennard, 1978).

RESIDENTIAL TREATMENT SETTING

For severe intractable asthma, an intensive residential treatment experience provides the opportunity to restructure the child's behavior and achieve medical control of the illness. Residential treatment programs have become more focused in their efforts to modify behavior; consequently, the length of stay on these units has decreased. This approach is indicated primarily for children with severe illness that has been resistant to conventional treatment. More recently, the cost effectiveness of residential treatment has been demonstrated in those children with the most severe form of asthma (Strunk, Fukuhara, LaBrecque, & Mrazek, 1989).

PSYCHOPHARMACOLOGICAL INTERVENTIONS

In the course of treating asthmatic children with psychotropic drugs, the general principle is that the underlying symptom is targeted. The use of antidepressant medication for asthmatic patients may have additional therapeutic benefits. However, since the anticholinergic properties of these agents may have a direct impact on bronchodilation, careful monitoring of cardiac rhythm is required, as the tachycardia associated with antiasthmatic medications may be exacerbated by tricyclic antidepressants. A particular caution with the use of any psychotropic medication is the possible inclusion of tartrazine as an inactive ingredient, as this substance can trigger an allergic reaction in asthmatic children who have a specific sensitivity.

Prevention

The prevention of asthmatic symptoms in children at genetic risk for developing the illness has recently become an empirically supported clinical objective. While it has long been acknowledged that early stressors are associated with the onset of symptoms in some patients, there has been little systematic evidence to support this association. Recent prospective longitudinal studies of children of asthmatic parents have demonstrated that early parenting difficulties were associated with an increase in the likelihood of developing symptoms (Mrazek, Klinnert, Mrazek, & Macey, 1991). Emotional stressors are probably best understood as one of several key risk factors for the onset of the illness. Other conditions or experiences associated with the onset of asthma in genetically vulnerable children include early respiratory infection and a propensity for allergy as measured by elevated levels of IgE. There is some evidence to suggest that prolonged early breast feeding may be a protective factor. There are several specific research objectives related to asthma prevention. One is the need to develop a better understanding of how specific alleles are modulated by specific environmental exposures. Another is the effectiveness testing of early intervention efforts designed to delay or ultimately prevent the initial onset of asthma.

Conclusions

Asthma is a common disease of childhood. Severe symptomatology has been associated with increased emotional and behavioral disturbances. A wide variety of therapeutic interventions have been designed and targeted to address these problems. With genetically at-risk children, emotional factors have been implicated in the initial onset of the illness and early intervention, targeted at environmental stressors, may lead to the delay or prevention of symptoms.

REFERENCES

Barnes, P. J. (1986). Asthma as an axon reflex. *Lancet, 1,* 242–245.

Clapham, H. I., & Sclare, A. B. (1958). Group psychotherapy with asthmatic patients. *International Journal of Group Psychotherapy, 8,* 44–54.

Cockcroft, D. W., Ruffin, R. E., Dolovich, J., & Hargreave, F. E. (1977). Allergen induced increase in non-allergic bronchial reactivity. *Clinical Allergy, 7,* 503–515.

Creer, T. L. (1970). The use of time out from positive reinforcement with asthmatic children. *Journal of Psychosomatic Research, 14,* 117–120.

Esquibel, K. P., Foster, C. R., Garnier, V. J., & Saunders, M. L. (1984). A program to help asthmatic students reach their potential. *Public Health Rep., 99,* 606–609.

Foreman, J. C. (1987). Neuropeptides and the pathogenesis of allergy. *Allergy, 42,* 1–11.

Goetzl, E. J., Chernov-Rogan, T., Furuichi, K., Goetzl, L. M., Lee, J. Y., & Renold, F. (1986). Neuromodulation of mast cell and basophil function. In A. D. Befus, H. Beinestock, & J. A. Denburg (Eds.), *Mast Cell Differentiation and Heterogeneity* (pp. 223–229). New York: Raven.

Graham, P. J., Rutter, M. L., & Pless, H. E. (1967). Childhood asthma: A psychosomatic disorder? Some epidemiological considerations. *British Journal of Preventive Social Medicine, 21,* 78–85.

Hock, R. A., Rodgers, C. H., Reddi, C., & Kennard, D. W. (1978). Medicopsychological interventions in male asthmatic children: An evaluation of psychological change. *Psychosomatic Medicine, 40,* 210–215.

Jessner, L., Lamont, J., Long, R., Rollins, N., Whipple, B., & Prentice, N. (1955). Emotional impact of nearness and separation of the asthmatic child and his mother. *Psychoanalytic Study of the Child, 10,* 353–375.

Juniper, E. F., Suda, W. L., Kinsman, R. A., Souhrada, J., & Spector, S. (1978). Reproducibility and comparison of responses to inhale histamine and methacholine, *Thorax, 33,* 705–710.

Kahn, A. U., & Olson, D. L. (1977). Deconditioning of exercise-induced asthma. *Psychosomatic Medicine, 39,* 382–392.

Kallenbach, J. M., Dowdeswell, R., Reinach, G., Millar, S., & Zwi, S. (1987). Reflex heart rate control in asthma evidence of parasympathetic overactivity. *Chest, 87,* 644–648.

Kashani, J. H., Konig, P., Shepperd, J. A. (1988). Psychopathology and self-concept in asthmatic children. *Journal of Pediatric Psychology, 13,* 509–520.

Lask, B. (1979). Emotional considerations in wheezy children. *Journal of the Royal Society of Medicine, 72,* 56–59.

Lask, B., & Matthew, D. (1979). Childhood asthma: A controlled trial of family psychotherapy. *Archives of Diseases of Children, 54,* 116–119.

Leff, A. R., Stimler, N. P., Shioya, T., Tallet, J., & Dame, C. (1986). Augmentation of respiratory mast cell secretion of histamine caused by vagus nerve stimulation during antigen challenge. *Journal of Immunology, 136,* 1066–1073.

Liebman, R., Minuchin, S., Baker, L., & Rosman, B. L. (1976). The role of the family in the treatment of chronic asthma. In P. J. Guerin, Jr., (Ed.), *Family*

Therapy: Theory and Practice. New York: Gardner Press.

MacQueen, G., Marshall, J., Perdue, M., Siegel, S., & Bienenstock, J. (1989). Pavlovian conditioning of rat mucosal mast cells to secrete rat mast cell protease II. *Science, 243,* 83–85.

McNichol, E. N., Williams, H. E., Allan, J. (1973). Spectrum of asthma in children. III: Psychological and social components. *British Medical Journal 1973,* 16–20.

Mrazek, D. A. (1985). Childhood asthma: The interplay of psychiatric and physiological factors. *Advances in Psychosomatic Medicine, 14,* 16–32.

Mrazek, D. A. (1988). Asthma: Psychiatric considerations, evaluation, and management. In E. Middleton, C. E. Reed, & E. F. Ellis (Eds.), *Allergy: Principles and Practice* (3rd ed.) (pp. 1176–1196). St. Louis: C. V. Mosby.

Mrazek, D. A. (1991). Chronic pediatric illness and multiple hospitalizations. In M. Lewis (Ed.), *Child and Adolescent Psychiatry: A Comprehensive Textbook* (pp. 1041–1050). Baltimore: Williams & Wilkins.

Mrazek, D. A. (1992). Psychiatric complications of pediatric asthma. *Annals of Allergy, 69,* 285–290.

Mrazek, D. A., Anderson, I. S., Strunk, R. C. (1984). Disturbed emotional development of severely asthmatic preschool children. *Journal of Child Psychology and Psychiatry (supplement 4),* 81–94.

Mrazek, D. A., & Klinnert, M. (1991). Asthma: Psychoneuroimmunological considerations. In R. Ader, D. L. Felten, & N. Cohen (Eds.), *Psychoneuroimmunology II* (pp. 1013–1035). Orlando: Academic Press.

Mrazek, D. A., Klinnert, M., Mrazek, P., & Macey, T. (1991). Early asthma onset: Consideration of parenting issues. *Journal of the American Academy of Child and Adolescent Psychiatry, 30,* 277–282.

Norrish, M., Tooley, M., & Godfrey, S. (1977). Clinical, Physiological, and psychological study of asthmatic children attending a hospital clinic. *Archives of Diseases of Children, 52,* 912–917.

Ollerenshaw, S., Karvis, D., Woolcock, A., Sullivan, D., and Scheibner, T. (1989). Absence of immunoreactive vasoactive intestinal polypeptide in tissue from the lungs of patients with asthma. *New England Journal of Medicine, 320,* 1244–1248.

Parmalee, A. H. (1989). The child's physical health and the development of relationship. In A. J. Sameroff & R. Emde (Eds.), *Relationship Disturbances in Early Childhood* (pp. 191–220). New York: Basic Books, Inc.

Payan, D. G., Levine, J. D., & Goetzl, E. J. (1984). Modulation of immunity and hypersensitivity by sensory neuropeptides. *Journal of Immunology, 132,* 1601–1604.

Rogerson, C. H. (1934). The role of psychotherapy in the treatment of the asthma-eczema-prurigo complex in children. *British Journal of Dermatology Syph. (complete title), 46,* 368.

Smith, J. M. (1988). Epidemiology and natural history of asthma, allergic rhinitis and atopic dermatitis (eczema). In E. Middleton, C. E. Reed, & E. F. Ellis (Eds.), *Allergy: Principles and Practice* (3rd ed) (pp. 891–929). St. Louis: C. V. Mosby.

Steinhausen, H., Schindler, H., & Stephan, H. (1983). Correlates of psychopathology in sick children. An empirical model. *Journal of the American Academy of Child Psychiatry, 22,* 559–564.

Strunk, R. C., Fukuhara, J. T., LaBrecque, J. F., & Mrazek, D. A. (1989). Outcome of long-term hospitalization for asthma in children. *Journal of Allergy and Clinical Immunology, 83,* 17–25.

Verstraeten, J. M. (1976). Is there a selective indication of a parasympatholytic (Atrovent) and for a B-sympathomimetic (Berotec) in asthma in asthmatic bronchitis? *Acta Tuberculosea et Pneumologica Belgica, 3–4,* 130–155.

28 / The Child or Adolescent with Cancer

Jonathan A. Sugar

The child and adolescent psychiatrist will encounter the pediatric cancer patient in any one of several contexts. In the outpatient setting, a patient in psychotherapy or being seen for another psychiatric reason may develop a malignancy. A child's behavior may change due to an undiagnosed malignancy, or a child with cancer may be brought to the child and adolescent psychiatrist because of concern about the cancer's effect on the child and family. In the consultation-liaison general hospital setting, such consultations may be frequent (e.g., 13% of the consultations on the pediatric consultation liaison service at the University of Michigan have been for children with cancer), whereas the child and adolescent psychiatrist in the general outpatient setting may encounter such patients only rarely. It is likely, however, that such patients will be encountered in any setting, as childhood cancer is the second leading cause of death among children (American Cancer Society, 1992; Hockenberry, Coody, & Bennet, 1990; Miller, 1989), with an estimated 7,200 new cases being diagnosed in 1992.

The brain is directly involved in the cancer itself or in the treatment for roughly 40% of the childhood cancers (American Cancer Society, 1992; Glazer, 1991; Miller, 1989; Poplack, 1989); these children will be at high risk for psychiatric and behavioral sequelae and complications. For other children with cancer, psychiatric considerations may come into play at several points: the child or family may have profound difficulty accepting the diagnosis; compliance with treatment may be a problem for other reasons; there may be psychiatric consequences to the treatment itself, including conditioned nausea or anxiety; the child may have difficulty in school functioning or with reintroduction into previous social realms; the patient's siblings or parents may develop psychiatric disorders or severe psychological distress while coping with the illness; and the child or family's emotional needs in preparation for death may warrant formal psychiatric attention. In addition, the psychiatrist may be asked to contribute to pain control efforts for the child. Finally, the psychiatrist may identify a need for, and offer, consultation to other health care providers on a case-by-case basis in order to help them cope with the difficult emotional tasks of caring for seriously ill and dying children.

In this chapter we seek to provide a brief overview of the general epidemiology of childhood cancers, review the psychiatric concerns and consequences of the disease to childhood cancer patients and their families, and discuss the ways in which the child and adolescent psychiatrist can be helpful to patients, their families, and the treatment team. Psychopharmacologic as well as psychotherapeutic aspects are discussed.

Epidemiology

Recent figures (Miller, 1989) estimate that about 6,550 children will develop cancer annually; of these, roughly 33% will die from the disease (as-suming current treatment response rates). Incidence differs by site and by age: roughly 33% of these cancers will be leukemias, about 19% will involve the brain and central nervous system, another 12% will be lymphomas, 8% will involve the sympathetic nervous system, 6.5% will be of soft tissue origin, 6.25% will involve the kidney, close to 5% will be bone cancers, 3% will be retinoblastomas, and about 10% of the total will be tumors in assorted other sites. Retinoblastoma occurs primarily in infancy and Wilms' tumor chiefly among toddlers; neuroblastomas peak at under 5 years, as do medulloblastomas; acute lymphocytic leukemia strikes children primarily from age 4 to age 10, while acute myelogenous leukemia is evenly distributed among children under 16. Other brain tumors are evenly distributed through the ages of childhood; the lymphomas and bone tumors occur primarily among adolescents.

Psychiatric Problems in Children with Cancer

As alluded to, psychiatric problems and distress may manifest themselves at myriad points in the sick child's course. It is useful to view problems as occurring acutely in the course of the child's diagnosis or active treatment or as long-term sequelae of cancer treatment and cure. In addition, it is important to note that absence of psychiatric disorder in a child or family with cancer does not imply absence of distress. This fact must be kept in mind when reviewing incidence and prevalence studies of psychiatric disorder in children.

Several authors have described the periodic nature of increased stress for children and their families in the course of cancer treatment (Chesler & Barbarin, 1987a; Pfefferbaum, 1990). Diagnosis, initiation of treatment, return to school during outpatient treatment, return to "healthy" or "cured" status, relapse and reinitiation of treatment, change in treatment, and treatment failure and death have all been identified as times of maximal stress. It must be kept in mind, however, that different members of a given family may find different stages of treatment more or less stressful. Thus, while the child and parents may uniformly find diagnosis very difficult, the child may experience significant distress and anxiety upon returning to school, while the parents may experience this stage with profound relief. (See Chesler & Barbarin, 1987a.)

It is axiomatic that a child's emotional response to cancer will be mediated by his or her developmental stage. It is useful in this regard to consider the child's symptoms and planned interventions in the context of age-appropriate concerns and developmental tasks for the patient. Rowland (1990) has proposed that the child's concerns fall into five broad areas (the 5 Ds): distance, disfigurement, dependence, disability, and death. The child's responses will be partly age-determined, but Rowland believes that these broad areas are always called into play for a child when the diagnosis is made.

For example, 3-year-old leukemia patients may be concerned that Mother will not be able to stay with them during the entire hospitalization, may harbor age-specific fantasies about how they contracted leukemia, and their understanding of what treatment will involve will be partly governed by their developmental cognitive capacity. Their concerns about "distance" from parents is different from the 16-year-old's fears of distance from friends. While the loss of a limb for the 7-year-old boy may call forth fears of castration, the manifest fears for the 16-year-old may involve such concerns but will also involve the public stigma of looking very different, concerns about sexual attractiveness, and, possibly, future job and independence prospects.

Similar age-mediated concerns are found in each of the 5 areas outlined by Rowland.

Cognitive development must be considered, including linguistic sophistication. It is important to note that while most research illuminating children's understandings of illness and death used healthy children as subjects, data suggest that sick children are different (Blos, 1978) and may have adultomorphic concepts of death as early as 3 or 4 years of age. On the other hand, the meaning of words for young children remains developmentally mediated (Donovan & McIntyre, 1990), such that "bone marrow transplant" may mean something entirely different to 4-year-olds than to doctors or family, and the children's understanding may be at root of some behavioral problems or tantruming during procedures. In essence, it is

paramount that the psychiatrist help the patient and other physicians understand the child's affective and cognitive developmental stage as it relates to the child's behavior in illness and treatment and to the manner in which the treatment is explained to the child and family (Barber, 1989).

Sanger found that 53% of the children in a sample of children with cancer manifested psychosocial symptoms worthy of professional attention based on parent questionnaire (Sanger, Copeland, & Davidson, 1991). In contrast, Kaplan et al. (1987) found lower levels of reported depression than in age-matched normals. Neither study, however, utilized direct interview material with children, and Sanger's criteria were clearly broader than Kaplan's. A further consideration, when reviewing studies of the epidemiology of psychiatric disorder in any chronically ill population, is the contribution of somatic symptoms resulting from the disease itself to the psychiatric criteria formulated on a nonmedically ill sample. If such somatic symptoms are not deleted from the criteria, the sensitivity of the instrument is inappropriately increased (i.e., there will be an increased Type I error, or false positive rate).

Lansky and Cairns (1987) provides an overview of commonly presenting problems among childhood cancer patients. Major problems include separation anxiety, often presenting as school phobia, adjustment disorders, noncompliance, oppositional behavior with family and medical staff, and treatment refusal on the part of the patient and/or family.

Pfefferbaum (1990), in an excellent overview, suggests that different psychiatric problems become manifest at different stages of the treatment. This is in line with Chesler and Barbarin's (1987a) findings that parents reported different levels of stress at various points in their child's illness. While it is true that the experience of childhood cancer and its treatment is invariably taxing to coping skills, vulnerability to significant decompensation by the child or family is not the norm.

Certain children and families are at significant risk (Pfefferbaum, 1990): those with preexisting psychiatric disease in the child or parents; those families with preexisting marital discord or difficult divorces; children with special needs, such as retarded or autistic children; or those with sensory deficits or language deficits. In a similar vein, particular problems may appear at given times in the treatment: self-injurious or suicidal behavior may become manifest in the older child or parent at diagnosis; anxiety and depression may complicate treatment; and mental status changes may occur because of the disease itself or its treatment. Adjustment problems may accompany return to school and "daily life," after treatment induction or termination. Indeed, adjustment disorder may appear at any point in the treatment itself. Specific problems in treatment include anxiety related to the disease or its treatment, conditioned anxiety, and nausea and vomiting, to specific treatment modalities such as chemotherapy or lumbar puncture, and pain control.

In many instances, patients come to the attention of the child and adolescent psychiatrist because a member of the oncology treatment team is concerned about their response to treatment. While, ideally, a child and adolescent psychiatrist would be a member of the team itself and get to know patients as they are diagnosed and move throughout their treatment, it is far more likely that these patients will be referred to the psychiatrist. The rate of referral is entirely dependent on the sensitivity of treatment team members to psychiatric disorder. If team members have a high threshold for distress in the patients, the level of anxiety or depression may be greater than if the staff members are acutely sensitive to dysphoria in their patients. This point notwithstanding, a referral indicates that something is de facto wrong for patients and/or in the care such that psychiatric help is needed. Note that the help may be needed by the treatment team instead of or as well as for the patient.

Adjustment disorders among these children commonly present with sleep disturbances, nausea and vomiting (often in anticipation of chemotherapy), or problems with elimination (Lansky & Cairns, 1987). In the course of evaluating children, it is important to broaden the inquiry to ascertain their general level of functioning at home, school, and with friends and family. Short-term psychotherapy, perhaps including specific symptom-reducing techniques such as relaxation, or adjunctive anxiolytics, is recommended.

Separation anxiety occurs at an increased rate among children with cancer, and, in school-aged children, often presents as school refusal or school phobia. While the general population prevalence of school refusal is estimated at 3% (Hersov,

1985), children being treated for cancer may show a prevalence of 12% (Lansky & Cairns, 1987) or higher.

Separation difficulties may become manifest for the parents as well as children; in fact, "symbiotic reactions" among mothers and their children have been noted. In these cases, found in 4% of the patients in one series (Lansky & Cairns, 1987), the mother and child become an isolated dyad, showing extreme mutual dependency. Such children have been noted, as teenagers in hospital, to adopt the fetal position with the mother in bed next to them. This became particularly problematic when treatment failed, and the mother and child totally withdrew from the rest of the family and the treatment team. Such mothers were unable to begin grieving their child's anticipated death, and acute grief reactions up to 3 or 4 years after the child's death were noted.

Oppositional behavior, directed at parents and treating physicians, may prompt a psychiatric referral. It must be kept in mind that such behavior may be developmentally appropriate, such as in teenagers in the midst of separation from their family, and that patients may have a limited domain in which to demonstrate their independence. Such behavior also may take the form of treatment noncompliance. Approaches to such oppositionality should take into account the children's developmental and social tasks, and domains in which they can safely assert their feelings and independence need be sought. Such oppositionality may be a response to overly rigid therapeutic regimens (with unnecessarily tight time schedules, etc.) or to disagreements not otherwise acknowledged between patients and the treatment team.

Noncompliance with treatment may be the rule, rather than the exception, once patients have left the hospital setting. One study found that 50% overall, and 68% of adolescents, among a sample of children with leukemia and lymphoma, did not fully adhere to a prescribed prednisone regimen (Lansky & Cairns, 1987). While factors traditionally thought to be of import in compliance, such as health beliefs and individual and family pathology, undoubtedly play a role, this study found that parental personality characteristics and patient gender were of major import.

Pain management, eating difficulties, and family responses to these concerns may become major problems during periods of illness and treatment.

In general, pediatric pain and dysphoria are unrecognized (Pfefferbaum, 1990; Pfefferbaum, Adams, & Aceves, 1990). Often medications are prescribed "prn," which staff may interprete to mean "use minimally, and only if absolutely necessary." Moreover, in response to pain, children may withdraw and become silent rather than voice complaints, further complicating pain relief efforts. Clearly, adequate pain coverage will do much to foster an alliance with the family of the pediatric cancer patient.

Medication Issues

The use of phenothiazines as antiemetic agents is well established, but the use of other psychotropes as adjunctive treatments for other problems in the cancer treatment of children is not as well known. Antidepressants, stimulants, and antianxiety agents may all have their place in the optimal treatment of childhood cancer. Furthermore, the psychiatrist consultant may be in the best position to identify the inadequate medication of pain.

Critical to the appropriate use of such medications, however, is specification of the problem being treated, different approaches to the problem, and criteria by which to measure the intervention's success. Social withdrawal while on the hospital ward, for example, may herald a major depression but may also be children's response to increased pain or fear (Barber, 1989; Grossman & Shidler, 1987; Redd, 1990). Anticipatory anxiety regarding bone marrow aspiration or other painful procedures may respond to distraction strategies, such as video games or storytelling, as well as to antianxiety medication (Redd, 1990).

Pain is mediated at the local, spinal, and supratentorial levels; thus, multimodal interventions have proved useful. Biofeedback, relaxation, and specific self-hypnotic techniques have all proved successful in particular patients with cancer pain, including children (Pfefferbaum, 1990). While cancer pain may persist for a long time, it has been conceptualized usefully as a variant of acute pain, in that it is due to tissue damage and invasion, is localizable, and responds to acute medication efforts (LeBel-Schwartz, 1990). Analgesic pharmacotherapy historically has been underutilized

although it can be most effective, and concerns about addiction generally have been unfounded. In general, it is recommended that nonnarcotic analgesia be tried first, affecting the pain at the local level (LeBel-Schwartz, 1990). While nonsteroidal antiinflammatory agents are effective analgesics and antiinflammatory agents, they should be used cautiously in children with altered blood counts, for they universally affect platelet function (Insel, 1990). Acetaminophen does not share this property, although it, too, must be used cautiously because of its hepatic metabolism and serious toxicity at high serum levels. Pain from cancer, however, may very well require additional medication. Opiate and opiatelike compounds can be usefully added to these nonopiate medications. Useful guidelines for the use of narcotic analgesia in pediatric cancer patients can be found in Grossman and Shidler (1987), LeBel-Schwartz (1990), and Pfefferbaum (1990).

The use of phenothiazines and phenothiazinelike drugs as antiemetics is well established, but their potential for extrapyramidal reactions and sedation may be underappreciated. Similarly, their anticholinergic potential, with the possibility of exacerbating stomatitis and adding to constipation or urinary retention, must be noted.

Methylphenidate may be empirically useful in moderately withdrawn, depressed, ill children (Wilens, 1990). They may respond immediately with improved mood and concentration, decreased withdrawal, and increased appetite. Starting with a low dose (5 milligrams [mg]) in the morning and titrating up is suggested in this population (Wilens, 1990).

Antidepressant agents may well prove useful in the treatment of depressive syndromes among pediatric cancer patients. Pfefferbaum (1990) recommends reserving antidepressant medications for persistent symptoms or symptoms that interfere with medical treatment or daily functioning. Clearly, obtaining baseline and periodic electrocardiograms as well as blood counts and liver function tests is warranted. Monitoring cardiac status is especially important in children receiving cardiotoxic chemotherapeutic agents such as adriamycin. It is equally important that the patient's and family's understanding and unambivalent support of a psychopharmacologic intervention for depressive symptoms obtained in order to assure compliance, especially as an outpatient.

These patients often respond to tricyclic doses lower than those required by their non-ill peers. Pfefferbaum (1990) suggests 1 to 2 mg per kilogram and provides evidence of the efficacy of such doses in an earlier paper (Pfefferbaum-Levine et al., 1983). In addition, there is some evidence that immediate responses occur to these medications, in contrast to the 2- to 4-week response delay commonly seen in non-ill children being treated pharmacologically for depression (Huessy, 1984; Pfefferbaum-Levine, Kumor, Cangir, Choroszy, & Roseberry, 1983; Wilens, 1990).

The specific agent chosen should depend, in large measure, on the side effect profile as it relates to patients' conditions. The tricyclics lower seizure threshold and should be used very cautiously or avoided in patients with seizure potential. The caveat given with respect to the antiemetic agents' anticholinergic potential applies also to the tricyclic antidepressants, particularly the tertiary amines amitriptyline and imipramine. While the use of nontricyclic agents, such as the serotonin reuptake inhibiting agents, is inviting because of the lack of cardiac effects, it must be noted that fluoxetine, amitriptyline, and desipramine were all found by Brandes et al. (1992) to stimulate tumor growth in rodents, when given in clinically relevant doses.

Antianxiety agents, such as the benzodiazepines, can be useful in the management of acute anxiety and anticipator anxiety, and as adjuncts in antiemetic therapy (Marshall, 1989; Pfefferbaum, 1987). It is this author's opinion, however, that they should be used adjunctively with behavioral and other psychotherapeutic approaches rather than as primary therapies, in order to facilitate children's potential for perceived mastery of symptoms and parts of the disease and treatment process and for the subsequent improvements in self-esteem.

Long-term Sequelae

Interest in the long-term adaptation of childhood cancer survivors has only recently become an area of extensive study, reflecting the increased survival of children with cancer. In 1960, only 4% of all children with acute lymphoblastic leukemia survived longer than 6 months; now more than 75% of these children survive over 5 years (Pfefferbaum, 1990). While not all childhood cancers have shown such dramatic improvement in prognosis, overall these children are being cured more frequently; the "cost" of survival in terms of long-term adjustment and adaptation for some of these children is now becoming apparent.

Any consideration of the long-term psychosocial well-being of children with cancer must take note of the substantial stigma and social obstacles still encountered by these children and families. Ostracism and lack of understanding by teachers and students in the school setting (Larcombe et al., 1990) remains a serious problem despite well-publicized advances in therapy and earlier return to daily living for these children. Many children and adults think cancer is contagious (McWhirter & Kirk, 1986), and this undoubtedly affects the social interactions of children with cancer. Moreover, the stigma attached to a disease such as cancer, while sometimes subtle, can be pervasive and socially powerful in terms of social institutions (many of these patients experience substantial difficulty obtaining health insurance or life insurance, despite years of disease-free survival) and identity (Goffman, 1963; Sontag, 1990).

Research findings on the overall well-being of childhood cancer survivors are contradictory, although recent authors have repeatedly stressed the point that most of these children "do well" (Chesler & Barbarin, 1987a; Fritz, Williams, & Amylon, 1987). Interpretation of all of these studies must be cautious, for the studies employ different criteria for "survival" (e.g., 2 years to 5 years after diagnosis, 2 years disease free, etc.); markedly different criteria are used to assess emotional well-being (clinician impression, unstructured psychiatric interview, parent only interview, parent questionnaire, etc.); and the sample sizes vary considerably. Nevertheless, as will be illustrated, the studies point out several aspects of pediatric cancer "cure" or "survival" worthy of psychiatric attention. Furthermore, the finding that "most" children and families do well should underscore the import of finding and providing treatment for those children and families most likely to suffer unduly.

Substantial attention has been paid to the long-term effects of cranial irradiation on two groups of pediatric cancer survivors: those with acute lymphoblastic leukemia and those with brain tumors. Cranial radiation was widely used in the treatment of acute lymphoblastic leukemia patients to prophylax against central nervous system recurrence up through the mid-1980s. As concern against the sequelae of this practice rose, the dosage of radiation and then the practice itself was discontinued, except for the roughly one-third of patients considered at "high risk" (R. Hutchinson, personal communication). Pediatric brain tumor patients still routinely receive therapeutic cranial irradiation.

In one of the first systematic studies of childhood cancer survivors, O'Malley et al. (1979) conducted psychiatric interviews on 114 children and their parents. Over half of the sample was thought to be "maladjusted," with 12% thought to be seriously impaired. Based on their interview data, the authors reported that well-adjusted survivors remembered reacting to news of their diagnosis with relief that the cancer was treatable; in contrast, the more impaired group reported primarily shock and distress at the diagnosis. These authors, like several others, also noted that denial was a commonly used and effective defense mechanism employed by these patients in talking about their cancer experiences.

Adolescents 2 to 8 years after treatment for cancer were found to have a prevalence of depression roughly equal to that found in general surveys, but they demonstrated enduring psychological concerns directly related to the cancer (Fritz & Williams, 1988). Over 1 in 5 were thought to be "counterphobic" regarding their bodies, and over 1 in 4 reported scrutinizing their bodies and being preoccupied with health issues. Fully 27% reported extreme difficulties with the opposite sex, and the same percentage of adolescents reported that their relationships with members of the opposite sex were totally platonic, free of dating, dancing, and without an identified boy- or girlfriend. The authors reported that serious adjustment problems were found primarily among those who had relapsed.

In an earlier study, Fritz et al. (1987) found that most childhood cancer survivors showed successful long-term adaptation, with "good" global adjustment and only rare problems with depression and academic or social malfunction. Communication patterns among family members and be-

tween family members and the medical staff were most predictive of psychosocial outcome, whereas severity of disease was not.

Friedman (Friedman & Mulhern, 1991) studied 183 childhood cancer survivors at least 2 years after completing treatment and at least 5 years after diagnosis. Over three-quarters of her sample had elevations greater than 1.5 standard deviations above the mean on one or more Child Behavior Checklist (Achenbach & Edelbrock, 1983) scales. Fifty-four percent of her sample had low social competency, and 42% had elevations on behavioral scales of the checklist. A two- to four-fold increased risk of school behavioral problems was found among children with enduring physical disability who had received a radiation treatment for leukemia, who were older than 12 years at the time of the survey, or who lived in a single-parent household.

Several studies have looked specifically at neuropsychological sequelae of radiation for these children. Reviewing these studies, Gamis and Nesbit (1991) found that IQ decrements among children with acute lymphoblastic leukemia who were treated with cranial irradiation were most prevalent among children younger than 8 years of age who also received intrathecal methotrexate. Similarly, one-third to three-quarters of childhood brain tumor survivors revealed below-average IQs when tested, and those below 7½ years of age who received whole brain irradiation were found to be at most risk. In the same vein, Peckham (1991), reviewing the learning sequelae among children treated for acute lymphoblastic leukemia (ALL) and brain tumors, found that:

Late sequelae in ALL children involved specific difficulties in attention, memory, and visual-motor integration;

Among children who had received 2400 cGy prophylactic brain irradiation, 8–10 years after treatment, students were 2.7 years below expected levels in reading and math. This decrement in performance was based on pretreatment test scores.

In general, these children reported difficulties with inner distractibility, memorizing, and sequencing tasks, especially under pressure.

LeBaron (LeBaron, et al., 1988) found that over half of the children who had posterior fossa tumors resected had later problems in academic, motor, sensory, cognitive, or emotional realms. Parent-completed Child Behavior Checklists revealed most problems on the somatic, depression, and social withdrawal subscales. The authors noted that over one-third of these cancer survivors "warranted" professional attention. The children most at risk for subsequent progressive cognitive deterioration were under the age of 6 to 8 years at the time of treatment and were treated with cranial irradiation and intrathecal methotrexate.

As noted, interpretation of these studies must be cautious, but several predictive risk factors do emerge. Brain cancer itself puts a child at risk for cognitive or socioemotional complications after successful treatment, as does cranial irradiation, especially among young children. Radiation and methotrexate combined dramatically increase the risk of neurobehavioral problems for children under 6 or 8. Family discord, functional disability, and poor communication among and between family members and the medical team also significantly increase the risk to a child of developing later emotional, cognitive, or behavioral problems. In contrast, cranial irradiation alone for older children, a degree of "optimal denial" throughout the disease and its treatment, and good family communication patterns seem to provide emtional and cognitive protection for these children.

Family Issues

Childhood cancer has been termed a "family disease," and recent work has begun to explore the effects on a family system of childhood malignancy. Family involvement in the child's journey through cancer treatment begins prior to diagnosis, and family functioning and style is critical to overall adjustment and psychosocial status of all family members. Research on the family aspects of cancer has focused on stability of coping styles, effects on marital functioning, and, to a limited extent, the effects on siblings of an index patient's disease. Some work has correlated family functioning with psychosocial outcome.

Empirical work with these families has shown that parental and sibling roles and responsibilities are significantly altered by the need to care for a child with cancer or other chronic diseases

(Chesler & Barbarin, 1987a; Fife, Norton, & Groom, 1987; Krener & Adelman, 1988). Family roles are changed in concrete ways—fathers may become involved in much more direct child care, siblings may become responsible for increased domestic duties, mothers commonly find themselves at their child's side 24 hours per day. Significant changes in responsibilities accompany these role changes, and individuals may find themselves increasingly isolated in the family system. In addition, parenting a child with chronic illness requires that parents adopt problematic parenting strategies (Krener & Adelman, 1988).

Krener notes how parenting a child with any chronic disease entails tasks for the parents that would otherwise interfere in their child's and family's development:

Parents must constantly recalibrate their expectations and demands to their child's needs, making it more difficult for them to appropriately assess and promote developmentally appropriate capacities.

Partial symbiosis, or a diffusion of the parent-child boundary, is a normal response of a parent-child dyad to acute illness in the child, but as the illness becomes chronic this symbiosis may serve to isolate the pair from others in and outside of the family.

Chronic illness highlights parents' worries that they cannot meet their child's needs, increasing the parents' sense of being "out of control."

Finally, repeated hospitalizations interfere with the parents' capacity to socialize the child to the outside world. (Krener & Adelman, 1988)

Parents commonly report their wish to shield their children from hurtful news, and this includes passing on the diagnosis of cancer. Fully 60% of the children in one sample were not told of their diagnosis at diagnosis (Chaflin & Barbarin, 1991). This same study found that younger children, as a rule, were told less than older children but that these younger children reported distress at least as great as the older subjects. Children in another study commonly reported that they did not wish to "burden" their parents with their concerns, worries, and fears about cancer and family life (Carpenter & Sahler, 1991). This is in line with the general finding that children are skilled at learning what is allowed in conversation in various settings and at respecting these "moral" limits (Wilkinson, 1988). The picture, then, is of individual members of a family becoming increasingly isolated out of a wish to protect other members from distress. While older children may wish to have some increased "time alone," this isolation is directly counter to younger children's needs to be with family members (Claflin & Barbarin, 1991).

Psychosocial "difficulties" and psychiatric symptoms increase for the siblings of children with cancer, although severity of these symptoms may fall short of diagnostic criteria. Breslau and Prabucki (1987) found increased rates of psychiatric symptoms, especially aggressive behavior and later depressive symptoms, among the siblings of children with chronic disease. The prevalence of children with symptoms increased in this sample over 5 years, to 15 to 18% (with a 12.1% prevalence of the same symptoms in a control sample). Carpenter (Carpenter & Sahler, 1991) found that over half of the siblings in their study reported emotional lability, negative attentional behavior, academic decrements, and social withdrawal. The children in Carpenter's study who supposedly did well reported the most open family communication patterns.

Family coping styles have been found to be stable over at least the first year postdiagnosis for children with acute lymphoblastic leukemia (Fife et al., 1987), and variation in the medical status of the child has little bearing on the coping strategies employed by parents (Chesler & Barbarin, 1987). Eight basic coping strategies have been identified: denial, optimism, acceptance, maintenance of emotional balance, information seeking, active problem solving, religion, and searching for social support (Chesler & Barbarin, 1987a,b). Interestingly, Chesler and Barbarin (1987) found that greater parental education is associated with the use of active information seeking, optimism, and poorer relationships with medical staff. This factor may play a role in some psychiatric referrals (Chesler & Barbarin, 1987), when oncology staff feel that parents are not accepting their recommendations appropriately.

Contrary to what might be assumed, recent research has found that divorce is not an increased risk, at least in the first years after a child's diagnosis, for families of children with cancer (Chesler & Barbarin, 1987). Barbarin, Hughes, and Chesler (1985) found that husbands and wives generally felt they were brought closer by their child's illness. Their perceptions of their spouse's support-

iveness decreased, however, as the number of hospitalizations for the child increased, and a wife's perception of her husbands' supportiveness was directly correlated with the husband's direct involvement in the sick child's care.

In general, the findings just outlined support the notion that most families do "well," with some families being at particular risk for increased psychosocial difficulties. Parental psychopathology along with adverse social and material family circumstances may mitigate effective family response to illness. Seemingly protective factors include open family communication patterns, somewhat fluid family roles that allow for accommodation to the sick child's needs for support and attendance, and a parental ability to allow "normalized" (as much as possible) developmental social milestones for their children.

The Role of the Child and Adolescent Psychiatrist

As alluded to earlier, the child and adolescent psychiatrist may be called upon to treat a child with cancer in inpatient or outpatient settings. The role of the pyschiatrist is, to a large extent, determined by the setting—for example, a consultation psychiatrist in a university medical center will be called on differently than a private practitioner in a university town—but certain generalities apply: First, in assessing a child's difficulties, the psychiatrist must consider neuropsychological as well as emotional responses to illness; second, the psychiatrist must have a thorough understanding of the child's cancer, its treatment, course, and prognosis, plus knowledge of the child's and family's understanding of the disease and its course; finally, the psychiatrist must attend to the patient and family throughout the assessment and treatment. Repeated studies have found family factors, including communication patterns and discord, to be instrumental in psychosocial outcome for these children.

Patients and families may feel the psychiatric referral is a punishment from their doctor for being a bad patient or a sign of failure in caring for their child (Krener & Adelman, 1988). Such stigma may apply to referring physicians, nurses, and social workers on oncology services, as well. Referral to a psychiatrist may be seen as appropriate only for severe mental illness and not for help with pain, adjustment, or other concerns. The experiences and views of psychiatry held by each staff member likely impacts his or her referral practices. Furthermore, the involvement of a psychiatrist may signify to the treatment team's members their own inadequacy to care for the patient, and referral may be resisted.

Medical staffs that treat children with cancer must routinely deal with death, grieving families, and disappointment, as well as with the elation of cure. Physicians and nurses involved in this endeavor must regularly subject children to painful procedures in the course of treating their disease. Pediatricians and nurses must learn to distance themselves from their patients' pain in order to function effectively, but some of these strategies may yield undue patient suffering and decrease therapeutic rapport and effectiveness (Barber, 1989). These aspects of pediatric cancer care impact on caregivers relentlessly, and the psychiatrist is in the unique position to notice, comment, and provide some support for these professionals (Sugar & Herzog, 1992). Clearly, contact between the psychiatrist and the oncologic treatment team is of potential benefit to the medical staff as well as the patient.

In the consultation-liaison setting, ideally, the psychiatrist should be integrated into the treatment team and introduced to the patient early in the patient's treatment. Doing so may be particularly important in certain treatment settings, such as bone marrow transplant, which involve significant potential trauma to the child and psychosocial isolation (Stuber, Nater, Yasuda, Pynoos, & Cohen, 1991). Such early integration of psychiatry

and pediatric oncology should do much to reduce the stigma and shame felt by patients and families with later referral for psychiatric input.

In the outpatient setting, it is recommended that the psychiatrist endeavor to communicate and integrate treatment plans with the oncology treatment team. Informing the team that the child is being seen, of any medication trials being undertaken, and of significant psychological concerns that become evident can only be beneficial in terms of coordinating treatment efforts. Being informed by the team of new chemotherapy trials, their concerns about the patient's psychological well-being and family stresses as well as physical changes will similarly benefit the psychiatrist's work.

In a broader sense, integration of child psychiatry and pediatric oncology has much to offer theoretically as well as clinically. Collaboration between oncology physicians and nurses and child psychiatrists allows the consideration of emotional and social considerations in the treatment of these children. It should help promote useful self-reflection on the part of caregivers that allows them to minimize countertransference interference in their work with cancer patients and their families. Involvement with these patients and families offers the child psychiatrist the opportunity to witness and participate in a child's and family's response to a life-threatening stressor that calls forth major coping capacities. It offers a chance to participate with other medical caregivers in life-saving and sustaining endeavors, and a chance to participate in the medical community. Finally, working with and studying children's emotional and neuropsychological responses to different cancers and treatments demands "biopsychosocial" integration on the part of the psychiatrist.

REFERENCES

Achenbach, T. M., & Edelbrock, C. (1983). *Manual for the Child Behavior Checklist and Revised Child Behavior Profile.* Burlington, VT: Thomas A. Achenbach.

American Cancer Society. (1992). *Cancer facts & figures—1992.* Author.

Barbarin, O. A., Hughes, D., & Chesler, M. A. (1985). Stress, coping and marital functioning among parents of children with cancer. *Journal of Marriage and the Family,* (473–480).

Barber, J. (1989). Suffering children hurt us. *Pediatrician, 16,* 119–123.

Blos, P. J. (1978). Children think about illness: Their concepts and beliefs. In E. Gellert (Ed.), *Psychosocial aspects of pediatric care* (pp. 1–17). New York: Grune & Stratton.

Brandes, L., Arron, R., Bogdanovic, R. P., et al. (1992). Stimulation of malignant growth in rodents by antidepressant drugs in clinically relevant doses. *Cancer Research, 50,* 3796–3800.

Breslau, N., & Prabucki, K. (1987). Siblings of disabled children. *Archives of General Psychiatry, 44,* 1040–1046.

Carpenter, P. J., & Sahler, O. J. Z. (1991). Sibling perception and adaptation to childhood cancer. In J. H. Johnson & S. B. Johnson (Eds.), *Advances in child health psychology* (pp. 193–205). Gainesville: University of Florida Press.

Chesler, M. A., & Barbarin, O. A. (1987a). Coping as a family. In M. A. Chesler & O. A. Barbarin (Eds.), *Childhood cancer and the family* (pp. 91–117). New York: Brunner/Mazel.

Chesler, M. A., & Barbarin, O. A. (1987b). Parent coping strategies. In M. A. Chesler & O. A. Barbarin (Eds.), *Childhood Cancer and the Family* (pp. 118–138). New York: Brunner/Mazel.

Claflin, C. J., & Barbarin, O. A. (1991). Does "telling" less protect more? Relationships among age, information disclosure, and what children with cancer see and feel. *Journal of Pediatric Psychology, 16,* 169–191.

Donovan, D. M., & McIntyre, D. (1990). *Healing the hurt child.* New York: W. W. Norton.

Fife, B., Norton, J., & Groom, G. (1987). The family's adaptation to childhood leukemia. *Social Science & Medicine, 24,* 159–168.

Friedman, A. G., & Mulhern, R. K. (1991). Psychological adjustment among children who are long-term survivors of cancer. In J. H. Johnson & S. B. Johnson (Eds.), *Advances in child health psychology* (pp. 16–27). Gainesville: University of Florida Press.

Fritz, G. K., & Williams, J. R. (1988). Issues of adolescent development for survivors of childhood cancer. *Journal of the American Academy of Child and Adolescent Psychiatry, 27,* 712–715.

Fritz, G. K., Williams, J. R., & Amylon, M. (1987). After treatment ends: Psychosocial sequelae in pediatric cancer survivors. *American Journal of Orthopsychiatry, 57,* 552—561.

Gamis, A. S., & Nesbit, M. E. (1991). Neuropsychologic (cognitive) disabilities in long-term survivors of childhood cancer. *Pediatrician, 18,* 11–19.

Glazer, J. P. (1991). Psychiatric aspects of cancer in childhood and adolescence. In M. Lewis (Ed.), *Child and adolescent psychiatry* (pp. 964–977). Baltimore: Williams & Wilkins.

Goffman, E. (1963). *Stigma.* Englewood Cliffs, NJ: Prentice-Hall.

Grossman, S. A., & Shidler, V. R. (1987). An aid to prescribing narcotics for the relief of cancer pain. *World Health Forum, 8,* 525–528.

Hersov, L. (1985). School refusal. In M. Rutter & Hersov (Eds.), *Child and adolescent psychiatry* (pp. 382–399). Boston: Blackwell Scientific Publications.

Hockenberry, M. J., Coody, D. K., & Bennet, B. S. (1990). Childhood cancers: Incidence, etiology, diagnosis, and treatment. *Pediatric Nursing, 16,* 239–246.

Huessy, H. R. (1984). Tricyclics for children with cancer [Letter to the editor]. *American Journal of Psychiatry, 141,* 472.

Insel, P. A. (1990). Analgesic-antipyretics and antiinflammatory agents; Drugs employed in the treatment of rheumatoid arthritis and gout. In A. G. Gilman, T. W. Rall, A. S. Nies, et al. (Eds.), *Goodman & Gilman's The Pharmacological Basis of Therapeutics* (pp. 638–681). New York: Pergamon Press.

Kaplan, S. L., Busner, J., Weinhold, C., et al. (1987). Depressive symptoms in children and adolescents with cancer: A longitudinal study. *Journal of the American Academy of Child and Adolescent Psychiatry, 26,* 782–787.

Krener, P., & Adelman, R. (1988). Parent salvage and parent sabotage in the care of chronically ill children. *American Journal of the Diseases of Childhood, 142,* 945–951.

Lansky, S. B., & Cairns, N. U. (1987). Psychiatric syndromes in pediatric oncology patients. *Psychiatric Medicine, 5,* 405–417.

Larcombe, I. J., Walker, J., Charlton, A., et al. (1990). Impact of childhood cancer on return to normal schooling. *British Medical Journal, 301,* 169–171.

LeBaron, S., Zeltzer, P. M., Zeltzer, L. K., et al. (1988). Assessment of quality of survival in children with medulloblastoma and cerebellar astrocytoma. *Cancer, 62,* 1215–1222.

LeBel-Schwartz, A. (1990). Pain management in children. In M. S. Jellinek & D. B. Herzog (Eds.), *Massachusetts General Hospital psychiatric aspects of general hospital pediatrics* (pp. 98–113). Chicago: Year Book Medical Publishers.

McWhirter, W. R., & Kirk, D. (1986). What causes childhood leukaemia. *Medical Journal of Australia, 145,* 314–316.

Miller, R. W. (1989). Frequency and environmental epidemiology of childhood cancer. In P. A. Pizzo & D. G. Poplack (Eds.), *Principles and practice of pediatric oncology* (pp. 3–18). Philadelphia: J. B. Lippincott.

O'Malley, J. E., Koocher, G., Foster, D., et al. (1979). Psychiatric sequelae of surviving childhood cancer. *American Journal of Orthopsychiatry, 49,* 608–616.

Peckham, V. C. (1991). Educational deficits in survivors of childhood cancer. *Pediatrician, 18,* 25–31.

Pfefferbaum, B. (1990). Common psychiatric disorders in childhood cancer and their management. In J. C. Holland & J. H. Rowland (Eds.), *Handbook of psychooncology* (pp. 544–561). New York: Oxford University Press.

Pfefferbaum, B., Adams, J., & Aceves, J. (1990). The influence of culture on pain in Anglo and Hispanic children with cancer. *Journal of the American Academy of Child and Adolescent Psychiatry, 29,* 642–647.

Pfefferbaum-Levine, B., Kumor, K., Cangir, A., Choroszy, M., & Roseberry, E. A. (1983). Tricyclic antidepressants for children with cancer. *American Journal of Psychiatry, 140,* 1074–1076.

Poplack, D. G. (1989). Acute lymphoblastic leukemia. In P. A. Pizzo & D. G. Poplack (Eds.), *Principles and practice of pediatric oncology* (pp. 323–366). Philadelphia: J. B. Lippincott.

Redd, W. (1990). Behavioral interventions to reduce child distress. In J. C. Holland & J. H. Rowland (Eds.), *Handbook of psychooncology* (pp. 573–581). New York: Oxford University Press.

Rowland, J. H. (1990). Developmental stage and adaptation: Child and adolescent model. In J. C. Holland & J. H. Rowland (Eds.), *Handbook of Psychooncology* (pp. 519–543). New York: Oxford University Press.

Sanger, M. S., Copeland, D. R., & Davidson, E. R. (1991). Psychosocial adjustment among pediatric cancer patients: A multidimensional assessment. *Journal of Pediatric Psychology, 16,* 463–474.

Sontag, S. (1990). *Illness as metaphor and AIDS and its metaphors.* New York: Anchor Books.

Stuber, M. L., Nater, K., Yasuda, P., Pynoos, R. S., &

Cohen, S. (1991). Stress responses after pediatric bone marrow transplantation: Preliminary results of a prospective longitudinal study. *Journal of the American Academy of Child and Adolescent Psychiatry, 30,* 952–957.

Sugar, J. A., & Herzog, D. B. (1992). Hospitals and LOS [Letter to the editor]. *Journal of the American Academy of Child and Adolescent Psychiatry, 31,* 566.

Wilens, T. E. (1990). Depression in the medically ill child. In M. S. Jellinek & D. B. Herzog (Eds.), *Massachusetts General Hospital psychiatric aspects of general hospital pediatrics* (pp. 263–271). Chicago: Year Book Medical Publishers.

Wilkinson, S. R. (1988). The form of dialogue. In S. R. Wilkinson (Ed.), *The child's world of illness* (pp. 10–32). Cambridge: Cambridge University Press.

---

29 / Cerebral Palsy: The Psychiatric Implications of a Motor Handicap

James C. Harris

Although long recognized by families and professionals, cerebral palsy (a static motor encephalopathy) was not distinguished from other motor handicaps until the 19th century, when William John Little attributed spastic rigidity to obstetrical complications and perinatal anoxia. In his classic report of 200 cases published in 1861, he suggested etiologies for spastic rigidity and thus offered the opportunity for prevention. As a result of his work, the condition was referred to as Little's disease (Accardo, 1989). Later William Osler introduced the term "cerebral palsy" (a contraction of the word "paralysis") in his 1889, book, *The Cerebral Palsies of Children*. In 1897 Sigmund Freud (Accardo, 1982; Freud, 1968), a child and adult neurologist before turning to psychoanalysis, published *Infantile Cerebral Paralysis*. In this work, he introduced an early clinical classification that provided a basis for the later classifications. Modern refinements in classification were introduced

and summarized in Crothers and Paine's *The Natural History of Cerebral Palsy* (1959). The current agreed-upon classification of the clinical motor disorders was adopted by the American Academy of Cerebral Palsy (Minear) in 1956.

The term "cerebral palsy" lacks specificity. It does not describe the severity or type of motoric deficit that is present and indicates simply that the cause of the motor deficit is thought to be the result of nonprogressive brain pathology, due to maldevelopment or to brain damage incurred during birth or in early life. Consequently, neurologists often prefer the term "static motor encephalopathy" and concurrently list the specific motor handicap and other associated disabilities. Like the terms "mental retardation," "learning disability," and "pervasive developmental disorder," it is the accepted general term for a handicapping condition that has a wide range of both psychological and social implications.

Efforts at prevention and early treatment were initiated at the beginning of the 20th century when programs in physical therapy were introduced. More recently, using noninvasive imaging tech-

This chapter has been adapted in part from J. C. Harris, "Cerebral Palsy," in *Developmental Neuropsychiatry: Assessment, Diagnosis, and Treatment of Developmental Disorders,* pp. *127–141.*

niques, additional information has been gained on clinicopathological correlates. Extensive efforts have been focused on therapy both for the movement disorder and for psychological adaptation by the child and family.

Definition

Cerebral palsy is a nonprogressive, but not unchanging, disorder of movement and posture that results from an injury to or a congenital anomaly of the immature brain (Hughes & Newton, 1992). It is recognized during the period of most rapid brain growth; it is associated with sensory, behavioral, and cognitive manifestations. The term "cerebral palsy," along with these associated features, designates a multiply handicapping disorder that may be mild, moderate, or severe. Although it is a static motoric disability, changes do occur as the central nervous system matures. The cerebral lesion is nonprogressive, but the peripheral physical symptoms may change over time with brain development. For example, a hypotonic infant may become a spastic child, and a child who is first diagnosed as choreoathetoid may later become dystonic and develop contractures. For some children, there is gradual improvement, but for others a plateau occurs in their functioning. Bracing and surgery may be required due to the severity of the disorder.

Because the stability of the diagnosis is less clear during infancy, there is disagreement about the age at which the cerebral palsy should be diagnosed. It has been suggested that brain damage that occurs before the age of 3 should be used as a guideline. If this were the standard, children with acquired cerebral palsy occurring from infection or trauma might be included.

Epidemiology

Cerebral palsy occurs with a prevalence estimated at 1.5 to 2.5 per 1,000 live births for moderate-to-severe forms (Kuban & Leviton, 1994). A declining but not statistically significant trend for incidence in the 20-year period from 1970 to 1989 has been found with better management of pregnancy, delivery, and care of the newborn (Meberg & Broch, 1995). When milder cases are included, prevalence may be 1 to 6 per 1,000. Spastic cerebral palsy, the most frequent type, accounts for approximately 50% of cases; it is followed by athetosis, 20%, and rigidity, ataxia, tremor, and mixed forms, which account for approximately 25% or more (Stanley & Alberman, 1984). The survival rate has remained high for children who live through the neonatal period and reached 88% in the 1940s and 1950s (Cohen & Mustacchi, 1966) and remains at that level. Chichton, MacKinnon, and White (1995) report a 30-year survival rate of 87%. Factors affecting survival include the type of cerebral palsy (prognosis is the worst for spastic quadriplegia), epilepsy, and severe or profound mental retardation. Longer term survival offers new challenges to both physical and psychological treatment.

Changes in the care of newborns have resulted in changes in morbidity. Summaries of earlier research from the 1940s and 1950s and the monograph by Crothers and Paine (1959) suggest that birth injury and developmental problems accounted for approximately 50% of reported cases at that time. In the 1990s cerebral palsy associated with prematurity has been more strongly represented, as smaller and smaller premature infants survive in neonatal intensive care units.

Etiology

The National Collaborative Perinatal Project (Nelson, 1988; Nelson & Ellenberg, 1986) concluded that recognition of important known antecedents of cerebral palsy failed to account for the majority of cases. A high rate of false positive identifications was noted and the authors found that the majority of cerebral palsy cases did not have a specifically defined cause. Like etiologically unidentified mental retardation syndromes and congenital malformations, they lacked a specific etiology. In 20 to 30% there is no known cause—there may have been unrecognized events during pregnancy or an unknown genetic abnormality.

Cerebral palsy does not have a single cause; the etiology of the various presentations is not identical. Early studies considered perinatal events as causative, but more recent investigations (Blair & Stanley, 1985) found asphyxia in only 6 to 8% of cases. In the Perinatal Collaborative study of National Institutes of Neurological and Communicative Disorder and Stroke (Nelson, 1988) 14% of quadriplegia was due to birth asphyxia. The relative contributions of prenatal, perinatal, and genetic factors in etiology must all be considered. Birth complications are the most common cause and generally involve reduced oxygenation to motor control areas; several brain regions are involved in the coordination of muscle activity, so a variety of areas may be involved. The most common cause is periventricular leukomalacia associated with prematurity (Kuban and Leviton, 1994). In early childhood, encephalitis, meningitis, stroke, head injury, or poisoning may be etiologic factors.

Mechanism

Developments in classification highlight how much there is to learn about the etiology of cerebral palsy. Powell, Pharoah, Cooke, and Rosenbloom (1988a,b) reported on 1,048 low-birthweight infants and identified 48 with cerebral palsy. Intrapartum events were associated with hemiplegia, but factors involved in the rate of fetal development were more prominent in diplegia, which is more often associated with prematurity. Central nervous system infections in the first year recently have been reported to account for 6% of cases (Naeye, Peters, Bartholomew, & Landis, 1989), and about 2% are attributed to genetic factors. In their early stages, other inherited disorders may mimic a static encephalopathy.

Care is necessary in attributing the etiology to hypoxic-ischemic brain injury. A full-term infant with hypoxic damage will show signs that include seizures, abnormalities in tone, an unusual degree of alertness, and primitive reflex patterns. Fetal distress with meconium staining and reduced Apgar scores may also be a product of other etiologies. Disorders of neuronal migration may account for some movement disorders. Neurons migrate to the cortical plate between 7 and 16 weeks of gestational age making this a vulnerable period. Since the neocortex is laid down from inside to outside, newly developing neuronal terminals pass through layers that have already developed. If abnormal migration occurs, association pathways may be affected, leading to motor dysfunction, seizures, and learning and behavioral problems. Localized migrational problems have been described in addition to the more severe forms, such as agyria, microgyria, and pachygyria. Both environmental factors at sensitive developmental periods and genetic disorders may affect development in this way.

Assessment

The evaluation of a child with cerebral palsy requires an integrated approach to treatment by an interdisciplinary team. The nature of the handicap often requires the involvement of pediatrics, neurology, psychiatry, orthopedics, ophthalmology, physiatry, and dentistry as well as physical, occupational, and speech therapy. Social workers, psychologists, and educators complete the team. The assessment is complicated by the child's multiple handicaps. Cognitive ability may be difficult to evaluate due to the extent of the motoric handicap and associated language disorders. Thus, standardized testing needs to be adapted to discern accurately the child's particular strengths and weaknesses. Following their assessments, team members meet to develop treatment plans and intervention tasks are assigned.

Motor delay is essential to the diagnosis of cerebral palsy. However, establishing whether there is a permanent movement disorder is difficult since early signs may improve or resolve. There is an understandable reluctance to diagnose cerebral palsy during the first 6 months of life since the handicap may not be clearly evident. Some motor delays will resolve with maturation in children of this age; they may also resolve in children between 6 and 18 months. Since one-third to one-half of very low-birthweight infants may have some type of developmental disability, follow-up should continue into the school-age years.

Besides the standard neurological examination, a neurodevelopmental examination is essential to evaluate motor development. This study involves a search for persisting primitive reflexes and for recognizing postural reactions. These include the asymmetric tonic neck reflex, the moro, and the tonic labyrinthine reflex (Capute & Accardo, 1991a; Capute et al., 1984). By 6 months of age, these primitive reflexes ordinarily are inhibited by higher cortical centers, and, in normal development, their disappearance is followed by postural reactions. The postural responses include head righting, the Landau reaction, and derotational righting. They appear before rolling over, sitting, and crawling emerge.

Advances in the use of noninvasive imaging techniques are now being utilized to improve and enhance assessment methods. Currently, ultrasound is used in early diagnosis of intraventricular hemorrhage, and magnetic resonance imaging may be utilized to evaluate structural changes and positron emission tomography (Chugani, 1992; Volpe, 1992; Sugimoto et al., 1995; Krageloh-Mann et al., 1995; Kucukali et al., 1995). In the future, assessments of metabolic activity, structural changes and regional cerebral blood flow using positron emission tomography may be utilized.

Classification of Types of Cerebral Palsy

A multiaxial classification is used to classify cerebral palsy (Bax, 1964; Minear, 1956); it includes the type and location of the dysfunction and associated conditions. The systems of classification are referred to as physiologic (pyramidal and extrapyramidal), topographic, and supplemental. Since all cerebral palsy has an early hypotonic phase, early classification is tentative until a clear presentation syndrome can be perceived. Cerebral palsy is then classified by the type of motor abnormality that is identified and the part of the body involved. The classification of an individual case may be difficult because of mixed features that may be demonstrated on the motor examination.

There are two main groups of dysfunction (physiological classification): the pyramidal or spastic and the extrapyramidal or nonspastic types. The spastic type is the most common and is characterized by increased muscle tone in the involved muscle groups. Because of the increased tone, there is a state of constant muscle contraction. These neurological findings are persistent and vary little with movement, with emotion, or during

TABLE 29.1
Classification of Cerebral Palsy

Symptom	% Occurrence
Hemiplegia	25–40
Spastic diplegia	10–33
Spastic quadriplegia	9–43
Extrapyramidal (athetoid, ataxic, dystonic)	9–22
Mixed	9–22

(From Nelson and Ellenberg, 1978)

sleep. Pathological reflexes are readily demonstrated in spastic forms. The frequency of occurrence of these types is shown in Table 29.1.

SPASTIC TYPES

The spastic subtypes are classified depending on the number of limbs involved. They are designated as monoplegia (1 limb), diplegia (2 limbs), triplegia (3 limbs), quadriplegia (4 limbs), and hemiplegia (an arm and a leg on the same side of the body). Because of their hypotonicity, infants with these types are often described as floppy. With increasing age, they show increased muscle tone and associated musculoskeletal deformities that may require orthopedic surgery. Furthermore, primitive reflexes, such as the tonic neck reflex, may persist, leading to problems in posture and movement. In hemiplegia, the upper limbs generally are more impaired than the lower ones. In diplegia, all 4 limbs may be involved, but the upper limbs may have only minimal involvement. In quadriplegia, the upper limbs may be less impaired, but there is generally severe dysfunction of all limbs. Monoplegia and triplegia are less common and are variations of hemiplegia and quadriplegia.

EXTRAPYRAMIDAL TYPES

Extrapyramidal forms are nonspastic types of cerebral palsy and are designated as choreoathetoid, ataxic, dystonic, and rigid forms. These groups can be recognized clinically but are less clearly linked to neuropathological findings. Increased movement symptoms in persons with extrapyramidal cerebral palsy are associated with activity, with emotions, and when active muscle tension is required. During sleep or relaxation, symptoms may be less intense. Abnormal involuntary movements increase with emotional stress, which may be evident in a psychiatric interview. Primitive reflexes are more apparent in the extrapyramidal forms.

Individuals with athetosis display involuntary movements that involve various muscle groups. Consequently, they may appear contorted, stiff, or in continuous motion. Their speech may be dysarthric, and hearing impairment may be an associated finding. Chorea may occur with athetosis: the individual is then described as choreoathetoid. Chorea consists of involuntary jerky movements involving the face, tongue, portions of the extremities (especially the distal portions), and, in some instances, the trunk. These movements are rapid and irregular and are more pronounced during voluntary movement. The dystonic form involves extreme athetoid movements where the body and/or the extremities are forced into fixed postures by muscle contraction.

Individuals with extrapyramidal forms of cerebral palsy of the dyskinetic type are thought to have damage to the basal ganglia and to cranial nerves. Since the cerebrum usually is not involved, there is less cognitive impairment than in the spastic types. However, it should be noted that both extrapyramidal and pyramidal forms may be present in the same individual.

The other types—ataxic, rigid, and atonic—are much less common. Ataxic cerebral palsy is rare and involves the cerebellum, so muscle tone is primarily affected. These children are hypotonic and show severe motor delays. As they get older, functioning may improve. The rigid and the atonic types are much rarer forms. Children with these forms have very poor muscle tone and may have associated bone deformities. Mixed types of extrapyramidal forms of cerebral palsy also exist.

mal stretch reflex, the earliest changes are resistance to movement of the forearm, ankle, and knee. For spastic diplegia, symptoms are first noted in the legs and may be associated with leg extension or scissoring when the child is vertically suspended and increased tone when the child is placed to walk. In spastic hemiplegia, symptoms are usually first noted in the arms, and unequal muscle tone may be noted along with tight fists and an unequal response to the parachute maneuver. Furthermore, poor feeding may become apparent. The duration of hypotonia is variable and may last 6 to 17 months or even longer; the longer it lasts, the greater the severity of the handicap. If it persists longer than 3 years, the term "hypotonic cerebral palsy" is used.

Changes in tone continue to be noted with ongoing development. The hypotonia may be followed by dystonia—for example, when the infant is first able to hold up his or her head—extensor decerebrate rigidity may become apparent as the head is extended. Dystonic episodes may be present from 2 to 12 months of age. Eventually rigidity appears. In extrapyramidal cerebral palsy, persistent hypotonia is accompanied by immature (primitive) postural reflexes. With extrapyramidal forms, the asymmetrical tonic neck reflex and the righting response persist longer than in those with spasticity. The earliest sign of extrapyramidal dysfunction is finger posturing, which becomes apparent when the infant reaches for an object. Finger/hand posturing may be seen by 9 months. With dyskinesis, the dyskinetic postures are elicited by sudden changes in the position of the head, trunk, or limbs. Some children with early signs may not show them on later examination. Capute and Accardo (1991b) describe this continuum of developmental disability and emphasize that up to one-third of those affected subsequently show perceptual problems and hyperactivity. With increasing age, the consequences of early birth injury are more variable, and cognitive, academic, and behavioral problems become more apparent.

Natural History

For children who experience perinatal asphyxia and have subsequent involvement of the motor system, sequential changes have been documented. As the child gets older, early hypotonia may progress to spasticity. As a result of an abnor-

Associated Handicaps

As the child matures, the problems associated with cerebral palsy may assume particular prominence. Speech and motor disability may be more apparent in the preschool years, whereas, on beginning school, learning disabilities may become apparent. Difficulties that may influence learning include visual perceptual problems, speech impairment, and hearing impairment. The most handicapping of the associated problems are cognitive difficulties. The recognition of these new difficulties means another readjustment for the family that already faces the continuing need for surgery, bracing, and the use of other adaptive equipment. Moreover, communication disorder is also a particularly important problem that demands intervention. Speech synthesizers and communication boards often are essential to facilitate interpersonal communication.

Thus associated nonmotoric handicaps that occur in children with cerebral palsy include mental retardation, sensory impairment of vision and hearing, learning disability, and language disorders. These associated handicaps, along with psychological and psychiatric problems, determine the extent of possible rehabilitation.

The extent of motor disability ranges considerably from mild spasticity, where the individual may be mentally retarded but where ambulation is possible, to athetoid conditions or mixed athetoid and spastic conditions, where the individual may be essentially nonverbal and dependent on family for care, yet has average or above-average intelligence, and requires special communication devices to interact with others.

Mental retardation occurs in approximately 60% (50 to 75%) of those with cerebral palsy. Affected nonretarded children are at risk for academic skills disorder or other cognitive impairment, visual and hearing deficits (6 to 16%), seizures (overall 20 to 30%; but in 70% with a spastic presentation and 20% with an athetoid presentation), strabismus (50%), sensory impairment (especially in hemiplegia), and social, emotional, and family dysfunction (Capute & Accardo, 1991a). Capute and Accardo (1991a) note that certain associated features accompany particular types of cerebral palsy. For example, spastic hemiplegia is more often associated with seizures, hemianopsia, growth arrest, and cortical sensory deficits (including a visual field abnormality). Spastic diplegia may be associated with strabismus and spastic quadriplegia with epilepsy, mental retardation, dysarthria, and strabismus. Choreoathetosis is associated with mental retardation, auditory impairment, and dysarthria.

MENTAL RETARDATION

Cognitive disability is among the most important considerations in cerebral palsy and leads to vulnerability to environmental stressors. The degree of cognitive impairment varies considerably and determines the child's educational level. Assessment of intelligence is particularly difficult due to the multiple physical disabilities that make full participation with testing problematic. A variety of tests are used. In their report on 1,000 6-year-olds, Blair and Stanley (1985) found an average IQ of 68; the range of IQ was broad and variable, broader, indeed, than in the general population. Those with ataxia showed the most variability; those with athetoid types displayed less impairment. The spastic group was more cognitively impaired than the athetoid group. The intellectual deficit was more severe in those with spastic quadriplegia when compared to those with paraplegia or spastic hemiparesis.

CENTRAL NERVOUS SYSTEM DYSFUNCTION

Brain damage is an important vulnerability factor in the establishment of psychiatric disorder in those with cerebral palsy. In the Isle of Wight study, Rutter, Graham, and Yule (1970) demonstrated that those children who were most affected cognitively were those who had a physical condition involving the brain. Yet the mechanism of how brain dysfunction results in behavioral abnormality remains unclear. Does brain dysfunction lead directly to behavioral disturbance, or does it increase the child's vulnerability to environmental stresses (Breslau, 1990)? Breslau suggests that brain dysfunction may lead to difficulty in inhibiting irrelevant environmental stimuli and subsequent misperceptions. In addition, brain damage may result in emotional lability, irritability, impulsiveness, limited social awareness, and attentional deficits resulting in personality disturbances.

ACADEMIC SKILLS DISORDER

Learning disability commonly is found in cerebral palsy as a consequence of deficits in visual perception, in auditory processing, and in information sequencing. Comprehensive neuropsychological testing is essential in the identification of strengths and weaknesses in learning.

Activities of Daily Living

The daily tasks of toileting, feeding, dressing, and transferring the disabled child from one place to another must be carried out for the child's comfort. Feeding may be a particular adjustment for the parent of a child with cerebral palsy, and parents may report prolonged feeding sessions of an hour or more. In the case of the infant, tongue thrust in the form of forceful tongue protrusion may interfere with the initiation of feeding. Tonic biting may be initiated when the gums are stimulated. The parent must be taught feeding techniques that position the infant to optimize tone by inhibiting extensor tone. This involves methods of introducing the nipple by supporting the jaw.

For the older child, management of incontinence is an ongoing concern. There may be many reasons for incontinence; psychological, cognitive, neurological, and neuromuscular factors must all be considered. The child or adolescent may be reluctant to participate in a toileting program. Family members and caregivers may not understand the reasons for the child's reluctance to participate, may become angry and require help with a behavior program. Incontinence may occur sporadically and be linked to spasticity of the bladder, resulting in intermittent voiding. Because the patient may not be believed, the behavior may be interpreted as showing a poor motivation. Children who do not understand the parental response may characterize themselves as lazy or feel hopeless about their lack of control in toileting.

Developmental Issues

Developmental phases are influenced by temperamental and physical aspects related to brain dysfunction; these, in turn, may interfere with parent/infant attunement and attachment (Cox and Lambrenos, 1992). Attunement between child and parent may be affected by cerebral palsy because ordinary coordination of body movement with mother's voice may not occur due to the movement disorder. The early practicing subphase described in Mahler's theory of separation-individuation may be disrupted by the inability of the child with cerebral palsy to move away from the parent and explore the environment. In addition, the child's limited ability to explore and return to a secure base, along with parent-child communication problems, also may affect separation-individuation. Older children with cerebral palsy may benefit from motorized wheelchairs to help explore the environment.

The inhibition of primitive reflexes is essential intervention to help the family deal with the developmental disorder. The tonic neck reflex, reflex arm extension when the head is turned, can be interpreted by the parent as an intentional movement to push them away. On other occasions, a child may produce a high-pitched cry associated with opisthotonic movements that elicits anxiety in the parent. Effective holding and handling to inhibit these primitive reflexes may enhance attachment.

In normal child development early attachment experiences result in the internalization of "working models" of the caregivers. To facilitate this developmental phase in children with cerebral palsy, communication devices are of particular importance. As children with cerebral palsy grow older, the motor disability becomes apparent to other children, and may lead to stigmatization. The higher-functioning group become increasingly aware of their difference and may be most affected by stimatization. More severely mentally disabled children may have cognitive deficits and may remain unaware. Positive internal working models are important in preparation for the early school years as a buffer to such experiences.

There are a series of developmental crises associated with life changes during each phase of development. These occur at the time of the diagnosis, during early phases of motor and language development, at the time of school entry, at the onset of adolescence, and at the time of leaving school.

Interview with the Parent

Since the parent is an active participant in the child's care and often functions as a cotherapist, it is essential that the parent is confident and fully informed about care requirements. The parent is burdened by the child's illness and needs regular support.

The difficulty in recognizing motor disability in the early months of life can be quite stressful for family members. Often parents are concerned about a floppy infant, but the physician may have to counsel waiting in order to clarify the nature of the condition. During this period, parents may shop, going from one physician to another for consultation. Furthermore, the parents may misinterpret the child's behavior. For example, when the tonic neck reflex persists, as mentioned, some parents may incorrectly interpret the reflex movement of the baby's arm toward them when the head is turned as an effort to push them away or reject them rather than simply as a motor reflex.

The use of early physical therapy can be extremely helpful to parents, particularly in teaching them to deal with primitive reflexes. An effective physical therapy intervention, utilizing postures that allow the reflexes to be inhibited, may allow the child to appear more normalized in the parents' company. When held and handled properly, the child may vocalize more appropriately. High-pitched screams from infants with cerebral palsy can be very disconcerting for parents and interfere with the process of attachment.

Cerebral palsy is a movement disorder that varies in its expression. This variability is affected by the parents' adjustment to the handicap. The psychiatric outcome must take into account the child in the family context. The first consideration is how the parents' adaptation influences the child's development. Since the developmental disability becomes apparent before the age of 3, it is essential that parents make an early adjustment to the child's handicap. A comprehensive support system of care is needed to facilitate this adjustment process. Associated brain damage, cognitive impairment, social stigma, and nonverbal learning disabilities all play a role in the beginning of a psychiatric disorder.

Any family history of previous psychiatric disturbance or of developmental disorder must also be elicited. Whether there is a past history of parental disturbance or not, parental adjustment to the child's handicap is a critical consideration. Most important among the psychological issues are denial of the handicap, self-blame, depression, projection, and dependency. To determine the degree of the parents' adaptation to the handicapping condition, a number of areas should be specifically covered as parents are interviewed regarding the child (MacKeith, 1976; Richmond, 1972). First, it is important to clarify the degree of denial; does the parent have a realistic appreciation of the nature of the handicap and its seriousness? Denial of the nature of the illness may place the child at risk. Second, whom does the parent talk to when he or she becomes upset about the child?; is there a close confiding relationship with a friend or is the parent psychologically isolated? The third area deals with excessive guilt. Who does the parent feel is to blame for the child's condition—is it the hospital staff, the parent him- or herself? Self-blame and the accompanying guilt are important to assess since these emotions may be linked to a depressive disorder. A sense of self-blame may emerge regarding their capacity at child rearing or the experience of shame for producing a handicapped child.

A fourth area of importance involves the caregiving staff. The parent is asked about the adequacy of the child's hospital care. Does he or she feel that the care staff can be trusted to carry out the procedures that the parent routinely does at home? Not uncommonly, parents criticize caregivers as an expression of their projected fears and anxiety and may benefit from the opportunity to vent these feelings. A fifth area focuses on the parent's sense of adequacy. Does the parent feel adequate to take care of the child, or has he or she become dependent on friends? Does the parent automatically follow directions from others and feel increasingly dependent? Is the overwhelmed parent dependent and passive or actively engaged in the child's care? When excessive dependency on caregivers occurs, the pediatrician may report a sense of frustration when the parent does not complete routine tasks of child care. When this occurs, the doctor often receives frequent telephone calls about minor illnesses and is asked to make more and more decisions for family members.

Finally, future plans for the child should be discussed. In discussing future plans, it is important to clarify whether there is a genetic basis for the condition and if so what do the parents believe are genetic implications to the diagnosis? The parents' ability to make future plans for their child and concurrently care for their spouse and the other children is an important aspect of the assessment.

Interview with the Child (Special Considerations)

In the interview with the child, the clinician must take into account both the child's developmental level and stage and his or her means of communication. At the first meeting, establishing confidence and cooperation is critical. Particular patience may be needed to comprehend the child's speech. In many instances, a letter board, speech synthesizer, or facilitated communication devices may be required. Assistance from a speech pathologist may be helpful at first, but, as familiarity with the communication equipment is established, such assistance is discontinued. Once emotional contact is established, the interview may proceed as with any child of equivalent mental age.

Adjustment Problems Related to Cerebral Palsy

With appropriate intervention, the child with cerebral palsy may have a productive school and family life. The availability of handicapped access to school and community facilities is a particularly crucial element. In the course of treatment, the following adjustment problems must be considered (Hurley & Sovner, 1987).

PASSIVITY AND DEPENDENCE ON OTHERS

Children with cerebral palsy often become dependent on others and show a lack of assertiveness and self care. Moreover, an attitude of dependency can be fostered by a parent's difficulty in adapting to the disability. Parental guilt may result in overprotection and an unwillingness to allow the child sufficient independence. Without adequate support, a child may then have difficulty initiating and following through on individual aspirations.

EXPERIENCES OF HOPELESSNESS AND FRUSTRATION

The inability to carry out tasks with fluidity of movement may lead to frequent frustration, particularly for the person with athetoid cerebral palsy. In addition, the sense of being deformed and different from others becomes more apparent with age. Children with cerebral palsy often feel they are victims of an uncurable condition.

DOUBTS REGARDING SOCIAL COMPETENCE

In children with cerebral palsy, the sense of hopelessness may be accompanied by a concern about their social competence. This concern may focus on the physical problems that are difficult to control—dribbling food and drooling saliva, urinary incontinence, and physical problems that socially isolate the child from others. In addition, social competence may be affected by social/emotional learning disabilities manifested by difficulty in attending to and understanding social cues. Potential problems with social perception and learning disabilities may lead to additional hazards in performing academic tasks and, ultimately, to school failure.

These disturbances of physical appearance, difficulty with activities of daily living, and lack of social awareness may combine to produce social stigma. Being stigmatized is an ongoing concern for the child's care. Furthermore, because of the physical handicap, higher-functioning children may be misdiagnosed as mentally retarded. Being considered mentally retarded leads to further stresses that may compound the child's difficulties.

With the onset of adolescence, peer group relationships assume additional importance, and social rejection may become a major issue. In adulthood, social rejection and discrimination, unfortunately, are not uncommon in the workplace.

GUILT AND SHAME

Like the parent, the child, too, may develop a sense of guilt or shame. With increasing self-awareness, children with cerebral palsy may become even more conscious of the burdens, both physical and financial, that their disorder causes other family members. In order for the youngsters to work through their feelings, a supportive parental attitude is crucial. Parental concern can lead to the use of appropriate counseling services to help the child maintain a more appropriate attitude. As the child grows older, the need for community services increases and the requirement for social support is greater for both child and parent.

Psychiatric Disorders Occurring in Persons with Cerebral Palsy

Psychiatric disorders fall into several categories: psychiatric conditions, such as adjustment disorder secondary to physical disability, personality trait disturbance, and difficulties in temperament. In addition, major psychiatric diagnoses may co-occur in a person with a movement disorder (dual diagnoses).

Brain damage is a predisposing factor to behavioral and emotional disorder. Persons with cerebral palsy are at risk for increased rates of emotional lability, irritability, attention deficits, impulsiveness, and limited skills in social problem solving. Breslau (1990) examined 157 children with cerebral palsy, myelodysplasia, or multiple handicaps along with 339 randomly selected controls. Both parent and child were interviewed. Increases in depressive symptoms and inattention were significantly associated with physical disabilities. In both groups, a troubled family environment was found to significantly heighten depression, but not inattention. This study demonstrates that parental/child problems alone or in combination with a difficult temperament in the child may lead to psychiatric disorder. In addition, children who have been overly protected may be at risk for separation anxiety disorder. Other children whose parents had difficulty setting limits may present with oppositional defiant disorder. Attention deficits are common and must be carefully assessed. Stress-related brief psychotic reactions may occur and must be distinguished from schizophrenia and mood disorder. Moreover, major mental illness, both in the form of mood disorder or schizophrenia, may present in adolescence and early adult life. Both conditions respond to psychotropic drug treatment. It is essential to review the family history for these conditions. Among these, mood disorder is a particular concern; a major depression may go unrecognized or be attributed to adjustment difficulties.

Comprehensive Therapy

A comprehensive treatment approach (Kohn, 1990) includes medical supervision, psychoeducational assessment and management, orthopedic management, and physical and occupational therapy (Bleck, 1987). Recent additions to the array of therapies are linked to advances in rehabilitation technology. Among these are orthotics (braces), robotics, mobility and seating devices, and computer interfaces for the regulating devices. Augmentative communication devices allow children early in life to make choices and understand cause-effect relationships. Guides to their use are available for parents (Blasco, Baumgartner, & Mathes, 1983). Intensive physiotherapy with specific measurable goals is essential to a successful outcome (Bower, McLellan, Arney, & Campbell, 1996).

Psychotherapy with individuals who have cerebral palsy requires adaptations to the particular handicap. In particular, psychotherapy must be tailored to the relevant features of the person's disorder. Of particular importance is the use of communication devices—communication boards and other special devices to facilitate language use. It is important to keep in mind that, although considerable patience is required, psychotherapeutic interventions can be effective with persons with disabilities just as with persons without disabilities, especially when the intervention involves both the child and family. Initial therapeutic goals focus on children understanding the presenting problem, their comprehension of the nature of their handicap, and their expression of their feelings about it. Later psychotherapeutic goals include better self-control, attributing responsibility for behavior to one's self, use of problem-solving techniques to understand consequences, developing a vocabulary of emotions, appreciating others' point of view as different from one's own, and recognition of the effect of one's behavior on others.

Crisis intervention techniques are essential for family members and include anticipatory guidance and preventive interventions. Anticipatory guidance is needed at times of predictable crisis: the time of diagnosis, adapting to the specific physical needs for child care, the time of school entry, entry into adolescence, and future family planning. Preventive interventions are essential throughout the crisis. For example, since mental retardation may become evident for the first time at the beginning of school, school entry can be particularly difficult. If parents demonstrate failure to adapt to the handicap during the initial parental interviews, then short-term therapy goals must be developed. These goals may focus on denial, guilt and self-blame, projection, and excessive dependency on others.

Pharmacotherapy is effective and should be utilized in keeping with the presenting diagnosis. The reason for the medication must be reviewed with the patient, and parent and the child should be actively involved in drug treatment. A careful baseline neurological examination is necessary before initiating neuroleptic or other drug treatment. Finally, the patient's cognitive level must be considered in monitoring side effects of medications.

Conclusion

Treatment for children and adolescents with cerebral palsy requires an understanding of the various types of cerebral palsy, the associated physical and psychological disabilities, and the family's adaptation to the handicap. Family crises are predictable at the time of diagnosis, during the preschool years, at school entry, during adolescence, and at the completion of schooling. With maturation, the extent of function and impairment may vary. Additional associated impairments may become more evident with age—for example, mental retardation and seizure disorders may become apparent and require treatment. Young children who were walking with crutches may become nonambulatory with growth and weight gain during adolescence. Sometimes parents may misinterpret the extent of the child's difficulty with feeding, toileting, or ambulation and attribute it to poor motivation.

Parental mastery of the problems associated with adjustment to the child's handicap is essential since the parents play a vital role in the child's psychological development. The joy of a loving presence, the frustration of not being able to communicate, and the sense of loneliness that is experienced by the handicapped child are movingly presented in the poems of Christy Brown (1971), a young man who had athetoid cerebral palsy. Through his poems, Christy Brown demonstrates the possibility of developing internal working models of interpersonal relationships despite the physically-challenging condition.

REFERENCES

Accardo, P. J. (1982). Freud on diplegia: Commentary and translation. *American Journal of Diseases of Children, 136,* 452–456.

Accardo, P. J. (1989). William John Little (1810–1894) and cerebral palsy in the nineteenth century. *Journal of the History of Medicine and Allied Sciences, 44,* 56–71.

Bax, M. C. O. (1964). Terminology and classification of cerebral palsy. *Developmental Medicine and Child Neurology, 6,* 295–297.

Blair, E., & Stanley, F. (1985). Interobserver agreement in the classification of cerebral palsy. *Developmental Medicine and Child Neurology, 27,* 615–622.

Blasco, P., Baumgartner, M., & Mathes, B. (1983). Literature for parents of children with cerebral palsy. *Developmental Medicine and Child Neurology, 25,* 642–647.

Bleck, E. (1987). Orthopedic management of cerebral palsy. *Clinics in Developmental Medicine* (No. 99/100). Oxford: Blackwell Scientific Publications.

Bower, E., McLellan, D. L., Arney, J., & Campbell, M. J. (1996). A randomised controlled trial of different intensities of physiotherapy and different goal-setting procedures in 44 children with cerebral palsy. *Developmental Medicine & Child Neurology, 38,* 226–237.

Breslau, N. (1990). Does brain dysfunction increase children's vulnerability to environmental stress? *Archives of General Psychiatry, 47,* 15–20.

Brown, C. (1971). *Come softly to my wake.* London: Secker and Warburg.

Capute, A. J., & Accardo, P. J. (1991a). Cerebral palsy: The spectrum of motor dysfunction. In A. J. Capute & P. J. Accardo (Eds.), *Developmental disabilities in infancy and childhood* (pp. 335–348). Baltimore: Paul H. Brookes Publishing Co.

Capute, A. J., & Accardo, P. J. (1991b). A neurodevelopmental perspective on the continuum of developmental disabilities. In A. J. Capute & P. J. Accardo (Eds.), *Developmental disabilities in infancy and childhood* (pp. 7–41). Baltimore: Paul H. Brookes Publishing Co.

Capute, A. J., Palmer, F. B., Shapiro, B. K., Wachtel, R. C., Ross, A., & Accardo, P. J. (1984). Primitive reflex profile. *Monographs in Developmental Pediatrics* (Vol. 1). Baltimore: University Park Press.

Chugani, H. T. (1992). Functional brain imaging in pediatrics. *Pediatric Clinics of North America, 39* (4), 777–796.

Cohen, P., & Mustacchi, P. (1966). Survival in cerebral palsy. *Journal of the American Medical Association, 195,* 462.

Cox, A. O., & Lambrenos, K. (1992). Childhood physical disability and attachment. *Developmental Medicine & Child Neurology, 34,* 1037–1046.

Crichton, J. U., Mackinnon, M., & White, C. P. (1995). The life-expectancy of persons with cerebral palsy. *Developmental Medicine & Child Neurology, 37,* 567–576.

Crothers, B. S., & Paine, R. S. (1959). *The natural history of cerebral palsy.* Cambridge, MA: Harvard University Press.

Freud, S. (1968). *Infantile cerebral paralysis.* Coral Gables, FL: University of Miami Press. (Originally published 1897.)

Hughes, I., & Newton, R. (1992). Genetic aspects of cerebral palsy. *Psychiatric Aspects of Mental Retardation Reviews, 6,* 1–6.

Hurley, A., & Sovner, R. (1987). Psychiatric aspects of cerebral palsy. *Psychiatric Aspects of Mental Retardation Reviews, 6,* 1–6.

Kohn, J. G. (1990). Issues in the management of children with spastic cerebral palsy. *Pediatrician, 17,* 230–236.

Krageloh-Mann, I., Petersen, D., Hagberg, G., Vollmer, B., Hagberg, B., & Michaelis, R. (1995). Bilateral spastic cerebral palsy—MRI pathology and origin. Analysis from a representative series of 56 cases. *Developmental Medicine & Child Neurology, 37,* 379–397.

Kuban, K. C. K., & Leviton, A. (1994). Cerebral palsy. *New England Journal of Medicine, 330,* 188–194.

Kucukali, I., DeReuck, J., Decoo, D., Strijckmans, K., Goethals, P., & Lemahieu, I. (1995). Positron emission tomography in spastic diplegia. *Clinical Neurology and Neurosurgery, 97,* 28–31.

Little, W. J. (1961–62). On the influence of abnormal parturition, difficult labors, premature birth, and asphyxia neonatorum, on the mental and physical condition of the child, especially in relation to deformities. *Transactions of the Obstetrical Society of London, 3,* 293–344. (Originally published 1861.)

MacKeith, R. (1976). The restoration of parents as a keystone of the therapeutic arch. *Developmental Medicine and Child Neurology, 18,* 285–286.

Meberg, A., & Broch, H. (1995). A changing pattern of cerebral palsy. Declining trend for incidence of cerebral palsy in the 20-year period 1970–89. *Journal of Perinatal Medicine, 23,* 395–402.

Minear, W. (1956). A classification of cerebral palsy. *Pediatrics, 18,* 841.

Naeye, R. L., Peters, E. C., Bartholomew, M., & Landis, R. (1989). Origins of cerebral palsy. *American Journal of Diseases of Children, 143,* 1154–1161.

Nelson, K. B. (1988). What proportion of cerebral palsy is related to birth anoxia? *Journal of Pediatrics, 112,* 572–574.

Nelson, K., & Ellenberg, J. (1978). Epidemiology of cerebral palsy. *Advances in Neurology, 19,* 421.

Nelson, K., & Ellenberg, J. (1986). Antecedents of cerebral palsy. *New England Journal of Medicine, 315,* 81–86.

Osler, W. (1889). *The cerebral palsies of children.* Philadelphia: P. Blakiston and Son.

Powell, T. G., Pharoah, P. O. D., Cooke, R. W. I., & Rosenbloom, L. (1988a). Cerebral palsy in low-birthweight infants. I. Spastic hemiplegia: Associations with intrapartum stress. *Developmental Medicine and Child Neurology, 30,* 11–18.

Powell, T. G., Pharoah, P. O. D., Cooke, R. W. I., & Rosenbloom, L. (1988b). Cerebral palsy in low-birthweight infants. II. Spastic diplegia: Associations with fetal immaturity. *Developmental Medicine and Child Neurology, 30,* 19–25.

Richmond, J. B. (1972). The family and the handicapped child. *Clinical Proceedings of Children's Hospital Medical Center, 8,* 156–164.

Rutter, M., Graham, P., & Yule, W. A. (1970). A neuropsychiatric study in childhood. *Clinics in Developmental Medicine* (No. 35/36). London: Spastics International Medical Publications in association with William Heinemann Books, Ltd.

Stanley, F., & Alberman, E. (1984). The epidemiology of cerebral palsy. *Clinics in Developmental Medicine* (No. 87) Oxford: Blackwell Scientific Publications.

Sugimoto, T., Woo, M., Nishida, N., Araki, A., Hara, T., Yasuhara, A., Kobayashi, Y., & Yamanouchi, Y. (1995). When do brain abnormalities in cerebral palsy occur? An MRI study. *Developmental Medicine & Child Neurology, 37,* 285–292.

Volpe, J. J. (1992). Value of MR in definition of the neuropathology of cerebral palsy in vivo. *American Journal of Neuroradiology, 13,* 79–83.

30 / Closed Head Injuries

Joan P. Gerring

Head injury is a major health problem in childhood and adolescence. Psychiatric sequelae of head injury occur frequently, are enduring, and may significantly alter the posttraumatic adjustment. As advances in biomedical technology, development of standardized assessment procedures such as the Glasgow Coma Scale, and use of statewide coordinated trauma retrieval systems have resulted in greatly increased patient survival, so the child psychiatrist will be asked to evaluate children and adolescents who have suffered mild, moderate, and severe head injuries. Child psychiatrists also will evaluate children with a variety of complaints who incidentally have a history of mild, moderate, or severe head injury. They may be asked to estimate the contribution of past head injury to present psychopathology.

Acute brain injury is the cause of approximately 100,000 pediatric hospital admissions per year in the United States (Kraus, Fife, & Conroy, 1987). The major causes of brain injury in children up to 15 years old are falls (35%), recreational activities (29%), and motor vehicle crashes (24%). Falls decrease with age as a cause of injury, while traffic-related accidents increase (Di Scala, Osberg, Gans, Chin, & Grant, 1991). The annual brain injury rate per 100,000 children is 185, 235 per 100,000 boys and 132 per 100,000 girls.

Head injury may be either open or closed. Open head or war injury occurs when the dura mater is penetrated, as, for example, with a missile. Open head injury is focal in nature, and psychiatric symptoms can be correlated with the location of injury. Loss of consciousness need not occur at the onset of the injury. Closed head injury is the most common type of civilian head injury and is the type most frequently seen in children and adolescents. Most of this chapter discusses closed head injury and its treatment. This injury occurs when a blow to the head does not penetrate the dura. Severe closed head injury frequently results in a sudden loss of consciousness. The resulting injury is multifocal throughout the brain. The presence of multiple lesions in gray and white matter makes it more difficult to correlate psychiatric symptoms with lesion location. In addition, the edema, ischemia, and problems in regulation of blood pressure, respiration, and electrolyte levels that may result from the primary injury probably contribute to early behavioral sequelae.

Injury severity can be measured by use of the Glasgow Coma Scale (GCS), a widely used, easily administered scale which measures eye opening, motor response and verbal response (Jennett & Teasdale, 1981). (See Table 30.1.) Scores range from 3 to 15, with a score of 3 indicating no eye opening, no motor response, and no verbal response and a score of 15 indicating full alertness. Persons with an initial score of 9 to 12 or those with initial scores of 13 to 15 who undergo brain surgery or who have an abnormal radioimaging procedure are considered to have moderate injuries. Other injuries are mild with initial scores of 13 to 15. It is hoped that these definitions of mild and moderate injury will replace the previously used designation of concussion. Concussion can refer to head injuries with momentary unconsciousness or up to 1 hour of unconsciousness. Using similar definitions of severity, Kraus's study of San Diego County hospital admissions noted 5% of pediatric head injuries to be severe, 3% to be moderate, and 93% to be mild (1987). Three percent died before arrival to the hospital, and 3% died in the hospital.

Prognostic Indicators

The duration of coma, the duration of posttraumatic amnesia, and age are three important prognostic indicators of outcome. It is important to obtain coma duration from the chart or from the recollection of family members. Coma is defined as the period of time when the patient is unable to obey simple commands, such as "stick out your

TABLE 30.1

Glasgow Coma Scale

EYE OPENING	
Spontaneous	E4
To Speech	3
To Pain	2
Nil	1
BEST MOTOR RESPONSE	
Obeys	M6
Localizes	5
Withdraws	4
Abnormal flexion	3
Extensor response	2
Nil	1
VERBAL RESPONSE	
Oriented	V5
Confused conversation	4
Inappropriate words	3
Incomprehensible sounds	2
Nil	1
COMA SCORE (E + M + V) = 3 to 15	

Note: From *Management of head injuries* by B. Jennett and G. Teasdale, 1981, Philadelphia: F. A. Davis. p. 78. Copyright 1981 by Jennett and Teasdale. Reprinted by permission.

tongue" or "hold up two fingers." This is an operational definition used by specialists in head injury; the termination of coma indicates that the patient is entering an active period of cognitive and motor rehabilitation. On the other hand, the neurologist defines coma differently, as a complete lack of psychologic responsiveness (Plum & Posner, 1987).

Posttraumatic amnesia is one of three types of amnesia associated with closed head injury. (See Table 30.2.) Retrograde amnesia, the first amnesia related to head injury, is the period of time prior to the injury for which the patient has no recollection. This period is usually measured in hours or days and tends to shrink with time. However, in more severe injuries, it rarely shrinks completely to encompass the actual memory of the accident event. As a consequence, these severely injured patients are not vulnerable to the development of a posttraumatic stress disorder. Anterograde amnesia occurs after the trauma and is a period of time during which the patient is unable to lay down continuous memories. The patient is also disoriented during this period and may appear confused. Islands of memory may be recalled later within the period of anterograde amnesia. These memories may be distortions of events or may clearly resemble events in which the patient participated. The anterograde amnesia may occur immediately after the trauma or may follow a period of coma after more severe injuries.

The posttraumatic amnesia consists of the period of anterograde amnesia plus the period of coma, if coma occurs. The duration of this posttraumatic amnesia can be elicited after its termination by asking the patients when they came back to their senses or when they felt like their old selves again. Or its termination can be determined by sequential administration of a test of orientation and memory. Posttraumatic amnesia ends when the patient achieves a certain score on an instrument such as the GOAT (Galveston Orientation and Amnesia Test) (Levin, Benton, & Grossman, 1982) or its childhood counterpart, the COAT (Childhood Orientation and Amnesia Test) (Ewing-Cobbs, Levin, Fletcher, Miner, & Eisenberg, 1990). (See Table 30.3.)

Age is an important prognostic indicator in

TABLE 30.2

Psychiatric and Neurologic Events that Follow Severe Closed Head Injury

	INJURY				
TIME	→				
PSYCHIATRIC EVENTS	*DSM–IV* Disorders		Delirium		*DSM–IV* Disorders
NEUROLOGIC EVENTS	Continuous Memories	Retrograde Amnesia	Posttraumatic Amnesia		Continuous Memories
			Coma	Anterograde Amnesia	

TABLE 30.3

Children's Orientation and Amnesia Test (COAT)

General Orientation:	Points:

1. What is your name? first (2) _____ (5) _____
last (3) _____

2. How old are you? (3) _____ When is your (5) _____
birthday? month (1) _____ day
(1) _____

3. Where do you live? city (3) _____ (5) _____
state (2) _____

4. What is your father's name? (5) _____ (10) _____
What is your mother's name? (5) _____

5. What school do you go to? (3) _____ (5) _____
What grade are you in? (2) _____

6. Where are you now? (5) _____ (5) _____
(May rephrase question: Are you at home now? Are you
in the hospital? If rephrased, child must correctly answer
both questions to receive credit.)

7. Is it daytime or nighttime? (5) _____ (5) _____

General Orientation Total _____

Temporal Orientation: (administer if age 8–15)

8. What time is it now? (5) _____ (5) _____
(correct = 5; < hr. off = 4; 1 hr. off = 3; > 1 hr.
off = 2; 2 hrs. off = 1)

9. What day of the week is it? (5) _____ (5) _____
(correct = 5; 1 off = 4; 2 off = 3; 3 off = 2; 4 off = 1)

10. What day of the month is it? (5) _____ (5) _____
(correct = 5; 1 off = 4; 2 off = 3; 3 off = 2; 4 off = 1)

11. What is the month (10) _____ (10) _____
(correct = 10; 1 off = 7; 2 off = 4; 3 off = 1)

12. What is the year? (15) _____ (15) _____
(correct = 15; 1 off = 10; 2 off = 5; 3 off = 1)

Temporal Orientation Total _____

Memory:

13. Say these numbers after me in the same order. (Discontinue when the
child fails both series of digits at any length. Score 2 points if both digits
are correctly repeated; score 1 point if only 1 is correct.)

3	5____	35296	81493____	(14) ____
58	42____	539418	724856____	
643	926____	8129365	4739128____	

14. How many fingers am I holding up? Two fingers (10) _____
(2) _____ three fingers (3) _____
10 fingers (5) _____

15. Who is on Sesame Street? (10) _____ (10) _____
(can substitute other major television show)

16. What is my name? (10) _____ (10) _____

Memory Total _____

OVERALL TOTAL _____

Note. From "The Children's Orientation and Amnesia Test: Relationship to severity of
acute head injury and to recovery of memory" by L. Ewing-Cobbs, H. S. Levin, J. M.
Fletcher, M. E. Miner, and H. M. Eisenberg, 1990, *Neurosurgery, 27* (5), p. 684.

TABLE 30.4

Sequelae of Closed Head Injury

MOTOR SEQUELAE
Spasticity
Ataxia
Decreased motor speed

NEUROPSYCHOLOGIC SEQUELAE
Decreased IQ, performance greater than verbal
Attentional deficits
Memory deficits
Visuomotor deficits
Visuoperceptual deficits
Executive dysfunction
Self-regulatory dysfunction
Decreased initiation

LANGUAGE SEQUELAE
Impaired confrontration naming
Word retrieval deficits
Disordered associations
Aphasia

PSYCHIATRIC SEQUELAE
Delirium—during posttraumatic amnesia
Amnestic and other cognitive disorders
Accentuation of premorbid psychiatric disorders
Personality change due to closed head injury

---

regard to general outcome, but there is no current evidence that age at injury bears any relationship to the risk of psychiatric disorder. There are suggestions from studies on cognitive outcome that younger children have a poorer outcome than older children. In a 1970 follow-up study of children with severe head injuries, children injured after the age of 10 had longer coma durations but higher posttraumatic IQs than children injured prior to age 10 (Brink, Garrett, Hale, Woo-Sam, & Nickel, 1970). Shaffer, Bijur, Chadwick, and Rutter (1980) studied children who had sustained compound depressed skull fractures at ages 4 through 12, which had been followed by a period of coma. These open head injuries had occurred at least 2 years before the follow-up reading evaluation. The prevalence of reading disorder in this sample was significantly higher in children with a longer duration of unconsciousness who had been injured before the age of 8.

Long-Term Sequelae

The severity of injury plays a significant role in the persistence of long-term sequelae. The most commonly observed sequelae after closed head injury are listed in Table 30.4. In the Kraus study (1987), the rate of moderate or severe disability, persistent vegetative state, or death was 100% with admission Glasgow Coma Scale scores of 3 or 4 and 65% with admission scores of 5 to 8. Only 1 of 18 children with a Glasgow Coma Scale score of 9 to 12 and 1 of 164 children with a score of 13 to 14 had a moderate or worse degree of disability. Functional recovery also may be correlated with duration of coma. Coma of more than 7 days usually is associated with some permanent motor, cognitive, or psychologic sequelae (Stover & Zeiger, 1976). Coma lasting longer than 90 days usually results in multiple severe motor, language, and cognitive sequelae (Kriel, Krach, & Sheehan, 1988). Coma durations less than 7 days may result in sequelae that are subtle or pronounced and short-lived or permanent, depending on variables such as injury location, lesion size, and nature of the injury.

Severe disability and persistent vegetative state are the worst outcomes of closed head injury. In the Kriel series of 26 patients under 19 years who were unconscious longer than 90 days, 20 children and adolescents regained consciousness, with 11 of these regaining the ability to communicate (1988). Severely disabled children are completely dependent on their caregivers and have disabilities that include immobility, muteness, and behavioral disinhibition. Persistently vegetative patients have preserved vegetative functions, including a sleep-wake cycle, but remain behaviorally unresponsive. Six patients of the 26 in the Kriel series who were unconscious longer than 90 days remained persistently vegetative.

MOTOR SEQUELAE

Incapacitating long-term motor sequelae, such as hemiparesis, quadriparesis or severe ataxia, usually occur only after prolonged coma. Although walking is the single most frequently impaired function (Di Scala et al., 1991), most severely injured patients leave the hospital walking. The most common motor sequelae are spasticity, ataxia, and combinations of these two. Lesser degrees of motor impairment, such as increased deep tendon reflexes and slight resistance to passive movement, are common but do not often lead to greatly impaired function (Brink et al., 1970).

NEUROPSYCHOLOGIC SEQUELAE

Severity of brain injury is directly related to the overall degree of neuropsychologic deficit. Neuropsychologic sequelae commonly seen after closed head injury include memory storage and retrieval deficits (Levin & Eisenberg, 1979); attentional deficits; visuospatial and visuomotor deficits (Chadwick, Rutter, Brown, Shaffer, & Traub, 1981); a diminution in the performance IQ (Chadwick, Rutter, Shaffer, & Shrout, 1981); and deficits in fine motor coordination, tactual-spatial functions, and verbal fluency (Winogron, Knights, & Bawden, 1984).

LANGUAGE SEQUELAE

Language dysfunction is common following closed head injury. Dysfunction in most patients is secondary to disruption of cognitive abilities, such as concentration, attention, conceptual organization, abstract thinking, and part/whole analysis and synthesis, although a specific language disorder may coexist. In other patients, a specific language disorder is predominant and cognitive impairment is minimal (Hagen, 1986). Impaired confrontation naming, word retrieval, and expressive organization of ideas over several sentences are language sequelae commonly seen after severe closed head injury in children. The associations of these children may be rambling, disconnected, tangential, and sometimes inappropriate (Ylvisaker, 1986).

Neuropsychologic and language deficits vary in degree and improve with time, most rapidly in the year following the injury. The patient may demonstrate a mild, moderate, or severe reduction from the previous level of performance. Children with moderate or severe neuropsychologic and language sequelae are most frequently placed in learning disability programs because they share deficits in common with the learning disabled population. However, adjustments need to be made for optimal placement because the predominant deficits and the pattern of deficits may differ for the two groups.

PSYCHIATRIC SEQUELAE

Contributing Factors: Severe closed head injury leads to a marked increase in the posttraumatic rate of psychiatric disorders (Brown, Chadwick, Shaffer, Rutter, & Traub, 1981), but psychiatric symptoms may contribute to functional disability with all severities of head injury. Psychiatric, neurologic, and psychosocial factors contribute to the onset of posttraumatic psychiatric disorders and determine their configuration. Whereas motor, neuropsychologic, and language deficits tend to progressively improve over several years' time, psychiatric disorders often appear or worsen in a sporadic manner (Johnston, 1991). The appearance and pattern of psychiatric sequelae are neurologically determined by the site, size, laterality, nature, and temporal course of the injury (Mesulam, 1986). Certain psychosocial factors contribute to the onset of psychiatric disorder. Included among these factors are: child not living with natural parents; sibship of at least four children; admission of the child into the care of local authorities; socially handicapping psychiatric disorder in the mother; paternal criminality; and a father with an unskilled or semiskilled job (Brown et al., 1981).

The pretraumatic psychiatric status is another determinant of the posttraumatic psychiatric status. Two pertinent observations emerge from Brown's prospective controlled study of 31 head-injured children between 5 and 14 years of age (Brown et al., 1981). The first is that children with pretraumatic psychiatric disorder are likely to manifest posttraumatic psychiatric disorder, and the second is that children without pretraumatic psychiatric disorder are more than twice as likely as controls to manifest a posttraumatic psychiatric disorder.

An assessment of pretraumatic psychiatric status has been performed on all severely head-injured children when they enter the Kennedy Krieger Institute Rehabilitation Program. This evaluation includes a psychiatric interview, a social work interview, and completion of the Child Behavior Checklist (Achenbach, 1991) by the parent. Experience with 400 children admitted over a 12-year period indicates that over 40% of the children had pretraumatic psychiatric disorders and/or learning disabilities. Disruptive behavior disorders were the most common pretraumatic diagnoses. In many instances, the trauma was the event that precipitated a first psychiatric evaluation. Often it emerged in the history taking that the parent had been urged by the teacher to obtain treatment for hyperactivity and inattention but had not followed that recommendation.

Early Sequelae: Posttraumatic psychiatric symptoms and disorders are divided into two groups according to their time of appearance. The temporal relationship between the psychiatric and the neurologic events that follow severe closed head injury is depicted in Table 30.2. Early posttraumatic psychiatric sequelae are symptoms and disorders that have their onset from the time of injury to the termination of the posttraumatic amnesia. In milder injuries, the patient may not have a period of coma, but only a period of disorientation or confusion that constitutes his or her posttraumatic amnesia. Psychiatric or behavioral symptoms that occur during this period are predominantly neurologically determined. Disorganized thinking, perceptual disturbances, disturbances of the sleep-wake cycle, and memory impairment are commonly seen. But most individuals traverse this period without increased psychologic distress or increased risk of harming others and so they do not require the attention of a psychiatrist. If psychiatric attention is merited for maladaptive behavior or for a pathologic emotional state and if diagnostic criteria are fulfilled, then the diagnosis is most frequently delirium.

Late Sequelae: Late posttraumatic psychiatric sequelae appear after the termination of the posttraumatic amnesia. These symptoms and disorders listed in the fourth edition of the *Diagnostic and Statistical Manual of Mental Disorders (DSM-IV)* (American Psychiatric Association, 1994) are the same as those found in the non–head-injured population. They include those symptoms and disorders that accompany other medical and neurologic diseases and include dementia, amnestic disorder, psychotic disorder, mood disorder, and anxiety disorder. Maladaptive personality or behavioral traits appearing after closed head injury are subsumed under the diagnosis of personality change due to closed head injury.

A 10- to 15-year follow-up of 40 patients injured between 15 and 44 years of age demonstrates the importance and persistence of psychiatric sequelae (Thomsen, 1984). Two-thirds of the patients had permanent changes in personality and emotion, including childishness, emotional lability, irritability, restlessness, and disturbed behavior. Severe head injury has been implicated as an important etiologic factor in patients who have severely aggressive delinquent behavior. Dorothy Otnow Lewis documented major neurologic dysfunction and a high incidence of severe physical abuse in the histories of 14 juveniles condemned to death for aggressive crimes (Lewis et al., 1988). In another study of 15 death row inmates, all of the inmates had histories of severe head injury, 5 had major neurologic impairment, and 7 others had less serious neurologic problems (e.g., blackouts, soft signs) (Lewis, Pincus, Feldman, Jackson, & Bard, 1986).

NEUROPSYCHOLOGIC AND LANGUAGE SEQUELAE AS CRITERIA OF MENTAL DISORDERS

Certain neuropsychologic and language sequelae after closed head injury may constitute criteria for mental disorders. Mental disorders with neuropsychologic and language criteria include mental retardation (cognitive deficits), attention deficit hyperactivity disorder (neuropsychologic symptoms of inattention and impulsivity), communication and pervasive developmental disorders (language and speech deficits), learning disorders (reading, mathematics, written expression), as well as delirium (neuropsychologic symptoms of inattention and memory impairment), dementia (global cognitive deficits), and amnestic disorder (memory deficits).

Type of Late Sequelae: What form do posttraumatic symptoms and disorders take in children with closed head injury? There are five possibilities.

1. The pretraumatic symptomatology is the same as the posttraumatic symptomatology.
2. The posttraumatic symptomatology is a diminished form of the pretraumatic symptomatology.
3. The posttraumatic symptomatology is an accentuation of the pretraumatic symptomatology.
4. The posttraumatic symptomatology constitutes a new organic psychiatric disorder.
5. The posttraumatic symptomatology constitutes a new nonorganic psychiatric disorder.

Brown (1981) described posttraumatic symptoms and disorders but did not compare these to the pretraumatic symptoms and disorders of the individual patients. It is hypothesized from clinical experience with the Kennedy Krieger rehabilitation patients that the pretraumatic symptoms and disorders remain the same or persist in an exaggerated form after the posttraumatic amnesia terminates.

Organic disorders may make their appearance after the posttraumatic amnesia terminates. The nature of the disorder is determined to a degree by the location of the lesion. The frontal and temporal lobes are areas of predilection for contusions, hematomas, intracerebral hemorrhage, and diffuse edema after closed head injury (Mattson & Levin, 1990). Lesions of the frontal and temporal lobes are associated with specific psychiatric symptoms. Maladaptive personality symptoms attributed to both of these locations are grouped together in the *DSM-IV* disorder of personality change due to closed head injury.

Psychiatric symptoms in adults are seen more frequently after focal frontal lobe damage than after damage to other cerebral areas. Rutter (1981) called attention to the similarity between disinhibited patterns of behavior seen in children after severe closed head injury and symptoms of frontal lobe syndrome seen in adults with focal brain disorders. He described a general lack of regard for social convention, overtalkativeness, carelessness in personal hygiene and dress, and impulsiveness in these children.

The frontal lobe syndrome, the designation used to describe the wide range of psychiatric and neurobehavioral symptoms seen after frontal lobe damage, is characterized by euphoria; lack of judgment, reliability, or foresight; disinhibition; childish behavior; and apathy (Lishman, 1968). This syndrome can be subdivided into two forms, orbital and mesial, according to lesion location and salient deficits. The clinical picture of orbital frontal psychopathology is dominated by major personality disturbances of drive and affect. Principal orbital symptoms are aggression, disinhibition, demandingness, childishness, and euphoria. Mesial frontal psychopathology is characterized by disturbances in the expression and experience of affect, in the initiation of activity, and in the ability to communicate. The principal mesial symptoms are apathy, bradykinesia, and mutism (Damasio, 1985). Criteria of personality change due to closed head injury attributed to frontal lobe damage are affective instability, recurrent outbursts of aggression or rage, markedly impaired social judgment, and marked apathy and indifference.

The criterion of personality change due to closed head injury attributed to temporal lobe damage is suspiciousness or paranoid ideation. Some evidence supports a personality disorder associated with chronic temporal lobe dysfunction (Guerrant et al., 1962; Pond & Bidwell, 1960), but a solid scientific foundation is lacking (Lishman, 1978). Personality symptoms seen in patients with temporal lobe epilepsy and other chronic temporal lobe disorders include suspiciousness or paranoid ideation, exaggerated aggressiveness, humorless verbosity, and religiosity (Herrington, 1969).

Focal temporal traumatic lesions, particularly on the left side, are associated with increased risk for the development of a psychotic disorder similar to schizophrenia (Hillbom, 1960). The Kluver-Bucy syndrome may occur rarely after acute bilateral temporal lobe injury. Psychiatric symptoms of this syndrome include placidity and loss of fear or anger, psychic blindness, persistent manual exploration of the environment with subsequent placement of objects into the mouth, and alterations in sexual behavior. All autopsied patients have had bilateral lesions of the medial, inferior, and anterior temporal cortex and, in most cases, damage to the temporal white matter (Lilly, Cummings, Benson, & Frankel, 1983).

IMPACT OF CLOSED HEAD INJURY ON PSYCHOLOGICAL DEVELOPMENT

There are no long-term follow-up studies on the effect of closed head injury at various ages on later psychological development. Overall prognosis is worse prior to the age of 2 in regard to motor, cognitive, and psychologic development. These younger children, depending on the coma duration and on location and extent of injury, are more likely to have multiple handicaps than individuals injured at another age. Judging from adult case studies of persons who suffered severe head injury at birth or during the perinatal period, it is surmised that early lesions of certain areas, specifically the frontal lobe, the anterior temporal lobe, the limbic system, and the anterior and dorsomedial thalami, are not compatible with normal development of intellectual abilities and affect (Damasio, 1985). For example, one study patient with a history of early brain injury had degeneration of the left frontal lobe and absence of the right frontal lobe surgically diagnosed at age 19. His childhood and adolescence was marked by severe behavioral problems in school and at home (Ackerly & Benton, 1948).

Those children who suffer severe head injury between 2 and 7 years of age fare less well cognitively than those children injured after the age of

7. This time period coincides with Piaget's stage of preoperational representation, that period when symbolic functions develop to enable the shift from the limited goals of concrete sequences of behavior to organization and contemplation of actions (Chess & Hassibi, 1978). In Freudian theory, this period encompasses the anal phase, the phallic phase, the oedipal complex, and the development of the superego. Disruption of these critical sequences of cognitive and psychosexual development by brain damage may lead to emotional and behavioral impairment, the nature of which is related to the location and severity of injury. Although the incidence of posttraumatic psychiatric sequelae is high after brain injury at any age, the onset is sporadic and is influenced by environmental determinants.

Children above the age of 7 probably have a better overall prognosis after brain injury compared to younger children. The IQs of older children do not fall as much after injury as those of younger children, but intelligence tests evaluate established information rather than the executive, self-regulatory, and social discourse functions that are believed to reside in the frequently injured frontal lobe. Evidence suggests that frontally mediated executive functions emerge in the first year of life and continue to develop at least until puberty (Welsh & Pennington, 1988).

At age 7 children enter Piaget's stage of concrete operations during which time they begin to organize and interpret thoughts and perceptions into a coherent system of intellectual functioning. Children at this stage can comprehend different viewpoints and can engage in reciprocal interactions (Chess & Hassibi, 1978). The psychosexual term for this stage is latency, that period when the material of the culture can be incorporated during a time of relatively little instinctual turmoil. Children injured between 7 and 11 may develop disruptive and disinhibited behaviors or maladaptive emotional responses that impede the progress of their psychological development.

Spurred by the biologic process of puberty, the child enters adolescence. Piaget's stage of formal operations is attained during this period. The adolescent can then understand the relationship between various propositions, can generalize from one set of solutions to another, and can devise abstract systems (Chess & Hassibi, 1978). Developmental tasks of adolescence include adjustment to a changing body image, progression toward independence from the family, creation of a mature identity, formation of realistic goals, development of the capacity to defer gratification, and the formation of caring and intimate relationships (Grob, 1986). Head injury can affect any of these tasks. Exacerbation of a previously existing mental disorder or the appearance of a new disorder, in combination with neuropsychologic deficits, may seriously hinder the adolescent with recent or past head injury. In addition, social isolation is a problem for the head-injured adolescent as former friends view him or her as a different person, sometimes slower or disinhibited or apathetic or with obviously inappropriate responses (Gerring, 1988).

Postconcussional Disorder

Postconcussional disorder occurs commonly after mild and moderate closed head injury in adults. Children and adolescents demonstrate many of the same symptoms after their injuries. The clinical symptomatology and natural history of postconcussional disorder in children and adolescents need to be clarified in order to estimate their contribution to the presenting psychiatric complaint of a child with a history of mild or moderate head injury. The syndrome includes somatic and cognitive symptoms of headaches, dizziness, fatigue, recent memory loss, emotional lability, impaired concentration, impaired judgment, disinhibition, photophobia, and hypersensitivity to sound (Jennett & Teasdale, 1981). Depression and anxiety also may accompany these symptoms, which persist during the time in which deficits of attention, concentration, memory, and judgment are present on neuropsychologic testing (Rimel, Giordani, Barth, Boll, & Jane, 1981; Rimel, Giordani, Barth & Jane, 1982).

At one year after injury, 10 to 15% of adult patients have not recovered from their concussive symptoms and many of these patients are more symptomatic than immediately after the injury. These patients suffer from persistent postconcussive syndrome (Alexander, 1995). The percentage of children and adolescents who develop this persistent condition is unknown.

Magnetic resonance imaging is able to detect focal brain lesions in up to 90% of patients admitted to the hospital for mild or moderate closed head injury. Levin et al. (1987) have demonstrated that resolution of magnetic resonance imaging lesion size in patients with mild and moderate closed head injury paralleled an improvement in performance on neuropsychologic testing administered at 1 and 3 months postinjury.

Family Adjustment

The occurrence of head injury is a family crisis. When the injury is severe, the overriding concern is the child's survival. This period of time, when the child's condition is critical, may extend from hours into days. Family members move from their ordinary life into a disrupted schedule of around-the-clock attendance in an intensive care unit. Their child may be comatose or appear physically disfigured. When the child attains medical stability, even though he or she may still be comatose, the child is moved into a less intense setting and a phase of acute rehabilitation commences. But uncertainty is continually present. If the child remains comatose for many days, the uncertainty concerns how long the coma will last. If the child has emerged from coma, the uncertainty concerns the existence and the extent of deficits. Even with mild and moderate injuries, when a child does not have coma, there is concern about the possibility of persistent cognitive and behavioral deficits.

The more severe the injury, the greater the family's need for effective coping strategies. This is true not only in the immediate postinjury period but also during acute and chronic rehabilitation, which may extend into months and years. Severely disabled children with multiple handicaps may need several outpatient services weekly, including occupational therapy, speech language therapy, and behavioral therapy. Families that adjust well to these difficult circumstances may positively influence their child's outcome (Gilchrist & Wilkinson, 1979). These families are able to resist feelings of discouragement and a tendency to project blame; to search out, assess, and carry out optimal treatments; to emotionally support their child dur-

ing his or her recovery; and then to accept the child as he or she will henceforth be. Beyond this, some family members possess altruistic defenses that enable them to assist and to support similarly afflicted people, either informally or through leadership in an organized advocacy group.

Maladaptive family coping is also seen. It occurs sometimes because of the extraordinary nature of the stress. Close relatives of the patient, those who witnessed the trauma, or those who participated in the circumstances of the trauma may develop a posttraumatic stress disorder. Head injuries often occur in a setting of high psychosocial adversity where family members may lack good coping skills or where they may lack the psychologic reserve to negotiate a further great stress.

Family members may demonstrate a variety of maladaptive defenses; projection and denial are commonly seen. Feelings of anger and blame are projected onto other family members and onto health professionals. This situation leads to conflict within the family, with marital separation and divorce sometimes an outcome. Anger and blame directed at health care professionals can lead to disrupted treatment plans for the child. Denial is another defense that may impede the course of recovery. While a degree of denial may be adaptive in allowing a parent to remain optimistic and to not get overly discouraged, the persistence of strong denial about a child's deficits may severely impede therapeutic efforts on the child's behalf.

Treatment Methods

The outcome of severe closed head injury ranges from good to persistently vegetative. The poorer the outcome, the greater will be the need for chronic interdisciplinary care, psychiatric care being but one aspect. But often psychiatric sequelae stand alone in needing therapeutic attention.

Four modalities constitute the psychiatric treatment of posttraumatic sequelae. The selection of one modality over the other is determined by the nature of the sequelae, their intensity, and the patient's psychosocial environment. Sometimes one modality will need to be replaced by another as the psychiatric status changes. And with severe psychiatric sequelae, it is frequently necessary to combine treatment modalities in order to achieve therapeutic benefit.

The first modality is behavioral therapy. Behavioral recommendations are important in the treatment of delirium. Redirection and creation of a structured environment that is not overly stimulating is a primary treatment for patients who are inattentive, hyperactive, and disoriented. These behavioral methods often are sufficient to help the patient through a delirious period, without ancillary use of medication.

Behavioral therapy also plays an important role in the therapeutic management of symptoms that occur after termination of delirium/posttraumatic amnesia. Methods that include positive reinforcement, planned ignoring, differential reinforcement, shaping, instructional training, and imitation training are used to treat patients who develop posttraumatic symptoms of aggression, disinhibition, apathy, and hyperactivity (Parrish & Reimers, 1988). Generalization of desirable behaviors is promoted across situations and across behaviors, and then parents and teachers receive training in the strategies that have been worked out. Whether the pretraumatic household was well structured or disorganized, the behavioral psychologist helps parents to compose a set of reasonable rules and guidelines for consistent enforcement.

Psychotherapy is the second modality in the management of posttraumatic psychiatric sequelae. The child or adolescent may experience the appearance of an affective or an anxiety disorder or the reappearance or accentuation of one of these disorders. If insight is present or preserved, he or she may benefit from a dynamic or a cognitive form of therapy. If insight is impaired, then a supportive type of therapy may be helpful.

Pharmacotherapy, the third component, is used most often in combination with behavioral therapy or psychotherapy. Once the child receives a psychiatric diagnosis, then medication may be chosen to alleviate his or her specific disorder. Medication has demonstrated usefulness in treating affective, anxiety, psychotic, and some behavioral disorders. Pharmacotherapy is most predictably beneficial in the treatment of mood, anxiety, and psychotic disorders. Its usefulness in the treatment of behavioral symptoms such as aggression and disinhibition is often unpredictable and usually incomplete. Medications that have demonstrated usefulness in treating aggressive symptomatology include carbamazepine, lithium, propranolol, and the neuroleptics. Sequential trials of several medications may need to be administered, with combinations of drugs sometimes necessary.

A psychosocial intervention, usually provided by a social worker, is the fourth treatment modality. This intervention is very frequently combined with one of the other therapeutic modalities. The social worker supports family members during the crisis of the injury and then intermittently during the course of rehabilitation. He or she helps to educate family members about head injury and its technologically complicated treatment. He or she assists in obtaining equipment and appropriate school and community placements. Also, the social worker may function as a case manager, coordinating and monitoring all necessary outpatient services.

REFERENCES

Achenbach, T. M. (1991). *Manual for the Child Behavior Checklist/4–18 and 1991 Profile.* Burlington, VT: University of Vermont Department of Psychiatry.

Ackerly, S. S., & Benton, A. L. (1948). Report of a case of bilateral frontal lobe defect. *Research Publication of the Association for Research in Nervous and Mental Disease, 27,* 479–504.

Alexander, M. P. (1995). Mild traumatic brain injury: pathophysiology, natural history, and clinical management. *Neurology, 45,* 1253–1260.

American Psychiatric Association. (1994). *Diagnostic and Statistical Manual of Mental Disorders, Fourth Edition.* Washington, DC.

Brink, J. D., Garrett, A. L., Hale, W. R., Woo-Sam, J., & Nickel, V. L. (1970). Recovery of motor and intellectual function in children sustaining severe head injuries. *Developmental Medicine and Child Neurology, 12,* 565–571.

Brown, G., Chadwick, O., Shaffer, D., Rutter, M., & Traub, M. (1981). A prospective study of children with head injuries: III. Psychiatric sequelae. *Psychological Medicine, 11,* 63–78.

Chadwick, O., Rutter, M., Brown, G., Shaffer, D., & Traub, M. (1981). A prospective study of children with head injuries: II. Cognitive sequelae. *Psychological Medicine, 11,* 49–61.

Chadwick, O., Rutter, M., Shaffer, D., & Shrout, P. E. (1981). A prospective study of children with head injuries: IV. Specific cognitive deficits. *Journal of Clinical Neuropsychology, 3,* 101–120.

Chess, S., & Hassibi, M. (1978). *Principles and practice of child psychiatry.* New York: Plenum Press.

Damasio, A. R. (1985). The frontal lobes. In K. Heilman & E. Valenstein (Eds.), *Clinical neuropsychology* (pp. 339–375). New York: Oxford University Press.

Di Scala, C., Osberg, J. S., Gans, B. M., Chin, L. J., & Grant, C. C. (1991). Children with traumatic head injury: Morbidity and postacute treatment. *Archives of Physical Medicine and Rehabilitation, 72,* 662–666.

Ewing-Cobbs, L., Levin, H. S., Fletcher, J. M., Miner, M. E., & Eisenberg, H. M. (1990). The Children's Orientation and Amnesia Test: Relationship to severity of acute head injury and to recovery of memory. *Neurosurgery, 27,* 683–691.

Gerring, J. P. (1988). Behavioral and emotional conditions of handicapped adolescents. In J. P. Gerring & L. P. McCarthy, *The psychiatry of handicapped children and adolescents: Managing emotional and behavioral problems* (pp. 73–99). Boston: Little, Brown.

Gilchrist, E., & Wilkinson, M. (1979). Some factors determining prognosis in young people with severe head injuries. *Archives of Neurology, 36,* 355–359.

Grob, C. (1986). Substance abuse: What turns casual use into chronic dependence? *Contemporary Pediatrics, 3,* 26–41.

Guerrant, J., Anderson, W. W., Fischer, A., Weinstein, M. R., Jaros, R. M., & Deskins, A. (1962). *Personality in epilepsy.* Springfield, IL: Charles C. Thomas.

Hagen, C. (1986). Language disorders in head trauma. In J. M. Costello & A. L. Holland, *Handbook of speech and language disorders* (pp. 245–281). San Diego: College Hill Press, Inc.

Herrington, R. N. (1969). The personality in temporal lobe epilepsy. In R. N. Herrington (Ed.), *Current problems in neuropsychiatry. British Journal of Psychiatry Special Publication No. 4.* Ashford, Kent: Headley Brothers.

Hillbom, E. (1960). After-effects of brain injuries. *Acta Psychiatrica et Neurologica Scandinavica, Supplement, 142* (35), 11–195.

Jennett, B., & Teasdale, G. (1981). *Management of head injuries.* Philadelphia: F. A. Davis Co.

Johnston, M. V. (1991). Outcomes of community reentry programmes for brain injury survivors, Part 2: Further investigations. *Brain Injury, 5,* 155–168.

Kraus, J. F., Fife, D., & Conroy, C. (1987). Pediatric brain injuries: The nature, clinical course, and early outcomes in a defined United States' population. *Pediatrics, 79,* 501–507.

Kriel, R. L., Krach, L. E., & Sheehan, M. (1988). Pediatric closed head injury: Outcome following prolonged unconsciousness. *Archives of Physical Medicine Rehabilitation, 69,* 678–681.

Levin, H. S., Amparo, E., Eisenberg, H. M., Williams, D. H., High, W. M., Jr., McArdle, C. B., & Weiner, R. L. (1987). Magnetic resonance imaging and computerized tomography in relation to the neurobehavioral sequelae of mild and moderate head injuries. *Journal of Neurosurgery, 66,* 706–713.

Levin, H. S., Benton, A. L., & Grossman, R. G. (1982). *Neurobehavioral consequences of closed head injury.* New York: Oxford University Press.

Levin, H. S., & Eisenberg, H. M. (1979). Neuropsychological outcome of closed head injury in children and adolescents. *Child's Brain, 5,* 281–292.

Lewis, D. O., Pincus, J. H., Bard, B., Richardson, E., Prichep, L. S., Feldman, M., & Yeager, C. (1988). Neuropsychiatric, psychoeducational, and family characteristics of 14 juveniles condemned to death in the United States. *American Journal of Psychiatry, 145,* 584–589.

Lewis, D. O., Pincus, J. H., Feldman, M., Jackson, L., & Bard, B. (1986). Psychiatric neurological, and psychoeducational characteristics of 15 death row inmates in the United States. *American Journal of Psychiatry, 143,* 838–845.

Lilly, R., Cummings, J. L., Benson, F., & Frankel, M. (1983). The human Kluver-Bucy syndrome. *Neurology, 33,* 1141–1145.

Lishman, W. A. (1968). Brain damage in relation to psychiatric disability after head injury. *British Journal of Psychiatry, 114,* 373–410.

Lishman, W. A. (1978). *Organic psychiatry.* Oxford: Blackwell Scientific Publications.

Mattson, A. J., & Levin, H. S. (1990). Frontal lobe dysfunction following closed head injury. *Journal of Nervous and Mental Disease, 178,* 282–291.

Mesulam, M. M. (1986). Editorial: Frontal cortex and behavior. *Annals of Neurology, 19,* 320–325.

Parrish, J. M., & Reimers, T. M. (1988). Behavioral approaches to the assessment and treatment of handicapped children and adolescents. In J. P. Gerring & L. P. McCarthy (Eds.), *The psychiatry of handicapped children and adolescents* (pp. 127–161). Boston: Little, Brown.

Plum, F., & Posner, J. B. (1987). *The diagnosis of stupor and coma 3d ed.* Philadelphia: F. A. Davis Company.

Pond, D. A., & Bidwell, B. (1960). A survey of epilepsy in fourteen general practices. II. Social and psychological aspects. *Epilepsia, 1,* 285–299.

Rimel, R. W., Giordani, B., Barth, J. T., Boll, T. J., & Jane, J. (1981). Disability caused by minor head injury. *Neurosurgery, 9,* 221–228.

Rimel, R. W., Giordani, B., Barth, J. T., & Jane, J. A. (1982). Moderate head injury: Completing the clinical spectrum of brain trauma. *Neurosurgery, 11,* 344–153.

Rutter, M. (1981). Psychological sequelae of brain damage in children. *American Journal of Psychiatry, 138,* 1533–1544.

Shaffer, D., Bijur, P., Chadwick, O. F. D., & Rutter, M. L. (1980). Head injury and later reading disability. *Journal of the American Academy of Child Psychiatry, 19,* 592–610.

Stover, S. L., & Zieger, H. E. (1976). Head injury in

children and teenagers: Functional recovery correlated with the duration of coma. *Archives of Physical Medicine Rehabilitation, 57,* 201–205.

Thomsen, I. V. (1984). Late outcome of very severe blunt head trauma: A 10–15 year second follow-up. *Journal of Neurology, Neurosurgery, and Psychiatry, 47,* 260–268.

Welsh, M. C., & Pennington, B. F. (1988). Assessing frontal lobe functioning in children: Views from developmental psychology. *Developmental Neuropsychology, 4* (3), 199–230.

Winogron, H. W., Knights, R. M., & Bawden, H. N. (1984). Neuropsychological deficits following head injury in children. *Journal of Clinical Neuropsychology, 6,* 269–286.

Ylvisaker, M. (1986). Language and communication disorders following pediatric head injury. *Head Trauma Rehabilitation, 1,* 1–16.

31 / Cystic Fibrosis

Gerald P. Koocher, Melanie L. McGrath, and Linda J. Gudas

Cystic fibrosis (CF) was first described as a syndrome in 1938 (Andersen, 1938). Today, it remains the most common lethal genetic disease affecting the Caucasian population (Orenstein & Wachnowsky, 1985) and the most common genetic killer of children. It is transmitted via an autosomal recessive genetic mechanism yielding a carrier rate in Caucasians of approximately 1 in 20, resulting in an incidence of an estimated 1 : 2000 live Caucasian births and 1 : 17,000 live births in the black population annually (Lewis et al., 1984; Matthews & Drotar, 1984). In the United States, approximately 1 : 20 individuals (5%) are carriers of the gene. Tests to identify carrier status have evolved following the discovery of genetic markers for the disorder on chromosome 7 (Roberts, 1988). Biological probes to detect carrier status by using the cystic fibrosis transmembrane regulator (CFTR) protein currently allow for a specific diagnosis. Unfortunately, as is the case with many if not most genetic diseases, a variety of mutations occur that complicate screening assays. Approximately 30% of mutations are not yet accounted for by the over 90 mutations reported to date (CF Genetic Consortium, 1991).

The gold standard for cystic fibrosis diagnosis remains the "sweat test," because one hallmark of the disease is an abnormally high sodium and chloride composition in the body sweat. Although the phenotypic manifestations of this disorder are variable in each individual patient (Matthews & Drotar, 1984), the disease process affects the pancreas and lungs. In the pancreas, secretions block the release of digestive enzymes, resulting in protein and fat malabsorption in 85% of all patients (Orenstein & Wachnowsky, 1985). Similarly, the respiratory system is compromised, providing fertile ground for bacteria and other organisms resulting in infections and the progressive obstructive lung disease.

The general goals of medical treatment are to control infection and facilitate removal of secretions in order to reduce pulmonary congestion, prevent pulmonary and digestive obstruction, and improve nutritional status. The three major components of the medical regimen are medication, chest physical therapy, and proper diet. The regimen requires taking multiple medications (including enzyme replacement and often more than 40 pills per day), daily chest physical therapy treatments and bronchodilator therapy, careful diet monitoring, and frequent outpatient medical visits and hospitalizations. Other interventions sometimes included in the treatment of individuals with cystic fibrosis are corticosteroid therapy, oxygen therapy, and newer pharmacologic treatments such as the use of DNAse.

Although current treatments focus on control of symptoms rather than cure, the effects of early vigorous, comprehensive medical treatment have dramatically improved both the length and quality of life in people with cystic fibrosis (Orenstein & Wachnowsky, 1985). Evaluation of this empirical approach and lack of treatment specificity is complicated by the lack of controlled longitudinal studies evaluating the efficacy of current therapies

(Mischler, 1985). With the recent advances in the detection of the gene, new therapies and new hope are emerging that will alter the course of the disease and the patients' lives.

Obviously, a disease that has such comprehensive effects for a child results in a number of areas of potential difficulty for the patient and family. The areas of impact we discuss in this chapter highlight some of the most important areas of difficulty and potential areas of intervention.

Adherence to the Medical Regimen

In all illness types, and especially in chronic disorders, patient adherence to medical advice has been found to be a serious and universal problem in both adults and children (Masek & Jankel, 1982). Whether adult or child, caregiver or patient, an individual's compliance or noncompliance is the result of multiple, highly complex behaviors, attitudes, and expectations (Haynes, 1976). In pediatric populations, the overall rate of compliance is estimated at approximately 50%, with a range of 20 to 80% (Litt & Cuskey, 1980; Rapoff & Christophersen, 1982). In the cystic fibrosis population, several issues relevant to this specific compliance problem are important to consider.

Consistent with the general literature, studies that have looked specifically at perceived severity of illness and compliance in people with cystic fibrosis have found the two factors highly correlated (Czajkowski, 1984; Passero, Remor, & Salomon, 1981). Cowen et al. (1984) and Czajkowski (1984) both report that minimization of severity of illness is more common in late adolescence and early adulthood than in earlier years, yet adherence to medical advice remains high (Czajkowski, 1984). However, in cystic fibrosis the parents' or child's perceptions of severity of the illness are complicated by the fact that actual severity of the disease varies markedly from patient to patient. Poor adherence to medical recommendations, despite individual beliefs and attitudes, has profound implications and potential consequences.

The role of optimism in adherence has been investigated recently with promising results. Czajkowski and Koocher (1986, 1987) reported a posi-

tive correlation between a health optimism score on the Medical Compliance Incomplete Stories Test (MCIST), a competency/coping skills assessment tool devised by Koocher and most recently revised by Koocher, Czajkowski, and Fitzpatrick (1987), and objective measures of medical adherence among adolescent patients with cystic fibrosis. Gudas, Koocher, and Wypij (1991) found that optimism was positively correlated with medication and chest physical therapy compliance and MCIST scores. Interactive effects between age and optimism were helpful in predicting medication adherence, with higher optimism leading to higher adherence, especially among older children. The optimistic or pessimistic behavioral patterns used by individuals in these studies may provide clues to facilitating adjustment to a host of life difficulties, such as physical impairment or serious illness.

Although many studies have reported that higher adherence levels are associated with illnesses regarded as serious, Gudas and her colleagues (1991) found that perceived severity was not a good predictor of medication or diet adherence. However, a negative correlation was found between perceived severity and chest physical therapy adherence. One possible reason for this finding is the fact that sicker children experience increasingly demanding medical regimens.

Patient and parent beliefs and expectations about the course of illness, its consequences, and its potential responsiveness to treatment are also important considerations but have not been specifically addressed in the literature. In a preliminary study with 80 people with cystic fibrosis conducted by McGrath, Gudas, and Koocher (1987), both the child's beliefs and those of his or her parent about the effectiveness of their treatment program were consistently among the highest predictor variables of adherence. More research in the area is needed.

Controversies in the medical community over uniform and objective guidelines for the major cystic fibrosis therapies occasionally lead to situations where medical instructions are altered or ignored by patients. A current example of treatment controversy for the people with the disease is the question of exercise as a substitute for chest physical therapy. Although that therapy has long been recommended as a mainstay of treatment, its benefit when used with patients having mild lung disease or as a prophylactic measure is unknown (Coates, 1987a). The benefits of an exercise program structured for people with cystic fibrosis may well complement or substitute for chest physical therapy sessions (O'Neill, Dodds, Phillips, Poole, & Webb, 1987). Studies of adherence among adolescents and young adults with cystic fibrosis have uncovered many patients substituting physical exercise for traditional chest physical therapy. Such changes have emerged, in part, from patients' attempts to balance an independent, flexible lifestyle against more rigid treatment regimens. Occasionally, lack of good patient-physician communication about such issues may lead to confusion regarding the optimal treatment regimen for any given patient. In fact, disagreement between physician and patient/parent report on the components of the treatment has been reported as high as 62% (McGrath, Gudas, & Koocher, 1987). Thus, good communication and exchange of information between the patient and physician is imperative.

Features of the medical regimen for people with cystic fibrosis include many of the factors that are identified in the health behavior literature as correlated with noncompliance, specifically, highly complicated medical treatments (Masek & Jankel, 1982), multiple treatments and recommendations, therapies that require extensive behavioral changes or impose changes or disruption in activities of daily living, and continuation of long-term treatment (Epstein & Cluss, 1982; Litt & Cuskey, 1980). Although Haynes (1976) suggests that adherence with one aspect of a regimen tends to be positively correlated with other components, adherence to one feature of a regimen does not, in fact, ensure adherence to other features or even the same feature at a later time. Different behaviors, skills, and demands are required for different treatments, as frequency and complexity vary (Meichenbaum & Turk, 1987).

The implications of these findings are significant when considering cognitive and behavioral factors related to improving the care of patients with cystic fibrosis. To begin with, it is important to recognize that noncompliance with (or at least less than total adherence to) the prescribed treatment regimen will be a way of life for many, if not all such patients. The more important issue is the degree to which individual variations from the ideal medical treatment program yield a quality of life and survival that are less than optimal.

Self-Management and Health Promotion

There has been a growing recognition by health care providers who treat people with cystic fibrosis, and by the medical community at large, that active involvement of the patient in the treatment process is essential (Anderson & Kirk, 1982). To what extent the patient should be involved, the role he or she should play, and how to encourage the patient to become involved are increasingly being addressed. Ultimately, the choice of medical treatment lies with the patient regardless of the physician's decision: If patients disagree with the recommendation, they will decide not to follow through. By actively bringing that decision-making process into the physician-patient relationship, the patient makes more informed choices and the physician can provide better care.

Self-management skills training has proven effective in a number of other chronic diseases (Youngren, 1981). Typically, such programs have included education, self-monitoring, self-regulation, problem solving, interpersonal skills training, and relapse prevention (Dunbar & Agras, 1980; Meichenbaum & Turk, 1987). Such treatment packages are important as they deal not only with the motivation to follow the recommendation but address the skills or ability of the individual to successfully follow the treatment recommendation. Given the demanding treatment regimens required of most people with cystic fibrosis, it is inevitable they will be faced with conflicts between normal life activities and treatment. The skills taught in self-management skills programs aid in the effective integration of the treatment regimen with the individual's lifestyle. For example, when faced with such a conflict, a patient's choice can interfere with social development and adjustment or with medical well-being unless he or she, or the parent, can effectively problem solve and arrange the situation such that there is neither psychological nor physiological sacrifice (McGrath, Gudas, & Koocher, 1987).

Training the patient in self-regulatory skills and evaluation of outcome is an important part of self-management: The patient becomes more involved in (and skilled at) self-management, the monitoring of symptoms, and the modification of the protocol in response to the data. Further, the individual's beliefs about the effectiveness of the treatment can be affected. As pointed out, belief in the effectiveness of the treatment has been identified as important in determining the degree to which patients carry out the treatment regimen. By systematically evaluating the effectiveness of individual components of the program, the patients can see what treatments are helpful. If a treatment does not appear helpful, its inclusion in the treatment regimen can be reevaluated.

In addition to encouraging self-management, the health care community is beginning to look at people with cystic fibrosis not only with a traditional disease-management eye but also from a health promotion point of view. What can we do to help these patients live a healthier, happier life? Much attention has been focused on diet and exercise as means for making people with cystic fibrosis healthier and more resilient. In the past, patients were told to avoid high-fat foods and endure restricted diets. Today, most physicians are not recommending restricting dietary fat; in fact, some recommend high-fat diets for higher caloric intake, increased weight, and increased growth. Similarly, because of the pulmonary component of cystic fibrosis, patients often were considered fragile and were discouraged from participating in sports. Today, much greater athletic participation is encouraged. There is controversy and excitement about the possibilities these two areas hold for the health of people with cystic fibrosis.

Exercise has been hypothesized to have numerous potential benefits for the individual with cystic fibrosis: helping to loosen and move mucous as an alternative to chest physical therapy, strengthening the ventilatory muscles, and learning to tolerate a higher degree of shortness of breath. Further, benefits in terms of general cardiopulmonary functioning and good health are thought to accompany regular, moderate exercise (Orenstein & Wachnowsky, 1985). Promising physiological and psychological results have been reported in terms of overall functioning. It should be noted that there are precautions to consider for people with cystic fibrosis intending to undertake an exercise regimen. Oxygen desaturation is a risk for those with advanced pulmonary disease, and a trial in an exercise laboratory to assess these effects is recommended (Coates, 1987b; Cropp, Pullano, Cerny & Nathanson, 1982). Further, patients should avoid excessive salt depletion and high altitudes when exercising (Coates, 1987b).

Given the documented caloric needs of 130 to 150% of recommended dietary allowance for individuals with cystic fibrosis, it is surprising that studies have shown that these patients typically consume less than the recommended dietary allowance for nonaffected individuals (Hodges et al., 1984). Initial attempts to improve the nutritional status of patients have been made with enteral nutrition; the results have been promising, indicating improved nutritional status, growth, and pulmonary functioning (Levy, Dury, Pencharz, & Corey, 1985). However, it is a relatively invasive procedure with associated psychological sequelae (Bayer, Bauers, & Kapp, 1983), and the effects are not maintained following discontinuation of the intervention. Behavioral programs using self-monitoring, reinforcement of appropriate feeding, and shaping and contracting to increase intake in children with cystic fibrosis have yielded preliminary positive results; increased caloric intake has been documented and reports of maintenance and effects on long-term medical outcome will follow (Stark, Knapp, Bowen, & Powers, 1993).

Symptom Management

Behavioral techniques have been effective in aiding patients in managing multiple aspects of chronic disease. For the patient with cystic fibrosis, the management of pulmonary symptoms, pain, headache, anxiety, and stress have been areas where the behavioral psychologist has been valued. Relaxation training and cognitive modification of stress-inducing thoughts and perceptions have helped patients with sleep disturbance, hyperventilation, bronchospasm, and anxiety (Spirito, Russo & Masek, 1984). Of course, a good behavioral analysis is always necessary to determine the most helpful program for each individual. The meaning of the symptoms for the patient and how the symptom functions must always be considered. With the aid of behavioral intervention, these patients can gain better self-control in a disease where increased dependence on others is often inevitable.

General Adaptation

Studies that look at qualitative differences in functioning in patients with cystic fibrosis have for the most part been limited to personality assessment. Initial research was based primarily on subjective psychiatric interviews and descriptive observations. This early research was embedded in the theoretical assumption that a chronic illness such as cystic fibrosis encouraged psychopathology and major illness-related life disruption. Specifically, intense preoccupation with death, excessive denial of illness, clinical depression, and poor school performance were identified (Lawler, Nakielny, & Wright, 1966; Meyerowitz & Kaplan, 1973; Tropauer, Franz, & Dilgard, 1970). Subsequent research, however, has challenged these findings.

Recent studies of people with cystic fibrosis find the majority to be functioning well at school, work, and home. Based on the results of objective, standardized psychological measures, these patients do not attitudinally differ significantly from healthy peers in trait anxiety, locus of control, or self-esteem (Borowitz, Humphrey & Kagan, 1987; Lavigne, 1983; Moise, Drotar, Doershuk, & Stern, 1987; Spirito et al., 1984). Compliance with medical treatment among these people has been shown to be higher than in the general population (Czajkowski, 1984; Orenstein & Wachnowsky, 1985). Intelligence seems to be normal, with several studies suggesting levels of IQ performance in the average or slightly higher range (Lavigne, 1983; Lewis et al., 1984).

Developmental Considerations

Having a life-threatening chronic illness with such a demanding treatment regimen clearly impacts normal developmental trajectories for both the child and family. The improved survival statistics for people with cystic fibrosis beyond early childhood have evolved only within the past 10 to 20 years, and the opportunity to study these patients' coping abilities and responses to medical therapies at different ages and stages of development did not exist previously. An entire lifestyle, revolving around the illness and its treatment, develops over the years of treatment (Barbero, 1973) and places exceptional demands on normal growth and developmental tasks, such as self-mastery, independence, and trust (Sawyer, Rosier, Phelan, & Bowes, 1995). Little information exists in the literature addressing the types of adherence issues and other problems that present at different age groups. An empirical investigation of the "normal ontogenetic" dynamics of compliance and noncompliance in this population, with age and stage-specific characteristics considered, was recently investigated (Gudas, Koocher & Wypij, 1991). Specifically, perceived compliance was found to be related to age, with 5- to 7-year-olds showing greater adherence to medical regimens than 8- to 11-year-olds or 12- to 15- and 16- to 20-year-old patients. The results of such investigations may lead to a comprehensive, developmental framework for designing new, more effective and specific behavioral and educational programs to enhance compliance and promote adjustment to medical therapies in people with cystic fibrosis at different stages of development.

Because little data exist regarding people who have cystic fibrosis across developmental stages, the following discussion will focus on general developmental knowledge, information about the impact of illness in general on childhood development, and our experiences over the years. It is important to note that several factors interact with development and can lead to various pressures and developmental outcomes across patients and families. In particular, the severity of illness is more varied in cystic fibrosis than in most other chronic illnesses. Consequently, every family may not be challenged intensely from birth. Thus, our discussion of the impact of the disease on normal developmental progression serves as a general guideline to be tailored to the specifics of each individual's and family's experience. As noted earlier, research has supported that people with cystic fibrosis do not evidence a higher degree of psychopathology than normals (Matthews & Drotar,

1984; Moise et al., 1987). Thus, our discussion does not imply that children and families will necessarily develop difficulties but instead highlights the developmental/behavioral challenges for these children and families.

In infancy and toddlerhood, a complex medical regimen with required compliance by the parents can lead to control and independence difficulties. The parents are faced with negotiating adherence to a medical regimen that the child usually does not wish to do, does not understand, and that serves as a constant reminder that their child has a life-threatening illness. As a result, parents may become lenient and compliance may not be optimal. This situation can sometimes result in parental guilt. If the parent is firm regarding medical treatment recommendations, the child may be faced with more demands for compliance and may experience stronger independence and control difficulties focused in other areas in an attempt to negotiate more independence successfully. Parents also may feel that because they require so much of the child regarding compliance to the medical treatment, they do not wish to set limits in other areas. This situation can lead to a variety of behavioral difficulties and an unrealistic expectation on the part of the child over how much control he or she has in the world. Parental inconsistency is also a risk for children who are seen as "vulnerable" by parents, resulting in parents not setting appropriate structure, limits, or behavioral expectations on the child.

The "vulnerable child" perception can lead to a high degree of monitoring by parents from infancy through adolescence. Many families, of necessity initially, may install monitoring systems so they may hear what is happening in the child's room. These parents have reported continuing not to sleep well and checking on the child for years after the need abated. They do this because of anxiety and fear for the child's life. This concern can be shared by the child over time, complicating the development of self-confidence and independence. Tasks such as separation for school or to play with peers becomes more difficult in such cases.

Once school age, a child faces separation from the parent, already discussed to be a challenge for some children, and the development of peer relationships. Children begin to affiliate with peers and want to be like them, which makes being "different" something they wish to avoid. However, the child with cystic fibrosis must take medication at school and will likely miss more school than other children. Also, if staying overnight with friends, other differences may be seen, and a discussion between parents may make the child's "differences" more open. During this age range, children and families make decisions on how to handle this issue, about how much to convey, and in what way, to the child's peers, teachers, and family friends. The way the family chooses to handle information sharing is linked to its predominant coping style.

The degree to which the child visits peers and affiliates is influenced by the still-developing level of independence and separation he or she has achieved from parents. Some families become very anxious when a child is away from home. There are multiple reasons for this fear, but a primary basis typically involves a fear that the child is more vulnerable when away from the parent who has protected him or her for so long. Thus, peer relationships may be inhibited by anxiety around separation. This anxiety also can be expressed to a lesser degree through parental overprotection. The parent who has been the primary caregiver may worry about every cold or the possibility of difficult situations when apart from the child; thus, the child may be kept home from school and prohibited from participating in sports. This situation highlights that the child is different, may cause the child to feel more vulnerable and less confident, and influences the development of peer relationships.

The concrete operational child's understanding of illness also changes from previous levels of understanding, because of greater ability to use observations of others in one's reasoning. Parents may therefore be asked more about cystic fibrosis during this time. These questions often focus on the reasons why the child is different and why specific treatments are necessary.

As the child with cystic fibrosis approaches adolescence, a combination of observable signs and symptoms, deviant growth patterns and physical limitations unique to the disease separate the patient from healthy peers (Lavigne, 1983). These signs may include: delay in development of secondary sex characteristics, short stature, lean body mass, barrel chest, discoloration of teeth, immature dental development, and digital clubbing. Patients also may experience labored breathing, chronic cough, fatigue, frequent loose foul-smelling stools, flatus, and a large appetite. Self-esteem and peer relationships may be affected by these characteristics. Moreover, with the tendency toward independence and rebelliousness, compliance with a complex medical regimen that marks them as "different" may be compromised. These same physical manifestations of cystic fibrosis may lead to concerns about body image and compromise the normal development of interpersonal intimacy so important in adolescent and young adult emotional development.

Another significant developmental issue is the transition from dependence as a child to independence as a young adult and back to dependence again as the disease progresses to the advanced stages. Negotiating the transition toward increased dependency is a difficult emotional and practical task, often accompanied by denial, avoidance, and significant reactive depression. Once again, acting out by virtue of nonadherence to medical advice and other expressions of rebellion may occur in the face of progressively distressing physical changes that the patient and medical team cannot control. Matters often are made worse by restrictive disability rulings imposed by employers on those patients who do work. For example, patients whose physical conditions would permit part-time but not full-time employment may be forced into choosing full-time disability status rather than risk losing company health insurance by virtue of part-time employment.

The Adult with Cystic Fibrosis

Reaching adulthood with cystic fibrosis is a relatively new but increasingly frequent phenomenon with its own subset of psychological concerns. The most pervasive among this new set of psychosocial issues is uncertainty regarding the future. Consider the relatively healthy high school student whose cystic fibrosis is manifest in only mild lung disease. How does this student plan for the future with respect to college, a career, marriage, and other normal life issues considering the uncertain future the disease provides? In their work with survivors of childhood cancer, Koocher and O'Malley (1981) described a kind of Damocles syndrome confronted by the children whose cancer treatment had been successful. The threat of recurrence and possible death hung over these patients and caused great continuing distress in some while being successfully ignored in others. Unlike cancer, however, cystic fibrosis cannot be cured, and the progression of the disease is inexorable. The psychological defenses used effectively by cancer patients, such as adaptive denial (Koocher & O'Malley, 1981), do not lend themselves well to use by people with cystic fibrosis. Denial of the threat of the disease could lead to less adherence to the medical regimen needed to maintain stable health status.

Marriage and sexuality issues are another area of concern, which was of little significance when most people with cystic fibrosis did not live past puberty. Most males with the disease are sterile as the result of anatomic changes associated with it, and while females with cystic fibrosis may be physically capable of child-bearing, the biological cost for them is greater than for a healthy woman without the pulmonary compromise. Counseling regarding these issues is an important but often neglected aspect of patient care. People with cystic fibrosis with children of their own are a relatively new but growing phenomenon. Genetic counseling for the children of people with cystic fibrosis will be important, since all will by definition be carriers of the cystic fibrosis gene. Decisions regarding childbearing for females with cystic fibrosis must include a recognition that they will produce children who carry the gene, and as a result these children will have an increased likelihood of having children of their own with the disease. Males with cystic fibrosis who wish to become parents must consider adoption or have a spouse who is willing to undergo artificial insemination. However, standard adoptions often are closed as options when one marriage partner has a terminal illness.

Because all mutations of the cystic fibrosis gene have yet to be identified, there is a significant need for genetic counseling services for the parents of people with the disease who would like information to assist them in future family planning, for siblings who would like to know whether they are carriers or not, and for amniocentesis screening.

Confronting the realities of being an adult with cystic fibrosis presents a new developmental crisis for patients. This was not as relevant an issue two decades ago, when few lived to adulthood. Today, however, planning for the future, both in terms of life goals and financial issues, is of great importance. The majority of young adults with cystic fibrosis will be able to complete their educations and enter the workforce. Along the way they may expect to encounter some degree of discrimination in securing both employment and insurance. As with any person having a chronic illness, the ability to earn a living and to secure and maintain health insurance will be of critical importance. Acquiring vocational counseling and familiarity with hiring practices and antidiscrimination laws will assist those patients who are able to work to secure their rights.

We also have noted that the current population of people with cystic fibrosis has changed significantly from the group studied a decade or more ago. There are now many children and adolescents with the disease who are medically stable, doing well, and are thus able to live more normalized lifestyles. Although these children and adolescents are at risk for emotional disturbance, their personality strengths have been shown to outweigh their difficulties (Matthews & Drotar, 1984). A subtle yet notable change in the approach of investigators who study group differences in children with cystic fibrosis and other chronic illnesses is emerging. Behaviors and personality characteristics once perceived as pathological are now viewed as adaptive coping responses within groups of individuals who are placed in an inordinate number of illness-related stressful situations. Future research might examine the interaction of personality variables and coping strategies in an effort to develop more effective intervention programs.

This same phenomenon is also true of older people with cystic fibrosis. Increasing numbers of people with the disease are living into their 30s and beyond. Choices regarding higher education, employment, marriage, childbearing or adoption, shifting one's medical care from a pediatric to an adult medical facility, and similar adult issues will demand new attention. Coping with progressive disability as a young adult also will be an increasingly frequent problem for people with cystic fibrosis who have been used to living and functioning independently. Further, the role of the mental health care provider in facilitating adaptation to this reality as well as in formulating and influencing social health policy regarding the numerous issues affecting this process is important.

Cystic Fibrosis and the Family

Obviously, the family of a child with cystic fibrosis is faced with stressors above what the typical family might face. The healthy siblings of a child with chronic illness often may need more mental health assistance than the identified patient. The time required of parents to care for the ill sibling can become a source of jealousy, and the child may then feel guilty for being jealous of their sick brother or sister. Parents may become emotionally drained in addition to the physical and financial difficulties they encounter. In particular, the family system frequently strives to balance around coping with the chronic illness. We have noted a pattern in cystic fibrosis families where if one parent is extremely anxious and protective of the child, the other parent may go to the other extreme to balance the tone of the family.

Many families also do not discuss the illness. The patient and the other children, however, often may have questions that they are afraid to ask—afraid that the parents may become upset and afraid of what the answer might be. Thus, they are left to imagine the answers to the questions. What a child imagines often can be worse than reality. Thus, many families need help with discussions of the illness and expectations. Intervention to assist in an understanding of genetic carrier status will be increasingly important for family members (Leonard, Bartholomew, Swank, & Parcel, 1995).

New Directions in Cystic Fibrosis Care

The relatively recent availability of heart-lung transplantation as a treatment option for some people with cystic fibrosis also presents an im-

337

portant new area for study. While the technique holds some promise, too few have been performed on people with the disease to report on the long-term medical outcome with certainty. In order to maximize chances for success, the transplant candidate must be relatively healthy. As a result, the decision involves a trade-off by the patient of a few remaining "good years" for a chance at a much longer life. Heart-lung transplantation remains an experimental treatment with a considerable degree of risk. The limited availability of potential donors and significant cost of the procedure are also significant restrictive factors. Far more patients will be seeking such surgery than can be accommodated, and this too will add to patients' stress levels.

Cystic fibrosis is a lifelong disease, and, thus, self-care and education is a lifelong process that must be adapted as the individual patient develops cognitively, physically, and emotionally. Often the bulk of education and training occurs at an early stage in the disease. However, this practice could allow early misconceptions or lack of information regarding new treatments to contribute to problems later on. Identification of critical points in the course of the illness could be important for selecting times at which to provide reeducation. Identification of such intervention points would be an important addition to the literature. For example, the level of understanding and self-care

requirements are different for a 10-year-old and a 20-year-old. New data can be used differently at each new level of cognitive development. Other points of reeducation could be identified by changes in physical status. For example, a patient who does not yet have severe lung involvement probably will not know much about that area of cystic fibrosis care or about strategies for integrating this care into his or her lifestyle. Thus, when pulmonary problems begin to occur with increasing frequency, reeducation on the entire area of physiology and aid in effective integration of new treatments are necessary in addition to emotional support around the issue of disease progression.

Replacing the psychopathological model of illness of past years is a more dynamic, psychosocial awareness of coping and adjustment behavior. A priority for future research would involve addressing how the behaviors, coping styles, and attitudes of patients differ at different developmental stages and in response to specific components of the disease regimen. Such applied research might best be directed toward measurable "target" outcomes, such as adherence with treatment protocols, rather than on global measures, such as personality adjustment. The most effective interventions will continue to be those that place emphasis on the patients' own goals and quality of life decisions.

REFERENCES

Andersen, D. H. (1938). Cystic fibrosis of the pancreas and its relation to celiac disease. *American Journal of Diseases of Children, 56,* 344–399.

Anderson, R. J., & Kirk, L. M. (1982). Methods of improving patient compliance in chronic disease states. *Archives of Internal Medicine, 142,* 1673–1675.

Barbero, G. J. (1973). The child, parent, and doctor in death from chronic disease. In P. R. Patterson, C. R. Denning, & A. H. Kutscher (Eds.), *Psychosocial aspects of cystic fibrosis* (pp. 76–83). New York: Columbia University Press.

Bayer, L. M., Bauers, C. M., & Kapp, S. R. (1983). Psychosocial aspects of nutritional support. *Nursing Clinics of North America, 1* (1), 119–127.

Borowitz, S., Humphrey, J., & Kagan, B. (Eds.). (1987). *Cystic fibrosis currents, 2.* (Available from McNeil Pharmaceutical, Dept. MC, Spring House, PA 19477).

Coates, A. L. (1987a, October). Behavior needed for successful management of cystic fibrosis; The role of the patient, the parent and the health professional. In A. L. Coates (Chair) *Behavioral Aspects of CF.* Symposium conducted at the North American Cystic Fibrosis Conference, Toronto, Canada.

Coates, A. L. (1987b, October). Exercise in CF: Does it help? Does it tell us anything? In M. Wall (Chair), *Controversies in CF Care.* Symposium conducted at the North American Cystic Fibrosis Conference, Toronto, Canada.

Cowen, L., Corey, M., & Keenan, N. (1985). Family adaptation and psychosocial adjustment to cystic fibrosis in the preschool child. *Social Science and Medicine, 20,* 553–560.

Cropp, G. J., Pullano, J. P., Cerny, F. J., & Nathanson, I. T. (1982). Exercise tolerance and cardiorespiratory adjustments at peak work capacity in cystic fibrosis.

American Review of Respiratory Disease, 126, 211–216.

Cystic Fibrosis Genetic Consortium Newsletter. (1991, May).

Czajkowski, D. R. (1984). *The use of a psychosocial competency/coping skills model to assess and predict the medical compliance of cystic fibrosis adolescents.* Unpublished doctoral dissertation, University of Virginia.

Czajkowski, D. R., & Koocher, G. P. (1986). Predicting medical compliance among adolescents with cystic fibrosis. *Health Psychology, 5,* 297–305.

Czajkowski, D. R., & Koocher, G. P. (1987). Medical compliance and coping with cystic fibrosis. *Journal of Child Psychology and Psychiatry, 28,* 311–319.

Dunbar, J. M., & Agras, W. S. (1980). Compliance with medical instructions. In J. M. Ferguson & C. B. Taylor (Eds.), *Comprehensive handbook of behavioral medicine* (Vol. 3). (pp. 253–268). New York: Spectrum Publications.

Epstein, L. H., & Cluss, P. A. (1982). A behavioral medicine perspective on adherence to long-term medical regimens. *Journal of Consulting and Clinical Psychology, 50,* 950–971.

Gudas, L. J., Koocher, G. P., & Wypij, D. (1991). Perceptions of medical compliance in children and adolescents with cystic fibrosis. *Developmental and Behavioral Pediatrics, 12,* 236–242.

Haynes, R. B. (1976). A critical review of the "determinants" of patient compliance with therapeutic regimens. In D. L. Sackett & R. B. Haynes (Eds.), *Compliance with therapeutic regimens* (pp. 26–39). Baltimore: Johns Hopkins University Press.

Haynes, R. B. (1979). Introduction. In R. B. Haynes, D. W. Taylor, & D. L. Sackett (Eds.)., *Compliance in health care* (pp. 1–7). Baltimore: Johns Hopkins University.

Hodges, P., Sauriol, D., Man, S. F., Reichert, A., Grace, M., Talbot, T. W., Brown, N., & Thompson, A. B. Nutrient intake of patients with cystic fibrosis. *Journal of the American Dietetic Association, 84,* 664–669.

Koocher, G., Czajkowski, D., & Fitzpatrick, J. (1987). *Manual for the Medical Compliance Incomplete Stories Test (MCIST).* Unpublished research instrument, Children's Hospital and Harvard Medical School, Boston, MA.

Koocher, G. P., & O'Malley, J. E. (1981). *The Damocles syndrome: Psychosocial consequences of surviving childhood cancer.* New York: McGraw-Hill.

Lavigne, J. V. (1983). Psychological functioning of cystic fibrosis patients. In J. Lloyd-Still (Ed.), *Textbook of cystic fibrosis* (pp. 419–432). Boston: John Wright PSG Inc.

Lawler, R. H., Nakielny, W., & Wright, N. A. (1966). Psychological implications of cystic fibrosis. *Canadian Medical Association Journal, 94,* 1043–1046.

Leonard, K. P., Bartholomew, L. K., Swank, P. R., & Parcel, G. S. (1995). A comparison of two approaches to education about carrier testing for cystic fibrosis. *Journal of Genetic Counseling, 4,* 97–113.

Levy, L. D., Dury, P. R., Pencharz, P. B., & Corey, M. L. (1985). Effects of long-term nutritional rehabilitation on body composition and clinical status in malnourished children and adolescents with cystic fibrosis. *Journal of Pediatrics, 107* (2), 225–230.

Lewis, M. I., Zaltzman, M., Reef, I., Pettifor, J. M., Kallenbach, J. M., & Zwi, S. (1984). Experience at an adolescent and adult cystic fibrosis clinic. *South African Medical Journal, 65,* 641–648.

Litt, I. F., & Cuskey, W. R. (1980). Compliance with medical regimens during adolescence. *Pediatric Clinics of North America, 27,* 3–15.

Masek, B. J., & Jankel, W. R. (1982). Therapeutic adherence. In D. C. Russo & J. W. Varni (Eds.), *Behavioral pediatrics: Research and practice* (p. 375–395). New York: Plenum Press.

Matthews, L. W., & Drotar, D. (1984). Cystic fibrosis—a challenging long-term chronic disease. *Pediatric Clinics of North America, 31,* 133–152.

Meichenbaum, D., & Turk, D. C. (1987). *Facilitating treatment adherence.* New York: Plenum Press.

Meyerowitz, J. H., & Kaplan, H. B. (1973). Cystic fibrosis and family functioning. In P. R. Patterson, C. R. Denning, & A. H. Kutscher (Eds.), *Psychosocial aspects of cystic fibrosis* (pp. 34–56). New York: Columbia University Press.

McGrath, M., Gudas, L., & Koocher, G. (1987, November). The role of means-end problem solving in compliance among patients with cystic fibrosis. In S. A. Hobbs (Chair), *Behavioral assessment and intervention with cystic fibrosis.* Symposium conducted at the annual convention of the Association for Advancement of Behavior Therapy, Boston.

Mischler, E. H. (1985). Treatment of pulmonary disease in cystic fibrosis. *Seminars in Respiratory Medicine, 6,* 271–284.

Moise, J. R., Drotar, D., Doershuk, C. F., & Stern, R. C. (1987). Correlates of psychosocial adjustment among young adults with cystic fibrosis. *Developmental and Behavioral Pediatrics, 8,* 141–148.

O'Neill, P. A., Dodds, M., Phillips, B., Poole, J., & Webb, A. K. (1987). Regular exercise and reduction of breathlessness in patients with cystic fibrosis. *British Journal of Diseases of the Chest, 81,* 62–69.

Orenstein, D., Franklin, B., Doershuk, C., Hellerstein, H., Germann, K., Horowitz, J., & Stern, R. (1981). Exercise conditioning and cardiopulmonary fitness in cystic fibrosis. *Chest, 80,* 392–398.

Orenstein, D. M., & Wachnowsky, D. M. (1985). Behavioral aspects of cystic fibrosis. *Annals of Behavioral Medicine, 7,* 17–20.

Passero, M. A., Remor, B., & Salomon, J. (1981). Patient reported compliance with cystic fibrosis therapy. *Clinical Pediatrics, 20,* 264–270.

Rapoff, M. A., & Christophersen, E. R. (1982). Compliance of pediatric patients with medical regimens: A review and evaluation. In R. B. Stuart (Ed.), *Adherence, compliance and generalization in behavioral medicine* (pp. 79–124). New York: Brunner/Mazel.

Roberts, L. (1988). Race for the cystic fibrosis gene nears end. *Science, 240,* 282–285.

Sawyer, S. M., Rosier, M. J., Phelan, P. D., & Bowes, G. (1995). The self-image of adolescents with cystic fibrosis. *Journal of Adolescent Health, 16,* 204–208.

Spirito, A., Russo, D. C., & Masek, B. J. (1984). Behavioral interventions and stress management training for hospitalized adolescents and young adults with cystic fibrosis. *General Hospital Psychiatry, 6,* 211–218.

Stark, L. J., Knapp, L. G., Bowen, A. M., & Powers, S. W. (1993). Increasing calorie consumption in children with cystic fibrosis: Replication with 2-year follow-up. *Journal of Applied Behavior Analysis, 26,* 435–450.

Tropauer, A., Franz, M. N., & Dilgard, V. W. (1970). Psychological aspects of the care of children with cystic fibrosis. *American Journal of Diseases of Children, 119,* 424–432.

Tyler, F. B. (1978). Individual psychosocial competence: A personality configuration. *Educational and Psychological Measurement, 38,* 309–323.

Youngren, D. E. (1981). Improving patient compliance with self-medication teaching program. *Nursing, 11,* 60–61.

32 / Psychosocial Aspects of Diabetes Mellitus in Children and Adolescents: Implications and Interventions

Stuart T. Hauser, Alan M. Jacobson, Karen A. Benes, and Barbara J. Anderson

Definition of Illness

Diabetes mellitus is caused by the body's inability to produce sufficient insulin or by the ineffective use of the insulin that is available. Insulin, a hormone produced by beta cells in the pancreas and secreted into the blood, facilitates entry of glucose to body cells. Without insulin, excess glucose accumulates in the blood. The cells, deprived of their main source of energy, turn to the body's energy reserves, beginning with glycogen, then proceeding to protein and ultimately fat, for sustenance. The burning of fat leads to the formation of highly acidic substances called ketones, which also accumulate in the blood. The kidneys work overtime in an effort to clear the blood of both the excess glucose and ketones, resulting in frequent urination. This leads to dehydration and concurrently losses of essential substances such as sodium. Left untreated, insulin-dependent diabetes leads inevitably to death caused by the metabolic consequences of insulin insufficiency. In essence, the cells "starve" in the presence of sufficient food-stuffs.

This work was in part supported by a grant from the National Institute of Arthritis, Diabetes, and Digestive and Kidney Diseases (DK27845) and NIMH Research Scientist Award 5K-03-MH-70178. Final scholarly contributions to the preparation of this chapter were provided by Dawn A. Obeidallah, Ph.D.

Prevalence and Clinical Aspects

Type I, insulin-dependent diabetes mellitus, mainly strikes children or adolescents and accounts for about 10% of all known cases of diabetes. In Type I diabetes, the pancreas eventually produces no insulin. This chronic disease, the most frequently occurring endocrine disorder for children and adolescents, occurs at a rate of 1.8 in 1,000 individuals from birth to age 20. Onset can occur anytime during the life span, but peaks between the ages of 5 and 6, and between the ages of 11 and 13 (Drash, 1981).

The exact cause of Type I diabetes is not known. It is known that Type I diabetes occurs after the pancreatic beta cells (insulin-producing) are destroyed by an autoimmune process. The triggers for the onset of this destructive process are unclear, but several factors, including heredity and viral infections, may lead to Type I diabetes (Turk & Speers, 1983).

Insulin, a polypeptide, can be taken only by injection. Type I diabetes requires daily multiple injections to compensate for the insulin's deficiency. Insulin injections must be balanced with food intake and energy expenditure on a daily basis. Medical treatment of diabetes strives to maintain blood glucose levels in a range that avoids wide swings leading to severe hyperglycemia and ketoacidosis or hypoglycemia. Blood glucose levels that are either too high or too low can cause disabling consequences and even death. Furthermore, Type I diabetes can cause a host of long-term complications, including retinopathy, nephropathy, neuropathy, impotence, cardiovascular disease, stroke, and peripheral vascular problems leading to gangrene.

The Influence of Psychosocial Factors on Diabetes-Specific Outcomes

A growing number of studies examine psychosocial dimensions that can be important determinants of children and adolescents' health status and adaptation to illness (Dimsdale et al., 1979; Turk, 1979; Sosa et al., 1980; Thomas & McCabe, 1980). Three broad psychosocial factors have been identified by these studies: stress, coping abilities, and social environment. These factors, separately and most often in combination, contribute to the young patients' problems and successes in maintaining health and handling chronic illness. Consequently, important health outcomes, such as adherence to the diabetic regimen, are influenced by stress, coping, and broader contextual processes. While these factors interact, each can be considered separately for purposes of review.

STRESS

Numerous investigators consider influences of emotionally stressful experiences on health status. For example, Rahe and colleagues (1964), using scaled measures of life events, found that acute medical illnesses tend to occur at times of change. Other studies suggest that stressful experience can be an important etiological factor in the pathophysiology of disabling chronic conditions, such as coronary vessel disease (Goldband, Katkin, & Morrell, 1979). The course of chronic illnesses, such as diabetes, also can be affected by stressful experience (Johnson & Sarason, 1979). These studies often emphasize the additive effects of

multiple stressful life events. In addition to number and intensity, the personal meaning of life events also contributes to their ultimate influence of health status (Bibring, 1956; Klerman & Izen, 1977; Johnson & Sarason, 1979).

Stress and Diabetes Onset: There has been long-standing interest in examining the role of psychological or environmental stressors in diabetes. Early reports (Stein & Charles, 1975) suggested that the onset of Type I diabetes may be triggered by psychological stress in a physiologically susceptible individual. Since psychological stress can alter activity in the sympathoadrenalmedullary systems, elevate plasma cortisol levels, and possibly enhance the secretion of glucagon and growth hormones, it is possible that one trigger for clinical manifestations of diabetes in patients with a partly destroyed beta cell mass could be psychosocial stress. Furthermore, ongoing research examining the effect of psychosocial stress in immune functions (Kiecolt-Glaser et al., 1987) suggests a possible pathway for stress to influence the start or continuation of autoimmune beta cell functions. Indeed, one recent animal study, using the BB rat as a model of Type I diabetes, indicates that increasing environmental stress shortens the time to onset of overt diabetes mellitus (Carter, Herrman, Stokes, & Cox, 1987). More research is needed to address this understudied area.

Stress and Metabolic Control: Extensive research considers the role of psychological stress in metabolic control among Type I patients. These studies have suggested interesting yet poorly documented relationships between emotionally stressful experiences and the diabetic metabolic states. The earliest work was performed by Hinkle and Wolf (1952). They demonstrated that stressful interviews, focused on personal problems and conflicts identified during prior psychotherapy sessions, usually led to decreases or increases in blood glucose. The blood glucose changes seemed to vary with the type of emotions that were elicited during these sessions. Experiences of anxiety and tension were associated with glucose decreases, while experiences of anger and resentment were associated with increases in blood glucose. Because the authors used a case study method, it is difficult to interpret the results of these first studies. Vandenbergh, Sussman, and Titus, (1966), using hypnotic suggestion to induce a stressful experience, also found that blood glucose usually dropped in response to stress. Eigler, Sacca, & Sherwin (1979) noted that the usual effect of these stress interviews has been a decrease in blood glucose. Moreover, in the most sophisticated study of the role of short-term psychological stress on metabolic control among Type I diabetic patients, Kemmer and colleagues (1986) report that short-term psychological stress, utilizing mental arithmetic tasks and public speaking experiences, did not lead to increases in blood glucose.

Gilbert, Johnson, Silverstein, & Malone (1989) compared groups of adolescents with diabetes in good control, poor control, and nondiabetics in terms of physiological, behavioral, and self-report assessments of anxiety and arousal administered during stressful manipulations. As stressors, a venipuncture and two public speaking tasks were used. The three groups did not differ in their psychological and physiological reactions to the stressors, and there was no evidence that the stressors used in the study had a significant impact on metabolic control. However, a surprising finding appeared. The diabetics in poor control showed a higher heart rate throughout the study, including baseline conditions, suggesting a link with autonomic and cardiac risk in this population. Delamater and colleagues (1988), in a similarly designed study, had a similar finding of increased autonomic and cardiac risk for adolescents in poor control.

Stabler and colleagues (1986) looked at individual differences in stress-sensitivity by comparing blood glucose levels between Type A and Type B diabetic children, whose ages ranged from 8 to 15 years, both before and after exposing them to a stimulating encounter with a video game. Five of the 6 of the Type A children showed an increase in blood glucose, while 6 out of 7 Type B children showed a decrease in blood glucose. Two other variables, heart rate and blood pressure, did not distinguish the two groups before, during, or after the video game.

In summary, there are intriguing suggestions from an initial study of animal models of diabetes that psychosocial stress may play a role in the onset of Type I diabetes. The application of a personality classification (Type A and Type B personality) from cardiovascular disease research has provided a useful method for subtyping diabetic patients who may be at special risk for the direct psychological impact on metabolic control difficulties (Stabler et al., 1987). While it is not yet clear whether psychosocial stress can directly alter metabolic control, many studies indicate that various psychosocial factors, including stress, may affect adherence behaviors, thereby having an indirect impact on metabolic control (Peyrot & McMurray, 1985; Hauser et al., 1990; Jacobson, Hauser, Anderson, & Polonsky, 1990).

COPING

Young patients' coping strategies have several connections with the course of their diabetes, affecting adherence, metabolic control, and overall adjustment (Helz & Templeton, 1990; Wertlieb, Jacobson, & Hauser, 1990). Higher self-esteem, for instance, may serve as a protective factor in a patient's adjustment to the vicissitudes of this complicated illness and to the potentially confusing, and at times inadvertently hurtful, responses of significant others, such as family members, close friends, and schoolmates. Along these lines, preadolescents and adolescents with lower levels of self-esteem express lower levels of adherence at the time of diagnosis and over time (Jacobson et al., 1987; Jacobson et al., 1990).

Another personality feature relevant to coping is the child's or youth's ego development. Level of ego development, reflecting the individual's maturation along the lines of impulse control, moral development, cognitive complexity, and interpersonal relationships, influences how the young patient may experience and respond to Type I diabetes (Jacobson, Hauser, Powers, & Noam, 1982; Hauser, Jacobson, Noam, & Powers, 1983). Barglow and colleagues (1983) found that ego development was the best predictor of an adolescent's responsiveness to a brief educative intervention designed to enhance adherence and glycemic control. In contrast, neither psychopathology nor self-esteem was associated with responses to this intervention. These findings suggest a patient's level of ego development can synergistically enhance the benefits of educational and medical interventions designed to improve metabolic control, adherence, or coping strategies. "A higher level of ego development may provide an individual with the cognitive and emotional maturity that is needed to deal effectively with the demands of having a chronic illness" (Silver et al., 1990, p. 309). Further research is needed to develop interventions tailored to significant development differences among diabetic children and adolescents (Hauser et al., 1979).

Links between specific adolescent coping styles and diabetes outcomes have also been followed (Hanson, Harris, et al., 1989a). Use of avoidant coping by diabetic youths was associated with poor adherence to treatment as well as with longer duration of the illness. In addition, patients used avoidant coping in the context of high stress and low family cohesion. In contrast, youths with short-duration Type I diabetes were more likely to cope through the use of personal and interpersonal resources (e.g., self-reliance, seeking social support).

SOCIAL ENVIRONMENT

Social environment is a third major psychosocial mediator of adaptation to chronic illness and maintenance of health (House, Landis, & Umberson, 1988). Friends, family, and health care providers may be important sources of support. Berkman and Syme (1979) have shown that the availability of friends and close family for support has a long-term effect on the mortality rates of individuals matched for age, sex, and health status. Men and women rated lowest in the availability of friendships were more than twice as likely to suffer a fatal illness in the course of the 9-year study than those rated highest. Yet it is too simple to assume that important other people are always positive influences. Disorganized and conflicted family relationships can negatively influence health status (Minuchin et al., 1975).

These studies are all based on adult samples and, together with clinical and theoretical considerations, they argue that the diabetic child's or adolescent's social surroundings will significantly affect the course of his or her illness (Hauser et al., 1990; Wertlieb, Jacobson, & Hauser, et al., 1990). Moreover, virtually all of these studies address one social environment, the family. While the focus on the family does not rule out influences from peer and other social groupings (e.g., religious groups, self-help groups), the most consistent evidence is based on family studies. It is important to keep in mind the likelihood that peer forces, and associated school settings, powerfully affect the adjustment, adherence, and clinical course of young patients'—especially adolescents'—diabetes.

FAMILY SETTINGS

Families of newly diagnosed children and adolescents with insulin-dependent diabetes experience the onset of this chronic illness in many ways (Patterson, 1988; Rolland, 1988). Mealtime routines, bodily care, and yearnings for independence are suddenly disrupted; family members' views of the young patient's longevity are unexpectedly questioned. Successful management of their son's or daughter's diabetes will require families to redistribute responsibilities, reorganize their daily routines, and renegotiate family roles (Hauser & Soloman, 1985). Not surprisingly, there has been considerable interest in the ways that family forces may influence patients' adaptation to their diabetes (Crain, Sussman, & Weil, 1966; Baker, Barcai, Kaye, & Haque, 1969, 1970; Koski, Ahlas, & Kumeto, 1976; Benoliel, 1977; Anderson & Auslander, 1980; Anderson, Miller, Auslander, & Santiago, 1981; Bobrow, Asruskin, & Siller, 1985; Hauser et al., 1985, Hauser et al., 1986; Wertlieb, Hauser, & Jacobson, 1986; Hanson & Henggler, 1987). Much of this research originally concentrated on the mother-child relationship and its effect on the young patient's adjustment (Pond, 1979; Anderson & Auslander, 1980; Stein, 1989). Attention then broadened to include the family unit and the ways it influences the youngster with diabetes, as investigations described the importance of maladaptive parenting styles (Stein, 1989), parental self-esteem (Grey, Genel, & Tamborlane, 1980), and marital satisfaction (Hanson et al., 1989b) and specific family orientations and relationships (Mendlowitz, 1983; Hauser, et al., 1986; Hanson & Henggler, 1987). Yet as Schafer, Glasgow, McCaul, & Dehrer (1983) observe, it is only very recently that empirical studies have focused on how families influence diabetes, such as the ways families facilitate and impede adherence to treatment.

Family influences can contribute to the child's and adolescent's adherence, metabolic control, early complications, and overall adjustment. While some studies consider the family with respect to metabolic control (Anderson et al., 1981) and the overall adjustment of the youngster with diabetes (Wertlieb et al., 1986), the largest corpus of work is devoted to identifying how family processes contribute to the child's or adolescent's adherence (Galatzer, Amir, Karp & Laren, 1982; Shouval, Ber & Galatzer, 1982; Schafer, Glasgow,

McCaul, & Dehrer, 1983; Bobrow, et al., 1985; Hanson & Henggler, 1987; Stein, 1989). Variables associated with adherence include family support, cohesion, expressiveness, conflict, and organization. In a recent 4-year follow-up study, perceived family cohesiveness at onset was found to be associated with more favorable short-term and long-term adherence by diabetic adolescents (Hauser et al., 1990). In the same study, when parents and youngsters perceived more family conflict, adolescents showed lower levels of adherence over the 4 years. These findings converge with previous cross-sectional studies describing deleterious impacts of family conflict on specific diabetes outcomes (Koski et al., 1976; Bobrow, Ausruskin, & Siller, 1985; Stein, 1989).

Waller and colleagues (1986) studied the relation between family support and metabolic control. Family warmth/caring and guidance/control were associated with better glycemic control for girls. Three specific family behaviors correlating significantly with glycemic control were whether: (1) the parent watched the child testing for glucose; (2) whether the parents wrote down results of the test; and (3) the child had someone in the family to talk with about diabetes. Children younger than 13 years old who tested their own blood and took major responsibility for self-care were in poorer metabolic control compared to adolescents who took some of the responsibility together with parents who observed the adolescent patients perform the glucose tests.

In addition to family cohesiveness and conflict, family organization (clear coordination and structure in planning family activities and responses) is associated with the adjustment and adherence of the diabetic patient. Anticipation and coordination is required for successful adherence. These individual strengths are probably enhanced in families where organization is valued and likely implemented in daily functioning. Parents' perceptions of family organization are associated with youngsters' higher self-esteem and more favorable adjustment to diabetes during the first year of illness (Hauser et al., 1985; Hauser et al., 1989). Moreover, parents' perceptions of family organization during the months following their child's diagnosis predict higher levels of adherence during the first year as well as over several years of follow-up (Hauser et al., 1990).

The next generation of family studies must advance knowledge on two fronts. First, there is the task of more precisely identifying family risk and protective factors. Once these dimensions and means for their assessment, are clearly delineated, we can design scientifically grounded family interventions that will promote optimal adjustment, adherence, and metabolic control of youngsters with diabetes. Second, it is important to determine how families can shape their young patients' adaptation and diabetes-specific outcomes (Hauser et al., 1986, 1989; Hauser, 1990). As we locate paths of action from family life to individual experience and behavior, we will be in an excellent position to identify specific family coping styles and interactions that may be most amenable to change, rather than pursuing more global, and elusive, family factors.

Psychosocial Impacts of Diabetes on Children and Adolescents

NEUROCOGNITIVE CONSEQUENCES

What effect, if any, does diabetes have on cognitive functioning? Six teams of investigators have found that while diabetic children and adolescents were as a group unaffected, certain subgroups tended to be at increased risk for selective neurocognitive impairment. Children diagnosed before age 5 performed more poorly on tests of visual-spatial and other aspects of neurocognitive functioning than controls or children who developed diabetes later (Ack, Miller, & Weil 1961; Hale et al., 1985; Holmes and Richman, 1985; Ryan, Vega, & Drash, 1985; Rovet, Ehrlich, & Hoppe, 1987, 1988; Hagen et al., 1990). It is possible that the greater incidence of hypoglycemic seizures or coma in younger diabetic children, and the hypersensitivity of the immature brain to physiological disturbances, may lead to cognitive impairments. One group has also noted impairments in verbal and conceptual abilities in the children with later-onset diabetes mellitus (Ryan, Vega, et al., 1985).

In contrast to these findings, Rovet, Ehrlich, and Czuchta(1990) conducted a 3 year longitudinal study to determine whether diabetic children are at risk for later neurocognitive impairment. Preliminary findings suggest no evidence of neurocognitive impairment in diabetic children at onset of disease or after 1 year of illness (Rovet, Ehrlich, & Czuchta 1990). In addition, there are no indications of negative impacts from mild or severe hypoglycemia. However, frequent hyperglycemia may adversely affect specific aspects of neurocognitive functioning (planning skills and part-whole perception) (Rovet, Ehrlich, & Czuchta, 1990).

The difference between Rovet and colleagues' (1990) preliminary findings and the others' findings is of particular interest since Rovet's study uses a prospective and longitudinal design. Because the other studies are retrospective and cross-sectional, causal attributions cannot be determined. On the other hand, repeated cognitive testing often leads to improved scores because subjects improve their test taking strategies. Thus, longitudinal repeated measure designs may underestimate cognitive deficits, especially mild ones.

Other studies indicate that children and adolescents with diabetes perform at lower levels of achievement in school (Gath, Smith, & Baum, 1980; Ryan, Longstreet, & Morrow, 1985). These decreased capacities on school achievement tests and in neuropsychological test batteries may represent neurological damage or demonstrate effects of diabetes on school absence rate (Ryan, Longstreet, & Morrow, 1985). In other words, children with the most impaired diabetic control, including repeated severe hypoglycemic episodes, could miss many days of classes, resulting in more achievement problems and associated neuropsychological dysfunctions.

PSYCHIATRIC CONSEQUENCES

A long-standing concern has been that Type I diabetes can place children and adolescents at greater risk for psychiatric disturbances. Early case reports (Slawson, Flynn, & Kollas, 1963; Swift, Seidman, & Stein, 1967; O'Leary, et al., 1983) described diabetic patients as expressing much psychopathology and concluded that Type I diabetes could lead to severe psychiatric consequences. Subsequent empirical investigations raise questions about this conclusion. Simonds (1976, 1977) assessed diagnosis, interpersonal conflict, and intrapsychic conflict in children with Type I diabetes. He found that the number of psychiatric diagnoses and levels of conflict were equivalent in diabetic and nondiabetic children.

Jacobson and colleagues, (1986) and Kovacs and colleagues, (1986) report that children at onset typically appear to experience, at most, mild transient situational disruptions without signs of early severe psychiatric pathology. Sullivan (1979) found mild increases in depression among adolescent campers, but no differences in the level of self-esteem in comparison to normative data. Ongoing prospective studies (Jacobson et al., 1986; Kovacs et al., 1986) are likely to soon provide data regarding longer-term psychological and psychiatric effects of Type I diabetes for children and adolescents. For example, several analyses indicate that, when compared with normal and recent acute illness adolescents, those with diabetes are functioning at lower levels of ego development (Hauser, Jacobson, Noam, & Powers, 1983; Hauser et al., 1992). Although statistically significant, the clinical meaning of this finding is not clear and awaits more detailed longitudinal studies (Hauser et al., 1992) that include diabetes-specific measures (e.g., metabolic control, compliance) as well as related psychological assessments (e.g., self-esteem, diabetes adjustment).

Some research has suggested that patients with diabetes experience a range of mood shifts with hyper- and hypoglycemic experience (Gonder-Frederick, Cox, Bobbitt, & Pennebaker, 1989). These can include periods of depression, euphoria, and irritability. It is possible that long-term poor glycemic control or extreme shifts in blood glucose could place certain diabetic individuals at higher risk for subsequent affective disorder.

There is a growing interest in examining the impact of Type I diabetes on the development of eating disorders. Results conflict; some studies suggest an increase in rates of symptoms related to anorexia nervosa and bulimia among female Type I diabetes patients. For example, Rosmark and colleagues (1986) studied 86 patients and a normal control sample. Using a standardized self-report questionnaire, they found that a greater proportion of the diabetic patients described eating-disorder symptoms when compared with the normal controls. Steel, Young, Lloyd, and Clarke, (1987) found a higher rate of clinically apparent eating disorders than would be expected from a community sample. Finally, Rodin and colleagues (1986) assessed 58 women with Type I diabetes using standardized diagnostic self-report interviews, based on *Diagnostic and Statistical Handbook of Mental Disorders-III* criteria. They

345

reported that 20.7% had a clinically significant eating disorder, 6.9% had anorexia nervosa, and 6.9% had bulimia. The rate of anorexia in this study was approximately 7 times that expected in a general population. Nielson, Borner, and Kabel (1987) also found approximately a sixfold increase in the prevalence of eating disorders at a tertiary center in Denmark. On the other hand, Birk and Spencer (1989) studied patients with Type I diabetes attending a large multispecialty group practice, using standardized self-report surveys. They studied 385 women ages 13 to 45 and reported far lower prevalence rates for anorexia (1%). The prevalence of bulimia was 10%. The authors concluded that their data contradicted previous studies since the prevalence of bulimia and anorexia nervosa was within the range considered to exist in the general population. Most recently, Fairburn (1988) and his group compared young women having Type I diabetes with a normative sample and found no difference in the prevalence of eating disorders, unlike some earlier studies (e.g., Rodin et al., 1986). This study used a comparison sample and seemed less likely to have a biased diabetic sample than a tertiary care center.

Our current state of knowledge about the psychiatric impact of Type I diabetes mellitus is at an early stage. Few studies have been performed using standardized criteria. Most studies have failed to use control samples. Furthermore, investigations frequently depend on samples of convenience and it is often not clear whether the control samples, when used, come from comparable populations. This is true of many studies done at tertiary care centers where patients may be preselected to come because of unusually severe problems with illness. Such special samples could consist of patients with higher than expected rates of psychiatric disturbances, such as anorexia, bulimia, and depression, since all of these can lead to secondary problems of glycemic control, thereby triggering referral to the specialized center for care.

DEVELOPMENT AND PERSONALITY

A burgeoning literature addresses how diabetes may affect personality and developmental outcomes among children and adolescents. Studies disagree as to whether diabetes has distinct impacts on aspects of personality and development (Dunn & Turtle, 1981). Several studies report no significant differences in self-esteem in comparing groups of children with and without diabetes (Jacobson, Beardslee, Hauser, & Noam, 1985; Jacobson et al., 1986; Ryan & Morrow, 1986; Wertlieb, Jacobson, & Hauser, 1990; Zeltzer et al., 1980). In contrast, there are findings of subtle developmental alterations in adolescents with Type I diabetes (Jacobson, Hauser, Powers, & Noam, 1982; Hauser, Jacobson, Noam, & Powers, 1983; Hauser, 1990). These studies consider the influence of diabetes on the child's or adolescent's psychological maturation and his or her ego development. As referred to earlier, two different, largely middle-class samples of adolescents with diabetes were found to be functioning at significantly lower levels of ego development (Hauser, Jacobson, Noam, & Powers, 1983; Hauser et al., 1992). In one instance, recently diagnosed patients with diabetes were longitudinally compared to a similar-age sample of patients with a recent acute illness (Hauser et al., 1992). Similar observations have been reported in studies of adolescents with longer and more variable durations of diabetes (Hauser et al., 1979; Jacobson, Hauser, Powers, & Noam, 1982; Hauser, Jacobson, Noam, & Powers, 1983). However, Silver and colleagues (1990), comparing a more heterogeneous sample of chronically ill adolescents that included 8 adolescents with diabetes (together with asthma, sickle cell anemia, arthritis, and chronic inflammatory bowel disease) with a comparable peer group, found no difference between the ego development of the two groups. The considerably lower social class of their sample, cross-sectional observations, and smaller number of adolescents with diabetes ($n = 8$), makes it difficult to interpret the extent to which their results differ from the previously reported cross-sectional and longitudinal findings.

One interpretation of the lower ego development of the patients with diabetes argues that these young patients are responding to the introduction and accumulation of many new stressors, such as diet changes and daily insulin injections. Rather than continuing normal psychological exploration and integration of inner experiences, perceptions, and relationships (all of which would be consistent with progressive ego development among adolescents), the new conflicts and preoccupations (e.g., "being different" or "getting complications") lead the diabetic adolescent to subtly withdraw from these developmentally appropriate tasks of adolescence to protect the now more vulnerable self (Hauser et al., 1992).

Other relevant personality and development findings are more scattered. Ingersoll, Orr, and Brink (1991) note that adolescents with Type I diabetes describe reduced health risk behaviors compared to adolescents without Type I diabetes. They speculate that underlying this finding are the life-threatening consequences of hypoglycemic seizures or diabetic ketoacidosis that could result from deviating from the strict treatment regimen associated with diabetes.

With respect to overall adjustment, self-esteem, and social adjustment, Zeltzer et al. (1980) find that diabetic adolescents report the lowest total overall impact of illness and fewer illness-related peer disruptions than their healthy counterparts.

FAMILIES

The onset and continued presence of diabetes in their child leads to a unique set of developmental stressors or strains for the family. The illness itself has a developmental course beginning at age of onset. The demands of diabetes interact with numerous developmental tasks for the diabetic child and his or her family, not only at onset but as he or she traverses the life cycle.

When diabetes is first diagnosed in a child, families are often shocked and grieve deeply (Wishner & O'Brien, 1978; Jacobson, Hauser, Powers, & Noam, 1982). Other feelings experienced and expressed by family members are anger, anxiety, and guilt. Besides the disturbing news, families have a vast amount of information to assimilate regarding management of the diabetes, new medical skills to master, and difficult medical decisions to make, such as choosing a specific doctor and treatment site. Some families seem to accept the illness relatively easily, incorporating the new diabetic regimen into their daily life; others adjust more slowly, continuing to deny the presence of the illness or maintaining a state of helplessness and sadness (Hauser & Soloman, 1985; Sargent, 1985; Stein, 1989). Certain aspects of diabetes are especially powerful influences. Because dietary control is such a basic feature of diabetes management, meal rituals are disrupted. The presence of diabetes exacerbates conflicts in families around such issues as independence and dependence in self-care tasks. The mother or the father of the diabetic child usually takes responsibility for the administration of insulin by injection. In adolescence, eventually youths self-inject. Overt parental concerns with the affairs of their adolescent's body, which ordinarily diminishes in adolescence, are heightened by this initial involvement in actual injections and continued attentiveness to this aspect of diabetes care. Parents are also drawn into greater engagement with the adolescent's bodily functions through concerns with metabolic control, as they inquire about urine or blood glucose. Moreover, the conscientious parent may also monitor the young child's physical activities outside the home, ensuring that he or she has the proper amount of exercise.

Much of the empirical research about how the onset and continued presence of the child's or adolescent's diabetes influences the family has focused on one or two relationships in the family (between parents, between parent and youngster) and on individual parental adjustment. Studies report that parents of diabetic children reveal greater marital strain and greater disagreement over child management issues than parents of nondiabetic children (Crain, Sussman, & Weil, 1966). Other studies consider the effect of the child's diabetes on the relationship between the parent and child. Parents may have difficulty dealing with their emotional reactions to the child, frequently responding in ways characterized as overprotective, overindulgent, or rejecting (Farrell & Hutter, 1984; Pond, 1979). In addition, parents may have more difficulty disciplining a child with diabetes, leading in turn to additional anxiety over their child rearing (Stein, 1989). Yet the family picture is not a completely bleak one. Studies also describe diabetic children as drawing much emotional support from their parents and feeling closer to them through coping with the illness (Farrell & Hutter, 1984).

Kovacs and colleagues (1990) looked at mothers of children with newly diagnosed Type I diabetes and periodically assessed them over the next 6 years. Most mothers initially responded to their children's diagnosis with mild depression and emotional distress. These initial reactions subsided in about 6 to 9 months. After initial adjustment, there were slight increases in mothers' depressive symptoms over the duration of their children's illness, although this effect was ameliorated by socioeconomic status (Kovacs et al. 1990). Overall psychological distress also increased over the course of the illness. As suspected, the initial response of mothers to their children's diagnosis was a strong predictor of the mothers' later symptomatology. Although symptoms increased, the stresses of having a diabetic child did not pose a risk for serious maternal depression. Mothers' symptoms were unrelated to medical aspects of Type I diabetes and levels of anxiety/depression reported by their children. The longer the children had the disease, the easier it became for the mothers to cope with it. The degree to which mothers considered Type I diabetes bothersome was associated with their overall levels of emotional distress.

Auslander, Anderson, Bubb, Jung, and Santiago (1990) in a longitudinal study found that diabetic children from African American and single-parent families are at higher risk for poor metabolic control than are children from white or two-parent families. They warn that definitive conclusions must be made cautiously because of the small number of children ($n = 11$) from African American and single-parent families. With regard to metabolic control, 2- and 3-year follow-up assessments reveal that the children remained in poorer control after the initial diagnosis of diabetes. These findings are of particular interest because the development of diabetic nephropathy is influenced by arterial hypertension, which is more common in African Americans (Auslander et al., 1990). Delamater (1985) reports that diabetes-specific family behaviors are better predictors of regimen adherence than global psychosocial variables and that conflict, whether indexed by general global measures or measures of family behavior related to the regimen, is associated with poor adherence and poor metabolic control.

An important direction of work considers the impact of Type I diabetes on the family as a total system. Family dimensions examined in relation to diabetes onset include role strain (Crain, Sussman, & Weil, 1966), family conflict (McCubbin & Patterson, 1982), activity orientation (Powers et al., 1984), family cohesion (Hauser et al., 1985), and enabling and constraining family interactions (Hauser, et al., 1986). For example, mothers of adolescents with recently diagnosed diabetes, in comparison to mothers of nondiabetic adolescents, were found to be more accepting and supportive of their spouses and their diabetic child in family discussions (Hauser et al., 1986). Fathers, however, were more judgmental and indifferent. These same families reported higher levels of or-

ganization and more shared activities than the comparison group (Hauser et al., 1989). Other studies describe an increase in conflict among families of diabetic children (Crain, Sussman, & Weil, 1966).

In summary, family studies portray multifaceted ways that the child and adolescent with diabetes can influence family life. Future studies in this area must address the important complexity of family effects, recognizing differences among families with diabetic youngsters, and systematically dissect sources of these differences. Only through such dissections will we be able to discover dimensions that underlie vulnerable and competent family adaptations to diabetes.

Recommendations for Psychosocial and Educational Interventions

Over the past decade, research on psychosocial and educational interventions with youths with diabetes has been increasing, yet a broad base of research knowledge is not available. Investigators in this area have confronted multiple problems that are barriers for intervention research efforts across pediatric chronic diseases: There are few theoretical plans (or testable conceptual paradigms) for guiding intervention methods and outcome variables (Harper, 1991); controlled experimental studies are difficult and expensive to implement and are not practical in many pediatric health care settings; adequate sample sizes of representative pediatric patients are not always available; and funding for research on psychosocial pediatric interventions has not been widely available.

Despite these barriers to research on psychosocial and educational interventions with youths with diabetes, the investigations of the past decade consistently indicate that the highest priority should be given to interventions focused on adolescents with Type I diabetes and their families. Few intervention research studies have focused on diabetic children before the adolescent years. In the only well-documented and evaluated study with preschool-age diabetic children, Golden, Russell, Ingersoll, Gray, & Hummer, at the University of Indiana (1985) evaluated the impact of an intensive program of individualized insulin therapy and blood sugar monitoring intervention with children diagnosed before the age of 5 years and their parents. The intervention, based on a strong educational program, included a psychosocial team member as an active player on the treatment team. Findings revealed that frequency of hospitalization and severe hypoglycemia can be successfully decreased in young children with diabetes. Frequent home blood glucose monitoring was critical. Extensive educational and psychosocial support were essential for families to cope successfully with the intensive individualized insulin treatment regimen.

A second intervention research effort with preadolescent diabetic children focused on a series of coping skills in training group programs with the 9 to 12-year age group (Gross, Anderson, Delcher, & Stiger, 1985; Gross, Johnson, Wildman, & Mullett, 1982). These group intervention studies focused on how to teach preadolescents to cope, verbally and non-verbally, with stressful social situations specific to diabetic children—that is, social situations in which children are tempted not to comply with their prescribed medical treatment regimen. Social skills training consisted of modeling and role-playing group activities. Assessments indicated that the training produced significant improvements in the ability of preadolescents to cope more effectively with social situations specific to their diabetes.

The vulnerability of adolescents with Type I diabetes to medical and psychosocial problems has been consistently documented (Anderson, Auslander, Jung, Miller, & Santiago, 1990; Daneman, Wolfson, Becker, & Drash, 1981; Report of the National Commission on Diabetes, 1976). In particular, many adolescents and parents have difficulty coping with both the lability of metabolic control characteristic of this age group (Amiel, Shervin, Simonson, Lauritano, & Tamborlane, 1986) and the constant need to renegotiate responsibilities for treatment. While not all diabetic adolescents display a disruptive medical course, there are identifiable adolescents who experience a cycle of dysfunction, with medical and interpersonal crises closely intertwined (Orr, Golden, Myers, & Marrero, 1983). These families are tyrannized by repeated hospitalizations, debilitating symptoms of chronic poor control, with concomitant school problems and family conflicts over treatment responsibility. Yet services for promoting self-care and effective family problem-solving

after initial diagnosis are lacking. A prime reason for this is that individualized professional mental health contact with adolescent patients is simply economically unfeasible. For these reasons, the majority of interventions have been group interventions focused on adolescent patients and their families.

There is convincing evidence that current health care delivery and educational approaches do not result in effective adolescent self-management. Studies by Ingersoll, Orr, Herrold, & Golden (1986) have shown that even older adolescents and their parents frequently do not participate in insulin self-adjustment. It has further been shown that both adolescents and parents often lack some basic diabetes knowledge and skills. There is a documented need for reeducating and updating the skills of diabetic adolescents who were diagnosed in early childhood, when parents assumed primary responsibility for treatment (Johnson, 1982). It is reasonable to believe that these potentially remediable deficiencies, in combination with the documented medical management problems that occur with the physiologic insulin resistance of the pubertal period, contribute to the deterioration in metabolic control.

Our review of the recent pediatric diabetes intervention literature indicates that the majority of studies have focused on group interventions with adolescents and their families. This does not imply that families necessarily cause management problems, for research has shown that chronic illness in general, and diabetes in particular, does not inevitably disrupt individual or family adjustment (Anderson, 1984; Drotar, Crawford, & Bush, 1984). Nor does a family-centered approach imply that families must change radically to solve disease-related problems. Often what is most critical is a reorientation of family members to the disease itself and a redistribution of responsibilities for disease management within the family (Coyne & Anderson, 1988).

In a series of well-controlled group interventions, Marrero and colleagues (1982a) focused specifically on adolescents in chronic poor metabolic control. The efficacy of their group model, emphasizing the development of coping skills, was reported across a full range of psychosocial variables. A successful replication resulted in a network of permanent clinical groups and courses to train therapists to work clinically with diabetic adolescents (D. G. Marrero, personal communication, 1988). As an extension of these studies, Golden, Herrold, & Orr, (1985a) conducted a series of interventions with adolescents repeatedly hospitalized due to diabetic ketoacidosis. Application of a stepwise intervention, progressing from biomedical evaluation and comprehensive educational program through escalating family and psychosocial interventions to ensure that insulin was appropriately administered, led to an elimination of recurrent ketoacidosis, underscoring the point that therapeutic approaches with this risk group must integrate psychosocial and biomedical care (Golden, Herrold, & Orr, et al., 1985).

Anderson, Wolf, Burkhart, Cornell, and Bacon (1989) demonstrated the effectiveness of integrating a problem-solving, group intervention into routine follow-up care for adolescents with Type I diabetes, utilizing coordinated parent-adolescent psychoeducational groups to prevent metabolic deterioration during the adolescent years. An 18-month intervention was carried out with young diabetic adolescents and their parents. Thirty-five adolescents were randomly assigned to the intervention and 35 to the comparison group or "standard care" condition. Groups were equated at baseline as to age, sex, disease duration, and metabolic control as indexed by glycosylated hemoglobin. At follow-up, adolescents in the comparison group revealed the expected deterioration in met-

abolic control, while the metabolic status of the intervention adolescents improved. Intervention adolescents did significantly more daily blood monitoring and adjustment of insulin and exercise than the comparison adolescents. However, despite an overall treatment effect, there was a subsample of adolescents with significant metabolic control and psychosocial problems for whom the scheduled intervention every 3 to 4 months proved insufficient. On an ad hoc basis, more regular, and perhaps individual, contact had to be provided to this subsample of at-risk adolescents. Citrin, La Greca, and Skyler (1985), and Brink (1987), have independently reported on several different approaches to and formats for group interventions with diabetic adolescents, although these were not as carefully documented and evaluated as those previously discussed.

Taken together, all of these intervention efforts indicate that by buffering some of the strong emotional responses of adolescents and parents to diabetes, and by building on emerging problem-solving abilities, adolescents can be encouraged to participate more actively and effectively in their own health care. It is also clear that a more potent, intense intervention is needed for families and patients facing more serious metabolic and psychosocial dysfunction.

REFERENCES

Ack, M., Miller, I., & Weil, W. B. (1961). Intelligence of children with diabetes mellitus. *Pediatrics, 25,* 264–770.

Amiel, S. A., Shervin, R. S., Simonson, D. C., Lauritano, A. A., & Tamborlane, W. V. (1986). Impaired insulin action in puberty: A contributing factor to poor glycemic control in adolescents with diabetes. *New England Journal of Medicine, 315,* 215–219.

Anderson, B. J. (1984). The impact of diabetes on the developmental tasks of childhood and adolescence: A research perspective. In M. Nattras, & J. Santiago, J. (Eds.), *Recent Advances in Diabetes* (pp. 165–171). London: Churchill Livingston.

Anderson, B. J., & Auslander, W. (1980). Research on diabetes management and the family: A critique. *Diabetes Care, 3,* 696–702.

Anderson, B. J., Auslander, W. F., Jung, K. C., Miller, J. P., & Santiago, J. V. (1990). Assessing family sharing of diabetes responsibilities. *Journal of Pediatric Psychology, 15,* 477–492.

Anderson, B. J., Miller, J., Auslander, W., & Santiago, J.

(1981). Family characteristics of diabetic adolescents: Relationships to metabolic control. *Diabetes Care, 4,* 586–594.

Anderson, B. J., Wolf, F., Burkhart, M., Cornell, R., & Bacon, G. (1989). Effects of peer-group intervention on metabolic control of adolescents with IDDM: Randomized outpatient study. *Diabetes Care, 12,* 179–181.

Auslander, W., Anderson, B., Bubb, J., Jung, K., & Santiago, J. (1990). Risk factors to health in diabetic children: A prospective study from diagnosis. *Health and Social Work, 15,* (2), 133–142.

Auslander, W., Haire-Joshu, D., Rogge, M., & Santiago, J. (1991). Predictors of diabetes knowledge in newly diagnosed children and parents. *Journal of Pediatric Psychology, 16* (2), 213–228.

Baker, L., Barcai, A., Kaye, R., & Haque, N. (1969). Beta-adrenergic blockade and juvenile diabetes: Acute studies and long-term therapeutic trial. *Journal of Pediatrics, 75,* 19–29.

Baker, L., Minuchin, S., & Rosman, B. (1976). Report,

National Commission on Diabetes, Appendix 33–43. Update. Washington, DC: U.S. Public Health Service.

Barglow, P., et al. (1983). Diabetic control in children and adolescents: Psychosocial factors and therapeutic efficacy. *Journal of Youth and Adolescence, 12,* 77–94.

Benoliel, J. Q. (1977). Role of the family in managing young diabetics. *Diabetes Educator, 5,* 8.

Berkman, L. F., & Syme S. L. (1979). Social networks, host-resistance, and mortality: A nine-year follow-up study of Alameda county residents. *Amerian Journal of Epidemiology, 109,* 186–204.

Bibring, G. (1956). Psychiatry and medical practice in a general hospital. *New England Journal of Medicine, 254,* 366–372.

Birk, R., & Spencer, M. L. (1989). Prevalence of anorexia nervosa, bulimia, and induced glycosuria in insulin-dependent diabetes mellitus females. *Diabetes Educator, 15,* 336–341.

Bobrow, E., Ausruskin, T., & Siller, J. (1985). Mother-daughter interaction and adherence to medical regimens. *Diabetes Care, 8,* 146–155.

Brink, S. (1987). Youth and parent support groups. In S. Brink (Ed.), *Pediatric and adolescent diabetes mellitus.* (pp. 359–368). Chicago: Year Book.

Carter, W. R., Herrman, J., Stokes, K., & Cox, D. J. (1987). Promotion of diabetes onset by stress in BB rat. *Diabetologia, 30,* 674–675.

Citrin, W. S., LaGreca, A. M., & Skyler, J. S. (1985). Group interventions in Type I diabetes mellitus. In P. I. Ahmed, & N. Ahmed (Eds.), *Coping with juvenile diabetes* (pp. 181–204). Springfield, IL: Charles C. Thomas.

Coyne, J. C., & Anderson, B. J. (1988). The "psychosomatic family" reconsidered: Diabetes in context. *Journal of Marital and Family Therapy, 14,* 113–123.

Crain, A. J., Sussman, M. B., & Weil, W. B. (1966). Effects of a diabetic child on mental interaction of related measure of family functioning. *Journal of Health and Human Behavior, 7,* 122–127.

Daneman, D., Wolfson, D. H., Becker, D. J., & Drash, A. L. (1981). Factors affecting glycosylated hemoglobin values in children with insulin-dependent diabetes. *Journal of Pediatrics, 99,* 847–853.

Delamater, A. (1985). Psychological aspects of diabetes mellitus in children. In A. E. Kazdin (Ed.), *Advances in Clinical Child Psychology* (Vol. 9, pp. 333–375). New York: Plenum Press.

Delamater, A. (In press). Adaptation of children to newly diagnosed diabetes. In C. S. Holmes (Ed.), *Neuropsychological and behavioral aspects of insulin and noninsulin dependent diabetes mellitus.* New York: Springer-Verlag.

Delamater, A., Bubb, J., Kurtz, S. M., Kuntze, J., Smith, J. A., White, N. H., & Santiago, J. V. (1988). Physiologic responses to acute psychological stress in adolescents with Type I diabetes mellitus. *Journal of Pediatric Psychology, 13* (1), 69–86.

Dimsdale, J. E., et al. (1979). The role of social supports in medical care. *Social Psychiatry, 14,* 175–180.

Drash, A. L. (1981). The child with diabetes mellitus, In H. Ritkin & P. Raskin (Eds.), *Diabetes mellitus,* 5. Bowie, MD: Prentice-Hall.

Drotar, D., Crawford, P., & Bush, A. (1984). The family context of childhood chronic illness: Implications for psychosocial intervention. In M. G. Eisenberg, L. C. Sutkin, & M. A. Jansen (Eds.) *Chronic illness and disability through the life span* (pp. 103–129). New York: Springer.

Dunn, S. T., & Turtle, J. R. (1981). The myth of the diabetic personality. *Diabetes Care, 4,* 640–646.

Eigler, N., Sacca, L., & Sherwin, R. (1979). Syngeristic interactions of physiologic increments of glucagon, epinephrine, and cortisol in the dog. *Journal of Clinical Investigations, 63,* 114–125.

Fairburn, C. G. (1988). The current status of the psychological treatments for bulimia nervosa. *Journal of Psychosomatic Research 32,* 635–645.

Farrell, F. Z., & Hutter, J. J. Jr. (1984). The family of the adolescent: A time of challenge. In M. G. Eisenberg, L. C. Sutkin, & M. A. Jansen (Eds.), *Chronic illness and disability through the life span: Effects on self and family.* New York: Springer.

Galatzer, A., Amir, S., Karp, M., & Laren, Z. (1982). Crisis intervention program in newly diagnosed diabetic children. *Diabetes Care, 5,* 414–419.

Gath, A., Smith, M. A., & Baum, J. D. (1980). Emotional, behavioral and educational disorders in diabetic children. *Archives of Diseases of Children, 55,* 371–75.

Gilbert, B., Johnson, S., Silverstein, J., & Malone, J. (1989). Psychological and physiological responses to acute laboratory stressors in insulin-dependent diabetes mellitus adolescents and non-diabetics controls. *Journal of Pediatric Psychology, 14* (4), 577–591.

Goldband, S., Katkin, E., & Morrell, M. (1979). Personality and cardiovascular disorder: Steps toward demystification. In I. Sarason & C. Spielberger (Eds.), *Stress and anxiety* (pp. 159–168). New York: Wiley.

Golden, M. P., Herrold, J. A., & Orr, D. P. (1985). An approach to prevention of recurrent diabetic ketoacidosis in the pediatric population. *Journal of Pediatrics, 107,* 195–200.

Golden, M. P., Russell, B. P., Ingersoll, G. M., Gray, D. L., & Hummer, K. M. (1985). Management of diabetes mellitus in children younger than 5 years of age. *American Journal of Diseases of Children, 139,* 448–452.

Gonder-Frederick, L. A., Cox, D. J., Bobbitt, S. A., & Pennebaker, J. W. (1989). Mood changes associated with blood glucose functioning in insulin-dependent diabetes mellitus. *Health Psychology, 8,* 45–49.

Grey, M. J., Genel, M., & Tamborlane, W. V. (1980). Psychosocial adjustment of latency-aged diabetics: Determinants and relationship to control. *Pediatrics, 65.*

Gross, A. M., Anderson, J. E., Delcher, H., & Stiger, M. (1985). Video teacher: Peer instruction. *The Diabetes Educator, 10,* 30–31.

Gross, A. M., Johnson, W. G., Wildman, H., & Mullett, N. (1982). Coping skills training with insulin dependent pre-adolescent diabetics. *Child Behavior Therapy, 3,* 141–153.

SECTION III / VARIETIES OF MEDICAL DISORDER

Hagen, J., Barclay, C., Anderson, B., Feeman, D., Segal, S., Bacon, G., & Goldstein, G. (1990). Intellective functioning and strategy use in children with insulin-dependent diabetes mellitus. *Child Development, 61,* 1714–1727.

Hale, D. B., Berenhaum, S. A., Traisman, H. S., Golden, M. P., Rosenberg, S. J., & Headen, S. (1985). Neuropsychological consequences of insulin-dependent diabetes in school-age children. *Journal of Clinical and Experimental Neuropsychology, 7,* 606.

Hanson, C., Harris, M., Relyea, G., Cigrang, J., Carle, D., & Burghen, G. (1989). Coping styles in youths with insulin-dependent diabetes mellitus. *Journal of Consulting and Clinical Psychology, 57* (5), 644–651.

Hanson, C., & Henggler, S. (1987). Social competence and parental support as mediators of the link between stress and metabolic control in adolescents with insulin-dependent diabetes mellitus. *Journal of Consulting and Clinical Psychology, 55,* 529–533.

Hanson, C., Henggler, S. W., Harris, M. A., & Burghen, G. A. (1989). Family system variables and the health status of adolescents with insulin-dependent diabetes mellitus. *Health Psychology, 8,* 239–253.

Harper, D. (1991). Paradigms for investigating rehabilitation and adaptation to childhood disability and chronic illness. *Journal of Pediatric Psychology, 16* (5), 533–542.

Hauser, S. T. (1990). The study of families and chronic illness: Ways of coping and interacting. In G. Brady & I. Sigel (Eds.), *Methods of family research* (pp. 59–86). New York: Plenum.

Hauser, S. T., Pollets, D., Turner, B. L., Jacobson, A., Powers, S., & Noam, G. (1979). Ego development and self-esteem in diabetic youth. *Diabetes Care, 2,* 465–471.

Hauser, S. T., Jacobson, A. M., Noam, G., and Powers, S. (1983). Ego development and self-image complexity in early adolescence: Longitudinal studies of diabetic and psychiatric patients. *Archives of General Psychiatry, 40,* 325–332.

Hauser, S. T., & Soloman, M. L. (1985). Coping with diabetes: Views from the family. In P. Ahmed & N. Ahmed (Eds.), *Coping with diabetes* (pp. 234–266). Springfield, IL: Charles C. Thomas.

Hauser, S. T., Jacobson, A. M., Wertlieb, D., Brink, S., & Wentworth, S. (1985). The contribution of family environment to perceived competence and illness adjustment in diabetic and acutely ill adolescents. *Family Relations, 34,* 99–108.

Hauser, S. T., Jacobson, A., Wertlieb, D., Weiss-Perry, B., Follansbee, D., Wolfsdorf, J. I., Herskowitz, R. D., Houlihan, J., & Rajapark, D. C. (1986). Children with recently diagnosed diabetes: Interactions within their families. *Health Psychology, 5,* 273–296.

Hauser, S. T., Jacobson, A., Wertlieb, D., Wolfsdorf, J., Herskowitz, R., Vieyra, M., & Orleans, J. (1989). Family contexts of self-esteem and illness adjustment in diabetic and acutely ill children. In C. Ramsey (Ed.), *Family systems in medicine.* New York: Guilford Press.

Hauser, S. T., Jacobson, A. M., Lavori, P., Wolfsdorf, J. I., Herskowitz, R. D., Milley, J. E., Bliss, R., Wert-lieb, D., & Stein, J. (1990). Adherence among children and adolescents with insulin-dependent diabetes mellitus over a four-year longitudinal follow-up: II. Immediate and long-term linkages with the family milieu. *Journal of Pediatric Psychology, 15* (4), 527–542.

Hauser, S. T., Jacobson, A. M., Milley, J., Wertlieb, D., Hershowitz, R., Wolfsdorf, J., & Lavori, P. (1992). Ego trajectories and adjustment to diabetes: Longitudinal studies of diabetic and acutely ill patients In L. Feagens, W. Ray, & E. Susman (Eds.), *Emotion and cognition in child and adolescent health and development.* Hillsdale, NJ: Lawrence Erlbaum Associates.

Helz, J. W., & Templeton, B. (1990). Evidence of the role of psychosocial factors in diabetes mellitus: A review. *American Journal of Psychiatry, 147,* 1275–1282.

Hinkle, L., & Wolf, S. (1952). A summary of experimental relating life stress to diabetes mellitus. *Journal of Mount Sinai Hospital, 19,* 567–570.

Holmes, C. S., & Richman, L. C. (1985). Cognitive profiles of children with insulin-dependent diabetes. *Development and Behavioral Pediatrics, 6,* 323–381.

House, J., Landis, K., & Umberson, D. (1988). Social relationships and health. *Science, 241,* 540–545.

Ingersoll, G., Orr, D., & Brink, S. (1991, April). *Behavioral and emotional risk among adolescents with diabetes.* Paper presented at the Biennial Meeting of the Society for Research in Child Development, Seattle, WA.

Ingersoll, G. M., Orr, D. P., Herrold, J. A., & Golden, M. P. (1986). Cognitive maturity and self-management among adolescents with insulin-dependent diabetes mellitus. *Journal of Pediatrics, 108,* 620–623.

Jacobson, A. M., Hauser, S. T., Powers, S., & Noam, G. (1982). Ego development in diabetes: A longitudinal study. *Pediatric Adolescent Endocrinology, 10,* 1–8.

Jacobson, A. M., Beardslee, W., Hauser, S., & Noam, G. (1985). Evaluating ego defense mechanisms using clinical interviews: An empirical study of adolescent diabetic and psychiatric patients. *Journal of Adolescence, 9,* 303–319.

Jacobson, A. M., Hauser, S. T., Wertlieb, D., Wolfsdorf, J. I., Orleans, J., & Vieyra, M. (1986). Psychological adjustment of children with recently diagnosed diabetes mellitus. *Diabetes Care, 9,* 323–329.

Jacobson, A. M., Hauser, S., Wolfsdorf, J., Houlihan, J., Milley, J., Herskowitz, R., Wertlieb, D., Watt, E. (1987). Psychologic predictors of compliance in children with recent onset of diabetes mellitus. *Journal of Pediatrics, 110,* 805–811.

Jacobson, A. M., Hauser, S. T., Anderson, B. J., Polonsky, W. (1990). Psychosocial Aspects of Diabetes for *Joslin's Diabetes Mellitus,* 13th Ed. Philadelphia: Lea Febiger Co.

Jacobson, A. M., Hauser, S. T., Lavori, P., Wolfsdorf, J. I., Herskowitz, R. D., Milley, J. E., Bliss, R., Gelfand, E., Wertlieb, D., & Stein, J. (1990). Adherence among children and adolescents with insulin-dependent diabetes mellitus over a four-year longitudinal follow-up: I. The influence of patient coping and adjustment. *Journal of Pediatrics Psychology, 15* (4), 511–526.

352

Johnson, J. H. & Sarason, I. G. (1979). Moderator variables in life stress research. In *Stress and Anxiety.* (pp. 159–168). I. Sarason and C. Spielberger, New York, Wiley, 159–168.

Johnson, S. B. (1982). Behavioral management of childhood diabetes. *New Directions for Mental Health Services, 15,* 5–18.

Kemmer, F. W., Bisping, R., Baar, H., & Steingruber, H. J. (1986). Psychological stress and metabolic control in patients with Type I Diabetes Mellitus. *New England Journal of Medicine, 314,* 1078–84.

Kiecolt-Glaser, J. K., Fisher, L. D., Ogrocki, P., Stout, J. C., Speicher, C. E., & Glaser, R. (1987). Marital quality, marital disruption and immune function. *Psychosomatic Medicine, 49,* 13–34.

Klerman, G. L., & Izen, J. E. (1977). Effects of bereavement and grief on physical health and general well-being. *Advanced Psychosomatic Medicine, 9,* 63.

Koski, L., Ahlas, A., & Kumeto, A. (1976). A psychosomatic follow-up study of childhood diabetes. *Acta Paedopsychiatrica, 42,* 12–25.

Kovacs, M., & Feinberg, T. (1982). Coping with juvenile onset diabetes. In A. Baum & J. Singer (Eds.), *Handbook of health and psychology* (Vol. 2, pp. 165–212). Hillsdale, NJ: Lawrence Erlbaum Associates.

Kovacs, M., Brent, D., Steinberg, T. F., Paulauskas, S., & Reid, J. (1986). Children's self-reports of psychologic adjustment and coping strategies during the first year of insulin-dependent diabetes mellitus. *Diabetes Care, 9,* 472–479.

Kovacs, M., Feinberg, T. L., Paulauskas, S., Finkelstein, R., Pollock, M., & Crouse-Novak, M. (1985). Initial coping responses and psychosocial characteristics of children with IDDM. *Journal of Pediatrics, 106,* 827–834.

Kovacs, M., Iyengar, S., Goldston, D., Obrosky, D. S., Stewart, J., Marsh, J. (1990). Psychological functioning among mothers of children with insulin-dependent diabetes mellitus: A longitudinal study. *Journal of Consulting and Clinical Psychology, 58* (2), 189–195.

Marrero, D. G., Golden, M. P., Kershnar, A., & Myers, G. L. (1982). Problem-focused versus emotion-focused coping styles in adolescent diabetics. *Pediatrics Adolescent Endocrinology, 10,* 141–146.

Marrero, D. G., Myes, G., Golden, M. P., West, D., Kershnar, A., & Lau, N. (1982). Adjustment of misfortune: The use of a social support group for adolescent diabetics. *Pediatrics Adolescent Endocrinology, 10,* 213–218.

Mattson, A. (1979). Juvenile diabetes: Impacts on life stages and systems. In B. Hamberg, L. F. Lipsett, G. E. Inoff, & A. L. Drash (Eds.), *Behavioral and psychosocial issues in diabetes* (pp. 43–56). Washington, DC: Government Printing Office.

McCubbin, H., & Patterson, J. (1982). Family adaptation to crises. In H. McCubbin, A. Cauble, & J. Patterson (Eds.), *Family stress, coping and social support* (pp. 169–188). Springfield, IL: Charles C. Thomas.

Mendlowitz, D. (1983). The relationship between level of metabolic control in children with juvenile onset diabetes and dimensions of family functioning. *Dissertations Abstracts International, 44.*

Minuchin, S., Baker, L., Rossman, B., Leibman, P., Milnan, L., & Todd, T. (1975). A conceptual model of psychosomatic illness in children. *Archives of General Psychiatry, 32,* 1031–1038.

Moos, R. H., & Moos, B. S. (1981). *Family Environment Scale.* Palo Alto, CA: Consulting Psychologists Press.

Nielson, S., Borner, H., & Kabel, M. (1987). Anorexia nervosa/bulimia in diabetes mellitus. *Acta Psychiatrica Scandinavica, 75,* 464–473.

O'Leary, D. S., et al. (1983). Effects of age on onset of partial and generalized seizures on neuropsychological performance in children. *Journal of Nervous and Mental Disorders, 171,* 624–629.

Orr, D. P., Golden, M. P., Myers, G., & Marrero, D. G. (1983). Characteristics of adolescents with poorly controlled diabetes referred to a tertiary care center. *Diabetes Care, 6,* 170–175.

Patterson, J. (1988). Chronic illness in children and the impact on families. In C. Chilman, E. Nunnally, & F. Cox (Eds.), *Chronic illness & disability.* Berkeley, CA: Sage Publications.

Peyrot, M., & McMurray, J. F. (1985). Psychosocial factors in diabetes control: Adjustment of insulin-treated adults. *Psychosomatic Medicine, 47,* 542–557.

Pond, H. (1979). Parental attitudes toward children with a chronic medical disorder: Special reference to diabetes mellitus. *Diabetes Care, 2,* 425–431.

Powers, S., Dill, D., Hauser, S. T., Noam, G. G., & Jacobson, A. M. (1984). *The coping strategies and psychosocial resources of seriously ill adolescents.* Presented at the Family Systems and Health Preconference Workshop, National Council on Family Relations, San Francisco, CA.

Rahe, R., Meyer, M., Smith, M., Kjaer, G., & Holmes, T. H. (1964). Social stress and illness onset. *Journal of Psychosomatic Research, 8,* 35–44.

Report of the National Commission on Diabetes. (1976). Vol. III: U.S. Dept. of Health, Education and Welfare, DHEW Publications No. (NIH) 76-1022.

Rodin, G. M., Johnson, L. E., Garfinkel, P. E., Daneman, D., & Kensholer, A. B. (1986). Eating disorders in female adolescents with insulin-dependent diabetes mellitus. *International Journal of Psychiatry Medicine, 16,* 49–57.

Rolland, J. (1988). A conceptual model of chronic illness and life threatening illness and its impact on families. In C. Chilman, E. Nunnally, & F. Cox (Eds.), *Chronic illness and disability.* Berkeley, CA: Sage Publications.

Rosmark, B., Berne, C., Holmgren, S., & Lago, C. (1986). Eating disorders in patients with insulin-dependent diabetes mellitus. *Journal of Clinical Psychiatry, 47,* 745–550.

Rovet, J., Ehrlich, R., & Czuchta, D. (1990). Intellectual characteristics of diabetic children at diagnosis and one year later. *Journal of Pediatric Psychology, 15* (6), 775–788.

Rovet, J., Ehrlich, R., & Hoppe, M. (1987). Intellectual deficits associated with early onset of insulin-dependent diabetes mellitus in children. *Diabetes Care, 10,* 510–515.

Rovet, J., Ehrlich, R., & Hoppe, M. (1988). Specific intellectual deficits in children with early onset diabetes mellitus. *Child Development, 59,* 226–234.

Ryan, C., & Morrow, L. (1986). Self esteem in diabetic adolescents: Relationship between age at onset and gender. *Journal of Consulting and Clinical Psychology, 54,* 730–731.

Ryan, C., Longstreet, C., & Morrow, L. (1985). The effects of diabetes mellitus on the school attendance and school achievement of adolescents. *Child Care, Health and Development, 11,* 229–240.

Ryan, C., Vega, A., & Drash, A. (1985). Cognitive deficits in adolescents who developed diabetes early in life. *Pediatrics, 75,* 921–927.

Sargent, J. (1985). Juvenile diabetes mellitus and the family. In P. Ahmed & N. Ahmed (Eds.), *Coping with juvenile diabetes.* Springfield, IL: Charles C. Thomas.

Satin, W., La Greca, A., Zigo, M., & Skyler, J. (1989). Diabetes in adolescence: Effects of multifamily group intervention and parent simulation of diabetes. *Journal of Pediatric Psychology, 14* (2), 259–275.

Schafer, L. C., Glasgow, R. E., McCaul, K. D., & Dehrer, M. (1983). Adherence to insulin-dependent diabetes mellitus regimens: Relationship to psychosocial variables and metabolic control. *Diabetes Care, 6,* 493–497.

Shouval, R., Ber, R., & Galatzer, Z. (1982). Family social climate and the health status and adaptation of diabetic youth. In Z. Laron (Ed.), *Psychosocial aspects of diabetes in children and adolescents.* New York: Basel Karger.

Silver, E. J., Bauman, L. J., Coupey, S. M., Doctors, S. R., & Boeck, M. A. (1990). Ego development and chronic illness in adolescents. *Journal of Personality and Social Psychology, 59,* 305–310.

Simonds, J. F. (1976). Psychiatric status of diabetic youth in good and poor control. *International Journal of Psychiatric Medicine, 7,* 133–151.

Simonds, J. F. (1977). Psychiatric status of diabetic youth matched with a control group. *Journal of the American Diabetes Association, 26,* 921–925.

Slawson, P. F., Flynn, W. R., & Kollas, E. J. (1963). Psychosocial factors associated with the onset and course of diabetes mellitus. *Journal of the American Medical Association, 185,* 166–170.

Sosa, R., Kennell, J., Klaus, M., Robertson, S., & Urrutia, J. (1980). The effect of a supportive companion on perinatal problems, length of labor, and mother-infant interactions. *New England Journal of Medicine, 303,* 597–600.

Stabler, B., Morris, M. A., Litton, J., Feinglos, M. N., & Surwit, R. S. (1986). Differential glycemic response to stress in type A and type B individuals with IDDM. *Diabetes Care, 9* (5), 550–552.

Stabler, B., Surwit, R., Laner, J., Morris, M. A., Litton, J., & Feinglos, M. N. (1987). Type A behavior pattern and blood glucose control in diabetic children. *Psychosomatic Medicine, 49* (3), 313–316.

Steel, J. M., Young, R. J., Lloyd G. G., & Clarke, B. F. (1987). Clinically apparent eating disorders in young diabetic women: Associations with painful neuropa-thy and other complications. *British Medicine Journal, 16,* 49–57.

Stein, J. (1989). *Family interaction and adjustment, adherence and metabolic control in adolescents with insulin-dependent diabetes.* Unpublished doctoral dissertation. Boston University.

Stein, S., & Charles, E. (1975). Emotional factors in juvenile diabetes mellitus: A study of the early life experiences of eight diabetic children. *Psychosomatic Medicine, 37,* 237–244.

Sullivan, B. J. (1979). Adjustment in diabetic adolescent girls: II. Adjustment, self-esteem, and depression in diabetic adolescent girls. *Psychosomatic Medicine, 41,* 127–138.

Swift, C., Seidman, F., & Stein, H. (1967). Adjustment problems in juvenile diabetes. *Psychosomatic Medicine, 29,* 555–571.

Thomas, G. B., & McCabe, O. L. (1980). Precursors of premature disease and death: Habits of nervous tension. *Johns Hopkins Medical Journal, 147:* 137–145.

Turk, D. (1979). Factors influencing the adaptive process with chronic illness. In I. Sarason & C. Spielberger (Eds.), *Stress and anxiety.* (Vol. 6, pp. 281–312). New York: Wiley

Turk, D. C., & Speers, M. A. (1983). Diabetes Mellitus: A cognitive functional analysis of stress. In T. Burnish & L. Bradley (Eds.), *Coping with chronic disease* (pp. 191–217). New York: Academic Press.

Vandenbergh, R. L. (1971). *Emotional aspects in juvenile-type diabetes and its complications.* Ed. K. E. Sussman. Springfield, IL: Charles C. Thomas, 411–438.

Vandenbergh, R. L., Sussman, K. E., & Titus, C. C. (1966). Effects of hypnotically induced acute emotional states on carbohydrate and lipid metabolism in patients with diabetes mellitus. *Psychosomatic Medicine, 28,* 382–390.

Waller, D., Chipman, J., Hardy, B., Hightower, M., North, A., Williams, S., & Babick, A. (1986). Measuring diabetes-specific family support and its relation to metabolic control: A preliminary report. *Journal of the American Academy of Child Psychiatry, 25* (3), 415–418.

Wertlieb, D., Hauser, S. T., & Jacobson, A. M. (1986). Adaptation to diabetes: Behavior symptoms and family context. *Journal of Pediatric Psychology, 11,* 463–479.

Wertlieb, D., Jacobson, A., & Hauser, S. (1990). The child with diabetes: A developmental stress and coping perspective. In P. T. Costa and G. R. VandenBos (Eds.) *Psychological aspects of serious illness: Chronic conditions, fatal diseases, and clinical care.* (pp. 61–102). American Psychological Association.

Wishner, W. J., & O'Brien, M. D. (1978). Diabetes and the family. *Medicine Clinics of North America, 62,* 849–856.

Zeltzer, L., Kellerman, J., Ellenberg, L., Dash, J., & Rigler, D. (1980). Psychological effects of illness in adolescence. II. Impact of illness in adolescent-crucial issues and coping styles. *Journal of Pediatrics, 97,* 132–138.

33 / End-Stage Renal Failure

John P. Kemph

When kidneys fail to perform their normal function of filtering and actively excreting substances from the circulating blood, the waste products of metabolism begin to accumulate in the tissues. Then various organs, including the brain, become dysfunctional because of the toxic accumulation of metabolites. One of the major causes of renal failure in children is obstructive uropathy. Even though the obstruction may be removed surgically, the resultant renal insufficiency may progress to end-stage renal disease (Warshaw et al., 1982). Other causes include glomerulonephritis, glomerulosclerosis, cystic disease, and other congenital defects and renal tumors. Rapoport and Cortesini (1987) estimate that there are 24,000 new cases of end-stage renal failure per year. This condition can occur at any age, from birth to old age, with congenital defects being more prevalent in childhood and glomerulonephritis occurring more frequently in adults. The signs and symptoms of renal failure are malaise, anorexia, nausea, vomiting, colitis, hypertension, edema, oliguria, hyperkalemia, acidosis, osteodystrophy, osteosclerosis, growth retardation, anemia, pericardial effusion, tremors, convulsions, and mental and emotional disorders (Kemph, 1982). Psychiatric symptoms reported in children are irritability, impulsivity, aggression, depression, inability to concentrate, loss of interest, delusions, and hallucinations (Sampson, 1975). The onset is often silent with very little symptomatology other than malaise or fatigue. As the renal function diminishes other symptoms develop.

One of the more insidious and more annoying childhood deficits resulting from end-stage renal disease is failure to grow at the normal developmental rate. This creates psychosomatic problems that add a physical reminder of being different, thus lowering the self-esteem of a child with an already lowered feeling of self-worth. Retardation of physical growth in children with renal insufficiency is well established, and the etiology is not entirely clear (Mehls, Ritz, Gilli, & Krenser, 1978; Rizzoni, Basso, & Setari, 1984). Among the etiologies considered for this growth retardation in renal failure are metabolic and hormonal problems (Holliday & Chantler, 1972), water and electrolyte imbalance (McSherry, 1978), and low caloric intake (Grupe, 1981). Crittenden and Holaday (1989) have demonstrated the complexity of the interrelationship between the various factors, including psychosocial ones, that may affect growth in these children, and also they note the difficulty in measuring these factors. Psychological factors and their relationship to compliance with medical regime were studied by Brownbridge and Fielding (1994), utilizing structured interview questionnaires and measures of anxiety, depression, and behavioral disturbance, weight gain, blood pressure, serum and blood levels, and dietitian surveys. Poor compliance was found to be related to anxiety and depression in children and parents, duration of dialysis, low family socioeconomic status, age (adolescents poorer than younger children), and family structure. The psychosocial factors interrelating with the metabolic and hormonal factors present opportunities for psychosomatic research. One of the most interesting aspects of this problem is that successful treatment of the renal failure per se often does not correct the growth failure.

Adult cognitive studies have shown that chronic renal insufficiency is related to decreased memory, attention, and IQ (Osberg, Meares, McKee, & Burnett, 1982; Teschan, Ginn, Bourne, Ward, & Hamel, 1979). These functions improve on dialysis and resolve on renal homotransplantation. Findings of studies on children differ. Children who fail to reach expected levels of development at an early age because of renal failure may exhibit only minimal if any growth or further development in other areas when renal failure is corrected by dialysis and short of normal or optimal development including stature with transplant.

It seems reasonable to assume that the earlier in life that end-stage renal disease occurs and the more severe and prolonged the condition, the greater would be the retardation of growth. Similarly, cognitive and emotional development would be expected to be more retarded with younger children who have more severe renal disease for more prolonged periods.

Some reports minimize the impact on development (Trachtman, Braden, Scerra, Brier, Weiss, 1984), while others find serious developmental problems (Rotundo et al., 1982). Wolff, Ehrich, Offner, & Brodell (1982, 1984) note that developmental problems tended to be transient and/or subtle until the uremic syndrome became severe enough to require dialysis. At that time, performance diminished and behavior problems developed. Grupe, Griefer, Greenspan, Leavitt, and Wolf (1986) concluded that children with chronic renal insufficiency are at no different risk for psychosocial or cognitive dysfunction than are those with other chronic illness.

However, Fennell, Fennell, Carter, Mings, and Klausner (1990) report a decrease in verbal abstracting ability (Similarities) and visual perceptual reasoning and visual-motor copying skills of patients in renal failure when compared with controls matched for age, sex, and race. Also impaired were immediate recall, memory, and learning; furthermore, testing performed at 6 months and 12 months after initiation of the study demonstrated either failure to improve as rapidly as controls or deterioration in these functions, thus indicating a progressive memory deficit with chronic renal disease. The patients developed renal disease early in childhood, suffering chronic exposure to metabolites deleterious to the developing brain. This may account for their finding that restoring renal function does not necessarily restore cognitive function.

In an excellent report by Garralda, Jameson, Reynolds, and Postlethwaite (1988), psychiatric problems were found more frequently among a group of children and adolescents with chronic renal failure than in a group of matched controls. Furthermore, they found more frequent and more severe psychiatric problems in subjects with more severe renal failure. They compared 3 groups, one group requiring dialysis, a second group with renal failure not requiring dialysis, and a third group of healthy matched controls, using a series of appropriate rating scales and interviews to determine the presence of psychiatric problems.

The major effort of children and adolescents is usually school related, and one of the major adaptational problems of children with renal insufficiency often is school adjustment. The school performance of children on continuous ambulatory peritoneal dialysis (CAPD) was compared with those who had received a kidney transplant, and also with healthy children. The children on CAPD had significantly more non-academic problems than those with transplants who had more such problems than healthy children (Fukunishi and Honda, 1995). In the same study, academic problems were more prevalent in children with transplants than those receiving CAPD, with the least prevalence occurring in healthy children. Thus, children being treated for end-stage renal disease have significantly more school problems in both academic and non-academic endeavors than their healthy peers. Their condition may prevent regular attendance at school, and their reduced capacity to function when they do attend school interferes with their learning process and relationships with peers. These children's experiences are much different from others in their peer group, and thus they find sharing experiences with peers difficult. This fact leads to isolation and loneliness. Having a special educator available who is trained to relate to and teach children with a variety of developmental deficits during prolonged periods of in-center hemodialysis not only provides an educational experience but avoids boredom and offers an opportunity to develop a rewarding supportive relationship, thus both reducing stress and increasing supports (Schultz, McVicar, & Kemph, 1974). Sander, Murray, and Robertson (1989) have proposed another approach to the school problem: provide dialysis after school and on Saturday mornings. With this change in schedule, significant improvement in academic performance and relationships with peers occurred in some cases.

Infancy

At birth, babies are born with their full complement of neurons, but dendrites and axons sprout throughout life. During the first year of life, brain growth occurs extremely rapidly. The human brain more than doubles in size in the first year, and this amounts to approximately 50% of the total postnatal brain growth (Lowrey, 1978). One of the most important events in brain development is synaptic proliferation. The number of synapses increases rapidly in the first year of life (Huttenlocher, 1984). Then the number of synapses begins to decline and by 11 years of age decreases to adult levels. This phase of reduction in synapses is called the "pruning back" phase, and it seems likely that it coincides with a period of intense learning. In addition to this phase of synaptic proliferation and reduction, there is an increase in specific neurotransmitters in various areas. Myelination starts before birth and continues as late as the fourth and the fifth decade of life, although the most dramatic phase of myelination occurs in the first 2 years of life (Yakovlev & LeCours, 1967).

Shortly after birth, infants seem to initiate interactions, not just respond. Although social smiling does not begin until around 6 weeks to 3 months, infants can produce smiles as well as other behavior long before this time; however, the related memory seems to extinguish rapidly without frequent stimulation. At 3 days of age, an infant can distinguish the mother's voice. These perceptual capacities are enhanced but not created by early experience. Infants have an unlearned preference for visual stimuli resembling the human face. They will mimic facial expressions within 36 hours after birth (visual-proprioceptive). Six-day-old infants can differentiate the odor of their mother's milk from that of another lactating woman. At this time of rapid development, the brain is particularly vulnerable to permanent damage even with only minimal stress (Dobling, 1974). Rotundo, Nevins, Lipton, Lockman, & Mauer (1982) have shown that children who developed decreased kidney function in infancy were found to have progressive encephalopathy. McGraw and Haka-Ikse (1985) have studied the development of 10 children who developed renal failure in infancy and found mild to severe developmental delay in gross and fine motor function, language, cognitive functions, and psychosocial skills. All had moderate or severe delays in at least some of these areas of development. Since all of these children had repeated prolonged hospitalization, it was not possible to evaluate psychosocial causes separately from nutritional, biochemical, and morphological causes.

Although no formal studies of the parents of these children were performed, it was the authors' clinical impression that the parents tended to be overprotective. Overprotection stifles infants' developing initiative, and if infants do not respond to the parental attempts at interaction, the parents may reject the infants.

CASE EXAMPLE

Renal Signs and Symptoms in Infancy: Within a few weeks after Herman was born, his mother was aware that he was much different from his older brother, who had been born 2 years and 3 months previously and had been a very active infant. Herman was apathetic, listless, rarely cried, and slept much of the time. The mother made several trips to the infant's doctor; finally, at 9 months of age, Herman was studied by a pediatric nephrologist, who found his blood urea nitrogen level (BUN) to be 80. The mother was told that her baby had an urethral obstruction, a small left kidney, and an enlarged right ureter. Attempts to dilate the urethral obstruction failed, but a cutaneous pyelostomy was successful, and Herman's BUN decreased from 80 to 30 in 1 month. His development in all areas had been delayed. At 11 months of age, he began to roll over and sit up. Within a few months he was able to pull himself upright and stand. His speech was slow to develop, using a few words at 2 years of age. This developmental progress, although still delayed, sparked new hope in the parents. Then at 21 months of age he developed grand mal seizures. A neurological examination identified a tremor of the upper extremities, which made it difficult for Herman to manipulate small objects and slowed development. The electroencephalogram initially was normal, but within 1 year it contained abnormal activity, for which the child received anticonvulsant medication. The mother was painfully aware of this child's being different and gave him much more attention than his older brother, who resented Herman. The father helped with Herman's care as much as his work permitted.

The Preschool-age Child

Although end-stage renal disease can occur at any age, often the renal problem has existed for a considerable time period before it is considered to be actually end stage. Until that time the condition is managed conservatively, utilizing appropriate diet and medication and procedures as necessary. Regardless of the cause for end-stage renal disease in very young children, the parents are confronted with four alternatives: hemodialysis, peritoneal dialysis, transplant, or conservative medical management for this terminal condition. Richard Fine (1982) has recommended that the physician "provide the parents with dispassionate information in order for them to make the ultimate, often painful, decision" (p. 755).

Some reports are encouraging, with survival results of transplant in children equaling those of adults (Krakauer, Grauman, McMullan, & Creede, 1983; Vollmer, Wahl, & Blagg, 1983). It also has been shown that children become more active, improve in fine and gross motor coordination, and grow more rapidly after transplant (Simmons, Klenin, & Simmons, 1977). Miller, Bock, Lum, Najarian, and Mauer (1982) have noted that children rarely develop a recurrence of disease in the graft, which is an advantage to transplant in the very young.

Although both hemodialysis and peritoneal dialysis offer life-supportive forms of treatment in young children, most centers are recommending transplant as a treatment of choice in young children (Blume, 1983; Fine, 1981). One reason for choosing transplant is the rapid improvement in cognitive power that results after the transplant (Fennell, Rasburu, Fennell, & Morris, 1984).

Many reports describe the physiological responses and pathological effects of transplants, immunosuppressive drugs as well as technical surgical data. Very few of them describe details of the "parameters of meaningful growth and development living" as proposed by John B. Reinhart (1970) and the quality of life of the child and his family (p. 506). It therefore seems appropriate to report in some detail the sociopsychological aspects of end-stage renal disease in very young children and their families to demonstrate the problems related to renal failure and the procedures used as treatment and their aftermath and also to show how the child psychiatrist may be helpful. Since the impact of dialysis was described elsewhere previously (Kemph, 1982; Kemph & Zrull, 1979), more attention will be given to renal transplantation in these cases.

CASE EXAMPLE

Herman: Herman's rate of development in all areas improved after surgically bypassing the obstruction, but he lagged considerably behind the age-expected levels. To further complicate his problems, he developed renal rickets at 2 years 7 months of age. Although medical treatment was initiated, it became necessary that he wear leg braces, which further complicated his already uncoordinated gait. Between the ages of 2 and 4 years his BUN level fluctuated sporadically with a very gradual overall increase. When he was 4½ years of age, it

became clear to the renal team of physicians that he was in end-stage renal disease. The various options for treatment were discussed with the parents, who decided to plan for a cadaveric transplant. At this point the child psychiatrist agreed to serve as consultant to the transplant team and to provide treatment for this family for as long as necessary. The mother managed her anxiety by reading much material in the medical literature about end-stage renal disease in children. She focused much of the family's energies into activities that allowed the patient to be a participant. The father, a skilled design technologist, was less verbal than the mother in his contact with doctors but was involved in the patient's care.

In preparation for the transplant, Herman was told that he would be going to the hospital for an operation soon to get a new kidney; he repeated that he was going to get a new kidney and he agreed that this would make him feel better. He repeated this statement without fear or any other emotion, apparently not realizing the implications or dangers of surgery, even though the mother and other physicians had explained this to him already. He was helped to play through hospital scenes depicting what would happen when he was admitted for transplant.

Both parents and the brother were interviewed to discuss the implications of the anticipated transplant. The mother had great hope that the transplanted kidney would function and that a minimum of immunosuppressive drugs would be necessary to prevent rejection of the new kidney. She tended to be cautiously optimistic. The father avoided discussing any alternative outcomes, retaining an overly optimistic attitude even when confronted directly with the possibility that a new kidney might not function.

The brother became emotionally involved in play therapy involving siblings. He was both sad and angry about his brother getting all the attention from his parents. He was interested in play that involved policemen, doctors, and ambulances with his being the object of the doctors' attention and the one the police were hunting.

The mother also noted that in his play with his brother, there was frequent talk about their stuffed animals dying during the play. An animal would become sick and have to go to the hospital and would die. The psychiatrist suggested to the mother that she get involved in the play and show how another animal got sick, went to the hospital, and got well at the same time, saying that some animals die and some animals get well when they go to the hospital but most of them get well. At other times in their play the patient had his brother's clothes catch on fire and have to go to the hospital and die. This seemed gratifying to both children but frightening to the mother.

Just before the transplant, the psychiatrist visited the patient and family in the hospital, playing with familiar objects and creating situations in which the patient could demonstrate autonomy and control.

For the first two postoperative days Herman slept often and complained of pain. On the third postoperative day he was walking around in his room and was much more alert than he had ever been before because the new kidney was functioning well (creatinine blood level decreased dramatically) but complaining about pain at the operative side. His mother was trying to help him to avoid the pain and cover up for it. The psychiatrist suggested that she acknowledge that he had pain, let him talk about it, reassure him that it would go away in a few days, and help him think about other things. While she was spending most of her time with the patient, she worried about his brother, who was with a sitter. Eighteen days following surgery there was a sudden increase in Herman's creatinine level, and his behavior became much more aggressive and less cooperative. It was ascertained that the renal vein from the new kidney had become obstructed and it was necessary to remove the kidney. The boy was prepared for the second surgery by telling him that the kidney had been working well but that it suddenly had stopped working and that it would be necessary to take it out to make him feel better. Later when the nurse attempted to tell him this again, Herman put his hand against her mouth to stop her from saying it. A day later he told his mother that the doctor was going to have to take his kidney out.

Immediately after the second surgery in which his transplanted kidney was removed, Herman responded in the same way that he had after the transplant, by sleeping much of the time. However, four days after surgery he demonstrated bursts of extremely angry behavior toward doctors, parents, and toys, kicking and striking out at people, stating that he was worried about losing his new kidney. At that point he was informed that the doctors were going to find him another new kidney after he went home and rested for a while. Within 2 months after the failure of the transplanted kidney, both parents were talking optimistically about the possibility of a second transplant.

The School-age Child

Many reports describe the physiological responses and pathological effects of transplants, immunosuppressive drugs, and technical or surgical data. Since the advent of more effective immunosuppressive drugs, such as cyclosporin, graft survival has improved dramatically (85% survival 1 year after cadaveric transplants) (Kahan, Kerman,

Wideman, Flechner, & Jarowenko, 1985). Even so, the side effects of this medicine, particularly kidney (Myers, Ross, Newton, Luetscher, & Perlroth, 1984) and liver toxicity (Lorber, Van Buren, Flechner, Williams, & Kahan, 1987), are serious and must be given due consideration, particularly when it is given to children. Usually transplant teams consider the immunosuppressive benefits to outweigh the ill effects of the drug.

Although there are many good results from dialysis and transplant, some poor results do occur. Poznanski, Miller, Salquero, and Kelsh (1978) reported several examples of children and their families whose quality of life was devastated by endstage renal disease and its treatment procedures. Children are less apt to be introspective regarding their quality of life than adolescents or adults. Furthermore, they are not effective in planning or achieving either passive or active suicide. This raises the ethical question of subjecting children to multiple transplant procedures that do not improve the quality of life. Winterborn (1983) has suggested that some children with end-stage renal disease should not be treated. Others (Reinhart & Kemph, 1988) suggest that restraint should be used when multiple procedures fail to improve the quality of life.

CASE EXAMPLE

Herman: The family decided that the mother would serve as donor for a second transplant for Herman. During the preparation for the second transplant, the mother continued to worry about her son's concerns about death. The father showed grave concerns about the risks to his wife as the donor. During this period, the brother became more rebellious toward his parents and had tantrums and crying spells with seemingly little provocation. Support was given through individual and family interviews to cope with these problems and to discuss preparation for the second transplant.

Immediately following the second transplant, for several days, the mother required frequent reassurance that the patient was getting medication administered via appropriate methods and that he was not being contaminated by his cloth comforter or toys. She also stated that she felt apprehensive about the success of the transplant. She had played her "hole card," which was her own kidney. What if it failed? She became moderately depressed during the first postoperative day and remained so much of the time for several months. She had little concern for her own welfare. Rather she was obsessed by the fear that the kidney she had donated would fail and that another kidney might never be found. She had experienced this type of anticipatory anxiety in crises throughout her life. She responded well to reassurance in the short term but quickly lost her resolve to think positively and tended to feel depressed again. Therefore, the child psychiatrist saw her for a series of psychotherapy sessions to assist her with her long-standing anxiety and recent depression.

The patient's BUN and creatinine levels returned to normal rapidly and he improved cognitively, achieving more complex thought processes than he had ever exhibited previously. He was making more purposeful movements, and the intricate fine movements of his fingers and hands were more deliberate and less clumsy than before the transplant. His speech was delivered much more rapidly and articulation was surprisingly improved.

After he arrived home from the hospital, his brother enjoyed playing with him for 2 days followed by greater resentment than ever before, in part because the patient was more capable and competitive with greater mental capacity and was much stronger physically. The brother began to have insomnia and nightmares, tantrums, behavioral problems at school, and was openly jealous of the attention Herman was getting. At its peak, the brother's hostility reached suicidal and homicidal proportions. The child psychiatrist then gave both brothers equal time in interviews, seeing them separately and together, encouraging the expression of them separately and together, encouraging the expression of rivalry through controlled games. The parents provided similar structure to their interaction at home and avoided unsupervised play. Herman and his family were treated by a child psychiatrist for a total of 4 years, when the boy was in third grade.

For several months after the second transplant, the mother continued to feel and appear depressed. Sensing her concern for the value of his new kidney, the patient would threaten to hurt the kidney if she didn't accede to his demands and wishes. With minimal provocation, he would run into his bedroom and attempt to impale himself on the bedpost, saying he would kill her kidney. This behavior devastated the mother. When she was preparing to leave home to take the patient to the clinic, the brother rolled on the floor complaining of abdominal pain, thus requiring that she take him along. These behaviors were beyond the mother's ability to manage. Her fear of injuring the patient and her guilt over the brother's complaints and her depression rendered her helpless at times.

Therefore, a program of behavioral modification was instituted for the family with the father responsible for the delivery of most of the aversive techniques. Both boys' behavior improved rapidly.

The mother's fear of the loss of the transplanted kidney was addressed directly in interviews in which she was encouraged to assume the kidney was lost or destroyed by the patient's actions. The potential treatment that would be available if the transplant failed was explored in the discussion, and all her fears surfaced and were openly discussed with anguish. After these discussions she became more comfortable.

Then it became necessary for Herman to use leg braces again, which he resisted violently. The mother was unable to keep him in his braces. Therefore, methylphenidate was prescribed temporarily to reduce his impulsivity. On this medicine he became much more compliant. He was able to attend kindergarten and passed to first grade.

The mother became deeply involved in a parent club of dialysis/transplant children and soon became the club's president. She found it helpful and gratifying to compare problems with other parents, some of whom had very similar concerns. Eventually she agreed to assume less responsibility for the patient's care, getting him to school and getting out of the house herself at least two evenings each week. She was requested to write her feelings on paper and bring them to the interviews. Some of the statements of feelings include: "I am tired of being strong for him." "I am tired of feeling afraid." "I don't think I can trust him with himself." "He is angry at restrictions placed on him by us and by his illness." "He is bitter." "I am angry at him for not being able to control himself." "The stress of reality doesn't hit him." "Things never seem to change for the better."

Through these efforts and others, the mother's depression gradually lifted. As she gained better control of her own feelings, she became more assertive in her control of the children.

The Adolescent

At a time when adolescents are attempting to invest in peers, their normal development is interrupted by illness that is usually accompanied by a regression in development. The most frequently reported symptoms of adolescents with end-stage renal disease are dependent-independent conflicts, depression, low self-esteem, and isolation (Denour, 1979; Poznanski, Miller, Salquerero & Kelsch, 1978). Beck, Nethercut, Crittenden, and Hewins (1986) have shown that the self-concept was lower in those patients whose condition was visible with the effects of end-stage renal disease and its treatment: stunted growth, cushingoid appearance, acne, and weight gain. They performed a study of 31 young adults, all of whom had end-stage renal disease during adolescence and were treated with dialysis or transplant or both. Several of them reported that they were particularly self-conscious about visible defects during their adolescent years. Later these patients established a more stable identity and increased self-esteem.

CASE EXAMPLE

A 16-year-old girl had been the recipient of a kidney donated by her 14-year-old sister. The referral was made to the child psychiatrist during a subsequent admission to the hospital 5 months after the transplant procedure, when it was discovered that the recipient had been putting immunosuppressive drugs in a drawer in the hospital instead of swallowing them. The family of five children and both parents were interviewed. The mother noticed that the recipient had become much more irritable and prone to sudden outbursts of anger since her transplant. The donor, who had discovered the hidden pills, felt that her sister, the recipient, seemed more emotionally distant since the transplant whereas previously they had a close relationship, sharing their thoughts and feelings. The recipient was quick to express her guilt over taking her sister's kidney. Her sister continued to have many friends while the recipient had lost many of her contacts with peers through her illness and had become much more dependent on her mother. Her appearance had changed from a slender body form and pretty face, to a typical cushingoid obese body with a moon face. She was ashamed of her appearance, and she was frustrated and angry with her lack of progress since the transplant because of four periods of hospitalization in a 5-month period because of mild to moderately severe rejection of the transplanted organ. She stated that she stopped taking her medicine deliberately to precipitate a final decision to send her home. This time the rejection was severe. She appeared hostile in her demeanor as she further elaborated rivalry with the donor for parental attention and affection. The psychiatrist saw the mother, donor, and recipient in a series of interviews extending over the period of a year to assist the recipient toward acceptance of the sister and her donated kidney and her concern over the constant threat of rejection of the transplanted organ. Gradually she became less hostile and more realistic. Furthermore, there was a slowing of the rejection of the transplanted organ and she became compliant with the medical regimen.

The child psychiatrist can be helpful in noncompliance, which is common with children and adolescents following transplant, particularly when steroids are used (Hesse, Roth, Knupperts, Wie-

nand, & Lilien, 1990). The role of the child psychiatrist in the cases described earlier was primarily to serve as a supportive therapist on an individual and family basis to the patients and their families and to some extent as a consultant to pediatrics and the transplant team. The child psychiatrist's role as liaison to the hemodialysis team was described previously (Kemph, 1982). When hemodialysis was performed at home, children formed close relationships with family and friends and therefore may have had less frequent need for psychiatric intervention (Brem, Brem, McGrath, & Spirito, 1988). However, when parents give dialysis at home, they are under much greater stress than the child because they are unable to express normal parental ambivalence toward their ill child. Being both medic and parent often leads to a contradiction of roles (LePontois, Moel, & Cohn, 1987). In this treatment program the parents may require more intervention than the child. Communication becomes essential between the treatment team and the family, and between the members of the interdisciplinary team. Meeting the information needs of the family may reduce the level of stress. Keeping the family informed and recommending parental respite through taking time away from the problems and parent support groups should be integral components of the long-term care of the children and their families (Watson, 1995). Summer camp has also been shown to provide respite for parents and to improve the self-esteem of the camper (Klee, 1992). In the decision-making process regarding the type of treatment to consider as a next step in the care of a patient, the child psychiatrist's expertise in communication with children should be helpful to provide the patient's perspective and to assist with an understanding of the emotional capacities of family members. In general terms, more children and adolescents function at higher levels with transplant than do the patients receiving home hemodialysis, who themselves function better than those receiving in-center hemodialyses or continuous ambulatory peritoneal dialysis (CAPD) (Evans et al., 1985; Fine, 1984). These large group studies do not account for widely varying individual differences and overlap between the groups, issues that need the psychiatrist's attention on an individual basis. Although ultimately a broad spectrum of assessments of physical and emotional attributes may become available to predict the appropriate type of treatment for each individual, the current status of our capability requires a multidisciplinary approach including psychiatry.

When symptoms of depression, anxiety, psychosomatic complaints, or psychosis develop, psychiatrists often are requested to provide consultation for the assessment and treatment of the patient with end-stage renal disease. The most common symptom is depression. In a literature search, figures on large groups of children and adolescents were not found but depression in children must be considered at least as difficult to diagnose as depression in adults.

Often the living related donor is given comparatively little postnephrectomy attention. Liounis, Roy, Thompson, Mau, and Sheil (1988) have reported in a follow-up study of 41 donors that nearly half felt they received inadequate attention and 25% of the donors became depressed after their nephrectomy. I have found that follow-up supportive psychotherapy helps to prevent or alleviate both donor and recipient depression. Reference to depression in donors and recipients is made throughout this review. Most authors seem to be referring to depressed mood without providing a diagnosis. In my experience, the most appropriate diagnosis is usually adjustment disorder with depressed moods.

REFERENCES

Beck, A. L., Nethercut, G. E., Crittenden, M. R., & Hewins, J. (1986). Visibility of handicap, self-concept, and social maturity among young adult survivors and end stage renal disease. *Developmental and Behavioral Pediatrics, 7* (2), 93–96.

Blume, E. (1983). Ambulatory dialysis: Special boon for children. *Journal of the American Medical Association, 249* (17), 2290–2291.

Brem, A. S., Brem, F. S., McGrath, M., & Spirito, S. (1988). Psychosocial characteristics and coping skills in children maintained on chronic dialysis. *Pediatric Nephrology, 2,* 460–465.

Brownbridge, G., & Fielding, D. M. (1994). Psychosocial adjustment and adherence to dialysis treatment regimens. *Pediatric Nephrology, 8* (6), 744–749.

Crittenden, M. R., & Holaday, B. (1989). Physical growth and behavioral adaptations of children with renal insufficiency. *American Nephrology Nurses Association Journal, 16* (2), 87–119.

Denour, A. K. (1979). Adolescents' adjustment to chronic hemodialysis. *American Journal of Psychiatry, 136,* 430–432.

Dobling, J. (1974). The later development of the brain and its vulnerability. In J. A. Davis & J. Dobling (Eds.), *Scientific foundations of pediatrics* (pp. 565–577). London: William Heinemann Medical Books.

Evans, R. W., Manninen, D. L., Garrison, L. R., Hart, L. G., Blagg, C. R., Gutman, R. A., Hull, A. R., & Lowrie, E. G. (1985). The quality of life of patients with end stage renal disease. *New England Journal of Medicine, 312* (9), 553–559.

Fennell, R. S., Fennell, E. B., Carter, R. L., Mings, E. L., Klausner, A. B., & Hurst, J. R. (1990). A longitudinal study of the cognitive function of children with renal failure. *Pediatric Nephrology, 4,* 11–15.

Fennell, R. S., Rasburu, W. C., Fennell, E. B., & Morris, M. (1984). Effects of kidney transplantation on cognitive performance in a pediatric population. *Pediatrics, 74* (2), 273–278.

Fine, R. N. (1981). The treatment of end stage renal disease in children. *Pediatric Annals, 10* (1), 65–73.

Fine, R. N. (1982). Renal transplantation in children. *Journal of Pediatrics, 100* (5), 754–755.

Fine, R. N. (1984). Choosing a dialysis therapy for children with end stage renal disease. *American Journal of Kidney Diseases, 4* (3), 249–252.

Fukunishi, I., & Honda, M. (1995). School adjustment of children with end-stage renal disease. *Pediatric Nephrology, 9* (5), 553–557.

Garralda, M. E., Jameson, R. A., Reynolds, J. M., & Postlethwaite, R. J. (1988). Psychiatric adjustment in children with chronic renal failure. *Journal of Child Psychology and Psychiatry and Allied Disciplines, 29* (1), 79–90.

Grupe, W. (1981). Nutritional considerations in the prognosis and treatment of children with renal disease. In R. Susskind (Ed.), *Textbook of pediatric nutrition* (pp. 577–534). New York: Raven Press.

Grupe, W., Greifer, I., Greenspan, S. I., Leavitt, A. L., & Wolf, G. (1986). Psychosocial development in children with chronic renal insufficiency. *American Journal of Kidney Diseases, 7* (4), 324–328.

Hesse, U. J., Roth, B., Knupperts, F., Wienand, P., & Lilien, T. V. (1990). Control of patient compliance in outpatient steroid treatment of nephrologic disease and renal transplant recipients. *Transplantation Proceedings, 22* (4), 1405–1406.

Holliday, M. A., & Chantler, C. (1978). Metabolic and nutritional factors in children with renal insufficiency. *Kidney International, 14,* 306–312.

Huttenlocher, P. R. (1984). Synapse elimination and plasticity in developing human cerebral cortex. *American Journal of Mental Deficiency, 88* (5), 488–496.

Kahan, B. D., Kerman, R. H., Wideman, C. A., Flechner, S. M., Jarowenko, M., & Van Buren, C. T. (1985). Impact of cyclosporin on renal transplant practice at the University of Texas Medical

School at Houston. *American Journal of Kidney Diseases, 5,* 288–295.

Kemph, J. P. (1982). End stage renal disease-dialysis. *Psychiatric Clinics of North America,* 5 (3), 407–417.

Kemph, J. P., & Zrull, J. (1979). The dialysis patient. In J. D. Noshpitz (Ed.), *Basic handbook of child psychiatry,* Vol. 1. (pp. 459–464). New York: Basic Books.

Klee, K. M. (1992). Benefits of a mainstreamed summer camp experience for teens with ESRD. *Advances in Peritoneal Dialysis, 8,* 423–425.

Krakauer, H., Grauman, M. S., McMullan, M. B. A., & Creede, C. C. (1983). The recent U.S. experience in the treatment of endstage renal disease by dialysis and transplantation. *New England Journal of Medicine, 308* (26), 1558–1563.

LePontois, J., Moel, D. I., & Cohn, R. A. (1987). Family adjustment to pediatric ambulatory dialysis. *American Journal of Orthopsychiatry, 57* (1), 78–83.

Liounis, B. L., Roy, L. P., Thompson, J. F., Mau, J., & Sheil, A. G. R. (1988). The living related kidney donor: A follow-up study. *Medical Journal of Australia, 148,* 436–444.

Lorber, M. I., Van Buren, C. T., Flechner, S. M., Williams, C., & Kahan, B. D. (1987). Hepatobilitory and pancreatic complications of cyclosporin therapy in 466 transplant patients. *Transplantation, 43,* 35–40.

Lowrey, S. H. (1978). *Growth and development of children* (7th ed.). Chicago: Year Book Medical Publishers.

McGraw, M. E., & Haka-Ikse, K. (1985). Neurologic-developmental sequelae of chronic renal failure in infancy. *Journal of Pediatrics, 106* (4), 579–583.

McSherry, E. (1978). Acidosis and growth in non-uremic renal disease. *Kidney International, 14,* 237–247.

Mehls, O., Ritz, E., Gilli, G., & Krenser, H. (1978). Growth in renal failure. *Nephron, 21,* 237–247.

Miller, L. C., Bock, G. H., Lum, C. T., Najarian, J. S., & Mauer, M. S. (1982). Transplantation of the adult kidney into the very small child: Long term outcome. *Journal of Pediatrics, 10* (5), 675–680.

Myers, B. D., Ross, J., Newton, I., Luetscher, J., & Perlroth, M. (1984). Cyclosporin-associated, chronic, nephropathy. *New England Journal of Medicine, 311,* 699–705.

Osberg, J. W., Meares, G. J., McKee, D. C., & Burnett, G. B. (1982). Intellectual functioning in renal failure and chronic dialysis. *Journal of Chronic Diseases, 35,* 445–447.

Poznanski, E., Miller, E., Salquero, C., & Kelsh, R. C. (1978). Quality of life for long term survivors of end stage renal disease. *Journal of the American Medical Association, 239,* 2343–2347.

Rapoport, F. T., & Cortesini, R. (1987). The past, present and future of organ transplantation with special references to current needs in kidney procurement and donation. *Transplant Proceedings, 17* (2), 3–10.

Reinhart, J. B. (1970). The doctors' dilemma. *Journal of Pediatrics, 77,* 505–507.

Reinhart, J. B., & Kemph, J. P. (1988). Renal transplantation for children: Another view. *Journal of the American Medical Association, 260* (22), 3317–3328.

Rizzoni, G., Basso, T., & Setari, M. (1984). Growth in children with chronic renal failure on conservative treatment. *Kidney International, 26,* 52–58.

Rotundo, A., Nevins, T. E., Lipton, M., Lockman, L. A., Mauer, M. S., & Michael, A. F. (1982). Progresive encephalopathy in children with chronic renal insufficiency in infancy. *Kidney International, 21,* 486–491.

Sampson, T. (1975). The child in renal failure. *Journal of the American Academy of Child Psychiatry, 14,* 462.

Sander, V., Murray, C., & Robertson, P. (1989). School and in center pediatric hemodialysis patient. *American Nephrology Nurses Association Journal, 16* (2), 72–74.

Schultz, M. T., McVicar, M. I., & Kemph, J. P. (1974). Treatment of emotional and cognitive deficits of the child receiving hemodialysis. In N. B. Levy (Ed.), *Living or dying: Adaptation to hemodialysis* (pp. 62–73). Springfield, IL: Charles C. Thomas.

Simmons, R. G., Klenin, S. D., & Simmons, R. L. (1977). *Gift of life, the social and psychological impact of organ transplantation.* New York: John Wiley & Sons.

Teschan, P. E., Ginn, H. E., Bourne, J. R., Ward, J. W., Hamel, B., Nunnally, J. C., Musso, M., & Vaughn, W. K. (1979). Quantitative indices of uremia. *Kidney International, 15,* 676–697.

Trachtman, M., Braden, K., Scerra, C., Brier, N., Weiss, R. A., & Greifer, I. (1983). Neuropsychological functioning in adolescents on chronic hemodialysis. In J. Brodehl & J. H. H. Ehrisch (Eds.), *Pediatric nephrology* (pp. 183–187). Berlin: Springer-Verlag.

Vollmer, W. M., Wahl, P. W., & Blagg, C. R. (1983). Survival with dialysis and transplantation in patients with end stage renal disease. *New England Journal of Medicine, 308* (26), 1553–1558.

Warshaw, B. L., Edellrock, H. H., Ettenger, R. B., Malekzadeh, M. H., Pennisi, A. J., Uttenbogaort, C. H., & Fine, R. N. (1982). Progression to end stage renal disease in children with obstructive uropathy. *Journal of Pediatrics, 100,* 183–187.

Watson, A. R. (1995). Strategies to support families of children with end-stage renal failure. *Pediatric Nephrology, 9* (5), 528–631.

Winterborn, M. H. (1983). Optimum treatment of end stage renal failure. *Archives of Disease in Childhood, 58,* 164–166.

Wolff, G., Ehrich, J. H. H., Offner, G., & Brodell, J. (1982). Psychosocial and intellectual development in 12 patients with infantile nephropathic cystinosis. *Acta Paediatrica Scandinavia, 71,* 1007–1011.

Wolff, G., Ehrich, J. H. H., Offner, G., & Brodell, J. (1983). Psychosocial problems in patients with infantile nephropathic cystinosis. In J. Brodell & J. H. H. Ehrich (Eds.), *Pediatric nephrology* (pp. 188–191). Berlin: Springer-Verlag.

Yakovlev, P. I., & LeCours, A. R. (1967). The myelogenetic cycles of regional maturation of the brain. In A. Minkowski (Ed.), *Regional development of the brain in early life* (pp. 3–70). Oxford: Blackwell.

34 / Deafness

Annie G. Steinberg

> I didn't have feeling. I didn't know feeling until
> I was age 9. Age 9 I went to deaf camp. There,
> I learned signs, "happy, sad, upset, angry, ugly."
> Age 9 I learned feelings.

The relationship of thought and language, the development of presymbolic and symbolic communication, and the essential sensory modalities involved in early attachment leading to an internalized self-representation are but several of the fundamental issues related to the impact of deafness on the development of a child. Work with the child who is deaf requires the integration of disciplines such as psychoanalysis, development, linguistics, anthropology, and education. Examination of deafness in infancy and childhood offers a unique opportunity to witness adaptation to profound perceptual impairment and resilience despite a disruption in dyadic and intrafamilial communication channels. Deafness need not impede normal development or place an individual at a functional disadvantage.

The child psychiatrist will be challenged to reexamine the emphasis on symbolic representation in the predominantly verbal linguistic tradition of psychiatry and to gather and integrate information regarding the individual child, the family, the home environment, and the larger social and cultural context of deafness. Providing preventive and interventional mental health services for this population demands a reappraisal of prior formulations of the "talking cure," neutrality, empathic attunement, and the boundaries of professional roles and responsibilities.

Deafness has been defined in several ways, with little consensus among professionals about basic terminology (Steinberg & Knightly, in press). Classifications of deafness in the medical community have generally considered etiologic factors, such as postmeningitic hearing loss, congenital deafness secondary to rubella infection during the first trimester of pregnancy, and aminoglycoside-induced hearing loss.

Audiologists assess hearing impairment by measuring decibel units of loss in the speech range and reduction in functional hearing. Hearing loss is described as mild, moderate, severe, or profound, based on the ability to perceive single tones at particular frequencies. Most audiologists reserve the term "deaf" for those individuals whose hearing loss is in the profound range; below that an individual would be called "hearing impaired" or "hard of hearing." Not all audiologic evaluations assess the ability to discriminate or understand the meaning of what is spoken or heard. By contrast, other measures such as the Gallaudet Hearing Scale have been developed to measure hearing problems ranging from difficulty hearing and understanding whispered speech, to being unable to hear any sounds whatsoever. Comparison of these scales and routine audiometric testing has demonstrated high levels of agreement (Schein, Gentile, & Haase, 1970).

Linguists and educators characterize deafness according to the time of onset; prelingual deafness occurs prior to and postlingual deafness occurs after the development of language. This characterization, when used broadly and not for an individual child, is limited by the imprecision of the timing of language acquisition as well as the lack of inclusion of variables, such as the etiology of hearing impairment or the extent of the hearing loss. It does highlight the important relationship of deafness and language acquisition.

Many hearing people consider deafness a disease or deformity. This understanding of deafness often justifies any intervention that can even partially ameliorate or obscure the disability. During the past decade, however, researchers, clinicians, and the deaf community have articulated a cultural view and definition of deafness. From this perspective, the major significance of hearing impairment is not primarily its medical or audiological symptoms; rather, it is best understood as a cultural phenomenon, with members of this cultural minority sharing historical, linguistic, intellectual, social, political, and educational dimensions (Vickrey Van Cleve & Crouch, 1989; Woodward, 1982).

The Deaf community (capitalized to underscore it as a discrete group) refers not only to persons with audiologic conditions affecting the capacity to hear but to hearing people who identify themselves as members of this group and who share a common language and culture. American Sign Language, the language of Deaf culture, has been recognized as an evolving, complex, and rich manual language vital to the integrity of group members (Woodward, 1972). Membership in the Deaf community does not relate to the degree of hearing loss but rather to an identification with Deaf culture and the sharing of language. This cultural view of deafness emphasizes the need for communication and contact with other community members. However, many infants and children who are deaf but have hearing parents may not have any contact with other individuals who are deaf until school years or even after secondary school graduation.

Controversy permeates even the definitional criteria of deafness. In 1991, the World Federation of the Deaf and the International Federation of Hard of Hearing People rejected the term "hearing-impaired" in favor of two distinct groups with different needs: the "deaf" and the "hard of hearing" (Joint Declaration, 1991). While individuals who are deaf rely on their visual skills for communication, hard-of-hearing persons seek ways to retain their listening and speaking skills. Both organizations recognized that individuals with hearing losses select their own group affiliation.

Prevalence

In 1994, an estimated 968,000 children and adolescents under the age of 18 years were hearing-impaired, representing 1.8% of the U.S. population (National Center for Health Statistics, 1994). The number of prelingually deafened children (defined as occurring before the acquisition of language) is difficult to ascertain. In a 1996 national survey of children identified as having a hearing impairment, more than 48,000 prelingually deaf children were identified (Center for Assessment and Demographic Studies, 1996). However, of those, 30,000 were identified at the known age of onset, while the age of onset for the remainder was unknown but presumed to be at

birth. The specific age of onset of deafness often is difficult to determine, particularly between birth and 3 years of age. In hard-of-hearing children, the loss may go undetected and/or misdiagnosed well into adolescence.

Data from the Department of Education indicate that the number of hearing-impaired students served by public education guaranteed by federal laws has decreased over the past decade (Annual Report to Congress, 1995). Since the implementation of two such laws, PL 94-142 and PL 89-313, the number of students below 21 years of age served by programs operating under these laws decreased from 88,732 in 1978–79 to 64,249 in 1993–94. These data should be interpreted with caution, given that detection, inclusion criteria, and access to services have changed for deaf students during this 10-year period. Many students who are currently "mainstreamed" in their local school system are not included in these surveys. In addition, changes in categorization of children by "primary handicapping condition" may have led to an apparent decrease in the number of deaf children, given that 30% of hearing-impaired children are "multiply handicapped" and have additional recognized conditions (Wolff & Harkins, 1986).

Etiology

Heredity and meningitis are the leading causes of deafness in school-age children (Newton, 1987). Individuals with genetic hearing loss vary widely with regard to the audiometric pattern of the hearing loss, the time of onset, and the nature of genetic transmission. They have a relatively low incidence of additional handicapping conditions. The proportion of hearing loss attributed to genetic causes has varied over time, influenced by prevailing environmental factors, increased recognition of the effects of intrauterine infections, and better identification of exogenous etiologies.

Bacterial meningitis is more likely to result in neurological sequelae than is viral meningitis. The incidence of meningitis related hearing loss is notable for its higher prevalence in minority populations, a fact that most likely is related to socioeconomic status and access to health care. With the recent introduction of the vaccine against Hemophilus Influenzae, it is anticipated that the prevalence of meningitis-related hearing loss will decline (Wolff & Brown, 1987).

Until recent years, maternal rubella was the leading cause of deafness, but when those affected by the rubella epidemic of 1963 to 1965 left school, the number of deafened youth with hearing loss due to rubella dropped sharply. Deafness secondry to intrauterine viral infections such as cytomegalovirus, rubeola, and rubella often have comorbid conditions including auditory, ocular, cardiac, and neurological sequelae such as seizure disorders, mental retardation, and panencephalitis due to viral reactivation. With the moderate resurgence of rubella and rubeola infections and the expected cyclic nature of rubella epidemics, the incidence of congenital deafness secondary to maternal rubella is increasing once again ("Increase in Rubella and Congenital Rubella Syndrome," 1991).

Much research remains to be done on the pathogenesis of hearing impairment secondary to severe problems in the perinatal period, such as hypoxia, hyperbilirubinemia, and sepsis. Reported etiologies of hearing loss after birth such as high fevers, infections, and trauma actually represent symptoms of several diseases. In summary, the etiology of hearing loss appears to be multifactorial, including variables as diverse as the course of epidemics, location, race, heredity, and socioeconomic factors.

Prevalence of Psychiatric Disorders

Estimates of the incidence of emotional disturbance among deaf children have ranged from 2 to 6 times greater than among their hearing counterparts (Meadow & Trybus, 1979; Robinson, 1971; Schlesinger & Meadow, 1972). Although no large epidemiological surveys have been performed, numerous case series consistently suggest a high risk of behavioral and emotional problems. Schlesinger and Meadow reported that 31.2% of the residential deaf students studied were judged by teachers to be emotionally disturbed compared to 9.7% of hearing students assessed by their

teachers in a large metropolitan school district. Chess, Corn, and Fernandez (1971) reported a disproportionately high rate of psychiatric disturbance in participants with hearing impairments in their longitudinal rubella study. Although past studies have attributed emotional or psychiatric problems to the hearing loss itself, many other factors, such as organicity and the systemic disorder that resulted in deafness, may be involved. A retrospective survey of outpatient child and adolescent evaluations found a strong relationship between emotional and behavioral disturbances and the inability of children to communicate with their family members in a shared language (Vanderbosch, 1989). The greater prevalence of psychiatric disturbance in deaf children and adolescents also may be attributed to the lack of accessible mental health services, comorbid conditions, and the inadequacy and inaccuracy of diagnostic and therapeutic regimens offered to this population with specialized communication and service needs. Many barriers to the accurate assessment of the prevalence of psychiatric disturbance in this population exist, including the absence of validated measures (such as structured clinical interviews or self-administered questionnaires) that are not dependent on spoken language or English literacy and the lack of consistency regarding the definition of the population. When a child presents with severe behaviors such as talking or signing to him- or herself, conversing with imaginary friends, and gaze aversion, the presenting symptoms can be manifestations of undersocialization and sensory deprivation, a comorbid developmental disorder or an acute psychiatric disorder. Inadequate language access, minimal knowledge of deafness, and inappropriate diagnostic criteria and nosology are some of the factors which have impeded the accurate assessment of the prevalence of psychiatric disorders in children and adolescents who are deaf.

Few studies have addressed the prevalence of emotional and behavioral problems among children with progressive or unilateral hearing loss. Also unclear is whether the increased reporting of emotional or behavioral problems in specialized programs for the deaf is a consequence of knowledgeable educators, an available group of peers for comparison, or self-selection, as those students who "fail" mainstreaming are often transferred to a special school for more focused attention and accessible programming.

Cognition, Language, and Deafness

The belief in the primacy of spoken language has pervaded both traditional perspectives of deafness and of psychiatry. Spoken language has been perceived as the main tool in the construction of an organized thought process. The preverbal child was felt to have some inner thoughts, but they were believed to be amorphous. A functional relationship between verbal language and cognition often was presumed, with verbal language hypothesized as the mediating symbol system of thought. In the past, children who were deaf were commonly viewed as cognitively "inferior" due to their language deprivation and inability to express themselves verbally. Spoken language was felt to be a primary modality of symbol formation crucial to adaptation and ego development. In contrast to these traditional assumptions, Piaget (1962) demonstrated rudimentary cognitive functioning prior to the development of language and symbolization's central role in cognitive functioning. Furth (1966) extended these observations and challenged the commonly accepted assumption that knowledge, consciousness, and language could be equated by examining the disparity between the concepts of knowledge, consciousness, and language in both deaf and hearing children. Language-lacking deaf children demonstrated symbolic skills and demonstrated knowledge through play, fantasy and gesture. Their inner thought processes were proven to be equivalent to that of hearing children, evidenced by the use of a symbolic code and meaningful use of objects in imaginative play by children who are deaf. This work recognized the inventive power of the human intellect and the resilience and adaptation of the child or adolescent who is deaf and who creates inner symbols and language in the absence of a continual auditory environmental supply. Vernon (1967) interpreted data from 31 research studies involving both language-rich and language-impoverished youths who were hearing-impaired. He observed that their cognitive functioning was the same and concluded that no functional relationship exists between verbal language and cognition—thought process—or between symbol formation and level of vocal language development. These studies demonstrated that vocal language was not the mediating symbol system of thought.

Despite nonverbal or performance test results that demonstrate the equivalence of the intellectual abilities of children who are deaf with their hearing peers, widely divergent academic achievement has led investigators to explore critical variables that impact on this outcome. Marschark (1993) reviewed the results of recent research examining the cognitive skills of children who are deaf and recognized differences in the processing (e.g., a greater reliance on visual-spatial short-term memory coding) and attentional strategies employed by deaf and hearing children which may account for the disparity in achievement across a wide variety of domains. Marschark underscored the need for a critical appraisal of significant research findings and cautioned that cognitive differences should not be equated with cognitive deficiencies.

Language Acquistion

Language is a tool used for communication, social interaction, learning, and creative outlets, acquired through a process involving biological maturation, cognitive preparedness, opportunities for interaction, and environmental exposure. While hearing children acquire language without special efforts, children who are deaf (born to parents who are hearing) must be helped to gain exposure to language through the use of sign language, amplified auditory stimuli, and/or oral training in lipreading and speech.

For years, most educators and parents believed that they needed to "teach" the deaf child language (language being equated with speech). During the past 30 years, linguists have demonstrated that deaf children and adults produce spontaneous manual language for their own communication. These manual or sign languages have been studied extensively and demonstrated to be rich complete languages, following all linguistic rules and presenting reality in an immediate visual form. In *The Signs of Language,* Klima and Bellugi (1979) demonstrated that American Sign Language not only has its own vocabulary, phonology, morphology, and syntax, but also the silent-language analog of poetry and song, wit and sign play, and slips of the hand. These allow for the visual demonstration of the signer's intuitive awareness and tremendous sensitivity to the range of expression in this linguistic format.

Deaf children with parents who are deaf are exposed to sign language from birth and utilize manual babbling. This babbling with the hands is similar to the vocal babbling of hearing infants and is related to the abstract linguistic structure of language and to developmentally appropriate expressive capacities (Petitto & Marentette, 1991). Studies of children who are deaf clearly demonstrate that the initiation of linguistic competence is independent of the modality of expression; children who are deaf with parents who are hearing produce isolated gestures spontaneously and at an early age (Goldin-Meadow & Mylander, 1990). However, American Sign Language, like all other languages, does not develop in isolation; without access to this language, significant delays occur in children who are deaf. As more than 90% of children who are prelingually deaf are born to hearing parents, many children are deprived of exposure to both spoken and visually accessible language. Even if the child has exceptional speech and lipreading capabilities, oral training is slow and difficult for the preschooler; therefore, the deaf child's usable language skills are typically less than optimal and result in communicative frustration and social isolation. Milestones in language acquisition are the same for speaking and signing children when they are exposed to sign language; furthermore, they traverse these milestones in the same sequence and at approximately the same time (Meier & Newport, 1990). Proficiency in sign language appears to be correlated not with length of experience with American Sign Language but with age at first exposure, a fact that corroborates Lennenberg's concept of a "critical period" for language acquisition in early childhood (Lennenberg, 1967; Newport & Supalla, 1990). Children who ultimately rely on visually accessible language but are not exposed to sign language until later school years are late language learners, with decreased sign language proficiency and difficulty articulating abstract concepts, values, and feeling states. These young children may be limited to the expression of only the most basic mood states (sad, happy, angry), while adolescents may continue to have difficulty distinguishing more subtle differences such as laziness and fatigue, sadness and depression, despair, and remorse. Despite the obvious advantage of maximal language exposure in childhood and the absence of data to support the need for a single communication modality or experience, objective guidelines for parents who face communication choices for their child and family have not been developed, and parental decision-making is often influenced by the individual philosophy of the professional(s) encountered (Rushmer, 1994).

Silence and Uncertainty

Although no children or adolescents who are deaf live in absolute silence, silence is a word often used in association with painful isolation and the presumed experience of deafness. Our knowledge of the impact and influence of silence on the inner world and ego functioning is quite limited. Shafii (1973) addressed this lack of knowledge and suggested that its roots lie in our ambivalent feelings and our traumatic experiences of silence in childhood. Silence may be associated with absence; with lack of understanding; with an inability to communicate; with separation; and with aloneness. Numerous factors contribute to the meaning of silence for each child who is deaf. Of perhaps equal importance is the meaning of silence to the parent of the deaf child and the manner in which the parenting experience may resonate with his or her own preverbal experiences of silence (as either complete communion with the object or abandonment and loneliness). Many adults cannot tolerate silence, keeping a radio, television, even a white noise machine operating through the day and night. Therapy with a child who is deaf requires a tolerance of one's own experience of silence and capacity to be with the child or adolescent through periods of uncertainty, doubt, and unknowing.

Affective Interchange, Symbolization, and Self-Representation

It is hypothesized that the nonverbal nature of the communication of basic affect allows the young deaf child adequate affective (not cognitive) interaction with parents, avoiding "a potentially fatal psychological deprivation" (Vernon, 1972, p. 361).

The growth and development of language in all young children occurs on the foundation of a highly developed nonverbal and prelinguistic communication system. It is unclear to what extent this is affected by prelingual deafness. Do young children who have never heard experience not hearing a soothing parental voice as deprivation? Likely much depends on the presence or absence of visual, tactile, and other sensory stimuli. Little is also known about the different features of the young toddler who has never heard versus the toddler who is suddenly cut off from auditory input as a result of an illness such as meningitis. Parents often report a dramatic change in behavior and temperament following an illness and sudden sensory loss, although numerous factors may contribute to this change.

An infant's hearing loss can disrupt the development of presymbolic and symbolic communication. However, the intense affective interchange between mother and child and the sensitivity and innate capacity of the child to sense the mother's mood through facial expression and body movement evolve into a complex dyadic exchange rich with meaning beyond words (Papousek & Papousek, 1979). Affective intuition, knowledge, and inner thought need not be altered by the lack of auditory input. Although most deaf children are exceptions to the rule of children learning verbal language from their parents, they are not deprived of the primal experience of nonverbal dyadic communication and understanding.

Loewald (1988) addressed the manner in which a parent immerses the infant in speech that becomes an integral part of the "global experience within the mother/child field" (p. 185). Parental speech conveys closeness at a distance and presence in absence. In later months, objects and words remain linked on a primitive, preconscious level and function as symbolizing bridges between the partners. Clearly, the linkage of words and objects may only occur if the language is accessible to the child.

The intersubjective exchange of affect and the reciprocal behaviors that make up social dialogues during the infant's first 9 months of life are notable for the mother's working within the same sensory modality and elaborating on the expression of her infant (Papousek & Papousek, 1979). A study of deaf mothers and their deaf infants demonstrated that deaf mothers had positive facial expressions for a larger portion of time than hearing mothers and engaged in "coactional duetting," a dialogue in which the mother and infant form the same facial expression simultaneously (Meadow-Orlans, 1987b). This may be similar to hearing mothers and infants matching each other's pitch and rhythm in sequences of vocal utterances. For the hearing parent with a deaf child, the intuitive knowledge of how and when to mirror the child's nonverbal language or give this nonverbal language a verbal symbolic form more familiar to the hearing parent is often difficult. Parents who are helped to be with their infant and child comfortably in a nonverbal modality may experience less discouragement, frustration, and deprivation regarding the lack of spoken words. Stern's (1985) description of affective attunement in which a parent begins to expand his or her behavior beyond true imitation into cross-modal matching, taking the experience of emotional resonance and recasting it in another form, raises interesting questions for the child who is deaf and the parent or therapist who is hearing. The reflection of the inner state of the infant or child occurs regardless of the hearing status of the parent and child; however, the degree to which hearing impairment impacts on maternal self-esteem, the capacity for empathy, and mirroring is variable and dependent on numerous factors.

Impact on the Child and Adolescent

INFANCY AND TODDLERHOOD

Over the past 20 years, research on the social, emotional, and cognitive development of prelingually deaf infants and children has included an examination of the mother/child relationship. Theoretical and clinical paradigms have emerged regarding the essential elements of this interpersonal experience and the creative modifications that must occur if caregivers and infants are to dialogue in a reciprocal fashion within a shared sensory modality. Schlesinger and Meadow (1972) examined mother/child interactions with both hearing and deaf children, describing variables specific to maternal behavior, child behavior, and reciprocal parent-child interaction. They found that hearing mothers of deaf children were less flexible, less approving, more didactic, and more intrusive than mothers of hearing children. Not surprisingly, the degree of communicative competence of hearing parents appeared also to be related to the deaf child's enjoyment, happiness, compliance, creativity, and pride in mastery of developmental tasks. They addressed the complex interplay of the factors involved, including the necessary alterations in communication with the deaf child, its accompanying frustration and discomfort, as well as the assimilation of often overwhelming and conflicting professional "advice." Hearing impairment was felt to exert a tremendous influence on important aspects of child-rearing behaviors as well as both the expressive and receptive components in parent/child interaction. In a later study, Greenberg (1980) examined the modality of dyadic communication (oral only vs. oral and manual combined, also referred to as "total communication") and the level of competence within that modality. He found that dyads augmenting oral communication with manual language demonstrated more complex social interactions, with more cooperation, positive affect, and less gaze aversion. These studies elaborated the manner by which not only deafness but also the form and level of communication impacted on the child's relationship with the caregiver.

Mothers have been observed to use communication either to control behavior or to generate communication (Newport, Gleitman, & Gleitman, 1977). Schlesinger (1987) addressed this in relation to a parental experience of powerlessness due to unresolved feelings generated by the diagnosis of deafness in the child. She examined dialogue strategies of mothers and deaf children and correlated this with later academic achievement. Mothers of deaf children with poor academic outcomes

were likely to be more controlling, less responsive to their child's behaviors or communications, to refer to visible concrete objects, and to ask more "test" questions. These maternal behaviors thwarted exploration or reciprocal, interactive linguistic stimulation. Researchers have examined the mother-child attachment and the quality of mother-infant behavior with somewhat disparate conclusions regarding the impact of deafness on this early relationship (Lederberg & Mobley, 1990). Research is needed to enhance our understanding of the father-child dyad and to generate interventions to decrease paternal disengagement and discomfort with his infant or child who is deaf.

CHILDHOOD

Unresolved grief, anger, guilt, helplessness, and denial often impede the acceptance and development of the most accessible (often manual) communication with parents of deaf children (Mindel & Vernon, 1971). As a result, in the absence of language fluency and without the usual option of vocal explanation, parents often must resort to punishment or overindulgence.

Although clinicians previously referred primarily to the intrapsychic conflicts and parental mourning reactions, cognitive factors required to parent on a nonintuitive basis are increasingly recognized. Attention to the family and community, with provision of professional and social supports for parents and primary caregivers, appears critical. Researchers have correlated stress with maternal controlling behavior and decreased responsiveness to the child, and mothers with deaf children receiving higher levels of support have been shown to have more positive mother-child interaction (Crnic & Greenberg, 1990; Meadow-Orlans & Steinberg, 1993).

Parents often express bewilderment as to how to establish reasonable behavioral expectations of their deaf children without the availability of verbal explanations. The child who is deaf misses significant interpersonal interactions and both the expressed and imbedded information transmitted in family conversations. Schlesinger and Meadow (1972) noted the manner in which this lack of meaningful reciprocal communication may lead to developmental delay/arrest prior to the formation of an autonomous self. Delayed toilet training, feeding problems, and imposition of stringent safety measures are common complaints of parents of children who are deaf. Desperately seeking a shared modality of communication, parental insistence on the child's production of spoken words may paradoxically lead to an oppositional resistance to later speech and language therapy. The development of initiative, too, may be affected by deafness, as much purposeful behavior, expression of intent, and the resultant reinforcement and encouragement are expressed through verbal language.

In the absence of verbal language or an alternative to it, children are left with motoric responses to their affective expression until shared communication channels are established. If a deaf child does not learn or use a language during his or her early years, not only are language skills inadequate, but the opportunity for open communication and exploration with family and peers is sorely missed. This inadequate communication between parents and children often leads to impulsive, motoric responses to vent frustration, disappointment, and anger by both parent and child. Earlier studies based on a high-risk population referred for psychiatric treatment reported characteristics such as emotional immaturity, shortened attention span, poor impulse control, and hyperactivity (Altshuler, 1974). Diagnoses such as attention deficit hyperactivity disorder or impulse control disorder must be differentiated from the motoric expression of a mood or affect such as frustration in a child who has had few opportunities to develop the language and cognitive skills necessary for impulse control. Studies of children with parents who are also deaf as well as those who have had early exposure to manual communication have demonstrated the positive correlation of language opportunity with measures of impulse control (Harris, 1978).

Children with unilateral hearing loss or with mild hearing loss are required to observe visual cues with a vigilance uncharacteristic of young children, and may appear to have attentional problems when fatigued; this may be exacerbated by increased degrees of hearing loss, particularly in the absence of a visually accessible, manual language. Additionally, deafness and attention deficit hyperactivity disorder are not mutually exclusive; numerous etiological factors such as rubella result in both and increase the risk of academic underachievement.

It is impossible to separate the linguistic and cognitive development of deaf children from their social and psychological development. Chess and Fernandez (1980) examined 4 personality characteristics previously ascribed to deaf children—impulsivity, hyperactivity, rigidity, and suspiciousness—but were unable to find a "typical" personality constellation in deaf children. Liben (1978) described the cognitive and social lags of the deaf child as they relate to experiential deficiencies. The social experience for the deaf child is notable for the lack of available role models; reduction in the transmission of information; decreased opportunity for communication among peers; and didactic, superficial, and less mutual communication with parents and teachers. Stika found that compared to their hearing peers, children who are deaf were significantly deficient in their abilities to analyze and interpret social situations and to take another person's perspective. This social-cognitive delay was not felt to be related to the ability to perceive and label situational cues nor to the ability to empathize. Stika (1989) described difficulty in gathering and processing information about the environment and an "inactive" style in which effective cognitive mediating strategies are not effectively utilized in selectively attending to the experience of the other person.

The libidinal drive development of the deaf child may be modified by communication deficits relating both to deafness and its sequelae. The parental ambivalence leading to inconsistent limit setting may leave the child with unrealistic and grandiose images of his or her power within the family and the environment (Brinich, 1981). A child who utilizes predominately nonverbal expression of aggressive impulses often may appear less sublimated and more out-of-control when miming destructive fantasies.

In a family denying a child's deafness, the child who relies on visually accessible language experiences an inevitable conflict between the ego seeking a modality of communication and expressive outlet and the ego ideal that denigrates the manual or signed communication. It is not uncommon to note an identification with the aggressor in that the deaf child will devalue deaf friends and deafness as if this feature were isolated from his or her self. Once nonverbal or manual communication skills are acquired, the child experiences intense ambivalence. Spoken language is often the link to the parents, with sign language a reminder of deafness and the parents' shame and intense narcissistic injury. Without auditory access to words or exposure to sign language, without a shared family language, the child is left without a container not only for his or her own internal experience but for the dyadic interchange, as well. The cumulative impact of this deprivation may lead to a profound affective or behavioral disturbance.

In therapy with deaf children or adolescents with a history of poor-to-absent shared communication with parents and dysfunctional object relationships, words and signs become symbolic representations of both the good and bad mother. The establishment of an empathic environment in which the child can be understood both linguistically and affectively is essential. Repetitive naming of objects, finger-spelling and reading names from a telephone book or dictionary, and find-the-word puzzle games may serve as enactments and the working through of conflicts with the good or bad object; words also may function as transitional objects.

Beyond the provision of a shared language in the therapy, empathic understanding may involve working through previously unexpressed affective experiences of frustration, isolation, loneliness, rage, and depression. The child who is deaf and who has experienced little shared language in the home often does not have an awareness of his or her own abilities. A celebration of the child's affective expression and previously unacknowledged cognitive abilities is a vital aspect of therapy. Optimally, the child psychiatrist should foster parental appreciation for the child's abilities and self.

The importance of the educational environment for the child who is deaf cannot be underscored enough; school provides an opportunity for the expansion and optimal achievement of social and communication potential. However, due to a bitter, two-century-long controversy among professionals about the recommended approach for communication and education of deaf infants and children, the educational arena is a battleground. School remains the locus of a heated conflict between proponents of oralism, who reject the use of sign language, and advocates of total communication, who support the use of both sign language and residual speech and hearing. This debate has been examined from historical, linguistic, philo-

sophical, cultural, economic, and psychological perspectives (Winefield, 1987). Parents often are besieged by advocates of the various philosophies and may choose an educational modality based on the most supportive and/or convincing individual rather than the most sensible alternative(s). Unfortunately, the definitive study has not been undertaken to date and the absence of consensus regarding appropriate outcome measures for the deaf child remains a daunting obstacle.

In recent years, the study of sign language and deaf culture has impacted on legislative and educational thinking about deafness. The recommendations of the 1988 Federal Commission on Education of the Deaf included the recognition of American Sign Language under the Bilingual Education Act. A position paper by Johnson, Liddell and Ertig (1989) recommended bilingual education in both English and American Sign Language for all deaf children and suggested that low academic achievement levels are related to the problems in the communication practices of teachers and the absence of accessible language in the classroom setting. The primary use of American Sign Language in the classroom, exposure of deaf children to deaf teachers and other adult role models, and instruction in English as a second language through reading and writing has been advocated in recent years. Instruction in American Sign Language and bilingualism are complex issues necessitating further research and practical examination; at the current time, there is an insufficient number of teachers who are either deaf or fluent in American Sign Language.

Although the future impact of these recommendations and educational trends remain to be seen, currently few deaf students are educated in a linguistically accessible environment. Varying amounts of sign language and speech are used in 59% of classrooms, and 38% of deaf students must learn using only residual auditory capacities and lipreading despite advances in assistive technologies and the training of increasing numbers of sign language and oral interpreters (Center for Assessment and Demographic Studies, 1989). In 1989, 22% of hearing-impaired children attended a residential school and 9% a day school. Fifty-seven percent were taught in a special education classroom in a public school and 4.7% in a regular classroom where no special educational services were offered. The remainder of the children attended school at a variety of sites, such as speech and hearing clinics.

Many conflicts regarding the education of deaf children involve mainstreaming. This phenomena has been rapidly increasing since the passage of public law 94-142 in 1975; however, this does not necessarily mean that children who are deaf are included in all or even many of the classes and activities with hearing children in the schools in which they are placed. Often, hearing-impaired children are isolated in a special education classroom in their local school and spend most or all of the day in this class with other hearing-impaired children, many of whom are multihandicapped and heterogeneous with respect to age, IQ, and educational level. Currently, the extent to which hearing-impaired students have truly entered the "mainstream" of education with nondisabled students appears to vary widely. Carefully controlled outcome studies of this significant educational trend are greatly needed.

ADOLESCENCE

Puberty brings great challenges for the adolescent who is deaf, who must develop a sense of identity and self-acceptance prior to becoming an autonomous individual. Rapid physical growth and sexual development usually occur without the benefit of adequate information regarding the normal maturation process. The ensuing confusion and sense of isolation may lead to a consuming preoccupation with normal developmental changes. During adolescence, the child must begin to consolidate a self-concept that integrates his or her deafness. Manifestations of this struggle include "practicing hearing" at the mirror, pretending to be hearing and that others are deaf, losing or refusing to use hearing aids, gaze avoidance and refusal to lipread or sign. The deaf adolescent's separation individuation often involves increased peer activities, which can be extremely threatening for nonsigning parents. This mirrors the experience of parents with their hearing adolescents' peer language but is more dramatic in that American Sign Language is completely incomprehensible to nonsigning parents and may be used by the adolescent to test limits and challenge parental authority and competence.

Although earlier childhood experiences have been demonstrated to exert a powerful impact on the depressive vulnerability of adolescents and young adults, the adolescent years provide an opportunity for reworking familial relationships and past experiences with a heightened awareness of the meaning of deafness to the individual within the family as well as the larger deaf community (Leigh, Robins, & Welkowitz, 1990). Disruptions in the first separation-individuation phase, often coinciding with the diagnosis of deafness, may be reflected during adolescence when adolescent ambivalence and/or parental discomfort with driving, dating, college departure, or independent living becomes apparent.

School experiences continue to have significant implications for the development of healthy peer relationships and a positive self-concept. Those students in residential settings have a greater opportunity to socialize with deaf friends, to be exposed to deaf role models, to participate in group activities, to assume positions of leadership, to have successful experiences, and to receive information from peers and counselors. Graduates of residential programs describe their social experiences as more positive than graduates of mainstream programs in which deaf students are enrolled in local schools rather than special residential or day schools for deaf children and adolescents (Mertens, 1989). Within mainstream programs, students who received appropriate educational assistance services, such as interpreters, do experience supportiveness in the academic environment to a greater extent than those without services. Students who transition from one educational setting to another often experience tremendous turmoil, identity confusion, and emotional maladjustment, and develop psychiatric symptomatology necessitating intervention (Lytle, Feinstein, & Jonas, 1987).

For all youngsters, adolescence is often a time of increased vulnerability for substance abuse; however, for the deaf adolescent, the use of alcohol or drugs offers a means of social integration with both deaf and hearing peers and family members. Indeed, many deaf individuals are initiated into the drug world by hearing siblings and peers.

Unfortunately, deaf students often leave high school with no work experience and unrealistic career goals. Parents may play a critical role both with participation and perceptions of their child's options with respect to postsecondary programs and vocational training (El-Khiami, 1987). The level of stressful personal and family events seems to be a critical factor in postgraduate outcome (Mowry, 1991). The perception of deafness as a disability warranting a monthly social security disability insurance payment has a profound impact on the young adult's perception of the need to work as well as his or her own vocational potential.

Impact on Family

Similar to the birth of any child with a disability, the birth of a deaf infant generates a grief response in hearing parents. Traversing this stage is related not only to the coping mechanisms of the extended and immediate family, the child's own adaptability, but also to the quality of professional assistance. Often the diagnosis follows months or years of anxiety and confusion, exacerbated by health care professionals who minimize the parents' intuition that "something is wrong." Parents often experience the information that their child is hearing-impaired as an intense narcissistic injury that disrupts their hopes and dreams for their lives and the life of their child. Guilt and reactive depression compound the intense frustration for both parent and child regarding their inability to communicate fully with one another as language becomes increasingly more central in achieving developmentally appropriate relationships. News of the deafness often serves as a catalyst for underlying marital discord, with blame, anger, resentment, and guilt as prominent features. Immediate financial expenditures for hearing aids and medical appointments as well as time lost from work serve as additional stresses to the family system. Frequently one parent (generally the primary caregiver) takes on the role of "interpreter" of the child's needs and wishes. Often this parent becomes responsible for accompanying the child to all appointments and school meetings, risking permanent loss of employment, which generates an overwhelming sense of burden and places additional stress on the marital dyad.

Grandparents and family elders are often the bearers of family and cultural myths regarding deafness, which may further the perception of deafness as a disability likely to be acccompanied by a life of isolation and deprivation. The involvement of these elders in parenting, overprotection, overindulgence, and sabotage of parental child rearing often further complicates matters. Siblings frequently provide a communication link with the deaf child and the family. Growing together and developing "home" signs unique to the sibling dialogue, these siblings often serve as family interpreters, sibling protectors, and caregivers in a parentified role, regardless of the siblings' relative ages.

The staff of day and, especially, residential schools also serve as extended family members, especially for students entering school while very young and remaining on campus continuously except during vacations and occasional weekends at home. Residential schools vary in the extent to which they seek parental involvement and coordination of child-rearing decisions. Frequent meetings and shared communication with parents may be difficult for practical reasons when schools are a great distance from the family residence. Anger and resentment may develop between these two sets of "parents" in a fashion similar to a dysfunctional marital relationship.

During later childhood and adolescence, families with deaf children and adolescents who communicate primarily in American Sign Language may be viewed as cross-cultural environments. There are many inherent difficulties in the initiation of adolescents into a culture that is foreign to and different from that of their parents. The development of a cross-cultural perspective and the instruction of bicultural skills to family members should heighten the awareness and comfort of both parents and deaf adolescents to the cultural values of their respective communities.

Interventions

An infant or young child with a possible hearing impairment should be referred immediately to a skilled audiologist for an evaluation. Once the diagnosis of a hearing impairment has been made, the child should be referred for placement in a multidisciplinary, comprehensive intervention program, including early child and family education. Early intervention has been shown to be valuable in improving the ultimate achievement of hearing-impaired children (Meadow-Orlans, 1987a). Following diagnosis, parents, often already in crisis, need to integrate conflicting expert opinions in their child-rearing decisions. Early intervention programs vary widely in philosophical orientation and often set the course for childhood experiences in elementary school and beyond. Early exposure to sign language and to adults who are deaf with highly developed language skills is one intervention with low risk and tremendous potential benefit, enhancing the effectiveness of any and all subsequent therapies.

The goals for a successful intervention include family adaptation to and acceptance of the child's special communication needs and the provision of a linguistically accessible home and school environment that enhances the child's self-esteem. Parents need support as they suddenly lack the usual language resources to communicate easily with their child, and they need to have confidence and joy restored to their parenting role. The heterogeneity of this small population creates many difficulties for effective intervention planning. Optimally, programs should be flexible in their orientation and able to utilize all family support systems, including sibling, friends, relatives, church members, and other neighborhood service providers. Parents are often overwhelmed with inconsistent information and the biases of professionals, and tension arises regarding the chosen communication approach. Parent education materials and national information centers are now available and can assist the parent and mental health professional in understanding the controversies in education, in selecting linguistically accessible educational settings, in recognizing that their options are neither mutually exclusive nor irreversible, and in achieving the child's potential for language acquisition. Family therapy can play an important role in resolving intrafamilial conflicts, working through unresolved grief, exploring choices regarding educational and vocational placement, and facilitating the achievement of independent living skills (Harvey, 1989).

Psychiatric diagnoses, prognostic impressions, and interventions with deaf individuals have been scrutinized in recent years. Examiner bias was suggested by Lane (1988), who reviewed journal articles and books on the psychology of the deaf from the past 20 years and assembled a list of trait attributions—aggressive, immature, stubborn, impulsive, and so on—and hypothesized that a significant variable is the paternalistic posture of the hearing diagnostician.

Child psychiatrists must be sensitive to special issues involved in the development of a therapeutic alliance with deaf children and adolescents— that is, to the primacy of negotiating an effective communication strategy. Rapport can be established with the presence of a sign language interpreter, special attention to lipreading, written modes of communication, and nonverbal behaviors such as gesture and play. If the child or adolescent communicates in American Sign Language, a certified interpreter will provide a safe, confidential, nonjudgmental environment in which to begin to explore feelings. Greater barriers to effective therapy are present when the "interpreter" is a family member already embroiled in the conflict precipitating the evaluation. In general, providing mental health services to deaf children and adolescents requires specialized knowledge and communicative skills (Steinberg, 1991).

An understanding of sign language and deaf culture is important in the assessment of an adolescent who communicates using a manual language. The use of written language with adolescents can be confusing in that sign language is syntactically very different from written English. American Sign Language may appear psychotic, loose, and illogical when translating literally or word-for-word by an unskilled interpreter. By and large, personality inventories and self-administered diagnostic questionnaires require a high level of English comprehension and are not useful adjuncts in evaluation, often resulting in invalid diagnoses of psychopathology.

The mental status examination also is vulnerable to erroneous interpretation when used with deaf children and adolescents. Nuances of facial expression, gesture, the force, quality, and speed of signing are easily missed by therapists inexperienced in sign language. Polite head nodding and affirmative gestures often belie underlying misunderstandings and confusion. Usual verbal modalities for assessing a capacity for abstraction must be discarded with patients who are deaf. Decreased attention span and low frustration tolerance in the diagnostic or therapeutic setting may be wrongfully assumed due to inadequate communication with a therapist unskilled in sign language.

Psychological evaluations should be obtained with a psychologist with extensive knowledge of deafness and familiarity with the complexity and testing limitations with deaf children and adolescents. Neuropsychological evaluations can offer vital information, particularly when the etiology of deafness is a systemic illness. Verbal neuropsychological instruments such as the Luria-Nebraska should not be used.

School-based interventions allow behaviors to be viewed from a developmental perspective and in the context of both the school and home environment. School-family collaboration enables school personnel to work more effectively with the child or adolescent, and allows for the examination of the symptom in a broad and contextually relevant fashion. Supportive services and modifications in the school environment can help the student to maintain a positive attitude about his or her own abilities. The consulting child psychiatrist may wish to examine the factors influencing the child or adolescent's ability to function optimally and recommend alterations in the seating, lighting, use of amplification devices, even the nature of the educational approach and school setting.

School-based interventions allow for the development of an intervention that may be implemented consistently in both environments. Many parents of children who are deaf utilize school staff when problems arise in the home, so the involvement of the consulting child psychiatrist may uncover underlying conflicts or inconsistencies in the expectations or responses of family and school staff and ultimately strengthen the school-family collaboration. Children and adolescents who are deaf are extremely responsive to group interventions with peers and/or group leaders who are also deaf; school settings are often the ideal milieu for group therapy addressing general interpersonal problem-solving and socialization skills or special problems related to victimization, parental addiction to drugs, and the like. Buddy and mentor programs can be vital in enhancing self-esteem and growth. The consulting child psychiatrist may be involved in curriculum development; the expansion of vocational, educational, interpersonal experiences; self-esteem enhancement; prevention of substance abuse and other self-destructive behaviors for the student body; as well as in conflict resolution among parents, teachers, and treatment teams. Importantly, consulting child psychiatrists also can help professionals to appreciate a child or adolescent who is deaf as a member of a cultural minority, often more restricted by societal expectations than deafness.

Child psychiatrists may also be called upon to participate in presurgical evaluations for cochlear implantation. This procedure was approved by the Food and Drug Administration in 1990 and involves the surgical implantation of electrodes and direct electrical stimulation of the cochlea. Despite its increased use across the country, there is little published data on the psychological, social, vocational, or educational outcomes for children with cochlear implants, and the procedure remains controversial. If cochlear implantation is offered to a child under the age of 18, it should be performed as an adjunct to standard beneficial treatments and in the context of a clinical trial with multidisciplinary team collaboration monitoring not only linguistic but also social and emotional outcomes.

Despite federal statutes mandating accessible mental health care for all persons, the mental health service needs of children and adolescents who are deaf or hard-of-hearing remain profoundly underserved. Child psychiatrists who provide these services must familiarize themselves with the linguistic heterogeneity and distinctiveness of the individual child who is deaf or hard of hearing; the nature of Deaf culture and the regional Deaf community; and the impact of deafness on the child's development, the family system, and the diagnostic and therapeutic process. Child psychiatrists new to this area of specialization should avail themselves of the expertise of organizations, institutions, and professionals experienced in providing mental health services to children and adolescents who are deaf and hard of hearing. Although demanding, work with children and adolescents who are deaf or hard of hearing is a unique challenge that is both compelling and highly rewarding.

REFERENCES

Altshuler, K. Z. (1974). The social and psychological development of the deaf child: Problems, their treatment and prevention. *American Annals of the Deaf, 119,* 365–376.

Annual Report to Congress on the Implementation of the Education of the Handicapped Act. (1995). Office of Special Education and Rehabilitative Services.

Brinich, P. M. (1981). Application of the metapsychological profile to the assessment of deaf children. *Psychoanalytic Study of the Child, 36,* 3–32.

Center for Assessment and Demographic Studies. (1989). Data from the *1988-89 annual survey of deaf and hard of hearing children and youth.* Washington, DC: Gallaudet University.

Center for Assessment and Demographic Studies. (1996). Data from the 1995-96 annual survey of deaf and hard of hearing children and youth. Washington, DC: Gallaudet University.

Chess, S., Corn, S. J., & Fernandez, P. B. (1971). *Psychiatric disorders of children with congenital rubella.* New York: Brunner & Mazel.

Chess, S., & Fernandez, P. (1980). Do deaf children have a typical personality? *Journal of the American Academy of Child Psychiatry, 19,* 654–664.

Crnic, K. A., & Greenberg, M. T. (1990). Minor parenting stresses with young children, *Child Development, 61,* 1628–1637.

Densham, J. (1995). *Deafness, children and the family.* Brookefield: Ashgate Publishing Company.

El-Khiami, A. (1987). The role of the family in the transition in young hearing-impaired adults. In G. B. Anderson & D. Watson (Eds.), *Innovations in the habilitation and rehabilitation of deaf adolescents.* (99–116). Little Rock, AK: National Deaf Adolescents Conference.

Furth, H. G. (1966). *Thinking without language: Psychological implication of deafness.* New York: Free Press.

Goldin-Meadow, S., & Mylander, C. (1990). Beyond the input given: A child's role in the acquisition of language. *Language, 66,* 323–355.

Greenberg, M. T. (1980). Social interaction between deaf preschoolers and their mothers: The effects of communication method and communication competence. *Developmental Psychology, 16* (5), 465–474.

Gregory, S., Bishop, J., & Sheldon, L. (1995). *Deaf young people and their families.* Cambridge: Cambridge University Press.

Harris, R. I. (1978). Impulse control in deaf children: Research and clinical issues. In L. S. Liben, *Deaf children: Developmental perspectives.* (137–156). New York: Academic Press.

Harvey, M. A. (1989). *Psychotherapy with deaf and hard-of-hearing persons: A systemic model.* Hillsdale, NJ: Lawrence Erlbaum.

Increase in rubella and congenital rubella syndrome—United States, 1988-1990 (1991). *Morbidity and Morality Weekly Report, 40,* (6), 93–99.

Johnson, R. E., Liddell, S. K., & Ertig, C. J. (1980). *Unlocking the curriculum: Principles for achieving access in deaf education.* Working Paper 89–3. Washington, DC: Gallaudet Research Institute.

Joint Declaration. "Deaf and hard of hearing." (1991). *Self Help for Hard of Hearing People, Inc. Journal, 12* (1), 6.

Klima, E. S., & Bellugi, U. (1979). *The signs of language.* Boston: Harvard University Press.

Lane, H. (1988). Is there a "psychology of the deaf?" *Exceptional Children, 55* (1), 7–19.

Lederberg, A. R., & Mobley, C. E. (1990). The effect of hearing impairment on the quality of attachment and mother-toddler interaction. *Child Development, 61,* 1596–1604.

Leigh, I. W., Robins, C. J., & Welkowitz, J. (1990). Of communication of depressive vulnerability in deaf individuals. *Journal of the American Deafness and Rehabilitation Association, 23* (3), 68–73.

Lennenberg, E. H. (1967). *Biological foundations of language.* New York: John Wiley & Sons.

Liben, L. S. (1978). Developmental perspectives on experiential deficiencies of deaf children. In L. S. Liben, *Deaf children: Developmental perspectives.* (195–215). New York: Academic Press.

Loewald, H. W. (1980). *Papers on Psychoanalysis.* New Haven, CT. Yale University Press, 185.

Lytle, R. R., Feinstein, C., & Jonas, B. (1987). Social and emotional adjustment in deaf adolescents after transfer to a residential school for the deaf. *American Academy of Child and Adolescent Psychiatry, 26* (2), 237–241.

Marschark, M. (1993). Intelligence and cognitive development. In M. Marschark, *Psychological Development of Deaf Children.* (128–149). New York: Oxford University Press.

Meadow, K. P., & Trybus, R. J. (1979). Behavioral and emotional problems of deaf children: An overview. In J. J. Branford & W. G. Hardy (Eds.), *Hearing and hearing impairment.* New York: Grune & Stratton.

Meadow-Orlans, K. P. (1987a). An analysis of the effectiveness of early intervention programs for hearing-impaired children. In M. J. Guralnick & F. C. Bennett (Eds.), *The effectiveness of early intervention for at-risk and handicapped children.* New York: Academic Press.

Meadow-Orlans, K. P. (1987b). *Interactions of deaf and hearing mothers with three and six month old infants.* Paper presented at the Society for Research and Child Development, Baltimore.

Meadow-Orlans, K. P., & Steinberg, A. G. (1993). Effects of infant hearing loss on maternal support on mother-infant interactions at 18 months. *Journal of Applied Developmental Psychology, 14,* 407–426.

Meier, R. B., & Newport, E. L. (1990). Out of the hands of babes: On a possible sign language advantage in language acquisition. *Language, 66,* 1–23.

Mertens, D. M. (1989). Social experiences of hearing-impaired high school youth. *American Annals of the Deaf, 134,* 15–19.

Mindel, E., & Vernon, M. (1971). *They grow in silence—the deaf child and his family.* Silver Spring, MD: National Association of the Deaf.

Mowry, R. (1991). *Social transition of deaf adolescents from high school: Results of a longitudinal study.* Poster presented at the American Deafness and Rehabilitation Association, Chicago.

National Center for Health Statistics. (1994). Data from the National Health Interview Survey, Series 10, No. 188, Table 1, 24–25.

Newport, E., Gleitman, L., & Gleitman, H. (1977). "Mother, I'd rather do it myself:" Some effects and noneffects of motherese. In C. Ferguson & C. Snow (Eds.), *Talking to children.*

Newport, E., & Supalla, T. (1990). Maturational constraints on language learning. *The Journal of Cognitive Science, 14,* 11–28.

Newton, B. E. (1987). Etiology of bilateral sensorineural hearing loss in young children. *The Journal of Laryngology and Otology* (Suppl. 19), 1–21.

Papousek, H., & Papousek, M. (1979). Early ontogeny of human social interaction: Its biological roots and social dimensions. In M. VonCranach, K. Foppa, W. Lepenies, & P. Ploog (Eds.), *Human ethology: Claims and limits of a new discipline.* Cambridge: Cambridge University Press.

Petitto, L. A., & Marentette, P. F. (1991). Babbling in the manual mode: Evidence for the ontogeny of language. *Science, 251,* 492–1496.

Piaget, J. (1962). *Play, dreams and imitation in childhood.* New York: W. W. Norton.

Robinson, L. S. (1971). *Sound minds in a soundless world.* HUB PUB ADM 77-560. Washington, DC: U. S. Department of Health, Education and Welfare.

Rushmer, N. (1994). Supporting families of hearing impaired infants and toddlers. *Seminars in Hearing, 15* (2), 160–172.

Schein, J. D., Gentile, A., & Haase, K. W. (1970). *Development evaluation of an expanded hearing loss scale questionnaire.* Series 2, No. 37, Rockville, MD: National Center for Health Statistics, Vital and Health Statistics, U. S. Government Printing Office.

Schlesinger, H. S. (1987). Effects of powerlessness on dialogue and development: Disability, poverty, and the human condition. In B. W. Heller, L. M. Flohr, & L. S. Zegans (Eds.), *Psychosocial interventions with sensorially disabled persons.* (1–27). New York: Grune & Stratton.

Schlesinger, H. S., & Meadow, K. (1972). *Sound and sign.* Berkeley: University of California Press.

Shafii, M. (1973). Silence in the service of ego: Psychoanalytic study of mediation. *International Journal of Psychoanalysis, 54,* 431–443.

Steinberg, A. (1991). Issues in provding mental health services to hearing-impaired persons. *Hospital and Community Psychiatry, 42* (4), 380–389.

Steinberg, A., & Knightly, D. (In press). Hearing. In M. L. Batshaw, *Children with disabilities.* Baltimore: Paul H. Brookes Publishing.

Stern, D. N. (1985). *The interpersonal world of the infant.* New York: Basic Books.

Stika, C. J. (1989). *Empathy and its enhancement in hearing impaired children—A multidimensional affective education program.* Doctoral dissertation, Syracuse University, Syracuse, NY.

Vanderbosch, J. E. (1989). *Prevalence of mental disorders in a sample of hearing impaired psychiatric outpatients.* Doctoral dissertation, Illinois School of Professional Psychology, Chicago.

Vernon, M. (1967). Relationship of language to the thinking process. *Archives of General Psychiatry, 16,* 325–333.

Vernon, M. (1972). Language development: Relationship to cognition, affectivity and intelligence. *Canadian Psychologist, 13* (4), 360–374.

Vickrey Van Cleve, J., & Crouch, B. (1989). *A place of their own: Creating the deaf community in America.* Washington, DC: Gallaudet University Press.

Winefield, J. (1987). *Never the twain shall meet: The communication debate.* Washington, DC: Gallaudet University Press.

Wolff, A. B., & Brown, S. C. (1987). Demographics of meningitis-induced hearing impairment: Implications for immunization of children against hemophilus influenzae type B. *American Annals of the Deaf, 131,* 26–30.

Wolff, A. B., & Harkins, J. E. (1989). Multihandicapped students. In A. N. Schildroth & M. A. Karchmer. *Deaf Children in America* (55–81). San Diego: College-Hill Press.

Woodward, J. (1972). Implications for sociolinguistics research among the deaf. *Sign Language Studies, 1,* 1–7.

Woodward, J. (1982). *How you gonna get to heaven if you can't talk with Jesus: On depathologizing deafness.* Silver Spring, MD: T. J. Publishers.

35 / Hereditary Bleeding Disorders

Åke Mattsson and Charles W. Daeschner III

The two major groups of inherited blood disorders, the hemolytic anemias and the coagulation disorders, usually have their onset of symptoms in early childhood. An early onset carries a perspective of a chronic hemorrhagic disorder with frequent periods of unforeseen and lengthy medical crisis. The occurrence of AIDS and chronic hepatitis have added the dimension of early death for many families. The children's physical growth and personality development may become delayed by their repeated experience of somatic dysfunction and psychological stress factors. The supportive functioning of their families, crucial for the children's optimal adaptation, also may falter under the burden of a familial chronic illness (Graham & Turk, 1996; Mattsson & Kim, 1982; Shakin & Thompson, 1991).

The hemolytic anemias are discussed in Chapter 40. This chapter reviews the biological and psychosocial aspects of the three major hereditary coagulation disorders with onset in childhood (DiMichele, 1996; Werner, 1996): hemophilia A (also named classic hemophilia), caused by clotting factor VIII deficiency; hemophilia B (also named Christmas disease), caused by clotting factor IX deficiency; and von Willebrand disease (often referred to as vWD and known earlier as pseudohemophilia or vascular hemophilia), caused by abnormality of the von Willebrand factor, a plasma protein necessary both for normal platelet function and normal plasma transport of clotting factor VIII.

Biological Aspects

Factor VIII deficiency and factor IX deficiency share similar clinical manifestations, screening test abnormalities (prolonged coagulation time and normal bleeding time), and recessive X-linked inheritance patterns. Factor VIII deficiency has an incidence of 4:50,000 newborn males, whereas the incidence of factor IX deficiency is 1:50,000. At least 25,000 males with factor VIII and factor IX deficiency live in the United States. Due to their genetic and clinical similarities, this chapter discusses the two types together, for the most part, under the term "hemophilia."

Each one of the two forms of hemophilia is transmitted as a sex-linked recessive trait on an X chromosome by a usually asymptomatic female carrier to her recipient son. A carrier with a defective gene for the production of factor VIII or factor IX will bear sons with a 50% chance of being

hemophiliacs and daughters with a 50% chance of being carriers of defective factor VIII or IX genes. All sons of a hemophilic male will be unaffected while all his daughters will be carriers due to a defective hemophilia gene on one of their X chromosomes. Recombinant DNA technology has made it possible to isolate the hemophilia genes and has refined the methods for carrier detection and for prenatal diagnosis of hemophilia (Miller, 1989). Female carriers of the hemophilias generally have factor VIII or IX levels higher than 50% of normal. In female carriers for X-linked traits, the X chromosome in each cell is inactivated in a random manner. Thus, some carrier females may have 100% factor VIII while others may have sufficiently decreased levels to cause symptoms if stressed with physical trauma, surgery, or childbirth (Miller, 1989).

Recent reviews of hundreds of pedigrees of hemophiliacs show that at least 60 to 70% of affected males have a family history of hemophilia. Thus, a significant incidence of gene mutations contributes to new cases of hemophilia (about 30%).

Boys with severe hemophilia (levels of factors VIII or IX less than 1% of normal) tend to show the first episodes of bruising and hemorrhages into soft tissues and joints during infancy. Throughout their childhood, such episodes frequently recur, at times "spontaneously." Repeated bleeding into the large joints and the musculature causes considerable pain and swelling and periods of enforced immobilization. Energetic replacement therapy with clotting factor products at the first signs of bleeding has diminished the risk for degenerative joint disease resulting from recurrent hemarthrosis (Hilgartner & Pochedly, 1989; DiMichele, 1996). Intracranial, retropharyngeal, and retroperitoneal bleeding may be life-threatening and require vigorous replacement therapy. Patients with moderate hemophilia (factor levels 2 to 5% of normal) and with mild hemophilia (factor level above 5%) rarely bleed spontaneously. However, they tend to have excessive bleeding following trauma, surgery, or dental procedures, which can be prevented with the use of factor concentrates. Patients with mild factor VIII deficiency also may benefit from an injection or use of an intranasal spray of desmopressin (DDAVP), which transiently raises factor VIII levels by releasing stored factor. Since DDAVP is a synthetic protein, the risk of exposure to plasma-derived concentrates is reduced. The use of fibrinolytic inhibitors such as epsilon aminocaproic acid (EACA) also may decrease the need for factor concentrates.

Von Willebrand disease, by now recognized as the most common of the inherited hemorrhagic disorders (Werner, 1996), is named after the Finnish physician who in 1931 published his observations of a 7-year-old girl with a severe bleeding disorder and the results of his examination of 65 of her relatives (Smith, 1989). Many of them, males as well as females, showed mild forms of a hemorrhagic disease, which usually involved skin and mucous membranes (e.g., epistaxis, gum bleeding, heavy menses, postpartum hemorrhage, poor hemostasis after surgery and physical trauma). The patients also had a prolonged bleeding time, another contrast to classic hemophilia, whose genetic and clinical characteristics had been known for centuries. Von Willebrand named the newly recognized disorder hereditary pseudo-hemophilia.

Sixty years later, molecular biology and genetic techniques have clarified the inheritance pattern of von Willebrand disease, the nature of the gene defect, and the interaction between von Willebrand factor and factor VIII (Miller, 1989; Smith, 1989). Von Willebrand disease is an autosomal dominant bleeding disorder with variable penetrance. It is caused by any of a number of known defects of the gene that controls the production of von Willebrand factor and is carried on chromosome 12. This factor is a plasma protein necessary for normal platelet aggregation at the sites of vessel wall injury, initiating the formation of a hemostatic plug. In addition, it binds to and stabilizes the transport of factor VIII in plasma. This fact explains the earlier difficulty in distinguishing many situations of von Willebrand disease from hemophilia A—the coagulant activity of both von Willebrand factor and factor VIII are depressed but only the former gene is defective. Three types of von Willebrand disease are currently recognized, each type with several subtypes. Type I has a quantitative defect in von Willebrand factor. The Type II variant has qualitative defects in the factor's structure. Factor VIII levels may be normal or only mildly suppressed in this variant. Type III von Willebrand disease is associated with very low factor VIII and von Willebrand factor levels and is a rare, severe hemorrhagic disorder, with markedly prolonged bleeding time.

In its common clinical forms (60–70%), von Willebrand disease is a heterozygous disorder, transmitted by either parent to—theoretically—50% of their children of either sex. However, due to its reduced penetrance, the actual chance is estimated at 33% (Miller, 1989). The clinical manifestations of bleeding are mild to moderate, as described. Surgery and dental procedures often cause the first hemorrhages that require medical attention. Women are frequently symptomatic because of profuse menorrhagia.

Type III von Willebrand disease shows a clinical picture similar to that of severe hemophilia. The patients are often homozygous for the von Willebrand factor gene defect, frequently due to parental consanguinity. Von Willebrand's original patient, probably homozygous, died in her early adolescence due to uncontrollable menstrual flow (Smith, 1989).

The major characteristics of the disease are often mild and highly variable symptoms even in patients within the same family. This fact provides an explanation for its long underrecognition by patients, families, and professionals.

Recent epidemiological studies have estimated prevalence rates of von Willebrand disease of about 1%. This high frequency of defective genes in the population warrants genetic testing and counseling of prospective spouses of known patients with the disease in order to determine the risk of a couple bearing a child homozygous for the von Willebrand factor deficiency (Miller, 1989; Werner, 1996).

Treatment Aspects

Current coagulation laboratory tests and recombinant DNA techniques allow for prompt diagnosis of the various hemophilias (type A, type B, von Willebrand disease), including their severity. The advances in genetic testing have greatly improved the accuracy of carrier detection and prenatal diagnosis of these disorders. During genetic counseling of families with a clotting deficiency, the results of genetic testing often are used in providing objective, sensible information about the many reproductive choices available to individuals at risk for transmitting a bleeding disorder (Handford & Mayes, 1989; Miller, 1989).

The ongoing medical care of hemophiliacs (including those with von Willebrand disease) of all ages saw dramatic progress in the 1960s when the first plasma clotting factor concentrates were introduced (Hilgartner & Pochedly, 1989). It became possible to use various concentrates, from cryoprecipitate to specific factor concentrates such as factor VIII and factor IX, in high dosages for replacement infusion at the first signs of a hemorrhagic episode. Equally important, they could be given prophylactically immediately after a physical trauma and before a dental or surgical procedure. In the 1970s home care management of bleeding episodes and of their prevention gained wide acceptance for young children and adolescents with hemophilia. Their parents were instructed about when and how to administer factor replacement and had easy phone access to the local hemophilia care team. Home care programs proved highly successful: Fewer hospital admissions, quicker recovery after acute hemorrhages, fewer absences from school and work, less crippling joint involvement were all noted (Hernandez, Gray, & Lineberger, 1989). In addition, there were marked psychological benefits for most families who became active, informed participants in the ongoing care of the hemophiliac (Mattsson & Kim, 1982). The establishment of federally supported hemophilia diagnostic and treatment centers, initiated in 1975 and by now present in all but 3 states, made comprehensive care available to most of the nation's hemophiliacs. The multidisciplinary staff of these centers include the mental health professions; genetic counseling; educational, vocational, and financial counseling; physical therapy; and, of course, all essential medical specialists and nursing services (Handford & Mayes, 1989; Shakin & Thompson, 1991).

The treatment advances just outlined resulted in significant improvement in the quality of life of most hemophiliacs and their families. By the early 1980s, the prognosis for child and adolescent patients seemed bright in terms of a likely normal life span, less disability from chronic joint disease, and rapid, often self-monitored medical control of hemorrhagic episodes.

Then, in 1982, the bright future was eclipsed by reports of the first cases of AIDS among hemophiliacs in the United States. Within a few years it was estimated that about 85% of hemophilia patients regularly treated with clotting factor concentrates before 1985 were seropositive for HIV (Agle, Gluck, & Pierce, 1987; Eyster, 1989). (In most Western European countries, only 15% to 25% were infected due to healthier donors and safer factor concentrate manufacturing.) The stunned hemophilia population began to question the safety of all factor replacement products, which led to a period of decreased use of factor concentrates, jeopardizing prompt management of hemorrhages. Many families of hemophiliacs understandably lost trust in their health care teams, were faced with the risk of transmission of HIV, and became ostracized in some unenlightened communities (Agle, Gluck, & Pierce, 1987; Handford & Mayes, 1989; Markova, Wilkie, Naji, & Forbes, 1990; White & Cunningham, 1991). The public confused many hemophiliacs with the high-risk groups of gay men and intravenous drug users. The patients' overriding fear, however, was one of a drastically shortened life span with little realistic hope for survival. A detailed account of the multifaceted psychosocial problems of HIV-infection and AIDS in pediatric age groups is given in Chapter 25.

Since 1985, children in the United States with a bleeding disorder have been increasingly protected against contracting HIV-infection from clotting factor replacement. Thanks to closely screened and tested donors and the use of heat-treated and pasteurized plasma products, the risk of HIV and hepatitis transmission is greatly reduced (Eyster, 1989; Schimpf et al., 1989). Recombinant DNA-derived clotting factors for factor VIII patients are available for clinical use and further reduce the risk of viral contamination. With the successful cloning of factor VIII and factor IX genes prompt and safe gene-addition therapy will soon be available for hemophilias A and B. Thus, these disorders will be amenable to preventive measures which will minimize hemorrhagic episodes. (Non-A–non-B hepatitis has remained a problem. The recent introduction of effective screening for hepatitis C, the major cause of non-A–non-B hepatitis, will greatly reduce this risk (DiMichele, 1966).

Psychosocial Impact on Children and Families

Here we apply a family open systems model to show the interrelationships between a growing

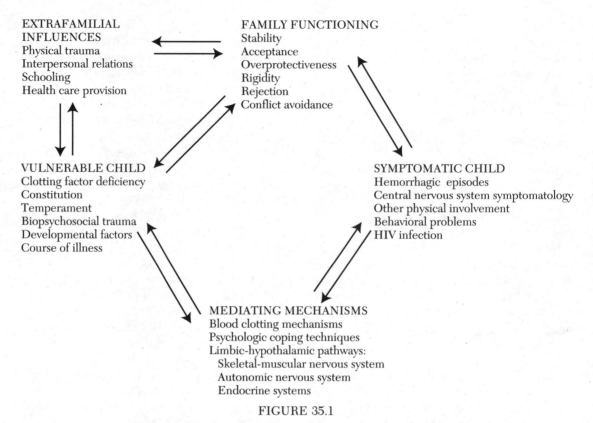

EXTRAFAMILIAL
INFLUENCES
Physical trauma
Interpersonal relations
Schooling
Health care provision

FAMILY FUNCTIONING
Stability
Acceptance
Overprotectiveness
Rigidity
Rejection
Conflict avoidance

VULNERABLE CHILD
Clotting factor deficiency
Constitution
Temperament
Biopsychosocial trauma
Developmental factors
Course of illness

SYMPTOMATIC CHILD
Hemorrhagic episodes
Central nervous system symptomatology
Other physical involvement
Behavioral problems
HIV infection

MEDIATING MECHANISMS
Blood clotting mechanisms
Psychologic coping techniques
Limbic-hypothalamic pathways:
    Skeletal-muscular nervous system
    Autonomic nervous system
    Endocrine systems

FIGURE 35.1

Open systems model of hemophilia in childhood and adolescence

child with a bleeding disorder, the family, and the health care team (Mattsson, 1984). This model also can provide the consultation-liaison psychiatrist with a useful biopsychosocial framework for clinical and research activities involving young hemophiliacs and their families (see Figure 35.1.)

The model shows how the genetically vulnerable child is influenced by and also influences the functioning of the family. The family interaction can be helpful or stressful to the child and undergoes many changes as the child grows—coping with hemophilia is a lifelong ordeal. Extrafamilial influences include physical trauma, peer relations, and schooling—the latter still reflects the public's reaction both to hemophilia and associated HIV infection. The ongoing provision of medical and psychosocial care is also a major influence on the growing hemophiliac (Handford & Mayes, 1989).

The vulnerable child responds to extrafamilial and intrafamilial influences by the activation of biological and psychophysiological mediating mechanisms (to be discussed later). As a result, the child may become "symptomatic" in the form

of an acute hemorrhagic crisis with pain and physical weakness, at times with central nervous system or joint involvement. "Symptomatic" also may denote secondary behavioral problems and symptoms related to HIV-AIDS. Whatever the symptoms, the hemophilic child and adolescent will interact differently with family and peers. Consequently, the functioning of his family is likely to change as its members strive to assist the ill child (Mattsson, 1984).

The open systems model illustrates how changes in any of its subsystems—the hemophiliac, the parents, the medical team—will reverberate within the total system. The model also calls attention to the unique biopsychosocial given of each family with a hemophilic member. It becomes important for clinicians to gain knowledge of the various components of the subsystems around the affected child—special vulnerabilities, family functioning, extrafamilial influences, the child's psychological coping techniques—and how medical crises cause psychosocial reverberations within the family.

VULNERABILITY FACTORS

In addition to the inherited clotting factor deficiency, the young hemophiliac (or von Willebrand patient) may show constitutional traits that shape personality development—high activity level, low anxiety threshold, marked shyness, or a cyclothymic disposition. Early psychosocial trauma or losses are known to impair any individual's ability to cope with a life-threatening illness. The developmental factors of hemophilic children include their cognitive abilities to comprehend the nature of the illness, the rationale of its management, and its long-term implications. In regard to the course of the illness, its complications may add to the patient's vulnerability; for instance, impaired intellectual functioning due to central nervous system involvement or chronic joint disease often interfere with normal physical activities, education, and peer relations.

MEDIATING MECHANISMS AND THE SYMPTOMATIC HEMOPHILIAC

The impact of physical and psychosocial stress factors on the vulnerable hemophiliac will engage various psychophysiologic mechanisms in mediating the responses to stresses as well as to any physical symptoms. First of all, the clotting factor deficiencies may lead to hemorrhaging. There is no conclusive evidence for psychophysiological influences on the plasma levels of factor VIII, factor IX, and von Willebrand factor (Mattsson, 1984). Nor do recent studies on large groups of hemophiliacs report a clear association between frequency of bleeding episodes and certain psychosocial variables such as personality profiles, major life events, and daily living stress (Cochran, Ahles, & Weiss, 1987).

Reports by some dentists, hematologists, and psychiatrists give empirical evidence that training in self-relaxation or application of mild trance may reduce the amount of bleeding during dental work as well as the number of bleeding episodes in certain hemophiliacs used as their own controls (Handford & Mayes, 1989; Lucas, 1975). These observations would be an example of how psychological mechanisms operating within the hemophiliac's "mind" or central nervous system, via limbic-hypothalamic pathways and the autonomic nervous system, might influence the peripheral vascular bed via neurohumoral agents. The end result would be diminished extravasation through capillary bleeding (Mattsson, 1984). The autonomic nervous system and the vascular bed also may relate to the so-called spontaneous or psychophysiological hemorrhagic episodes. Many hematologists, parents of hemophiliacs, and patients themselves describe how certain states of emotional arousal, positive or negative, seem associated with an increased bleeding tendency without clear evidence of physical trauma (Agle, 1984; Mattsson & Gross, 1966). One speculative explanation would be that emotional arousal, via the autonomic nervous system, may lead to increased vascular permeability. This mechanism would be similar to the one proposed in causing the bruising and ecchymoses in patients with psychogenic purpura and in individuals showing religious stigmata (Agle, 1984; Mattsson & Agle, 1979).

Recent studies on healthy subjects have documented that physical activities, acute mental stress associated with cognitive problem solving, and adrenaline infusion cause an activation of plasma coagulation factors, platelet aggregation, and fibrinolysis (Jern, Wadenvik, Mark, Hallgren, & Jern, 1989). It is unlikely that these findings have clinical relevance for severe hemophiliacs and von Willebrand patients due to their low clotting factor levels.

PSYCHOLOGICAL STRESS FACTORS AND COPING BEHAVIORS: A DEVELOPMENTAL REVIEW

Many emotional stress factors repeatedly impinge on children with hemophilia and severe von Willebrand disease. Bleeding, pain, immobilization, and absence from normal school and leisure activities are common occurrences. A developmental approach is necessary to delineate the expected coping behaviors of hemophiliacs as they age. Positive, adaptive coping behaviors assist the patients' mastery of their distress; these behaviors enable the patients to prevent their distress from interfering with their cognitive functioning, interpersonal relations, and cooperation with medical management. The salient coping behaviors are cognition including the use of psychological defenses, motor activity, and emotional expression.

Preschool Patients: In preschool children with hemophilia, the most common behavioral response to pain, malaise, and fears is one in which their emotional arousal induces physical activity involving the neuromuscular-skeletal and the autonomic nervous systems. (See Figure 35.1.) Irritability, crying, fighting, and resisting medical interventions are often noted. Such responses are seen mainly among preschoolers not yet able to comprehend the cause-and-effect relationship of their symptoms, the reasons for injections and other painful procedures and for separations from home and parents. The egocentric, preoperational style of thinking, characteristic of this age group, seems to place these children at "the center of the universe" (Elkind, 1974). They often see themselves as responsible for unpleasant, painful events such as an illness. There are no impartial, natural reasons for a hemorrhage, swollen joint, or a concentrate infusion even when given by the parents at home. Consistent empathetic reassurance and handling by parents and medical staff is essential to the prevention of psychological trauma for children at this stage of development. Child life programs in inpatient and outpatient settings can provide these patients with structured outlets for dysphoric affects and stressful experiences, allowing for mastery through therapeutic play.

School-age Patients: By age 5 to 7, children begin to make great strides in their cognitive reasoning abilities. They have entered the stage of concrete operational thinking, which implies improved mastery of words and concrete concepts. Able to think about representations of objects and events, they can link episodes of their illness and its treatment in a cause-and-effect manner. Furthermore, children of this age can conceptualize time and comprehend the principle of conservation of reversible quantities such as size, weight, and volume. This new ability makes explanations by staff and parents of procedures—for instance, about the way plasma infusion increases the concentration of clotting factors in the blood—more comprehensible. Hemophiliacs of school age also can operationally recall many of their previous bleeding crises and their treatment. They become able to report the early signs of trauma or hemorrhage and begin to be cautious in physical activities. Finally, they also are ready to assist in medical procedures, such as home therapy.

Repeated explanations, using pictures and timetables related to causes and treatment of the bleeding disorder, begin to pay off for school-age hemophiliacs. The parents and the health team reinforce their work with these patients by using similar phrases, illustrations, and realistic reassurances. At times of acute bleeding and other painful events, even well-adapted school-age children may show regressive, angry, and despondent behavior. The family and the medical staff should expect this release of natural distress and the children should be allowed to verbalize and share their anguish.

School-age children increasingly use more adult types of psychological defense mechanisms that will support adaptation to a chronic illness when they are not overutilized. Among hemophiliacs, the mechanism of denial of future painful crises and setbacks is ubiquitous. When overused, denial may result in poor reality testing, careless behaviors, and lack of cooperation with medical management. Other common defense mechanisms are isolation of feelings, intellectualization about their illness (also referred to as "control through thinking"), rationalization, and identification with other hemophiliacs and with various health professionals.

One major coping technique of most well-adapted young hemophiliacs is their use of medically safe physical activities. These are of great importance to strengthen muscles and increase joint stability. In addition, participation in exercise, sports, and play benefits these children's confidence and self-image. The cognitive strides of this age group make it possible for them to understand the risks involved in many body contact sports and why activities such as baseball, swimming, sailing, tennis, and hiking are preferred.

Adolescent Patients: Most hemophilic patients who reach adolescence have achieved a satisfactory mastery of their illness. The common emotional lability of adolescence is unlikely to interfere with medical compliance and reliable self-care. Yet for a small group of teenagers, the management of their illness will suffer due to their overall poor coping with the tasks of puberty and adolescence. Their parents usually feel at a loss to provide consistent yet flexible guidance. The dysfunction of families with a teen-age hemophiliac often reflects a lack of knowledge of the normal adolescent tasks. Health professionals attending to the hemophiliac must explain these tasks, which include: adjustment to the biological changes with the rise in sexual and assertive drives; achievement of psychosocial independence and a sense of one's own individuality and identity; loosening of the childhood ties to the family, which often leads to states of aloneness and feeling like a stranger at home; and coping with the common states of self-preoccupation and unpredictable mood swings. The burden of a chronic disorder adds to the reasons for an adolescent's shaky self-image and depressive mood. The possibility of repeated hemorrhages and physical disability looms repulsive at an age when issues of immortality, physical strength and attractiveness, and creative planning for the future are common themes. At times, adolescent hemophiliacs attempt to suppress feelings of low self-esteem and despondency by engaging in rebellious, daring acts and in alcohol or drug abuse (Agle, 1984).

The intensity of these distressing emotional states among some adolescents is due partly to their state of cognitive development. Most teenagers gain the ability to conduct formal, abstract operational thinking. This gain usually assists them in adaptive coping with a chronic disorder. At times, however, it contributes to poor adaptation. The ability to "think about one's thoughts," to be introspective, to form theoretical propositions in a hypothetical-deductive manner, is responsible for the normal state of adolescent egocentrism (Elkind, 1974). When overused, this ability can turn adolescents' attention to their body and cognition in a pathological manner. Young hemophiliacs may become overly sensitive and self-conscious, at times appear "paranoid," and experience marked self-doubts and despondency. The concept of "the personal fable" among adolescents derives from their egocentrism and exaggerated belief in their uniqueness (Elkind, 1974). For instance, a hemophiliac may think he cannot get hurt even when engaging in dangerous daredevillike activities because he is "special," invulnerable, unlike other hemophiliacs. He often challenges established treatment routines and the hemophilia team members. The team and the parents should be prepared to anticipate these likely expressions of adolescent uniqueness and egocentrism so they are ready to discuss treatment modifications and compromises with the adolescent hemophiliac.

STRESSES ON THE FAMILY AND FAMILY ADAPTATION

The open systems model of hemophilia in childhood and adolescence emphasizes the role of the family in supporting optimal psychosocial adaptation of the growing hemophiliac. A family with the hemophilia trait faces an especially stressful period when informed that one of its members—usually a young boy—suffers from an inherited bleeding disorder. In addition to initial shock, disbelief, fears, sadness, and anger, the genetic nature of the illness often causes special concerns in the mother and sisters of the hemophiliac. The mother always struggles with some self-accusatory feelings, as she is the carrier of the defective gene. Eventually the daughters of the family will realize that they also may be carriers and then have to face the issue of reproductive choices as they become young adults. All family members experience a sense of helplessness before they begin to accept that it is possible to raise a "severe" hemophiliac to become an independent, productive citizen.

In terms of initial maladaptive family reactions, the most common one shows overprotective, at times martyrlike attendance to the young hemophiliac. This behavior may lead to social isolation of parents and older siblings. Financial stress on the family is caused by the demanding management of hemophilia and the need for the parents to provide home care of their child. The unforeseeable, episodiclike nature of hemophilia constitutes another ongoing stress factor.

The optimal family functioning around the child with hemophilia provides the patient with a safe and stable environment that will encourage an ongoing discussion about the illness, its management, and the uncertain future. All family members will benefit from information about the emotional and cognitive aspects of the developmental stages of childhood and adolescence.

Dysfunctional families of hemophilic children and adolescents are unable fully to assist the patients' optimal psychosocial development. One major dysfunctional family type is characterized by overprotectiveness and enmeshment, where everyone is overinvolved with one another. Such a family tends to discourage the hemophiliac's striving for autonomy, competence, and responsibility for his own care. A second common type of family dysfunctioning is one of rigidity, where change and personality growth are difficult to accept. For example, new treatment approaches and new health care providers are unduly questioned. A rigid family system is slow to recognize the adolescent's increased need for independence, decision making, and choosing of friends and activities. There is a danger that such inflexible family attitudes will precipitate rebellious and risk-taking behaviors in the hemophilic teenager.

A third dysfunctional family type is characterized by overtly rejecting and negligent parents. These parents may have turned their backs on an ill child because of intellectual limitations or serious psychopathology. Another reason for rejecting attitudes stems from some parents' long-standing inability to master their feelings of anger, fear, and guilt related to their fate of having to raise a "defective" child. The past histories of such parents often show that they grew up with a disabled sibling or that they lost a child or a sibling due to a serious illness (Mattsson & Gross, 1966).

A final, common group of dysfunctioning families are characterized by long-standing marital conflicts or conflicts between parents and children where the hemophilic child serves as a "conflict avoidance tool" or scapegoat. Long-standing family problems have become "hidden" behind the child with a serious illness. A common example of this family constellation is the dyad of a concerned mother and her hemophilic son being allied in a firm coalition against the father. The excluded father then often withdraws and serves as a poor role model for his son, who, in turn, later on may rebel against and leave the overly involved mother.

improved sense of well-being (Hernandez, et al., 1989; Rosendaal et al., 1990; Shakin & Thompson, 1991).

Long-term assessments of school-age and adolescent patients with hemophilia and of healthy controls utilizing standardized parent, teacher, and patient questionnaires report no higher occurrence of psychological disturbances among the hemophiliacs despite the evidence of HIV infection among some of them (Kvist, Kvist & Rajantie, 1990; Logan et al., 1990; Rosendaal et al., 1990). It should be noted that these hemophilic populations were receiving ongoing comprehensive care.

In this country, Handford and associates have conducted several studies on hemophilic boys up to age 19, assessed with personality inventories, and compared them to norms for healthy male age mates (Handford & Mayes, 1989). The hemophiliacs were rated as more intelligent, stable, and secure. Boys with severe hemophilia seemed more self-controlled, serious, and submissive compared to those with mild to moderate hemophilias.

A longitudinal study by Handford's group reported significant relationships between parental acceptance and evidence of emotional stability, security, and intelligence in their hemophilic sons (Mayes, Handford, Kowalski & Schaefer, 1988).

Thus, it appears that hemophilia, like any other chronic disorder, does not necessarily lead to serious psychological problems among patients. Significant psychosocial maladaptation often is related to crippling physical handicaps, including central nervous system involvement. In addition, the interference of family dysfunction will jeopardize the hemophiliac's normal personality development. Most studies of the psychosocial adaptation among patients with bleeding disorders have included biased samples—the patients have been enrolled in comprehensive treatment programs.

Outcome Studies

The past decade has seen a number of longitudinal studies regarding the medical course of young hemophiliacs and their psychosocial and vocational adaptation. Several authors confirm the increased longevity of hemophiliacs, their decreased school and work absences, less use of inpatient and outpatient hospital facilities, and an overall

Comprehensive Care Role
of the Psychiatrist

Most hematology teams that provide comprehensive care of children and adolescents with bleeding disorders include a part-time psychiatrist in addition to the essential services of social workers, psychologists, and educational and vocational specialists (Handford & Mayes, 1989). The role of the consulting psychiatrist should be twofold—educational and therapeutic—with the overall goal of assisting hemophiliacs, their families, and the health care team in maintaining mastery of the many stressful situations associated with the chronic disorder. As an educator, the psychiatrist may use an open systems model to show the medical staff and the parents the characteristics of a hemophilic patient in the areas of physical and psychosocial vulnerabilities, family strengths and weaknesses, and coping techniques of the patient and family members. It is also helpful to explain the stage of the patient's cognitive development. The attainment of adaptive coping behaviors depends on the maturation of cognitive, emotional, and physical attributes.

The consulting psychiatrist is also asked to serve as a therapist, providing individual or family therapy in those circumstances where prolonged psychosocial maladaptation interferes with medical compliance, personality development, or both. This chapter has emphasized the often fruitful role of family therapy in regard to maladaptive family functioning around the young hemophiliac (Handford & Mayes, 1989; Mattsson, 1984; Shakin & Thompson, 1991). A common aim of family therapy is to remove the hemophiliac as the major symptom bearer of the family, decreasing his centrality and power to manipulate the family. Group therapy with parents of hemophiliacs has proven useful in terms of education and a forum for parents to share common practical and emotional concerns. In many instances these parents can later serve as lay counselors of inexperienced families with young hemophiliacs (Mattsson & Agle, 1972).

Behavioral approaches to pain control, relaxation, positive imagery, and self-induced trance are usually in the purview of the hemophilia team's psychologist. Such techniques increase the patient's sense of being able to control many manifestations of their disorder.

The psychiatrist is often asked to evaluate the possibility of central nervous system dysfunction due to evidence of intracranial hemorrhages or complications of AIDS. Such evaluations usually require neuropsychological assessment and electroencephalogram and brain imaging studies (Shakin & Thompson, 1991).

Mood disorders of a depressive nature are not uncommon among young hemophiliacs. In reactive types of depression—an adjustment disorder with depressed mood—individual psychotherapy that may include cognitive techniques usually alleviates the symptoms in a short period of time. The psychiatrist may want to facilitate recovery by the use of a tricyclic-type antidepressant. (Monoamine oxidase inhibitors should be avoided due to their potential risk of causing hypertensive crises.) When a young hemophiliac is severely depressed, a trial period of an antidepressant drug usually is called for. Such medication, however, is no substitute for individual and family psychotherapeutic interventions. It is well known that adolescents are less responsive to antidepressant medication than other age groups.

Narcotic analgesics and benzodiazepines are rarely prescribed to young hemophiliacs. Current factor replacement techniques usually yield rapid control of acute hemorrhagic episodes. It is important to avert any risk for drug dependence among hemophiliacs.

The special problems related to hemophiliacs with an HIV infection and signs of AIDS are discussed in Chapter 25. The current AIDS epidemic has drastically added to the biopsychosocial problems of young hemophiliacs and their families. The hemophilia treatment centers and the National Hemophilia Foundation have responded to the HIV-related needs for psychosocial services in an energetic manner (National Hemophilia Foundation, 1992).

As noted earlier, the HIV plague affecting patients with bleeding disorders is leveling off. The long-term prognosis for hemophiliacs diagnosed after 1985 is good.

REFERENCES

Agle, D. (1984). Hemophilia—psychological factors and comprehensive management. *Scandinavian Journal of Haematology, 33* (Suppl. 40), 55–63.

Agle, D., Gluck, H., & Pierce, G. F. (1987). The risk of AIDS: Psychologic impact on the hemophilic population. *General Hospital Psychiatry, 9,* 11–17.

Cochran, C. D., Ahles, T. A., & Weiss, A. E. (1987). Psychological factors and bleeding frequency in hemophilia. Lack of association. *American Journal of Pediatric Hematology/Oncology, 9,* 136–139.

DiMichele, D. (1996). Hemophilia 1996. New approach to an old disease. *Pediatric Clinics of North America, 43,* 709–736.

Elkind, D. (1974). *Children and adolescents: Interpretive essays on Jean Piaget* (2nd ed.). New York: Oxford University Press.

Eyster, M. A. (1989). Natural history and transmission of hemophilia-associated human immunodeficiency virus (HIV) infections. In M. Hilgartner and C. Pochedly (Eds.), *Hemophilia in the child and adult* (3rd ed., pp. 263–274). New York: Raven Press.

Graham, P. J., and Turk, J. (1996). Psychiatric aspects of pediatric disorders. In M. Lewis (Ed.), *Child and Adolescent Psychiatry. A comprehensive textbook* (2nd ed.), pp. 989–1005.

Handford, H. A., & Mayes, S. D. (1989). The basis of psychosocial programs in hemophilia. In M. Hilgartner & C. Pochedly (Eds.), *Hemophilia in the child and adult* (3rd ed., pp. 195–212). New York: Raven Press.

Hernandez, J., Gray, D., & Lineberger, H. P. (1989). Social and economic indicators of well-being among hemophiliacs over a 5-year period. *General Hospital Psychiatry, 11,* 241–247.

Hilgartner, M. W., & Pochedly, C. (1989). *Hemophilia in the child and adult* (3rd ed.). New York: Raven Press.

Jern, C., Wadenvik, H., Mark, H., Hallgren, J., & Jern, S. (1989). Haematological changes during acute mental stress. *British Journal of Haematology, 71,* 153–156.

Kvist, B., Kvist, M., & Rajantie, J. (1990). School absences, school achievements and personality traits of the haemophilic child. *Scandinavian Journal of Social Medicine, 18,* 125–132.

Logan, F. A., Maclean, A., Howie, C. A., Gibson, B., Hann, I. M., & Parry-Jones, W. L. (1990). Psychological disturbance in children with haemophilia. *British Medical Journal, 301,* 1253–1256..

Lucas, O. N. (1975). The use of hypnosis in hemophilia dental care. *Annals of the New York Academy of Sciences, 240,* 263–266.

Markova, I., Wilkie, P. A., Naji, S. A., & Forbes, C. D. (1990). Self- and other-awareness of the risk of HIV/AIDS in people with haemophilia and implications for behavioral change. *Social Science and Medicine, 31,* 73–79.

Mattsson, A. (1984). Hemophilia and the family: Lifelong challenges and adaptation. *Scandinavian Journal of Haematology, 33* (Suppl. 40), 65–74.

Mattsson, A., & Agle, D. (1972). Group therapy with parents of hemophiliacs: therapeutic process and observations on parental adaptation to chronic illness in children. *Journal of the American Academy of Child Psychiatry, 11,* 558–571.

Mattsson, A., & Agle, D. (1979). Psychophysiologic aspects of adolescence: Hemic disorders. *Adolescent Psychiatry, 7,* 269–280.

Mattsson, A., & Gross, S. (1966). Social and behavioral studies on hemophilic children and their families. *Journal of Pediatrics, 68,* 952–964.

Mattsson, A., & Kim, S. P. (1982). Blood disorders. *Psychiatric Clinics of North America, 5,* 345–356.

Mayes, S. D., Handford, H. A., Kowalski, C., & Schaefer, J. H. (1988). Parent attitudes and child personality traits in hemophilia: A six-year longitudinal study. *International Journal of Psychiatry in Medicine, 18,* 339–355.

Miller, C. H. (1989). Genetics of hemophilia and von Willebrand's disease. In M. Hilgartner and C. Pochedly (Eds.), *Hemophilia in the child and adult* (3rd ed., pp. 297–345). New York: Raven Press.

National Hemophilia Foundation. (1992, April). *Index of AIDS updates.* New York: National Hemophilia Foundation.

Rosendaal, F. R., Smit, C., Varekamp, I., Bröcker-Vriends, A., Van Dijck, H., Suurmeijer, T. P., et al. (1990). Modern hemophilia treatment: Medical improvements and quality of life. *Journal of Internal Medicine, 228,* 633–640.

Schimpf, K., Brackmann, H., Kreuz, W., Kraus, B., Haschke, F., Schramm, W., et al. (1989). Absence of anti-human immunodeficiency virus types 1 and 2 seroconversion after the treatment of hemophilia A or von Willebrand's disease with pasteurized factor VIII concentrate. *New England Journal of Medicine, 321,* 1148–1152.

Shakin, E. J., & Thompson, T. L. (1991). Psychiatric aspects of hematologic disorders. In A. Stoudemire & B. Fogel (Eds.), *Medical psychiatric practice* (pp. 193–242). Washington, DC: American Psychiatric Press.

Smith, P. S. (1989). Von Willebrand's disease: Pathophysiology, diagnosis, and treatment. In M. Hilgartner & C. Pochedly (Eds.), *Hemophilia in the child and adult* (3rd ed., pp. 275–295). New York: Raven Press.

Werner, E. J. (1996). von Willebrand disease in children and adolescents. *Pediatric Clinics of North America, 43,* 683–707.

White, R., & Cunningham, A.-M. (1991). *Ryan White. My own story.* New York: Dial Books.

36 / Borderline Intellectual Functioning and Mild Mental Retardation

Anne S. Walters, Carl B. Feinstein, and Rowland P. Barrett

This chapter presents an overview of children and adolescents with borderline and mild retardation, including a brief summary of the developmental and psychosocial challenges facing these youngsters. Children and adolescents with borderline or mild mental retardation are not categorically different from their nonretarded peers. In the sense that intellectual abilities are a major underpinning of adaptive strength and that a certain level of cognitive skills is required to succeed at certain activities, particularly those stressed by the educational process, youngsters with borderline or mild retardation are significantly disadvantaged. The potential range of developmental outcomes for the developing child and family coping with this disadvantage is quite wide, however, depending on a complex array of familial and sociologic variables, and personal attributes.

Intelligence is a complex entity that may be impaired in a variety of ways. Numerous possible cognitive profiles, combining deficits and relative strengths in attention, memory, linguistic, spatial, motoric, and other skills, may result in an overall intellectual impairment that meets criteria for borderline or mild mental retardation. What may superficially appear as a straightforward diagnosis of retardation may describe only poorly the particular strengths and weaknesses of a given individual. Other aspects of the child's endowment, such as gender, temperament, appearance, and the presence or absence of other disabilities, interact during development with family attributes and responses, sociological status, cultural values, social stereotypes, and a wide variety of social and educational services. Many psychosocial outcomes are possible, although the psychiatric risk for children with borderline or mild mental retardation is far higher than that for the child with normal intelligence (Koller, Richardson, Katz, & McLaren, 1982; Rutter, Tizard, & Whitmore, 1970).

Dr. Feinstein's work was supported by Child and Adolescent Mental Health Academic Award 1K07MH00766 from the National Institute of Mental Health.

Diagnosis of Mental Retardation

PROBLEMS IN THE DEFINITION OF BORDERLINE INTELLECTUAL FUNCTIONING AND MILD MENTAL RETARDATION

Changes in the definition of mental retardation during the past 50 years have served to emphasize the relative rather than categorical nature of this impairment. In 1959, the Heber Committee of the American Association of Mental Deficiency set the upper limit of mental retardation at one standard deviation below the mean, thus including 16% of the population within the range of mental retardation (Edgerton, 1988). In 1973, the boundaries were shifted to include only those with IQ scores 2 standard deviations below the mean. This change in criteria of 15 points in IQ reclassified almost 26 million relatively low IQ individuals as nonretarded (Edgerton, 1988). In 1983, the Grossman committee recommended that clinical judgment be employed in diagnosing mental retardation in individuals whose IQ falls within a few points of the IQ cut-off (Grossman, 1983). Thus, in 14 years, an individual with an IQ of 71 would have been included, excluded, and possibly included again among those labeled as mildly mentally retarded. These shifts highlight the fact that decisions about who is retarded are often administrative and/or fiscal rather than in accordance with an absolute standard.

Further complicating matters is the uncertainty regarding how much more impaired an individual with an IQ of 65 is than someone with an IQ of 70. Edgerton (1988) has noted that, in the mild and borderline ranges of mental retardation, IQ is a poor prognostic variable in the absence of other factors that might more reliably predict adjustment and comments: "we must also realize that the prevalence of mild mental retardation can and does vary as a function of social circumstances and cultural beliefs, and it is to these social circumstances and beliefs that we must look if we also wish to prevent or reverse the prevalence rate of mental retardation" (p. 340). In summary, although diagnosing the milder ranges of mental retardation may appear to involve simple application of an absolute standard, it is in fact a vexingly murky endeavor. This is unfortunate, since the impairments directly related to low IQs, the effects of labeling, and the cut-offs for special service provisions that flow from the diagnosis of mental retardation all have profound effects on the lives of individuals on whom one label or another is applied or not applied.

CURRENT DIAGNOSTIC CRITERIA FOR BORDERLINE INTELLECTUAL FUNCTIONING AND MILD MENTAL RETARDATION

Current criteria for mental retardation emphasize both standardized IQ scores and assessment of adaptive behavior, as defined by the American Association of Mental Deficiency: "Mental retardation refers to significantly subaverage general intellectual functioning resulting in or associated with concurrent impairments in adaptive behavior and manifested during the developmental period" (Grossman, 1983, p. 11).

"Subaverage" intellectual functioning is defined as scores less than 70 (2 standard deviations below the mean) on a standardized test of intellectual functioning. Standardized intelligence tests refer to assessment instruments that measure general cognitive ability in an individual and compare their results with those of other individuals of the same age. Examples are the Wechsler scales (the revised Wechsler Intelligence Scale for Children and the revised Wechsler Adult Intelligence Scale) and the Stanford Binet Intelligence Test, Fourth Edition, but the choice of instrument depends on such factors as age and cultural background for all children and physical or sensory impairments for some.

The determination of adaptive behavior deficits required for diagnosis has proven to be a complex and often unreliable process (Sattler, 1988). The inclusion of adaptive behavior deficits in the diagnostic criteria expands the definition of mental retardation beyond IQ to reflect the more pervasive impairment in functioning considered to be a defining characteristic of persons who truly have mental retardation. The purpose of considering adaptive behavior is to ensure that children are not classified as mentally retarded by an IQ test

alone, when poor test scores might result from school maladjustment, lack of educational opportunity, or cultural deprivation. Such factors could well reduce a child's performance on intelligence tests while leaving intact his or her ability to function adaptively in the developmentally appropriate psychosocial domains (home, neighborhood, school, peer group, etc.).

The critical behaviors that form the basis of evaluating adaptational competence vary with the age of the individual. For example, personal responsibility and/or vocational skills are important areas to assess in a young adult, academic skills and peer relationships are key areas for the school-age child, and communication and social responsiveness are critical for the preschooler. The use of a new generation of standardized scales such as the Vineland Adaptive Behavior Scales (Sparrow, Balla, & Cicchetti, 1984) has enhanced our ability to assess adaptive behavior reliably. The Vineland assesses currently performed adaptive behaviors in the domains of communication, socialization, daily living, and motor skills.

Classification of *level* of mental retardation is generally based solely on IQ score, except in cases where the score is close to the cusp and adaptive behavior is discrepant with the IQ estimate. Specifically, individuals are classified as borderline intellectual functioning with a Full Scale IQ score between 70 and 79 on the Wechsler Scales or a composite score between 68 and 78 on the fourth edition of the Stanford Binet. Individuals are classified as mildly mentally retarded with scores between 55 and 69 on the Wechsler Scales and between 52 and 67 on the Stanford Binet. For both of these levels of cognitive functioning, adaptive behavior must be commensurate with or lower than expected for IQ. In instances where IQ scores and adaptive behavior scores are widely discrepant, both must be reported and clinical judgment employed in characterizing level of retardation.

Epidemiology

Approximately 7.4% of individuals assessed with standardized intelligence tests score in the borderline and mildly retarded ranges. The overall prevalence rate for mental retardation utilizing standardized IQ scores alone would be approximately

3% of the population. However, this appears to be an overestimate of actual affected individuals. When adaptive behavior is also used as a criteria, the number is likely to be reduced to closer to 1% or even lower (Baroff, 1986). This projected prevalence rate of 1% has recently received strong empirical support from a population-based federal survey of the Metropolitan Atlanta area, utilizing a multiple source method (Yeargin-Allsopp, Murphy, Oakley, & Sikes, 1992). Of this 1% of the population who meet full criteria for mental retardation (currently corresponding to 2.5 million individuals in the United States), 89% fall into the mildly retarded range (Sattler, 1988). An additional 6% fall into the borderline range. Thus, the vast majority of individuals with retardation fall into the borderline or mild range of deficiency.

Higher rates of mental retardation have been reported in school-age boys than girls at the upper end of the range of mental retardation, particularly in the borderline range. These ratios range from 1.94:1 to 4.18:1 (Richardson, Koller, & Katz, 1986). For all levels of retardation, the ratio of males to females is probably close to 1.6 to 1 (Rowitz, 1991). Some researchers maintain that this difference varies with age, peaking in the 15- to 19-year-old group (Kiely, 1987), and may be due to such diverse factors as overidentification in males or overrepresentation of biological causes (X-linked disorders) of mental retardation in males.

The prevalence of mental retardation is thought to increase with age until early adulthood, at which point there is a decrease. The higher prevalence rate in children stems from the fact that failure to achieve academically at the expected level triggers the process of assessment and diagnosis during the school years. Stated otherwise, school places adaptive demands on children with mental retardation, which leads to diagnosis. Adjustment to work, community, and social expectations (the adaptive demands of adulthood) is more easily achieved by adults with borderline or mild retardation.

Etiology

MODES OF TRANSMISSION

Most borderline and mild retardation is idiopathic or multifactorial in etiology (Rowitz, 1991).

In contrast, known genetic disorders account for approximately half of individuals with IQs under 50 (Abuelo, 1991) and consist of three types: chromosomal, single gene, and multifactorial. Since single-gene and chromosomal anomalies tend to produce children with more severe levels of retardation, they will be discussed in detail in Chapter 37. Only 4.3 to 7.8% of individuals with mild retardation have known chromosomal anomalies. Single-gene defects are also relatively uncommon in this group.

Multifactorial transmission refers to a combination of genetic, social, and environmental factors. According to McLaren and Bryson (1987), 11.0 to 23.4% of cases of mild mental retardation are due to multifactorial prenatal causes, 14.7% are associated with histories of abuse and/or neglect, and 18.6% are associated with perinatal hypoxia. Furthermore, although more severe retardation is evenly distributed across socioeconomic classes, mild mental retardation occurs far more commonly in lower social class groups. Kiely (1987) quotes the results of a study in Scotland suggesting that environments of children with mild retardation were associated with "overcrowding, endemic disease, high birth rate, and symptoms of social disorganization" (p. 209). Zigler, Balla, and Hodapp (1984) discuss the notion of two peaks in the distribution of IQ for the retarded population, one corresponding to multifactorially determined retardation and the other to chromosomal, genetic, or other clearly defined biologically based retardation. Estimates of the "reaction range"— that is, the variation in IQ due to environmental rather than genetic causes—suggest that benign or enriched environments have the potential to raise functioning from the mild range into the normal ranges of intellectual functioning (Zigler, Balla, & Hodapp, 1984).

Nature of Borderline and Mild Mental Retardation

Research on cognition among persons with mental retardation has focused on differences in cognitive processes between them and normally developing individuals. Brookes, McCauley, and Merrill (1988) note that knowledge appears to be organized in a similar fashion for both groups, suggesting some basic similarities in learning processes. Currently there appear to be three somewhat overlapping perspectives regarding the ways in which mentation is impaired in people with retardation: structuralist, process, and developmentalist (Hale & Borkowski, 1991). The structuralist perspective assumes that fixed and primary defects in memory and cognitive systems (including attention, memory, and problem solving) underlie deficits in learning ability (Ellis & Cavalier, 1982). The process theory emphasizes the role of inefficient overall cognitive or information-processing strategies and/or deficits in higher-level functions such as metamemory rather than specific deficits (Detterman, 1987). The developmentalist position holds that cognitive deficits in individuals with retardation are related to slower rates of development (rather than fixed deficits) and to a ceiling in overall capacity (Zigler, 1969).

Developmental Challenges

At various developmental psychosocial stages, commonly occurring themes and developmental challenges faced by children with retardation and their families can be identified. The response of family and child to these challenges has a major impact on how optimally and adaptively the child progresses as well as on the quality of family life.

INFANCY TO PRESCHOOL: THE EARLY DIAGNOSTIC CRISIS AND ATTACHMENT

The need for infants to develop secure, trusting relationships with others and also to be an object of attachment constitutes one challenge faced in this early period of life. The parents' natural responses of denial, disappointment, anxiety, anger, and grief when they first notice or confirm earlier predictions of developmental delay in their infant or child greatly stresses their relationship with that child. The process by which the parents acknowledge the reality of the developmental delays and search for a diagnosis and prognosis can, especially if they receive contradictory opinions by different specialists, undermine their morale, attack their self-esteem, create numerous frustrations, and compromise their emotional availability to their child. Furthermore, this parental grief response is likely to return at later developmental stages, as the child diverges from deeply held parental images and aspirations for their offspring (as a school-age child, teenager, young adult, etc.).

CASE EXAMPLE

Early Diagnosis: A young middle-class, college-educated couple brought their firstborn 21-month-old son for evaluation because of his failure to speak and his unresponsiveness to verbal communication. They felt panicked and embattled as they, along with friends and extended family, increasingly noticed lags in their child's development compared with expectations. In the evaluation, the boy presented as an active toddler with significant language delays and subdued social behavior. It was obviously difficult for his parents to recognize the fleeting social cues he presented during the family interview. Neither parent trusted their perception of him and both tended to react tensely or intrusively to him. Both mother and father were frightened and tearful at the possibility that their child might be below average or even retarded.

Diagnostic Follow-up: A working-class couple at a different point in the process of coming to grips with their son's development were seen for a reevaluation of their 5-year-old son, H. H presented with attentional deficits, language delays, and motor control difficulties. The parents had first brought him for evaluation when he was 3. They had found a good early intervention program, such that H had made substantial social and communicative gains. It had become clear, however, despite these excellent efforts, that H still lagged cognitively and behaviorally behind his peers. The mother now expressed much uncertainty about her ability to "discipline" H, fearing, on the one hand, that she was not firm enough, yet afraid, on the other, of losing her temper. She was clearly struggling with both impatience and grief regarding his disabilities. There was also much friction in the marriage as a result of differing expectations about H's abilities and the sharing of responsibility for his care. The father tended to deny that H had any problem, but clearly favored the boy's younger sibling.

SCHOOL-AGE CHILDREN: ENGAGING SUPPORT SERVICES AND COPING WITH DIFFERENCE AND STIGMATIZATION

For school-age children with mental retardation and their families, the transition to educational settings may bring to the fore discomfort, shame, or fear of stigmatization. The youngster of this age with mild retardation first begins to recognize that he or she is "different." Many parents have difficulty communicating with their child or his or her siblings about the disability. For many children with mild developmental disabilities, education involves a range of easily identifiable special education services, from resource assistance within a mainstream classroom to a combination of self-contained and mainstream classes. The child or his or her siblings may have questions about the special school bus, the different classroom, and/or other "special" arrangements. The directness and comfort with which parents can talk with the child about "differences," "special needs," "slow learning," and the like is critical if the child with retardation is to accept his or her limitations yet maintain self-esteem. Enormously complicating this process, however, is the near ubiquity in most communities of pejorative attitudes or discomfort with mental retardation. The child with mild retardation, yearning to be like other children, will almost certainly encounter painful episodes of name-calling, teasing, or rejection by peers or older children. Parents of older children with retardation may attempt to shield them from such experiences by keeping them at home. Doing so, however, promotes social withdrawal and interferes with the child's social learning and coping repertoire. Thus, the mental health professional must be prepared to work with child and family on the meaning of "mental retardation" and on means of coping and maintaining self-esteem in a problematic social climate.

CASE EXAMPLE

Coping with Differences: C was a 10-year-old girl with mild retardation who began to ask questions about her disabilities when she transferred from a totally self-contained classroom to partial mainstreaming. At home there was a regression to perseverative behavior, distractibility, and tantrums. She struggled a great deal with questions such as why she had attended a "special" school from age 3, her difficulty making friends, and why she attended a different school from her younger sister.

Stigmatization: A 10-year-old boy, G, with an IQ of 65, was referred due to "immaturity" and extreme social isolation in his mainstream classes at public school as well as in his neighborhood. On several occasions, he

had thrown rocks at a group of boys. When asked to identify three wishes, he said "a huge fort, lots of arrows to shoot at bad guys, and a giant noisemaker." The interview revealed that the giant noisemaker would drown out the boys when they called him names; the arrows were so that he could shoot them from far away; and the fort was a place he would be safe from attack. It gradually emerged from multiple sources that G had been rejected repeatedly by this group of boys, some of whom had been on his Little League baseball team. G had disrupted several of their games by behavior such as refusing to acknowledge that he had been called out while baserunning, leaving the game inappropriately, and batting out of turn. Some of his teammates blamed him for games that the team had lost. When G tried to crash neighborhood group activities, the boys had called him "retard" and "weirdo." G was preoccupied with getting back at the group and was vaguely aware that he felt badly about himself.

ADOLESCENCE: OVERCOMING OBSTACLES TO INDEPENDENT FUNCTIONING AND PEER RELATIONSHIPS

For adolescents with mental retardation, one of the more painfully negotiated developmental challenges is that of loosening the parental ties that have been a primary support at earlier ages while simultaneously developing rewarding peer relationships outside the family. By this age, teenagers with mild retardation are aware that they cannot keep up in many ways with peers or cognitively intact siblings and have experienced numerous painful social rejections. Many such teenagers cling with increasing despair to the hope of participating in milestone events, such as proms, driver's license, and class trips. For parents, it is a struggle to find spheres within which they can allow their child more independence and participation in age-appropriate social activities in the face of intense and often realistic worry about safety, exposure to ridicule/abuse, and/or harmful sexual contact.

CASE EXAMPLE

Social Isolation: K was a mildly retarded 16-year-old girl in a partially mainstreamed high school program, referred for separation anxiety and social withdrawal that had escalated to school refusal. Upon meeting with the family, it was clear that K's world had become narrow and sheltered subsequent to puberty as a result of her mother's concerns about her sexuality and safety, K's extreme self-consciousness about her appearance, daily struggles about what clothing to wear, and many worries shared by K and her parents about being teased by peers. Much of the therapeutic intervention with the family involved identifying extracurricular activities where K's relative aptitude for crafts would allow experiences of success and in overcoming parental reluctance to entering K in a regionally based weekend program for teenagers with mild retardation. K went on to develop close and sustaining friendships with peers in the regional club, including an appropriate boyfriend relationship.

Adolescent Independence: S, a 17-year-old boy with mild retardation who had a disfiguring orthopedic handicap, was referred for psychiatric care after threatening to harm his sister with a knife. It soon became clear that S was struggling with intense envy of his developmentally intact teenage sister's friends and activities. In addition, his relationship with his mother was problematic, as she was unable to stand up to his numerous coercive tantrums. Another major problem was that teasing and name-calling over the years had led to his view of himself as a "monster" and to the development of compensatory grandiose fantasies (being a surgeon, rock star, or a professional basketball player) complete with arrogant, off-putting social behavior. The multidisciplinary treatment program developed for S focused on his emotional acceptance of handicaps and the development of strategies to cope with the stigma of having both mental retardation and a physical handicap. Occupational therapy enabled him to accomplish critical personal self-care skills independently. Group therapy focused on fostering the use of peers for support and problem solving and confronted his self-destructive arrogant style. Family therapy ultimately enabled the mother to send her son to a very advantageous rehabilitative program away from home.

YOUNG ADULTHOOD: LEAVING THE FAMILY OF ORIGIN AND FUTURE PLANNING

For young adults, one of the primary challenges is moving from educational settings to work settings, and sometimes, from residence with the family to residential group homes or supported independent living. Finding appropriate programs and access to services can be difficult, time-consuming, and anxiety-provoking for all involved. In addition, this period may involve planning for financial and residential needs in anticipation of parental disability and/or death, with the goal of avoiding the long-range trauma of unplanned placement.

CASE EXAMPLE

Transition to Adulthood: R was a 22-year-old woman with mild retardation who had been living at home as part of a close-knit family. During adolescence, she became increasingly avoidant of school. Her parents, who were dissatisfied with her educational programming and pained by her poor self-esteem and experiences of failure, eventually supported her decision to leave school at 16. She remained at home without major problems until she was 21. At that time her older sister became engaged and subsequently married. This precipitated severe depression, a suicide attempt, and eventual hospitalization for R. The tasks for R and her family were to cope with the loss of a significant portion of her already diminished network (her sister), to help her deal emotionally with the realization that she might never get married, and to begin a process of realistic vocational appraisal aimed at helping her to develop meaningful activity and social contacts outside of the home. Although R responded well to treatment and was able to become involved in a sheltered employment setting, with the goal of eventual transition to community work, both parents continued to deny or reject the need to help R develop social relationships outside the family and the need for future planning for independent living.

Risk Factors for Psychiatric Disorders

The rate of psychiatric disorders in youngsters with retardation has been found repeatedly to be 4 to 6 times greater than that for cognitively normal peers (Koller et al., 1982; Matson & Barrett, 1982; Rutter et al., 1970). This is the case even when socioeconomically matched samples of youngsters with and without retardation are compared (Koller et al., 1982).

As the preceding case examples suggest, a wide variety of individual circumstances affect the risk status for psychiatric disorders in youngsters with borderline or mild retardation. Recent research findings, however, indicate a few especially high-risk factors within this population. Boys have somewhat higher rates of psychiatric disorder than girls. Boys with the highest IQs within the mild to borderline range have significantly higher rates of disorder than boys or girls in any other IQ grouping within the range of retardation. For girls, variation in IQ within this range is not significantly related to the rate of psychiatric disorder.

Adverse family backgrounds and low socioeconomic status increase the risk of psychiatric disorder for youngsters with borderline or mild retardation. When a cohort of such youngsters seen earlier in childhood was reevaluated at ages 16 to 22, it was found that psychiatric disorder was more likely to be present at this age if it had been previously diagnosed in childhood (Richardson, Koller, & Katz, 1985a). Among this cohort of youngsters, findings of psychiatric disorders both in childhood and at follow-up were strongly related to an adverse family environment. Interestingly, neurologic status (evidence of central nervous system disorder versus no abnormality) as measured by a systematic neurological examination was not correlated with psychopathology (Richardson, Koller, & Katz, 1985b), although 30% of the cohort did have positive findings by physical examination. A significant shortcoming of this research is that the cohort studied was predominantly of lower socioeconomic status. Since it is known that lower social class is itself associated with increased rates of mild and borderline mental retardation, the findings apply to a large proportion of youngsters with mental retardation. Available data concerning family adjustment to having a child with retardation suggests that middle- and upper-class families tend to experience greater stress in response to having a child with mild retardation than do lower-class families (Richardson et al., 1985b). However, this effect may be overshadowed by the much higher rate of mild retardation in the higher-risk socioeconomically lower portion of the population.

Common Pitfalls in the Recognition and Assessment of Psychiatric Disorder in Children and Adolescents with Retardation

While this chapter does not deal specifically with psychopathology in youngsters with borderline and/or mild retardation, since the rate of psychiatric disorders in this population is so high, it is critical that certain pitfalls in recognition, assessment, and treatment response be mentioned. First is a phenomena that has been termed diagnostic overshadowing (Reiss, Levitan, & Szyszko, 1982). This refers to a tendency to regard all abnormal behavior observed in persons with retardation as secondary to the mental retardation itself. Two serious problems result from this common tendency: failure to properly diagnose *DSM* Axis I disorder and inappropriate minimization of the complex subjective mental and affective life of the person with borderline or mild retardation.

Failure to recognize a psychiatric disorder that is essentially of the same type found in cognitively unimpaired children or adolescents denies appropriate treatment to youngsters with mild retardation. Failure to inquire about or respond to their youngster's subjective mental life leads to premature reliance on pharmacotherapeutic or more mechanistic behavioral approaches and neglects both the contribution of psychosocial precipitants to the problem and the possible usefulness of interpersonal psychotherapeutic treatments. A second common pitfall that can lead to improper diagnosis is that of assuming that all emotional or behavioral problems in youngsters with retardation stem directly from brain damage or dysfunction. While this may be the case at times, for the range of borderline and mild retardation, psychosocial factors commonly play an important role (Richardson, Koller, & Katz, 1985a). It is certainly the case that growing up with retardation is associated with a distinctive and painful array of psychosocial stressors and stigmatizations that, in and of themselves, increases the risk of psychiatric disorder (Feinstein & Levoy, 1991).

A third pitfall to note is the assumption that, because of cognitive limitations, youngsters with a diagnosis of retardation cannot provide useful diagnostic information from a clinical interview. Abundant clinical experience suggests that youngsters with borderline or mild retardation often may be capable of providing valuable clinical information, whether about precipitating factors known only to them, subjective distress, fears and fantasies, affective symptoms, or characterologic style. The psychiatric assessment of youngsters with borderline or mild retardation should always include a clinical interview. Treatment for emotional or behavioral problems should not be instituted until after a diagnostic process that includes an interview and a careful review of the psychosocial forces that contribute to the patient's condition.

REFERENCES

Abuelo, D. K. (1991). Genetic disorders. In J. L. Matson, & J. A. Mulick (Eds.), *Handbook of mental retardation* (2nd ed., pp. 97–114). New York: Pergamon Press.

Baroff, G. S. (1986). *Mental retardation: Nature, causes, and management* (2nd ed.). Washington, DC: Hemisphere Publishing Company.

Brookes, P. H., McCauley, C. M., & Merrill, E. M. (1988). Cognition and mental retardation. In F. J. Menolascino & J. A. Stark (Eds.), *Prevention and curative intervention in mental retardation* (pp. 295–318). Baltimore: Paul H. Brookes.

Detterman, D. K. (1987). Theoretical notions of intelligence and mental retardation. *American Journal of Mental Deficiency, 92,* 2–11.

Edgerton, R. B. (1988). Perspectives on the prevention of mild mental retardation. In F. J. Menolascino & J. A. Stark (Eds.), *Preventive and curative intervention in mental retardation* (pp. 325–342). Baltimore: Paul H. Brookes.

Ellis, N. R., & Cavalier, A. R. (1982). Research perspectives in mental retardation. In E. Zigler & D. Balla (Eds.), *Mental retardation: The developmental-difference controversy* (pp. 121–152). Hillsdale, NJ: Lawrence Erlbaum.

Feinstein, C., & Levoy, D. (1991). Pharmacotherapy of severe psychiatric disorders in mentally retarded individuals. In A. Stoudemire & B. S. Fogel (Eds.), *Medical psychiatric practice* (pp. 507–537). Washington, DC: American Psychiatric Press.

Grossman, H. J. (Ed.). (1983). *Classification in mental retardation.* Washington, DC: American Association on Mental Deficiency.

Hale, C. A., & Borkowski, J. G. (1991). Attention, memory, and cognition. In J. L. Matson & J. A. Mulick (Eds.), *Handbook of mental retardation* (2nd ed., pp. 505–528). New York: Pergamon Press.

Kiely, M. (1987). The prevalence of mental retardation. *Epidemiologic Reviews, 9,* 194–218.

Koller, H., Richardson, S. A., Katz, M., & McLaren, J. (1982). Behavior disturbance in childhood and the early adult years in populations who were and were not mentally retarded. *Journal of Preventive Psychiatry, 1* (4), 453–468.

Matson, J. L., & Barrett, R. P. (1982). *Psychopathology in the mentally retarded.* New York: Grune & Stratton.

McLaren, J., & Bryson, S. E. (1987). Review of recent epidemiological studies of mental retardation: Prevalence, associated disorders, and etiology. *American Journal of Mental Retardation, 92* (3), 243–254.

Reiss, S., Levitan, G. W., & Szyszko, J. (1982). Emotional disturbance and mental retardation: Diagnostic overshadowing. *American Journal of Mental Deficiency, 86,* 567–574.

Richardson, S. A., Koller, H., & Katz, M. (1985a). Continuities and change in behavior disturbance: A follow-up study of mildly retarded young people. *American Journal of Orthopsychiatry, 55* (2), 220–229.

Richardson, S. A., Koller, H., & Katz, M. (1985b). Relationship of upbringing to later behavior disturbance of mildly mentally retarded young people. *American Journal of Mental Deficiency, 90* (1), 1–8.

Richardson, S. A., Koller, H., & Katz, M. (1986). A longitudinal study of numbers of males and females in mental retardation services by age, IQ, and placement. *Journal of Mental Deficiency Research, 30,* 291–300.

Rowitz, L. (1991). Social and environmental factors and developmental handicaps in children. In J. L. Matson & J. A. Mulick (Eds.), *Handbook of mental retardation* (2nd ed., pp. 158–165). New York: Pergamon Press.

Rutter, M., Tizard, J., & Whitmore, K. (Eds.). (1970). *Education, health and behaviour.* London: Longman.

Sattler, J. M. (1988). *Assessment of children* (3rd ed.). San Diego: Jerome M. Sattler.

Sparrow, S., Balla, D. A., & Cicchetti, D. V. (1984). *Vineland Adaptive Behavior Scales.* Circle Pines, MN: American Guidance Service.

Yeargin-Allsopp, M., Murphy, C. C., Oakley, G. P., & Sikes, R. K. (1992). A multiple-source method for studying the prevalence of developmental disabilities in children: The Metropolitan Atlanta Developmental Disabilities Study. *Pediatrics, 18* (4), 624–630.

Zigler, E. (1969). Developmental vs. difference theories of mental retardation and the problem of motivation. *American Journal of Mental Deficiency, 73,* 536–556.

Zigler, E., Balla, D., & Hodapp, R. (1984). On the definition and classification of mental retardation. *American Journal of Mental Deficiency, 89* (3), 215–230.

37 / Moderate to Profound Mental Retardation

Jean A. Frazier, Rowland P. Barrett, Carl B. Feinstein, and Anne S. Walters

This chapter provides an overview of moderate to profound mental retardation in children and adolescents. Unlike children with borderline intellectual functioning and mild mental retardation, children with moderate to profound mental retardation differ in significant ways from their nonretarded peers. Not only are children in this grouping at a greater cognitive disadvantage, but a large number also suffer from physical and/or neurologic handicap. The combination of cognitive and physical impairments makes attempts at normal adaptive functioning extremely difficult. As a result, in contrast to their peers with mild mental retardation, children with moderate to profound mental retardation often require more dependent care situations. It is important to note, however, that children with moderate to profound mental retardation may experience a varied range of developmental outcomes, depending on a number of biological, psychological, and social factors. These factors include individual characteristics, such as the presence or absence of physical disabilities and comorbid psychiatric conditions, family support, social (peer) support, quality of education, cultural values, and the availability of medical and dental care. Although mental retardation represents a deviation from normal development, the developmental outcome for these children is not fixed per se. The development of children with mental retardation is subject to the same contextual influences responsible for shaping development in the general child population (Sameroff, 1982). Therefore, it may be favorably or unfavorably affected by the range of advantages and disadvantages commonly acknowledged as impinging on the development of all children and adolescents.

Dr. Feinstein's work was supported by Child and Adolescent Mental Health Academic Award 11K07MH00766 from the National Institute of Mental Health.

Diagnosis of Mental Retardation

The American Psychiatric Association (1994) has established three essential criteria that must be satisfied when making a diagnosis of mental retardation. First, an individual must present with significantly subaverage general intellectual functioning, based on the results of a standardized, individually administered intelligence (IQ) test. Second, concurrent deficits or impairments in adaptive behavior must be observed. Third and finally, the conditions of subaverage intellectual and adaptive functioning must be manifest during the developmental period (i.e., onset prior to age 18 years).

For the purposes of diagnosis, subaverage intellectual functioning is defined as an IQ of less than 70, or 2 standard deviations below the established mean IQ for the test employed. Cognitive abilities of school-age children usually are measured using standardized instruments such as the third edition of the Wechsler Intelligence Scale for Children and the fourth edition of the Stanford-Binet. These instruments, particularly the Stanford-Binet, also are viewed as appropriate tests for use with children and adolescents who function in the moderate range of mental retardation. The Leiter International Performance Scale is commonly used to assess the more profoundly mentally retarded or nonverbal children within the population. Unfortunately, most standardized instruments lack the sensitivity to test intellectual functioning at the lower end of the scale (Kinsbourne, 1985), making the measurement of IQ in the population of children with moderate to profound mental retardation difficult and often imprecise. Consequently, the importance of accurately assessing adaptive behavior increases in proportion to decreases in measured IQ. The lower the child's IQ, the more important it becomes to establish valid skill levels in a variety of adaptive areas that represent the activities of daily living (i.e., communication, socialization, eating, dressing, toileting). The two instruments most commonly used to evaluate adaptive functioning are the Vineland Adaptive Behavior Scale (Sparrow, Balla, & Cicchetti, 1984) and the American Association on Mental Deficiency Adaptive Behavior Scale for Children and Adults (Nihira, Foster, Shellhaas, & Leland, 1975).

Mental retardation, in general, is divided into four specific diagnostic categories or subtypes that depict the severity of the disorder:

Mild: IQ from 50–55 to 70.
Moderate: IQ from 35–40 to 50–55.
Severe: IQ from 20–25 to 35–40.
Profound: IQ ≤ 20 or 25

To meet criteria for each subtype, a child's adaptive functioning must be either equivalent to what is expected of a given IQ or somewhat lower than expected. Although IQ is an important consideration in diagnosing the severity or subtype of mental retardation, differential classification according to subtype requires clinicians to consider adaptive functioning with great care. A differential diagnosis of moderate vs. profound mental retardation is usually readily apparent; however, there are many important and subtle differences in adaptive ability that distinguish both the child with moderate mental retardation from a child with severe mental retardation and the child with severe retardation from one with profound mental retardation (e.g., communication skills, self-help skills). Special education, the principal form of therapy encountered by the vast majority of children with mental retardation across their lifetimes, can be dramatically enhanced by an appropriate classroom placement based on an accurate depiction of cognitive and adaptive ability (i.e., subtype classification).

Epidemiology

Mental retardation is the most common and widely known of the neuropsychiatric disorders. Several authors have suggested that, based on expectations of a normal distribution of intelligence, mental retardation exists in 2 to 3% of the school-age population (Cook & Leventhal, 1992). Others, including the American Psychiatric Association (1994), estimate that within the general population, the prevalence is closer to 1%. In any case, approximately 85% of the mentally retarded population falls within the category of mild retardation; the remainder (those with IQs less than 50), comprise the group discussed in this chapter.

In a review of the prevalence of mental retardation, Kiely (1987) found that most studies reported prevalence rates for moderate to profound mental retardation of 3 to 5 per 1,000 of population. According to McLaren and Bryson (1987), the prevalence rate of moderate mental retardation is approximately 2 per 1,000, while the rate for severe mental retardation is 1.3 per 1,000, and the rate for profound mental retardation is 0.4 per 1,000.

Lifelong prevalence of mental retardation tends to vary with age, sex, and socioeconomic status (Kiely, 1987; McLaren & Bryson, 1987; Rutter, Tizard, Yule, Graham, & Whitmore, 1976). This prevalence seems to increase from the preschool years to adolescence (Kiely, 1987), followed by further increases with age until early adulthood, when it decreases from approximately 5 to 4 per 1,000 (McLaren & Bryson, 1987). The highest male-to-female ratio (1.94:1) is seen among those who fall within the mild range of mental retardation (Richardson, Koller, & Katz, 1986). The ratio remains slightly in favor of males (1.5:1) among those in the severe to profound range of mental retardation (Rowitz, 1991). The reasons why more males have cognitive deficits are unknown. They might be due to a prejudicial cultural tendency to label boys as mentally retarded or to an overrepresentation of X-linked disorders, such as fragile X syndrome (McLaren & Bryson, 1987; Richardson et al., 1986).

Studies examining the relationship between mental retardation and socioeconomic status indicate that mild mental retardation is grossly overrepresented at the lower end of the economic continuum (Bregman & Hodapp, 1991; Kiely, 1987; Zigler, Balla, & Hodapp, 1984). Moderate to profound mental retardation appears to be more equitably distributed across the socioeconomic strata and bears fewer social implications.

Etiology

Approximately 25% of the population with mental retardation has a known biologic etiology. Known etiologies can be divided into prenatal, perinatal, and postnatal mechanisms. A specific etiology is less likely to be identified in children with borderline intellectual functioning and mild mental retardation and much more likely to be known among those individuals falling within the moderate to profound range of mental retardation (Rowitz, 1991). For children diagnosed with moderate to profound subtypes of mental retardation, prenatal factors account for approximately 25 to 30% of the cases; perinatal factors account for 11%; and postnatal factors for anywhere from 0.8 to 12.8% (McLaren & Bryson, 1987). There is no known etiology for 25 to 40% of children with IQs less than 50 (McLaren & Bryson, 1987). Chromosomal abnormalities are significantly more common in these groups (Abuelo, 1991), with Down syndrome (Trisomy-21) cited as the most common single factor (Abramowitz & Richardson, 1975; Bregman & Hodapp, 1991).

Prenatal factors that may lead to mental retardation include infection (rubella, toxoplasmosis, cytomegalovirus, herpes simplex, hepatitis, human immunodeficiency virus, syphilis), X-ray exposure, street drugs (heroin), alcohol, maternal mercury poisoning, genetic abnormalities (chromosomal, specific single-factor inheritance, unfavorable polygenic combinations), metabolic abnormalities (low T4), prescribed drug treatments (anticonvulsants, thalidomide, chemotherapy) (Kaufman, 1990), and maternal illness (diabetes, malnutrition, anemia, emphysema) (Kaplan & Sadock, 1991). Common perinatal factors include asphyxia, prematurity, and mechanical birth injury. Postnatal factors include bacterial infections (hemophilus influenza, diplococcus pneumonia, viral encephalitis), head trauma, and lead intoxication.

In children with IQs falling below 50, known genetic disorders account for approximately 50% of the prenatal etiologies of their mental retardation (Abuelo, 1991). Chromosomal abnormalities give rise to a relatively small portion of genetic disorders. Some genetic disorders are caused by specific single-gene anomalies; the majority, however, result from unfavorable and complicated polygenic combinations (Kinsbourne, 1985). Common autosomal chromosomal abnormalities include Down syndrome (Trisomy-21), Trisomy-13, -14, and -15. The incidence of Down syndrome in the general population is approximately 1 in 1,000 (Kinsbourne, 1985). Sex chromosome abnormalities include fragile X syndrome (Xq27.3), Turner syndrome (45XO), Klinefelter syndrome (47XXY), and Multiple X (47XXX). Fragile X syndrome is considered the second most frequent chromosomal cause of mental retardation after Down syndrome (Goldson & Hagerman, 1992).

Nature of Moderate to Profound Mental Retardation

Physical, sensory, and neurologic handicaps are commonly identified in children with moderate to profound mental retardation (Barrett, Walters, Mercurio, Klitzke, & Feinstein, 1992). Approximately 10% of children with moderate mental retardation have seizure disorders (Rivinus, Grofer, Feinstein, & Barrett, 1989). The number of associated physical disorders tends to increase in proportion to the severity of the mental retardation. Epilepsy, for example, is diagnosed in 50% of children and adolescents with severe or profound mental retardation (Corbett, Harris, & Robinson, 1975). In comparison to the general population, many more children with severe and profound mental retardation are blind (30:1) and deaf (20:1) (Baroff, 1986). Ultimately, children in the severe to profound range of mental retardation are significantly more likely to die in childhood or adolescence (Eyman, Grossman, Tarjan, & Miller, 1987). Approximately 50% of profoundly mentally retarded children live only until age 20 years (McLaren & Bryson, 1987), while survival rates to age 20 years are 98% for children with moderate to mild mental retardation (Herbst & Baird, 1983).

Cognitively, children with moderate to profound mental retardation often experience decreased language capacity. Impairments in language may be due to a variety of factors. Some are biological and attributable to an essential cognitive deficit; others may be social and reflect decreased maternal verbal stimulation during a period of adjustment to the handicapped child. Children with IQs below 50 show marked deficits in information processing and tend to have more difficulty with problem solving (Brooks, McCauley, & Merrill, 1988), largely because of the conceptual nature of the strategies and social skills required for problem resolution. The development and acquisition of social skills and cognitive problem-solving abilities are among the most important adaptive achievements challenging children and adolescents with moderate mental retardation (Barrett et al., 1992).

Children with moderate mental retardation also tend to suffer much more social ostracism and peer rejection than their mildly mentally retarded age mates. As a disability, moderate mental retardation of organic etiology often is accompanied by physical handicaps, and the combination can readily lead to social isolation. Interestingly, the majority of children and adolescents with mild mental retardation have siblings with subaverage IQs; however, most children with IQs of less than 50 have developmentally and cognitively intact siblings. As a result, children in the moderate range of mental retardation are at increased risk for the social and emotional difficulties that may arise from not being like everybody else, including members of their own families.

Developmental Challenges

Numerous cognitive, physical, emotional, social, and behavioral challenges face individuals with mental retardation and their families during the course of development. The way in which the family system responds to the child, and the way the child within the system responds to the family, will shape the developmental pathway. Children with mental retardation tend to develop more slowly and, by definition, reach a final level of development that is less than that of their developmentally intact peers. However, it is important to note that the course of their overall cognitive and social development is subject to many of the same contextual influences that challenge and shape development in the general population. Develop-

mental challenges for children and adolescents with mental retardation can be anticipated and satisfactorily addressed, if adequate planning has been undertaken and the proper family, social, and special education supports are available.

INFANCY

Often the early secure attachment for an infant that is born with mental retardation is in jeopardy because of the stress the parents experience in adjusting to a child with developmental delays. Parents frequently experience varying and sometimes lengthy periods of denial, anger, and sorrow (Lewis & MacLean, 1982). Parents often struggle with their acceptance of their child's mental retardation. This can lead to their decreased emotional availability to the child as well as to each other and the rest of the family. Following the birth of a child with mental retardation, it is not unusual for parents and family members to experience an ongoing chronic grief process that waxes and wanes with each developmental milestone that is or is not reached.

CASE EXAMPLE

Lindsey was the third pregnancy of her then 34-year-old mother. She has one older brother, who is developmentally intact. Mother's first pregnancy was miscarried. The parents' marriage is intact. Both parents are college educated and well traveled. Father is professionally employed, and the family enjoys an upper middle class lifestyle. There is no evidence of psychiatric illness, alcoholism, or learning disability in the maternal extended family. Father's younger brother is autistic.

Mother's pregnancy with Lindsey was planned and wanted. The pregnancy was 38 weeks. Delivery was by cesarian section following detection of fetal distress. Birthweight was 6 pounds, 9 ounces. Apgars were 9 and 8, at 1 and 5 minutes, respectively. Lindsey received supplemental oxygen therapy during the first 36 hours. A pneumothorax was noted to resolve within 48 hours. Mother and baby were discharged from obstetric care after a routine hospital stay.

Mother reported that the first 2 weeks were remarkable for the baby's inactivity and lack of responsiveness. It was hard to wake Lindsey for feedings. She was slow to arouse and had difficulty sucking. By age 1 year the parents were concerned about the possibility of developmental delay. At age 15 months, she was evaluated at the local medical college, where developmental motor and speech milestones were noted as significantly delayed. It was recommended that Lindsey be enrolled in an early intervention special education center.

By age 30 months, the parents were concerned that Lindsey's developmental progress was significantly more impaired than they had envisioned. Her special education teacher confirmed that Lindsey appeared capable of achieving more but, for whatever reason, was unable to make progress developmentally. Lindsey was unable to walk independently, showed an unbalanced and awkward gait with support, blinked her eyes frequently, and was unable to sustain attention even with obviously preferred objects.

Lindsey was referred for neurological evaluation; the results of a computed tomography scan were unremarkable, but an electroencephalogram study indicated petit mal status epilepticus. Anticonvulsant medication was started and, within several weeks, developmentally early motor milestones were acquired, motor coordination improved, and Lindsey learned to walk.

In the course of her preschool and early elementary school years, behavioral difficulties involving oppositional behavior, temper tantrums, and aggression emerged. Although Lindsey remained enrolled in special education, her parents involved her in a number of less than traditional treatment approaches (auditory training, spinal manipulations) with the hope of facilitating developmental growth (viz. normalcy) and resolving her behavioral difficulties. Additionally, they enrolled Lindsey's older brother at a boarding school, ostensibly to ensure his safety and protect him from the household stress created by his sister. The parents stated that Lindsey's behavior made them feel like "prisoners in their own home", and that it was "not a healthy environment for a normal boy to grow up in." They also noted that the boarding school placement allowed them to spend more time working with Lindsey.

Currently, Lindsey is 8½ years old and an inpatient at a medical school–affiliated hospital specialty program for autistic and mentally retarded children with serious behavior disorders. Prior to her admission, she had been dismissed from special education programming by two separate centers, both of which cited extremely disruptive and aggressive conduct that could not be safely managed within the classroom setting.

The parents have rightly questioned their role in the development of Lindsey's oppositionality and aggression. They noted that while they have always tried to set limits on her misbehavior, they have been inconsistent and rarely successful. Since learning of her mental retardation in infancy, they have somehow felt responsible for her disability and were very uncomfortable disciplining her "over every little thing that she did or didn't do." In her parents' words: "It was hard enough on Lindsey that she was retarded. We felt that she deserved a break. It made us feel good to give her a break. It

was something that we could do for her. Most of the time, letting her have her own way about things seemed to quiet her down, which was a great relief to us. We know now that we let it go too far, and we're paying for it in spades. So is Lindsey. Her behavior is worse than it's ever been."

PRESCHOOL

Often the effort required for diagnosis, treatment, and subsequent interventions in the home and school can be draining on a family in terms of time, energy, and finances. Ultimately, many families must face the difficult challenge of deciding if the child can live at home or will require out-of-home placement.

CASE EXAMPLE

Brandon was the third pregnancy of his then 20-year-old mother. No information regarding his two older siblings is known, other than that they have been adopted. Mother's pregnancy with Brandon was unplanned and full term. The prenatal period was remarkable for her extensive use of alcohol and cocaine as well as tobacco and marijuana. There is no record of mother receiving any form of prenatal health care. Upon admission to the maternity suite of a community hospital, mother was observed to have multiple weeping skin lesions and a large number of tattoos. It was noted that her membranes had ruptured approximately 20 hours earlier and that she had inhaled cocaine 1 hour prior to arriving at the hospital. Delivery was normal vaginal. Birthweight was 5 pounds, 15 ounces. Upon delivery, Brandon was observed to be "jittery" and breathing rapidly. He was transferred to the neonatal intensive care unit following detection of a systolic heart murmur.

Brandon was placed in incubation for 1 week and spent an additional week in the special care nursery. During the neonatal period he displayed difficulty sucking, vomiting, a weak cry, irritability, sleep difficulties, deliberate arching of the back, and sudden twitching or stiffening of the back and arms. Drug withdrawal was apparent. In addition, Brandon was diagnosed with an enlarged heart and a (benign) ventriculoseptal defect. An electrocardiogram study was unremarkable, and an earlier possible diagnosis of sepsis was ruled out.

Social services determined the biological mother to be unable to provide for Brandon adequately and, upon discharge from hospitalization at age 1 month, he was placed in foster care.

At age 2 months, Brandon was readmitted to hospital care with chief complaints of continuing feeding and swallowing difficulties, wheezing, unexplained episodes of breath holding, irritability, tremors of the arms and legs, and cyanosis. An electroencephalographic study identified a left temporal focus. Results of a computed tomography scan were unremarkable. Anticonvulsant medication was not prescribed. Brandon was diagnosed with colic and responded favorably to treatment.

At age 4 months, Brandon presented with tonic-clonic movements and phenobarbital was prescribed. He also was enrolled in an early intervention program for at-risk infants. At age 8 months, he was hospitalized for a third time for treatment of dehydration secondary to a viral infection. At age 10 months, Brandon contracted varicella, after which he refused to eat solid (pureed) foods. Eating difficulties persisted through age 20 months and required enrollment in a hospital-based feeding evaluation and treatment program. Sleep difficulties also were prominent during this period, with reports of as little as 13 hours of sleep in any given week. Reports of irritability and hyperactivity led to a discontinuation of the phenobarbital; however, this did not favorably affect Brandon's behavior, as anticipated.

By age 3 years, Brandon was actively involved in a preschool special education program. Developmental motor milestones were reported as achieved with delay, and he was observed to be nonverbal. Severe mental retardation was diagnosed. Eating and sleep problems, hyperactivity, labile mood, and oppositional-aggressive behavior continued to be observed on a daily basis. At age 3½ years, he was admitted to inpatient status at a medical school–affiliated hospital with a special program for autistic and mentally retarded children and adolescents with severe behavior problems. Among the chief complaints of family members was the fear that he was unsafe in the home setting and that his medical and behavioral difficulties were unrelenting and overwhelming.

Brandon responded most favorably to treatment. After a 120-day hospital course, he was observed to eat solid foods, maintain a normal sleep schedule, present with a stable mood, and show little oppositional-aggressive behavior. Although he was highly active, the use of close observation, a structured routine, and alternative communication programming effectively circumvented many potential problems.

Upon his discharge from hospitalization, the foster parents who had cared for Brandon since birth and had later formally adopted him into their family at age 1 year voluntarily relinquished their parental rights to social service. They stated that they had a full understanding of the treatment conditions responsible for Brandon's progress and that they were unable to replicate them in their home. Brandon was then placed with a second foster family.

SCHOOL AGE

Rarely, children in the upper range of moderate mental retardation may remain undiagnosed until they reach school age, when they are first noted to lag behind peers. At this stage, the child with mental retardation and his or her family require professional support and uncomplicated access to special education services. The child's cognitive delays often become more readily apparent as the youngster begins to engage in the academic process. By age 16 years, the child with moderate mental retardation is generally viewed as capable of achieving a mental age comparable to that of a 5- to 8-year-old. These children can manage many of their own basic needs and may acquire elementary academic and social skills through schooling. In terms of cognitive development, children with severe mental retardation tend to be more limited, showing mental ages of between 3 and 5 years by midadolescence. They require supportive, highly structured special education schooling, with an emphasis on communication skills training and the development of self-help skills for eating, dressing, toileting, and recreation. The child with profound mental retardation usually has a rudimentary ability to communicate, with a mental age in the range of 1 to 3 years.

Certainly, children in the upper range of moderate mental retardation become aware that somehow, cognitively and socially, they are different. It is frequently observed that moderately retarded children tend to have the same knowledge base about social relationships as do their nonretarded peers (Brooks et al., 1988). As the school years advance, peer rejection tends to become an issue of increasing importance. Families have to deal with the prospects and realities of their own tensions, fears, discomfort, and shame. At the same time, they must cope with the psychological reactions of their disabled child, as the child is exposed to increasingly demanding academic and social circumstances. As the result of ostracism encountered at school, in the neighborhood, or at home, it is not uncommon to observe decreases in the child's motivation, accompanied by social withdrawal.

Family and, particularly, parents' comfort and adaptation to the presence of a mentally retarded child can influence the child's ability to adapt to and accept the challenges of the all-too-obvious disabilities.

CASE EXAMPLE

Webster was the first pregnancy of his then 21-year-old mother. A younger brother is developmentally intact. Webster's parents are divorced. Although mother does not drink, the maternal and paternal extended family histories are remarkable for alcoholism. There is no history of mental retardation or learning disability in either extended family.

Mother's pregnancy with Webster was planned and wanted. The prenatal period was unremarkable. Routine prenatal health care was provided. Labor was spontaneous after full term, but a breech presentation required cesarian section. Birthweight was 8 pounds 10 ounces. Apgars were 9 and 9, at 1 and 5 minutes, respectively. Neonatal jaundice resolved without treatment within 24 hours. Developmental motor and speech milestones were reported as achieved within normal limits. Webster walked independently by age 8 months and used words meaningfully in sentences by age 18 months. A febrile seizure was observed at age 11 months, with a second seizure at age 13 months. Anticonvulsant medication was not prescribed. Development progressed normally through age 3 years.

At age 3½ years, Webster displayed attentional difficulties and slightly slurred speech. He was enrolled in Head Start and, later, at age 4 years, was transferred to a preschool special education program to address emerging learning and behavioral difficulties described as "hyperactivity." Stimulant medication was not prescribed. Approximately 1 year later, at age 4½ years, an increased slurring of speech was noted followed by a significant decrease in oral language. An electroencephalographic study indicated a seizure disorder. Results of a computed tomography scan and magnetic resonance imaging study were unremarkable. Anticonvulsant medication was started. By age 5, Webster presented with progressive seizure activity that was difficult to manage. For a 2-month period, he averaged 9 generalized seizures per day, and for the next 2 months, an average of 1 generalized seizure per day. Oral language was reduced to a few noun labels, and attentional skills were severely impaired. Generalized seizure activity was observed approximately every 6 to 8 weeks thereafter.

At age 5½ years, Webster was placed in a day special education program for several months; ultimately, concerns about seizure management and progressively worsening hyperactive, agitated, and aggressive behavior forced the school to pursue a program of homebound instruction. At approximately age 7, Webster returned to a school-based special education program, where he was observed to be entirely nonverbal, highly distractible, inattentive, oppositional, hyperactive, and aggressive. At this point, generalized seizure activity was rare. However, as this type of seizure activity came under increasingly better control, mother reported that she had now begun to notice frequent staring spells.

Accordingly, Webster was referred for further diagnostic evaluation and treatment for his severe behavioral difficulties, lack of oral speech, and failure to progress developmentally secondary to attentional deficits. A recommendation for long-term residential placement was anticipated by the mother, who noted that she was "completely in the dark . . . and overwhelmed" by her son's behavior, which included "terrifying his younger brother." The findings of the evaluation indicated the presence of Landau-Kleffner syndrome (acquired epileptic aphasia), along with an active absence seizure disorder. Treatment centered on additional anticonvulsant therapy; alternative communication skills training; intensive positive reinforcement programming for compliant, helpful, and prosocial behavior; and family therapy. Webster responded favorably to treatment, with marked improvements in attention and behavior as well as a recovering (minimal) ability for speech. Along with the medication, a parent education and family therapy program was designed both to assist mother and younger brother in understanding Webster's unique developmental disorder as well as to offer them skill training in effective child behavior management. These components were viewed as central to the ultimately favorable clinical outcome in this case.

Currently, Webster lives at home with his mother and younger brother and attends a hospital-based special education day program that also provides professional in-home support during afterschool hours and on weekends.

ADOLESCENCE

Social (peer) acceptance and separation from family are two important issues for adolescents. Most teenagers with mental retardation, particularly those with IQs of less than 50, have experienced peer rejection and social isolation. Not only do these teenagers have cognitive deficits, but they also often appear different physically. Many have both weight-control and complexion problems and may frequently display an awkward physical appearance and gait (Shapiro & Friedman, 1987).

Teenagers with moderate mental retardation range from being partly to entirely dependent on

403

caregivers; they never are able to separate from their families in the same way and for the same reasons as their siblings. Brothers and sisters grow older and leave the family to attend college, enter military service, marry, or accept an out-of-town job. For adolescents and young adults with moderate to profound mental retardation, separation may be "forced" on families, as parents are required to consider long-term future planning for their developmentally disabled son or daughter.

Within the context of being partially dependent, the adolescent with moderate mental retardation needs help with establishing areas of personal and social independence. Teenagers with moderate mental retardation can and should be supported and educated to develop a preferred vocational skill. Through the mastery of vocational tasks, adolescents and young adults who have moderate mental retardation can develop feelings of personal usefulness, social constructiveness, and a sense of being a part of things.

Sexuality is an important issue for all adolescents, including the adolescent with mental retardation. Teenagers with mental retardation clearly have typical levels of sexual desire and interest. What they tend to lack is sexual knowledge. It is critically important to provide sex education to adolescents with mental retardation, particularly the moderately retarded teenager. Many embarrassing and difficult social situations, as well as potentially dangerous and life-threatening circumstances, may be avoided if the adolescent with mental retardation is well educated in the facts and responsibilities of sexual behavior and conduct. Teenagers with mental retardation, especially those with lower IQs, are quite vulnerable sexually. They are likely to experience verbal ridicule and often are subject to physical abuse and sexual abuse. Issues of safety are paramount and should be supported, without reservation, as a part of the special educational curriculum for all students with mental retardation.

CASE EXAMPLE

Karen is a 17-year-old with moderate mental retardation. Despite a mild articulation disorder, she has good oral language ability. She lives at home with her parents and two brothers, one older and one younger, each of whom is developmentally intact. Karen is a socially eager teenager and displays a relatively keen awareness of the basic social interests of teenage girls. She is aware that teenagers drive cars, that driving a car ". . . is cool," that teenagers have part-time jobs, and ". . . make money," and that teenagers go to college after high school, ". . . like my brother." Moreover, she is aware of the opposite sex and describes herself as "boy crazy." Karen is unaware, however, of the skills and responsibilities required to operate a motor vehicle and work in a competitive employment setting, nor does she grasp the purpose of higher education. Moreover, she is grossly undereducated with respect to sex and has only a vague notion of her own sexuality and sexual interest: "I like boys to kiss them . . . If you like a boy, you kiss him a lot . . . if you don't like a boy, you don't kiss him."

Karen's social skills have always appeared to be ahead of her general cognitive ability. Her attractiveness, gregariousness, and eagerness to please were considered social assets. Consequently, an attempt was made to include her in normal high school nonacademic activities such as art, music, and physical education.

After one semester of mainstreaming, Karen was referred for outpatient psychiatric evaluation and treatment because of uncharacteristically labile moods, social withdrawal, and severe trichotillomania. The parents reported that Karen had first started hair-pulling after she failed to make the girls' basketball team. Although it was negotiated that she could serve as the team's manager, Karen was further frustrated by her inability to grasp that the "team manager" went to practices and games but didn't receive a uniform and never actually played. Her parents' attempt to mollify Karen's irritability and quiet her relentless pleading to learn to drive resulted in increased hair-pulling when the car ". . . just [didn't] drive like it does for other people." A third disappointment came when she learned that she could not work for her father during high school, like her older brother, because the work was too dangerous. Shortly thereafter, Karen asked her "boyfriend" to a school dance and was rejected. Additional contributing factors in the onset and maintenance of her irritable mood, social withdrawal, and trichotillomania included: increasing jealousy of students who were observed to drive to school, some insensitive teasing from peers about her speech, sexually provocative advances in response to chiding from older boys, and the frustration of attending a school honors assembly where she was not among those students called to the stage amid applause to receive ". . . a gift."

ADULTHOOD

Many young adults with moderate to profound mental retardation remain dependent on family and caregivers throughout their lives. Often adults with moderate mental retardation can live in supervised, community-based group homes and work in sheltered workshops and supported employment settings. The adult with severe and profound mental retardation requires ongoing structured dependent care. Inevitably, the level of such care can be complicated by medical and psychiatric illness.

Adults with mental retardation and IQs of less than 50 are at particular risk of undiagnosed medical and psychiatric illness because of communication skill deficits and the phenomenon of "diagnostic overshadowing" (Reiss, Levitan, & Szyszko, 1982), wherein changes in mental status, mood, and behavior are wrongly attributed to the individual's status as mentally retarded.

CASE EXAMPLE

John is a 42-year-old man with moderate to severe mental retardation. He is nonverbal and communicates basic needs through pointing and a few natural gestures. His receptive language ability appears to function clearly in advance of his minimal expressive skills. Throughout his school years, John lived at home and attended special education programming within a self-contained classroom. Currently he resides in a community-based group home and commutes daily to a sheltered worksite. Overnight visits to his parents' home occur each weekend and during holidays. John's parents strove diligently across the years to attain adequate educational and vocational training services to meet the special needs of their son. They remained actively involved with John during his adulthood in order to ensure that his residential and continuing vocational needs were met, as well.

John was referred for outpatient psychiatric evaluation by his parents, after significant urging by the staff at his worksite and group home. The chief complaints involved bouts of "hyperactive" motor behavior accompanied by stereotyped self-injury in the form of repeatedly slapping and scratching his cheeks. He had failed to respond to a variety of behavioral interventions. Although John presented with impressive bruising and swelling of his face, the parents were nonplussed and almost apologetic about the recommendation for evaluation. They were genuinely concerned about John's health and sincerely wished that he could stop hurting himself, but they had been advised long ago to ". . . expect this sort of thing." John, they noted, had always had "fast cycles" and bouts of hurting himself, even as a child. "As you know, Doctor, he is mentally retarded and probably a little autistic, too. These things come with the territory."

After several "educational" therapy sessions outlining the nature of John's psychiatric disorder and the treatment options, the parents agreed to a pharmacotherapy trial. John responded most favorably.

Comorbid Psychiatric Disorders

In general, children with mental retardation have more emotional and behavioral problems (Matson & Barrett, 1993) and are thought to be at greater risk for developing psychopathology at some point during their life than the general child population (Lewis & MacLean, 1982; Matson & Frame, 1986; Rutter et al., 1976). The lower the child's IQ, the greater the tendency toward behavioral problems and psychopathology. Consequently, behavioral disturbance has the greatest probability of occurrence in the profoundly mentally retarded population with seizure disorder or neurologic findings (Bregman, 1991).

According to Bregman (1991), 30 to 60% of the mentally retarded population may present with comorbid psychopathology. This psychopathology may be expressed somewhat differently from that commonly observed in the general population due to both poorer communication skills and the tendency of children with mental retardation to communicate depression, anxiety, agitation, and frustration in more primitive forms, such as self-injurious behavior, stereotyped rocking, aggression, and self-stimulation (Lewis & MacLean, 1982).

Children and adolescents with mental retardation have a decreased capacity to process and self-manage the demands of life; as a result, they are generally more susceptible to behavioral disturbance and mental illness. This increased risk is due to limitations imposed by physical, sensory, and neurologic handicaps that make the child unable to understand and respond adaptively to the demands of environment. A decreased ability to express needs effectively, the tendency to underinterpret or misinterpret life events, the many issues associated with being different, societal nonacceptance, and other cultural-familial factors (Lewis & MacLean, 1982) frequently operate synergistically to increase the risk of behavioral or emotional disturbance for such youngsters.

Comorbid psychiatric conditions often are difficult to diagnose in the population of children with mental retardation due to the child's inability to report symptoms, secondary to general cognitive and language deficits. However, the phenomenon of "diagnostic overshadowing" (Reiss et al., 1982), wherein inappropriate behavior is wrongly attributed to cognitive deficit, is giving way in view of the development of specialized diagnostic instruments that have been standardized and validated for this population (Aman, 1991; Reiss, 1993).

The following psychiatric disorders may be more or less commonly observed in the mentally retarded children and adolescents with mental retardation: affective disorder (including major depression, dysthmia, and bipolar disorder), anxiety disorder, oppositional disorder, attention deficit hyperactivity disorder (ADHD), intermittent explosive disorder, posttraumatic stress disorder, stereotypy/habit disorder with self-injury, pica, obsessive-compulsive disorder, and Tourette's disorder (Barrett et al., 1992). Autism and pervasive developmental disorder co-occur in about one-third of the population with mental retardation. Many investigators have found that approximately one-half of the sample with mental retardation in their studies had experienced an affective disorder, while approximately 2 to 3% satisfied diagnostic criteria for comorbid schizophrenia, and 10 to 20% presented with ADHD (Bregman, 1991). Chronic family disturbance is overrepresented in households of mentally retarded children and adolescents (Barrett et al., 1992), making family therapy a priority for a favorable treatment outcome.

Diagnosis of Central Nervous System Abnormalities and Psychopathology

Early in the life of a child with mental retardation, a basic physical examination and medical/developmental history should be completed. Laboratory tests including thyroid function tests, electrolytes/BUN/CRE, glucose, lead level, serum zinc, magnesium, complete blood count, urinalysis, urinary amino acids, and chromosomal studies should be pursued. Subsequent genetic counseling should occur, and a careful neurological examination, with electroencephalogram, computed tomography scan, and magnetic resonance imaging studies should be completed, as indicated, to rule out treatable progressive neurologic disorders.

Diagnosis of comorbid physical conditions in the child with mental retardation requires careful developmental observation and workup. Because these children are limited in their verbal capacity to report symptomatology, the clinician is dependent on laboratory-based methods of screening and diagnosis and must rely heavily on information from parents, family members, and other caregivers. A careful mental status examination also is important.

Identification of central nervous system abnormalities often can be achieved through neuroimaging (Bregman, 1991). Magnetic resonance imaging, for example, is indicated if an individual has had a recent change in mental status, a traumatic head injury, or a recent unexplained loss in ability to function (Cook & Leventhal, 1992). Computed tomography scans also can be helpful. Although positron emission tomography scans have limited clinical utility, participation in an appropriate research protocol may be helpful in investigating further the relationship between brain and behavior for any given patient (Popper, 1988).

Treatment

Once diagnosis of a comorbid psychiatric condition is made, the question of selecting a treatment approach must be addressed. Operant behavioral interventions often are very helpful in treating the behavior problems common to persons with mental retardation (Barrett, 1986). Intensive programs that utilize differential reinforcement techniques may be of particular value (Cook & Leventhal, 1992). Behavior therapy has been used very effectively for decreasing aggression, extinguishing a variety of maladaptive behaviors, and increasing prosocial behavior.

Cognitive behavioral therapy and psychotherapy can be particularly useful for children and adolescents in the mild range of mental retardation; these also have been helpful for adolescents and young adults diagnosed with moderate mental retardation (Barrett et al., 1992).

A good rule of thumb is that psychopharmacologic interventions should not be used as a first approach to treatment. However, if target symptoms persist, clinicians should not hesitate to consider such approaches. Importantly, where a patient already is receiving medication, the drug(s) must be reviewed and consideration given to the possibility that the target symptoms might be the result of the current medication regimen (Feinstein & Levoy, 1991). Many clinicians have reported that the child and adolescent population with mental retardation requires lower doses than usually prescribed and seems much more prone to untoward effects (Aman & Singh, 1988). Indeed, in these cases, polypharmacy, drug interaction effects, and dose titration are more likely to emerge as confounding variables. Titrating youngsters with mental retardation off behavior-modifying drugs (and select antiepileptic drugs) must be accomplished slowly, with the understanding that this population is particularly prone to withdrawal and rebound symptomatology.

Of course, clinicians also must consider whether the patient is being undermedicated. Enough drug must be used over a long enough period of time to allow for a valid assessment of its therapeutic value. A good rule of thumb is to make dose changes correspond to four times the drug half-life and to commit to a 15- to 30-day period of behavioral observation once a therapeutic level of the drug has been achieved. Although in the past the population with mental retardation has been subjected to generally poor and frequently abusive drug practices, this sad history should not unduly influence clinicians to avoid the practice of responsible pharmacotherapy. Once an accurate psychiatric diagnosis is made, pharmacotherapy may be extremely helpful in enhancing the capability of youngsters with mental retardation for self-regulation and allowing them to access other forms of therapy, including psychotherapy, behavior therapy, and special education.

Overall, the goal of treatment for children and adolescents with mental retardation and comorbid psychiatric/neurologic disorders is to decrease inappropriate behavior, relieve symptomatology, and enhance affective, behavioral, and cognitive self-regulation. The aim is to create conditions that lead to optimal adaptive functioning, facilitate development, and result in an improved quality of life for the children and their families.

REFERENCES

Abramowicz, H. K., & Richardson, S. A. (1975). Epidemiology of severe mental retardation in children: Community studies. *American Journal of Mental Deficiency, 80* (1), 18–39.

Abuelo, D. K. (1991). Genetic disorders. In J. L. Matson & J. A. Mulick (Eds.), *Handbook of mental retardation* (2nd ed., pp. 97–114). New York: Pergamon Press.

Adams, R. D., & Victor, M. (1985). *Principles of neurology* (3rd ed.). New York: McGraw-Hill.

Aman, M. G. (1991). *Assessing psychopathology and behavior problems in persons with mental retardation: A review of available instruments.* Rockville, MD: U.S. Department of Health and Human Services.

Aman, M. G., & Singh, N. N. (1988). *Psychopharmacology of the developmental disabilities.* New York: Springer-Verlag.

American Psychiatric Association. (1994). *Diagnostic and statistical manual of mental disorders* (4th ed.). Washington, DC: Author.

Baroff, G. S. (1986). *Mental retardation: Nature, cause,* *and management* (2nd ed.). Washington, DC: Hemisphere Publishing Corporation.

Barrett, R. P. (1986). *Severe behavior disorders in the mentally retarded: Nondrug approaches to treatment.* New York: Plenum Press.

Barrett, R. P., Walters, A. S., Mercurio, A. F., Klitzke, M. G., & Feinstein, C. (1992). Mental retardation and psychiatric disorders. In V. VanHasselt & D. J. Kolko (Eds.), *Inpatient behavior therapy for children and adolescents* (pp. 113–149). New York: Plenum Press.

Bregman, J. D. (1991). Current developments in the understanding of mental retardation. Part II: Psychopathology. *American Academy of Child and Adolescent Psychiatry, 30* (6), 861–872.

Bregman, J. D., & Hodapp, R. M. (1991). Current developments in the understanding of mental retardation. Part I: Biological and phenomenological perspectives. *American Academy of Child and Adolescent Psychiatry, 30* (5), 707–719.

Broman, S., Nichols, P. L., Shaughnessy, P., & Kennedy, W. (1987). *Retardation in young children.* Hillsdale, NJ: Lawrence Erlbaum.

Brookes, P. H., McCauley, C. M., & Merrill, E. M. (1988). Cognition and mental retardation. In F. J. Menolascino & J. A. Stark (Eds.), *Prevention and curative intervention in mental retardation* (pp. 295–318). Baltimore: Paul H. Brookes.

Cook, E. H., & Leventhal, B. L. (1992). Neuropsychiatric disorders of childhood and adolescence. In S. C. Yudofsky & R. E. Hales (Eds.), *Neuropsychiatry* (2nd ed., pp. 641–644). Washington, DC: American Psychiatric Press.

Corbett, J. A., Harris, R., & Robinson, R. (1975). Epilepsy. In J. Wortis (Ed.), *Mental retardation and developmental disabilities* (Vol. 7, pp. 79–111). New York: Brunner/Mazel.

Eyman, R. K., Grossman, H. J., Tarjan, G., & Miller, C. R. (1987). *Life expectancy and mental retardation.* Washington, DC: American Association on Mental Deficiency.

Feinstein, C., & Levoy, D. (1991). Pharmacotherapy of severe psychiatric disorders in mentally retarded individuals. In A. Stoudemire & B. S. Fogel (Eds.), *Medical psychiatric practice* (pp. 507–537). Washington, DC: American Psychiatric Press.

Fryers, T. (1984). *The epidemiology of severe intellectual impairment: The dynamics of prevalence.* Orlando, FL: Academic Press.

Goldson, E., & Hagerman, R. J. (1992). The fragile X syndrome. *Developmental Medicine and Child Neurology, 34,* 826–832.

Herbst, D. S., & Baird, D. A. (1983). Nonspecific mental retardation in British Columbia as ascertained through a registry. *American Journal of Mental Deficiency, 87,* 506–513.

Kaplan, H. I., & Sadock, B. J. (1991). *Synopsis of psychiatry.* Baltimore: Williams & Wilkins.

Kaufman, D. M. (1990). *Clinical neurology for psychiatrists* (3rd ed.). Philadelphia: W. B. Saunders.

Kiely, M. (1987). The prevalence of mental retardation. *Epidemiologic Reviews, 9,* 194–218.

Kinsbourne, M. (1985). Disorders of mental development. In J. H. Menkes (Ed.), *Textbook of child neurology* (3rd ed., pp. 768–774). Philadelphia: Lea & Febiger.

Lewis, M. H., & MacLean, W. E., Jr. (1982). Issues in treating emotional disorders. In J. L. Matson & R. P. Barrett (Eds.), *Psychopathology in the mentally retarded* (pp. 1–36). New York: Grune & Stratton.

Matson, J. L., & Barrett, R. P. (Eds.). (1993). *Psychopathology in the mentally retarded.* (2nd ed.). Boston: Allyn & Bacon.

Matson, J. L., & Frame, C. L. (1986). *Psychopathology among mentally retarded children and adolescents.* Beverly Hills, CA: Sage Publications.

McLaren, J., & Bryson, S. E. (1987). Review of recent epidemiological studies of mental retardation: Prevalence, associated disorders, and etiology. *American Journal of Mental Retardation, 92* (3), 243–254.

Menolascino, F. J. (1990). The nature and types of mental illness in the mentally retarded. In M. Lewis & S. M. Miller (Eds.), *Handbook of developmental psychopathology* (pp. 397–408). New York: Plenum Press.

Nihira, K., Foster, R., Shellhaas, M., & Leland, H. (1975). *AAMD Adaptive Behavior Scale.* Washington, DC: American Association and Mental Deficiency.

Peterson, H. (1992). Mental retardation. In D. M. Kaufman, G. E. Solomon, & C. R. Pfeffer (Eds.), *Child and adolescent neurology for psychiatrists* (pp. 220–227). Baltimore: Williams & Wilkins.

Popper, C. W. (1988). Disorders usually first evident in infancy, childhood, or adolescence. In J. A. Talbott, R. E. Hales, & S. C. Yudofsky (Eds.), *The American Psychiatric Press textbook of psychiatry,* (pp. 702–711). Washington, DC: American Psychiatric Press.

Reiss, S. (1993). Assessment of psychopathology in persons with mental retardation. In J. L. Matson & R. P. Barrett (Eds.), *Psychopathology in the mentally retarded* (2nd ed., pp. 17–40). Boston: Allyn & Bacon.

Reiss, S., Levitan, G. W., & Szyszko, J. (1982). Emotional disturbance and mental retardation: Diagnostic overshadowing. *American Journal of Mental Deficiency, 86,* 567–574.

Richardson, S. A., Koller, H., & Katz, M. (1986). A longitudinal study of numbers of males and females in mental retardation services by age, IQ, and placement. *Journal of Mental Deficiency Research, 30,* 291–300.

Rivinus, T. M., Grofer, L. M. Feinstein, C., & Barrett, R. P. (1989). Psychopharmacology in the mentally retarded individual: New approaches, new direction. *Journal of the Multihandicapped Person, 2* (1), 1–23.

Rowitz, L. (1991). Social and environmental factors and developmental handicaps in children. In J. L. Matson & J. A. Mulick (Eds.), *Handbook of mental retardation* (2nd ed., pp. 158–165). New York: Pergamon Press.

Rutter, M., Tizard, J., Yule, W., Graham, P., & Whitmore, K. (1976). Research report Isle of Wight Studies 1964–1974. *Psychological Medicine, 6* (2), 313–332.

Sameroff, A. J. (1982). The environmental context of developmental disabilities. In D. Bricker (Ed.), *Intervention with at risk and handicapped infants: From research to application* (pp. 141–152). Baltimore: University Park Press.

Shapiro, E. S., & Friedman, J. (1987). Mental retardation. In V. B. VanHasselt & M. Hersen (Eds.), *Handbook of adolescent psychology* (pp. 381–397). New York: Pergamon Press.

Sparrow, S., Balla, D. A., & Cicchetti, D. V. (1984). *Vineland Adaptive Behavior Scales.* Circle Pines, MN: American Guidance Service.

Tanguay, P. E., & Russell, A. T. (1991). Mental retardation. In M. Lewis (Ed.), *Child and adolescent psychiatry* (pp. 508–516). Baltimore: Williams & Wilkins.

Zigler, E., Balla, D., & Hodapp, R. (1984). On the definition and classification of mental retardation. *American Journal of Mental Deficiency, 89* (3), 215–230.

38 / Seizure Disorder

Wun Jung Kim

Seizures are discrete clinical events that reflect a temporary physiological dysfunction of the brain, characterized by excessive and hypersynchronous discharge of cortical neurons (Scheuer & Pedley, 1990). Seizures are a common symptom of disturbed brain function due to acute and chronic neurologic disorders or metabolic abnormalities. Many types of seizures are "symptomatic," secondary to the known causes of brain dysfunction, and are usually self-limited. Febrile seizures that are common during early childhood are such an example. "Idiopathic" implies that no known cause of recurrent seizures can be uncovered. Epilepsy is usually referred for these recurrent, unprovoked seizures. This chapter deals primarily with psychiatric and developmental aspects of idiopathic seizures and pseudoseizures. Like psychiatric disorders, genetic, neurochemical, neuroanatomic, and electrophysiological factors have been postulated as etiological. The interplay of genetic, acquired pathophysiological, and psychosocial factors is as important as in understanding such an interplay in psychiatric disorders, thus warranting biopsychosocial perspectives. The current classification scheme developed by International League Against Epilepsy employs phenomenological approaches rather than etiological or anatomical classification systems used in the past. Many conditions mimic epilepsy, including psychogenic seizures, and several different types of seizures may coexist in the same patient. Accurate diagnosis requires meticulous attention to clinical and laboratory findings and medical investigation for a differential diagnosis (Morrell, 1993).

Epidemiology

The lifetime prevalence rate of epilepsy was reported to be about 6% for a single afebrile seizure and about 4% for recurrent seizures (Hauser & Kurland, 1975). Febrile convulsions occur in 3% of children under age 5, but only a minority of them later develop recurring seizures. A conservatively estimated prevalence rate of active epilepsy in the United States is about 6 per 1,000, which is translated into at least 1.5 million people. The most reliable study in England (Rutter, Graham, & Yule, 1970) and in the United States (Cowan, Bodensteiner, Leviton, & Doherty, 1989) demonstrated a prevalence rate of 4 to 6 per 1,000 in children and adolescents. Different epidemiological studies of the general population have reported that at least 75% of epilepsy begins before the age of 20, and 50% of childhood-onset epilepsy occurs during the first 5 years of life (Cowan et al., 1989; Gudmundsson, 1966; Silanpää, 1973). Indeed, epilepsy is primarily a disorder of childhood and adolescence. About 70% of children with epilepsy are considered idiopathic. A good portion of these children with idiopathic seizures also have coexisting minor to gross physical deficits that are not the cause of seizure. A great deal of variation exists in the different studies regarding the type of seizures, due to problems with the reliability of the classification system. Generalized seizures seem to be the most frequent type (about 50%) followed by partial seizures and other types. The male-female ratio is 1.1 : 1.2. The study by Cowan et al. (1989) also pointed to a higher rate in blacks than in whites, consistent with the findings of several other U.S. studies.

The prognosis of epilepsy varies widely, depending on underlying neurological and mental handicap, the age of diagnosis, the type of seizure and the degree of initial seizure control (Brorson & Wranne, 1987). The reported remission rates range from one-third to three-quarters depending on the type of seizure studied and on the number of years of follow-up (Annegers, Hauser, Elveback, & Kurland, 1980; Brorson & Wranne, 1987; Lindsay, Ounsted, & Richards, 1980; Tennison, Greenwood, Lewis, & Thorn, 1994). The absence seizures appear to have the best prognosis, followed by the generalized tonic-clonic seizures and others. Factors favoring remission include the absence of a definable cause, a normal neurological examination, normal intelligence, a less abnormal electroencephalogram, and a low rate of seizure occurrence (Callaghan, Garrett, & Goggin, 1988; Matricardi, Brinciotti, & Benedetti, 1989). At the opposite end of the spectrum, the mortality rates during childhood and early adult life range from about 20% in children with neonatal seizures and infantile spasms to about 6 to 10% in children with different childhood epilepsies (Callaghan et al., 1988; Silanpää, 1973). Thus, the outlook for an epileptic condition at its onset varies more widely than for any other medical illness, a fact that sets the scene for interesting psychological ramifications for epileptic children and their families.

Psychiatric and Learning Complications

Since epilepsy involves the central nervous system, it not only results in psychosocial problems of adjusting to a chronic illness but also in increased cognitive and behavioral problems associated with central nervous system dysfunction (Deonna, 1993). In addition, the family's adjustment problems, social prejudice, and cognitive/behavioral toxicity of antiepileptic drugs also complicate the epileptic child's psychosocial adjustment. Rutter et al. (1970) reported that in comparison to a 6.6% rate of psychiatric disorder for the general population of 5- to 14-year-old children, the rate for children with neuroepileptic disorders was 34.3%. The rate of psychiatric disorder for idiopathic epilepsy was 28.6%, while the rate for epilepsy with central nervous system lesion was much higher, 58.3%. Focal electroencephalogram abnormalities and temporal lobe epilepsy have been associated with a higher rate of psychiatric disorders.

As to the relationship between epilepsy and specific psychiatric syndrome, the fallacy of "epileptic personality" in children and adolescents has been disputed, while interest in such a distinctive personality—showing hyperemotionality, viscosity, dissociation, and religiosity—remains in adults with temporal lobe epilepsy. Schizophrenialike psychosis, especially in the left temporal lobe epilepsy and depressive disorders have been studied

more in adult epileptics, but such an association has not been established in epilepsies of childhood and adolescence. However, there is a trend of higher incidence of psychosis and hyperkinetic syndrome in children and adolescents with epilepsy and central nervous system lesion/mental retardation. Although there is a report of overrepresentation of epilepsies in children and adolescents who attempted suicide (Brent, 1986), no study indicates epilepsy in childhood and adolescence as a risk factor in completed suicide. In adult literature (Mathews & Barabas, 1981), it is estimated that the suicide risk among adult epileptics is 4 to 5 times higher than in the general population.

Among different childhood psychiatric syndromes, disruptive behavior or impulse control disorders have been most frequently cited in relation to epilepsy. Attention deficit hyperactivity disorder, conduct disorder, and symptoms of such disorders—inattentiveness, overactivity, aggression, rage attacks, and antisocial behaviors—have been identified by numerous studies (Ounsted & Lindsay, 1981), especially in boys with temporal lobe epilepsy. These symptoms or syndromes were thought to be inherently associated with epilepsy, not solely attributable to the effect of antiepileptic drugs or as an adjustment reaction of chronic illness. Related to these impulsive, disruptive behavioral problems, educational underachievement and learning deficits are found in many epileptic children of normal intelligence.

Some reports based on referred samples indicate that 50% of epileptic children have school problems and are in need of a remedial educational program. They are behind grade level in reading, spelling, and arithmetic and exhibit a greater variability of intelligence than normal children (Rutter et al., 1970). In addition, overactivity, inattentiveness, perceptual/motor coordination problems, type and severity of seizure (Holdsworth & Whitmore, 1974; Stores, 1978; Stores & Hart, 1976), and toxicity of the antiepileptic drugs (Addy, 1987; Reynolds, 1975; Trimble & Cull, 1988) are mediating factors for these academic deficits. Researchers have investigated and debated whether there are intellectual degenerative processes at work in epilepsy (Dodrill, 1986; Lesser, Lüders, Wyllie, Dinner, & Morris, 1986; Pedersen & Dam, 1986). Intellectual deterioration does not take place in the majority of epileptic children (Bourgeois, Prensky, Palkes, Talent, & Busch, 1983; Ellenberg, Hirtz, & Nelson, 1985), only in about 10%, who may suffer from early onset, severe type of seizure, brain damage, and toxicity of antiepileptic drugs.

Seizure, Pseudoseizure, and Electroencephalograms in Child Psychiatry Practice

Ever since German neuropsychiatrist Hans Berger developed the electroencephalogram (EEG) in the 1920s, it has been utilized extensively in the investigation of childhood psychiatric disorders in an attempt to find a causal relationship. There have been reports of specific and nonspecific EEG abnormalities in hyperactivity, conduct disorder, learning disability, and child psychosis. Children and adolescents with autism and aggressive juvenile delinquents have been found to have a much higher incidence of epilepsy than control groups (Lewis, Pincus, Shanok, & Glasev, 1982; Volkmar & Nelson, 1990). While attempts to correlate specific EEG patterns with different childhood psychiatric syndromes have not been successful, evidence of relationships between temporal lobe dysfunction and aggressive behavioral disorders seems to be converging. Several studies have reported that nonepileptic children with temporal lobe EEG abnormalities tended to have high rates of aggressive and delinquent behaviors. Laterality (left temporal lobe) and sex (male) have been reported to play a part in increasing vulnerability in both epileptic and nonepileptic children. Advanced EEG technology by use of computerized EEGs, brain electric activity mapping, evoked response potential, and sleep polysomnography may prove to be useful in understanding brain physiology and diagnosis of certain childhood psychiatric syndromes such as depression, attention deficit hyperactivity disorder, and psychosis (Kuperman, Johnson, Arndt, Lindgren, & Wolraich, 1996). While autism and autisticlike childhood neuropsychiatric disorders, such as Rett syndrome, Landau syndrome, and fragile X syndrome, are frequently associated with epilepsy, childhood psychiatric disorders are not of epileptic origin. Yet episodic or paroxysmal outbursts of children's behavioral problems often raise a high index of suspicion for possible epileptic origin. In the absence of clinical seizure, the value of routine EEGs is rather limited. Both false positive and false negative rates are quite high, up to 15% and 30 to 70%, respectively (Ajmone Marsan & Zivin, 1970; Eeg-Olofsson, 1970). A high false negative rate becomes an especially perplexing problem in the diagnosis and management of pseudoseizure.

Pseudoseizure may be a symptom manifestation of a primary psychiatric disorder or psychiatrically complicated epilepsy. Differential diagnosis is very difficult, and misdiagnosis of epilepsy as pseudoepilepsy and vice versa is not unusual. Pseudoseizure has been called psychogenic seizure, hysterical seizure, conversion seizure, pseudoepileptic seizure, and nonepileptic seizure, each of which has been labeled from different conceptual perspectives. A study of adolescents and young adults reported that the psychopathology of patients with hysterical seizure was largely of depressive, suicidal, and borderline symptoms rather than histrionic symptoms (Stewart, Lovitt, & Stewart, 1982). In children, anxiety symptoms were reported to be more prevalent than depressive symptomatology (Goodyer, 1985). Hysterical seizures in children and adolescents are not uncommon and occur more commonly in adolescents and in girls. Patients with mixed epileptic seizures and pseudoseizures, and nonepileptic patients who are misdiagnosed as epileptic are very difficult groups to manage and often receive inappropriate kinds and doses of antiepileptic drugs. Intensive EEG monitoring, serum prolactin monitoring (no postictal rise in pseudoseizure), and careful psychiatric evaluation would help in differential diagnosis.

Developmental and Family Perspectives

Using epilepsy as an example, Taylor (1979) conceptualized three components of sickness: disease, illness, and predicament. Disease represents the pathological lesion; illness, the manifestations of the lesion; and predicament, the impact on the individual and the family from psychological and sociological perspectives. These three components of epilepsy will be discussed in relation to the developmental tasks of different age groups and the family.

INFANCY AND EARLY CHILDHOOD

During the early period of life, epilepsies often present with underlying perinatal trauma, brain damage, and gross mental and physical handicaps. Developmental tasks of achieving attachment, basic trust, autonomy, and separation/individuation will be hard to accomplish in children who have underlying neurodevelopmental deficits. Overprotection, inconsistent parenting, and dependency of the child are frequently observed in the early parent-child relationship. During this early period of evolving personality formation, children with neuroepileptic disorders may show the characteristic of *difficult* temperament, which is a predictable variable for later personality and psychosocial dysfunction (Hertzig, 1983). Exposure to antiepileptic drugs during the vulnerable periods of early life may increase the risk for physiological adversity, such as hepatotoxicity with valproate and cognitive impairment with phenobarbital.

LATER CHILDHOOD

A high rate of regressive behaviors in school children with epilepsy, such as nail-biting, thumbsucking, stuttering, enuresis, and encopresis, has been reported. These behaviors may be viewed as regression in relation to increasing stresses and/ or continuation of early neurodevelopmental immaturity. Entering school and the task of academic learning and socialization add stresses to epileptic children, as does the fear of unexpected loss of self-control in public. These children often have significant learning, motor coordination, and other physical deficits, too, causing prejudice and rejection. Disappointment and frustration by their own underachievement and rejection by peers will reinforce their early doubt and shame about themselves. The Eriksonian task of initiative and industry during this stage of child development may be seriously compromised.

ADOLESCENCE

The discrepancy between physical and emotional maturity seen in a normal adolescent, which is a source of conflicts and problems, may be more glaring in epileptic adolescents who have not been able to build up competencies in the earlier developmental stages. The normal adolescent identity search includes movement toward emancipation from the parents, toward sexual identity, and toward vocational identity. However, adolescents with epilepsies may not have been well prepared for these tasks. They are poorly adjusted to the social milieu of teenagers—less involved in competitive sports or other extracurricular activities, restricted in driving a car. There is also a tendency to shorten the period of education for epileptic adolescents. Viberg, Blennow, and Polski (1987) reported that adolescents with epilepsy had a larger discrepancy between the observed self-image and the ideal self-image than the control group. They were also found to have poor body and self-image and unstable sexual identity, and to feel threatened by the unknown and by risk of acting out.

ADULT OUTCOME

Considering the cumulative stresses and incomplete acquisition of developmental competencies in the early developmental stages, it is not surprising to find many reports depicting poor adult outcome of epileptic children and adolescents. Occupational disadvantages are manifested in lower-paid and unskilled work and a higher rate of unemployment. There is a high incidence of psychosexual disorders and a lower rate of marriage among epileptic adults than among the general population (Levin, Banks, & Bers, 1988). Consequently, epileptic adults have a low sense of psychosocial well-being. They are at a higher risk to develop depression and suicide.

FAMILY

The burden of raising epileptic children and coping with accompanying psychosocial complications rest with the immediate family, parents and siblings. Although there have been reports of a high divorce or separation rate in the parents of epileptic children, poor marital adjustment in the parents of children with chronic illness in general and with epilepsy in particular is a controversial issue. The negative influences on the family also have been examined in the psychopathology of the immediate family members. Both parents and siblings of epileptic children have a higher incidence of psychiatric morbidity than the general population or other comparison groups (juvenile diabetics) (Hoare, 1984). However, in addition to a stress reaction, there may be genetic and other confounding factors that increase the incidence of psychopathology in parents and siblings. Interactive and systems approaches would be more useful in understanding dynamic interplays within the family of the epileptic child (Ritchie, 1981) than a monodimensional stress reaction model. Hoare (1987) proposed that the family of an epileptic child may be studied using Minuchin's psychosomatic family model. Earlier psychoanalytic views still exert strong influences on clinicians' understanding of interactions of parents and epileptic children. The mourning processes of loss, denial, anger, depression, and guilt have been applied to the parents' reaction to the child's epileptic condition. This kind of neurotic response gives rise to a wide range of parental attitudes ranging from overprotection and overindulgency to rejection, resulting in further compromise in the development of the epileptic child, many of whom are already developmentally disadvantaged.

Psychopharmacology

PSYCHOTROPIC EFFECTS OF ANTIEPILEPTIC DRUGS

Studies have consistently pointed to a greater frequency of behavioral/cognitive side effects with the older class of drugs, such as phenobarbital and phenytoin. Epilepsy itself is accompanied by an increase of behavioral and cognitive impairments, which are further complicated by the adverse effects of these drugs. Phenobarbital is well known for its excitable side effects such as hyperactivity, irritability, insomnia, and tantrums (Wolf & Forsythe, 1978). A recent prospective study (Farwell, Lee, Hirtz, Sulzbacher, Ellenberg, & Nelson, 1990) unequivocally illustrated that phenobarbital caused stunting of intellectual growth in young

children. Phenytoin also has been reported to cause cognitive deterioration—"pseudodegenerative disease" and "encephalopathy" manifested in cerebral (confusion, delirium, psychosis) and cerebellar signs. While the newer class of drugs, such as carbamazepine and valproate, are increasingly becoming popular for the treatment of various psychiatric disorders in adults as well as in children and adolescents, these drugs also may cause irritability, hyperactivity, and labile mood. However, the side effects are much less frequent than those of phenobarbital and phenytoin (Berg, Butler, Ellis, & Foster, 1993). The risk of behavioral toxicity by antiepileptic drugs is related to earlier onset of epilepsy, brain damage, long-term use of a drug, and use of multiple drugs, medical negligence, and metabolic variation (Reynolds, 1975). Differential effects on behavior and cognition by different blood levels of drugs are an interesting but little-studied area. Examples are excited behavioral problems at low levels of phenobarbital and primidone, difficulties of motor coordination at high valproate levels, and the improved speed of performance at high carbamazepine levels. In general, pharmacokinetic studies have shown greater interpatient variability in children than in adults. Recent interests in relationship between pharmacokinetics and cognitive function indicate a more stable path of cognitive functioning when serum concentration of antiepileptic drugs fluctuates less by use of a controlled-release preparation (Aldenkamp, Alpherts, Dekker, & Overweg, 1990).

EPILEPTOGENIC SIDE EFFECTS OF PSYCHOTROPIC DRUGS

Epileptogenic side effects of psychotropic drugs are rather rare in psychiatric patients without underlying risk for epilepsy. However, psychotropic drugs invariably produce EEG changes and may induce subclinical or clinical seizures in nonepileptic patients who are vulnerable to seizure. Psychotropic drugs also may aggravate preexisting epileptic conditions. Risk factors for seizure precipitation by psychotropic drugs include a family history of seizure, pretreatment EEG irregularities, a history of epilepsy, presence of organic brain pathology, a history of brain damage, polypharmacy, a sudden rapid change of dose and/or a high dose regimen, and individual hypersensitivity (Itil & Soldatos, 1980). For instance, the occurrence of seizures was reported in about 0.5% of patients receiving low to moderate doses of phenothiazines and in about 10% of patients receiving large doses of phenothiazines. The use of psychotropic drugs in epileptic children and in nonepileptic children with neuromaturational deficits and abnormal EEGs poses dilemmas and challenges to the psychiatrist. In general, epileptogenic side effects of neuroleptics are related linearly with their sedative properties and inversely with their extrapyramidal side effects, except that piperazine phenothiazines are less epileptogenic than other phenothiazines. Antidepressants are generally less epileptogenic than neuroleptics. Tricyclic antidepressants are more epileptogenic than newer nontricyclic antidepressants. While lithium may cause a significant increase of paroxysmal and focal EEG abnormalities, its safe and effective use in epileptic patients and in children with aggressive conduct disorder, most of whom had abnormal baseline EEGs, (Campbell, Small, Green, Jennings, Perry, Bennett, & Anderson, 1984) also has been reported. Human and animal research indicates that dopamine antagonists are antipsychotic and mildly epileptogenic, and dopamine agonists, such as levo-dopa, apomorphine, and amphetamine, are psychotogenic and mildly antiepileptic (Trimble, 1977). Thus, theoretically, stimulant drugs used for attention deficit hyperactivity disorder should have some antiepileptic property, although no clinical research data support such a proposition (Kim, 1991). As hyperactivity and attentional problems are the most common psychiatric symptoms of epileptic children, this area should be studied further.

Psychiatric Treatment

In sum, at least one-third of children and adolescents with epilepsy manifest various difficulties—seizure control, academic, emotional, behavioral, and family problems. As a group, they have a much higher rate of psychiatric disorder than healthy children and children with other chronic illnesses (Hoare, 1987). This increased vulnerability is associated with several factors, including the type of neurological lesion (brain damage, site of origin and type of epilepsy, chronicity, seizure frequency, etc.), the individual characteristics of the child (age, gender, temperament, cognitive

ability, etc.), psychiatric disturbance in other family members, and the adverse effects of antiepileptic drugs. Some of these vulnerability factors are interrelated and mediate various outcomes of epilepsy—seizure control, learning problems, and a host of psychosocial adjustment areas in addition to psychopathology. As with any childhood psychiatric disorder, psychiatric disorders of epileptic children appear to be multifactorially determined, with neurological factors, intellectual and educational factors, and sociofamilial influences all playing a part in causation. Similarly, the type of psychiatric disorder manifested in epileptic youths is not uniquely different from the range of psychiatric disorder found in the general population or in children with chronic mental illnesses. However, disruptive behavioral disorders, such as attention deficit hyperactivity disorder and conduct and aggressive behavioral disorders tend to occur more often, especially in boys.

In view of the multihandicapping nature of epilepsy in children and ample evidence for increased psychiatric risk, therapeutic and preventive psychiatric interventions are justified. Developmental assessments of intellectual, academic, social, and emotional progress should be a routine part of management of epilepsy in the young population. How the epileptic youth is progressing in terms of disease, illness, and predicament should be assessed periodically. Impairments of control and competency in epileptic children and their families are the major long-term complication. The mastery of developmental tasks in both the child and the family may be interrupted or lag behind. A cognitive coping strategy model applied to chronic sickness of children by Compas (1987) is a useful model in enhancing the mastery and competency of various developmental tasks and thus in promoting overall successful adaptation. M. A. Lewis and colleagues (1990, 1991) reported on the impact of a child-centered, family-focused supportive educational and counseling program for children with epilepsy and for their parents. Increased knowledge and social competency and reduced anxiety were observed in both children and parents. The authors stressed, that changing children's self-attributed labels from "epileptic and disabled" to "competent and socially skilled" may have a profound effect on the lives of children with severe disorders.

Diagnostic and psychotherapeutic skills would be of great value when assisting children with epilepsy and their family members who present with complex management problems, in order to accurately ascertain the nature of the problem and to provide educational and supportive counseling initially. Arrangement of a special educational program for some or counseling for teachers and parents is often indicated to clarify the children's gross or subtle learning handicap and to combat the lack of understanding and increase appropriate expectations by the teachers and parents (Long & Moore, 1979). Behavior modification treatment, psychodynamically oriented psychotherapy (Sperling, 1978), and family systems interventions have been proposed to lessen seizures and improve conditions associated with epilepsy. Psychotropic drugs can be used judiciously and effectively for psychiatric disorders of epileptic youths. These children and adolescents should not be deprived of the benefits of modern pediatric psychopharmacotherapy just because of their epilepsy. The psychiatrist also can play an important role in detecting behavioral and cognitive side effects of antiepileptic drugs and should work closely with the neurologist. The magnitude and the extent of problems in epileptic youths are well suited for clinical and research investigations by clinicians who are biopsychosocially and developmentally oriented.

REFERENCES

Addy, D. P. (1987). Cognitive function in children with epilepsy. *Developmental Medicine and Child Neurology, 29,* 394–396.

Ajmone Marsan, C., & Zivin, L. S. (1970). Factors related to the occurrence of typical paroxysmal abnormalities in the EEG records of epileptic patients. *Epilepsia, 11,* 361–381.

Aldenkamp, A. P., Alpherts, W. C. J., Dekker, M. J. A., & Overweg, J. (1990). Neuropsychological aspects of learning disabilities in epilepsy. *Epilepsia, 31* (Suppl. 4), S9–S20.

Annegers, J. F., Hauser, W. A., Elveback, L. K., & Kurland, L. T. (1980). Remission and relapses of seizures in epilepsy. In J. Wada & J. Penry (Eds.), *Advances in epileptology: The tenth International Epilepsy Symposium* (pp. 143–147). New York: Raven Press.

Berg, I., Butler, A., Ellis, M., & Foster, J. (1993). Psychiatric aspects of epilepsy in children treated with carbamazepine, phenytoin or sodium valproate: A random trial. *Developmental Medicine and Child Neurology, 35,* 149–157.

Bourgeois, B. F. D., Prensky, A. C., Palkes, H. S., Talent, B. K., & Busch, S. G. (1983). Intelligence in epilepsy: A prospective study in children. *Annals of Neurology, 14,* 438–444.

Brent, D. A. (1986). Overrepresentation of epileptics in a consecutive series of suicide attempters seen at a children's hospital, 1978–1983. *Journal of the American Academy of Child Psychiatry, 25,* 242–246.

Brorson, L. O., & Wranne, L. (1987). Long-term prognosis in childhood epilepsy: Survival and seizure prognosis. *Epilepsia, 28,* 324–330.

Callaghan, N., Garrett, A., & Goggin, T. (1988). Withdrawal of anticonvulsant drugs in patients free of seizures for two years. *New England Journal of Medicine, 318,* 942–946.

Campbell, M., Small, A. M., Green, W. H., Jennings, S. J., Perry, R., Bennett, N. G., & Anderson, L. (1984). Behavioral efficacy of haloperidol and lithium carbonate: A comparison in hospitalized aggressive children with conduct disorder. *Archives of General Psychiatry, 120,* 650–656.

Compas, B. E. (1987). Coping with stress during childhood and adolescence. *Psychological Bulletin, 98,* 310–357.

Cowan, L. D., Bodensteiner, J. B., Leviton, A., & Doherty, L. (1989). Prevalence of the epilepsies in children and adolescents. *Epilepsia, 30,* 94–106.

Deonna, T. (1993). Annotation: Cognitive and behavioral correlates of epileptic activity in children. *Journal of Child Psychology and Psychiatry, 34,* 611–620.

Dodrill, C. B. (1986). Correlates of generalized tonic-clonic seizures with intellectual, neuropsychological, emotional, and social function in patients with epilepsy. *Epilepsia, 27,* 399–411.

Eeg-Olofsson, O. (1970). The development of the electroencephalogram in normal children and adolescents from the age of 1 through 21 years. *Acta Paediatrica Scandinavica* (Suppl. 208).

Ellenberg, J. H., Hirtz, D. G., & Nelson, K. B. (1985). Do seizures in children cause intellectual deterioration? *Annals of Neurology, 18,* 389.

Farwell, J. R., Lee, Y. J., Hirtz, D. G., Sulzbacher, S. I., Ellenberg, J. H., & Nelson K. B. (1990). Phenobarbital for febrile seizures—Effects on intelligence and on seizure recurrence. *New England Journal of Medicine, 322,* 364–369.

Goodyer, I. M. (1985). Epileptic and pseudo-epileptic seizures in childhood and adolescence. *Journal of the American Academy of Child Psychiatry, 24,* 3–9.

Gudmundsson, G. (1966). Epilepsy in Iceland. *Acta Neurologica Scandinavica, 43* (Suppl. 25), S124–S129.

Hauser, W. A., & Kurland, L. T. (1975). The epidemiology of epilepsy in Rochester, Minnesota, 1935 through 1967. *Epilepsia, 16,* 1–66.

Hertzig, M. E. (1983). Temperament and neurological

status. In M. Rutter (Ed.), *Developmental neuropsychiatry* (pp. 164–180). New York: Guilford Press.

Hoare, P. (1984). Psychiatric disturbance in the families of epileptic children. *Developmental Medicine and Child Neurology, 26,* 14–19.

Hoare, P. (1987). Children with epilepsy and their families. *Journal of Child Psychology and Psychiatry, 28,* 651–655.

Holdsworth, L., & Whitmore, K. (1974). A study of children with epilepsy attending normal schools. I: Their seizure patterns, progress and behavior in school. *Developmental Medicine and Child Neurology, 16,* 746–758.

Itil, T. M., & Soldatos, C. (1980). Epileptogenic side effects of psychotropic drugs: practical recommendations. *Journal of the American Medical Association, 244,* 1460–1463.

Kim, W. J. (1991). Psychiatric aspects of epileptic children and adolescents. *Journal of the American Academy of Child and Adolescent Psychiatry, 30,* 844–866.

Kuperman, S., Johnson, B., Arndt, S., Lindgren, S., & Wolraich, M. (1996). Quantitative EEG differences in a nonclinical sample of children with ADHD and undifferentiated ADD. *Journal of the American Academy of Child and Adolescent Psychiatry, 35* (8), 1009–1017.

Lesser, R. P., Lüders, H., Wylie, E., Dinner, D. S., & Morris, H. H., III (1986). Mental deterioration in epilepsy. *Epilepsia, 27,* (Suppl. 2), S105–S123.

Levin, R., Banks, S., & Berg, B. (1988). Psychosocial dimensions of epilepsy: a review of the literature. *Epilepsia, 29,* 805–816.

Lewis, D. O., Pincus, J. H., Shanok, S. S., & Glaser, G. H. (1982). Psychomotor epilepsy and violence in a group of incarcerated adolescent boys. *American Journal of Psychiatry, 139,* 882–887.

Lewis, M. A., Matton, C. L., Salas, I., Leake, B., & Chiofalo, N. (1991). Impact of the children's epilepsy program on parents. *Epilepsia, 32* (3), 365–374.

Lewis, M. A., Salas, I., de la Sota, H., Chiofalo, N., & Lenke, B. (1990). Randomized trial of a program to enhance the competencies of children with epilepsy. *Epilepsia, 31* (1), 101–109.

Lindsay, J., Ounsted, C., & Richards, P. (1980). Longterm outcome in children with temporal lobe seizures. 4. Genetic factors, febrile convulsion and the remission of seizures. *Developmental Medicine and Child Neurology, 22,* 429–440.

Long, C. G., & Moore, J. R. (1979). Parental expectations for their epileptic children. *Journal of Child Psychology and Psychiatry, 20,* 299–312.

Matricardi, M., Brinciotti, M., & Benedetti, P. (1989). Outcome after discontinuation of antiepileptic drug therapy in children with epilepsy. *Epilepsia, 17,* 245–256.

Matthews, W., & Barabas, G. (1981). Suicide and epilepsy: A review of the literature. *Psychosomatics, 22,* 515–524.

Morrell, M. J. (1993). Differential diagnosis of seizures. *Neurological Clinics, 11,* 737–754.

Ounsted, C., & Lindsay, J. (1981). The long-term outcome of temporal lobe epilepsy in childhood. In E. Reynolds & M. Trimble (Eds.), *Epilepsy and psychiatry* (pp. 185–215). London: Churchill Livingston.

Pedersen, B., & Dam, M. (1986). Memory disturbances in epileptic patients. *Acta Neurologica Scandinavica, 74* (Suppl 109), 11–14.

Reynold, E. H. (1975). Chronic antiepileptic toxicity: A review. *Epilepsia, 16,* 319–352.

Ritchie, K. (1981). Research note: Interaction in the families of epileptic children. *Journal of Child Psychology and Psychiatry, 22,* 65–71.

Rutter, M., Graham, P., & Yule, W. (Eds.). (1970). A neuropsychiatric study in childhood. *Clinics in Developmental Medicine* (pp. 1–257). London: Heinemann/Spastics International Medical Publications.

Scheuer, M. L., & Pedley, T. A. (1990). The evaluation and treatment of seizures. *New England Journal of Medicine, 323,* 1468–1474.

Silanpää, M. (1973). Medico-social prognosis of children with epilepsy: Epidemiological study and analysis of 245 patients. *Acta Paediatrica Scandinavica, 62* (Suppl. 237), 3–104.

Sperling, E. (1978). Epilepsy, psychodynamics and therapy. In E. Sperling (Ed.), *Psychosomatic disorders in childhood* (pp. 285–307). New York: Jason Aronson.

Stewart, R. S., Lovitt, R., & Stewart, M. S. (1982). Psychopathology associated with hysterical seizures. *American Journal of Psychiatry, 139,* 926–929.

Stores, G. (1978). School children with epilepsy at risk for learning and behavior problems. *Developmental Medicine and Child Neurology, 20,* 502–508.

Stores, G., & Hart, J. (1976). Reading skills of children with generalized or focal epilepsy attending ordinary school. *Developmental Medicine and Child Neurology, 18,* 705–716.

Taylor, D. C. (1979). The components of sickness: Diseases, illnesses and predicaments. *Lancet, 2,* 1008–1010.

Tennison, M., Greenwood, R., Lewis, D., & Thorn, M. (1994). Discontinuing antiepileptic drugs in children with epilepsy. *The New England Journal of Medicine, 330,* (20), 1407–1410.

Trimble, M. R. (1977). The relationship between epilepsy and schizophrenia: a biochemical hypothesis. *Biological Psychiatry, 12,* 299–304.

Trimble, M. R., & Cull, C. (1988). Children of school age: The influence of antiepileptic drugs on behavior and intellect. *Epilepsia, 29* (Suppl. 3), S15–S19.

Viberg, M., Blennow, G., & Polski, B. (1987). Epilepsy in adolescence: Implications for the development of personality. *Epilepsia, 28,* 542–546.

Volkmar, F. R., & Nelson, D. S. (1990). Seizure disorders in autism. *Journal of the American Academy of Child and Adolescent Psychiatry, 29,* 127–129.

Wolf, S. M., & Forsythe, A. (1978). Behavioral disturbance, phenobarbital and febrile seizures. *Pediatrics, 61,* 728–731.

39 / Severe Burns

Frederick J. Stoddard

Infants, children, and adolescents suffer burn injuries worldwide, and have throughout history. Most are from preventable accidents, and for many years accidents have been the commonest cause of death for children ages 1 to 15 years (Crawford, 1990). Burns result from scalds, house fires, war, gasoline, electrocution, volcanos, abuse or self-abuse, other causes, and toxic epidermal neurolysis, which is much like a burn. Many children with severe burns die, but most survive because of remarkable progress in wound management (e.g., artificial skin), anesthesia, nutrition, metabolism, and infection control (Ryan, Sheridan, Tompkins, 1996; Tompkins et al., 1988). The severity of a burn involves not only its size, but also its meaning, location, associated pain, and residual functional loss and disfigurement. Responses to disfigurement vary in different cultures. In a few cultures there is public acceptance and legal recognition of the special needs of burn patients, while in most cultures, stigmatization occurs. Advances in plastic and reconstructive surgery such as facial and hand reconstruction, microsurgery, tissue expanders, breast reconstruction, and staged flap procedures have vastly improved cosmetic and functional outcomes, lessening stigma.

Burn psychiatry, often involving children and adolescents, has an illustrious history. Stanley Cobbs and Erich Lindemann wrote classic studies of grief after the Coconut Grove fire in 1943. Other studies have broken new ground in areas as varied as military psychiatry, psychiatric epidemiology, burn delirium, child abuse, undertreatment of pain, endorphins, pharmacokinetics, hypnosis, posttraumatic stress disorder, self-immolation, stigma and disfigurement, long-term outcomes, parent posttraumatic stress disorder, and staff stress and burnout. Much more research is needed.

In the United States, approximately 2 million people are burned annually, 70% of whom are children under 5. Of the thousands hospitalized, about 68% are under 19 years of age, and of those more than half are under 4. McKay, Halpern, McLaughlin, Locke, and Crawford (1979) showed there was a fivefold greater incidence of burns in census tracts where the median income was at poverty level compared to more middle-class census tracts of the same cities. Many infants and toddlers are burned, especially by scalding, and skills in infant psychiatry are very helpful on pediatric burn units. Large burns have been proven to cause more pain (Figure 39.1), disproving the notion that larger burns destroyed pain sensation.

The principal burn units for severely burned children are the Shriners Burns Institutes in Bos-

THE EFFECT OF BODY SURFACE AREA (BSA) BURNED ON THE MEAN PAIN SCORES OF PATIENTS DURING BURN DRESSING CHANGES (BDC's)

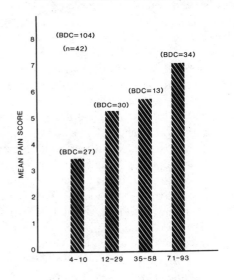

% BODY SURFACE AREA BURNED

FIGURE 39.1

The mean pain scores of 42 acutely burned children (8 to 18 years old) during 104 burn dressing changes, ordered by the extent of body surface area involved. Scores were obtained at 1-minute intervals at least. (Patients volunteered changes in scores between the minute queries). Source: Atchison, Osgood, Carr, & Szyfelbein, 1991.

ton, Cincinnati, Galveston and Sacramento, and several in children's hospitals or public general hospitals in major cities. Many children are treated in burn units that include adults, and most are treated as outpatients. The American Burn Association is the national scientific organization for all medical and allied disciplines involved in burn treatment. The Phoenix Society is the very active international self-help organization.

Body Image

The subject of body image development in burned children and adolescents is central to the consultative process with burned children (Stoddard, 1982). The mother of the newly burned infant expresses acute grief over the loss of her unblemished child and often needs help with her guilt and the disruption in her attachment to her child. Effective psychotherapeutic intervention through the crisis can help her sustain her infant, rather than abandoning or overprotecting the child. Body image as defined by Schilder (1950) is the concept or mental scheme of the body that each person has, involving interpersonal, environmental, and temporal factors. A more complex definition by Shontz (1990) that has been helpful with burn patients expands the concept of body image to the functions that it serves and the developmental levels at which it operates. The functions it serves are sensory register, instrument of action, source of drives, stimulus to the self (aoursal, pain proprioception), stimulus to others through attractive or unattractive appearance, expressive instrument through nonverbal communication, and a private world (the experience of the self). Body image is a relatively stable aspect of self-concept by 18 to 30 months and is modified by growth, puberty, trauma, and aging. It is usually integrated by age 3 to 4 and reflects pleasurable and painful, active and passive bodily experiences such as seeing and being seen, holding and being held, motor activity, feeding, toileting and arousal states.

Disorders in body image functioning may occur at any level of body image experience, including the basic neurological body image–body schemata, body self, body fantasy, or body concept—the highest level of body image and the most susceptible to cognitive intervention. A classic example of a body schemata disorder might be the occurrence of phantom limb phenomena following amputation. An extreme example of a disturbance of body self might be the sense of loss of personality that patients with severe facial burns may experience when they look at themselves in the mirror for the first time. An example of a body fantasy is of the child maintained on a respirator who over time incorporates the nasopharyngeal tube into her body image, and without it becomes panicked she will die regardless of the actual danger. A body concept disturbance may appear to the clinician to be simply a misunderstanding—for example, when a young adolescent is told he will have plastic surgical repair of a deformed hand and he believes that the hand will be fixed with "plastic" to appear just as it did before he was injured. Factors involved in such a misunderstanding may be anxiety interfering with comprehension of explanations, denial, omnipotent fantasies about doctors, limited education, and cognitive immaturity.

CASE EXAMPLES

The following case examples will illustrate some of the developmental, body image, posttraumatic, and sociocultural aspects that are common in burn injuries.

An 11-Month-Old with a Scald Burn to His Face: Dennis was an 11-month-old boy who suffered 32% scalds to his face, chest, back, and neck as a result of pulling a cup of coffee onto himself. He is one of seven children and his mother was diagnosed with depression one year earlier. He became agitated and received sedatives. His medications included intravenous morphine (1.5 to 3 milligrams [mg] per hour), chloral hydrate (500 mg twice), and midazolam (Versed) (1 mg as needed). His parents maintained contact only by phone during the initial 2 weeks of treatment, although the maternal grandparents visited once. Psychological care included a consistent nurse and soothing tactile and vocal "holding" to attempt to lessen the separation reaction he was presumed to be having.

A 30-Month Old with 20% Chemical Burns to Trunk, Buttock, and Leg: Laura, a 30-month-old black girl, was admitted with burns anteriorly to her right and left trunk, buttock, and leg. She was reported to have spilled RamOut Liquid Plumber over herself. She presented for weeks as withdrawn and pain insensitive, and the nursing staff were concerned that she may have been abused. The history did not indicate this, but a child abuse/neglect petition was filed; child protective screening was done 10 days after admission, and allegations by medical personnel of possible abuse were not substantiated. Despite her continued withdrawal, sad appearance, and lack of crying, discharge plans were made since she had nearly healed. Just before scheduled discharge, another hospital called to report that the mother was being treated for a severe beating by the father. Although the mother was embarrassed and said this was the first time, the child's discharge was postponed pending completion of the reopened child abuse investigation.

A Girl with Burns to Her Perineal Area: Erica was a 4½-year-old with a 10% scald to her abdomen and thighs from Dunkin' Donuts Coffee in a bag. The bag was trapped in the safety belt over her lap and the coffee soaked into her jogging outfit, scalding her. She was extremely pain sensitive. She was a large overweight girl whose mother described her as "shy" and "standoffish," but was less so with an oral psychotherapeutic group for burned children. At first she was withdrawn, but with encouragement she described how her burn happened and talked (in displacement) of feeling afraid, not of burn dressing changes but rather of a black scary dog that she had feared would bite her and had licked her face. When asked to draw the scary image, she drew a black scribbled circle and then scratched it out. As she healed, her anxiety decreased, and since she did not actually have a genital burn, her parents were reassured. (Note: Most genital burns heal well.)

An Adolescent with Burns from a Cabin Fire: Mark was a 15½-year-old boy who suffered 86% burns to his face, hands, and trunk, including his perineal area and penis, and was placed in a sterile tent. Pain was managed with background intravenous morphine (8 mg/hr) and 15 mg boluses when needed; anxiety with 1 mg lorazepam (Ativan) every 6 hours intravenously. A friend died in the fire and another boy was severely burned but Mark denied grief, focusing more upon his bodily losses. He complained of nightmares of the fire and had waking flashbacks. He yearned for a private room instead of the embarrassment of being exposed on

the open burn unit. His mother was intellectually limited, emotionally regressed, and could not tolerate his pain; she removed his splints against medical orders on several occasions. His denial of his severe hand burns was evident in his wish to hand wrestle and feeling that he "looked fine." After 6 weeks he was more aware that he had suffered irreparable losses, sadly saying "my hair can grow back but my hands can't," as he watched the tips of his fingers slowly auto-amputate. Despite such losses, he (together with his mother) gradually recovered psychologically, while his wounds healed through further surgery, intensive physical therapy, discharge, and reentry to his home and school.

Acute and Long-Term Diagnostic Assessment

Coping following burns, as after other trauma, is impaired by presence of emotional or behavioral disorders, preexisting or caused by the burn experience. Table 39.1 shows the range of psychiatric disorders that occur near the time of burn injury.

TABLE 39.1

Common Diagnoses with Acutely Burned Children

Pain syndromes

Delirium

Acute stress and anxiety states

Sleep disorders

Grief

Posttraumatic stress disorder

Child neglect

Child abuse (physical, sexual)

Adjustment disorders

Preexisting disorders:
- Learning disabilities
- Attention deficit hyperactivity disorder
- Conduct disorders
- Depression
- Substance abuse

Children usually survive and are left with scarring to various body parts. Failure to thoroughly evaluate children psychiatrically often leads to underrecognition of serious disturbance and undertreatment of burned children. Research indicates that those with massive burns or with visible disfigurement, such as to the face or hands, may be more likely to suffer negative interpersonal, emotional, and vocational consequences from burn injuries. However, many children with burns progress well with supportive family and school and do not necessarily manifest long-term problems.

Tragically, some children do not survive. When a burned child is dying, staff communication should be close to support the patient, family, and burn team and to reduce stress. Ethical issues should be addressed within the team and outside consultation sought when needed (Stoddard, 1990). After a death, follow-up outreach to the family may assist them in their grief.

What range of disorders are commonly seen on follow-up of burn patients? A few well-designed studies have been done both with patients whose burns have not been severe (approximately under 30%) and those who have had extremely severe burn injuries.

Reviews of the outcome literature of children (Stoddard, 1996; Tarnowski & Rasnake, 1994) and adults (Patterson et al., 1993) conclude that most patients function well despite burn injuries, and burn size does not seem to be correlated with psychopathology. However, most studies prior to 1985, which constitute a majority of those reviewed, and some since then, used non-random or poorly characterized samples, mainly those with small burns; lacked current diagnostic instruments; used mainly mailed questionnaires; and did not have comparison groups. This author concludes that it is premature to dismiss findings of long-term psychopathology due to burns in a substantial minority of patients, or to attribute those findings wholly to preexisting psychopathology. A few studies suggest that those with small burns may suffer more emotional disturbances than those with large burns. The meanings that the injury has for those patients are important since patients with similar injuries respond differently. Both anxiety and depressive disorders are common, but many children have them acutely but

not chronically. More severe injuries are associated with more severe and lasting sequelae, but not always. For example, one boy with a 95% burn at age 7 survived, has had over 30 operations and 10 years of weekly psychotherapy. He is very independent, reads voraciously, has a dry sense of humor, has friends, is sexually active, and will soon enter college.

The disorders that have been found in studies of children burned years earlier include a range of anxiety disorders, especially phobias, depression, posttraumatic stress disorder, enuresis, conduct disorder, and attention deficit disorder, as well as no disorders (Stoddard, Norman, Murphy, & Beardslee, 1989) (Figure 39.2).

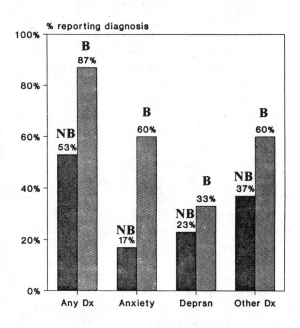

NB = NONBURNED

B = BURNED

FIGURE 39.2

DSM-III *lifetime diagnoses for children after recovery from burns, and nonburned children. Rates of any diagnosis and of anxiety disorders for the burned sample compared to the nonburned sample are significantly elevated. In addition, elevations in depression and other diagnoses are evident. Source: Stoddard, Norman, Murphy, & Beardslee, 1989.*

Probably certain disorders found in psychiatric research with burned children and adolescents, such as phobias, enuresis, and most depression, are manifestations of posttraumatic stress disorder. One study documented that over a third of survivors of childhood burns went on to marry, and many had children (Knudson-Cooper & Thomas, 1988).

Evaluation and Treatment

A range of interventions (Table 39.4) are quite helpful in managing problems of burned children. Child psychiatric management objectives are: to identify the problems, preexisting and new, and plan appropriate individual psychotherapeutic, psychopharmacologic, and family treatment from the acute through the rehabilitation phases. The burn team should include a child and adolescent psychiatrist, psychologist, and social worker. These people should be interested, specially trained, and available to assist in meeting the psychosocial goals. Past social and psychiatric history often includes unique circumstances around the injury, developmental change, disruptive or learning disorders, child neglect or abuse, or parental divorce, depression, or substance abuse. Pain should be carefully assessed (Table 39.2) and managed based on that assessment (Carr, Osgood, & Szyfelbein, 1993). It should be alleviated based on the patient's self-ratings of pain, which usually reflect beta-endorphin levels, as shown in Figure 39.3, which shows higher pain ratings with beta-endorphin levels in burned children.

A series of three studies with children showed that preparing them and allowing them to participate in their dressing changes dramatically reduced the psychological problems associated with their treatment (Lasoff & McEttrick, 1986).

Important methods of pain relief also include opiates, sometimes at high doses, other intravenous analgesics, benzodiazepines (see Table 39.3), relaxation techniques, and hypnosis. Pain relief methods should be selected and documented in the chart of each patient.

When a child is critically burned, there should be especially close team communication and support for the patient and family in order to reduce

TABLE 39.2
Assessment of Burn Pain: Relevant Factors

SUBJECTIVE AND OBJECTIVE MEASURES:	Self-ratings Observer ratings/staff attitudes Scales/checklists
PHYSICAL: *Burn Characteristics* *Treatments*	Type Location Extent and depth Burn dressing changes Tubbing Silver nitrate Silver sulfadiazene (Silvadene) & other applications
Neurochemical Factors	Endorphin levels Analgesic or antianxiety drug effects, toxicity
BEHAVIORAL:	Hypermetabolism/drug excretion Vocal and behaviors Responsivity to pain relief Appetite Sleep
PSYCHOLOGICAL:	Temperament Developmental stage Locus of control Past experience with pain Presence of parent Relationship with nurse Guilt Preexisting psychopathology Hypnotizability
SOCIAL/CULTURAL:	Poverty Social sanction for expression of pain response Response to intensive care unit Fluency in language used by caregivers

stress. Following the acute phase, child psychiatric reevaluation can assess needs for longer-term treatment. When such treatment is not needed, it is important to clarify this with the parents since many assume their child is emotionally damaged. Treatment should include diagnostic evaluation, crisis intervention, parent counseling, and appropriate pharmacotherapy. Since most pediatric

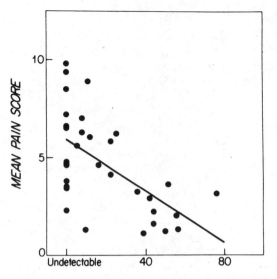

FIGURE 39.3

The relationship of the initial (before analgesic and BDC) beta-endorphin plasma immunoactivity and mean pain score for the time of burn dressing change: Scores obtained at intervals of 1 minute or less throughout the BDC (I = 0.60, p < 0.001, n = 33). Source: Szyfelbein, Osgood, & Carr, 1985.

TABLE 39.3

Commonly Used Psychotropic Drugs

	Drug [half-life in hours]
ANALGESICS: OPIATES	Morphine
	Oxycodone
	Codeine
ANXIOLYTICS: BENZODIAZEPINES:	Midazolam (Versed) [1–12.3]
	Lorazepam (Ativan) [10–20]
	Diazepam (Valium) [20.50]
	Triazolam (Halcion) [1.6–5.4]
	Clonazepam (Klonopin) [18–50]
	Flurazepam (Dalmane) Metabolites [2–4 and 47–100]
SEDATIVES:	Benadryl
	Chloral hydrate

TABLE 39.4

Treatment Interventions

Separation anxiety/abandonment reactions:
- Consistent parent surrogate
- Photos, audiotapes, familiar stories
- Monitor infant's responsivity to interventions

Pain and sleep assessments:
Pain-relieving methods—Psychological
- Provide familiar objects
- Encourage parent room in
- Increase patient's control: relaxation methods, hypnosis, biofeedback methods

Pharmacological:
- NSAIDS Nonsteroidal antiinflammatory drugs (e.g., acetaminophen [Tylenol])
- Opiates
- Benzodiazepines
- Patient-controlled analgesia
- Assess recurrent biological factors, especially sleep deprivation

Anxiety/Panic/Posttraumatic Stress Disorder:
- Short-term psychotherapy
- Benzodiazepines, especially midazolam, lorazepam
- Group therapy (young child; adolescent)

Depression:
- Psychotherapy
- Assess biological factors
- Antidepressants

Parent Anxiety and Grief:
- Parent education and therapy groups
- Establish consistent relationship
- Identify stage of adaptation
- Facilitate affective expression of grief
- Prepare for rehabilitation phase

burn units have very limited mental health consultation, patients with the most acute needs should be made a priority. From early in treatment, patient and family should be educated about burn rehabilitation and encouraged to think realistically and hopefully about the future (see Table 39.4).

Parents and family members often need counseling or psychotherapy to relieve grief and guilt before they can help their child. In most units, social workers provide this crucial intervention. Family, school, and community agencies need to be encouraged not to overprotect the child, who usually is able to return to previous levels of functioning after leaving the hospital. Return to school rather than home tutoring lessens isolation from peers and stigmatization and usually enhances self-esteem. School visits by hospital staff, phone calls, correspondence, and a videotape of the child for the school all lessen fears and stigma associated with burns and disfigurement for teachers and classmates. Reentry after recovery is a phase in which disability can be lessened (Cahners & Kartiganer, 1990). Over the long term, a psychiatric consultant should be available at future crisis points such as further surgery, bodily growth, rejection by a peer, puberty and sexual functioning, school or social problems, or inability to function in some way because of a burn-related impairment.

Stress Within the Burn Team

Enabling staff members to express their feelings, such as grief, anger, or humor, within a safe context is essential to their empathic functioning on a pediatric burn unit rather than developing burnout. Simply being on a burn unit is so painful visually, and traumatic in other sensory ways, as to qualify as a stressor for posttraumatic stress. Therefore, to a degree, witnessing burned children's disfigurement and the smell of their burned, bleeding, and infected flesh can cut through the feelings of the best-defended nurse, surgeon, or psychiatrist and expose deep emotional and visceral reactions (Ravenscroft, 1982). Despite such stresses, the satisfactions make work on a burn team worthwhile. It is rewarding for staff to treat injured children, to relieve their pain, and to aid and see their physical and emotional recovery.

Often it is helpful to prepare new nurses, surgeons, or psychiatrists on a burn unit for the normal responses that they may feel: sadness, nightmares, and guilt about children being angry with them for causing pain. It can also be useful for doctors or nurses to observe and remember that their own initial confused, irritated, or sad traumatic reactions mirror what may be felt by the patient or family. It is important for team members to monitor their own levels of stress and tension and to see what affects this and in what ways it does so. It is important for staff to work with the patient's family and respond to and ac-

knowledge—but not get caught up in—their feelings of guilt, anger, and helplessness, which may be displaced onto the medical staff. Since insomnia, irritability, and depression can occur among staff, supportive meetings—in crises or weekly—led by the consultant to the burn team is often beneficial. Bedside consultations, rounds with the medical staff, and going into the operating room to talk with the surgeons similarly builds the consultative relationships.

Emerging Research

The area of pain mechanisms and pain management is expanding rapidly. There are hundreds of articles and many new books regarding ways of measuring pain, the genetics controlling endorphin secretion, and pharmacological interventions helpful in decreasing or eliminating pain (Schechter, Berde, & Yaster, 1993). There is hope that the pain of burns may become less psychologically traumatic than it has been by improved pharmacological and psychological methods of pain relief.

An area in need of study involves psychopharmacological intervention with burned children. There has been little formal research despite extensive use of potent analgesic and antianxiety drugs with burn children. A recent study of clonazepam use for anxiety revealed that it decreased anxiety at both low and high doses, and that over sedation was an undesirable side effect at high doses in interaction with morphine. Children with acute burns are a good group to study because of the widespread use of benzodiazepines to manage their severe anxiety and of other agents to manage pain and agitation. Antidepressants (e.g., desipramine, fluoxetine, sertraline) are used more commonly now, mainly after recovery from the acute burn (Stoddard, Stroud, & Murphy, 1992). Side effects and toxic effects of psychotropic and analgesic drugs have not been studied in burned children. There is little scientific basis to guide clinical psychopharmacological care of burned children.

Another area for research is in outcome studies of the families of burn children. Recent studies indicate that parents may be more traumatized by their experience of a burn than the child (Rizzone,

Stoddard, Murphy, & Kruger, 1994). They have witnessed their treasured child becoming damaged and must adapt to the new appearance of the child—the "new child"—their own feelings of guilt, and the child's new needs for specific support and sustenance, but not overprotection. In addition, enduring such a trauma can challenge a marriage, and siblings also must receive needed attention. Further studies in these areas are needed as well as developmental studies looking at large cohorts of children of specific ages and their similar or dissimilar responses to comparable burns.

Conclusion

Progress in surgical treatment of acute burns and surgery after recovery has outpaced progress in psychosocial treatments for burned children and their families. There is new understanding of the psychology of body image and disfigurement, pain mechanisms, and psychological outcomes. The time is appropriate for more psychotherapeutic and psychopharmacological study and for increased psychiatric services to burn units and burned children.

REFERENCES

Atchison, N. E., Osgood, P. F., Carr, D. B., & Szyfelbein, S. K. (1991). Pain during burn dressing change in children: relationship to burn area, depth, and analgesia regimen. *Pain, 47,* 41–45.

Cahners, S., & Kartiganer, P. (1990). In *Acute management of the burned patient* (pp. 306–319). Philadelphia: W. B. Saunders.

Carr, D. B., Osgood, P. F., & Szyfelbein, S. K. (1993). Treatment of pain in acutely burned children. In N. Schechter, C. B. Berde, & M. Yaster (Eds.), *Pain in infants, children and adolescents.* Baltimore: Williams & Wilkins.

Cobb, S., Lindemann, E. (1943). Neuropsychiatric observations after the Cocoanut Grove fire. *Annals of Surgery, 117* (6), 814–824.

Crawford, J. (1990). Accident prevention and management. In M. Jellinek & D. Herzog (Eds.), *MGH handbook of general hospital pediatrics* (pp. 291–297). Chicago: Yearbook Medical Publishers.

Knudson-Cooper, M., & Thomas, C. M. (1988). Psychosocial care of the severely burned child. In H. F. Carvajal, & D. H. Parks (Eds.), *Burns in children* (pp. 345–362). Chicago: Yearbook Medical Publishers.

Lasoff, E. M., & McEttrick, M. A. (1986). Participation versus diversion during dressing changes: Can nurses' attitudes change? *Issues of Comprehensive Pediatrics in Nursing, 9,* 391–398.

McKay, A., Halpern, J., McLoughlin, E., Locke, J., & Crawford, J. D. (1979). A comparison of age-specific burn injury rates in five Massachusetts communities. *American Journal of Public Health, 69,* 1146.

Osgood, P. A., & Szyfelbein, S. K., & Martyn, J. A. J. (Eds.). Management of pain. In *Acute management of the burned patient* (pp. 201–216). Philadelphia: W. B. Saunders.

Patterson, D. R., Everett, J. J., Bombardier, C. H., Questad, K. A., Lee, V. K., & Marvin, J. A. (1993). Psychological effects of severe burn injuries. *Psychological Bulletin, 113* (2), 362–378.

Ravenscroft, K. (1982). The burn unit. *Psychiatric Clinic of North America, 5,* 419–432.

Rizzone, L., Stoddard, F. J., Murphy, J. M., & Kruger, L. J. (1994). Posttraumatic stress disorder in mothers of burned children and adolescents. *Journal of Burn Care & Rehabilitation, 15,* 158–163.

Ryan, C. M., Sheridan, R. L., Tompkins, R. G. (1996). A simplified model for early prediction of outcome from burns in the 1990s. American Burn Association 28th Annual Meeting.

Schecter, N., Berde, C. B., & Yaster, M. (Eds.). (1993). *Pain in Infants, Children and Adolescents.* Baltimore: Williams and Wilkins.

Schilder, P. (1950). *The image and appearance of the human body.* New York: International Universities Press.

Shontz, F. C. (1990). Body image and physical disability. In T. F. Cash & T. Pruzinsky (Eds.), *Body images: Development, deviance and change* (pp. 157–161). New York: Guilford Press.

Stoddard, F. J. (1982). Body image development in the burned child. *Journal of the American Academy of Child Psychiatry, 21* (5), 502–507.

Stoddard, F. J. (1990). Psychiatric management of the burn patient. In J. A. J. Martyn (Ed.), *Acute care of the burn patient* (pp. 256–272). Philadelphia: W. B. Saunders.

Stoddard, F. J. (1996). Care of infants, children, and adolescents with burn injuries. In M. Lewis (Ed.), *Child and Adolescent Psychiatry* (pp. 1016–1033). Baltimore: Williams and Wilkins.

Stoddard, F. J., Norman, D., Murphy, J. M., & Beardslee, W. E. (1989). Psychiatric Outcome of burned children. *Journal of the American Academy of Child and Adolescent Psychiatry, 28,* 589–595.

Stoddard, F. J., Stroud, L., & Murphy, J. M. (1992). Depression in burned children. *Journal of Burn Care & Rehabilitation, 13,* 340–347.

Stoddard, F. J., & Wilens, T. (1990). Delerium. In M. Jellinek & D. Herzog (Eds.), *MGH handbook of general hospital pediatrics* (pp. 254–259). Chicago: Yearbook Medical Publishers.

Szyfelbein, S. K., Osgood, P. A., & Carr, D. B. (1985). Assessment of pain and plasma β-endorphin immunoactivity in burned children. *Pain, 22,* 173.

Tarnowski, K. J., & Rasnake, L. K. (1994). Long-Term Psychosocial Sequelae. In *Behavioral Aspects of Pediatric Burns* (pp. 81–118). New York: Plenum Press.

Tompkins, R. G., Remensnyder, J. P., Burke, J. F., Tompkins, D. M., Hilton, J. F., Schoenfeld, D. A., Behringer, G. E., Bondoc, C. C., Briggs, S. E., & Quimby, W. C. (1988). Significant reductions in mortality for children with burn injuries through the use of prompt eschar excision. *Annals of Surgery, 208* (5), 577–585.

40 / Sickle Cell Anemia

Joseph Fischhoff and Dorothy Stevenson Jenkins

Sickle cell anemia is a hereditary blood disease caused by a basic defect in a mutant, autosomal gene. It mainly affects the black population in the United States and parts of Africa. Ethnic groups from the Mediterranean and Middle and Near Eastern areas also are affected. Heterozygous occurrence of the sickle gene, which is called sickle cell trait, usually is benign. Rarely, entering into a state of shock or flying at high altitudes in unpressurized aircraft may result in hypoxia and produce vaso-occlusive phenomena in a carrier. Other than that, the heterozygous individual does not develop signs and symptoms. By the way of contrast, children who are homozygous for this gene suffer from sickle cell disease, a severe, chronic hemolytic anemia. Deoxygenation results in a change that facilitates stacking of deoxygenated sickle hemoglobin molecules into monofilaments; these aggregate into elongated crystals, distorting the red cell membrane and forming the sickle cell (Behrman & Vaughn, 1987). Such a cell is viable for only 15 to 25 days.

Two major consequences follow when the sickle cells are rapidly destroyed or when conditions allow the occurrence of sickling. First, the body recognizes that the sickle cells present abnormal shapes and rapidly removes them. This rapid destruction causes jaundice. The body strives to compensate by producing new red blood cells as quickly as possible; the rate of regeneration is limited, however, and patients with sickle cell disease will have only one-half to one-third as many red cells as a normal individual. Second, the elongated cells are very rigid and cannot easily pass through small blood vessels. As a result they form logjams that often deprive vital organs, tissues, and muscles of blood and oxygen. This kind of vaso-occlusive phenomenon is traditionally called a crisis and is marked by a considerable degree of pain. Such vaso-occlusion can occur in any organ of the body.

Signs and Symptoms of the Disease

Like other patients who have anemia, children with sickle cell anemia often suffer from chronic fatigue. Jaundice and swollen, painful extremities are not uncommonly present. The "hand-foot syndrome," or sickle cell dactylitis, may be the initial manifestation of sickle cell anemia in infancy but can occur at any age. This is characterized by swollen, warm, and painful extremities. Other symptoms that characteristically afflict younger children are irritability, fussiness, distention of the abdomen, repeated fever, poor appetite, vomiting, slow weight gain, and jaundice. Vaso-occlusion of the spleen is also a noticeable problem at this developmental level, with infarction resulting in severe abdominal pain; other abdominal structures may be similarly involved.

The authors acknowledge support by National Institutes of Health Sickle Cell Center Grant HL16008.

Young children with sickle cell anemia are quite susceptible to infections and, in general, are felt to be at much greater risk than are their nondiseased contemporaries. Repeated vaso-occlusion involving the head of the femur may result in aseptic necrosis, with accompanying symptoms of persistent pain and a limp. Progressive impairment of liver function occurs from infancy on due to vaso-occlusion, and gallstones have occurred in children as young as 3 years. Vascular blockage also may result in a stroke or in pulmonary and renal infarctions (Behrman & Vaughn, 1987).

Patients with sickle cell disease also may experience an aplastic crisis, which can last for 10 to 20 days, thus placing the afflicted person in a life-threatening position. The symptoms include lethargy, weakness, and fainting. The hyperhemolytic crisis in which the already-rapid destruction of red blood cells is further accelerated causes pallor, jaundice, faintness, and lethargy. In childhood, most children with sickle cell anemia are underweight and smaller in stature than are their peers; as they come into adolescence, puberty frequently is delayed (Behrman & Vaughn, 1987).

Literature Review

In 1974 Whitten and Fischhoff could write that "there are apparently no published studies" on the psychosocial effects of sickle cell anemia (p. 681). Federal funding then became available for treatment, education, and research into sickle cell anemia, and psychosocial studies have evolved gradually, with findings reported in the literature or at the annual conference on sickle cell disease. (See also Allen, 1976; Conyard et al., 1980; Goldberg, 1981; Moore, Waugh, & Whitten, 1974; Nishiura & Whitten, 1980, 1981; Tetrault, 1981; Vavassur, 1977). Early reports revealed that parents of children with sickle cell anemia often knew little about the disease or had erroneous information—for example, 50% felt that the child needed "special" food, and 80% did not know why the anemia occurred. Several years later, a survey revealed that parents in 50% of the families saw the disease as a problem only from time to time and that 25% of the children were concerned about

their small stature and were the objects of teasing. Almost 25% used the disease to avoid chores, 40% were concerned about delayed sexual maturation, and 50% were behind in school. They had frequent extended absences from school because of illnesses, and they experienced limitations in physical ability due to fatigue.

Some studies have pointed to a greater tendency to withdrawal from relationships; lower self-esteem; an increase in dependency, fear of illness, depression, and anxiety; and, sometimes, a preoccupation with death (Conyard, Dosik, & Krishnamurthy, 1980; Nishiura & Whitten, 1981). Conversely, other studies have reported that although children with sickle cell anemia may have a greater tendency to withdraw because of frequent episodes of illness, when compared to children with other chronic diseases, they did not differ in their global, personal, and social adjustment (Allen, 1976). Problems were not a function of physical illness but low socioeconomic status associated with poverty and minority status. Interactions occurred between medical and environmental factors (Lemanek, Moore, Gresham, Williamson, & Kelley, 1986). Intelligence was not affected by the disease except in those instances where a stroke occurred that damaged a specific area of the brain; however, academic problems due to frequent illnesses and absences were of real concern. Clinical accounts of adolescents report greater than normal difficulty with separation and achieving independence and intensified concerns with body image and sexual identity (Goldberg, 1981). Adolescents with sickle cell disease reported less satisfaction with their bodies. They also spent less time in social and nonsocial activities and were less successful in school (Morgan & Jackson, 1986). There were problems in a range of adjustment variables, particularly for adolescent males, especially in the areas of social adjustment and behavior problems (Hurtig & White, 1986). Some investigators report depression to be more frequent (Conyard et al., 1980). Presentations about treatment have focused on family stress and pathology; individual, group, and family therapy; parent education; and special academic supports, including home teaching programs, vocational training and rehabilitation, camping programs, and community education programs (Tetrault, 1981; Vavassur, 1977; Whitten & Fischhoff, 1974).

Psychosocial Effects of the Disease

The child or adolescent with sickle cell anemia has to cope with and adapt to a numer of manifestations of the disease: pain, fatigue, jaundice with "yellow eyes," the possibility of a cerebrovascular accident, enuresis, thin and small stature, delayed puberty with concern over sexuality, frequent school absences and "running to catch up," unpredictable periods of hospitalization, and repeated transfusions (which may in turn demand treatment for excess iron storage).

The way an individual adapts to a chronic illness involves a number of factors: his or her existing personality structure with its strengths, ego functions, and defenses; the family's attitudes and behavior; and the community's responses and resources. At any given time, one factor may play a greater role than the others, but overall, it is the character of the interactions among the individual, family, and community that is critical. The following discussion seeks first to identify these aspects of sickle cell anemia that can be stressful, then to clarify the multiple influences and the interrelations that determine the eventual level of adjustment, and finally to recommend mechanisms designed to prevent maladjustment. A developmental or maturational approach to personality development and coping techniques is utilized.

Effects on the Child

As is true of any illness, the symptoms of sickle cell anemia arouse feelings of helplessness and fear of abandonment in the affected children. This does not mean abandonment in the literal sense; rather, it is a fear that the youngsters will not be taken care of but left to experience the illness without appropriate help, intervention, or psychological support. These feelings have to be met with reassurance and positive behavior by the adults who are significant in those children's lives. When youngsters have pain, for example, they need to feel that caregivers are available at all times who will respond in a sympathetic, reassuring, and positive manner. This tends to diminish their fear of abandonment.

Part of the feeling of helplessness generated in children with sickle cell anemia is related to another aspect of hospitalization, the exposure to painful procedures inherent in medical care. Since hospitalization and the attendant medical procedures are frightening, efforts should be made to minimize the untoward effects by preparing children (and parents) for this experience. If little is done to interpret the world of the hospital to children, particularly to explain when painful procedures are going to occur, hospitalized children can live in constant fear of the unknown. Moreover, resentment of the unpleasant aspects of hospitalization can augment resentment over having the disease.

The provision of support is not the only way to relate to youngsters' fear of helplessness and abandonment. If children can communicate their feelings, they are less likely to develop a sense of isolation. Children with sickle cell anemia should be permitted and encouraged to talk about their fear of pain, fatigue, or helplessness. No area of the disease or their feelings should be off limits. If any aspects of the condition are forbidden for discussion, feelings of loneliness and abandonment will tend to increase. Children will quickly sense the adult's reluctance or disinterest in discussing certain areas and may then comply with the adult's desires so that they can continue to remain close even though their needs are not being met.

Parents need to be counseled on how to encourage their child to talk about fears and feelings about being sick. Many parents believe children will be upset if they speak about their illness when, in reality, it is the parents who are disturbed and wish to avoid talking about it. Parents can be told that children always have feelings and throughts about their illness and that while some of their thoughts and observations are accurate, others are likely to be misconceptions. If parents are advised that their child wishes and needs to communicate thoughts and feelings but that he or she needs their permission and support to do so, most parents will be able to speak with their child.

Parents should be told that among other things, children may cry, express anger, say that they are unloved, express jealousy toward siblings who are not ill, and talk about fears and misconceptions about their illness. Parents should respond by being supportive but not overprotective. If the children are anxious, they should be assured that the parents will care for them. If they are depressed, parents should let them know that the feeling is not unreasonable. If they are angry that fate, often represented by the parents, has dealt them an unfair blow, parents can agree that it is unpleasant, but they should not accept blame for the illness. As the parents hear the children out, they should give verbal approval for what they have been able to say and encourage children about the future.

In these discussions, illness and its manifestations, such as pain, need to be explained in terms of the children's frame of reference. If they are not given clear, honest simple explanations, they are forced to create answers for themselves. Often these will be erroneous. Children will create a cause-and-effect relationship because this is the natural mode of thought in childhood. They may firmly believe that their illness or pain are forms of punishment for "bad" thoughts or past behavior. They may hope or imagine that if they are "good," they will be subjected to fewer symptoms or acute exacerbations of their illness. They also may believe that if they are good and complaint, they will not lose those on whom they depend.

Younger children's concerns are related to pain, helplessness, and abandonment rather than death because they imagine death not as a permanent condition but as one in which they are alone, unprotected, without parents to care for them. Parents can be guided in how to talk to children in a reassuring manner about these issues. School-age children become aware that death is irreversible and perhaps that another child has died of sickle cell anemia. The psychiatrist should provide anticipatory guidance so that parents will acknowledge the children's questions about death but say that death from the illness is not usual or frequent, that the doctors are finding new ways of treatment, and that many people with sickle cell anemia live a long life. Hope should never be taken away from children, and in reality medical advances are being made. Of course adolescents are more aware than children that death is a possibility, but they also are aware that adults who have sickle cell disease live productive lives and that some have lived to be over 60 years old. If the adolescents have had good emotional support as children, they are not preoccupied with the possibility of death. They are concerned with the pain they have during a sickle cell crisis, the possibility of a stroke, and the physical limitations imposed by the disease.

Although no specific time should be set aside to discuss the illness, if parents encourage children to talk, at times the conversation will take such a turn naturally or spontaneously. For example, after a sudden episode of illness has subsided, a child can more easily share feelings and thoughts with those who have been providing supportive care.

If parents say their child has never spoken about the illness, they should be told that he or she may need their permission to do so.

A well-adjusted adult is capable of functioning independently. Sickle cell anemia, like all chronic childhood illnesses, creates longer and more intense psychological dependency on adults and thus makes it more difficult for the child to learn to function independently. Therefore, throughout childhood, it is essential that all areas of functioning that promote autonomy and independence be emphasized and encouraged. Parents of children with sickle cell anemia should be informed that, when the children have severe pain, they will be completely dependent on them psychologically and will need total care. However, when the acute phase has passed, children should be encouraged and expected to do as much as they are capable of doing. For example, depending on the children's age, they should be required to dress themselves, help to straighten up their room, be responsible for specific chores, and be disciplined appropriately and consistently. If children are making a successful adaptation to their illness, they wish to be up and about as much as possible, to engage in activities, to play with their friends, and to continue in school. One indication of a poor adjustment is the desire to continue in a dependent role after the pain crisis.

Another essential characteristic of a well-adjusted adult is a sense of self-esteem. This is developed in childhood in part through the concrete mastery of situations. Certain features of sickle cell anemia pose barriers to the development of a sense of mastery over the disease. In a number of chronic illnesses, such as diabetes, some of the manifestations can be controlled by acts of the person with the disease. In contrast, victims of sickle cell anemia are powerless to influence the fatigue or the time of onset, frequency, duration, or intensity of pain. Although they cannot control the symptoms, involved children may develop a sense of mastery by becoming less fearful of the illness and by learning to do well in studies, hobbies, or games. We have indicated how parents can help children be less fearful. Parents also must help children with sickle cell anemia to find areas where they can excel.

There is another aspect of chronic illness that can undermine children's ego devleopment; this involves the interruption of critical normal activities. When pain crises occur, children may be unable to attend school. If this occurs frequently enough and home tutoring is not available, children's academic performance can fall below that of classmates and thereby further threaten their sense of self-worth. Absences can be frequent enough to lead to actual failure. To foster children's sense of competence, mastery, and self-esteem, they should continue to study at home. This means that periodic home tutoring is essential. The school should be informed that the children may be absent frequently; a continuance plan should be available, one that can be implemented whenever they have to be out of school for any length of time. If they are absent for a short time, parents or others might help with studies, but homebound teaching is critical when children with sickle cell anemia must be out of school for long periods. This is a form of primary prevention. It minimizes the possibility of children becoming so frustrated and discouraged about falling behind peers that they actually drop out of school.

The tendency of these children to tire easily imposes realistic limitations on their activities. These limitations also can undermine the development of self-esteem and should be approached via primary prevention. Since the youngsters may not want or be able to engage fully in all of the activities of their playmates, a wide range of activities should be made available that they might perform at a slower pace or while sitting down. For instance, they can be encouraged to develop sedentary hobbies such as crafts, building models, working with wood or metal, photography, sewing or tailoring, and cooking. Tabletop competitive games also should be encouraged. In school, if children do not wish to or cannot engage in gym activities, they should have an opportunity to work with audiovisual materials, help in the library, or serve as an aide in the office. Some older children may enhance their self-esteem by helping younger children who are having difficulty with their studies.

This is not to suggest that these children should not engage in more strenuous physical activities, such as playing ball or riding bicycles. However, likely they will not do as well as their peers in these activities. Many children want to go to gym both because they enjoy it and because they do not want to be treated as if they are different. They can and should be permitted to engage in sports until they tire. In most instances, the children themselves are the best judges of their tolerance; children soon learn their physical limitations and abide by them.

No child likes to be smaller than his or her friends, but many a child must face the fact that growth retardation does occur in sickle cell anemia. The children are not expected to like this feature (or any other aspect of the disease), but if they feel that they are capable in some realm, it will be easier for them to cope. Some of the techniques that can be utilized to develop their sense of competency have been described already. If the emphasis has been on identifying and developing abilities rather than dwelling on the disadvantages of the disabilities, the smaller size becomes less important.

Other children may tease the child who is smaller and fatigues easily, and adults may treat such children as if they are much younger than they are. These practices can be devastating to children's egos. Children should be taught how to use "one-upmanship" in response to the teasing, and parents must strive not to permit other adults to relate to the children inappropriately. The children should not be allowed to degrade themselves.

PARENTAL RESPONSES

As we have indicated, the parents' responses to children's illness are a major determinant of their adjustment. The parents will have many concerns. They will worry about the future of the children with respect to their ability to achieve social and economic success; they will experience resentment at having children whose care may be demanding and frequently will inconvenience them; there will be disappointment and guilt over being responsible for the children's illness; and there will be recurrent episodes of anxiety about the potential for early death. There also may be anger over economic problems related to frequent hospitalizations as well as feelings of embarrassment, shame, and displeasure because of the children's size. The parents may react by being unduly restrictive and overprotective (not permitting children to be as active and independent as they are capable of being), by pressing for accomplishments beyond the children's abilities, by being unduly permissive, by neglecting the children, or by rejecting them outright.

One study found that the primary parent experiences additional emotional strain, but only in single-parent families was there some evidence of an adverse impact on the relationship between the parent and the chronically ill child. The parents with more knowledge about the illness and more social support appear to cope better. The more psychosocial stressors within the family, the less effectively the child copes with the illness and the treatment regimen (Burlews, Evans, & Oler, 1989; Melne, 1990). Severity of illness as a factor in affecting adjustment was less significant than socioeconomic structure, family structure, and support systems (Hurtig, Koepke, & Park, 1989).

Most parents require counseling in order to manage so ill a child in an appropriate manner. If their feelings are raised early and discussed in an open, supportive manner, these emotions will exert much less force. In addition to working with their reactions in the counseling sessions, parents should learn the facts of the disease and what to expect on a day-to-day basis. Above all, however, they must be encouraged to express their feelings and communicate their problems. To accomplish this, they need to be made aware that none of these reactions is unusual or forbidden. In time they will then gain confidence that the clinician is there to support them; and this, in turn, will help them develop coping techniques for specific problems and learn the importance of developing their child's self-esteem.

In addition to the frequent occurrence of pain, the ubiquitous fatigue, and the recurrent need for hospitalizations, parents should be prepared to face a number of additional aspects of the disease. They should be alerted in advance that their children may wet the bed frequently, have a poor appetite, exhibit growth retardation, and experi-

ence a delay in adolescent development. In this connection, it is important to consider the nature of anticipatory guidance. This should not be thought of as a single session in which questions are asked and all explanations are given or even understood. Instead it must be regarded as a process that extends over time. Through the years, parents may need to have these areas reexplained many times and clarified over and over in ever greater detail. The first time such material is presented, they may not fully understand what is explained, or they may wish to minimize or deny the reality of what they hear. If those events most likely to occur are explained clearly to the parents, they will be less anxious, they can spell out what is happening to the child, and they will be able to plan rather than merely live from crisis to crisis. This all increases the parents' feeling of competence, which in turn is transmitted to the child.

ADOLESCENT RESPONSE

Normal adolescent development is characterized by sexual maturation, psychological separation from the parents, and the need to be increasingly independent, all of which takes place over a span of years. If the patient and the family have not related to the illness appropriately by the time the children reach adolescence, they may be afraid to take the steps necessary to become autonomous individuals and may continue to remain in a passive, dependent relationship to their parents. The children's view of life and of their own potential may be constricted, and gradual withdrawal from normal relationships may occur. Their motivation and aspirations to succeed in any area are likely to be limited and their self-esteem inadequate. Emotionally, they would tend to feel depressed, helpless, fearful, and they may be preoccupied with death. Such youngsters are prone to become hypochondriacal and experience more pain and fatigue than can be accounted for by their physical condition. Slight changes in their physical state may evoke a great deal of anxiety. They may lack the dreams and aspirations universal to adolescence. A girl with sickle cell anemia once said: "If you had a stroke, it's like living with a gun at your head because you never know when you will have another one."

Adolescents with sickle cell anemia who have

had a stable supportive background may experience adolescence in much the same way as an adolescent without an illness. But it is not unusual for teenagers with a chronic illness, even if they are well adjusted, to find the years from age 13 to 16 somewhat stressful. During this time, they may want to feel that they have no limits or "imperfections." This is typical of all adolescents. However, youths with sickle cell disease may thrust themselves into stressful situations in order to prove that they are like other teens. The net result is that for a time they may exacerbate the illness.

During this teenage period, a strong supportive relationship with an adult is often helpful. The relationship may be used only intermittently, and, in fact, there may be more telephone contacts than face-to-face discussions. Nonetheless, the knowledge that the adolescents have someone to turn to is often sufficient.

It is troublesome for many youths to confront the fact that they cannot compete in physical activities. They probably will be disappointed and resent physical limitations; nonetheless, adolescents who are coping with sickle cell anemia in a satisfactory fashion often find pleasure in those things that they can do.

As mentioned, adolescents with this disease may encounter a delay in the onset of puberty. Boys and girls may tease those who are slow to develop and thereby make them feel inferior, resentful, and rejected. All adolescents need to feel accepted by their peers, and if acceptance is not forthcoming, they may withdraw from social relationships. However, for the well-adjusted child, delayed sexual development in adolescence, while it may be a source of unhappiness, does not in itself lead to social isolation.

All teenagers need to ponder career goals, be they vocational or professional. This is especially true for teenagers with chronic illness. Adolescents with sickle cell anemia need not make specific commitments concerning future occupations, but they need to be aware of the wide range of realistic possibilities. They usually have only a vague conception of what specific occupations demand. Such youths will have great hopes and aspirations for the future, and their fantasies may very well be similar to those of adolescents without illness. The realities gradually become apparent to these young people through the ease with which

they become tired. This fact may serve to direct their interest to occupations that do not require great physical endurance. But the majority will need vocational counseling and guidance, both in terms of their need to select a sedentary type of occupation and in respect to the opportunities that are available.

Studies of adults indicated that they may have significant psychosocial distress in the areas of employment and finances, sleeping and eating, and performance of normal daily activities. Fear and anxiety regarding body deterioration and lack of assertiveness in social situations suggest that depression may be a common problem (Barrett et al., 1988). However, another study found no significant relationships between psychosocial impairment and the presence or absence of physical complications (Damilouji, 1982).

Pain Management

Pain is a significant component of sickle cell anemia. Adolescents need to control situations in which they find themselves, and pain management contracts may be helpful to aid adolescents with sickle cell disease cope better in a crisis (Burghardt-Fitzgerald, 1989). Coping strategies are important predictors of pain and adjustment. Individuals high on negative thinking and passive adherence have more severe pain, are less active and more distressed, and use more health care services (Gil, Abrams, Phillips, & Keefe, 1989). Dysfunctional adaptation to the recurrent pain is due to inadequate resolution of essential developmental conflicts.

Coping behaviors, not the reported intensity or duration of pain, mediate the functional levels of the individuals. Other factors noted were social isolation and school absenteeism and failure, and being overly dependent on parents and the medical system. Emphasis in treating these children should be placed on the team approach, the meaning of the pain, family, school setting, teaching relaxation, guided imagery, hypnosis, and cognitive restructuring (Walco & Dampier, 1987).

Involvement with job, school, group activities, and family and community relationships lead to more frequent home management of sickle cell disease pain. Also helpful is biofeedback, progressive relaxation, self-hypnosis, and cognitive strategies. Multidisciplinary programs, family conferences, counseling, education, and group therapy can prove to be most beneficial (Gil, 1989).

There has been a rapid expansion of sickle cell centers and programs. These centers offer families a multidisciplinary approach that includes medical treatment; family, individual, and group therapy and counseling; vocational counseling and rehabil-

itation; and educational sessions and literature. Taken in aggregate, these modalities present the facts of sickle cell anemia accurately and dispel those myths and misinformation that still exist (although they are less prevalent than in the past). As is true with other chronic diseases, when these centers and programs have offered expertise and excellence, they have proven repeatedly to be the best way to treat families and children who have sickle cell anemia.

REFERENCES

Allen, J. (1976). Anxiety, self-concept, and personal and social adjustments in children with sickle cell anemia. *Journal of Pediatrics, 88,* 859–863.

Barrett, D. H., Wisotzek, I. E., Abel, G. G., Rouleau, J. L., Platt, A. F., Pollard, W. E., Eckman, J. R. (1988). Assessment of psychosocial functioning of patients with sickle cell disease. *Southern Medical Journal, 81,* 745–750.

Behrman, R. E., & Vaughn, V. C. (1987). *Nelson textbook of pediatrics* (13th ed.). Philadelphia: W. B. Saunders.

Burghardt-Fitzgerald, D. C. (1989). Pain behavior contracts: Effective management of the adolescent in sickle cell crisis. *Journal of Pediatric Nursing, 4,* 320–324.

Burlew, A. K., Evans, R., & Oler, C. (1989). The impact of a child with sickle cell disease on family dynamics. *Annals of the New York Academy of Sciences, 565,* 161–171.

Conyard, S., Dosik, H., & Krishnamurthy, M. (1980). Psychosocial aspects of sickle cell anemia in adolescents. *Health and Social Work, 5,* 20–26.

Damilouji, N. (1982). Social disability and psychiatric morbidity in sickle cell anemia and diabetes patients. *Psychosomatics, 23,* 925–931.

Gil, K. M. (1989). Coping with sickle cell disease pain. *Annals of Behavioral Medicine, 11,* 49–51.

Gil, K. M., Abrams, M. R., Phillips, G., & Keefe, F. J. (1989). Sickle cell disease pain: relation of coping strategies to adjustment. *Journal of Consultant and Clinical Psychology, 57,* 725–731.

Goldberg, R. T. (1981). Toward an understanding of the rehabilitation of the disabled adolescent. *Rehabilitation Literature, 42,* 3–4.

Hurtig, A. L., Koepke, D., & Park, K. B. (1989). Relation between the severity of chronic illness and adjustment in children and adolescents with sickle cell disease. *Journal of Pediatric Psychology, 14,* 114–132.

Hurtig, A. L., & White, L. S. (1986). Psychosocial adjustment in children and adolescents with sickle cell disease. *Journal of Pediatric Psychology, 11,* 411–427.

Lemanek, K. L., Moore, S. S., Gresham, F. M., Williamson, D. A., & Kelley, M. D. (1986). Psychological adjustment of children with sickle cell anemia. *Journal of Pediatric Psychology, 11,* 397–410.

Melne, R. I. (1990). Assessment of care of children with sickle cell disease. *British Medical Journal, 6721,* 371–374.

Moore, A., Waugh, D., & Whitten, C. F. (1974). Unmet needs of parents of children with sickle cell anemia. *Proceedings of the First National Symposium on Sickle Cell Disease* (pp. 275–276). Washington, DC: Howard University.

Morgan, S. A., & Jackson, J. (1986). Psychosocial and social concomitants of sickle cell anemia in adolescents. *Journal of Pediatric Psychology, 71,* 429–440.

Nishiura, E., & Whitten, C. F. (1980). Psychosocial problems of families of children with sickle cell anemia. *Urban Health, 9,* 32–35.

Nishiura, E., & Whitten, C. F. (1981). *Psychosocial effects of sickle cell anemia: employment and sickle cell conditions.* Paper presented at the annual conference on sickle cell disease, St. Louis, MO.

Tetrault, S. M. (1981). The student with sickle cell anemia. *Today's Health: The Journal of the National Educational Association, 70,* 52–57.

Vavassur, J. (1977). A comprehensive program for meeting the psychosocial needs of sickle cell anemia patients. *Journal of the National Medical Association, 69,* 335–339.

Walco, G. A., & Dampier, C. D. (1987). Chronic pain in adolescent patients. *Journal of Pediatric Psychology, 12,* 215–225.

Whitten, C. F., & Fischhoff, J. (1974). Psychosocial effects of sickle cell disease. *Archives of Internal Medicine, 133,* 681–689.

41 / An Overview of Childhood Speech and Language Disorder

Joseph H. Beitchman, Jennifer Wild, and Robert Kroll

There is compelling evidence for an association between speech and language impairment and psychiatric disorder in childhood. Given the centrality of language to human communication and development, this association is not surprising. To be diagnostically comprehensive and therapeutically effective, clinicians working with children need to understand the relation between speech and language impairment and developmental and psychiatric disorders.

This chapter provides an overview of speech and language disorders in childhood. It begins with a definition of terms and a review of early language development. Disorders of language and peak ages of onset are described, followed by a review of the epidemiological literature. Next, the correlates of speech and language impairment are summarized. Familial and genetic factors, neuroanatomical findings, and disturbances with biological underpinnings are discussed. A review of psychiatric disorders associated with language impairment, and language outcomes in children with early speech and language delay, concludes the chapter. Clinical examples are presented throughout to illustrate the problems commonly found in the speech/language impaired child.

Definitions

Language is a systematic means of communication. It is fundamental to sociability, thinking, feeling, learning, and behaving. The grammar of language is a set of rules that defines the system of signals used to communicate ideas. Grammar includes phonology, syntax, semantics, and pragmatics. Phonology describes how to combine sounds into words; syntax describes how words are combined into sentences; semantics describes the meaning of words and sentences; and pragmatics describes how to participate in a conversation, how to sequence sentences, and how to anticipate information required by a listener. Language is used to signal needs, intentions, and feelings. It is also used for self-talk and the mediation of thought processes. In broad terms, language is differentiated into expressive and receptive forms. Expressive language includes speech, or the articulation of sounds. Receptive language refers to the understanding of what has been heard.

Early Speech and Language Development

The beginnings of speech are seen at birth. The first sounds that are produced in infancy are those of undifferentiated cries. These sounds are purely reflexive. Among these sounds, mothers can distinguish between cries of hunger and those of discomfort. Differentiated vocalization begins to occur during the second month of life. Infants begin to produce noncrying sounds such as cooing and gurgling. Speechlike vowels and consonants are produced; however, these are not yet restricted to the language of a baby's home. At this early age infants will start responding to human sound by turning toward the speaker or displaying searching and scanning behavior and producing additional cooing.

The period from 3 to 6 months of age is typically referred to as the babbling stage. Here, the coos and gurgles from the previous stage increase until some identifiable sounds are heard. At the same time there is a marked increase in awareness of others. During this stage babies show a random

This is a revised and expanded version of an earlier paper entitled "Childhood Speech and Language Disorders" by J. H. Beitchman & E. B. Brownlie in *Do They Grow Out of It? Long Term Outcomes of Childhood Disorders*, (p. 225–253) ed. L. Hechtman (Washington, DC: American Psychiatric Press, 1996).

The authors would like to thank Alison Inglis for her assistance in the preparation of this manuscript and Suzanne Martin for the provision of clinical vignettes.

display of different sounds in a continuous and experimental fashion. At this stage babies are not yet using speech to communicate meaning but rather as an activity associated with physiological needs and emotions. Babies are producing a greater variety of sounds than will ever be produced during the true speech period. The babbling stage represents a training period for later meaningful articulated utterances.

At approximately 8 months the process of self-imitation begins. This stage, sometimes referred to as "lalling," results in repetitiouslike utterances such as "ba-ba," "ga-ga," and the like. During this stage, the first melodic or intonational patterns of the language are detected. This is felt to be the first characteristic of a true linguistic feature. Children now make fewer sounds but are engaged in a process of duplication and are preparing themselves for the imitation of sounds produced by others. Children may appear to be producing meaningful words but in most cases these are simply random syllable repetitions that resemble real words, such as "da-da." The final prelingual stage, occurring between 9 and 12 months of age, is referred to as the echolalic period. Here children show parrotlike repetitions of sounds, sound combinations, or words spoken by others. The purpose of this stage is to build children's phonetic or sound repertoire specific to the language of their home environment.

True speech occurs when children assign meaning to the words that they utter. The first words are usually duplicated syllables, such as "ma-ma." At this early stage they can use language only to identify things in their immediate presence. Some have called this period, which usually occurs between 12 and 18 months of age, the "identification language" period.

By the middle of the second year, children are intentionally using language to bring about an event. They are now learning that language can be used to manipulate physical and social environments. At this stage children typically will have about 50 meaningful words in their vocabulary. These single words and their intonational patterns are usually operating as full thoughts or sentences; thus, this period has been called the "holophrastic" stage of development.

From the age of 3 there is a steady growth of vocabulary, sentence length, and syntactic complexity. Children can now communicate most of their needs and wants; they are operating as full partners in their linguistic community. Children are now understood by listeners and can be conversational partners. With the sophistication of their syntax, children can now create an infinite number of novel utterances. They have mastered even the function words of their language, such as prepositions, articles, and conjunctions. By about the age of 5, children have incorporated all of the morphologic, syntactic, and semantic rules of language. The development of speech articulation continues until about the age of 7, at which point children master the complete sound system.

Speech and Language Disorders

Childhood speech disorders include problems in speech production that may reflect stuttering or voice abnormalities. Speech production difficulties are due to an inability to articulate sound segments even if there is no disorder in the ability to follow the rules of the sound system, either in production or discrimination. Such disorders may occur in normal children or in those children with other developmental disabilities such as autism, mental retardation, or hearing impairment.

Childhood language disorders may involve impairment in the central cognitive processes associated with syntax, semantics, or pragmatics. These processes are component parts of linguistic functioning and include auditory memory, comprehension, discrimination and integration.

Generally, language impairment is a heterogenous condition. For example, language impairment may involve problems with auditory comprehension, phonological discrimination, and/or syntax. Unless the precise nature of the deficit can be specified, it is impossible to know which linguistic function or group of functions may be affected.

A number of researchers have attempted to define distinct linguistic impairments among children identified with speech and language disorders. Fundudis, Kolvin, and Garside (1979) identified three different groups of language-delayed children. However, these were based on the age the child achieved different motor milestones as well as on the presence or absence of medical conditions, such as cerebral palsy, autism, and others. Other researchers have defined distinct linguistic subtypes among the speech/language impaired. Wolfus, Moscovitch, and Kinsbourne (1980), using a very small clinic sample, identified two groups of language-impaired children; one group was impaired in the production of syntax and phonology and the other in phonological discrimination, digit span, and semantics. Cantwell, Baker, and Mattison (1980) have described a group of children with pure speech problems and another group with language processing problems. Beitchman et al. (1989a) described four groups of children obtained from a community sample: children with poor auditory comprehension but normal on other language tests, children displaying poor articulation but normal on other language tests, children with impaired performance on a variety of expressive and receptive language tests, and children performing above average on a variety of language tests.

Speech/language disorders are typically among the earliest signs of developmental dysfunction. The first peak in the detection of speech and language disorders occurs in infancy. Delayed onset of speech sounds may be the most obvious symptom. Children may show little evidence of babbling, cooing, and other forms of protolanguage indicative of developmental speech/language delay. Children may show various speech sound substitutions or articulation errors. Many speech-sound substitutions are developmentally appropriate—for instance, the 3-year-old who says "wabbit" instead of "rabbit"—so that identifying those that are developmentally inappropriate or that persist beyond the expected age may require an assessment by a speech/language pathologist. Children may show immaturities in grammar, using a statement form with a rising intonation to indicate a question rather than using the more mature interrogative. For example, "Have cookie, please?" "Please" ends in a rising intonation, compared to "Can I have a cookie, please?"

Problems of comprehension are more subtle and can begin in infancy. Although children may not speak or have very limited expressive language, their comprehension is expected to exceed their spoken language. Diagnosing language comprehension disorders or delays is difficult. They should be suspected in any child with autisticlike symptoms or any child who seems "spacey," lost, or odd.

A second peak in the detection of speech/language problems occurs during the preschool years. Typically, once children are among their peer group, preschool teachers and other caregivers inform the parents of problems with the language that they may have failed to notice themselves. Behavioral problems and symptoms associated with attention deficit hyperactivity disorder are frequently noticed at this time, as they frequently co-occur with speech/language impairment. Parents also contribute to this peak period of impaired speech/language detection by waiting until a child's third birthday before concluding that his or her language is delayed or that the child needs an assessment.

The third peak occurs on formal entry to kindergarten. The more formal nature of a school setting increases expectations of children's language abilities. They must now be able to attend to story time, follow more complex oral instructions, and verbally express their own wants and needs. Under these demanding circumstances, problems with auditory memory and auditory discrimination may manifest for the first time. Children may have difficulty making themselves understood and consequently shy away from interactions requiring verbal expression. Children may become restless and fidgety, and their teachers may soon identify them as having a behaviour problem. Two clinical examples illustrate some of these points:

CASE EXAMPLE

A 7-year-old boy was asked to tell a story based on a picture. His difficulties sequencing a story are apparent.

"Once upon a time there was a big white house. But when their mother was cleaning the kitchen, she walked to a puddle was the dripping of and then the dad started falling off the stool and breaked all the cans and fall and things they all fell down and broke. But suddenly, somebody stopped and then somebody said, 'Can somebody help me get out of this hole?' But nobody understand. But he said, 'Wow, what was that?' Well, they said, 'Maybe this is not a good day.' He said, 'Maybe it will be better . . . .'"

It is apparent that this child's language skills are seriously compromised. Everyone with whom he communicates will have difficulty understanding all but the simplest of his statements. School, because of its emphasis on language arts, will be a major challenge for this youngster. Unless he is identified and given special attention, emotional and behavioral problems are likely to interfere with his willingness to attend school and his ability to learn and participate in the school curriculum.

CASE EXAMPLE

Another common but less severe form of language problem involves word-finding difficulties. A 9-year-old boy talking about a toy says:

"They got balls like . . . um . . . soccer ball, no, not soccer balls . . . and there's um . . . what's it called again? Um . . . oh . . . oh . . . um . . . oh yeah. It's like a police set. It's like a police set like guns and handcuffs. It's not actually a game . . . I don't know what it is actually . . . It's just a play game. Like it's like a thing you have to hook up."

Clearly, this youngster is struggling to make himself understood. While an adult may be sufficiently patient to help and encourage him to find the missing word, few of his peers will be willing to do so. It is apparent that his self-esteem and peer relationships will suffer, although perhaps not as severely as the youngster previously described.

Epidemiology

A broad range of prevalence rates, between 3 and 15%, has been reported by various authors (Fundudis et al., 1979; Jenkins, Bax, & Hart, 1980; Silva, McGee, & Williams, 1983; Stanovich, 1982). Generally, these prevalence rates are based on surveys of preschool-age children, since this is the age when speech and language problems first present. Stevenson and Richman (1976) administered a variety of standardized language tests to 705 3-year-old children (a 1-in-4 community sample). They estimated that the prevalence rate of expressive language delay was 3.1%.

Fundudis et al. (1979) surveyed the health records of 3,300 children. Using a crude definition of language problems as recorded by public health nurses (failure at 36 months to coherently string 3 or more words together), they calculated a 4% rate of language delay among their sample, very similar to the rate provided by Stevenson and Richman (1976), who used different measures and definitions.

Jenkins et al. (1980) used a community sample to determine the types of behavior problems found in preschool-age children. They found that 36 out of 168 children (21.6%) between the ages of 2 and 5 years displayed probable or definite speech *and* language problems as defined by standardized language tests.

Silva et al. (1983) surveyed language problems in a community sample of 3-year-old children. They defined language delay as deficits in verbal comprehension, expression, or both, as measured by a standardized language test. Using this definition, they reported a 7.6% prevalence for language delay in their sample of 1,027 children.

Beitchman, Nair, Clegg, Ferguson, and Patel (1986) reported higher prevalence rates in their community survey of 5-year-old children. Using standardized speech and language tests, they reported a prevalence rate of 19% for both speech and language disorders.

The discrepancies among prevalence rates are a function of sample selection (such as varying age ranges or community versus clinic samples), measurement techniques, and both the types of disorder being investigated and their definitions (Beitchman, 1985). A review of language intervention literature found that, in a 6-year period, there was great variability between articles on standardization and comprehensiveness of language assessment procedures (Werner & Smith 1982). This affects the types of speech and language disorders assessed and reported and the prevalence figures cited. Beitchman, Nair, Clegg, Ferguson, et al. (1986) found that when cut-off scores for defining disorder were adjusted to reflect 1 or 2 standard deviations from the mean, prevalence rates of speech, language, and speech and language disorders in 5-year-old children dropped from 19% (1 standard deviation below the mean) to 9.6% (2 standard deviations below the mean).

The Correlates of Speech and Language Disorders

SOCIOECONOMIC STATUS

The association between lower socioeconomic status (SES) and speech and language disorders is a robust finding and has been described by several investigators (Baker & Cantwell, 1983; Fundudis et al., 1979; Silva, McGee, Thomas, & Williams, 1982). Beitchman, Peterson, and Clegg (1988) found a significant association between speech and language impairment and different components of SES (family income, occupational status, or parental education level). However, no one has identified the aspects of SES that are relevant to this association (Puckering & Rutter, 1987). Although various components of SES are correlated with speech and language disorders, these components simply reflect different ways of measuring SES. Low SES is associated with many forms of disadvantage, which further complicates the relationship between low SES and language impairment. These various forms of disadvantage include marital discord, single-parent status, fewer educational and employment opportunities, lower income, parental mental illness, and pre- and perinatal complications.

PARENTAL MARITAL STATUS

Very little is known about the relation between speech/language disorders and parental marital status. Beitchman et al. (1988) found a higher percentage of single-parent families among speech- and language-impaired children than among normal-language children. Parental marital status is known to have a broad range of influences on child development, but how marital status influences language development is unclear. There is evidence that enhanced linguistic development may result from intense interchange between mother and child (Puckering & Rutter, 1987). Some effects of single-parent status are likely to be expressed in reduced opportunities for maternal-child interaction. Single-parent status is also associated with reduced income, a feature of low SES correlated with speech and language disorder.

FAMILY SIZE AND BIRTH ORDER

Firstborn status appears to be associated with language competence (Beitchman, Nair, Clegg, & Patel, 1986; Butler, Peckham, & Sheridan, 1973; Tomblin, Hardy & Hein, 1991). Beitchman (1985) have reported that compared to controls, language-impaired children are more commonly second- and later born. Tomblin et al. (1991), in a survey of 662 children between 2.5 years and 5 years of age, found that the strongest predictor of poor language development was birth order. Later-born children had substantial increases in the probability of having poor language skills. Butler et al. (1973) and Kolvin, Fundudis, and Scanlon (1979) also have reported similar findings. Belmont and Marolla (1973) and Breland (1974) reported birth-order effects for higher verbal skills. These findings, however, have been challenged because the reported studies have failed to control for family size and socioeconomic status. For instance, Tomblin (1990) showed that when family size and SES were controlled, the birth-order effect was no longer significant.

Because birth-order effects are related to both SES and family size, it is not known whether they act independently through such variables as the intrauterine environment (Gualtieri & Hicks, 1986) or are secondary to the language environment in which the child is raised. It is likely that second- and later-born children are exposed to less adult language than are firstborns. As family size increases, each child receives proportionately less exposure to adult language. Beitchman et al. (1987) noted that the family's mean number of children was significantly greater for speech- and language-impaired children than for control children. Baker and Cantwell (1985) reported that speech- and language-impaired children tended to come from large families. Storfer (1990) found a negative effect of close sibling spacing (more likely in large than small families) on the development of linguistic abilities—the closer the spacing, the poorer the linguistic abilities. There is evidence for both birth-order and family size effects, although it is unknown if these are independent effects or whether they are mediated to some extent through environmental or biological factors.

PREGNANCY AND BIRTH COMPLICATIONS

The association between pregnancy and birth complications and speech and language disorders is unclear. McGee, Silva, and Williams (1984) found that being small for gestational age (as measured by birthweight and head circumference) was related to delayed verbal functioning in early childhood. However, as their sample was predominantly disadvantaged socioeconomically, it is impossible to discern the relative effects of birth complications and those of disadvantaged SES. The relative effects of these variables are inconclusive.

Perinatal complications appear to be related to impaired physical and emotional development, but only in combination with disadvantaged environments (Werner, 1989; Werner & Smith, 1982). Preterm infants' language development was more affected by environmental influences than was full-term infants' development (Siegel, 1982). The specific mechanism that mediates the association between SES and language impairment may be related in part to prenatal stress and length of gestation. Beitchman et al. (1984) reported higher levels of prenatal stress and early or late delivery dates among speech/language-impaired children; however, these children were also more likely to come from lower SES families than were normal language controls. Lower SES families report higher incidence of prenatal stress and of pregnancy and birth complications.

HEARING LOSS

Hearing impairment in children is associated with speech and language retardation (Baker & Cantwell, 1977; Beitchman, 1985; Beitchman, Hood, Rochon, Peterson, Mantini, & Majumdar, 1989; Bishop & Edmundson, 1986; Silverman, 1971). Beitchman (1985) found that speech/language-impaired children were more likely to fail a hearing test compared to matched controls. Beitchman, Hood, Rochon, Peterson, Mantini, and Majumdar (1989) compared four groups of children classified according to linguistic profile: high speech/language skills overall, low speech/language skills overall, poor articulation, and poor auditory comprehension. Hearing impairment significantly differentiated children in the high versus low overall groups.

Silva, Chalmers, and Stewart (1986) found that bilateral otitis media with effusion had long-term adverse effects on children. Compared to subjects without bilateral otitis media, these children gained significantly lower (average) scores in tests of verbal comprehension and expression, speech articulation, and reading abilities. In an earlier study of these children, Silva et al. (1982) found that the children with otitis media failed to differ from children without otitis media in terms of background characteristics. However, they were significantly disadvantaged in speech articulation, verbal comprehension, motor development, and intelligence. These findings support the view that hearing loss is related to speech and language difficulties.

IQ

The relationship between IQ and speech and language disorders has generated some controversy. In part, the relationship is a natural and expected one because language is a necessary component of most psychometric tests of intelligence. Consequently, it is not surprising to find that low IQ and speech/language disorders are correlated (Silva, 1987). However, it also has been found that speech/language-disordered children fall within normal IQ ranges (Baker & Cantwell, 1983). In fact, Beitchman et al. (1989a) found that low versus normal IQ scores characterize different types of speech and language problems. Children with articulation or speech disorders, but without other language delays, show normal IQs (Beitchman et al., 1989a). Children with more general language delays show lower IQ scores, supporting the conclusion that IQ is more strongly correlated with general language delays than specific ones (Beitchman, Hood, Rochon, Peterson, Mantini, & Majumdar, 1989a; Silva, 1987).

IQ is also correlated with SES. It is difficult to say whether SES is generally related to overall cognitive ability as measured by IQ tests or more specifically associated with speech and language problems (Puckering & Rutter, 1987; Silva, 1987). As yet, no research parcels out the general or specific associations between SES and cognition versus language (Puckering & Rutter, 1987).

FAMILIAL AND GENETIC FACTORS

It is a common clinical observation that speech and language disorders tend to run in families. As part of their longitudinal study of language-impaired children, Tallal, Dukette, and Curtiss (1989) were able to show that families of language-impaired children are more likely than families of controls to report a positive family history. George and Kolvin (1979) report significantly more family members with histories of stutter, stammer, and delayed speech development in a speech-retarded group compared with controls. In the only epidemiologically based community sample with a control group, Beitchman, Nair, Clegg, and Patel (1986) were able to show increased rates of positive family histories of speech, language, and learning problems in the speech/language-impaired group compared to the controls. It is estimated that from 24% to as high as 45% of children have speech and language disorders that are thought to be of familial origin (Ingram, 1959; Neils & Aram, 1986; Silver, 1971).

Stuttering is thought to be transmitted via a sex-modified inheritance (Scarr & Kidd, 1983), and it appears to occur more among boys than girls (Kidd, Kidd, & Records, 1978). Kidd et al. (1978) also found that girls have more affected relatives than boys, and more of these affected relatives are males. It is unknown if other speech and language disorders have similar patterns of familial transmission (Beitchman, Hood, Inglis, 1992). The familiality of phonological disorders also has been investigated. Significantly more family members of phonologically disordered children than normal children are reported to have speech/language disorders, stuttering, and dyslexia. Lewis (1990) has examined the pedigrees of 4 children with a severe phonological disorder demonstrating three generations of members with speech/language disorders. Studies of normal twin pairs (Locke & Mather, 1987; Matheny & Bruggemann, 1973) have demonstrated greater phonetic concordance in monozygotic than dizygotic twins, which supports a genetic explanation for articulation and phonological skills in normal individuals.

Additional support for the role of genetic factors comes from studies of dyslexics. Recent reports from the Colorado Reading Project (DeFries, Olson, Pennington, & Smith, 1991) lend strong support to the notion that phonological processing problems may be the heritable precursor to the deficit in phonological coding of written language. In other words, some forms of dyslexias may be traced to an underlying language deficit. Pennington (1990) has concluded that dyslexia is a developmental language disorder that mainly affects the phonological domain of language. Phonological coding of written language is a prerequisite for skill in single-word recognition and spelling. Heritable differences in certain spoken language skills, especially the awareness of phonemic segments in words, lead to problems in this area of phonological coding. The results of segregation and linkage analyses support the not-too-surprising conclusion that dyslexia is genetically heterogeneous. Attempts to identify specific chromosomes, such as chromosome 15, as the location of the gene or genes responsible for some forms of dyslexia have failed to be replicated (DeFries, 1992). Genetic models that have been suggested for reading disability include polygenic, oligogenic, and single-gene inheritance. While these ideas are unable to be translated wholesale to speech/language disorders, there may be enough overlap between dyslexias based on phonological processing problems and speech/language disorders for the heritability models of dyslexia to have heuristic value in the study of speech/language disorders.

NEUROANATOMICAL FINDINGS

With the advent of sophisticated neuroimaging technology in the past 20 years, it has become possible to study brain morphology in children and adults with language disorders without the restriction of postmortem samples. This area of rapidly advancing knowledge has shown intriguing findings but few conclusive results. Most information available on the neuroanatomical correlates of language impairment is based on studies of developmental dyslexia. These studies of developmental dyslexia have focused on known language areas, such as Wernicke's area and Broca's area, and whether hemispheric asymmetries reveal abnormalities in these structures (Filipek & Kennedy, 1991). There have been less than a dozen neuroimaging studies of developmental dyslexia (Filipek & Kennedy, 1991) and even fewer of speech and language impairment.

Some early studies (Leisman & Ashkenazi, 1980; LeMay, 1981) have reported a reversal of the normal hemispheric asymmetry with a wider right posterior hemisphere in dyslexics (Filipek & Kennedy, 1991). Historically, the left insular region has been associated with language disturbance (Hynd, Semrud-Clikeman, Lorys, Novey, & Eliopulos, 1990). Hynd, Semrud-Clikeman, Lorys, Novey, & Eliopulos (1990) reported bilateral shorter lengths of the insular regions of dyslexic brains when compared with controls. In addition, the dyslexic subjects demonstrated a reversal of the usual, left larger than right, asymmetry in the posterior temporal region that includes the planum temporale.

The planum temporale also has been found to lack the expected asymmetry in children with language and learning disorders (Galaburda, 1991). Reduced volumes of the left perisylvian region in language/learning-impaired children (Jernigan, Hesselink, Sowell, & Tallal, 1991) or symmetrical perisylvian configurations (Hynd, Semrud-Clikeman, Lorys, Novey, & Eliopulos, 1990; Rumsey et al., 1986) have been reported in language-impaired children. Plante (1991) reported atypical perisylvian asymmetries in the majority of parents of language-impaired boys, suggesting that atypical perisylvian asymmetries reflect a transmittable biological factor. Although these findings remain inconclusive, the evidence suggests that hemispheric specialization of function may be anomalous in this population (Jernigan et al., 1991).

The search for anatomical specificity among children with speech and language disorders may, however, be misplaced. Recent work with aphasia in adults has led to a profound change in the conceptualization of the neural systems thought to underlie complex functions such as language and memory. These are now thought to be the result of synchronized activity in vast neuronal networks, made up of many functional regions in the cerebral cortex and subcortical nuclei. Numerous pathways are thought to interconnect these regions in reciprocal fashion (Damasio, 1992). Any one of many interconnecting neural networks could be implicated in populations of children with nonspecific speech/language impairments.

Damasio and Damasio (1992) describe 3 interacting sets of neural structures related to language function. The first, a large collection of neural systems in both the right and left hemispheres, represents nonlanguage interactions between the body and its environment. The brain categorizes these nonlanguage representations and creates another level of representation that forms the basis for abstraction and metaphor. The second, a smaller number of neural systems generally located in the left cerebral hemisphere, represent phonemes, phoneme combinations, and syntactic rules for combining words. These systems assemble word forms and generate sentences to be spoken or written; they also perform the initial processing of auditory or visual language signals. A third set of structures, also located largely in the

left hemisphere, mediates between the first two. These structures can take a concept and stimulate the production of word forms, or they can receive words and cause the brain to evoke the corresponding concepts. Many of these neural structures are located in the region of the sylvian fissure. They also include the classic language areas of Wernicke and Broca. Because language function is concentrated in the left hemisphere in the region of the sylvian fissure, it is not surprising that in samples of children with impaired language function, this region of the brain is most often found to be abnormal in relation to normals.

Because of the extensive interconnections between the various language areas and the higher conceptual areas, deficits in any of these structural areas or in their interconnections will likely result in some speech or language problem. For example, adult patients with lesions in the left posterior temporal and inferior parietal cortex retain access to their concepts but show an inability to produce proper word morphology; they produce phonemically distorted color names, saying "buh" for "blue." Lesions in the anterior and middle regions of both temporal lobes impair the brain's conceptual system (Damasio & Damasio, 1992).

Given this conceptualization of the neural systems that underlie language function, it is unlikely that heterogeneous groups of speech/language-impaired children will be likely to show anatomical specificity. As stated before, any one of many interconnecting neural networks could be implicated in populations of children with nonspecific speech/language impairments. Homogeneous subtypes of speech/language-impaired children will need to be defined so that some specificity in the underlying neuroanatomy can be found.

Speech and Language Disorders With Underlying Biological Disturbance

MENTAL RETARDATION

Medical disorders suggestive of organic brain damage, particularly mental retardation, often are associated with speech and language delays (Cantwell & Baker, 1977; Chapman & Nation, 1981;

Rutter, Graham, & Yule, 1970). Baker and Cantwell (1987a) compared psychiatrically ill and well groups of speech- and language-impaired children. They found that the psychiatrically ill group was more likely to have chronic medical disorder or disorder suggesting central nervous system damage. Mental retardation was the single most common cause of serious language delay.

An impoverished vocabulary is characteristic of mentally retarded children, who also have difficulty with abstraction. These children use fewer verbs and more nouns than normals (O'Connor & Hermelin, 1963). When compared with normal peers, mentally retarded children consistently show deficits in phonology, especially articulation defects (Beitchman & Peterson, 1986; Yoder & Milleder, 1972). Mentally retarded children fail to achieve communicative clarity to the same degree as normal children; they often use shorter sentences, less complex sentence structures, and take less advantage of syntactic options, such as predicate elaboration and subordinate and relative clauses, than normal children (Bloom & Lahey, 1978; Jordan, 1967; Naremore & Dever, 1974). In general, mentally retarded children show delays across a broad variety of language functions.

While the speech and language characteristic of mental retardation are usually indistinctive, several recently described syndromes in which speech and language are sufficiently unusual are noteworthy.

FRAGILE X SYNDROME

A fragile site break on the long arm of the X chromosome in males and on the two X chromosomes in females results in the fragile X syndrome. Four-fifths of affected males show cognitive defects, and about one-third of carrier females are mentally retarded. Fragile X accounts for approximately 10% of all boys with severe mental retardation of no obvious cause and 6 to 10% of unexplained mild mental retardation. Fragile X individuals are particularly prone to autism. This disorder also may be associated with hyperactivity and conduct disorder. Reading and spelling skills are relatively advanced in contrast with poor arithmetic performance (Kemper, Hagerman, & Altshui-Stark, 1988). In relation to speech and language, Hanson, Jackson, and Hagerman (1986) found that the speech of fragile X individuals is often cluttered with frequent dysfluent, rapid, tangential remarks and poor topic maintenance. The language delays found among children with other sex chromosome abnormalities, such as Turner's syndrome, Klinefelter's syndrome, and XXY syndrome, are regarded as indistinctive.

COCKTAIL PARTY SYNDROME

A language disorder characteristic of some hydrocephalic children who exhibit excessive chatter and illogical thinking has been called the "cocktail party syndrome." These children use long, complicated sentences incorporating sophisticated vocabulary, but the content of their language is empty or irrelevant, and formal testing reveals poor comprehension (Bishop & Rosenbloom, 1987; Tew, 1979; Tew & Lawrence, 1979). This disorder suggests that mastery of the form of language (syntax and phonology) can occur despite limited cognitive ability (Bishop & Rosenbloom, 1987). Poor abstract reasoning, visual perceptual, and academic skills are characteristic of the cocktail party syndrome (Hurley, Dorman, Laatsch, Bell, & D'Avignon, 1990). The disorder is more common in girls and although it occurs among hydrocephalic children, many of these children display no features of cocktail party syndrome.

WILLIAMS SYNDROME

Williams syndrome is a rare metabolic neurodevelopmental disorder of unknown etiology, resulting in mental retardation and occurring in approximately 1 in 25,000 live births (Reilly, Klima, & Belugi, 1990; Udwin & Yule, 1991). Its features include distinctive "elfinlike" faces, renal and cardiovascular abnormalities, growth retardation, and developmental delay (Martin, Snodgrass, & Cohen, 1984; Udwin & Yule, 1991; Udwin, Yule & Martin, 1987). Published and unpublished case studies and assessments confirm that most children with Williams syndrome are language delayed, hypersensitive to noise, learning disabled, and have emotional and behavioral disturbances. No one has yet identified auditory abnormalities to explain the children's hypersensitivity to noise. However, Klein, Armstrong, Greer, and Brown (1990) found high prevalence rates for hyperacusis (95%) and otitis media (61%).

Language abilities develop slowly in these children during the preschool years. By school age, however, they show fluent and articulate speech that is verbose and pseudomature (Meyerson & Frank, 1987; Reilly et al., 1990; Udwin & Yule, 1991). On both production and comprehension tasks, Williams syndrome subjects evidence a remarkable preservation of linguistic knowledge in the context of otherwise widespread general cognitive impairment. They demonstrate good command and frequent utilization of affective prosodic devices and semantic clustering strategies in verbal memory tasks. The spontaneous language of these adolescents often includes unusual word choices, such as "The bees abort the beehive" (Bellugi, Wang, & Jernigan, 1994). The majority of children with Williams syndrome have moderate to severe learning difficulties, and overall their verbal abilities are markedly superior to their visuospatial and motor skills. Despite their spatial cognitive dysfunction, the Williams subjects show preservation of the ability to discriminate unfamiliar faces (Jernigan & Bellugi, 1992).

Speech/Language Impairment and Psychiatric Disorders

Sufficient data demonstrate that speech- and language-impaired children are at increased risk for developing psychiatric disorders of all kinds (Baker & Cantwell, 1987b; Beitchman, 1986; Cantwell & Baker, 1977; Cantwell & Baker, 1985; Chess & Rosenburg, 1974; Grinnell, Scott-Hartnet, & Glasier, 1983; Gualtieri, Koriath, Van Bourgondien & Saleeby, 1983; Kotsopoulis & Boodoosingh, 1987; Stevenson & Richman, 1978). Whether one starts with a psychiatric sample or a language-impaired sample, it is clear that language impairment and psychiatric disorders occur together.

Although there are fairly extensive data with regard to the prevalence of speech and language impairment and its association with psychiatric disorders, the specific types of linguistic impairment associated with various psychiatric disorders have not yet been cataloged. In the following section, specific psychiatric disorders and the corresponding linguistic deficit(s) are described. For some conditions, specific relationships are identi-

fied; for others, only general statements are possible.

HYPERACTIVITY

There is good evidence that attention deficit hyperactivity disorder is associated with language impairment. Beitchman, Nair, Clegg, Ferguson, et al. (1986) reported a prevalence of 30% attention deficit hyperactivity disorder in their sample of language-impaired 5-year-old children. Baker and Cantwell (1987b) found hyperactivity to be the preponderant diagnosis among the language impaired. Using empirical clustering techniques, Beitchman, Hood, Rochon, and Peterson (1989) were able to show not only that attention deficit hyperactivity disorder was the most common psychiatric diagnosis but that it was associated with global deficits in speech and language. The deficits included articulation, language comprehension, and language expression. There are no other studies of which the authors are aware that have looked at attention deficit and the specifics of language function.

Beitchman (1989b) proposed that an underlying neurodevelopmental immaturity may be the antecedent condition responsible for both hyperactivity and language impairment. In a more recent study of language-impaired preschool children, Tallal et al. (1989) found that language-impaired children performed poorly on tasks assessing attention, perception, and motor functions. Poor performance on these tasks is suggestive of neurodevelopmental dysfunction. It is also commonly found to differentiate hyperactive children from normal controls (Barkley, 1990). Tallal's findings, then, support the hypothesis that neurodevelopmental dysfunction or delay may predispose a child to both language impairment and behavior disorder. In a seven-year follow-up study, Beitchman and colleagues found results also consistent with a neurodevelopmental immaturity model of language impairment. Findings revealed that children's cognitive, academic, and developmental delays paralleled their delays in language functioning (Beitchman, Wilson, Brownlie, Walters, & Lancee, 1996).

A case example may help demonstrate some of the language and communication problems found among children with attention deficit disorder, in particular, their frequent inability to stay on topic.

CASE EXAMPLE

A 10-year-old boy was asked to retell a story:

"They were building a house and they had no place to live so they're going to find a house. And some people don't have a house, they live outside. But people live in a house."

Asked "What happened after they built the house?" the boy replied:

"They were sad because it was thunderstorm . . . (singing) la la la la, I am walking to go to BiWay because I love it . . . (refocused on task) 'cause they were sleeping and they were crying they were sad. Anyways! (laughter) I don't like this story."

It is apparent that this boy has difficulty remaining on task. Although the emotional content of the story may have affected his willingness and ability to tell the story, this difficulty is typical of children with attention deficit disorders. The manifest problem of topic maintenance may be due to underlying language problems, such as poor auditory memory, attentional problems, or, as is illustrated in this case, the emotional content of the story itself. Whatever the reason, these children have problems with storytelling, a task that is central to one's ability to communicate.

EMOTIONAL DISORDERS

Socioemotional disorders are also more prevalent among the language impaired than among controls. Beitchman, Nair, Clegg, Ferguson, et al. (1986) reported a 12.8% prevalence of emotional disorders among the language impaired compared to 1.5% among controls. The differences in prevalence rates were particularly marked among females when teacher reports of emotionality were considered. Baker and Cantwell (1987a) found an association among language impairment, emotional disorder, and being female. Tallal et al. (1989) found that preschool language–impaired girls scored significantly higher on the social withdrawal scale of the Child Behavior Checklist (Achenbach & Edelbrook, 1983) than did control girls. For reasons as yet unknown, language-impaired girls seem to be more prone to emotional disorders than language-impaired boys. One speculation worth investigating is that neurodevelopmental immaturity in boys is more likely to emerge as hyperactivity, whereas in girls it appears as withdrawn, avoidant, or anxious behaviors. To some extent, differential socialization in boys and girls may reinforce these behaviors.

ELECTIVE MUTISM

Rutter and Lord (1987) report that elective mutism is about equally divided between boys and girls, with possibly a slight excess of girls. Some recent evidence suggests that electively mute children may be delayed in the onset of language and may show immaturities in communication (especially articulation) as late as 6 to 10 years of age (Kolvin & Fundudis, 1981; Lerea & Ward, 1965). Children who overcome their elective mutism may continue to show speech/language impairment.

Immaturities among the electively mute are common (Krolian, 1988). In a review of 24 cases of elective mutism, Kolvin and Fundudis (1981) found delayed speech milestones, articulation disorders, electroencephalographic immaturities, and associated developmental problems of soiling and enuresis. Mild cognitive delays also have been found in children initially diagnosed as electively mute (Parker, Olsen, & Throckmorton, 1960; Reed, 1963). Wilkin (1985), in a comparison of 24 elective mutes with controls, found that one-third of the elective mutes had delayed speech development or problems with articulation. Although speech/language immaturities fail to be a necessary precondition for elective mutism, they coexist in about one-third to one-half of cases (Kolvin & Fundudis, 1981; Wilkin, 1985). These immaturities appear to be a logical precursor to elective mutism and may play some causal or contributory role.

LEARNING DISABILITIES

Learning disabilities are a heterogeneous group of disorders in which educational attainment falls below that expected on the basis of IQ and is not due to inadequate instruction. Learning disabilities are often also referred to as dyslexia. Three models of dyslexia have been described: an auditory-verbal subtype, a visuospatial subtype, and a mixed subtype. The auditory-verbal subtype is thought to be the most common.

Children with speech/language impairment are found to have academic problems; the reported prevalence ranges from 45% (Baker & Cantwell, 1987b) to 90% (Stark, Bernstein, & Condino,

1984). Conversely, children with learning disabilities are found to exhibit speech and language problems (Benton, 1975; Vellutino, 1979). Barkely (1990) reported that 60% of children with reading disabilities had associated language disorders. Deficits in specific aspects of linguistic functioning among the reading disabled, including verbal encoding and labeling, are common (Denckla & Rudel, 1976; Vellutino, Smith, Steger, & Kaman, 1975).

Phonologic processing (using phonologic information in the processing of written and oral language) has been reported as an important causal factor in the acquisition of reading skills (Wagner & Torgesen, 1987). It is also known that phonologic processing is highly correlated with general measures of language function, such as educational attainment and visuospatial abilities (Lewis, Ekelman, & Aram, 1989). Consequently, it would be natural to find increased rates of reading disabilities and educational failure among the speech- and language-impaired. Baker and Cantwell (1987b) observed a 28% incidence of learning disabilities among their sample of speech- and language-impaired children, and Aram and Nation (1980) found high rates of reading problems among 63 preschool children with language difficulties.

Several investigators have noted that the more pervasive the language impairment, the worse the academic outcome in terms of reading ability. Silva, Williams, and McGee (1987) observed that children with general language delay had more reading dificulties than children with specific delays. Childs and Angst (1984) observed that children with articulation and language problems had more reading difficulties than those with articulation problems alone. Furthermore, in a group of reading-disabled children ages 3 to 11 years, language skills were reported to decline with age. The authors viewed this decline as a partial result of their reading difficulties (Share & Silva, 1987).

Problems with phonological processing are illustrated with the following example.

CASE EXAMPLE

A 9½-year-old youngster is talking to an examiner:

Examiner: Say "block." Now say it again, but don't say /b/.
Child: ock.

Examiner: Say "smile." Now say it again, but don't say /s/.
Child: ile.

These children have difficulty recognizing the blended consonants, such as "bl" and "sm." If they have trouble hearing these sounds, they usually will have difficulty reading them. These kinds of phonemic analysis problems are common among poor readers.

AUTISM

Disturbances of language and communication have long been held to be one of the hallmarks of autism. Most children with autism show delays in the development of language, with comprehension deficits being especially marked (Lord, 1984; Tager-Flusberg, 1981). Abnormalities in the use of language are associated with autism throughout childhood, and autistics usually are unable to use language in a flexible and reciprocal conversational manner. Immediate echolalia—repeating back what someone has just said—although common in autism, is not specific to it (Rutter, 1966). On the other hand, delayed echolalia, in which the child repeats something that was said minutes to months before, is thought to occur almost exclusively in children with severe social deficits or autism (Bartak, Rutter, & Cox, 1975). Pronominal reversal, the tendency to say you instead of I, also is thought to be associated with autism (Bartak & Rutter, 1974).

The failure to use gesture, facial expression, or normal intonal patterns to express a variety of intentions is also considered a communication deficit associated with autism. One interesting aspect of the language dysfunction of autistics is that certain aspects of speech and language remain intact, unlike language disturbances in most other disorders (e.g., hyperactivity). For instance, in autistics, phonology and syntax may be relatively unimpaired, but semantics and pragmatics may be severely affected (Tager-Flusberg, 1981).

It is important to recognize that some of the language behaviors associated with autism, such as echolalia and delayed echolalia, are understandable within the context of developmental communicative behavior. Prizant and Wetherby (1986) have described a developmental sequence of intentional communicative behavior, suggesting that immediate and delayed echolalia can be understood as transitional phenomena toward communicative language. Controlling for receptive language age, the language and communication of autistics may not be demonstrably different from those of dysphasics, for instance. A study comparing sentence comprehension strategies of autistic, normal, and language-impaired subjects found that children with autism and those with specific language impairment responded to a sentence comprehension task in a manner similar to that used by normal children at similar levels of comprehension ability. The study concluded that the language processing deficits seen in autism may be less unique to the syndrome than previously believed (Paul, Fischer, & Cohen, 1988). The differences between the language and communication of the developmental receptive dysphasics and autistics may be a matter of degree and possibly a manifestation of the developmental level of intentional communicative social behavior.

When comparing the language and communication of autistics and those of both the mentally retarded and the receptive language dysphasics, it must be ensured that these groups are equivalent in terms of receptive language age. Differences in mental age (Siegel, Vukicevie, Elliot, & Kramer, 1989) or receptive language age (Sigman & Ungerer, 1984) can account for differences between autistics and the mentally retarded. The studies of Bartak et al. (1975) and Bartak and Rutter (1974) are commonly cited as showing differences in the language and communication of autistics and dysphasics; however, these studies compared groups that were not equivalent in receptive language age. Despite the vast literature on language disturbances in autism, the specific and unique features of these disturbances remain to be defined.

The Outcome of Early Speech/Language Impairment

Clinic-based samples of speech/language-impaired children report continued speech/language problems in 40 to 88% of cases at follow-up (Aram & Hall, 1989). However, clinic cases are subject to referral biases limiting generalizability

of findings. Furthermore, few studies tested the children at follow-up; instead they depended on secondary sources such as parents for evidence of communication problems. The true rate of continued speech/language impairment can be obtained only from community studies utilizing representative random selection methods with well-defined criteria and appropriate controls (Beitchman & Brownlie, 1996).

In the only well-defined community sample with a control group, 81% of children with both a speech *and* language disorder at 5 years of age were still speech and or language impaired at 12.5 years. In contrast, sixty-five percent of children with a speech problem at 5 years were impaired at 12.5 years, and 72% of language-impaired children were still language impaired at 12.5 years (Beitchman, Brownlie, Inglis, Wild, Mathews, Schachter, Kroll, Martin, Ferguson, & Lancee, 1994).

Children with more pervasive problems show poorer outcomes compared to children with isolated problems (Bishop & Edmundson, 1987). Disorders confined to speech or the phonological aspects of language have a more favorable outcome than disorders involving other or more general aspects of language (Beitchman, Brownlie, Inglis, Wild, Mathews, Schachter, Kroll, Martin, Ferguson, & Lancee, 1994). The outcome of children with both receptive and expressive language delays is worse than that of children with either one alone. Additionally, there is evidence that in some language-impaired samples, nonverbal IQ is an important predictor of eventual language performance (Aram, Ekelman, & Nation, 1984; Griffiths, 1969; Paul & Cohen, 1984).

In very young children (2 to 3 years old), the smaller the child's vocabulary, the more irregular the child's eating, and the less time engaged in quiet activities with mother, the more persistent the language deficit (Fischel, Whitehurst, Caulfield, & DeBaryshe, 1989).

Early childhood speech/language impairment significantly increased the risk for learning disabilities compared to non–language-impaired children. Not all the increased risk of learning disabilities was due to the speech/language impairment; some was attributable to the associated lower IQ, lowers SES, less educated mothers, and birth status (second- or later-born) associated with speech/language impairment. However, speech/language

445

impairment independently predicted learning disabilities, even after controlling for these other variables (Beitchman et al., 1993).

The middle childhood and young adolescent outcome of early language impairment shows clearly the increased risk of psychiatric and behavioral problems. Children with more pervasive problems were at higher risk for psychiatric problems than those with more circumscribed problems. For instance, the risk of psychiatric disorder associated with language delays was greater than that associated with speech delays. The risk is increased when receptive language is more severely compromised than expressive language. For children with language comprehension problems, social relations appear more affected than other behavioral dimensions. Psychiatric disorder in late childhood was associated with early speech/language delays even when the speech/language delay improved (Beitchman & Brownlie, 1996).

While there is evidence that early childhood speech and language delays increase the risk of psychiatric disorder and learning disabilities in middle and later childhood, there is virtually no information on the risk of disorder in adulthood. This is a serious gap in our knowledge that requires further study.

Summary and Conclusions

Speech/language disorders are common and are associated with psychiatric disorders such as attention deficit hyperactivity disorder, anxiety, depression, autism and learning disabilities. The reason for the increased rates of psychiatric disorders among speech/language-impaired children has generated many hypotheses. It is possible that speech/language-impaired children have some increased vulnerability based on neurodevelopmental impairments that raises the risk for disorders of various kinds. In the presence of certain temperamental characteristics and an inhospitable or insensitive environment, psychiatric disorder can become manifest. It is also possible that the speech/language impairment acts secondarily through such phenomena as school failure, peer rejection, and scapegoating, which, in turn, leads to behavioral disturbance. There also may be cognitive impairments based on the speech/language disturbance that limit the child's ability to use language to modulate emotions, express feelings and ideas, delay action, and control his or her own and other people's behavior. Under these circumstances, the child will be prone to behavioral outbursts on the one hand and withdrawal on the other. The complex mechanisms that mediate the relation between speech/language impairment and psychiatric problems is poorly understood and clearly in need of further investigation.

The etiology of speech/language impairment is unknown but associated with many variables. These include large family size, lower socioeconomic status, later-born status, and hearing impairment. In addition, evidence suggests that familial and genetic factors are implicated in the transmission of speech/language impairment. Birth and pregnancy variables, medical disorders suggestive of organic brain damage, and mental retardation are also known to be associated with speech/language disorders.

Sophisticated imaging technology has been used to describe the neuroanatomical basis for some cases of speech/language impairment. The planum temporale has been found to show reversed asymmetries or the lack of the expected asymmetry (normally left is greater than right); reduced volumes of the left perisylvian region also have been noted in language-impaired children. However, recent changes in the conceptualization of the neural systems thought to underlie complex functions such as language and memory make it unlikely that heterogeneous groups of speech/language-impaired children will show neuroanatomical specificity. Homogeneous subtypes of such children will need to be defined to achieve some underlying neuroanatomical unity.

Language is not a unitary phenomenon, however, and some system of classifying speech/language disorders is an important prerequisite to further advances in clarifying their neuroanatomy and the relation between speech/language impairment and psychiatric disorders. For instance, the components of the linguistic system are differentially impaired among children with diverse psychiatric disorders. Among autistics, syntax and phonology typically are spared, but semantics and pragmatics usually are affected. Attention deficit hyperactivity disorder has been associated with

446

specific impairments in auditory memory and discrimination and more general impairments in receptive and expressive language. Recent evidence suggests that phonological processing problems are common precursors of learning disabilities. To date the nature of the language impairment found among other psychiatric disorders has not been identified, but it represents a potentially fruitful line of enquiry.

The practitioner needs to be alert to speech/language problems for many important reasons. Many children thought to be willfully disobedient, oppositional, or hyperactive may be suffering from problems with auditory memory, auditory discrimination, or auditory comprehension. Unless these deficits are recognized, attempts to treat these children may be misplaced and end in failure. The language skills of withdrawn, depressed children also need to be examined, since language deficits are found among children with emotional disorders. Furthermore, language deficits may intensify poor peer skills and tendencies to social isolation. The clinician always should suspect problems with language comprehension in any child who seems odd, who says things that appear out of context, and who may seem spacey or autisticlike. The proper planning of the child's academic program depends on an appropriate understanding of the child's linguistic capabilities. Psychotherapeutic encounters must, of necessity, be in tune with the child's language skills in order to be maximally beneficial and effective. It is possible that many psychotherapeutic failures can be traced to unrecognized language impairments.

There have been many reports of the short-term and intermediate outcome of speech and language delays but no methodologically acceptable studies of the adult outcome of speech/language impairment to adulthood (Beitchman & Brownlie, 1996). Those studies reporting on the outcome to middle childhood and early adolescence demonstrate substantial levels of morbidity in speech/language development, behavioral adjustment, and learning. To what extent these difficulties continue into adulthood and affect vocational outcome, psychosocial functioning, and mental health more generally is not yet known but should be considered a priority for future investigations.

Given the persistent nature of speech/language impairment and the high rates of associated psychiatric morbidity, continued research into the etiology, treatment, and prevention of this impairment and associated disorders is strongly recommended. Although early intervention programs with enriched language environments for young children at high risk now exist, the effects of these types of programs remain insufficiently studied and inadequately understood. No one can confidently describe the specific outcomes of speech/language intervention (Nye, Foster, & Seaman, 1987) or the effects of language intervention on coexisting behavior problems. Careful evaluation and long-term follow-up are essential to properly assess the effects of these types of programs. This information is of theoretical and practical importance, as it will assist in directing scarce treatment resources and aid in clarifying the relation between language impairment and psychiatric disorders. This clarification will assist in the understanding of human development from infancy to adulthood.

REFERENCES

Achenbach, T. M., & Edelbrook, C. S. (1983). *Manual for the Child Behavior Checklist and Revised Child Behavior Profile.* Burlington: University of Vermont.

Aram, D. M., Ekelman, B. L., & Nation, J. E. (1984). Preschoolers with language disorders: 10 years later. *Journal of Speech and Hearing Research, 27,* 232–244.

Aram, D. M., & Hall, N. E. (1989). Longitudinal follow-up of children with preschool communication disorders: Treatment implications. *School Psychology Review, 18,* 487–501.

Aram, D. M., & Nation, J. E. (1980). Preschool language disorders and subsequent language and academic difficulties. *Journal of Communication Disorders, 13,* 159–170.

Baker, L., & Cantwell, D. P. (1977). Psychiatric disorder in children with speech and language retardation. *Archives of General Psychiatry, 34,* 583–591.

Baker, L., & Cantwell, D. P. (1983). Developmental, social and behavioral characteristics of speech and language disordered children. In S. Chess & A. Thomas (Eds.), *Annual progress in child psychiatry and child development* (pp. 205–216). New York: Brunner/Mazel.

Baker, L., & Cantwell, D. P. (1985). Psychiatric and learning disorders in children with speech and language disorders: A critical review. In K. Gadow (Ed.), *Advances in learning and behavioral disabilities* (pp. 1–28), London: JAI Press.

Baker, L., & Cantwell, D. P. (1987a). Comparison of well, emotionally disordered, and behaviorally disordered children with linguistic problems. *Journal of the American Academy of Child and Adolescent Psychiatry, 26,* 193–196.

Baker, L., & Cantwell, D. P. (1987b). A prospective psychiatric follow-up of children with speech/language disorders. *Journal of the American Academy of Child and Adolescent Psychiatry, 26,* 546–553.

Barkely, R. (1981). Learning disabilities. In E. Mash & L. Terdal (Eds.), *Behavioral assessment of childhood disorders* (pp. 441–482). New York: Guilford Press.

Barkely, R. (1990). Attention deficit disorders: History, definition, and diagnosis. In M. Lewis & S. M. Miller (Eds.), *Handbook of developmental psychopathology* (pp. 65–76). New York: Plenum Press.

Bartak, L., & Rutter, M. (1974). Use of personal pronouns by autistic children. *Journal of Autism and Childhood Schizophrenia, 4,* 217–222.

Bartak, L., Rutter, M., & Cox, A. (1975). Comparative study of infantile autism and specific developmental receptive language disorder: I. The children. *British Journal of Psychiatry, 126,* 127–145.

Beitchman, J. H. (1985). Speech and language impairment and psychiatric risk: Toward a model of neurodevelopmental immaturity. *Psychiatric Clinics of North America, 8,* 721–735.

Beitchman, J. H., Nair, R., Clegg, M., Ferguson, B., & Patel, P. G. (1986). Prevalence of psychiatric disorders in children with speech and language disorders. *Journal of the American Academy of Child Psychiatry, 25,* 528–535.

Beitchman, J. H., Nair, R., Clegg, M., & Patel, P. G. (1986). Prevalence of speech and language disorders in 5-year-old kindergarten children in the Ottawa-Carleton region. *Journal of Speech and Hearing Disorders, 51,* 98–110.

Beitchman, J. H., & Peterson, M. (1986). Disorders of language, communication, and behavior in mentally retarded children: Some ideas on their co-occurrence. *Psychiatric Clinics of North America, 9* (4), 689–698.

Beitchman, J. H., Peterson, M., Rochon, J., Hood, J., Majumdar, S., & Mantini, T. (1987). *Language impairment and psychiatric risk: Further explorations.* Ottawa, Ont.: Final Report, Health & Welfare Canada.

Beitchman, J. H., Peterson, P., & Clegg, M. (1988). Speech and language impairment and psychiatric disorder. *Child Psychiatry and Human Development, 18,* 191–207.

Beitchman, J. H., Hood, J., Rochon, J., Peterson, M., Mantini, T., & Majumdar, S. (1989). Empirical classification of speech/language impairment in children. I. Identification of speech/language categories.

American Academy of Child and Adolescent Psychiatry, 28 (1), 112–117.

Beitchman, J. H., Hood, J., Rochon, J., & Peterson, M. (1989). Empirical classification of speech/language impairment in children. II. Behavioral characteristics. *American Academy of Child and Adolescent Psychiatry, 28* (1), 118–123.

Beitchman, J. H., Hood, J., & Inglis, A. (1992). Transmission of speech and language impairment: A preliminary investigation. *Canadian Journal of Psychiatry, 37* (3), 151–156.

Beitchman, J. H., Ferguson, B., Schachter, D., Brownlie, E. B., Inglis, A., Wild, J., Lancee, W., Kroll, R., Mathews, R., Brunshaw, J., Walters, H., & Martin, S. (1993). *A seven year follow-up of speech/language impaired and control children.* Ottawa, Ont.: Final Report, Health and Welfare Canada.

Beitchman, J. H., Brownlie, E. B., Inglis, A., Wild, J., Mathews, R., Schachter, D., Kroll, R., Martin, S., Ferguson, B., & Lancee, W. (1994). A seven year follow-up of speech/language impaired and control children: Speech/language stability and outcome. *Journal of the American Academy of Child and Adolescent Psychiatry, 33* (9), 1322–1330.

Beitchman, J. H. & Brownlie, E. B. (1996). Childhood Speech and Language Disorders. In L. Hechtman (Ed.), *Do they grow out of it? Long-term outcomes of childhood disorders* (pp. 225–253). Washington, DC: American Psychiatric Press.

Beitchman, J. H., Wilson, B., Brownlie, E. B., Walters, H., & Lancee, W. (1996). Long-term consistency in speech/language profiles: I. Developmental and academic outcomes. *Journal of the American Academy of Child and Adolescent Psychiatry, 35,* 804–814.

Beitchman, J. H., Patel, P. G., Nair, R., Ferguson, B., Pressman, E., Smith A., Clegg, A., & Hrnchiar, C. (1984). *Speech and language disorders among 5-year-old Ottawa-Carleton kindergarten children.* Ottawa, Ont.: Final Report, Health and Welfare Canada.

Bellugi, U., Wang, P., & Jernigan, T. (1994). Williams syndrome: An unusual neuropsychological profile. In S. H. Broman & J. Grafman (Eds.), *Atypical cognitive deficits in developmental disorders: Implications for brain function* (pp. 23–56). Hillsdale, NJ: Lawrence Erlbaum.

Belmont, L., & Marolla, F. A. (1973). Birth order, family size, and intelligence. *Science, 182,* 1096–1101.

Benton, A. L. (1975). Developmental dyslexia: Neurological aspects. In W. J. Friedlander (Ed.), *Advances in neurology* (pp. 1–47). New York: Raven Press.

Bishop, D. V. M., & Edmundson, A. (1986). Is otitis media a major cause of specific developmental language disorders? *British Journal of Disorders of Communication, 31,* 321–338.

Bishop, D. V. M., & Edmundson, A. (1987). Language-impaired 4-year-olds: Distinguishing transient from persistent impairment. *Journal of Speech and Hearing Research, 52,* 156–173.

Bishop, D. V. M., & Rosenbloom, L. (1987). Childhood language disorders: Classification and overview. In

W. Yule & M. Rutter (Eds.), *Language development and disorders* (pp. 16–41). Philadelphia: Mac Keith Press.

Bloom, L., & Lahey, M. (1978). *Language development and language disorders.* New York: John Wiley & Sons.

Breland, H. M. (1974). Birth order, family configuration, and verbal achievement. *Child Development, 45,* 1011–1019.

Butler, N. R., Peckham, C., & Sheridan, M. (1973). Speech defects in children aged 7 years: A national study. *British Medical Journal, 3,* 253–257.

Cantwell, D. P., & Baker, L. (1977). Psychiatric disorder in children with speech and language retardation: A critical review. *Archives of General Psychiatry, 34,* 583–591.

Cantwell, D. P., & Baker, L. (1985). Psychiatric and learning disorders in children with communication disorders. Part II: Methodological approach and findings. In K. D. Gadow (Ed.), *Advances in learning and behavioral disabilities* (Vol. 4, pp. 29–47). Greenwich, CT: JAI Press.

Cantwell, D., Baker, L., & Mattison, R. (1980). Psychiatric disorders in children with speech and language retardation: Factors associated with development. *Archives of General Psychiatry, 37,* 423–426.

Chapman, D. L., & Nation, J. E. (1981). Patterns of language performance in educable mentally retarded children. *Journal of Communication Disorders, 14,* 245–254.

Chess, S., & Rosenburg, M. (1974). Clinical differentiation among children with initial language complaints. *Journal of Autism and Childhood Schizophrenia, 4,* 99–109.

Childs, P. J., & Angst, D. M. (1984). Description of an ongoing special education preschool program. *Language, Speech and Hearing Services in Schools, 15,* 262–266.

Damasio, A. R. (1992). Aphasia. *New England Journal of Medicine, 326* (8), 531–539.

Damasio, A. R., & Damasio, H. (1992). Brain and language. *Scientific American, 267* (3), 89–95.

DeFries, J. C. (1992, May). *Genetic studies of reading disabilities.* Paper presented at the language conference of the University of Toronto, Division of Child Psychiatry, Toronto, Ont.

DeFries, J. C., Olson, K., Pennington, B. F., & Smith, S. D. (1991). Colorado Reading Project: An update. In D. D. Drake & D. B. Gray (Eds.), *The reading brain: The biological basis of dyslexia* (pp. 53–87). Parkton, MD: York Press.

Denckla, M. B., & Rudel, R. (1976). Naming of pictured objects by dyslexic and other learning disabled children. *Brain and Language, 39,* 1–15.

Filipek, P. A., & Kennedy, D. N. (1991). Magnetic resonance imaging: Its role in the developmental disorders. In D. D. Duane & D. B. Gray (Eds.), *The reading brain: The biological basis of dyslexia* (pp. 133–160). Parkton, MD: York Press.

Fischel, J. D., Whitehurst, G. J., Caulfield, M. B., & DeBaryshe, B. (1989). Language growth in children with expressive language delay. *Pediatrics, 82,* 218–227.

Fundudis, T., Kolvin, I., & Garside, R. (1979). *Speech retarded and deaf children: Their psychological development.* London: Academic Press.

Galaburda, A. (1991). Anatomy of dyslexia: Argument against phrenology. In D. D. Drake & D. B. Gray (Eds.), *The reading brain: The biological basis of dyslexia* (pp. 53–87). Parkton, MD: York Press.

George, G. S., & Kolvin, I. (1979). Speech retardation: Environmental and social factors. In T. Fundudis, I. Kolvin, & R. F. Garside (Eds.), *Speech retarded and deaf children: Their psychological development.* London: Academic Press.

Griffiths, C. (1969). A follow-up study of children with disorders of speech. *British Journal of Disorders of Communication, 4,* 46–56.

Grinnell, S. W., Scott-Hartnet, D., & Glasier, J. L. (1983). Language disorders (Letter to the editor). *Journal of the American Academy of Child and Adolescent Psychiatry, 22,* 580–581.

Gualtieri, C. T., Koriath, W., Van Bourgondien, M., & Saleeby, N. (1983). Language disorders in children referred for psychiatric services. *Journal of the American Academy of Child and Adolescent Psychiatry, 22,* 580–581.

Gualtieri, T., & Hicks, R. E. (1986). An immunoreactive theory of selective male affliction. In S. Chess & A. Thomas (Eds.), *Annual progress in child psychiatry and child development* (pp. 221–258). New York: Brunner/Mazel.

Hall, P. K., & Tomblin, J. B. (1978). A follow-up study of children with articulation and language disorders. *Journal of Speech and Hearing Disorders, 43,* 220–226.

Hanson, D. M., Jackson, A. W., & Hagerman, R. J. (1986). Speech disturbances (cluttering) in mildly impaired males with the Martin-Bell/Fragile X syndrome. *American Journal of Medical Genetics, 23,* 195–206.

Hurley, A. D., Dorman, C., Laatsch, L., Bell, S., & D'Avignon, J. (1990). Cognitive functioning in patients with spina bifida, hydrocephalus, and the "cocktail party" syndrome. *Developmental Neuropsychology, 6* (2), 151–172.

Hynd, G., Semrud-Clikeman, M., Lorys, A., Novey, E., & Eliopulos, D. (1990). Brain morphology in developmental dyslexia and attention deficit disorder/hyperactivity. *Archives of Neurology, 47,* 919–926.

Ingram, T. T. S. (1959). Specific developmental disorders of speech in childhood. *Brain, 82,* 450–467.

Jenkins, S., Bax, M., & Hart, H. (1980). Behavior problems in preschool children. *Journal of Child Psychology and Psychiatry, 21,* 5–17.

Jernigan, T. L., & Bellugi, U. (1994). Neuroanatomical distinctions between Williams and Down syndromes. In S. H. Broman & J. Grafman (Eds.), *Atypical cognitive deficits in developmental disorders: Implications for brain function* (pp. 57–66). Hillsdale, NJ: Lawrence Erlbaum.

Jernigan, T. L., Hesselink, J. R., Sowell, E., & Tallal, P. A. (1991). Cerebral morphology on MRI in language/learning-impaired children. *Archives of Neurology, 48,* 539–545.

Jordan, T. E. (1967). Language and mental retardation: A review of the literature. In R. Schiefelbusch, R. Copeland, & J. Smith (Eds.), *Language and mental retardation* (pp. 20–38). New York: Holt, Rinehart, and Winston.

Kemper, M. B., Hagerman, R. J. & Altshui-Stark, D. (1988). Cognitive profiles of boys with the Fragile X syndrome. *American Journal of Medical Genetics, 30,* 191–200.

Kidd, K. K., Kidd, J. R., & Records, M. A. (1978). The possible causes of the sex ratio in stuttering and its implications. *Journal of Fluency Disorders, 3,* 13–23.

King, R. R., Jones, C., & Laskey, E. (1982). In retrospect: A fifteen-year follow-up report of speech-language-disordered children. *Language, Speech, and Hearing Services in Schools, 13,* 24–32.

Klein, A. J., Armstrong, B. L., Greer, M. K., & Brown F. R. III. (1990). Hyperacusis and otitis media in individuals with Williams syndrome. *Journal of Speech and Hearing Disorders, 55,* 339–344.

Kolvin, I., & Fundudis, T. (1981). Elective mute children: Psychological development and background factors. *Journal of Child Psychology and Psychiatry, 22,* 219–232.

Kolvin, I., Fundudis, T., & Scanlon, E. (1979). Early development, type and prevalence. In T. Fundudis, I. Kolvin, & R. Garside (Eds.), *Speech retarded and deaf children: Their psychological development* (pp. 3–20). London: Academic Press.

Krolian, E. B. (1988). "Speech is silver, but silence is golden." Day hospital treatment of two electively mute children. *Clinical Social Work Journal, 16,* 355–377.

Leisman, G., & Ashkenazi M. (1980). Aetiological factors in dyslexia: IV. Cerebral hemispheres are functionally equivalent. *Neuroscience, 11,* 157–164.

LeMay, M. (1981). Are there radiological changes in the brains of individuals with dyslexia? *Bulletin of the Orton Society, 31,* 135–141.

Lerea, L., & Ward, D. (1965). Speech avoidance among children with oral-communication defects. *Journal of Psychology, 60,* 265–270.

Lewis, B. A. (1990). Familial phonological disorders: Four pedigrees. *Journal of Speech and Hearing Disorders, 55,* 160–170.

Lewis, B. A., Ekelman, B. L., & Aram, D. M. (1989). A familial study of severe phonological disorders. *Journal of Speech and Hearing Research, 32,* 713–724.

Locke, J. L., & Mather, P. L. (1987, November). *Genetic factors in phonology: Evidence from monozygotic and dizygotic twins.* Paper presented at the annual convention of the American Speech-Language-Hearing Association. New Orleans, LA.

Lord, C. (1984). Language comprehension and cognitive disorder in autism. In L. Siegel & F. J. Morrison (Eds.), *Cognitive development in atypical children* (pp. 67–82). New York: Springer-Verlag.

Martin, N. D. T., Snodgrass, G. J. A. I., & Cohen, R. D. (1984). Idiopathic infantile hypercalcaemia—a continuing enigma. *Archives of Disease in Childhood, 59,* 605–613.

Matheny, A. P., & Bruggemann, C. E. (1973). Children's speech: Heredity components and sex differences. *Folia Phoniatrica, 25,* 442–449.

McGee, R. O., Silva, P. A., & Williams, S. M. (1984). Perinatal, neurological, environmental, and developmental characteristics of seven year old children with stable behavior problems. *Journal of Child Psychology and Psychiatry, 25,* 573–586.

Meyerson, R., & Frank, R. (1987). Language, speech and hearing in Williams syndrome: Intervention approaches and research needs. *Developmental Medicine and Child Neurology, 29,* 258–270.

Naremore, R., & Dever, R. (1974). Language performance of educable mentally retarded and normal children at five age levels. *Journal of Speech and Hearing Research, 18,* 82–95.

Neils, J., & Aram, D. M. (1986). Family history of children with developmental language disorders. *Perceptual and Motor Skills, 63,* 655–658.

Nye, C., Foster, S. H., & Seaman, D. (1987). Effectiveness of language intervention with the language/learning disabled. *Journal of Speech and Hearing Disorders, 52,* 348–357.

O'Connor, N., & Hermelin, B. (1963). *Speech and thought in severe subnormality.* Oxford: Pergamon.

Parker, E. B., Olsen, T. F., & Throckmorton, M. C. (1960). Social casework with elementary school children who do not talk in school. *Social Work, 5,* 64–70.

Paul, R., & Cohen, D. J. (1984). Outcomes of severe disorders of language acquisition. *Journal of Autism and Developmental Disorders, 14,* 405–421.

Paul, R., Fischer, M. L., & Cohen, D. J. (1988). Brief report: Sentence comprehension strategies in children with autism and specific language disorders. *Journal of Autism and Developmental Disorders, 18,* 669–679.

Pennington, B. F. (1990). The genetics of dyslexia. *Journal of Child and Adolescent Psychiatry, 31,* 193–201.

Plante, E. (1991). MRI findings in the parents and siblings of specifically language-impaired boys, *Brain and Language, 41,* 67–80.

Prizant, B. M., & Wetherby, A. M. (1986). Communicative intent: A framework for understanding sociocommunicative behavior in autism. *Journal of the American Academy of Child and Adolescent Psychiatry, 26,* 472–479.

Puckering, C., & Rutter, M. (1987). Environmental influences on language development. In W. Yule & M. Rutter (Eds.), *Language development and disorder* (pp. 103–128). London: Mac Keith Press.

Reed, G. F. (1963). Elective mutism in children: A reappraisal. *Journal of Child Psychology and Psychiatry, 4,* 99–107.

Reilly, J., Klima, E. S., & Bellugi, U. (1990). Once

more with feeling: Affect and language in atypical populations. *Development and Psychopathology, 2,* 367–391.

Rumsey, J. M., Dorwart, R., Vermess, M., Denckla, M., Kruesi, M., & Rapoport, J. (1986). Magnetic resonance imaging of brain anatomy in severe developmental dyslexia. *Archives of Neurology, 43,* 1045–1046.

Rutter, M. (1966). Behavioral and cognitive characteristics of a series of psychotic children. In J. K. Wing (Ed.), *Early childhood autism* (pp. 51–81). London: Pergamon Press.

Rutter, M., Graham, P. & Yule, W. (1970). *A neuropsychiatric study in childhood.* Lavenham, Suffolk: Lavenham Press.

Rutter, M., & Lord, D. (1987). Language disorders associated with psychiatric disturbance. In W. Yule & M. Rutter (Eds.), *Language development and disorder* (pp. 206–233). London: MacKeith Press.

Scarr, S., & Kidd, K. K. (1983). Developmental behavior genetics. In P. H. Mussen (Ed.), *Handbook of child psychology, Vol. 2: Infancy and developmental psychobiology* (pp. 345–433). New York: John Wiley & Sons.

Share, D. L., & Silva, P. A. (1987). Language deficits and specific reading retardation: Cause or effect? *British Journal of Disorders of Communication, 22* (3), 219–226.

Siegel, B., Vukicevie, J., Elliot, C. R., & Kramer, H. C. (1989). The use of signal detection theory to assess DSM-III-R criteria for autistic disorder. *Journal of the American Academy of Child and Adolescent Psychiatry, 28,* 542–548.

Siegel, L. S. (1982). Reproductive, perinatal, and environmental factors as predictors of the cognitive and language development of preterm and full-term infants. *Child Development, 53,* 963–973.

Sigman, M., & Ungerer, J. A. (1984). Cognitive and language skills in autistic, mentally retarded, and normal children. *Developmental Psychology, 20,* 293–302.

Silva, P. A. (1987). Epidemiology, longitudinal course and some associated factors: An update. In W. Yule & M. Rutter (Eds.), *Language development and disorder* (pp. 1–15). London: Mac Keith Press.

Silva, P. A., Chalmers, D., & Stewart, I. (1986). Some audiological, psychological, educational and behavioral characteristics of children with bilateral otitis media with effusion: A longitudinal study. *Journal of Learning Disabilities, 19* (3), 165–169.

Silva, P. A., McGee, R. O., Thomas, J., & Williams, S. M. (1982). A descriptive study of socio-economic status and child development in Dunedin five year olds: A report from the Dunedin Multidisciplinary Child Development Study. *New Zealand Journal of Education Studies, 17,* 133–139.

Silva, P. A., McGee, R. O., & Williams, S. M. (1983). Developmental language delay from three to seven years and its significance for low intelligence and reading difficulties at age seven. *Developmental Medicine and Child Neurology, 25,* 783–793.

Silva, P. A., Williams, S. M., & McGee, R. O. (1987). A longitudinal study of children with developmental language delay at age three: Later intelligence, reading and behaviour problems. *Development and Medicine and Child Neurology, 29,* 630–640.

Silver, L. B. (1971). Familial patterns in children with neurologically based learning disabilities. *Journal of Learning Disabilities, 3,* 349–358.

Silverman, S. R. (1971). Hard of hearing in children. In L. E. Travis (Ed.), *Handbook of speech pathology and audiology* (pp. 341–440). New York: Appleton-Century-Crofts.

Stanovich, K. (1982). Individual differences in the cognitive processes of reading: I. Word decoding. *Journal of Learning Disabilities, 15,* 485–493.

Stark, R. E., Bernstein, L. E., & Condino, R. (1984). Four-year follow-up study of language impaired children. *Annals of Dyslexia, 34,* 50–69.

Stevenson, J., & Richman, N. (1976). The prevalence of language delay in a population of three year old children and its association with general retardation. *Developmental Medicine and Child Neurology, 18,* 431–441.

Stevenson, J., & Richman, N. (1978). Behaviour, language and development in three-year-old children. *Journal of Autism and Childhood Schizophrenia, 8,* 299–313.

Storfer, M. D. (1990). *Intelligence and giftedness.* San Francisco: Jossey-Bass.

Tager-Flusberg, H. (1981). On the nature of linguistic functioning in early infantile autism. *Journal of Autism and Developmental Disorders, 11,* 45–46.

Tallal, P., Dukette, D., & Curtiss, S. (1989). Behavioral/emotional profiles of preschool language impaired children. *Developmental Psychopathology, 1,* 51–67.

Tew, B. (1979). The cocktail party syndrome in children with hydrocephalus and spina bifida. *Journal of Disorders of Communication, 14,* 89–101.

Tew, B, & Lawrence, K. M. (1979). The clinical and psychological characteristics of children with the "cocktail party syndrome." *Zeitschrift für Kinderchirurgie, 28,* 360–367.

Tomblin, J. B. (1990). The effect of birth order on the occurrence of developmental language impairment. *British Journal of Disorders of Communication, 25,* 77–84.

Tomblin, J. B., Hardy, J. C., & Hein, H. A. (1991). Predicting poor-communication status in preschool children using risk factors present at birth. *Journal of Speech and Hearing Research, 34,* 1096–1105.

Udwin, O., & Yule, W. (1991). A cognitive and behavioral phenotype in Williams syndrome. *Journal of Clinical and Experimental Neuropsychology, 13* (2), 232–244.

Udwin, O., Yule, W., & Martin, N. (1987). Cognitive abilities and behavioral characteristics of children with idiopathic infantile hypercalcaemia. *Journal of Child Psychology and Psychiatry, 28,* 297–309.

Vellutino, F. R. (1979). *Dyslexia: Theory and research.* Cambridge, MA: MIT Press.

Vellutino, F. R., Smith, H., Steger, J. A., & Kaman, M. (1975). Reading disability: Age differences and the perceptual-deficit hypothesis. *Child Development, 46,* 487–493.

Wagner, R. K., & Torgesen, J. K. (1987). The nature of phonological processing and its causal role in the acquisition of reading skills. *Psychological Bulletin, 101,* 192–212.

Werner, E. E. (1989). High risk children in young adulthood: A longitudinal study from birth to 32 years. *American Journal of Orthopsychiatry, 59,* 72–81.

Werner, E. E., & Smith, R. S. (1982). *Vulnerable but not invincible: A longitudinal study of resilient children and youth.* New York: McGraw-Hill.

Wilkin, R. (1985). A comparison of elective mutism and emotional disorders in children. *British Journal of Psychiatry, 146,* 198–203.

Wolfus, B., Moscovitch, M., & Kinsbourne, M. (1980). Subgroups of developmental language impairment. *Brain and Language, 10,* 152–171.

Yoder, D. E., & Milleder, J. F. (1972). What we may know and what we can do: Input toward a system. In J. E. McLean, D. E. Yoder, & R. L. Schiefelbusch (Eds.), *Language intervention with the retarded* (pp. 89–107). Baltimore: University Park Press.

42 / Tourette's Disorder and Tic Disorders

Donald J. Cohen, James F. Leckman, and Mark Riddle

Motor tics are rapid, rhythmic, purposeless, "involuntary" movements of muscle groups; vocal tics are sounds, words, or phrases that are emitted out of the context of normal discussion and without normal communicative intent. Tics are more easily recognized than precisely defined, clearer to the eye and ear than to formal specification. The diversity of phenomena lumped under the label "tics" conceals their remarkable heterogeneity. Tics include simple twitchlike muscle movements, such as eye blinking, which last up to a few hundred milliseconds; sustained tensing of a group of muscles, as in dystonic tics, lasting well over a few seconds; paroxysms of movements, with multiple, orchestrated jerks and complicated acts, continuing for minutes; meaningless sounds such as humming, sucking, and hawking; and explosive phrases or full sentences with a well-directed aggressive content (Cohen, Leckman, Shaywitz, 1985; Cohen, Bruun, Leckman, 1988; Cohen, Leckman & Towbin, 1989; Leckman & Cohen, 1988).

We appreciate the collaboration of our colleagues in the Child Study Center Tourette Syndrome Research Group, particularly Drs. David Pauls, George Anderson, Kenneth Kidd, Robert King, Phillip Chappell, Paul Lombroso, and Ms. Sharon Ort, Ms. Maureen Hardin, and Mr. Larry Scahill. This work was supported in part by grants MH30929 and MH44843 from the National Institute of Mental Health and RR00125 and HD03008 from the National Institutes of Health; the Gateposts Foundation; and the Tourette Syndrome Association.

This chapter was written in 1992.

The Tic Disorder Spectrum

Disorders involving tics are divided into categories according to age of onset, duration of symptoms, and the presence of vocal, or phonic, tics in addition to motor tics.

The simple, *transient tics of childhood* begin during the early school years and occur in about 10% of all children. Common transient motor tics include eye blinking, nose puckering, grimacing, and squinting. Transient vocalizations, such as coughing, throat clearing, humming, or other distracting noises, are less common. Childhood tics sometimes are complex and odd, such as pulling faces, arm waving, or genital pinching. A childhood tic, such as making a fish mouth or eye rolling and squinting, may be brought out by excitement, such as watching television; worry, as during oral reading; or fatigue. These tics may occur from a few to many times a day, persist for weeks or a few months, and affect boys more often than girls. When they persist, tics sometimes will lead families to various medical consultations with their pediatrician, allergists, and ophthalmologists, and, on occasion, children will be misdiagnosed and treated for disorders such as allergic rhinitis. Often there appears to be a family history of tics in sibs or one parent, but since tics are so prevalent this is to be expected. By definition, transient tic disorder does not persist for more than a year (American Psychiatric Association, 1994), but this is an arbitrary, diagnostic convention, and it is not uncommon for a child to have a series of transient tics over the course of several years. We do not know which children will have just one or a few episodes of transient tics and who will go on to many years of tic symptoms. Nor, from a clinical perspective, is it clear how best to define the troubles of a child who has a sudden onset of multiple motor and vocal tics that have lasted only a few months. Is this the beginning of Tourette's disorder or just childhood tics? A family history of Tourette's should, of course, alert the clinician. Transient tics do not, in general, seem to be associated with specific behavioral or school problems, but a long-standing impression among clinicians, which is reinforced by some cases, associates tics with anxious, serious, and bookish children.

Chronic motor or vocal tic disorders persist for many years, and the morphology of the tics may be relatively unchanging. Perhaps one in 200 individuals has chronic tics, but there are no firm epidemiological data. While transient tics tend to appear and disappear—nose twitches being replaced by lip puckering, clapping by finger snapping—chronic tics, such as pulling the mouth to one side or squinting, may be a permanent tic signature. The line between chronic tics and other movement disorders, such as blepharospasm, may be hard to draw; persistent eye tics may interfere with reading, but usually the major problems with chronic tics are cosmetic.

When an individual has both motor and vocal tics for more than 1 year, the diagnostic convention for Tourette's disorder is met (Shapiro, Shapiro, Young, & Feinberg, 1988). *Tourette's disorder* is characterized by multiform, frequently changing, motor and phonic tics and a range of behavioral symptoms. In its full-blown form, Tourette's may affect up to one individual in 2,500, with several times more males than females; in milder forms, the incidence may be one in 1,000 or more (Burd, Kerbeshian, Wilkenheiser, & Fisher, 1986; Caine et al., 1988). Since its first description 100 years ago, the modal age of onset is 7 years, with some cases starting as early as age 2 or as late as 18. The purposeless motor movements affect multiple muscle groups, singly and in orchestrated sequences; the multiple vocal tics include sounds, words, and phrases, with perhaps 10 to 20% (de-

pending on the clinical series and severity of cases) having the pathognomonic symptom of coprolalia, the sudden, explosive utterance of sexually obscene or aggressive words, phrases, or sentences. Tics are emitted in clusters, with refractory periods between bouts. The overall severity (frequency and disruptiveness) of tics tends to vary between contexts (worse at home and far better controlled in "public" or in new situations, such as during school or at a consultation with a physician); also, tics may be related to states of arousal (more tics when there is excitement or emotionality and fewer tics when concentrating on a task, such as reading). Many patients display clear-cut waxing and waning over weeks to months; it is sometimes possible to find a trigger in a major life event or seasonal change, but this is usually unconvincing.

While young children often seem unaware of their tics, the majority of older children and adolescents describe premonitory experiences before the emission of tics. These feelings are described as a tension, irritation, or uncomfortable sensation (like an itch or the feeling before a sneeze) combined with an urge to act, localized to a part of the body that will be the site of the tic (the nose or shoulders) or in the vocal tract; the patients feel a mounting crescendo of the sensation and may try to divert themselves from doing the tic by a mental operation (by focusing attention on something) or a physical act (by exerting a counterforce, such as clenching the fingers into a fist). Or the patients may try to reduce the tension and satisfy the urge by emitting a compromise symptom (saying "ff" instead of "fuck"). Most often, the patients cannot sustain the mounting tension. They give in and do the tic or make the sound, which may then leave them in a refractory state for a shorter or longer time; inevitably, the tension returns, to the same or another site. This cycle of progressive tension and self-awareness, giving in, doing the tic, and brief respite, gives tics a quality that is somewhere between "volitional" and "involuntary" in nature. In any case, individuals find their tics "undesirable" and uninvited. Metaphysical terms such as "voluntary" do not capture the phenomenology underlying the experience of having one's inner world taken over by impulses that one tries, without success, to resist and that lead to great emotional and social cost.

The clinical criteria for Tourette's disorder do not convey the whole clinical story, in particular the internal state of patients whose life may be captured by their tics and the full range of behavioral difficulties, such as obsessions, compulsions, and attentional problems, that so often complicate the tic disorder.

Associated Conditions

Patients with Tourette's often have behavioral difficulties that would justify another psychiatric diagnosis. Comorbidity is of importance clinically as well as in relation to understanding the basic underlying dysfunction. In clinical series, half the patients have other diagnosable conditions. The ways in which these conditions are related to Tourette's are currently being studied, using genetic, natural history, and epidemiological approaches; areas of study include whether the presence of additional disorders represents the fact that patients with more severe illness or multiple problems are more likely to seek help; whether Tourette's causes emotional distress, as would any other chronic and visible disorder, and thus more disorder, or whether the conditions reflect the same underlying, neurobiological diathesis. While there is still uncertainty about which associated difficulties are intrinsic to Tourette's and represent alternate or the fullest expressions of the vulnerability, newer genetic evidence suggests that obsessions and compulsions, including obsessive-compulsive disorder (OCD), are manifestations of the underlying, genetic Tourette's disorder diathesis and that attentional disorders probably are closely related to it (Comings & Comings, 1987; Pauls & Leckman, 1986; Pauls, Raymond, Stevenson & Leckman, 1991).

Many Tourette's patients are burdened with *obsessions and compulsions*, which are quite similar to those seen in the standard, clinical form of OCD. They do and redo, put things in order, worry about cleanliness and contamination, wash their hands, experience mental slowness and doubting, worry about harm they might have caused inadvertently, and the like. A possibly distinctive feature is that Tourette's patients more often feel the need for symmetry (if they touch something with the right hand they must touch it with the left; if they look up they need to look down) and the need to do things in "just the right way" or with "just the right feel." These "motoric" concerns may be related to the role of the basal ganglia in Tourette's and the centrality of these brain structures in monitoring motor activity and bringing actions into alignment with intent: it is as if the Tourette's patient cannot satisfy the motor program sufficiently, so there is a reverberating circuit of trying to do the act again, in just the right way, to satisfy the intention.

Within the families of patients with Tourette's disorder, there is a marked increase in the prevalence of OCD, with up to 10% of all first-degree relatives afflicted; some of these relatives themselves have tics, but many do not. Similarly, studies of patients with OCD reveal an increase in their personal and family histories of tic disorders. These data suggest a genetic association between Tourette's and OCD, with some cases of OCD representing an alternate manifestation of the gene(s) that underlie Tourette's. Phenomenologically, it appears as if, for some individuals, tics are motor obsessions and obsessions are mental tics; from a metapsychological perspective, the association is particularly interesting, with the hyperkinetic tic disorder and the hypokinetic, inhibited obsessive disorder exemplifying the way in which superficially distinct impairments may reflect alternate manifestations of a dysfunction in a process involving impulse regulation and inhibition. It is further tempting to speculate about the possible adaptive function of compulsive modes of organization in relation to a basic underlying deficit in inhibition, but the relationship between these two domains of psychological disturbance remains open for future study.

At least 50% of children seen clinically for Tourette's disorder satisfy the diagnostic criteria for attention deficit hyperactivity disorder (ADHD). Symptoms of distractibility, impulsivity, and hyperactivity may originate early in the preschool years and precede the onset of tics. These difficulties also seem to reflect the underlying psychobiological dysfunction involving inhibition; problems with attention also may be exacerbated by the strain in attending to the outer world while working hard to remain quiet and still. Yet genetic data have been less convincing that ADHD is an alternate manifestation of the vulnerability to

Tourette's disorder, as is OCD. Since ADHD is such a common problem of childhood, it is to be anticipated that some Tourette's children will, by chance alone, also have ADHD; also, since ADHD makes children more visible and difficult for parents and teachers to manage, it is possible that those children with ADHD and Tourette's are more likely to come for clinical care than those with Tourette's alone. Indeed, epidemiological evidence suggests that only about 10% of Tourette's patients are ever diagnosed; those who are not seem to have a lower rate of ADHD and other problems. However, the natural history of ADHD and its merging into Tourette's disorder, and the high rate of ADHD in some families and in the clinic, lead us to believe that ADHD's relations with Tourette's may be deeper. In any case, those children with ADHD tend to have a more difficult long-term adjustment. While Tourette's children without ADHD tend to lag somewhat in social skills, those with both disorders as a group are substantially more immature.

Even for children without ADHD, school functioning is impaired by the disruption produced by their symptoms, difficulties in attention, and the interference of certain specific symptoms. About a third of children receiving treatment for Tourette's disorder have serious school performance handicaps that require special intervention. Areas of particular difficulty are penmanship (graphomotor skills) and subjects involving visual imagery of spatial relations (visual apraxia). Obsessive-compulsive symptoms may lead a child to write and rewrite the same word, wearing out the paper; get stuck and have to return to read the same paragraph; block in writing down an answer that is known; hold the pencil in an odd manner; or worry about touching a book used by others. Thus, even bright children with Tourette's may feel uncomfortable in school and fall behind academically.

Natural History

Behavioral difficulties, such as irritability, frustration, or attentional problems, emerge during the late preschool years; these problems are prodromal to or may be accompanied by a few tics.

Around first or second grade, more persistent tics emerge that are followed by other motor and phonic symptoms. The children also may be unusually sensitive to touch, the feel of clothes, or particular sensory experiences in the body or outside. During this phase, the children may feel that their mind has been invaded; they cannot control what they know is originating from within themselves; the impulses they express feel alien and unwanted and mark them out as odd and socially deviant. As parents themselves do not understand what their child is experiencing, they may scold and reprimand and tell the child to stop. The negative, intrusive interaction may, in turn, lead children to feel guilty for what they know they cannot control (Cohen et al., 1988).

Over time, the children may be led to focus more and more of their time and energy on the urges within their body, on the tics that pop out or on the acts and sounds that they feel, in some way, they actively emit. They will become progressively more aware of what tics they are having at any period, of how "bad" their tics are on any given day, and of which tics are most embarrassing or distasteful to self and others; they will work, to a greater or lesser degree, to hold back or to camouflage the tics. They also will become experts on recognizing their impact on others as well as on knowing where they can feel safer in just "letting go." To a far greater extent than normal, children with Tourette's will spend time monitoring their bodily states of tension and self-generated gratification; just like starving children hypercathect food and images of satiation, children with Tourette's will increasingly be aware of their bodily states and images of being free of tics. They also will be more sensitive than others to the nuances of how others react to them. Through the reactions of others and their own self-criticism, these children may be led to feel that they are secret co-conspirators with the compelling urges to tic that arise from within: that they are surrendering to the tics' demands rather than bravely resisting, that they are satisfying themselves rather than choosing the morally superior road of abstinence. They thus may feel disloyal to their family and to themselves; they also may feel angry at themselves and others for the conflicts they experience within, which they then project outwardly. Their self-image becomes tainted by what they suffer in the privacy of their own body.

Along with other children who have chronic illnesses, children with Tourette's disorder irrationally may feel guilty for having the disorder, as if they brought it on themselves by something they thought or did, and for the troubles it brings the family; but, unlike most other conditions, children with tics may feel the additional guilt that accompanies the sense that they have a hand, however weak, in the tics' expression. Thus, recurrent multiple tics may become a distorting influence on children's sense of their body as a source of pleasure and of their mind as the agent for expression or control of instinctual urges. In varied and individualized ways, tics become enmeshed in their relations with family and peers, in the inner world of fantasy, and in the children's sense of self as autonomous individuals where desires are balanced by values and controls (Cohen, 1990, 1991).

A rostrocaudal progression of motor tics is seen in some children, with eye blinking and other facial tics followed by shoulder shrugging, arm movements, truncal symptoms, and leg movements. Simple tics are followed by complex motor tics, which sometimes may be quite elaborate and orchestrated. In turn, phonic symptoms usually follow the simple motor tics by months or a year, and then are followed by complex phonic symptoms. The most flamboyant motor symptoms—compulsions, rituals, and self-destructive acts—and the most dramatic phonic symptoms—graphic descriptions of sexual acts, rude descriptions, and argumentativeness—usually emerge several years or more after the onset of the simple tics (Bruun, 1988). Mirror phenomena (the need to do what one has just seen or say what one has heard) and perseverative symptoms (saying and doing the same thing over and over) usually appear in children with the most severe tics after they have had the syndrome for a few years. Obsessions and compulsions tend to develop around age 11 or 12 or later, sometimes while the tics are waning. For the most severely afflicted patients, OCD may become the major source of impairment. The majority of patients experience some decrement in tics and other symptoms during or after adolescence. For a minority of patients, however, Tourette's disorder can be a totally disabling illness in which they are plagued by incessant, complex, and intrusive motor and vocal symptoms and their mind is controlled by nonstop thoughts and preoccupations that are meaningless but compelling. Self-injurious symptoms (such as eye gauging and head banging) may lead to serious medical problems, including blindness or fractures, which may further ostracize people with Tourette's and increase their self-loathing.

The range of severity of tic symptoms among patients with Tourette's is quite broad. Most children with Tourette's generally have mild tic symptoms; they never come for clinical diagnosis and generally do not require therapeutic intervention. For those who are diagnosed, ultimate social adaptation may be more a function of behavioral and attentional difficulties than of tic symptom severity. Many patients with severe tics achieve adequate social adjustment in adult life, although usually with considerable emotional pain. The factors that appear to be of importance with regard to social adaptation include the seriousness of attentional problems, school achievement, intelligence, degree of family support, and the severity of complex motor and phonic symptoms. Thus, while the majority of Tourette's disorder patients have no or little impairment from their childhood, self-limited symptoms, for other patients the disorder takes over their entire lives and they become, in the fullest sense, "victims of Tourette's" (Cohen, 1990).

Pathogenesis

Family genetic studies suggest that an alteration of a single gene that is transmitted as an autosomal dominant may manifest as chronic tics, Tourette's disorder, and/or OCD. Sex hormones operating in the prenatal or later periods appear to make an important modification of the expression of the gene. Males with the gene are more likely to express some symptoms (chronic tics, full-blown Tourette's, or OCD), with a penetrance of about 0.9 for the gene; females are less likely to express the gene in any way (with a penetrance of about 0.7). However, females are more likely to have OCD than Tourette's. These observations help explain the often-repeated observation that males are more likely to have Tourette's than females, by a ratio of over 3 : 1. When females with Tourette's and its alternate manifestation of OCD are added together, the ratio narrows to about

1.2 : 1, closer to the predictions from an autosomal dominant gene (Pauls et al., 1990). While the genetic factor(s) appears to exert a powerful influence in the etiology of Tourette's disorder, a family history is not found in all cases nor is it known through what mechanism(s) the genetic diathesis operates. Even if the gene(s) underlying the disorder is identified, it will be necessary to explicate its molecular mode of action and to identify specific risk factors that may cause this vulnerability to be expressed.

Multiple neurochemical systems have been implicated in Tourette's, particularly dopaminergic, serotonergic, noradrenergic, and opiate peptide (Chappell, Leckman, Pauls, & Cohen, 1990; Leckman, Walkup, Riddle, Towbin, & Cohen, 1987). However, there is not a sufficient body of scientific data to support a clear role for any particular neurotransmitter system in the etiology or pathophysiology of this disorder. Several lines of study have suggested that the basal ganglia are importantly involved in the pathogenesis of Tourette's disorder (Chappell et al., 1990). A heuristic hypothesis is that the multiple, varying symptoms reflect disruptions in the functioning of the parallel pathways and microcircuits that link together cortex, thalamus, and basal ganglia (Alexander, Delong, & Strick, 1986; Leckman, Knorr, Rasmusson, Cohen, 1991).

Multiple environmental risk factors may influence the course and severity of symptom expression. Those that have received the most attention include exposure to stimulant or neuroleptic medication and chronic intermittent stress (Leckman et al., 1984). More research is needed to clarify the contributions of such risk factors to symptom expression and the overall severity of the illness.

Differential Diagnosis

The differentiation of Tourette's disorder from other tic syndromes may be no more than semantic since recent genetic evidence links Tourette's with multiple tics. Transient tics of childhood are best defined in retrospect. Usually they disappear or are benign; rarely, they are the precursors for full-blown Tourette's. Tourette's is unlikely to be confused with any other disorder. The wild thoughts and uncontrolled expression of ideas, in word and action, in patients sometimes suggest a psychotic disorder, but Tourette's patients maintain a painful awareness of what they are doing and feeling, and they recognize the "craziness" of their thoughts and actions. While they may feel that thoughts pop into their mind, they do not have the same experience of thought insertion as found in schizophrenia: they recognize the thoughts as their own.

On occasion, it may be difficult to distinguish children with extreme ADHD from those with Tourette's. Restlessness, fidgety movements, impulsive behavior, out-of-context statements, diffuse hyperactivity, fingering and touching objects, and other symptoms in children with severe ADHD are also found in those with Tourette's; some ADHD children, on close examination, have a few tics and grimacing and noises that can pass for them. As noted earlier, some ADHD children may have variant forms of Tourette's. Further biological and genetic research is needed to make this differentiation in difficult cases.

Autistic and retarded children may display the entire gamut of Tourette's symptoms, including simple and complex motor and phonic tics, echolalia, palilalia, and coprolalia. Autistic children's needs to preserve sameness in their environment and routines, stereotypic hand flapping and other movements, and bizarre posturing also are reminiscent of Tourette's. Some autistic children have elaborate compulsions. Whether an autistic individual requires the additional diagnosis of Tourette's may remain an open question until there is a biological or other diagnostic test. On the side of diagnosing Tourette's would be a positive family history, characteristic age of onset and progression of tics, severity of simple motor and phonic tics, compulsions, and the presence of coprolalia. We have seen Tourette's in association with a number of other developmental, neurological, and medical disorders, and it is possible that central nervous system trauma or deviations may predispose a child to the expression of the disorder, particularly if there is a genetic history, or may convert the vulnerability into a full expression of Tourette's.

Innumerable neurological diseases have motor symptoms, including disorders of the basal ganglia and various degenerative conditions. In practice, their clinical history, symptom profiles, and physical findings (spasticity, chorea, seizures, or deterioration) distinguish Tourette's from central nervous system disorders such as Wilson's disease or dystonia. Laboratory tests are rarely needed for diagnosis of Tourette's, and available methods (computed brain tomography, magnetic resonance imaging, electroencephalography, blood tests, etc.) are unrevealing.

By prevailing diagnostic criteria, all children who for at least 1 year have suppressible multiple motor and phonic tics, however minimal, should be diagnosed as having Tourette's disorder. In practice we deviate from this rigorous research approach. In talking with families, and thinking about the disorder as clinicians, we tend to consider severity and associated features (particularly complex motor and phonic symptoms as well as attentional problems and general disinhibition) in the diagnosis. For the meticulous, hardworking boy, we are willing to use the term "nervous habits," to cover his throat clearing, facial grimacing, and occasional shrugging. Corporate headquarters, the halls of Congress, and the faculties of law and medical schools are filled with such boys grown up into successful men. Although their symptoms may meet formal criteria for the diagnosis of Tourette's disorder, conveying this formally seems, to us, to stretch the diagnosis beyond the best interests of the patient. However, since there are genetic implications, and some families and patients wish to have full disclosure of the physician's thoughts, the clinician may want to raise the possible relationship between the patient's symptoms and Tourette's. While not everything that twitches is Tourette's, without definitive diagnostic tests it is hard to draw the line between tics, eccentricities and habits, on one side, and Tourette's disorder, on the other. In the course of research, clear diagnostic criteria with appropriate specification of severity and associated features must be followed: such work has revealed that most often Tourette's is a mild disorder.

Treatment Guidelines and Options

The decision about whether to treat will depend not only on the primary diagnosis but on the degree to which the varied tic symptoms interfere with the child's normal development (Cohen, 1990; Cohen et al., 1988). The primary emphasis in management of Tourette's must be on helping children to navigate the normal developmental tasks—for school-age children to feel competent in school, develop friendships, experience trust in parents, and enjoy life's adventures. Many children with multiple tics and Tourette's do well in moving onward with development; for them, treatment to ameliorate the tics generally is not indicated. Natural parental upset about the tics requires lengthy, calm discussion and education about available treatments. If the child, family, and physician decide upon treatment, developmental issues must be reassessed constantly.

MONITORING

Unless there is a state of emergency, the clinician usually can follow a patient for several months before a specific treatment plan is organized. The goals of this first stage of treatment are to establish a baseline of symptoms; define associated difficulties in school, family, and peer relationships; obtain necessary medical tests; monitor the range and fluctuations in symptoms and the specific contexts of greatest difficulty; and establish a relationship.

REASSURANCE

It may become apparent that a child's tics are of minimal functional significance. Even if a child satisfies the criteria for Tourette's, he may have good peer relationships, school achievement, and sense of himself, and no treatment may be needed. If parents have read about the disorder, they may be worried about the child's future. In general, Tourette's severity announces itself within a short period following its appearance; by the time a child has had the disorder for 2 to 3 years, the clinician can guess with reasonable accuracy how severe the disorder ultimately will be. Thus, the clinician can reassure the family of a 13-year-old boy with mild Tourette's that first appeared at age 7 that it probably will become no worse than what they have already seen. In such cases, we tend to tell families that while their child can be diagnosed as having Tourette's, it is not the same severity or type of disorder as what they might hear about in regard to the disorder. For transient single tics, such reassurance is fully appropriate. Because of the clear genetic factors involved, families deserve to know about the emerging knowledge in this area even if they are reassured about the nature of their child's disorder.

PSYCHOTHERAPY

Individual or group psychotherapy may be useful for children with Tourette's disorder, just as for children with other medical problems who have personality and adjustment difficulties, difficult peer relationships, depression, anxiety, and the like. As a rule, tics are not responsive to psychotherapy. Some families of children with Tourette's will benefit from support groups and family therapy. Behavior modification, hypnotherapy, and relaxation methods have been tried with patients with little sustained success. Adolescents and adults sometimes are able to learn methods of self-control as well as camouflage, which they utilize in public situations.

SCHOOL INTERVENTIONS

Children with attentional and learning problems require educational interventions similar to those used in the treatment of other forms of ADHD and learning disabilities. Tourette's patients may require special tutoring, a learning laboratory, a self-contained classroom, or a special school, depending on the severity of school and associated behavioral problems. Since Tourette's is an uncommon disorder, schools need to be informed about the symptoms, the children's inability to suppress symptoms, the ways in which they might deal with bouts of tics (e.g., by leaving the room), the use of prosthetic devices (such as a computer for poor handwriting), and the puzzling nature of OCD symptoms that may block or interfere with a child's performance.

Children with Tourette's sometimes are kept as homebound students because their symptoms (e.g., touching other children, coprolalia, or explosive yelling) are too disruptive for the classroom. Phonic and behavioral symptoms are most difficult for schools. If a child is homebound, we consider this an emergency situation demanding intensive medical and legal intervention. At home and deprived of school, symptoms are likely to exacerbate, as the child exerts less control over symp-

toms, is bored and without outside diversions, and, frequently, is locked in intense, often negative or ambivalent interactions with parents. A chain reaction may be set up: bad symptoms lead to worse symptoms and increasing isolation from normal forces of socialization. Even more than tics, school difficulties and appropriate school placement require prompt clinical intervention, sometimes including inpatient hospitalization.

HOSPITALIZATION

Short-term hospitalization may be of use during extreme crises. However, Tourette's patients may be unwelcome on an inpatient neurology or psychiatry service because of disruptive and bizarre behavior. The availability of an inpatient service willing to accept such patients in crisis can be reassuring for both them and the physician.

PHARMACOTHERAPY

There are several effective, pharmacological treatments for tic disorders and associated conditions. In deciding on the use of medication, the benefits for the children in relation to the reduction of tics must be weighed against short- and long-term problems, both biological and developmental, to which medication may expose them. The presence of severe tics may limit children's social sphere, impair their sense of control over what is inside, and lead to painful social and emotional scarring. The use of medication may have considerable positive impact on children's emerging sense of self-control, self-esteem, and social acceptance. Yet medication may alter how children's bodies feel to them and how they experience the working of their minds; medication may single children out in school, alter their daily schedule, and focus parental and other adult concern on small changes in symptoms and side effects.

Medications used to treat tics include haloperidol, pimozide, clonidine, and various neuroleptics. For many children and adolescents with Tourette's, ADHD is at least as impairing, or more troubling, than the tic symptoms. Medications used to treat the symptoms of ADHD—inattention, impulsivity, and hyperactivity—include clonidine, desipramine, and the psychostimulants methylphenidate and dextroamphetamine. Serotonin reuptake inhibitors, including clomipramine, fluoxetine, fluvoxamine, and sertraline, reduce the severity of obsessive-compulsive symptoms in patients with "primary OCD." These medications may also alleviate OCD symptoms in patients with Tourette's. Details about specific medications may be found elsewhere (Cohen, Riddle, & Leckman, 1992).

Conclusions

Tourette's disorder is a chronic and usually lifelong disorder in which the simple motor and phonic tics may interfere less with development than complex tics and associated obsessive-compulsive, attentional, and behavioral problems. Clinical evaluation must include careful attention to personality development and school achievement; intervention includes reassurance and support, medication if needed, and guidance and advocacy in relation to appropriate school placement. Throughout the assessment and treatment, target symptoms should include not only motor and phonic symptoms but each child and adolescent's full range of functioning and development. The major goal of treatment is to help the child succeed in moving along the various lines of development. The use of medication that interferes with these achievements runs the risk of creating patients who are socially more disadvantaged than had they been left undiagnosed. Being maintained on psychoactive medications for many years poses many medical and behavioral toxicological risks that require careful scrutiny.

Family therapy, psychotherapy, and behavior modification approaches have limited value in regard to the motor and phonic tics, but they may help children deal with the behavioral and psychological problems that may compound the disorder or be elicited in a family because of the stress of a chronic neuropsychiatric disorder. As with any chronic disorder, periods of exacerbation are likely to lead to anxiety and stress, which may further exacerbate the condition. The clinician's availability and a long-standing relationship are especially important at such times. One reassuring fact for families and patients is that Tourette's disorder has become an area of active clinical research interest. The detection, cloning, and understanding of the gene(s) underlying this complex developmental disorder should lead to a profound increase in our knowledge of the pathogenesis and treatment of it.

REFERENCES

Alexander, G. E., DeLong, M. R., & Strick, P. L. (1986). Parallel organization of functionally segregated circuits linking basal ganglia and cortex. *Annual Review of Neuroscience, 9,* 357–381.

American Psychiatric Association. (1987). *Diagnostic and statistical manual of mental disorders* (3rd edition, rev.). Washington, DC: Author.

American Psychiatric Association. (1994). *Diagnostic and statistical manual of mental disorders* (4th ed.). Washington, DC: Author.

Bruun, R. (1988). The natural history of Tourette's syndrome: In D. J. Cohen, R. D. Bruun, & J. F. Leckman (Eds.), *Tourette's syndrome and tic disorders: Clinical understanding and treatment* (pp. 21–40). New York: John Wiley & Sons.

Burd, L., Kerbeshian, L., Wikenheiser, M., & Fisher, W. (1986). A prevalence study of Gilles de la Tourette syndrome in North Dakota school-age children. *Journal of the American Academy of Child and Adolescent Psychiatry, 25,* 552–553.

Caine, E. D., McBride, M. C., Chiverton, P., Bamford, K. A., Rediess, S., & Shiao, S. (1988). Tourette syndrome in Monroe County school children. *Neurology, 38,* 472–475.

Chappell, P., Leckman, J., Pauls, D., & Cohen, D. (1990). Biochemical and genetic studies of Tourette's syndrome. In S. I. Deutsch, A. Weizman, & R. Weizman (Eds.), *Application of basic neuroscience to child psychiatry* (pp. 241–260). New York: Plenum Medical Book Company.

Cohen, D. J. (1990). *Tourette's syndrome: Developmental psychopathology of a model neuropsychiatric disorder of childhood.* Paper presented at the 27th annual Institute of Pennsylvania Hospital Award Lecture in memory of Edward A. Strecker, Philadelphia.

Cohen, D. J. (1991). Finding meaning in one's self and others: clinical studies of children with autism and Tourette's syndrome. In F. Kessel, M. Bornstein, & A. Sameroff (Eds.), *Contemporary constructions of the child: Essays in honor of William Kessen* (pp. 159–175). Hillsdale, NJ: Lawrence Erlbaum.

Cohen, D. J., Bruun, R. D. & Leckman, J. F. (Eds.).

(1988). *Tourette's syndrome & tic disorders: Clinical understanding and treatment.* New York: John Wiley & Sons.

Cohen, D. J., Leckman, J. F., & Shaywitz, B. A. (1985). The Tourette syndrome and other tics. In D. Shaffer, A. Ehrhardt, & L. Greenhill (Eds.), *The clinical guide to child psychiatry* (pp. 3–28). New York: Free Press.

Cohen, D. J., Leckman, J. F., & Towbin, K. E. (1989). Tic disorders: Phenomenology, diagnosis and assessment. In T. B. Karasu (Ed.), *Treatments of psychiatric disorders* (pp. 687–714). Washington, DC: American Psychiatric Association.

Cohen, D. J., Ort, S. I., Leckman, J. F., Riddle, M. A., & Hardin, M. T. (1988). Family functioning in Tourette's syndrome. In D. J. Cohen, R. D. Bruun, & J. F. Leckman (Eds.), *Tourette's syndrome and tic disorders: Clinical understanding and treatment* (pp. 179–196). New York: John Wiley & Sons.

Cohen, D. J., Riddle, M. A., & Leckman, J. F. (1992). Pharmacotherapy of Tourette's syndrome and associated disorders. *Psychiatric Clinics of North America, 15,* 109–129.

Comings, D. E., & Comings, B. G. (1987). A controlled study of Tourette syndrome. I. Attention-deficit disorder, learning disorders, and school problems. II. Conduct. *American Journal of Human Genetics, 41,* 701–760.

Leckman, J. F. & Cohen, D. J. (1988). Descriptive and diagnostic classification of tic disorders. In D. J. Cohen, R. D. Bruun, & J. F. Leckman (Eds.), *Tourette's syndrome and tic disorders: Clinical understanding and treatment* (pp. 3–20). New York: John Wiley & Sons.

Leckman, J. F., Cohen, D. J., Price, R. A., Minderaa, R. B., Anderson, G. M., & Pauls, D. L. (1984). The pathogenesis of Gilles de la Tourette's syndrome. A review of data and hypothesis. In A. B. Shah, N. S. Shah, & A. G. Donald (Eds.), *Movement disorders* (pp. 257–272). New York: Plenum Press.

Leckman, J. F., Knorr, A. M., Rasmusson, A. M., Cohen, D. J. (1991). Basal ganglia rersearch and Tourette's syndrome. *Trends in Neuroscience, 14,* (3), 94.

Leckman, J. F., Walkup, J. T., Riddle, M. A., Towbin, K. E., & Cohen, D. J. (1987). Tic disorders. In H. Y. Meltzer (Ed.), *Psychopharmacology: The third generation of progress* (pp. 1239–1246). New York: Raven Press.

Pauls, D. L., & Leckman, J. F. (1986). The inheritance of Gilles de la Tourette syndrome and associated behaviors: Evidence for autosomal dominant transmission. *New England Journal of Medicine, 315,* 993–997.

Pauls, D. L., Pakstis, A. J., Kurlan, R., et al. (1990). Segregation and linkage analysis of Gilles de la Tourette's syndrome and related disorders. *Journal of the American Academy of Child and Adolescent Psychiatry, 29,* 195–203.

Pauls, D. L., Raymond, C. L., Stevenson, J. F., & Leckman, J. F. (1991). A family study of Gilles de la Tourette. *American Journal of Human Genetics, 48,* 154–163.

Shapiro, A. K., Shapiro, E. S., Young, J. G., & Feinberg, T. E. (1988). *Gilles de la Tourette syndrome* (2nd ed.). New York: Raven Press.

---

43 / **Transplants**

Margaret L. Stuber

Pediatric organ transplantation, only recently reviewed as experimental, is now the treatment of choice for a number of life-threatening illnesses. This change has been a result of a number of technologic advances. In 1983 the introduction of cyclosporin A for immunosuppression dramatically decreased problems with rejection, making heart and liver transplantation practical (Kocosuis, Tzakis, Todo, Neyls, & Noun, 1993). Improved histocapability matching and the availability of computer banks for matching unrelated marrow donors has expanded accessibility of bone marrow transplantation (Santos, 1990). Kidney transplantation, already established with living related donors, also has become more available since reduced rejection made use of cadaveric kidneys more feasible (Rosenthal, Ettenger, Ehrlich, & Fine, 1990). Organ transplantation has become the treatment of choice for many types of pediatric illness. Between 1987 and 1993, 1,269 children and adolescents received heart transplants, 3,804 received kidney transplants, and 2,877 received liver transplants in the United States (United Network for Organ Sharing database, 1995). Pediatric patients accounted for 8.25% of all organ trans-

This work was supported in part by American Cancer Society Clinical Oncology Career Development Award #91-192.

plants in the United States in 1993. The overall 1-year survival rate for pediatric solid organ transplantation is now over 70%, with a 1-year survival rate for liver transplantation of 85% (Dousett & Houssin, 1992). Between October 1987 and December 1992, survival rates at 1, 2, and 3 years post-transplant were at least 90% for both cadaveric and living-related kidney transplants for all but the neonates, whose numbers were slightly lower (United Network for Organ Sharing database, 1993).

The impact of organ transplantation on families is enormous regardless of the age of the recipient. However, additional factors add to the material burden in the case of pediatric transplantation. First, many of these children are very young (see Table 43.1). Two-thirds of the pediatric liver transplants in the United States are performed on children less than 5 years of age. Pediatric heart transplant recipients are even younger, with over 40% less than one-year old at the time of transplant (United Network for Organ Sharing database, 1995). These children must depend upon their mothers to provide care, explain and comfort during procedures, and make treatment decisions. Second, almost 50% of the kidney transplant donors were living relatives, often parents. For those who are not able to use the organ of a living donor, the wait for a cadaveric donor can be lengthy and dangerous. The median wait for a pediatric liver is approximately 3 to 4 months, a heart 1 to 3 months, and a kidney 9 to 18 months (United Network for Organ Sharing database, 1995).

Despite the improved access just described, donor organs, particularly those small enough for pediatric recipients, are in scarce supply. The United Network for Organ Sharing estimates that 10% of all those waiting for solid organ transplants will die before receiving an organ (see Tables 43.3 and 43.4). Since the major indications for pediatric heart and liver transplantation are congenital illnesses, small organs are in significant demand. This demand has led to controversial innovations, such as the use of organs from anencephalic newborns (Holzgreve, Beller, Buchholz, Hanzman, & Kohler, 1987). Ethical concerns also were raised recently when a couple in their 40s reversed a vasectomy to conceive a child who could potentially be a bone marrow donor to treat the chronic myelogenous leukemia of their adolescent daughter (Chang, 1991). Recent success with transplantation of partial livers into small children has allowed sharing of adult cadaveric livers or use of living related donors (Alonzo, Whittington, Broelsch, Emond, & Thislethwaite, 1989). These "split livers" raise many of the issues encountered with kidney and bone marrow transplantation, which have historically used living related donors: use of minor donors, problems obtaining truly informed consent in such emotional settings, and the possibility of family coercion (Simmons, Klein, & Simmons, 1977; Singer et al., 1989; Goldman, 1993).

The criteria for selection as a transplant recipient have changed dramatically over the past 15 years, with many who would have previously been viewed as medically ineligible now receiving life-saving treatment. For example, UCLA Medical Center, which did over 1,000 liver transplants between 1984 and 1994, reports that refusal for medical unsuitability was reduced from 31% in the first 100 patients to 4% for transplants number 800 through 1,000. Operative time, intensive care unit stay, and hospital stay were all significantly reduced in the later group of patients. Survival was also significantly improved, with 1-year survival of 73% in the first 100 and 88% in the more recent 200 (Busuttil et al., 1994). Despite these encouraging data, the tremendous cost and the limited availability of donor organs have raised questions as to whether organ transplantation is affordable on a societal level. There has even been some move to restrict access to organ transplantation by the state of Oregon, although this has met with limited success (Welch & Larson, 1988).

TABLE 43.1

Children and Adolescents on the National Transplant Waiting List as of 9/30/93

Age	Kidney	Liver	Heart
0–5 years	74	239	63
6–10 years	117	86	18
11–17 years	433	73	36

Source: UNOS OPTN and scientific registry data.

Nonadherence to
Medical Instructions

The primary psychosocial or behavioral concern of organ transplant teams has been adherence to regimens of medication and medical follow-up. Nonadherence to medical recommendations, especially regarding use of immunosuppressive drugs to prevent rejection of the donor organ, has been identified as a prime cause of organ failure in kidney transplant recipients (Didlake, Dreyfus, Kerman, Van Buren, & Kahan, 1988). In addition to the immunosuppressive medications which must be taken daily for the rest of their lives, post-transplant care requires regular assessments, some of which are painful or intrusive (e.g., myocardial biopsies). A recent study found that adult organ transplant recipients with significant psychiatric disorders, such as depression or anxiety, that would be classified as Axis I by the Diagnostic and Statistical Manual of the American Psychiatric Association (1994), were more likely to report distress after transplant than those who did not have these major psychiatric problems. However, it was the presence of psychiatric disorders that would be classified as Axis II or personality disorders that predicted difficulty with adherence to medical instructions (Chacko, Harper, Kunik, & Young, 1996).

Nonadherence to medical instructions has been found to be significantly higher in patients less than 20 years old compared to those greater than 40 ($p = 0.001$) (Rovelli, Plameri, Vessler, Bautus, Hull, & Schweizer, 1989). The health belief model suggests that this ultimately self-destructive behavior is a result of a weighing of the costs and benefits of recommended procedures (Siegal, Hanson, Viswanathan, Margolis, & Butt, 1989). Initially, the transplant is seen as an almost miraculous second chance at life, and adherence is generally good. However, over time, the discrepancy between the child's and family's expectations and the reality of life with a donor organ leads to dissatisfaction and, in some cases, the belief that the cost-benefit ratio is not sufficient to continue treatment. Despite efforts to educate recipients and families about organ transplantation, most re-cipients expect a "cure." Often they are dismayed to discover that post-transplant care still requires taking medications that have significant side effects, regular medical procedures (e.g., biopsies) and occasional hospitalizations. One study found that recipients took a mean of 3.0 medications a day postliver transplant, compared to 4.7 a day prior to the transplant (Zitelli et al., 1987). The hirsutism of cyclosporin and the cushingoid features resulting from steroids are often quite distressing, leading recipients to modify or even stop their medications.

An additional problem is the normal separation-individuation process of adolescence. This development phase leads to experimentation or even outright defiance of adult instructions, sometimes with disastrous consequences. Symptoms of rejection can be quite subtle in the initial phases and not detected until the graft is beyond medical salvage. Thus, there is little medical warning to family or physicians of the recipient's nonadherence, making careful monitoring essential in recipients with psychiatric indicators of high risk (Stuber, 1993a).

Pretransplant Illness

Considerations of the psychologic impact of transplantation on the child or adolescent recipient must always include the indications for transplant or the underlying disease process. For some, this is an acute event, such as when a previously well child contracts a viral cardiomyopathy. For others, the acute event has a psychiatric component, such as when an adolescent overdoses on acetaminophen, resulting in liver toxicity. However, most pediatric organ transplants are performed for chronic, if not congenital, illnessses. These children and adolescents are often small for their age, have been unable to participate fully in peer activities, and have delays in motor development. The psychiatric issues thus include those common to children and adolescents with chronic illnesses.

The overwhelming psychiatric issue, however, is the life-threatening nature of the illness by the time transplantation is contemplated. Most pediatric patients and families feel the transplant offers the only chance for long-term survival and rarely feel they have much choice about undergoing transplantation. Some, more skeptical of high-tech approaches or weary after the long illness, question whether transplantation offers enough to justify the ordeal. Most, however, focus on the ends rather than the means, particularly since it is difficult for them to fully understand what a transplant entails.

The Transplant Evaluation

Instruments have been developed which use pretransplant assessment of psychosocial factors to predict the types of services that will be needed by adult transplant patients (Twillman et al., 1993; Levenson & Olbrisch, 1993). Predictors of nonadherence have been suggested as indicators for preventative interventions or as contra-indications to selection in adult organ transplant candidates (Olbrisch & Levenson, 1996). However, despite widespread knowledge of these predictors, and some uniformity in the types of information gathered at transplant center across the United States, the selection process and criteria vary widely both by transplant center and by organ (Olbrisch & Levenson, 1996).

No such validated measures are available for psychosocial assessment of pediatric organ transplant candidates. Any such instrument would have to differ in significant ways from the adult measures. Given the extreme youth of the majority of pediatric organ transplant recipients, parental variables are obviously important. In one study of 38 families six months post-liver transplantation, successful adaptation was correlated with intact marriage of parents, private insurance coverage, less subjective financial stress, and higher intellectual and developmental functioning in the children (Kennard, Petrik, Stewart, Waller, & Andrews, 1990). High levels of family stress have been found to be related to poor medication adherence in pediatric kidney transplant recipients (Foulkes, Boggs, Fennell, & Skibinski, 1993). The basic components of a pediatric pretransplant psychosocial assessment are described in Table 43.2.

Zitelli et al. (1987) have suggested that the in-

TABLE 43.2
Transplant Evaluation

• Understanding	Does the child and family clearly understand what a transplant requires and why it is necessary?
• Commitment	Are the children and family committed to the transplant and the long-term care?
• Support	What social support is available to the child and family? Are there friends, a church, relatives?
• Adherence	What is the history of adherence to medical instructions? Have there been serious problems?
• Psychopathology	Is there significant psychopathology in the child or family? Is this treatable? How much has this interfered with functioning?

ability to understand or accept the procedure be considered a contraindication to pediatric liver transplantation, comparable to medical contraindications such as unresectable extrahepatic malignancy. However, various transplant centers give more or less weight to these factors; their importance is determined largely by the experience of that particular group. The younger the child, the more a psychosocial evaluation assesses the parents rather than the child. A thorough pretransplant assessment should allow the psychiatric consultant to have a clear sense of the issues likely to emerge before, during, and after the transplant hospitalization and to develop a plan for appropriate interventions.

Waiting

Once a child has been evaluated and found suitable for transplantation, he or she is put on the list of candidates. If a living related donor is to be used, scheduling of the transplant can then proceed, limited only by finances and availability of hospital facilities. However, if cadaveric organs are to be used, transplantation scheduling is dependent on the availability of an organ of the correct size and blood type. A national organization exists to facilitate matching of donors and recipients. Since each available organ could potentially match a number of waiting candidates, a computerized registry system has been established that gives the sickest suitable person on the list priority over the others. The weeks or months of waiting are often extremely stressful for both patients and parents who know that death can be prevented only with a procedure that may not be available in time. Psychiatric intervention during the waiting period can be extremely useful in assisting the parents and child with adaptive coping. Tours of the facilities, relaxation training, supportive psychotherapy, or medical play can help reduce anxiety, increase hope, and improve cooperation.

The briefer wait for a living related transplant also can be used to prepare the donor. It is easy for families to emphasize the importance of the donation to the point that the donor feels personally responsible for the outcome of the transplant (Wiley, Lindamood, & Pfefferbaum-Levine, 1984). This pressure can be minimized by active work with the donor and the family during the waiting period. Sibling donors particularly need explanations at a developmentally appropriate level and an opportunity to actively work with their natural fears and anxiety. Kinrade's guidelines for preparation of sibling bone marrow donors can be used as a basis for such work (Kinrade, 1987). (See Table 43.3.)

Transplant Hospitalization

The admission for transplantation, while the most dramatic aspect of organ transplantation, is often the briefest phase of the transplant process. Psychologic issues emerging during this hospitalization are similar to those of other children admitted for major procedures. Protective isolation can be disturbing to children, particularly in hospitals that use masks and gowns, since these reduce the number and types of interactions possible for the child. The presence of trusted adults with them in the hospital provides reassurance for most young children as they deal with pain, confusing machines, lines and drains, and frequent procedures. Psychiatric consultants must be alert to the tendency to underdiagnose (and therefore undertreat) pain and delirium in children, since the behavioral manifestations are not always clearcut (Ross &

TABLE 43.3

Preparation of Sibling Donor for Bone Marrow Transplant

Step 1: Donor's Adaptive Assessment	Step 2: Situational Assessment	Step 3: Interventions
Beliefs ("It will hurt")	Birth order of donor and recipient	Education (picture book)
Attitudes ("I don't want to")	Developmental level of the donor	Preparatory play (medical equipment)
Affect (anxiety, grief)	Relationship of siblings	Encourage pride but not total responsibility
Understanding (confusion)	Recipient's medical status	Identify and use emotional supports available
Adaptation (school problems)	Recipient's prognosis	Plan (games, food, clothes for hospital)
	Family circumstances	Address guilt (especially regarding graft vs. host reactions)

Source: Loosely based on L. C. Kinrade (1987), "Preparation of Sibling Donor for Bone Marrow Transplant Harvest Procedure," *Cancer Nursing, 10* (2): 77–81.

Ross, 1988; Trzepacz, DiMartini, & Tringali, 1993b; Smith, Balitbant, & Platt [in press]). Many of the drugs commonly given to transplant recipients have definite or potential psychotropic activity (Trzepacz, DiMartini, & Tringali, 1993a). Although a full discussion of psychopharmacology in transplantation is beyond the scope of this chapter, the transplant psychiatrist must have a working knowledge of pain management and the diagnosis and treatment of delirium in children.

Posttransplantation

The majority of medical problems in the posttransplant period have to do with graft failure or rejection (Gersony, 1990; Kocosuis, Tzakis, Todo, Neyes, & Nour, 1993). Recurrence of the underlying disease and toxicity of medications are also major sources of morbidity and mortality in the first 2 years after transplantation. Longer-term, chronic immunosuppression has been found to increase the probability of cancer, particularly lymphoma, in transplant survivors (Pennington, Sarafian, & Swartz, 1985). Bone marrow transplant recipients, exposed to large doses of chemotherapy, antibiotics, and sometimes radiation, also have been found to have a higher incidence of growth failure, infertility, cataracts, learning difficulties, cardiac difficulties, and hearing loss (Trigg, 1988). Cyclosporin also has been associated with seizures in liver, kidney, and bone marrow transplant recipients (Adams, et al., 1987).

Quality of life for pediatric transplant recipients has been assessed in a variety of ways, including relatively extensive psychological assessments of heart transplant recipients in both the United States (Lawrence & Frricker, 1987) and Great Britain (Wrat, Radley-Smith, & Yacoub, 1992). Long-term survivors of pediatric kidney transplantation are much improved over their pretransplant situations, and fall within norms for age, although they rate themselves lower than healthy controls (Almond, et al., 1991). Long-term follow-up studies of pediatric liver and heart transplant recipients have found normal growth, return to school, and an absence of significant complications (Gersony, 1990; Stewart, et al., 1991). The child's appearance is generally improved over the imme-

diate pretransplant time, but may not resemble the premorbid state, due to steroid-related weight gain and the hirsutism and gum hyperplasia associated with cyclosporin A. Similarly, although it appears that children do better cognitively after transplantation than before, there still may be deficits, particularly in children who had cyanotic heart disease (Stewart, Kennard, Waller, & Fixler, 1994; Hobbs & Sexson, 1993).

There have been few consistent medical predictors of functional outcome identified, despite some studies of reasonable size. However, clinically it appears that the previous functional level and age of onset of illness are important. Children with congenital illnesses, who have never been healthy, will have had a very different life experience and expectations than those who have acute onset of fulminant organ failure. Post-transplant medications appear less burdensome to those who have always taken medication than to those who expected a return to their previous lives (Stuber, 1993b). Previous functional level will also play a prominent role in the ability of the child to adapt following the transplant. Children who had never attended school will be at a disadvantage regardless of an intact central nervous system (Stewart, et al., 1991).

Some recent studies of children and adults have found evidence that medical life threat can be sufficient to precipitate post-traumatic stress symptoms, which persist for years in both survivors and their parents (Kazak, et al., in press; Pelcovitz, et al., 1996; Alter, et al., 1996). Parents report more symptoms than children, and appear to influence the perceptions of life threat of their children (Stuber, et al., 1994).

A long-term follow-up of 10 adolescent survivors, 2 to 10 years after bone marrow transplant, found few residual symptoms of posttraumatic stress at that point. However, these adolescents felt the transplant had changed their lives in a variety of ways, attributing to it reduced career goals (felt "not as smart" since the transplant), altered personality (acquired characteristics of the sibling donor), and altered worldview (small things less important). There was also evidence of reluctance to ask for or accept information about possible medical sequelae of the transplant, especially regarding infertility (Stuber and Nader, 1995). Although this line of research has been fruitfully pursued with bone marrow transplantation (Pot-

Mees, 1989; Stuber, Nader, Yasuda, Pynoos, & Cohen, 1991; Stuber & Nader, 1995; Stuber, Nader, Housekamp, & Pynoos, in press), similar studies have yet to be done with survivors of solid organ transplants or their parents.

Impact on the Family

The high amount of parental involvement in pediatric transplants makes assessment of parental understanding, commitment, adherence, and psychopathology essential in pretransplant evaluations, although it rarely serves as a contraindication for transplant. Parents must make the initial decision to proceed with transplantation and are generally responsible for getting the child to outpatient appointments before and after the transplant as well as for administering medications. This can be extremely time-consuming, resulting in lost days from work or job resignations. The stress and anxiety, coupled with the financial and time obligations, take a toll on both parents and on their relationship. In one study of parents of children undergoing bone marrow transplant, 12 of 15 mothers and 6 of 8 fathers reported persistent distress and depression in the pretransplant phase. During the transplant hospitalization, the 17 parents who stayed in the hospital with their children became intermittently extremely anxious, complaining of sleep disturbances, fatigue, and "claustrophobic feelings" (Pot-Mees & Zeitlin, 1987). Parents may experience conflict due to altered roles in the family, such as when a mother's increased comfort in a decision-making role or a father's new ease as a caregiver threatens the couple's established division of responsibilities (Freund & Siegel, 1986). When parents are differentially involved in day-to-day care, their interpretations of and emotional responses to specific events may differ considerably, hindering communication and leading to stress and isolation (Slater, 1994). Some attempts to deal with these issues have included support groups for parents of transplant patients (Patenaude, Levinger, & Baker, 1986). However, these generally focus on the hospitalization phase of transplantation. Preliminary findings of a prospective study of parents of pediatric bone marrow transplant patients suggest that anxiety persists at least 1 year after transplantation, even when the children appear to be doing well (Yasuda, Stuber, & Nader, 1990). Parents deal with continued medical expenses, long-term side effects of medications, and concerns about the future, including medical insurance for their children and whether they will ever have grandchildren (Gold, Kirkpatrick, Fricker, & Zitelli, 1986). The divorce rate in parents of 65 pediatric liver transplant recipients followed up to 5 years posttransplant was only 12%, lower than the national average, and similar to that reported in studies of families of chronically ill children (Zittelli et al., 1988).

The impact of transplantation on siblings can be quite significant. Those who are selected as donors often feel responsible for the results of the transplant, while those who are not feel left out, albeit relieved (Carr-Gregg & White, 1987; Stewart, Kennard, DeBolt, Petrik, Waller, & Andrews, 1993). Behavioral difficulties, including school problems, have been noted in siblings of kidney transplant recipients (Poznanski et al., 1978). Although identical twins present the least biologically complicated donor-recipient pairs, they may be the most complex psychologically (Wiley et al., 1984).

Impact on Staff

Organ transplantation raises powerful issues for staff, as well. Nursing staff are stressed by the patient care needs as well as the philosophical, ethical, and interpersonal aspects of transplantation (Stutzer, 1989). Allocation of staff time and hospital facilities as well as organs raise difficult issues for staff attempting to make selection decisions (Omery & Caswell, 1988). In one study of liver transplant nurses at the initiation of the transplant program and 5 years later, only a minority felt they received adequate support from social work or psychiatry in dealing with the psychologic issues raised by transplant patients and their families (Stuber, Caswell, Cipkala-Gaffin, & Billet, 1995). Members of a transplant team must struggle with the promises, both overt and covert, made to the patient and family, as demonstrated in an interesting ethnographic study of a pediatric bone marrow transplant team (Marsden, 1988). The psychiatric consultant can help in deliberations that often reach into areas previously unexplored (Stuber & Reed, 1991).

Recommendations

The psychiatric consultant to a transplant serivce should be an integral member of the team (Wolcott & Stuber, 1992). Psychiatric involvement is needed in the pretransplant evaluation to establish the needs and plan interventions for candidates and their families. Careful documentation of the

psychosocial predictors of successful transplantation will be needed as selection criteria are refined in response to economic pressures. Good pediatric consultation skills during the transplant hospitalization are needed to provide both adequate support and appropriate diagnosis and treatment of behavioral problems as well as the less common chronic pain or delirium. Consultation with the staff is an important component of both the pretransplant and hospital phases. After the transplant, psychiatric intervention is needed to deal with the serious problems of medical nonadherence. Further research will help us to know what psychiatric price these survivors pay for their second chance of life.

REFERENCES

Adams, D. G., Gunson, B., Honigberger, L., Buckels, J., Ponsford, S., Boon, A., Williams, A., Elias, E., & McMaster, P. (1987). Neurological complications following liver transplantation. *Lancet, 1*, 949–951.

Almond, P. S., Morell, P., Matas, A. J., Gillingham, K. J., Chan, K. S., Brown, A., Kasutan, C. E., Mauen, S. M., Cuauans, B., & Nevins, T. E. (1991). Transplanted children with long-term graft function have an excellent quality of life. *Transplantation Proceedings, 23* (1 PT 2), 1380–1381.

Alter, C. L., Pelcovitz, D., Axelrod, A., Goldenberg, B., Harris, H., Meyers, B., Grobois, B., Mandel, F., Septimus, A., Kaplan, S. (1996). Identification of PTSD in cancer survivors. *Psychosomatics, 37,* 137–143.

Alonzo, E. M., Whitington, P. F., Broelsch, C. E., Emond, J. C., & Thislethwaite, J. R. (1989). "Split liver" orthotopic liver transplantation (OLT). *Pediatric Research, 25,* 107 (Abstract).

American Psychiatric Association. (1994). *Diagnostic and Statistical Manual, Version IV.* Washington, DC: APA Press.

Beck, D. E., Fennel, R. S., Yost, R. L., Robinson, J. P., Geary, D., & Richards, G. A. (1980). Evaluation of an educational program on compliance with medication regimens in pediatric patients with renal transplants. *Journal of Pediatrics, 96* (6), 1094–1097.

Busuttil, R. W., Shaked, A., Millis, J. M., Junim, A., Colquhoun, S. D., Snackleton, C. R., Nuassa, B. J., Csete, M., Goldstein, L. I., McDiarmid, S. U. (1994). One thousand liver transplants. The Lessons Learned. 219 (5), 490–497.

Carr-Cregg, M., & White, L. (1987). Siblings of paediatric cancer patients: A population at risk. *Journal of Medical and Pediatric Oncology, 15,* 62–68.

Chacko, R. C., Harper, R. G., Kunik, M., & Young,

J. (1996). Relationship of psychiatric morbidity and psychosocial factors in organ transplant candidates. *Psychosomatics, 37,* 100–107.

Dousset, B., & Houssin, D. (1992). Liver transplantation: The challenges of the 1990s. *Biomedicine and Pharmacotherapy, 46* (2–3), 79–83.

Chang, I. (1991, June 5). Baby girl's bone marrow transplanted into sister. *Los Angeles Times,* pp. 1.

Craven, J., & Rodin, G. M. (Eds.) (1992). *Psychiatric aspects of organ transplantation.* Oxford, UK: Oxford University Press.

Didlake, R. H., Dreyfus, K., Kerman, R. H., Van Buren, C. T., & Kahan, B. D. (1988). Patient noncompliance: A major cause of late graft failure in cyclosporin-treated renal patients. *Transplantation Proceedings, 20* (3), 63–69.

Ettinger, R. B., Rosenthal, J. T., Mark, J. L., Malekzadem, M., Forsythe, S. B., Kamil, E. S., Salusky, I. B., & Fine, R. N. (1991). Improved cadaveric renal transplant outcome in children. *Pediatric Nephrology, 5,* 137–142.

Foulkes, L. M., Boggs, S. R., Fennell, R. S., & Skibinski, K. (1993). Social support, family variables, and compliance in renal transplant children. *Pediatric Nephrology, 7* (2), 185–188.

Freund, B. L., & Seigel, K. (1986). Problems in transition following bone marrow transplantation: Psychosocial aspects. *American Journal of Orthopsychiatry, 56* (2), 244–252.

Gersony, W. M. (1990). Cardiac transplantation in infants and children. *Journal of Pediatrics, 116,* 266–268.

Gold, L. M., Kirkpatrick, B. S., Fricker, F. J., & Zitelli, B. J. (1986). Psychosocial issues in pediatric organ transplantation: The parents perspective. *Pediatrics, 77* (5), 738–744.

Goldman, L. S. (1993). Liver transplantation using liver donors: Preliminary donor psychiatric outcomes. *Psychosomatics.*

Gutkind, L. (1988). Life after transplantation. *Transplantation Proceedings, 20* (10) (Suppl. 1), 1092–1099.

Hobbs, S. A., & Sexson, S. (1993). Cognitive development and learning in the pediatric organ transplant recipient. *Journal of Learning Disabilities, 26,* (2), 104–113.

Holzgreve, W., Beller, F. K., Buchholz, B., Hanzmann, M., & Kohler, K. (1987). Kidney transplantation from anecephalic donors. *New England Journal of Medicine, 316* (17), 1069–1070.

Kazak, A. E., Barakat, L. P., Meeske, K., Christakis, D., Meadows, A. T., Casey, R., Penati, B., & Stuber, M. L. (In press). Post-traumatic stress symptoms, family functioning, and social support in survivors of childhood leukemia and their mothers and fathers. *Journal of Clinical and Consulting Psychology.*

Kennard, B. D., Petrik, K., Stewart, S. M., Waller, D. A., & Andrews, W. S. (1990). Identifying factors in post-operative successful adaptation to pediatric liver transplantation. *Social Work in Health Care, 15,* 19–33.

Kinrade, L. S. (1987). Preparation of sibling donor for bone marrow transplant harvest procedure. *Cancer Nursing, 10* (2), 77–81.

Kocosuis, S. A., Tzakis, A. G., Todo, S., Neyes, J., & Nour, B. (1993). Pediatric liver transplantation: History, recent innovations, and outlook for the future. *Clinical Pediatrics, 32,* 386–392.

Korsch, B. M., Fine, R. N., & Negrete, V. F. (1978). Noncompliance in children with renal transplants. *Pediatrics, 61,* 872–876.

Levenson, J., & Olbrisch, M. (1993). Psychosocial evaluation of organ transplant candidates: A comparative study. *Psychosomatics, 34,* 314–323.

Marsden, C. (1988). Caregiver fidelity in a pediatric bone marrow transplant team. *Heart & Lung, 17* (6), 617–625.

Olbrisch, M. E., Levenson, J. H., & Hammer, R. (1989). The PACT: A rating scale for the study of clinical decision-making in psychosocial screening of organ transplant candidates. *Clinical Transplantation, 3,* 164–169.

Olbrisch, M. E., & Levenson, J. H. (1996). Psychological assessment of organ transplant candidates. *Psychosomatics, 36,* 236–243.

Omery, A., & Caswell, D. (1988). A nursing perspective of the ethical issues surrounding liver transplantation. *Heart & Lung, 17,* 626–631.

Patenaude, A. F., Levinger, L., & Baker, K. (1986). Group meetings for parents and spouses of bone marrow transplant patients. *Social Work in Health Care, 12* (1), 51–65.

Pelcovitz, D., Goldenberg, B., Kaplan, S., Weinblatt, M., Mandel, F., Meyers, B., & Vinciguerra, V. (1996). Post-traumatic Stress Disorder in mothers of pediatric cancer survivors. *Psychosomatics, 37,* 116–126.

Pennington, D., Sarafian, J., & Swartz, M. (1985). Heart transplantation in children. *Journal of Heart and Lung Transplantation, 4,* 290–292.

Piers, E. V. (1977). The manual for the Piers-Harris Self-Concept Scale (Cassette recording). Nashville, TN: Cousellor Recordings and Tapes.

Pot-Mees, C. C., & Zeitlin, H. (1987). Psychosocial consequences of bone marrow transplantation in children: A preliminary communication. *Journal of Psychosocial Oncology, 5* (2), 73–81.

Pot-Mees, C. (1989). The psychosocial effects of bone marrow transplantation in children. CW Delft, Netherlands, Eubron, Delft.

Reinhart, J. B., & Kemph, J. P. (1988). Renal transplantation for children: Another view. *Journal of the American Medical Association, 260* (22), 3327–3328.

Rosenthal, J. T., Ettenger, R. B., Ehrlich, R. M., & Fine, R. N. (1990). Technical factors contributing to successful kidney transplantation in small children. *Journal of Urology, 144,* 116–119.

Ross, D. M., & Ross, S. A. (1988). *Childhood pain, current issues, research, and management.* Baltimore: Urban & Schwarzenberg.

Rovelli, M., Plameri, D., Vossler, E., Bartus, S., Hull, D., & Schweizer, R. (1989). Noncompliance in organ transplant recipients: Evaluation by socioeconomic groups. *Transplantation Proceedings, 21* (1), 833–834.

Santos, G. W. (1990). Bone marrow transplantations in hematologic malignancies. *Cancer, 65,* 786–791.

Serrano, J. A., Verougstraete, C., & Ghislain, T. (1987). Psychological evaluation and support of pediatric patients and their parents. *Transplantation Proceedings, 19,* 3358–3362.

Siegal, B. R., Hanson, P., Viswanathan, R., Margolis, R., & Butt, K. M. H. (1989). Renal transplant patients' health beliefs. *Transplantation Proceedings, 21* (6), 3977–3978.

Simmons, R. G., Klein, S. D., & Simmons, R. L. (1977). *Gift of life: The psychological and social impact of organ transplantation.* New York: John Wiley & Sons.

Singer, P. A., Siegler, M., Whittington, P. F., Lantos, J. O., Emond, J. C., Thistlewaite, J. U. R., & Boelsch, C. E. (1989). Ethics of liver transplantation with living donors. *New England Journal of Medicine, 321* (9), 620–622.

Slater, J. A. (1994). Psychiatric aspects of organ transplantation in children and adolescents. *Child and Adolescent Psychiatric Clinics of North America, 3* (3), 557–598.

Smith, M. J., Braitbart, W. & Platt, M. (In press). A critique of instruments and methods to detect, diagnose and rate delirium. *Journal of Pain and Symptom Management.*

Stewart, S. M., Vavy, R., Waller, D., Kennard, B. D., Bensser, M., & Andrews, W. S. (1989). Mental and motor development, social competence, and growth one year after successful pediatric liver transplantation. *Journal of Pediatrics, 114,* 574–581.

Stewart, S. M., Hiltebeitel, C., Nici, J., Waller, D. A.,

Uauy, R., & Andrews, W. S. (1991). Neuropsychological outcome of pediatric liver transplantation. *Pediatrics, 87* (3), 367–376.

Stewart, S. M., Kennard, B. D., DeBolt, A., Petrik, K., Waller, D. A., & Andrews, W. S. (1993). Adaptation of siblings of children awaiting transplantation. *Children's Health Care, 22* (3), 205–215.

Stewart, S. M., Kennard, B. D., Waller, D. A., & Fixler, D. (1994). Cognitive function in children who receive organ transplantation. *Health Psychology, 13* (1), 3–13.

Stuber, M. L. (1993a). Psychologic care of adolescents undergoing transplantation. In E. R. McNarney, R. E. Kreipe, D. P. Orr, & G. D. Comerci (Eds.), *Textbook of adolescent medicine* (pp. 1138–1142). Philadelphia: W. B. Saunders.

Stuber, M. L. (1993b). Psychiatric aspects of organ transplantation in children and adolescents. *Psychosomatics, 34* (5), 379–387.

Stuber, M. L., Nader, K., Yasuda, P., Pynoos, R. S., & Cohen, S. (1991). Stress responses after pediatric bone marrow transplantation: Preliminary results of a prospective, longitudinal study. *Journal of the American Academy of Child and Adolescent Psychiatry, 30,* 952–957.

Stuber, M. L., & Reed, G. (1991). Never been done before: Consultative issues in innovative therapies. *General Hospital Psychiatry, 13,* 337–343.

Stuber, M. L., Caswell, D., Cipkala-Gaffin, J., & Billet, B. (1995). Nursing concerns regarding liver transplantation: A case for more nursing involvement. *Nursing Management, 26,* 62–70.

Stuber, M. L., & Nader, K. (1995). Psychiatric sequelae in adolescent bone marrow transplant survivors: Implications for psychotherapy. *The Journal of Psychotherapy Practice and Research 4* (1), 30–42.

Stuber, M. L., Nader, K. O., Houskamp, B. M., & Pynoos, R. S. (In press). Acute trauma responses of children undergoing bone marrow transplantation. *Journal of Traumatic Stress.*

Stutzer, C. A. (1989). Work-related stresses of pediatric bone marrow transplant nurses. *Journal of Pediatric Oncology Nursing, 3,* 70–78.

Trigg, M. E. (1988). Bone marrow transplantation for treatment of leukemia in children. *Pediatric Clinics of North America, 35,* 933–948.

Twillman, R. K., Manetto, C., Wellisch, D. K. et al. (1993). The transplant evaluation rating scale: a revision of the psychosocial levels system for evaluating organ transplant candidates. *Psychosomatics, 34,* 133–154.

Trzepacz, P. T., DiMartini, A., & Tringali, R. (1993a). Psychopharmacologic issues in organ transplantation. Part I: Pharmacokinetics in organ failure and psychiatric aspects of immunosuppressant and anti-infectious agents. *Psychosomatics, 34,* 199–207.

Trzepacz, P. T., DiMartini, A., & Tringali, R. (1993b). Psychopharmacologic issues in organ transplantation. Part II: Psychopharmacologic medications. *Psychosomatics, 34,* 290–298.

United Network for Organ Sharing data base, 1993, 1995.

Welch, H. G., & Larson, E. B. (1988). Dealing with limited resources: The Oregon decision to curtail funding for organ transplantation. *New England Journal of Medicine, 319,* 171–173.

Wiley, F. M., Lindamood, M. M., & Pfefferbaum-Levine, B. (1984). Donor-patient relationship in pediatric bone marrow transplantation. *Journal of the Association Pediatric Oncology Nurses, 1* (3), 8–14.

Wolcott, D., & Stuber, M. L. (1992). Bone marrow transplantation. In J. Craven & G. M. Rodin (Eds.), *Psychiatric aspects of organ transplant* (pp. 189–204). Oxford, UK: Oxford University Press.

Wolcott, D., & Stuber, M. L. (1992). Bone marrow transplantation. In J. Craven & G. Rodin (Eds.), *Psychiatric aspects of organ transplant* (pp. 189–204). Oxford, UK: Oxford University Press.

Wrat, J., Radley-Smith, R., Yacoub, M. (1992). Effect of cardiac or heart-lung transplantation on the quality of life of the paediatric patient. *Quality of Life Research, 1* (1), 41–46.

Yasuda, P., Stuber, M., & Nader, K. (1990, November). *Parental responses to pediatric bone marrow transplantation.* Paper presented at the annual meeting of the Academy of Psychosomatic Medicine, Phoenix, AZ.

Zitelli, B. J., Gartner, J. C., Malatack, J. J., Urbach, A. H., Miller, J. W., Williams, L., Kirkpatrick, B., & Breinig, H. M. (1987). Pediatric liver transplantation: Patient evaluation and selection, infectious complications and life-style after transplantation. *Transplantation Proceedings, 19* (4), 3309–3316.

Zitelli, B. J., Miller, J. W., Gartner, J. C., Malatack, J. J., Urbach, A. H., Belle, S. H., Williams, L., Kirkpatric, B., & Starzyl, T. E. (1988). Changes in life-style after liver transplantation. *Pediatrics, 82* (2), 173–180.

SECTION IV
Varieties of Culture and Ethnicity

44 / Cultural Competence in Child Psychiatry

Andres J. Pumariega and Terry L. Cross

Relevance of Cultural Competence

Child and adolescent psychiatry as a field has had a strong tradition of interest in cross-cultural issues impacting on children and families, as witnessed by the work of pioneers such as Erickson (1963) and Berlin (1983, 1987). However, the attitude of most individuals in the field, and in society in general, has been neglectful at best to the importance of these issues. Recent demographic changes in the United States, however, have served to underscore the significance of these issues. In the past 20 years, there has been a remarkable growth in what have been termed "minority" groups; they are growing at a much faster rate than the majority, European-origin population. In many areas of the United States the total minority population will outnumber the majority population by the year 2000. Most of this growth has been in the under-18 age group, both as a result of higher birth rates and increased immigration by people of color. Minority youth will constitute 30% of the population under the age of 18 by the year 2000 and close to 40 percent by 2020 (U.S. Bureau of the Census, 1986). Consequently, these trends are particularly important for child and adolescent psychiatrists.

Currently minority groups are multiply discriminated against in the U.S. mental health system. A number of barriers to access to mental health care exist for minorities, including the lack of minority practitioners, lack of culturally appropriate services, lack of knowledge and skill among majority practitioners around cross-cultural issues, and persistent lack of public child and adolescent mental health services. The morbidity and mortality resulting from such neglect has resulted in high social and financial costs for our society at large as well as high personal costs for minority children and their families. Such problems as high homicide and suicide rates, the substance abuse epidemic, homelessness, teenage pregnancy, school dropout and illiteracy, and penal or psychiatric institutionalization are at least partially results of these barriers and the policies that have created them.

Concepts of Culture and Cultural Values

In order to begin to understand the special needs of minority-group individuals, a working conceptual framework of the role of culture in human development and behavior is necessary. Spiegel (1971) and Kluckhorn (1953) have contributed the basis for such a framework. They define culture as part of a transactional field that influences human behavior and is made up to a series of interdependent levels or foci. Culture is the focus or interface between a society and the greater physical universe where the meaning of social behavior and knowledge of the meaning and function of guidelines for the maintenance of the social system, linguistic systems, and systems of beliefs and values are found. (See Figure 44.1.) According to Spiegel and Kluckhorn, basic cultural values at-

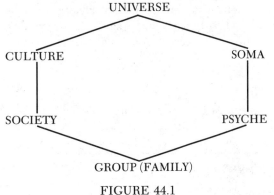

FIGURE 44.1

Foci within the Transactional Field.

Adapted from: Spiegel (1971), p. 42.

473

TABLE 44.1

Value Domains and Orientations/Preferences

Domains	Orientations/Preferences		
Man-Nature	Subjugation	Harmony	Mastery
Time	Past	Present	Future
Activity	Being	Being-in-becoming	Doing
Relational	Lineal	Collateral	Individual

Adapted from: Spiegel (1971), p. 163.

tempt to define human' relationships to 4 basic domains: nature, time, activity, and relationships. Different cultures define these relationships in ways that are adaptive according to the group's environmental and relational context. Tables 44.1 and 44.2 give examples of the different value orientations generally found within these domains and examples of how they are expressed in different cultures.

Such guidelines, beliefs, and values have particular importance for clinicians attempting to interact clinically with children from diverse cultural backgrounds. They help define psychosocial developmental norms and expectations, role functioning in different contexts (gender, family, occupational), and acceptable patterns for interpersonal communication. They also serve to define which behaviors or behavioral patterns are seen as adaptive or maladaptive. They influence attributional beliefs about mental illness and stress, which influence an individual or family's attitudes and responses. They define the role that the "sick" individual is to fulfill within both the family and the greater society. (For example, the individual with a mental illness may be expected to behave in a fragile manner or like an invalid, to carry on normal responsibilities,

or to serve a special spiritual role within the society.) Finally, such values and beliefs also influence patterns of help-seeking behavior and the orientation of healers sought out by the group, be they traditional (folk) healers or from the medical establishment.

Cultural Competence in Clinical Care

Cross, Bazron, Dennis, and Isaacs (1989), in their monograph titled *Towards A Culturally Competent System of Care,* set out to define the prerequisites for culturally appropriate or "competent" services for minority children and their families. The cultural competence model is defined as a set of congruent behaviors, attitudes, and policies that are found in a system, agency, or a group of professionals which enables them to work effectively in cross-cultural situations. The authors identify a spectrum of cultural competence that has been demonstrated by society at large and institutions in particular, ranging from cultural destructiveness (immigration quotas, services that break up fami-

TABLE 44.2

Contrasting Value Orientations Among Different Cultural Groups

Subculture	Man-Nature	Time	Activity	Relational
Hispanic	Subjugated	Present	Being	Linear
Anglo-Amer.	Mastery	Future	Doing	Individual
Oriental	Harmony	Past	Being-in-Bec.	Linear
Afro-Amer.	Subjugated	Present	Doing	Collateral

Adapted from: Spiegel (1971), p. 170.

lies), cultural blindness ("equal" treatment for all patients), cultural precompetency (provision of token services), cultural competence, and cultural proficiency (provision of innovative services and research.)

Cross et al. (1989) have gone on to define the particular qualities that culturally competent practitioners and agencies must embody and achieve. For individual practitioners, the qualities include: being aware and accepting of difference, awareness of their own culture, understanding the dynamics of working cross-culturally, developing cultural knowledge, and adapting practice skills to fit the client's cultural context. Cross draws on the work of Wilson (1982), who summarizes the qualities to be developed in the areas of attitude, knowledge, and skill. (See Tables 44.3, 44,4, and 44.5.) Many do not differ from those qualities found in good therapists; but others are specific to the needs of minority children and families. They also define four main qualities to be demonstrated by culturally competent agencies of institutions: valuing and adapting to cultural diversity; ongoing organizational self-assessment understanding and managing of the dynamics of difference; the institutionalization of cultural knowledge through training, experience, and literature; and instituting service adaptations to better serve minority patients. They go on to specify that such

TABLE 44.3

Personal Attributes Essential for Cultural Competence

* Personal qualities that reflect genuineness, accurate empathy, non-possessive warmth, and a capacity to respond flexibly to a range of possible solutions.
* Acceptance of ethnic difference between people.
* A willingness to work with clients of different ethnic minority groups.
* Articulation and clarification of the therapist's personal values, stereotypes, and biases about their own and others' ethnicity and social class, and ways these may accommodate or conflict with the needs of ethnic minority clients.
* Personal commitment to change racism and poverty.
* Resolution of feelings about one's professional image in fields which have systematically excluded people of color.

From: Wilson (1982).

TABLE 44.4

Areas of Knowledge Essential for Cultural Competence

* Knowledge of the culture (history, traditions, values, family systems, artistic expressions) of ethnic minority clients.
* Knowledge of the impact of class and ethnicity on behavior, attitudes, and values.
* Knowledge of the help-seeking behaviors of ethnic minority clients.
* Knowledge of the role of language, speech patterns, and communication styles in ethnically distinct communities.
* Knowledge of the impact of social service policies on ethnic minority clients.
* Knowledge of the resources (agencies, persons, informal helping networks, research) that can be utilized on behalf of ethnic minority clients and communities.
* Recognition of the ways that professional values may conflict with or accommodate the needs of ethnic minority clients.
* Knowledge of power relationships within the community, agency, or institution and their impact on ethnic minority clients.

From: Wilson (1982).

adaptations include addressing barriers to care (cultural, linguistic, geographic, or economic), levels of staffing that reflect the composition of the community being served, needs assessment and outreach, training in communication or interviewing skills, and modifications in actual assessment and treatment procedures and modalities.

Cultural Competence in Development

The concept of cultural competence also can be applied to the assessment of the psychosocial functioning of the individual child within his or her sociocultural context. An individual could be considered to be culturally competent if he or she can develop a strong sense of ethnic identification so as to respond effectively to cultural expectations for role functioning, interpersonal relationships, communication patterns, and behavioral norms. Another important aspect of individual cultural

TABLE 44.5

Areas of Skill Essential for Cultural Competence

* Techniques for learning the cultures of ethnic minority client groups.
* Ability to communicate accurate information on behalf of ethnic minority clients and their communities.
* Ability to openly discuss racial and ethnic differences and issues and to respond to culturally based cues.
* Ability to assess the meaning ethnicity has for individual clients.
* Ability to differentiate between the symptoms of intrapsychic stress and stress arising from the social structure.
* Interviewing techniques reflective of the therapist's understanding of the role of language in the client's culture.
* Ability to utilize to concepts of empowerment on behalf of ethnic minority clients and communities.
* Capability of using resources on behalf of ethnic minority clients and their institutions.
* Ability to recognize and combat racism, racial stereotypes, and myths in individuals and institutions.
* Ability to evaluate new techniques, research, and knowledge as to their validity and applicability in working with ethnic minorities.

From: Wilson (1982).

competence is the capacity to value and function comfortably within a context of cultural diversity. These characteristics and skills are acquired early in the course of individual development and parallel the acquisition of other cognitive and emotional characteristics.

ETHNIC IDENTIFICATION

The development of ethnic identification begins in the preschool period (ages 3 to 5 years). It is at this time that ethnic awareness begins in children, with beginning awareness of color differences and early differentiation of other's ethnicity (Goodman, 1964; Katz, 1976; Porter, 1971). However, self-misidentification is quite common in children, as evidenced by their selection of the wrong color doll when asked to pick one out like them (Aboud, 1977). Minority children, in fact, develop ethnic awareness and self-awareness earlier since they are confronted with this issue at an earlier age (Goodman, 1964). However, all throughout this period, the child is acquiring and consolidating culturally prescribed social skills and attitudes.

During early latency (ages 5 to 8), children begin to develop a stronger sense of ethnic orientation. They begin to demonstrate strong social preferences for individuals from their own group and to develop a sense of group concept and affiliation (Aboud, 1977; Porter, 1971). It is toward the end of this period that children are able to acquire the concept of "conservation of ethnic identity." Up to age 7 or 8 years, children cannot see their own ethnic identity as unchangeable if they dress or assume another characteristic from another group (Aboud, 1987). During the late latency-age period (ages 8 to 10 years), children begin to crystallize their attitudes about their own ethnic group and to develop curiosity about other groups.

In adolescence, externally defined roles and characteristics are integrated and synthesized into a unique definition of self, or identity (Erickson, 1968). Adolescents develop a subjective identification with an ethnic group, assimilating into their self-concept ethnic characteristics that are seen as their own, and refine their social identity. At the same time, they come in contact with more individuals of other ethnic or cultural groups, which serves to reinforce the "external boundaries" of their ethnic self-definition. These external boundaries are further reinforced if their ethnic/cultural group maintains strong traditions and institutions, such as social and educational organizations. However, those lacking these external reinforcers have greater degrees of assimilation (Rosenthal, 1987). The few studies so far on the developmental changes of ethnic identity indicate that late adolescents with a stronger ethnic identity have a greater awareness of cultural cohesion and preoccupation with such issues as retention of traditions, endogamy, and rejection of assimilation (Giles, Llado, McKirnan, & Taylor, 1979).

ADAPTATION TO DIVERSITY

The development of adaptation to diversity has received little attention from researchers in spite of its importance in an increasingly multicultural society. Attitudes about other ethnic/racial groups appear to be formed at a very early age and, whether positive or negative, become more intense as children become older (Brand, Ruiz &

Padilla, 1974). Although older children may appear less prejudiced than younger children, they are also more aware of socially "correct" responses and are more able to mask prejudice (Prozshansky, 1966). A number of environmental factors early in development appear to contribute to the development of prejudice, such as proximity and frequency of contact with other ethnic groups, degree of familial vertical mobility, and parental attitudes (LeVine & Campbell, 1972). Ethnic/racial prejudice appears to be associated with adverse developmental consequences. Children who show more prejudice tend to be more socially constricted, cynical, suspicious, and less secure than children who are more tolerant (Gouch, Harris, Martin, & Edwards, 1972). Prejudiced children are also more likely to be rigid and moralistic, to dichotomize their view of the world, to externalize conflict, and to have a high need for definiteness (Allport, 1954). Adolescents who are more secure in their own identity are less apt to have negative attitudes toward other ethnic/racial groups (Rosenthal, 1987).

DEVELOPMENTAL PROBLEMS

Inability to develop these adaptational characteristics results in a number of patterns with adverse psychological consequences. These include marginalization resulting from reification or mummification of the culture of origin, overidentification with the mainstream culture, and resultant identity diffusion or negative identity formation as defined by Erikson (1968). Many of these problems develop in the context of cultural conflict that is either internalized or externalized between generations in the family (Szapocznik, Scopetta, & Tillman, 1978). Next we present brief vignettes illustrating these unique adaptational problems and their potential mental health consequences.

CASE EXAMPLES

Marginalization: Maria was a 14-year-old youngster of Mexican origin who was referred by the local middle school to the community mental health center for increasing withdrawal as well as frequent fights with peers. Upon interviewing her, she described how her peers made fun of her conservative dress as well as her aversion to peer activities and interests, such as popular music. She vigorously denied such interests herself and believed that the other girls in her school were "imma-

ture." She was clearly dysphoric, but lacked vegetative symptoms of depression and described being able to function well within her family. However, further examination of her family context provided much insight into her problems. She was the oldest of seven children, including four brothers and two sisters. Her mother spent much of her time caring for her own elderly and infirm mother in Mexico, and her father was a strict disciplinarian and head of household. Father, who hardly spoke any English in spite of living in the United States for most of his adult life, indicated that he crossed the border to Mexico to look for a "traditional girl" to marry, and his expectations of his children included unfailing obedience and dedication to the family. He indicated that Maria had asked to have girlfriends from school over a couple of times, but he dissuaded her since they "do not believe in these kinds of friendships" until Maria was ready to marry.

Overidentification: Tamera was a 17-year-old African American youngster who was brought by her family to a university medical center to evaluate her refusal to eat and obsession with her weight and appearance. She presented with classic symptoms of anorexia nervosa, which had begun at age 15 but had worsened over the past 6 months and necessitated hospitalization. When examining her idealization of fashion magazine models in her psychotherapy sessions, it became evident that all of these idealized images were white. After this was brought out in her psychotherapy sessions, she proceeded to share openly her intense rejection of almost everything black, making derogatory remarks about the appearance, dress, speech, and behavior of African Americans, particularly black women. This intense rejection of her ethnic background was associated with a similarly intense hatred of her family, whom she saw as "lazy" and "cold." She was the youngest of two daughters in this middle-class family, with her mother working as an administrative assistant with a state agency and her father working as a supervisor at a local manufacturing concern. Her parents had worked hard to provide a much higher standard of living for their children than they had experienced and had expectations of higher education for both girls. The older daughter, however, became pregnant out of wedlock and dropped out of high school at about the time that Tamera's symptoms began, and the parents continued to provide her support in the hope that she could continue with her education. They expressed concern about Tamera's continual criticism of the family and its values and behaviors, such as her sister's pregnancy and mother's penchant for a weekly night out to play bingo. They were concerned for her health, but felt that Tamera was now acting "uppitty" and could no longer fit into the family.

Identity Diffusion: José and Gloria were 10- and 7-year-old Hispanic children referred by the local protective services agency to the child psychiatry clinic due to José's physical aggression toward Gloria, reported by their mother. The mother currently lived with a boyfriend who had taken her in after she left the children's natural father due to his physical abuse of her. She was quite distressed about José's behavior and noted that in many respects he reminded her of her former husband in his aggressive approach toward her and his sister. She acknowledged that Gloria was special to her and that in many ways she did not know how to relate to José outside of a disciplinary crisis. However, José's disruptive behavior was confined primarily to the home, with him making good grades and having few behavioral problems at school. In examining the mother's own developmental history, it became evident that she herself had a stormy relationship with her father, whom she described as abusive and alcoholic. She was able to gain insight as to how this influenced both her earlier marriage as well as her relationship with José. She was openly rebellious toward her father in her adolescent years, going out with adult men, which he disapproved of. Later, as a young adult, she concealed her Mexican origins, perfecting her English and telling people that she was a distant Hispanic descendant. José had a close alliance with his Mexican-origin male therapist but avoided any mention of their shared background. After his mother was able to explore her own cultural identification problems, José spontaneously began to ask his therapist not only about what a Mexican was but also about various idioms in Mexican Spanish. At the same time, he made marked progress in his behavioral self-control.

Negative Identity Formation: Jeannie was a 16-year-old Caucasian female who presented with a 2-year history of depressive symptoms and school refusal. She lived in a working-class neighborhood in an industrial Southern town that had been undergoing a strong transformation toward becoming multiethnic. She very much wanted to complete high school and go on to college to study fine arts, for which she received little support from her family. She was the youngest daughter of four siblings; the three oldest already had married and left home as late teens, finishing high school only later. They had settled close to their parents. Her father had a skilled job at a local factory, at which he worked long hours on demand out of fear of getting laid off. Her parents openly bemoaned the transformation of their community and increasing feelings of isolation and expressed their prejudice against the blacks and Hispanics who were moving into their neighborhood. As Jeannie began to recover from her depressive symptoms, she began to socialize primarily with minority youth from her high school art classes, but she was sharply rebuked for this by her parents. This led to her going out with gang members, breaking curfew rules, and absenting herself from the household. Her dress changed to a disheveled "punk" look from her previous "preppy"

style, and she began to speak in a distinctly non-Southern accent. In individual sessions, she spoke about her increasing resentment for her family, seeing them as uneducated "country bumpkins" and seeing herself as "different" from them.

It is important not to view the lack of development of a stable cultural/ethnic identity in minority youths as a disorder, but as developmental tasks that youths can achieve given the proper environmental support and opportunities, which are often lacking in the difficult socioeconomic and social circumstances in which they grow up. Remarkably, many do develop them in spite of very adverse circumstances, including poverty and discrimination. Sue (1981) suggests that the process of ethnic identity formation can be assessed effectively and that therapeutic interventions can be designed to facilitate the development of a healthy bicultural adjustment. However, behaviors that may be offensive to the larger society are likely to be exhibited during identity development, causing many helpers to see a healthy but painful process as pathologic. Inappropriate responses may inhibit healthy outcomes and contribute to role confusion and identity diffusion. It is important to note that, as illustrated in Jeannie's case, these are issues that are increasingly faced by youths from the majority culture as they develop in a multicultural milieu, and they require the attention of clinicians who can help both the youth and his or her family address them in an adaptive manner.

BICULTURAL COMPETENCE

The achievement of bicultural competence can be viewed as the optimal adaptation for minority and majority youths in a multicultural society. This competence implies the ability to function in two different cultures by alternating between two or more different sets of values and attitudes. It also may mean acquiring attributes of other cultures besides one's own, such as norms, attitudes, and language and behavioral patterns. However, this does not imply having a bicultural or multicultural self-identification or identity. In fact, bicultural or multicultural competence can be accomplished only after the attainment of a stable cultural/ethnic identity. It was presumed for many years that, for minority youths, bicultural competence was the result of a forced choice between the dominant culture and the culture of origin, with negative consequences such as identity diffusion, insecurity, and defensiveness (Goodman, 1964; Stevenson & Stewart, 1958). However, later studies have demonstrated that youths who are biculturally competent demonstrate greater flexibility in roles and cognitive style as well as adaptability to use the cultural norms appropriate for a given context or situation. Biculturally competent youth also have a higher self-esteem, greater understanding of others, and higher achievement (Ramirez, 1983).

Application of Cultural Competence in the Clinical Setting

The concept of cultural competence has direct applications in the clinical setting, at the interface between the child and adolescent psychiatrist and the child and his or her family. Next we present how these concepts are applied at different stages of clinical work.

BARRIERS TO CARE

Even before the child and family actually present for a clinical visit, the clinician must be aware of how cultural differences can impact on access to the care desired. The clinic or facility may have inadvertently developed barriers, such as how the telephone referral is handled over the phone (e.g., either too formal or impersonal or not sufficiently respectful), the geographic location of the clinic (away from accessible transportation or the neighborhoods), and the appointment hours available (which may not match the work and activity hours of the family). The clinic setting and decor may not reflect the cultural values of the populations being served, such as having sufficient room for extended family or kin. In fact, some clinics may actively discourage attendance by such related individuals during initial visits, even though they may have critical information for the diagnostic process. Registration and financial procedures also may serve to enhance an atmosphere of impersonality and mistrust. Studies suggest that such barriers result in significantly lower levels of mental health services by minority children and youth (Mason & Gibbs, 1992; Coffe, Waller, Cuccaro, Pumariega, & Garrison, 1995; Pumariega, Glover, Holzer, & Nguyen, in press).

BUILDING A THERAPEUTIC ALLIANCE

Once the child and family present for their initial appointments, the clinician must be attentive to how his or her nonverbal and verbal cues and those of the family are perceived within their cultural context and impact on the establishment of a therapeutic alliance. For example, even the manner in which a handshake is approached can have vastly different meanings in different cultures. Among many tribes of Native Americans, a soft handshake is the appropriate sign of respect and trust with either gender. On the other hand, Hispanic males expect a firm handshake, while females expect a softer one. Avoidance of eye contact, which majority clinicians may misperceive as a sign of dishonesty or even psychopathology, is a sign of respect among Orientals and a self-protective adaptational stance among African Americans. It may be important to establish quickly who is the main spokesperson for the family and to direct inquiries through that individual, at least initially.

A number of factors may impinge on the minority family's motivation for clinical assistance. It is important to establish whether the motivation is primarily their own or enforced by some outside agent or agency (e.g., school, welfare department); the latter impetus may lead to resentment and disinterest. If the referral resulted from the failure of a traditional cultural healer to address the problem, the family may be dealing with demoralization and frustration. Whether such care is sanctioned by the family elders/decision makers, such as grandparents, is very important, and they should be involved as soon as possible. The clinician should ascertain the degree of stigma associated with mental illness and seeking psychiatric help in the culture and how this could impact on the family's comfort with the consultation. It is important to determine the family's expectations and hoped-for outcomes early in the evaluation so that they may be dealt with openly to prevent misconceptions or disappointment.

DIAGNOSTIC ISSUES

Cultural factors also are involved in the reporting and assessment of symptomatology. Differences in language and idiomatic expressions can determine how different symptoms are identified. Symptoms also may take on different meanings in different cultural contexts. For example, the term "blue" may have clinical significance to a psychiatrist but to an African American, it may reflect a state resulting from chronic oppression, while to a Hispanic, it may not make any sense at all since it would be interpreted literally (feeling a color). Cultural values also may dictate who are reliable reporters and observers as well as where it is appropriate to discuss different symptoms and problems. For some time it was assumed that Orientals suffered more somatic symptoms than other people, but recent research has demonstrated that they report somatic symptoms to physicians, while they are able to identify emotional responses and symptoms only to close friends and family. Specific culture-bound syndromes defy the diagnostic categories we work under, which were developed primarily with a Euro-American focus, as well as different clusters of symptoms that may vary among different groups. For example, many fewer Africans than Britons identified as depressed meet criteria for major depression cited in the *Diagnostic and Statistical Manual of Mental Disorders*. Such differences in the interpretation of emotional experiences, the labeling and interpretation of symptomatology, and degree of self-disclosure affect the cross-cultural and cross-ethnic validity of most diagnostic instruments utilized in clinical assessment, since the large majority of these were normed with primarily Anglo-American populations. Results from any such instruments require interpretation within the youngster's sociocultural context and support by careful clinical observation (Draguns, 1984).

The cultural and family context of symptomatology also must be considered in the assessment of a minority child. Symptomatology may be occurring in the context of a culturally normative period of transition, such as a grief/mourning period or a maturational stage. Clinicians also must assess whether cross-cultural dynamics may play a role in the symptomatology, such as intergenerational conflicts around acculturation, discrimination, and margination from the majority culture

or the youth's own culture. The impact of such unique experiences as poverty and deprivation or traumatic immigration experiences should be considered, as well.

In assessing the behavior and psychosocial development of minority children, clinicians consider that their expected norms may differ considerably among different cultural groups, with different psychological and cognitive skills being reinforced according to different cultural values. Minority children also are exposed to different family structures, role expectations, and communication patterns than majority children. When minority children are evaluated against the norms for the majority, Euro-American culture, they may be erroneously found to be deficient or abnormal. For example, African-American children are frequently overrepresented in the disruptive behavior diagnoses, (Fabrega, Ulrich, & Mezzich, 1993; Kilgus, Pumariega, & Coffe, 1995) but the greater emphasis on motoric development in Afro-centric cultures is not taken into account in coming to such diagnostic conclusions. Another misconception, that African-American children have lower levels of self-esteem than whites, was proven erroneous by a number of studies that found that they actually had higher levels of self-esteem and used each other as models for comparison. Native American children often are assessed as quiet or lacking in social skills due to being socialized to use longer pauses between turns at conversation. When the Native American child pauses for a polite silence of up to 30 seconds after the previous speaker, children or adults of other cultures usually break the silence, leaving the Native child out of the conversation. In the diagnostic interview, this behavior is often misinterpreted. In fact, particular sources of stress for minority children are the conflicting developmental expectations from within and outside their families and communities, with the risk of being labeled as dysfunctional by either (Gibbs and Huang, 1989; Philips, 1983; Powell, Yamamoto, Romero, & Morales, 1983).

In order to ascertain more accurately the role of culture and cultural values in the functioning of minority children, the clinician must become knowledgeable about the developmental norms and child-rearing patterns of the populations that he or she serves. Although there are excellent resource materials for reference, the best source of such information is the family itself. The traditional diagnostic interview must be modified for this purpose. The techniques utilized often are termed ethnographic interviewing; the best overall reference is the article "Teaching Ethnographic Methods to Social Service Workers" by Green and Leigh (1989). Green and Leigh have adapted the work of James Spradley (1979) to allow human service professionals to have a window on the reality experienced by their clients. In general, such techniques involve having a family member serve as the cultural guide for the clinician by making a series of open-ended inquiries about different cultural aspects of family life. For example, the clinician might ask the parent or grandparent about the usual expectations for behavior or self-control by asking "How are boys supposed to behave and mind in your community?" The clinician might need to mark a transition from the typical psychiatric interview and actively enlist the cooperation of the family member in this task. He or she also might incorporate some of these techniques in the interview with the child to evaluate his or her understanding of cultural expectations. In addition, the clinician should, as much as possible, include in the interview or the interview area symbols significant to the child's culture so as to facilitate expression of conflicts in culturally syntonic ways. This might include having dolls and figures of the appropriate racial group, wall hangings depicting traditional scenery, or reading materials that could elict cultural themes.

TREATMENT PLANNING AND IMPLEMENTATION

The treatment planning and interpretive process are critical in the effective treatment of the minority child. The minority family may feel a strong power differential between themselves and the professional; this is often the case when dealing with agents of the majority culture. Often they may choose to acquiesce passively and later not follow recommendations. It is important to address this perception and empower the family in making treatment decisions for their child. The clinician must ensure that a true consensus is developed with the family around the understanding of the child's problems and possible illness. Doing so may involve using terminology and concepts acceptable in their cultural belief system. It is also important to present treatment options in a demystifying manner understandable to family members but in a manner that is not condescending to them. Such options should include cultural or folk practitioners and consultants whenever indicated as well as the option not to pursue treatment at all. Modalities that focus on immediate needs and problems and have a present orientation are more acceptable and practical than those emphasizing insight and a future orientation.

Although pharmacotherapy may seem to be the most straightforward modality to be utilized cross-culturally, it does involve some special considerations. In order to obtain optimal treatment compliance, it is important to educate and obtain true informed consent from the family decision makers or elders. This also involves demystifying the use of medications and addressing misperceptions based both on traditional cultural beliefs as well as on the perceived power differential with the clinician (e.g., the medication will "control the child's thinking"). Discussion of biological and genetic factors also can serve to alleviate feelings of guilt on the part of family members, who often may feel responsible for the child's illness or problems as a result of their socioeconomic limitations.

In individual psychotherapy, the clinician must address the dynamics of cultural difference and power differential with the child as clearly as with the family. The presence of identity or role confusion as a result of acculturation conflicts should be addressed empathetically but in a way that empowers the child to make his or her own flexible choices around cultural values and identification. It is important to address specific areas of cultural conflict, such as role pressures on the child to serve as a "cultural broker" with the family, pressures to not "betray" the culture, and negative identification against the culture of origin. A value-neutral approach, where the clinician models openness to the diverse cultural influences that the child is exposed to, is quite effective in achieving these goals. Therapists who have experienced any of these conflicts in their own experience also can use judicious self-disclosure with the child. It is important to address issues of confidentiality in psychotherapy so the clinician is not perceived as "driving a wedge" between the patient and his or her family or is not used by the patient as a means of resisting dealing with family issues (Gibbs & Huang, 1989).

All treatment of minority children must have a

family focus in order to address cultural issues effectively. The therapist must respect culturally established means of communication and family role functioning, but at the same time foster flexibility on the part of the family to accommodate differing points of view that might be espoused by the more bicultural offspring. This involves addressing parental fears of "abandonment" by their acculturating child, while also facilitating the family in their role of transmission of traditional cultural values and beliefs in a nonconflictual fashion. The family can also accept greater acculturation by the child if empowered in dealing with the majority culture more effectively. They can be encouraged to utilize community resources and groups to facilitate both the enhancement of their traditions and the introduction into new cultural viewpoints. The utilization of a cultural consultant in therapy, with the family's consent, can be useful in dealing with issues around the interpretation of traditional beliefs and values as well as potential distortion of these issues for dysfunctional purposes.

The Application of Cultural Competence in Child and Adolescent Psychiatry Training

Perhaps the most important area of application of the principles of cultural competence is in the training of future child and adolescent psychiatrists. This is the stage during which the development of attitudes, knowledge, and skills concerning serving minority youth and their families can best be established.

A specific cross-cultural seminar should be a standard component of the curriculum of every child and adolescent psychiatry residency program. It should include conceptual and research literature in the normal development, family structure/function, and psychiatric issues of children from the main, underserved U.S. ethnic minority groups, as it is likely any graduate will encounter children and families from these groups at some point in his or her professional life. These readings should be supplemented by some from the popular literature of some cultures being studied and visiting lecturers or presenters from minority groups in the local community. Such semi-

nars should deal with attitudinal issues through open discussion of viewpoints presented in the readings as well as exercises through which the residents can explore and express their own cultural biases (Valle, 1986).

Clinical rotations should include traditional settings with diverse populations, rotations in underserved areas with predominantly minority populations, and rotations in alternative mental health programs tailored to particular cultural groups. In these rotations, residents can attend to issues such as institutional barriers to care and the impact of culturally sensitive/competent versus incompetent services.

Skills development can best be accomplished in the context of clinical supervision. While it is important that resident caseloads include a diversity of cultural groups, cases with clear cross-cultural issues are very important. In the process of supervision, the instructor can help the resident develop insight around how his or her cultural values may bias understanding of patients. It is also in supervision that diagnostic and intervention skills consonant with a multicultural outlook can be developed.

Such training best takes place within the context of institutions and agencies where culturally competent policies have already been instituted. Institutional cultural competence is critical to the training and development of culturally competent professionals, since an atmosphere that includes culturally diverse colleagues and faculty/role models further enhances the residents' appreciation of these principles. Minority faculty are rare commodities who need much support and nurturance, since they are invaluable in fostering an academic approach to cross-cultural issues, particularly research. Majority-group individuals selected to train in child and adolescent psychiatry should possess attitudinal qualities which are consistent with cultural competence given the numbers of minority children whom they will likely serve. Minority residents need special support and mentoring, especially around the issues of maintaining their own cultural identities while acculturating to the culture of the profession. Additionally, every effort should be made to recruit minorities into child and adolescent psychiatry, especially given their disproportionately low numbers (at most 7 to 10 percent) in comparison to the growing population of minority children and families and their unique needs and challenges.

REFERENCES

Aboud, F. E. (1977). Interest in ethnic information: A cross-cultural developmental study. *Canadian Journal of Behavioral Science, 9,* 134–146.

Aboud, F. E. (1987). The development of ethnic self-identification and attitudes. In J. S. Phinney & M. J. Rotheram (Eds.), *Children's ethnic socialization: Pluralism and development.* Newbury Park, CA: Sage Publications.

Allport, G. W. (1954). *The nature of prejudice.* Cambridge, MA: Addison-Wesley.

Berlin, I. N. (1983). Prevention of emotional problems among Native American children: Overview of developmental issues. In S. Chess & A. Thomas (Eds.), *Annual progress in child psychiatry and development* (pp. 320–333). New York: Brunner/Mazel.

Berlin, I. N. (1987). Anglo adoptions of Native Americans: Repercussions in adolescence. *Journal of the American Academy of Child and Adolescent Psychiatry, 17,* 387–388.

Brand, E. S., Ruiz, R. A., & Padilla, A. M. (1974). Ethnic identification and preference: A review. *Psychological Bulletin, 81,* 860–890.

Cross, T. L., Bazron, B. J., Dennis, K. W., & Isaacs, M. R. (1989). *Towards a culturally competent system of care.* Washington, DC: CASSP Technical Assistance Center, Georgetown University Child Development Center.

Coffe, S. P., Waller, J., Cuccaro, M., Pumariega, A. J., & Garrison, C. Z. (1995). Race and gender differences in the treatment of psychiatric disorders in young adolescents. *Journal of the American Academy of Child & Adolescent Psychiatry, 34* (11), 1536–1543.

deAnda, D. (1984). Bicultural socialization: Factors affecting the minority experience. *Social Work, 29,* 101–107.

Draguns, J. G. (1984). Assessing mental health and disorder across cultures. In P. B. Peterson, N. Sartorious, & A. J. Marsella (Eds.), *The cross-cultural context. Vol. 7: Cross-cultural research and methodology series* (pp. 31–58). Beverly Hills, CA: Sage Publications.

Erikson, E. H. (1963). *Childhood and society.* New York: W. W. Norton.

Erikson, E. H. (1968). *Identity, youth, and crisis.* New York: W. W. Norton.

Fabrega, H., Ulrich, R., & Mezzich, J. E. (1993). Do Causasians and Black adolescents differ at psychiatric intake? *Journal of the American Academy of Child & Adolescent Psychiatry, 32* (2), 407–413.

Gibbs, J. T., & Huang, L. N. (1989). A conceptual framework for assessing and treating minority youth. In J. T. Gibbs & L. N. Huang (Eds.), *Children of color: Psychological interventions with minority youth* (pp. 1–29). San Francisco: Jossey-Bass.

Giles, H., Llado, N., McKirnan, D. H., & Taylor, D. M. (1979). Social identity in Puerto Rico. *International Journal of Psychology, 14,* 185–201.

Goodman, M. E. (1964). *Race awareness in young children* (rev. ed.). New York: Collier.

Gouch, H., Harris, D. B., Martin, W. E., & Edwards, M. (1972). Children's ethnic attitudes: I. Relationships to certain personality factors. In A. Brown (Ed.), *Prejudice in children.* Springfield, IL: Charles C. Thomas.

Green, J. W., & Leigh, J. W. (1989). Teaching ethnographic methods to social service workers. *Practicing Anthropology, 11,* 8–10.

Katz, P. A. (1976). The acquisition of racial attitudes in children. In P. A. Katz (Ed.), *Towards the elimination of racism.* New York: Pergamon Press.

Kilgus, M. D., Pumariega, A. J., & Coffe, S. P. (1995). Race and diagnosis in adolescent psychiatric inpatients. *Journal of the American Academy of Child & Adolescent Psychiatry, 34* (1), 67–72.

Kluckhorn, F. R. (1953). Dominant and variant value orientations. In C. Kluckhorn & H. A. Murray (Eds.), *Personality in nature, society, and culture.* New York: Knopf.

LeVine, R., & Campbell, D. (1972). *Ethnocentrism: Theories of conflict, ethnic attitudes, and group behavior.* New York: John Wiley & Sons.

Mason, M. A., & Gibbs, J. T. (1992). Patterns of adolescent hospitalization: Implications for social policy. *American Journal of Orthopsychiatry, 62* (3), 447–457.

Philips, S. U. (1983). *The invisible culture.* New York: Longman.

Porter, J. D. R. (1971). *Black child, white child: The development of racial attitudes.* Cambridge, MA: Harvard University Press.

Powell, G. J., Yamamoto, J., Romero, A., & Morales, A. (Eds.). (1983). *The psychosocial development of minority group children.* New York: Brunner/Mazel.

Prozshansky, H. (1966). The development of intergroup attitudes. In L. W. Hoffman & M. L. Hoffman (Eds.), *Review of child development research* (Vol. 2) New York: Russell Sage.

Pumariega, A. J., Glover, S., Holzer, C. E., & Nguyen, H. (In Press). Utilization of mental health sciences in a tri-ethnic sample of addresses. *Community Mental Health Journal.*

Ramirez III, M. (1983). *Psychology of the Americas: Mestizo perspectives on personality and mental health.* New York: Academic Press.

Rosenthal, D. A. (1987). Ethnic identity development in adolescents. In J. S. Phinney & M. J. Rotheram (Eds.), *Children's ethnic socialization: Pluralism and development.* Newbury Park, CA: Sage Publications.

Spiegel, J. (1971). *Transactions: The interplay between individual, family, and society,* ed. J. Papajohn. New York: Science House.

Spradley, J. (1979). *The ethnographic interview.* New York: Holt, Reinhart, and Winston.

Stevenson, H. W., & Stewart, E. C. (1958). A developmental study of racial awareness in young children. *Child Development, 29,* 399–409.

Sue, D. W. (1981). *Counseling the culturally different.* New York: Wiley Interscience.

Szapocznik, J., Scopetta, M. A., & Tillman, W. (1978).

What changes, What remains the same, and what affects acculturation in Cuban immigrant families. In J. Szapocznik & M. C. Herrera (Eds.), *Cuban Americans: Acculturation, adjustment, and the family*. Washington, DC: COSSMHO.

U.S. Bureau of the Census. (1986) *Statistical abstract of the United States: 1987* (107th ed.) Washington, DC: U.S. Department of Commerce.

Valle, R. (1986). *Cross-cultural competence in minority communities: A curriculum implementation strategy*. (1986). In M. R. Miranda & H. H. L. Kitano (Eds.), *Mental health research and practice in minority communities: Development of culturally sensitive training programs*. Rockville, MD: National Institute of Mental Health, ADAMHA.

Wilson, L. (1982) *The skills of ethnic competence*. Unpublished manuscript, University of Washington, Seattle.

45 / The African American Child

Ruth L. Fuller

Definitions and Epidemiology

African American children and adolescents are defined in the United States as those young people who include among their ancestors individuals who came from various African countries and/or cultural groups. There are approximately 9.6 million African American children (under age 18) representing 32% of the total African American population of the United States. Although this diverse ethnic group is distributed across the entire country, the highest concentrations are found in large metropolitan areas along the East Coast (from Massachusetts to Florida), the Gulf states, the West Coast (especially California), and in the middle of the country (in Chicago, Detroit, Memphis, etc.) (U.S. Bureau of the Census, 1992).

Economically, recently more African Americans have moved into the upper-middle income range of over $50,000 per year, even with a decrease in those numbers between 1990 and 1991. The overall picture is more sobering when African Americans' share of the country's wealth is considered. In 1990, the median income of all households in the United States was $29,943, with $31,231 for white households and only $18,676 for African American households (U.S. Bureau of the Census, 1992).

At any given income level, African American families generally have less disposable income than their white counterparts. These families also have less income than white families at any given educational level. The poverty line varies yearly and by the size of the family. In 1990, the poverty rate for white families was 14.1% but 50% for African American families.

In addition to the tasks of daily living, African Americans have been and still are reconsidering the larger American society's view of them and their own view of themselves. As a result of this reflectiveness, in recent years, increasing numbers of African Americans have been embracing the term "African American" as preferable to the historically important term "black." This development is seen as part of an evolutionary process in which this American group, which has been defined by skin color, would be defined by familial, historic, and geographic points of origin plus citizenship, as other American groups are defined. "African American" is used in lieu of a more specific localization because, with rare exceptions, U.S. history has erased the links between the contemporary African American population and their precise African ancestral roots (McAdoo, 1988). More recently arrived Americans of African descent are able to define themselves as coming from a very specific country and cultural heritage. Some individuals prefer using the older term "Afro-American" or its newer variation, "African-American." Some families from the West Indies or Caribbean islands, or Central or South America, may prefer to define themselves in terms of the specific islands and/or countries from which the families migrated—for example, Jamaican American. Still other individuals feel that their family is best defined as persons of color. It is the task of the clinician to be clear about such preferences.

The History of African Americans in the United States: Facts and Myths

FACTS OF AFRICAN HISTORY

In his history of Africans, Harris (1987) presents an overview of the geography of Africa, the second largest continent, three times the size of the United States. The continent includes tropics, desert, mountain ranges, plains, large rivers, and lakes. Among others, Hughes, Meltzer, and Lincoln (1983) note that within this large expanse of land, there are hundreds of African cultural groups with a wide range of physical types. By size, the range varies from the four-and-a-half- to five-foot Pygmy groups to the seven-foot Watusis. In complexion, one finds dozens of skin tones, from ivory through mahogany to ebony. In world history, African history may be as old as 1.75 million years or more. Wilford (1996) summarized the finding of anthropological evidence that modern human beings evolved in the Olduvai Gorge in the Serengeti Plain of northern Tanzania, East Africa [3.18 million years ago] and, most recently, in the Hadar badlands of northern Ethiopia [2.3 million years ago].

The Dorling Kindersdley History of the World (Fry, 1994) and *The Times Atlas of World History* (Stone, 1989) note cultural developments during the period, 40,000 to 1200 B.C. such as: Aboriginals arrive in Australia c. 40,000; Cro-Magnon humans reach Europe from Africa c. 38,000; Hunter-gatherers make settlements in Zaire c. 18,000; the first crossings over the Bering Strait to the future Americas c. 13,000; the first two towns appear [in Turkey and Israel] c. 6000; the first civilization, Sumer [Iraq], developed about 5000 and is followed by Egypt about 3100; and the development of other civilizations, in China and Greece for example, by 1200. In later centuries, other African empires include: the Kushite kingdom [in Sudan] [300 B.C. to 350 A.D.]; Ghana [55 A.D. to c. 1100]; Mali [c. 1225 to c. 1450]; and Songhai [to power c. 1460 to 1591]. These empires existed with complex social orders.

A broader view of Africans and their descendants shows that they have been globally dispersed as explorers, traders, warriors, and slaves to Europe, Asia, and the Americas throughout centuries of ancient and modern history.

MYTHS

The African and his or her descendants have been portrayed in stereotypes throughout the history of black-white relations, and stereotypes continue to exist in many minds. From Greek and Roman writings in the sixth-century B.C. regarding Ethiopians, through treaties by 18th-century explorers and historians, to contemporary "research" in human development, the physical characteristics of darker skin color, broad features, and nonstraight hair texture have been used as obvious evidence of the inferiority of Africans and their descendants. These features were described as ugly. The characteristic qualities assigned to persons with these features include stupidity, laziness, licentiousness, lying, thievery, savage dangerousness, a limited capacity for affect, excessive affect, and shallowness in interpersonal relations.

Another myth presents Africans, and therefore their descendants, as having no history, culture, or civilization other than that presented by Europeans. Some historical writers, such as C. G. Seligman, concluded that Egypt's development was due to ancient European immigrants (Eastern Hamites) and, therefore, that the peoples of the Sahara were not Africans (Harris, 1987).

HISTORY OF THE CONTINENTAL UNITED STATES

The earliest known Africans in the United States came with explorers in the 1500s, reflecting African dispersal into Europe, particularly through Portugal (starting in 1440). The most detailed history of African Americans begins with "the peculiar institution" of the world's most widespread, profitable, and organized system of slavery (1619 to 1863) (Hughes et al., 1983).

The continuous agrarian economics of the southern American colonies demanded a steady source of cheap, controlled labor to raise sugar, tobacco, rice, coffee, and, later, cotton. Slavery was less rewarding in the northern colonies. Negroes, as Africans were called, were highly desirable. Their physical appearance allowed for ready identification. They were dislocated from familiar terrain. Zinn (1980/1990) notes that although 1 million slaves had been delivered to the Caribbean and South America by 1619, by 1860, 10 to 15 million had arrived in the Americas (approximately one-third of those seized in Africa). The trade triangle consisted of a start in British ports loaded with goods, to the Guinea (Slave) Coast in West Africa for "Black Gold," to the American colonies and a return to Europe with agricultural products (Harris & Levey, 1975).

Not all African Americans were slaves. In the colonies and later in the United States, there were free persons of color and runaway slaves. Some former slaves found sanctuary among receptive Native American Indian groups in remote areas of the country or later to the North. Slave insurrections also occurred, but for most African Americans, slavery continued until the Civil War, and myths and stereotypes about African American inferiority were perpetuated. After a brief reconstruction period, the postslavery period saw the rise of legal segregation of the races in which the caste system of slavery could persist. The Civil Rights Movement of the 1950s through the 1970s challenged the segregation laws of the land. Most authors contend that to this day African Americans still struggle for social equity in spite of legal, political, and economic gains (Bell, 1987; McAdoo, 1988). Coner-Edwards and Edwards (1988), among others, underscore the diversity and strengths of the African American children and their families.

FAMILY STRUCTURES

Incorrect assumptions about "proper" family structures, roles, and relationships have led to other misconceptions about African American families. Although sometimes debated as an all-or-none phenomenon, contemporary authors view African American family and community structure as reflecting both African traditions and adaptations to life in the United States. Historian John Hope Franklin (1988) offers historical overviews of the centrality of consanguine (kin) relationships for African American families. Devotion to family survived despite threatened and real separations of spouses and children through slavery, reconstruction, segregation, massive urban migrations, and extensive poverty. The importance of kin relationships over marital ones is one of a number of values different from those of the general American culture. Other differing values include language, ways of relating to important persons in the family's life, a generous expression of affect, communalism, spirituality, and task-oriented

views of time, values that are in opposition to the values of the general American culture. As a result of these differences, biculturality is a fact of life for African American families. A workable resolution of biculturality, and the dissonance it often causes, is a task for each child. The child is required to negotiate a daily life in which one set of behaviors is perceived as desirable by one culture and undesirable by the other. For example, behavior seen as reasonably assertive in one culture may be seen as crudely aggressive, if not dangerous, in the other.

The myth of the disorganized, inadequate, single-parent family as the usual experience for African American children appeared before the 1960s when 75% of the families had two parents present. Single-parent families are not necessarily disorganized or dysfunctional. Among African Americans, the number of single mothers is of concern (64% of births by 1989) as well as the number of young teenage mothers. Overall societal support of single mothers with dependent children has moved many young families into individual households in which the young mothers receive financial support but may or may not receive or accept emotional support. This arrangement does not replace the complex emotional and educational support that had been characteristic of continuous, often multigenerational, extended and/or augmented family living. Although dependent children must have their needs met, and American society continues to struggle with the question of how best to address those needs, these new patterns of more isolated living represent a profound shift away from historical mores of communal living and shared responsibility for child rearing (Fuller, 1990).

Positive educational and economic gains have resulted in similar shifts toward nuclear family life in African American middle-class families. Career demands, the utilization of promising geographic moves, and upward mobility have tended to create more conjugally based nuclear family units. For those families that have moved toward this general American ideal of family, the parental generation and the next generation of children are not focused on kinship as the prime force in relationships. Across economic lines, the potential stress of relative isolation is a real factor to consider in the mental health of African American children (Spurlock & Booth, 1988).

486

The Impact of Sociocultural Factors: A Biopsychosociocultural Frame of Reference

Numerous theoretical frames of reference have been put forth as tools to be used in addressing transcultural issues (Chunn, Dunston & Ross-Sherriff, 1983; Gaw, 1993; Ho, 1992; Vargas & Koss-Chioino, 1992). A biopsychosociocultural frame of reference suggests viewing a person as a physical being who:

- lives in a particular geographic area, and at a particular point in history
- has an internal emotional, psychological, and spiritual life
- interacts with an intimate environment that is peopled by family members (parents, siblings, great-grandparents, aunts, uncles, cousins, etc.) and friends-like-family
- also lives in a society (a country) that may or may not support the values of the more intimate environment
- has, therefore, a commonality with his or her historical past and a uniqueness within his or her geopolitical present
- is met at a particular developmental stage, in which there are particular risk factors as well as potential resources (Fuller, 1984)

INFANCY THROUGH ADULTHOOD

Prenatal and Perinatal Influences: Influences of socioeconomic class hold across many cultural lines. An unplanned pregnancy in a poor, single adolescent has higher risk factors for less or no prenatal care, lower-birthweight infants, more perinatal complications, and higher infant mortality rates. A planned, wanted pregnancy in a middle-class, married woman in her 20s decreases risk factors. However, compared to white babies, African American babies are twice as likely to be born with no prenatal care, live with neither parent, or be supported by public funds. Additionally, an African American baby is three times more likely to have a teenage mother, have a single parent, have the mother die in childbirth, or to be taken home to substandard housing. Every other African American child is born into poverty compared to 20% of white children (Edelman, 1985; U.S. Census Bureau, 1992).

The future influence of such factors as maternal nutrition or malnutrition, anemia, and timing of prenatal care have been debated as to their significance in the development of any one particular African American child. The biological influence of toxic factors, such as tobacco, alcohol, drugs, lead, and HIV exposure, is debated less. The relatively high incidence of, for example, HIV-exposed infants in the African American population is expected to increase in the next decade.

It has been noted that parents of any socioeconomic background anticipate the birth of a baby with a wide range of hopes, expectations, and some worries. To a lesser degree than in past generations, African American parents include among their thoughts about the physical characteristics of their baby ideas about the physical match between baby and parents. Skin tones have not yet reached a point of neutral valence in our general society. In human thinking, a baby's variant physical appearance raises transient questions about genetic backgrounds, particularly paternity. If an older generation is available to the mother and father, potential anxieties about paternity can be addressed with generations of observations and folklore plus newer research about the appearance of newborn African American babies (Fuller & Geis, 1985). Due to the existence of hundreds of gene sites influencing skin color and genetic plurality, babies may be born showing much less melanin (and lighter skin tones) than they will have in later months. Occasionally babies exhibit more pigmentation. Along with hair texture and facial features, parents are reworking their past experiences with racism, among other issues. Coping skills learned from these experiences with racism are included in the parental knowledge bank and will be part of the child's socialization, to a greater or lesser degree, throughout childhood (Boykin & Tomas, 1985; Peters, 1985).

Infancy and Toddlerhood: In family organizations that include traditional extended or augmented membership, child care is shared. Multiple parents had been assumed to be undesirable, or even critically detrimental, by many white clinicians, until more than 50% of all U.S. mothers entered the workforce (1978) (Fuller, 1990). Child development investigators then proposed that a full generation would be needed for study before conclusions about multiple parenting could be reached. Currently, there is increasing concern that many middle-class African American families have become geographically and socially isolated from this system of traditional extended child care, thus taking early child care out of the larger African American family circle. Another increasing question for child development researchers is the influence of motor development in this period on overall psychic development. For example, African American babies walk sooner than white babies. What can be understood about this shift from horizontal to vertical travel at 7 to 10 months of age rather than later? Since walking is a developmental milestone, marking the move from infancy to toddlerhood, does this motoric gift contribute to the shorter childhood of African American children (Norris & Spurlock, 1993)?

The Child: Investment in hard work, education, and upward mobility are values that African Americans share with other striving and middle-class American families. However, African American parents struggle with the question of how to prepare their children for the encounters that they will have with overt or covert, individual or institutional discrimination and the shifting forms of that discrimination. In 1987, Phinney and Rotherdam published a volume that noted that racial differences are perceived as early as 2 years of age. Families begin early to teach the child a sense of African American history, kinship, and religious beliefs in order to support his or her clear sense of self, self-esteem, and sense of belonging to a rich heritage (Sudarkasa, 1988).

At the same time, an African American child is twice as likely to have the head of household be a high school dropout, have disciplinary actions in school, and to function below grade level. A white child is twice as likely to be seen as gifted and one-third as likely to be assessed as mentally retarded. African American families may have more ambivalence about schools and school systems and their ability to succeed in educating African American children.

For those families that have reconciled the tensions of biculturality, are financially secure, and maintain a loving, nourishing, peaceful home environment, the children tend to do well. The components of a sense of self-worth as a valued person need to be in place so that the child's encounters with stressors in the larger society are met as realities of life but are understood as inaccurate reflections of his or her own worth.

African American children are more likely to experience medical illness but to be seen in crisis rather than on a preventive basis. Incomplete immunizations, elevated lead blood levels, and tuberculosis are all more common in African American children than in White children.

Of possible congenital disorders, sickle cell anemia deserves special mention. This condition requires diligent care concerning immunization, prophylactic antibiotic therapy, monitoring anemia, relieving pain associated with episodes of sickling, and vigorously treating infections (Wright & Phillips, 1988). Sickle cell trait (heterozygous gene) is present in 8% of the African American population but is not exclusive to this population. There are other hemoglobinopathies to consider. Hemoglobin C is found at a rate of 2%, beta-thalassemia at 0.5%, and hemoglobin S-beta-thalassemia (Behrman & Vaughn, 1987).

Mental retardation may be suggested too readily when behaviors in school are disruptive, different, or puzzling, but not considered soon enough when the broader spectrum of developmental disabilities comes to be considered.

The Adolescent: The African American adolescent has potentially escalating stressors. African American male teenagers are 10 times as vulnerable as white teenagers to die as a homicide. When encounters with the law occur, the African American adolescent is twice as likely to be channeled into the justice system versus the mental health system. Alcohol and substance abuse, earlier and unprotected sexual activity, potential exposure to HIV infection, and the potential appeal and/or pressure of gangs are other risk factors that are disproportionately high. The higher death rate for African American male adolescents shifts somewhat compared to white adolescents. Vehicular accidents and suicide result in more white male teen deaths (U.S. Bureau of the Census, 1992).

Identity issues in adolescence may have another dimension for African American teens. If more privileged, they may feel guilty. If they are able to continue with their education while friends from grade school are dropping out, there may be feelings of loss, grief, and confusion (Rankin, 1988). In recent years, a return of increased racism on some college campuses has been noted. For those adolescents who have not been prepared for the fact that their worth may be judged by their skin color, first encounters with such hate have been a disorganizing experience. The shattering of the illusion of equality can lead to greater demands on campus student mental health services.

Adulthood: The middle-class adult must negotiate career and relationship demands as well as those of upward mobility in a climate of varying and variable receptivity. There is the daily demand to assess the environment accurately and to negotiate discrimination. Adults may be socially isolated in higher education, work, or living situations in which there is little or no contact with other African Americans.

In later adulthood, medical problems seen more often in African Americans include hypertension (20 to 30% of all adults), lupus and sarcoidosis (14 times higher) (Johnson, 1988). Total life expectancy is lower for African Americans than whites (1990 births, 66 years as compared to 72.6 years). African American males have a shorter life expectancy than females. Even correcting for income, African Americans get less vigorous medical care when seen (Abraham, 1991).

COGNITIVE EFFECTS

It is helpful to view cognitive issues in a developmental framework. The biological effects of genetic disorders, inadequate nutrition, alcohol and substance exposure, infections, and exposure to toxic substances are not unique to African American children. However, they may encounter these factors more often, and the factors may take a greater toll on cognitive development. Experiences of understimulation and overstimulation need to be considered. The massive Headstart effort has brought millions of African American children to a place of equal readiness for grade school as white children. However, as primary and secondary students, the same children are likely to experience decreasing success as they move to higher grades. Formal assessment of a youngster's functioning brings up, or reemphasizes, the question of the use of culture-free or culturally relevant frames of reference. For example, in assessing cognitive development, the inclusion of styles of thought is very important but seldom done. The daily life of many African American children requires a greater investment in divergent thinking (considering shifting possibilities) rather than convergent thinking (reaching "the" answer). Similarly, teleological thinking (seeing the opposite

possibility in a situation) is necessary for the maintenance of a positive self-image in a hostile world.

Clinical Implications

In treating African American children, the clinician is required to become familiar with a cultural history including values, styles of thinking, modes of relating, forms of communication, stressors, coping strategies, and misconceptions that he or she may not have previously pursued in an organized, focused manner.

For example, if the clinician is not part of a visible ethnic group, experience with regular assaults of prejudice is limited. Similarly, he or she may not be aware of potential stereotypes in which African American children are seen as aggressive or cognitively impaired (rather than depressed), unreflective (rather than cautious), or unmotivated (rather than conflicted or following an inner schedule). Such stereotypes will influence the accuracy of assessment and treatment recommendations. Understanding is reached by a combined effort of: (1) study, such as reading scientific and culturally important literature, becoming familiar with traditions, languages, arts, music, food, religions, time, and the handling of life events; (2) discussion with knowledgeable colleagues; and (3) experience. A clinician's clearest view of similarities and differences in any individual child and family makes for a more definitive and useful clinical experience for the child and family.

Clinical Interventions

African American children and adolescents can be addressed by any of our modalities of treatment, and clinical interventions are selected on an individual basis. Individual African American children and adolescents have found family, group, activity group, cognitive, behavioral, individual supportive or psychodynamic, psychoanalytic, and psychopharmacological therapies helpful. Family therapy offers the opportunity to address a youngster's issues in the context of family stressors and coping strategies, and important community and cultural traditions. Many clinicians have found family therapy particularly useful. For other youngsters, individual, private time to process problems and reach new possible solutions is efficiently and diligently used. When the clinician perceives the general concepts of goal-directed treatment and task-oriented thinking as compatible with his or her general technique, such familiarity with values can be helpful. Psychoeducational techniques are recommended by many. The place of expectations and the potential for not having those expectations met are important in the mental life of African American children. African American children have a shorter childhood and are expected to mature sooner. They are to achieve more than their parents, assist those following them, and continue the collective struggle toward equality.

Ethnic differences between the therapist and the child need to be addressed, usually earlier rather than later. The clinician may need to use the real relationship with the child initially, in a stance closer to the supportive environment. Anger may appear quickly and with intensity, but less obvious anxiety and tenderness need to be defined with the child.

As the fields of pediatric psychopharmacology and ethnopsychopharmacology expand, it would be expected that the field of pediatric ethnopsychopharmacology will develop in the very near future (Lin, Poland, & Nakasaki, 1993).

Cultural Meanings of Psychiatric Syndromes, Psychiatry, and Psychiatric Services

PSYCHIATRIC SYNDROMES

Culture-bound syndromes or culture-related patterns are not usually reported as occurring among African Americans, but they do exist. Voodoo illnesses, hexes, or spells can be presented by families in any part of the country. These illnesses are seen as being caused by an evil, supernatural force that is invoked, or conjured, by another person. This force is combated by a root or conjure doctor, a person who is accepted in the community

as being knowledgeable about cures for such illnesses. Some parents of African American children and adolescents will present their daughter or son with a complaint of having been hexed or of being the victim of root work. A therapeutic effort that includes this belief would be more effective than one that does not.

Although sometimes seen as debatable, another syndrome is falling-out or blackout and reported as a chief complaint. These seizurelike episodes have been described as being limited to residents in southeastern states (Simons & Hughes, 1993). Clinically, it is helpful to consider a greater geographic distribution of the syndrome. The clinician needs to consider factors of migration and multigenerational transmission of beliefs, say from grandparent, to parent, to grandchild.

Although today more African American children and adolescents and their families seek treatment for diverse psychiatric difficulties earlier, still more families are most familiar with psychiatric syndromes related to crises with major mental illness. Such acute episodes often lead to precipitous hospitalization or rehospitalization of the family member with a diagnosis of schizophrenia or alcohol/substance abuse. Major mental illness has been perceived by many African American families as hopeless. Griffith and Baker (1993) review issues of misdiagnosis in African Americans. The diagnosis of schizophrenia has been used much more frequently than epidemiological findings would support. As more bipolar disorders are diagnosed and treated in the African American population, greater familiarity with these diagnoses will follow.

Depression and anxiety in African American children can be more difficult to appreciate. The field of psychiatry has moved from teaching that African Americans are too limited to become depressed (Griffth & Baker, 1993). Continuing quality improvement reviews and outcomes studies should support or refute anecdotal reports that clinicians unfamiliar with some of the complexities involved in assessing and treating African American children and adolescents may still misdiagnose depressive or anxious disorders or disruptive (particularly in large adolescent males).

Reminders of the complex interplay of internal and external factors operating in the lives of African American children and adolescents can be summarized as follows: (1) individual variation; (2) stoicism as a valued, traditional, African American coping style; (3) religious traditions in the family and the community; (4) hopelessness, with or without dangerous behavior, as a response to separations, loss, racism, upward mobility, and/or violence. Loss, grief and grieving are very familiar to African American families. Parents do attend to their child's pain but they may expect their usual resources of other family members, friends, and religious institutions to suffice in time (Norris & Spurlock, 1993).

PSYCHIATRY

Psychiatric resources are used selectively and vary with the family's overall use of physicians and psychological services. Growing numbers of African American families view psychiatry as one helpful resource to children and families in pain. Contact with psychiatrists in familiar, community settings helps families to change their views of psychiatry as alien, or as a resource of last resort for desperate, dangerous, or hopeless situations, or as a self-indulgent resource in an overly specialized field.

PSYCHIATRIC SERVICES

Views of psychiatric services may be clearer to the clinician if an organization of the African American family is kept in mind. When distressed, adults are more likely to seek out a family member, extended family member, friend, or religious leader. Since distress frequently has physical symptoms, they may go on to see their family physician. They seek out familiar, helpful individuals. If personal experience has introduced psychological experts, a counselor, social worker, or psychologist may be contacted. A psychiatrist is usually not a familiar person. Of course, some families are familiar with psychiatrists and psychiatric services. In my experience, it is more common for parents to contact known or recom-

mended individual clinicians in any one of the mental health fields. For many parents, the ability to understand the nature of an illness is crucial. The expectation is that the clinician is competent, no matter what the formal training. Similarly, institutions are assessed as reliable (or not) based on past individual and collective experience. Experience with a hospital, for example, more likely would have been with the emergency room, obstetrical service or pediatrics. If these initial experiences are positive, other specialists within the institution enjoy increased credibility. In the life of many families, child psychiatric services are used more when they are available within and/or endorsed by familiar settings that are used more often. The child and adolescent psychiatrist who becomes a familiar face in hospitals, schools, neighborhood recreation programs, and religious centers is seen as part of the community (Fuller, 1987). For this reason, collaborative and/or consultation needs may continue to increase. One question is how will these needs be met.

Diverse views exist about psychiatric services for children and adolescents. Distressed parents more readily seek out and accept services for children with serious disturbances. For children with less serious disorders, parents tend to see their own usual resources as more than adequate. A collective opinion from the extended family or friends that more professional help is necessary is a profoundly important factor for parents. A child's symptoms may allow for entry into the family's difficulties such as financial strain or marital discord; otherwise, unless finances are secure, psychiatric treatment for a child may be viewed as a luxury rather than a medically indicated need that has priority over other pressing demands of daily life. African American children and adolescents and their families are diverse, resourceful, resilient, and creative. As clinicians, it is our task to work with these strengths creatively and accurately.

REFERENCES

Abraham, L. (1991, January 7). Blacks' poorer health has many causes. *American Medical News*, 26.

Behrman, R. E., & Vaughn III, V. C. (Eds.). (1987). *Nelson textbook of peadiatrics* (13th ed.). Philadelphia: W. B. Saunders.

Bell, D. (1987). *And we are not saved: The elusive quest for racial justice*. New York: Basic Books.

Boykin, A. W., & Tomas, F. D. (1985). Black child socialization: A conceptual framework. In H. P. McAdoo & J. L. McAdoo (Eds.), *Black children: Social,* educational, and parental environments (pp. 33–52). Newbury Park, CA: Sage Publications.

Chunn II, J. C., Dunston, P. J., & Ross-Sherriff, F. (Eds.). (1983). Mental health and people of color. Washington, DC: Howard University Press.

Coner-Edwards, A. F., & Edwards H. E. (1988). The black middle class: Definitions and demographics. In A. F. Coner-Edwards & J. Spurlock (Eds.), Black families in crisis: The middle class (pp. 1–9). New York: Brunner/Mazel.

Edelman, M. W. (1985). The sea is so wide and my boat is so small; Problems facing black children today. In H. P. McAdoo & J. L. McAdoo (Eds.), Black children: Social, educational, and parental environments (pp. 72–84). Newbury Park, CA: Sage Publications.

Franklin, J. H. (1988). A historical note on black families. In H. P. McAdoo (Ed.), Black familes (2nd ed.) (pp. 23–26). Newbury Park, CA: Sage Publications.

Fry, S. (1994). The Dorling Kindersley history of the world. London: Dorling Kindersley Limited; New York: Dorling Kindersley Publishing, Inc.

Fuller, R. L. (1984, July). Mental health educational processes for minority (black) populations. In Center for Clinical Personnel Development, Division of Human Resources, National Institute of Mental Health, Minority mental health education processes: A report of a workshop. Bethesda, MD: National Institute of Mental Health (pp. 142–179).

Fuller, R. L. (1987). The impact of the therapist's pregnancy on the dynamics of the therapeutic process. Journal of the American Academy of Psychoanalysis, 15, 9–28.

Fuller, R. L. (1990). Working mothers. In J. Spurlock & C. Rabinowitz (Eds.), Women's progress: Promises and problems (pp. 91–108). New York: Plenum Publishing.

Fuller, R. L., & Geis, S. (1985). The significance of skin color of a newborn infant. American Journal of Diseases of Children, 139, 672–673.

Gaw, A. C. (Ed.) (1993). Culture, ethnicity and mental illness. Washington, DC: American Psychiatric Press.

Griffith, E. E. H., & Baker, F. M. (1993). Psychiatric care of African Americans. In A. C. Gaw (Ed.), Culture, ethnicity and mental illness (pp. 147–173). Washington, DC: American Psychiatric Press.

Harris, J. E. (1987). Africans and their history (rev. ed.) New York: Mento/New American Library/Penguin Books.

Harris, W. H., & Levey, J. S. (Eds.) (1975). The new Columbia encyclopedia. New York: Columbia University Press.

Ho, M. D. (1992). Minority children and adolescents in therapy. Newbury Park, CA: Sage Publications.

Hughes, L., Meltzer, M., & Lincoln, C. E. (1983). A pictorial history of black Americans (5th rev. ed.). New York: Crown Publishers.

Johnson, C. E. (1988). Psychological aspects of some major physical disorders: The role of physicians in treatment. In A. F. Coner-Edwards & J. Spurlock (Eds.), Black families in crisis: The middle class (pp. 163–169). New York: Brunner/Mazel.

Lin, K.-M., Poland, R. E., & Nakasaki, G. (Eds.) (1993). Psychopharmacology and psychobiology of ethnicity. Washington, DC: American Psychiatric Press.

McAdoo, H. P. (Ed.) (1988). Black families (2nd ed.). Newbury Park, CA: Sage Publications.

Norris, D. M., & Spurlock, J. (1993). Separation and loss in African American children: Clinical perspectives. In A. C. Gaw (Ed.), Culture, ethnicity and mental illness (pp. 175–188). Washington, DC: American Psychiatric Press.

Peters, M. F. (1985). Racial socialization of young black children. In H. P. McAdoo & J. L. McAdoo (Eds.), Black children: Social, educational, and parental environments (pp. 159–173). Newbury Park, CA: Sage Publications.

Phinney, J., & Rotherdam, M. (Eds.) (1987). Children's ethnic socialization: Pluralism and development. Newbury Park, CA: Sage Publications.

Rankin, F. E. (1988). Identification of responses to emotional stress. In A. F. Coner-Edwards & J. Spurlock (Eds.), Black families in crisis: The middle class (pp. 157–162). New York: Brunner/Mazel.

Simons, R. C., & Hughes, C. C. (1993). Culture-bound syndromes. In A. Gaw (Ed.), Culture, ethnicity and mental illness (pp. 75–100). Washington, DC: American Psychiatric Press.

Spurlock, J., & Booth, M. B. (1988). Stresses in parenting. In A. F. Coner-Edwards & J. Spurlock (Eds.), Black families in crisis: The middle class (pp. 79–89). New York: Brunner/Mazel.

Stone, N. (Ed.) (1989). The Times atlas of world history (3d. ed.). London: Times Books. [First published in 1978].

Sudarkasa, N. (1988). Interpreting the African heritage in Afro-American family organization. In H. P. McAdoo (Ed.), Black families (2nd ed.) (pp. 27–43). Newbury Park, CA: Sage Publications.

U.S. Bureau of the Census. (1992). Statistical abstract of the United States: 1990 (112th ed.). Washington, DC: Author.

Vargas, L. A., & Koss-Chioino, J. D. (Eds.) (1992). Working with culture: Psychotherapeutic interventions with ethnic minority children and adolescents. San Francisco, CA: Jossey-Bass.

Wilford, J. N. (1996). 2.3 million-year-old jaw extends human family tree. Rocky Mountain News [from the New York Times], November 19, p. 2A.

Wright, H. H., & Phillips, L. G. (1988). Psychosocial issues in sickle cell disease. In A. F. Coner-Edwards & J. Spurlock (Eds.), Black families in crisis: The middle class (pp. 170–187). New York: Brunner/Mazel.

Zinn, H. (1990). A people's history of the United States. New York: Harper Perennial. (Originally published 1980.)

46 / The Anglo-Saxon Child

Allen Oliver and Paul Adams

The term "WASP" is a familiar one—white Anglo-Saxon Protestant. It connotes privilege and power, and conjures images of society's elite. A WASP is one who has money, education, and control of the political system. He or she has a sense of entitlement that comes from being part of the ruling majority.

WASPs are Caucasian by race and Protestant by nature. According to the Venerable Bede, the Anglo-Saxons sprang from three Germanic peoples: the Angles, the Saxons, and the Jutes, who invaded England in the mid-fifth century A.D. (Stenton, 1967). Inexorably, they conquered the Britons, native Celts, and dominated the island until the Norman invasion under William the Conqueror. Initially pagan, by the seventh century these peoples had clothed themselves uneasily in Christianity, fitting it to their own sense of the eternal (Blair, 1977).

The American WASP of the 20th century, or the New Anglo-Saxon of the 21st, is a direct descendant of the Anglo-Saxons who invaded England late in the fifth century. Despite the intervening generations, wide geographic dispersion, and a natural adaptive process, the essence of the ancient culture remains and fills its people today. Likely it will be passed to yet another generation. However, because of transformations now taking place, this group likely will be known not as WASPs but as New Anglo-Saxons.

The Anglo-Saxon Ethos

In the first section of this chapter we outline critical elements of the persistent Anglo-Saxon ethos and how it informs the personalities and behaviors of those latter-day descendants of the early Anglo-Saxons. In the second section we suggest ways in which the therapist might engage the ethos in treatment.

FAMILISM

The foundation of the Anglo-Saxon system was "blood and kin," with family as the essential unit (Churchill, 1956, p. 67). The family of the Anglo-Saxon was unusual for its time. It represented more of a true partnership between men and women than in any other society (Fell, 1984). Within 100 years, this would be lost to the English as a whole as a result of the Norman Conquest and the rising dominance of the Latin church. However, in pre-Norman England, the family flourished, and within the hearts of the Anglo-Saxons, it managed to survive the Conquest. It must be admitted, however, that the vivid colors of this wonderful mosaic faded with time. The available evidence from Anglo-Saxon England indicates that women were then more nearly the equal companions of their husbands and brothers than at any other period (Stenton, 1957).

In Old English, the word *"mann"* was equally used for male and female (Fell, 1984). Such a one was a *gesith,* a whole person, worthy of respect and full companionship (Fell, 1984; Hodgkin, 1967; Stenton, 1957).

Mann denoted personhood. Males and females all shared in this in equal portions. From both the family sprang, and by both was it sustained. The names given to men and women denoted the division of labor required in the work of sustenance. Woman was *wifeman,* likely weaving-man, while man was *waepman,* weaponed man.

Sexual equality was taught to the children from birth (Fell, 1984). Both male and female children were nurtured and schooled by the family, and there is no evidence to suggest that child rearing fell exclusively to one or the other parent. What evidence does exist indicates that these responsibilities were shared by both mother and father.

RACISM

The Anglo-Saxon community was racist and has continued to be so throughout its history. This racism has been tempered by time and experience, but it has not been extinguished. Anglo-Saxon princes traced their lineages to Wotan, chief of the gods (Blair, 1977).

To them, the blood link was certain and true, and was not to be violated. It was the source of power and identity. Sadly, this Aryan mystique still survives. Even today, candidates of respectable political parties give voice to ancient hatreds in Anglo-Saxon terms.

From the beginning, the Anglo-Saxons were disdainful of the Britons and other inhabitants of England (Fell, 1984). Despite the fact that the Romans left cities, towns, and villages intact, the Anglo-Saxons did not make any immediate attempt to inhabit them or to adopt the Romano-British lifestyle (Blair, 1977). To them, the local inhabitants were *wealisc*—foreign and worthy only of contempt (Fell, 1984).

The racism of the Anglo-Saxon is of a particularly violent strain. "Of all the Germanic tribes, none was more fierce than the Saxons. Their very name, which spread to the whole confederacy of Northern tribes, was supposed to be derived from the use of a weapon, the *seax*, a short one-handed sword" (Churchill, 1958, p. 65). Carrying the blood of the gods and knowing no kinship but that of family and tribe, they sought to extinguish fully the Britons and any others who would contest their hegemony.

Tight family bonds, rarely broken by intimate contact with other races, were intensified by a hunger for homeland. Not enough can be made of the fact that the Anglo-Saxons were a rootless people. Despite the fact that they peopled England and dominated it, their hold on the land was tenuous. The Britons resisted them for two centuries. Then the Anglo-Saxons were required to face one challenger after another—the Danes, the Vikings, and finally the Normans. The latter finally wrested the island from them and returned them to the status of the disinherited.

Their struggle for the land elevated the racism of the Anglo-Saxons to xenophobia. So powerful was it that it imbued the whole of English society, even after the Conquest, and fed the colonialism of this insular people.

Xenophobia is the most pathological aspect of the Anglo-Saxon ethos. It springs from an ancient fear of extinction, drunk in with mother's milk and nourished in a warrior's soul. The problem has been exacerbated by a belief in private justice. Among Anglo-Saxons, when the justice system failed, the family had both a right and an obligation to seek private justice. This led to the blood feud. Likewise, it gave rise to vigilantism. It is only a short step within Anglo-Saxonism to night riders, cross burnings, and lynching.

FRIEND, COMPANION, STEWARD

As a result, the Anglo-Saxon people have no peace. They are at war without and within. That they desire peace is evidenced in some of their most cherished concepts—companion, friend, and steward.

The principle of *comitatus,* companion, meant that one had an intimate into whose hands one's life could be trusted. He would fight and die to preserve that life. At a later time, he would say "I pledge my life, my fortune, and my sacred honor."

The concept of friend is as powerful as that of companion. Originally, the word is a form of the verb *freogan,* meaning to like, to love, or to honor. An Anglo-Saxon retainer referred to his lord as his *winedrihten,* his "friend-lord" (Fell, 1984). The term also is used in relationships between husband and wife or between lovers. It is a powerful bond that transcends kinship and can have all of the intimacy of a sexual relationship. It can bind men to men, women to women, and men to women. It even can have a religious connotation.

CLASS DISTINCTIONS

Anglo-Saxon culture was and is a class-bound culture (Hodgkin, 1967; Stenton, 1957). While a certain respect is accorded to each class, the distinctions are sharply made and strongly maintained. Still, it contains a flexibility that has allowed it to persist. This flexibility rests on two pillars, freedom of the individual and nobility of service.

Society consisted of *ethling* (member of the royal family), *eorl* (earl or nobleman), and *ceorl* (ordinary freeman), but each *mann* (all men) was free and had voice within the society. The lowly *ceorl* had the freedom to associate with any lord of his choosing, and every lord had to maintain the approbation of his followers. The *folk-moot* (people's court) was the place where voices were raised on the issues facing the village. Here decisions were made, and each *mann* was free to participate. Later in New England, the *folk-moot* would be seen again in the form of a town meeting.

A person was ennobled not only by birth but also by great service. This service was invariably rendered to a victorious war-chief who in turn granted great rewards to his companions. This nobility of service carried with it a name associated with prowess. The noble who gained his status by service was a doer of great deeds, and worthy of songs and general acclaim. Such nobility exists today, although there is disagreement as to what constitutes great service. Is it academic enlightenment? Government service? Business success? Athletic prowess? Regardless, those who are so ennobled receive great rewards and great wealth (Hodgkin, 1967; Stenton, 1957).

It should be noted that among genuine Anglo-Saxon people, wealth itself is not ennobling, nor does it even signify social status. Throughout Anglo-Saxon history, many who were considered noble were of mean estate monetarily. The concept of service has been corrupted to imply that wealth is ennobling, which is not true. Ennoblement comes by birth or service, not wealth. Consequently, the Anglo-Saxon community cannot be stratified by economics to gain a true picture of social class. At best, such stratification provides only an approximation. Wealthy people may be of a lower class, while poor people may still be seen as genteel. Of the two, birth persists longer and is more resistant to changes in social standing. Consequently, it may be preferred among true Anglo-Saxons. One's place is more important than what one has. Nobility affords dignity, while wealth offers only comfort.

While the concept of nobility of service can degenerate into *noblesse oblige,* and should be employed gingerly, it also has the power to override racist tendencies and to moderate rigid class distinctions. Certainly it has often been well used by VISTA and the Peace Corps. Therapists are encouraged to consider how it might be utilized in the clinical setting to advance the emergence of mental health of the New Anglo-Saxon. An intimate involvement with one's fellows modifies one's culture and mind-set. The nature of today's American society has shattered any attempts to remain insular. Healthy engagement and thoughtful reflection among a people who generally cherish such a process can accelerate the inevitable.

Much has been written by scholars about the effects of economic stratification. It cannot be denied that the ease of life grows with wealth. However, the ethos that is currently under discussion is very resistant to the changes that can be wrought by economic forces. If economics could eradicate these cultural traits, they would have been destroyed in the centuries that immediately followed the Norman Conquest. Most of the Anglo-Saxon community was reduced to abject poverty, even servitude, not for one but for repeated generations. Still, these values were nurtured in the hearts of *ethling* and *ceorl* alike, and passed along with the memory of what had been. One of the great triumphs of the race was that they Saxonized their conquerors despite their mean estate.

At Runnymede, on June 15, 1215, the descendants of the great Norman warriors who had subdued the Anglo-Saxon knights at Hastings in 1066, compelled their king, John, to overturn the commands of the Conqueror and their own forefathers and to return to the Anglo-Saxon ways of organizing society. Wealth and power thus had yielded to the force of culture. This last is critical in understanding the "myth of the majority." The Anglo-Saxons were successful in Saxonizing their conquerors. These Anglo-Normans in their turn colonized and sought to Saxonize the world. To some extent they succeeded. Consequently, to this day all white Protestants of English or even Northern European descent are seen as Anglo-Saxons.

PROTESTANTISM

The key elements of Protestantism are: (1) individualism, (2) lay control (as opposed to clerical control), (3) emphasis on personal salvation and awareness of self, and (4) an appeal to the Bible or individual conscience as a higher authority than ecclesiastical pronouncements (Bowie & Ginger, 1965). In the more than 250 sects and denominations of Protestantism, these key items intermingle in a richly varying combination, and, once combined, they form a set of assumptions and expectations that underlies the Anglo-Saxon child's view of existence.

All Protestants are not alike. They vary on theological, regional, and class lines. They range from the zealous snake handler to the biblical fundamentalist, to the relatively dispassionate, tolerant secularist and humanist who is barely "religious" for want of a belief system. The rural Free-Will

Baptist in Georgia definitely is set apart from the New England town-dwelling Unitarian or Congregationalist. As a general rule, the Protestant sects are made up of lower-class people, while the denominations—such as Methodist or Presbyterian—include more people of middle- and working-class membership. The ecclesiastical groups, such as Anglican or Episcopalian, seldom include lower- and working-class persons (Pope, 1942).

Protestantism has always been native soil for the Anglo-Saxons. These were a pagan people who uneasily clothed themselves in Christianity and struggled hard against Romanization. It took an ecclesiastical council at Whitby to bring any kind of agreement among Anglo-Saxon Christians, and there remained a strong minority party whose agreement was but grudging, at best. With the Conquest and the strong partnership between the Normans and Rome, protest was inevitable. The church supported the Conquest and so began to lose the support of its English adherents. Just as they did politically, the Anglo-Saxons pushed against their conquerors' religious ideas and, in the end, Saxonized them.

The theological keys to the Protestantizing of England lie in the Anglo-Saxon emphasis on the freedom of the individual, personal allegiance to a warrior-king, and subscription to the rule of law. Protestantism tapped these values with the concepts of the priesthood of all believers, the individual's relationship with *Christus Victor,* and the primacy of the scriptures. Regardless of the variety of Protestant, these themes ring out clearly today.

The Christianizing of the Anglo-Saxons was truly a conversion. It seemed to come as a result of the power of both the message and the messengers. Certainly the winning of the kings and lords pressed it forward. The Protestantizing of the Anglo-Saxons was only a reaffirmation of their native values in the face of the changes that Christianity had required of them. It may be that even today Anglo-Saxons are still pagans with a thin veneer of Christianity. Certainly they affirm the earth, hunger for celebration, cherish their own personal histories, and long for the age of the heroes. While many Christians may lay claim to one or more of these elements, they long preceded Christianity, with their origins lying somewhere far beyond time out of mind.

Psychologism and privatism frequently are found among Protestants. Psychologism occurs whenever the attitude is propounded that the inner world takes precedence over the outer world of overt actions. Psychologism attends the Protestant spirit like an alter ego. Privatism, a pattern that holds one uninvolved until oneself or one's immediate world is touched or encroached upon, also lives wherever the spirit of Protestantism reigns. The earlier pagan spirit may well be antidotal to these.

THE MYTH OF THE MAJORITY

One of the great myths associated with Anglo-Saxons is that they are in the majority. They are not a majority anywhere and have not been since the Norman Conquest, except perhaps for a time in the early history of America. They controlled society not by power of numbers but by setting the rules of society. When William the Bastard defeated the Anglo-Saxons, he left the entire legal system, many of the political structures, and the basic sociocultural premises intact. It was like Brer Fox throwing Brer Rabbit back into the briar patch—the Anglo-Saxons thrived.

The American Revolution, and the time preceding it, may well have been an Anglo-Saxon renaissance, the first time they were in the majority since 1066. Certainly it was bracing for Thomas Jefferson, a direct lineal descendant of Alfred the Great. In his roles as revolutionary, legislator, governor, diplomat, president, and elder statesman, Jefferson bent all his efforts to designing the rules of the game until he and his friends accomplished the task. The sage of Monticello and his most intimate companions held the position of chief executive from its inception until 1828. By then the die was cast. The basic rules were set, and they had survived the challenges of war and insurgency. Once again the Anglo-Saxon community had created the national framework out of their cultural ethos, and they were guaranteed a powerful position within the society. However, by that time another die was cast. The slave ships had transported thousands of unwilling immigrants, and the siren call of American opportunity bade a host of other non-Saxon people to come to the United States. Once again the Anglo-Saxons found themselves in the minority.

496

While this assertion flies in the face of common wisdom, it is no less true. Those of Anglo-Saxon descent are in the minority, a fact of which they are aware, even if the rest of society is not. Having been a minority people for so long, their racial distinctiveness often has been compromised, diluting the ethos and reducing the stock. Still, they are a separate and distinct ethnic group.

Clinical Implications of the Anglo-Saxon Ethos

CHARACTERISTICS ANGLO-SAXON EMOTIONAL DISTURBANCES

Earlier psychodynamic theories postulated built-in, phylogenetically programmed conflicts and complexes. Freudians saw the Oedipus complex as instinctive and universal. Carl Jung saw collective unconscious archetypes as part and parcel of the mental life of all children throughout the human species. Only the Adlerians and the post-Freudians turned their attention to experiential and social variables, thereby paving the way for the study of psychopathological states that vary across cultures and subcultures, and are thus relative to the specific and intimate culture of the child's experience. Harry Stack Sullivan, Karen Horney, Erich Fromm, and Clara Thompson were leaders in this tendency to see child development, whether healthy or pathologic, from a social standpoint. Hence, the matter of emotional vulnerabilities within particular ethnic, religious, or racial subgroups of children is an issue that is alive only for the holder of a post-Freudian, sociopsychiatric perspective. Logically, Anglo-Saxon distinctiveness is important, but regrettably there is little clear-cut empirical work to confirm logical expectations. The field of psychohistory, as it pertains to the history of childhood, represents an important endeavor in studying white Anglo-Saxon Protestant child rearing as well as that of other cultural groups. Likewise, the older social anthropology concerned with "culture and personality studies" and the sociology of childhood, taken along with transcultural studies of familiar and exotic culture-specific syndromes, make for immense steps for-

ward in a multidisciplinary field that remains embryonic. This survey of early Anglo-Saxon cultural formation coupled with more modern manifestations makes hesitant steps in this direction.

The following discussion is necessarily selective, speculative, and truncated; for details, the reader is referred to other chapters in this volume containing descriptions of the different psychopathological syndromes, particularly of character malformations. Interestingly, Brookhiser (1991) notes six features of the archetypal Anglo-Saxon character: conscience, industry, success, civic-mindedness, use, and antisensuality. Such orienting concepts of Anglo-Saxonism focus on the individual person—values, identity, integrity, relations with others—that is, on the realm of neuroses and character problems. Table 46.1 summarizes the ways in which positively valued Anglo-Saxon traits can, by extension to rigidity or absurdity, become symptoms.

Absent more serious psychopathology, the long-range effects of the character structures of Anglo-Saxonism will include the neuroses and character problems of adult life, with the potentiality of decompensation under grave stress to a psychotic disorder. Probably the most frequent consequence of Anglo-Saxonism driven to absurdity is conventionality just short of symptom formation. As has been formulated by Jung, Otto Rank, Fromm, and others, it is the problem of an unfulfilled, "unlived life." In some ways, it is an outcome that might be less happy than neurosis, and certainly less interesting. The Protestant enthronement of Logos and devaluation of Eros may be useful in mass bureaucratic society, but they make for an imbalance, a lack of wholeness, that, since it is unconscious, continues unrecognized. The Jungians—and Jung came out of a Protestant heritage—have stressed the "shadow" that is unconscious, unaccepted, and projected, filled with insufficiently developed functions (thinking, feeling, sensation, intuition) and subliminal perceptions. The dark Anglo-Saxon shadow of candor is sanctimoniousness; of compassion, inverted self-pity; of humility, inferiority; of loyalty, obstinacy; of considerateness, hypocrisy; and of generosity, a grand mixture of inimitable fecklessness with corrupt calculation. Anglo-Saxon living is well-endowed with shadow, compensations, and reaction formations.

497

TABLE 46.1

Anglo-Saxon "Virtues" and Their Related "Symptoms" at Various Ages

Stage	Virtue Propounded	Symptom Picture
Oral	Do not spoil child	Neglect, inadequate "mothering"
Oral	Trust in others	Overdependence
Anal	Self-control	Overinhibition, phlegm, fear and shame
Anal	Independence	Compulsion, scruple, responsibility, overwork, accountability, officiousness
Anal	Let conscience guide	Self-righteousness, guilt, rigidity
Anal, oedipal	Be own person	Oppositionalism
Oedipal	Self-starting energy	Narcissism of the "self-made"
Latency	Self-awareness	Introversive isolation, quiet, self-criticism
Latency	Self-assertion	Tension discharge disorder
Latency	Fair play	Sentimentalism
Latency	Hard work	Acute anxiety, compulsion, judgmentalism, self-depreciation
Preadolescence, adolescence	Group belonging	Pseudomutuality, overconformism
Preadolescence, adolescence	Self-reliance	Mistrustfulness
Adolescence	Identity	Ethnocentrism, intolerance
Adolescence	Success	Triumphalism, materialism, destructiveness
Adolescence	Civic-mindedness	Social control, individual neglect, relentless conformity

COPING DEVICES AMONG ANGLO-SAXON CHILDREN

Anglo-Saxon culture does provide children with certain kinds of defenses, notably reaction formations and a sublimating love of hard work. The Protestant work ethic has some residual utility for coping in the contemporary world. From a favorable perspective, it can be said to enhance life, but from an unfavorable or detracting perspective, it must be said to induce a rather grim, serious outlook. Being white, Anglo-Saxon, and Protestant is not always an agonizing ordeal for the Anglo-Saxon children. Some of their attributes may be considered as special competencies: a hustling industriousness, a feeling of stewardship, a strong sense of self (in identity, worth, control, assurance, study, help, enlargement or improvement, and even in transcendence), a willingness to take the rap if failure occurs after "giving it an old school try," a willingness to experiment, to make and to take changes, to take risks. The learning of Anglo-Saxon children is frequently unhampered and joyous as a result of the Anglo-Saxon ethos already outlined (although it may be a recurrent anguish of inferiority).

In general, the Anglo-Saxon image has had good press agents who have, in fact, often oversold the product behind the image. Likewise, for Anglo-Saxons to prosper in a pluralistic society, there need be no "special arrangements" or "affirmative action"—unless these cultural traits come to be considered special: political democracy, feminism, guarantees of individual rights and liberties, trial by one's peers, respect for "different drummers," and a nation concerned for human welfare, even for the welfare of young children.

DEVELOPMENTAL ISSUES AND CORRESPONDING THERAPEUTIC APPROACHES

Anglo-Saxon values, like all other values, are implanted by precept and example as early as the neonatal maintenance and feeding stage. In their most vital aspect, they are learned implicitly and assumptively, not overtly and verbally. Yet mothers often verbalize sturdy capitalist-Protestant virtues such as "waste not, want not" while bottle-feeding their newborn babies. A special mystique surrounds Anglo-Saxon mothering and the bond between infant and mother. It may have arisen following the Norman Conquest, where the nursery was the last bastion of cultural or ethnic defense. Regardless, the bond is reinforced further today by the fact that among affluent Anglo-Saxons, a familial awareness spanning many generations is present. In this regard the thinking of Murray Bowen is a helpful frame. In fact, it may be said that much of the foregoing is based on Bowen's concept of multigenerational transmission (Bowen, 1966). While Bowen has a tendency to devalue cultural or environmental characteristics as a determinative for the individual, we believe that the position of the Anglo-Saxon people on the human family tree is distinctive enough to warrant it as being seen as a single, extended family. Therefore, the Anglo-Saxon child is part of a continuous natural process in which the generations press against one another so intimately that they are one and the transactions of then and now are quite similar.

The Anglo-Saxon infant learns, if circumstances are ideal-typical, that he or she is immersed in a sea of caring, loving interdependence. Then, if not held in bondage to symbiotic infantile patterns, the child grows with the imprint of a model of altruistic optimism, savoring all the face-to-face relationships to be experienced throughout life. Such a child has a zesty self-confidence and feeling of self-worth that can be observed readily in the toddler, nursery school, and elementary school phases. He or she feels like a good egg, hatched and grown according to a good plan. If the ideal infantile-maternal relationship does not occur, as may happen in Anglo-Saxon households of both the lower- and upper-middle classes, the child will be more defensive, less secure, and less trusting of others. If full dependence during infancy is not relished and acknowledged, a fear of domination will shadow the growing child's existence. Or, if the Anglo-Saxon child does not progress beyond infancy, he or she will retain a mother-fixated immaturity that Southern writers have described often and clearly.

The preceding discussion covers the twin issues of fusion and differentiation (Bowen, 1966). The healthy Anglo-Saxon progresses well through the process of differentiation while the troubled child becomes fused with its source. The modern Anglo-Saxon child who is moving forward in the process of differentiation knows him- or herself to be a person of worth with rights and responsibilities, a message likely given to the child by both parents. He or she usually is grounded in the past and well oriented toward the future. Male and female have a strong sense of entitlement and a firm belief in their potential to accomplish. They are quick to mark out their turf and will defend it with a vengeance. These children have an expectation of adequate material resources and often are able to develop a clear plan for acquiring and sustaining those resources. This is true regardless of milieu. The Yuppie girl of the urban Northeast and the farm boy of rural Kentucky both resonate with the same favorable sense of self.

The therapist who will make inroads in treating the troubled Anglo-Saxon child will of necessity be familiar with family therapy. The child can neither be treated nor understood apart from the transgenerational extended family. In fact, the child cannot even be approached without the full approbation of the current senior representatives of that family, particularly if child and family are highly fused. The therapist must be seen to understand the family system and be able to join with it. Structural change will have to come from within, and the therapist must be seen as a companion and friend in the process. He or she must be an accomplished time traveler, able to reach backward and forward in the history of the family in order to grasp and shape the dynamics of both the individual and the family.

Models of family therapy are systems-based. They recognize the interconnectedness of all the players: the individual, other family members, and the social milieu. A family therapy perspective views clinical problems as derivatives of interpersonal processes (Feldman, 1992). In emphasizing family therapy, we are advocating the blending of both interpersonal and intrapsychic perspectives in working with the Anglo-Saxon child. This is consistent with the earliest psychiatric roots of the family therapy movement (Ackerman, 1938, 1958; Adler, 1917; Bowen, 1976; Bowlby, 1949; Flugel, 1921; Freud, 1912; Midelfort, 1957; Moreno, 1940, 1952; Wynne, 1961). We believe that successful treatment of the Anglo-Saxon child will require both interpersonal and intrapsychic changes. The blending of family therapy and personal psychotherapy offers the best opportunity to accomplish these changes. This is because they are both complementary and synergistic (Feldman, 1992).

Feldman (1992) offers a model for the blending of family therapy and individual psychotherapy, the Integrative Multilevel Model. In its development, Feldman has drawn from analytic, cognitive, behavioral, and family systems theory.

We have asserted that the most common pathologies of the Anglo-Saxon structure are extreme conventionality, neuroses, and character problems. Accompanying these, at the Axis I level, are depression and anxiety, expressed either singly or in tandem. These relate to the process of cognition. Indeed, a good case can be made that, for the Anglo-Saxon child, they arise in that process. Regardless, it has been our clinical experience that the Anglo-Saxon child responds well to cognitive-behavioral therapy.

The cognitive-behavioral approach rests on the belief that pathology arises out of a dysfunctional cognitive process in which there exist either deficiencies or distortions. Consequently, interventions are developed that attend especially to the patient's process of cognition, with an eye to restoring it to right functioning (Beck, 1976; DiGiuseppe & Bernard, 1983; Kendall, 1977, 1991; Spivack & Shure, 1982). Of late, this work also has included the place of the family in both functional and dysfunctional aspects of the cognitive process (Stark, Rouse, & Livingston, 1991), an effort that we applaud.

Central to cognitive-behavioral treatment is the assumption that the patient can and will be an active participant in the therapeutic process (Stark, Rouse, & Livingston, 1991). A review of the virtues in Table 46.1 will illustrate why we believe that the Anglo-Saxon child is primed for cognitive-behavioral work. These virtues all support a self-actualized, rational, problem-solving approach to the resolution of difficulties which have effective cognition at their base. However, at the same time, these virtues, pushed to the extreme, will make remediation quite difficult because massive cognitive distortions will arise. This situation likely will be exacerbated still further because of the interlocking nature of the virtues

and their warped counterparts. Still, if one is familiar with the virtues, their formation, and their basic message, then what has been done can be undone by therapeutic interventions that drive the patient away from the extreme edge back along the same continuum to a safer range of expression.

We maintain that those who will work with the New Anglo-Saxon will see a renaissance of the equality of male and female. Denigration of the female was not native to the Saxon culture. It too came with the Conquest. Those who have maintained closest connections with the ancient ethos show marked differences from the common culture, which has kept women as second-class citizens. Farm families and highly sophisticated urban families give ample illustration. Therapy that aids in unleashing this ancient practice will move these people toward health.

Here the therapist can gain insight from the work currently being pursued by feminist therapists (Gilbert, 1980; Greenspan, 1983; Marecek & Hare-Mustin, 1987; Rawlings & Carter, 1977; Sturdivant, 1980; Worell & Remer, 1992). Feminist therapists hold that the clients' social, political, economic, and cultural environments play in the problems that they are experiencing (Worell & Remer, 1992). This is certainly consistent with our assertions regarding the Anglo-Saxon ethos. They would further declare that many sexist approaches are "androcentric," that is, based on male norms (Worell & Remer, 1992). Cognitive-behavioral therapy would be one such approach and we would agree. This is why we applaud the latest attempts to blend family therapy with cognitive-behavioral treatment. It corrects this androcentrism by adding a much-needed relational element. We believe that because of the accretions from cultures other than Anglo-Saxon ones, initially an empowerment model of feminist therapy is needed (Worell & Remer, 1992). However, when that basic equality inherent in the Anglo-Saxon ethos is fully freed, then a more androgynist approach would become more appropriate. The empowerment model revolves around three foci—"the Personal Is Political," "Egalitarian Relationships," and "Valuing the Female Perspective" (Worell & Remer, 1992). The first of these foci seeks to separate the external from the internal, to reframe pathology in light of this separation, and to initiate a program of social as well as personal change. The second seeks to empower the client, to balance power in relationship, and to affirm the individual woman. The last seeks to throw off the androcentric definitions of womanhood and lead women to redefine themselves, and to hold for the value of these definitions and their associated characteristics with the society at large.

The anal and phallic oedipal phases create expected crises for Anglo-Saxon children. The familism of the Anglo-Saxon household has some drawbacks, for familial and tribal pride frequently have been the basis of arrogance and provincialism, as manifested early (for example) in schoolchildren who derogate others who lack strong family roots. In preadolescence, the Anglo-Saxon most frequently finds an Anglo-Saxon from a similar family for a beloved chum, and development thus proceeds in a salutary way, validating worth and forestalling loneliness. Only in adolescence may Anglo-Saxon youths undertake a first rebellious reinspection of the family pride package on which they were enculturated, and this undertaking gives pungency to the search for an identity of their own.

Anglo-Saxon parents show ambivalence about their children's freedom. On the one hand, they know that it is not what they enforce on the children, but only what the children discover directly and experientially, that will serve to develop a conscience of their own. Hence the parents are torn between their wish to have individuality unfold and, at the same time, their wish to civilize by extracting obedience. The children are caught in this ambivalence, concluding that they must be both conformist and reformer, or even if radical, "respectable." The children must be dutiful stewards, industrious and rather joyless, learning to stand alone. One Eastern Kentucky coal miner told his children, "You must learn to rise above the babble of the rabble," and then administered the lessons with a strong hand.

The children learn the subtleties of when and where and in what measure they can assert themselves. Anglo-Saxon children are often pleasantly surprised that they are "allowed" considerable autonomy by parents and siblings and encouraged to experiment and take risks. At the same time, at latency the children may become so compulsively duty-bound that naturalness and spontaneity suffer. The Anglo-Saxon and Protestant threads interweave to strengthen the children's growing sense of autonomy and accountability. On the Protestant side, the universal priesthood of believers is actualized, and all persons stand accountable for their own decisions, commitments, and choices, without intermediary or interceder. The immediate encounter with "the indwelling Christ" is deeply felt and personal. Private prayer and devotional exercises are stressed. Closely akin to these religious values are political values concerning liberty for the person, equality for any and all beliefs to be expressed, and a sense of civic responsibility and duty. Children are to make their own decisions if that coincides often enough with the godliness of adults and their life of stewardship.

The latency period is enshrined in Protestantism. If Protestants hold life seriously, and the purpose of Christian living is to set one's conscience aright, then it is an easy transition to the view that wasting time is sinful and earning money is a God-given warrant of virtue. Albert Schweitzer learned as a Protestant child that carefree, lucky people must feel called to diminish the pain of others. Nearly any kind of work or duty comes to be thought better of than fun and play, although one is counseled to enjoy what one does. From puritanism to capitalism is not a giant step, as Max Weber explained and Herbert Hoover exemplified. By adulthood, the Anglo-Saxon has been enculturated into an industriousness and seriousness that make for a good citizen and parent, if "times are good." But if racism, economic collapse, and civil disorder characterize the times, the obverse side, the shadow of all Anglo-Saxon virtues, comes to the fore with bigotry, authoritarianism, exploitation, and violence—the dark side of whiteness, Protestantism, and Anglo-Saxon culture. Violence has a very human face, and the Anglo-Saxon face is very human.

Once again, the thinking of Murray Bowen (1966) may be helpful in constructing interventions to work with the Anglo-Saxon child as he or she traverses the way through these very powerful cultural or family messages toward independence. Coupled with these are the thoughts being propounded by feminist therapists. Work on the family of origin, controlled confrontation, individuating, power analysis, assertiveness training, detriangulating, consciousness raising, reframing and relabeling, and therapy demystification may all prove helpful.

The Anglo-Saxon American of today is, like early forebears, essentially xenophobic and so capable of standing in the face of overwhelming evidence and power, and hurling a multiplicity of racial epithets at supposed enemies. Such a one may even challenge the therapist's ability to understand and help. As painful or problematic as it is to confess, ethnic heritage can be a major block in establishing a therapeutic rapport with an Anglo-Saxon client and should be addressed as a therapeutic issue early in treatment.

The therapist who can harness the ancient concepts of companion and friend and drive them beyond the bounds of race can make great headway against the xenophobia of the Anglo-Saxon. Although therapists should not have close relationships with their clients, they must be able to convey to Anglo-Saxon patients that they possess what might be called "the spirit of a friend." To these therapists the work of treatment is more than simply a job and patients are more than cases. To accomplish this task therapists must possess a firmly grounded professional identity that allows them to convey a sense of intimacy while maintaining proper boundaries.

In addition to the ancient cultural concepts of companion and friend, another Protestant belief can be of service in the treatment-resistance of the xenophobic Anglo-Saxon child: the concept of stewardship. Within Protestant theology is the often-repeated belief that no human has claim to title to the land. It is all to be held in stewardship. Such stewardship is to be gentle and protective, and the land to be surrendered on demand to God, to whom it belongs. Stewards do not need a homeland. Home is where they hang their hat. The general societal climate is right to give power to this concept and make it valuable in treatment.

FAMILIAL REACTIONS TO ANGLO-SAXONISM

Anglo-Saxon children derive support from the very fact that people of their cultural type are hegemonic, although in a community where differences are allowed, if not always praised. The children often believe that their family does not have the shame or defensiveness that are so often elicited from minorities in majority-ruled democratic societies. However, the truth is that the family has that deep anxiety that belongs to a minority holding tenuous control over the majority. As pluralism comes to supplant the majority-minority system, Anglo-Saxonism, because of its

premiums on individual diversity and the primacy of the individual's conscience, may be expected to give New Anglo-Saxon families a sense of merit without imparting the arrogance historically associated with Anglo-Saxon dominance of national life.

When treating Anglo-Saxon youths, insightful therapists will understand the linkages between the youths' basic xenophobia, their certain knowledge of minority status, and the belief that the system that they have constructed is in jeopardy. Theirs is a powerful *angst* that may need to be addressed if treatment is to be wholly successful. The youths may not be able to articulate the underlying causes but will feel the *angst* as deeply as will their parents. Parallels can be seen in the white communities of Zimbabwe or South Africa. What the New Anglo-Saxons will come to discover, but now simply lack the needed insight, is that the power of their ideas about human organization are such that they will survive without manipulation and that they as a people will prosper within a pluralistic society. They have always done so (Brookhiser, 1990).

CULTURAL REACTIONS TO ANGLO-SAXONISM

A prevailing form of radical or liberal chic during the past three decades has tended to ridicule Anglo-Saxon attributes, even those of children, while extolling the features of almost all other ethnic groups. That situation is in stark contrast to an earlier worshipful definition of "American" in a strictly Anglo-Saxon model. The ideology of Americanization and the melting pot was one that stacked the cards in favor of Anglo-Saxon ways. Culture change already has occurred in the power, status, and advantage formerly associated in the United States with whiteness, Anglo-Saxonism, and Protestantism. It would seem likely that these changes will advance apace as various other ethnic groups intensify their rhetoric and their effective instrumentalities for obtaining greater equality in the United States. The Anglo-Saxon establishment is dying, but its successor will, in all probability, retain certain of the external and some of the inner features of the Anglo-Saxon way of life, which stamped the ethos of American life throughout most of the first bicentennium of the nation's existence. Within this milieu the New Anglo-Saxon will emerge.

REFERENCES

Ackerman, N. W. (1938). The unity of the family. *Archives of Pediatrics, 55,* 51–62.

Ackerman, N. W. (1958). *The psychodynamics of family life.* New York: Basic Books.

Ackerman, N. W., Beatmon, F. L., & Sherman, S. N. (Eds.). *Exploring the base of family therapy.* New York: Family Service Association of America.

Alder, A. (1917). *The neurotic constitution.* Trans. Bernard Blueck & John E. Lund. New York: Moffatt, Yard, & Co.

Albers, R. H. (1995). *Shame: A faith perspective.* Binghamton, NY: Haworth Press.

Barker, P. (1996). *Psychotherapeutic metaphors: A guide to theory and practice.* New York: Brunner/Mazel.

Beck, A. T. (1976). *Cognitive therapy and the emotional disorders.* New York: International Universities Press.

Beck, J. S. (1995). *Cognitive therapy: Basics and beyond.* New York: Guilford Press.

Blair, P. H. (1977). *An introduction to Anglo-Saxon England.* Cambridge: Cambridge University Press.

Bowen, M. (1966). The use of family theory in clinical practice. *Comprehensive Psychiatry, 7,* 345–374.

Bowen, M. (1976). Family therapy and family group therapy. In D. H. L. Olson (Ed.), *Treating relationships.* Lake Mills, IA: Graphic Press.

Bowen, M. (1978). *Family therapy in clinical practice.* New York: Jason Aronson.

Bowie, W. R., & Giniger, K. S. (Eds.). (1965). *What is Protestantism?* New York: Franklin Watts.

Bowlby, J. (1949). The study and reduction of group tension in the family. *Human Relations, 2,* 123–128.

Branden, N. (1996). *Taking responsibility: Self-reliance and the accountable life.* New York: Simon & Schuster.

Brookhiser, R. (1991). *The way of the WASP.* New York: Free Press.

Chazan, S. (1995). *The simultaneous treatment of parent and child.* New York: Basic Books.

Churchill, W. (1956). *History of the English-speaking peoples: The birth of Britain.* New York: Dodd, Mead, & Company.

Davidson, J. K., & Moore, N. B. (1996). *Marriage and family: Change and Continuity.* Needham Heights, MA: Allyn & Bacon.

DiGiuseppe, R., & Bernard, M. E. (1983). Principles of assessment and methods of treatment with children: Special consideration. In. A. Ellis & M. E. Bernard (Eds.), *Relational emotive approaches to the problems of childhood* (pp. 45–88). New York: Plenum Press.

Ellis, A. (1971). *Growth through reason.* Hollywood, CA: Wiltshire Books.

Feldman, L. (1992). *Integrating individual and family therapy.* New York: Brunner/Mazel.

Fell, C. (1984). *Women in Anglo-Saxon England.* Bloomington: Indiana University Press.

Flugel, J. C. (1921). *The psycho-analytic study of the family.* London: Hogarth Press.

Freud, S. (1958). Recommendations for physicians on the psychoanalytic model of treatment. In J. Strachey (Ed. and trans.), *The standard edition of the complete psychological works of Sigmund Freud.* (Vol. 12, pp. 109–120). London, England: Hogarth Press. (Original work published in 1912).

Gilbert, L. A. (1980). Feminist therapy. In A. M. Brodsky & R. T. Hare-Mustin (Eds.), *Women and psychotherapy* (pp. 245–265). New York: Guilford Press.

Goldenberg, I., & Goldenberg, H. (1996). *Family therapy: An overview* (4th ed.). Pacific Grove, CA: Brooks/Cole.

Greenspan, M. (1983). *A new approach to women and therapy.* New York: McGraw-Hill.

Gustafson, J. P. (1995). *Brief versus long psychotherapy: When, why, and how.* Northvale, NJ: Jason Aronson.

Harkness, S., & Super, C. M. (Eds.) (1996). *Parents' cultural belief systems: Their origins, expressions, and consequences.* New York: Guilford Press.

Hodgkin, R. H. (1967). *A history of the Anglo-Saxons* (3rd ed., Vol. 1). London: Oxford University Press.

Jacobson, N. S., & Gurman, A. S. (eds.) (1995). *Clinical handbook of couple therapy.* New York: Guilford Press.

Kendall, P. C. (1977). On the efficacious use of verbal self-instructional procedures with children. *Cognitive Therapy and Research, 1,* 331–341.

Kendall, P. C. (1991). *Child and adolescent therapy.* New York: Guilford Press.

Kimball, M. M. (1995). *Feminist visions of gender similarities & differences.* Binghamton, NY: Harrington Park.

Kopp, R. R. (1995). *Metaphor therapy: Using client-generated metaphors in psychotherapy.* New York: Brunner/Mazel.

Madanes, C., & Haley, J. (1977). Dimensions of family therapy. *Journal of Nervous and Mental Diseases, 165,* 88–98.

Marecek, J., & Hare-Mustin, R. T. (1987). *Feminism and therapy: Can this relationship be saved?* Unpublished manuscript.

Midelfort, C. F. (1957). *The family in psychotherapy.* New York: McGraw-Hill.

Moreno, J. L. (1940). Psychodramatic treatment of marriage problems. *Sociometry, 3,* 1.

Moreno, J. L. (1952). Psychodrama of a family conflict. *Group Psychotherapy, 5,* 20–37.

Nichols, W. C. (1996). *Treating people in families: An integrative framework.* New York: Guilford Press.

Phares, V. (1995). *Fathers and developmental psychopathology.* New York: John Wiley & Sons.

Pope, L. (1942). *Millhands and preachers.* New Haven, CT: Yale University Press.

Rawlings, E. I., & Carter, D. K. (1977). *Psychotherapy for women: Treatment toward equality.* Springfield, IL: Charles C. Thomas.

Spivack, G., & Shore, M. B. (1982). The cognition of social adjustment: Interpersonal problem-solving thinking. In B. B. Lahay & A. E. Kaydin (Eds.),

Advances in clinical child psychology (Vol. 5, pp. 323–372). New York: Plenum Press.

Stark, K. N., Rouse, L. W., & Livingston, R. (1991). Treatment of depression during childhood and adolescence: Cognitive behavioral procedures for the individual and family. In P. C. Kendall (Ed.), *Child and adolescent therapy* (pp. 165–206). New York: Guilford Press.

Stenton, D. M. (1957). *The English woman in history*. London: Oxford University Press.

Stenton, F. (1967). *Anglo-Saxon England* (2nd ed.). London: Oxford University Press.

Sturdivant, S. (1980). *Therapy with women: A feminist philosophy of treatment*. New York: Springer.

Worell, J., & Remer, P. (1992). *Feminist perspectives in therapy: An empowerment model for women*. Chichester, England: John Wiley & Sons.

Wynne, L. (1961). The study of intrafamilial alignments and splits in exploratory family therapy. In N. W. Ackerman, F. L. Beatmon, & S. N. Sherman (Eds.), *Exploring the base for family therapy*. New York: Family Service Association of America.

47 / Foreign Culture, Geographic Mobility, and Children's Mental Health

Peter S. Jensen and Jon A. Shaw

As modern society has become more mobile and international, increasing concerns have been raised about the effects of living in different cultures on children and adolescents. Many of these reports, predominantly anecdotal, have suggested that living in different cultures is associated with psychiatric disorders and/or psychosocial dysfunction in children and adolescents. David and Elkind (1966) described the intense stresses and pressures impacting upon U.S. families living abroad, including the effects of foreign schools systems on children, the relative resistance of foreign schools to parental input, and the loss of supportive friends and kinship networks. Werkman (1972) detailed a variety of difficulties in rearing children overseas, including exposure to foreign caregivers, unusual cultural practices, and even the relative loss of association with the child's own mother and father (who may be caught up in work-related issues or other circumstances related to their adaptation to the new environment). Other authors have sounded similar concerns (Bower, 1967) and have suggested that such problems are particularly pronounced for children and adolescents of mili-

tary and diplomatic personnel (Aisenstein, 1988). Interestingly, such children may exhibit additional difficulties in readjusting to their own culture upon the return home later.

Similar to these reports and concerns about the effects of transcultural experiences on children and adolescents, other clinicians and researchers have described an association between children's emotional problems and any form of geographic mobility (Puskar & Dvorsak, 1991; Stubblefield, 1955).

Clinical Relevance

The effects of transcultural adaptation and geographic mobility are relevant to clinicians for several reasons. Times of transition, geographic mobility, and transcultural adjustment form a natural demarcation in time and space when, by virtue of the extensive relocation, old habits and patterns of adaptation are interrupted and new ones are established. Such stressful transitions may be destabilizing for many children, adolescents, and their families, and can set in motion a time of emotional upheaval or behavioral difficulties. Quite possibly, the common resistance to seeking out mental health care may be somewhat lessened

The opinions and assertions contained in this chapter are the private views of the authors and are not to be construed as official or as reflecting the views of the Department of Health and Human Services, the National Institute of Mental Health, or the University of Miami School of Medicine.

during such periods, not just by virtue of increased emotional and behavioral difficulties in a child but as a result of the effects of the broader transition on the values and attitudes of parents as well as the general loss of other supportive network structures.

Accordingly, the clinician must carefully consider a number of possibilities concerning the relationship among the child's transcultural adaptation, geographic mobility, and the reasons for referral at this point in time. Is the exposure to new and different life experiences somehow directly related to the child's current difficulties, and hence the clinical referral, or is the association by chance alone? Or is a third factor, set in motion by the changes of the relocation and the transcultural adaptation, responsible for the child's clinical presentation, while the move and foreign cultural experience in and of itself is merely epiphenomenal? For example, Hendershott (1989) examined the relationships among self-concept, self-esteem, depression, and geographic mobility, and found that mobility was unrelated to adolescent self-esteem. However, recent geographic mobility in the absence of support from family and friends was associated with increased depression and lower self-esteem. Thus, the effects of the social network may be a critical mediating factor in determining the nature and effects of geographic mobility or foreign culture exposure on children and adolescents. In this vein, based on data from extensive school observations, home interviews, and self-reports, Vernberg (1990) noted that mobile adolescents more commonly experienced "rejection experiences"; these effects were particularly pronounced for boys compared to girls.

These findings suggest that geographic mobility and foreign cultural adaptation may not be harmful in and of itself, although it may be associated with temporary increases in emotional and behavioral problems in the presence of other stressful conditions (e.g., loss or absence of social supports, rejection experiences, etc.). Similarly, other evidence suggests few effects of transcultural experiences and geographic mobility on the development of mental disorders in children and adolescents. Pedersen and Sullivan (1964) compared 27 children referred to a psychiatric clinic with 30 children referred to a pediatric clinic, in terms of the number of moves experienced by the child and family as well as family attitudes toward

the military. Interestingly, the actual number of moves did not differ between the two groups, although the psychiatric clinic children and their parents had significantly more negative attitudes and perceptions about mobility. Similarly, McKain (1973) studied 80 military families' perceptions of personal, family, and marital problems and found significant correlation between mothers' sense of alienation from the military and their levels of personal, family, and marital problems. Although the problems were unrelated to recency and frequency of moves, highly alienated wives attributed their problems more frequently to mobility. Such data indicate that parental, child, and family attributions about mobility comprise important self-explanatory constructs and may shape further family perceptions of the relationships among mobility, foreign culture adaptation, and psychological adjustment, even in the absence of a direct causal relationship.

Thus, the clinician must carefully tease out the actual etiologic role of foreign culture adaptation, life changes, and mobility on the child's psychosocial and behavioral difficulties from the larger array of other potentially confounding influences. These influences may include family perceptions and attributions about the move, the potential likelihood of self-referral for problems unrelated and preexisting to the actual transition, and the association between the child's difficulties and a third co-occurring factor that mediates the relationship between child adjustment and foreign cultural experiences (e.g., loss of previously available time or support from parents, rejection experiences at school, etc.).

Although the move or transcultural life experience may have set in motion a number of emotional conflicts and dilemmas, the clinician's awareness of the relationship between social and environmental factors and the child's adaptation is critical for the development of an adequate treatment plan. It may be important that the clinician consider treatment interventions that will assist the child form new friendships and social supports during the time of the child's transition and adjustment. Reestablishment of familiar family contacts and ties may be appropriate if these have been disrupted. Examination of potentially extraneous, new, and stressful experiences that have occurred since the move may be appropriate (e.g., exposure to foreign caregivers with quite different or even problematic caregiving practices). If the child's difficulties center predominantly around language concerns in a foreign school, consideration of alternative school experiences or tutoring may be appropriate. The loss of an important central attachment figure from the child's family of origin (e.g., a grandparent) and the child's resulting sense of loss and grief for this figure may suggest the need for and benefit of that person visiting the child in the new environment or increased letter and phone contacts with the missed person.

In developing a treatment plan, the clinician also should consider that the highly mobile child or one living in a foreign culture may have somewhat different treatment needs as a result of past exposure to frequent moves. For example, Shaw (1982) noted that children with a history of high geographic mobility saw themselves as somewhat more changeable, boring, and distant than adolescents with less frequent moves. Thus, even if a move is unrelated in time and space to the child's clinical presentation and current problems, the child with frequent or significant moves or foreign cultural experiences may require somewhat different treatment approaches, to the extent that personality formation may have been shaped by past mobility and foreign life experiences.

Etiologic Role

It should be clear that transcultural experiences and geographic mobility may impact children quite differently from their parents. Thus, for some families, an overseas move may mean promotion and new job activities, but for the child, it may mean the loss of friends, school or social contacts in an established peer group, as well as the cessation of cherished objectives or life goals. Certainly these attributions and expectations may powerfully shape the child's and family's adaptation to foreign cultures. A number of studies of military families living overseas have shed an important light on these phenomenon. Garrett and colleagues (1978) noted that military wives overseas reported higher levels of boredom and increased use of alcohol since deployment overseas. Much of these changes were thought to be related

to increasing difficulties and changes in the marital relationship and loss of employment and other opportunities for the spouses. Similarly, Manning and DeRouin (1981) studied overseas spouses and determined that employed spouses of military personnel had higher levels of adaptation and happier marriages than nonemployed spouses. Presumably such factors as marital happiness and parental satisfaction-dissatisfaction may be related to child adjustment. Of course, it is not clear that in every case what is good for the parent is also good for the child.

CULTURAL SIMILARITY

Quite possibly, adaptation to foreign life and culture is made easier by the degree of similarity between the original home environment and the new environment to which the family moves. For example, the stresses and adaptation needs may be relatively modest for many U.S. military families where a "Little America" has been created abroad. Military communities overseas are generally indistinguishable from military posts on the U.S. mainland. In such overseas settings, abundant social activities, community sports, and available similar persons with similar values and backgrounds are the rule rather than the exception. Further data supporting this conclusion have been provided by Shaw and Pangman (1975), who reported that children living overseas who were referred to a military child guidance clinic actually had fewer moves than a control group of schoolchildren. Their findings indicated little consistent or meaningful relationships between children's emotional or behavioral problems and geographic mobility. They concluded that, given the similar values and cultures to which the child moves within the military setting, overseas moves and adaptation for military children are probably not intrinsically pathogenic.

The potential role that cultural similarity plays in aiding child and adolescent foreign cultural adaptation likely applies to nonmilitary settings, as well: Sam and Eide (1991) surveyed 310 foreign students from various countries enrolled at a university in Norway and found that students from non-Western nations had the greatest difficulties and levels of psychiatric symptoms, while Americans and other Scandinavians reported fewest difficulties. Most available data are consistent with the hypothesis that the degree of cultural similarity between the home and foreign countries enables a more ready adaptation to the potential "culture shock" entailed in cultural adaptation.

A more complete understanding of the relationship among geographic mobility, exposure to foreign environments, and psychosocial adjustment is provided through interactional models of human development. Shaw and Pangman (1975) suggest that crisis theory is more consistent with actual data than a simple cause-effect model. A geographic move or a period of foreign cultural life may provide a pivotal growth experience for some children (Tooley, 1970), while other children who do not have adequate coping resources to master the challenge may fall victim to a sequence of increasing difficulties. Thus, the fit among personality, the individual repertoire of adaptive capacity, and life experience as well as the environmental demands must be carefully considered (Stokols & Shumaker, 1982). In a related vein, the extent to which the family has some control over the move and its timing may be critical factor in adaptation (Marsh, 1976).

POSITIVE EFFECTS OF FOREIGN CULTURAL
EXPOSURE AND MOBILITY

In contrast to the concerns that geographic moves and overseas adaptation may be intrinsically harmful, a number of studies have suggested that those with higher numbers of geographic moves during childhood may actually be better prepared for adulthood (O'Connell, 1981; Stroh & Brett, 1990). For example, Mann (1972) observed 69 college students, measuring anxiety in test and nontest situations, and found significant relationships between decreased anxiety and residential mobility, indicating that those with more frequent childhood moves showed less anxiety and more social maturity in a variety of situations.

Transcultural experiences and geographic mobility are not harmful for most children and adolescents per se. Such events probably constitute meaningful growth opportunities, even though adjustment attendant to foreign cultural life and mobility may be associated with temporary emotional and behavioral symptoms and, in a few instances, clinical referral. While families and children may attribute symptoms to geographic mobility and overseas adaptation, empiric data does not support

a major cause-effect relationship. The better-conducted studies indicate that persons' attributions about the move are more important than the actual circumstances of the move. When embedded in a supportive context or meaning, moves may have quite positive consequences (Steinglass, Weisstub, & De-Nour, 1989).

Conclusions

Children and adolescents do not usually favor moving from friends or known, comfortable surroundings, yet they generally note the positive nature of travel and the value of exposure to other cultural experiences that accompany such mobility (Darnauer, 1976). Although they rate mobility as a "negative life experience," it usually ranks as only modestly negative (Lewis, Seigel, & Lewis, 1984). In general, studies with the most empirical data-oriented approach to the question have found little or no geographic effects on children and adolescents (Hendershott, 1979; Lewis et al., 1984; Mann, 1972; McKain, 1973; Pedersen & Sullivan, 1964; Sam & Eide, 1991; Shaw & Pangman, 1975; Stokols & Shumaker, 1982). In contrast, those reports citing the negative impact of overseas life and geographic mobility consist mostly of anecdotal reports, poorly drawn clinical samples, or case reports (Aisenstein, 1988; Puskar & Dvorsak, 1991; Stubblefield, 1955; Werkman, 1972).

In designing a treatment plan for a child who presents for clinical evaluation and treatment, when that child currently lives in a foreign culture or has otherwise been very "mobile," the clinician should consider the potential etiologic role of the geographic or foreign life experiences. However, a healthy degree of skepticism about any etiologic role is warranted. If the child's presentation seems clearly linked to the move or foreign cultural experiences, consideration of the likelihood of the transient nature of the child's symptoms may be sensible. The design of the treatment plan should first and foremost be based around the child's clinical condition and primary disorder. When and if there seems to be overwhelming evidence that the child's difficulties are related to the transcultural experience or geographic mobility, careful consideration of environmental manipulations should be considered as an option of first choice. This strategy failing, the clinician should consider the possibility of a more serious underlying and primary

condition as explaining the nature of the child's current difficulties rather than any significant etiologic role played by the move or foreign cultural experiences.

REFERENCES

Aisenstein C. (1988). Stress and psychopathology in children of international employees. *Child Psychiatry and Human Development, 19,* 45–59.

Bower, E. M. (1967). American children and families in overseas communities. *American Journal of Orthopsychiatry, 37,* 787–796.

Cole, J., Allen, F., & Green, J. (1980). Survey of mental health of overseas students. *Social Science in Medicine 15,* 627–631.

Darnauer, P. (1976). The adolescent experience in career army families. In H. I. McCubbin, B. B. Dahl, & E. J. Hunter (Eds.), *Families in the military system* (pp. 42–66). Beverly Hills, CA: Sage Publications.

David, H. P., & Elkind, D. (1966). Family adaptation overseas: Some mental health considerations. *Mental Hygiene, 50,* 90–99.

Furnham, A., & Trezise, L. (1983). The mental health of foreign students. *Social Science in Medicine 17,* 365–370.

Garrett, G. R., Parker, B., Day, S., Ven Meter, J. J., & Cosby, W. (1978). Drinking and the military wife: A study of married women in overseas base communities. In E. J. Hunter & D. S. Nice (Eds.), *Military families: Adaptation to change* (pp. 222–235). New York: Praeger Publishers.

Hendershott, A. B.: (1989). Residential mobility, social support, and adolescent self-concept. *Adolescence, 24,* 217–232.

Jensen, P. S., Lewis, R. L., & Xenakis, S. N. (1986). The military family in review: Context, risk, and prevention. *Journal of the American Academy of Child Psychiatry, 25,* 225–234.

Lewis, C. E., Siegel, J. M., & Lewis, M. A. (1984). Feeling bad: Exploring sources of distress among preadolescent children. *American Journal of Public Health, 74,* 117–122.

Mann, P. A. (1972). Residential mobility as an adaptive experience. *Journal of Consulting and Clinical Psychology, 39,* 37–42.

Manning, F. J., & DeRouin, E. M. (1981). Employed wives of US Army members in Germany fare better than those unemployed. *Military Medicine, 146,* 726–728.

Marsh, R. M. (1976). Mobility in the military: Its effect upon the family system. In H. I. McCubbin, B. B. Dahl, & E. J. Hunter (Eds.), *Families in the military system* (pp. 92–111). Beverly Hills, CA: Sage Publications.

McKain, J. L. (1973). Relocation in the military: Alienation and family problems. *Journal of Marriage and Family, 35,* 205–209.

O'Connell, P. V. (1981). *The effect of mobility on selected personality characteristics of ninth and twelfth grade military dependents.* Ph.D. dissertation, University of Wisconsin-Milwaukee.

Pedersen, F. A., & Sullivan, E. J. (1964). Relationship among geographic mobility, parental attitudes, and emotional disturbance in children. *American Journal of Orthopsychiatry, 34,* 575–580.

Puskar, K. R., & Dvorsak, K. G. (1991). Relocation stress in adolescents: Helping teenagers adjust. *Pediatric Nursing, 17,* 295–298.

Reed, D., McGee, D., & Yano, K. (1984). Psychosocial processes and general susceptibility to chronic disease. *American Journal of Epidemiology, 119,* 356–370.

Sam, D. L., & Eide, R. (1991) Survey of mental health of foreign students. *Scandinavian Journal of Psychology, 32,* 22–30.

Shaw, J. A. (1982). Adolescents and the mobile military community. In G. Feinstein (Ed.), *Adolescent psychiatry* (pp. 85–98). Chicago: University of Chicago Press.

Shaw, J. A. (1988). Children in the military. *Psychiatric Annals, 17,* 539–534.

Shaw, J. A., & Pangman, J. (1975). Geographic mobility and the military child. *Military Medicine, 140,* 413–416.

Steinglass, P., Weisstub, E., & De-Nour, A. K. (1989). Perceived personal networks as mediators of stress reactions. *American Journal of Psychiatry, 145,* 1259–1264.

Steinhausen, H. C., Edinsel, E., Fegert, J. M., & Gobel, D. (1990). Child psychiatric disorders and family dysfunction in migrant workers and military families. *Euoropean Archives of Psychiatric and Neurologic Science 239,* 257–262.

Stokols, D., & Shumaker, S. A. (1982). The psychological context of residential mobility and well-being. *Journal of Social Issues, 38,* 149–171.

Stroh, L. K., & Brett, J. M. (1990). Corporate mobility: After the move, what do the children think? *Children's Environments Quarterly, 7,* 7–14.

Stubblefield, R. L. (1955). Children's emotional problems aggravated by family moves. *American Journal of Orthopsychiatry, 25,* 120–126.

Tooley, K. (1970). The role of geographic mobility in some adjustment problems of children and families. *Journal of the American Academy of Child Psychiatry, 9,* 366–378.

Vernberg, E. M. (1990). Experiences with peers following relocation during early adolescence. *American Journal of Orthopsychiatry, 60,* 466–472.

Ward, L. (1967). Some observations of the underlying dynamics of conflict in a foreign student. *Journal of the American College Health Association, 10,* 430–440.

Werkman, S. L. (1972). Hazards of rearing children in foreign countries. *American Journal of Psychiatry, 128,* 992–997.

Willis, B., & Power, P. (1985). Counselors as a resource for teachers in overseas schools. *Elementary School Guidance Counseling, 19,* 291–299.

48 / **The Central American Child**

Luis D. Herrera and Andres J. Pumariega

Central Americans comprise the most recent of Hispanic immigrant groups to settle in the United States and are perhaps the fastest growing. According to the U.S. Census (Bureau of the Census, 1990), 1.11 million Central Americans reside in the United States. Since many Central Americans emigrate into the United States illegally, this figure is probably an underestimate. Due to their high rates of immigration and reproduction, there is also likely to be a continued high growth rate and a high percentage of children and youth. Central Americans are close to becoming the second largest Hispanic group in the United States, thus surpassing Puerto Ricans and second only to the large Mexican American population with whom they are often confused and combined. Central American communities have been established in such large U.S. cities as Los Angeles, Houston, Miami, and New York.

Central American immigrants originated primarily from the wartorn and politically unstable nations of this region, including Nicaragua, El Salvador, Honduras, Guatemala, and Panama. The plight of these nations has been well publicized in the American press, but the special characteristics, cultural values, traditions, and special needs of this significant group of Americans are poorly understood both by mainstream America and even by the other Hispanic groups in the United States. It is hoped that this chapter will provide a useful overview of this growing segment of our population and will depict their special developmental and mental health needs.

Historical and Political Background

In order to understand the Central American child and family in the United States, it is important to be aware of the historical and political forces that shaped their cultures of origin. It is important to keep in mind that Central Americans are themselves immensely heterogeneous, not only in terms of their nationalities but also in respect to their racial, subcultural, and socioeconomic differences. In fact, there may be more similarities between a Guatemalan or Costa Rican upper-middle-class adolescent and a Caucasian counterpart from any major U.S. city than between these teenagers and their native counterparts within their own nations. Prior to the arrival of the Spanish conquerors in the 1500s, the region was originally dominated by Maya culture and similar native subcultures. The Spanish attempted to eradicate these native influences and proceeded to enslave or indenture the indigenous populations en masse. Missionaries converted over 90% of the population to Catholicism, but the cultural and socioeconomic differences between the Caucasian Spanish immigrants and the much more numerous native population have remained to this day. Although the majority indigenous population speaks Spanish, for the most part they are illiterate and communicate primarily in their native languages. For example, in Guatemala, with a population of 9.7

million inhabitants, 5.2 million primarily speak indigenous Maya languages. On the other hand, in Costa Rica, with a population of 3.2 million, only 10,000 speak the native Chibcan languages. The Spanish domination of close to 250 years finally gave way to independence for most of these nations in the first quarter of the 1800s. However, the families of Caucasian Spanish descendants have remained the upper elite of the population, breeding continued resentment among the much poorer native inhabitants.

Much of the political unrest in the region is due to these continued sociocultural differences and inequities, which are often inflamed by opportunistic political leaders. The region's strategic location, bridging North and South America, also has led to the involvement of outside forces in these long-standing conflicts. Examples of such involvement range from the inception of Panama to the struggles in the 1970s and 1980s over Nicaragua and El Salvador. Panama was originally a part of Colombia, but in the early 1900s the United States instigated its secession in order to pursue the building of a cross-oceanic canal. The more recent stresses were between Soviet/Cuban supported and U.S.-supported factions. A notable exception to this pattern is Costa Rica, which has had the second longest successful democracy in the hemisphere. Here, over the past century, a series of progressive governments have sought to address the social inequities within their nation, with incremental results (and much lower immigration rates into the United States).

The continued unrest in these nations is characterized by long-running cycles of political violence involving both paramilitary groups and rural insurgency/guerrilla armies that has touched most families in the affected nations. To a considerable extent, it is this pattern that has driven the large Central American immigration into the United States. This is different from the primarily economic forces that have driven Mexican immigration. For the most part, the Central American immigration is largely comprised of impoverished, poorly educated native families escaping from both poverty and continued violence; however, it also includes better-educated middle-class and upper-middle-class opponents of regimes in power escaping political persecution. The region's political unrest and violence has had an overwhelming impact on the mental health of the chil-

dren and families who inhabit it. For example, as a result of government-sponsored counterinsurgency "tactics" in Guatemala, approximately 400 Maya villages were brutally attacked and destroyed, leaving thousands of native children orphaned, mutilated, and terrorized (Melville & Lykes, 1992). At the most recent celebrations for the International Day of the Child in Guatemala City, there was a large march of indigenous children representing relatives of about 45,000 *desaparecidos* (missing persons) as a result of political violence. On the same day, over 5,000 children and adolescents, most of them orphaned as a result of the political violence in their nation, marched through the streets of the capital city of El Salvador, demanding both services for their basic needs and a definitive halt to the cycle of political violence (PRO-NIÑO, 1994). It is hard to separate the impact of violence and unrest per se from that of the resulting economic deprivation and lack of basic services for many of the children in the region, particularly those from remote rural areas. In Costa Rica, the infant mortality rate is 14 per 1,000 live births, while in strife-torn Guatemala it is 43 per 1,000 live births. However, in Costa Rica, 25% of primaparous births and 40% of all births are to girls under 18 years of age (Caja Costarricense de Seguro Social, 1993).

Although the mental health impact of these conditions is significant, many more of these children are likely to die from measles than suicide, or to be impaired developmentally from lack of a basic education than from the lack of a child psychiatrist to diagnose and treat them. Due to the magnitude of the problems facing Central American nations and the multitide of basic health and social needs not being met, mental health and psychopathology are not seen as national priorities. As a result, the number of mental health professionals in these nations, particularly for children, is minimal, as is the exposure of typical families to mental health services. Although psychiatric services are organized primarily under the ministries of health and social security in these nations, most of the available services are located in the capital cities and thus are not accessible to the large rural populations. Some national governments operate child psychiatric units in their national psychiatric hospitals, but these serve children with severe neuropsychiatric disorders or mental retardation, and primarily provide custodial care. Table 48.1 sum-

TABLE 48.1

Number and Population Ratios for Child and Adolescent Psychiatrists in Central America and the United States

Country	Number of Child Psychiatrists	Population under 15	Ratio per 100,000
Guatemala	3	4,409,702	0.053
El Salvador	1	2,399,895	0.041
Honduras	2	2,296,008	0.087
Nicaragua	1	1,944,840	0.051
Costa Rica	5[a]	1,267,200	0.39
Panama	6	891,924	0.67
United States	6,500	56,550,837	11.5

Note. Data collected from national medical and surgical associations and psychiatric associations from throughout Central America.
[a]Only 5 of the 11 registered in Costa Rica actually practice child and adolescent psychiatry.

marizes estimates of the numbers and ratios of child and adolescent psychiatrists in the region as obtained from regional professional organizations; this does not include practitioners who choose to serve children without formal training. These child and adolescent psychiatrists are not only extremely few in number, they are also poorly trained to deal with the multiplicity of problems that these children present. At this time, the promotion of mental health and the prevention of emotional disturbance/mental illness must have a higher priority in these nations than the provision of clinical services (Arroyo, 1992).

Family Organization and Child Rearing

Three family structures and constellations are common among Central Americans. Nuclear families are quite frequent, especially in urban areas, primarily as a result of the low divorce rate in Central America as compared to the United States. These nuclear families are rather large, with four to five children on average. This may well be a useful survival strategy in the face of chronically high rates of infant mortality. Extended families are more traditional in this region, with grandparents and uncles/aunts being actively involved in child rearing and limit-setting. This

situation is especially true in nations where the native population is predominant (such as Guatemala). The extended family is very important in terms of the management of disruptive behavioral problems in children and in helping to buffer or cushion families from internal conflicts or crises. Most of these families are formally patrilineal, although women are important carriers of culture and are responsible for maintaining family traditions and communication.

In some large segments of the population (particularly those of lower socioeconomic background), there is a third type of family organization. These are families with a female head of household who may or may not have established a legal relationship with the father of the children. The father may help financially, most of the time irregularly, and may live with his children only intermittently and for short periods. At times the mother may have children by multiple partners who "drop by" alternately. For example, in the northern part of Costa Rica, as many as 60% of families fit this pattern. In the past few years, due to several socioeconomic factors, there is an increasing number of youngsters in the streets of the main Central American cities. These children live in shanty towns around the city, are not attending school and go to the street to beg, sell flowers, candy, commit minor thefts, and the like. An increasing but unknown number of adolescents are sexually exploited in what seems to be a rapidly growing nightlife business, mostly for tourists.

Children in Central America are commonly perceived as "less of a person" than an adult; this is particularly true in rural areas but occurs to some extent in all sociodemographic groups (Zurcher, 1994). This situation facilitates what could be called a "collective projective identification" of parents toward their children. Children receive positive attention and often overprotective care, but only to the extent that the child satisfies the parent's narcissistic emotional needs. Inasmuch as children express different degrees of emotional autonomy or do not fulfill parental expectations, they are criticized, ridiculed, or even punished, both physically and emotionally. Expressions of assertiveness by the child are often perceived as a threat to parental authority, especially in more traditional families.

However, in rural areas, due to the need for economic survival, children are often pressed to abandon their childhood and prematurely assume adult responsibilities. Many cannot continue their schooling because they are required to help their parents as farm laborers, in the fields if males and in the household if females. Many children enter the workforce at about 10 years of age. In addition, as a result of this process, adolescents often take on parental roles with their younger siblings. This phenomenon determines a different developmental course for these children, possibly resulting in the personality traits commonly associated with Central American adults. These present a facade of *machismo* and self-sufficiency, which masks underlying dependent, immature traits in marital and family relationships. On the other hand, this early exposure to adversity and the demand for self-sufficiency breed a high degree of resiliency in the face of continued adversity.

Finally there is a child-rearing pattern that is not unique to Central American culture but is seen more commonly in this population than in others; in this constellation, the parents split the nurturing and disciplinary roles, especially along gender lines. Thus, for example, a disruptive 8-year-old child will be asked to behave by his mother with no effect whatsoever but, out of frustration, will then be threatened with report of his behavior to the father. The child will take his or her chances and often continue the behavior. Upon the father's arrival, he learns of the misbehavior and quickly, and often severely, punishes the child. The mother then will either intervene to stop the punishment or will approach the child later on and console and nurture him or her, motivated by guilt and remorse. Through these interactions, children develop a pattern of expectations of fathers as provider/disciplinarians and mothers as nurturant/protectors. As a result, it is very common for children to develop manipulative coping strategies in order to avoid responsibility for their behavior and to deflect blame or consequences. This pattern also may contribute to coping characteristics of conflict avoidance and indirect means of confrontation that are common among Central Americans.

Characteristic Mental Health Issues

There are no epidemiological, population-based studies documenting the prevalence of psychiatric disorders among Central American children either in their homelands or in the United States. The following observations are based on the experience and data collected by the first author through several years of practicing child and adolescent psychiatry in Costa Rica. We present a suggested distribution of child psychiatric disorders derived from 100 consecutive intake evaluations of children over a period of 3 years. These included a clinical psychiatric interview and data from the Child Behavior Checklist (Achenbach, 1987) completed by parents. The data were collected at the Hospital Nacional de Ninos of Costa Rica, which has the largest child and adolescent service in the region, with an average of 8,000 visits per year and 45 patients seen daily. The initial primary diagnoses were distributed as follows:

Disruptive disorders: 43%. Hyperactivity (attention deficit hyperactivity disorder), oppositional, aggressive, and impulsive behavioral profiles.
Anxiety disorders: 31%. Separation anxiety, overanxious, and avoidant anxiety disorders profiles.
Depressive disorders: 10%. Adjustment reactions, dysthymia, and major depression.
Somatoform disorders: 8%. Somatization, hypochondriasis, and conversion symptoms.
Sexual problems: 5%.
Others: 3%. Pervasive developmental disorders, psychoses, tics, and eating disorders.

Notwithstanding the existence of some difference in prevalence of disorders and how they are understood and handled by families and communities, the disorders seen among Central American children are similar to those seen in most other nations (Quay & Werry, 1986). What is definitely different is the way that these disorders are regarded in terms of attributed causes and in respect to their nature. These are largely governed by traditional cultural beliefs. For example, a bipolar adolescent in an agitated, delusional manic phase may be considered a witch or clairvoyant. A conversion symptom in a young boy may be attributed to sorcery. Strong religious prohibitions serve as injunctions against self-destructive behaviors, with adolescent suicide almost unheard of in comparison to the United States. Such beliefs, in addition to a strong stigma associated with mental illness and lack of familiarity with mental health services, contribute to familial reluctance to seek such services. Since the few services available are mostly government-sponsored, families, based on years of repressive regimes, also are naturally suspicious of them. Counseling by native healers or the clergy is seen as a safe and effective alternative. These attitudes persist when families emigrate to the United States, and lead to greater resistance among Central Americans to receiving formal mental health services than other Hispanic immigrant groups.

Other differences in symptomatic expression and interpretation are worth noting. In Central American cultures, it is very common to express mental distress through somatic complaints. This is encouraged from early childhood. For example, toddlers receive more positive attention for being "good eaters" than for prosocial behaviors. This fact is usually associated with an unexpected prevalence of childhood obesity, which in adverse economic circumstances has survival value. Immediate attention is also given to youngsters if they complain of headaches, stomachaches, or fatigue. Since most of the population has limited formal education, they lack the ability to eloquently articulate their psychological suffering, and they find it easier to express such distress somatically. Adolescents often suffer from dissociative disorders and children suffer from functional neurological symptoms, such as paralysis and paresthesias.

The diagnosis of conduct disorder, as conceptualized in the fourth edition of the *Diagnostic and Statistical Manual of the American Psychiatric Association* (American Psychiatric Association, 1994) is seldom made or considered in these countries. The reasons for this difference is unknown, but at least two factors may help to explain it. In Central America, there is a clearer distinction between the legal and mental health systems than in the United States. Therefore, many youths who would be referred to mental health agencies in the United States would be considered plainly delinquent according to Central American societal standards; and accordingly, they are referred to the large and primarily punitive legal/correctional system. On the other hand, families in Central America are both more intact and more effective in containing behaviors, thus buffering the adolescent against his or her impulsive and aggressive impulses. Finally, it is likely that many adolescents are not referred for treatment for their delinquent or disruptive behaviors because these behaviors frequently are seen as a "bad phase" that the children will grow out of; this, in turn, fosters more tolerance and less emotional reaction by adults. For example, in Costa Rica, this situation has contributed to an absence of inpatient adolescent facilities. This may well be a wise approach, since some researchers have documented that most delinquent adolescents do not become adult criminals (Rutter & Giller, 1988).

Effects of War and Immigration on Central American Children

The continual political violence and insurgency that Central American children and adolescents have been exposed to have led to thousands of them being killed, orphaned, and tortured. In addition, they also have been exposed to other levels of trauma. Many adolescents and even children have been pressed into service as combatants. Furthermore, children are also victims of the aftermath of warfare in terms of unemployment of their parents, worsening of health care and social services, destruction of schools, and geographic dislocation.

It is difficult to make generalizations about the effect of political violence and warfare on children due to the wide differences in exposure. It is very different, for example, for a child to be exposed to random bombing of civilians than to witness the murder or torture of his or her parents. Several international organizations (including Redd Barna and UNICEF) and researchers have been involved in relief efforts and have studied Central American children affected by political violence. However, most studies have been hampered by a multitude of difficulties involved in the accurate assessment of psychological symptoms in children exposed to political violence, such as culturally inadequate instruments or the loss of subjects to follow-up. In the United States and other developed nations, many researchers (Arroyo & Eth, 1985; Richman, 1993; Summerfield, 1987) have reported the psychological sequelae of such experiences on small groups of refugees from Central America. However, these may be select groups with different characteristics (socioeconomically, educationally, or even in terms of personality structure) than the great majority whose families choose not to leave their countries. These differences are further confounded by the psychological impact of immigration itself, including the loss of extended family support, the pressure to understand a new language and new customs, and the struggle to survive economically.

Of greatest relevance, perhaps, is the fact that the medical diagnostic model employed to assess the psychological effects of political violence may be inadequate. Children process their experiences, traumatic or not, on the basis of mental constructs developed within a social context specific to their society, culture, community, and family (Dawes, 1992). The manner in which they understand the experience of exposure to political violence may be very different from what is assumed by clinicians and researchers, based on their own different sociocultural context. It may well be that children from different cultural contexts may develop a variety of mental constructs of their experiences that may make them more resilient, in part supported by the ideological concepts emphasized by the warring factions. They also may subordinate and sublimate the expression of distress resulting from political violence toward the satisfaction of more basic needs, such as food,

shelter, schooling, and work (Punamaki, 1992). These basic needs are "givens" for most children and adolescents in developed societies where such clinical constructs as posttraumatic stress disorder have been elaborated, so their relative importance is greater for children and families in Third World contexts. This may explain why these clinical conditions are not reported more frequently under such difficult conditions. Perhaps when the child and his or her family emigrate out of such circumstances (and move into a different sociocultural context), there may be more complete expression of such symptomatology.

However, for those children who do become symptomatic, some basic findings can be outlined. Some symptoms are acute and do not last very long, such as intense anxiety, sleep disturbance, and panic attacks. Others are long-term reactions to the challenging environment (whether it takes the form of violence or immigration to a new culture), such as hypervigilance, fear of survival, irritability, regression, and increased dependency. For some, the effects are congruent with the phenomenology of posttraumatic stress disorder such as hyperarousal, avoidance of reminiscent stimuli, reenactment, and other manifestations of incomplete processing of emotional experiences. Somatization of stress, which is culturally facilitated in Central America, is very common; various forms of dysthymia due to dramatic and frequent losses that are not fully expressed in the context of adverse circumstances are also frequent (Turner & Gorst-Unsworth, 1990).

Clinicians in the United States need to keep these various factors in mind as they work with Central American children and their families. Work with these children and families will involve simultaneously addressing multiple aspects of their psychosocial adaptation, such as cultural transition, residual traumatization, adaptation to new demands in a more complex society, and retainment of their individual and cultural identity. As with other Hispanic immigrant groups, family-focused, child-centered approaches are more culturally syntonic and effective, emphasizing family strengths and culturally acceptable approaches to dealing with stress and trauma.

REFERENCES

Achenbach, T. (1987) *Manual for the Child Behavior Checklist and Behavior Profiles*. Burlington: University of Vermont.

American Psychiatric Association. (1994) *Diagnostic and statistical manual of mental disorders* (4th ed.) Washington, DC: Author.

Arroyo, J. (1992). Programas de salud mental en el nino en el nivel comunitario. In I. Levav, (Ed.). *Temas de salud mental en la comunidad* (p. 43). Organizacion Panamericana de la Salud.

Arroyo, W., & Eth, S. (1985). Children traumatized by Central American warfare. In S. Eth, & R. Pynoos (Eds.). *Post-traumatic stress disorder in children* (pp. 103–120). Washington, DC: American Psychiatric Press.

Caja Costarricense de Seguro Social. (1993). *Programa de atencion integral en salud de los adolescentes*. San Jose, Costa Rica: Ministerio de Salud y Caja Costarricense de Seguro Social.

Dawes, A. (1992, January). *Political and moral learning in the context of political conflict*. Paper presented at the conference entitled "The Mental Health of Refugee Children Exposed to Violent Environments," Refugee Studies Programme, Oxford University, England.

Melville, M. B., & Lykes, M. B. (1992) Guatemalan Indian children and the sociocultural effects of gov-ernment-sponsored terrorism. *Social Sciences in Medicine, 34*, 533–548.

PRO-NIÑO. (1994). *Ninos de Guatemala demandan la paz* San Jose, Costa Rica: Fundacion Paniamor.

Punamaki, R. L. (1992, January). Natural healing processes & experiences of political violence. Paper presented at the conference entitled "The Mental Health of Refugee Children Exposed to Violent Environments," Refugee Studies Programme, Oxford University, England.

Quay, H. C., & Werry, J. S. (1986). *Psychopathological disorders of childhood*. New York: John Wiley & Sons.

Richman, N. (1993). Annotation: Children in situations of political violence. *Journal of Child Psychology and Psychiatry, 34*, 1286–1302.

Rutter, M., & Giller, H. (1988). *Delinquencia juvenil*. Barcelona: Ediciones Martinez Roca.

Sumerfield, D. (1987). Nicaragua: War and mental health. *Lancet, 2*, 914.

Turner, S., & Gorst-Unsworth, C. (1990). Psychological sequelae of torture: A descriptive model. *British Journal of Psychiatry, 157*, 475–480.

U.S. Bureau of the Census. (1992). *Statistical abstract of the United States*. Washington, DC: U.S. Government Printing Office.

Zurcher, J. (1994). Ninez y desarrollo. *PRO-NIÑO, 1*, 25–26. San Jose, Costa Rica: Fundacion Paniamor.

49 / The Cuban American Child

Andres J. Pumariega and Pedro Ruiz

Among the recent immigrant groups that have entered the United States, the Cubans have enjoyed perhaps the most recognition and the most rapid success socioeconomically. Cuban Americans now total 1.1 million, or approximately 4.9%, of the nation's Hispanics. They have achieved rough socioeconomic and educational parity with the predominant Euro-American population over a relatively short time. According to the 1990 census, the median household income for Cuban Americans was $27,890 per year, with 20.7 percent of households earning over $50,000. This compares to a $28,906 median household income and 23.5% earning over $50,000 for the total population, while the Hispanic population as a whole earned a $21,922 median household income and 13.8% earned over $50,000. While 22.4% of Cuban American families were headed by someone who was not a high school graduate, this was true for 22.5% of households in the total population and 33.2% of all Hispanic-origin households (U.S. Bureau of the Census, 1991). As a group, Cuban Americans have made a significant impact in a number of areas of U.S. life disproportionate to their relative numbers. These include economic development (particularly in Florida, the Northeast, and Puerto Rico), art and music, science and medicine, and politics and foreign affairs (Bernal, 1982).

Although Cubans and Cuban Americans reside primarily in the South Florida and northeast sections of the United States, they are also found in smaller numbers in all areas of the country. Clinicians should have knowledge and special consideration for the unique characteristics that distinguish this group even from other U.S. Hispanics. In fact, Cubans themselves are an amalgam of different cultural, racial, and ethnic groups that emigrated to the island over its nearly 500-year recorded history. Iberian and African influences predominate within the culture, with relatively little native influence (as opposed to other Hispanic American groups), since the island's inhabitants were exterminated within the first century of colonization by Spain. However, later immigrants included Chinese and Eastern Europeans in this century. Cuba's close proximity to the United States also led to perhaps the greatest cultural influence on Cubans in the past century, prior to the Castro era. This fact partially explained the rapid integration and success demonstrated by Cuban emigrees, particularly in the early post-Castro years. As we discuss later, this affinity to U.S. culture was not absolutely protective during the process of adaptation and acculturation; a number of mental health implications arose from this process.

Waves of Immigration

It is important to note that, since the 1820s, there have been numerous waves of immigration from Cuba to the United States, usually in response to periods of political instability on the island. However, the most significant migration of Cubans to the United States occurred in the last 30 years in response to the totalitarian Castro regime. Even within the exodus, the characteristics of immigrants arriving in the United States varied greatly according to their time of arrival. The earliest to arrive were from upper-class families that were able to take at least some of their financial resources with them. The group that left during the first decade of migration comprised the island's middle class, which were well educated and were forced to leave all their worldly possessions by the Castro government. These immigrants had a much harder time economically and culturally, since they had no support systems upon their ar-

rival other than limited governmental and church assistance. However, this is the group that was primarily responsible for the "economic miracle" commonly associated with the Cuban migration. This group banded together, for the most part setting aside political and other differences, and built a strong sociocultural support system from which later, less-educated immigrants were able to benefit.

Many of these families had to deal not only with a sharp drop in socioeconomic standing but also with separation from loved ones and the stress of the journey itself. In fact, during the early period of exile, approximately 15,000 children came to the United States without their parents as a result of parents panicking and sending their children ahead of them and the U.S. government allowing them to come over on visa waivers. Many of these children were never reunited with their families and were settled with relatives or in orphanages and foster homes throughout the United States. Although Cuba is only 90 miles from U.S. shores, political obstacles led to many having to flee in small boats and rafts over the dangerous waters of the Florida Straits and others through third countries such as Spain and Mexico (Rumbaut & Rumbaut, 1976).

Cultural Traits and Values

A number of cultural characteristics define the Cuban character and are particularly important in the development of the Cuban American child. Cubans are guided in their interpersonal relations by the principle of *personalismo*, which assigns greater value and trust to extended family and kinship networks than to impersonal institutions and structures. It also implies a concern for personal dignity and a person-oriented approach to social relations. Cuban Americans, for example, spend more of their leisure time in social pursuits than in activities oriented to personal growth as their Anglo counterparts. Being *simpatico* (affable, charming) and *esplendido* (generous) are highly valued, while being *pesado* (disagreeable or cold) and *tacano* (stingy or frugal) are considered cultural sins. Most interactions, even of a business or legal nature, are interpreted on a personal basis. Such values lead to a natural mistrust of agencies and established authorities, which are perceived as looking out for their personal gain and being uncaring. There are even formal and informal tenses by which people are addressed that define whether they belong within or outside the individual's kinship network: the pronoun "you" can be expressed either as *tu* in the informal tense or *usted* in the formal tense. It is difficult for Cuban Americans to achieve consensus on sociopolitical issues given these attitudes, as witnessed by the long history of political instability and the proliferation of factional groups, even in the United States.

Cubans strongly identify with the image of the *criollo*, or creole, who were the second generation and beyond of the Spanish settlers in Cuba, often with a strong African background due to the introduction of slavery. The criollo personality is one that is carefree and unabashedly hedonistic, with much open expression of emotion and enjoyment of sensual experiences. It is reflected in Cuban music, art, literature, and food, all of which have a celebratory nature to them. It is also reflected in the spoken language, which is rapid, loud, and punctuated with colloquialisms and liberal use of curse words. In fact, the same Cuban Americans who may speak in very rational, businesslike English become highly expressive when they convert to Spanish. At the same time, the criollo is fiercely proud, achievement-oriented, and has a sense of self-confidence and superiority over Spanish forebears. These traits were accentuated in the process of migration and acculturation in the United States, contributing to the remarkable success the Cuban Americans have experienced and their ability to retain their cultural heritage. The traits also can be easily misperceived by outsiders as arrogance. As a result of the mixed Spanish (traditionalist/linear) and African (egalitarian) influences, Cuban Americans are perhaps not as egalitarian as Anglo-Americans but not as hierarchical as Spaniards (Queralt, 1984).

In spite of their individualism, pride, and achievement orientation, Cuban Americans have a fatalistic outlook on life, as expressed by many linguistic expressions that make allusions to destiny and God's will. However, their outlook is also an optimistic one, with a propensity to attribute responsibility to external causes and factors. Cuban Americans are also more present-oriented than Anglo-Americans, attaching more importance to the task or experience at hand than time parameters and future concerns. It could be argued that this unusual mix of values and characteristics may have served Cuban Americans well in the arduous task of successfully adapting to a difficult environment and uncertain circumstances (Queralt, 1984).

Spiritual beliefs have had a very strong influence in Cuban culture. However, unlike some of the other Hispanic groups, which adhere rigidly to the dogma of the Catholic church, Cuban Americans approach their spiritual life in the same individualistic manner as they approach other issues. A common saying among Cuban Americans characterizes their attitude: When asked if they are Catholic, they respond *"Soy Catolico a mi manera"* (I'm Catholic in my own way). In fact, Cuban culture contains an amalgam of religions, including traditional Catholic beliefs and beliefs and practices of the Lucumi religion, commonly referred to as Santeria, which was imported by African slaves brought from West Africa during Cuba's colonization. In fact, the Lucumi religion was disguised using Catholic symbols to protect its practitioners from persecution. Although there are purist practitioners of each of these traditions, most Cubans adhere to elements of both. This fact is reflected in the veneration of saints who symbolize African deities (although they were decanonized by the Catholic church) and in such common beliefs as *mal de ojo* (evil eye) and the medicinal use of herbs originally used in African rituals (Ruiz, 1982).

Another unique characteristic of Cuban culture that is relevant to their acculturation is the long-standing ambivalent relationship that Cuba has had with the United States. This is ambivalence in the true sense, with strong positive identification with many American values and ideals (independence, democracy, freedom of expression, achievement orientation) but with strong negative feelings about the role that the United States has played in Cuban history (ambivalent in itself, as reflected in its shift from previous interventionism to the current hands-off approach to Castro). This ambivalence is heightened by the conflicting experiences that Cuban emigrees have had in the

United States (great freedom and opportunity but also discrimination and stereotyping) and the Cuban family's common fear of their offspring losing their cultural heritage and becoming "Americanized" (Rumbaut & Rumbaut, 1976).

Development of the Cuban American Child

The Cuban American child grows up in the pre-latency years primarily within the very protective environment of his or her family, which often includes grandparents and other extended family. It is common for the Cuban American child to become as bonded to grandparents or other close relatives as to his or her parents. The role of women in Cuba was already more emancipated than in most of Latin America prior to immigration, with a higher level of participation in the workforce and in political life. With the necessity for two-job or career families in order to advance economically in the United States, the extended family also becomes the caregiver of preference. Therefore, it is rare for the Cuban American child to encounter children outside their extended family until kindergarten. Cousins are often the child's first playmates and best friends. Furthermore, the Cuban American child is frequently first fluent in Spanish.

Machismo is still evident in parental roles, with the father's authority being foremost in importance while the mother (or mother surrogate) is idealized as the source of affection, nurturance, and virtue. It also influences early child-rearing practices and the early establishment of gender roles, with girls dressed in frilly, lacy garments from early on and boys openly encouraged to engage in rough-and-tumble play outside the home. Much more emphasis is placed on the development of strong familial ties and *respeto* (respect for parents and elders) than on physical independence and autonomy. Therefore, a Cuban American child is rewarded much more for obedience and familial loyalty than for physical independence. By Anglo standards, a Cuban American child would be considered quite spoiled, with many of his or her wants and needs being readily attended to by family members with as little frustration as possible. There is also much open expression of affection, both physically and verbally, between family members, even of the same gender. Such affection is sometimes expressed through nicknames, either original ones or derived from the diminutive tense of the child's name (e.g., Roberto would be called "Robertico") which often persist throughout the individual's life. However, there are strong prohibitions around the disclosure of "family business" to outsiders (Bernal, 1982).

During latency, Cuban American children often make their first real-life encounter with American culture through teachers and peers. (However, this assumes that the children attend public or parochial schools in an integrated neighborhood. It is not uncommon for many Cuban American children to attend Hispanic private schools or to live in almost exclusively Hispanic areas, where such contact is limited.) As a result of this exposure, they quickly become bicultural and begin to show interest in some of the activities and customs of Anglo children. A proverbial tug-of-war now begins between the attraction of the majority culture and the often intense efforts of their grandparents, parents, and relatives to reinforce Cuban customs and the Spanish language so they do not become too "Americanized." In fact, Cuban American parents whose children are not fluent in Spanish are openly looked down upon as not doing a "good-enough" job in parenting.

Personal responsibility is not emphasized in terms of chores and self-care, with household chores and allowances being only a recent development. However, the Cuban American child does experience a good deal of pressure to achieve academically and socially beginning in elementary school. To have an intelligent or a popular child is the pride and joy of a Cuban American family. *Respeto* continues to be emphasized in relation to elders, but the child is given increasing freedom to participate in family discussions, which are often quite raucous but rarely lead to any lasting repercussions.

During adolescence, Cuban American children increasingly develop a strong bicultural orientation, feeling equally at home in either their culture of origin or the majority culture. Peer pressure now contributes to this finely balanced outcome. Youths who too strongly identify with Cuban culture are looked down upon by their Cuban American peers, with those tending to the Cuban extreme being labeled "Cubanazos" or "Marielitos" (slang terms for a stereotypical super-Cuban or a recent arrival from the Mariel boatlift, respectively). On the other hand, family pressure to retain their Cuban heritage is further intensified. One manifestation of this are the often lavish celebrations for the Cuban American girls' *quince*, or fifteenth birthday. The latter has been traditionally individual celebration of "coming-out" into dating and young adulthood. In Cuba, families celebrated according to their economic means, with lavish parties reserved for the very wealthy. In the United States, it is not uncommon for working-class Cuban families to take out $10,000 loans to put on a lavish *quince* celebration, complete with limousine, formal attire, and choreographer for the traditional waltz. In a sense, this is not only a celebration of the daughter's coming of age but also the family's success in the United States as well as an instillment of traditional values. On the other hand, such practices as chaperoned dating for adolescents have succumbed to peer and cultural pressures (Bernal, 1982). Cuban American adolescents have eclectic tastes in music, being as likely to attend a rock concert as a Latin salsa dance hall and pursue as active a social life as their Cuban forebears. Their expensive tastes in brand-name clothing and entertainment finally lead the family to support their increasing financial and social independence.

The traditional role of Cuban American women has undergone further transformation in the United States, providing new role models for adolescent girls. The emphasis on achievement and education in Cuban American families is now equivalent for both genders, with a strong expectation for college education and careers (Queralt, 1984). In general, although a strong bond is maintained with the nuclear and extended family into adulthood, there is now greater tolerance for Cuban American young adults to live geographically away from their families to pursue their education or career goals, whereas traditionally the child (male or female) was expected to live at home until marrriage. Expectations of early marriage for females and tolerance of a "double standard" of male and female sexual behavior also have diminished with greater acculturation (Bernal, 1982). There is also greater acceptance for intercultural

dating and marriage. However, the stereotypes of Americans (or more acculturated youth) as "fast" and "loose" still persist within many Cuban families. This reflects the intense pride they feel in their heritage, with fears of intermarriage "diluting" the culture, as well as resistance to adopt American moral values.

The Acculturation Process

In spite of their obvious success, Cuban Americans have experienced a number of stressors related to their adaptation to a new environment. Cuban immigrants have experienced a number of losses stemming from the Castro takeover and subsequent flight to the United States, including loss of their previous status, possessions, and even careers; separation and loss of family ties resulting from obstacles to travel and communication as well as imprisonment and disappearance by the Castro regime; and traumatic departures to the United States, which at times have been illegal and treacherous. Rumbaut and Rumbaut (1976) described the process of adaptation for the newly arrived immigrants, which begins with mild paranoia that is a carryover from living in a totalitarian regime, then a sense of transient relief and even euphoria at having left the conditions in Cuba, and finally a slow realization of the long struggle ahead to adapt and survive in the new country, which is accompanied by emotional distress.

Once in the United States, first- and second-generation Cuban Americans have faced stressors related to the acculturation process. These have included pressure, especially fueled by the media, to adopt American customs and values, to adopt the English language to the exclusion of Spanish, and even to adopt a generic form of "Hispanic" identity that conforms to American stereotypes. The older generations have felt obligated to maintain Cuban traditions and values in the face of such pressures, which has created some strain with the younger generations of American-born and even immigrant Cubans. Rumbaut and Rumbaut (1976) hypothesize that the pressure to achieve among Cuban Americans could be a form of overcompensation to the prolonged feeling of helplessness and uprootedness.

However, it is important to note that, in general, Cuban Americans have been remarkably successful in maintaining their cultural identity while being able to function effectively in both American culture and among other Hispanic Americans in the United States (Rumbaut & Rumbaut, 1976). This is especially true when compared to the other main Hispanic groups in the United States. Mexican Americans have had more difficulty with biculturality given their poorer socioeconomic backgrounds and their greater cultural difference with American culture, while Puerto Ricans' open access and contact with their homeland exerts a very strong cultural influence. Cuban Americans have had little access to their homeland and have felt freer to adopt American values, but have relied on the development of strong support systems to maintain their cultural heritage. As a result, Cuban Americans often have assumed positions in business and government as liaison between the United States and Latin America. In a sense, they are models for the successful bicultural adaptation referred to by authors in the cross-cultural mental health field (deAnda, 1984). Cuban Americans actually should be considered a unique cultural group, quite different from their immigrant forebears, Anglo-Americans, and their counterparts in Cuba (who have undergone another cultural transition as a result of Soviet influence). When asked, most Cuban Americans readily admit that they do not wish to return to Cuba if it is liberated from the Castro regime.

Another, less openly acknowledged source of stress faced by Cuban Americans is that of discrimination. They have had to contend with much jealousy and suspicion as a result of their rapid success. These reactions have come both from the majority population, which have found them incompatible with their stereotype of the "lazy" and "passive" Hispanic, and from various minority groups, which resent what they perceive as the Cubans' "special place" among minority groups (not unlike the recent experiences with Oriental minority groups). This situation has led to much interethnic tension between Cuban Americans and other groups such as African Americans and Jews. There is also discomfort with Cuban Americans' open, spontaneous expression of affect, whether positive or negative, which in itself leads to stereotypes of impulsivity and the "hot Latin

temper" and results in underestimation of their interpersonal and analytic capabilities.

Another challenge has come from the arrival of the more recent Cuban immigrants. The experience with the 1980 Mariel boatlift, where hundreds of incarcerated and mentally ill Cubans were slipped into the United States by Castro, served to create negative attitudes about the recent immigrants. However, beyond these new stereotypes, more recent immigrants face real differences and difficulties. Not only are they less educated and less familiar with U.S. culture, but they are also less familiar with traditional Cuban values due to their 30 years' experience within a totalitarian regime. This leads them to feel less comfortable with open affective expression and assertiveness and more comfortable with external forms of control (such as the government). Because of their lack of rootedness in either cultural tradition (Cuban or U.S.), these individuals experience more marginalization, hopelessness, and internal distress and are more susceptible to pressures for rapid assimilation through consumerism and even substance abuse (Bernal, 1982).

Mental Health Issues

Particular maladaptive patterns in dealing with these stressors can be identified in Cuban American individuals and families. One is a pattern of "cultural mummification" where the customs and values of pre-1959 Cuba are idealized to the exclusion of any American or newer Cuban perspectives, leading to social marginalization and even Spanish monolingualism (although not necessarily economic marginalization due to the strong Cuban ethnic economy). In such circumstances, people often experience unresolved grief over losses incurred in the process of immigration. On the other hand, another pattern can be identified where the individual or family (usually younger or recent immigrant) completely rejects the Cuban identity and overidentifies with U.S. cultural beliefs and practices, particularly materialism. This pattern is usually associated with experiences of discrimination and identity crisis.

Greater acculturation is accompanied by changing patterns of psychiatric synmptomatology. While older Cuban Americans have tended to experience adaptational anxiety (including post-traumatic stress disorders) and depression (particularly in the elderly) in response to the stresses of acculturation, younger Cuban Americans tend to demonstrate symptoms of substance abuse, at times accompanied by depression and suicidality (Ruiz, 1982; Vega, Warheit, Apospori & Zimmerman, 1993). Investigators have identified a pattern of significant intergenerational acculturation conflict associated with disruptive behavioral symptoms, substance abuse, and poor school performance in Cuban American adolescents (Szapocnik, Scopetta & King, 1978; Sokol-Katz & Ulbrich, 1992). In these circumstances, the parents are inflexible in their strict adherence to traditional Cuban values, while the adolescents develop a negative identification with Cuban values and passionately adhere to all things American. Pumariega (1986) found that as many Cuban American adolescent girls score abnormal on the Eating Attitudes Test as American girls and found that degree of acculturation to American customs was significantly correlated with more abnormal eating attitudes, indicating a rise in eating disorders in this population. There has also been a change in patterns of substance abuse. While alcohol and minor tranquilizer abuse have been more prevalent in older Cuban Americans, younger Cuban Americans have gravitated more to cocaine and other street drugs (National Institute of Drug Abuse, 1987).

Conflicts related to gender role definition also predominate. Ruiz (1982) described a pattern of family conflict arising from exposure to the different gender role expectations in the United States and greater freedoms afforded to women, particularly for families headed by older, more traditional Cuban Americans. He points out that, if these conflicts are not handled by a therapist sensitive to the difficulties involved in acculturation and the transitioning of gender roles, adverse outcomes in therapy are probable. Another group affected by the strict definition of gender roles among Cuban Americans are male homosexuals. The greater freedom afforded in Anglo society clashes with the strict prohibitions against homosexuality traditional in Cuban machismo. This often results in the cut-off of male homosexuals from their families and greater risk for internal conflict and depression (Ruiz, 1982).

With acculturation, Cuban Americans' beliefs and attitudes about mental illness also have changed significantly. Traditionally, beliefs centered around the two main religious traditions, either "sin/guilt" based (Catholic) or "hex/retribution" based (Santeria/Afro-Cuban). Particular culture-bound syndromes have been associated with these traditions, including hysterical dissociative phenomena with acute decompensations commonly called *ataques de nervios*. In Cuba, the upper and middle classes had access to traditional psychiatric treatment, principally psychoanalytic in orientation. The lower classes sought out folk healers or provided home care rather than pursuing the alternative, which was internment in the national psychiatric hospital in Habana, which had very inhumane conditions. More recently, with the rise in psychiatric problems related to migration and acculturation stressors, greater numbers of Cuban Americans have sought out both traditional psychiatric help and traditional *santeros*. As a result, there has been a rapid destigmatization of mental illness among Cubans, with very open discussion of these mental health issues in public and in the Cuban American media. In fact, more Cubans seek out psychiatric care than any other Hispanic group in the United States. This is also featured by Cuban American's higher socioeconomic status and access to insurance coverage (Ruiz, Venegas-Samuels, & Alarcon, 1995).

A number of cultural considerations arise in the treatment of Cuban American children and adolescents. Family participation is essential for the accurate assessment of culturally related stressors, for successful engagement in the treatment process, and for effective intervention, no matter which modality is considered. Paternal consent and involvement is necessary, but usually not difficult to obtain, but the mother's role in the facilitation of communication is also crucial. Extended family members are also very important, especially grandparents, since they can further support treatment and provide much historical and cultural information. It is important to obtain a full history on the family's immigration experience and particular stressors and losses they faced that have shaped their experience and perception. The exploration of intergenerational issues is also a must, since acculturation conflicts usually are played out against this background (Bernal, 1982).

The child psychiatrist working with a Cuban American child needs to be sensitive to traditional Cuban values, such as strong pride, mistrust of established authority, and emphasis on personal and kinship ties. This means that initially a great deal of respect and formality in interactions is indicated, but as the family indicates comfort with the clinician, a more informal style is required. Entry into family issues needs to be gradual, with no undue burden placed on any member to be an "informant." However, once conflictual issues are revealed, intense affect expressed should not be misinterpreted as loss of control or pathological as long as it is not accompanied by behavioral disruption. The child psychiatrist also should be reasonably expressive of some affect, or else he or she may be misjudged as cold or indifferent to the child's condition. Both the child and the family should be directly educated as to the process and expected outcome of whichever treatment modality is used, since it is a safe assumption that family members will "compare notes" and inconsistencies will be cause for mistrust and premature termination. However, adherence to these approaches should lead to successful treatment outcomes, given Cuban Americans' relative openness to psychiatric and psychological approaches.

REFERENCES

Bernal, G. (1982). Cuban families. In M. McGoldrick, J. K. Pearce, J. Giordano (Eds.), *Ethnicity & family therapy* (pp. 187–207). New York: Guilford Press.

de Anda, D. (1984). Bicultural socialization: Factors affecting the minority experience. *Social Work, 29,* 101–107.

National Institute of Drug Abuse. (1987). *Use of selected drugs among Hispanics: Mexican-Americans, Puerto Ricans, and Cuban-Americans. Findings from the Hispanic Health and Nutrition Survey.* Rockville, MD: Alcohol, Drug Abuse, and Mental Health Administration.

Pumariega, A. J. (1986). Acculturation and abnormal eating attitudes. *Journal of the American Academy of Child and Adolescent Psychiatry, 25*(2), 269–275.

Queralt, M. (1984). Understanding Cuban immigrants: A cultural perspective. *Social Work, 29,* 115–121.

Ruiz, P. (1982). Cuban-Americans. In A. Gaw (Ed.), *Cross-cultural psychiatry* (pp. 75–86). Boston: John Wright-PSG.

Ruiz, P., Venegas-Samuels, K., & Alarcon, R. D. (1995). The economics of pain: Mental health care costs among minorities. *Cultural Psychiatry, 18*(3), 659–670.

Rumbaut, R. D., & Rumbaut, R. G. (1976). The family in exile: Cuban expatriates in the United States. *American Journal of Psychiatry, 133,* 395–399.

Sokol-Katz, J. S., & Ulbrich, P. M. (1992). Family structure & adolescent risk-taking behavior: A comparison of Mexican, Cuban, & Puerto-Rican-Americans. *The International Journal of the Addictions, 27*(10), 1197–1209.

Szapocznik, J., Scopetta, M. A., & King, O. E. (1978). Theory and practice in matching treatment to the specific characteristics and problems of Cuban immigrants. *Journal of Community Psychology, 6,* 112–122.

U.S. Bureau of the Census. (1991). *Current population reports, series P-20, No. 449. The Hispanic population in the United States: March, 1990.* Washington, DC: U.S. Government Printing Office.

Vega, W. A., Warheit, G., Apospori, E., & Zimmerman, R. (1993). The relationship of drug use to suicide ideation & attempts among African-American, Hispanics, & white non-Hispanic adolescents. *Suicide and Life-threatening Behavior, 23*(2), 110–119.

50 / The Puerto Rican Child

Ian A. Canino and Glorisa Canino

Puerto Ricans now constitute 11% of the total Latino population in the continental United States. They have the highest poverty rates (particularly in persons under 18 years of age), the lowest median household incomes ($16,169.00), the highest percent of female-headed families, the highest unemployment rates among men (10.3%), and the lowest labor participation rates when compared to Mexicans, Cubans, Central and South Americans, and other Latinos residing in the United States. Among a total population rate of 21.4%, the total percent completing four years of college was 10.1% (Garcia & Montgomery, 1991). Puerto Ricans in Puerto Rico have a gross per capita income of $4,600.00 (Informe Economico al Gobernador, 1988) and the official unemployment rate as of 1989 was 14.4% (Encuesta de Vivienda, 1989). During the 1987–1988 period, 7.7% of males and 7.5% of females finished college (Informe Anual, 1987–1988).

These demographic characteristics are different but certainly not significant between these two groups of Puerto Ricans. They share a common heritage and social profile and certainly a past but not a recent history. Their recent history diverged because increasingly they have been exposed to a host of different economic and political transitions, to a variety of different cultures and languages, and to different degrees of stress caused by migration, family disorganization, acculturation, and discrimination.

The impact of island versus stateside politics and economics on mental health policy and resource allocation is likely to create different service utilization rates and a variety of service delivery patterns for these two groups. The added exposure of stateside Puerto Ricans to other cultures and languages will certainly affect the style of symptom expression and the level of need and type of socioculturally relevant diagnostic and treatment interventions. Finally, but not least, the degree, type, and frequency of stressful life events that these two populations are exposed to may determine the timing of disease expression, the frequency of exacerbations and remissions, and certainly the long-term prognosis for those members of these populations at risk or already suffering from mental disorders.

Unfortunately, there is a paucity of studies investigating the differences between these two groups of Puerto Ricans; even fewer studies address the relevance and impact of these issues on Puerto Rican children and adolescents. It will be assumed, until further data are available, that these two groups share some similarities but may have some significant differences.

For populations with different cultural patterns and concomitant social stressors, it is particularly difficult to differentiate what is cultural and what is socially determined. The term "sociocultural" is utilized throughout this chapter to address this issue. Furthermore, it may be necessary to refer to some findings in the adult Puerto Rican population and extrapolate their potential impact on Puerto Rican children. Within these limitations, this chapter reviews some of the existing literature and suggest some important guidelines for the clinician treating Puerto Rican children exposed to difficult environments.

Epidemiology

PUERTO RICAN CHILDREN IN PUERTO RICO

In spite of the obvious advantages of epidemiological research for child psychiatry, there is still a relative paucity of research in this area. As in adult psychiatric epidemiology, past studies of the prevalence of childhood disorders did not describe the frequency of discrete psychiatric conditions in children but of global maladjustment or maladaptive behavior (Gould, Wunsch-Hitzig, & Downrenwend, 1980; Links, 1983; Verlhurst, Akerhuis, & Althaus, 1985). More recently a number of child psychiatry epidemiological surveys in different regions of the world such as Canada (Offord, et al., 1987), New Zealand (Anderson, Williams, McGee, & Silva, 1987), the United States (Costello, et al., 1988; Cohen, et al., 1989), and Puerto Rico (Bird, et al., 1988) have been conducted. All these studies made use of structured diagnostic interview schedules to ascertain discrete psychiatric disorders based on criteria from the third edition of the *Diagnostic and Statistical Manual of Mental Disorders* (DSM-III).

Although all these studies used the same diagnostic criteria, they differed on the decision rules used in the estimation of prevalence rates. For example, Puerto Rico added a global measure of impairment—the Child Global Assessment Scale (C-GAS) by Shaffer and associates (1983)—that was utilized separately by the clinician and incorporated into the decision rule for determining prevalence rates. In Canada, clinicians were instructed to consider impairment in making their clinical judgments. When considering impairment in the definition of "caseness," most regions had similar prevalence rates, fluctuating between 17% (18% in Puerto Rico) to 22% in Canada and some regions of the United States. In Puerto Rico, when prevalence rates were estimated using *DSM-III* criteria alone (through either clinical judgment of indigenous child psychiatrists or the computer algorithms of the Diagnostic Interview Schedule for Children) (Costello, Edelbrock, Dulcan, & Kalas, 1987), approximately half (49% to 52%) of the population of children ages 4 to 16 years of the island met diagnostic criteria. Prevalence rates were estimated using the computer algorithms of the Diagnostic Interview Schedule for Children (DISC) administered by child psychiatrists. Rates were also estimated based on the clinical judgment of these same psychiatrists who administered the DISC. Using both methods of case ascertainment, the rates of psychiatric disorder were equally high. Nevertheless, most of the children who met *DSM-III* criteria, but were not functionally impaired, were not considered to be in need of mental health services by either the child psychiatrist who evaluated them, their parents, or their teachers (Bird, Yager, Staghezza, Gould, Canino, & Rubio-Stipec, 1990). Prevalence rates were significantly lowered to 17% when moderate to severe impairment (as ascertained by the C-GAS) in addition to *DSM-III* criteria was used in the definition of caseness. The high prevalence rate of disorder in the Puerto Rican children population was accounted for mainly by high prevalence rates of separation anxiety, oppositional disorders, and simple phobias (Bird et al., 1988).

Recent data from four sites (Georgia, Connecticut, New York, and Puerto Rico), reported by the the Collaborative Agreement for Methodologic Research for Multi-Site Epidemiologic Surveys of Mental Disorders in Child and Adolescent Populations study (MECA), showed similar results to those obtained in Puerto Rico (Shaffer, et al., 1996). The data from both studies and the four different communities studied suggest that many or most of the children who meet criteria for *DSM-III-R* disorders may not be functionally impaired and that a measure of impairment is imperative in the estimation of population prevalence rates for children. The data also suggest that prevalence rates of overall psychopathology in children do not seem to vary cross-culturally. Other studies in which both *DSM* criteria and impairment in functioning were used to estimate prevalence rates have also reported rates ranging from 16 to 20% (Anderson, McGee, Silva, & Williams, 1987; Costello, 1989; Costello et al., 1988; Offord et al., 1987; Velez & Ungermack, 1989; Verhulst, Koot, & Berden, 1990; Verhulst, Berden, & Sanders-Woudstra, 1985).

While it seems that overall prevalence is similar across studies, cultural differences in the rates of specific disorders, specific areas of symptomatology, and the associated risk factors of specific disorders need to be evaluated. For example, in the 1985 Puerto Rico study, prevalence rates of alcohol and drug use, as well as conduct disorders in the child and adolescent population, were considerably lower than those obtained in other epidemiological studies on the mainland or other parts of the world. These findings were confirmed several years later (1992) when data from Puerto Rico were compared to three other sites as part of the MECA study (Shaffer et al., 1996). This study employed the same methodology, such as identical case ascertainment methods (the DISC 2.3), and a household probability sample, in an attempt to reduce the influence of local variables (Lahey, et al., 1996). In spite of the methodological similarities, Puerto Rican children had substantially lower rates of substance abuse and conduct disorders. Their lower rates were attributed to cultural and contextual factors related to strong family ties and parental and community supervision typical of Puerto Rican families with children ages 9 to 17 and not as common in the U.S. communities studied.

In a comparison between the same study previously referenced and a similar epidemiological study carried out in the United States, mean scores on both the Child Behavior Checklist and the Teacher Report Form among nonreferred Puerto Rican children were significantly higher than those observed in the normative sample of United States children (Achenbach et al., 1990). On the other hand, mean scores on the Youth Self Report were lower; Bird, Gould, Rubio-Stipec, Staghezza, and Canino (1991) state that this could be explained in part by a cultural tendency among Puerto Rican adolescents, as part of an authoritarian family structure, to keep their opinions to themselves.

Other important findings from this epidemiology study showed that only 16% of the children who met criteria for a probable or definite psychiatric condition, as defined by meeting criteria for a *DSM-III* diagnosis and having a C-GAS score between 61 and 70, were receiving mental health services; of these 16% who received services, 61% were received in schools (Staghezza, Bird, Gould, & Canino, 1995).

The correlates of mental disorders in the Puerto Rican children also were identifed as part of the study. Male children, children of low socioeconomic class, those between the ages of 6 to 11, children from dysfunctional family systems, children with a history of physical illness, and those who came from families with many life stressors were at more risk for mental disorders (Bird, Gould, Yager, Staghezza, & Canino, 1989).

The relationship between parental psychiatric disorder and parental alcoholism and risk for maladjustment in the offspring also has been investigated with Puerto Rican children. The data were obtained from the merging of the data sets of the child epidemiological study (Bird et al., 1988) and an adult psychiatric epidemiology survey (Canino, et al., 1987). Both surveys used the same sampling frames. Results indicated that significantly more children of disturbed parents were functionally impaired and had higher total behavior scores on the parent and youth Child Behavior Checklist (Achenbach & Edelbrock, 1987) as compared to children of normal parents. These associations were maintained even after accounting for an adverse family environment, suggesting a strong relationship between parental and childhood psychopathology as well as a mediating influence of environmental adversity (Canino, Bird, Rubio-Stipec, Bravo, & Alegria, 1990). On the other hand, besides creating an adverse family environment, parental alcoholism had an affect on the relative risk for maladjustment in the offspring as measured by the Child Behavior Checklist; an increased risk also was observed for internalizing symptoms, particularly depressive symptoms. Similar findings were obtained for the children of parents with other psychiatric disorders, suggesting that the effects of parental alcoholism in children ages 4 to 16 may not be different from

the consequences of parental mental illness per se (Rubio-Stipec, Bird, Canino, Bravo, & Alegria, 1991).

PUERTO RICAN CHILDREN IN THE UNITED STATES

Limited data are available concerning Puerto Rican children in the United States. Langner, Gerstein, and Eisenberg (1974) studied 1,034 children ages 6 to 18 randomly selected from a cross-section of Manhattan households and consisting of 56% white, 29% Spanish-speaking (many came from Puerto Rican households), and 14% African American children. Information was obtained through interviews with mothers. Hispanic and African American children were found to experience more stressors than did white children. Compulsivity, toilet training difficulties, isolation, and weak group membership were more common in the Hispanic group. When this randomly selected group was compared to a sample of welfare-dependent families, the Spanish-speaking children tended to be the most impaired of the three ethnic groups in the sample. The Hispanic Research Center collected data from 16,000 New York City Department of Mental Health intake forms and compared Hispanic children (overrepresented by Puerto Rican children) to white and African American children who were serviced by the outpatient mental health facilities in the city. The rates of admissions to all local facilities were highest for Hispanic children. Puerto Rican children reported higher rates of sleep problems, anxiety, fears, and phobias than did African Americans. Slightly larger percentages of interviewed Puerto Rican and African American children were diagnosed as transient situational and behavior-disordered than of white children (Canino, Early, & Rogler, 1980). In a study of 147 Hispanic and African American children attending an outpatient clinic in New York City and utilizing inventory forms that provided standardized information on symptomatology, psychiatric diagnosis, and the presence of family and psychosocial stressors, the authors found that a higher proportion of Hispanic (mainly Puerto Rican) children than African American children entered the clinic through the emergency services and had symptoms of depression, fears and phobias, anxiety and panic, school refusal, and disturbances of relationships with other children. On Axis V Hispanic children were more likely to have poor levels of adaptive functioning; they did not differ in the frequency of the other diagnostic axes and associated abnormal psychosocial situations. High proportions of both Hispanic and African American children had Axis III diagnoses (physical disorders and conditions) and came from dysfunctional families with a high frequency of mental illness (Canino, Gould, Prupis, & Shaffer, 1986).

In one of the few studies comparing Puerto Rican children in Puerto Rico with those on the mainland, Velez and Ungermack (1989) studied all children 10 to 12 years of age in two schools in New York City, known for the high percentage of Puerto Rican children attending them, and matched them, on socioeconomic class, to children in two schools in Puerto Rico. Four distinct groups were considered: children of Puerto Rican parents born in New York, children born in New York of Puerto Rican parents who migrated back to Puerto Rico, children born in Puerto Rico who immigrated to New York, and children born in Puerto Rico who never left the island. The authors found that boys in general were more likely to use drugs except for the group immigrating to New York, where girls outnumbered boys; this variation apparently resulted from a higher susceptibility among girls previously educated in a very rigid society. The children born in New York and attending school there were at a higher risk to use drugs than the group immigrating into New York, which in turn were at higher risk than the children who migrated to the island. Length of stay in New York and broken homes seemed to increase the risk.

Clinical Issues

CHILD-REARING PRACTICES

Even though the impact of child-rearing practices may or may not have long-term consequences (Quinton, 1980), some authors have suggested that it can influence the pace and timing of developmental processes (DeVries & Sameroff, 1984; Thomas & Chess, 1980). Child-rearing practices are sensitive to social class levels and expectations and the impact of the media, and they certainly can vary according to the degree of exposure to other cultural groups. The clinician must assess the degree to which child-rearing practices have been consistent, malleable, or syntonic to the demands of the environment in which the child is being reared as well as their suitability to the child's particular temperamental style.

Many reports have addressed the importance of child-rearing practices in the Puerto Rican population. The utilization of toys for amusement and not for educational purposes in poor families, the inculcation of respect for the elderly, the clear demarcation of sexual roles, the strict adherence to parental commands and less emphasis on independence, little participation by children in decision making, and the fostering of early sociability and cooperativeness have been described in the past (Gannon, 1975; Rogler & Santana-Corney, 1984; Thomas, Chess, Sillen, & Mendez, 1974).

Even though child-rearing practices alone may not cause psychiatric disorders, they may affect their presentation and outcome. Parents may label certain behaviors as deviant or as normal to their culture. They may thus punish certain behaviors and reinforce others. Parental expectations, in turn, are affected by their level of education, number of other children in the household, marital status, and their own previous experiences as children. Child-rearing practices and family norms that openly conflict with the environmental demands and expectations can produce paradoxical messages to the child and eventually cause symptoms of distress.

In the case of Puerto Rican children, child-rearing practices may place them in jeopardy in some cases and fortify them in others. A child in a small traditional community in Puerto Rico will need to learn to be cooperative, conform, depend on the extended network, and be respectful to the elderly. Thus, a third-generation Puerto Rican child raised in New York and returning to a small community in Puerto Rico will experience many difficulties. On the other hand, a Puerto Rican child in the inner city of New York needs to be self-assertive and reliant, reach early independence, and relate to adults more equally. Recently arrived children from Puerto Rico who are raised to be dependent on the family and attached to the mother until they are older may develop separation anxiety symptoms if the inner-city environment demands that they be independent and streetwise much earlier in their development.

An adolescent girl in a traditional Puerto Rican family is expected to follow clearly demarcated sexual roles; in a large urban area, she is expected to act and behave within a more flexible framework. Should she find herself exposed to these conflicting messages, she may opt to rebel, may act out sexually, or may develop identity conflicts and low self-esteem (Rotheram-Borus, 1989). Not yet clear about what is expected of her by her non-Puerto Rican peers and upset about her perceived and internalized parental rules, she may feel guilty and develop symptoms of anxiety and depression. Should the family conflicts be in the area of disciplinary approaches, disruptive and externalizing symptoms may occur. Rodriguez and Zayas (1990) suggest that Hispanic adolescents may be at high risk for antisocial behavior due to the combined effect of a disadvantaged status (low income, social discrimination) and an antisocial family environment (a family inefficient in their disciplinary function).

SYMPTOM EXPRESSION
AND HELP-SEEKING BEHAVIOR

Different cultural groups express distress in particular forms, have different beliefs of what causes mental illness in their children, and have their own patterns of help-seeking behaviors. Additionally, differences have been found within cultures when factors such as intelligence, personality, attitudes and behaviors, and social class have been measured. Unfortunately, the research methodology still have many limitations. For example, instruments developed and calibrated in a given social group often are translated and used in groups that differ not only culturally but socially. Attitudes and behavior do not have a one-to-one correspondence in different languages and certain experiences are not available in certain cultures (Guthrie, 1984).

In terms of Puerto Rican adults, Dohrenwend and Dohrenwend (1969) found them to report a significantly greater number of psychiatric symptoms than their social class counterparts in other ethnic groups. They stated that the observed differences may have been due to methodological factors, such as cultural differences in response style, language used to express psychological distress, and concepts of socially desirable behavior. Canino et al. (1992) found that Puerto Ricans reported the highest level of somatic symptoms when compared to three other ethnic groups. This finding seemed independent from possible sociodemographic confounders. They postulate that a possible explanation of this phenomena is that Puerto Ricans find this style of expressing distress more culturally accepted or as providing a more effective access to health services that may otherwise be unavailable. Research needs to be done in terms of how symptom reporting of Puerto Rican parents affects the symptom reporting on their children and how their symptom choice patterns affect patterns of distress expression by their children. In the meantime, the clinician must be cognizant of these patterns in the parents and thus must avail him- or herself of other sources of information during the assessment of these children. In view of the possible learned patterns of distress expression through somatic symptoms, the clinician must always investigate for these symptoms in Puerto Rican children and thoroughly review their pediatric charts.

As Puerto Ricans are exposed and educated to the mental health needs and difficulties of their children and learn to utilize the health resources in their communities, their beliefs and health utilization patterns will more closely resemble those of the general population. Those who have not found relief within the existing health delivery system may utilize other resources. In a study of island Puerto Ricans, Canino et al. (1987) found that among those who met criteria for the Diagnostic Interview Schedule/*DSM-III* disorders, only 17% utilized the mental health sector or a specialist in mental health, whereas 47% visited a nonpsychiatrist physician and 21% used both the health sector and spiritualists for their mental health problems. In a study analyzing health-seeking behavior of Hispanics in New York (the largest group being Puerto Rican), Rodriguez (1987) found that acculturated Hispanics were more likely than unacculturated ones to use mental health services. Other reports have been published about the utilization of native healers or *espiritistas* among stateside Puerto Rican adults (Garrison, 1977; Harwood, 1977).

There has been a paucity, nevertheless, of reports on Puerto Rican children. It is not known how many Puerto Rican children with psychiatric problems are seen by other health professionals such as pediatricians. In terms of those attending *espiritistas,* Bird and Canino (1981) interviewed 50 Puerto Rican mothers attending an outpatient clinic in New York and found that 24% admitted to have consulted a spiritualist about their child during the previous year. A large proportion of children were directly involved by the parents in the folk religious practices. These consisted of bathing in herbal water, wearing special articles of clothing, reciting prayers, and sacrificing a pigeon. The mothers took their children to the *espiritistas* because of behavior problems, academic difficulties, and sleep disturbances. Even though these are small numbers and may not reflect or be representative of all Puerto Rican children, the clinician must be aware of these patterns and ask the family for what reason and to what extent were these alternative services utilized. Manuel, a 13-year-old schizophrenic boy, is an illustrative example. After a brief hospitalization, family therapy and medication were recommended as part of the treatment plan. Many months occurred with little family cooperation until a culturally sensitive consultant was called. She was able to identify immediately the fact that the family practiced *espiritismo.* The family felt the child's problems were spiritual in nature and would be healed only through seances. These seances had started while the child was in weekend passes at home. The family felt that family therapy as well as medication were not relevant and thus were not following the treatment recommendations. They had not notified the clinician about this because their previous experiences had taught them that clinicians would feel they were "ignorant" and "crazy." The consultant explained that there was a physical part to the disease that needed medical care as well. After talking to the staff and to the family and clarifying their mutual misunderstandings, a combined and effective treatment plan was instituted.

Finally, in order to bring Puerto Ricans to our mental health services, these have to be accessible, multidisciplinary, and culturally sensitive (Costantino, Malgady, & Rogler, 1988; Rosado, 1986; Zayas et al., 1984). Costantino et al. (1988) developed a culturally sensitive approach for these children where folk tales were read, discussed, and replayed, and where parents, mainly mothers, participated. This *cuento* (storytelling) therapy showed a significant decrease in aggressive and anxious behaviors and an increase in social judgment capacity. A "hero/heroine" therapy was used with adolescents where art, sports, and folk heroes were used as models, and a detailed description of their struggles and achievements was highlighted. The adolescents showed an increase in ethnic pride and a decrease in anxiety symptoms.

CLINICAL DIMENSIONS

Utilizing conceptual frameworks from the literature addressing culturally sensitive research instruments (Bravo, Canino, Rubio-Stipec, & Woodbury-Farina, 1991; Flaherty, 1987), this section addresses the need of the clinician to be aware of three dimensions when evaluating Puerto Rican children.

The first dimension is the semantic equivalence of the clinician's verbal interventions. This dimension is meant to ensure that, during translation, the meaning of each item is similar in the language of each culture. An example offered by Bravo, Woodbury, and Canino (1993) is the translation of the word "worry." The word in Spanish is *preocupacion,* which may mean both to anxiously worry as well as to be appropriately concerned. A clinician evaluating a Puerto Rican child or eliciting a history from the parent must address this subtlety in meaning before concluding that the child comes from an overly anxious family or has anxiety symptoms.

The second dimension is content equivalence. This dimension addresses whether the content of an item is relevant to a given population. An example of this would be in assessing a dysphoric Puerto Rican adolescent for a history of seasonal depressive episodes while she lived in Puerto Rico. As Puerto Rico is a tropical island, there are no striking differences in the length of the days during the year and no environmental changes during the various seasons.

The third dimension is conceptual equivalence. This addresses the fact that theoretical concepts may be interpreted differently in different cultures. For example, the presence of visual hallucinations or visions in a child in Puerto Rico may be interpreted there as a culturally accepted behavior; in the United States, it may be interpreted as a symptom of a mental illness. The clinician thus must be careful not to underestimate or overestimate the difference between behaviors that may be seen as normative in a given culture from those that may be truly symptomatic.

Conclusion

Epidemiological findings are useful to clinicians inasmuch as they caution them against utilizing diagnostic criteria alone to classify disorders in Puerto Rican children from the island. It is clear from the data that if diagnostic manuals are going to be used by clinicians, addressing the section on global assessment of impairment is crucial. In addition, these studies indicate the high risk for psychopathology of Puerto Rican children of psychiatrically disturbed parents. This suggests that if a reduction of child mental disorders is to be achieved, preventive interventions with children whose parents are disturbed are necessary.

Puerto Rican children from Puerto Rico as well as those residing in the United States express distress through internalizing and emotional symptoms. Furthermore, study findings suggest that Puerto Rican children at risk are those with physical illnesses and those from dysfunctional family environments exposed to concomitant and frequent social stressors. For those Puerto Rican children who express distress through externalizing behaviors, migration patterns and acculturation stressors have to be considered as well.

In view of the reported child-rearing, symptom expression, and help-seeking patterns of Puerto Rican adults, the clinician must consider these patterns in assessment and treatment approaches of Puerto Rican children. The clinician needs to determine the impact of the rearing environment to the individual child, seek other informants, review pediatric charts to identify past somatic complaints, and identify other relevant help resources and belief systems in the family. In addition, the clinician must be aware of the semantic, contextual, and conceptual dimensions affecting the evaluation of these children.

Finally, further studies investigating the long-term impact on behavior and cognition of child-rearing practices and cultural beliefs, further research on the validity of diagnostic instruments and criteria across different cultures, and the creation of more ethnically sensitive treatment approaches are still necessary.

REFERENCES

Achenbach, T. M., Bird, H. R., Canino, G., Phares, V., Gould, M. S., & Rubio-Stipec, M. (1990). Epidemiological comparisons of Puerto Rican and U.S. mainland children: parent, teacher, and self reports. *Journal of the American Academy of Child and Adolescent Psychiatry, 29* (1), 84–93.

Achenbach, T. M., & Edelbrock, C. S. (1983). *Manual for Child Behavior Checklist and Revised Child Behavior Profile.* Burlington, VT: University Associates in Psychiatry.

Achenbach, T. M., & Edelbrock, C. S. (1987). *Manual for the youth self report and profile.* Burlington, VT: University Associates in Psychiatry.

American Psychiatric Association. (1980). *Diagnostic and Statistical Manual of Mental Disorders* (3rd. Ed.). Washington, DC: Authors.

Anderson, J. C., Williams, S., McGee, R., Silva, P. A. (1987). DSM-III disorders in preadolescent children. *Archives of General Psychiatry, 44* (1), 69–80.

Bird, H., & Canino, I. (1981). The sociopsychiatry of espiritismo; findings of a study in psychiatric populations of Puerto Rican and other hispanic children. *Journal of the American Academy of Child and Adolescent Psychiatry, 20,* 725–740.

Bird, H., Canino, G., Rubio-Stipec, M., Ribera, J., Sesman, M., Woodbury, M., Huertas, S., Pagan, A., Sanchez-Lacay, A., & Moscoso, M. (1988). Estimates of the prevalence of childhood maladjustment in a community survey in Puerto Rico. *Archives of General Psychiatry, 45,* 1120–1126.

Bird, H., Gould, M. S., Rubio-Stipec, M., Staghezza, B., & Canino, G. (1991). Screening for childhood psychopathology in the community using the Child Behavior Checklist. *Journal of the American Academy of Child and Adolescent Psychiatry, 30,* 116–123.

Bird, H., Gould, M. S., Yager, T., Staghezza, B., & Canino, G. (1989). Risk factors of maladjustment in Puerto Rican children. *American Academy of Child and Adolescent Psychiatry, 28,* 847–850.

Bird, H., Yager, T. J., Staghezza, B., Gould, M. S., Canino, G., & Rubio-Stipec, M. (1990). Impairment in the epidemiological measurement of childhood psychopathology in the community. *American Academy of Child and Adolescent Psychiatry, 29* (5), 796–803.

Bravo, M., Canino, G., Rubio-Stipec, M., & Woodbury-Farina, M. (1991). A cross-cultural adaptation of a psychiatric epidemiological instrument: The Diagnostic Interview Schedule's adaptation in Puerto Rico. *Culture, Medicine and Psychiatry, 15,* 1–18.

Bravo, M., Woodbury, M. A., & Canino, G. J. (1993). The Spanish translation and cultural adaptation of the Diagnostic Interview Schedule for Children (DISC) in Puerto Rico. *Culture, Medicine and Psychiatry, 17,* 329–344.

Canino, G., Bird, H., Rubio-Stipec, M., Bravo, M., & Alegria, M. (1990). Children of parents with psychiatric disorders in the community. *American Academy of Child and Adolescent Psychiatry, 29* (3), 398–406.

Canino, G., Bird, H., Shrout, P., Rubio-Stipec, M., Bravo, M., Martinez, R., Sesman, M., & Guevara, L. M. (1987). The prevalence of specific psychiatric disorders in Puerto Rico. *Archives of General Psychiatry, 44,* 727–735.

Canino, I., Early, B., & Rogler, L. (1980). *The Puerto Rican child in New York City: Stress and mental health.* monograph No. 4, Bronx, NY: Hispanic Research Center, Fordham University.

Canino, I., Escobar, J., Canino, G., & Rubio-Stipec, M. (1992). Functional somatic symptoms: A cross-ethnic comparison. *American Journal of Orthopsychiatry, 62* (4), 605–612.

Canino, I., Gould, M., Prupis, S., Shaffer, D. (1986). A comparison of symptoms and diagnoses in Hispanic and black children in an outpatient mental health clinic. *Journal of the Academy of Child Psychiatry, 25* (2), 254–259.

Chess, S. (1980). Developmental theory revisited. In S. Chess & A. Thomas (Eds.), *Annual Progress in Child Psychiatry and Child Development* (pp. 3–20). New York: Brunner Mazel.

Cohen, P., Cohen, J., Kasen, S., Velez, C. N., Hartmark, C., Johnson, J., Rojas, M., Brook, J., & Struening, E. L. (1993). An epidemiological study of disorders in late childhood and adolescence: I Age and gender-specific prevalence. *Journal of Child Psychology and Psychiatry, 34,* 851–867.

Costantino, G., Malgady, R. G., & Rogler, L. H. (1988). Folk hero modeling therapy for Puerto Rican adolescents. *Journal of Adolescence, 11,* 155–165.

Costello, E. J. (1989). Developments in child psychiatric epidemiology. *American Academy of Child and Adolescent Psychiatry, 27,* 836–840.

Costello, E. J., Costello, A. J., Edelbrock, C., Burns, B., Dulcan, M., Brent, D., & Janiszewski, S. (1988). Psychiatric disorders in pediatric primary care: Prevalence and risk factors. *Archives of General Psychiatry, 45,* 1107–1116.

Costello, A. J., Edelbrock, C., Dulacan, M. K., Kalas, R., & Klaric, S. (1987). *Testing of the NIMH Diagnostic Interview Schedule for Children (DISC) in a clinical population: Final report.* Rockville, MD: Center for Epidemiological Studies, NIMH.

DeVries, M. W., & Sameroff, A. J. (1984). Culture and temperament: Influence on infant temperament in three East African societies. *American Journal of Orthopsychiatry, 54* (1), 83–96.

Dohrenwend, B. P., & Dohrenwend, B. S. (1969). *Social status and psychological disorder: A causal inquiry.* New York: John Wiley & Sons.

Encuesta de Vivienda (1989). Departamento de Trabajo. San Juan, Puerto Rico. (Household Survey by the Department of Labor).

Flaherty, J. A. (1987). Appropriate and inappropriate research methodologies for Hispanic mental health. In M. Gaviria & J. D. Arana (Eds.), *Health and behavior: Research agenda for Hispanics* (pp. 117–186). Chicago: University of Illinois at Chicago.

Gannon, S. (1975). *Behavioral problems and temperament in middle class and Puerto Rican five-year-old boys.* Unpublished master's thesis. New York: Hunter College.

Garcia, J., & Montgomery, P. (1991). The Hispanic population in the United States: March, 1991. Current Population Reports, Series P-20, No. 455. Washington, DC: U.S. Bureau of the Census.

Garrison, V. (1977). Doctor, espiritista or psychiatrist? Mental health seeking behavior in a Puerto Rican neighborhood of New York city. *Medical Anthropology, 1,* 65–180.

Gould, M. S., Wunsch-Hitzag, R., & Dohrenwend, B. P. (1980). Formulation of hypotheses about the prevalence, treatment and prognostic significance of psychiatric disorders in children in the U.S. In B. P. Dohrenwend, M. S. Gould, & B. Link (Eds.), *Mental illness in the U.S.: Epidemiological estimates* (pp. 9–44). New York: Praeger.

Guthrie, G. M. (1984). Problems of measurement in cross cultural research. In J. E. Mezzich and C. E. Berganza (pp. 87–99). *Culture and Psychopathology.* New York: Columbia University Press.

Harwood, A. R. (1977). *Rx.: Spiritists as needed: A study of Puerto Rican community mental health resources.* New York: John Wiley & Sons.

Informe Anual. (1987–1988). San Juan, Puerto Rico: Division de Estadisticas. Departamento de Educacion.

Informe Economico al Gobernador. (1988). Junta de Planificacion de Puerto Rico. Estado Libre Asociado de Puerto Rico. San Juan, Puerto Rico: Oficina del Gobernador.

Lahey, B. B., Flagg, E. W., Bird, H. R., Schwab-Stone, M., Canino, G., Dulcan, M. K., Leaf, P. J., Davies, M., Brogan, D., Bourdon, K., Horwitz, S. M., Rubio-Stipec, M., Freeman, D. H., Lichtman, J., Shaffer, D., Goodman, S. H., Narrow, W. E., Weissman, M., Kandel, D. B., Jensen, P. S., Richters, J. E., & Regier, D. A. (1996). The NIMH methods for the epidemiology of child and adolescent mental disorder (MECA) study: Background and methodology. *Journal of the*

American Academy of Child and Adolescent psychiatry, 35 (7), 855–864.

Langner, T., Gerstein, J., & Eisenberg, J. (1974). Approaches to measurement and definition in the epidemiology of behavior disorders: Ethnic background and child behavior. *International Journal of Health Services, 4,* 483–501.

Links, P. S., (1983). Community surveys of the prevalence of childhood psychiatric disorders: A review. *Child Development, 54,* 531–548.

Offord, D. R., Boyle, M. H., Szatmari, P., Rae-Grant, N. L., Links, P. S., Cadman, D. T., Byles, J. A., Crawford, J. W., Blum, H. M., Byrne, C., Thomas, H., & Woodward, C. A. (1987). Ontario child health study: II. Six month prevalence of disorder and rates of services utilization. *Archives of General Psychiatry, 44,* 832–836.

Quinton, D. (1980). Cultural and community influences. In M. Rutter (Ed.), *Scientific Foundations of Developmental Psychiatry* (pp. 77–91). London: Heinemann Medical Books.

Rodriguez, O. (1987). *Hispanics and human services: Help seeking in the inner city.* Monograph No. 14. New York: Hispanic Research Center, Fordham University.

Rodriguez, O., & Zayas, L. H. (1990). Hispanic adolescents and antisocial behavior: Sociocultural factors and treatment implications. In A. R. Stiffman, & L. E. Davis (Eds.), *Ethnic Issues in Adolescent Mental Health.* (pp. 147–171). Newbury Park, CA: Sage Publications.

Rogler, L. H., Malgady, R. G., & Rodriguez, O. (1989). *Hispanics and mental health: A framework for research.* Melbourne, Florida: Robert E. Kriger Publishing.

Rogler, L. H., & Santana-Corney, R. (1984). Puerto Rican Families in New York city: Intergenerational Processes. Maplewood, NJ: Waterfront Press.

Rosado, J. W., Jr. (1986). Toward an interfacing of Hispanic cultural variables with school psychology service delivery systems. *Professional Psychology: Research and Practice, 17,* 191–199.

Rotheram-Borus, M. J. (1989). Ethnic differences in adolescents' identity status and associated behavior problems. Special issue: adolescent identity: An appraisal of health and intervention. *Journal of Adolescence, 12* (4), 361–374.

Rubio-Stipec, M., Bird, H., Canino, G., Bravo, M., &

Alegria, M. (1991). Children of alcoholic parents in the community. *Journal of Studies of Alcohol, 52* (1), 78–88.

Shaffer, D., Fisher, P., Dulcan, M., Davis, D., Piacentini, J., Schwab-Stone, M., Lahey, B., Bourdon, K., Jensen, P., Bird, H., Canino, G., & Regier, D. (In press). The NIMH Diagnostic Interview Schedule for Children (DISC 2.3): Description, acceptability, prevalences, and performance in the MECA study. *Journal of the American Academy of Child and Adolescent Psychiatry, 35* (7), 865–877.

Shaffer, D., Gould, M. S., Brasic, J., Ambrosini, P. J., Fisher, P., Bird, H. R., & Aluwahlia, S. (1983). A Children's Global Assessment Scale (C-GAS). *Archives of General Psychiatry, 40,* 1228–1231.

Staghezza-Jaramillo, B., Bird, H. R., Gould, M. S., & Canino, G. (1995). Mental health service utilization among Puerto Rican children ages 4 through 16. *Journal of Child Family Study, 4* (4), 399–418.

Thomas, A., Chess, S., Sillen, J., & Mendez, O. (1974). Cross cultural study of behavior in children with special vulnerabilities to stress. In *Life History Research in Psychopathology.* Minneapolis: University of Minnesota Press.

Thomas, A., & Chess, S. (1980). *The Dynamics of Psychological Development.* New York: Brunner Mazel.

Velez, C. N., & Ungermack, J. (1989). Drug use among Puerto Rican youth: An exploration of generational status differences. *Social Sciences and Medicine, 29,* 779–789.

Verlhust, F. C., Akerhuis, G. W., & Althaus, M. (1985). Mental health in Dutch children: I. A cross-cultural comparison. *Acta Psychiatrica Scandinavica* (Suppl. No. 323), *72,* 1–108.

Verlhust, F. C., Berden, G. F., & Sanders-Woudstra, J. (1985). Mental health in Dutch children: (II) The prevalence of psychiatric disorder and relationship between measures. *Acta psychiatrica Scandinavica,* (Suppl. No. 324), *72,* 1–45.

Verlhust, F. C., Koot, H. M., Berden, G. F. (1990). Four-year follow-up of an epidemiological sample. *Journal of the American Academy of Child and Adolescent Psychiatry, 29,* 440–448.

Zayas, L. H., & Bryant, L. H. (1984). Culturally sensitive treatment of adolescent Puerto Rican girls and their families. *Child Adolescence Social Work Journal, 1,* 235–253.

51 / The Mexican American Child

William Arroyo and Richard C. Cervantes

There are unique sociocultural factors that require special attention by children mental health service providers, other children service providers, investigators, advocates, and others who share the common interest of improving the lives of Mexican American children and adolescents (hereafter children). This is especially true in the provision of services for Mexican American children who suffer from mental disorders. These factors include culture, linguistic abilities, education, acculturation, economics, and general child development. Such sociocultural factors may influence their clinical presentation, diagnosis, and treatment.

Population Definition

GROUP TERMS

The terms and definitions used by authors in reference to people of Mexican descent in both the medical and social science literature have changed throughout the 20th century. Terms used by the U.S. Census Bureau have undergone similar change (Hernandez, Estrada, & Alvirez, 1973). People of Mexican descent are frequently subsumed under the global terms "Hispanic," "Hispanic White," "Latino," and "Latino American" among others. These umbrella terms connote one homogeneous group, thereby minimizing the ethnic, racial, cultural, and linguistic variation among the numerous groups that are subsumed under them. "Hispanic" is also often associated with federal bureaucratic expediency and is perceived as primarily emphasizing European roots as opposed to native Latin American roots. "Latino," on the other hand, which is derived from the popular "Latino Americano" and used by Latin Americans for self-identification, emphasizes native Latin American roots. For this reason, the term "Latino" will be used in this chapter to refer to all people of Latin American descent. The practice of subsuming the various Latino groups under one rubric often has resulted in erroneous assumptions

by the mental health planner (Hayes-Bautista, 1983), the clinician, and the investigator; this, in turn, has led to the design of nonresponsive clinical services and to faulty study comparisons (Lampe, 1984).

"Chicano," "Mexican," and "Mexican American" are the terms used specifically to refer to people of Mexican descent. "Mexican" is generally used to refer to native Mexicans while "Chicano" is primarily associated with the political movements of people of Mexican descent during the 1960s and early 1970s. Lampe (1984) emphasizes the importance of nativity; he, therefore, recommends terms that distinguish among these various groups. For purposes of this chapter and uniformity, the term "Mexican American" will be used to refer to all people of Mexican descent who reside in the United States.

POPULATION STATISTICS

According to the U.S. Census Bureau (U.S. Department of Commerce News, 1991), the 1990 census figures indicate that the Latino (Hispanic White) population is 22.3 million, an increase of 50% since 1980. Latinos account for 9% of the U.S. population and are expected to be the largest ethnic minority group by the year 2000 (Macias, 1977). Almost 70% of the Latino population in the United States is divided among four states, California, Texas, Florida, and New York. More than 34% of the nation's Latino population lives in California. Nearly 63% of the Latino population, or 14.0 million Latinos in the United States, are of Mexican origin (U.S. Department of Commerce, 1990). Legal immigration accounts for the major portion of the increase; during the 1980s Mexico led all sources of immigration, with nearly 1 million. Estimates of undocumented entrants of Mexican descent are inaccurate. Mexican Americans with a median age of 23.3 years comprise the youngest of the several Latino groups, a fact that has implications for population growth; the non-Latino median age is 33.2 years. Approximately

39.1% (5.5 million) of Mexican American children are below the age of 18 years compared to 26.0% of the non-Latino population.

EDUCATION

According to a 1991 report of the American Council on Education (1991), Latinos are grossly underrepresented at every school level. The proportion of Latino students completing high school dropped from 60.1% in 1984 to 55.9% in 1989 while the rate for Euro-American (Anglo or non-Hispanic whites) students dipped to 82.1% in 1989. These findings cannot be attributed to the influx of immigrant students, since American-born Latinos have considerably lower education levels than non-Latinos. Several factors are conjectured to contribute to this problem, including the lack of access to equal educational resources, the culture of poverty, a pattern of poor educational facilities in predominantly minority communities, shrinking public educational funding, low performance expectations on the part of the schools and the students themselves, lack of effective ways to involve the students' parents, and possibly language fluency. In 1989, only 3% of all bachelor's degrees were awarded to Latinos, which further underscores the crisis of education and Latinos.

ECONOMICS

Latino Americans have made minor economic gains during the last decade; however, many remain impoverished. The 1990 census data (U.S. Department of Commerce, 1990) revealed that 37.6% of all Latino (37.8% of all Mexican American) children live below the federally established poverty level compared to 17.3% of all non-Latino U.S. Children. Economic disadvantage has been correlated with child psychiatric disorders (Offord, 1990).

Cultural Meaning of Mental Illness and "Culture-Bound" Syndromes

Fabrega (1990) challenges investigators and clinicians alike to examine the degree of applicability of what he terms "establishment psychiatry" to Latino populations (p. 339). He defines establishment psychiatry as that which "constitutes the dominant professional perspective about mental health problems and is seen to reflect a universalist focus and a biological determinism."

The prescription of mental health interventions for Mexican Americans should reflect their (child and family's) perceptions of mental illness, of therapeutic expectations, and of general health beliefs. According to Karno and Edgarton (1969), Mexican American adults perceive and define mental illnesses similarly to Euro-Americans. In their study, however, Mexican Americans more frequently believed that mental disorders began in childhood than did their Euro-American counterparts. Mental health-seeking behavior might include consultation with a highly respected family or community member, a family physician, a religious minister, a nonmental health service agency, and more rarely a folk healer (a *curandero*).

The therapeutic expectations of children and their families vary. Acosta (1979) found that low-income adult Mexican Americans expected their therapist either to actively engage them in dialogue or to take on a listening role; a minority of the sample expected the clinician to give specific instructions to resolve the presenting problem. Falicov (1982) proposes that lower-socioeconomic families respond better to a brief and problem-oriented approach that redefines the problem as a function of the parent-child relationship. More recently, Cervantes (1993) argues that therapeutic approaches for Latinos must include identification of culturally specific stress events. Such events have been correlated with increased symptomatology, including depression, anxiety, and somatization (Cervantes, Padilla, & Salgado de Snyder, 1992).

A study (Mull & Mull, 1981) of general health beliefs among Mexican American women has implications for psychotropic prescribing practices. Results indicate that the respondents' prominent beliefs include: injections are more helpful than oral medications; good physicians prescribe injections for their patients; oral medication that does not relieve symptoms within 3 days is not going to work; and having blood drawn weakens one's body. Castro, Furth, and Karlow (1984) found that minimally, bicultural, and highly acculturated women endorsed at least mild acceptance of Latino folk beliefs. All three groups held hot-cold illness relationship beliefs, while only the low-acculturated woman was more likely to believe that God, chance, or the physician were powerful external agents that could affect one's health status.

Mexican Americans recognize at least a few syndromes that have been referred to as "culture-bound" syndromes or folk diseases (Martinez & Martin, 1966). They may mimic several psychiatric disorders. The lay "*Nervios* (literally nerves) syndrome" can be a signal to Latinos of family difficulties and a sense of personal dyscontrol (Low, 1981). *Susto* (literally fright) (Klein, 1978) is caused by life-threatening events. *Mal Puesto* (Martinez & Martin, 1966) is primarily viewed as being a victim of a hex. *Mal de Ojo* (Martinez & Martin, 1966) refers to the syndrome by which a child develops both somatic and emotional symptoms as a result of being observed in a covetous fashion. Specialized folk treatments, folk healers, and specially trained community members may become additional treatment resources for intervention especially if the family desires them and can be considered as another facet of intervention.

Epidemiology

Although several epidemiologic surveys on the prevalence of mental illness among Mexican American adults have been undertaken (Karno et al., 1987), there is a paucity of comparable studies in Mexican American children and adolescents. The lone extensive epidemiologic study of Latino youngsters is one involving Puerto Rican children and adolescents (Bird et al., 1988). The prevalence of psychiatric disorders among Mexican American youths is unknown.

Arrest data or delinquency rates falsely suggest that there is a high prevalence of conduct disorder among Latino youths (primarily Mexican American) in California. Furthermore, there is differential treatment of Latinos and whites by the health service agencies and the juvenile justice systems (Chambliss & Nagasawa, 1969).

The information on rates of substance and alcohol abuse as psychiatric syndromes among Mexican American children and adolescents is minimal

(Gilbert & Alcocer, 1988). Research problems include the common error of inadequately defining "Hispanic"; combining subjects of various ethnic and racial origins; and not matching for age and sex. However, there is evidence (Mata, 1986) to suggest that both Euro-American males and females consume more alcohol than Mexican American males and females of comparable ages, with the greater disparity between females than males. Other evidence suggests that the more acculturated Latino male tends to have higher levels of substance abuse (Hispanic Health and Nutrition Examination Survey, 1987). Karno et al. (1987) found a higher lifetime prevalence of drug abuse/dependence among adult Euro-American males than among Mexican Americans and a higher alcohol abuse/dependence among the Mexican American male group. They also found sharp differences among the women with respect to age including Euro-Americans having 50% higher rates for any Diagnostic Interview Schedule disorder than Mexican Americans in the under age 40 group. Alcohol abuse/dependence and substance abuse/dependence was also greater in adult Euro-American females. Risk factors include intrafamilial substance or alcohol abuse, family disintegration, and diminished religiosity.

According to a recent review of general health among Latino youth (Amaro, Messinger, & Cervantes, 1996), there are three common indicators that are used to compare mortality between Latinos and white non-Latino youth: leading cause of death, years of potential life lost, and death rates for selected causes of death. Data show that the leading causes of death among Latino youth (15–24) years of age is homicide. Chronic medical conditions, asthma, diabetes, cardiovascular disease, infectious disease, and substance use are other causes of death among the same group. Data from the National Center on Health Statistics also indicate that overall death rates for Latino youth exceed those of white non-Latinos. The 1990 death rate for homicide and legal intervention among Latino youth (43.4 per 100,000) greatly exceeded those of white non-Latinos (22.3). High mortality rates due to homicide, suicide, and legal intervention (43.4) among Latino youth exceeded the years of potential life lost (YPLL) when compared to white non-Latinos (22.3 per 100,000). Other challenging health problems among Latino youth include low health care utilization. In studies conducted by the Centers for Disease Control and the National Survey of Family Growth, Latino children were reported to be the least likely to see a physician for a number of childhood illnesses and Latino adolescents were the least likely to use family planning services and mental health services compared to white non-Latinos.

Obviously greater efforts are needed to determine the prevalence of psychiatric disorders among Mexican American children. The authors argue that these children do suffer from psychiatric disorders at rates similar to those of other ethnic and racial groups. The phenomenology of these disorders may vary depending on the various sociocultural factors. The need for mental health services for Mexican American children and their families appears to be at least equal to the needs of other children. However, the design of specialized and responsive services for this population is challenging in light of the absence of prevalence data.

Immigration and Acculturation

Issues related to immigration can be sources of stress. For example, those experiences of a newly arrived undocumented (so-called illegal) person can be very different from that of a fourth-generation Mexican American. Relevant studies of adults (Cervantes & Castro, 1985) do exist, while those for Mexican American children and adolescents are rare (Padilla, 1988). Padilla's study of first-generation Mexican American adolescents revealed that the main sources of stress were "living in a neighborhood where there is crime" and other disruptions to family unity such as "having a family member arrested." The latter source is a remarkable contrast to studies on adolescents of the dominant society, who tend to report more personalized life events as creating the highest sources of stress (Yeaworth, York, Hussey, Ingu, & Gordman, 1980). The lack of English proficiency (Padilla, 1988), especially when having to negotiate services for a family member from an agency, was another frequently cited source of stress. More experience with stressful events on the part of the recently immigrated adolescents did not appear to lessen their reported level of stress. Female respondents tended to acknowledge their stresses more openly than males.

The experience of migration itself often can be traumatic for some Mexican American children. Migration often means separation from familiar surroundings, school, friendships, and sometimes family members. Multiple family separations and reunifications can engender fears of abandonment, deportation anxiety as well as hostile feelings toward caregivers.

Acculturation refers to the internal process by which new immigrants adapt to the customs of the host society. Despite the fact that people of Mexican descent do acculturate, they often maintain elements of their original culture. Different levels of acculturation are often evident within the same community and the same family. The level of acculturation can play a crucial role in areas of psychological functioning and the manifestations of psychopathology (Olmedo & Padilla, 1978). Instruments designed to measure acculturation of Mexican Americans have been primarily used with adults (Burnam, Telles, Karno, Hough, & Escobar, 1987); a few of them are used with adolescents (Olmedo, Martinez, & Martinez, 1978; Olmedo & Padilla, 1978). Only recently have two scales for children been developed (Franco, 1983; Martinez, Norman, & Delaney, 1984). Some investigators (Rueschenberg & Buriel, 1989) have focused on family acculturation patterns. Important stress differences related to urban-rural acculturation may be readily apparent when children who work in the fields are compared to urban youngsters.

Family Structure, Values, and Customs

It is falsely assumed that there exists in our society a "typical family system." This false assumption also applies to the Mexican American family. The numerous misconceptions or stereotypes that have been promoted in the social science literature regarding Mexican American families include having a patriarchal structure, rural family values, and "culture of poverty traits" (Lewis, 1966).

These latter traits include "fatalism," "machismo," "superstitiousness," "religiosity," and "female submissiveness." Cultural contrasts between Euro-American and Mexican American families often have been made as if they were mutually exclusive cultures; in such comparisons Mexican American traits have been viewed as deficits or weaknesses, implying that the Euro-American traits are ideal (Mejia, 1983). Apart from these negative stereotypes, traditional Latinos often have been characterized as having very strong values regarding family unity and family relationships.

Familism, or the sharing of family functions, among Mexican Americans is practiced intergenerationally and laterally. Such functions include caregiving and disciplining of children, companionship, financial responsibility, emotional support, and problem solving. As a result, extended family members often have far-reaching decision-making influences on a family. Family organizational patterns are variable, although a common one is related to age and sex, with older males tending to have more authority (Falicov, 1982).

Many families, especially immigrant and second-generation ones, emphasize certain values and customs. These include the concept of *respeto* (literally respect), which connotes an emotionalized respect and deference toward parents, adults, and other authority figures. Children are expected to be very polite and behave in a dignified manner. Such behavior toward a clinician may be misinterpreted as distant, unfriendly, unassertive, nonaggressive, and lacking spontaneity.

Compadrazgo (literally coparenting) is an important custom among many Mexican American families and is related to the practice of Roman Catholicism. Baptism, for example, establishes two sets of important relationships, one between the *padrinos* or godparents and the child's parents and the other between the godchild and the godparents. Some godparents become important sources of support for the family and the godchild, in particular. On occasion including a godparent in a family-focused intervention may prove advantageous, especially when one of the aims of intervention is to mobilize supportive resources for a child.

Quinceaniera, or fifteenth birthday, is another cultural/religious (Roman Catholic) milestone for many Mexican American females. These celebrations are similar to those of a debutante.

Machismo is a term that has lost its original connotation in the lay American literature to the point of having almost an exclusively negative connotation. The original connotation refers to a man's source of pride derived from raising a family, having the responsibility for a family, a strong sense of personal honor, a sense of loyalty, love for his children, and respect for the aged. Many Mexican American male teenagers may share these attitudes. Instead of making an erroneous assumption, a clinician might explore the significance of machismo in a family or particular youngster. A clinician who is eager to enlist the father of a child patient might consider appealing to father's sense of machismo.

Sex roles of Mexican Americans also have been stereotyped in the literature (Vasquez & Gonzalez, 1981). In one study, middle-class Mexican American and Euro-American parents' perceptions of the father's role demonstrated more similarity between the two groups than dissimilarity (Mejia, 1973), dispelling the stereotyped standard of an authoritarian-traditionalist extended family and the submissive wife concept. A literature review (Senour, 1977) on Mexican American women describes the stereotypes as women suffering more from oppression, exhibiting lower self-esteem, condoning higher family status to males, being less defined intrapsychically, being more prosocial, being less competitive, and being less achievement-oriented than the men. Baca-Zinn (1980) points out that in contrast to past family-role and gender-role research, which focused primarily on cultural factors as the major determinant of role-related behavior, studies must extend beyond a traditional-modernistic continuum to include social and economic factors. Numerous research methodological flaws are common in the literature.

Several areas regarding sexual practices and attitudes (Padilla & Baird, 1991) of teenage Mexican Americans have implications for clinical treatment. Most youths of both sexes in the study believed that the responsibility of birth control belonged to the female, that it was important to have children, that females should be virgins at marriage, and that sex was not acceptable if two people were not in love.

Impact of Mexican American Culture on Child Development

Cultural values, beliefs, and attitudes together are an important cornerstone of child development, particularly as related to socialization patterns and child-rearing practices. These socialization and child-rearing practices influence the extent to which development occurs in the areas of ethnic identity, language development, and cognitive development. Unfortunately, few research studies have examined the impact of culture on child development as this relates to the development of health versus maladaptive patterns of behavior among Mexican American children (Cervantes & Castro, 1985).

Clinical research suggests that a myriad of sociocultural factors influence personality development among Mexican American children. Garza and Lipton (1982) have presented an interactional "socioecological" model of personality development. They suggest that personality is determined by a continuous interaction of the person with social, cultural, and socioecological factors. Individual personality characteristics are said to be developed and expressed in a person's attitudes, beliefs, and customs. While previous writers and researchers in the area of culture often fell victim to stereotypic descriptions of Mexican American children and families, more recent research and clinical work suggest that each individual's level of acculturation varies with his or her duration of and level of intensity of exposure to a particular host culture. Garza and Lipton (1982) suggest that the truly "bicultural" individual is capable of functioning effectively under two separate sets of sociocultural milieus. The development of a bicultural style of personality is an area that merits further investigation.

With respect to child development, it can be said that more "traditional" (poorly defined in the literature) Mexican American families place a heavy emphasis on the importance of family-centered values, the value of personal relationships (i.e., cooperative versus competitive behavior), and religious values. Immigrant Mexican American children tend to develop these values.

In a review of developmental research, Zepeda and Espinosa (1988) contend that there is virtually no research on early socialization influences of Mexican American children. The authors indicate that this is a distressing state of affairs, given that it is during the early years that children begin to formulate a sense of self, primarily through their interaction with parents. For example, the primary language of a child is determined by the extent to which the family uses a dominant language within the home. Language development is an important aspect of childhood socialization. It has been suggested that in a predominantly Spanish-speaking environment, children generally develop a positive loyalty to Spanish language as well as to their culture of origin. The Mexican American adult who had early and consistent exposure to Spanish is likely to develop a greater appreciation for language as a cultural expression. Thus, the development of Spanish-language skills becomes an important aspect of a child's ethnic identity and cultural awareness. The extent to which Spanish-language skills are fostered in these children determines the degree to which they develop an egosyntonic sense of cultural identity. In a recent study by Bernal, Knight, Garza, Ocampo, and Cota (1990), children's use of Spanish at home was strongly correlated with several ethnic identity components, including the number of correct ethnic labels used by children, correct grouping of Mexican American peers, use of ethnic role behaviors, ethnic knowledge, and ethnic preferences.

The development of ethnic and racial awareness and identity in children of Mexican descent is rarely addressed in the scientific literature. African American and Euro-American youngsters demonstrate the ability to identify members of their own groups at ages 3 to 5; however, the recognition of ethnic groups occurs later (Fox & Jordan, 1983). In their study of Mexican American children, Bernal et al. (1990) conclude that they can identify their ethnic group at age 6 to 7; however, constancy of ethnic identification does not emerge until age 8 or later (Semaj, 1980).

The literature on cognitive development primarily addresses issues related to field dependence/independence. Earlier research strongly suggests Mexican American children to be more field-dependent when compared to non–Mexican American children. More recent research, however, suggests that when a level of acculturation is considered, Mexican American children who are second generation or later score very close to Anglo-American norms in terms of field independence. Buriel (1975) suggests that cognitive development in the areas of field-dependence, independence, and internal versus external locus of control is greatly influenced by the level of acculturation of a particular Mexican American family.

Studies on intelligence and IQ testing among Mexican American children have been debated intensely. The major problem of determining the extent to which culture influences intelligence is related to the absence of tests that reliably and validly measure intelligence; many of these tests have been standardized with Euro-American children. For example, Dunn (1987) reviewed numerous studies that show that Mexican American and other Latino children score approximately 10 to 12 points below Euro-American children on various IQ tests. Such differences persist despite the translation of tests and use of alleged culturally appropriate instruments. Mercer (1988) suggests that intelligence testing of Mexican American children be expanded to include children's adaptive functioning. In a series of studies, she found that when adaptive psychosocial functioning is considered, Mexican American children are found to be comparable to their non-Latino counterparts. It is important that clinicians recognize the variable connotations of intelligence and their implications between and among Latino and non-Latino groups. Such connotations may be associated with other elements of their respective cultures.

Clinical Implications of Culture and Development

Clinicians who treat Mexican American children face the challenge of integrating cultural and developmental contextual issues. One of the more important aspects in working with a Mexican American child is the initial assessment of his or her level of acculturation. This level serves to form the basis for selection of appropriate therapeutic approaches and techniques (Acosta, Yamamoto, & Evans, 1982).

The extent to which cultural conflicts within the Mexican American family disrupt the various lines of child development has not been addressed in the literature. The clinical work of the authors, however, suggests that the identification of potential sources of cultural conflict for any child is important. For example, among Mexican American immigrant families, it is not uncommon to find parents whose values and beliefs are much different from those of the developing child. While parents may adhere rigidly to traditional beliefs and customs, the developing child, who is being socialized in a predominantly non-Mexican social milieu, may adopt beliefs and values that are distinctly different and devalued by the child's parents. These cultural differences within the family system may give rise to childhood behavior problems that become reflected in symptomatic behaviors at home as well as in the school setting. In their work with Cuban American families, Szapocznik and colleagues (1989) have developed an approach toward working with families. In conducting Bicultural Effectiveness Training, Szapocznik attempts to develop in both child and parents an appreciation for the differences in cultural values held by various family members. The resolution of the cultural conflicts appears to help clarify the individuals' ethnic identity and reduce the problematic behaviors.

Work with parents becomes extremely important for clinicians who conduct treatment with Mexican American children and adolescents. The inculcated values of family unity and family integrity compel a clinician to include at least one parent in the treatment of the child. Differences in child-rearing practices between the new and old cultures, developmental issues, ethnic identity, bilingualism, and other values are common concerns of both parents and children.

Separation and individuation issues during adolescence may be manifested differently in the Mexican American family, especially in families that encourage interdependency. A clinician may inadvertently encourage a teenager to individuate more assertively than is clinically indicated given the cultural context. If an adolescent in a "traditional" household is very defiant, the behavior may be a manifestation of serious family problems.

Sibling rivalry may be minimal in many families due to a common parental practice of inculcating their children with the value of cooperative behavior (Kagan, 1977). This effort promotes the value of family primacy. A clinician may inadvertently interpret sibling interdependence and support as psychopathological.

Special problems in the area of child development may arise with respect to immigrant children. For example, newly immigrated adolescents may become acutely aware of the disparity between their level of social "independence" relative to their very "individualized" non-Latino peers. Their reaction may be to continue to abide by the traditional dependent role and therefore be perceived as "weird" by classmates or to plunge into the new customs, thereby alarming their parents, who now perceive the adolescents as rebellious.

Personalismo (literally personalism), often a highly desirable quality, reflects a preference for person-to-person interchange as opposed to an interchange with an institution or a formal impersonal structure. It connotes an attitude of empathy, warmth, and kindliness in the interpersonal exchange. A clinician with personalismo can be very effective therapeutically (Chavez, 1975).

Clinical Assessment/Interventions

Many authors have recommended that "culturally sensitive" services be provided to culturally diverse populations (Rogler, Malgady, Costantino, & Blumenthal, 1987). Rogler's group (1987) reminds clinicians that the ultimate aim of mental health interventions should be relief from psychological distress and facilitating the adaptation of the Latino client to the new society. Several authors (Rogler et al., 1987) controversially suggest that, on occasion, the goal of an intervention may be to change a culturally prescribed behavior if it interferes with therapeutic goals. Lopez and Hernandez (1986) warn that not only is it important to consider culture but, also, it must be considered accurately and appropriately.

The concept of "cultural competence" (Cross, Bazron, Dennis, & Isaacs, 1989) expands the concept of "cultural sensitivity" to include the dimensions of effectiveness or competence in the provision of mental health services. This concept of cultural competence is applicable not only to the clinician but also to an entire service system. The

guidelines for developing culturally competent services include the concepts of family-focused intervention; services driven by culturally preferred choices; the incorporation of cultural knowledge into practice and policy making; the acknowledgment that all minority groups are at least bicultural; the incorporation of the natural, informal helping network of the minority community into the actual service delivery; minority community participation in decision-making bodies; and staffing patterns that reflect the cultural composition of the minority community. Special considerations for services targeting Mexican Americans include Spanish-language capability and assurance that the agency does not interface with the Immigration and Naturalization Service. Specialized training for clinicians who are neither bicultural nor bilingual should be provided. Spanish-speaking clinicians cannot be assumed to be bicultural; the clinician's ethnic origin may not be Mexican.

Other misconceptions that have implications for interventions include the ideas that impoverished Mexican Americans do not want psychotherapy (Acosta, 1979), that they do not conceptualize mental health problems as do the members of the dominant society (Karno & Edgarton, 1969), that the majority seek help for mental disorders via a folk healer, and that Mexican Americans are generally prejudiced against Euro-American psychotherapists (Acosta & Sheehan, 1976).

Clinicians who engage in family therapeutic interventions should assume a flexible concept of family, with boundaries extending beyond the nuclear family. It behooves clinicians to include those family and extended family members who are influential in the decision-making process when an intervention may have extensive family ramifications or when the support of influential family members would facilitate the prescribed intervention.

It is not uncommon to have treatment abruptly interrupted by summer vacations to Mexico, when those who continue to have close ties to relatives in Mexico leave the United States for several weeks despite having minimal financial means. The opportunity for such departures is much more readily available to this population due to Mexico's relatively close proximity to the United States than it is for other ethnic groups. This pattern often serves to refuel travelers with emotional support from family members in Mexico and to reconfirm their Mexican customs and values.

Cervantes and Arroyo (1995) caution clinicians about cultural considerations that should be made when using *DSM-IV* (American Psychiatric Association, 1994). Those criteria which directly relate to communication (including language), socialization of children, and standardized testing should be considered in a cultural context since these areas may be strongly influenced by cultural factors.

Psychological testing conducted with Mexican Americans of all ages has been an ongoing focus of controversy. Generally, however, culture has been found to be an important mediator of IQ and personality testing for Latinos (Cervantes & Acosta, 1992). The small body of clinicial research provides minimal direction for psychological testing or test interpretation. The following issues are crucial in psychological testing: the child's primary language, his/her nativity, the skills (verbal versus nonverbal) required for the specific test, the normative data used to standardize the specific test, the clinician's primary language, and the clinician's knowledge of the subject's culture. The clinical work of these authors strongly suggests that any testing assessment of a particular Mexican American child must include an assessment of that child's behavior. Both the Conners Behavior Rating Scale (Goyette, Conners, & Ulrich, 1978) and the Achenbach Child Behavior Checklist (Achenbach & Edelbrock, 1983) have been found useful for testing Mexican American children. Adaptive psychosocial functioning also should be assessed (Mercer, 1988); the Vineland Social Maturity Index Scale (Doll, 1965) has been used in this regard.

Psychological test data, particularly cognitive and intellectual testing material, must be interpreted with extreme caution. Many test data interpretations are used for treatment planning as well as educational interventions. As such, the interpretation of test data can greatly facilitate or impede the treatment process with the Mexican American child. The authors' clinical experience suggests that, in general, the reliability of the test data is directly related to the child's level of acculturation. The impact of culture on the reliability and validity of personality testing has been documented across several studies with Hispanic adults (Greene, 1987).

The use of translators for testing or psychotherapy can be problematic with some Mexican American families. The choice of the identified child patient as a translator can inadvertently serve to undermine the parental authority role. This can unduly lead to intrafamilial conflict. The child, on the other hand, may experience distress at being placed in a position of brokering services for the family, a role that the child also views as a parental role. A young child in this position is rarely an effective advocate for his or her family. Furthermore, the identified child patient may be tempted to unilaterally edit the clinicial information on his or her behalf. Interpreters specially trained in mental health issues, development, and sexual matters can be very useful in child psychiatric settings.

Recently immigrated families tend to view schoolteachers as a more authoritative and knowledgeable than do families in the general community. This perception lends itself to effective collaboration with the patient's teacher, especially if the teacher is knowledgeable about the youngster's culture. School systems that incorporate elements of the child's culture will elicit more parental participation.

Conclusion

In summary, Mexican American children are now one of the fastest-growing segments of youth in the United States. The limited mental health research on this population suggests that Mexican American youths suffer from a range of mental disorders not unlike that found in other populations. Furthermore, the need for child and family mental health services for Mexican Americans appears at least equal the mental health needs of youth of other ethnic and racial groups. Mental health professionals are likely to be confronted with the challenge of providing services to Mexican American children and must consider their ethical responsibility of providing culturally competent services.

In order to effectively help or accurately study children and families of Mexican descent, it is imperative that, in addition to the psychological symptoms, many other sociocultural aspects be considered. These include the child's linguistic ability, degree of acculturation, generation in the United States, education, impact of cultural factors on the child development, and the ancestral country of origin. The family's cultural context as well as its perception of the presenting clinical problem is equally important. The developmental standard to which the child is compared should ideally be normative data based on a cultural peer group. Future research in these areas will help develop more effective services and clinical instruments to be used with this population of children and families.

REFERENCES

Achenbach, T. M., & Edelbrock, C. S. (1983). *Manual for the Child Behavior Checklist and Revised Child Behavior Profile.* Burlington: University of Vermont Department of Psychiatry.

Acosta, F. X. (1979). Barriers between mental health services and Mexican Americans: An examination of a paradox. *American Journal of Community Psychology, 7* (5), 503–516.

Acosta, F. X., & Sheehan, J. G. (1976). Preferences toward Mexican American and Anglo American Psychotherapists. *Journal of Consulting and Clinical Psychology, 44,* 272–279.

Acosta, F. X., Yamamoto, J., & Evans, L. A. (Eds.) (1982). *Effective psychotherapy for low-income and minority patients.* New York: Plenum Press.

Amaro, H., Messinger, M., Cervantes, R. C. (1996). The health of Latino youth: Challenges for disease prevention. In Kagawa-Singer, Katz, Taylor, & Vanderryn (Eds.), *Health Issues for Minority Adolescents* (pp. 80–115). Lincoln, NE: University of Nebraska Press.

American Council on Education, Office of Minorities in Higher Education. (1991). *Ninth annual status report: Minorities in higher education.* Washington, DC: Author.

American Psychiatric Association. (1994). *Diagnostic and Statistical Manual of Mental Disorders,* 4th ed. Washington, DC: American Psychiatric Press.

Baca-Zinn, M. (1980). Employment and education of Mexican American women: The interplay of modernity and ethnicity in eight families. *Harvard Educational Review, 50* (1), 47–62.

Bernal, B. E., Knight, G. P., Garza, C. A., Ocampo, K. A., & Cota, M. K. (1990). The development of ethnic identity in Mexican-American children. *Hispanic Journal of Behavioral Sciences, 12* (1), 3–24.

Bird, H. R., Canino, G., Rubio-Stipec, M., Gould, M. S., Ribera, J., Sesman, M., Woodbury, M., Huertas-Goldman, S., Pagan, A., Sanchez-Lacay, A., Moscoso, M. (1988). Estimates of the prevalence of childhood maladjustment in a community survey in Puerto Rico. *Archives of General Psychiatry, 45,* 1120–1126.

Buriel, R. (1975). Cognitive styles among three generations of Mexican American children. *Journal of Cross-Cultural Psychology, 6,* 417–429.

Burnam, M. A., Telles, C. A., Karno, M., Hough, R. L., & Escobar, J. I. (1987). Measurement of acculturation in a community population of Mexican Americans. *Hispanic Journal of Behavioral Sciences, 9* (2), 105–130.

Castro, F. G., Furth, P., & Karlow, H. (1984). The health beliefs of Mexican, Mexican American, and Anglo women. *Hispanic Journal of Behavioral Sciences, 6* (4), 365–384.

Cervantes, R. C. (1993). The Hispanic Family Intervention Program: An empirical approach to substance abuse prevention. In B. Kail, R. Mayer, & T. Watt, (Eds.), *Hispanic substance abuse* (pp. 101–114). Newberry Park, CA: Sage Publications.

Cervantes, R. C., & Acosta, F. X. (1992). Psychological testing for Hispanic Americans. *Journal of Applied and Preventive Psychology, 1,* 209–219.

Cervantes, R. C., & Arroyo, W. (1995). Cultural considerations in the use of DSM IV with Hispanic children and adolescents. In A. Padilla (Ed.), *Hispanic Psychology: Critical Issues in Theory and Research* (pp. 131–147). Thousand Oaks, CA: Sage Publications.

Cervantes, R. C., & Castro, R. G. (1985). Stress, coping, and Mexican American mental health: A systematic review. *Hispanic Journal of Behavioral Sciences, 7,* 1–73.

Cervantes, R. C., Padilla, A., & Salgado de Snyder, N. S. (1992). The Hispanic stress inventory: A culturally relevant approach towards psychosocial assessment. *Psychological Assessment: A Journal of Consulting and Clinical Psychology, 3* (3), 438–447.

Chambliss, W., Nagasawa, R. (1969). On the validity of official statistics: A comparative study of white, black, and Japanese high school boys. *Journal of Research on Crime and Delinquency, 6,* 71–77.

Chavez, N. (1975). *Mexican Americans' expectations of treatment, role of self and of therapist: Effects on utilization of mental health services.* Unpublished doctoral dissertation, University of Denver, CO.

Cross, T. L., Bazron, B. J., Dennis, K. W., & Isaacs, M. R. (1989). *Towards a culturally competent system of care: A monograph on effective services for minority children who are severely emotionally disturbed.* Washington, DC: Georgetown University Child Development Center.

Doll, E. A. (1965). Vineland Maturity Scale: Condensed manual of directions. Circle Pines, MN: American Guidance Service.

Dunn, L. M. (1987). *Bilingual Hispanic children on the U.S. mainland: A review of research on their cognitive, linguistic, and scholastic development.* Circle Pines, MN: American Guidance Service.

Fabrega, Jr., H. (1990). Hispanic mental health research: A case for cultural psychiatry. *Hispanic Journal of Behavioral Sciences, 12* (4), 339–365.

Falicov, C. J. (1982). Mexican families. In M. McGoldrick, J. K. Pearce, & J. Giordano (Eds.), *Ethnicity and family therapy* (pp. 134–165). New York: Guilford Press.

Fox, D. J., & Jordan, V. D. (1983). Racial preference and identification of Black, American Chinese, and White children. *Genetic Psychology Monographs, 88,* 229–286.

Franco, J. N. (1983). An acculturation scale for Mexican American children. *Journal of General Psychology, 108,* 175–181.

Garza, R. T., & Lipton, J. P. (1982). Theoretical perspectives on Chicano personality development. *Hispanic Journal of Behavioral Sciences, 4* (4), 407–432.

Gilbert, M., & Alcocer, A. M. (1988). Alcohol use and Hispanic youth: An overview. *Journal of Drug Issues, 18* (1), 33–48.

Goyette, C., Conners, C. K., & Ulrich, R. (1978). Normative data on Revised Connors Parent and Teacher Rating Scales. *Journal of Abnormal Child Psychology, 6,* 221–236.

Greene, R. L. (1987). Ethnicity and MMPI performance: A review. *Journal of Consulting and Clinical Psychology, 55,* 497–512.

Hayes-Bautista, D. (1983). On comparing studies of different Raza populations. *American Journal of Public Health, 73* (3), 274–276.

Hernandez, J., Estrada, L., & Alvirez, D. (1973). Census data and the problem of conceptually defining the Mexican American population. *Social Science Quarterly, 53,* 671–864.

Hispanic Health and Nutrition Examination Survey (HHANES). (1987). *Use of selected drugs among Hispanics: Mexican Americans, Puerto Ricans, Cuban Americans.* Rockville, MD: U.S. Department of Health and Welfare.

Jessor, R., & Jessor, S. L. (1977). *Problem behavior and psycho-social development: A longitudinal study of youth.* New York: Academic Press, 1977.

Kagan, S. (1977). Social motives and behaviors of Mexican-American and Anglo-American children. In J. L. Martinez, Jr. (Ed.), *Chicano psychology* (pp. 45–86). New York: Academic Press.

Karno, M., & Edgarton, R. B. (1969). Perception of mental illness in a Mexican-American community. *Archives of General Psychiatry, 20,* 233–238.

Karno, M., Hough, R. L., Burnam, A., Escobar, J. I., Timbers, D. M., Santana, F., & Boyd, J. H. (1987). Lifetime prevalence of specific psychiatric disorders among Mexican Americans and non-Hispanic Whites in Los Angeles. *Archives of General Psychiatry, 44,* 695–701.

Klein, J. (1978). Susto: The anthropological study of diseases of adaptation. *Social Science and Medicine, 12,* 23–28.

Lampe, P. E. (1984). Mexican Americans: Labeling and mislabeling. *Hispanic Journal of Behavioral Sciences, 6* (1), 77–85.

Lewis, O. (1966, October). The culture of poverty. *Scientific American, 215,* 19–25.

Lopez, S., & Hernandez, P. (1987). When culture is considered in evaluations of psychopathology. *Journal of Nervous and Mental Disease, 176,* 598–606.

Low, S. (1981). The meaning of nervios. *Culture, Medicine and Psychiatry, 5,* 350–357.

Macias, R. F. (1977). Hispanics in 2000 A.D.—Projecting the number. *Agenda, 7,* 16–20.

Martinez, C., & Martin, H. W. (1966). Folk diseases among urban Mexican-Americans. *Journal of the American Medical Association, 196* (2), 147–150.

Martinez, R., Norman, R. D., & Delaney, H. E. (1984). A children's Hispanic Background Scale. *Hispanic Journal of Behavioral Sciences, 6,* 103–112.

Mata, A. (1986). Alcohol use among rural South Texas youth. Austin: Texas Commission on Alcohol and Drug Abuse.

Mejia, D. A. (1973, April 14–19). *The Spanish-speaking child in the United States: Culture, class and ethnic differences.* Paper presented at the 14th Interamerican Congress of Psychology, São Paolo, Brazil.

Mejia, D. A. (1983). The Development of Mexican-American Children in G. J. Powell (ed.) The Psychosocial Development of Minority Group Children, pp 77–114, New York: Brunner/Mazel.

Mercer, J. R. (1988). Ethnic differences in IQ scores: What do they mean? (A response to Lloyd Dunn). *Hispanic Journal of Behavioral Sciences, 10* (3), 199–218.

Mull, J. D., & Mull, D. S. (1981). Residents' awareness of folk medicine beliefs of their Mexican patients. *Journal of Medical Education, 56,* 520–522.

Offord, D. R. (1990). Social factors in the aetiology of childhood disorders. In B. Tonge, G. Burrows, & J. Werry (Eds.), *Handbook of studies on child psychiatry* (pp. 55–68). Amsterdam, The Netherlands: Elsevier.

Olmedo, E. L., Martinez, J. L., & Martinez, S. R. (1978). Measure of acculturation for Chicano adolescents. *Psychological Reports, 42,* 159–170.

Olmedo, E. L., & Padilla, A. M. (1978). Empirical and construct validation of a measure of acculturation for Mexican Americans. *Journal of Social Psychology, 105,* 179–187.

Padilla, A. M. (1988). Life experiences, stress, and adaptation of immigrant adolescents. In J. W. Berry & R. C. Annis (Eds.), *Ethnic psychology: Research and practice with immigrants, refugees, native peoples, ethnic groups and sojourners* (pp. 135–146). Boulder, CO: Westview Press.

Padilla, A. M., & Baird, T. L. (1991). Mexican-American

adolescent sexuality and sexual knowledge: An exploratory study. *Hispanic Journal of Behavioral Sciences, 13* (1), 95–104.

Rogler, L. H., Malgady, R. G., Costantino, G., & Blumenthal, R. (1987). What do culturally sensitive mental health services mean? The case of Hispanics. *American Psychologist, 42* (6), 565–570.

Rueschenberg, E., & Buriel, R. (1989). Mexican family functioning and acculturation: A family systems perspective. *Hispanic Journal of Behavioral Sciences, 11* (3), 232–244.

Semaj, L. (1980). The development of racial evaluation and preference: A cognitive approach. *Journal of Black Psychology, 6* (2), 59–79.

Senour, M. N. (1977). Psychology of the Chicana. In J. L. Martinez (Ed.), *Chicano psychology* (pp. 329–342). New York: Academic Press.

Szapocznik, J., Santisteban, D., Rio, D., Perez-Vidal, A., Santisteban, D., & Kurtines, W. M. (1989). Family effectiveness training: An intervention to prevent drug abuse and problem behavior in Hispanic adolescents. *Hispanic Journal of Behavioral Sciences, 11* (1), 4–27.

U.S. Department of Commerce, Bureau of the Census. (1990). *Current population report* (P-20, No. 444, 10-23). Washington, DC: U.S. Government Printing Office.

U.S. Department of Commerce News, Bureau of the Census. (1991, March 11). Press Release, CB91-100.

Vasquez, M., & Gonzalez, A. (1981). Sex roles among Chicanos: Stereotypes, challenges, and changes. In A. Baron, Jr. (Ed.), *Explorations in Chicano psychology* (pp. 50–70). New York: Praeger.

Yeaworth, R., York, J., Hussey, M., Ingu, M., & Gordman, T. (1980). The development of an adolescent Life Change Event Scale. *Adolescence, 15*, 93–97.

Zepeda, M., & Espinosa, M. (1988). Parental knowledge of children's behavioral capabilities: A study of low income parents. *Hispanic Journal of Behavioral Sciences, 10* (2), 149–159.

52 / The Middle Eastern/Arabic Child

Fady Hajal

Arab Americans have very diverse origins. They come from 21 countries stretching from Asia's Fertile Crescent and the Arabian Peninsula, across the Red Sea, and over North Africa to the shores of the Atlantic. "Arab" refers to people whose primary language is Arabic and who share the values and beliefs of Arab culture irrespective of religious affiliation or national origin.

Precise figures about Arabs in the United States are not available because there are no reliable ways of identifying U.S. citizens or residents of Arab extraction. It is estimated that 3 million people in the United States are of Arab extraction. This number includes American citizens, residents on permanent visa, and sojourners on temporary status to study or work in the United States.

Arab Americans are scattered throughout the United States, with significant clusters in large cities such as Detroit, New York, and Los Angeles. The Detroit Arab community is likely the largest in North America. According to a 1985 estimate, there were about 78,000 of people of Middle Eastern ancestry in the tricounty area around Detroit; it was further estimated that by 1990, their number might approach 100,000 (Kulwicki, 1989), or even 300,000 (Eisenlohr, 1988).

Arab emigration to the United States began in the last two decades of the 19th century and occurred in three major waves: the first wave prior to World War I, the second after World War II, and the third and largest wave from the year 1967 on. This last wave has been promoted by political turbulence in the Middle East. These three cohorts differed in a number of ways: in their pattern of emigration, in their sociodemographic profile, and in their approach to, and eventual integration into, American society and culture.

The first wave came primarily from Lebanon, Syria, and Palestine. Single individuals fled the political, religious, and economic hardships created by Ottoman rule in what was then Greater Syria. Mostly rural and Christian, these pioneers worked as peddlers at first and later entered commerce. Eventually they became fully integrated into the American way of life.

The waves that occurred after World War II,

and especially that after the 1967 Arab-Israeli War, were more cosmopolitan. Arabs from all Middle Eastern countries were represented, notably Palestine and Jordan, Iraq, Yemen, Saudi Arabia, Kuwait, Egypt and other North African Arab countries, in addition to those emigrating from Syria and Lebanon. Their religious affiliations and their educational and occupational backgrounds were diverse. These waves included Moslems and Christians (with all denominations represented), rural and urban Arabs, educated as well as illiterate, blue collar and professional, poor, middle class, and wealthy. As a result, there is much greater heterogeneity in the Arab American community today than existed in earlier decades. In spite of the diversity, however, the "Arabism" of these Arab Americans, as expressed in a common language and in a set of customs, beliefs, and social characteristics, tends to transcend religious, political and national affiliations (Meleis & Sorrell, 1981; Patai, 1973).

Common features relevant to child development and psychiatric practice include Arabic family structure and relationships; the status of women and its impact on the upbringing and socialization of girls; and traditional popular beliefs regarding causation of physical and psychological illness, including beliefs regarding healing practices.

The Family in Arab Culture

Among Arabs, the family is the central unit of social organization and comprises the most durable and influential social institution of the Middle East. Family and personal relations figure, along with religion, as the principal axes around which an Arab's life is organized. Indeed, family sentiment in the Middle East has been called "a passion" (Prothro, 1967), and such blood relations fulfill many of the Arabs' affiliative needs (Lipson & Meleis, 1983).

The extended patriarchal, patrilineal, and patrilocal family is the predominant form of family structure in the Arab World. When children, particularly sons, marry, they are encouraged or even expected to go on living with their parents. If they cannot continue residing within the same physical household, they are pressured to remain at least in geographical proximity to their family of origin.

The extended family plays a number of important functions. It helps provide physical, psychological, and economic support and security for its members. Arabs rely on family connections for career advancement, for social influence, for status and power. Socially, the extended family plays a major role in the maintenance and transmission of crucial cultural values, including those involved in child rearing. All family members participate in the upbringing and socialization of the children. As a result, the extended family plays a central role as a psychosocial bonding structure.

The traditional Arab family, authoritarian and patriarchal, is organized along a strict hierarchical order: the elder rule over the younger, males over females. The father is the uncontested head of the family; his authority often is described as dictatorial, even tyrannical. He is expected to provide materially for the family and to be a strict disciplinarian as well as a provider of affection and love. He is expected to strengthen the family by reinforcing its cohesiveness and resolving conflicts among its members. Respect for and obedience to the father and other elders are paramount values. Children are shamed or punished whenever they annoy, disturb, or otherwise fail in their duties toward their parents. Paying respect and honor to parents is supposed to bring about prosperity and happiness (El-Islam, 1983; Sharabi & Ani, 1977).

Traditionally, a marriage is a contract between two families rather than the union of two individuals. Therefore, parents have not only a right but an obligation to arrange marriages for children of both sexes. Even in more "liberal" or "modern" families, where prospective grooms and brides are granted a greater role in choosing their mates, parents continue to play a decisive role in this respect. Early arranged marriages are still favored in traditional families, particularly rural ones. Marriages to cousins are preferred because they strengthen family ties. Arab society has a long historic tradition of endogamy. Husband and wife are expected to come from equal-status families. Throughout the life cycle, filial relationships are considered more important than marital relationships.

The status of Arab women is generally described as low. Traditionally, women are not only subordinate to men in the family (and in society), they also are segregated away from the company of men. When it comes to male-female relationships, Arab society, both Moslem and Christian, enforces a strict double standard. In the socialization of girls, there is a strong emphasis on submissiveness and dependency. A woman's function is above all to bear and rear children, preferably male children. This has traditionally been a major source of identity and self-esteem for Arab women (El-Islam, 1975, 1983; Meleis & Sorrell, 1981). Women's sexuality is permitted only in marriage. An extremely high premium is given to premarital virginity as well as to sexual purity throughout the life cycle. In the Arab Middle East, as in other Mediterranean societies, the honor of men and their kin has rested upon the sexual purity of their women. Arab girls are taught early on to practice rigid self-control in the sexual area in order to prevent them from bringing shame and dishonor on their fathers (and families) by engaging in premarital or extramarital activities. According to some, this obsession with virginity is a major cause of sexual problems among Middle Eastern women (Eisenlohr, 1988). Women's chastity is jealously guarded, sometimes through veiling and seclusion, and their infidelities are severely condemned and punished, at times by death (Prothro & Diab, 1974).

Polygamy, although permitted by Islamic code, has been increasingly frowned upon recently. Its practice is now curtailed or even banned in a number of Arab countries. Where it is still practiced, it is at times identified as a source of marital stress resulting in symptom formation (Chaleby, 1986).

Divorce remains easy to obtain and, to a large extent, is still the prerogative of husbands. Following divorce, a woman is supposed to return to her family of origin, with authority over her reverting to her father or oldest brother. Her children will remain in the custody of their father and his family.

Under the pressure of socioeconomic, cultural, and political factors, traditional structures within the Arab family are beginning to give way. In Middle Eastern countries, Arab society is undergoing major transformations that greatly impact individuals as members of families. Different sets of relationships are emerging, such as a trend toward nuclear (as against extended) families, and new patterns of marriage and divorce. Yet, despite

all these changes, "relatives generally remain closely interlocked in a web of intimate relationship that leave limited room for independence and privacy" (Barakat, 1985, p. 37). On the other hand, weekly visiting among family members has been described not only as a means of keeping in touch and reinforcing norms and values among family members but also as a mechanism for managed change in these rough and turbulent times for Arab families (Meleis & Sorrell, 1981).

Child-Rearing Practices in Arab Culture

In the Arab world, large families are strongly preferred and children are highly valued. The parental role is an expected and important transition in the marriage relationship. A marriage is not firmly secure until a child is born. Among Moslem Arabs, for example, sterility in a woman is a legitimate cause for divorce.

Children are generally treated with fondness, affection, warmth, and indulgence, especially in the early years. Arab parents promote dependency in their children by encouraging them to rely extensively on the family and its various members. They believe in the importance of controlling their children and of providing for their security within a tightly knit family-kinship group. Children are taught to be grateful to their parents, who often compete for the exclusive affection and allegiance of their children. Arabs frown on aggression against parents; the good child is obedient and polite. Disobedience, toward the father in particular, is severely punished. Arab children are more closely oriented toward parents and kin than to their peers. As they grow older, they remain more concerned about parental disapproval than about peer approval. As a result, Arab children grow up feeling more responsible and obligated toward the family than toward the society in which they live (Abu-Saad, 1984; Sharabi & Ani, 1977).

The traditional Arab family emphasizes sex-role differentiation from an early age; this is evident in gender-specific tasks, play, and dress. Arabs prefer male children, because they carry the family name and are expected to provide security to their parents in old age. Girls are generally seen as liabilities. While the birth of a boy is cause for loud celebrations, that of a girl is often greeted with plaints and embarrassment. This preference translates itself into a number of behaviors: Boys are nursed longer than girls, and they are sent to school more often than girls. More boys survive their first year of life than girls, presumably as a reflection of better dietary treatment (Adlakha & Suchindran, 1985; Racy, 1970). Arab infants are generally breast-fed until weaning at age 18 to 24 months.

The high degree of indulgence lavished on Arab children in the first years of life is drastically curtailed as they approach their third birthdays. The interruption of indulgence accompanies walking, weaning, and usually the birth of a sibling. This withdrawal of attention and gratification has been described as traumatic. Often it is accompanied by parental encouragement of sibling rivalry, which is considered a means of achieving toughness and character (Racy, 1970). Toilet training is usually carried out in a variable and lax manner. It may start early but is pursued erratically and eventually achieved late.

Circumcision among Moslems is carried out between the ages of 5 and 7 or even later in some parts of the Arab world (for instance, on wedding day among certain tribes in the Arabian peninsula). In some North African countries, clitoridectomy may be performed, leading at times to devastating effects on women's sexual adjustment (Mays & Stockley, 1983). There have been no studies of the impact of circumcision of boys at the various ages in which it is practiced. Observers of this practice in the Arab context have generally "commented on the function of male circumcision as a test of manliness, bravery and courage which fills the boy who passes it with a feeling of self-importance and achievement" (p. 123). In contrast, the circumcision of girls is not considered a test of courage. Carried out in privacy or even surreptitiously, it is "calculated to impress the girl with her own inferiority in relation to boys." (p. 124). The main goal of the operation is to "intimidate the girl's sexuality" and reduce the woman's sexual desire (Patai, 1973, p. 124).

In traditional families, sexual matters are never openly discussed. The parents do not provide any sexual instruction or education. In Arab culture, the concept of sexuality is strongly masculine in orientation, with great emphasis on power, prowess, and prestige. Sex is thought to be man's business (Racy, 1970).

Various authors have stressed the intensely close relationship that exists between mothers and their sons. The first male child is the family's, and his mother's, "most precious possession." Much attention is lavished on him and on other male children. This special position is a double-edged sword, however, for, according to Sharabi and Ani (1977), the Arab male child ends up being smothered by his mother and oppressed by his father. They argue that, as a result of being accorded less attention than boys, girl children mature more quickly and become better able to deal with frustration than boys. Boys, on the other hand, may be hurt by overdependence and overministering. As a result they develop a sense of helplessness, self-centeredness, and social timidity, which may be expressed in various forms of asocial behavior. Barakat (1985) concurs, stating that Arab "parents are usually overprotective and restrictive, and children grow up to feel secure only on familiar ground. They avoid taking risks and trying new ways of doing things, for independence of mind, critical dissent, and adventure beyond the recognized limits are constantly and systematically discouraged by parents and other older members of the family" (p. 36).

In traditional Arab culture, male and female roles are quite distinct and rigidly defined. Girls are socialized to be dependent and submissive. Cultural expectations for them are to be docile, calm and dignified, serious and quiet. They must never show aggressiveness. They are brought up to tolerate high levels of frustration and to express very little in the way of opinion during decision making (El-Islam, 1982). Arab girls are expected to manifest modesty in their dress, to be bashful, humble, retiring, and timid when interacting with men and with strangers (Cederblad, 1968; Meleis & Sorrell, 1981). If they do not comply with these expectations, they may be treated harshly with slaps, blows, or grounding. While Arab parents generally value education for their children, it is not as highly valued for girls as for boys, for it is not seen as necessary for marriage and procreation. Boys, on the other hand, are expected to be strong, physically brave, generous, polite, assertive, and above all respectful to older people. They are expected to take responsibility for the family and, in later years, to help support the family economically.

Boys and girls are allowed to play together during early and middle childhood. By age 9 to 10, however, they are increasingly reared apart. Girls are kept indoors, busy with housebound, domestic activities, while boys are given more freedom to explore the outside world (Abu-Saad, 1984). At puberty, girls' movement outside the home is severely restricted, and relationships with men outside the family forbidden (Eisenlohr, 1988).

Traditional Arab child rearing instills behavior oriented toward accommodating conformity, cooperation, and interdependence, rather than behavior oriented toward individuation and independence (El-Islam, 1982). Arab culture is characterized by a set of moral codes, social values, customs, and rituals of behavior maintained and enforced by, among other pressures, the authoritarian, hierarchical extended family. The demand for conformity applies not only to general values and rules; it extends as well to minor rituals practiced in day-to-day living (Chaleby, 1987). In the course of child rearing, there is an intense focus on prohibitions and on correcting children's negative behavior. This results in a high level of criticism in Arab families, where parents expend much time chastising their children and reflecting on the things they do not want them to do. Adadow Gray pointed out that the disproportionate emphasis placed on correcting and shaming in Arab families, instead of supporting and praising, inhibits the development of playful interactions and the establishment of an atmosphere of enjoyment of one another (Abed, Abu-Laban, Adadow Gray, Bibi, & Mobarak, 1990).

Emphasis on obedience, conformity, and respect for authority all work toward binding the individual ever more closely to the family group. These values are enforced through the use of strict discipline supported by shaming as well as by corporal punishment. Many in Arab culture favor use of corporal punishment, particularly when it comes to correcting the misbehavior of boys. In this regard, girls are more leniently treated.

Arab culture is generally described as a shame culture, one in which moral actions are governed by a need to "save one's face" and to avoid experiencing feelings of shame. These feelings arise when and if one's unacceptable behavior becomes known to others. Arab families believe in the primacy of shame as a mechanism of discipline and social control.

This use of shame as a mechanism of social control and a major motivator of behavior results in an overemphasis on pride, secrecy, loyalty to one's kinship group, favoritism, and open display of prowess and hospitality (Racy, 1970). Saving face is a dominant theme; it pervades much male behavior, from the individual and familial levels all the way to the national level.

Arab child rearing has been described as inconsistent. Punishments and rewards are administered in an arbitrary manner according to the moods of the parents. Limit-setting is carried out in an impulsive, sometimes unpredictable, way, with lack of follow-through. Prohibitions or threats are not applied or carried out systematically. This manner of upbringing interferes with good internalization of parental standards of behavior and results in what has been described as a weak superego in Arab individuals (Cederblad, 1968).

Affiliation-oriented and shame-based child rearing has been blamed for deficits in the psychological development of Arab children, such as the stifling of imaginative and creative effort. Deficits in superego development have been attributed to the cultivation of obedience and of moral behavior based on fear of others' criticism and shame, instead of the promotion of guilt as a mechanism of moral regulation. The promotion of a sense of individual responsibility and the development of a self-critical faculty (via the inculcation of guilt-inducing mechanisms), typical in Western superego formation, are often lacking in the upbringing of Arab children (El-Islam, 1982). Some writers have attributed the weakness of the superego to the extended nature of the family structure; the fact that a number of people are closely involved in the child's upbringing weakens attachments between children and parents (Cederblad, 1968).

Some researchers have linked the prevailing use of shame in the upbringing of children to a particular type of adult personality structure, called Fahlawi personality (*fahlawi* is a Persian word meaning a "sharp-witted, clever person") considered to be prevalent in Egypt and other Arab countries (Ammar & Al-Azm, cited in Patai, 1973). This Fahlawi personality shares a number of features with forms of narcissistic personality described in the West. It includes the following characteristics: (1) ready adaptability, which is expressed in genuine flexibility to changing, variable situations but also in "a readiness to express superficial agreement and fleeting amiability"; (2) quick wit; (3) a tendency toward exaggerated self-assertion, a sense of self-importance, and a need to demonstrate one's superior powers (may lead to recklessness, excess, scorn for others, the habit of flourish in behavior and speech); and (4) an emphasis on virility and honor. The Fahlawi does not fear failure itself as much the shame and disgrace in case it becomes known. According to Ammar, "What motivates the Fahlawi is not dedication to duty, nor a wish for self-realization, but rather the desire for reward or the fear of punishments" (p. 110). Both Al-Azm and Ammar believe this personality structure to be grounded on feelings of inferiority, which are concealed because this type of individual is "dominated by the concept of shame and the fear of shame more than he adheres to reality and objectivity" (Patai, 1973, p. 110).

Changing Nature of Family Structures and Relations: Adolescence and Intergenerational Conflict

Sharabi and Ani (1977) have described the intergenerational tensions present during adolescence in the traditional Arab family. The Arab boy, they write, is all but crushed by a feeling of personal inadequacy. Given the hierarchical nature of family relations, he experiences a sense of impotence and insignificance; he is "starved for recognition, status and power." The Arab male child yearns to break out of the dependency, the severe restrictions, and the sexual and emotional repression imposed by his environment. They pointed out that "resentment grows stronger during the period of adolescence, the period of greatest strain and frustration for the Arab child, male or female" (p. 247).

Thus, during the years of late adolescence and young adulthood, the stage is set for a parent-child confrontation. In recent years, this confrontation has been intensified by the process of large-scale societal and cultural changes taking place in the Arab world. Major socioeconomic changes, including a substantial rise in educational, informational, and material opportunities (in the Arabian Peninsula in particular), have led to changes in both family life and the nature of family relations (Barakat, 1985; El-Islam, 1983; Meleis, 1979; El Sendioni, Abou el-Azaem, & Luza, 1977).

Exposure to foreign influences and better education for the younger generation are leading Arab youths to adopt more radical attitudes toward the issues of parental control and their own independence. Socialization of children now takes place outside the family. Formal, Western-type education of children has grown more widespread. The influence of schools, mass media, and increased contact with foreigners abroad or within Arab countries are all new and powerful vectors making for socialization and cultural change. One net effect of these developments, which provide Arab youths with "nontraditional value orientations," is a weakening of parental authority. Thus, in the course of developing their sense of self and crystalizing their value system, young Arabs can choose from coexisting yet often conflicting value orientations. The conflict between parental attitudes and values introjected during childhood and the new values and life choices to which they are exposed, and to which they often find themselves drawn, can be intense and mystifying. Ultimately, intergenerational conflicts in contemporary Arab families can be traced to parents' attempts to direct their children's lives and careers in accordance with their own aspirations rather than in keeping with the children's interests, and all this at a time when this traditional approach is strongly challenged. In past generations, feelings of anger and hostility arising within the family may have been projected onto supernatural objects or external scapegoats, eliciting cohesive support from family members; currently, however, educated youths more readily attribute such feelings to parental control, giving rise to confrontation and crisis (El-Islam, 1982, 1983).

In modern Arab families, intergenerational conflict centers mainly on patterns of family relationships, on attitudes toward education and career choices (including, most prominently, the question of higher education for women), on the rigidity of sexual roles, on methods of mate selection and marriage, and on issues raised by the emancipation of women from their unequal and subordinate position. The intergenerational gap is greater for Arab women than it is for Arab men. For women, the areas of marriage and education are the most important conflict areas. Many families view education of Arab women positively. From the parents' perspective, higher education for their daughters may help them to get a better marriage partner or to obtain a prestigious job, thus unburdening the family, according to El-Guindi, from "the stigma from paid employment and the goal of protecting women from being in subordinate positions to strange men" (Seginer, 1988, p. 752). Educated women are increasingly challenging the traditional limitations of their role in marriage and mothering, demanding increasing freedom of choice in choosing their mate and pursuing traditional as well as new career paths (de Costa, 1985). As a result, sex-role differences had become less apparent in many major Arab cities (Abu-Saad, 1984). On the other hand, several Arab countries have experienced a resurgence of traditional Islamic values and practices regarding the role of women and their place in family and society. This return to tradition is advocated by Moslem fundamentalists and, in some cases, has been put into practice in countries where they have gained political dominance. Many notable steps made by women toward the attainment of fairness and equality have been challenged and, in some countries, erased. Women's rights remains a central battleground in this period of cultural flux and political polarization.

Another area of conflict during adolescence is that of leisure activities. During adolescence, cultural norms and differences between the sexes in this area become salient. Adolescent boys in particular strive to detach themselves from the family in favor of stronger links with the peer group; adolescent girls are confined at home to do chores. Florian and Har-Even, comparing Arab and Jewish youths in Israel, found a greater dissatisfaction among Arab boys and girls in the way they spend their leisure time as compared to their Jewish peers (Florian & Har-Even, 1984).

New values, role models, and social realities—some progressive, others regressive—are constantly emerging, creating an increased chasm between parents and children in the Arab world. Parents often wonder whether their old values

could survive the effect on their children of, among other things, various cultural "invasions," some from the West, others from the East (Iran, for instance). Furthermore, since traditional respect for parental authority prevents an open discussion of these cultural-developmental tensions between children and parents, parents are increasingly alienated from their children. As a result, young Arabs turn to their peers for support, validation, and definition of identity (El-Islam, 1983).

Traditional parents usually perceive the process of separation from the family during adolescence in negative terms: as a sign of an "anticulture," antiparent revolt, to be resisted and crushed, rather than as a sign of a normative developmental progression to be supported by the older generation. To complicate matters further, many older people envy modern educational and occupational opportunities that their own generation did not have. This is true not only in the Arab Middle East and North Africa, where some countries experienced a phenomenal rise in wealth in less than two generations, but also among Arabs transplanted to Western countries, where they find themselves surrounded by a plethora of educational, career, and life opportunities. Having worked hard themselves to attain their middle- or upper-class status, Arab parents expect much from their children and at times are disappointed by the weak efforts their offspring make to achieve and excel. The children, having grown up in more affluent circumstances, lack, in their parents' opinion, constructive attitudes toward work (El-Islam, 1983).

These generational, interpersonal conflicts in turn generate a number of intrapsychic conflicts in both adults and youths. Members of the older generation may envy the wide range of life opportunities available to the young; indeed, some parents blame themselves for providing their children the education that drew them away from their family and culture. For their part, the young may feel guilty about abandoning introjected parental values and transgressing religious rules. Fears, or even guilt, aroused by these felt transgressions may impede the progress of the young adult toward a true or smooth integration of the new, culturally alien yet intellectually accepted values (El-Islam, 1983).

Because of its supportive, security-providing role, the extended family has the potential to help its members cope with intergenerational conflict and resulting emotional upheavals. Yet educational and occupational opportunities attract the younger generation away from the fold of a functional extended family system. As the nuclear family is, nearly everywhere, slowly replacing the traditional extended family, a major source of support and enculturation is being lost, thus weakening the cohesiveness of Arab families and threatening their integrity.

Issues Confronting Arab American Families

While the pioneers of Arab immigration to the United States came as unattached individuals, more recent immigrants have tended to emigrate as families. As a result, these newer arrivals are finding it harder to adjust to their new environment. Arab families feel the flux and reorganization that come with immigration intensely, and conflict in a number of areas often arises. Clashes between traditional and "American" marital values and between secular and religious values are almost universally present. Conflicts between Arab traditional and American "psychological" values in child rearing are very prevalent. In addition, these families lack the community support they had in the home country, particularly that of the extended family. As a result, they close ranks and increase their dependence on each other and on others of similar outlook. This clustering exacerbates their isolation and their sense of differentness. It contributes to the development of an intense sense of ethnicity, which impedes a smooth integration into the mainstream culture.

Parents often experience as painful the competing claims on their children's socialization by various social and public agencies, by schools, and by the media. They perceive these claims to be challenges to their worldview, their value system, and their authority. A wider generation gap and a more intense intergenerational conflict are the inevitable results. Challenge to parental authority may begin at a younger age than in the home country. Three areas of conflict are likely to develop for Arab children growing up in the United

States: conflicts between children and their parents, conflicts between children and the larger American society (peers who ridicule and stereotype them, for example), and, finally, conflicts between parents and the larger society (Abu-Laban, Adadow Gray, Becharra, & Suleiman, 1990).

In reporting on a number of studies carried out in the United States, Suleiman noted the problems faced by Arab-American families. These issues included questions and conflicts around sex-role socialization and practices; intersectarian and interethnic dating and marriage; divorce and remarriage; juvenile problems; language difficulties; and the impact of prejudice on the sense of self and sense of cultural identity (Abu-Laban et al., 1990).

Arab American youths often complain that their parents do not trust them and try to control them too much. Parents do not allow their children to choose their own friends, nor do they encourage their young to try different things on their own and to learn from their errors if need be. Parents also do not allow their children increasing levels of independence as they mature, thereby adjusting parental expectations to the developmental level of the child. Adolescents complain about unsolicited advice from their parents, which they often perceive as criticism (Mobarak, in Abed et al., 1991).

These problems are particularly acute for Arab American girls. A number of factors have a very negative impact on the sense of self of Arab American girls and women, including the double standard for females, the preference for male progeny, and the fact that males are supported and encouraged in their career development efforts whereas females are encouraged to get education but not to have a career. In both the Arab world and among Arab Americans, wife and mother remain the only culturally condoned life róles for women. Marrying off their daughters as early as possible remains a major objective for Arab families (for their mothers in particular). In this regard, a girl's reputation is a highly prized commodity, based primarily on her chastity and avoidance of any hint of impropriety in the area of intimate relationships (Eisenlohr, 1988). To many Arab immigrants, the dating system in the United States is particularly "shocking" and incomprehensible.

Growing up Arab American leads to a kind of double identity, as the individual is torn between the pull of assimilation into the mainstream culture on the one hand and the wish to retain his or her Arab cultural heritage on the other. The smaller world of family and home, where Arabic language and ancestral values are maintained more or less intact, confronts the larger world of American society, which has no use for either. In the small domestic world, strong bonds among relatives are maintained. Children have a sense of belonging and identify with their parents' values and heritage. As the young move into the wider society, however, a pattern of rejection of the smaller society, of its values and its heritage, becomes apparent. First, there is rejection of the language. Children perceive their parents pushing Arabic language and culture on them. This pressure conflicts with the children's wish to be similar to their mostly American peer group and to the many others in their environment, who often look down on Arabic language and culture. An increasing desire to conform at school and among peers leads children to gradually reject the family's traditional values (Abu-Laban, in Abed et al., 1991).

American society is essentially ethnocentric: There is an expectation that all immigrants should assimilate and conform to the mainstream Anglo-Saxon culture. Biases toward different immigrant groups are expressed through various means of discrimination and stereotyping. Arab Americans have felt particularly targeted in the United States. Negative stereotypes of Arabs are widespread and are constantly reinforced by television, movies, and songs (Abu-Laban & Suleiman, 1989). As Slade observed, "the Arabs remain one of the few ethnic groups who can still be slandered with impunity in America" (Abraham, 1989, p. 20). They remain one of the most disparaged ethnic groups in the United States. Inevitably, this constant bombardment gives rise to a sense of being inferior. In this unfriendly climate, it is no wonder that Arab American children often wish to reject their cultural heritage and their identity as Arabs.

At times embarrassment about one's Arab identity is reinforced by the family's behavior and attitudes. As often happens, immigrant parents react defensively to the ethno-cultural threat by reinforcing the most traditional aspects of their background; predictably, however, this stands to exacerbate the conflict. As Abu-Laban put it aptly: "they think in 50 years ago's mentality!" El-Islam (1982) noted with irony that after migrating out-side the Arab world, young Arabs "adhere strongly to the very cultural identity they would have struggled against had they continued to live in their home countries." In their strictness, they end up manifesting only the negative aspects of the culture, instead of emphasizing its many useful and adaptive aspects (Abed et al., 1991). Parents' fear that they are going to lose their children to people and influences outside the culture may lead them to isolate themselves from the societal mainstream in a ghettoized fashion: They socialize exclusively with other Arabs and deal with Americans only for business purposes.

According to Abu-Laban, the emergent identity problems faced by Arab American youths are compounded by the fact that their parents are not adequate teachers about Arabic culture, since they themselves are not experts in many of its crucial aspects. While at first, children's questions about Arab culture grow out of curiosity, later on, in their teen years, such questions may become a vehicle for testing and challenging their parents' omniscience as well as their cultural attitudes and practices. If parents are unable to provide good explanations about religious and other aspects of the culture, children will be at risk for drifting away from many Arabic beliefs and values and from Moslem religious principles in particular. This may lead to an exacerbation of parent-child conflicts and, among the youth, to a sense of impoverishment (Abed et al., 1991).

Thus, in these families, a cultural gap aggravates the generation gap. Parents find it difficult to refrain from culturally driven responses, which for some become an almost instinctive reaction. In these families, communication ceases to be a two-way street and further alienation ensues, sometimes complicated by acting-out behavior, symptom formation, and/or family conflict and dysfunction. This cultural gap is reduced when parents recognize and explicitly acknowledge positive values in both cultures. Rather than holding their children back, children will then experience their parents as enhancing their advancement in American life (Bibi, in Abed et al., 1991).

Suleiman reported on a number of coping strategies used by Arab American youths to deal with some of these culture conflicts. They include: rationalization ("I do this because I'm an Arab"); fantasy (such as being a different kind of person in the future, or in another place); suppression or repression; and deviousness (avoiding what parents think one should do; not telling parents).

The youths Suleiman reported on had a number of suggestions for their parents to assist in smoothing the road from childhood and adolescence to young adulthood in the Arab American community. They urged their parents to keep up with changes in American culture, to remember that things have changed from the old ways, and especially to remember that their children are growing up in the United States, not in the old country. They also advised their parents to trust them, not to underestimate their potential, to listen and talk to them, and to avoid saying no to them all the time. Another important area of concern was peer relationships. These youths wished their parents to let them do things with their friends and, above all, not to prevent them from developing friendships (Abu-Laaban et al., 1990). Ultimately, children bridge cultures more easily than do their parents; still, the more positive their parents' attitude toward American culture and the more comfortable they are in it, the easier it is for their children to overcome the cultural gap and mend the identity split.

Intermarriage between Arabs and Americans has become very common. In these families of mixed heritage, children inevitably lean more toward the American parent and identify with American rather than with Arabic culture (Abu-Laban et al., 1990).

Attitudes Toward Psychiatric Treatment

In general, Arabs have a basically negative attitude toward psychiatry. While they are not adverse to seeking help for "nervous" conditions, they would rather consult neurologists, internists, or even local healers than be caught in a psychiatrist's office (Lipson & Meleis, 1983). Meleis and LaFever (1984) pointed out that "For the immigrant Arab American, seeking psychiatric care is the last resort after everything else fails, after all resources for physical health care have been exhausted" (p. 72). The family of the Arab American patient is often disappointed at its own failure to take care of its kin. Patients are angry for being sent to the "lunatic house" when they need to be psychiatrically hospitalized. Admission to a psychiatric hospital is regarded as a source of embarrassment and shame for the family as well as cruel to the patient, to be avoided at all cost. It is thought to seriously jeopardize the chances of marriage not only of the patient but also of his or her siblings. In the Arab world, families generally tolerate mental disorders unless they are expressed in unprovoked violence, in sexually shameful behavior, or in uncontrollable motor overactivity (Al-Issa & Al-Issa, 1969). Misconceptions concerning mental illness and fear of social stigma as well as culturally supported denial often delay beneficial early treatment (Der-Karabetian, Kadi, Elmasian, & Yetenekian, 1975). This, in turn, leads to exacerbations of psychopathology and the emergence of more severe forms of psychiatric or psychosocial disturbances; eventually, referral is "forced" upon families.

There are no systematic studies of the incidence or prevalence of psychiatric illnesses among American Arabs. However, some studies carried out in the Middle East may give us some sense of the prevailing psychiatric disorders among Arabs (Al-Issa & Al-Issa, 1969; Baker, 1990; Chaleby, 1986; El Sayed, Maghraby, Hafeiz, & Buckley, 1986; Karam, 1994; Katchadourian, 1974; Katchadourian & Racy, 1969; Okasha, Kamel, & Hassan, 1968; Osman, 1992; Pattison, 1986).

In a study carried out in Saudi Arabia in the psychiatric clinic of a university medical center over a period of 6 months, 324 patients attended the clinic (total clinic attendance of 2,157, out of a provincial population of approximately 1 million inhabitants): 55% were men and 45% were women. In terms of diagnoses: 26% had affective psychosis, 21% were diagnosed with anxiety neurosis, 10% were schizophrenic patients, 10% were diagnosed as epileptic, and 8% as hysteric; 25% of the sample were grouped as "other" (El Sayed et al., 1986). Katchadourian and Racy's study (1969), carried out in Lebanon in the mid-1960s, showed a pattern of distribution of mental disorders essentially similar to that in the Western world with a few differences. Psychotic disorders constituted the bulk of the disorders for which patients sought or for which patients were in treatment. Males predominated in the schizophrena group and females in the affective disorders group. These two categories accounted for most of the hospitalized patients in their point prevalence group. Other notable features were the relatively higher rates of conversion reactions and the low rate of alcoholism among Moslems (Katchadourian, 1974). (The rate of drug addiction is somewhat higher among Moslem Arabs compared to Christian Arabs; the latter tend to show a higher rate of alcoholism.) Similar findings were reported by other investigators (Okasha et al., 1968; Pattison, 1984). Chaleby (1986) noted some Saudi women's susceptibility to marital and family stresses originating in the male-dominated nature of Saudi families, which relegate women to a more passive role, thus setting up "a typical model of learned helplessness" (p. 169). Chaleby (1987) also reported a high incidence of social phobia among young, educated, and professional Saudi males. He related it to the highly structured and ritualized nature of social interactions in Saudi culture where strict rules apply to minor social rituals and where "there are traditions or rituals for every social situation." Susceptible individuals "less willing to conform with a ritualistic social milieu" may develop social phobia as a response (p. 169). Even though the rates of depression seem to be on the rise, related to modernization, migration, dislocation of the extended family and of traditional support system, suicide remains rare.

Middle Easterners hold common cultural belief systems regarding causation of illness, whether physical or psychological. Emotional disturbances are generally defined in somatic terms and expressed in body language. The symptoms are usually attributed to a neighboring organ. Arabs are particularly preoccupied with processes of ingestion and elimination; in their perception of health and illness, the condition of the alimentary tract has priority over other systems. Somatic symptoms, on the other hand, are rarely if ever attributed to psychological disturbances. Anxiety or depression are typically somatized. Social and interpersonal problems often cannot be expressed as such and are disguised as somatic, emotional, or behavioral problems. This situation provides fertile ground for the growth of "iatrogenic hypochondriasis" and doctor-shopping; through repeated physical examinations and laboratory investigations, patients seek assiduously for a confirmation of their belief in the somatic basis of their emotional ailment (El-Islam, 1975, 1982; Okasha et al., 1968).

At times, emotional and behavioral problems are explained away in terms of delusory cultural beliefs. One belief system, for example, relates to the role of supernatural agents such as the devil, jinns, and sorcery in the causation of disease (El-Islam & Malasi, 1985). The word *Wiswas*, for instance, can refer both to the devil and to worrying thoughts. *Junun* is both insanity and possession by a jinn (a supernatural being). El-Islam (1982) observes that "unacceptable wishes, feelings, and acts are liable to be projected onto the devil, and ruminations involving aggressive or unacceptable sexual impulses are also attributed to him, enabling people to doubt or to disavow these and to avoid guilt feelings respecting them" (p. 6).

Another popular disease-causation theory involves belief in the evil eye, which is thought to be cast when jealous or hostile people wish misfortune upon the objects of their envy or anger. Thus, unexpected misfortunes, including illness, are explained in a supernatural yet personalized way. This type of harm is believed to occur commonly, as many situations seem to arouse envy in Arabs. Where others may be spurred into action and competition by somebody else's success or talent, Arabs (and other Middle Easterners) often attribute such attainments to luck or fate rather than to effort and achievement, and react to them with envy (including, for some, ill-wishing). The belief in the evil eye and in the power of envy and ill-wishing leads Arabs to fear others, especially outsiders. For example, Arab parents will refrain from making public comments on the good qualities of their children for fear that they might elicit envious reactions, thus making their offspring a target for the evil eye. In fact, in order to protect the youngsters from the evil eye, parents make modest or even disparaging remarks about them in public. This protective disguising of their true feelings often confuses and misleads the children who, when young, are unable to grasp the meaning of or the reasons behind the parents' behavior. Infants are generally protected from the evil eye by the wearing of amulets, gold jewelry, blue beads, and/or verses of the Qur'an.

Even though Western medicine is generally sought after and widely practiced in the Middle East, beliefs in the role of the evil eye, of hot and cold, and of digestive disturbances as contributory to or even causative factors in promoting ill health are widespread. Their invocation, however, is partly dependent on the socioeconomic and educational levels of the family. While they are more widespread among rural populations, city dwellers have been known to invoke them when an illness becomes chronic or where a condition unexpectedly takes a turn for the worse. El-Islam and Malasi (1985) found that educated patients were just as likely as the less educated to involve traditionally held supernatural forces in their psychotic delusions, suggesting that, notwithstanding their past period of education, these patients resorted to cultural beliefs to explain their morbid experiences. All types of disturbances in children are attributed to the evil eye.

In the United States, Arab Americans seek mental health services for a number of reasons, including marital problems leading at times to separation and divorce and for problems and symptoms related to immigration and separation from kin and country. Most prominently, however, they come for family crises, in particular those involving parent-child problems (Laffrey, Meleis, Lipson, Solomon, & Omidian, 1989). Parents seek assistance regarding ineffective or too-harsh disciplinary practices. They come hoping to gain information about alternative child-rearing and discipline methods, which will help them check or prevent abusive or neglectful behaviors within the family. They also consult mental health professionals for cultural and generational conflicts that result in school problems, running away, acting out, and/or drug use by youths.

Embarrassment regarding coming for assistance often causes families to delay or avoid seeking help altogether. Additional reasons for the insufficient penetration of health care services into the Arab population (in deprived areas especially) include cultural and language barriers, fragmentation of services, lack of public or private transportation, limited health care insurance, poverty, and a lack of awareness of existing services (Kulwicki, 1989).

Regarding Arabs in Israel—yet his remarks could be generalized to Arabs elsewhere, including Arab Americans—Gorkin (1986) warns us that there is a general perception that "Arab patients are not sufficiently sophisticated or psychologically minded to benefit from insight-oriented psychotherapy" (p. 71). He observes that while it is true that many Arab patients enter treatment with expectations of receiving advice, directives, and concrete forms of help, "these expectations are not rigid and unchangeable" and that it is "inaccurate to portray Arab patients as incapable of introspection or psychological mindedness" (p. 71).

When a child is ill or disturbed, the basic attitude of Arab parents and families is one of extreme concern. Immediate family members as well as close relatives and neighbors offer advice and help on how to manage the illness. While American families cope with the stress of illness by means of problem solving and information seeking, Arabs depend in a crisis on other people for advice, counsel, and guidance. For instance, when Arab children were asked how they coped with physical pain, they showed a preference for talking about their pain and having friends close by to cheer them up. The same study showed that when in physical pain, most Arab children were more likely than their American counterparts to feel better in the presence of their mother or others. This finding is consistent with cultural expectations that in addition to "nursing" the ill child, family and friends provide comfort and solace by their presence. When a child is hospitalized, visits to the hospital by relatives as well as acquaintances are expected. These visits have the important function of helping the family cope with a major stress (Abu-Saad, 1984).

A number of social properties shared by Middle Easterners, including Arab Americans, affect their behavior when they enter the health care system as patients (Lipson & Meleis, 1983; Meleis & La Fever, 1984; Wagner, 1991). The Arabs' affiliative needs, already highly developed, are intensified during illness. Given their strong commitment to family ties, Arab patients will turn first to their kin and friends for help and sustenance. They may thus exclude health care professionals, even at those times when they desperately need medical or nursing help.

Decisions regarding health care typically are made by the family group. They are not seen as the responsibility of the individual. Hence, a common misperception arises among health care professionals, who see these families "meddling" or being intrusive. In fact, they are merely carrying out their familial responsibilities as prescribed by their Arab value system. The physician is still expected, however, to be the ultimate decision maker and will be held responsible for the outcome of his or her decisions.

Arabs value privacy and guard it vehemently. Hence, when asked to go through a comprehensive health assessment inquiry, they may show various degrees of uncooperativeness. For example, a formal interview in English may yield answers designed to please the interviewer, or to save face, and/or to absolve the family from responsibility for the illness.

At the hospital, staff members are likely to find the family "overbearing" and the patient seemingly too docile. Behaviors that may be considered perfectly normal within the patient's cultural context will be perceived by the staff as "bizarre." These behaviors may include a patient's overdependence on the family, a family's overprotection of the patient, an overpossessive mother-child relationship, a patient's reluctance to be touched by a member of the opposite sex, a patient's silence or staring. Staff members sometimes tend to respond to the patient by misinterpreting and labeling behavior (e.g., labeling family members as "anxious" and "intrusive") and by setting limits on family visits and interactions. Staff members often perceive the actions of family members as "overindulging" their hospitalized relative and creating a major interference in the patient's care. Indeed, the staff members may become exasperated by the behavior and actions of the patient and relatives, to the point of rejecting them outright. Arabs have developed a reputation as chronic and unpopular patients (Meleis & LaFever, 1984).

According to Meleis and LaFever (1984), health care professionals face the following questions when treating Arab patients:

1. How much should the patient's family be involved?
2. What constitutes invasion of privacy (will touching a female patient for a physical examination or even asking certain questions be perceived as unacceptable intrusions on the patient's privacy)?
3. How far should one guide or encourage the patient toward self-help, inner reliance, and independence, instead of reliance on the family?
4. Which of the many therapeutic modalities are best suited to the patient's cultural biases and expectations? For instance, Arab patients assume that medication by intrusive methods (e.g., injections) will be more effective than pills. On the other hand, they do not expect work on interpersonal relationships to be helpful. In addition, patients and families expect instant cure.

Language is an additional barrier, and so too is the absence of mutually understood symbols. For example, the Arabic concept of time differs from that prevalent in Western cultures. Arabs show little or no preoccupation with time; they are not anxious to meet deadlines, nor do they plan meetings by set clock time. For most Arabs, the focus is on interpersonal interactions and human relations rather than on tasks and instrumentalities (Lipson & Meleis, 1983; Meleis & LaFever, 1984). They prefer to talk around issues instead of addressing the business at hand directly and efficiently.

Planning for discharge is particularly complex for Arab American patients. As pointed out by Meleis and her collaborators, Arabs view a complete termination of physician-patient contacts or relationship as tactless and inconsiderate. Termination of any relationship to an Arab patient means stress. As a result, health professionals sometimes see Arab Americans as procrastinating over the final details of discharge. Often it helps to reassure patients of a continuing relationship whenever possible: instead of a dry and final "good-bye," substituting "see you again sometime" may provide the reassurance that strengthens rapport and promotes compliance (Meleis & LaFever, 1984; Meleis & Jonsen, 1983).

At the time of an Arab American's admission to treatment, health care professionals need to clarify roles, expectations, and cultural differences with family and patient. Perceptions of mental illness and hospitalization require additional clarification. The family should be enlisted as a major coping device. There may be a need for ongoing staff meetings with an Arabic-culture consultant to increase understanding of the patient's behavior and to alleviate staff frustration and feelings of failure and rejection.

Conclusion

A basic principle in the psychiatric assessment and treatment of a patient who is ethnically and culturally different is to be sensitive to the particular circumstances of the individual and the family. In order to evaluate Arab individuals accurately and plan for their treatment, it is essential to remember both the central position families occupy in their life and the network of obligations and expectations the culture has woven around them. Any slip-up in upholding norms of behavior prescribed by the culture, any "betrayal" of the kinship group, triggers intense reactions of shame and fear of public opprobrium and rejection. Arabs are particularly sensitive to transgressions in the areas of sexual role differentiation, of gender relations, and of hierarchical power relations. A rejected, socially isolated individual is threatened with psychological as well as physical withering. Seeking psychiatric treatment for a defined emotional or mental disturbance evokes precisely such shameful, socially embarrassing, even dishonoring feelings. The repercussions of such a condition do not overwhelm the affected individual alone but engulf the whole family, as well. Hence, when dealing with Arab Middle Eastern patients and families, it is critical to show extra sensitivity in order to avoid exacerbating their sense of individual and group shame. An additional challenge for mental health professionals is to find an optimal way of mobilizing around their patients the most elaborate social network possible. Doing so will have as good a potential for promoting rehabilitation and healthy functioning as any of the therapeutic measures currently available.

REFERENCES

Abed, I., Abu-Laban, B., Adadow Gray, N., Bibi, H., & Mobarak, A. (1991, October 20). *The Arab-American family dealing with change.* Symposium presented by the Egyptian American Professionals Society in White Plains, NY.

Abraham, N. (1989). Arab-American marginality: Mythos and praxis. In B. Abu-Laban & M. Suleiman (Eds.), *Arab-Americans: Continuity and change* (p. 20). Belmont, MA: Association of Arab-American University Graduates.

Abu-Laban, B., Adadow Gray, N., Becharra, G., & Suleiman, M. (1990). Issues confronting Arab-American families. A roundtable discussion at the 10th anniversary convention of the American-Arab Antidiscrimination Committee.

Abu-Laban, B., & Suleiman, M. W. (Eds). (1989). *Arab-Americans: Continuity and change.* Belmont, MA: Association of Arab-American University Graduates.

Abu-Saad, H. (1984). Cultural components of pain: The Arab-American child. *Issues in Comprehensive Pediatric Nursing, 7,* 91–99.

Adlakha, A. L., & Suchindran, C. M. (1985). Factors affecting infant and child mortality. *Journal of Biosocial Science, 17,* 481–496.

Baker, A. M. (1990). The psychological impact of the Intifada on Palestinian children in the occupied West Bank and Gaza: An exploratory study. *American Journal of Orthopsychiatry, 60* (4), 496–505.

Barakat, H. (1985). The Arab family and the challenge of social transformation. In E. W. Fernea (Ed.), *Women and the family in the Middle East* (pp. 27–48). Austin, TX: University of Texas Press.

Cederblad, M. (1968). A child psychiatric study on Sudanese Arab children. *Acta Psychiatrica Scandinavica* [Suppl. 200].

Chaleby, K. (1986). Psychosocial stresses and psychiatric disorders in an outpatient population in Saudi Arabia. *Acta Psychiatrica Scandinavica, 73,* 147–151.

Chaleby, K. (1987). Social phobia in Saudis. *Social Psychiatry, 22,* 167–170.

de Costa, C. (1985). Adolescent pregnancy. *Medical Journal of Australia, 142,* 490.

Der-Karabetian, A., Kadi, Z., Elmasian, S., & Yetenekian, A. (1975). Attitudes toward mental illness in Lebanon: An initial report. *Lebanese Medical Journal, 28,* 297–306.

Eisenlohr, C. J. (1988). *The dilemma of adolescent Arab girls in an American high school* (Unpublished Ph.D. diss.). Ann Arbor, MI: University Microfilm International.

El-Islam, M. F. (1975). Culture-bound neurosis in Qatari women. *Social Psychiatry, 10,* 25–29.

El-Islam, M. F. (1982). Arabic cultural psychiatry. *Transcultural Psychiatric Research Review, 19,* 5–14.

El-Islam, M. F. (1983). Cultural change and intergenerational relationships in Arabian families. *International Journal of Family Psychiatry, 4,* 321–329.

El-Islam, M. F., & Malasi, T. H. (1985). Delusions and education. *Journal of Operational Psychiatry, 16,* 29–31.

Florian, V., & Har-Even, D. (1984). Cultural patterns in the choice of leisure time activity frameworks: A study of Jewish and Arab youth in Israel. *Journal of Leisure Research, 16* (4), 330–337.

Glidden, H. W. (1972). The Arab world. *American Journal of Psychiatry, 128* (8), 984–988.

Gorkin, M. (1986). Countertransference in cross-cultural psychotherapy: The example of Jewish therapist and Arab patient. *Psychiatry, 49,* 69–79.

Al-Issa, I., & Al-Issa, B. (1969). Psychiatric problems in a developing country: Iraq. *International Journal of Social Psychiatry, 16,* 15–22.

Karam, E. G. (1996). The nosological status of bereavement-related depressions. *British Journal of Psychiatry, 165,* 48–52.

Katchadourian, H. (1974). A comparative study of mental illness among the Christians and Moslems of Lebanon. *International Journal of Social Psychiatry, 20,* 56–67.

Katchadourian, H., & Racy, J. (1969). The diagnostic distribution of treated psychiatric illness in Lebanon. *British Journal of Psychiatry, 115,* 1309–1322.

Kulwicki, A. (1989). Infant mortality among Arab Americans. *Michigan Nurse, 62,* 12–15.

Laffrey, S. C., Meleis, A. I., Lipson, J. G., Solomon, M., & Omidian, P. A. (1989). Assessing Arab-American health care needs. *Social Science and Medicine, 29,* 877–883.

Lipson, J., & Meleis, A. I. (1983). Issues in health care of Middle Eastern patients. *Western Journal of Medicine, 139,* 854–861.

Mays, S., & Stockley A. (1983). Victims of tradition. *Nursing Mirror, 156,* 19–21.

Meleis, A. I. (1979). The health care system of Kuwait. *Social Science and Medicine, 13A,* 743–749.

Meleis, A. I., & Jonsen, A. (1983). Ethical crises and cultural differences. *Western Journal of Medicine, 138,* 889–893.

Meleis, A. I., & LaFever, C. W. (1984). The Arab American and psychiatric care. *Perspectives in Psychiatric Care, 22* (1), 72–86.

Meleis, A. I., & Sorrell, L. (1981). Arab-American women and their birth experiences. *American Journal of Maternal and Child Nursing, 6,* 171–176.

Okasha, A., Kamel, M., & Hassan, A. H. (1968). Preliminary psychiatric observations in Egypt. *British Journal of Psychiatry, 114,* 949–955.

Osman, A. A. (1992). Substance abuse among patients attending a psychiatric hospital in Jeddah: A descriptive study. *Annals of Saudi Medicine, 12* (3), 289–293.

Patai, R. (1973). *The Arab Mind.* New York: Scribners.

Pattison, E. M. (1986). War and mental health in Lebanon. *Journal of Operational Psychiatry, 15,* 31–38.

Prothro, E. T. (1967). *Child rearing in the Lebanon.* Middle Eastern Monograph Series No. 8. Cambridge, MA: Harvard University Press.

Prothro, E. T., & Diab, L. N. (1974). *Changing family patterns in the Arab East.* Beirut: American University of Beirut.

Racy, J. (1970). Psychiatry in the Arab East. *Acta Psychiatrica Scandinavica* [Suppl. *211*].

El Sayed, S. M., Maghraby, M. M., Hafeiz, H. B., & Buckley, M. M. (1986). Psychiatric diagnostic categories in Saudi Arabia. *Acta Psychiatrica Scandinavica, 74,* 553–554.

Seginer, R. (1988). Adolescents' orientation toward the future: Sex role differentiation in a sociocultural context. *Sex Roles, 18* (11/12), 739–757.

El Sendioni, M. F. M., Abou el-Azaem, M. G. M., & Luza, F. (1977). Culture change and mental illness. *International Journal of Social Psychiatry, 23,* 20–25.

Sharabi, H., & Ani, M. (1977). Impact of class and culture on social behavior: The feudal-bourgeois family in Arab society. In L. Brown & N. Itzkowitz (Eds.), *Psychological dimensions of Near Eastern studies* (pp. 240–256). Princeton, NJ: Darwin Press.

Wagner, R. (1991). Cultural differences should be considered in treating Arab-Americans. *The Psychiatric Times* (April 1991), 15.

53 / Psychiatric Disorders in American Indian and Alaska Native Children and Adolescents

Donald W. Bechtold and Spero M. Manson

Clinical Population

The designation "American Indian and Alaska Native" recently has supplanted "Native American" as the preferred identification for this segment of the population. This designation is, in fact, more

Partial support for the preparation of this chapter was provided by Grant Number T01 MH19156-02, K02 MH00833-01, RO1 MH 42473-05, and R01 DA06076-01, from NIMH.

accurate insofar as it distinguishes the population in question from native Hawaiians, who constitute a distinct sociocultural subgroup and must be discussed separately from American Indians and Alaska Natives. The 1990 U.S. Census revealed that American Indian and Alaska Native people comprise 0.8% of the total U.S. population and number almost 2 million. More than 25% of these individuals are children and adolescents; in fact, the Indian and Native population is remarkably young. The median age for the population is 19.4

years, compared with 29 years for the U.S. population in general (May, 1982). This discrepancy may be accounted for by the fertility rate of Indian and Natives, which is the highest of any major group in the United States and is approximately twice as high as that of the country at large (May, 1982). In addition, this population suffers from an excessively high death rate among certain age groups, such that fewer Indian and Native people live to their more senior years (Yates, 1987). For these reasons, then, Indian and Native people comprise the fastest-growing minority group in the United States and include a disproportionately greater representation of youths (May & Broudy, 1980).

The American Indian population is also noted for its remarkable cultural heterogeneity. There are over 300 reservations and 505 federally recognized tribes (Bureau of Indian Affairs, 1988). Approximately 200 tribal languages are still spoken today (LaFromboise, 1988). This diverse population is comprised of not only rural/reservation residents but also of a large number of urban dwellers. In fact, as much as 60% of the Indian and Native population resides in urban areas. Hence, a discussion of Indian or Native culture must occur in the context of a particular tribal group. Clinical and developmental implications derive from such issues as tribal affiliation, formal enrollment as a member of the tribe, urban or rural/reservation residence, and tribal specific values. Failure to recognize this cultural heterogeneity may result in stereotyping that is both inaccurate and stigmatizing. Consider the stereotype of the "suicidal Indian." In the aggregate, Indian and Native suicide rates exceed those of the general population. However, rates among certain tribes prove to be much lower and rates among other tribes much higher than national averages (Shore, 1975). Hence, it is clearly inaccurate to assume that an individual's risk for suicide is excessive simply due to being Indian or Native. While practicality mandates that Indian and Native people be considered as a distinct ethnic group so that clinical and developmental issues may be discussed, it must be remembered that this "distinct" ethnic group actually encompasses hundreds of diverse subgroups.

In general, Indian and Native people comprise a low-income, highly stressed population that suffers from extensive physical and mental health problems. In spite of the high incidence of health-related problems, however, remarkably few epidemiologic studies have been completed in this population (Manson, Shore, Bloom, Keepers, & Neligh, 1989; Shore, Manson, Bloom, Keepers, & Neligh, 1987). The existing ones typically suffer from one of two types of problems. The first is that serious flaws may be noted in the sampling methods, diagnostic systems, and cultural sensitivity of many of these studies. Second is that social systems and conditions have changed considerably in the 20 years or more since the majority of these studies were performed. As a result, caution must be exercised in any discussion of the epidemiology of alcohol, drug, and mental disorders among Indian and Native people. Some population-based data on alcohol and drug use in these populations is available, particularly in regard to adolescents. Little such data exist for other mental disorders defined according to current diagnostic systems (the fourth edition of the *Diagnostic and Statistical Manual of Mental Disorders* [DSM-IV], American Psychiatric Association, 1994), or for the co-occurrence of mental disorders with substance abuse. Much of the older literature amounts to no more than a handful of small epidemiologic or quasi-epidemiologic studies, mainly concerning Eskimo communities. Anecdotal evidence, however, derived from these older studies as well as from the impressions of service providers and community members suggests that Indian and Native people are at least as heavily impacted by the entire range of alcohol, drug, and mental disorders as any other group, and perhaps significantly more so. Information about the prevalence and distribution of specific disorders, associated functional impairment, and issues of service utilization and access analogous to the information collected by the Epidemiologic Catchment Area studies is badly needed.

Developmental Considerations

Human development occurs along a continuum that spans an entire lifetime. Behavior has long been understood as relating not only to immediate stimuli but to antecedent events that occur much earlier in the developmental progression of the individual. Current thinking likewise recognizes that throughout this developmental continuum, behavioral outcomes are the result of a complex interplay among an individual's biologic/genetic endowment, psychologically significant experiences that are assigned unique meanings in the context of personal histories, and the social milieu of the individual, which includes family, peer group, culture, and various dimensions of affiliative status. This biopsychosocial model of development is an especially appropriate one by which to consider the developmental progression of American Indian and Native children and adolescents. According to this model, development may be viewed longitudinally as a series of potential crises at a number of developmental phases, from conception through early adulthood.

FETAL DEVELOPMENT

The first stage of risk occurs in utero. Indian and Native individuals are among the most severely socioeconomically disadvantaged populations in the United States (U.S. Senate Select Committee on Indian Affairs, 1989). Nutrition is typically substandard among impoverished and disadvantaged people; the sequelae of prenatal nutritional deficiencies may include both physical and mental changes.

Accessibility of medical services tends to relate directly to one's socioeconomic level: the more severe the level of poverty, the less accessible are medical care and related services. The earlier in pregnancy during which prenatal care is established, and the more regular its maintenance throughout gestation, the greater the benefit to the developing fetus. Through the Indian Health Service, which is a branch of the Public Health Service, competent medical care is available to a number of Indian people who could not otherwise afford to purchase such services. Nonetheless, large numbers of Indian people live outside the services areas of Indian Health Service, and other individuals within the service area fail to utilize the available resources. Consequently, many Indian and Native babies develop in utero without the advantage of adequate prenatal care or nutrition.

Intrauterine development is also recognized as a stage of risk for Indians and Natives insofar as the developing fetus is highly susceptible and vulnerable to the toxic effects of a variety of chemical substances. Substance use and abuse begins at an earlier age among many Indian people than in the U.S. population at large, progresses more rapidly to stages of abuse, and involves the use of a greater number of substances (Beauvais, Oetting, & Edwards, 1989). It is not surprising, then, that Indian babies may be at increased risk for developmental anomalies associated with chemical use and abuse throughout pregnancy. Tobacco utilization during pregnancy has been shown to result in small-for-gestational-age babies. A host of behavioral, developmental, physiologic, and anatomic anomalies are known to occur in fetal alcohol syndrome and fetal alcohol effect as a result of the toxic impact on the fetus of alcohol ingestion during early pregnancy. High rates of fetal alcohol syndrome have been documented among a number of tribal groups (May & Hymbaugh, 1983; May, Hymbaugh, Aase, & Sarnet, 1983). Furthermore, these rates are increasing among a number of Indian and Native groups such as the Navajo and Pueblo communities (May et al., 1983).

Maternal variables such as age, marital status, environmental support, and desire for the pregnancy also affect the intrauterine environment. Perinatal complications clearly increase in young mothers with little or no environmental support who are ambivalent or hostile toward their pregnancy. Teen pregnancy rates have increased dramatically among Indian and Native youth such that greater numbers of teenagers are producing more babies and at younger ages than in times past. Logically, in many cases, their developing babies are at increased risk.

While the stage of risk associated with in utero development most directly relates to biologic factors, psychologic and social dimensions cannot be overlooked. Many factors affect the developing fetus, including the psychological state of the mother. The process of parent/child bonding begins during the in utero phase. Issues such as whether the pregnancy was planned or not, desired or not, the status of the relationship between the parents, parental preference for fetal gender, socioeconomic status of the parents, and availability of social supports impact the establishment of the parent/child bond. Hence, while disorders of bonding and attachment are expressed during later phases of development, their origins may be traced in part to the psychological state of the parents from conception forward and to the availability and adequacy of social supports during this period of development. Again, the prevalence of psychiatric disorder and the social disorganization and dysfunction common to many Native individuals place their unborn children at increased risk.

INFANT DEVELOPMENT

The next phase of development to consider is infancy. This phase, too, carries an attendant set of risks for Indian and Native individuals, namely disorders of bonding and attachment. As has been discussed previously, the origin of disorders of bonding and attachment may be traced in part to prenatal maternal and paternal variables. Infant issues such as gender, health, developmental normality, and temperament likewise impact on the establishment of the attachment relationship. Disorders of bonding and attachment assume a variety of manifestations, among which Indian and Native children are heavily represented. This is not surprising, given the degree of risk experienced by Indian and Native people related to the variables mentioned earlier. Insofar as Indian parents tend to be socioeconomically disadvantaged, to have experienced histories of significant social and familial disruption, and to experience high rates of a variety of alcohol, drug, and mental disorders, their ability to establish healthy parent/child bonds may be adversely affected. Likewise, high rates of physical disorders among Native infants— such as otitis media, birth defects including those associated with fetal alcohol syndrome and fetal alcohol effect, and cognitive and psycholinguistic developmental disorders—also may interfere with the establishment of healthy parent/child bonds. Clearly, then, Indian and Native children are at increased risk for a variety of disorders of bonding and attachment.

Nonorganic failure to thrive represents an attachment disorder in which the parents fail to provide adequately for the most basic needs of the child. True prevalence rates of this disorder among Indian/Native children are most likely greater than current estimates due to underreporting as well as to underutilization/unavailability of medical and social services. Other dimensions of child abuse and neglect also may be understood as a phenomenon rooted in disordered bonding

and attachment insofar as the exploitation of a developmentally vulnerable child represents a significant failure in the development of empathy in the parent/child relationship. High rates of abuse and neglect are reported among Indian children (Lujan et al., 1989; Piasecki et al., 1989). Bureau of Indian Affairs data reflect that a minimum of 1 percent of Indian children in Bureau service areas may have been abused or neglected in a single year (U.S. Department of the Interior, Bureau of Indian Affairs, 1989). Sadly, Bureau data are known to underestimate the extent of abuse and neglect of Indian children for a number of reasons. They do not include urban Indians; neither does the Bureau have unlimited jurisdiction in all cases of abuse and neglect among Native children. Rather, numerous cases are handled through county and state social service agencies. Finally, abuse and neglect among all populations of children are known to be seriously underreported.

Anaclitic depression as described by Spitz (Spitz & Wolf, 1946) occurs in certain infants when an attachment relationship is broken during a sensitive phase of development. Indian and Native children are known to be at substantially increased risk for disruption of attachment relationships. This disruption may be the result of actual loss of the attachment figure due to death, parental separation, or abandonment, all of which occur at increased frequency among many Native families. It also may be due to the psychological absence of the parent due to depression, addiction, or other mental disorder; again, these are prevalent conditions among many Native families. In fact, high prevalence rates for depressive disorders among Indian and Native adults may be due both to a genetic predisposition for affective illness (Neligh, 1990) and to the establishment of a "depressive core" deriving in part from a disrupted attachment relationship in early development.

Reactive attachment disorder of infancy or early childhood is a disorder in which children manifest either inadequate or excessive and indiscriminate social interactions. The etiology derives from a severely pathologic parent/child relationship. Few data exist on the prevalence rate for this condition among Indian and Native children; however, many Indian children would be expected to be at increased risk. Caution must be exercised in establishing this diagnosis with Indian and Native families. The culturally insensitive observer may misinterpret the stoicism encouraged by Native culture, and which is transmitted intergenerationally to the young, as an avoidant, resistant, or unattached child or as a detached, disinterested, or uninvested parent.

SCHOOL-AGE DEVELOPMENT

The next developmental phase to consider is that of latency, or the school-age child. During this phase of development, Indian and Native children may experience a well-described and frequently recognized phenomenon known as "academic crossover," which represents the primary stage of risk for the school-age Native child (Beiser & Attneave, 1982; Bryde, 1967). School-age Indian/Native children are, in fact, at risk for a variety of educationally handicapping conditions. They experience high rates of mental retardation, sensory impairment, emotional/behavioral dysfunction, and learning disabilities, even more so than their Asian, Hispanic, black, or Anglo counterparts (O'Connell, 1987).

Concerns relating to the education of Indian and Native youth date at least as far back as 1928 with the issuance of *The Problem of Indian Administration,* more commonly known as the Meriam Report (Meriam, 1928). This report highlighted a series of school-related issues concerning the physical and emotional well-being of Indian/Native youth. It concluded that educational deficiencies derive from the impoverished standard of living of the Indian child, the cultural irrelevance of curriculum created primarily for the Anglo child, the small number and poor quality of schools and school personnel for Indian children, and the low self-esteem commonly observed among Indian children. In 1969, the Senate Special Subcommittee on Indian Education, in a document that became known as the Kennedy Report, cited "a dismal record of absenteeism, dropouts, negative self-image, low achievement, and, ultimately, academic failure" (U.S. Senate, 1969 p. 21) among Indian and Native youth. At approximately the same time, the concept of academic crossover was first introduced (Bryde, 1967). While Native youth typically begin the first grade somewhat ahead of national academic norms, by the fourth grade, on average, they fall half a year behind in academic achievement; their performance continues to decline in subsequent years. Developmental factors must be considered in attempting to understand this phenomenon. School-age years are ones in which the child undertakes a variety of activities spanning a number of domains in the service of development of a sense of competence, mastery, and efficacy within the environment. School assumes a particularly important role during this phase of development. While early school years are oriented more to the visual and motor abilities of the student, later years require the student to demonstrate increasing aptitude in verbal and conceptual skills. Traditional Indian/Native culture, however, is more visual than verbal, more experiential than conceptual. Major discrepancies in the verbal/performance subscales of the revised Wechsler Intelligence Scale for Children are commonly seen among Native children and speak to this distinct cognitive style. Hence, one dimension of crossover relates to the culturally insensitive application of educational techniques that are inappropriate to the cognitive style of the Indian child. Unfortunately, as academic failures accumulate, Indian children are likely to perceive themselves as inadequate and ineffectual agents within their environment, rather than understanding that it is the educational system that has failed them.

ADOLESCENT DEVELOPMENT

During later school years, the Indian child begins to negotiate adolescent issues of identity formation and consolidation. One dimension of identity is that of educational identity. To the extent that children perceive education as valued in their culture and valuable for their future, it becomes positively incorporated into their identity. Many Indian children, however, are denied this vantage point; education is less often seen as valued or valuable. Student dropout rates and adult unemployment rates may reach as high as 85% on some reservations (Sack, Beiser, Clarke, & Redshirt, 1987). In the face of such high dropout rates, it is understandable that many Indian children fail to perceive education as valued within their culture. Likewise, with such dramatic elevations of unemployment rates, the Indian child may perceive education as irrelevant and futile insofar as it does not ultimately affect outcome in terms of meaningful employment. Hence, a second dimension of academic crossover relates to the perception of education as meaningless and irrelevant.

As Native youths continue along the developmental continuum, they must negotiate issues related to other dimensions of identity, as well. It is inaccurate to consider identity as a single, unified concept. Rather, each of the various dimensions that contributes to the formation and consolidation of identity among Native people must be addressed. In addition to education, these include social, cultural, religious, sexual, and vocational aspects of the self.

Establishment of sociocultural identity is a complex process for Indian and Native children, as it is for children of other ethnic minority groups. Reservation-based children are confronted with issues specific to rural lifestyle and geographic isolation. Urban Indian children face a different set of issues, insofar as their unique status as an ethnic minority emerges at an early age. In both cases, the children are confronted with the need to establish a balance between the maintenance of traditional Indian ways, customs, and beliefs and the ability to function effectively within the dominant culture. Traditionality assumes many forms among Indian and Native children. Religious practices; maintenance of tribal language; preference for certain foods and styles of food preparation; usage of particular plants, herbs, or woods; style of dress; hair length and hairstyle may indicate high degrees of traditionality. Establishment of sociocultural identity is clearly enhanced when Indian adolescents are able to develop and maintain a level of traditionality consistent with their family and community standards and can at the same time function and compete successfully in a social, educational, and vocational environment dominated by the majority culture. By contrast, neither extreme is desirable. The highly traditional Native adolescent with no skills for survival in the non-Indian world cannot live in a vacuum, isolated from the dominant culture. Likewise, the highly acculturated Native youth seldom can flee from or escape the traditional wisdom of his or her people and their past, as this often represents a necessary foundation for subsequent development of a sociocultural identity. Clearly, the child who is neither facile nor

comfortable with either traditional beliefs and practices or those of the dominant culture is least prepared to meet the developmental demands of identity formation.

Establishing a religious identity also is complicated for Indian and Native adolescents. All adolescents struggle with the issue of, first, *if to believe*, and, second, specifically *what to believe*. For Indian youths, religion is even more intrinsically bound to traditional culture. Consequently, what to believe becomes the preeminent question, and has been complicated in recent days by not only the dichotomy between the Native American churches and those of the dominant culture but also by the impact of various cult and occult influences that increasingly pervade the culture of the young.

Indian youths also must negotiate the various dimensions of sexual identity during the adolescent stage of development. While core gender identity is established early in childhood, sexual preference becomes solidified during adolescence. Indian and Native youths are no different in this regard. Neither do Indian youths differ in regard to the tumult and vicissitudes so commonly observed during the developmental transition from the primary task of identity consolidation to the establishment of the capacity for intimacy, mutuality, and reciprocity in a relationship. Evidence for this tumult may be seen among Native youths in the form of excessive and growing rates of both teen pregnancies and sexually transmitted diseases.

The establishment and consolidation of identity among Indian and Native youths is complicated by an additional factor that the clinician must anticipate. For many Indian and Native youths, adolescence may represent the first developmental phase in which they personally and directly experience the impact of racism, prejudice, and discrimination. Adults may buffer the impact of this social ill for younger children. Adolescents, however, must negotiate its impact from a number of perspectives. As has already been described, Indian adolescents must successfully negotiate an educational system that may be irrelevant to important dimensions of their culture and prejudiced toward their cognitive and learning style. They may, for the first time, experience the personal effect of racism in the context of taboos, prohibitions, or sanctions against cross-ethnic dating. They may ultimately find themselves inadequately prepared for successful competition in the workforce or may be victimized by the oppression of massive rates of unemployment. Nevertheless, during adolescence Indian and Native youths become acutely aware that their ethnic identity at times encounters obstacles of prejudice that must be addressed, negotiated, and surmounted.

TRANSITION TO ADULTHOOD

As Indian adolescents enter early adulthood, they must negotiate a final stage of risk. Clearly, the seeds for this stage of risk have been sown throughout earlier development. Young Indian adults are at high risk for a variety of self-injurious behaviors. Included among these are elevated rates of suicide, substance abuse, and various manifestations of disregard for health through noncompliance with medical care. Indian youths who experience themselves as competent and effective within their environment develop a comfortable sense of identity in its various dimensions, overcome the prejudice that may attend their ethnic identity, and establish the capacity for intimate, empathic, mutually gratifying interaction are likely to make a successful transition to early adulthood. However, many Indian youths face a number of hurdles during development that may render them vulnerable during this phase of transition to early adulthood. Failure to negotiate earlier developmental tasks successfully or completely leaves young Native adults ill-prepared for the escalating demands of adulthood. Self-injurious behaviors that bespeak despondence, futility, and despair may be viewed both as manifestations of failure during earlier phases of development and as attempts to avoid future failures in the developmental tasks of adulthood.

Cultural Variation in the Phenomenology of Psychiatric Syndromes

One of the most salient feature of psychiatric disorders, for children as well as adults, is a distinction between psyche and soma that reflects a long Western intellectual history of mind-body dualism. This distinction is particularly evident in the formulation of major depressive episode, dysthymia, generalized anxiety disorder, and posttraumatic stress disorder, which revolve around particular affects—dysphoria, represented by depressed mood or loss of interest or pleasure, and anxiety, principally described as excessive worry or apprehension—and associated somatic symptoms, notably appetite and weight change, sleep disturbances, psychomotor agitation or retardation, fatigue, difficulty concentrating, recurrent thoughts of death, motor tension, autonomic hyperactivity, and vigilance. The latter, like many physical experiences, are relatively easy to ascertain across cultures, although their elicitation depends on understanding local idioms for expressing such distress. The greatest difficulty lies in determining the presence of dysphoria and anxiety, as defined by Western experience, largely because of the attendant assumptions about emotion and its phenomenology.

Definitions of the self vary along a continuum between "egocentric" and "sociocentric" (Shweder & Bourne, 1984). The former, best exemplified in Western, industrialized populations, characterize the person as unique, separate, and autonomous. The latter, found in many non-Western cultural traditions, depict the person in relational terms, as part of an interdependent collective, defined by kinship and myth (Geertz, 1984). In the United States, such differences often distinguish American Indians and Alaska Natives from white, middle-class Americans (Trimble, Manson, Dinges, & Medicine, 1984). It should not be surprising, then, that the location and experience of emotions vary along similar lines. In other words, they are not necessarily *just intra*psychic phenomena. Hence, diagnostic criteria that depend on eliciting individualistically oriented, contextless self-statements of dysphoria—such as "*I* feel blue," "These things no longer mean anything to *me*"—or worry—such as "I am bothered by things that usually do not bother *me*," "*I* fear things that *I* do not normally fear"—may be constrained, intrinsically, from discovering other ways of feeling and expressing the same affect.

Numerous studies underscore the rich and varied lexicons of emotion in non-Western cultures such as American Indians. Establishing the semantic equivalence of the terms by which Indian/

Native children, adults, and families refer to the same affect typically is approached through a translation/back-translation process. The results are seldom unequivocal, reflecting the indeterminacy of meaning that typifies human language (Good & Good, 1986; Robins, 1989). For example, guilt, shame, and sinfulness, which often are closely linked in Western experience—and, indeed, comprise a single question on the Diagnostic Interview Schedule intended to assess feelings of worthlessness—can be translated into Hopi but are conceptualized quite differently and evoke attributions that are both distinct from one another as well as those implied by their English counterparts within a Judeo-Christian framework (Manson, Shore, & Bloom, 1985).

Then, too, the words "depressed" and "anxious" are absent from the languages of some cultures, certain American Indians and Alaska Natives among them (Manson et al., 1985; Terminsen & Ryan, 1970). However, their absence does not, in and of itself, preclude the existence of related affect, or even analogous categories of illness. Manson et al. (1985) demonstrate that the *DSM-III* formulation of major depressive disorder in the third edition of the *DSM* (*DSM-III*) does not correspond directly to any of the categories of illness indigenous to the Hopi. Instead, symptoms of the former distribute differentially across the latter, which are characterized by distinct etiologies and treatments. This particular example depicts the problem of category validity described by Good and Good (1986).

Such variation in the phenomenology as well as language of emotion suggests that cultures selectively emphasize and elaborate these experiential domains. Drawing from the ethnographic literature on anger, Jenkins, Kleinman, and Good (1990) illustrated the dramatic degree to which different cultures may contrast with one another in this regard. Whereas Eskimos seldom display anger, others employ elaborate and complex means of expressing anger (Briggs, 1970). Likewise, other cultures (i.e., Iranians) encourage (Good, Good & Moradi, 1985) or discourage (i.e., Navajos; Miller & Schoenfeld, 1971) displays of extreme sadness and sorrow.

Within-group differences also are evident along these lines, most notably in terms of social class and gender, especially for dysphoria and excessive worry. This appears to be true among mainstream

Americans (Hirschfeld & Cross, 1982; Weissman & Klerman, 1981) as well as ethnic minorities such as Indians and Natives (Ackerson, Dick, Manson, & Baron, 1990; Baron, Manson, Ackerson, & Brenneman, 1990; Manson, Ackerson, Dick, Baron, & Fleming, 1990).

Not only may culture place differential emphasis on particular emotions; it also can assign unique attributions to the intensity of their experience as well as expression. Thus, distinguishing among mood, symptom, and disorder, which are presumed to vary along a continuum, is not as simple as it might seem (Kleinman & Good, 1985). Current diagnostic operations assume that such experiences are unidimensional, linear, and additive in nature, not unlike a ruler. The cross-cultural literature suggests that the "markers" on the ruler may vary from one group to another akin to the difference between metric and nonmetric systems of measurement. Not only may the scale of measurement differ in terms of minimal unit(s)—for example, millimeter versus 1/32 of an inch—but the significant categories of aggregation may not correspond as well—as in centimeter and meter versus inch, foot, and yard. Assessing the degree to which subjective conditions such as dysphoria and anxiety are present in cross-cultural settings, then, is not straightforward, as elegantly demonstrated by McNabb (1990) in his article on determining the accuracy and meaning of self-reported "satisfaction" among the Eskimo.

Let us assume that ways are developed to translate from one "ruler" to another, by no means an easy task, even in the simplest form of the problem. This accomplishment does not take into account the normative uncertainty of psychiatric ratings (Chance, 1963; Manson et al., 1985; Murphy & Hughes, 1965). Specifically, the threshold at which "normal" is demarcated from "abnormal" may vary by gender and cultural group. For example, the persistently higher prevalence of depressive *symptoms* reported among females than males and among American Indians than white, middle-class Americans may represent culturally patterned variations in the experiential levels of these phenomena and not necessarily higher rates of *disorder*. Consequently, such normative differences imply different "cutoff points" for distinguishing common, unremarkable episodes of mood from those that are unusual and noteworthy. Returning to the "ruler" analogy, if such "cutoff points" were solely a function of intensity or severity, then female and Navajo thresholds between normal and abnormal dysphoria, for example, might fall much farther along (or "out" or "up," depending on its orientation) the "ruler" than male and white middle-class thresholds.

The *DSM*, however, employs more than just intensity or severity in rendering such judgments. Duration often figures into the diagnostic calculus, as in 2 weeks of persistent dysphoria to meet criterion for major depressive episode or 1 month for posttraumatic stress disorder. Nevertheless, the same logic applies. For example, among the Hopi, sadness and worry are so common and widespread that periods of 1 month or more may be required to reach a level of significance for the individual *and* fellow community members equivalent to that presupposed by the *DSM* (Manson et al., 1985). Even then, it appears as if duration is but a "proxy" measure of functional impairment: The sadness or worry experienced by a Hopi person becomes a concern when he or she begins to fail to meet deeply ingrained social expectations.

There is no magic way by which to gain access to these aspects of an Indian or Native child's experience. The clinician needs to focus on the process of inquiry, the way in which one elicits the story of his or her illness (Kleinman, 1988). This process should emphasize careful clinical description. It must take into account the social contexts and cultural forces that shape an Indian child's everyday world, that give meaning to interpersonal relationships and life events. Effective and relevant psychiatric care, then, will follow from this insight.

Clinical Implications

The relative contribution of the biologic, psychologic, social, and cultural dimensions vary from one condition to another; significant cross-tribal variation exists in terms of prevalence rates for particular disorders. Nonetheless, it is generally true that Indian and Native children and adolescents are at increased risk for a number of alcohol, drug, and mental disorders. Indian youths themselves speak clearly to this increased vulnerability. In May 1987 more than 300 Indian and Native youths representing 53 tribes in 21 states convened under the auspices of the United National Indian Tribal Youth as part of the Youth 2000 Campaign. They identified their most pressing concerns in descending order as (1) substance abuse, (2) suicide, (3) teen pregnancy, (4) preservation of traditional tribal culture, (5) communication with tribal government, (6) higher education, (7) self-esteem, (8) school dropout rates, (9) recreation, and (10) unemployment. The available data support these concerns.

DEVELOPMENTAL DISORDERS

High rates of mental retardation, learning disabilities, emotional disabilities, sensory disabilities, and multiple handicaps have been identified among Navajo youths (Joe, 1980). Neurosensory disorders and certain developmental disabilities occur from 4 to 13 times more frequently for American Indians than for the population at large (Native American Rehabilitation and Training Center, 1979). For the nation as a whole, American Indians have the highest rate of learning disabilities, the second highest rate of mental retardation, and exceed the national averages for speech impairment and multiple handicaps, as well (O'Connell, 1987). Hence, many Indian and Native youths clearly are at increased risk for a variety of developmental disorders.

MOOD DISORDERS

The data likewise support high rates of affective illness among Indian and Native youths. One study indicated that depression was the most common specific diagnosis assigned teenage girls in the Mental Health Branch of the Indian Health Service (Beiser & Attneave, 1982). A 1983 survey of service utilization patterns reported that depression was diagnosed in approximately 3% of all young people between the ages of 10 and 19 seen as outpatients in the Albuquerque area of the Indian Health Service (May, 1983), and these figures may significantly underrepresent the true prevalence of depressive disorders among these children. Three recent studies completed by the National Center for American and Alaska Native Mental Health Research involved administration of a 20-item scale developed by the Center for Epidemiologic Studies (CES-D) (Beals, Manson, Keane, & Dick, 1991; Dinges & Duong-Tran,

1993; Manson et al., 1990). The surveys sought to identify depressive symptoms and were administered in a tribally operated boarding school, a boarding school operated by the Bureau of Indian Affairs, and a cohort including Indian and Native students from across 5 major universities. A CES-D score of 16 or greater suggests high risk for major depression; the scores for the 3 cohorts were 19.28, 19.53, and 17.75, respectively. While more rigorous epidemiologic research is clearly indicated, these preliminarily support the assertion that Indian and Native youths are at increased risk for depressive disorders.

ANXIETY DISORDERS

High rates of anxiety-related conditions also are reported among Indian and Native youths. Beiser and Attneave (1982) observed rates of anxiety disorders approximately equal to those of depressive disorders. The aforementioned 1983 report identified anxiety disorders in up to 13% of young people between the ages of 10 and 19 seen as outpatients (May, 1983). Again, these figures probably underestimate the true prevalence. At least three separate dimensions of anxiety have been suggested among Indian and Native youth: physiologic anxiety reactions, phobic anxiety reactions, and performance anxiety reactions (Beals et al., 1991; Dinges & Duong-Tran, 1993). Specifically, such conditions as panic disorder, overanxious disorder, generalized anxiety disorder, school avoidance, and separation anxiety disorder are diagnosed by service providers. In addition, given the high rate of exposure to loss, violence, abuse, neglect, and other manifestations of psychic trauma, high rates of posttraumatic stress disorder should be expected and have been reported anecdotally among these youths as well.

PSYCHOACTIVE SUBSTANCE USE DISORDERS

Numerous studies indicate that young Indian and Native people manifest higher rates of use and abuse for most drugs, including alcohol (Beauvais & Laboueff, 1985; Beauvais, Oetting, & Edwards, 1985a; Beauvais, Oetting, & Wolf, 1989; Oetting, Beauvais & Edwards, 1988; Oetting & Goldstein, 1979). Differences in rates are particularly dramatic for stimulants, marijuana, inhalants, and alcohol (Beauvais et al., 1985; Beauvais, Oetting, & Wolf, 1989). Rates of inhalant use by Indi-

ans have been reported to be almost twice the national average in the 12- to 17-year-old group (Oetting & Goldstein, 1979). Inhalant use, however, tends to decrease as substances such as marijuana and alcohol become more available. The data also suggest that Indian youths begin abusing various substances at a younger age than do their non-Indian counterparts, and that alcohol consumption and problem drinking are extending to progressively younger youths (Young, 1988). Likewise, Indian youths have been reported to escalate to problematic substance abuse more rapidly and to tend more strongly toward polysubstance use and abuse (Weibel-Orlando, 1984). There is little doubt that substance use and abuse poses one of the greatest threats to Indian and Native youths today.

SUICIDE

Elevated rates of suicide during the adolescent and young adult years are particularly well documented among Indian/Native youths. In 1987, suicide rates for Indian and Native youths ages 10 to 14, 15 to 19, and 20 to 24 were reported to be 2.8, 2.4, and 2.3 times greater than national averages, respectively (May, 1987). In fact, the peak incidence of suicide among Indian and Native people occurs among the young, as opposed to among the elderly, as is the case for the population at large (McIntosh & Santos, 1981). The preponderance of completed suicides among young Indian and Native males exceeds that for the population at large. In addition, there appears to be a strong association of substance abuse, usage of highly lethal means such as guns or hanging, and an absence of strongly held traditional values with suicide (Shore, 1974). Indian and Native youths have been reported at increased risk for suicide due to interpersonal conflict, unresolved grief over past losses, familial instability, depression, unemployment, and family history of psychiatric disorder, especially alcoholism, depression, and suicide (Dizmang, Watson, May, & Bopp, 1974; Jilek-Aall, Jilek, & Flynn, 1978; National Task Force on Suicide in Canada, 1987; Ross & Davis, 1986; Shore, Bopp, Walter, & Dawes, 1972; Spaulding, 1985). Sociocultural variables such as multiple home placements, social disintegration, and acculturation pressures also have been cited as risk factors for suicide among Indian and Native youths (Berlin, 1986; Hochkirchen & Jilek, 1985;

Levy & Kunitz, 1971). As these findings suggest, the etiologic pathways to suicide are many. Nonetheless, the sum total of this myriad of influences is that many young Indian and Native people are at substantially increased risk for death by suicide.

BEHAVIOR DISORDERS

Although not formal psychiatric syndromes, a number of other clinical issues are of interest, as well. The available literature suggests that Indian and Native youth dropout of school at rates 2 to 3 times those of the general population (Developmental Associates, 1983; Grant, 1975; U.S. Department of the Interior, 1976). High rates of delinquency—characterized by a preponderance of petty offenses and misdemeanors and found to be more common among males than among females—have been documented among Indian and Native youths (Forslund & Cranston, 1975; May, 1983). In addition, running away from home and delinquency are strongly related among Indian and Native youths. The modal Native runaway has been described as having a history of academic dysfunction, socioeconomic disadvantage, and an absence of strongly traditional values (Indian Center, 1986). Family problems, legal problems, substance abuse, and peer pressures are commonly reported, as well. Runaway youths typically support themselves through illegal means, such as theft and prostitution, and have extensive arrest records.

CHILD ABUSE AND NEGLECT

The nature and extent of child abuse and neglect vary widely across Indian and Native communities; yet high rates have been documented consistently by numerous reports. Interpersonal conflict, marital disruption, parental substance abuse, attachment problems, parental unemployment, and violent death are common among many abused and neglected Indian children (Fischler, 1985; Ishisaka, 1978; Oakland & Kane, 1973; White & Cornely, 1981; Wischlacz, Lane, & Kempe, 1978). Indian and Native youths also have been reported at risk for child abuse and neglect due to sociocultural shifts such as a transition away from traditional values, changes in gender roles and expectations, and the changing nature of the extended family in Native culture (Beiser, 1974; Grayburn, 1987; Hauswald, 1987). Additional data

suggest that histories of abuse and neglect render young Native people more vulnerable to a variety of psychiatric disorders. Significantly higher rates of depressive, sleep, anxiety, conduct, drug use, schizotypal, and developmental disorders have been reported among abused and neglected Indian and Native youths (Piasecki et al., 1989).

Clinical Interventions

While it is true that Indian and Native youths are at increased risk for a variety of disorders, it does not necessarily follow that intervention and treatment hold no hope for this population. Rather, a continuum of treatment modalities offers considerable promise at all levels of prevention and intervention.

In 1988, under a contract with the Indian Health Service, 850 providers and agencies were surveyed regarding the nature of ongoing prevention and intervention activities in Indian and Native communities (Manson et al., 1989). One hundred ninety-four programs were identified that actively engaged in prevention and intervention activities. Approximately one-quarter of the programs were school-based; the remainder were located mainly in other human service and community settings. Tribal sponsorship was present in about half of the programs. Range of services included psychotherapy, suicide prevention, substance abuse intervention, training, recreation, and cultural activities. Most often the programs were aimed at mental health promotion, identification of at-risk individuals, and promotion of cultural identity.

INDIAN HEALTH SERVICE

A closer look at the system that delivers mental health care services to Indian and Native young people reveals two central agencies. The Indian Health Service is a branch of the Public Health Service, which itself is a branch of the Department of Health and Human Services of the U.S. Government. Two branches of the Indian Health Service play key roles in the delivery of services to Native children and youth: the Mental Health Programs Branch and the Alcoholism/Substance Abuse Programs Branch. The mandate of the

Mental Health Programs Branch is to provide access for all Indian persons to high-quality and culturally appropriate mental health services that are appropriate to the nature and severity of their mental illness (U.S. Congress, 1990). The distribution of resources within the Indian Health Service varies considerably from one area to the next—particularly with regard to specialty trained child and adolescent clinicians, although every service area experiences a critical shortage. A 1989 survey revealed a total of only 17 child and adolescent trained mental health professionals in the Indian Health Service (U.S. Department of Health and Human Services, 1989), only 5 of whom were child and adolescent psychiatrists. Given the shortage of mental health care providers, the relative absence of specialty trained child and adolescent providers, and the primary emphasis on acute health care services of the Indian Health Service, primary care practitioners are, de facto, the principal resource for the diagnosis and treatment of mental health problems for Indian children and adolescents.

The delivery of substance abuse services to Native youths was greatly enhanced through the 1986 Omnibus Drug Act, which led to the development of a youth services component within the Substance Abuse Programs Branch of the Indian Health Service the following year. The youth services component seeks to intervene in terms of prevention, outpatient treatment, and residential treatment. In 1988, a commitment to the provision of community-based aftercare and to the full integration of alcohol and drug abuse treatment services into the health care system was added to its substance abuse programming as well (U.S. Department of Health and Human Services, 1988). The Indian Health Service concluded, however, that the key to improvement in the problem of Indian and Native substance abuse resided within the community commitment to change rather than within its various treatment resources.

BUREAU OF INDIAN AFFAIRS

While less directly involved than the Indian Health Service, the Bureau of Indian Affairs is no less crucial to the delivery of mental health services to Indian and Native children and adolescents. Established in 1824 as part of the War Department, the Bureau became a part of the United States Department of the Interior in 1849. It works closely with tribal governments at the community level and interfaces with the mental health needs of the community in a number of ways. It augments publicly and privately available schools with additional educational resources. Included in its educational role is the provision of assistance for college expenses, vocational training, and continuing adult education. Schools funded by the Bureau of Indian Affairs include curricular foci aimed at alcohol and substance abuse prevention and intervention as well as at the identification, assessment, and intervention of mental health problems of the student population. At present, the Bureau funds almost 200 schools, which serve approximately 20% of all Indian and Native children (U.S. Department of the Interior, 1988).

In collaboration with local tribal governments and the Indian Health Service, the Bureau is also active in social services and child protective services, particularly in reservation-based communities. Central to these human services is Bureau support of the Indian Child Welfare Act Programs, which are managed at the tribal level and which address such issues as child abuse and neglect, parent training, child custody, foster care, and adoption. Often, Indian child welfare workers from the Bureau of Indian Affairs play a primary role in identifying Indian and Native children and adolescents in need of mental health services. Unfortunately, a lack of treatment resources and providers remains a barrier, even after identification has been established.

The role of the Bureau in the law enforcement and criminal justice systems on many reservations overlaps significantly with the delivery of mental health services to children and adolescents. Frequently, this overlap occurs in such areas as the detention and diversion of substance abusing adolescents, delinquent youth, truant youth, and runaway youth. A joint Bureau of Indian Affairs—Indian Health Service Organizational Management Action Plan calls for substantial increases in this collaborative linkage (U.S. Department of the Interior & U.S. Department of Health and Human Services, 1988).

OTHER MENTAL HEALTH SERVICES

In addition to the Indian Health Service and the Bureau of Indian Affairs, mental health services are delivered to Indian and Native youths through a number of other agencies. As a result of Public Law 93-638, the Indian Self-Determination and Education Assistance Act, there has been a trend toward the assumption by tribes of varying levels of control over local health programs. Mental health services, however, are rare or even absent in a number of these programs, and the special needs of children and adolescents are seldom addressed in an explicit manner (U.S. Department of Health and Human Services, 1987).

Since their inception in 1972, urban Indian health programs have continued to develop, although they tend primarily to provide acute care services. Unfortunately, these programs are specifically denied mental health funding through the Indian Health Service; such funds have been limited to providing mental health services to Indian people remaining on or near reservations (U.S. Congress, 1990). Some urban programs have overcome this obstacle by obtaining funding through resources other than the Indian Health Service. Nonetheless, even in these programs the funding specified for mental health services is only a small fraction of the overall budget, and the specialty needs of children and adolescents are, at best, managed through referral to other metropolitan agencies (American Indian Health Care Association, 1988).

Indian and Native children and adolescents also may receive mental health services through community and state agencies and facilities. Little information exists as to the extent of utilization of these resources by Native people. Most likely, the greatest utilization occurs in urban communities. The data suggest that the treatment available through these resources tends to suffer from cultural insensitivity and that follow-through after the initial visit is adversely affected (Sue, 1977).

There is little doubt that the delivery of mental health services to Indian and Native children and adolescents would benefit from the establishment of a community-based, comprehensive continuum of services. In such a system, each element in the continuum performs a unique function determined by the intensity and acuity of need of the individuals at that level. Such a continuum of care minimally would include a psychiatric hospital, a residential treatment center, a partial hospital program, outpatient services, and prevention programming. While certain elements of the continuum can be identified in various communities, the full range of services is seldom accessible to most Indian and Native individuals.

Successful examples of prevention programming in Indian communities can be cited, however. Prevention programs in Indian communities have been shown to increase reporting and self-referrals for cases of child abuse and neglect; reduce foster home placements; reduce risks for a variety of adolescent psychiatric disorders including depression, substance abuse, and antisocial behavior; reduce risk of suicide; and promote the likelihood of health maintenance activities and healthy life choices (Beiser & Manson, 1987). Although longer-term and more carefully controlled outcome studies are clearly indicated, these preliminary results engender optimism that appropriately selected and applied prevention technology will impact favorably the mental health of Indian and Native children and adolescents.

SPECIFIC THERAPEUTIC MODALITIES

Data also exist that support the efficacy of outpatient intervention with Indian and Native children and youth. While these reports are infrequent in number and tend toward anecdotal observation, they suggest nonetheless that a variety of individual therapies are of benefit to certain Indian youth. Successful applications of psychoanalytic, behavioral and learning therapies have all been described (Boyer, 1964; Devereux, 1950, 1951; Duran, 1984; Galloway & Mickelson, 1971; Goldstein, 1974; Jilek-Aall, 1976).

While conventional wisdom previously asserted that group psychotherapy is not indicated for Indian and Native people due to distinct cultural reasons, the utilization of group therapies among Indian and Native children and youths is known to be on the increase (Edwards & Edwards, 1984). In particular, single-issue groups that focus on such topics as incest or parental alcoholism and self-help groups that focus on such issues as the development of self-esteem and social skills or addictive problems are common. Additional programs provide conventional family therapies in the context of the nuclear family, while others employ network therapies including the extended family and kinship members, as well. Network therapies appear particularly well suited to Native families insofar as family and kinship relationships assume primary importance in the development of socialization within Native culture (Red Horse, 1980; Shattuck & Hoffman, 1981).

Examples of recreational and outdoor therapies

serving Indian and Native youths have been identified (Beiser & Manson, 1987). Typically, these programs emphasize healthy peer relationships, personal mastery, and self-esteem. While little outcome data are available, the naturalistic approach of many of these programs is readily integrated within traditional Native culture.

An additional trend that has been identified within a number of outpatient programs is the integration of traditional Native practices such as the four circles, the talking circle, and the sweat lodge with more conventional Western psychotherapeutic techniques (Dinges, Trimble, Manson, & Pasquale, 1981; Manson, Walker, & Kivlahan, 1987). The four circles refers to a process through which a person's significant relationships are visualized and analyzed, employing a series of concentric circles. The talking circle may be viewed as a culturally specific form of group therapy in which the participants foster one another's ability to cope with life stresses and conflicts. The sweat lodge is a modality that combines elements of the traditional (individual meditation and prayer) with the conventional (group therapy). Most commonly such culturally specific interventions are found within tribally sponsored programs.

Mandate for the Future

Unfortunately, the continuum of care for most Indian and Native children and adolescents has, until quite recently, ended at the level of outpatient services (U.S. Congress, 1990). There are no inpatient psychiatric treatment facilities dedicated to Indian children or adolescents. Indeed, there is only one such resource for adult Indians: a 12-bed program in Rapid City, South Dakota. The 1986 Drug Omnibus Bill gave rise to a series of Indian adolescent residential treatment programs, of which there are now 10. However, these facilities are designed primarily for the treatment of substance abuse disorders and, with few exceptions, seldom include professional mental health staff. Such intensive levels of care require the mobilization of extremely scarce resources, and in the case of reservation youths, usually requires their removal and isolation from family, community, and other supports. In part, these limitations spring from the rural, isolated environments typically associated with Indian communities. An additional barrier, however, is the complex, multi-agency nature of the system, which is not always negotiated successfully.

Not only is the continuum of mental health services for Native children and adolescents largely devoid of the more intensive levels of intervention, it is also typically deficient in the wider range of ancillary and supportive services that augment the basic elements of the continuum. Such services include therapeutic foster homes, group homes, structured recreational activities, before- and after-school programs, case management, respite programs, and a variety of home-based interventions. Rarely are such supportive services available in Indian or Native communities (U.S. Congress, 1990).

The potential of current mental health therapeutic technology far exceeds the actual level of practice in most Indian and Native communities today (Neligh, 1990). If the latter is to catch up with the state of the art, a number of obstacles must be overcome. The first encompasses a variety of cross-cultural issues including a long-standing history of cultural distrust, language and communication barriers, and culturally insensitive application of clinical techniques. The second entails the critical manpower shortage, particularly of specialty trained child and adolescent clinicians available to serve Indian and Native people. The last is the level of complexity of the federal system, which includes multiple agencies and frequently unclear boundaries surrounding such key issues as jurisdiction and service obligations.

REFERENCES

Ackerson, L. M., Dick, R. W., Manson, S. M., & Baron, A. E. (1990). Depression among American Indian adolescents: Psychometric characteristics of the Inventory to Diagnose Depression. *Journal of the American Academy of Child and Adolescent Psychiatry, 29* (4), 601–607.

American Indian Health Care Association. (1988). Mental health services delivery: Urban Indian health programs. St. Paul, MN: unpublished report.

American Psychiatric Association. (1994). *Diagnostic and statistical manual of mental disorders* (4th ed.). Washington, DC: Author.

Baron, A. E., Manson, S. M., Ackerson, L. M., & Brenneman, D. L. (1990). Depressive symptomatology in older American Indians with chronic disease: Some psychometric considerations. In C. Attkinsson & J. Zich (Eds.), *Screening for depression in primary care* (pp. 217–231). (New York: Routledge, Chapman and Hall, 1990).

Beals, J., Manson, S. M., Keane, K. M., & Dick, R. W. (1991). The factorial structure of the Center for Epidemiologic Studies depression scale among American Indian college students, *Psychological Assessment 3* (4), 623–627.

Beauvais, F., & Laboueff, S. (1985). Drug and alcohol abuse intervention in American Indian communities. *International Journal of the Addictions, 20* (1), 139–171.

Beauvais, F., Oetting, E. R., & Edwards, R. W. (1985a). Trends in drug use of Indian adolescents living on reservations: 1975–1983. *American Journal of Drug and Alcohol Abuse, 11* (4), 209–229.

Beauvais, F., Oetting, E. R., & Edwards, R. W. (1985b). Trends in the use of inhalants among American Indian adolescents. *White Cloud Journal, 3* (4), 3–11.

Beauvais, F., Oetting, E. R., & Wolf, W. (1989). American Indian youth and drugs, 1976–87: A continuing problem. *American Journal of Public Health, 79* (5), 634–636.

Beiser, M. (1974). Hazard to mental health: Indian boarding schools. *American Journal of Psychiatry, 131*, 305–306.

Beiser, M., & Attneave, C. L. (1982). Mental disorders among Native American children: Rate and risk periods for entering treatment. *American Journal of Psychiatry, 139* (2), 193–198.

Beiser, M., & Manson, S. M. (1987). Prevention of emotional disorders in Native North American children. *Journal of Preventive Psychiatry, 3* (3), 225–240.

Berlin, I. N. (1986). Psychopathology and its antecedents among American Indian adolescents. *Advances in Clinical Child Psychology, 9*, 125–152.

Boyer, L. B. (1964). Psychoanalytic insight in working with ethnic minorities. *Social Casework, 45* (4), 519–526.

Briggs, J. (1970). *Never in anger: Portrait of an Eskimo family.* Cambridge, MA: Harvard University Press.

Bryde, J. F. (1967). The Sioux Indian student: A study of scholastic failure and personality conflict. *Cumulative Reports in Education.* Pine Ridge, SD: ERIC Document Reproduction Service No. ED 018289.

Bureau of the Census (1992). *1990 census of population: General population characteristics* (1990 CP-1-1). Washington, DC: U.S. Government Printing Office.

Chance, N. (1963). Conceptual and methodological problems in cross-cultural health research. *American Journal of Public Health, 52*, 410–417.

Development Associates. (1983). *Final report: The evaluation of the impact of the Part A entitlement program funded under Title IV of the Indian Education Act.* Arlington, VA: Author.

Devereux, G. (1950). *Reality and dreams: Psychotherapy of a Plains Indian.* New York: International Universities Press.

Deveraux, G. (1951). Three technical problems in the psychotherapy of Plains Indian patients. *American Journal of Psychotherapy, 5*, 411–423.

Dinges, N. G., Trimble, J. E., Manson, S. M., & Pasquale, F. (1981). Counseling and psychotherapy with American Indians and Alaska natives. In A. J. Marsella & P. Pederson (Eds.), *Cross-cultural counseling and psychotherapy* (pp. 241–275). New York: Pergamon Press.

Dinges, N. G., & Duong-Tran, Q. (1993). Suicide ideation and suicide attempt among American Indian and Alaska Native boarding school adolescents. In C. Duclos & S. M. Manson (Eds.), Calling from the rim: Suicidal behavior among American Indian & Alaska Native adolescents (pp. 167–182). Niwot, CO: University Press of Colorado.

Dizmang, L. H., Watson, J., May, P. A., & Bopp, J. (1974). Suicide in the American Indian. *Psychiatric Annals, 4* (9), 22–28.

Duran, E. (1984). *Archetypal consultation: A service model for Native Americans.* New York: Peter Lang.

Edwards, E. D., & Edwards, M. E. (1984). Group work practice with American Indians. *Social Work with Groups, 7* (3), 7–21.

Fischler, R. (1985). Child abuse and neglect in American Indian communities. *Child Abuse & Neglect, 9*, 95–106.

Forslund, M. A., & Cranston, V. A. (1975). A self-report comparison of Indian and Anglo delinquency in Wyoming. *Criminology, 13* (2), 193–197.

Galloway, C. G., & Mickelson, N. I. (1971). Modification of behavior patterns of Indian children. *Elementary School Journal, 72*, 150–155.

Geertz, C. (1984). From the native's point of view: On the nature of anthropological understanding. In R. Shweder & R. Levine (Eds.), *Culture theory: Essays on mind, self, and emotion* (pp. 123–136). Cambridge, MA: Harvard University Press.

Goldstein, G. S. (1974). Behavior modification: Some cultural factors. *Psychological Record, 24* (2), 89–91.

Good, B. J., & Good, M.-J. (1986). The cultural context of diagnosis and therapy: A view from medical anthropology. In M. Miranda & H. Kitano (Eds.), *Research and practice in minority communities.* (pp. 1–27). Washington, DC: U.S. Government Printing Office.

Good, B. J., Goo, M.-J., & Moradi, R. (1985). The interpretation of Iranian depressive illness and dysphoric affect. In A. Kleinman & B. J. Good (Eds.), *Culture and depression.* (pp. 369–428). Berkeley: University of California Press.

Grant, W. V. (1975). Estimates of school dropouts. *American Education, 11* (4), 42.

Grayburn, N. (1987). Severe child abuse among the Canadian Inuit. In N. Scheper-Hughes (Ed.), *Child survival.* (pp. 211–225). Norwell, MA: Kluwer Academic Publications.

Hauswald, L. (1987). External pressure/internal change: Child neglect on the Navajo reservation. In N. Scheper-Hughes (Ed.), *Child survival.* (pp. 145–164). Norwell, MA: Kluwer Academic Publications.

Hirschfeld, R. M., & Cross, C. (1982). Epidemiology of affective disorders: Psychosocial risk factors. *Archives of General Psychiatry, 39,* 35–46.

Hochkirchen, B., & Jilek, W. (1985). Psychosocial dimensions of suicide and parasuicide in American Indians of the Pacific Northwest. *Journal of Operational Psychiatry, 16* (2), 24–28.

Indian Center, Inc., and University of Nebraska Lincoln, Department of Sociology, Bureau of Sociological Research. (1986, July). *The Native American adolescent health project: Report on interview surveys of runaways, parents, community leaders and human service workers.* Unpublished report, Lincoln, NE.

Ishisaka, H. (1978). American Indians in foster care: Cultural factors and separation. *Child Welfare, 57* (5), 299–308.

Jenkins, J. H., Kleinman, A., & Good, B. J. (1990). Cross-cultural studies of depression. In J. Becker & A. Kleinman (Eds.), *Advances in mood disorders.* (pp. 67–99). Hillsdale, NJ: Lawrence Erlbaum.

Jilek-Aall, L. (1976). The western psychiatrist and his non-western clientele. *Canadian Psychiatric Association Journal, 21* (6), 353–359.

Jilek-Aall, L., Jilek, W. G., & Flynn, F. (1978). Sex role, culture, and psychotherapy: A comparative study of three ethnic groups in Western Canada. *Journal of Psychological Anthropology, 4,* 473–488.

Joe, J. R. (1980). Disabled children in Navajo society, unpublished Ph.D. dissertation. University of California, Berkeley.

Kleinman, A. (1988). *The illness narratives.* New York: Basic Books.

Kleinman, A., & Good, B. (Eds.). (1985). *Culture and depression.* Berkeley: University of California Press.

LaFromboise, T. D. (1988). American Indian mental health policy. *American Psychologist, 43* (5), 388–397.

Levy, J., & Kunitz, S. (1971). Indian reservations, anomie, and social pathologies. *Southwestern Journal of Anthropology, 27* (2), 97–128.

Lujan, C., DeBruyn, L. M., May, P. A., & Bird, M. E. (1989). Profile of abused and neglected American Indian children in the southwest. *Child Abuse and Neglect, 13,* 449–461.

Manson, S. M., Shore, J. H., & Bloom, J. D. (1985). The depressive experience in American Indian communities: A challenge for psychiatric theory and diagnosis. In A. Kleinman & B. Good (Eds.), *Culture and Depression.* Berkeley, CA: University of California Press.

Manson, S. M., Ackerson, L. M., Dick, R. W., Baron, A. E., & Fleming, C. M. (1990). Depressive symptoms among American Indian adolescents: Psychometric characteristics of the CES-D. *Journal of Consulting and Clinical Psychology, 2* (3), 231–237.

Manson, S. M., Shore, J. H., Bloom, J. D., Keepers, G., & Neligh, G. (1989). Alcohol abuse and major affective disorders: Advances in epidemiologic research among American Indians. In D. L. Spiegler, D. A. Tate, S. S. Aitken, & C. M. Christian (Eds.), *Alcohol use and abuse among U.S. ethnic minorities,* National Institute on Alcohol Abuse and Alcoholism Monograph Series, No. 18, (ADM) 89-1435. (pp. 291–300). Washington, DC: U.S. Government Printing Office.

Manson, S. M., Walker, R. D., & Kivlahan, D. R. (1987). Psychiatric assessment and treatment of American Indians and Alaska Natives. *Hospital and Community Psychiatry, 38* (2), 165–173.

May, P. A. (1982). Substance abuse and American Indians: Prevalence and susceptibility. *International Journal of the Addictions, 17,* 1185–1209.

May, P. A. (1983). *A survey of the existing data on mental health in Albuquerque Area.* Unpublished report prepared under Contract No. 3-200423.

May, P. A. (1987). Suicide and self-destruction among American Indian youths. *American Indian and Alaska Native Mental Health Research, 1* (1), 52–69.

May, P. A., & Broudy, D. W. (1980). *Health problems of the Navajo and suggested interventions,* 2nd ed. Window Rock, AZ: Navajo Health Authority.

May, P. A., & Hymbaugh, K. J. (1983). A pilot project on fetal alcohol syndrome for American Indians. *Alcohol, Health, and Research World, 7,* 3–9.

May, P. A., Hymbaugh, K. J., Aase, J. M., & Sarnet, J. M. (1983). Epidemiology of fetal alcohol syndrome among American Indians of the Southwest. *Social Biology, 30* (4), 374–387.

McIntosh, J. L., & Santos, J. F. (1981). Suicide among minority elderly: A preliminary investigation. *Suicide and Life Threatening Behavior, 11* (3), 151–166.

McNabb, S. L. (1990). Self-reports in cross-cultural contexts. *Human Organization, 49* (4), 291–299.

Meriam, L. (1928). *The problem of Indian administration.* Baltimore, MD: Johns Hopkins University Press.

Miller, S. I., & Schoenfeld, L. S. (1971). Suicide attempt patterns among the Navajo Indians. *International Journal of Social Psychiatry, 17,* 189–193.

Murphy, J. M., & Hughes, C. C. (1965). The use of psychophysiological symptoms as indicators of disorder among Eskimos. In J. M. Murphy & A. H. Leighton (Eds.), *Approaches to cross-cultural psychiatry.* (pp. 108–160). Ithaca, NY: Cornell University Press.

National Task Force on Suicide in Canada. (1987). *Suicide in Canada.* Ottawa, Ontario: Health and Welfare Canada.

Native American Rehabilitation and Training Center. (1979). Unpublished program report, University of Arizona, Tucson, AZ.

Neligh, G. (1990). Mental health programs for American Indians: Their logic, structure and function. *American Indian and Alaska Native Mental Health Research, 3* (Monograph 3).

Oakland, L., & Kane, R. (1973). The working mother

and child: Neglect on the Navajo reservation. *Pediatrics, 51,* 849–853.

O'Connell, J. C. (Ed.). (1987). *A study of the special problems and needs of American Indians with handicaps both on and off the reservation.* Report submitted to the U.S. Department of Education, Office of Special Education and Rehabilitative Services.

Oetting, E., Beauvais, F., & Edwards, R. W. (1988). Alcohol and Indian youth: Social and psychological correlates and prevention. *Journal of Drug Issues, 18,* 87–101.

Oetting, E. R., & Goldstein, G. S. (1979). Drug use among Native American adolescents. In G. Beschner & A. Friedman (Eds.), *Youth drug abuse.* (pp. 119–135). Lexington, MA: Lexington Books.

Piasecki, J. M., Manson, S. M., Biernoff, M. P., Hiat, A. B., Taylor, S. S., & Bechtold, D. W. (1989). Abuse and neglect of American Indian children: Findings from a survey of federal providers. *American Indian and Alaska Native Mental Health Research, 3* (2), 43–62.

Red Horse, J. (1980). Family structure and value orientation in American Indians. *Social Casework, 61* (8), 462–467.

Robins, L. N. (1989). Cross-cultural differences in psychiatric disorder. *American Journal of Public Health, 79* (11), 1479–1480.

Ross, C. A., & Davis, B. (1986). Suicide and parasuicide in a Northern Canada Native community. *Canadian Journal of Psychiatry, 3,* (4), 331–334.

Sack, W. H., Beiser, M., Clarke, G., & Redshirt, R. (1987). The high achieving Sioux Indian child: Some preliminary findings from the Flower of Two Soils project. *American Indian and Alaska Native Mental Health Research, 1* (1), 37–51.

Shattuck, A., & Hoffman, F. (Eds.). (1981). *The American Indian family: Strengths and stress.* Isleta, NM: American Indian Social Research and Development Associates.

Shore, J. H. (1974). Psychiatric epidemiology among American Indians. *Psychiatric Annals, 4* (11), 56–66.

Shore, J. H. (1975). American Indian suicide—fact and fantasy. *Psychiatry, 38,* 86–91.

Shore, J. H., Bopp, J. E., Walter, T. R., & Dawes, J. W. (1972). A suicide prevention center on an Indian reservation. *American Journal of Psychiatry, 128* (9), 1086–1091.

Shore, J. H., Manson, S. M., Bloom, J. D., Keepers, G., & Neligh, G. (1987). A pilot study of depression among American Indian patients with research diagnostic criteria. *American Indian and Alaska Native Mental Health Research, 1* (2), 4–15.

Shweder, R., & Bourne, E. (1984). Does the concept of the person vary cross-culturally? In R. Shweder & Levine (Eds.), *Culture theory: Essays on mind, self, and emotion.* (pp. 158–199). Cambridge, MA: Harvard University Press.

Spaulding, J. M. (1985). Recent suicide rates among ten Ojibwa Indian bands in northwestern Ontario. *Omega, 16* (4), 347–354.

Spitz, R., & Wolf, K. (1946). Anaclitic depression: An inquiry into the genesis of psychiatric conditions in early childhood. *Psychoanalytic Study of the Child, 2,* 313–342.

Sue, S. (1977). Community mental health services to minority groups: Some optimism, some pessimism. *American Psychologist, 32* (8), 616–624.

Terminsen, J., & Ryan, J. (1970). Health and disease in a British Columbian community. *Canadian Psychiatric Association Journal, 15,* 121–127.

Trimble, J. E., Manson, S. M., Dinges, N., & Medicine, B. (1984). American Indian concepts of mental health: Reflections and directions. In P. B. Pedersen, N. Sartorius, & A. J. Marsella (Eds.), *Mental health services: The cross-cultural content.* (pp. 199–220). Beverly Hills: Sage Publications.

U.S. Congress, Office of Technology Assessment. (1990). *Indian Adolescent Mental Health,* OTA-H-446 Washington, DC: U.S. Government Printing Office.

U.S. Congress, Senate. (1989). Select Committee on Indian Affairs, Special Committee on Investigations. *Final report and legislative recommendations,* Report 101-216 Washington, DC: U.S. Government Printing Office.

U.S. Department of Health and Human Services, Public Health Service, Health Resources and Services Administration, Indian Health Service, Office of Health Program Development. (1987, May). Final report: Descriptive analysis of tribal health systems.

U.S. Department of Health and Human Services, Public Health Service, Indian Health Service, Mental Health Programs Branch. (1989, June 26). *A national plan for Native American mental health services.* 10th draft, unpublished report, Rockville, MD.

U.S. Department of Health and Human Services, Public Health Service, Indian Health Service. (1988). *A progress report on Indian alcoholism activities: 1988.* Rockville, MD.

U.S. Department of the Interior. (1976). *BIA, Research and evaluation report series,* No. 42.00.

U.S. Department of the Interior, Bureau of Indian Affairs. (1988). *American Indians today.* Washington, DC: U.S. Government Printing Office.

U.S. Department of the Interior, Bureau of Indian Affairs. (1989, February 21). Fiscal year 1988 child abuse and neglect data. Unpublished table.

U.S. Department of the Interior, Bureau of Indian Affairs, and U.S. Department of Health and Human Services, Public Health Service, Indian Health Service. (1988, October 18). Organizational management action plan responsibilities (areas). Revision no. 1.

U.S. Senate. (1969). *Indian education: A national tragedy—a national challenge.* Committee on Labor and Public Welfare, Special Subcommittee on Indian Education.

Weibel-Orlando, J. (1984). Substance abuse among American Indian youth: A continuing crisis. *Journal of Drug Issues, 14* (2), 313–335.

Weissman, M., & Klerman, G. (1981). Sex difference and the epidemiology of depression. In E. Howell & M. Baynes, (Eds.), (pp. 130–152). *Women and mental health.* New York: Basic Books.

White, R., & Cornely, D. (1981). Navajo child abuse and neglect study: A comparison group examination of abuse and neglect of Navajo children. *Child Abuse and Neglect, 5*, 9–17.

Wischlacz, C., Lane, J., & Kempe, C. (1978). Indian child welfare: A community team approach to protective services. *Child Abuse and Neglect, 2*, 29–35.

Yates, A. (1987). Current status and future directions of research on the American Indian child. *American Journal of Psychiatry, 144* (9), 1135–1142.

Young, T. J. (1988). Substance use and abuse among Native Americans. *Clinical Psychology Review, 8*, 125–138.

54 / Mental Health of Chinese American Youths

Luke Y. Tsai

In recent years the popular press has described Asian American youths as exceptionally successful in school (Butterfield, 1990). This chapter, however, is concerned mainly with the need for investigation of mental health issues in Asian American youths, focusing on the Chinese segment. Historical and traditional factors that have shaped Chinese American culture are described because of their potential impact on mental health, now and in the future, as well as because effective prevention and treatment of mental disorders depend on an understanding of the underlying culture.

Studies concerning relationships between ethnicity and behavioral patterns traditionally assume a degree of cultural homogeneity, that is, members of the ethnic or racial group studied are treated as if they possess a relatively uniform set of attitudes, beliefs and behaviors (Hessler et al., 1980). However, in the study of mental health in Chinese American youths, such an assumption is an unwarranted stereotype that can lead to faulty conclusions. A brief review of the history of Chinese immigration to the United States exposes the fallacy of cultural homogeneity.

Historical Background

A few Chinese were known to have arrived in the United States as early as 1785. By 1849, there were about 800 Chinese in San Francisco, including two women. By 1852, more than 20,000 had arrived to look for a better life in the new world. Except for those who had jobs in San Francisco, they settled in the mining districts. The number of Chinese immigrants increased steadily in subsequent years. Chinese laborers were invited to the United States by railroad agents who had gone to China, promising them plentiful work, high wages, and free passage. In the 1860s, the Chinese population reached 50,000. In October of 1876, a joint committee of Congress reported a figure of 117,449. The arrival of such great numbers of Chinese aroused the concern of many Americans (McClellan, 1971). The concerns of the host group gradually turned into fear, then animosity and even led to atrocities. This was particularly so after the Central Pacific Railway met with the Union Pacific Railway in Utah in 1869 and the Nevada mines collapsed in 1878. In the minds of most Californians, the presence of the Chinese had suddenly changed from a blessing to a curse (McClellan, 1971).

It was during this period that ethnic slurs began. Unwelcome immigrant Chinese were being referred to as "Chinamen," "Yellow lepers," "the Yellow peril," or "Chinks." In 1882, the first Chinese Exclusion Act sealed the gates in order to keep the Chinese from entering the United States. Faced with racial prejudice and discrimination from the host society, Chinese immigrants began to withdraw from competitive labor and sought to enter occupations that other immigrants eschewed. They moved into the cheaper housing districts of urban centers. They kept to themselves, living in extremely crowded conditions. For example, in the 1960s, the Chinese population in the New York metropolitan area was about 25,000, with approximately 8,000 living in and around New York City's Chinatown. The presence of the Chinese community was feared, because the part of the city or town where they congregated was soon assigned the character of a foreign settlement. It is against this historical backdrop of discrimination, alienation, and ghettoization that the characters in the drama of Chinese family life play their parts (Huang, 1976).

In the 1940s, many Chinese students arrived in the United States for advanced studies. However, during the 1950s, the changing political regime in mainland China made it impossible for many of them to return to their homeland. As a result, most of these individuals completed their education and became U.S. citizens with professional careers. By the 1970s, many had become grandparents to American-born children.

During the 1960s and 1970s, Chinese immigrants to the United States came primarily from Hong Kong and secondarily from Taiwan. These two islands were highly urbanized, industrialized, and Westernized. The residents had been exposed to the English language, to Western technology, and to American culture through publications, films, and personal travels. Therefore, the transition from Hong Kong and Taiwan to the United States was not as great a cultural shock as for those who came from mainland China. The latter had been highly insulated from Western culture (Sung, 1987).

According to the U.S. Bureau of the Census, in 1980, the population of ethnic Chinese population living in the United States numbered 812,000. In 1990, this number had increased to 1.5 million; according to a projection made by the Population Reference Bureau in Washington, D.C., by the year 2000 that number may be close to 1.7 million. This phenomenal increase will come mostly from immigration. The large number of immigrants coming to the United States has and will continue to produce an increasing disparity between the later generations of American-born Chinese living in this country who have become acculturated and the recently arrived foreign-born Chinese. Some Chinese American youths jokingly group their fellow Chinese by their site of birth and the length of time they have been in the United States. Names (usually in the form of acronyms) are given to

each group for distinction, such as ABCs (American-born Chinese), FOBs (Fresh off the boat), HIPs (Hong Kong Instant Product), and MITs (Made in Taiwan). It certainly indicates some sort of division if not discrimination among the Chinese themselves. When bullied by other minority neighborhood groups, however, all the "varieties" of Chinese youths often rally together in gangs to protect themselves (*Newsletter of the Midwest Chinese Student and Alumni Services*, 1969).

On the other hand, even though children and youths under the age of 19 comprise one-fourth of the Chinese immigrants and refugees, no specific mental health research has ever been carried out in this particular group of youngsters. Indeed, these children often are considered as appendages of adults. They are not viewed in a separate light, they go wherever their parents take them, and they live wherever their parents decide. Nevertheless, these children do have concerns of their own and do react differently. Their experiences deserve to be delineated and considered separately, especially when they exhibit unusual characteristics (Sung, 1987).

Characteristic of Chinese American Youths

Although Chinese American youths should not be viewed as a homogeneous group, there are certain characteristics that they tend to share in common.

SOCIALIZATION

Chinese parents often take their children to almost every kind of social gathering. They do not feel comfortable leaving their children at home with baby-sitters or other adults. Having thus spent much time in the company of adults, Chinese children are quite aware of socially approved patterns of behaviors and know what is expected of them. As a result, Chinese young people, even those born in the United States, tend to be socially more conservative and less aggressive than their Caucasian friends (Huang, 1976). In his study, Sollenberger (1968) found that 74% of Chinese parents demanded that under no circumstances should their children show any aggression. Parents never urged their children to defend themselves, nor did they punish them for running home for help in case of attacks by other children. Sibling rivalry and aggression too were generally discouraged. Such rearing practices encourage one to give in during a quarrel or to yield in favor of someone else.

In the household, Chinese culture rewards being silent and inconspicuous, while it punishes outspoken behavior. Verbal communication between parents and children has been noted to be rather limited. This observation has been used to explain the Chinese American students' tendency to score lower in the verbal sections of their college entrance examination than do their American counterparts (Huang, 1976).

Sue and Kirk (1973) found Chinese American students at the University of California at Berkeley to be more comfortable in well-structured situations, less autonomous, less independent from parental controls and authority figures, more obedient, conservative, conforming, inhibited, socially introverted, and more likely to withdraw from social contacts. In terms of socialization within the American context, the passive and noncompetitive Chinese American youths are at a disadvantage.

ATTITUDES TOWARD SEX

Most Chinese families, whether foreign-born or American-born, do not engage in open discussions of sex with their children. Many Chinese from Taiwan or mainland China did not begin dating before they were 20 or even older. They were brought up with the concept that early dating was not beneficial. This attitude has influenced their American-born children. For example, in the American dating game, young Chinese American males are characterized as "inadequate," "shallow," "egocentric," "childish," and "sexually inept" (Weiss, 1969).

AFFECTION

It is characteristic of the Chinese family that its members do not express overt affection to one another. Many Chinese children have never seen their parents kiss or hug one another openly. The Chinese are seldom seen embracing or kissing one another at airports or railroad stations, either when

seeing relatives off or when welcoming them. Instead, there is a great deal of smiling and handshaking accompanied by shouts of joy at greeting or polite verbal expressions of farewell at leavetaking. Open expressions of affection tend to embarrass the Chinese, both professional and nonprofessional, American-born and foreign-born (Huang, 1976). Chinese American youths generally show restrained emotion and affect; they tend to be seen as "shy," "quiet," "cold," "distant," and "timid."

ETHIC AND VALUES

Chinese families believe and practice the Confucian ethic, which emphasizes the centripetal family. People work not just for themselves, but for the honor of the family. It is quite common among Chinese American youths that their families still come first in their lives, and it is not unusual for them to choose a career according to their parents' desires. Confucianism also teaches that man can be perfected through practice. Like other Asian American youths, Chinese American youths work harder than Caucasian American youngsters. The Chinese American students spend more hours doing homework and preparing for tests. Their parents are willing to devote time to helping the children with homework and are able to instill in them a much greater motivation to work hard. Another factor that contributes to academic success among Chinese American youths is that their parents expect a high level of academic performance. Since the family is central in their lives, the children do not want to let their parents down.

In recent years, an inordinate number of Chinese immigrant youths have been the recipients of prestigious scholarships. A primary reason why the parents emigrated to the United States was to open up a brighter future for their children. It appears that the combined effort of parents and children has led these youngsters to success. One question now being asked is whether Chinese American youths will continue their record of achievement, as they become more assimilated into the American society. Sanford M. Dornbusch, a professor of human biology, sociology, and education at Stanford University, has found that the more English spoken in the Asian American high school students' homes—indicating a greater degree of assimilation into American life—the poorer they tended to do in school (Butterfield, 1990).

FAMILY CONFLICTS

Despite the fact that culture in China has undergone great changes, the traditional practices that were brought over by early immigrants in the last century carry on among many Chinese Americans. Many parents of Chinese American youths are eager to instill a knowledge of Chinese history and culture in their children; accordingly they send their children to Chinese schools in the evenings or on weekends. Since the 1970s, many Chinese parents, professionals and otherwise, have been sending their teenage children back to Taiwan and/or mainland China, either for the summer months or for the whole year, for the purpose of getting acquainted with Chinese culture. However, no matter how eager the parents are to retain the Old World values, the young Chinese are growing up in a brand-new world. These youngsters are caught in between the culture in which they live and the one that their parents have brought with them. Because of the strong emphasis on filial piety and obedience toward parents in the Chinese family, the conflicts between the Chinese-born parents and American-born children are relatively subtle and hidden. However, cultural conflict and the inconsistency experienced by the younger generation cannot be denied. Finding their parental generation full of obsolete precedents and out-of-date responses, many youths resort to looking for new models among their peers (Huang, 1976).

General Adjustment of Chinese American Youths

School performance is the most convenient and reasonable index to use in evaluating the adjustment or maladjustment of Chinese American youths. Generally, newly arrived Chinese immigrants tend to have more difficulties than do American-born Chinese youngsters. This is particularly true among children from mainland China (Sung, 1987). On the other hand, although the later generations of American-born Chinese closely resemble Caucasian Americans in their outlook and values, consistent and persistent personality differences still remain (Sue & Sue, 1987). Being racially different from the Caucasian host group, most Chinese Americans find themselves isolated and find it difficult to be totally accepted by the host society. The reality is that Chinese Americans are always regarded by others as foreigners in their own country. Despite the fact that many generations of one's family have lived in the United States, and notwithstanding how American one feels, Chinese Americans are often asked, "How long have you been in this country?" or "Where do you come from?" Even thoroughly assimilated Chinese American citizens are said to suffer from the "banana" syndrome, yellow on the outside and white on the inside (Yee, 1974).

In a study on the changing personality traits of second-generation Orientals in America, Smith (1928) classified them into three types: the conformist type, the rebellious type, and the philosophic type. The conformist group consists of those who are very conservative, living close to their parents, accepting their ideas and traditions and venturing no change. The rebellious group tends to react against the old system but has not yet worked out any consistent scheme of behavior. To be freed from the old seems to be their important goal; they want some changes in their lives. The philosophic group consists of those who appreciate both their parents' values as well as those of the American culture. They serve as mediators between the two cultures, neither rejecting the culture of their parents nor adopting everything American. They are able to embrace elements from both cultures and thus to adjust themselves with considerable success.

Mental Disorders in Chinese American Youths

Large-scale epidemiological surveys of mental disorders in Chinese American youths have not yet been done. No systematic study specifically looks into the mental health problems of Chinese American youths. Although there are some data from various mental health clinics and hospitals, these studies tend to find that Chinese Americans are relatively well adjusted and they have low rates of psychopathology (Sue & Sue, 1987). A study specifically examined Chinese immigrant children in New York City, and found that these immigrant children and teenagers in Chinatown have exhibited extraordinary resilience, courage, and stamina in their transplantation from Chinese to American soil (Sung, 1987). On the other hand, Lorenzo and Adler (1984) noted that at a community mental health center, Chinese American children and adolescents had a low incidence of behavior problems but a high incidence of affective and anxiety disorders. Nevertheless, it must be borne in mind that Chinese Americans tend not to seek mental health services. Thus, all the data obtained from these sources must be reviewed as preliminary information.

Future Development

The reported 51% incidence of interracial marriages among Asians (Kikumura & Kitano, 1973) suggests that intermarriage between second-generation Chinese and non-Chinese will continue to increase, despite the fact that most Chinese parents prefer their children to marry Chinese. This rejecting of parental desires may evoke conflicts and guilt in the offspring. It is not clear whether the mental health of the children born from these interracial marriages will be affected. It is hoped that by increasing racial awareness through encouraging Chinese parents to become more active participants of school-sponsored activities, this potential mental health problem can be minimized.

Many young Chinese Americans have begun to realize through historical records that the earlier Chinese Americans had suffered prejudice and discrimination silently. The current generation of Chinese American youths shows a conviction that it is time to get organized in order to fight for equal rights and justice as citizens of the United States. Today, most of the larger universities have Asian American Faculty and Student Associations. In the 1980s, Asian American youths all over the United States, on university campuses and in some high schools, began to organize the Yellow Power Movement. The objectives of the movement consist of reeducating the white majority and raising the consciousness of all Asian Americans. The movement may therefore reduce the psychological alienation of Asian Americans, as it strives to promote the social and economic welfare of disenchanted minority groups through political participation (Huang, 1976).

Conclusion

A number of gaps exist in the research on the mental health of Chinese American youths. For one, there is a paucity of systematic studies on the prevalence of mental disorders among the members of this group. Two other points also must be stated. First, whereas some Chinese immigrants left their homeland for economic purposes, many recent immigrants have left because of political reasons. Thus, they have widely varied backgrounds. Some of the immigrants are well-educated, middle-class or upper-class professionals; others have had little education, are very poor, and speak little if any English (Hsia, 1988). There has been no research exploring how these different family backgrounds affect the children's adaptation to their new environments. Second, the 1980 census showed that over 10% of the Chinese families in the United States were headed by single-mothers. Little is known about the causes of such a family constitution or its effect on children's mental development.

The Chinese community in the United States is changing and growing at a rapid pace. Conditions that hold true today may be outdated tomorrow. There is an urgent need for more information on this population, whose increase is fed mainly by the immigrant stream from the Far East. Although this chapter offers some insight into the mental health issues affecting present-day Chinese American youths, it raises more questions than it answers. With the increased availability of bilingual Chinese American mental health investigators, future mental health research projects may yield further understanding of this particular topic.

REFERENCES

Butterfield, F. (1990). Why they excel. *Parade Magazine* (January), 4–6.

Hessler, R. M., Nolan, M. F., Ogbru, B., & New, P. K. M. (1980). Intraethnic diversity: Health care of the Chinese-American. In R. Endo, S. Sue, & N. N. Wagner (Eds.). *Asian-Americans: Social and psychological perspectives* (Vol. 2, pp. 36–63). Ben Lomand, CA: Science and Behavior Books.

Hsia, J. (1988). *Asian Americans in higher education and at work*. Hillsdale, NJ: Lawrence Erlbaum.

Huang, L. (1976). The Chinese American family. In C. Mindel & R. Habenstein (Eds.), *Ethnic families in America, patterns and variations* (pp. 124–147). New York: Elsevier.

Kikumura, A., & Kitano, H. H. L. (1973). Interracial marriage: A picture of the Japanese Americans. *Journal of Social Issues, 29*, 67–81.

Lorenzo, M. K., & Adler, D. A. (1984). Mental health services for Chinese in a community health center. *Social Casework, 65*, 600–609.

McClellan, R. (1971). *The heathen Chinese*. Athens: Ohio University Press.

Newsletter of the Midwest Chinese Student and Alumni Services. (1969, Winter). 12.

Smith, W. (1928). Changing personality traits of second-generation Orientals in America. *American Journal of Social Psychology, 23*, 922–929.

Sollenberger, R. (1968). Chinese American child rearing practices and juvenile delinquency. *Journal of Social Psychology, 74*, 13–23.

Sue, D. W., & Kirk, B. A. (1973). Differential characteristics of Japanese-American and Chinese-American college students. *Journal of Counseling Psychology, 20*, 142–148.

Sue, D., & Sue, S. (1987). Cultural factors in the clinical assessment of Asian American. *Journal of Consulting and Clinical Psychology, 55*, 479–487.

Sung, B. L. (1987). *The adjustment experience of Chinese immigrant children in New York City*. New York: Center for Migration Studies.

Weiss, M. S. (1969, April). *Interracial romance: The Chinese Caucasian dating game*. Paper presented at the Southwestern Anthropological Association, Las Vegas, NV.

Yee, L. (1974 meeting of the summer). "Banana." *Newsletter of the Midwest Chinese Student and Alumni Services, 16* (4).

55 / Japanese American Children

Joe Yamamoto, Joyce Wu Yeh, May Yeh, and S. Sumiko Hifumi

In 1970, Japanese Americans were the most numerous Asians in the United States. However, by 1980, their number had been surpassed by a great increase in the number of Filipinos, Chinese, Southeast Asian refugees, and Koreans. In the 1990 census, Japanese Americans in the United States numbered 847,562, accounting for 0.34% of the country's population (Japanese American National Museum, 1991).

In viewing the development of Japanese American children, the relevance of factors such as ethnicity (compared to other Asians), generation and social class are very apparent. Around the turn of the century, the first migration of Japanese to the United States was made up of waves of young men who left Japan to earn a fortune in America and who then planned to return to their homeland as rich men. Most of these men came prior to 1924, when the Oriental Exclusion Act was passed (Kitano, 1976).

There are historical differences in the Japanese population. At the outset, the Japanese were not treated as badly as were the Chinese, perhaps because Japan had won a war against Russia just after the turn of the century. Despite their more favorable treatment in the state of California, there were nonetheless many discriminatory acts against the Japanese, such as laws prohibiting land ownership, denial of citizenship, and segregation of residential areas. Discrimination was widespread, and in that day there were no fair employment acts. Compared with the Chinese and Filipi-

This study was supported in part by the National Research Center on Asian American Mental Health (NIMH #R01 MH44331 and MH47525).

nos, however, there was one important difference, namely: The Japanese men were permitted to bring their brides to the United States.

World War II made a tremendous difference in the treatment of Japanese Americans. In particular, 120,000 Japanese Americans, whether citizens or noncitizens, were "relocated" into ten camps in the heartland of America during the war (Yamamoto, Machizawa, & Steinberg, 1986): Gila River and Poston, Arizona; Granada, Colorado; Heart Mountain, Wyoming; Jerome and Rohwer, Arkansas; Manzanar, Minidoka, and Tule Lake, California; and Topaz, Utah (Armor & Wright, 1988). This experience was a turning point. Until the beginning of World War II on December 7, 1941, Japanese Americans had for the most part lived in ethnic islands, such as Little Tokyo in Los Angeles and Terminal Island, or in farming communities. With the advent of World War II, however, heightened anti-Japanese racism became prevalent all along the Pacific Coast. The Japanese were "relocated" and the order of their lives shattered. Among other things, this process disrupted the normal flow of family authority.

Before World War II, the first generation to come to the United States (*issei*) were the authority figures, with the father heading the household. Just as in Japan, the father was treated with respect and deference and awarded the customary courtesies of authority. Like the Chinese and Koreans, the Japanese also were influenced by the teachings of Confucius, who advocated loyalty between lord and subject, order between senior and junior, propriety between husband and wife, intimacy between father and son, and trust between friends (Herbert, 1950). After the wartime relocation center experience, the traditional patriarchs were rendered helpless, and the power in the Japanese American families passed to the second generation (*nisei*) who could speak English and communicate with camp administrators.

Prior to World War II, because of the racism directed against Asians on the West Coast, college graduates had difficulty obtaining middle-class and upper-middle-class jobs. In the wake of the wartime relocation center experience, some Japanese Americans left the camps to work, to go to school, and to continue their lives away from the Pacific Coast. As a result, this cohort underwent a more rapid acculturation. Since the war, two

additional generations have been born, the third generation (*sansei*) and fourth (*yonsei*).

In recent years, only a limited number of Japanese have arrived in the United States. Most have come as employees of Japanese corporations, assigned to spend 3 to 5 years in the United States representing their home companies. In contrast to the previous wave of immigrants from Japan, these company men plan to go back to Japan. Their futures are brighter because of their experience in a foreign land. With a clearer understanding of the different culture of the United States, they will be able to work more efficiently for their companies.

At the same time, there have been changes among the Japanese within Japan itself. The study by Kono, Towle, and Harford shows that in Japan men drank much more heavily than did the Japanese American men in Oahu, Hawaii, and Santa Clara, California. The number of Japanese women who are drinking, some heavily, also has increased (however, not as much as in the United States). The Japanese in Japan are also changing. Just as the Japanese Americans have changed with acculturation, in some ways, the Japanese in Japan are becoming more cosmopolitan while remaining traditional in other ways.

In Asia, the cultures are evolving rapidly toward industrialization. However, changes toward a more democratic and egalitarian family structure have been less rapid. The teachings of Confucius are still held in high esteem, with great emphasis on filial piety, the differences between male and female, and the ideology of primogeniture (Herbert, 1950).

The Acculturation Process

Within the United States, many changes have occurred due to acculturation (Yamamoto & Wagatsuma, 1980). Intermarriage has increased tremendously. In Los Angeles County, the percentage of marriages to non-Japanese varied from 51 to 63%, remaining at approximately 51% in the most recent study (Kitano, Fujino, & Takahashi, in press). An interesting phenomenon is the fact that women tend to outmarry more often than men. For example, in 1977, 60.6% of Japanese American women outmarried versus 39.4% of the men; in 1984, 60.2% of the women outmarried versus 39.8% men; and in 1989, the figures were 58.3% for the women versus 41.7% for the men (Kitano et al., in press).

Japanese Americans have changed considerably, with each cohort's characteristics depending on their generation. The first generation Japanese Americans were an ethnically homogenous group, and there was very little outmarriage among their immediate offspring. However, since the third and fourth generation, the outmarriage rates have increased tremendously, so that there has been a discernable dilution of the original Japanese cultural values.

There may be a similar weakening of the strong family ties that were once the hallmark of Japanese Americans. Today, for example, it is less likely that the elderly will be taken care of by their children. One author recalls being socialized to want to take care of his parents so that when he was 5, he said to his mother, "When I grow up, I'm going to buy a Cadillac car so I can drive you around." Third- and fourth-generation Japanese Americans do not retain these values. However, along with the more traditional Japanese, they do accept the importance of filial piety and helping take care of their parents to a much greater extent than the average American.

In order to understand Japanese Americans who are not acculturated, it is important to consider the much greater emphasis on family ties in the Japanese culture (Kitano, 1976; Lebra, 1976; Roland, 1988; Yamamoto & Wagatsuma, 1980). One example is how Japanese families will help a family member to attend college. All family members will contribute so that the one member may have this advantage. To most Japanese Americans family ties are important, and the relationship among family members is stronger, on average, then among European Americans.

Since Japanese Americans are Asians, they cannot participate in the melting pot. As long as the physical ideal is that of a European American, someone with an Asian physiognomy does not fit that ideal. To that extent, the acculturation of Japanese Americans is hindered. This situation is changing in two states in the United States. Hawaii had undergone this transformation a long time

ago, so that in recent years, the governor, senators, and congresspersons are all Asians. In California, with the state's changing demography and, in particular, with 10% of the state Asian Americans it is much more possible for Asians to become political and industrial leaders. However, the possibility is all too often not a reality, and the frustrations and disappointments related to the glass ceiling may cause enough stress to lead to some cases of depression among Asian Americans. (Although there are no data to support this contention, we offer it as a reasonable assumption.) Some marginal Japanese Americans may participate in Asian gangs, a phenomenon that is an increasing problem in California. Currently, Japanese Americans participate in such gangs at a lower rate than the newer Asian immigrant population.

Development of Japanese American Children

Since Japanese Americans were discussed by Kitano (1976) and Yamamoto and Iga (1983), the picture has changed, mainly because of the high level of intermarriage among the young of this group. By and large, outmarriages occurred with Americans (European Americans, Hispanic Americans, Asian Americans, American Indians, and African American.); ultimately, they had the effect of diluting the traditional cultural values and led to more rapid acculturation. Of course, where Asian Americans married Asians, the movement toward acculturation may have been diminished. At any rate, the situation is quite diverse and complicated. The authors hope that the emerging diversity will perpetuate some of the strengths of the Japanese American cultural values such as strong family ties, respect for the elderly, an emphasis on education through diligence, and an emphasis on empathy and interpersonal relationships.

The first and second names of a Japanese American child give a cue as to the degree of acculturation of the family. The first generation had only Japanese given names. The second generation often had both an American and a Japanese given name; in the third and fourth generations, the customs have varied tremendously. In general, the more acculturated the family, the more American the given names.

As noted, the Japanese are very family oriented. They are also very hierarchical and sexist in orientation. The MacArthur Constitution, which was imposed on the Japanese after World War II, tried to make the situation more equal for men and women. To some extent, it has succeeded; nonetheless, as in many cultures in Asia, the authority structures are vertical, hierarchical, and sexist. If you ask first-generation or second-generation Japanese Americans what they value, they will respond in terms of the strong family ties, importance of diligence and perseverance, the ability to withstand negative stressors, and the capacity to persist toward achievement for one's family and one's self. In addition, honesty, reliability, and the avoidance of difficulties that would reflect adversely on the Japanese-American community have long been valued.

The development of Japanese American children may be affected by the close family ties and the Asian attitude about the importance of diligence in educational progress (Stevenson, 1992; Yamamoto & Iga, 1983; Yamamoto & Kubota, 1983). Inevitably, conflicting demands will be made on the Japanese American children, depending on their generation; in the nature of things the third-, fourth-, and fifth-generation Japanese Americans are likely to be increasingly acculturated and much more "American" in their values. What will be preserved? The answer to this question will have to await future research. Our belief is that some of the Japanese values about diligence will be maintained, tempered, however, by such American cultural values as the importance of individuality, recreation, and social activities.

Mental Health Issues

The prevalence of mental disorders among Japanese Americans is not known. There have been two studies of the effects of the relocation center experience; these revealed issues related to the aversive effects of being incarcerated (Leonetti,

1983; Yamamoto et al., 1986). In a nonrepresentative study of elderly Japanese Americans who recalled the relocation center experience during World War II, it was found that a high percentage, approximately 10%, presented a symptom profile that led to the diagnosis of major depression (Yamamoto et al., 1986). In addition, approximately one-third recalled the wartime relocation experience as having had adverse effects on them (Yamamoto et al., 1986). Perhaps a logical explanation would be that a bad experience, such as being incarcerated, may predispose a person to major depression (just as women who are raped subsequently often experience a major depression).

Among Asians generally, the high stigma associated with mental illness has led them to avoid mental health care, both in Asia and in the United States (Hwu, Yeh, & Chang, 1986; Sue, 1977). However, as the Japanese acculturate, those who need mental health services may more appropriately use them as do other Americans, albeit still at a somewhat lesser rate. For example, in Los Angeles County, the use of mental health services by Asian Americans (the figures are not available specifically for Japanese Americans) is about 40% of their proportion in the population (Mochizuki, 1975). Since no major epidemiological study has been done in Japan, we cannot even turn to results from the homeland. However, a still-to-be published telephone survey using a portion of the National Institute of Mental Health's Diagnostic Interview Schedule Version III in Japan reveals that the prevalence of major depression there was approximately 5% (Yamamoto & Machizawa, 1993). This is comparable to the prevalence in the United States, higher than the prevalence in Korea (3.5%) (Lee et al., 1990a,b), and much higher than in Taiwan (0.9%) (Hwu et al., 1986).

One of the important mental health issues is the high prevalence of suicide among elderly Japanese males and females (Yamamoto, 1989). A study by Annie Diego and Joe Yamamoto shows that the hypothesis that suicides among elderly Asian women were related to cultural conflicts with the younger generation was not true (Diego, Yamamoto, Nguyen, & Hifumi, 1994). The women who committed suicide were well connected with their children but committed suicide because they were depressed, chronically physically ill, or for other reasons unrelated to culture conflicts.

Kari Yoshimura completed an interesting study

entitled "Acculturative and Sociocultural Influences on the Development of Eating Disorders in Asian American Females" (1992), which examines, among other things, the relationship between symptoms of eating disorders and acculturation. The 31 Asian American females who participated in this study indicated that they had experienced symptoms of eating disorders (anorexia nervosa or bulimia), either currently or in the recent past. Their ages ranged from 16 to 39 years with an average of 23.1 years. Ten were Japanese Americans, 9 were Chinese Americans, 6 were Korean Americans, 4 were Filipino Americans, and 2 were Vietnamese Americans. Eleven were first generation, 7 were second generation, 9 were third generation, and 4 were fourth generation. Twenty-seven were single, 3 were married, and 1 was divorced. Twenty were students, 3 were semiprofessionals, 2 were in sales or clerical work, 2 were in professional or high-level administrative work, and 4 in other work not specified in the questionnaire.

The issue of antisocial acting out is an important one. In the past, the Japanese were socialized to be exquisitely aware of behavior that might have an adverse impact upon the Japanese community (Kitano, 1976). Now, with increasing acculturation, and outmarriage, the behavioral norms have changed more toward the behavioral norms of Americans generally. The fact that the emphasis on education and diligence has permitted Japanese Americans to advance educationally and, therefore, socioeconomically has been a positive factor.

A study of 800 children to determine whether they were seriously emotionally disturbed had very few Asian-Japanese American members (Q. James, personal communication, 1993). Compared to the low divorce rate among the first generation of Japanese Americans, the prevalence of divorce has increased dramatically. This situation will certainly have an impact on the children, for divorce may be dangerous to their mental health.

There are no systematic studies of the mental health of Japanese American children. One can only speculate about the nature of the significant variables. One important issue may be that in the past, when the first and second generation Japanese Americans lived in the United States, they occupied ethnic islands which were havens of safety for them, since the students in the schools were Japanese-Americans (the teachers were not), and their associations were essentially in a Japanese-American community. Indeed, the first generation Issei parents could live and die in Little Tokyo without learning to speak English. With the advent of fair housing, and the dispersion of the Japanese Americans from totally Japanese communities to neighborhoods with greater representation of Americans of European, Hispanic, African, American Indian and Asian backgrounds, all this has changed. This is progress in a sense, but with a diminishment of the social supports and solidarity which were present in the past.

There are no epidemiological data about the development of Japanese American children, or about the prevalence of such emotional disorders as might beset them. The only relevant data are studies of the elderly Japanese done by Yamamoto et al., (1985). Using the Diagnostic Interview Schedule Version III, the figures demonstrated that the prevalence of psychiatric disorders was substantially lower than among young American adults and comparable to the findings among elderly Euro-Americans in the Epidemiological Catchment Area studies. There were two significant findings, namely: the prevalence of cognitive impairment in very old (over 80 years of age) Japanese Americans and a high prevalence of major depression among those Japanese American elderly who had been relocated during World War II. One-third of them still recalled the injustices with bitterness, resentment, and feelings that their health had been impaired (Yamamoto et al., 1985).

Data on Japanese American children seen in the Los Angeles County Mental Health system during the years 1982 to 1988 may provide a picture of the distresses in this population that present for mental health services. The 153 first-time child clients in this sample ranged in age from 3 to 17 with a mean age of 12.9 and a modal age of 16. Forty-six percent of the sample were female and 54% were male. Adjustment disorder (26.1%), child conduct disorder (19.0%), other child/adolescent disorder (11.8%), nonpsychiatric condition (7.8%), major depression (7.2%), and affective/other disorder, atypical (7.2%) were the six most common admission diagnoses given, totaling 79.1% of the population. Comparison with the Caucasian population yields both similarities and differences. The Caucasian sample ranged from 0 to 17 years in age with a mean age of 11.6, which was significantly lower than that of the Japanese American sample ($p < .0001$). The modal age of this population was 15. Japanese American diagnoses differed somewhat from that of the Caucasian child population, where adjustment disorder (34.1%), child conduct disorder (15.0%), other child/adolescent disorder (11.2%), affective/other disorder, atypical (9.9%), deferred diagnosis (5.1%), and anxiety disorder (4.3%) were the six most common admission diagnoses, totaling 79.6% of the population. The percentage of female and male clients in the Caucasian sample did not differ significantly from the Japanese American population, with 43% female clients and 57% male clients.

Differences in Conceptualization of the Self

Increasing evidence suggests that the conceptualization or definition of self differs in Japanese and in Western society (Landrine, 1992; Roland, 1988). Roland introduced the familial self as an additional psychic structure among the Japanese, a formulation that goes beyond the Western conceptualized individuated self. Landrine differentiated the referential self from the indexical self, which, Landrine proposed, does not exist independently from relationships and contacts and which more closely approximates how Asians perceive the self.

Markus and Kitayama (1991) proposed two construals of the self: independent and interdependent. The independent construal of the self is mostly prevalent in the Western cultures while the interdependent construal of the self is more relevant to and descriptive of the Asian cultures. Markus and Kitayama cited a study by S. Cousin (1989) that found a clear difference between the concept of self among American and Japanese students. In completing statements starting with "I am . . ." Japanese students defined themselves more on the basis of roles and relationships. For example, they would make statements such as "I am the third son." American students described themselves more with personal attributes, such as "I am intelligent." Furthermore, the proportion of attributes in their self-descriptions increases in the Japanese students when the "I am . . ." statements are qualified with specific situations.

All these studies seem to indicate that there is a difference between Japanese and Americans in their concept of the self. Differences in social structure, family values, and child-rearing practices no doubt contribute to the development of this difference. The Japanese Americans have preserved some of their traditional values, but, as the number of generations increases, they are also acculturating. There is evidence of a changing style of child rearing among the Japanese Americans (Kitano, 1976). It would be most interesting to see how the progressive changes affect the development of the self-concept among the Japanese American children.

A clinical case may shed some light on the development of the self in a Japanese American boy.

CASE EXAMPLE

Kevin (fictitious name) is a *sansei* Japanese American. At the age of 16, he presented serious acting-out behavior and emotional problems; among other things, despite at least average intelligence, he was also failing school. Inpatient treatment temporarily arrested his problems, but after discharge, he quickly relapsed. Both Kevin and his family members were extremely resistant to mental health services for fear of stigma and being shamed, and they believed that strict discipline was the solution. After the legal system forced them into treatment, however, the whole extended family became involved and were very supportive of Kevin. Because of his resistance, denial, and low ability to express himself verbally, a nonverbal therapeutic technique, sand play therapy, was employed. As the representation of his self emerged in the play, it was always accompanied by representations of his family members. It was not until the last stage of the 2-year treatment that Kevin's more individuated self appeared in the play as a competitive athlete along with his peers. This symbolized his eventual adaptation to American society.

REFERENCES

Armor, L., & Wright, P. (1988). *Manzanar.* New York: Times Books.

Cousins, S. (1989). Culture and selfhood in Japan and the U.S. *Journal of Personality and Social Psychology, 56,* 124–131.

Diego, A., Yamamoto, J., Nguyen, L. H., & Hifumi, S. S. (1994). Suicide in the elderly: Profiles of Asians and Whites. *Asian American and Pacific Islander Journal of Health, 2* (1), 49–57.

Herbert, E. A. (1950). *Confucian notebook.* London: Butler and Tanner.

Hwu, H. G., Yeh, E. K., & Chang, L. Y. (1986). Chinese diagnostic interview schedule. *Acta Psychiatrica Scandinavica 73,* 225–233.

Japanese American National Museum. (1991). *United States of America population 1990 U.S. Census Data.* Los Angeles: Japanese American National Museum.

Kitano, H. H. L. (1976). *Japanese Americans: The evolution of a subculture* (2nd ed). Lexington, MA: Ginn Press.

Kitano, H. H. L., Fujino, D. C., & Takahashi, J. S. (in press). Interracial marriages: Where are the Asian Americans and where are they going? In N. Zane & L. Lee (Eds.), *Handbook of Asian American Psychology.* Sage Publications.

Kono, H., Towle, L. H., & Harford, T. C. (1991). *Alcohol consumption patterns and related problems in the United States and Japan: Summary report of a Joint United States–Japan alcohol epidemiological project.* Rockville, MD: National Institute on Alcohol Abuse and Alcoholism.

Landrine, H. (1992). Clinical implications of cultural differences: The referential versus the indexical self. *Clinical Psychology Review, 12,* 401–415.

Lebra, T. S. (1976). *Japanese patterns of behavior.* Honolulu: University of Hawaii Press.

Lee, C. K., Kwak, Y. S., Yamamoto, J., Rhee, H., Kim, Y. S., Han, J. H., Choi, J. O., & Lee, Y. H. (1990a). Psychiatric epidemiology in Korea. Part I: Gender and age differences in Seoul. *Journal of Nervous and Mental Disease, 178* (4), 242–246.

Lee, C. K., Kwak, Y. S., Yamamoto, J., Rhee, H., Kim, Y. S., Han, J. H., Choi, J. O., & Lee, Y. H. (1990b). Psychiatric epidemiology in Korea. Part II: Urban and rural differences. *Journal of Nervous and Mental Disease, 178* (4), 247–252.

Leonetti, D. L. (1983). *Nisei aging project report.* Seattle: University of Washington.

Markus, H. R., & Kitayama, S. (1991). Culture and the self: Implications for cognition, emotion, and motivation. *Psychological Review, 98* (2), 224–253.

Mochizuki, M. (1975). Discharge and units of service by ethnic origin: Fiscal year 1973–1974 (Vol. 3, Report No. 11). In *Los Angeles County Department of Health Services* (E & R Rows and Columns). Los Angeles: County of Los Angeles Department of Health Services, Mental Health Services.

Roland, A. (1988). *In search of self in India and Japan.* Princeton, NJ: Princeton University Press.

Stevenson, H. W. (1992, December). Learning from Asian schools. *Scientific American,* 70–76.

Sue, S. (1977). Community mental health services to minority groups: Some optimism, some pessimism. *American Psychologist, 32,* 616–624.

Yamamoto, J. (1989). Suicide among the Chinese and Japanese. In Group for the Advancement of Psychiatry Committee on Cultural Psychiatry (Eds.), *Suicide and ethnicity in the United States* (pp. 58–71). New York: Brunner/Mazel.

Yamamoto, J., Alboran, N., Araki, F., Cater, R., Cabrera, J., Chen, C. T., Leung, J., Machizawa, S., Nguyen, B. V., Reece, S., Yap, J., & Steinberg, A. (1985). Elderly Asian Americans in Los Angeles. In *Proceedings, International Symposium on Psychiatric Epidemiology* (in Taipei, Taiwan, April 26–28, 1985) (pp. 141–156). Republic of China: Department of Health, Executive Yuan.

Yamamoto, J., & Iga, M. (1983). Emotional growth of Japanese-American children. In G. Powell, J. Yamamoto, A. Romero, & A. Morales (Eds.), *The psychosocial development of minority group children* (pp. 167–178). New York: Brunner/Mazel.

Yamamoto, J., & Kubota, M. (1983). The Japanese-American family. In G. Powell, J. Yamamoto, A. Romero, & A. Morales (Eds.), *The psychosocial development of minority group children* (pp. 237–247). New York: Brunner/Mazel.

Yamamoto, J., & Machizawa, S. (1993). *Major depression in Asia and in America.* Manuscript.

Yamamoto, J., Machizawa, S., & Steinberg, A. (1986). The Japanese American relocation center experience. *P/AAMHRC Research Review, 5* (3/4), 17–20.

Yamamoto, J., & Wagatsuma, H. (1980). The Japanese and Japanese Americans. *Journal of Operational Psychiatry, 11* (2), 120–135.

Yoshimura, K. (1992). *Acculturative and sociocultural influences on the development of eating disorders in Asian American females.* Doctoral dissertation, Alhambra, CA: Library of California School of Professional Psychology.

56 / Cultural and Psychopathology in Pacific/Asian Children

James E. Dillon and Veronica Ichikawa

For many reasons Pacific/Asian cultures are important to child mental health professionals in the West. First, over 7 million Asian Americans, including East Indian Asians, were counted in the 1990 United States census, representing just under 3% of the total population. Since 1960, this population has increased sevenfold, making it the fastest-growing minority in the United States. Second, because of the stresses associated with immigration and minority status. American children of Pacific/Asian descent face unique adaptive hurdles requiring modification of routine clinical practice. Third, the rapid growth of Pacific rim economies has led to increasing transcultural and economic exchanges between the East and the West. Clinicians in the United States and other Western countries are frequently called upon to examine children from Japan, Korea, Hong Kong, Taiwan, China, and other Eastern nations during extended educational or business sojourns in the West. Fourth, the comparative study of culture and race promises important insights about social and biological influences on development. Formerly the exclusive province of anthropology and public health, cross-cultural studies of behavior can now benefit from systematic application of recent advances in psychiatric research methodology.

Asian Populations

In the United States, the term "Asian" refers to peoples of extremely heterogeneous racial, geographic, ethnic, and linguistic heritages; indeed, their principal commonality is the tendency of Euro-Americans to stereotype them as a group. According to Lee, (1992) "In the totality of American perception, all Asians are somehow lumped together into one racial group, devoid of distinctive ethnic and cultural differences. As one person

said to me, it doesn't matter what you are—Chinese, Korean, or Japanese—you'll always be seen as a 'chink' in this country." (p. VII) Stereotyping of Asians has encouraged the emergence of a *political* group within the United States, whose chief unifying characteristic is its historical experience as an immigrant racial minority. This increasingly influential political affiliation is remarkably unified despite centuries of ethnic and national conflict among its constituent groups. The Chinese and Japanese, for example, have fought repeatedly during the past century and hold ethnic prejudices every bit as virulent as the animus between racial groups in the United States; yet abroad they form a natural coalition, their former animosities evaporating in the crucible of American racial tensions.

Although the problem of stereotyping is hardly solved by refining the stereotype, heuristically it is useful to distinguish several major geographic groups within Asia and the Pacific Islands that define broad, culturally related populations. The expression "Pacific/Asian," it should be noted, derives only loosely from the geographic entity called Asia, in that it includes the widely scattered islands of the Pacific, far removed from the Asian continent, while it excludes many peoples of the former Soviet Union living in Asia proper.

East Asia, formerly called the "Far East," includes China, Mongolia, Korea, Japan, and Eastern Siberia, and sometimes refers to countries more precisely situated in Southeast Asia, including Vietnam, Cambodia, Thailand, Laos, Malaysia, Indonesia, and the Philippines. To the southwest are the nations of the Indian subcontinent, including India proper, Sri Lanka, Pakistan, Bangladesh, Bhutan, and Nepal. Eastward from the Philippines and Indonesia are the Pacific Islands, comprised of Polynesia, including Hawaii, Easter Island, Samoa, and Tonga; Micronesia, including Guam and the Marshall Islands; and Melanesia, including Fiji, Papua New Guinea, and the Solomon Islands. In this chapter we focus on groups who have immigrated to the United States in substantial numbers from the "Pacific/Asian" nations, by which we mean countries of the Pacific rim including the Pacific Islands but excluding Australia, New Zealand, and the Indian subcontinent. More detailed discussions of specific national subgroups from China, Japan, Korea, and Cambodia appear elsewhere in this volume.

Peoples of Asia and the Pacific Islands reflect diverse religious, philosophical, and ethnic traditions. Confucianism and Buddhism, blended with local traditions such as Shinto in Japan and Taoism in China, predominate in East and Southeast Asia. South and east of the Indochinese peninsula, in Malaysia and Indonesia, Islam is the prevailing religious influence. Indonesian peoples represent over 300 different ethnicities speaking over 25 distinct languages and 200 dialects. Singapore is a cosmopolitan blend of racial, ethnic, and religious elements from other parts of Asia, the Pacific Islands, and the West.

The Pacific Islands are scattered widely throughout the tropical central and south Pacific; they consist of thousands of volcanic peaks and small coralline atolls, most of which are uninhabited. Thirty thousand years ago peoples from Indonesia and the Malay peninsula migrated to the islands over land bridges to become the ancestors of present-day Pacific Islanders. The economies of the less developed islands are primitive by Western standards and depend largely on subsistence agriculture. Christianity, emblematic of Western influence in the modern era, has become the dominant religious influence in many Pacific islands and the Philippines.

Both Western and local political influences have dramatically altered the conditions under which many Pacific/Asian children are raised. The war in Southeast Asia and its aftermath, for instance, decisively influenced the adaptation of recent generations of Vietnamese, Cambodian, and Laotian children, both in their native countries and in their adopted Western homelands. In Communist China, political and economic pressure on families to have only one child has created a generation of "only children," a unique sociological event that many predicted would produce a nation of "little emperors" (Falbo & Poston, 1993). Although this fear has not materialized (Wan, Fan, Ling, & Jing, 1994), the state's assumption of responsibility for providing lifelong economic security to Chinese citizens, traditionally the domain of multigenera-

tional families, has resulted in changing parental rationales for raising children (Tseng et al., 1988). Culture is thus a dynamic concept: What can be said about Asian peoples in any particular place at any particular time represents a limited, cross-sectional view of heterogeneous social systems in continuous flux.

Economics is also important in understanding differences among and within Asian cultures. Attitudes about material achievement, education, and employment among Japanese, whose gross domestic product is $19,000 per capita, are much more like those of Americans than like those of Laotians, whose gross domestic product is $200 per capita. Poverty has degraded long-standing social values in some Asian countries. For example, in Thailand, where commercial sex among girls and young women flourishes, 3% of late primary/early secondary school children live with a "female sex worker," and 12% consider prostitution a normal occupation (Sittitrai, Joladsakul, Norral, & Brown, 1992). Similarly, economic differences among social strata from nominally similar cultures may be of enormous significance in shaping norms and values. A vast cultural gap thus separates the educated children of wealthy Filipino and Singaporian (Isralowitz & Hong, 1990) society from youth of the agrarian and urban lower classes (Reyes, Valdecanas, Reyes, & Reyes, 1990), to mention only two striking examples.

Since 1521, when Magellan "discovered" Guam, Western colonialism has profoundly shaped social, economic, and political development in Asia and the Pacific. England, France, Holland, and Russia were already playing major roles in regional politics by the middle of the 19th century, when Commodore Matthew Perry led an expedition that would terminate 200 years of Japanese national seclusion and trigger the period of modernization known as the Meiji Restoration. The Allied victory in World War II resulted in American stewardship of the democratized Japanese nation and U.S. leadership in the postwar development of the Philippines, South Korea, and parts of the Pacific Islands, including Hawaii. The British in Hong Kong and India, the French (and later the United States) in Vietnam and Cambodia, and the Soviet Union in China had comparable influences in the postwar era.

The impact of Western culture is most pronounced among affluent and educated Asians with ready access to information from abroad. Among Vietnamese emigrants, government officials and professionals educated in the French curriculum were able to adopt Western values and customs more readily than those who emigrated later as "boat people." Similarly, Chinese students stranded in the United States during the cultural revolution represent completely different cultural patterns from Chinese driven by financial incentives to enter the United States as construction workers and laundry shop owners.

East Asian Philosophy

If there is a "mother" nation that has influenced the culture of most Eastern and Indochinese peoples, that nation is surely China. The peoples of Japan and Korea routinely study Chinese writing and history as part of their standard education. Japan's oral language is in the Altaic family, suggesting origins in northern Asia; yet the system of Japanese writing called Kanji consists of traditional characters understood by most literate Chinese and Koreans. The influence of Chinese culture on its neighbors in Japan, Korea, and Indochina can be likened to the influence of European culture on the United States.

In the fifth century B.C., Asian personal virtue and social values were codified in the writings of China's great secular philosopher, Confucius. In the service of interpersonal harmony, the core value of the Confucian moral system, group cohesion and welfare take precedence over individual rights and interests. Family and tradition are fundamental, representing special instances of harmony within intergenerational groups. Virtuous character is that which promotes group harmony and cohesion: "There are five things and whoever is capable of putting them into practice . . . is certainly 'benevolent.' . . . They are respectfulness, tolerance, trustworthiness in word, quickness in acting to achieve results, and generosity" (Confucius, 1979, p. 144).

Good breeding is evinced by respect for the ways of the parents: "Observe what a man has in mind to do when his father is living, and then observe what he does when his father is dead. If, for three years, he makes no changes to his father's

ways, he can be said to be a good son" (Confucius, 1979, pp. 60–61).

The virtues modeled in family relationships are extended to other groups, as well: "A young man should be a good son at home and an obedient young man abroad, sparing of speech but trustworthy in what he says, and should love the multitude at large but cultivate the friendship of his fellow men" (Confucius, 1979, pp. 59–60).

Humility and respect may camouflage brilliance. The polite and taciturn demeanor of an Asian student can be mistaken for dullness. "I can speak to Hui all day without his disagreeing with me in any way. Thus he would seem to be stupid. However, when I take a closer look at what he does in private after he has withdrawn from my presence, I discover that it does, in fact, throw light on what I said. Hui is not stupid after all" (Confucius, 1979, p. 64).

The motto "less talk, more action" could easily have been Confucian: "The gentleman is ashamed of his word outstripping his deed" (Confucius, 1979, p. 128).

Thus, Asians from the Confucian tradition seek high attainment without being demonstrative: "Only when the cold season comes is the point brought home that the pine and the cypress are the last to lose their leaves" (Confucius, 1979, p. 100).

Like Confucianism, Taoism and Buddhism are seminal traditions shaping Asian cultural values. Lao Tzu, a contemporary of Confucius, advocated a subjective spirituality transcending the distinction of self from other:

It lies in the nature of Grand Virtue
To follow the Tao and the Tao alone
                    · · ·
Throughout the ages Its Name has been preserved
In order to recall the Beginning of all things.
How do I know the ways of all things at the Beginning?
By what is within me. (Lao Tzu, 1990, pp. 30–31)

Although sometimes antagonistic to Confucianism, Taoist philosophy enshrines many similar personal virtues:

The highest form of goodness is like water.
Water knows how to benefit all things without striving for them.
                    · · ·
In dealing with others, know how to be gentle and kind.
In speaking, know how to keep your words.

In governing, know how to maintain order.
In transacting business, know how to be efficient.

. . .

If you do not strive with others,
You will be free from blame. (Lao Tzu, 1990, p. 10)

The rejection of outward worldly virtues, in favor of simplicity and modesty, promotes interpersonal harmony:

By not exalting the talented you will cause the people to cease from rivalry and contention.
By not prizing goods hard to get, you will cause the people to cease from robbing and stealing.
By not displaying what is desirable, you will cause the people's hearts to remain undisturbed. (Lao Tzu, 1990, p. 4)

Almost contemporaneously with the Chinese philosophers, the historical Buddha in India developed a religion that would eventually separate into two main branches: Hinayana Buddhism, which teaches the attainment of personal enlightenment (Nirvana); and Mahayana Buddhism, which emphasizes the salvation of all beings. The former became the predominant influence in nations of southern Asia, such as Myanmar (Burma), while the latter evolved in China, Tibet, Japan, and Korea. Bodhidharma, the 28th patriarch in the line of succession from the Buddha Shakyamuni, brought Buddhism to China in the fifth century C.E., where it blended with native Taoism to form Ch'an Buddhism; this, in turn, evolved to its pinnacle in Japan and Korea as Zen Buddhism. Strict discipline and spare living are hallmarks of Zen that underlie the orderliness, self-sacrifice, and self-abnegation characteristic of Japanese and Korean cultures, as indicated in this passage from the work of Dogen, the Japanese progenitor of Soto Zen Buddhism:

Another time, Jooshuu said, "Out of all those who have renounced the world is there anyone who lives the way I do? I sleep on the earthen floor on a torn mat without a cover and with only a wooden pillow. No incense is offered before the Buddha-image; instead, there is the smell of manure chips."
We can see from the above illustrations how poor Jooshuu's life was. We should all follow his example. . . . All of the ancient Buddhas lived like Jooshuu. (Dogen, 1975, p. 301)

Asian cultures are child centered, as indeed they must be to bring about the degree of conformity and discipline required of children. Cross-cultural research on education demonstrates clearly that parents of Japanese and Taiwanese children, both in their native lands (Lee, Ichikawa, & Stevenson, 1987) and in the United States, have higher performance standards and take a greater personal role in the education of their children than do their American counterparts (Azuma, Kashiwagi, & Hess, 1981; Stevenson, Lee, & Stigler, 1986). Immigrant parents of Indochinese origin, despite a background of economic deprivation and political turmoil, also stress high standards of academic achievement in their children.

Developmental Psychopathology in Pacific/Asian Children

The scientific study of development and psychopathology in Pacific/Asian nations and peoples has burgeoned with the advent of research instruments and techniques adapted from British and American sources (Morita, Suzuki, Suzuki, & Kamoshito, 1993; Takeuchi & Kitamura, 1991). Although it is beyond the scope of this chapter to review this body of research comprehensively, a brief survey may be useful.

DEVELOPMENT

Differences between Asian and Caucasian infants are apparent soon after birth and may reflect constitutional differences. Lewis, Ramsay, and Kawakami, (1993), for instance, found significant differences between Japanese and Caucasian American infants at 4 months of age in response to routine inoculations. Caucasian infants showed a more vigorous behavioral and affective response and required longer to become quiet than did Japanese infants, who showed a more robust cortisol response to the same stimulus. This finding may foreshadow the predominance of emotional over behavioral disturbances in Asian children and adolescents that has been identified in some surveys.

Differences between American and Asian populations in maternal speech and responsiveness to infants also have been documented. American mothers, for example, use speech that is more information-oriented and ask more questions of

3-month-old infants than do their Japanese counterparts (Toda, Fogel, & Kawai, 1990). Whereas American mothers tend to label objects for older infants, Japanese mothers use objects to engage infants in social routines (Fernald & Morikawa, 1993). Variations in response to infant looking (Bornstein et al., 1992) and maternal role perceptions (Shand, 1985) also have been noted. Characteristics of young Japanese children, whether of cultural and/or biological origin, appear to be quite enduring. Tseng, Ebata, Miguchi, Egawa, and McLaughlin (1990) interviewed Japanese orphans left in China at the end of World War II and reared as culturally Chinese. On return to Japan as adults, they continued to exhibit social behaviors and personality traits characteristic of Japanese.

CROSS-CULTURAL COMPARISONS
OF CHILD PSYCHOPATHOLOGY

In Japan, mainland China, Taiwan, Thailand, and Malaysia, the development of Asian-language adaptations of Western research instruments has permitted the epidemiological study of child psychiatric disorders. A limited literature comparing children from various Asian nations to children from Europe and the United States suggests that Asian youths have types and rates of psychiatric disorder that are substantially similar to those of Caucasians in America and Europe; these findings, however, may be artifacts of crude methodology. Cross-national comparisons are complicated by culturally mediated rating biases. Thus, Indonesian and Chinese clinicians are more likely to rate a given behavior as "hyperactive-disruptive" than are U.S. clinicians (Mann et al., 1992). American mothers tend to overrate whereas Japanese and Taiwanese mothers tend to underrate academic success and innate ability, as measured by objective tests (Lee, Ichikawa, & Stevenson, 1987). Furthermore, teacher and parent checklists employing Likert scales for judgments of behavioral deviance elicit judgments based on cultural norms rather than on objective criteria. If Asian children in general exhibit less behavioral disturbance, minor degrees of misbehavior (by Western standards) would be endorsed as significant by Asian raters. Such instruments are therefore apt to *underestimate* differences between cultural groups.

Some investigators, however, have been undaunted by the difficulties inherent in cross-cultural studies. Weisz et al. (1987) compared behavioral and emotional problems in 600 American and 360 Thai school-age children from comparable urban, suburban, and semirural settings. Total problem scores on the Achenbach Child Behavior Check List showed small but statistically significant group differences, with the Thai children scoring slightly higher than the Americans. Modest differences were similarly found in 54 specific problem areas. Substantial differences, however, were found in only 6: Thai children had higher scores on "doesn't eat well," "constipated," "feels dizzy," "underactive, lacks energy," and "sulks a lot"; American children had moderately higher scores on the item "self-conscious." On the "overcontrolled" factor (derived from principal components analysis of American samples), Thai children scored higher than Americans, while on the "undercontrolled" factor, no differences were observed. Male-female differences, such as higher "undercontrolled" scores for boys, were similar across cultures.

Iwawaki, Sumida, Okuno, and Cowen (1967) assessed 451 children from Japan, France, and the United States with the Children's Manifest Anxiety Scale. Japanese children scored lowest of the three groups on both anxiety and lie scales, in contrast to studies showing high levels of anxiety in Japanese adults (Ohmura & Sawa, 1957) and college students (Cattell & Scheier, 1961).

Xin, Chen, Tang, Lin, and McConville (1992) followed 3,000 consecutive births at a maternity center in Shanghai and studied the children at ages 4 to 5 using Chinese versions of the Achenbach Child Behavior Check List, the Denver Developmental Screening Test (Revised), a semistructured mental status examination, and a measure of intelligence. Unfortunately, fatal arithmetic errors in the data analysis make interpretation of their results difficult. It appears, however, that the Shanghai sample had total problem scores comparable to French-Canadian and Chilean but higher than Dutch and American samples. Somatic problems and social withdrawal were common among girls while aggressive and delinquent behaviors were prevalent in boys. Only 4 of the 3,000 children displayed severe developmental delays. Parental health and family relationship problems were common in somatizing children, whereas aggression and delinquency were associated with risk factors such as poor parental health, living in nuclear families, delivery complications, father's level of education, family income, and marital problems. Girls displayed predominantly internalizing symptoms, while boys exhibited a preponderance of externalizing symptoms. In a 4-year follow-up of a subgroup of the Shanghai sample, children with problems showed little improvement and were likely to have developed superimposed hyperactivity.

PSYCHOPATHOLOGY: CHINA

The Shanghai study (Xin et al., 1992) is one of several conducted in mainland China and Taiwan. Another group of Chinese investigators (Tseng et al., 1988) used an adaptation of the Child Behavior Check List as part of a home-visit survey of child development and behavior in 3- to 6-year-olds from Nanjing and the surrounding countryside. The sample of 697 children, drawn disproportionately from rural settings, was not representative of China as a whole. Mean parental ages were 34 years for fathers and 32 years for mothers; fewer than 1% of couples were divorced or separated. Ninety-nine percent of the children were raised in infancy by either their parent or grandparents, and 68% had no siblings. Only 1 child in the survey had his own bedroom, and 89% shared a bed with their parents. Factor analysis of CBCL items for boys and girls separately yielded factors that differed considerably from those derived from Achenbach's American sample. This is difficult to interpret, however, since the authors included 3- and 4-year-olds in the same analysis, failed to specify the parameters of analysis, and employed a sample size that was inadequate for the multivariate analyses. On each of the derived factors, boys raised as only children were indistinguishable from those with sibs, whereas girls without siblings tended to be more depressed and moody. Boys cared for primarily by their grandparents had slightly more conduct problems than those raised principally by their parents. Rural "only" girls had more "temper" problems than their urban counterparts, a difference the authors attribute to parental favoritism toward rural boys, who are valued for their capacity to participate in farm labor.

Using both parent- and teacher-rated Chinese adaptations of the Children's Behavior Questionnaire (Rutter, 1967), Ekblad (1990) studied 248 sixth graders in a primary school connected to the Chinese Academy of Sciences in Beijing. Correlations between teacher and parent ratings were low, the parents generally reporting more symptoms than teachers. According to the mothers, 55.5% of boys and 60.8% of girls had psychosomatic symptoms, while 50.0% of boys and 56.7% of girls had tantrums. The Chinese children generally had higher frequencies of behavioral symptoms than children in comparable studies from other developed and developing nations. Using Rutter's cut-off score of 13 (Rutter, Tizard, & Whitmore, 1970), 22% of boys and 13% of girls were rated deviant by their mothers. In contrast, teacher ratings showed low rates of deviance, compared both to the parent ratings in this study and to teacher ratings in other populations. In both teacher and mother ratings of boys, hyperactivity and aggression were prominent and were associated with low academic achievement.

In another Chinese study (Luo, 1992) of 1,428 children under age 14 from Fuzhou, 7% were found to have "abnormal" mental health. These children tended to come from less educated families, and "the emotion between their parents is always not so harmonious."

Using the Conners' Teacher's Rating Scale, Wang, Chong, Chou, and Yang (1993) studied the prevalence of attention deficit hyperactivity disorder among 4,290 randomly selected Taiwanese primary school children. Optimal cut-off points for the scale were determined in a subsample diagnosed by child psychiatrists using criteria from the third revised edition of the *Diagnostic and Statistical Manual of Mental Disorders*. In the larger sample, 9.9% of children were identified as having attention deficit hyperactivity disorder on the Conners' questionnaire, the boys outnumbering girls by a ratio of approximately 3:1.

PSYCHOPATHOLOGY: JAPAN

Japanese studies benefit from the ethnic homogeneity of the population and the uniformity of educational practices throughout the island nation. Suzuki, Suzuki, and Morita (1990) described an epidemiological investigation of psychiatric diagnosis in 592 Japanese students, ages 10 to 15, from elementary and junior high school. Rutter's teacher and parent questionnaires were employed after the instruments had been validated against diagnoses made by pediatricians. The overall rate of psychiatric disorder, excluding a single case of mental retardation, was estimated to be 17%. In another sample of 1992 children from five junior high schools (Morita et al., 1993; Suzuki, Morita, & Kamoshita, 1990), the estimated prevalence of psychiatric disorder was 14.8%. Among these children, 20.1% of boys and 8.3% of girls merited diagnosis (ratio of 2.4 : 1). The ratio of emotional disorder to conduct disorders was 1.9 : 1, but conduct disorders were much more likely to be diagnosed among boys. Apart from teacher interventions, only one child judged to have psychiatric disorder had received professional help.

Since Japanese business relationships customarily involve frequent and heavy use of alcohol, substance abuse among Japanese children is of particular interest (Suzuki et al., 1991). A survey of 12,892 Japanese adolescents revealed high rates of alcohol and tobacco use (Kawabata et al., 1991). Among male students in the third year of senior high school, for example, 37% smoked and 59% used alcohol on at least a monthly basis. In another survey, 1,062 high school students demonstrated even higher rates of alcohol use: 21.4% were abstainers, 60.9% nonproblem drinkers, 12.6% "misusers," and 0.9% "alcoholiclike drinkers." Use of tobacco and organic solvents increased the risk of alcohol use. These rates are much higher than those obtained in a similar survey 10 years earlier.

School refusal which occurs in about 0.5% of Japanese junior high school students (Kobayashi, 1993), is among the most salient psychiatric complaints. This syndrome, which is distinct from both truancy and separation anxiety disorder, affects primarily adolescents (Inomata, Yamazaki, Mizoguchi, & Watanabe, 1991; Okazaki, Onoda, Inagaki, & Kodaki, 1980). Academic stress is especially severe in high school, as reflected in the General Health Questionnaire (Nagata, Okubu, Moji, & Takemoto, 1993), since the acquisition of skills needed for college entrance examinations ultimately determines the student's career, social status, and economic success. Treatment of school refusal is rarely successful, since the affected children generally perceive it as a solution rather than as a problem. Affluent families can purchase correspondence courses or send students to high school abroad, where academic pressures are milder.

Historically, Japanese girls have been at high risk for suicide (Iga, Yamamoto, & Noguchi, 1975), although the rate of youth suicide in Japan declined during the 1980s. More recently, weight and dieting concerns, comparable to those reported in Western populations, have been documented in Japanese adolescent females (Mukai, Crago, & Shisslak, 1994; Suematsu, 1985). Changing social patterns in postwar Japan also have seen increasing rates of delinquency involving shoplifting, glue sniffing, and automobile and bicycle theft. Innovative treatments, including family residential treatment, have been employed in efforts to manage this population (Inomata, Yamazaki, Tsuji, Kobayashi, & Sakuta, 1990).

PSYCHOPATHOLOGY: KOREA, MALAYSIA, AND THE PHILIPPINES

Suicidal behavior in adolescents is increasingly important in Korea. Juon, Nam, and Ensminger (1994) administered a detailed questionnaire to 9,886 8th and 11th graders from a randomly selected sample of junior and high school students living in Seoul and other urban and rural areas of Korea. Suicide attempts were reported in 4.4% of subjects, and serious suicidal ideation was reported in 7.2%. Suicidal ideation was more common among girls and 11th graders than in boys and 8th graders. Suicide attempts, however, were most frequent among 11th-grade males, with a reported rate of 5.1%. The authors speculate that this finding is related to academic pressure on males who are anticipating college entrance examinations. Correlates of suicidal behavior included academic stress, depression, hostility, and alcohol use. Such variables as family background and social integration were not strongly associated with suicidality. The link among suicide, depression, and substance use replicates findings from the West, but the importance of academic stress as a risk factor may be more critical in Asian groups.

Using the 10-item Research Questionnaire for Children, Kasmini, Kyaw, Krishnaswamy, Ramli, and Hassan (1993) looked for evidence of psychopathology among 507 children living in a rural village on the western coast of Malaysia. Children who were symptomatic on the questionnaire were then interviewed in a semistructured format by a psychiatrist. Thirty-one children, representing 6.1% of the village population ages 1 to 15, were identified as having modified mental disorders diagnosed according to the ninth edition of the *International Classification of Diseases* (*ICD*-9). Neurotic and emotional disorders were diagnosed in 1.8% of the population; 2.3% were mentally retarded, and 1.4% had such symptoms as enuresis, stuttering, and sleep disturbance. Conduct disorder, hyperkinetic disorder, and personality disorder were each diagnosed in only one child. Excluding cases of mental subnormality and children under 3 years old, the prevalence of *ICD*-9 diagnoses was 5.4%.

On the same questionnaire administered in a primary care setting in the Philippines, at least one symptom was present in 36% of the children studied (Giel et al., 1981). Despite a high rate of behavioral problems, mental health treatment in the Philippines is reserved for severely handicapped children. In one large survey of clinic populations (Layug, 1989), for example, all children under age 5 receiving mental health services had organic brain syndromes. Political detention of fathers has affected many Filipino children, although no formal diagnostic study of this group has been conducted.

On the Pacific Islands, mental health services, sponsored by the World Health Organization, emphasize community treatment. We are not aware of any psychiatric epidemiologic studies among Pacific Islander children.

Although the several studies of psychiatric disorder in Asian children vary in quality and in comparability to Western studies, they persuasively document the occurrence of mental disorder in a substantial fraction of children from every population studied. The relatively greater externalizing psychopathology in boys and internalizing psychopathology in girls match findings from other cultural groups; in short, no systematic differences from studies in Western populations clearly emerge. Owing to methodological weaknesses in many of the studies, however, the validity of these comparisons, is at best, uncertain.

Asians in the United States

The Asian groups of greatest interest to English-speaking peoples are those that have migrated in large numbers to the West. In 1990, the population of foreign- and U.S.-born persons of Asian ancestry numbered as follows: Chinese, 1.6 million; Filipino, 1.4 million; Japanese, Asian Indian, and Korean, each about 0.8 million; Vietnamese, 0.6 million; Cambodian, 0.4 million; Hawaiian 0.2 million; and Lao, 0.15 million. Groups representing between 50,000 and 90,000 persons include the Thai, Hmong, Samoan, and Guamanian.

The first wave of Asian immigrants were Chinese attracted by gold in California and by employment in the rapidly developing American West of the mid-19th century. Because these early settlers were forbidden to bring wives, only a few fifth- and sixth-generation descendants of these settlers live in the United States today. The 1882 Exclusion Act ended Chinese immigration until the end of World War II, when limited quotas for Chinese were established. The 1965 Immigration Act, which ended racial quotas, resulted in a third wave of Chinese immigrants.

Coinciding with exclusion of the Chinese, Japanese settlers first came to the United States in the 1880s, having been actively recruited for work on Hawaiian sugar plantations and mainland farms. This migration ended with the Immigration Act of 1924. Unlike their Chinese counterparts, the Japanese men were permitted to have wives, resulting in the emergence of Japanese American generational cohorts known as the *issei* (first generation, born in Japan), *nissei* (second generation), *sansei* (third generation), and *yonsei* (fourth generation). By virtue of these multigenerational families and frequent intermarriage with Caucasians, the Japanese are perhaps the best assimilated group of Asian Americans. Thousands of Japanese women came to the United States after World War II as war brides, producing a large group of biracial Japanese Americans. Whereas the Isseis concentrated in the Japanese ghettos on the West Coast—"Japan town" in San Francisco and "Little Tokyo" in Los Angeles—the war brides melted into the communities all over the United States with little help and support from peers.

Filipino immigration began early in this century but was curtailed in the 1930s by a quota permitting only 50 Filipino immigrants annually. The American colonial and military presence in the Philippines, promoting widespread knowledge of the English language and familiarity with American culture, made the United States an attractive haven for oppressed Filipinos after 1965, when immigration restrictions were eased. Koreans, like the Filipinos, had a brief wave of migration early in the century, but most contemporary Korean Americans came to the United States after 1965.

Migration of Southeast Asians—Vietnamese, Cambodian, and Laotian—followed the debacle of the Vietnam war. This group, the newest and perhaps least assimilated cohort of Asian Americans, presents special mental health issues arising both from the circumstances of their departure from Indochina and from their relative unfamiliarity with American culture.

Pacific/Asian American Children: Psychopathology and Adaptation

To the best of our knowledge, no large-scale epidemiological studies of psychopathology in Asian American children have been conducted to date. A well-designed British epidemiologic study (Newth & Corbett, 1993) of 3-year-old Anglo-Asians of Indian and Pakistani descent found that, compared with Caucasian controls from the same birth cohort and born in the same hospital, Asian children had fewer sleep difficulties and were less difficult to control. The available U.S. data, by contrast, come largely from clinic populations; since Asians are known to seek mental health care less readily than Caucasians, such data are probably not comparable to non-Asian clinical populations. Furthermore, the Asian American population represents a composite of racial and ethnic groups at various stages of assimilation to the host culture, each of which displays unique problems and coping styles. A study of first- second-, and third-generation Japanese Americans, for example, showed the anticipated increasing acculturation of subjects from one generation to the next (Masuuda, Matsumoto, & Meredith, 1970). Although formal studies comparing mental disorder across generations are unavailable, we would expect a similar intergenerational contrast in forms and rates of psychopathology.

Asian Americans are usually perceived as having fewer emotional problems than their non-Asian peers. Whether this reflects cultural stereotyping of the "model minority" (see, e.g., Uba, 1994, pp. 158–195) or an extraordinary resilience in the face of uncommon stress (Sung, 1987) cannot be resolved on the basis of existing data. There is little doubt, however, that with respect to educational success, an important index of adaptation in children, Asian children, both in America and abroad (Lee, Ichikawa, & Stevenson, 1987) have performed dramatically better than their Caucasian and African American counterparts. At the same time, Asian Americans exhibit less disruptive and antisocial behavior but more anxiety and depression than their Euro-American counterparts (Lorenzo & Adler, 1984).

Ethnic differences in psychiatric diagnosis among subgroups of Asian American adolescents were studied retrospectively using records of 529 males and 425 females evaluated at clinics affiliated with the Los Angeles County department of Mental Health. Compared to Caucasians, Asians were more likely to receive nonpsychiatric diagnoses, although Asian females were more likely to be diagnosed as depressed than Caucasian females. Chinese and Japanese Americans differed from Korean and Vietnamese Americans in their patterns of psychiatric morbidity. Generalizability of the findings is impossible, however, since 75% of the population received public assistance, making the subjects unrepresentative of the Pacific/Asian American population as a whole.

McKelvey, Mao, and Webb (1992, 1993; McKelvey, Webb, & Mao, 1993) showed that Amerasian Vietnamese youth with multiple background risk factors, such as a history of missing school and frequent hospitalizations, were more likely to display psychiatric symptoms, especially depression, after removal from Vietnam to a Philippine refugee center. Children raised continuously by their biological mothers had better outcomes than those reared by multiple surrogates (McKelvey & Webb, 1993). Among refugee Cambodian adolescents who have experienced war traumata and resettlement difficulties, high rates of posttraumatic stress disorder and low rates of antisocial behavior are well documented (Clarke, Sack & Goff, 1993; Sack, Clarke, & Seeley, 1996). Sack, McSharry, and Dickason discuss this population in detail in Chapter 58.

Although little research is available on psychopathology in the heterogeneous and rapidly changing population of Pacific/Asian American children, there are sufficient data to document major problems requiring further research and clinical attention.

Special Considerations for the Practitioner in America

Accurate assessment and sensitive treatment are impossible without a respectful appreciation of the ethnic values and cultural norms that inform approaches to child rearing:

Social workers burst into their homes and upset the usual routine of their lives, opening windows, undressing children, giving orders not to eat this and that, not to wrap babies in swaddling clothes. . . . The mother of five or six children may, with some reason, be inclined to think that she knows a little more about how to bring up children than the young-looking damsel who insists upon teaching her how to do it. (Sartorio, 1918, quoted in Seller, 1981)

Hsu, Tseng, Ashton, McDermott, and Char (1985) report a study involving 12 Japanese American and 12 Caucasian American families, selected for their apparent *normalcy*. The two groups were compared on measures of family and marital functioning derived from Western family theory. It turned out that well-trained but ethnically diverse raters of family function were unreliable, casting doubt on the measures used. The Japanese American families exhibited inferior functioning (i.e., scores closer to the pathological range) on virtually all measures, thus demonstrating the cultural limits of the family assessment instruments and their underlying theories of normative family function.

In a study by Matsushima and Tashima (1982), Asian American therapists ranked the importance of cultural values and ethnic issues in psychotherapeutic practice. Among the most important considerations mentioned by these clinicians were: family problems; shame and guilt; status and role considerations; immigration experiences; and cultural conflicts in values and lifestyle. According to Uba (1994), the therapist needs to explain aspects of psychotherapy that may conflict with cultural expectations. She observes that Asian Americans (and by extension, the parents of Asian American children) anticipate treatment that involves, first, rapid diagnosis without intrusive questioning; second, brief interventions with rapid symptom relief; and third, attention to the stated complaint rather than to "underlying" problems. Solutions based on willpower and self-discipline are more likely to resonate positively with Asian families than are abstract psychodynamic hypotheses, while imperatives of family integrity and honor may contraindicate a direct focus on family pathology. Asian parents are more apt to accept concrete and practical advice from a relatively active and senior therapist.

The second author's experiences are illustrative of the problems that even a culturally sensitive therapist may encounter in treating Asian Americans. During her internship, for example, she discovered that her Japanese patient had feigned a hypnotic trance in order to spare the young trainee the indignity of technical failure. Another Japanese patient, by way of expressing gratitude and trust, attempted to arrange a marriage between her nephew and the author.

Mental health treatments generally last longer with therapists who are ethnincally and linguistically matched with their patients (Sue, Fujino, Hu, Takeuchi, & Zane, 1991). Therapy may end prematurely if the therapist greets the wrong person first, thereby insulting the family patriarch. If the therapist is boisterous in manner or given to loud speech, a Vietnamese patient may regard her as disrespectful. On the other hand, if her style is not friendly and ingratiating, she may have difficulty forming an alliance with a garrulous Filipino patient. If she talks too little, she may be regarded as incompetent; but if she talks too much, her patient may, out of respect, remain silent and disclose nothing. Translations, even when correct, may be imperfect in capturing meaning. Thus, a Japanese patient saying "yes," the usual translation of the word "hai," may intend to convey "I hear what you're saying but I don't necessarily agree." The inexperienced therapist may overpathologize an Asian patient who smiles "inappropriately" (by American standards) while discussing disturbing issues; or may misinterpret culturally acceptable behavior, such as the tardy arrival of a Southeast Asian family, as resistance. Some foibles can only be avoided by a therapist prepared with a specific knowledge of folk beliefs. What Western therapist would anticipate, for example, that publicly complimenting a Mien child would seem like a hostile act intended to invoke evil spirits?

The therapist who reports an international business executive to child protective services for bathing nude with his 8-year-old daughter belies his ignorance that such behavior is common and acceptable in Japan. Similarly, Chinese parents may be mistakenly accused of physical abuse for applying traditional medical remedies that entail bruising, such as pinching the throat or rubbing the child's body with the back of a spoon.

On the other hand, the therapist willing to attribute any manner of strange behavior to cultural diversity, or any sign of psychopathology to racism, will fail to address real problems adequately. We had occasion to interview a Japanese child living in the United States who had been diagnosed and treated for attention deficit hyperactivity disorder. The child's poor English after three years in the United States was attributed to his Japanese origin; in fact, a careful history revealed significant delay in acquisition of his native tongue indicative of a language disability and possible pervasive development disorder.

Similar problems may develop just as easily for the Asian therapist treating a Western patient. For instance, a psychiatric resident of our acquaintance, a practitioner of the Hindu faith who had recently emigrated from India, announced that his new patient would require hospitalization and neuroleptic medication. The patient was obviously delusional, for she had averred that, after death, she would rise to heaven and meet her God.

Cultural sensitivity is thus more than a benevolent state of mind; it is a skill that requires knowledge and experience along with goodwill.

Treatments deeply rooted in Western culture, such as psychodynamic psychotherapy and structural family therapy, may be inappropriate or impossible to implement effectively with Asian families. In the Eastern tradition, responsibility for the welfare and behavior of young children falls almost exclusively to the parents and extended family. Teachers and spiritual masters, who also may function as healers, play increasing roles as the child matures; but nowhere in this scheme is there an obvious place for the psychotherapist of Western medicine.

Indigenous Eastern therapies, in contrast to the secular therapies of the West, are apt to be explicitly spiritual, deriving from Buddhist and Taoist principles. Sitting meditation (*zazen*), for example, shares with psychodynamic therapies the goal of profound insight; and it bears at least a superficial technical resemblance to the Western techniques of hypnosis, relaxation, and autogenic training. In Japan, Morita therapy blends Western psychiatric concepts of mental hygiene and psychotherapy with the unmistakably Buddhist goal of "accepting things as they are" (*aru ga mama ni*). Patients are exhorted to concentrate on immediate, concrete experience, including manual work, and to abandon self-preoccupation and verbal conjecture. Such treatments, although rarely applied to children, suggest how Western techniques might be adapted for use with Asian populations.

Thus, Western psychotherapies that employ an active therapist, offer prescriptive advice, and endorse techniques of persuasion have more in common with traditional Asian approaches than do psychodynamically based treatments. From the broad palette of techniques relied on by Western therapists, behavioral and cognitive-behavioral therapies, which are typically brief, focused, and structured, and which include explicit guidance for patient participation, are the approaches most likely to be effectively utilized by Asian families.

Biological treatments, on the other hand, may be received more favorably than talking cures, owing to the long tradition of Chinese medicine, practiced widely throughout the East. Based on the functional anatomy of the life force, *chi,* traditional Chinese medicine is "holistic," eschewing the mind-body dualism of Western medicine. Herbal treatments seek to manipulate and modify *chi* through the use of agents that alter *yin* (feminine) and *yang* (masculine) energies in target organs. Since the mind and body are viewed as a single, integrated entity, little distinction is drawn between problems described in the West in the separate categories of psychiatric and somatic. Herbal preparations, breathing routines (*qigong*), meditation, physical exercise (e.g., *t'ai chi chuan* and *kung fu*), traditional dietary practices, and acupuncture all address spiritual, mental, and physical aspects of health at once. Within China, traditional and Western medical practices often are employed together, without conflict, sometimes by practitioners trained in both models. Fortunately, most Chinese are familiar with modern medical practices, although some may entertain notions of health and behavior that are quite alien to Western health care professionals.

Several studies have documented that Asian adults are more sensitive than Caucasians to the effect of some psychotropic drugs (Okuma, 1981) and may display more side effects, such as extrapyramidal symptoms (Binder & Levy, 1981), for similar surface area–adjusted doses. These observations have been attributed both to pharmacokinetic differences reflected in higher blood levels for equivalent drug doses (Potkin et al., 1984) and to pharmacodynamic differences (Lin et al., 1989). At similar blood levels of haloperidol, for example, Asians demonstrate a more robust prolactin response than do Caucasians. As in Caucasian populations, Asian adults exhibit huge interindividual variations in their metabolism of tricyclic antidepressants (Shimoda, Minowada, Noguchi, & Takahashi, 1993) and neuroleptics (Someya et al., 1990). Comparable studies in children, unfortunately, are unavailable. There also may be racial differences in delayed drug effects, such as tardive dyskinesia. Asian patients receiving chronic neuroleptic treatment generally have exhibited relatively low rates of tardive dyskinesia (e.g., Chiu, Shum, Lau, Lam, & Lee, 1992). but some studies have shown the opposite (Koshino et al., 1992). Given the extreme paucity of pediatric data, an initial conservative approach to medication of Asian children is prudent.

Summary and Future Directions

Pacific/Asian Americans comprise an important and growing population sector in the United States but represent very heterogeneous cultural and linguistic groups. Cross-national comparisons have tended to show more similarity in psychopathological profiles than have cross-ethnic comparisons within the United States, a contrast that may result from methodologic difficulties. Psychiatric problems in Asian American children have multiple roots, related to native culture, to the stresses compelling migration, to the stress of immigration and acculturation per se, to racism within the host country, and possibly to biological differences in temperament and treatment response. The study of psychiatric problems in Asian pediatric populations has just begun, but the rate of cultural change in diverse groups entering a global society is so rapid that even an aggressive research program cannot keep pace with the questions deserving attention. The research agenda therefore must be selective and thoughtful. In our view, the most pressing needs now are threefold. First, methodologies are needed that provide valid cross-national and cross-cultural comparisons in rates and quality of descriptive psychopathology in children. Second, treatments appropriate for various cultural groups need to be developed, and the cultural biases underlying current conceptions of psychotherapy need to be reexamined. Third, biological factors affecting differential psychopathology and treatment response among cultural and racial groups should be studied. The safe and effective extension to Asian populations of rapidly developing biological treatments in child psychiatry depends on expanded research in ethnopharmacology. Given the multiplicity and complexity of cultural, ethnic, and linguistic factors that contribute to psychopathology and its treatment, the training of a cadre of child psychiatrists and therapists specializing in transcultural mental health may be needed in order to address the neglected mental health problems in the Pacific/Asian American pediatric population.

REFERENCES

Azuma, H., Kashiwagi, K., & Hess, R. D. (1981). Hahaoya no Taido Koudo to Kodomo no Chiteki Hattatsu [The effect of mother's attitude and behavior on the cognitive development of the child: A U.S.-Japanese comparison]. Tokyo: Tokyo University Press.

Binder, R. L., & Levy, R. (1981). Extrapyramidal reactions in Asians. *American Journal of Psychiatry, 138,* 1243–1244.

Bornstein, M. H., Tamis-LeMonda, C. S., Tal, J., Ludemann, P., Toda, S., Rahn, C. W., Pecheux, M. G., Azuma, H., & Vardi, D. (1992). Maternal responsiveness to infants in three societies: The United States, France, and Japan. *Child Development, 63,* 808–821.

Cattell, R. B., & Scheier, I. H. (1961). *The Meaning and Measurement of Neuroticism and Anxiety.* New York: Ronald Press, 1961.

Chiu, H., Shum, P., Lau, J., Lam, L., & Lee, S. (1992). Prevalence of tardive dyskinesia, tardive dystonia, and respiratory dyskinesia among Chinese psychiatric patients in Hong Kong. *American Journal of Psychiatry,* 149, 1081–1085.

Clarke, G., Sack, W. H., & Goff, B. (1993). Three forms of stress in Cambodian adolescent refugees. *Journal of Abnormal Child Psychology, 21,* 65–77.

Confucius. (1979). *The Analects.* Trans. D. C. Lau. London: Penguin Books.

Dogen, Z. (1975). *Shooboogenzoo [The eye and treasury of the true law].* Trans. K. Nishiyama. Tokyo: Nakayama Shoboo Japan Publications.

Ekblad, S. (1990). The children's behaviour questionnaire for completion by parents and teachers in a Chinese sample. *Journal of Child Psychology and Psychiatry, 31,* 775–791.

Falbo, T., & Poston, D. J. (1993). The academic, personality, and physical outcomes of only children in China. *Child Developments, 64,* 18–35.

Fernald, A., & Morikawa, H. (1993). Common themes and cultural variations in Japanese and American mothers' speech to infants. *Child Development, 64,* 637–656.

Giel, R., d'Arrigo Busnello, E, Climent, C. E., Elhakim, A. S., Ibrahim, H. H., Ladrido Ignacio, L., & Wig, N. N. (1981). The classification of psychiatric disorder. A reliability study in the WHO collaborative study on strategies for extending mental health care. *Acta Psychiatrica Scandinavica, 63,* 61–74.

Hsu, J., Tseng, W. S., Ashton, G., McDermott, J. F., & Char, W. (1985). Family interaction patterns among Japanese-American and Caucasian families in Hawaii. *American Journal of Psychiatry, 142,* 577–581.

Iga, M., Yamamoto, J., & Noguchi, T. (1975). Vulnerability of young Japanese women and suicide. *Suicide, 5,* 207–222.

Inomata, J., Yamazaki, K., Mizoguchi, K., & Watanabe, R. (1991). Consultation-liaison psychiatric approach for school-refusal students in Hiratsuka City, Kanagawa Japan. *Tokai Journal of Experimental Clinical Medicine, 16,* 89–95.

Inomata, J., Yamazaki, K., Tsuji, R., Kobayashi, M., & Sakuta, T. (1990). Family therapy for juvenile delinquents in a reformatory, K-1 Institute. *Keio Journal of Medicine, 39,* 91–96.

Isralowitz, R. E., & Hong, O. T. (1990). Singapore youth: The impact of social status on perceptions of adolescent problems. *Adolescence, 25,* 357–362.

Iwawaki, S., Sumida, K., Okuno, S., & Cowen, E. L. (1967). Manifest anxiety in Japanese, French, and United States children. *Child Development, 38,* 713–722.

Juon, H. S., Nam, J. J., & Ensminger, M. E. (1994). Epidemiology of suicidal behavior among Korean adolescents. *Journal of Child Psychology and Psychiatry, 35,* 663–676.

Kasmini, K., Kyaw, O., Krishnaswamy, S., Ramli, H., & Hassan, S. (1993). A prevalence survey of mental disorders among children in a rural Malaysian village. *Acta Psychiatrica Scandinavica, 87* (4), 253–257.

Kawabata, T., Minagawa, K., Nishioka, N., Nakamura, M., Mochizuki, Y., Takahashi, H., Ichimura, K., Okajima, Y., Iwai, K., Nozu, Y., et al. (1991). Standardization of definitions concerning smoking behavior among Japanese adolescents—results from the Japan Adolescent Smoking Survey (JASS). *Nippon Koshu Eisei Zasshi, 38,* 859–867.

Kim, L. S., & Chun, C. A. (1993). Ethnic differences in psychiatric diagnosis among Asian American adolescents. *Journal of Nervous and Mental Disease, 181,* 612–617.

Kobayashi, R. (1993). Characteristics of those who refuse to attend school in Fukuoka City: An analysis based on teachers' reports. *Japanese Journal of Psychiatry and Neurology, 47,* 545–553.

Koshino, Y., Madokoro, S., Ito, T., Horie, T., Mukai, M., & Isaki, K. (1992, February). A survey of tardive dyskinesia in psychiatric inpatients in Japan. *Clinical Neuropharmacology, 15,* 34–43.

Lao Tzu. (1990). *Tao Teh Ching.* Trans. J. C. H. Wu. Boston: Shambhala.

Layug, M. E. (1989). Behavior disorders among Filipino children. *Philippine Journal of Psychology, 22,* 37–45.

Lee, J. F. J. (1992). *Asian Americans.* New York: The New Press.

Lee, S., Ichikawa, V., & Stevenson, H. W. (1987). Beliefs and achievement in mathematics and reading: A cross-national study of Chinese, Japanese, and American children and their mothers. *Advances in Motivation and Achievement: Enhancing Motivation, 5,* 149–179.

Lewis, M., Ramsay, D. S., & Kawakami, K. (1993). Differences between Japanese infants and Caucasian American infants in behavioral and cortisol response to inoculation. *Child Development, 64,* 1722–1731.

Lin, K., Poland, R., Nuccio, I., Matsuda, K., Hathuc, N., Su, T., & Fu, P. (1989). A longitudinal assessment of haloperidol doses and serum concentrations in Asian and Caucasian schizophrenic patients. *American Journal of Psychiatry, 146,* 1307–1311.

Lorenzo, M. K., & Adler, D. A. (1984). Mental health services for Chinese in a community health center. *Social Casework, 65,* 600–609.

Luo, W. (1992). [Epidemiological study of children's mental health in Fuzhou]. *Chung Hua Shen Ching Ching Shen Ko Tsa Chih, 25,* 175–178.

Mann, E. M., Ikeda, Y., Mueller, C. W., Takahashi, A., Tao, K. T., Humris, E., Li, B. L., & Chin, D. (1992). Cross-cultural differences in rating hyperactive-disruptive behaviors in children. *American Journal of Psychiatry, 149,* 1539–1542.

Masuuda, M., Matsumoto, G. H., & Meredith, G. M. (1970). Ethnic identity in three generations of Japanese Americans. *Journal of Social Psychology, 81,* 199–207.

Matsushima, N. M., & Tashima, N. (1982). *Mental health treatment modalities of Pacific/Asian American practitioners.* San Francisco: Pacific Asian Mental Health Research Project.

Matsuura, M., Okubo, Y., Kato, M., & Kojima, T. (1989). An epidemiological investigation of emotional and behavioral problems in primary school children in Japan: The report of the first phase of a WHO collaborative study in Western Pacific Region. *Social Psychiatry and Psychiatric Epidemiology, 24,* 17–22.

Matsuura, M., Okubo, Y., Kojima, T., Takahashi, R., Wang, Y. F., Shen, Y. C., & Lee, C. K. (1993). A cross-national prevalence study of children with emotional and behavioural problems—a WHO collaborative study in the Western Pacific Region. *Journal of Child Psychology and Psychiatry, 34,* 307–315.

McKelvey, R. S., Mao, A. R., & Webb, J. A. (1992). A risk profile predicting psychological distress in Vietnamese Amerasian youth. *Journal of the American Academy of Child and Adolescent Psychiatry, 31,* 911–915.

McKelvey, R. S. Mao, A. R., & Webb, J. A. (1993). Premigratory expectations and mental health symptomatology in a group of Vietnamese Amerasian youth. *Journal of the American Academy of Child and Adolescent Psychiatry, 32,* 414–418.

McKelvey, R. S., & Webb, J. A. (1993). Long-term effects of maternal loss on Vietnamese Amerasians. *Journal of the American Academy of Child and Adolescent Psychiatry, 32,* 1013–1018.

McKelvey, R. S., Webb, J. A., & Mao, A. R. (1993, March). Premigratory risk factors in Vietnamese Amerasians. *American Journal of Psychiatry, 150,* 470–473.

Morita, H., Suzuki, M., & Kamoshita, S. (1990). Screening measures for detecting psychiatric disorders in Japanese secondary school children. *Journal of Child Psychology and Psychiatry, 31,* 603–617.

Morita, H., Suzuki, M., Suzuki, S., & Kamoshita, S. (1993). Psychiatric disorders in Japanese secondary school children. *Journal of Child Psychology and Psychiatry, 34,* 317–332.

Mukai, T., Crago, M., & Shisslak, C. M. (1994). Eating attitudes and weight preoccupation among female high school students in Japan. *Journal of Child Psychology and Psychiatry, 35,* 677–688.

Nagata, K., Okubo, H., Moji, K., & Takemoto, T. (1993). Difference of the 28-item general health questionnaire scores between Japanese high school and university students. *Japanese Journal of Psychiatry and Neurology, 47,* 575–583.

Newth, S. J., & Corbett, J. (1993). Behavioral and emotional problems in three-year-old children of Asian parentage. *Journal of Child Psychology and Psychiatry, 14,* 333–352.

Ohmura, M., & Sawa, H. (1957). Taylor's anxiety scale in Japan. *Psychologia, 1,* 123–126.

Okazaki, T., Onoda, K., Inagaki, T., & Kodaki, N. (1980). [An epidemiological approach to school refusal in Shimane prefecture.] *Japanese Journal of Child & Adolescent Psychiatry, 21,* 333–342.

Okuma, T. (1981). Differential sensitivity to the effects of psychotropic drugs: psychotics vs. normals; Asians vs. Western populations. *Folia Psychiatrica Neurol Jpn, 35,* 79–81.

Potkin, S. G., Shen, Y., Pardes, H., Phelps, B. H., Zhou, D., Shu, L., Korpi, E., & Wyatt, R. J. (1984). Haloperidol concentrations elevated in Chinese patients. *Psychiatry Research, 12,* 167–172.

Reyes, M. R., Valdecanas, C. M., Reyes, O. L., & Reyes, T. M. (1990). The effects of malnutrition on the motor, perceptual, and cognitive functions of Filipino children. *International Disabilities Studies, 12,* 131–136.

Rue, D. S. (1993). Depression and suicidal behavior among Asian whiz kids. In, H. Kwon & S. Kim (Eds.), *The emerging generation of Korean-Americans* (pp. 91–106). Seoul, Korea: Kyung Hee University Press.

Rutter, M. (1967). A children's behaviour questionnaire for completion by teachers: preliminary findings. *Journal of Child Psychology and Psychiatry, 8,* 1–11.

Rutter, M., Tizard, J., & Whitmore, K. (1970). *Education, health, and behaviour.* London: Longman.

Sack, W. H., Clarke, G. N., & Seeley, J. (1996). Multiple forms of stress in Cambodian adolescent refugees. *Child Development, 67,* 107–116.

Sartorio, E. (1918). *Social and religious life of Italians in America.* Boston: Christopher Publishing Company.

Seller, M. S. (1981). *Immigrant women.* Philadelphia: Temple University Press.

Shimoda, K., Minowada, T., Noguchi, T., & Takahashi, S. (1993). Interindividual variations of desmethylation and hydroxylation of clomipramine in an Oriental psychiatric population. *Journal of Clinical Psychopharmacology, 13,* 181–188.

Sittitrai, W., Joladsakul, P., Norral, C., & Brown, T. (1992). Commercial sexual culture: The next generation. *International Conference on AIDS, 8,* D498 (abstract no. PoD 5657).

Someya, T., Takahashi, S., Shibasaki, M., Inaba, T., Cheung, S. W., & Tang, S. W. (1990). Reduced haloperidol/haloperidol ratios in plasma: Polymorphism in Japanese psychiatric patients. *Psychiatry Research, 31,* 111–120.

Stevenson, H. W., Lee, S. Y., & Stigler, J. W. (1986). Mathematics achievement of Japanese, Chinese, and American children. *Science, 231,* 693–699.

Sue, S., Fujino, D., Hu, L., Takeuchi, D., & Zane, N. (1991). Community mental health services for ethnic minority groups: A test of the cultural responsiveness hypothesis. *Journal of Consulting and Clinical Psychology, 59,* 533–540.

Suematsu, H. (1985). Seito ni okeru sessyoku syougai [Eating disorders among students]. *Seishin Igaku to sono Kinsetsu Ryouiki, 26,* 92–97.

Sung, B. L. (1987). *The adjustment experience of Chinese immigrant children in New York City.* New York: Center for Migration Studies.

Suzuki, K., Matsushita, S., Muramatsu, T., Muraoka, H., Yamada, K., Shigemori, K., Takagi, S., & Kono,

599

H. (1991). [Problem drinkers among high school students in Japan]. *Arukoru Kenkyuto Yakubutsu Ison, 26*, 142–152.

Suzuki, M., Morita, H., & Kamoshita, S. (1990). [Epidemiological survey of psychiatric disorders in Japanese school children. Part III: Prevalence of psychiatric disorders in junior high school children]. *Nippon Koshu Eisei Zasshi, 37*, 991–1000.

Suzuki, M., Suzuki, S., & Morita, H. (1990). [Epidemiological survey of psychiatric disorders of Japanese school children]. *Nippon Koshu Eisei Zasshi, 37*, 146–152.

Takeuchi, M., & Kitamura, T. (1991). The factor structure of the General Health Questionnaire in a Japanese high school and university student sample. *International Journal of Social Psychiatry, 37*, 99–106.

Toda, S., Fogel, A., & Kawai, M. (1990). Maternal speech to three-month-old infants in the United States and Japan. *Journal of Child Language, 17*, 279–294.

Toupin, E. A., & Son, L. (1991). Preliminary findings on Asian Americans: "The model minority" in a small private East Coast college. *Journal of Cross-Cultural Psychology, 22*, 403–417.

Tseng, W. S., Ebata, K., Miguchi, M., Egawa, M., & McLaughlin, D. G. (1990). Transethnic adoption and personality traits: A lesson from Japanese orphans returned from China to Japan. *American Journal of Psychiatry, 147*, 330–335.

Tseng, W. S., Kuotai, T., Hsu, J., Jinghua, C., Lian, Y., & Kameoka, V. (1988). Family planning and child mental health in China: The Nanjing survey. *American Journal of Psychiatry, 145*, 1396–1403.

Uba, L. (1994). *Asian Americans: Personality patterns, identity, and mental health.* New York: Guilford Press.

Wan, C., Fan, C., Lin, G., & Jing, Q. (1994). Comparison of personality traits of only and sibling school children in Beijing. *Journal of Genetic Psychology, 155U*, 377–388.

Wang, Y. C., Chong, M. Y., Chou, W. J., & Yang, J. L. (1993). Prevalence of attention deficit hyperactivity disorder in primary school children in Taiwan. *Journal of the Formosa Medical Association, 92*, 133–138.

Weine, A. M., Phillips, J. S., & Achenbach, T. M. (1995). Behavioral and emotional problems among Chinese and American children: Parent and teacher reports for ages 6 to 13. *Journal of Abnormal Child Psychology, 23*, 619–639.

Weisz, J. R., Chaiyasit, W. Weiss, B. (1995). A multimethod study of problem behavior among Thai and American children in school: Teacher reports versus direct observations. *Child Development, 66*, 402–415.

Weisz, J. R., Sigman, M., Weiss, B., & Mosk, J. (1993). Parent reports of behavioral and emotional problems among children in Kenya, Thailand, and the United States. *Child Development, 64*, 98–109.

Weisz, J. R., Suwanlert, S., Chaiyasit, W., Weiss, B., Achenbach, T. M., & Eastman, K. L. (1993). Behavioral and emotional problems among Thai and American adolescents: Parent reports for ages 12–16. *Journal of Abnormal Psychology, 102*, 395–403.

Weisz, J. R., Suwanlert, S., Chaiyasit, W., Weiss, B., & Jackson, E. W. (1991). Adult attitudes toward over- and undercontrolled child problems: Urban and rural parents and teachers from Thailand and the United States. *Journal of Child Psychology and Psychiatry, 32*, 645–654.

Xin, R., Chen, S. K., Tang, H. Q., Lin, X. F., & McConville, B. J. (1992). Behavioural problems among preschool age children in Shanghai: analysis of 3,000 cases. *Canadian Journal of Psychiatry, 37*, 250–258.

57 / Korean Immigrant Children

Wun Jung Kim

The first Korean immigrants to the United States were a group of 101 Koreans admitted to the Hawaiian islands in 1903. By 1905, a total of 7,226 Korean immigrants had arrived to labor in the sugarcane fields of Hawaii. From the Korean war of 1950 until 1965, Korean orphans and wives of U.S. servicemen were the majority of Korean immigrants. The third, much larger, wave of Korean immigrants began with the Immigration and Naturalization Act of 1965, leading to an average of 30,000 Korean immigrants annually entering the United States in the 1970s and 1980s. About half of them settled in the Pacific Coast states, and more than 50% of those moved to the metropolitan areas of Los Angeles, Chicago, and New York, adding new ethnic neighborhoods and creating retail businesses in the depressed sections of the cities.

The 1990 U.S. Census reported that 798,849 Korean Americans reside in the United States, representing more than a 100% increase from the 1980 U.S. Census count of 357,393 and a 1,000% increase from the 1970 Census count of about 70,000. However, a 1990 unofficial survey by the Korean Embassy and Consulates in the United States estimated that a total of 1,240,197 Koreans or Korean Americans reside in this country, including 174,335 Koreans in transit for graduate studies, business, and diplomatic affairs. Of this total, about one-third are children and adolescents.

Background of Koreans and Korean Immigrants

Some Westerners believe that Koreans are hybrid or mixed-blood Japanese and Chinese. Almost 90% of college students in one U.S. university class did not have any knowledge of Koreans, nor could they differentiate Koreans from Japanese or Chinese (Hurh, 1980). Historians believe the Korean people are descendants of several Mongol tribes. They have developed and preserved their own history, language, and culture in spite of the repeated invasions by neighboring countries, thus fostering a strong sense of pride and national/ethnic identity. The beginning of Korean history is often dated to 2333 B.C., and many kingdoms had risen and fallen before the Japanese occupation in 1910. The defeat of Japan and superpower politics in 1945 divided the land into North and South Korea at the 38th parallel. The Communist North Korea and the democratic South Korea engaged in a tragic war between 1950 and 1953 in search of unification and hegemony of the Korean peninsula. Since the temporary ceasefire of 1953, millions of displaced and separated families have been waiting to return home and to be reunited with their families. As North Korea does not have diplomatic relations with the United States, no one from North Korea has ever been admitted to this country as an immigrant. However, many Korean immigrants from South Korea were actually born in North Korea and still have immediate family members and relatives there.

Both North and South Korea have made tremendous efforts to rebuild their part of the country and have become important players in international politics and business. South Korea has a population of 42.8 million, and per capita income is $7,670, ranking 12th in the world (*Korea Update*, 1995). The population and the gross national product of North Korea are each about one-half of that of South Korea. The Korean peninsula is about the size of Minnesota or of England and Scotland combined. Until recently, rapid population growth in such a small land as South Korea during the poverty-stricken, politically unstable postwar years made U.S. immigration an incredibly enviable opportunity. Many professionals who came to the United States for graduate studies and advanced training did not return to Korea because better professional and economic opportunities were available in the United States. Besides the political instability under the threat of a recurring North–South Korean conflict, the rigidity of Korean society characterized by provincialism, elitism, and meritocracy made many young people seek to emigrate. The mean age of the most recent Korean immigrants is 27.3 years. Most come from urban, middle-class backgrounds, and about half are college graduates who held professional, technical, or managerial jobs in Korea before migration (Hurh & Kim, 1988). These young immigrants place great value on the achievement of their children through good education and occupational success while the majority of the parents engage in labor-intensive work, such as dry cleaning, small groceries, and restaurants, thus downgrading their occupational status in the new land.

Social/Cultural Influences on Family and Development

About 60 to 70% of the new immigrants attend Korean ethnic Christian churches in the United States for social and psychological support in addition to religious functions (Hurh & Kim, 1988). Christianity has gained phenomenal acceptance among Koreans in the short time since the Korean war. However, Taoism (mostly Buddhism) and Confucianism are the religious and ethical teachings that influence Koreans most. Postwar Western influence, especially during the rapid modernization period of the 1970s and 1980s, has shaken up old beliefs and mores. Opposing Korean and Western values coexist, sometimes harmoniously but often in conflict, in Korean families living in both Korea and the United States. It is very important for clinicians to understand that these old values are still operating, consciously and subconsciously, in the behaviors and emotions of Korean immigrants, even though some of them may appear to be very much acculturated on the surface.

FAMILY

In traditional Korean families, the hierarchy and boundaries are very clear. The man is in charge of the household in the nuclear family, and the grandfather is the man to be revered in the extended family. Ancestral worship and inheritance to the first son are emphasized. Both generational and gender roles are clearly defined and practiced. The Korean model of kinship is that of father-son dominance with the attributes of continuity, inclusiveness, authority, and asexuality, whereas American kinship is the husband-wife dominance dyad with the attributes of discontinuity, exclusiveness, volition, and sexuality (C. Kim, 1989). The Koreans' preference for sons has a lot to do with the old-age security value of children (Kagitcibasi, 1982). Male chauvinism has long been institutionalized and still is prevalent in Korea's changing society. For instance, child rearing is considered strictly a woman's responsibility. Korean fathers have shown a great reluctance to participate in child care. However, many Korean fathers in the United States contribute significantly to child care and help their wives (Yu & Kim, 1983). Changes also have occurred in intergenerational relations and living arrangements for older Koreans in the United States. Korean elders and their adult children help each other to form Korean retirement communities and accept a pattern of coexistence more characteristic of the United States than of Korea (Koh & Bell, 1987). This situation may change the greater role grandparents traditionally have held in the upbringing of Korean children.

Another important characteristic is a strong family identity in the context of a long history of family pedigree and clan loyalty. Individuality or individual identity often is overlooked in such a family atmosphere or group identity. Individual misfortune is a family disgrace, and individual success is a source of family pride. For example, Korean mothers of mentally retarded children are more worried about having to admit that their children are mentally retarded, while mothers with mentally retarded children in other cultures are more concerned about the children's educational placement (Y. S. Kim, 1986). Clan networking in social, business, and political arenas and promotion of common interests by marriage have resulted in cronyism, sectarianism, and corruption in the past and still, to a degree, in modern Korean society. On the positive side, kinship is a very important resource and often is viewed as being as important as friendship. Kin assistance, both financial and nonfinancial, is essential to the premigration preparation and postmigration adjustment for many nonprofessional Korean immigrants (Min, 1984).

DEVELOPMENTAL PERSPECTIVES

Children are valued very much by the family not only out of love but also as the bearers of the family name and procreators of the family. While genetic aspects of human development are heeded, as evidenced by the very meticulous mating practices of probing each other's family illnesses designed to promote a healthy genetic pool, the Koreans have subscribed to the "nurture" school, as well. In adulthood, parenting is the duty of utmost importance. A great deal is invested in children's education, and it starts very early in life. Parents and child target specific tasks for accomplishment; in the process, they sometimes overlook developmental perspectives and continuities in psychosocial areas. Whether Korean children living in the United States are more like Korean children living in Korea or American children with respect to developmental and psychosocial features is a question that has not been addressed. A clue may be sought through a very informative study on the transitional object. Hong and Townes (1976) reported that 53.9% of American children, 34% of Korean American children, and 18.3% of Korean children had transitional objects. The kind of attachment objects and their use also were significantly different. These differences were explained by different sleeping arrangements (Korean children sleeping in the parents' bedroom versus American children sleeping in their own room) and different baby-sitting arrangements (Korean children by familiar people, often by grandparents, versus American children by strangers). In these respects, Korean American children fell between the Korean and American children.

Infancy and Early Childhood: As a general rule, Korean parents and grandparents indulge and overprotect children. For example, it is an old custom not to visit a newborn for the first 21 days, due to fear of outside contamination and the desire to allow both baby and mother to adjust and recuperate to a new life and to bond. Feeding and weaning schedules are liberal. Infants and young children sleep in the same room with the parents. If baby-sitting has to be arranged, leaving the children with strangers is avoided as much as possible. Grandparents often travel from Korea to the United States to care for grandchildren, and sometimes infants are sent to Korea to be cared for by grandparents or other relatives. There is a great deal of physical contact and emotional nurturing, thus fostering dependence of the child. This may result in the development of basic trust and object relations but slower development of initiative and separation/individuation (Yu & Kim, 1983).

Later Childhood: As children enter formal schooling, early indulgence begins to shift to a demanding and disciplined path of development. Achievement-oriented growth and development call for obedience and conformity on the part of the child and demand a good deal of parental involvement. Yu and Kim (1983) reported school teachers' somewhat stereotypic descriptions of Korean pupils in U.S. classrooms as being "quiet, obedient, respectful, studious and likable" (p. 153). Some teachers noted that they are less verbally expressive, less assertive, more sensitive to approval, and less self-confident than their Caucasian counterparts. In general, they are viewed as emotionally stable and thriving on academic work, and responding well to concrete and specific instructions. The Korean children's low verbal expression may have to do with both language as well as cultural factors. Almost all first-generation Korean parents speak Korean at home. In addition, they associate, sometimes exclusively, with fellow countrymen and relatives rather than participating in mainstream community affairs. Thus, Korean children usually begin to learn English only as they enter the formal educational system.

Moreover, in Korean homes there is a relatively low level of verbal communication and more reliance on nonverbal implicit modes of communication between children and parents.

Adolescence: The second separation/individuation process may be as unencouraging to the child as the first one. Adolescents may be pulled to an "adhesive mode of adaptation" (Hurh, 1990, p. 22) by the family, which is eager to maintain Korean customs, culture, and networking, while adolescents have to develop peer relationships and self-identity in the dominant culture. Thus, adolescent developmental drives of autonomy and independence must confront the parent-child relationship dominated by parental authority. Adolescents who have not been adequately guided in asserting themselves, expressing different opinions, and dealing with anger or aggression will face disadvantages in dealing with the sexual, impulsive, and aggressive drives of adolescence. Sexuality and dating are not openly discussed in the traditional Korean culture. Rather, they are issues to be discouraged.

A great many Korean American children also have to maintain a basic proficiency in the Korean language in order to communicate with their parents. However, the language barrier may prevent sophisticated, abstract discussions with the parents. Bilingualism and biculturalism may eventually become assets, but they also add to the ambivalence many teenagers have about their families and identities. While parents may have attained financial and occupational stability, they may not be good social role models because of their poor command of English and lack of an active or leadership role in the mainstream society. Role models and support from the Korean American community are not readily available because of the short history of Korean immigration. Korean American adolescents are left to ponder and experiment on their own in dealing with these important developmental tasks while their parents demand that their children achieve high academic standards. Both parents and youngsters may take different defensive postures in reacting to this shift and threat, a spectrum ranging from acting out to conscious/subconscious suppression and inhibition.

Young Adulthood: As mentioned before, separation/individuation, independence, and autonomy typically have not been encouraged in Korean children. Entrance to college often opens the door for many Korean youths to complete such tasks somewhat later than their American counterparts. In traditional, authoritarian, age-graded Korean culture, researchers have found the same developmental sequence but at a different pace for other kinds of developmental tasks, such as Kohlberg's stages of moral development (Park & Johnson, 1984). Despite the physical separation, close family ties are still maintained when children leave home. They often receive full financial support from the parents for higher education, which is felt to be one of the last duties of parents (next to a wedding). As they enter college or the workforce, away from the family, these young adults may feel isolated and become more acutely aware of their minority status. Many U.S.-born or immigrant young Korean adults may blend themselves well into the mainstream society, but socialization and finding their own place in a competitive and sometimes hostile environment may become very stressful. Interracial marriage or even dating often causes a family crisis. They are caught in two opposing value systems—a traditional Korean pursuit of homogeneity versus the diverse idealistic pursuits of an open U.S. society.

In the early 1980s, the new term "1.5 generation" emerged from the Korean communities of the United States. It refers to older adolescents and young adults who were born in Korea and came to this country during their formative growing years. The 1.5 generation poignantly depicts the dilemma they confront. They have to work harder to "succeed" as Korean, Korean American, or American. These abstract, confusing ethnic identities are hard to grasp and reconcile internally. These people attain a higher degree of bilingualism and biculturalism than the first, second, or third generation, but a limited assimilation into either culture. This kind of structural marginality influences the personality of the 1.5 generation to produce two possible modes of adaptation—the cosmopolitan and the marginal personalities (Hurh, 1990). The cosmopolitan personality type emerges from the positive resolution of biculturalism and displays creativity, motivation, leadership potential, and active participation in both the ethnic and mainstream community and a strong sense of Korean American ethnic identity. The marginal personality type is a product of the negative resolution of the external pressure and internal conflicts, and exhibits ambivalent personal identity, inferior-

ity conflicts, hypersensitivity, social isolation, and feelings of powerlessness.

Cross-Cultural Psychosocial Studies

There is a paucity of cross-cultural studies in general, and data on children and adolescents are even scarcer. This section summarizes what has been learned, including adult studies of a largely descriptive nature, for the purpose of suggesting future directions for research.

A large psychiatric epidemiological study using the same methodology of the Epidemiologic Catchment Area contrasted prevalence rates between Korea and St. Louis, Missouri (Lee et al., 1990). The prevalences of different disorders were roughly comparable between the two sites although the rates in Korea tended to be lower, except for alcoholism and somatization disorder. The higher prevalence of alcohol abuse in men, but not in women, in Korea was thought to be related to social stresses caused by rapid modernization, cultural acceptance of heavy drinking in a male-oriented society, and social sanctions against female drinking (Helzer et al., 1990). On the other hand, the rate of suicide in Korea is somewhat lower than in the United States, which may be due to differences in reporting and documenting rather than true differences. In 1986, the suicide rate of the general population was 8.8 per 100,000 in Korea versus 12.9 in the United States. The rate for the 15- to 19-year-old group in Korea was 7.4 versus 10.2 per 100,000 in the United States (W. Kim, 1988). A high prevalence of depression and anxiety has been reported in Korean adults living in the United States (Kuo, 1984; Pang, 1992). Hwa-Byung (Lin, 1983) is perhaps the only culturally bound syndrome known for Koreans; it is a Korean manifestation of a spectrum of affective and somatization disorders prevalent among married women. It literally means "anger syndrome," attributed to the suppression of anger, and it occurs very much in the context of family conflicts. According to the fourth edition of the *Diagnostic and Statistical Manual of Mental Disorders* (American Psychiatric Association, 1994), the symptoms include insomnia, fatigue, panic, fear of impending death, dysphoric affect, indiges-

604

tion, anorexia, dyspnea, palpitations, generalized aches and pains, and a feeling of a mass in the epigastrium.

In a World Health Organization collaborative study of emotional and behavioral problems in primary school children in Korea, Japan and China, Matsuura et al. (1993) reported higher rates of deviant scores on the teachers' and parents' scales of Rutter's questionnaires among the Korean children (14.1 and 19.1%, respectively) than the Japanese and Chinese children. While deviance of the antisocial type was more frequent than the neurotic type in Japan and China, both types were almost equally frequent in Korea. The prevalence of deviance was higher in boys and also higher in those children with poor school achievement. While the prevalence of deviance was higher in Korea than its neighbor nations, the overall rates of deviance in Korean children were comparable to the rates from other studies such as from England and New Zealand, except for a higher rate of somatic complaints. Various childhood psychiatric disorders prevalent in the United States were also observed in Korea in similar proportions in a clinic setting, including infantile autism, disruptive behavior disorders, and emotional disorders (Hong, 1982). It appears that, in general, Korean children and adolescents manifest similar kinds of psychopathology as those observed in the United States and other Western countries, but these may present different dynamics and characteristics due to genetic and cultural factors, for example, higher somatization tendencies.

Clinical Implications

Are Korean immigrant children and adolescents a vulnerable group? If so, is it because they are Koreans, because of immigration, or because they live in the United States? First of all, there is no comprehensive epidemiological data on the extent of developmental and psychiatric problems among Korean youths in the United States. Korean children are underrepresented in a clinic setting (L. Kim, 1992) and among juvenile delinquents of Hawaii (Voss, 1963). As to being a Korean, epidemiological studies in Korea do not indicate a higher prevalence of any psychiatric disorders ex-

cept adult male alcoholism and somatization of children, both of which are due to cultural rather than genetic reasons. Migration into the United States poses more complex questions. Immigration is a stressful event and can add a risk to already vulnerable individuals. However, immigration also can be a positive experience for some. Thus, immigration is not a uniform experience to all. The Ontario Child Health Study (Munroe-Blum, Boyle, Offord, & Kates, 1989) reported a general observation that immigrant children are not at increased risk for psychiatric disorders or poor school performance. The culture of the host country, culture of the native land, and its interactive dynamics may play a significant role in the child's and the family's psychosocial adjustment. Due to the newness of their arrival, research on Koreans in the United States is still in an exploratory stage. However, several studies described family violence, alcoholism, alienation of the elderly, marital and intergenerational conflicts, and mental disorders.

In a family-oriented culture, it is worth noting a few epidemiological studies on Korean immigrant adults. Kuo (1984) reported that Koreans as a group in the Seattle area exhibited the highest depression scores compared to those of Chinese, Japanese, and Filipino Americans. Kuo attributes this finding to a shorter length of residence in the United States, higher rates of underemployment (higher educational status but lower-prestige jobs), limited proficiency in English, and a higher concentration in small businesses located in high-risk minority districts. Hurh and Kim (1990b) described gender differences in the dynamics of depression: While Korean males who are married and employed in a high-status occupation showed better subjective mental health than others, no distinctive set of variables accounted for the female respondents' mental health. Two-thirds of Korean women sampled in the Chicago area were employed, and most of the employed wives carried a double burden of performing the household tasks and working outside the home. In a survey of 150 Korean women residing in Chicago, 60% were reportedly battered by their husbands/partners, 75% of them within 3 to 5 years of immigration (Song-Kim, 1992). Female employment in Korea, especially for married mothers, is very rare, and the mother's employment (for economic necessity and better opportunity) undoubtedly affects the family dynamics and parent-child relationship. Child neglect/abuse or relative deprivation may increase as young couples move to the United States and struggle to settle in a new land. As seen in Korean adults (Hurh & Kim, 1990a), the first few years seem to be an especially vulnerable period for children, as well.

Timing of immigration in relation to the developmental stage of children will affect their adjustment and development. For instance, the younger the age at immigration (especially before puberty), the higher the level of the immigrant's proficiency in English and American culture. On the other hand, the younger the age at immigration, the less likelihood that true bilingualism and biculturalism will develop. Language deprivation following immigration to the United States during later childhood years can initially cause withdrawal and despondency (Marcos, 1982) before adaptive integration. Parents' erroneous expectations of the community and educational system of the United States may leave the needs of school-age children unmet and leave the parents disappointed and bewildered; for example, children in Korea learn not only academic skills but principles of moral behavior through the educational system. Some families have come to the United States ostensibly because of the educational advantage in the land of opportunity; 80% of parents in Korea want to send their children to college and beyond, but due to a very competitive entrance examination, only 39% of children are actually allowed to enter college.

Adolescence is a very difficult time to move to a different culture, leaving social and peer networks and support behind. As a result, some youths may maintain their traditional culture, reject the new culture, and suffer rejection from classmates at school. Yet parents preoccupied with their own survival may not be available to children for continued nurturing and guidance. Many youths turn to their peer groups for support, often to a group of other rejected youths, which sometimes leads to the development of gangs in response to the sense of alienation from parents and community. The same dynamic is applicable to adolescents who were born in the United States or migrated in the early years of their life. Identity conflicts and the lack of sense of belonging to family, community, and the country contribute to a strong pull by a gang or other kind of group identification

process—such as religions and extreme political movements. In the New York and Los Angeles metropolitan areas, Korean community leaders have focused much attention on the activities of Korean youth gangs. Korean American psychiatrists and family practitioners often encounter withdrawn, depressed, and suicidal Korean adolescents. Regardless of whether they exhibit externalizing or internalizing behavioral problems, the underlying dynamics of intergenerational tension, alienation between parents and adolescents, and identity conflicts are evident. The marital conflicts of parents due partly to the changing gender role dynamics in the process of acculturation and to disruptions in the continuity of family life also play a role.

SPECIAL ISSUES

Child Abuse and Neglect: There are no data about child maltreatment in Korean families residing in the United States. A survey of 1,142 third and fourth graders in two schools in Seoul, South Korea, revealed that 8.2% of them had been "seriously battered" at least once in a 1-year period, constituting child abuse according to the authors (K. Kim & Ko, 1990). These children came from broken families and families of low socioeconomic status. Boys were far more likely to be battered than girls (42 versus 24%). It is estimated that over 90% of children in Korea are subjected to physical methods of discipline by parents and teachers. Corporal punishment has been a well-accepted method of disciplining in Korean culture. Therefore, child maltreatment is not easy to distinguish from legitimate physical discipline by caring and concerned parents. Child abuse is rarely reported to the authorities in Korea and seems to be viewed as a family affair rather than a social issue (Chun, 1989). However, a cross-cultural study of U.S. and Korean children found no differences in the use of physical punishment and related symptoms of anxiety, such as nail-biting and nightmares (Englehart & Hale, 1990).

As mentioned before, children in the first few years of immigration are at risk for maltreatment and relative deprivation due to parents' acculturation and survival stresses. Strict discipline, parental overreaction out of anxiety in response to the foreign culture, and the demand of academic endeavors without balanced recreational activities may give an impression of child abuse. However, the cultural differences and the child's perceptions of parental discipline should not be overlooked. In sharp contrast to the findings among North American youths, Korean youths' perceptions of parental control are correlated positively with perceived parental warmth and low neglect (Rohner & Pettengill, 1985). Similarly, expectations of girls assuming more household responsibility than boys at relatively young ages and physical touching, even touching of young boys' genitalia by older people (as a sign of affection and adoration of a male gender), should be viewed in light of cultural customs. Child protective services must be aware of and sensitive to the practice of delegating responsibilities to children and issues of dominance and submission when dealing with Korean families, just as they must recognize differences among other ethnic minority groups (Gray & Cosgrove, 1985).

Korean Adoptees: Unlike the transracial adoption of black children, transracial adoption of Asian children has not been the subject of much scientific attention or controversy. Even though the Korean war ended in 1953 and Korea has made noticeable progress economically, the number of Korean children adopted by American families continued to increase until recently. During the 10-year period following the Korean war, Korean children adopted by American families amounted to about 20% of all foreign adoptions in the United States. Yet between 1976 and 1986, the proportion increased to 50 to 60% (W. Kim, 1995). In 1986 alone, 6,150 Korean children were adopted, representing 59% of all foreign children adopted in the United States. The reasons for the increase of Korean adoptees are many. Historically, in Korea, adoption has been viewed as a means of continuing family lines rather than as a means of aiding children in need of a permanent home. Intercountry adoption has been used as an alternative way of meeting children's needs. Because many war orphans were adopted, the infrastructure was in place for reliable and efficient adoption of Korean children, which contributed to the popularity of these adoptions in the United States. Improving images of Asian countries and Asians in the United States and the stereotypic perceptions of Asians as quiet, trouble-free, intelligent, and high achieving also may have contributed to the increasing popularity of Korean

children. However, the number of Korean children available for international adoption began to decrease markedly from 1988, the year of the Olympics, when the world, especially the United States press, cynically made an issue of Korean adoption practice (e.g., the article "Babies for Export" in the April 21, 1988, *New York Times*). By 1994, the annual number of Korean children adopted fell to 1,795, less than one third of the pre-Olympic level. The decrease has to do with the Korean government's arbitrary discouragement of intercountry adoption rather than a decrease in the number of adoptable children or alternative solutions to meeting their needs.

Although the number is decreasing now, about 100,000 Korean children have been adopted by American families. How have they fared in the United States and what are the issues concerning them? Studies done in both Europe and the United States have shown that most adopted Korean children have adjusted well. Some studies have indicated that Korean adoptees have done even better than intraracially adopted white children of the United States and other internationally adopted children of Europe, in general and even during the turbulent adolescent period (Feigelman & Silverman, 1984; Verhulst, Althaus, & Versluis-den Bieman, 1990). Results of a study of adopted Korean adolescents (D. Kim, 1977) and a 10-year follow-up study of adopted Korean adolescents and young adults (Lydens & Snarey, 1989) are especially encouraging. These authors reported development of a positive self-concept and positive social adjustment.

A few factors might explain such surprising findings. First, the majority of Korean children are adopted during infancy. For instance, in 1989, 2,778 out of 3,552 (78%) were adopted before the age of 1. There is ample evidence of a higher risk of behavioral and emotional problems in children adopted at a later age. Good prenatal and neonatal care in most Korean children through efficient adoption agencies has reduced the incidence of malnutrition, abuse, and neglect. For cultural reasons in Korea, more girls than boys have been available for adoption. Child psychiatric epidemiological studies have consistently shown a higher risk of emotional and behavioral problems in boys than girls. It also can be speculated that parents who opt for transracial adoption tend to be liberal and may place fewer demands on the success and achievement of their adopted children. Parental demand or overexpectation has been cited as a frequent source of conflict in the parent/child relationship of adoptive homes. While studies indicate that Korean children are "successfully" mainstreamed into American culture, there has been little investigation into their development of ethnic identity. It appears that a genuine interest in the unique qualities of their ethnicity, while facilitating a competitive, compensating acculturation in this society, should also be stimulated, in order to foster historical continuity and social linkage with the children's background.

Biracial Korean Children: Korea has been the fourth leading contributor of foreign spouses after Mexico, the Philippines, and England between 1980 and 1985 (Thornton, 1992). Between 1945 and 1985, 68,296 Koreans had been admitted to the United States as spouses of U.S. citizens, mostly to U.S. servicemen stationed in Korea. Including children from interracial marriage by the second- and third-generation Koreans and more recent immigrants, there are well over 100,000 biracial Korean children in the United States. Many Korean women who were married to U.S. servicemen come from the disadvantaged segments of Korea and may have been traumatized before coming to the United States. They have been described as a high-risk group because of the language differences, the Korean value of suppression of feelings, and high expectations of spouses and their families (Ratliff, Moon, & Bonacci, 1978). Consequently, there is a high rate of marital failure and marital conflict in this group (B. L. Kim, 1977).

There are no data on biracial Korean children. The traditional Asians' attitudes against "mixed-blood" biracial children are well known, and the Koreans are no exception. In Korea, biracial children are often teased by peers and suffer from social ostracization. The social gap does not seem to change among Koreans even after immigration to the United States. Biracial children are not well accepted by and seem to shy away from the Korean communities of this country. As ethnic identities do not seem to involve conscious selection (abstract) and emerge from individuals' social interactions with members of their heritage group (experiential), biracial Korean children may overly identify with the race of their fathers (black or white). As mentioned before, since the parents'

marriage seems to be at high risk, children may lose the benefits of mixed-heritage status, such as increased contact with members of two heritage groups, enjoyment of two cultures, facility in language spoken by both heritage groups, and intergroup tolerance (Stephan, 1992).

Treatment Considerations

It is easy for misunderstandings to occur from an ethnocentric perspective, and these misunderstandings are unlikely to be in the minority group's favor. A good example is case management of child abuse/neglect by child protective services (Gray & Cosgrove, 1985). The importance of awareness of and sensitivity to cultural underpinnings of child-rearing practices, views of mental illness, and help-seeking behaviors cannot be overemphasized in the evaluation of immigrant children and their families.

KOREANS' VIEWS OF MENTAL ILLNESS AND MENTAL HEALTH SERVICE

In a study of psychiatric patients at the Seoul National University Psychiatric Clinic, Rhi (1973) reported that two-thirds had previously tried Eastern healing methods, including shamanistic sessions, faith-healing endeavors, and Chinese medicine in various combinations. Shamanism and a hybrid of Shamanism and religion are still practiced in rural parts of Korea. As opposed to possession by evil spirits or devils, Korean Shamanism regards misfortune or ill health as a result of the wrath of "spirits" or a bad relationship with the spirits. So shamanistic rites different from Western religious exorcism are desired to mend the relationship with spirits or soothe the spirits through a *goot* (ceremonial rite) by a *mudang* (a shaman). Faith healing, religious counseling, special prayers, and fasting also have been widely practiced even as Christianity gained rapid acceptance in Korea. Families of severely disturbed adults and adolescents frequently seek out mountaintop prayer centers and some kind of closed facilities under the auspices of alleged religion in remote rural areas. Chinese herbal medicines and acupuncture are still popular for all kinds of medical conditions, and especially for neurasthenic, psychosomatic, and emotional disorders.

Although psychiatry and psychology were introduced to Korea in the early 20th century, and psychotherapy and biological therapy have been practiced for the past four decades, psychiatric services are underutilized in Korea (Barcus, 1982; Chang & Kim, 1973). Fear of chronic mental illness and shame make families hesitant or resistant to seeking evaluation and treatment. There is a great deal of secrecy about the mental illness of family members. Although more educated and more acculturated Korean Americans become more cognizant of the need for psychological help and more tolerant of the "stigma" associated with such help, Koreans, like other Asians, tend to be less receptive to mental health services (Atkinson & Gim, 1989). Underutilization may mean that treatment facilities have not responded to the needs of these groups (Sue & McKinney, 1975).

CLINICAL SUGGESTIONS

There are some important clinical caveats for clinicians to consider when treating Korean American families and their children. First, the notion of "evaluation" needs to be emphasized in dealing with initial resistance and shame. Stage-specific developmental tasks are important concerns to parents, and evaluation of psychopathology in the context of overall developmental assessments would be more readily acceptable. Once initial contact is made, it is essential to understand different stages of transition in the postimmigration adjustment of the family, from a conventional, paternalistic, authoritarian family to a more egalitarian, nuclear family (Yun, 1976). With a traditional Korean family, appropriate communication style in terms of manners and choice of words and seeking the approval of the father would be very important. The therapist also may establish authority and become directive initially, as some traditional parents and their child would expect; doing so fosters rapid development of positive transference on the part of the patient and confidence in the therapist as psychoeducationalist (L. Kim, 1993). The ethnicity and gender of the therapist will have a great influence on the course of treatment. For instance, while Korean American clinicians may be preferred over clinicians of other ethnic origins for easier and more affective communication, the therapy may become overly ethnocentric. Clinicians of other ethnic origins may have the advantage of being more objective and neutral, yet the family may view them as "foreigners," and splitting by the youngster can become a source of conflict or premature termination of therapy.

Koreans, like other ethnic parents, may view the use of psychotropic drugs in children and adolescents with mixed emotions. But Korean families will view as justifiable a physician's authoritative, direct explanation of the diagnosis as a medical condition and the prescription of drugs as necessary. However, more compliance problems may arise in terms of dose adjustments because in Korea, patients and pharmacists sometimes make dose adjustments without a doctor's supervision. Studies of psychotropic drugs for Asian adults have indicated different sensitivity to side effects, different dose requirement, and different pharmacokinetics (Lin, Poland, & Chien, 1990). However, scant knowledge regarding these drugs exists for Asian children in general and Korean children in particular.

Future Directions

Despite the dearth of research on Korean immigrant children, it appears that they are not any more vulnerable than other ethnic American children. Even the most vulnerable group, such as transcontinentally and transracially transplanted Korean adopted children, have fared very well. In a study comparing Korean children with black children in an urban school district, Chang (1975) found that Korean American children in third to sixth grades scored higher in behavior, intellectual and school status, and happiness and satisfaction on Piers-Harris Self-Concept Scale, but scored lower in physical appearance attributes and popularity than black children. Boys showed higher anxiety than girls in both ethnic groups. While gender identity disorder and homosexuality seem to be less prevalent in the Korean culture, which defines and practices clear gender roles, Korean American boys may be viewed as effeminate, and they may struggle with body image and related self/gender concept and peer/heterosexual relationships. Korean American girls tend to do better in this area. Normative developmental data in relation to different ethnic groups need to be accumulated for better understanding of intricate gender, migration, and cultural dynamics. Culturally sensitive mental health services also need to be developed to increase utilization for this traditionally underserved group, focusing on early identification of developmental deviation on the basis of appropriate normative data and preventive interventions.

REFERENCES

American Psychiatric Association. (1994). *Diagnostic and statistical manual of mental disorders* (4th ed.). Washington, DC: Author.

Atkinson, D. R., & Gim, R. H. (1989). Asian-American cultural identity and attitudes toward mental health services. *Journal of Counseling Psychology, 36,* 209–212.

Babies for export. (1988). *New York Times* (April 21).

Barcus, R. A. (1982). Clinical psychology and mental health in South Korea. *Clinical Psychologist, 35,* 16–19.

Chang, S. C., & Kim, K. (1973). Psychiatry in South Korea. *American Journal of Psychiatry, 130,* 667–669.

Chang, T. S. (1975). The self-concept of children in ethnic groups: Black American and Korean-American. *Elementary School Journal, 76,* 52–58.

Chun, B. H. (1989). Child abuse in Korea. *Child Welfare, 68,* 154–158.

Englehart, R. J., & Hale, D. B. (1990). Punishment, nail-biting, and nightmares: A cross-cultural study. *Journal of Multicultural Counseling and Development, 18,* 126–132.

Feigelman, W., & Silverman, A. (1984). The long-term effects of transracial adoption. *Social Service Review, 58,* 588–602.

Gray, E., & Cosgrove, J. (1985). Ethnocentric perception of childbearing practices in protective services. *Child Abuse and Neglect, 9,* 389–396.

Helzer, J. E., Canino, G. J., Yeh, E., Bland, R. C., Lee, C. K., Hwu, H., & Newman, S. (1990). Alcoholism—North America and Asian. *Archives of General Psychiatry, 47,* 313–319.

Hong, K. M. (1982). *Children psychiatric disorders in Korea.* Paper presented at the annual meeting of the American Academy of Child Psychiatry, Washington, DC (October).

Hong, K. M., & Townes, B. D. (1976). Infant's attachment to inanimate objects. *Journal of the American Academy of Child Psychiatry, 15,* 49–61.

Hurh, W. M. (1980). Towards a Korean-American ethnicity: Some theoretical models. *Ethnic and Racial Studies, 3,* 444–463.

Hurh, W. M. (1990). The "1.5 Generation": A paragon of Korean-American pluralism. *Korean Culture,* 21–31.

Hurh, W. M., & Kim, K. C. (1988). *Uprooting and adjustment: A sociological study of Korean immigrants' mental health.* Final Report to the National Institute of Mental Health.

Hurh, W. M., & Kim, K. C. (1990a). Adaptation stages and mental health of Korean male immigrants in the U.S. *International Migration Review, 24,* 456–479.

Hurh, W. M., & Kim, K. C. (1990b). Correlates of Korean immigrant's mental health. *Journal of Nervous and Mental Disease, 178,* 703–711.

Kagitcibasi, C. (1982). Old age security value of children and development: Cross-national evidence. *Journal of Comparative Family Studies, 13,* 133–142.

Kim, B. L. (1977). Asian wives of U.S. servicemen: Women in shadows. *Amerasia Journal, 4,* 91–115.

Kim, C. (1989). Attribute of "asexuality" in Korean kinship and sundered Koreans during the Korean war. *Journal of Comparative Family Studies, 20,* 309–325.

Kim, D. S. (1977). How they fared in American homes: A follow-up study of adopted Korean children. *Children Today, 6* (2), 2–6.

Kim, K., & Ko, B. (1990). An incidence survey of battered children in two elementary schools of Seoul. *Child Abuse and Neglect, 14,* 273–276.

Kim, L. (1993). Psychiatric management of Korean-American patients. In A. Gaw (Ed.), *Culture, ethnicity and mental illness* (pp. 347–376). Washington, DC: American Psychiatric Press.

Kim, W. (1988). *Overview of adolescent suicide.* Paper presented at the annual meeting of Korean Neuropsychiatric Association, Taegu, Korea (October).

Kim, W. (1995). International adoption: A case review of Korean children. *Child Psychiatry and Human Development, 25,* 141–154.

Kim, Y. S. (1986). A comparative survey of anxiety in mothers of mentally retarded children in Tokyo and Seoul. *Japanese Journal of Special Education, 24,* 1–16.

Koh, J. Y., & Bell, W. G. (1987). Korean elders in the U.S.: International relations and living arrangement. *Gerontologist, 27,* 66–71.

Korea Update. (1995). *Economic News, 6* (2), 4.

Kuo, W. H. (1984). Prevalence of depression among Asian-Americans. *Journal of Nervous and Mental Disease, 172,* 449–457.

Lee, C. K., Kwak, Y. S., Yamamoto, J., Rhee, H., Kim, Y. S., Han, J. H., Choi, J. O. & Lee, Y. H. (1990). Psychiatric epidemiology in Korea, Part 1: Gender and age differences in Seoul. *Journal of Nervous and Mental Disease, 178,* 242–246.

Lin, K. M. (1983). Hwa-Byung: A Korean culture-bound syndrome? *American Journal of Psychiatry, 140,* 105–107.

Lin, K., Poland, R. E., & Silver, B. (1993). Overview: The interface between psychobiology and ethnicity. In K. Lin, R. E. Poland, & G. Nakasaki (Eds.), *Psychopharmacology and psychobiology of ethnicity* (pp. 11–36). Washington, DC: American Psychiatric Press, Inc.

Lydens, L., & Snarey, J. (1989, April). *Identity development among cross-cultural adoptees: A longitudinal study.* Paper presented at the biannual meeting of Society for Research in Child Development, Kansas City, MO.

Marcos, L. R. (1982). Adults' recollection of their language deprivation as immigrant children. *American Journal of Psychiatry, 139,* 607–610.

Matsuura, M., Okubo, Y., Kojima, T., Takahashi, R., Wang, Y.-F., Shen, Y.-C. & Lee, C. K. (1993). A cross-national prevalence study of children with emotional and behavioral problems—A WHO collaborative study in the Western Pacific Region. *Journal of Child Psychology and Psychiatry, 34* (3), 307–315.

Min, P. G. (1984). An exploratory study of kin ties among Korean immigrant families in Atlanta. *Journal of Comparative Family Studies, 15,* 58–75.

Munroe-Blum, H., Boyle, M. H., Offord, D. R., & Kates, N. (1989). Immigrant children: Psychiatric disorder, school performance, and service utilization. *American Journal of Orthopsychiatry, 59,* 510–519.

Pang, K. Y. (1992, May). *Depression among Korean elderly immigrants.* Paper presented at the 145th annual meeting of the American Psychiatric Association, Washington, DC.

Park, J. Y., & Johnson, R. C. (1984). Moral development in rural and urban Korea. *Journal of Cross-Cultural Psychology, 15,* 35–46.

Ratliff, B. W., Moon, H. F., & Bonacci, G. A. (1978).

Intercultural marriage: The Korean-American experience. *Social Casework, 59,* 221–226.

Rhi, B. Y. (1973). A preliminary study of the medical acculturation problems in Korea. *Neuropsychiatry,* (Seoul, Korea), *12,* 2.

Rohner, R. P., & Pettengill, S. M. (1985). Perceived parental acceptance-rejection and parental control among Korean adolescents. *Child Development, 56,* 524–528.

Song-Kim, Y. I. (1992). Battered Korean women in urban United States. In S. M. Furuto, R. Biswas, D. K. Chung, K. Murase, & F. Ross-Sheriff (Eds.), *Social work practice with Asian Americans* (pp. 213–226). Newbury Park, CA: Sage Publications.

Stephan, C. W. (1992). Mixed-heritage individuals: Ethnic identity and trait characteristics. In M. P. P. Root (Ed.), *Racially mixed people in America* (pp. 50–63). Newbury Park, CA: Sage Publications.

Sue, S., & McKinney, H. (1975). Asian Americans in the community mental health care system. *American Journal of Orthopsychiatry, 45,* 111–118.

Thornton, M. C. (1992). The quiet immigration: Foreign spouses of U.S. citizens, 1945–1985. In M. P. P. Root (Ed.), *Racially mixed people in America* (pp. 64–76). Newbury Park, CA: Sage Publications.

Verhulst, F. C., Althaus, M., & Versluis-den Bieman, H. J. M. (1990). Problem behavior in international adoptees: I. An epidemiological study. *Journal of the American Academy of Child and Adolescent Psychiatry, 29* (1), 94–103.

Voss, H. L. (1963). Ethnic differentials in delinquency in Honolulu. *Journal of Criminal Law and Criminology, 54,* 322–327.

Yu, K. H., & Kim, L. (1983). The growth and development of Korean-American children. In G. J. Powell (Ed.), *The psychosocial development of minority group children* (pp. 147–158). New York: Brunner/Mazel.

Yun, H. (1976). The Korean personality and treatment considerations. *Social Casework, 57* (3), 173–178.

58 / **Children of Pacific Asians: Cambodia**

William H. Sack, Shirley McSharry, and Dan Dickason

In his book, *The Twentieth Century Book of The Dead,* Gil Elliot (1979) documents the unspeakable arithmetic of the 110 million people, ". . . a nation of the dead," who have been murdered by organized governments since 1900. No more tragic an example of this phenomenon in the last half of this century exists than in Cambodia. Yet Cambodia's ordeal seems to have outlasted the attention of everyone except its victims. From 1969 onward, Cambodia has undergone an uninterrupted succession of disasters that have killed millions, uprooted millions more, devastated the country's land and spirit, and all but extinguished its culture (Issacs, 1988).

In 1969, the Vietnam war spilled over into neighboring Cambodia. Partly as a result of the internal political repercussions, by 1975, the country had fallen under the control of a fanatical Communist group of Cambodians named the Khmer Rouge, whose leader was known as Pol Pot. The Pol Pot regime launched a radical, bizarre attempt to eradicate all "Western influence" and convert the entire nation to an extreme fundamentalist form of Marxist communism. This task was undertaken mercilessly, with complete disregard for humanitarian considerations or, indeed, for human life. During the years 1975 to 1979, between 1 and 2 million of the country's 7 million people died (Ablin & Hood, 1987; Becker, E., 1986; Jackson, 1989; Ponchaud, 1977; Shawcross, 1985).

David Hawk (1982) describes the Pol Pot regime as a three-tiered structure of murder by government. At the top of this metaphoric pyramid of death was the prison system, which systematically tortured and executed so-called political prisoners. The central security prison in Phnom Penh was called Tuol Sleng. Of the 15,000 people incarcerated there, only 7 survived.

The second tier of this pyramid of death was a series of massacres that were directed at particular social, political, economic, and ethnic groups. These victims were considered remnants of the old feudal society that was to be transformed. Buddhist monks, civil servants, army officers, and anyone with a Western education were targets. This included physicians and "capitalists." Reliable sources (S. Ka, 1991, personal communication) estimate that only 43 out of 487 physicians survived. The ranks of dentists, pharmacists, nurses, and other caregivers were similarly decimated.

Children often were bribed with food to spy on their adult family members and relatives and to report to the Khmer Rouge. Those showing any "subversive" ideas would be summarily executed. One study subject estimates that she unknowingly may have been responsible in this way for as many as 200 adult deaths. Later, when the revolution did not progress satisfactorily, the Khmer Rouge executed members of its own party, as well.

The bottom, largest layer of this pyramid of death were those who died from a combination of exhaustion, starvation, and disease as the result of forced marches into the countryside and forced labor in collective farms. Children over the age of 6 often were separated from their parents and forced to work in camps. The Pol Pot regime fractured all of the normal social networks among its people: familial, religious, and commercial. In early 1979, the Khmer Rouge finally were driven from power by their former political ally (but longstanding traditional enemy), the Communist Vietnamese.

It soon became apparent that an enormous wave of Cambodians were fleeing their country, mostly on foot, and without adequate food supplies. Eventually, more than half a million people had crossed the mined border with Thailand, many sustaining injury during their escape. At first, the Thai government did not grant them refugee status, and they were contained in primitive "holding camps" just across the border by the Thai military. There they suffered continuing attacks, and thousands died during forced "repatriation" to Cambodia.

Fortunately, their plight shocked the world, and many international organizations and voluntary agencies mounted a major relief effort. Somewhat safer refugee camps were then established with the cooperation of the Thai government, and basic food and medical aid were supplied. Some 50,000 of these people with the most pressing reasons for departure had been permitted to resettle in other countries, including the United States. However, in 1982 there were still some 90,000 Cambodians existing in Thailand with no visible future prospects. At that time, first France and then the United States announced their willingness to resettle Cambodians who had connections with their countries (DeVecchi, 1982). Under this sponsored resettlement movement, by 1990, 148,200 Cambodian refugees had come to live in the United States (Gordon, 1991).

Tragically, the withdrawal of Vietnamese occupation forces from Cambodia in 1990 resulted in the outbreak of internal hostilities again and precipitated the exodus of a further wave of refugees into Thailand. More than 350,000 "displaced persons" waited hopelessly in border camps (Crisp, 1991). Most of these were women and children. Finally, in 1994, a resettlement program was begun. Now all the refugee camps are closed and the Cambodians who languished there have returned to their homeland. Their ultimate adjustment remains to be determined as the Khmer Rouge still control some territory in the country and periodic violence continues.

Over the past 10 years the tragedy of Cambodia has been followed by other wars, most recently the Bosnian conflict. Studies of children surviving this ordeal showed similar effects of war trauma (Zwac, 1993; Morrisseau, 1994; Weine et al., 1995). The literature on children as victims of war has been reviewed both by Jensen and Shaw (1993) and more recently by Saigh and Fairbank (In press).

Emigration of Cambodian refugees to the United States dwindled from a peak in 1980 to 1982 to a few hundred in 1990. Since resettlement, there has been a great deal of secondary migration within the country, resulting in the largest refugee enclave existing in California.

Children remaining in their own country have fared poorly. At the end of the disastrous decade of the 1970s, Cambodia's economy had been destroyed, its cities had been emptied, and its schools and public services were nonfunctional. The health and nutritional status of women and children was precarious. Cambodia then had the highest infant mortality rate in the world, and the majority of the surviving population was severely undernourished.

In addition, the prolonged armed conflict has given rise to thousands of children and adults with amputated limbs. Children will have to grow up trying to bear the sufferings of their shattered bodies and lives with Buddhist stoicism (UNICEF, 1990). The suffering of Cambodian children continues, and the extent of damage to their mental health is unknown.

The provision of psychiatric services within Cambodia is minimal and colored by cultural concepts of what constitutes mental disorder. The Khmer people certainly recognize psychosis as major mental illness, but tend to include in that category only levels of disorder that result in serious social dysfunction. For them, such flagrant dysfunction carries a very strong stigma, as they see it as casting shame on their family. Since all helping systems have essentially broken down now, it seems that the current generation of mentally and physically injured individuals in Cambodia remains without care.

Cultural Traditions

For Cambodian refugees, the traumas of the last 15 years have involved a continuing series of losses: human, material, and symbolic. In one study, Kinzie, Sack, Angell, Manson, and Ben (1986) found that 80% of a community convenience sampler of Khmer adolescents had lost at least one family member; the average number lost, either dead or missing, was three members of the nuclear family. The Khmer people also lost their means of livelihood, previous social status or social role, not to mention their homeland and many of their rich and centuries-old cultural traditions (Boehnlein, 1987). Clinicians treating transcultural populations need to be aware of differences in customs and value systems, of which a few necessary examples follow.

Cambodia, like other Southeast Asian cultures, has been a culture of high family continuity (Benedict, 1938). Traditionally in such cultures, people work alongside their parents as children and then alongside their children as parents. Family ties are enormously important (Tobin & Friedman, 1984). Ngor and Warner (1988) contrast the traditional Khmer lifestyle with that of urban American life.

The Cambodian way of life was much simpler than that of America. There was no Social Security, Welfare, daycare centers, old-age homes or psychiatrists. All we needed were our families and the monks. Most households had three generations living together. The grandparents helped raise their grandchildren. The adults in the middle put food on the table. When there were problems and arguments, the monks helped take care of them (p. 47).

Khmer children are thought to be independent at birth and then are wooed into a sense of interdependency by attentive (and by Western standards, indulgent) child-rearing practices by extended family members. Parents become increasingly strict in their expectations for conformity and responsibility after the age of 7. Compliance is based not only on emotional ties but also on respect for authority. Responsibility for honoring the family name is learned early. Adolescence in traditional Cambodian families usually is not accompanied by overt emancipation struggles. Respect for elders' authority is undiminished, even as the youths are apprenticed into adult status by work or marriage. Age itself serves as an important social organizing principle (Tobin & Friedman, 1984).

Equally important is the need to maintain smooth interpersonal relationships with others, both inside and outside the family. It is important to "save face" and not to embarrass or offend others in interpersonal situations.

The Khmer culture has been shaped by both Hindu and Buddhist traditions, intermixed with varying amounts of folk religion. The Buddhist temple serves not only as a religious institution but as an important social center. Many refugees in the United States attend both a Christian church and the temple for traditional holidays. A central tenet of the Buddhist tradition is reincarnation, the belief that current life successes or failures may have depended on events in a previous life. In some refugees, this may lead to what by Western standards seems a passive acceptance of suffering (rather than "talking it out" or "fighting" against past injustice).

Interwoven with mainstream Buddhist traditions are folk religions that have a strong supernatural focus. Suffering also can be viewed from this vantage point, as having been brought on by supernatural events rather than by natural events (Spiro, 1967). Some Khmer people believe that spirits of the deceased can return and cause illness when ignored or angered by the misdeeds of descendants. A number of Khmer subjects have reported to us being visited at night by the spirit of a deceased family member. While these experiences can have a hallucinatory quality, they should not be confused with the hallucinations of a major mental illness.

Traditionally, marriages are arranged by the families of the bride and groom. Education and economics are important considerations in these arranged marriages. Dating is a foreign concept to traditional Khmer families. Adolescent females are kept close to home and may not be allowed out, even to attend school social functions, without considerable family worry. Premarital sexual activity can bring heavy shame on families, particularly if it results in an out-of-wedlock pregnancy. Often marriages are arranged hastily in such cases, and then a separation and divorce follows after the child is born. It is important to determine which strata of society a Khmer refugee comes from. A "middle-class" adolescent will usually have high

respect for education and be a diligent, conscientious student. Refugees from rural backgrounds may not have been exposed to much formal education, as their traditional farming tasks have not necessitated the mastery of academic skills. These people often are illiterate in their own language, and the task of adapting to the academic expectations of an American high school can be overwhelming.

Psychopathology: The Traumatic After-Effects from a Developmental Perspective

ADULTS

Since 1978, the Department of Psychiatry at the Oregon Health Sciences University has maintained a clinic for Indochinese refugees. As the Khmer refugees were seen over the first several years, Dr. Kinzie and his colleagues slowly began to identify symptoms of both posttraumatic stress disorder and depression in many who had survived this massive trauma and dislocation (Kinzie, Frederickson, & Ben, 1984). In adult refugees, the posttraumatic stress disorder symptoms tended to fluctuate over time but ran essentially a chronic course. Many intrusive symptoms improved on antidepressant medication, but the avoidant symptoms of the disorder proved resistant to intervention (Boehnlein, Kinzie, & Ben, 1985; Kinzie, 1986). All adult refugee patients remained vulnerable to intermittent stress. Even minimal stress could reactivate a full display of posttraumatic stress disorder symptoms.

ADOLESCENTS

Work with adolescents commenced in 1983 when the Department of Psychiatry at Oregon Health Sciences University was approached by a staff member from a Portland high school for assistance in understanding unusual behaviors exhibited by some Khmer students. For instance, several students felt they were under gunfire attack when firecrackers were set off on the school grounds. One student began screaming uncontrollably when she dug up a dog bone during a school field trip to study plants. With the cooperation of school officials, a systemic study was undertaken in which 46 of the 52 Cambodian students received a semistructured psychiatric interview as well as teacher classroom assessments and a home inventory (Kinzie et al., 1986; Sack, Angell, Kinzie, & Ben, 1986).

Six of the 46 students had left Cambodia before Pol Pot and therefore suffered no major traumas and had no posttraumatic stress disorder symptoms. Of the remaining 40 students (average age 17), 50% received a diagnosis of posttraumatic stress disorder (based on criteria from the third edition of the *Diagnostic and Statistical Manual of Mental Disorders*). Depressive disorders, usually of a mild or intermittent type, were also present in 53% of this group. While this was a nonclinical sample, 6 students had received some form of prior mental health care. No cases of drug or alcohol abuse, psychoses, or antisocial or conduct disorders were found.

A strong relationship was found between the current living situation and the psychiatric diagnosis. Thirteen of 14 students (unaccompanied minors) living in a foster home received a psychiatric diagnosis, while those living with at least one other family member fared much better. Living with a family member seemed a significant protective factor for these Khmer adolescents.

Students who had a psychiatric diagnosis were more likely to be rated by their teacher as withdrawn or "daydreamers," but not disruptive. Home interviews revealed that many parents had similar posttraumatic stress symptoms (poor sleep, startle responses), as well, but frank discussions between teenager and parent about their prior "Pol Pot" experience was the exception rather than the rule. The school seemed to be a critical acculturation experience for these students. Their teachers played a number of important roles in introducing them to life in the United States (Sack et al., 1986).

A 3-year follow-up study of these same students was undertaken by the same authors (Kinzie, Sack, Angell, Clarke, & Ben, 1989) and revealed the same overall prevalence (50%) of posttraumatic stress disorder as in the original study. However, those students who qualified for this diagnosis were not necessarily the same as in Time 1, confirming the clinical impression that this condition waxes and wanes over time. Despite the high rates of posttraumatic stress disorder and depression, the functional status of these students was quite good. Many were working or enrolled in a local community college. Few had drug and/or alcohol problems. Such early findings may change as Cambodian youths come into closer and more sustained contact with the harsh urban environment of the United States.

A 6-year follow-up study of these same students (Sack et al., 1993) showed that the course of the two main diagnoses (PTSD and depression) was moving in different directions. While depression had dropped precipitously to a prevalence rate of 6%, PTSD showed a nonsignificant drop from 50% to 38%. No new cases of PTSD had appeared between 3 and 6 years. A 12-year follow-up of this sample is currently underway. Thus, it appears that symptoms of PTSD tends to endure over periods of time and across important developmental nodal points.

CHILDREN

At this time, young children seen in our clinics rarely show signs of posttraumatic stress disorder as an aftermath of having survived the Pol Pot regime. Fortunately, most preschool children were not separated from their parents from 1975 to 1979. Rather, the clinical problems are more a reflection of cultural child-rearing conflicts. Cambodian parents can be baffled and disheartened by the amount of "freedom" they see American children as having. As the Cambodian children become acculturated, they begin to pressure their parents for the same kind of freedom. Giving their children such freedom seems, to these parents, to willfully neglect their traditional child-rearing practices. Not knowing what to do, their self-confidence and their authority in the family is undermined. Had such a problem arisen while they were living in Cambodia, a respected uncle would be called in to appraise the situation and offer advice. Yet most times this is not possible in the United States. As a result, Cambodian children often present with oppositional symptoms. One of the roles of the clinician is to help parents regain control and authority in the family, while also helping them be more flexible and comfortable with some "American" practices, such as allowing the child to visit peers outside the home after school, attend school events, and so on.

At times the war *did* cut off parents and their children, with reunification of families occurring only after the war. Children in such families may present with conduct disorder symptoms and/or antisocial behavior. The underlying pathology can be attachment problems between parent and child. Some of the very behaviors that fostered survival during the war or in a refugee camp (stealing, aggression, etc.) are now no longer needed, but remain. These children do not show the traditional respect for parental authority. In fact, they may try to "run" their families with threats. Such problems are more serious, and the prognosis is uncertain. A delinquent outcome is a real possibility.

Clinical experience has confirmed findings from these studies. Symptom profiles seem related not only to the prior massive trauma but to the resettlement and acculturation stresses of life in a new country, as well. The vulnerability of traumatized Khmer refugees to intercurrent stressors of any form is an important clinical concept to recognize. Moreover, since children and adolescents often undergo a more rapid rate of acculturation than do their parents, family tensions over what is acceptable behavior frequently arise.

Despite the number of traumas and stresses they have experienced, Cambodians have extraordinary strengths, as well. While they are serious about life, they often have an infectious sense of humor that is instrumental in their coping ability.

Assessment

In addition to taking a current history of the presenting problem, the clinician assessing a Khmer child or adolescent needs to pay special attention to the family's past life in Cambodia, particularly under the Khmer Rouge. A careful assessment of past trauma is crucial in understanding the current symptom profile.

Second, an assessment of the degree to which each family member has undergone acculturation in this country is also critical. The greater the acculturation disparity across generational lines, the more opportunity for family strife.

The clinician who knows something of Khmer culture should not expect children or adolescents to disagree or confront their elders openly. Many will smile politely and defer to whatever the clinician says in order to maintain smooth relations with a respected professional. A more traditional medical model is quite compatible with Khmer tradition. The family expects the psychiatrist to be authoritative and direct in his or her advice. Khmer families can be confused by nondirective approaches or by therapists who place too great an emphasis on intrapsychic reflection.

In taking a history, the clinician should be aware of the immediate setting. The possibilities of simulating past interrogation sessions should be kept in mind. In Cambodia, knowledge of a person's identity during the Pol Pot era could have meant instant death (Kinzie, 1989). Thus, the clinical process of a history taking can, in itself, be potentially threatening.

Interviewing Through an Interpreter

Many clinical interviews with Khmer families and/or youths will be conducted with an interpreter. In the Oregon Health Sciences University Indochinese Psychiatric Clinic and research programs, the Khmer interpreters have extensive prior training in their roles and are carefully supervised. With experience, some become able to provide direct clinical services themselves. Careful selection of these people is crucial, for the work requires them to be sensitive to nuances of expression and emotion, to be able to interpret the cultural context to the interviewer, to be sufficiently skilled in English so that the translation is accurate, and to endure the stress of hearing very painful stories. These individuals thus do more than simply interpret; they often function as a cultural consultant (Freed, 1988; Westermeyer, 1990). The confidentiality of their role is stressed continually.

Clinicians need to be aware that even though a Khmer child, adolescent, or adult seems fluent in conversational English, his or her understanding of concepts and ideas can be quite limited. Interpreters may be needed in such situations. Clarke, Sack, and Goff (1992) gave the Peabody

Picture Vocabulary Test and the vocabulary section of the Stanford-Binet to 27 Khmer adolescents. Even though most could speak fluent English, they scored surprisingly low on these tests. Their average vocabulary skill level was between grades 3 and 4 (Clarke, Sack, Ben, Lantham, & Hun, 1993).

In addition to issues of language, certain constructs of emotion can be very difficult to translate. For instance, no comparable word for "depression," per se, exists in the Khmer language. For our research purposes, we developed specific illustrations for several psychological concepts so that these concepts would be explained to the subject in a consistent fashion by the interpretor.

Therapy

Khmer adolescents share the same concerns about seeing a mental health professional as do their American counterparts. They do not want to be thought of as being "crazy." Khmer parents often are baffled about how to apply traditional Cambodian family rules in a new culture. Some may "give up," withdraw, and allow their offspring much more freedom than is healthy. They may be surprised when the therapist endorses their role as an authority figure and limit-setter since they may feel that all American children are allowed to "run wild." Others need assistance in gently loosening controls over their children and adolescents while still retaining their authority and respect in the family.

For those adolescents and adults suffering from posttraumatic stress disorder and/or depression, the role of the therapist should be both active and supportive (Boehnlein et al., 1988). Patients' sense of helpless rage, guilt, and loss needs to be endorsed as a normal reaction to a devastating experience over which they had no control. The stress of these traumatic stories can be considerable for the therapist, also. As Terr (1988, personal communication) and Kinzie (1991) point out, at some level, therapists treating the traumatized patient become traumatized themselves. The experienced therapist will make provision for handling this form of countertransference.

The therapist should keep in mind that Cambodian refugee youths and their parents all have a story to tell. This story often contains experiences of past trauma, the stress of starting afresh in a new country, and the huge uncertainties of the future. Facilitating the retelling of these stories is often therapeutic for the patient and informational and powerful for the therapist.

Antidepressants have proven to be a useful adjunct to treatment of both the intrusive posttraumatic stress symptoms and the associated depression. Kinzie and Leung (1989) have found clonidine, in combination with antidepressants, to be particularly useful in Khmer adults. Medication is more easily accepted as a concrete form of help, although patients often are noncompliant in the continued use of psychotropic medications and so require careful monitoring. The need for the therapist's interest and support cannot be overemphasized. Many of these supportive relationships become long term, since some patients are very vulnerable to intercurrent stress.

Often all therapeutic approaches seem shallow when faced with the existential questions involved in the meaning of life after one has witnessed meaningless trauma and death. At times no words can deal with the experience the patient has lived through. This painful sharing between patient and therapist involves a search, a search in which the therapist is a privileged, yet burdened, observer (Kinzie, 1989).

REFERENCES

Ablin, D., & Hood, M. (Eds.) (1987). *The Cambodian agony.* New York: M. E. Sharpe.

Becker, E. (1986). *When the war was over: The voices of Cambodia's revolution and its people.* New York: Simon and Schuster.

Benedict, R. (1938). Continuities and discontinuities in cultural conditioning. *Psychiatry, 1,* 161–167.

Boehnlein, J. (1987). Clinical relevance of grief and mourning among Cambodian refugees. *Social Science Medicine, 25* (7), 765–772.

Boehnlein, J., Kinzie, J. D., & Ben, R. (1985). One year follow-up study of post traumatic stress disorder among survivors of Cambodian concentration camps. *American Journal of Psychiatry, 142,* 956–960.

Clarke, G., Sack, W., & Goff, B. (1992). *English language skills in Cambodian adolescent refugees.* Unpublished manuscript.

Clarke, G., Sack, W., Ben, R., Lantham, K., & Hun, C. (1993). English language skills in a group of previously traumatized Khmer adolescent refugees. *Journal of Nervous and Mental Disease, 181,* 454–456.

Crisp, J. (1991). Coming back from the border. *Refugees, #84,* Public information service of the United Nations high commissioner for refugees (UNHCR).

DeVecchi, R. P. (1982). Pollitics and policies of "first asylum" in Thailand. *World Refugee Survey.* US Committee for Refugees.

Elliot, G. (1979). The twentieth century book of the dead. New York: Charles Scribner's Sons.

Freed, A. O. (1988). Interviewing through an interpreter. *Journal of the National Association of Social Workers, 33* (4), 315–319.

Gordon, L. (1991). *Refugee Reports, 11* (1), 11.

Hawk, D. (1982). The killing of Cambodia. *New Republic, 187,* 17–21.

Issacs, A. R. (1988, March 21). Cambodia's nonstop ordeal. *New York Times.*

Jackson, K. D. (1989). Cambodia 1975–1978: Rendezvous with death. Princeton, NJ: Princeton University Press.

Jensen, P. S., & Shaw, J. (1993). Children as victims of war: Current knowledge and future research needs. *Journal of the American Academy of Child & Adolescent Psychiatry, 32,* 697–708.

Kinzie, J. D. (1986), Severe post traumatic stress syndrome among Cambodian refugees: Symptoms, clinical course and treatment approaches. In J. Shore (Ed.), Disaster stress studies, pp. 123–140. Washington, DC: American Psychiatric Press.

Kinzie, J. D. (1989). Therapeutic approaches to traumatized Cambodian refugees. *Journal of Traumatic Stress, 2* (1), 75–91.

Kinzie, J. D. (1991). Counter-transference in the treatment of southeast Asian refugees. In J. P. Wilson & J. Lindy (Eds.), *Beyond empathy: Managing affect and counter-transference in the treatment of post traumatic stress disorder* (pp. 249–362). The Guilford Press.

Kinzie, J. D., Frederickson, R. H., & Ben, R. (1984). Post traumatic stress disorder among survivors of Cambodian concentration camps. *American Journal of Psychiatry, 141,* 645–650.

Kinzie, J. D., & Leung, P. (1989). Clonidine in Cambodian patients with post traumatic stress disorder. *Journal of Nervous and Mental Diseases, 177* (9), 546–550.

Kinzie, J. D., & Sack, W. H. (1991). Severely traumatized Cambodian children: research findings and clinical implications. In F. L. Ahern & G. L. Atry (Eds.) *Refugee children: Theory, research, & practice.* Baltimore, MD: University Press.

Kinzie, J. D., Sack, W. H., Angell, R., Clarke, G., & Ben, R. (1989). A three-year follow-up of Cambodian young people traumatized as children. *Journal of the American Academy of Child and Adolescent Psychiatry, 28* (4), 501–504.

Kinzie, J. D., Sack, W. H., Angell, R. H., Manson, S., & Ben, R. (1986). The psychiatric effects of massive trauma on Cambodian children: The children. *Journal of the American Academy of Child Psychiatry, 25* (3), 370–376.

Mollica, R. F., & Jalbert, R. R. (1989). *Community of confinement: The mental health crises in site two.* Unpublished report, The World Federation for Mental Health, Committee on Refugees and Migrants.

Morrisseau, L. (1994). Guerre et separation en ex-Yugoslovie. *Neuropsychiatric de l' enfance, 42* (8), 604–607.

Ngor, H. S., & Warner, R. (1988). *A Cambodian odyssey.* New York: Macmillan.

Ponchaud, F. (1977). *Cambodia year zero.* New York: Holt, Rinehart, and Wilson.

Sack, W. H., Angell, R., Kinzie, J. D., & Ben, R. (1986). The psychiatric effects of massive trauma on Cambodian children: Part II. The family, the home, and the school. *Journal of the American Academy of Child Pyschiatry, 25* (3), 377–383.

Sack, W., Clarke, G., Hun, C., Dickason, D., Goff, B., Lantham, K., & Kinzie, J. D. (1993). A six-year follow-up of Cambodian youth traumatized as children. *Journal of the American Academy of Child & Adolescent Psychiatry, 32,* 431–437.

Saigh, P. A., Fairbanks, J. A. (In press). War related posttraumatic stress disorder among children and adolescents in stressful life events. (2d ed.), T. Miller (Ed). Madison, CT: International Universities Press.

Shawcross, W. (1985). *The quality of mercy.* New York: Simon and Schuster.

Spiro, E. M. (1967). *Burmese supernaturalism.* Englewood Cliffs, NJ: Prentice-Hall.

Tobin, J. J., & Friedman, J. (1984). Intercultural and developmental stresses confronting southeast Asian refugee adolescents. *Journal of Operational Psychology, 15,* 39–45.

UNICEF. (1990). *Cambodia: The situation of children and women.* United Nations Children's Fund, Office of Special Representative, Phnom Penh.

Weine, S., Becker, D. F., McGlashan, T. H., Vojuoda, D., Hartman, S., & Robbins, J. R. (1995). Adolescent survivors of ethnic cleansing: Observations on the first year in amencor. *Journal of the American Academy of Child & Adolescent Psychiatry, 34* (9), 1153–1159.

Westermeyer, J. (1990). Working with an interpreter in psychiatric assessment and treatment. *Journal of Nervous & Mental Disease, 178,* 745–749.

Zwic, J. (1993). Emotional reactions of children to war stress in Croatia. *Journal of the American Academy of Child & Adolescent Psychiatry, 32,* 709–713.

59 / Immigrant and Refugee Children

Stuart A. Copans

The Importance of Immigration

During the next few decades, it will be especially important for child psychiatrists to understand the process of immigration and the effects it has on children and families. Legal immigration into the United States increased drastically in the 1980s, to a level higher than it had been in any decade since the 1900s, and it is predicted to increase still further in the 1990s and beyond.

Immigration is not just increasing but is changing, as well. As a result, it is essential that clinicians and planners have some general understanding of the process, so that as we are faced with new groups of immigrants, we are prepared to develop preventive and therapeutic interventions for both the new immigrants and their children. In addition, many of the new immigrants have a history of trauma; their adequate treatment requires an understanding of the effects of trauma, of the effects of immigration, and finally, of their culture.

Because of the changing ethnic patterns and educational attainments of the new waves of immigrants, prejudice against new groups of immigrants has increased. Child psychiatrists in the 1990s and the 21st century must have the data and understanding that will enable them to speak out against such prejudice and discrimination, which only can impair the healthy development of all children, whether native born or newly arrived.

One additional reason for studying immigration and the effects it has on children is that it may provide a valuable model for understanding the effects of sociocultural change on the functioning of families and the emotional growth and development of children. Given the increasing rate of change, both in American society and in the world as a whole, any child born in these waning years of the 20th century will be faced with the task of adapting, as an adult, to a very different world from the one in which he or she was raised.

An increased understanding of those children and families whose behavioral and emotional difficulties are in part the result of their migration from one culture to another through space may help us prevent and heal such difficulties when they occur as a result of migration from one culture to another through time.

The Changing Face of Immigration

The history of America is a history of immigrants, dating back to the successive crossings of the Bering Straits by those we now call Native Americans and to the little-understood or documented visits of the Vikings to North America. In any case, since the opening up of the Americas to European exploitation and settlement in the 15th century, there have been successive waves of immigration, for religious, political, or economic reasons. Some people came to seek a better life; others came to escape an oppressive one. Some came voluntarily; others, particularly blacks, were brought here against their will. While a detailed history of the successive waves of immigration and of the contribution of different immigrant groups to American life and to the shaping and definition of the American culture is clearly beyond the scope of this chapter, it is important to note that not only has immigration to America more than doubled since the 1950s and 1960s, but there have been major shifts in the reasons for immigration and in the ethnic backgrounds and educational attainments of the new immigrants (Hutchinson, 1956).

Recent waves of legal immigrants have included fewer Europeans and significantly more Southeast Asians and Spanish-speaking peoples. While immigrants in the 1950s and 1960s were better educated than the U.S. population, the new immigrants are now less educated than the general American population. While those earlier immigrants came primarily because of increased economic or educational opportunities, increasing numbers of recent immigrants are refugees, fleeing political, religious, or ethnic persecution. At the present time, one-quarter of all workers in the United States without high school diplomas are immigrants.

Common Misconceptions about Immigrants

The romantic image is of the immigrant as poor, uneducated, and coming from a backward rural area to the gleaming cities of America. In fact, in the 1950s, the average immigrant had one more year of education than his or her American counterpart. People often think of immigrants in groups based on country of origin. In fact, different waves of immigrants from a given country or ethnic background may differ greatly in education, economic background, reason for emigrating, history of exposure to violence or persecution, and consequently in the stress of the immigration process and in the psychiatric illnesses seen. Studies of the adaptation of Vietnamese immigrants (Ganesan, Fine, & Lin, 1989) have distinguished four separate waves of immigration with different histories, different backgrounds, and consequently different clinical characteristics. Kinzie and Sack (1991) described different developmental disruptions and consequent behavioral symptoms in different groups of Cambodian refugee children.

People think of immigration as a process that involves one or at most two generations. In fact, the process of successfully integrating elements from the old and new cultures often takes at least three generations, and when people remain in separate ethnic and linguistic neighborhoods, it may not take place for several generations, if at all. The Japanese American community actually has three words to describe Japanese Americans: one for a first-generation immigrant, one for the second generation, and one for the third.

People think of immigrants as moving from one nation to another, but internal migrations within nations share many of the characteristics of migrations that cross national boundaries. The novel

The Grapes of Wrath provides as clear a picture of the process of migration as any book about immigrants to the United States. People think of immigrants as being at greater risk of mental disorder, whereas studies have shown that the risk for mental disorder actually may be lower among some communities of immigrants than among the native population of a region. Such studies may provide important clues about what the most useful approaches to primary prevention of psychiatric illness might be.

The Process of Immigration

The process of immigration has been described in many ways. Ebaugh (1988) suggests that immigration is similar to other role changes and suggests that any significant role change involves four stages: first doubts, seeking and weighing of alternatives, turning points, and, finally, establishing a new identity. She also identified several significant variables that can affect the way people move through the process of immigration, including:

1. Whether it is a forced migration or an elective choice
2. The centrality of the national identity being exited
3. The reversibility of the migration
4. The duration of the migration, if reversible
5. The degree of control over the process of migration, both of leaving the country of origin and of entering the new country
6. Individual migration versus migration as part of a family, an extended family, a village, or a whole region
7. Whether the immigration involves only a change in country of residence or whether it involves changes in multiple roles, such as occupation or social class
8. Whether the immigrants are accepted and granted high status in their new country or are stigmatized and discriminated against
9. The degree to which the status of "immigrant" is recognized and given support in the new country
10. The degree of awareness of the conditions they will experience after immigration
11. The number of stages in the process of migrating from one country to another

Sluzki (1979) focuses specifically on the immigration process and its effects on the family. He identified five stages: (1) the preparatory stage; (2) the act of migration; (3) an early period of overcompensation before the family comes to grip with the effects of the migration; (4) a period of decompensation when the family is temporarily overwhelmed by the changes necessary to adapt to the new culture; and (5) a gradual working out of the rules the family will use for blending what they bring from their old culture into what they will incorporate from the new. This process, Sluzki points out, may be worked out over several generations.

Developmental Effects of Immigration

It is useful, in considering the developmental effects of immigration, to integrate two different but complementary vantage points. First we consider that of Erikson (1963), who proposed a sequential set of child-parent (or child-other) interactions that led to the development of relatively persistent characteristics or outlooks on the self and the world. Second, we consider the ideas suggested by a number of contemporary systems theorists, who point out that particular interactions between parent and child around particular developmental issues have the potential to set up stable patterns of parent-child interaction that are extremely difficult to interrupt or change.

Trust, Erikson's first stage, is most likely to be affected by traumatic events during the first year of life, by early separation from the family, or by early affective unavailability of the mother. A number of studies of immigrant children have suggested that family functioning, especially maternal functioning, after migration has a powerful effect on the functioning of the migrant children.

Autonomy, Erikson's second stage, roughly ages 2 to 4, is intimately connected with the learning of language and of the rules of society. This period is most likely to be disrupted by a move to a different culture with different rules or to a situation in which a new language is the language spoken, so that the child loses early success at understanding and being understood.

Initiative, Erikson's third stage, actually may be strengthened in some children by the role reversal that places them as intermediaries between the family and society. Children learn both language and the rules of the new society more quickly than adults, and so may be empowered by the family at a young age. This empowerment may persist and may lead to high levels of achievement but also to later interpersonal difficulties.

Industry also may be an area of particular strength in some immigrant children, both as a result of a parent who models hard work as a way of succeeding and sometimes as a result of the child's early work being powerfully supported and encouraged by a hardworking and upwardly mobile family. Sung (1985), in a paper focusing on the differences between the Chinese and American value systems, shows how Chinese values may lead to high levels of academic achievement.

Identity and intimacy are both areas of potential difficulty for the immigrant child, since they are so closely interconnected, and since they force the child to define his or her relationship to both the culture of origin and the new culture.

Generativity is likely to depend heavily on the adult's success in negotiating the earlier stages, while integrity, Erikson's last stage, is likely to depend heavily on the immigrants' ability to integrate successfully both old and new culture into a coherent whole.

Home, Community, and Objects

When children immigrate, they leave behind not just relationships and a culture but physical objects, as well: their home, their neighborhood, their community, and many of their toys and possessions.

The importance of the home and of special objects to the child's development has been ignored by most child development theorists, with the notable exception of Winnicott (1971).

Anyone who has visited the museum at Ellis Island cannot help being struck by the power of seemingly trivial objects carried great distances with great effort as a way of preserving some sense of stability and connection with the mother country. A more detailed discussion of the importance of home, place, community, and objects, and the effects of their loss can be found in Chapter 60.

The Mediating Effect of the Mother

A number of studies on immigrant children point out the powerful effects of family and maternal functioning. Maternal depression is a powerful predictor of behavioral and emotional dysfunction in immigrant children, and maternal depression in immigrant mothers has been shown to be powerfully affected by a number of factors, including communication with husband, continued interaction with members of the culture of origin, and presence of discrimination.

Sociocultural Change and Emotional Development

Hughes (1965) suggested that increased psychiatric illness resulted from 10 particular sociocultural situations, in particular those that interfered with feelings of: physical security; being able to obtain recognition; being able to give love; being able to secure love; being able to express hostility; being able to secure sexual satisfaction; being able to express spontaneity; being aware of one's place in society and of the place of others; belonging to a moral order and doing right with what one does; and being a member of an identifiable human group.

Peseschkian (1987), a Persian psychiatrist trained in West Germany, Switzerland, and the United States, has developed a system of psychotherapy based on his work with immigrants and his analysis of cultural differences and the conflicts that arise in families and individuals as a result. He has identified a series of what he calls "actual capacities" that are dealt with differently in different cultures and has developed a way of assessing these in individuals, to better define some of the roots of interpersonal and interpersonal conflicts. He lists several "actual capacities" that often are the source of conflicts in bicultural couples or families: punctuality, cleanliness, obedience, courtesy, honesty/candor, faithfulness, diligence/achievement, thrift, reliability, precision, conscientiousness, love, modeling, patience, time, sexuality, trust—confidence, hope, faith/religion, doubt, certitude, and unity.

Peseschkian's theory is particularly interesting in light of the data cited by Totman (1979) showing that it is the first generation born in the United States that appears to be most heavily stressed and that their level of stress (as estimated on the basis of physiological variables) is exceeded only by those children who have one immigrant and one American-born parent.

Assessment of the Immigrant Child and Family

Before planning clinical interventions for the immigrant child, it is important to supplement the usual history of the present illness, child mental status examination, family history, and developmental history with a comprehensive history of the immigration process, including preimmigration and immigration stressors, an assessment of cultural discontinuities and conflicts, and a Meyerian life chart of significant events and moves. A home visit can be especially helpful in assessing the degree of acculturation, the ties to the culture of origin, the current environment, and the current functioning of the family.

Tables 59.1, 59.2, and 59.3 present an outline for a home visit, a Meyerian life chart, and a comprehensive sociocultural loss and immigration stress interview.

Clinical Summary

In reviewing the variety of studies looking at children of immigrant families, it seems clear that the simple act of moving from one country to another is less crucial than a number of other variables,

TABLE 59.1

Home Visit Outline

Procedure: Explain to the family that as part of the assessment, you will come to their house for dinner and for a tour of their house and neighborhood. Explain that you would like to join them for dinner on an evening when the entire family will be present, and that as part of the home visit you will arrive roughly 30 minutes before dinner so that the child (or the child and his/her parents) can give you a tour of the house and neighborhood. Explain that you would like them not to make anything special for dinner because you are coming but to have an ordinary family dinner as much as possible. Work out a mutually convenient date and time for the home visit. Be sure to get detailed instructions on how to get there.

When driving to the home visit, allow enough time to arrive 15 minutes to 30 minutes early. This will allow for difficulty finding the house and also will enable you to spend some time driving around the neighborhood to get a sense of what it is like.

After you arrive, ask for a tour of the house. Notice which objects the family is particularly proud of. Ask the child to show you his/her room and ask to see toys. Ask the child if he/she has any special things or places he/she would like you to see.

Observations:
  I. The Neighborhood
        Physical characteristics: urban, rural, nearby areas for play
        Socioeconomic characteristics
        Sociocultural characteristics
        Ethnic characteristics of the neighborhood
 II. The House or Apartment
        Physical description
        Number of rooms
        Condition of the house or apartment
III. Specific rooms
        The child's room
        Common rooms
        Kitchen
        Bathroom
        Other rooms
 IV. Special objects
        Family objects
        Preimmigration objects
        Newly acquired objects
  V. The Meal
        The menu
        Seating at the table
        The discussion during the meal
        Family interaction
 VI. Impressions
        Family functioning and dynamics
        The identified child's role in the family
        Relationship of the family and child with the culture of origin
        Degree of acculturation of the family and child
        Sociocultural stresses
        Stresses related to the immigration process
VII. Hypotheses
         Relationship of observations and impressions to the presenting problem

Note. Adapted from the Dartmouth Child Psychiatry Training Program, Lectures and supervision of Ray Sobel, 1974 to 1977.

TABLE 59.2

The Sociocultural History: The Immigrant Child Assessment Questionnaire

I. History of immigration
   A. The preimmigration stage
      1. When did the idea of emigrating first occur?
      2. How long did it take you (or the family) to decide and what alternatives did you consider?
         a. Who insisted on the move?
         b. Was someone rescued by the move?
         c. Who experienced the greatest loss in the move?
      3. What events helped you finally decide?
      4. What were the reasons for your migration?
         a. economic
         b. religious
         c. educational
         d. political
         e. illness-related
         f. other
      5. Were they positive (to find a better life) or negative (to escape a miserable situation)?
      6. Once you had decided, what did you have to do in order to emigrate?
      7. How long did it take?

II. History of traumatic events and losses
   A. Inventory of traumatic experiences
      1. Before or during the process of immigration, did you ever feel your life was endangered?
         a. What were the circumstances?
         b. Were others killed at the time?
         c. How did you survive?
      2. Were you ever put in prison or tortured?
         a. What were the circumstances?
         b. Were others tortured at the time?
         c. How did you survive?
      3. Were you ever beaten or threatened with injury?
         a. What were the circumstances?
         b. Were others beaten at the time?
         c. How did you survive?
      4. Were you ever forced to do things you now regret?
         a. What?
         b. What would have happened if you hadn't done them?
   B. Inventory of losses
      1. Have you lost contact with any family members between the time you first thought of emigrating and the present?
         a. by death or relocation
         b. violent or nonviolent
         c. witnessed or not witnessed
         d. if witnessed, by whom, when; what was their immediate reaction?
         e. did family members get to say good-bye to them?
      2. Home
         a. Can you describe the home you lived in before emigrating?
         b. What do you miss most about it?
      3. Important objects
         a. Were there any important objects you brought with you? Can you tell me what they were and what made them important to you?
         b. Were there any important objects you left behind? Can you tell me what they were and what made them important to you?
      4. Community
         a. Can you tell me about the community you left behind?
      5. Language
         a. Do you understand your new language?

TABLE 59.2 (*Continued*)

      6. Culture
         a. What do you miss most from your old country?
         b. Are there foods you miss? Celebrations? Music? Other activities?
      7. Friendships
         a. Are there friends you left behind when you moved?
         b. Tell me about them. What do you miss about them?
  C. Presence of survivor guilt
      1. Do you have dreams about emigrating?
      2. Do you feel guilty about leaving your old country? About things that happened in the process of leaving?
      3. How clearly do you remember things that happened in your old country?
  D. Communication with the past
      1. Do you remember what it was like with your family in your homeland?
      2. Do you feel as if things that happened with you and your family in the past are still with you?
      3. Do you have any continuing experiences with ghosts or spirits from the past?
  E. Do you feel angry about things that led up to your immigrating?
  F. What are your current feelings about your homeland?
  G. What helps you deal with the losses you've experienced?
      1. Do you get comfort from religious beliefs? Which beliefs?
      2. Do you get comfort by practicing religious rituals?

III. The act of migration
  A. How did you get here?
  B. Did the family come together or separately?
  C. What events occurred during the process of immigration?
  D. Where did you arrive?
  E. Who met you?
  F. What was the first day like?

IV. The period of overcompensation
  A. What were the first six months like?
  B. What did the family do to get along in the new country?

V. The period of decompensation
  A. Did the family have a particularly difficult time sometime during the first year after immigration?
  B. What family rules and customs had to be changed to adapt to the new country?
  C. How did the family work out the rules for making changes?

VI. The culture of origin
  A. Where did you originally live?
      1. Was it urban or rural?
      2. What was the climate?
      3. What was the transportation system?
  B. What race and religion were most of the people in that area?
  C. What language or languages did people speak?
  D. What did you do for work there?
  E. How far had you gone in school?
  F. Were you involved in the religious activities of the community?
  G. How were you involved in the social life of the community?

VII. History of adjustment and acculturation (establishing a new identity)
  A. Can you tell me the history of your moves and job changes since migration?
  B. Can you tell me about your current community?
      1. Area
         a. Do you live in a city or in the country?
      2. Living quarters
         a. Do you live in a house or in an apartment?
         b. Do you rent or own?
         c. How are the rooms used in your house or apartment?
         d. What are the living arrangements for the child you are concerned about?

3. What is the transportation system where you live?
4. Do others of same national or racial background live in your community?
   a. What religious institutions do you belong to or participate in?
   b. Do you belong to any national social clubs?
   c. Do you participate in any ethnic celebrations or festivals?
   d. Do you get to spend time with others who speak your native language?
   e. Do you live near members of your extended family or from the same village or area?
5. Acceptance by the community
   a. Do you have to deal with ethnic, religious, or racial prejudice or discrimination?
      —in your community?
      —in the larger society?
   b. Are you in conflict or competition with other ethnic, religious, or racial groups?
   c. What is your social network?
      —In what social, religious, or educational organizations do you participate?
   d. What is the racial/ethnic and social class composition of your neighborhood and school?

C. Economics
1. What is your current socioeconomic status?
   a. How does this compare with your status prior to immigration?
2. What is the socioeconomic status of your neighborhood?

D. Current cultural adjustment
1. How does your family feel about what it is like in America?
   a. Is your family part of a religious community?
      —Is religion important in your family?
      —How often do you have contact with that religious community?
   b. Does your family participate in any rituals or celebrations?
      —Do you have regular mealtimes?
      —Who eats together?
      —Do you have any special meals during the week or year?
      —Do you celebrate holidays and birthdays? If so, how they are celebrated?
      —Are there other family rituals, celebrations, repetitive seasonal activities that are part of your family life?
   c. What are your family's attitudes toward health?
      —What are your attitudes toward physical health?
      —What do you think being healthy means?
      —Do you use healers from your native culture for care of physical problems?
      —Do you use physicians and Western medicine for physical problems?
      —What are your attitudes toward mental health?
      —How can you tell if someone is mentally healthy?
      —Do you use healers from native culture for mental health problems?
      —Do you get help from psychiatrists, psychologists, or counselors for mental health problems?
   d. How does your family feel about schools and the educational system in America?
   e. What does your family think children and adolescents should do as part of the family?
   f. How do you think children and adolescents change as they grow?
   g. What are your beliefs about how children should be raised?
      —How much should children depend on their parents?
      —When should they learn to be on their own?
      —How should children be disciplined?
      —How should children show respect to their parents?
      —How are boys and girls different?
      —Do you expect different things from your sons and daughters?
      —What should your children do when they are angry?
      —How should your children go about making friends?
   h. What are your family's attitudes about death and illness?
   i. What are the best things about your family?
   j. How does your family deal with difficulties or tragedies?

626

TABLE 59.2 *(Continued)*

2. How comfortable does your family feel in your new environment?
    a. How do they deal with food?
        —What does your family eat and not eat?
            °At home
            °Outside the home
    b. How do they deal with the new language?
        —What language is spoken by the parents?
            °At home
            °Outside the home
        —What language is spoken by the child?
            °At home
            °Outside the home
    c. What kind of clothes do people wear?
        —What kind of clothes are worn by the parents?
            °At home
            °Outside the home
        —What kind of clothes are worn by the children?
            °At home
            °Outside the home
    d. Who does your family admire?
        —Who do the parents admire?
        —Who do the children admire?
    e. What occasions does the family celebrate?
        —At home
        —Outside the home
    f. Who in the family sees themselves as American?
        —the parents
        —the child
    g. If each member of the family could save one special object, what would they save? What makes each object special?

VIII. Transgenerational phenomena
    A. What conflicts are there and have there been between the children and the immigrant parents reflecting cultural conflicts?
        1. Have there been conflicts over behavior and limits?
        2. Have there been conflicts over dependence and independence?
        3. Have there been conflicts over values?
        4. Have there been conflicts over norms?
        5. Have there been conflicts over mores?

Note. Based on the work of Canino (1988); Ebaugh (1988); Eisenbruch (1990); and Sluzki (1979).

including: a history of traumatization and/or separation from the family; loss of significant family members; the effect of the move on the parents' functioning, particularly the mother; the father's ability to provide ongoing support for the mother; the presence of cultural or racial hostility and/or discrimination; marginal employment or unemployment; and the involvement of the parents, and most particularly the mother, in religious and or social groups that provide her with relationships and support (Westermeyer, 1989).

Some data suggest that immigrant families moving to an area where there are others of similar background may more easily establish support networks and hence have a more stable sense of who they are and be less susceptible to depression.

Clinical Interventions

Therapeutic interventions for immigrant children and families may be designed at a number of different levels—that of the individual child, the family, the school, or the community. At whatever

TABLE 59.3

The Meyerian Life Chart

The Meyerian life chart can be particularly helpful in conceptualizing the effects that trauma and immigration have had on immigrant children. The data gathered in the sociocultural history are displayed in a tabular time line, usually beginning at the time of conception of the identified patient.

Insert in the following chart all significant life events, including moves, birth of siblings, traumatic events, significant transitional events (going to school, moving to a new school). Note the date and age of the child at the time of the event. Also note any behavioral or physical changes that followed the event. The achievement of developmental landmarks (such as crawling, walking, toilet training, speaking) are entered in their own column, along with any instances in which previously achieved developments are lost (e.g., the loss of toilet training after a move).

The time line here runs from top to bottom; however, you may wish to display your data with the chronology running from right to left across the page.

Child's Name_____

Date	Age of Child	Place of Residence	Significant Life Events	Child's Behavior	Physical Illnesses	Developmental Landmarks

level the intervention, however, it is important for any therapist working with an immigrant child or family to be aware of any significant discrepancies between his or her own worldview and that of the family and of any major differences between his or her therapeutic goals and the family's goals.

Clinical interventions for individual immigrant children must be designed to take into account the health beliefs of the family and the degree to which these beliefs mirror those from the culture of origin, from the new culture, or are some amalgam of these two. The use of drawings has proven an effective way of intervening with traumatized children, and may prove equally effective with those immigrant children whose preimmigration history includes a significant history of trauma or exposure to trauma. In cases where children have been separated from their families, every effort must be made to reunite the children with any surviving family members.

In designing clinical interventions for families, it is essential first to assess the contribution of the immigration, preimmigration trauma, and sociocultural change to the presenting problem. Given the high rate of depression and psychosomatic illness reported in some groups of immigrants, and the correlation among child behavior problems, school and peer difficulties, and parent depression or psychosomatic illness, an assessment of the parent's mental health and the provision of appropriate treatment, if indicated, must be included as part of the evaluation and treatment of any immigrant child presenting for a child psychiatry evaluation.

Interventions with the family most often will need to focus on issues related to unresolved losses (Eisenbruch, 1990) and, according to Sluzki (1979), will be needed most often during the phase of family decompensation. The tasks of these interventions must be twofold: (1) to assess what losses each member of the family has experienced and to help them begin to work through these losses; and (2) to help the family formulate rules that will help them negotiate the changes they must make to adapt to their new society. There is some conflict in the literature between those who advocate working actively and early with immigrant families to help them adapt to and develop ties within their new culture, and those—most notably Stein (1984)—who suggest that a working through of earlier unresolved issues of separation and individuation should precede any attempts to become actively involved in the new culture. In fact, a combination of these approaches may be helpful and synergistic. As family members begin to work through their losses, they may have more energy available for investing in new connections, and as they begin to develop new supports and relationships, working through earlier losses may become easier.

In designing any clinical intervention, either at a family or an individual level, it may be important to understand how the parents conceptualize the child's problems and to explain the intervention in a way that makes it understandable to the parents.

Collaboration with healers from the family's culture of origin may prove to be helpful.

Interventions with the school may aim at helping school personnel understand the child's history and cultural background and at educating other children there about some of these differences. In some cases supplementary classes or tutoring may be helpful, or the assigning of a "big brother" or "big sister" who can help the new child learn the rules and connect with the other children.

Community interventions may aim at helping the family develop a support network or at educating the community about the immigrant culture, and the specific immigrant families and what they bring to the community.

Preventive Interventions

Like therapeutic interventions, preventive interventions for immigrant children and families may be designed at a number of different levels: the individual child, the family, the school, the community, or the culture.

Preventive interventions at the individual level may include the use of art and projective drawings in preventive work with these children. In addition, the therapist may alert school personnel that these children may be at risk and that their parents may be less likely to seek help from the mental health system, so the school may need to function as a screening and referral source. It will also be important to begin exploring the mental health beliefs of the immigrant child's culture before assistance is needed, so that if help is required, it can be conceptualized and presented in a way acceptable and understandable to the parents.

Family interventions have four aims: (1) minimizing the experience of parental loss and separations; (2) helping the family foresee and anticipate periods of loneliness and rootlessness; (3) helping the family find mechanisms that will ensure the maintenance of contact with people from the culture of origin; and (4) helping the family make connections and become part of their new community and culture.

Schools should set up programs to ensure that the immigrants learn the language of the new country as soon as possible; at the same time, they should provide support for active participation in sports, art, and music, which do not depend primarily on verbal skills. Schools may want to educate nonimmigrant schoolchildren about the culture, history, and customs of the new child's country of origin and, when there are a significant number of immigrant children from the same culture, may wish to develop a special class or even a summer camp for the immigrant children to focus on their culture of origin and to help them begin to negotiate their new identity.

Community interventions may include providing new and potential immigrants with prior information about the practical realities and social rules of their new community, either through personal communication or a community guidebook; providing new immigrants with support for keeping intact parts of their old cultures while incorporating the new, through such things as community ethnic festivals, in which members of the immigrant group share their food and culture with members of the community, or through making arrangements for ethnic food vendors to be part of the community farmer's market; or providing immigrants with surrogate extended families through a system of community or church sponsorship of immigrant families.

Williams (1991) cites a particularly innovative program in which unaccompanied Cambodian refugee children were placed in ethnically similar foster homes and participated in three different Cambodian Buddhist ceremonies, a memorial for absent family members held in the home of their foster parents, a communitywide family reunion of living and dead relatives, and a religious observance for absent family members. These ceremonies were carried out with the aid of Buddhist monks and had the goal of helping these children deal with grief for their lost and absent relatives

and with the traumatic events that often resulted in the death of family members.

Societal interventions involve working on a larger scale to help change the attitudes toward immigrant groups through the use of television, radio, newspapers, and magazines to educate the larger society about new immigrant groups and what they contribute. Such programs can help validate the identity of the newcomers by educating others about their customs, values, foods, philosophies, child-rearing ways, and language, and can help fight racial or ethnic prejudice against these groups. In addition, a country can provide institutionalized structures and supports that help new immigrants with the processes of assimilation and acculturation. In the United States such support generally has come through private, nonprofit agencies, while in other countries, such as Israel, a variety of government-supported programs provides new immigrants and their children with food and housing, special language instruction, and special children's programs during the period immediately following immigration.

Conclusion

As child psychiatrists living in a country composed largely of immigrants and their offspring, it is important that we contribute our skills to help make the transition and acculturation process less traumatic for new immigrants and their children. We should take on this task eagerly, because of our role as advocates for children and families, because of the contributions immigrants have made and continue to make to our country (Light & Bonacich, 1988), and as a way of repaying our debt to the country that welcomed our ancestors, however many generations ago that was.

REFERENCES

Ahearn, F. L., Jr., & Athey, J. L. (Eds.). (1991). *Refugee children: Theory, research, and services.* Baltimore: Johns Hopkins University Press.

Canino, I. A. (1988). The transcultural child. In C. J. Kestenbaum & D. T. Williams (Eds.), *Handbook of*

clinical assessment of children and adolescents (pp. 1024–1042). New York: New York University Press.

Ebaugh, H. R. F. (1988). *Becoming an EX: The process of role exit.* Chicago: University of Chicago Press.

Eisenbruch, M. (1990). The cultural bereavement interview: A new clinical research approach for refugees. *Psychiatric Clinics of North America.* 13 (4), 715–735.

Erikson, E. H. (1963). *Childhood and society.* New York: Norton.

Ganesan, S., Fine, S., & Lin, T. Y. (1989). Psychiatric symptoms in refugee families from South East Asia: Therapeutic challenges. *American Journal of Psychotherapy,* 93 (2): 218–228.

Hughes, C. C. (1965). The life history in cross-cultural psychiatric research. In J. M. Murphy & A. H. Leighton (Eds.), *Approaches to cross-cultural psychiatry* (pp. 285–328). Ithaca, NY: Cornell University Press.

Hutchinson, E. P. (1956). *Immigrants and their children, 1850–1950.* New York: John Wiley & Sons.

Kinzie, J. D., & Sack, W. (1991). Severely traumatized Cambodian children: Research findings and clinical implications. In F. Ahearn L. & J. L. Athey (Eds.), *Refugee children: Theory, research, and services* (pp. 92–105). Baltimore: Johns Hopkins University Press.

Light, I., & Bonacich, E. (1988). *Immigrant entrepreneurs: Koreans in Los Angeles 1965–1982.* Berkeley: University of California Press.

Peseschkian, N. (1987). *Positive psychotherapy.* Berlin: Springer-Verlag.

Sluzki, C. E. (1979). Migration and family conflict. *Family Process, 18* (4), 379–390.

Stein, H. F. (1984). The emotional separation syndrome among recent Oklahoma migrants: Description, explanation and clinical implications. *Oklahoma State Medical Association Journal, 77,* 152–157.

Sung, B. L. (1985). Bicultural conflicts in Chinese immigrant children. *Journal of Comparative Family Studies, 16* (2), 255–269.

Totman, R. (1979). *Social causes of illness.* New York: Pantheon Books.

Westermeyer, J. (1989). *Psychiatric care of migrants: A clinical guide.* Washington, DC: American Psychiatric Press.

Williams, C. L. (1987). *An annotated bibliography on refugee mental health.* Rockville, MD: U.S. Department of Health and Human Services.

Williams, C. L. (1991). Toward the development of preventive interventions for youth traumatized by war and refugee flight. In F. L. Ahearn, Jr., & J. L. Athey (Eds.), *Refugee children: Theory, research, and services* (pp. 201–217). Baltimore: Johns Hopkins University Press.

Winnicott, D. W. (1971). *Playing and reality.* London: Tavistock Publications.

---

60 / **When Children Relocate**

Stuart A. Copans

Demographics

Every year roughly 40 million Americans move. From 15 to 20% of the children enrolled in public school eary year are transfers from another school in another town or neighborhood. Sell (1983) reported 147 million moves over 5 years. Of the 147 million moves, 8 million local movers and half a million migrants were forced to move, and 15 million had job-imposed relocation; 25% of mobility and 40% of migration occurred under conditions of substantial constraint.

I would like to acknowledge the particular assistance of Audrey McCollum and Nadia Jensen during my preparation of this chapter. Our collaboration on a guide for relocating adults and families has helped enrich and enlarge the scope of this chapter.

Reasons for Moving

It is important, before looking at the effects of a move, to distinguish between various groups of movers. Some children and families are part of a migratory culture—for example, Gypsies or migrant farm workers. Others move as a result of economic pressures, as when large numbers of families and individuals migrate from an area with high unemployment to an area where jobs are available. In some cases moves are caused not by economic necessity but because of occupational requirements—for example, military families, families of executives in multistate or multinational companies, or physician's families during the years of school and residencies.

Sell (1983) suggested that the usual distinction

between forced and voluntary moves was an over-simplification and listed 24 different reasons why people move, divided into 3 main categories: forced, imposed, and preference dominated. He further subdivided imposed moves into employment related and family related (marriage, divorce, separation, death), and subdivided preference-dominated moves into employment related, housing and family related, neighborhood related, and other.

One particular type of move not identified or commented on in most studies of moving is the psychologically motivated move. While the fantasy of the "geographic cure" is well described in the literature on alcoholics and alcoholic families, it is also seen in families with other psychiatric problems. Couples acting on the fantasy that a move from an urban to a rural area will resolve their marital difficulties are seen frequently in rural outpatient psychiatry and child psychiatry clinics.

Individuals may move as a way of distancing themselves from a painful relationship or as part of an attempt to achieve separation and individuation from their family of origin.

A particular clinical concern is children living with frequently moving, psychiatrically ill single parents. Children growing up in such psychologically motivated, frequently moving families often have few or no close relationships outside of the parental relationship, and as a result of the distortions in mirroring in the parent-child relationship and the lack of other mirroring relationships, often present with severe identity problems as well as other severe psychiatric problems. In these cases, if an area of strength and stability can be detected, it is often the result of an earlier relationship with a grandparent, uncle, or aunt; the reinvolvement of the child with this source of stability and support may significantly improve the prognosis.

The Effects of Geographic Moves on Children

In order to understand the effects of moving on children, it is important to understand a variety of factors that play a part in the effects of a move. These include the meaning and significance of the home; the importance of place, neighborhood, pets, objects, and peers; and the effects of the move on the parents, on the marital relationship, and, most important, on the mother with the consequent secondary effects on these factors on the children.

THE MEANING AND SIGNIFICANCE OF THE HOME

For most children, the home in which they spend their childhood years acquires powerful emotional meanings. Bachelard, the French phenomenologist, suggested in 1964 that human memories were inextricably linked with settings, and suggested the need for the study of what he called "topoanalysis . . . the systemic psychological study of the sites of our intimate lives." "Our house," Bachelard went on to say, "is our corner of the world. As has often been said, it is our first universe, a real cosmos in every sense of the word. . . . Memories of the outside world will never have the same tonality as those of home. . . . All our lives we come back to [memories of our first house]" (p. 4).

Marc (1977) reiterated Bachelard's emphasis on the importance of the house. "To build a house is to create an area of peace, calm, and security, . . . where we can leave the world and listen to our own rhythm; it is to create a place of our very own, safe from danger. For once we have crossed the threshold and shut the door behind us, we can be at one with ourselves" (p. 14).

Csikszentmihalyi, whose early studies focused primarily on the relationship of adults and children with the objects in their homes, noted that "The proper function of the home is to be a safe haven of recognition" (Csikszentmihalyi & Rochberg-Ralton, 1981). "Much of what makes a home such a warm and familiar place," he went on to say, "is that it embodies all our prejudices and habitual idiosyncrasies and allows us to 'vegetate' when we must."

The home, then, in many ways functions for children as what Winnicott would term a holding environment. It allows them to feel safe, to take a time out, to retreat from the vicissitudes of the world.

McCollum (1990), in her study of the effects of moving on women, pointed out the importance of the home and the relationship of the home to women's sense of self. "Because so many elements of the self can permeate a dwelling—taste and values, personal and family history—the pain of leaving can be intense" (p. 67). The home also played an important part, McCollum found, in defining relationships and boundaries, both inside and outside the family. "In important ways, dwellings shape relationships. They foster closeness or they allow needed distance between family and the outside world. . . . Dwellings define boundaries within the family as well, offering secret nooks and crannies, shelters from the friction and irritations of daily life" (pp. 68–69).

Not only does a home reinforce the notion of the self, McCollum suggests, but by giving a sense of history and continuity, it may help reinforce a stable sense of self. "By embodying personal and family history, home reinforces a woman's sense of continuity" (p. 69).

THE MEANING AND SIGNIFICANCE OF PLACE

Part of our sense of who we are, and the stage on which, as children, we act our parts, is the region and community that surround our home (Walter, 1988). Most contemporary adults live in a world which is decentered. Our identity as child psychiatrists, as alumni of a particular college and medical school and training program, as Republicans or Democrats, may seem far more important to us than our sense of ourselves as residents of Packers Corners, or Green River, or the 400 block of 7th Avenue. "The ability of humans to control and manipulate their environment," Entrikin (1991) points out, "is related to a secular, scientific world view that has standardized and desacralized space and time. Unlike the 'centered' spaces of religious and mythical thought that ordered the universe around one's group, the objective space-time of modern science is a 'decentered' space" (pp. 62–63). This decentering is not without cost, however. "The weakening of the social and cultural glue that binds individuals to groups and groups to places," Entrikin points out, "has put a greater burden on the individual to construct meaning in the world" (p. 63).

Children however, "live [their] lives in place and have a sense of being part of place, but . . . also view place as something separate, something external. [Their] neighborhood is both an area centered on [themselves] and [their] home, as well as an area containing houses, streets and people

that [they] may view from a decentered or an outsider's perspective. Thus place is both a center of meaning and the external context of [their] actions" (Entrikin, 1991, p. 7). As a result, children "cannot conceive [themselves] as independent . . . , as bearers of selves wholly detached from [their] . . . attachments . . . [They] are partly defined by the communities [they] inhabit . . . The story of [their] life is always embedded in the story of those communities from which [they] derive [their] identity— whether family or city, tribe or nation, party or cause" (Entrikin, 1991, p. 9).

If we think back to our childhood, we discover that our thoughts are less of ideas and more of places. When we think back to our memories of childhood friends, we often find them connected with remembered places. "Each one of us, then," Bachelard suggests, "should speak of his roads, his crossroads, his roadside benches; each one of us should make a surveyors map of his lost fields and meadows. Thoreau said that he had the map of his fields engraved in his soul" (p. 11).

Seamon (1980) suggests that the importance of place, and the loss we feel when we move, goes beyond conscious memories and meanings and is at least partially the result of what he terms "the habitual nature of everyday movement." "Many movements," he suggests, "are conducted by some preconscious process which guides behaviors without the person's need to be consciously aware of their happening" (p. 153). These movements may coalesce to form what Seamon calls time-space routines and space-ballets. The child walking home from school may stop everyday and throw some rocks in a stream, say hello to the man who sits on the porch of the nursing home, and bark at the dog in the green house, as precisely as if it were choreographed, but without conscious awareness of the fixed nature of his behaviors. When children move, Seamon suggests, part of what they miss are these preconsciously guided behaviors that they may not even have been consciously aware of.

NEIGHBORHOODS

Children live in and grow up in gradually expanding neighborhoods. As they grow up, the area surrounding their house where they feel free to wander and explore gradually increases.

Bryant (1985) studied children's relationships with their neighborhoods by accompanying children on walks through their neighborhoods and questioning them about their sources of support. He found that the most common sources of support included pets, grandparents, places where they could be by themselves, siblings, peers, and nonrelative adults. Twenty-three percent of the children listed at least one nonrelative adult among their top-10 supportive adults. In this same study, Bryant found that the extent of a child's neighborhood network of support predicted his or her social-emotional functioning.

In McCollum's study of women and moving (1990), she found that while 1 in 3 of the recently moved women she studied felt at home in their homes 2 years after their move, less than 1 in 6 felt positively connected to their neighborhood.

While children become connected to their neighborhoods more quickly, as a result of both their comfort with exploration and their contacts with other children in school, the loss of neighborhood can represent a significant stressor for both school-age and adolescent movers.

THE IMPORTANCE OF OBJECTS

Csikszentmihalyi has studied the relationship of both children and adults with objects and points out that "The importance of objects for the normal development of young children has been recognized in the past two decades" (Csikszentmihalyi & Rochberg-Ralton, 1981).

"Every object," Marc (1977) pointed out earlier, "strikes a chord deep within us, 'symbolizing' an aspect of ourselves, and thus making up part of it" (p. 29).

Csikszentmihalyi points out that in the past, individuals were largely defined by the tools of their trade—the blacksmith by his hammer and anvil, the doctor by his black bag and stethoscope, the mason by his trowel. In our modern world, he goes on to suggest, adults, and to a large extent children, "now define [them]selves through objects of consumption rather than production"; however, "The objects children cherish share a proclivity for action" (p. 96).

"Objects affect what a person can do," Csikszentmihalyi points out, "either by expanding or restricting the scope of that person's actions and thoughts. And because what a person does is largely what he or she is, objects have a determining effect on the development of the self, which is why understanding the type of relationship that exists between people and things is so crucial" (p. 53).

The objects that children bring with them when they move, and the objects they acquire after they move, help them in defining who they are, and can help us, as child psychiatrists, in assessing their cultural identity and conflicts.

The Effects of Relocation on Mothers

McCollum (1990) reviewed the literature dealing with the effects of moving on women's physical and mental health. She cites a number of studies reporting increased separation anxiety, shame, sadness, depression as well as increased physical symptoms in women following a move. While some symptoms are reported in men, as well, it appears that these symptoms are more common in women.

The Effects of Relocation on Child and Adolescent Mental Health

A variety of studies have looked at whether moving adversely affects the mental health of children and adolescents. Some studies seem to show positive effects from moving, while others seem to show negative effects. Unfortunately, moves often follow other stressors, such as divorce, death, or loss of a job, and this is almost never controlled. In addition, when studies are done using nonmobile classmates as a control group, the apparent beneficial or deleterious effects of mobility may be an illusion created by the demographics of the control group.

Despite these cautions, certain studies strongly suggest that moves can at least contribute to pathological outcomes in some children and adolescents.

Knudson-Cooper and Leuchtag (1982) reported that children who had recently moved were significantly overrepresented in their sample of seriously burned children and that children appeared most vulnerable to burn accidents 2 to 5 months after a move.

A variety of studies of migrant families (Barankin, Konstantareas, & de Bosset, 1989; Monroe-Blum, Boyle, Offord, & Kates, 1989; Steinhausen et al., 1990) have found that the strongest predictor of behavioral and emotional disturbance in a child was impairment of the physical and mental health of the parents, and most particularly of the mother.

Barankin et al. (1989), in a study of Soviet Jewish immigrants to Canada, found that immigrants with depression and psychosomatic illness reported greater behavior, academic, peer interaction, and child-parent difficulties in their children.

Monroe-Blum et al. (1989), studying children born outside of Canada, found that while these children were indeed at increased risk for child psychiatric disorder, a majority of this increased risk could be accounted for by family dysfunction, poverty, living in subsidized housing, and older child age.

Brown and Orthner (1990), studying early adolescents, found that frequent moves were not associated with well-being among males but were associated with increased depression among females.

de Wilde, Kienhorst, Diekstra, and Wolters (1992), in a study relating adolescent suicidal behavior and life events, found that it took multple "insults" to precipitate suicidal behaviors and that relocation was but one of them, and not the most important.

Two recent studies have used data from the 1988 National Health Interview Survey of Child Health, in which data was collected on a nationally representative sample of approximately 10,000 children. Wood, Halfon, Scarlata, Newacheck, and Nessim (1993) compared infrequent movers with frequent movers and found that "frequent relocation was associated with higher rates of all measures of child dysfunction; 23% of children who moved frequently had repeated a grade vs. 12% of children who never or infrequently moved. Eighteen percent of children that moved frequently had four or more behavioral problems vs 7% of children who never or infrequently moved" (p. 1334). At the same time, children who moved

frequently "were no more likely to have had delays in growth or development or a learning disorder."

Simpson and Fowler (1994), using the same data, compared children who had moved three or more times with those who had never moved. Those who had moved three or more times "were 2.3 times more likely to have had emotional/behavioral problems, 2.2 times more likely to have received psychological help, 1.7 times more likely to have repeated a grade, and 1.9 times more likely to have been suspended or expelled from school compared with children who had never moved" (p. 303). In their analysis, Simpson and Fowler controlled for key sociodemographic variables, such as mother's marital status, mother's education, poverty level, and race/ethnicity, that had been shown to be related to children's emotional behaviors or to the number of times children move. They recommend that information about family relocations, both recent and throughout life, be included on screening or intake questionnaires and that a finding of recent and frequent moves should trigger additional inquiry and referral to available support systems. They also suggest that school-based programs may represent an ideal locus of preventive intervention for relocating families.

DEVELOPMENTAL CONSIDERATIONS

One important factor determining the effect a move has on a child is the child's age and developmental status. The child's ability to adequately conceptualize the move, the child's object relations, and the child's achievement of previous developmental tasks all help determine the outcome of a given relocation.

Newborns are most likely to be affected secondarily, by the effect the move has on the mother's ability to provide milk and nurturing. Toddlers are more likely to be affected by loss of alternate caregivers or, occasionally, by the loss of a transitional object during the chaos of the move.

In latency, children remain extremely vulnerable to the effects of the move on their parents but also are likely to mourn the loss of close friends or of neighborhood adults with whom they have a close relationship. Often latency-age children may have sources of support in their neighborhood of which their parents are unaware.

For adolescents, moving may be difficult because it temporarily increases their dependence on their parents at a time when they are striving for additional independence. At times the compensatory need to move rapidly toward more independence from parents after a move may lead to a rapid and inappropriate choice of peer groups.

MITIGATING INFLUENCES

Given that moves disrupt so much of what is important in children's lives and that so many children move each year, it is important to consider why more pathology resulting from these geographic dislocations is not seen. A number of factors seem to contribute to children's resiliency in the face of moves, both voluntary and involuntary. These include the rapidity with which children adjust and learn new languages and habits, the structure and contact provided by school, the structure and support provided by an intact family with intact family rituals, and the relative uniformity of much contemporary television-mediated children's culture.

Hendershott (1989), in a study of 205 students, found that social support from parents and peers attenuated the negative effect of mobility on specific measures of self-concept.

Moilanen and Myhrman (1989) suggested that the factors protecting children during migration were good family relationships, good peer relationships, verbalization ability, good cognitive abilities, high school achievement, and, when children move to an area where a different language is spoken, a clear linguistic identity.

Migratory Cultures

In migratory cultures, the community may migrate as a whole, as in the case of carnival or circus workers, or may migrate as a family unit, as in the case of Gypsies (Gmelch, 1986) or migrant farm workers (Diaz, Trotter, & Rivera, 1989). In some cases, especially for migrant farm workers and circus or carnival workers, there is often a "home base" consisting of a small piece of land or a small house.

Some recent theorists, on the basis of updated and expanded versions of Kurt Lewin's field theory (Lewin, 1951), have suggested that in the case of migratory communities such as a carnival or a circus, the field may be thought of as moving, with the individuals or families remaining in relatively stable positions within the changing field. In fact, stories of carnival life suggest that those traveling with the carnival end up setting up their booths or trailers in similar positions in each new location.

While there has been some recent interest in the structure of both Gypsy and carnival workers' lives and families, the most extensively studied migratory group is migrant farm workers, at least partially as a result of Coles's pioneering studies of migrant farm children (1967) and the subsequent federal legislation providing services for these families and children.

Larson, Doris, and Alvarez (1987) reported that "the incidence of child maltreatment rate among migrate farm worker families, as perceived by migrant educators, was substantially higher than the rate observed for the population as a whole or even for families with approximately the same socioeconomic status." They also pointed out that of the three federally defined categories of migrant farm workers—interstate, intrastate, resettled—only the interstate workers are eligible for most federally funded services, including health, legal, educational, and child care services.

Risk factors for child abuse among the migrant population include chronic unemployment, economic insecurity, isolation from formal and informal support systems, parental history of being abused, use of harsh discipline to induce conformity, and use of punishment to achieve compliance. The rate of maltreatment (110.6 children per 1,000) in this population is 10 times the rate for the U.S. population (10.5 children per 1,000) and 4 times the rate of people from the same socioeconomic status (27.3 children per 1,000).

Preventive Interventions

Puskar and Dvorsak (1991) suggest the development of a school-based health-promotion program for relocated adolescents. They suggest assessing the adolescents' perceptions of the move, concurrent stresses, coping skills, and support systems, and then intervening by providing education and support, linking the adolescent with potential natural support groups, and referring the adolescent for evaluation and treatment when appropriate.

At least two children's books about moving may be helpful in explaining upcoming moves to preschool or young elementary school children (Berenstain, 1981; Rogers, 1987). Going over the schedule of the move, what will be moved, how it will be moved, where it will be stored, when it will arrive and be unpacked can all be helpful in preparing all children for upcoming moves.

McCollum, Jensen, and Copans (1996) devote three chapters in their book on the emotional aspects of relocation to strategies that can help children and adolescents relocate successfully.

Among the preventive strategies are premove preparations to help minimize the effects of the move; helping children stay in touch with their premove friends through visits, phone calls or correspondence; whenever possible letting children have some say in which objects and/or pets are brought along; and providing specific supports for moving mothers to help them cope with the stresses of the move. Although it may be painful at the time, helping children say good-bye to friends is an important step in a successful relocation.

It also can be helpful to provide education to moving parents about the stresses involved in a move, about the possibility of regression in children following a move, and about the importance of providing extra family support to all children, even older adolescents who claim not to need it.

Identifying children's areas of interest and strength before the move can be helpful, since these may help facilitate their involvement in natural support groups, such as sports, band, cheerleaders, or church groups. Taking photographs of their old house and making a scrapbook about special places and people, which can be viewed after the move, can help with the transition.

Working with school principals or guidance counselors to help ensure the child's placement in an appropriate classroom or appropriate classes can be particularly important in easing the transition to a new community.

Some parents have described setting aside money before a move so their children could purchase some new clothes that "fit in" in the new community.

Simple awareness of the difficulties that follow a move may be of significant help both to children and parents.

Conclusion

Although we cannot predict the effects of a single move on the mental health of children, there is little question that moves represent a significant stressor for both parents and children and that repetitive moves significantly increase the risk of both academic and behavioral problems.

It is also clear that an adequate psychiatric history should include a history of relocations and of the responses to them.

In the past, relocation often has been the precipitant of therapy termination. Data in this chapter would suggest that when child patients relocate, the therapist should help the parents and child find ways to minimize potential ill effects of the move. The establishment of a new relationship with a therapist should be strongly encouraged, since the parents' distress following the move may well interfere with their ability to recognize and get help for their child's postrelocation distress.

REFERENCES

Bachelard, G. (1964). *The poetics of space*. New York: Orion Press.

Barankin, T., Konstantareas, M. M., & de Bosset, F. (1989). Adaptation of recent Soviet Jewish immigrants and their children to Toronto. *Canadian Journal of Psychiatry, 34* (6), 512–518.

Berenstain, S., & J. (1981) *The Berenstain bears' moving day*. New York: Random House.

Brown, A. C., & Orthner, D. K. (1990). Relocation and personal well-being among early adolescents. *Journal of Early Adolescence, 10* (3), 366–381.

Bryant, B. K. (1985). The neighborhood walk: Sources of support in middle childhood. *Monographs of the Society for Research in Child Development, 50,* (3, Serial No. 210), 1–122.

Buttimer, A., & Seamon, D. (Eds.). (1991). *The human*

experience of space and place. New York: St. Martin's Press.

Coles, R. (1967). *Migrants, sharecroppers, mountaineers.* Boston: Little, Brown.

Csikszentmihalyi, M., & Rochberg-Ralton, E. (1981). *The meaning of things.* New York: Cambridge University Press.

de Wilde, E. J., Kienhorst, I. C. W. M., Diekstra, R. F. W., & Wolters, W. H. G. (1992). The relationship between adolescent suicidal behavior and life events in childhood and adolescence. *American Journal of Psychiatry, 149,* 45–51.

Diaz, J. O. P., Trotter, R. T., II, & Rivera, V. A. J. (1989). *The effects of migration on children: An ethnographic study.* State College, PA: Centro de Estudios Sobre la Migracion.

Eisenbruch, M. (1988). The mental health of refugee children and their cultural development. *International Migration Review, 22* (2), 282–300.

Entrikin, J. N. (1991). *The betweenness of place.* Baltimore: Johns Hopkins University Press.

Gmelch, S. B. (1986). Groups that don't want in: Gypsies and other artisan, trader, and entertainer minorities. *Annual Review of Anthropology, 15,* 307–330.

Hendershott, A. B. (1989). Residential mobility, social support and adolescent self-concept. *Adolescence, 24* (93), 217–232.

Knudson-Copper, M. S., & Leuchtag, A. K. (1982). The stress of a family move as a precipitating factor in children's burn accidents. *Journal of Human Stress, 1,* 32–38.

Larson, O. W., III, Doris, J., & Alvarez, W. F. (1987). Child maltreatment among U.S. East Coast migrant farm workers. *Child Abuse and Neglect, 11,* 281–297.

Lewin, K. (1951). *Field theory in social science.* Chicago: University of Chicago Press.

Marc, O. (1977). *Psychology of the house.* London: Thames and Hudson.

McCollum, A. T. (1990). *The trauma of moving.* Newbury Park, CA: Sage Publications.

McCollum, A. T., Jensen, N., & Copans, S. A. (1996). *Smart moves: Your guide through the emotional maze of relocation.* Lyme, NH: Smith and Kraus.

Moilanen, I., & Myhrman, A. (1989). What protects a child during migration. *Scandanavian Journal of Social Medicine, 17,* 21–24.

Monroe-Blum, H., Boyle, M. H., Offord, D. R., & Kates, N. (1989). Immigrant children: Psychiatric disorder, school performance, and service utilization. *American Journal of Orthopsychiatry, 59* (4), 510–519.

Puskar, K. R., & Dvorsak, K. G. (1991). Relocation stress in adolescents: Helping teenagers cope with a moving dilemma. *Pediatric Nursing, 17* (3), 295–298.

Rogers, F. (1987). *Moving,* New York: G. P. Putnam's Sons.

Seamon, D. (1980). Body-subject, Time-space routines, and place-ballets. In A. Buttimer & D. Seamon (Eds.), *The human experience of space and place* (pp. 148–165). New York: St. Martin's Press.

Sell, R. R. (1983). Analyzing migration decisions: The first step—Whose decisions. *Demography, 20* (3), 299–311.

Simpson, G. A., & Fowler, M. G. (1994). Geographic mobility and children's emotional/behavioral adjustment and school functioning. *Pediatrics, 93* (2), 303–309.

Steinhausen, H. C., Edinsel, E., Fegert, J. M., Gobel, D., Reister, E., & Rentz, A. (1990). Child psychiatric disorders and family dysfunction in migrant workers' and military families. *European Archives of Psychiatry and Neurological Sciences, 239,* 257–262.

Walter, E. V. (1988). *Placeways: A theory of the human environment.* Chapel Hill, NC: University of North Carolina Press.

Wood, D., Halfon, N., Scarlata, D., Newacheck, P., & Nessim, S. (1993). Impact of family relocation on children's growth, development, school function, and behavior. *Journal of the American Medical Association, 270* (11), 1334–1338.

SUBJECT INDEX

Runaway, adolescent, *(continued)*
  epidemiology, 139–140
  gender, 140
  health problems, 141
  HIV, 142–143
  indications of mental health problems, 142–143
  legal issues, 143
  living situations, 141
  mental health interventions, 144–145
  pregnancy, 142
  risk factors for mental health problems, 140
  school, 143
  sexual abuse, 141
  street kids, 139
  substance abuse, 143
  suicide, 142
  system kids, 139
  throwaway kids, 139
  trading sex for money or drugs, 143
  victimized children, 139–140
Rural residence
  adolescent, 220–227
    clinical implications, 223–224
    clinical interventions, 226–227
    cognitive development, 223
    development, 222–223
    epidemiology, 220–221
    misconceptions, 221
    service delivery, 225–226
  child, 220–227
    clinical implications, 223–224
    clinical interventions, 226–227
    cognitive development, 223
    development, 222–223
    epidemiology, 220–221
    misconceptions, 221
    service delivery, 225–226
  child abuse, 224
  minority group, 221
  poverty, 221
  school, 224

School-age child
  adoption, 6–7
  borderline intellectual functioning, 392–393
  end-stage renal failure, 359–360
  mild mental retardation, 392–393
  only child, 164
  seizure disorder, 412
  sibling position, 245
  stepfamily, 48

Seizure disorder, 409–415
  adult, 412
  antiepileptic drug, 413
  developmental issues, 411–413
  early childhood, 412
  electroencephalogram, 411
  epidemiology, 409–410
  family, 412–413
  infant, 412
  learning complications, 410–411
  psychiatric complications, 410–411
  psychiatric treatment, 414–415
  psychopharmacology, 413–414
  school-age child, 412
Self-care, 155–161. *See also* Latchkey children
  adolescent, 158
  child, 157–158
  television, 158
Self-concept
  homosexual parent, 149–150
  Japanese American child, 584
Self-esteem
  homosexual parent, 149–150
  religion, 213–214
  sickle cell anemia, 428–429
  stepfamily, 49
Self-representation, deafness, 369
Separation
  adoption, 9
  Mexican American child, 538
Separation anxiety disorder, bereavement, 36–37
Sexual abuse, 97, 141
  children of alcoholics, 174–175
  parental alcohol use, 174–175
Sexuality
  adoption, 8
  religion, 211–212
Shame, Middle Eastern child, 547
Sibling
  birth order. *See* Sibling position
  divorce, 103
  Mexican American child, 538–539
  of psychiatrically disordered child, 228–236
    clinical implications, 232–235
    clinical interventions, 235–236
    developmental impact, 229–232
    environmental influences, 229–231
    family variables, 229–231
    genotypical influences, 231–232
    phenotypical influences, 231
    sociocultural variables, 231

NAME INDEX

Aase, J. M., 172, 173, 559
Abed, I., 547, 550, 551
Abel, E. L., 172, 173
Abel, G. G., 431
Ablin, D., 612
Abou el-Azaem, M. G. M., 548
Aboud, F. E., 476
Abraham, L., 489
Abraham, N., 551
Abramowicz, H. K., 399
Abrams, M. R., 431
Abu-Laban, B., 547, 550, 551, 552
Abu-Saad, H., 545, 547, 549, 554
Abuelo, D. K., 391, 399
Accardo, P. J., 115
Aceves, J., 307, 310, 312
Achenbach, T., 300, 512
Achenbach, T. M., 443, 524, 525
Ack, M., 344
Ackerly, S. S., 325
Ackerman, N. W., 499
Ackerman, R. J., 183
Ackerson, L. M., 564
Acock, A. C., 209
Acosta, F. X., 533, 538, 539, 540
Adadow Gray, N., 547, 550, 551, 552
Adams, D. G., 466
Adams, D. W., 83
Adams, J., 300
Adams-Greenly, M., 68, 70
Adams-Taylor, S., 197, 198, 199
Addy, 410
Adelman, R., 303, 304
Adlakha, A. L., 546
Adler, B. N., 237
Adler, B. R., 288
Adler, D. A., 578, 594
Adnopoz, J., 25
Adrian, C., 66, 67
Affleck, G., 264
Agbayewa, M., 180
Agle, D., 381, 383, 385, 387

Agras, W. S., 332
Agyei, Y., 150
Ahlas, A., 343, 344
Ahles, T. A., 383
Ahmed, F., 212
Ahn, H. N., 120
Ainsworth, M. D., 193, 199
Aisenstein, C., 504, 507
Ajmone Marsan, C., 411
Akerhuis, G. W., 523
Akiskal, H. S., 35
Al-Issa, B., 552
Al-Issa, I., 552
Alarcon, R. D., 521
Alberman, E., 308
Albert, V., 117
Albisser, A. M., 260
Albiston, C. R., 100
Alboran, N., 583
Alcocer, A. M., 534
Aldenkamp, A. P., 413
Aldridge, M. H., 117
Alegria, M., 525
Alexander, G. E., 457
Alexander, M. P., 326
Alfaro, J., 121
Allan, J., 291
Allen, D. A., 263
Allen, D. M., 143
Allen, G. D., 212, 215
Allen, J., 426
Allison, P. D., 104, 106
Allport, G. W., 208, 477
Almond, P. S., 466
Alonzo, E. M., 462
Alpert, B., 158
Alpert-Gillis, L. J., 107
Alpherts, W. C. J., 413
Alter, C. L., 466
Alterman, A. I., 174, 175, 176, 177
Althaus, M., 523, 607
Altman, R., 121
Altschuler, K. Z., 371
Altshui-Stark, D., 441
Aluwahlia, S., 523, 524
Alvarez, M., 281
Alvarez, W. F., 636
Alvino, J., 129

Alvirez, D., 532
Aman, M. G., 406, 407
Amaro, H., 198, 534
Amato, P. R., 102, 103, 104, 105, 108
Ambrosini, P. J., 523, 524
Amiel, S. A., 349
Amir, S., 343
Amparo, E., 327
Amylon, M., 263, 301, 302
Anderson, A. R., 164, 238
Anderson, B., 344
Anderson, B. J., 342, 343, 348, 349, 350
Anderson, D. H., 332
Anderson, E., 46, 47, 51, 200
Anderson, E. R., 102, 103, 104, 106, 107, 108
Anderson, G. M., 457
Anderson, I. S., 291
Anderson, J. C., 523, 524
Anderson, J. L., 115
Anderson, L., 220, 223, 414
Anderson, S. L., 245, 246
Anderson, W. W., 325
Andreski, M. A., 54
Andrews, W. S., 464, 466, 467
Androkites, A., 263
Angell, R., 55, 56, 615
Angell, R. H., 613, 615
Angst, D. M., 237, 444
Ani, M., 544, 545, 546, 547
Annegers, J. F., 409
Anthony, S., 72, 77
Anyan, L. L., 171, 182, 183
Apospori, E., 521
Appelbaum, M. I., 288
Araki, A., 310
Araki, F., 583
Aram, D. M., 439, 444, 445
Arasteh, J., 46
Argyle, M., 208, 209, 212
Armistead, L., 104, 107
Armor, L., 580
Armstrong, B. L., 441
Arndt, S., 411
Arnett, C., 222

Arney, J., 316
Arroyo, J., 511
Arroyo, W., 54, 55, 56, 514, 540
Arthur, B., 34
Asarnow, J. R., 71, 72
Ash, P., 90, 91, 95, 96
Asher, S. J., 101
Ashkenazi, M., 439
Ashton, G., 599
Aspinwall, L. G., 65, 69
Assadullahi, T., 288
Atchison, N. E., 417
Atkinson, D. R., 609
Attneave, C. L., 561, 565, 566
Auld, P., 198
Auslander, W., 343, 348
Ausruskin, T., 343, 344
Austin, J. K., 260
Axelrod, A., 466
Ayalon, A., 60
Azuma, H., 589, 590

Baar, H., 342
Babani, L., 254, 266
Babick, A., 344
Babor, T. F., 177
Baca-Zinn, M., 536
Bach, G. R., 42
Bach, J., 164, 238
Bachrach, C. A., 29
Bacon, G., 344, 350
Baden, R. K., 159
Baghurst, P., 263
Baider, L., 69
Bailey, J. M., 150
Bailey, J. S., 160
Bain, M., 40, 43
Baird, D. A., 399
Baird, T. L., 536
Bakeman, R., 194
Baker, A. M., 54, 55, 59, 552
Baker, F. M., 490
Baker, K., 467
Baker, L., 294, 343, 435, 437, 438, 440, 441, 442, 443, 444

665

670

684